DEMOCRACY

An Introduction to

HBJ

HARCOURT BRACE JOVANOVICH, INC.

New York   San Diego   Chicago   San Francisco   Atlanta
London   Sydney   Toronto

DEMOC

An Introduction

MILTON C. CUMMINGS, JR.

The Johns Hopkins University

DAVID WISE

Author and political analyst

UNDER PRESSURE

the American Political System

FOURTH EDITION

Copyright © 1981, 1977, 1974, 1971 by Harcourt Brace Jovanovich, Inc.

DEMOCRACY UNDER PRESSURE
An Introduction to the American Political System
FOURTH EDITION

ISBN: 0-15-517343-X

Library of Congress Catalog Card Number: 81-80036

Printed in the United States of America

Cover photo: Copyright © Claude Chassagne 1981

Illustrations: EH Technical Services, Inc.

ACKNOWLEDGMENTS AND COPYRIGHTS
Textual Material

The Associated Press. For excerpt from "Federalism: It Doesn't Always Work," The *Washington Post,* September 4, 1973. Also for excerpt from "The Guns of March," The *Washington Post,* March 30, 1973. Also for excerpt from the *San Francisco Chronicle,* August 25, 1977.

Atheneum Publishers, Inc. For excerpt from *A Very Personal Presidency: Lyndon Johnson in the White House* by Hugh Sidey, published by Atheneum and by Andre Deutsch Ltd.

The *Christian Science Monitor.* For excerpt quoted by permission from the article, "Auto repairs sputter, miss" in the *Christian Science Monitor.* © 1970 The Christian Science Publishing Society. All rights reserved.

Columbia Broadcasting System, Inc. For excerpt from the transcript of the television news special, "LBJ: Why I Chose Not to Run," December 27, 1969.

Congressional Quarterly, Inc. For excerpt from *Weekly Report,* November 1, 1980, the Reagan-Carter Debate. Used with permission.

Dailey and Associates. For text of a political advertisement by Peter Dailey. Reprinted by permission.

Doubleday & Company, Inc. For excerpt from *Sexual Politics* by Kate Millett, copyright 1969, 1970 by Kate Millett. Reprinted by permission of Doubleday & Company, Inc., and by permission of Rupert Hart-Davis Ltd. Also for excerpt from Arthur Bernon Tourtellot, *The Presidents on the Presidency* (Doubleday, 1964).

E. P. Dutton & Co., Inc. For excerpts from the book *Plunkitt of Tammany Hall* by William Riordon. Introduction by Arthur Mann. Introduction copyright © 1963 by Arthur Mann. Dutton Paperback edition. Published by E. P. Dutton & Co., Inc. and reprinted with their permission. Also for excerpt from the book *Justice: The Crisis of Law, Order and Freedom in America* by Richard Harris. Copyright © 1970 by Richard Harris. Published by E. P. Dutton & Co., Inc. and reprinted with their permission and by permission of the author.

Esquire Magazine. For excerpt from article by James Farmer in *Esquire* Magazine, May 1969. Reprinted by permission of *Esquire* Magazine. © 1969 by Esquire, Inc.

Harper & Row, Publishers, Inc. For excerpt from *Lyndon Johnson and the American Dream* by Doris Kearns (Harper & Row, 1976). Reprinted by permission.

Holt, Rinehart and Winston, Inc. For excerpt from Robert Sam Anson, *McGovern: A Biography by Robert Sam Anson* (Holt, Rinehart and Winston, 1972).

Houghton Mifflin Company. For excerpts from Arthur M. Schlesinger, Jr., *A Thousand Days* (Houghton Mifflin, 1965).

Inquiry Magazine. For an excerpt from an article June 26, 1978. Reprinted by permission.

Alfred A. Knopf, Inc. For excerpt from Carl L. Becker, *The Declaration of Independence* (Alfred A. Knopf, 1942).

Little, Brown and Company. For excerpt from Catherine Drinker Bowen, *Miracle at Philadelphia* (Little, Brown, 1966). Also for excerpt from William H. Riker, *Federalism: Origin, Operation, Significance.* Copyright © 1964 by Little, Brown and Company. Also for excerpt from *White House Years* by Henry Kissinger. Copyright © 1979 by Henry A. Kissinger. By permission of Little, Brown and Company.

Los Angeles Times Syndicate. For excerpts from *Los Angeles Times;* by Bill Drummond (10/27/78), Bryce Nelson (9/29/77), Michael Seiler (1/1/78), Robert Scheer (8/7/78), and Laurie Becklund (2/15/79); © 1977/78/79 by the Los Angeles Times Syndicate. Reprinted by permission.

McGraw-Hill Book Company. For excerpts from *Storm Over the States* by Terry Sanford. Copyright 1967, McGraw-Hill, Inc. Used with permission of McGraw-Hill Book Company.

The Nation. For an excerpt from an article September 30, 1978. Reprinted with permission.

National Journal. For excerpts © 1977/78/80 by the *National Journal.* Reprinted by permission.

The New American Library. For excerpt from George E. Reedy, *The Twilight of the Presidency* (The New American Library, 1971).

The New York Times Company. For excerpts from The *New York Times.* © 1958/69/70/72/73/74/77/78/79/80 by the New York Times Company. Reprinted by permission.

Newsweek Magazine. For excerpt © 1975 by Newsweek, Inc. All rights reserved. Reprinted by permission.

Pantheon Books. For excerpt from Richard M. Elman, *The Poorhouse State* (Pantheon Books, 1966).

Rand McNally & Company. For excerpt from Lester Milbrath, *The Washington Lobbyists,* © 1963 by Rand McNally & Company, Chicago.

Acknowledgments and copyrights for textual material and for illustrations continue on page 651, which constitutes a continuation of the copyright page.

PREFACE

There is, without doubt, no better experience than revising a college text in government and politics to remind one of the astonishing pace of change that takes place within the American political system.

With the publication of this fourth edition in the spring of 1981, it has been just ten years since *Democracy Under Pressure* first made its appearance. And what an extraordinary ten years they have been. The decade saw the end of the long war in Vietnam, the resignation of the Vice President of the United States, the Watergate trauma and the impeachment inquiry, the resignation and pardon of the President of the United States, and the increasing burden of inflation and unemployment. There was, in addition, the election of Jimmy Carter, an "outsider," to the Presidency, the energy crisis and the congressional response, the seizure of the American hostages in Iran, the Soviet invasion of Afghanistan, the shift away from détente, at least for a time, in the nation's post-Vietnam foreign policy, the failure of Edward M. Kennedy's quest for the Presidency in 1980, and, finally, a sea change—the election and inauguration of Ronald Reagan, a conservative Republican President pledged to increasing the nation's military strength while cutting a broad range of social programs.

This fourth edition of *Democracy Under Pressure* has been thoroughly and extensively revised not only to reflect these kaleidoscopic events, but to focus as well on the broader trends and on the newer interpretations of the American political system.

A number of new features and topics are incorporated in this edition. Although, as in the past, the making of public policy is discussed throughout the book (and particularly in Part Three, "The Policymakers"), a new section introducing the student to policy analysis has been added to Chapter One. This introduction to the policy process follows, in logical progression, the discussion of the concept of a political system.

The impact of single-issue groups in American politics and the dramatic rise in the number, influence, and expenditures of political action committees (PACs) are treated in detail in this edition. The 1980 election is also analyzed in a new case study.

Many new issues are also discussed. For example, we have expanded the arguments for and against a federal system and explained the new changes in the revenue-sharing program. We have included many of the key recent decisions of the Burger Court in such areas as "affirmative action," censorship, closed trials, libel and privacy, search and seizure, and the rights of criminal defendants. We have greatly expanded our discussion of the role of women in American politics. We have included new census data reflecting changes in the political landscape, and we have added new material on Hispanic Americans and their political role.

The discussion of public opinion, of political socialization, and of the manipulation of public opinion has been broadened. The continuing decline of party loyalties, the 1980 national conventions, and the recent trends in voting behavior of various groups in the political system are also discussed, as are the 1980 televised debates, and the use of commercials, professional campaign managers, and sophisticated polling methods in the 1980 presidential election. The paradox of presidential power is re-examined in the light of events of the recent past, and the question is raised of whether the American Presidency has become an arena for failure. Much new work by scholars is reflected in the chapter on Congress, which explores such topics as the effects of change in the seniority system, the subcommittee explosion and the resultant fragmentation of Congress, the growth of congressional staff, and the resurgence of Congress in the field of foreign policy.

We have added new material on the concept of "triangles" among the bureaucracy, Congress, and interest groups. And we have added material on the reorganization of the civil service system, the deregulation of industry, and on "whistle-blowing" in the bureaucracy. Among the other new topics in this edition are the crisis in Iran (discussed in the context of post-Vietnam foreign policy), the Panama Canal treaties, and the establishment of diplomatic relations with China.

Several new structural features have been added. A Perspective at the end of each chapter, beginning with Chapter Two, provides a summary of key points for the reader. Also, for the first time, we have included a Glossary. As before, the Constitution is included, along with a list of the Presidents of the United States and the vote they received.

Once again, a study guide, keyed to the text, is available for those who wish to use it. It has been revised and updated to parallel the changes in the content of the fourth edition.

As the title of this book indicates, the authors recognize that the American political system is under pressure, that its ability to cope with the problems facing the nation is being questioned by many individuals and groups in our society. In such a time, we continue to believe it useful to provide a book that focuses not only on the very considerable achievements of the American system of government but on its shortcomings too—a book that focuses on the reality as well as the rhetoric of American democracy. We have tried to do this in a textbook designed for the '80s.

In writing this book, we set three goals. First, we believe that a textbook should be lively and stimulating to read. So we have attempted to provide a text that is as clear and readable as possible without sacrificing scholarship or content.

Second, although we present American governmental and political institutions in their historical context, we have sought to relate politics and government to contemporary issues. At the same time, we have attempted to relate those contemporary issues to larger concepts. We have also included case studies on a number of topics.

Third, as we have indicated, we have attempted to focus on the gaps, where they exist, between American myths and American realities, between the political system's promise and its performance. Students and other citizens may not be disillusioned with the principles of American democracy, but they do ask that the political system practice those principles.

In examining the structure and processes of American politics and government, we have tried to ask: How is the political system supposed to work? How does it actually work? What might be done to make it work better? Each chapter is organized around a series of basic questions about the workings of the political system. The book does not, in every case, provide ready answers to those questions, but it raises them for the student's consideration and, if desired, for classroom discussion. At the same time, the book emphasizes the importance of each individual citizen for the quality of American society and American government. It provides examples of participation in the political process by students and other citizens. It examines the responsibilities as well as the rights of citizens in a democracy.

The authors deeply appreciate the assistance of the many people who helped to produce this book. We must begin with M. J. Rusk-Pierce, who provided expert research and editorial assistance at every stage in the preparation of the revised manuscript for this fourth edition. We also wish to thank Norma J. Elliott, our principal research assistant for the first edition (1971), and Thomas A. Horne, whose research contribution was also invaluable; Freda F. Solomon, the research assistant for the second edition (1974); and Nancy D. Beers, who provided research and editorial assistance for the third edition (1977). We also wish to express our appreciation to Emily S. Webb, who kept our reference files up to date; to Wayne P. Kelley, Executive Editor and Publisher of *Congressional Quarterly;* to Jean Woy, of the book department of *Congressional Quarterly;* and to John Fox Sullivan, Publisher of the *National Journal.*

We are grateful as well to the many persons who gave us the benefit of their advice and assistance along the way. That list is long, and it includes Frederick L. Holborn, of the School of Advanced International Studies, The Johns Hopkins University; Dom Bonafede, Senior Editor of the *National Journal;* as well as the many other scholars and colleagues whose help was acknowledged in the first and second editions and to whom we remain indebted.

The authors are also grateful to those who read and commented on portions of the book, assisting us in the preparation of the third edition: Henry J. Abraham, University of Virginia; Herbert E. Alexander, Citizens' Research Foundation; W. Lance Bennett, University of Washington; Charles Hamilton, Columbia University; Barbara Hinckley, University of Wisconsin; Robert Lineberry, Northwestern University; Alpheus T. Mason, Princeton University, retired; Frederick C. Mosher, University of Virginia; Daniel Nimmo, University of Tennessee; Judith Parris, Congressional Research Service of the Library of Congress; Michael Reagan, University of California, Riverside; James Sundquist, the Brookings Institution; and H. Bradford Westerfield, Yale University.

For this fourth edition, the authors especially wish to thank the following scholars who offered their comments: Henry J. Abraham, University of Virginia; W. Lance Bennett, University of Washington; Margaret Conway, University of Maryland; George C. Edwards III, Texas A & M University; W. Robert Gump, Miami University; M. Kent Jennings, University of Michigan; Alpheus T. Mason, Princeton University, retired; Daniel Nimmo, University of Tennessee; Robert Peabody, The Johns Hopkins University; Michael Preston, University of Illinois; James Rosenau, University of Southern California; Michael Reagan, University of California, Riverside; Francis Rourke, The Johns Hopkins University; and James Sundquist, The Brookings Institution.

A number of professors teaching the introductory American government course also offered us invaluable chapter-by-chapter comments on the third edition that helped us to plan the fourth edition: Roscoe C. Adkins, North Texas State University; Eugene J. Alpert, Texas Christian University; Kevin E. Bailey, North Harris County College; Dean O. Barnum, Kellogg Community College; John P. Bradley, North Texas State University; Lynn R. Brink, Northlake College; Gary W. Burbridge, Grand Rapids Junior College; Faye Carroll, Western Kentucky University; Greg Casey, University of Missouri, Columbia; Forrest Cook, San Antonio College; C. Jeremy Curtoys, Tarleton State University; Doris Daniels, Nassau Community College; Louise W. Dengler, University of South Alabama; William A. de Rubertis, Los Angeles Pierce College; Brian K. Dille, Odessa College; Howard T. East, Jr., Menlo College; Charles Elliott, East Texas State University; William A. Giles, Mississippi State University; A. O. Grant, Tarleton State University; J. C. Horton, San Antonio College; Frank Kessler, Missouri Western State College; Elias

Kottoulas, Moraine Valley Community College; John E. Lampe, Southwest Texas Junior College; Bob Little, Brookhaven College; William Loiterman, Los Angeles Harbor College; Douglas A. Neal, Northern Virginia Community College; Ted Neima, Los Angeles Pierce College; Charldean Newell, North Texas State University; Jerry C. Petersen, Kellogg Community College; Waino M. Peterson, College of the Sequoias; Donald Ranish; Allen K. Settle, California Polytechnic State University, San Luis Obispo; Robert Sindermann, San Antonio College; Herbert Smith, Western Maryland College; John Smith, Kellogg Community College; David Stroud, Kilgore College; John J. Stuart, Paris Junior College; Richard J. Sullivan, John Tyler Community College; Stanley Thames, North Texas State University; Christopher Thompson, Saint Olaf College; Neal Wise, Saint Edward's University; and Kenneth D. Yeilding, Odessa College. The comments of all these reviewers were consistently helpful; at the same time, responsibility for the final draft, including any errors or shortcomings, is ours.

Finally, we wish to express out thanks to members of the College Department of Harcourt Brace Jovanovich: William A. Pullin, Senior Editor, who first proposed this project to us and gave it his continued support; Everett M. Sims, Director; Eben W. Ludlow, Executive Editor; and Joanne D. Daniels, Political Science Editor, all of whom provided invaluable editorial guidance. We shall always owe a special debt of gratitude to Virginia Joyner, our manuscript editor for the first two editions. For this new edition we are deeply grateful to Susan M. Tuttle, our dedicated and talented manuscript editor, whose skills added greatly to the clarity of the text. This new edition benefited enormously as well from the expert copy editing of Sandra Lifland. Tracy K. Cabanis, Production Manager, efficiently saw the book through the various stages of production. Art editor Elaine Bernstein, with the assistance of Richard Lewis, skillfully supervised the selection of the many photographs in this edition. And designer Harry Rinehart applied his creative talent to integrate the whole, type and graphics, into a result that captures in visual form the spirit and purpose of our examination of *Democracy Under Pressure*.

Milton C. Cummings, Jr.
David Wise

CONTENTS

Part One   The American Democracy

1   GOVERNMENT AND PEOPLE, 4

2   THE CONSTITUTIONAL FRAMEWORK, 26

3   THE FEDERAL SYSTEM, 60

Part Two   Politics U.S.A.

Part Four Government in Operation

Part Five   The American Community

DEMOCRACY UNDER PRESSURE

An Introduction to the American Political System

FOURTH EDITION

Part One

THE AMERICAN DEMOCRACY

GOVERNMENT AND PEOPLE

President and
Mrs. Reagan,
Inauguration Day, 1981

On January 20, 1981, Ronald Reagan raised his right hand and took the oath of office as the fortieth President of the United States.

In the winter sunlight, against the backdrop of the stark, white Capitol dome, the new President stood before the television cameras and the crowd overflowing onto the mall and swore to "preserve, protect, and defend the Constitution of the United States." The words and the ritual were familiar. Yet, the inauguration of Ronald Reagan, who had defeated Jimmy Carter for the Presidency, symbolized more than an ordinary change in the national leadership.

For Reagan's philosophy varied sharply from that of most of his modern predecessors. Once an actor, later governor of California, he was a conservative Republican who promised a new approach to the governing of America. He had been elected on a pledge to reduce the reach and the scope of the federal government in the daily lives of Americans, while increasing the nation's military strength and cutting taxes. These were the themes he emphasized in his inaugural address, which envisioned "an era of national renewal," a government that would "stand by our side, not ride on our back," and a military establishment with "sufficient strength to prevail if need be."[1]

Extraordinary drama surrounded the inauguration of the new President and Vice President George Bush. At 12:25 P.M., as Reagan was concluding his

[1] *New York Times,* January 21, 1981, p. B1.

inaugural address, two jet planes took off from Iran carrying the fifty-two Americans who had been held hostage in that country for 444 days. That night, television viewers in the United States watched the former prisoners debark at a stopover in Algeria, and the next day, Jimmy Carter flew to Wiesbaden, West Germany, to greet them personally.

But there were other reasons, above and beyond the freeing of the hostages and the fact that the voters had chosen a conservative to lead them, that made 1981 different from the past. America's perception of itself was changing. The almost boundless confidence of a nation that had pushed westward to the Pacific across a land of seemingly unlimited resources had given way, by 1981, to a more cautious appraisal of America's ability to solve its problems.

At home, double-digit inflation and high unemployment were impairing the economy and for several years had defied government solutions. The energy crisis was reflected in spiraling prices for gasoline and home heating oil. And

Vice President
George Bush

President Reagan: "Government Is the Problem"

These United States are confronted with an economic affliction of great proportions.

We suffer from the longest and one of the worst sustained inflations in our national history. It distorts our economic decisions, penalizes thrift and crushes the struggling young and the fixed-income elderly alike. It threatens to shatter the lives of millions of our people.

Idle industries have cast workers into unemployment, causing human misery and personal indignity.

Those who do work are denied a fair return for their labor by a tax system which penalizes successful achievement and keeps us from maintaining full productivity.

But great as our tax burden is, it has not kept pace with public spending. For decades we have piled deficit upon deficit, mortgaging our future and our children's future for the temporary convenience of the present. To continue this long trend is to guarantee tremendous social, cultural, political and economic upheavals. . . .

In this present crisis, government is not the solution to our problem; government is the problem. . . . Our government has no power except that granted it by the people. It is time to check and reverse the growth of government which shows signs of having grown beyond the consent of the governed.

It is my intention to curb the size and influence of the federal establishment . . . the federal government did not create the states; the states created the federal government.

Now so there will be no misunderstanding, it is not my intention to do away with government. It is rather to make it work — work with us, not over us; to stand by our side, not ride on our back. . . .

So, with all the creative energy at our command, let us begin an era of national renewal. Let us renew our determination, our courage, and our strength. And let us renew our faith and our hope.

—President Ronald Reagan, Inaugural Address, January 20, 1981.

Inauguration Day, 1981

past shortages demonstrated that Americans could no longer be certain there would always be enough fuel for the family car.

The effect on American society of continued economic problems during a period of declining or scarce resources was not yet clear. But these realities at least raised the questions of whether the political system could cope with the problems facing it, and whether American society would hold together in the face of these strains.

Special interest groups, often well financed and supporting a single issue, seemed more and more a dominant feature of the nation's politics. Indeed, these groups had played a key role in helping to elect President Reagan. They had also helped to elect a Republican-controlled Senate for the first time in more than a quarter of a century. Other trends were visible: the nation's political parties appeared to be declining in importance, and public confidence in the institutions of government was low.

Abroad, American influence and military power, while still enormous, did not always seem capable of being applied effectively. The fifty-two American hostages were finally free, in exchange for an agreement by the United States to unfreeze several billion dollars in Iranian assets. But the Americans had been held in Iran under adverse conditions for more than fourteen months. And, increasingly, Americans realized they were all hostages to the price of oil set by the Organization of Petroleum Exporting Countries (OPEC).

Left: Iran, November 1979: American hostages are seized at U.S. embassy in Teheran. *Right:* January 1981: The freed hostages come home.

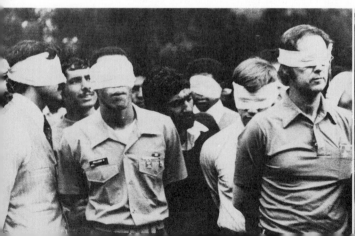

Sheik Ahmed Zaki Yamani, Saudi Arabia's Minister of Petroleum, attends meeting of OPEC nations, 1980.

President Jimmy Carter was the second incumbent Chief Executive in a row to be defeated. Carter himself had ousted President Ford four years before his own loss to Ronald Reagan in 1980.

Had the Presidency become a revolving door, an arena for failure? Had the strains and pressures on the American political system become so great that no President could lead? Was the system unmanageable, the nation ungovernable? The fact that these questions were even being asked reflected the new political atmosphere as the Reagan administration came to power.

B. Kliban from *Tiny Footprints,* Workman

It was a time not only of uncertainty and reappraisal, but of rapid, kaleidoscopic change. Ronald Reagan assumed office at a moment in history when the American nation had passed through an extraordinarily turbulent period of assassination, civil unrest, war, abuse of presidential power, economic distress, and challenges to America's power in the world. The murder of President John F. Kennedy had been followed within two years by explosions of anger in the black areas of the nation's cities, by eight years of war in Vietnam, by the Watergate scandal and the resignation and pardon of Richard Nixon, by the painful

The Limits of Presidential Power

Presidents find it harder and harder to induce foreigners to behave as Americans want them to behave. The President cannot prevent the rise in the price of oil, the fall of Saigon, the revolution in Iran, the invasion of Czechoslovakia or Afghanistan, or any of a dozen other unwelcome shifts in the political situation, here, there, or anywhere in Africa, Asia, or Latin America. . . . Gone are the days when he could impose American standards or values even on friendly countries. He cannot be sure of persuading his European allies to do what he wants. . . . At home, the President cannot seriously hope to persuade Congress to pass more than a wretched fragment of his legislative program, itself carefully

tailored down from what he would have liked to see voted into law in a perfect world. He cannot hope to carry out more than a fraction of the program he campaigned and was elected on. . . . He will be lucky if he can cope with some of the most urgent items on the national agenda. . . . He cannot end inflation. He cannot bring about a serious reduction in energy consumption or make more than a token start on the search for alternative energy sources. Still less can he hope to attack structural social or economic problems. Whether he is liberal or conservative, or even if — as seems increasingly inevitable — he is both at once, he is unlikely to be able to achieve his goals or to fulfill his promises.

—Godfrey Hodgson, *All Things to All Men: The False Promise of the Modern American Presidency.*

Miami, 1980   An American in Vietnam

combination of inflation and unemployment that marked the 1970s and continued into the start of the 1980s, and by the seizure of American hostages in Iran.

The swirling currents of these events, over a period of two decades, had brought change not only to America but to the way that Americans perceived their government and their political system. To some extent, at least, the coming to power of Ronald Reagan coincided with a new national mood.

Some observers saw in Reagan's election, and in the Republican victory in the Senate, a sharp turning to the right by the American electorate. Others interpreted Reagan's election as a vote against the policies of President Carter. Voter discontent with both major-party candidates was high in 1980, so high in fact that it helped to give rise to the independent candidacy of Representative John B. Anderson of Illinois, who received nearly 7 percent of the popular vote.

But in campaigning against the federal government's power over the lives of the people, Reagan had clearly struck a responsive chord. Well before 1980, many liberals and conservatives alike were questioning the effectiveness of government solutions to some social problems. Five decades earlier, President Franklin D. Roosevelt had ushered in an era of great social reform through federal government programs. John F. Kennedy and Lyndon Johnson had followed in his path. But many of the programs of Johnson's "Great Society" had not worked as their architects had envisioned, and in 1980 Reagan successfully assailed the "bureaucracy" and the government in Washington.

Four years earlier, Carter had promised in his campaign to revitalize various federal social programs and to restructure the executive branch. But Carter never won the confidence of the people for a sustained period. He was regarded by many people as a "decent" but ineffective leader. He had been elected as an outsider campaigning against the establishment in Washington. But once in power, he often seemed to lack the experience and the political skills to deal with Congress and the other actors in the capital, including the press and the bureaucracy. Inflation, unemployment, and the Iranian crisis undermined his popularity in the long run, and in the end, he was brought down by another "outsider" who campaigned against the government, much as Carter himself had done in 1976.

Despite the problems facing both individuals and the nation as a whole in the 1980s, there were encouraging signs as well. The American political system had weathered the storm of Watergate, and that great crisis had been resolved within the framework of the Constitution. In the aftermath, at least a measure of reform had occurred; a new campaign finance law had been enacted to try to regulate the abuses of political contributions, and the law also provided for public financing of presidential campaigns. And Congress and the nation had finally begun to shape an energy policy and to focus on the problem of resources for the future.

President Reagan might or might not succeed in achieving his goals and carrying out his campaign promises. But beyond the policies of a particular President, broader questions were raised by the problems experienced by the nation over the past two decades. After some two hundred years, was the American political system capable of meeting the needs of the American people? Were the nation's institutions outmoded and irrelevant to the times? Or was the American democracy still workable and merely being subjected to unusual pressures?

These and other questions will be explored in this book, but first it might be useful to examine the general relationship between people and government in a democratic system.

The Reciprocal Nature of Democratic Power

In July 1945 a small group of scientists stood atop a hill near Alamogordo, New Mexico, and watched the first atomic bomb explode in the desert. At that instant the traditional power of government to alter the lives of people took on a terrifying new dimension. Since the onset of the nuclear age and the development of intercontinental ballistic missiles, people have lived less than thirty minutes away from possible self-destruction. That is all the time it would take for ICBMs to reach their targets, destroying whole cities and perhaps entire nations.

Today, the President of the United States is often described as a person with his finger "on the nuclear button." The existence of such chilling terminology, and of nuclear weapons, reflects the increasingly complex, technological, computerized society in which Americans live. As America has changed through the development of science, technology, and industrialization, government has changed along with it. Government has expanded and grown more complex; it is called on to perform more and more tasks.

Obviously, government can affect the lives of students or other citizens by sending them overseas to fight in a war in which they may be killed. Less obvious, perhaps, are the ways in which government pervades most aspects of daily life, sometimes down to minute details. For example, the federal government regu-

The Impact of Government on People

Wounded American soldiers
in Vietnam

lates the amount of windshield that the wipers on a car must cover and even the *speed* of the windshield wipers. (At the fast setting, wipers must go "at least 45 cycles per minute.")[2]

College students driving to class (perhaps over a highway built largely with federal funds) are expected to observe local traffic regulations. They may have to put a dime in a city parking meter. The classroom in which they sit may have been constructed with a federal grant. Possibly they are attending college with the aid of federal loans or grants made available by the Higher Education Act of 1965. By fiscal 1981, for example, the federal government was spending $4 billion a year on loans and grants to 3.5 million college and graduate students.

Clearly government's impact is real and far-reaching. Americans normally must pay three levels of taxes—local, state, and federal. They attend public schools and perhaps public colleges. They draw unemployment insurance, welfare benefits, Medicare, and social security. They must either obey the laws or pay the penalty of a fine or imprisonment if they break them and are caught and convicted. Their savings accounts and home mortgages are guaranteed by the federal government. Their taxes support the armed forces, police, fire, health, and sanitation departments. To hunt, fish, marry, drive, fly, or build they must have a government license. From birth certificate to death certificate, government accompanies individuals along the way. Even after they die, the government is not through with them. Estate taxes must be collected and wills probated in the courts.

In the United States, "government" is extraordinarily complicated. There are federal, state, and local layers of government, metropolitan areas, commissions, authorities, boards and councils, and quasi-governmental bodies. Many of the units of government overlap. And all have an impact on the lives of individuals.

The Impact
of People
on Government

Just as government affects people, people affect government. The American system of government is based on the concept that power flows from the people to the government. Jefferson expressed this eloquently when he wrote in the Declaration of Independence, "to secure these rights, Governments are instituted among men, deriving their just powers from the consent of the governed." Abraham Lincoln expressed the same thought when he spoke in his

[2] Motor Vehicle Safety Standards 104–3 (1969).

Gettysburg Address of "government of the people, by the people, for the people."

These are ideals, statements embodying the principles of democracy. As we shall note at many points in this book, the principles do not always mesh with the practices. Yet, it remains true that if government in the United States has very real and often awesome powers over people, at the same time people, both individuals and the mass of citizens together, can have considerable power over the government.

The reciprocal nature of democratic power is a basic element of the American political system. As the late V. O. Key, Jr., the distinguished Harvard political scientist, has put it: "The power relationship is reciprocal, and the subject may affect the ruler more profoundly than the ruler affects the subject."[3] Described below are several ways that people influence government.

Voting. The first and most important power of the people in America is the right to vote in free elections to choose those who govern. At regular intervals, the people may, in the classic phrase of Horace Greeley, the nineteenth-century journalist and politician, "turn the rascals out." The fact that a President, member of Congress, governor, mayor, or school board member may want to stand for re-election influences his or her performance in office. The knowledge of officials that they serve at the pleasure of the voters usually tends to make those officials sensitive to public opinion.

But isn't one person's vote insignificant when millions are cast? Not necessarily. That the individual's vote does matter even in a nation as big as the United States has been illustrated many times in close presidential elections.

Presidents are elected by electoral votes, but these are normally cast by the electors in each state for the candidate who wins the most popular votes in the state.[4] In 1960 a shift from John F. Kennedy to Richard M. Nixon of only 9421 voters in Illinois and Missouri would have prevented either candidate from gaining a majority in the electoral college. And in 1968 and 1976 shifts of relatively small numbers of voters in a few states would have changed the outcomes of the presidential elections in those years.

Party Activity. The political party is basic to the American system of government because it provides a vehicle for competition and choice. Without these, "free elections" would be meaningless. For the most part, the two-party system has predominated in the United States. Since candidates for public office, even at the presidential level, are usually selected by their parties, people can influence government, and the choice of who governs, by participating in party activities. Whether political campaigns offer meaningful alternatives on the issues depends in part on who is nominated. And that in turn may be influenced by how many people are politically active. Political participation can take many forms, from ringing doorbells to running for local party committees or for public office.

Public Opinion. Candidates and elected officials are sensitive to what the public is thinking. This has been particularly true since the Second World War when sophisticated methods of political polling and statistical analysis were

Drawing by Stevenson
© 1980 The New Yorker
Magazine, Inc.

"And don't waste your time canvassing the whole building, young man. We all think alike."

[3] V. O. Key, Jr., *Politics, Parties, and Pressure Groups*, 5th ed. (New York: Crowell, 1964), p. 3.
[4] See the description of the electoral college in Chapter 9.

developed. But citizens do not have to wait around to be polled. They can make their opinion felt in a variety of ways: by participating in political activities, talking to other people, writing to their representatives in Congress, telephoning the members of their city council, writing to their newspapers, or testifying at public hearings. Even by reading the newspapers and watching television news broadcasts (or by not doing those things) people may indirectly influence government. A citizen who carefully follows public issues in the news media and magazines of opinion may help to influence government, since a government is less likely to attempt to mislead when it knows it is dealing with an informed public.

Interest Groups. When people belong to groups that share common attitudes and make these views felt, or when they organize such groups, they may be influencing government. These private associations, or interest groups, may be unions, business and professional organizations, racial and religious groups, or organizations of such groups as farmers or veterans. An interest group does not have to be an organized body. Students, for example, constitute a highly vocal interest group, even when they do not belong to a formal student organization.

Direct Action. In the late 1960s and early 1970s, as had happened before in American history, people sought to influence government by civil disobedience and sometimes by militant or violent action. Some civil rights leaders and student activists practiced "the politics of confrontation." The idea of direct and often disruptive action to achieve political ends appeared to have grown in part out of the civil rights movement (beginning with peaceful "sit-ins" to desegregate lunch counters in the South) and in part out of the organized opposition to the war in Vietnam. Demonstrations, marches, sit-ins, campus strikes, picketing, and protest characterized those years. With the end of the war in Vietnam, this type of direct political action diminished considerably, but plainly it could return again if tensions in American society increased.

Direct action: Anti-nuclear demonstration in New York City, 1979

What Is Government?

The words "government," "politics," "power," and "democracy" ought to be clearly defined. The difficulty is that political scientists, philosophers, and kings have never been able to agree entirely on the meanings of these terms.

The ancient Greek philosopher Plato and his pupil Aristotle speculated on their meaning, and the process has continued up to the present day. Bearing in mind that no universal or perfect definitions exist, we can still discuss the words and arrive at a *general* concept of what they mean.

Even in a primitive society, some form of government exists. A tribal chief emerges with authority over others and makes decisions, perhaps in consultation with the elders of the tribe. The tribal leader is governing.

Government

Government, then, even in a modern industrial state, can be defined on a simple level as the individuals, institutions, and processes that make the rules for society and possess the power to enforce them. But rules for what? To take an example, if private developers wish to acquire a wildlife preserve for commercial use, and environmental groups protest, government may be called on to step in and settle the dispute. In short, government makes rules to decide who gets what of valued things in a society.[5] It attempts to resolve conflicts among individuals and groups.

David Easton, a political scientist at the University of Chicago, has written:

Even in the smallest and simplest society someone must intervene in the name of society, with its authority behind him, to decide how differences over valued things are to be resolved.

This authoritative allocation of values is a minimum prerequisite of any society. . . . Every society provides some mechanisms, however rudimentary they may be, for authoritatively resolving differences about the ends that are to be pursued, that is, for deciding who is to get what there is of the desirable things.[6]

Easton's concept has come to be broadly accepted by many scholars today. In highly developed societies the principal mechanism for resolving differences is government. Government makes binding rules for society that determine the distribution of valued things.

Benjamin Disraeli, the nineteenth-century British Prime Minister and novelist, wrote in *Endymion* that "politics are the possession and distribution of power."

Politics

Disraeli's definition of *politics* comes very close to our definition of *government*. Disraeli was ahead of his time, for many political scientists today would agree in general with his definition, and they would add that there is little difference between politics and government.

For example, V. O. Key, Jr., equates politics with "the process and practice

[5] A definition close to that suggested by the title of Harold D. Lasswell's *Politics: Who Gets What, When, How* (New York: McGraw-Hill, 1936).
[6] David Easton, *The Political System, An Inquiry into the State of Political Science* (New York: Knopf, 1953), pp. 136–37.

of ruling" and the "workings of governments generally, their impact on the governed, their manner of operation, the means by which governors attain and retain authority."[7] In other words, politics may be defined as the pursuit and exercise of power.

Such a definition might be confusing to those Americans who tend to look at politics as the pursuit of power, and government as the exercise of power. The conventional notion is that people engage in politics to get elected. But, in fact, those who govern are constantly making *political* decisions. It is very difficult to say where government ends and politics begins. The two terms overlap and intertwine, even if their meanings are not precisely the same.[8]

Power

Boss Tweed

Power is the possession of control over others. People have sought for centuries to understand the basis of power, why it exists, and how it is maintained. Authority over others is a tenuous business, as many a deposed South American dictator can attest.

A century ago Boss Tweed, the leader of Tammany Hall, the Democratic party machine in New York City, reportedly expressed a simple, cynical philosophy, "The way to have power is to take it." But once acquired, power must be defended against others who desire it. For seven years Nikita Khrushchev appeared to be the unquestioned ruler of the Soviet Union. One day in October 1964, he was summoned back to Moscow from his Black Sea vacation retreat and informed by his colleagues in the Presidium of the Communist party that he was no longer Premier of the Soviet Union. It was reported that those who deposed him changed all the confidential government and party telephone numbers in Moscow, so that Khrushchev could not attempt to rally support among elements still loyal to him.[9] Khrushchev was helpless, cut off from the tremendous power that was his only twenty-four hours before.

It is a truism that power is often destructive of those who hold it. Lord Acton, nineteenth-century British peer and historian, said that "power tends to corrupt and absolute power corrupts absolutely." The eighteenth-century French philosopher Montesquieu expressed a similar idea in *The Spirit of the Laws:* "Every man who has power is impelled to abuse it."

As Key has observed, power is not something that can be "poured into a keg, stored, and drawn upon as the need arises."[10] Power, Key notes, is *relational*—that is, it involves the interactions between the person who exercises power and those affected by that exercise of power.

If people, even in a primitive state, find it necessary to accept rulers who can authoritatively decide who gets what, then it follows that whoever governs possesses and exercises power in part because of that position. In other words, power follows office. To some extent, we accept the power exercised over us by others because we recognize the need to be governed.

[7] Key, *Politics, Parties, and Pressure Groups,* p. 2.
[8] Of course, the word "politics" can also refer to a process that occurs in a wide variety of nongovernmental settings—in fact, in every form of social organization where different people, with competing goals and differing objectives, interact. Thus, one sometimes speaks of politics in the local PTA, the politics of a garden club, or the politics in the newsroom of a campus newspaper. In this book, however, we are talking about politics as it is more commonly understood, in its governmental setting.
[9] *Observer* (London), November 29, 1964, p. 2.
[10] Key, *Politics, Parties, and Pressure Groups,* p. 2.

Democracy is a word that comes from two Greek roots, *demos,* the populace, and *kratia,* rule—taken together, rule by the people.[11] The Greeks used the term to describe the government of Athens and other Greek city-states that flourished in the fifth century B.C. In his famous *Funeral Oration,* Pericles, the Athenian statesman, declared: "Our constitution is named a democracy, because it is in the hands not of the few, but of the many."

All governments make decisions about the distribution of valued things. As was noted earlier, in a democratic government, power, in theory, flows from the people as a whole. This is one of the ideals on which the American democracy was founded. But the United States is too big for every citizen to take part in the deliberations of government, as in ancient Athens, so the distinction is sometimes made that America is a *representative* democracy rather than a direct one. Leaders are elected to speak for and represent the people.

Government by the people also carries with it the concept of *majority rule.* Everyone is free to vote, but normally whoever gets the most votes wins the election and represents *all* the people, including those who voted for the losing candidate. But in a system that is truly democratic, minority rights and views are also recognized and protected.

Every schoolchild knows the phrase from the Declaration of Independence, "We hold these truths to be self-evident, that all men are created equal." The concept of *equality*—that all people are of equal worth, even if not of equal ability—is also basic to American democracy. So are basic *rights* such as freedom of speech, press, religion, assembly, the right to vote, and the right to dissent

[11] There are, of course, many possible definitions of the word "democracy." The Greek word *demos* meant the populace, or the common people; hence democracy in this sense means government by the mass of people, as distinguished from those with special rank or status.

from majority opinion. The idea of *individual dignity* and the importance of each individual is another concept basic to American democracy. And, American government is *constitutional*—the power of government is limited by a framework of fundamental written law. Under such a government—in theory—the police power of the state should not be used illegally to punish individuals or to repress dissent.

These are the ideals, noble, even beautiful, in their conception. But, this is not always what really happens. Blacks and other minorities in America are still struggling for full equality; a person may dissent from the dominant political view but lose his or her job as the price of nonconformity; the probing questions asked of people on welfare may leave them with little individual dignity; the police sometimes have their own views on freedom of assembly; and, as the Watergate scandal revealed, the White House committed many abuses in the name of national security.

American democracy is far from perfect. "This is a great country," President John F. Kennedy once declared, "but it must be greater."[12] Every American has to judge for herself or himself how far America falls short of fulfilling the principles on which it was founded. Nevertheless, the ideas endure; the goals are there if not always the reality.

The Concept of a Political System

In today's electronic world, most people have listened to a stereo. Suppose for a moment that a visitor from outer space dropped in and asked you to describe a stereo set. You might say, "This is a turntable, this thing with all the knobs is an amplifier, and these big boxes over here are what we call speakers." Perhaps you might take the trouble to describe the details of each component at some length. At the end of your elaborate explanation, the visitor from space would still not know what a stereo was.

A better way to describe the set would be to explain that it is a *system for the reproduction of sound,* consisting of several parts, each of which performs a separate function and relates to the others. Having said that, you might turn on the stereo and play a record. Now the visitor would understand.

A Dynamic Approach

In the same way, it is possible either to describe people, government, politics, and power as isolated, static elements, or to look at them as interacting elements in a *political system.* The concept of a political system may provide a useful framework, or approach, for understanding the total subject matter of this book. Just as in the case of the stereo system, a political system consists of several parts that relate to one another, each of which performs a separate, vital function. If we think in terms of a system, we visualize all the pieces in motion, acting and interacting, dynamic rather than static. In other words, something is happening—just as when the record is playing.

[12] "Remarks of Senator John F. Kennedy, Street Rally, Waterbury, Connecticut, Novermber 6, 1960," in *The Speeches of Senator John F. Kennedy, Presidential Campaign of 1960* (Washington, D.C.: U.S. Government Printing Office, 1961), p. 912.

As David Easton says, "we can try to understand political life by viewing each of its aspects piecemeal," or we can "view political life as a system of interrelated activities."[13] One of the problems of trying to look at a political system is that government and politics do not exist in a vacuum — they are embedded in, and closely related to, many other activities in a society. But it is possible to separate political activity from other kinds of activity, at least for purposes of study.

Just as the stereo is a system for the reproduction of sound, a political system also operates for a purpose: it makes the binding, authoritative decisions for society about who gets what.

We may carry the analogy of a stereo to a political system even further. A sound system has *inputs, outputs,* and sometimes a loud whistling noise called *feedback.* Those are precisely the same terms used by political scientists in talking about a political system.

Inputs, Outputs, and Feedback

The *inputs* of a political system are of two kinds: demands and supports.

"Demands," as the word indicates, are what people and groups want from the system, whether it be health care for the aged, loans and grants for college students, equal opportunity for minorities, or higher subsidies for farmers.

"Supports" are the attitudes and actions of people that sustain and buttress the system at all levels and allow it to continue to work. They include everything from the patriotism drilled into schoolchildren to public backing for specific government policies.

The *outputs* of a political system are chiefly the binding decisions it makes, whether in the form of laws, regulations, or judicial decisions. Often such decisions reward one segment of society at the expense of another. The millionaire dowager on New York's Park Avenue may be heavily taxed to clothe slum children on the South Side of Chicago. Or she may benefit from a tax loophole enacted by Congress for the rich and pay no taxes at all. The freeway that runs through an urban ghetto may speed white commuters from the suburbs but dislocate black residents of the inner city. These decisions are "redistributive" measures in that something of value is reallocated by the political system. Sometimes even a decision *not* to act is an output of a political system. By preserving an existing policy, one group may be rewarded while another group is not.

Feedback in a political system describes the response of the rest of society to the decisions made by the authorities. When those reactions are communicated back to the authorities, they may lead to a fresh round of decisions and new public responses.

The concept of a political system is simply a way of looking at political activity. It is an approach, an analytical tool, rather than a general theory of the type developed to explain the workings of scientific phenomena. It enables us to examine not only the formal structure of political and governmental institutions, but also how these institutions actually work.

[13] David Easton, "An Approach to the Analysis of Political Systems," *World Politics,* Vol. 9 (April 1957), pp. 383–84. Our discussion of the concept of a political system relies chiefly on Easton's work, although it should not be read as a literal summary of his approach. For example, the analogy to a stereo system is the authors' own; and Easton's analysis of a political system is both much more detailed and broader in scope than the outline presented here.

Public Policymaking

There is a tendency in the study of American politics and government to concentrate on the institutions of government, such as the Presidency, Congress, and the courts, and on the role of political parties, campaigns, and voters.

The *analysis of public policy* is another way of looking at government and politics. Instead of examining only institutions, policy analysis looks at what the institutions do.

A policy is a course of action decided upon by a government—or by any organization, group, or individual. It involves *a choice among competing alternatives.* When policies are shaped by government officials, the result is called *public policy.*

The analysis of public policy, therefore, focuses on how choices are arrived at and how public policy is made. It also focuses on what happens afterward. How well or badly is a policy carried out? What is its impact in its own domain? And what effect does it have in other policy areas?

As Robert L. Lineberry has put it, policy analysts "focus, in systems language, on the outputs of the political system and their impact on the political, social, and economic environment."[14] But as Lineberry and other scholars have pointed out, if a problem does not get on the *public agenda*—the subjects that government policymakers try to deal with—no policy or output will be framed to deal with the problem. "Political issues emerge from contending definitions of a policy problem."[15] Thus, some people feel marijuana should be legalized, but unless a federal or state government acts, its possession and sale remain illegal.

But what happens when an issue does get on the public agenda and results in the creation of a public policy? Sometimes nothing. In 1964 President Lyndon Johnson declared his "war on poverty." A major new federal program was launched to try to deal with the problem. But almost two decades later, poverty had not been eradicated, or even dramatically reduced, in America.

"Bills are passed, White House Rose Garden ceremonies held, and gift pens passed around by the President. At that point, when attention has waned, when the television cameras are gone and the reporters no longer present, the other face of policy emerges."[16] This second face of policy analysis, as Lineberry has suggested, is concerned with *implementation, impact,* and *distribution.*

Implementation is the action, or actions, taken by government to carry out a policy. "When policy is pronounced, the implementation process begins. What happens in it may, over the long run, have far more impact . . . than the intentions of the policy's framers."[17]

The *impact* of a policy can be measured in terms of its consequences, both in its immediate policy area and in other areas. For example, a government decision to combat inflation by tightening credit and raising interest rates may result in the closing of automobile plants and worker layoffs because consumers have less money to use to buy cars. (The closing of the auto plants may, in turn, lead to layoffs in the steel industry, since steel is a major supplier of the auto industry.)

[14] Robert L. Lineberry, *American Public Policy: What Government Does and What Difference It Makes* (New York: Harper & Row, 1977), p. 3.
[15] *Ibid.,* p. 24.
[16] *Ibid.,* p. 69.
[17] *Ibid.,* p. 71.

Distribution is concerned with the question of who wins and who loses from a given public policy. When the government builds post offices or maintains national parks, its policies are distributive, and people assume that everyone benefits. But a *re*distributive policy takes something away from one person and gives it to someone else. A welfare program that taxes more affluent members of society to assist the poor would be an example of such a policy. It is here in the area of redistributive policies that many of the major political battles are fought.

Public policies and policymaking are discussed throughout this book, and are the subject, in particular, of Part Four, "Government in Operation."

Democratic Government and a Changing Society

A political system relates to people, and the size of the population affects the outputs of the system. Of equal importance is the qualitative nature of the population: who they are, where they live, how they work, how they spend, how they move about. How the political system works, in other words, is affected to some extent by the surrounding social, economic, and cultural framework. As society changes, the responses of government are likely to change. Government reacts to basic alterations in the nature of a society; it tries to tailor programs and decision making to meet changing needs and demands. Population changes are also important politically; for example, the 1980 census data confirmed that the American population balance had shifted dramatically from the Northeast to the South and West. As a result, Southern and Western states were expected to gain about seventeen seats in Congress in 1982.

226,000,000 Americans

In 1980 federal census takers fanned out across America, counting the population, as the Constitution requires every ten years. By the end of the year, 226.5 million people had been counted. The Census Bureau estimates that by the year 2000 the figure may conceivably rise as high as 283 million.[18]

According to one study of population patterns in the United States, if the projections of some experts were realized, "we would have close to *one billion* people in the United States one hundred years from now."[19] Although the authors of the study add that birth control and other factors make it unlikely that such a staggering total will be reached by that time, they estimate that the United States *could* support a population of one billion without people pushing one another into the ocean.

How the nation has expanded from a population of about 4 million in 1790, and what the future may hold, can be charted with Census Bureau statistics and projections to the year 2000, as shown in Table 1-1.

This dramatic increase in numbers of people — the "population explosion" — is taking place around the world. It raises questions that governments must

[18] U.S. Bureau of the Census, *Current Population Reports,* Projections of the Population of the United States: 1977 to 2050, Series P-25, No. 704, July 1977, p. 3.
[19] Ben J. Wattenberg in collaboration with Richard M. Scammon, *This U.S.A.* (New York: Doubleday, 1965), p. 18. Population projections have been lowered since this study was published.

Profile of the United States Population, 1790–2000

Table 1–1

| | Population (in millions) | | | | | | |
| | Actual | | | | | Projected | |
	1790	1870	1920	1960	1970	1980	2000
Total population	4	39	106	179	203	226.5†	260
Urban	—*	10	54	125	149	NA‡	NA
Rural	4	29	52	54	54	NA	NA
Nonwhite	1	5	11	20	25	31	41
White	3	34	95	159	178	192	219
Median age (years)	NA	20	25	30	28.1	30	36
Primary and secondary school enrollment	NA	7	23	42	53	47	NA
College enrollment	NA	—*	.6	3	7	10	NA

* Less than 200,000.
† Actual.
‡ NA: Not Available.
Source: U.S. Bureau of the Census. Projected totals are the most likely estimates as of 1977. Population figures rounded.

ponder. Will there be enough food to eat? Enough room to live? Enough oil and other natural resources to meet humanity's future needs? Will the environment be destroyed?

An interesting profile of the American public can be sketched with statistics that answer the question "Who are we?" (See Table 1-2.) A portrait of national origins can also be drawn. The great successive waves of immigration placed a stamp of diversity on America; even third- and fourth-generation Americans may think of themselves as "Irish" or "Italian." A 1973 census survey indi-

Who Are We?*

Table 1–2

113.9 million	females
108.2 million	males
16.0 million	under five years
24.9 million	sixty-five and over
191.6 million	white
30.6 million	nonwhite
123.0 million†	married, divorced, or widowed
160.2 million	old enough to vote
10.0 million†	in college
47.9 million†	in other schools
49.3 million†	white-collar workers
32.1 million†	blue-collar workers
145.4 million†	urban dwellers
50.3 million‡	homeowners

* Projected data for 1980 except as otherwise noted.
† Data for 1979.
‡ Data for 1978.
Source: U.S. Bureau of the Census.

cated that the national origin of Americans includes the following countries: Great Britain, 14.4 percent; Germany, 12.5 percent; Ireland, 8 percent; Spain, 4.5 percent; Italy, 4.3 percent; France, 2.6 percent; Poland 2.5 percent; and Russia, 1.1 percent.[20]

The United States is also a nation of more than 73 million Protestants, 49.6 million Catholics, and 5.8 million Jews.[21] Sometimes, prevailing notions about America's population are incorrect. For example, we are generally thought to be a nation of white, Anglo-Saxon Protestants. That group is influential in many areas of our national life. But as the national origin figures indicate, a majority of Americans stem from other than Anglo-Saxon stock.[22]

Although the accent in America is on youth, the median age of Americans is not eighteen or twenty-one but about thirty, and likely to go up as a result of a decline in the birth rate during the 1960s, combined with greater life expectancy.

A political system reacts not only to shifts in population totals but also to the *movement* of people, geographically, socially, and economically.

The Mobile Society

For example, farm population declined from 30.5 million in 1930 to a little more than 8 million in 1978.[23] As the nation changed from a predominantly rural to an urban society (see Table 1-1), the importance of the "farm bloc" decreased. By the 1980s Congress, although still concerned with price supports for wheat, was focusing more of its attention on such issues as sources of energy and defense spending.

Americans move about a great deal. According to the Census Bureau, about 18 percent of Americans change their residence each year. In 1964 California surpassed New York as the most populous state in the Union. As a result, presidential candidates now spend more time than they used to campaigning in California. And in three of four recent presidential years, 1968, 1972, and 1980, Californians were elected President.

During and after the Second World War, as blacks migrated to Northern cities, many whites in the central cities were moving to the suburbs. All these shifts and changing population patterns affect the American political system. The migration of millions of black citizens to Northern cities resulted in the election of black mayors in several large cities by the mid-1970s and in the election of more black members of Congress. And the population shift from the cities to the suburbs increased the political power of suburbia. More members of Congress and state legislators now represent suburban areas than in the past, because lawmakers are apportioned according to population.

[20] Citizens of these origins made up 49.9 percent of the total United States population. In addition, 41.6 percent of the population was classified as "other," and 8.6 percent as not reporting. Under "other" the Census Bureau included persons of mixed national origin, blacks, Asians, American Indians, and all countries not listed above. Source: U.S. Bureau of the Census, *Current Population Reports,* Characteristics of the Population by Ethnic Origin: March 1972 and 1971, Series P–20, No. 249, p. 19.

[21] The Census Bureau does not ask the religion of Americans in the decennial census, which has been taken every ten years in years that end in zero, but religious groups estimate their own membership. These are rounded figures based on the *Yearbook of American and Canadian Churches, 1980,* Constant H. Jacquet, Jr., ed. (Nashville, Tenn.: Abingdon Press, 1980).

[22] See Wattenberg and Scammon, *This U.S.A.,* pp. 45–46.

[23] U.S. Bureau of the Census, *Statistical Abstract of the United States: 1979* (Washington, D.C.: U.S. Government Printing Office, 1979), p. 681.

Technological, Economic, and Social Change

In addition to the population explosion, America has experienced a knowledge explosion. Science and technology, computers, electronics, and high-speed communications are reshaping American society. We have split the atom and traveled to the moon and back. We listen for signals from other galaxies in outer space, and explore the inner space of the human brain. There appear to be no limits to technological potential—except the inability of human beings to control their own nature.

Technological change is soon reflected within the political system. Consider for a moment a single innovation of the electronic age: television. Prior to the Second World War, television did not exist for the mass of Americans. Today, political candidates spend millions of dollars to purchase television time. Presidential nominees may deplore the "packaging" of political candidates by Madison Avenue, but they hire advertising agencies to do just that. Commercials are produced and Presidents and candidates sold in the manner of detergents.

A considerable amount of the technology of the electronic age is the by-product of defense research and development. In his farewell address to the nation in 1961, President Eisenhower, although himself a career soldier, warned of the dangers to liberty and democracy of the "military-industrial complex." What Eisenhower feared was that the Pentagon and the defense contractors who produce weapons for the military would gain "unwarranted influence" in the political system.

In the view of economist John Kenneth Galbraith, there already exists a "close fusion of the industrial system with the state," and in time "the line between the two will disappear." As a result of the technological revolution, Galbraith contends, a few hundred huge corporations are shaping the goals of society as a whole.[24] But government, too, exercises great power in the modern industrial state. Government is expected to help prevent either periodic economic recession or depression. Although economists argue over the best

[24] John Kenneth Galbraith, *The New Industrial State* (Boston: Houghton Mifflin, 1967), pp. 7–9, 392–93.

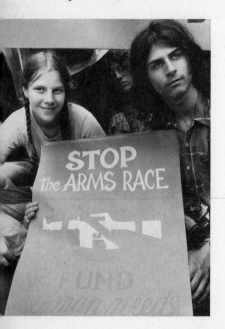

The space shuttle:
". . . no limits to technological potential . . ."

"And I say one bomb is worth a thousand words."

Drawing by Dana Fradon
© 1980 The New Yorker Magazine, Inc.

methods of managing the economy, they generally agree that the government has the major responsibility in promoting prosperity and full employment.

The past two decades have also been a time of rapid social change in America. At almost every level, wherever one looks, the change is visible — in manners and morals, in civil rights, in the increased emphasis on youth, in the theater, in literature, and in the arts. These social changes have been accompanied by new political concerns. By the 1970s and 1980s, increasing numbers of people were disturbed over the pollution of the natural environment that has resulted from technological advance. Many American cities are blanketed in smog. Some rivers are cleaner as a result of environmental legislation, but many are polluted by industrial and human waste. Pesticides are killing our wildlife.[25] Oil spills from tankers and offshore drilling are fouling our beaches. The gasoline engine, power plants, and other industries pour smoke and chemicals into the atmosphere.

It is not only a matter of esthetics, of preserving the natural beauty of the land. Air and water pollution damage health and upset the delicate balance of nature, the total relationship between human beings and their environment. They raise serious questions about whether humanity will be able to survive the damage it is inflicting on the earth that sustains all life.[26]

The energy crisis, and the fuel shortage experienced during the winter of 1973–1974 and again in 1979, underscored the fact that environmental problems are, in the end, political problems. They pose for America questions of priorities and values. For example, are people willing to use their cars less to conserve energy and reduce pollution? Do voters favor relaxation of environmental standards to increase the supply of oil and other energy sources? Thus the environment and the energy shortage have created conflicting choices for individual citizens, for political leaders, and for society as a whole.

There were many other areas of conflict and change. Back in the 1960s, for example, to any white American who cared to listen, the message of the times was clear: black Americans would wait no longer to obtain the equality and freedom that are the right of everyone under the American political system. This was the message preached peacefully by Dr. Martin Luther King, Jr., and expressed violently in the burning black ghettos of the nation's cities.

[25] See Rachel Carson, *Silent Spring* (Boston: Houghton Mifflin, 1962).
[26] We shall examine the problem of environmental pollution in more detail in Chapter 15.

It is not possible to discuss or even list in a few pages all the social, economic, and cultural factors that are influencing the American political system in the 1980s. Suggested here are simply some of the major changes, currents, and conflicts that have placed enormous pressures on American democracy. In later chapters, these will be taken up in more detail.

The Consent of the Governed

One of the characteristics of a viable political system is that it adapts to change. More than 200 years after its creation, the ability of the American political system to adapt to relentless change, and to cope with political crisis, was being severely tested.

Vietnam and Watergate were followed by a new atmosphere of questioning of presidential power by the public and by Congress. That kind of questioning is appropriate in a democracy. President Kennedy declared, in a speech at Amherst College in 1963, less than a month before his death, "men who create power make an indispensable contribution to the Nation's greatness, but the men who question power make a contribution just as indispensable."[27]

And yet, by the 1980s, Americans were also asking whether the Presidency was strong enough to govern. No one could predict what the Reagan-Bush years would mean for America. But the consent of the governed, to be freely given, required that the nation's political leaders earn and merit the trust of the people. In the long afternoon shadows of the twentieth century, such a bond of trust appeared to offer the best hope for the survival in America of democracy, a system that Winston S. Churchill once described as "the worst form of government except all those other forms that have been tried from time to time."[28]

[27] John F. Kennedy, "Remarks at Amherst College," October 26, 1963, in *Public Papers of the Presidents of the United States, John F. Kennedy, 1963* (Washington, D.C.: U.S. Government Printing Office, 1964), p. 816.

[28] *Parliamentary Debates,* House of Commons, Fifth Series, Vol. 444 (London: His Majesty's Stationery Office, 1947), pp. 206–07.

"Then we agree! We're doing the best job that can be done considering that the country's ungovernable."

Drawing by Dana Fradon
© 1978 The New Yorker Magazine, Inc.

Easton, David. *The Political System: An Inquiry into the State of Political Science,* 2nd edition* (Knopf, 1971). (Originally published in 1953.) The first edition was an early statement of the systems approach to the study of politics developed by Easton. See also his *A Framework for Political Analysis** (University of Chicago Press, 1979) and *A Systems Analysis of Political Life** (University of Chicago Press, 1979).

Galbraith, John Kenneth. *The New Industrial State,* 3rd edition* (Houghton Mifflin, 1978). A very readable account of changes in the nature and role of the large corporation in the modern state. These changes, Galbraith argues, have had a major effect on political and social life in highly industrialized countries such as the United States.

Helfrich, Harold W., Jr., ed. *The Environmental Crisis** (Yale University Press, 1970). A series of essays, written by authorities in a variety of fields, examining problems of ecology, including air and water pollution and population growth.

Key, V. O., Jr. *Public Opinion and American Democracy* (Philadelphia Book Company, 1961). An important work in which the pre-1961 findings concerning public opinion and mass attitudes toward politics are analyzed in terms of their consequences for the actual workings of government.

* Available in paperback edition

Lineberry, Robert L. *American Public Policy: What Government Does and What Difference It Makes** (Harper & Row, 1977). A lucid, concise analysis of the making of public policy, its implementation, and its impact. Provides a useful introduction to policy analysis, illustrated by specific case studies.

Nicholas, H. G. *The Nature of American Politics** (Oxford University Press, 1980). A survey of major features of the American political system, written by a perceptive English observer. Contains a thoughtful discussion of what the author identifies as the special national style of politics in America.

Schattschneider, Elmer E. *The Semisovereign People** (Holt, Rinehart and Winston, 1975). (Originally published in 1960.) A lively and revealing analysis of the role of American interest groups and political parties in bringing public demands to bear on political officials.

Tocqueville, Alexis de. *Democracy in America,* Phillips Bradley, ed. (Vintage Books, 1945). (Available in many editions.) A classic analysis of American political and social life as seen through the eyes of a nineteenth-century French observer.

Wattenberg, Ben J. *The Real America** (Doubleday, 1974). A provocative and interesting examination of economic and social trends in American society, based on a detailed analysis of the 1970 census data.

THE CONSTITUTIONAL FRAMEWORK

Every evening in Washington an unusual ceremony takes place in the great domed Exhibition Hall of the National Archives. There, beneath a gold eagle in the ornate hall, are displayed the Declaration of Independence, the Constitution, and the Bill of Rights. The faded parchments are sealed in protective bronze and glass cases containing helium and a small amount of water vapor for preservation.

When the last visitor has left the building, a guard pushes a button. With a great whirring noise, the documents slowly sink into the floor. An electric mechanism gently lowers them into a "fireproof, bombproof vault" of steel and reinforced concrete twenty feet below. A massive lid clangs shut and the documents are safely put to bed for the night. The whole eerie process takes one minute.

Ideas, of course, cannot be preserved in a vault, but documents can. The documents, and the mystique that surrounds them, are part of what Daniel J. Boorstin has called the "search for symbols."[1] The quest for national identity, in which such symbols play a role, is a continuing process in America.

But the Constitution is much more than a symbol. The Constitution established the basic structure of the American government and a *written set of rules* to control the conduct of that government; in its own words, the Constitution is

[1] Daniel J. Boorstin, *The Americans: The National Experience* (New York: Random House, 1965), pp. 325ff.

"the supreme Law of the Land." The United States was, in fact, the first nation to have a written constitution. It is a charter that has been continually adapted to new problems, principally through amendment and judicial interpretation by the Supreme Court—changes that often reflect the prevailing political climate.

Yet, today, the American political system is sometimes attacked for what its critics see as a failure to respond to urgent national problems. The growth of presidential power in the twentieth century, the use of the machinery of the executive branch against political enemies—symbolized by the Watergate scandal—and the resignation of a President under threat of impeachment have, in recent years, placed great strains on the system of constitutional government. Even though the Constitution is reinterpreted to meet changed conditions, does that process take place fast enough? Is the constitutional framework that was constructed in 1787 sufficiently flexible to meet the needs of a complex, urban society in the 1980s? Why, for example, did it take nearly one hundred years after the Civil War for the Supreme Court to apply the Constitution to outlaw racial discrimination in public accommodations? Or why did 131 years pass after the nation was founded before the Constitution recognized the right of women to vote?

We will be exploring these questions, and such others as: Who were the framers of the Constitution? What political ideas influenced them? Were they merely interested in protecting their own economic position? What political bargains were struck by the framers? Why does the United States have a federal system of government, and what does that mean? How did the Supreme Court acquire its power to interpret the Constitution? How does the Constitution affect people's lives in the 1980s?

The Constitution and the Declaration of Independence

The lines began to form before dawn outside the Supreme Court of the United States on July 24, 1974. The spectators were there to hear arguments in one of the most momentous cases to come before the Court in modern times. The very name of the case, *United States* v. *Nixon,* captured the essence of the drama.

The highest tribunal in the land was meeting to decide whether President Richard Nixon must turn over the tape recordings of sixty-four White House

The Constitution Today

conversations for use in the criminal trial of his former subordinates. They had been charged with covering up the Watergate burglary, in which a group of men working for the re-election of Nixon, a Republican, had broken into the Democratic party's headquarters in the Watergate office building in Washington in 1972. During Senate hearings on the affair, the nation was startled to learn that Nixon had secretly tape-recorded his conversations in the Oval Office. Now those tape recordings had become the battleground of his struggle to remain in power, for Nixon knew that they contained proof that he had participated in the cover-up. Even as the Supreme Court met, the Committee on the Judiciary of the House of Representatives was preparing to begin debate on the articles of impeachment of the President. Nor was it entirely certain that if the Court ruled that Nixon must yield the tapes, he would obey.

The chamber of the Supreme Court was packed as Chief Justice Warren Burger began reading the historic 8–0 opinion.[2] He spoke in a soft voice, but his words were like drumbeats to a listening nation. For the first time, the Court recognized the claim of "executive privilege," which Nixon had invoked in refusing to turn over the tape recordings to the Watergate special prosecutor. But the Court held that "neither the doctrine of separation of powers, nor the need for confidentiality of high-level communications" gave the Chief Executive "an absolute, unqualified presidential privilege of immunity" under all circumstances. Nixon was not basing his claim of privilege on the grounds that the tapes contained "military or diplomatic secrets." Permitting a President to withhold evidence "that is demonstrably relevant in a criminal trial would cut deeply into the guarantee of due process of law." Executive privilege must therefore yield to the "specific need for evidence in a pending criminal trial." Nixon, the Court held, must give up the tapes.

Chief Justice Burger—who had been appointed by Nixon—reaffirmed that it was the role of the Supreme Court to interpret the law and resolve conflicts between the branches of government. He reached back 171 years and quoted the celebrated case of *Marbury* v. *Madison,* in which the Court had ruled that it was the duty of the Supreme Court "to say what the law is."[3]

For eight hours the President at his home in California would not say whether he would obey the unanimous ruling of the justices.[4] Then his attorney, James D. St. Clair, announced that the President would comply with the decision "in all respects." The President would obey the Supreme Court.

One of the tapes included the President's conversations of June 23, 1972, in which he had personally ordered the cover-up of the Watergate break-in. Less than two weeks after the Supreme Court's ruling, Nixon released the transcripts of this tape. Four days later, on August 9, 1974, Richard Nixon became the first President of the United States to resign his office.

The rule of law had prevailed and a President had relinquished his power because the Supreme Court in 1974 interpreted the Constitution to mean that even the most powerful official in the land could not withhold evidence from a criminal trial. The case arose and was decided within the overall framework of the Constitution.

August 9, 1974: Richard Nixon prepares to leave the White House after announcing his resignation.

[2] *United States* v. *Nixon,* 418 U.S. 683 (1974).
[3] *Marbury* v. *Madison,* 1 Cranch 137 (1803).
[4] Justice William H. Rehnquist, whom Nixon had appointed to the Court, disqualified himself and did not take part in the decision because he had served in the Justice Department under Attorney General John N. Mitchell, one of the defendants in the cover-up trial.

School busing in Boston, 1974   Allan Bakke in medical school

The Constitution directly affects many other facets of American life and politics. When in 1954 the Supreme Court outlawed officially supported segregation in the public schools, it did so on the grounds that "separate-but-equal" schools violated the Constitution.[5] The enforcement of that constitutional decision—particularly as it related to the busing of schoolchildren—was still being contested in the political arena and the courts in the 1980s.

Abortion, another controversial political issue, has also been affected by Supreme Court rulings. In 1973 the Supreme Court ruled that state laws restricting abortions during the first three months of pregnancy were unconstitutional.[6] The Constitution, the Court held, recognized certain areas of personal privacy that government could not regulate. (The Court's rulings on abortion are discussed on pp. 107, 147–49.)

Five years later, the Court upheld college admission programs that helped remedy past discrimination by giving preference to blacks and other minorities. Properly drawn "affirmative action" programs did not violate the Constitution, the Court ruled in the historic *Bakke* case.[7]

As these selected examples illustrate, constitutional government affects the quality of American society here and now, today and tomorrow. Yet it is a story that has been unfolding for two centuries; it began, as much as anywhere, in the city of Philadelphia in June 1776.

[5] *Brown* v. *Board of Education of Topeka et al.,* 347 U.S. 483 (1954).
[6] *Roe* v. *Wade,* 410 U.S. 113 (1973); *Doe* v. *Bolton,* 410 U.S. 179 (1973).
[7] *Regents of the University of California* v. *Allan Bakke,* 438 U.S. 265 (1978).

Jefferson's draft of the Declaration of Independence originally included an attack on slavery, and sought to blame that "execrable commerce" on King George III. But the Continental Congress cut the passage out of the final document in deference to the wishes of South Carolina and Georgia, and, Jefferson suspected, those Northerners who profited from carrying slaves in their ships. Had the passage remained in, the Declaration would have included these words:

he has waged cruel war against human nature itself, violating it's most sacred rights of life &

liberty in the persons of a distant people who never offended him, captivating & carrying them into slavery in another hemisphere, or to incure miserable death in their transportation thither. This piratical warfare, the opprobrium of infidel *powers, is the warfare of the* Christian *king of Great Britain.* Determined to keep open a market where MEN should be bought & sold. . . . *suppressing every legislative attempt to prohibit or to restrain this execrable commerce . . . he is now exciting those very people to rise in arms among us, and to purchase that liberty of which* he *has deprived them, by murdering the people upon whom* he *also obtruded.*

—Carl L. Becker, *The Declaration of Independence.*

We Hold
These Truths . . .

Early in May 1776, Thomas Jefferson rode down the mountain on horseback from Monticello, his Virginia home, and headed north to take his seat in the Continental Congress at Philadelphia. It had been just over a year since the guns blazed at Lexington and Concord, but the thirteen American colonies, although at war, were still under the jurisdiction of the British crown.

Independence was in the air, however, nourished by the words of an Englishman only recently arrived in America. His name was Thomas Paine, and his pamphlet, *Common Sense,* attacked George III, the British monarch, as the "Royal Brute." Paine's fiery words stirred the colonies.

On June 7 Richard Henry Lee, one of Jefferson's fellow delegates from Virginia, introduced a resolution declaring that the colonies "are, and of right ought to be, free and independent States." Four days later, after impassioned debate, the Continental Congress appointed a committee of five, including Jefferson, to "prepare a declaration."

At thirty-three Jefferson was already known, in the words of John Adams of Massachusetts, as a man with a "peculiar felicity of expression," and the task of writing the declaration fell to him. Jefferson completed his draft in about two

Left: Thomas Jefferson. *Right:* Jefferson composed the first draft of the Declaration of Independence on this portable writing desk.

weeks. Sitting in the second-floor parlor of the house of Jacob Graff, Jr., a German bricklayer, Jefferson composed some of the most enduring words in the English language. His draft, edited somewhat by Benjamin Franklin and John Adams, was submitted on June 28.

On July 2 the Continental Congress approved Richard Henry Lee's resolution declaring the colonies free of allegiance to the crown. The Declaration of Independence is not the official act by which Congress severed its ties with Britain. Lee's resolution did that. Rather, the Declaration "was intended as a formal justification of an act already accomplished."[8]

For two days Congress debated Jefferson's draft, making changes and deletions that Jefferson found painful. No matter; what emerged has withstood the test of time:

> We hold these Truths to be self-evident, that all Men are created equal, that they are endowed by their Creator with certain unalienable Rights, that among these are Life, Liberty, and the Pursuit of Happiness — That to secure these Rights, Governments are instituted among Men, deriving their just Powers from the Consent of the Governed, that whenever any Form of Government becomes destructive of these Ends, it is the Right of the People to alter or to abolish it, and to institute new Government . . .

The Continental Congress approved the Declaration on July 4 and ordered that it be "authenticated and printed." Although the fact is sometimes overlooked, Jefferson and his colleagues produced and signed a treasonable document. They were literally pledging their lives.

Dr. Benjamin Rush of Philadelphia, one of the signers, asked John Adams many years later: "Do you recollect . . . the pensive and awful silence which pervaded the house when we were called up, one after another, to the table of the President of Congress to subscribe what was believed by many at that time to be our own death warrants?"[9]

The solemnity of the moment was breached only once. It is said that Benjamin Harrison of Virginia, whom Adams once described as "an indolent and luxurious heavy gentleman of no use in Congress or committee," turned to Elbridge Gerry of Massachusetts, a skinny, worried-looking colleague, and cackled: "I shall have a great advantage over you, Mr. Gerry, when we are all hung for what we are now doing. From the size and weight of my body I shall die in a few minutes, but from the lightness of your body you will dance in the air an hour or two before you are dead."[10]

The Political Foundations

Although Jefferson later said he had "turned to neither book nor pamphlet" in writing the Declaration of Independence, he was certainly influenced by the philosophy of John Locke (1632–1704) and others, by his British heritage, with its traditional concern for individual rights, and by the colonial political experience itself.

John Locke

[8] Carl L. Becker, *The Declaration of Independence* (New York: Vintage Books, 1942), p. 5.
[9] David Hawke, *A Transaction of Free Men* (New York: Scribner's, 1964), p. 209.
[10] *Ibid.*

The Influence of John Locke

John Locke's philosophy of *natural rights* was political gospel to most educated Americans in the late eighteenth century. Jefferson absorbed Locke's writings, and some of the English philosopher's words and phrases emerged verbatim in the Declaration.[11]

Locke reasoned that human beings were "born free" and possessed certain natural rights when they lived in a state of nature before governments were formed. People contracted among themselves to form a society to protect those rights. All persons, Locke believed, were free, equal, and independent, and no one could be "subjected to the political power of another, without his own consent."[12] These dangerous ideas—dangerous in an age of the divine right of kings—are directly reflected in the language of the Declaration of Independence, written nearly a century later.

The English Heritage

The irony of the American Revolution is that the colonists, for the most part, rebelled because they felt they were being deprived of their rights as *English citizens.* Many of the ideas of the Declaration of Independence in 1776, the Constitution, framed in 1787, and the Bill of Rights, added to the Constitution in 1791, evolved from their English heritage. The political and intellectual antecedents of the American system of government included such British legal milestones as the Magna Carta, issued by King John at Runnymede in 1215, in which the nobles confirmed that the power of the king was not absolute; the Habeas Corpus Act (1679); and the Bill of Rights (1689).

From England also came a system of *common law,* the cumulative body of law as expressed in judicial decisions and custom rather than by statute. The men who framed America's government were influenced by the writings of Sir Edward Coke, the great British jurist and champion of common law against the power of the king, and Sir William Blackstone, the Oxford law professor whose *Commentaries on the Laws of England* (1765–1769) is still an indispensable standard reference work for law students and attorneys.

If the *ideas* embodied in the American system of government are to be found largely in the nation's English heritage, it is also true that American *institutions* developed to a great extent from colonial foundations. The roots of much of today's governmental structure can be found in the colonial charters.

The Colonial Experience

Even before they landed at Plymouth in 1620, the Pilgrims—a group of English Puritans who had separated from the Church of England—drew up the Mayflower Compact. The Pilgrims had sailed from Holland, intending to settle in the area that is now New York City, but landed instead just north of Cape Cod. In the cabin of the *Mayflower* forty-one male adults signed the compact, declaring that "we . . . doe by these presents solemnly & mutualy in the presence of God, and one of another, covenant & combine our selves togeather into a civill body politick."

The Mayflower Compact, as Samuel Eliot Morison noted, "is justly regarded as a key document in American history. It proves the determination of

[11] For example, the phrase "a long train of abuses."
[12] Peter Laslett, ed., *Locke's Two Treatises of Government* (Cambridge: Cambridge University Press, 1960), p. 348.

the small group of English emigrants to live under a rule of law, based on the consent of the people, and to set up their own civil government."[13]

A year earlier at Jamestown, Virginia, a group of settlers had established the first representative assembly in the New World. Puritans from the Massachusetts Bay Colony and another group from London framed America's first written constitution in 1639—the Fundamental Orders of Connecticut. The Massachusetts Body of Liberties (1641) embodied traditional English rights, such as trial by jury and due process of law (later incorporated into the Constitution and the Bill of Rights).

The political forms established by the Puritans contributed to the formation of representative institutions. Beyond that, Puritanism shaped the American mind and left its indelible stamp on the American character. The English Puritans who came to America were influenced by the teachings of John Calvin, the sixteenth-century French theologian of the Protestant Reformation. Theirs was a stern code of hard work, sobriety, and intense religious zeal. Even today, with rapidly changing, increasingly liberal sexual and moral codes, Americans do not always seem to be able to enjoy their new freedom entirely. The Puritan heritage is not easily forgotten.

John Calvin

The Colonial Governments. The thirteen original colonies, some formed as commercial ventures, others as religious havens, all had written charters that set forth their form of government and the rights of the colonists. All had governors (the executive branch), legislatures, and a judiciary.

The eight *royal* colonies were New Hampshire, New York, New Jersey, Virginia, North Carolina, South Carolina, Georgia, and Massachusetts. They were controlled by the king through governors appointed by him. Laws passed by their legislatures were subject to approval of the crown. In the three *proprietary* colonies—Maryland, Delaware, and Pennsylvania—the proprietors (who had obtained their patents from the king) named the governors, subject to the approval of the crown; laws (except in Maryland) also required the crown's approval. Only in the two *charter* colonies, Rhode Island and Connecticut, was there genuine self-government. There, freely elected legislatures chose the governors, and laws could not be vetoed by the king.

Except for Pennsylvania, which had a unicameral legislature, the colonial legislatures had two houses. The members of the upper house were appointed by the crown or proprietor (except in Connecticut and Rhode Island, where both houses were elected), and the members of the lower house were elected by the colonists. Appeals from the colonial courts could usually be taken to the Privy Council in London.

The Paradox of Colonial Democracy. Democracy, in the modern sense, did not exist in colonial America. For example, by the 1700s every colony had some type of property qualification for voting. Women and blacks were not considered part of the electorate. In 1765, of the 1,850,000 estimated population of the colonies, 400,000 were blacks, almost all of them slaves. Consequently, "whatever political democracy did exist was a democracy of white, male property owners."[14]

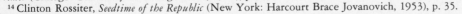

[13] Samuel Eliot Morison, "The Mayflower Compact," in Daniel J. Boorstin, ed., *An American Primer* (Chicago: University of Chicago Press, 1966), p. 19.
[14] Clinton Rossiter, *Seedtime of the Republic* (New York: Harcourt Brace Jovanovich, 1953), p. 35.

In addition, many white persons were indentured servants during the colonial period. These were English, Scotch-Irish, and Western Europeans, including many convicts, who sold their labor for four to seven years in return for passage across the sea.

Even aside from slavery and indentured servitude, there was little social democracy. A tailor in York County, Virginia, in 1674 was punished for racing a horse since "it was contrary to law for a labourer to make a race, being a sport only for gentlemen."[15] In colonial New York, the aristocracy "ruled with condescension and lived in splendor."[16]

Nine of the thirteen colonies had an established, official state church. Although the colonists had, in many cases, fled Europe to find religious freedom, they were often intolerant of religious dissent. The Massachusetts Bay Colony executed four Quakers who had returned there after being banished for their religious convictions. In Virginia, the penalty for breaking the Sabbath for the third time was death.[17] And although the colonial press and pamphleteers developed into a powerful force for liberty, the first newspaper to appear in America, *Publick Occurrences*, was immediately suppressed.[18]

Numb: 1,

PUBLICK
OCCURRENCES

Both *FORREIGN* and *DOMESTICK*.

Boston, Thursday Sept. 25th. 1690.

Yet, despite their shortcomings, the colonial governments provided an institutional foundation for what was to come. Certain elements were already visible: separation of powers, constitutional government through written charters, bicameral legislatures, elections, and judicial appeal to London, which foreshadowed the role of the Supreme Court. Equally important, in their relationship with England, the colonies became accustomed to the idea of sharing powers with a central government, the basis of the federal system today. It was, in Clinton Rossiter's apt phrase, the "seedtime of the republic."

British tax stamps

The American Revolution

"The Revolution," John Adams wrote in 1818, "was effected before the war commenced. The Revolution was in the minds and hearts of the people."[19]

[15] *Ibid.,* p. 87.
[16] *Ibid.,* p. 88.
[17] Nat Hentoff, *The First Freedom: The Tumultuous History of Free Speech in America* (New York: Delacorte Press, 1980), pp. 160–61.
[18] The newspaper was published in Boston on September 25, 1690.
[19] In Charles Francis Adams, ed., *The Works of John Adams,* Vol. X (Boston: Little, Brown, 1856), p. 282.

In the eyes of the crown, the American colonies existed chiefly for the economic support of England. Economic conflicts with the mother country, as well as political and social factors, impelled the colonies to revolt.

The British had routed the French from North America and provided military protection to the colonies; England in turn demanded that its subjects in America pay part of the cost. At the same time, the colonies were expected to subordinate themselves to the British economy; ideally they would remain agricultural, develop no industry of their own, and serve as a captive market for British manufactures.

The colonists had no representatives in the British Parliament. They resented and disputed the right of London to raise revenue in America. Whether or not James Otis, the Boston patriot, cried, "Taxation without representation is tyranny!"—and there is reason to think he did not—the words reflected popular sentiment in the colonies.[20]

A series of laws designed to give the mother country a tight grip on trade, restrict colonial exports, and protect producers in England proved to be the economic stepping stones to revolution. In 1772 Samuel Adams of Massachusetts formed the Committees of Correspondence to unite the colonies against Great Britain. This network provided an invaluable political communications link for the colonies. Letters, reports, and decisions of one town or colony could be relayed to the next.

The committees resolved to hold the First Continental Congress, which met in Philadelphia in September 1774. The war began in April 1775. The Second Continental Congress met the following month, and by June 1776 Thomas Jefferson was busily writing in the second-floor parlor of the bricklayer's house in Philadelphia.

The Declaration of Independence had proclaimed the colonies "free and independent states." During the war all the colonies adopted new constitutions or at least changed their old charters to eliminate references to the British crown. Seven of the new constitutions contained a bill of rights, but all restricted suffrage. All provided for three branches of government, but their dominant features were strong legislatures and weak executives. Governors were elected by the people or by legislatures, and their powers were reduced. For the first time, the colonies began to refer to themselves as "states."

When Richard Henry Lee offered his resolution for independence in June 1776, he had also proposed that "a plan of confederation" be prepared for the colonies. The plan was drawn up by a committee and approved by the Continental Congress in November 1777, a month before George Washington withdrew with his troops for the long hard winter at Valley Forge. The Articles were ratified by the individual states by March 1, 1781, and so were already in effect when the war ended with the surrender of Cornwallis at Yorktown that October. The formal end to hostilities came with the conclusion of the Peace of Paris in February 1783.

Article III of the Articles of Confederation really established a "league of friendship" among the states, rather than a national government. There was no

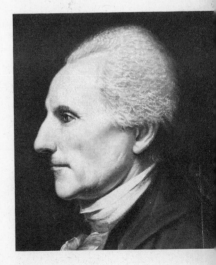

Richard Henry Lee

[20] Otis supposedly uttered his famous line in a speech to the Massachusetts Superior Court in 1761. But as Daniel J. Boorstin points out, the line does not appear in the original notes of the speech taken by John Adams. See Boorstin, *The Americans: The National Experience*, pp. 309, 360–61.

35

The Constitutional Framework

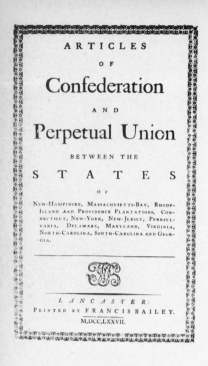

executive branch, no President, no "White House." Instead, Congress, given power to establish executive departments, created five: foreign affairs, finance, navy, war, and post office. Congress had power to declare war, conduct foreign policy, make treaties, ask for—but not demand—revenues from the states, borrow and coin money, equip the navy, and appoint senior officers of the army, which was made up of the state militias. Congress was unicameral, and each state, regardless of size, had only one vote. The most important actions by Congress required the consent of nine states. There was no national system of courts.

While these were not inconsiderable powers, the most significant fact about the government created under the Articles was its weakness. Congress, for example, had no power to levy taxes or regulate commerce—the colonies had seen enough of these powers under English rule. Above all, Congress could not enforce even the limited powers it had. The functioning of government under the Articles depended entirely on the good will of the states. Because unanimous agreement of the states was required to amend the Articles, but in practice could never be obtained, there was no practical way to increase the powers of the government; the Articles were never amended.

By 1783 the American states had achieved their independence not only from Great Britain but also from each other. They had won their freedom, but they had been unable to form a nation. Yet the Articles did represent the idea of some form of national government, for under them, "Congress waged war, made peace, and kept alive the idea of union when it was at its lowest ebb."[21] As historian Merrill Jensen has emphasized, the Articles "laid foundations for the administration of a central government which were to be expanded but not essentially altered in function for generations to come."[22]

Toward a More Perfect Union

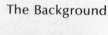
The Background

Under the inadequate government of the Articles of Confederation, the states came close to losing the peace they had won in war. They quarreled among themselves over boundary lines and tariffs. For example, New Jersey farmers had to pay heavy fees to cross the Hudson River to sell their vegetables in New York. With no strong national government to conduct foreign policy, some states even entered into negotiations with foreign powers. General Washington worried that Kentucky might join Spain.[23] There was real concern over possible military intervention by European powers.

By 1786 severe economic depression had left many farmers angry and hungry. Debtor groups demanded that state governments issue paper money. The unrest among farmers and the poor alarmed the upper classes. There was fear, in today's terms, of a revolution of the left. These political and economic factors, combined with fear of overseas intervention, generated pressure for the creation of a new national government.

James Madison

---

[21] Alpheus T. Mason, "America's Political Heritage: Revolution and Free Government—A Bicentennial Tribute," in M. Judd Harmon, ed., *Essays on the Constitution of the United States* (Port Washington, N. Y.: Kennikat Press, 1978), p. 17.

[22] Merrill Jensen, *The New Nation* (New York: Knopf, 1950), pp. 347–48.

[23] William H. Riker, *Federalism: Origin, Operation, Significance* (Boston: Little, Brown, 1964), pp. 18, 20.

Virginia, at the urging of James Madison, had invited all the states to discuss commercial problems at a meeting to be held at Annapolis, Maryland, in September 1786. The Annapolis conference was disappointing. Representatives of only five states turned up. But one of those delegates was Alexander Hamilton, a brilliant, thirty-one-year-old New York attorney who was one of a small group of men pushing for a convention to create a stronger government. There had been talk of such a meeting since 1780, when Hamilton wrote to a friend listing the "defects of our present system."[24]

At Annapolis, Hamilton and James Madison persuaded the delegates to call upon the states to hold a constitutional convention in Philadelphia in May 1787. In the interim a significant event took place. In western Massachusetts late in 1786, angry farmers, unable to pay their mortgages or taxes, rallied around Daniel Shays, who had served as a captain in the American Revolution. They were seeking to stop the Massachusetts courts from foreclosing the mortgages on their farms. Armed with pitchforks, the farmers marched on the Springfield arsenal to get weapons. They were defeated by the militia. Fourteen ringleaders were sentenced to death, but all were pardoned or released after serving short prison terms. Shays escaped to Vermont.

Shays's Rebellion, coming on the eve of the Philadelphia Convention, had a tremendous effect on public opinion. Aristocrats and merchants were thoroughly alarmed at the threat of "mob rule." The British were amused at the American lack of capacity for self-government. The revolt was an important factor in creating the climate for a new beginning at Philadelphia.

Alexander Hamilton

[24] Letter to James Duane, in Clinton Rossiter, *1787: The Grand Convention* (New York: Macmillan, 1966), p. 53.

Shays's Rebellion, 1786

The Philadelphia Convention

On February 21, 1787, Congress grudgingly approved the proposed Philadelphia Convention "for the sole and express purpose of revising the Articles of Confederation." Beginning in May, the Founding Fathers met and, disregarding Congress' cautious mandate, worked what has been called a "miracle at Philadelphia."[25]

The Delegates. Because the story of how a nation was born is in large part a story of people, it might be useful to focus briefly on some of the more prominent delegates who gathered at Philadelphia. First was George Washington, who had commanded the armed forces during the Revolution. A national hero, a man of immense prestige, Washington was probably the only figure who could have successfully presided over the coming struggle in the convention. After Washington was Benjamin Franklin, internationally famous as a scientist-diplomat-statesman. Now eighty-one and suffering from gout, he arrived at the sessions in a sedan chair borne by four convicts from the Walnut Street jail. Alexander Hamilton was there, as a delegate from New York, but he took surprisingly little part in the important decisions of the convention. From Virginia came James Madison, often called the "Father of the Constitution," who had long advocated a new national government. A tireless notetaker, Madison kept a record of the debates. Without him there would be no detailed account of the most important political convention in the nation's history.

Gouverneur Morris, a colorful man who stumped about on a wooden leg, shatters the image of the Founding Fathers as stuffy patriarchs. His wit offended some, but his pen was responsible for the literary style and polish of the final draft of the Constitution. From Massachusetts came Elbridge Gerry and Rufus

[25] Catherine Drinker Bowen, *Miracle at Philadelphia* (Boston: Little, Brown, 1966).

George Washington

Benjamin Franklin

Gouverneur Morris

King, a lawyer with a gift for debating; from South Carolina, John Rutledge, a leading figure of the revolutionary period and later a justice of the Supreme Court, General Charles Cotesworth Pinckney, Oxford-educated war hero and aristocrat, and his second cousin, Charles Pinckney, an ardent nationalist.

Twelve states sent delegates to Philadelphia. Only Rhode Island boycotted the convention; an agrarian party of farmers and debtors controlled the Rhode Island state legislature and feared that a strong national government would limit the party's power. Of the fifty-five men who gathered at Philadelphia in the Pennsylvania State House (now Independence Hall), eight had signed the Declaration of Independence, seven had been chief executives of their states, thirty-three were lawyers, eight were businessmen, six were planters, and three were physicians. About half were college graduates.[26] The delegates, in sum, were generally men of wealth and influence; the Constitution was not drafted by small farmers, artisans, or laborers.

It was a relatively young convention. Jonathan Dayton of New Jersey, at twenty-six, was the youngest delegate. Alexander Hamilton was thirty-two. Charles Pinckney was twenty-nine. James Madison was thirty-six. The average age of the delegates was just over forty-three. (At eighty-one, Franklin pulled the average up.)

Elbridge Gerry

The Setting. The Convention of 1787 had many of the earmarks of a modern national political convention but for one factor: to preserve their freedom of debate, the delegates worked in strictest secrecy. The press and public were not allowed in. In other respects the setting would be a familiar one today: the weather was intolerably hot, the convention hall stuffy, and the speeches interminable. And just as in a modern convention, a plush tavern and inn, the Indian Queen, soon became a sort of informal headquarters.

The convention opened on May 14, 1787, but it was not until May 25 that a quorum of delegates from seven states was reached. The delegates gathered in the East Room of the State House, the same chamber where the Declaration of Independence had been signed eleven years before. "Delegates sat at tables covered in green baize—sat and sweated, once the summer sun was up. By noon the air was lifeless, with windows shut for privacy, or intolerable with flies when they were open."[27] For almost four months the stuffy East Room was to be home.

The Great Compromise. On May 29 Edmund Randolph, the thirty-three-year-old governor of Virginia, took the floor to present fifteen resolutions that stunned the convention. The resolutions, which Madison had helped to draft, went far beyond mere revision of the Articles—they proposed an entirely new national government under a constitution. Randolph was moving swiftly to make the Virginia Plan, as his proposals are known, the main business of the convention.

As John P. Roche has noted, the plan, drafted by James Madison and the Virginia delegation, "was a political masterstroke. Its consequence was that once business got underway, the framework of discussion was established on Madison's terms. There was no interminable argument over agenda; instead the dele-

Edmund Randolph

[26] Charles Warren, *The Making of the Constitution* (New York: Barnes & Noble, 1967), pp. 55–60.
[27] Bowen, *Miracle at Philadelphia*, p. 23.

gates took the Virginia Resolutions—'just for the purposes of discussion'—as their point of departure."[28]

The Virginia Plan called for:

1. A two-house legislature, the lower house chosen by the people and the upper house chosen by the lower. The legislature would have the power to annul any state laws that it felt were unconstitutional.
2. A "national executive"—the makeup was not specified, so there might have been more than one President under the plan—to be elected by the legislature.
3. A national judiciary to be chosen by the legislature.

The convention debated the Virginia Plan for two weeks. As the debate wore on, the smaller states became increasingly alarmed. It had not taken them long to conclude that the more heavily populated states would control the government under the Virginia Plan.

On June 15 William Paterson of New Jersey, a lawyer, rose to offer an alternative plan. He argued that the convention had no power to deprive the smaller states of the equality they enjoyed under the Articles of Confederation. He proposed what became known as the New Jersey Plan, which called for:

1. Continuation of the Articles of Confederation, including one vote for each state represented in the legislature. Congress would be strengthened so that it could impose taxes and regulate trade, and acts of Congress would become the "supreme law" of the states.
2. An executive of more than one person to be elected by Congress.
3. A Supreme Court, to be appointed by the executive.

The Paterson plan would have merely amended the Articles. The government would have continued as a weak confederation of sovereign states. But many of the delegates at Philadelphia were determined to construct a strong *national* government, and for this reason the Paterson plan was soon brushed aside. As both the weather and tempers grew warmer, the convention swung back to consideration of the Virginia Plan. But little progress was made.

The fact was that the convention was in danger of breaking up. "I *almost* despair," Washington, presiding over the deadlock, wrote to Hamilton in New York.

[28] John P. Roche, "The Founding Fathers: A Reform Caucus in Action," *American Political Science Review*, Vol. 55, No. 4 (December 1961), p. 803.

An American King

Charles Pinckney rose . . . to urge a "vigorous executive." He did not say a "President of the United States." It took the Convention a long while to come around to *President*. Always they referred to a chief executive or a national executive, whether plural or single. James Wilson followed Pinckney by moving that the executive consist of a single person; Pinckney seconded him.

A sudden silence followed. "A considerable pause," Madison wrote . . . *A single executive!* There was menace in the words, some saw monarchy in them. True enough, nine states had each its single executive—a governor or president—but everywhere the local legislature was supreme, looked on as the voice of the people which could control a governor any day. But a single executive for the national government conjured up visions from the past—royal governors who could not be restrained, a crown, ermine, a scepter!

—Catherine Drinker Bowen, *Miracle at Philadelphia*.

The impasse over the makeup of Congress was broken on July 16 when the convention adopted the Great Compromise, often called the Connecticut Compromise because it had been proposed by Roger Sherman of that state. As adopted after much debate, the Connecticut Compromise called for:

1. A House of Representatives apportioned by the number of free inhabitants in each state plus three-fifths of the slaves.
2. A Senate, or upper house, consisting of two members from each state, elected by the state legislatures.

The plan broke the deadlock because it protected the small states by guaranteeing that each state would have an equal vote in the Senate. Only in the House, where representation was to be based on population, would the larger states have an advantage.

Catherine Drinker Bowen has suggested that the delegates might never have reached agreement "had not the heat broken." On Monday, July 16, the day the compromise was approved, "Philadelphia was cool after a month of torment; on Friday, a breeze had come in from the northwest. Over the weekend, members could rest and enjoy themselves."[29]

With the large state versus small state controversy resolved by this compromise, the convention named a committee to draft a constitution. Then the convention adjourned for eleven days, and General Washington went fishing.

On August 6 the convention resumed its work. The committee brought in a draft constitution that called for a "congress," made up of a house of representatives and a senate; a "supreme court"; and a "president of the United States of America."

The broad outline of the Constitution as it is today was finally clear. But much work remained. All through August and into September the draft constitution was debated, clause by clause.

The Other Compromises. The convention made other significant compromises. Underlying the agreement to count three-fifths of all slaves in apportioning membership of the House of Representatives was a deep-seated conflict between the mercantile North and the agrarian South, where the economy was based on slave labor. The men of the North argued that if slaves were to be counted in determining representation in the House, then they must be counted for tax purposes as well. In the end, the South agreed.

The slave trade itself was the subject of another complicated compromise. On August 22 George Mason of Virginia attacked "the infernal traffic" and its evil effect on both individuals and the nation. Slavery, he said, would "bring the judgment of heaven on a Country. As nations can not be rewarded or punished in the next world they must in this. By an inevitable chain of causes & effects providence punishes national sins, by national calamities."[30]

Charles Cotesworth Pinckney of South Carolina warned that his state would not join the union if the slave trade were prohibited. The issue was settled by an agreement that Congress could not ban the slave trade until 1808.

A Republic—If You Can Keep It

When the delegates to the Constitutional Convention at Philadelphia ended their long and difficult task in September of 1787 it is said that a lady approached Benjamin Franklin and asked:

"Well, Doctor, what have we got—a republic or a monarchy?"

"A republic," was the reply, "if you can keep it."

—Adapted from "Debates in the Federal Convention in 1787," in *Documents Illustrative of the Formation of the Union of the American States*.

[29] Bowen, *Miracle at Philadelphia*, p. 186.
[30] In Carl Van Doren, *The Great Rehearsal* (New York: Viking Press, 1948), p. 153.

This compromise is contained in Article I of the Constitution, which obliquely refers to slaves as "other persons."[31]

In yet another compromise the South won certain trade concessions. Southerners were worried, with reason, that the Northern majority in Congress might pass legislation unfavorable to Southern economic interests. Because the South relied almost entirely on exports of its agricultural products, it fought for, and won, an agreement forbidding the imposition of export taxes. Even today, the United States is one of the few nations that cannot tax its exports.

We the People. On September 8 a Committee of Style and Arrangement was named to polish the final draft. Fortunately it included Gouverneur Morris. Morris, probably aided by James Wilson,[32] drafted the final version, adding a new preamble that rivals Jefferson's eloquence in the Declaration of Independence: "We the People of the United States, in Order to form a more perfect Union, establish Justice, insure domestic Tranquility, provide for the common defence, promote the general Welfare, and secure the Blessings of Liberty to ourselves and our Posterity, do ordain and establish this Constitution for the United States of America."

On September 17 the long task was finished. The day was cold, and the trace of autumn in the air must have reminded the delegates of how long they

---

[31] Acting on President Jefferson's recommendation, Congress did outlaw importation of slaves in 1808. But the illegal slave trade flourished up to the Civil War. Perhaps 250,000 slaves were illegally imported to America between 1808 and 1860. The slavery issue was not settled until Appomattox and the ratification on December 18, 1865, of the Thirteenth Amendment, which declared that "neither slavery nor involuntary servitude, except as a punishment for crime whereof the party shall have been duly convicted, shall exist within the United States."

[32] Warren, *The Making of the Constitution,* pp. 687–88.

The Government of the United States
Figure 2–1

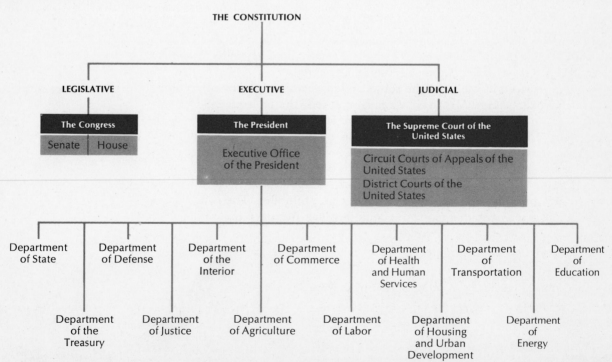

had labored. Thirty-nine men signed the Constitution that afternoon. Benjamin Franklin had to be helped forward to the table, and it is said that he wept when he signed. According to Madison's notes, while the last members were signing, Franklin observed that often, as he pondered the outcome during the changing moods of the convention, he had looked at the sun painted on the back of Washington's chair and wondered whether it was rising or setting. "But now at length I have the happiness to know," Franklin declared, "that it is a rising and not a setting sun."[33]

The Constitution was not perfect, but it represented a practical accommodation among conflicting sections and interests, achieved at a political convention. And the central fact of the Constitution is that it created the potential for a strong national government where none had existed before, and a written framework to control the power and operation of that government.

The Constitutional Framework

The Federal System. The structure of the government created by the Constitution is deceptively simple at first glance, yet endlessly intricate. Article VI declares that the laws passed by Congress "shall be the supreme Law of the Land." This important *supremacy clause* means that federal laws are supreme over any conflicting state laws. But the states also exercise control within their borders over a wide range of activities.

The Constitution thus brought into being a *federal system,* also known as *federalism,* in which the powers and functions of government are divided between the national government and the states. This system is discussed in detail in Chapter 3.

The National Government. The Constitution divided the national government into three branches—legislative, executive, and judicial. It created a government, therefore, based on the principles of *separation of powers* and *checks and balances.* Each of the three branches is constitutionally equal to and independent of the others. In this way the framers thought to prevent any single branch from becoming too powerful. (In fact, however, the twentieth century has seen the Presidency become the most powerful branch of the federal government, at least in foreign affairs.)

In creating a government based on these ideas, the Founding Fathers were influenced by the French political philosopher Baron de Montesquieu (1689–1755). In *The Spirit of the Laws,* published in 1748, Montesquieu advocated a separation of powers into legislative, judicial, and executive branches. "When the legislative and executive powers are united in the same person, or in the same body of magistrates, there can be no liberty," he wrote.[34]

Yet, the term "separation of powers" is somewhat misleading. Although the Constitution established institutional checks and separated powers, the United States is also a government of *shared powers.* The branches of the government are separated, but their powers and functions are fused or overlapping. The Constitution provided many ways in which the three branches would interact. For example, although Congress makes the laws, the President submits legisla-

---

[33] In Van Doren, *The Great Rehearsal,* p. 174.
[34] Baron de Montesquieu, *The Spirit of the Laws,* Vol. I (New York: Hafner, 1949), p. 151.

tion to it, and he may convene Congress in special session. The President may also veto bills passed by Congress. Clearly, the President is involved in the legislative function.

Similarly, Congress is involved in the executive process by its watchdog functions and through its power to create federal executive agencies and to advise on and consent to the appointment of high-level federal officials. Since Congress appropriates money to run the federal government, it may delve deeply, through its committees, into the operations of executive agencies.

Through the process of *judicial review,* the courts decide whether the laws passed by Congress or actions taken by the President are constitutional. (See pp. 474–76 for a detailed discussion of judicial review.) President Woodrow Wilson called the Supreme Court "a kind of Constitutional Convention in continuous session." The President participates in the judicial process through his power to nominate federal judges, including members of the Supreme Court.

The notion of three separate-but-equal branches of government has been eroded by the pressures of the twentieth century. In the past, American Presidents have, at varying times, exercised great powers, as did Lincoln during the Civil War. But in modern times, power, especially military-diplomatic power, has been largely concentrated in the hands of the President. The power of Congress to declare war, for example, has greatly diminished in importance since the Second World War. And in a nuclear attack the President would obviously have no time to consult Congress. But even in the case of protracted conflicts, such as in Korea (1950–1953) and Vietnam (1964–1973), Congress never did declare war. Frustration in Congress over the President's ability to wage war without congressional approval led in 1973 to the passage of the War Powers Resolution, which sets a time limit on the use of combat forces abroad by a President.

In other areas as well, the lines between the three branches of government have become blurred. Today, for example, the complex task of managing the economy has been delegated in part to independent regulatory commissions and agencies that do not fall neatly into any of the three categories — legislative, executive, and judicial — envisioned under the Constitution and in fact exhibit features of all three.

In sum, although the three branches of government are based upon separated powers, they also share powers. And among the three branches (as among human beings) there is a never-ending tug of war for dominance, a process that Alpheus T. Mason has called "institutionalized tension."[35]

The "Great Silences" of the Constitution. Some issues were so difficult and potentially divisive that the framers did not attempt to settle them at all. Since they were trying to construct a political document that stated general principles, they chose to avoid some sensitive problems.

The framers compromised over the vital moral and political issue of whether to abolish the importation of slaves while forming "a more perfect union"; the underlying question of whether to abolish slavery itself was not faced at Philadelphia. Five Southern states might not have ratified the Constitution if the framers had abolished the slave trade in 1787. The delegates compromised in order to achieve enough unity to form a new nation, but America

[35] Alpheus T. Mason, *The Supreme Court: Palladium of Freedom* (Ann Arbor, Mich.: University of Michigan Press, 1962), p. 8.

paid a high moral and political cost. The question of slavery, avoided at Philadelphia, led in time to a bloody civil war. And today, two centuries later, black men and women in America are still struggling for the full freedom and equality denied to them by the framers.

The framers also made no explicit statement in the Constitution defining the full scope of the powers of the national government. The history of the Supreme Court is the history of whether the Constitution is to be loosely or strictly interpreted.

But even the Supreme Court's power of judicial review is nowhere expressly provided for in the Constitution. The power of the Supreme Court to declare acts of Congress unconstitutional was not established until 1803, when the Court ruled in the case of *Marbury* v. *Madison*.[36] Chief Justice John Marshall, in his historic opinion, argued that since the Constitution was clearly "superior" to an act of Congress, "It is emphatically the province and duty of the judicial department to say what the law is. . . . A law repugnant to the Constitution is void."

The Constitution says nothing whatever about how candidates for office shall be chosen. The development of political parties, nominating conventions, and primaries all occurred outside the formal constitutional framework.

Similarly, the cabinet is not specifically established in the Constitution but has evolved through custom, beginning during Washington's first administration. As Richard F. Fenno, Jr., has noted, the cabinet is "an extralegal creation," limited in power as an institution by the very fact that it has no basis in law.[37]

Motives of the Framers. Were the framers of the Constitution selfless patriots who thrust aside all personal interests to save America? Or were they primarily rich men who were afraid of radicals like Daniel Shays? In short, did they form a strong government to protect themselves and their property, or did they act from nobler motives?

The debate has raged among scholars. More than half a century ago, the historian Charles A. Beard analyzed in great detail the economic holdings of the framers and concluded that they acted to protect their personal financial interests. The Constitution, said Beard, was "an economic document drawn with superb skill by men whose property interests were immediately at stake."[38]

Later scholars, reacting to Beard, have reached opposite conclusions. Forrest McDonald has asserted that of the fifty-five delegates, "a dozen at the outside, clearly acted according to the dictates of their personal economic interests." He concluded that an "economic interpretation of the Constitution does not work" and that it is "impossible to justify" Beard's analysis.[39] Similarly, Robert E. Brown has suggested that "we would be doing a grave injustice to the political sagacity of the Founding Fathers if we assumed that property or personal gain was their only motive."[40]

[36] *Marbury* v. *Madison* (1803).
[37] Richard F. Fenno, Jr., *The President's Cabinet* (Cambridge, Mass.: Harvard University Press, 1959), pp. 19–20.
[38] Charles A. Beard, *An Economic Interpretation of the Constitution of the United States* (New York: Macmillan, 1935), p. 188. Originally published in 1913.
[39] Forrest McDonald, *We the People* (Chicago: University of Chicago Press, 1958), pp. vii, 350, 415.
[40] Robert E. Brown, *Charles Beard and the Constitution* (Princeton, N. J.: Princeton University Press, 1956), p. 198.

The Constitution: Jefferson's View

In questions of power, then, let no more be heard of confidence in man, but bind him down from mischief by the chains of the Constitution.

—Thomas Jefferson, 1798, in Paul Leicester Ford, ed., *The Works of Thomas Jefferson*.

John Adams

Was It Democratic? The argument is sometimes advanced that the Constitution was framed to guard against popular democracy. "The evils we experience flow from the excess of democracy," Elbridge Gerry of Massachusetts told the convention.[41]

The word "democracy" today generally has a favorable, affirmative meaning, but to the framers of the Constitution, it was a term of derision. "Remember," John Adams warned, "democracy never lasts long. It soon wastes, exhausts, and murders itself. There never was a democracy yet that did not commit suicide."[42]

From a contemporary viewpoint some of the provisions of the Constitution appear highly undemocratic. For example, because the Constitution leaves voting qualifications to the states, persons without property, women, and many blacks were long disenfranchised. Until the passage of the Seventeenth Amendment in 1913, senators were elected by state legislatures, although by 1912 in at least twenty-nine states, an attempt was made to reflect popular choice.[43] The framers had deliberately avoided direct election of senators, for the Senate was seen as a check on the multitudes. Madison assured the convention that the Senate would proceed "with more coolness, with more system, and with more wisdom, than the popular branch." And, of course, the Constitution interposed an electoral college between the voters and the Presidency.

But to stress only these aspects of the Constitution would be to overlook the basically representative structure of the government it created—particularly in comparison with other governments that existed in 1787—and the revolutionary heritage of the framers. The Constitution perhaps originally reflected some distrust of popular rule, but it established a balanced institutional framework within which democracy could evolve.

The Fight over Ratification

When the convention had finished its work, a successful outcome was by no means certain. The political contest over ratification of the Constitution lasted for more than two and a half years, from September 1787 until May 29, 1790, when Rhode Island finally joined the Union. But the Constitution went into effect in June of 1788 when it was ratified by nine states.

The Articles of Confederation had required that any amendment be approved by Congress and the legislatures of all thirteen states. No such unanimity could ever be achieved. In effect this created a box from which the framers could not climb out. So they chose another route—they simply ignored the box and built an entirely new structure. Defending the convention's action, Madison reminded his countrymen of the right of the people, proclaimed in the Declaration of Independence, to alter or abolish their government in ways "most likely to effect their safety and happiness."[44]

[41] Elbridge Gerry, Edmund Randolph, and George Mason were the only three framers who refused to sign the Constitution. Much later, Gerry gave his name to a famous but undemocratic practice. While he was governor of Massachusetts in 1812, the legislature carved up Essex County to give maximum advantage to his party. One of the districts resembled a salamander. From then on, the practice of redrawing voting districts to favor the party in power became known as "gerrymandering." (See p. 435.)

[42] Charles Francis Adams, ed., *The Works of John Adams,* Vol. VI (Boston: Little, Brown, 1851), p. 484.

[43] Edward S. Corwin et al., eds., *The Constitution of the United States of America, Analysis and Interpretation* (Washington, D.C.: U.S. Government Printing Office, 1964), p. 1356.

[44] James Madison, "The Federalist, No. 40," in Edward Mead Earle, ed., *The Federalist* (New York: Random House, Modern Library), p. 257.

Article VII of the Constitution states that "ratification of the Conventions of nine States shall be sufficient for the Establishment of this Constitution." Why conventions and not legislatures? Since the Constitution took power away from the states, the framers reasoned that the state legislatures might not approve it. Second, if the Constitution were approved by popularly elected conventions, it would give the new government a broad base of legitimacy.

The great debate over the Constitution soon divided the participants into two camps—the Antifederalists, who opposed it, and the Federalists. Although the debate was vigorous, relatively few people actually participated in the ratification process. The voters could not vote for or against the Constitution. Their choice was confined to selecting delegates to the state ratifying conventions. Only an estimated 160,000 persons voted for delegates to the ratifying conventions, out of a total population of about 4,000,000.

Some historians tend to pay more attention to the Federalists—since they won—but the men opposed to the Constitution had a strong case. The convention, after all, had met in complete secrecy, in a "Dark Conclave," as the Philadelphia *Independent Gazetteer* termed it. What is more, the Constitution, as its opponents argued, was extralegal. The framers had clearly exceeded their mandate from Congress to revise the Articles of Confederation. Above all, the Constitution included no bill of rights.

The Federalists argued that the states faced anarchy unless they united under a powerful central government. The omission of a bill of rights was difficult to justify, however. The question had not been raised until near the end of the Philadelphia Convention, and the weary delegates were not inclined to open a new debate. Furthermore, many delegates felt that a bill of rights would be superfluous since eight states had bills of rights. Hamilton argued that "the Constitution is itself . . . a Bill of Rights."[45]

But during the struggle over ratification, the Antifederalists warned that without a bill of rights in the new Constitution, individuals in the states would have no protection against a powerful national government. Ultimately, as the price of winning support in the state conventions, the Federalists had to promise to enact a bill of rights as the first order of business under a new government.

Richard Henry Lee's *Letters of the Federal Farmer* was among the most effective of the various Antifederalist attacks circulated among the states. In New York, Hamilton, Madison, and John Jay, writing as "Publius," published more than eighty letters in the press defending the Constitution. Together in book form they are known today as *The Federalist,* the classic work explaining and defending the Constitution.

By January 9, 1788, a little over three months after the Philadelphia Convention, five states had ratified the Constitution: Delaware, Pennsylvania, New Jersey, Georgia, and Connecticut. Massachusetts, a key and doubtful state, ratified next, thanks to the efforts of Sam Adams and John Hancock. Maryland and South Carolina followed suit, and on June 21, 1788, New Hampshire became the ninth state to ratify.

The Constitution was now in effect, but Virginia and New York were still to be heard from. Without these two powerful states, no union could succeed. Washington, Madison, and Edmund Randolph, who finally decided to support the Constitution that he had not signed, helped to swing Virginia into the Federalist camp four days later. In part because of *The Federalist* papers, New

---

[45] Alexander Hamilton, "The Federalist, No. 84," in Earle, ed., *The Federalist,* p. 561.

York ratified on July 26 by a narrow margin of three votes. North Carolina finally ratified in 1789 and Rhode Island in 1790. (See Table 2–1.) By that time George Washington was already serving as President of the United States of America.

The Ratification of the Constitution

Table 2–1

State	Date	Vote in the Ratifying Convention
Delaware	December 7, 1787	Unanimous
Pennsylvania	December 12, 1787	46–32
New Jersey	December 19, 1787	Unanimous
Georgia	January 2, 1788	Unanimous
Connecticut	January 9, 1788	128–40
Massachusetts	February 6, 1788	187–168
Maryland	April 28, 1788	63–11
South Carolina	May 23, 1788	149–73
New Hampshire	June 21, 1788	57–47
Virginia	June 25, 1788	89–79
New York	July 26, 1788	30–27
North Carolina	November 21, 1789	194–77
Rhode Island	May 29, 1790	34–32

America: A Case Study in Nation Building

"The United States was the first major colony successfully to revolt against colonial rule," Seymour Martin Lipset has written. "In this sense, it was the first 'new nation.' "[46]

The Declaration of Independence and the success of the American Revolution influenced the philosophers and political leaders of the French Revolution. Jefferson's words were translated into many languages, influencing liberals during the nineteenth century in Germany, Italy, and South America. Even today, the ideas expressed in the Declaration of Independence have relevance in a world in which millions of persons are groping toward political freedom.

Problems of a New Nation

The turmoil that has accompanied the growth of the new countries of Africa and Asia demonstrates that independence does not necessarily bring political maturity and peace. From Vietnam to Zimbabwe, as colonialism has given way to the forces of nationalism, political independence has often been accompanied by political instability. Yet America had a successful revolution. And, despite the Civil War, two world wars, a depression, Vietnam, Watergate, and the energy crisis, inflation, and other issues that confront the nation in the 1980s, it has survived. How did the revolutionary leaders of America carve out an enduring new nation where none had existed before?

[46] Seymour Martin Lipset, *The First New Nation* (New York: Basic Books, 1963), p. 2.

The process was slow and difficult. As Lipset has observed:

A backward glance into our own past should destroy the notion that the United States proceeded easily toward the establishment of democratic political institutions. In the period which saw the establishment of political legitimacy and party government, it was touch and go whether the complex balance of forces would swing in the direction of a one- or two-party system, or even whether the nation would survive as an entity. It took time to institutionalize values, beliefs, and practices, and there were many incidents that revealed how fragile the commitments to democracy and nationhood really were.[47]

The United States, in other words, went through growing pains similar to those of the new nations of Africa and Asia today. For example, some have criticized the emergence in new nations of charismatic leaders such as Kwame Nkrumah, who was the President of Ghana until his ouster in 1966. Yet a charismatic leader may be necessary in a nation with no past, for, in Lipset's words, "he legitimizes the state." Americans may forget that "in his time, George Washington was idolized as much as many of the contemporary leaders of the new states."[48] Americans hung portaits of Washington over their hearths, and he was regarded as more of a patron saint than President.

And, if some contemporary new nations have encountered difficulty in establishing political freedom and democratic procedures, so did America. The Federalists under President John Adams wanted no organized political opposition and used the Alien and Sedition acts, passed in 1798, to suppress their opponents. At least seventy persons were jailed and fined under the Sedition Act, which made almost any criticism of the government, the President, or Congress a crime.

Lucian Pye has conceived of the process of nation building as a series of crises: identity, integration, penetration, participation, and distribution.[49]

The first crisis in the making of a new nation, as Pye views it, is for a people to gain "a sense of common *identity* as either subjects or citizens of a common political system."[50] For many years most colonists probably thought of themselves as Englishmen, or as New Yorkers or Virginians, rather than as Americans. And it took time and a series of conflicts between the colonies and the British government before a developing sense of American nationhood emerged.[51]

By then the process of *integration* was also underway. Integration, in this sense, describes the way that minority and other groups in the nation relate to one another and to the national governmental system. In the prerevolutionary period, integration was taking place rather rapidly; the Committees of Correspondence, which enabled the colonists to coordinate their responses to the British, served as a significant integrating device.

Penetration is the ability of a government to reach all layers of society in order to carry out public policies, to act directly on the people. Since 1789 the

The Process
of Nation Building

[47] *Ibid.,* p. 16.
[48] *Ibid.,* p. 18.
[49] Lucian W. Pye, "Transitional Asia and the Dynamics of Nation Building," in Marian D. Irish, ed., *World Pressures on American Foreign Policy* (Englewood Cliffs, N.J.: Prentice-Hall, 1964), pp. 154–72.
[50] *Ibid.,* p. 162.
[51] Richard L. Merritt, *Symbols of American Community* (New Haven: Yale University Press, 1966).

scope and importance of the national government's penetration has increased greatly, as every individual who has submitted a federal income tax form is aware.

Participation, or bringing increasing numbers of people into the political process, began in the 1780s and has continued ever since. The proportion of the population who were actively involved in the enactment of the new Constitution was fairly small. But it provided a base of popular support for the new government. Since 1787, through successive broadenings of the franchise and other measures, the scope of popular participation in the national government has been enlarged substantially, although not always peacefully. Women, blacks, and other groups have often had to fight for the right to participate in the political system.

Distribution describes the government's control over the outputs of the political process: "What are the rewards of the political system, and who is to receive them?"[52] When the framers prohibited export taxes in the Constitution, they were concerned with problems of distribution. Distribution lies at the very heart of the process of government and politics.

It is, of course, difficult to pinpoint just when a nation passes through these various crises. Nevertheless, the processes Pye has identified can be observed in the American experience. As a result, the historical development of the American nation — with all its crises and problems — remains relevant to the emerging nations in today's world.

The Constitution Then and Now

Chief Justice John Marshall, in *McCulloch* v. *Maryland,* said of the Constitution that it was "intended to endure for ages to come, and consequently to be adapted to the various crises of human affairs."[53] This opinion, delivered in 1819, embodied the principle of loose or *flexible construction* of the Constitution; that is, the Constitution must be interpreted to meet changing conditions.

The members of the Supreme Court have generally reflected the times in which they have lived. Successive Supreme Courts have read very different meaning into the language of the Constitution. But the Court is not the only branch of the government that interprets the Constitution. So does Congress when it passes laws. So does the President when he makes decisions and takes actions. In addition, the Constitution has been amended twenty-six times. The inputs of the American political system have resulted in a continual process of constitutional change. (The Constitution is found on pp. 641–49 of this book.)

What It Says   *The Legislative Branch.* Article I of the Constitution vests all legislative powers "in a Congress of the United States, which shall consist of a Senate and House of Representatives." This article spells out the qualifications and method of election of members of the House and Senate. It gives power of impeachment to the House but provides that the Senate shall try impeachment cases. It empowers the Vice President to preside over the Senate with no vote, except in the case of a tie.

[52] Pye, "Transitional Asia and the Dynamics of Nation Building," p. 167.
[53] *McCulloch* v. *Maryland,* 4 Wheaton 316 (1819).

It provides that all tax legislation must originate in the House. It allows the President to sign or veto a bill and Congress to override his veto by a two-thirds vote of both houses.

Section 8 of this article gives Congress the power to tax, provide for the "general welfare" of the United States, borrow money, regulate commerce (the "commerce clause"), naturalize citizens, coin money, punish counterfeiters, establish a post office and a copyright and patents system, create lower courts, declare war, maintain armed forces, suppress insurrections and repel invasions, govern the District of Columbia, and make "all necessary and proper laws" (sometimes called the "elastic clause") to carry out the powers of the Constitution.

Section 9 provides certain basic protections for citizens against acts of Congress. For example, it says that the writ of *habeas corpus* shall not be suspended unless required by the public safety in cases of rebellion or invasion. One of the most important guarantees of individual liberty, the writ is designed to protect against illegal imprisonment. It requires that a person who is detained be brought before a judge for investigation so that the court may literally, in the Latin meaning, "have the body."

The article also prohibits Congress or the states from passing a "bill of attainder"—legislation aimed at a particular individual—or "ex post facto" laws, imposing punishment for an act that was not illegal when committed. It provides that Congress must appropriate money drawn from the Treasury, a provision that is the single most important check on presidential power. The article also outlaws titles of nobility in America.

The Executive Branch. Article II states, "The executive Power shall be vested in a President of the United States of America." The framers did not provide for

"Congress of the United States . . . shall consist of a Senate and House of Representatives."

"The executive Power shall be vested in a President of the United States of America."

Aaron Burr

direct popular election of the President. Rather, they established the electoral college, with each state having as many electors as it had representatives and senators. The electors choose the President and Vice President. Alexander Hamilton argued that by this means the Presidency would be filled by "characters preeminent for ability and virtue." The electors, he thought, being "a small number of persons, selected by their fellow-citizens from the general mass, will be most likely to possess the information and discernment requisite."[54]

The election of 1800 was thrown into the House of Representatives because Jefferson and his vice-presidential running mate, Aaron Burr, although members of the same party, each received the same number of electoral votes. On the thirty-sixth ballot, the House chose Jefferson as President. Afterward, the electoral system was modified by the Twelfth Amendment to provide that electors must vote separately for President and Vice President.

The rise of political parties meant that in time the electoral college became largely a rubber stamp. As it works today, the voters in each state choose between slates of electors who usually run under a party label. All the electoral votes of a state normally go to the candidate who wins the popular vote in that state; electors on the winning slate routinely vote for their party's candidates for President and Vice President. But the electors do not *have* to obey the will of the voters. For a variety of reasons (discussed in Chapter 9), there has sometimes been pressure to modify or abolish the electoral college system. However, a proposed constitutional amendment to provide for direct, popular election of the President failed to pass the Senate in 1970 and again in 1979.

The Constitution makes the President Commander in Chief of the armed forces, gives him the right to make treaties "with the Advice and Consent" of two-thirds of a quorum of the Senate, to appoint ambassadors, judges, and other high officials, subject to Senate approval, and to summon Congress into special session.

The Judiciary. Article III states, "The judicial Power of the United States, shall be vested in one supreme Court, and in such inferior Courts" as Congress may establish. It also provides for trial by jury. The Supreme Court's vital right of judicial review of acts of Congress stems from both the *supremacy clause* of the Constitution (see below) and Article III, which asserts that the judicial power applies to "all Cases . . . arising under this Constitution."

Other Provisions. Article IV governs the relations among the states and between the states and the federal government. Article V provides methods for amending the Constitution and for ratifying these amendments. Article VI states that the Constitution, laws, and treaties of the United States "shall be the supreme Law of the Land." This is the powerful *supremacy clause* by which laws of Congress prevail over any conflicting state laws. Article VII declares that the Constitution would go into effect when ratified by conventions in nine states.

The Amendment Process

The framers knew that the Constitution might have to be changed to meet future conditions. It had, after all, been created because of the need for change. So they provided two methods of proposing amendments: by a two-thirds vote of

[54] Alexander Hamilton, "The Federalist, No. 68," in Earle, ed., *The Federalist,* pp. 441–42.

Amending the Constitution

Figure 2–2

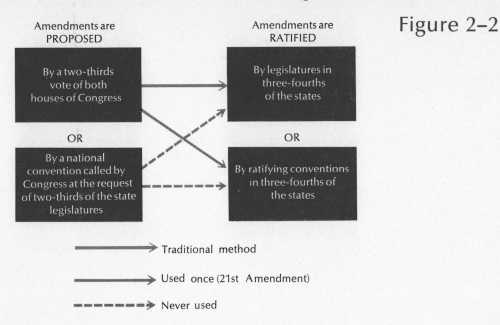

Amendments are
PROPOSED

By a two-thirds
vote of both
houses of Congress

OR

By a national
convention called by
Congress at the request
of two-thirds of the state
legislatures

Amendments are
RATIFIED

By legislatures in
three-fourths
of the states

OR

By ratifying conventions
in three-fourths of
the states

→ Traditional method

→ Used once (21st Amendment)

- - -→ Never used

both houses of Congress, or by a national convention called by Congress at the request of legislatures in two-thirds of the states.

Once proposed, an amendment does not take effect unless ratified, either by the legislatures of three-fourths of the states or by special ratifying conventions in three-fourths of the states.

No amendment has ever been *proposed* by the convention method. But in the mid-1960s, the late Senator Everett McKinley Dirksen of Illinois, the Republican Senate leader, encouraged the states to petition Congress to call a constitutional convention. The general purpose was to amend the Constitution to overturn the Supreme Court's "one person, one vote" decisions that had forced the reapportionment of state legislatures.[55] By 1970 thirty-three state legislatures, only one short of the required two-thirds, had petitioned Congress to call a convention. Dirksen's campaign failed, but the large number of petitions led several senators and legal scholars to warn that a constitutional convention might run wild and make sweeping changes in the structure of the federal government, since there is no precedent for setting an agenda of such a convention.

Similar warnings were voiced a decade later when a movement began to amend the Constitution to require a balanced federal budget. By 1980, thirty state legislatures had petitioned Congress for a convention. President Carter cautioned that such a conclave would be "completely uncontrollable." Nevertheless, the Constitution clearly permits a convention to be held if thirty-four state legislatures should request it.

Of the twenty-six amendments ratified by 1980, only the Twenty-first Amendment, repealing Prohibition, was ratified by state conventions; the rest

[55] See discussion in Chapter 9, pp. 336–39.

were ratified by state legislatures. Some of the amendments add to the Constitution; others supersede or revise the original language of the Constitution.

The amendments to the Constitution fall into three major time periods. The first twelve, ratified between 1791 and 1804, were remedial amendments designed to perfect the original instrument. The next three grew out of the great upheaval of the Civil War and were designed to deal with the new position of the blacks as free men and women. Amendments in the third group were all passed in the twentieth century and deal with a wide range of subjects, in part reflecting more recent pressures toward change in American society.

The first ten amendments are the Bill of Rights.[56] The provisions of the first four are freedom of religion, speech, press, assembly, and petition (First Amendment); the right to bear arms (Second Amendment); protection against quartering of soldiers in private homes (Third Amendment); and protection against unreasonable search and seizure of people, homes, papers, and effects, and provision for search warrants (Fourth Amendment).

The Fifth Amendment provides that no person can be compelled "to be a witness against himself" or to stand trial twice for the same crime. It also lists other rights of accused persons, including that of indictment by a grand jury for major crimes and the general provision that no person shall "be deprived of life, liberty or property, without due process of law." The Sixth Amendment calls for a speedy and public trial by jury in criminal cases and sets forth other protections, including the right to have a lawyer.

The Seventh Amendment provides for jury trial in civil cases, and the Eighth Amendment bars excessive bail or fines, or cruel and unusual punishment. The Ninth Amendment provides that the enumeration of certain rights in the Constitution shall not deny other rights retained by the people, and the Tenth Amendment reserves to the states, or to the people, powers not delegated to the federal government.

These ten amendments were designed to protect Americans against the power of the *federal* government. Nothing in the Constitution specifically provides that *state* governments must also abide by the provisions of the Bill of Rights. But in interpreting the Fourteenth Amendment, passed in 1866 after the Civil War, the Supreme Court in the twentieth century gradually has extended the protection of almost all of the Bill of Rights to apply to the states.

The Eleventh Amendment (1795)[57] was added to guarantee that a sovereign state would never again be hauled into federal court by a private citizen or foreign citizen. In *Chisholm* v. *Georgia*,[58] the Supreme Court had ruled for two South Carolina citizens who had sued the state of Georgia on behalf of a British creditor to recover confiscated property.

The Bill of Rights

The Later Amendments

[56] Some scholars regard only the first eight or nine amendments as the Bill of Rights. The first ten amendments were passed by the First Congress on September 25, 1789, and went into effect when ratified by three-fourths of the states on December 15, 1791. The Bill of Rights is discussed in detail in Chapter 4.

[57] Date after each amendment refers to date of ratification.

[58] *Chisholm* v. *Georgia*, 2 Dallas 419 (1793). However, citizens can sue states in *state* courts if they are deprived of their rights under the Constitution or federal laws, and states can appeal such cases to the federal courts. *Scheuer* v. *Rhodes*, 416 U.S. 232 (1974); *Maine* v. *Thiboutot*, 100 S. Ct. 2502 (1980).

The Twelfth Amendment (1804), as already discussed, was adopted after the deadlocked election of 1800. It provided that presidential electors vote *separately* for President and Vice President.

The next three amendments resulted from the Civil War. The Thirteenth Amendment (1865) forbids slavery. It also outlaws involuntary servitude in the United States and its territories except as punishment for a crime. Its purpose was to free the slaves and complete the abolition of slavery in America. Lincoln's Emancipation Proclamation, which was issued during the war, applied *only* to areas in rebellion and under Confederate control and therefore did not actually free any slaves.

The Fourteenth Amendment (1868) was adopted to make the former slaves citizens. But it has had other unintended and far-reaching effects. The amendment says that no state "shall abridge the privileges or immunities of citizens"; nor "deprive any person of life, liberty, or property, without due process of law"; nor deny anyone "the equal protection of the laws." The famous "due process" clause of the amendment has been used by the Supreme Court to protect the rights of individuals against the police power of the state in a broad spectrum of cases. The "equal protection of laws" provision was the basis for the landmark 1954 Supreme Court decision outlawing segregation in public schools.

The Fifteenth Amendment (1870) barred the federal and state governments from denying any citizen the right to vote because of race, color, or previous condition of servitude. It did not, however, prevent some states from disenfranchising blacks by means of restrictive voting requirements, such as literacy tests.

Forty-three years elapsed after the adoption of the Fifteenth Amendment before another was ratified. The Sixteenth Amendment (1913) allowed Congress to pass a graduated individual income tax, based in theory on ability to pay. The tax is, of course, the largest single source of federal revenue.

The Seventeenth Amendment (1913) provided for direct election of senators by the people, instead of by state legislatures.

The Eighteenth Amendment (1919) established Prohibition by outlawing the manufacture, sale, or transportation of alcoholic beverages. It provides a classic instance of an output of government doomed to failure because ultimately the input of popular *support* was lacking. Prohibition led to the era of bathtub gin, "flappers," speakeasies, and bootlegging. It was marked by widespread defiance of the law by otherwise law-abiding citizens and by the rise of organized crime, which quickly moved to meet public demand for illicit liquor. Partly as a result of Prohibition, organized crime remains entrenched in America today, exercising political influence in some areas of the country. Prohibition was repealed in 1933.

The Nineteenth Amendment (1920) guaranteed women the right to vote. Women voted in many states even before the amendment was proposed, but it provided a constitutional basis. Even so, it may seem surprising today that female suffrage was not constitutionally adopted until 1920, in time for that year's presidential election.

Under the Twentieth (or "lame duck") Amendment (1933), the terms of the President and Vice President begin on January 20 and the terms of members of Congress on January 3. Prior to that time a President and congressmen defeated in November would continue in office for four months until March 4 (formerly the date of presidential inaugurations). Injured by the voters, the defeated incumbents sat like "lame ducks."[59] The amendment also provides alternatives in case of the death of the President-elect before Inauguration Day or in case no President has been chosen.

The Twenty-first Amendment (1933) repealed Prohibition but permitted states to remain "dry" if they so desired.

The Twenty-second Amendment (1951) limits Presidents to a maximum of two elected terms. It was proposed after President Franklin D. Roosevelt had won a fourth term in 1944. Before then, through hallowed tradition established by George Washington, no President had been elected more than twice.

The Twenty-third Amendment (1961) gives citizens of the District of Columbia the right to vote in presidential elections; they did so for the first time in 1964. When the amendment was adopted, the capital had a population of 800,000 — larger than that of thirteen of the states.

The Twenty-fourth Amendment (1964) abolished the poll tax as a prerequisite for voting in federal elections or primaries. It applied to only five Southern states that still imposed such a tax, originally a device to keep blacks (and in some cases poor whites) from voting.

The Twenty-fifth Amendment (1967) was spurred by President Dwight D. Eisenhower's 1955 heart attack and by the murder of President Kennedy in Dallas, Texas, on November 22, 1963. It defines the circumstances under which a Vice President may take over the leadership of the country in case of the mental or physical illness or disability of the President. It also requires the President to nominate a Vice President, subject to majority approval of Congress, when that office becomes vacant for any reason. The amendment was used for the first time in October 1973 when President Nixon nominated House Republican leader Gerald R. Ford to replace Vice President Agnew. Congress confirmed Ford in December. When Nixon resigned in August 1974, Ford became President, again under the amendment. The amendment was used a third time when President Ford that same month nominated Nelson A. Rockefeller of New York to be Vice President. Congress confirmed Rockefeller in December 1974.

The Twenty-sixth Amendment (1971) gave persons eighteen years of age or older the right to vote in all elections — federal, state, and local. The amendment was proposed by Congress in March 1971 and ratified in June. As a result, 1972 was the first presidential election year in which persons eighteen through twenty were able to vote in elections at every level of government.

The proposed Twenty-seventh Amendment, designed to guarantee equal rights for women under the law, was approved by Congress in March 1972 and sent to the states for ratification by 1979. "Equality of rights under the law shall not be denied or abridged by the United States or by any State on account of sex," the amendment reads. It was proposed to nullify the many state laws that discriminate against women in jobs, business, marriage, and other areas.

---

[59] The phrase apparently originated as London stock exchange slang. It was used to describe a stock jobber or broker who could not make good his losses and would "waddle out of the alley like a lame duck." Abraham Lincoln is sometimes credited with introducing the phrase in America. When a defeated senator called on Lincoln and asked for a job as Commissioner of Indian Affairs, Lincoln was quoted as saying afterward: "I usually find that a Senator or Representative out of business is a sort of lame duck." George Stimpson, *A Book about American Politics* (New York: Harper & Row, 1952), pp. 527–28.

After an initial burst of support, the Equal Rights Amendment (ERA) ran into increasing difficulty. Although twenty-three states ratified the ERA in 1972, the bandwagon slowed considerably thereafter, and by January 1977, only thirty-five states—three short of the necessary thirty-eight—had approved the amendment.[60] With time running out, Congress extended the deadline for ratification to June 30, 1982. Unless ratified by then, the amendment would not become part of the Constitution.

In 1978 Congress approved and sent to the states a proposed constitutional amendment that would treat the District of Columbia as a state for purposes of representation in Congress and the electoral college. The Twenty-third Amendment gave district residents the right only to vote for President, and a 1970 law permitted the district a nonvoting delegate in the House. By 1980, nine states had ratified the proposed amendment.

"The Constitution belongs to the living and not to the dead," Thomas Jefferson wrote. He added:

> Some men look at constitutions with sanctimonious reverence and deem them like the ark of the covenant, too sacred to be touched. They ascribe to the men of the preceding age a wisdom more than human, and suppose what they did to be beyond amendment. . . . Laws and institutions must go hand in hand with the progress of the human mind. . . . As new discoveries are made, new truths disclosed, and manners and opinions change . . . institutions must advance also, and keep pace with the times.[61]

A Document
for the Living . . .

[60] Confusing the picture further, several states attempted to rescind their approval of the amendment.

[61] "Letter to Samuel Kercheval, 1816," in Saul K. Padover, ed., *The Complete Jefferson* (New York: Duell, Sloan & Pearce, 1943), p. 291.

Through a variety of ways, including amendments and judicial review, the oldest written national constitution in the world remains the vital framework of the American political system. But are constitutional principles enough? Today, many Americans are asking that the nation's institutions fulfill the promise of its ideals, and that principles be translated into reality. Constitutional democracy was born at Philadelphia, but, in a real sense, the work was only begun.

Perspective

The Constitution and the Bill of Rights provide the basic framework of American government. The Constitution established the structure of the government and a written set of rules to control the conduct of the government. The Declaration of Independence, approved by the Continental Congress on July 4, 1776, proclaimed that "all men are created equal" and that government derived its just powers from "the consent of the governed." Many of the ideas contained in these documents were drawn from the colonists' English heritage.

Before the Constitution was framed, a weak central government had been established under the Articles of Confederation. During the Constitutional Convention of 1787, the Virginia Plan, favored by the large states, and the New Jersey Plan, favored by the small states, were debated. The Great Compromise, also called the Connecticut Compromise, was finally adopted as an alternative. That compromise provided for a House of Representatives, to be based on population in each state, and a Senate, to consist of two members from each state—a solution that satisfied both the large and small states. The convention also compromised over the slavery issue by delaying a ban on the importation of slaves until 1808 and by counting three-fifths of all slaves in apportioning the House of Representatives.

The Constitution divided the national government into three branches: legislative, executive, and judicial. The government is based on the principles of separation of powers and checks and balances, even though in practice many powers and functions overlap and are shared. The Constitution also created a federal system, in which the powers and functions of government are divided between the national government and the states. The Constitution was ratified in 1788, but only after a long debate and political struggle between the Federalists and the Antifederalists. In 1791 the states ratified a Bill of Rights intended to protect individuals from the power of the federal government. These first ten amendments to the Constitution included provisions for freedom of religion, speech, press, assembly, and petition; the right to bear arms; protection against unreasonable search and seizure; the right to a speedy and public trial by jury in criminal cases; the right to due process of law; and protection against self-incrimination, double jeopardy, and cruel and unusual punishment. Through 1980, the Constitution had been amended twenty-six times. The Supreme Court interprets the Constitution. Exercising judicial review, the Supreme Court decides whether laws passed by Congress and acts of the President are constitutional.

Suggested Reading

Beard, Charles A. *An Economic Interpretation of the Constitution of the United States** (Macmillan, 1935). (Originally published in 1913.) The classic argument suggesting that delegates to the Philadelphia Convention were influenced primarily by economic motives in framing the Constitution. A number of later scholars have taken issue with Beard's interpretation.

Becker, Carl L. *The Declaration of Independence** (Knopf, 1966). (Originally published in 1942.) A perceptive discussion of the Declaration of Independence and the events leading up to it.

Boorstin, Daniel J. *The Americans: The Colonial Experience** (Random House, 1958). An analysis of the impact of the colonial period on U.S. political ideas and institutions.

Corwin, Edward S., et al., eds. *The Constitution of the United States of America, Analysis and Interpretation* (U.S. Government Printing Office 1964). A comprehensive and detailed line-by-line exposition of the Constitution. See also Corwin, revised by Harold W. Chase and Craig R. Ducat, *The Constitution and What It Means Today,** 14th edition (Princeton, 1978).

Earle, Edward Mead, ed. *The Federalist** (Random House, Modern Library). A classic collection of essays written by Alexander Hamilton, James Madison, and John Jay, prominent supporters of the proposed Constitution during the struggle over ratification. *The Federalist* papers were published in the press under the pseudonym "Publius"; they remain an important exposition of the structure of the federal government.

Farrand, Max. *The Framing of the Constitution of the United States** (Yale University Press, 1913). A good general account of the Constitutional Convention by the scholar who compiled in four volumes the basic documentary sources on the proceedings of the convention.

Harmon, M. Judd, ed. *Essays on the Constitution of the United States* (Kennikat, 1978). A collection of eight essays by different authors examining the continuity and stability of the principles upon which the Constitution was founded. Based on a series of lectures presented during 1976, the Bicentennial year.

Kelly, Alfred H., and Harbison, Winfred A. *The American Constitution: Its Origins and Development,* 5th edition (Norton, 1976). A good general history of American constitutional development beginning with the colonial period.

* Available in paperback edition

Lipset, Seymour Martin. *The First New Nation** (Norton, 1979). An important historical and sociological study of America that seeks to trace the relationship between a nation's values and the development of stable political institutions. Compares the early American experience with that of today's emerging nations.

Mason, Alpheus T., ed. *The States Rights Debate: Antifederalism and the Constitution,* 2nd edition* (Oxford University Press, 1972). A valuable series of essays and documents tracing the historical tension between states' rights and national supremacy in the federal system, as it was reflected in the Constitutional Convention and in the fight over ratification.

Rossiter, Clinton. *Seedtime of the Republic* (Harcourt Brace Jovanovich, 1953). A penetrating analysis of American political and social history in the colonial and revolutionary periods, with emphasis on the political ideas that were to condition the formation of the American nation.

Rossiter, Clinton. *1787: The Grand Convention* (Macmillan, 1966). A very readable account of the Philadelphia Convention, the battle for ratification of the Constitution, and the first years of the new republic. Makes interesting observations on the personal characteristics and objectives of the framers of the Constitution.

Rutland, Robert A. *The Birth of the Bill of Rights, 1776–1791** (Macmillan, 1962). A study of how Americans came to rely on legal guarantees in an effort to preserve their personal freedom. English common law, colonial charters and statutes, and specific events in the thirteen colonies are discussed as important factors that led to the Bill of Rights.

THE FEDERAL SYSTEM

It used to be said that the French Minister of Education could, by glancing at the clock in his office, tell at any given moment what book was being read by every schoolchild in France.

The tale may be a bit exaggerated, but no official in Washington could even begin to perform the same feat. France has a centralized, *unitary* system of government. The nation is divided into administrative units called departments, uniformly administered from Paris. Educational and other policies are set by the central government.

In contrast, the United States has a *federal* system of government, in which power is constitutionally shared by a national government and fifty state governments. Within the states, of course, are thousands of local governments—and schools are controlled by local and state governments or independent school districts. The constitutional sharing of power by a national government and regional units of government (states in the case of the United States) characterizes and defines a federal system or *federalism*. The terms "federalism" and "the federal system" are used interchangeably to describe this basic structure of government in the United States. (These terms should not be confused with "the federal government," which simply refers to the national government in Washington.)

To say that power in America is shared by the national and state governments may, at first glance, seem merely to be stating the obvious. Yet no prin-

ciple of American government has been disputed more than federalism. Should that be doubted, one need only recall that more than 500,000 died during the Civil War settling problems of federalism.

The question of *how* power is to be shared in the federal system is central to the political process in the United States. It is a subject of continuing political debate. It has been reflected in many important decisions of the Supreme Court. The migrant worker in the lettuce fields of California, the family on welfare in New York, the West Virginia coal miner, the spouse seeking a Nevada divorce, the murder suspect fighting extradition, the slum dweller hoping for an apartment in a federal housing project—none may think of their problems in terms of the federal system. Yet the relationship among national, state, and local governments vitally touches their lives. To a considerable extent, federalism affects who wins and who loses as a result of governmental decisions in American society. It affects the outputs of the political system.

Federalism is one answer to the problem of how to govern a large nation. Although there are all sorts of institutional arrangements in the 163 nations of the world, governments tend to be either centralized and unitary, or federated. In the twentieth century, federalism has become a popular style of government. By 1964, one study concluded, "well over half the land mass of the world was ruled by governments that with some justification, however slight, described themselves as federalisms."[1] The list of federal systems includes the Soviet Union, Switzerland, Canada, Australia, Mexico, India, and West Germany. Unitary systems, in which all power is vested in a central government, include Britain, France, Israel, and South Africa.

Federalism: The Pros and Cons

What are the arguments for and against a federal system? Federalism permits diversity. Since problems and circumstances vary from one community to another, the argument can be made that a number of governments dealing directly with local problems, and accountable to local voters, may perform better than a single, remote bureaucracy. Local governments, by this reasoning, may have a better idea than the national government of how to cope with local problems.

[1] William H. Riker, *Federalism: Origin, Operation, Significance* (Boston: Little, Brown, 1964), p. 1.

Another argument advanced for a federal system of government is that it allows more levels of government, more points of access to the government, and as a result, more opportunities for political participation. Because Americans have a federal system, they may vote at frequent intervals for mayors, council members, school boards, governors, other state officials, and members of the House of Representatives and senators elected from the states.

Some analysts also argue that because power is diffused and fragmented among many different units in a federal system, there is better protection for individual rights than in a highly centralized government. Concentrated power is dangerous, supporters of federalism often maintain.

Advocates of a federal system also stress that the existence of many units of government allows for more experimentation and innovation in solving problems. New social programs are sometimes originated in one state, for example, and then adopted in another, or even nationally.

In addition, advocates of federalism argue that it is well suited to the United States, a nation covering a large geographic area with a highly diversified population of more than 226 million people.

But a federal system also has distinct disadvantages. Federalism may serve as a mask for privilege and economic or racial discrimination.[2] In some areas of the South, and in other sections of the country as well, the federal system has permitted state and local governments to repress blacks. Inequalities may occur when special interests exercise considerable influence on the politics and economy of a state or locality; for example, West Virginia, although the nation's second leading coal producer, is a relatively poor state, a fact usually attributed in part to its dependence on a single industry. Along with abandoned strip mines, pockets of poverty scar the hillsides; in 1978 West Virginia ranked thirty-ninth

[2] *Ibid.*, pp. 152–53.

The Federal System

Table 3-1

Scholars and political leaders alike have debated the relative merits and drawbacks of federalism since the founding of the republic. Here are some of the major arguments that have been made:

Advantages	Disadvantages
Permits diversity and diffusion of power	Makes national unity difficult to achieve and maintain
Local governments can handle local problems better	Local governments may block national policies
More access points for political participation	May permit economic inequality and racial discrimination
Protects individual rights against concentrated government power	Law enforcement and justice are uneven
Fosters experimentation and innovation	Smaller units may lack expertise and money
Suits a large country with a diverse population	May promote local dominance by special interests

The American Democracy

One does not decide on the merits of federalism by an examination of federalism in the abstract, but rather on its actual meaning for particular societies. . . .

The main beneficiary throughout American history has been the Southern whites, who have been given the freedom to oppress Negroes, first as slaves and later as a depressed caste. Other minorities have from time to time also managed to obtain some of these benefits; e.g., special business interests have been allowed to regulate themselves, especially in the era from about 1890 to 1936, by means of the judicial doctrine of dual federalism, which eliminated both state and national regulation of such matters as wage rates and hours of labor. But the significance of federal benefits to economic interests pales beside the significance of benefits to the Southern segregationist whites. The judgment to be passed on federalism in the United States is therefore a judgment on the values of segregation and racial oppression.

—William H. Riker, *Federalism: Origin, Operation, Significance.*

in the nation in per capita income.[3] Although the energy shortage increased the price of coal and brought greater prosperity to the state, industry pressures tended to keep taxes low. That in turn affected West Virginia's ability to provide social services for its residents.

Critics argue that under the federal system, local or special interests — white supremacists in Mississippi, for example, or the automobile industry or the oil companies — have often been able to frustrate efforts to solve national problems like school desegregation, poverty, pollution, and the energy crisis. The same local officials whose understanding of local problems is often cited as a benefit of federalism may be in a position to thwart national policies. Government that is "closer to the people" may not serve all the people equally. Nor is it necessarily the case that local governments can solve problems more efficiently; they may lack the national government's skill and money. In fact, because the federal government collects most of the taxes in America, it can be argued that the system of federalism has often left cities and states unable to pay for local services.

Other arguments are sometimes made against a federal system: its very diversity may make it difficult to achieve and maintain national unity; it can be more difficult and costly to make a complex system work; and law enforcement and justice may be administered unevenly.

The relations between the states and the federal government are thus a source of continuing conflict and controversy in the American political system and raise a number of questions of fundamental importance. Who benefits and who loses under the federal system? Does federalism restrict progress in solving national problems? Do the advantages of federalism outweigh the price of fragmented government? Why does the United States have a federal system? What are the problems it has created? Can programs like revenue sharing help? What are the consequences of federalism in American politics? In the performance of the states?

[3] U.S. Department of Commerce, *Survey of Current Business* (Washington, D.C.: U.S. Government Printing Office, August 1979), pp. 30–31.

The Checkerboard of Governments

Average Americans complain that they are being squeezed by high taxes on at least three levels of government — national, state, and local. They are confronted by a bewildering checkerboard of overlapping governments and local districts. One study of the federal system found that a resident of Park Forest, Illinois, paid taxes to eleven governmental units, starting with the United States of America and ending with the "South Cook County Mosquito Abatement District."[4]

The Census Bureau has counted a total of 79,913 governments in the United States: some 3000 counties, 18,900 municipalities, 16,800 townships, 15,200 school districts, 26,000 special districts (for fire protection, water supply, and other services), 50 states, and 1 national government.[5]

But knowing how many governments exist in America tells little about how the federal system operates — how the various levels of government relate to one another. One way to visualize the system as a whole was suggested by Morton Grodzins:

> The federal system is not accurately symbolized by a neat layer cake of three distinct and separate planes. A far more realistic symbol is that of the marble cake. Wherever you slice through it you reveal an inseparable mixture of differently colored ingredients. There is no neat horizontal stratification. Vertical and diagonal lines almost obliterate the horizontal ones, and in some places there are unexpected whirls and an imperceptible merging of colors, so that it is difficult to tell where one ends and the other begins. So it is with federal, state, and local responsibilities in the chaotic marble cake of American government.[6]

Cooperation —
and Tension

Is the American federal system essentially cooperative — or is it competitive? In fact, federalism can be seen both as a rivalry between the states and Washington and as a partnership. A system of 79,913 governments could not operate without a substantial measure of cooperation, but a great tension is built into the system as well.

In 1975, for example, New York City was in deep financial trouble; there was a real possibility that the city would default on its bonds. The administration of President Gerald R. Ford at first declined to help. New York State took control of the city's finances, but the specter of default remained. Finally, Ford relented and recommended to Congress that it aid New York City. Congress passed a bill providing billions in federal loans for the city. Ultimately, the federal government did not permit the nation's biggest metropolis to go broke, but the political struggle over aid to New York City was protracted and bitter.

There have been other dramatic examples of tension within the federal system. Three times in recent decades the President of the United States has deployed armed federal troops in Southern states. In 1957 President Eisenhower sent troops into Little Rock, Arkansas, to enforce court-ordered integra-

---

[4] Morton Grodzins, *The American System* (Chicago: Rand McNally, 1966), pp. 3–4.

[5] U.S. Bureau of the Census, *1977 Census of Governments*, Governmental Organization, Vol. 1, No. 1, p. 1. The total represented the actual number of governments in 1977; the other figures are rounded.

[6] Morton Grodzins, "Centralization and Decentralization in the American Federal System," in Robert A. Goldwin, ed., *A Nation of States* (Chicago: Rand McNally, 1963), pp. 1–4.

tion of the previously all white Central High School. In the fall of 1962 two men were killed on the campus of the University of Mississippi at Oxford during rioting over the admission of James H. Meredith, a black student. President Kennedy deployed 16,000 federal troops in Mississippi to enroll Meredith and protect him as he attended classes. In June 1963 Governor George Wallace carried out a campaign pledge to "stand in the schoolhouse door" to try to prevent two black students from entering the University of Alabama. Wallace backed down after President Kennedy federalized the state's national guard to enforce the order of a federal court.

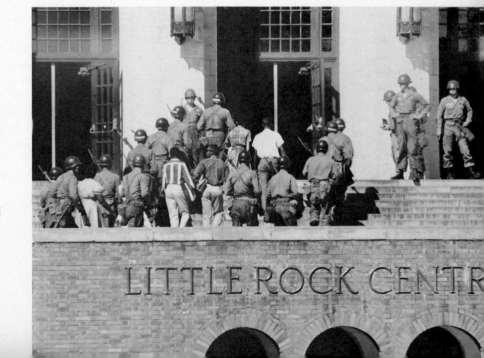

"A great tension is built into the system . . .": Federal troops on guard at Central High School in Little Rock, Arkansas, September 1957

LITTLE ROCK CENTR

BOOTHBAY HARBOR, MAINE, Sept. 3 (AP)—A seal that lay wounded on a beach for 14 hours . . . because of a dispute between state and federal officials died early today. The animal, which had been shot in the stomach, died at the laboratory of the State Department of Sea and Shore Fisheries. State wardens said they couldn't aid the seal because a new federal law placed jurisdiction for marine mammals with the U.S. Marine Fisheries Service.

At the Newagen Inn, a resort near where the seal was beached . . . guests tried to get help, but failed. . . . Several of the guests placed a towel under the seal and then . . . kept placing water on the towel to keep the seal moist. . . . The harbor seals killed in Maine this summer were probably shot by fishermen who complain that the seals tear holes in their nets.

—*Washington Post,* September 4, 1973.

Although Presidents tend to use the rhetoric of cooperation when they talk about federal-state relations, there is clearly an underlying tension among competing levels of government. Sometimes the tensions arise from social issues, as in the armed confrontations over racial desegregation. Often, as in the case of the "bailout" of New York City, they are rooted in disagreements over how tax revenues should be shared or used.

There are political and ideological tensions as well—between those who look to the federal government to solve major national social and economic problems (chiefly Northern Democrats and liberal Republicans), and those who tend to see the government in Washington as a threat to individual liberty and initiative and regard the states as a bulwark against an expanding federal "octopus" (chiefly Southern Democrats and conservative Republicans).

The Changing Federal Framework

The federal system has been viewed differently at different times. During much of the nineteenth century and until 1937, the concept of *dual federalism* was accepted, in which the Supreme Court saw itself as a referee between two competing power centers—the states and the federal government, each with its own responsibilities.

1935: President Franklin D. Roosevelt signs the Social Security Act.

This orthodox view of the federal system prevailed until the New Deal of Franklin D. Roosevelt. During the 1930s the Roosevelt administration responded to the Great Depression with a series of laws establishing social welfare and public works programs. In 1937 the Supreme Court began holding these programs constitutional. With the federal government thrust into an expanded position of power, a new view of federalism emerged, that of *cooperative federalism.* In this view, the various levels of government are seen as related parts of a single governmental system, characterized more by cooperation and shared functions than by conflict and competition. For example, the federal government provides most of the money to build major highways, but the program is administered by state and local governments. Some scholars have argued that, historically, the American federal system has always been characterized by such shared functions at the federal, state, and local levels.[7]

[7]Grodzins, *The American System;* Daniel J. Elazar, *American Federalism: A View from the States* (New York: Crowell, 1966); Daniel J. Elazar, *The American Partnership* (Chicago: University of Chicago Press, 1962).

One student of the federal system, Michael D. Reagan, has suggested that it no longer makes sense to think of federalism "as a wall separating the national and state levels of government." Rather, he maintains, extensive federal financial aid to the states has created *a nationally dominated system of shared power and shared functions.*"[8]

President Lyndon Johnson coined the term *creative federalism* to describe his own view of the relationship between Washington and the states. During his administration, Congress enacted "Great Society" legislation that further expanded the role of the federal government. President Nixon launched what he termed the *new federalism,* designed to return federal tax money to state and local governments.

All these changes in the patterns and language of federalism reflect the fact that the United States has to a great extent become a national society. People often look to Washington to solve problems. In the 1980s, for example, most people expect the national government—not their mayor or town council members—to deal with energy shortages and inflation.

But the need for solutions to major national problems has not resolved the larger question of how to make a federal system work. As one study viewed the problem,

> The basic dilemma . . . is how to achieve goals and objectives that are established by the national government, through the action of other governments, state and local, that are legally independent and politically may be hostile. Those state and local governments are subject to no federal discipline except through the granting or denial of federal aid. And that is not very useful, because to deny the funds is in effect to veto the national objective itself.[9]

The Historical Basis of Federalism

"A Middle Ground"

In April 1787, a month before the Constitutional Convention opened at Philadelphia, James Madison set forth his thoughts on the structure of a new government in a letter addressed to George Washington.

Madison argued that while the states could not each be completely independent, the creation of "one simple republic" would be "unattainable." "I have sought for a middle ground," Madison wrote, "which may at once support a due supremacy of the national authority, and not exclude the local authorities wherever they can be subordinately useful."[10]

Essentially, Madison had forecast the balanced structure that emerged from a compromise five months later. The bargain struck at Philadelphia in 1787 was a federal bargain. The Constitutional Convention created the federal system, with its sharing of power by the states and the national government. The delegates to the convention agreed to give up some of the states' independence in order to achieve enough unity to create a nation. Yet, America probably got a federal system of government because no stronger national government would have been acceptable to the framers or to the states.

[8] Michael D. Reagan, *The New Federalism* (New York: Oxford University Press, 1972), pp. 4, 145.
[9] James L. Sundquist with David W. Davis, *Making Federalism Work* (Washington, D.C.: The Brookings Institution, 1969), p. 12.
[10] Letter to George Washington, April 16, 1787, in Saul K. Padover, ed., *The Complete Madison* (New York: Harper & Brothers, 1953), p. 184.

There are a number of reasons why a stronger central government would have been unacceptable. First, public opinion in the states almost certainly would not have permitted adoption of a unitary form of government. Loyalty to the states was strong. The Articles of Confederation showed just about how far people had been willing to go in the direction of a central government prior to 1787—which was not very far. The diversity of the American people, regional interests, even the state of technology—transportation was slow and great distances separated the colonies—all militated against the establishment of a central government stronger than the one framed at Philadelphia. Finally, federalism was seen as an effective device for limiting national power by distributing authority between the states and the national government.

A Tool for Nation Building

The collapse of European colonial empires since the Second World War confronted successful rebels in Africa and Asia with an urgent problem: how to organize their new nations. William H. Riker holds that large emerging nations face two alternatives: they can unite under a central government, in which case they have "merely exchanged one imperial master for a lesser one"; or they can join "in some kind of federation, which preserves at least the semblance of political self-control." He adds, "In this sense, federalism is the main alternative to empire as a technique of aggregating large areas under one government."[11]

One rationale of federalism is that it protects diversity of interests within regional units while allowing a national political system to develop. On the other hand, the terrible civil war in Nigeria, touched off in 1967 by Biafra's secession from the central government, is a reminder that a federal system does not guarantee political stability. And it should not be forgotten that the United States also experienced a tragic civil war that threatened its federal system.

Yet the framework of federalism in the United States first permitted a disunited people to find a basis for political union and then allowed room for the development of a sense of national identity. As a result, "The United States of America" is not only the name of a country—to an extent, it is also a description of its formal governmental structure.

The Constitutional Basis of Federalism

Federal Powers: Enumerated, Implied, Inherent, and Concurrent

The Constitution established the framework for the American federal system. Under it, the three branches of the federal government are granted certain specifically *enumerated powers*. Congress, for example, has the power to coin money; the President is Commander in Chief of the armed forces.

In addition, the Supreme Court has held that the national government also has broad *implied powers*. These flow from its enumerated powers and the "elastic clause" of the Constitution, which gives Congress power to make all laws "necessary and proper" to carry out its enumerated powers. For example, the right of the United States to establish a national banking system is an implied power flowing from its enumerated power to collect taxes and regulate commerce.[12]

[11] Riker, *Federalism: Origin, Operation, Significance,* pp. 4–5.
[12] *McCulloch* v. *Maryland,* 4 Wheaton 316 (1819).

The Supreme Court has also held that the national government has *inherent powers* that it may exercise simply because it exists as a government. One of the most important inherent powers is the right to conduct foreign relations. Since the United States does not exist in a vacuum, it must, as a practical matter, deal with other countries, even though the Constitution does not spell this out. The Court made clear in the *Curtiss-Wright* case that the "war power" of the United States government is an inherent power. It said, "The power to declare and wage war, to conclude peace, to make treaties, to maintain diplomatic relations with other sovereignties, if they had never been mentioned in the Constitution, would have vested in the federal government as necessary concomitants of nationality."[13]

Finally, the federal government and the states also have certain *concurrent powers,* which they exercise independently. The power to tax, for example, is enjoyed by both the federal and state governments. Of course, a state cannot exercise a power that belongs only to the federal government under the Constitution, nor can a state take actions that conflict with federal law.

These various powers are complex concepts. They developed slowly as the nation grew and found it necessary to adapt the Constitution to changing conditions.

The Supreme Court serves as an arbiter in questions of state versus national power. The federal system could not function efficiently without an umpire.

The Supreme Court as Umpire

The Court's attitude has changed radically over the decades; sometimes the Court has supported states' rights, and sometimes it has supported expanded federal power. But in every period, the Court has served as a major arena in which important conflicts are settled within the federal framework.

McCulloch v. *Maryland.* The most important of these Supreme Court decisions was that of Chief Justice John Marshall in *McCulloch* v. *Maryland* in 1819. His ruling established the doctrine of implied powers and gave the federal government sanction to take giant steps beyond the literal language of the Constitution.

James W. McCulloch might otherwise not have gone down in American history. But as it happened he was cashier of the Baltimore branch of the National Bank of the United States, which had been established by Congress. The National Bank had failed to prevent a business panic and economic depression in 1819, and some of its branches were managed by what can only be termed crooks. As a result, several states, including Maryland, tried to force the banks out of their states. Maryland slapped an annual tax of $15,000 on the National Bank. McCulloch refused to pay, setting the stage for the great courtroom battle of the day. Daniel Webster argued for the bank, and Luther Martin, Attorney General of Maryland, for his state.

The first question answered by Marshall in his opinion for a unanimous Court was the basic question of whether Congress had power to incorporate a bank. Marshall laid down a classic definition of national sovereignty and broad constitutional construction. "The government of the Union ... is emphatically and truly a government of the people. In form and substance it emanates from

Chief Justice John Marshall: "Let the end be legitimate . . ."

[13] *United States* v. *Curtiss-Wright Export Corp.,* 299 U.S. 304 (1936).

them. Its powers are granted by them, and are to be exercised directly on them, and for their benefit."[14]

Marshall conceded that the Constitution divided sovereignty between the states and the national government but said that "the government of the Union, though limited in its powers, is supreme within its sphere of action." Although the power to charter a bank was not among the enumerated powers of Congress in the Constitution, he said, it could be inferred from the "necessary and proper" clause. In short, Congress had "implied powers."

"Let the end be legitimate," Marshall wrote, "let it be within the scope of the Constitution, and all means which are appropriate, which are plainly adapted to that end, which are not prohibited, but consist with the letter and spirit of the Constitution, are constitutional." Congress, said Marshall, had the right to legislate with a "vast mass of incidental powers which must be involved in the Constitution, if that instrument be not a splendid bauble."

On the second question of whether Maryland had the right to tax the National Bank, Marshall ruled against the state, for "the power to tax involves the power to destroy." No state, he said, possessed that right because this implied that the federal government depended on the will of the states. Marshall ruled the Maryland law unconstitutional.

Thus, at a very early stage in the history of our nation, Marshall established the key concepts of implied powers, broad construction of the Constitution, and national supremacy. More than one hundred years were to pass before these powers were exercised fully, but the decision laid the basis for the future growth of national power.

The Division of Federal and State Power. Under the Tenth Amendment, "The powers not delegated to the United States by the Constitution, nor prohibited by it to the States, are reserved to the States respectively, or to the people."

At first glance, this amendment might seem to limit the federal government to powers *specifically* enumerated and "delegated" to the federal government by the Constitution. But in deciding *McCulloch* v. *Maryland,* Chief Justice Marshall emphasized that the Tenth Amendment (unlike the Articles of Confederation) does not use the word "expressly" before the word "delegated."

This omission was not accidental. In 1789, during the debate on the first ten amendments, James Madison and others blocked the attempt of states'-rights advocates to limit federal powers to those "expressly" delegated.[15] During the debate, Madison objected to insertion of the key word "because it was impossible to confine a Government to the exercise of express powers; there must necessarily be admitted powers by implication, unless the Constitution descended to recount every minutia."[16]

The Supreme Court that followed the Marshall Court took a much narrower view of the powers of the federal government. Under Roger B. Taney, who served as Chief Justice from 1836 to 1864, the Court invoked the Tenth Amendment to protect the powers of the states. And in 1871 the Supreme Court

---

[14] *McCulloch* v. *Maryland* (1819).

[15] Alfred H. Kelly and Winfred A. Harbison, *The American Constitution* (New York: Norton, 1955), p. 176.

[16] In Walter Berns, "The Meaning of the Tenth Amendment," in Goldwin, ed., *A Nation of States,* p. 138. For a spirited defense of the opposite view, see "The Case for 'States' Rights'" by James J. Kilpatrick in the same volume.

ruled that the amendment meant that the federal government could not tax the salaries of state officials.[17]

For two decades after the First World War, the Court invoked the Tenth Amendment to invalidate a series of federal laws dealing with child labor and regulating industry and agriculture. And in 1935 the Court cited the amendment in declaring unconstitutional the National Industrial Recovery Act, a major piece of New Deal legislation designed to reduce unemployment.[18]

But in the watershed year of 1937, the Court swung around and upheld the Social Security program and the National Labor Relations Act as valid exercises of federal power.[19] And in 1941 it specifically rejected the argument that the Constitution in any way limited the power of the federal government to regulate interstate commerce. The decision upheld the Fair Labor Standards Act. Speaking for the Court, Chief Justice Harlan Fiske Stone called the Tenth Amendment "a truism that all is retained which has not been surrendered."[20]

Thus, more than 120 years after *McCulloch* v. *Maryland,* the Supreme Court had finally swung back to John Marshall's view of the Constitution as an instrument that gave the federal government broad powers over the states and the nation. Those powers are not unlimited, however. In 1976 the Supreme Court, in a 5–4 decision, struck down a federal law extending federal minimum-wage and maximum-hour provisions to some 3.4 million state and municipal workers. The Court held that Congress had infringed too far upon "the separate and independent existence" of the states.[21] Despite this case, the Supreme Court has generally upheld the right of the federal government to intervene in state and local affairs.

Nevertheless, many advocates of a states'-rights position continue to rely on the Tenth Amendment as the constitutional foundation for their argument. In general, they see the Constitution as the result of a compact among the states. A more widely accepted view today is that the national government represents the *people,* and that sovereignty rests not with the states but with "we the people," who created the Constitution and approved it.

The *supremacy clause* of the Constitution (Article VI, Paragraph 2) makes it clear that the Constitution and the laws and treaties made under it are supreme over state constitutions or laws.

In addition, the Constitution places many restrictions on the states: they are forbidden to make treaties, coin money, pass bills of attainder or ex post facto laws, impair contracts, grant titles of nobility, tax imports or exports, keep troops or warships in peacetime, engage in war (unless invaded), or make interstate compacts without congressional approval. The Bill of Rights, as interpreted by the Supreme Court, and the Fourteenth and Fifteenth amendments place additional restrictions on the states (see Chapter 4, pp. 123–25).

Local governments derive their powers from the states and are subject to

Restrictions on the States

[17] *Collector* v. *Day,* 11 Wallace 113 (1871). This decision was overruled by the Supreme Court in 1939 in *Graves* v. *O'Keefe,* 306 U.S. 466 (1939).
[18] *Schecter Poultry Corporation* v. *United States,* 295 U.S. 495 (1935).
[19] *Steward Machine Co.* v. *Davis,* 301 U.S. 548 (1937); *National Labor Relations Board* v. *Jones & Laughlin Steel Corp.,* 301 U.S. 1 (1937).
[20] *United States* v. *Darby,* 312 U.S. 100 (1941).
[21] *The National League of Cities* v. *Usery,* 426 U.S. 833 (1976).

the same constitutional restrictions as are the states. If a state cannot do something, neither can a locality, since "in a strictly legal sense it must be understood that all local governments in the United States are creatures of their respective states."[22]

Federal Obligations to the States

The Constitution (in Article IV) defines the relations of the federal government to the states. For example, the United States must guarantee to every state "a republican form of government." In addition, the federal government must protect the states against invasion and against domestic violence on request of the governor or legislature. Presidents have, on several occasions, intervened in the states with force either at the invitation of, or over the objections of, the governor.

Congress may admit new states to the union, but the Constitution does not spell out any ground rules for their admission. In practice, when a territory has desired statehood, it has applied to Congress, which has passed an "enabling act" allowing the people of the territory to frame a constitution. If Congress approved the constitution, it passed a joint resolution recognizing the new state. (If in the future Congress should admit another state, it could follow this procedure, or adopt a new one.) As the frontier expanded westward, Congress steadily admitted new states until 1912, when New Mexico and Arizona, the last contiguous continental territories, became states. The forty-eight states became fifty in 1959 with the admission of Alaska and Hawaii—the only states of the union that do not border on another state.

Interstate Relations

Article IV of the Constitution also requires the states to observe certain rules in their dealings with one another.

First, states are required to give "full faith and credit" to the laws, records, and court decisions of another state. In practice, this simply means that a judgment obtained in a state court in a civil (not a criminal) case must be recognized by the courts of another state. If, for example, a person in New York loses a lawsuit and moves to California to avoid paying the judgment, the courts there will enforce the New York decision.

Sometimes, however, states fail to meet their obligations to one another. For example, a couple legally married in one state might not be legally married in another. In the famed *Williams* v. *North Carolina* cases[23]—the dispute went up to the Supreme Court twice—a man and a woman left their respective spouses in North Carolina, went to Nevada, got six-week divorces, and married each other. When they returned home, the state of North Carolina successfully prosecuted them for bigamy.[24]

Second, the Constitution provides that the citizens of each state are en-

[22] Daniel J. Elazar, *American Federalism: A View from the States,* p. 164.

[23] *Williams* v. *North Carolina,* 317 U.S. 287 (1942), 325 U.S. 226 (1945).

[24] Despite the confusion of the divorce laws, the situation had improved somewhat since an earlier landmark case, *Haddock* v. *Haddock,* 201 U.S. 562 (1906). In the words of one constitutional scholar: "The upshot [of that Supreme Court decision] was a situation in which a man and a woman, when both were in Connecticut, were divorced; when both were in New York, were married; and when the one was in Connecticut and the other in New York, the former was divorced and the latter married," in Edward S. Corwin et al., eds., *The Constitution of the United States of America, Analysis and Interpretation* (Washington, D.C.: U.S. Government Printing Office, 1964), p. 750.

titled to "all privileges and immunities" of citizens in other states. As interpreted by the Supreme Court, this hazy provision has come to mean that one state may not discriminate against citizens of another. But in practice, states do discriminate against persons who are not legal residents. For example, a state university often charges higher tuition fees to out-of-state students. States usually charge nonresidents much higher fees for fishing and hunting licenses than they do residents.

Finally, the Constitution provides for extradition of fugitives who flee across state lines to escape justice. A state may request the governor of another state to return fugitives, and normally the governor will comply with such a request. But in several instances, Northern governors refused to surrender blacks who had escaped from chain gangs or prisons in the South.

One famous example arose in the Scottsboro case, which began in 1931 when nine black youths were pulled off a freight train in Alabama by a mob and accused of raping two white girls. There was considerable doubt that the crime had even been committed. The Supreme Court reversed death sentences imposed on eight of the defendants, but all drew long prison terms. In 1948 one defendant, Haywood Patterson, escaped from an Alabama prison and fled north. He was arrested in Detroit by the FBI, and the state of Alabama demanded his return. Governor G. Mennen Williams of Michigan refused to extradite him.[25]

The Constitution permits the states to make agreements with one another with the approval of Congress. These *interstate compacts* were of minor importance until the twentieth century, but the spread of metropolitan areas—and metropolitan problems—across state borders and the increasing complexity of modern life has brought new significance to the agreements.

Interstate Compacts

The Port of New York Authority was created by an interstate compact between New York and New Jersey and approved by Congress in 1921. The powerful and quasi-independent authority operates, among other things, John F. Kennedy International Airport and La Guardia Airport in New York and Newark Airport in New Jersey. It also controls and runs the bridges and tunnels leading into Manhattan, and the world's largest bus terminal, near Times Square. Air and water pollution, pest control, toll bridges, and transportation are items on which states have entered into agreements with one another, with varying degrees of success.

The Growth of Strong National Government

The late Senator Everett McKinley Dirksen of Illinois, a legislator noted for his Shakespearean delivery and dramatic flair, once predicted sadly that the way things were going, "The only people interested in state boundaries will be Rand McNally."[26]

[25] Patterson was later charged with stabbing a man, went to prison, and died there in 1953. The other Scottsboro prisoners were freed on parole by 1950. Clarence Norris, believed to be the last survivor of the nine defendants, was finally pardoned by the state of Alabama in 1976.
[26] *New York Times*, August 8, 1965, Section IV, p. 2.

While this may be an exaggerated view of trends in the American federal system, Dirksen's remark reflected the fact that the national government *has* been gaining increased power. The formal structure of American government has changed very little since 1787, but the balance of power within the system has changed markedly.

The Rise of Big Government

A century ago, the federal government did not provide social security, medical insurance for some 27,000,000 citizens, vast aid to public and private education, or billions of dollars in welfare payments. Nor did it have independent regulatory agencies to watch over various segments of the economy.

As American society has grown more complex, as population has surged, the national government's managerial task has enlarged. People demand more services and government grows bigger in the process. Five cabinet departments— Housing and Urban Development; Transportation; Energy; Health and Human Services; and Education—were created within the past three decades.

The power to tax and spend for the general welfare is a function of the national government that has expanded enormously in the twentieth century. The government's role in the regulation of interstate and foreign commerce has also vastly increased.

Much of the growth of big government and of federal social welfare programs took place during the New Deal in the 1930s and during Lyndon Johnson's "Great Society" in the 1960s. Although conservatives periodically attack these programs as "creeping socialism," the major programs are so well established that no new administration in Washington is likely to be able to abolish them. President Reagan, however, came into office in 1981, determined to make substantial cuts in federal spending in the field of social welfare. He had repeatedly pledged to do so in his campaign for the Presidency.

Big Government and Foreign Policy

The responsibility of the federal government for the conduct of foreign affairs in the nuclear age has increased the size of the national government. In fiscal 1981, for example, the defense budget request totaled $147 billion, a substantial 24 percent of the total federal budget, and the largest single item.[27] The State Department, the Central Intelligence Agency, the International Communications Agency, the National Security Agency, and related agencies have expanded along with the Pentagon.

The Impact of Federalism on Government and Politics

America's governmental institutions and its political system developed within a framework of federalism, and they reflect that fact. Federalism has also placed its stamp on a broad range of informal activities in American society, including the operations of many private groups.

---

[27] Military spending is the largest single category if social security funds are excluded from the budget of the Department of Health and Human Services. In the actual federal budget, social security funds are included in the HHS budget, so that the HHS total exceeds that of the Pentagon.

The nature of representation in Congress reflects the impact of federalism. Each state, no matter how small, has two senators who represent the constituents of their state. Members of the House represent districts within the states, but they also comprise an informal delegation from their states. Senators and representatives, when elected, must reside in the states they represent. In the event of a deadlock in the electoral college, the House of Representatives votes by state to select the President, with each state having one vote. Congress, in short, provides an institutional basis for federalism.

Federalism also affects the court system. State and local courts exist side by side with federal courts in the United States and handle the vast majority of cases. But even the federal district courts and circuit courts are organized along geographic lines that take into account state boundaries. And, under the custom of "senatorial courtesy," before the President appoints a federal district or circuit court judge, he privately submits the name to the senators representing the home state of the nominee. If the state has a senator from the same party as the President, and that senator objects, the name is usually dropped.[28]

Many powerful interest groups are in a sense federations of state associations and groups. This is true, for example, of the American Medical Association, the American Bar Association, and to some extent the American Federation of Labor-Congress of Industrial Organizations (AFL-CIO).

Federalism and Government

In October 1979 President Carter flew to Chicago, hoping to receive the political endorsement of Mayor Jane Byrne. Carter at the time was being strongly challenged by Senator Edward M. Kennedy for the 1980 Democratic presidential nomination. Before 12,000 guests at the largest fund-raising dinner in the city's history, the mayor announced she would not hesitate to vote "to renominate our present leader for another four years."

Carter left Chicago, confident that he had secured the support of Mayor Byrne and the powerful Cook County Democratic organization. He may not have known, however, that the mayor had first decided to go into politics after hearing a campaign speech by presidential candidate John F. Kennedy in 1960. Or that the day of the dinner for Carter, Mayor Byrne had received a telegram from Senator Kennedy that read: "I have known you and loved you and Chicago longer."[29]

Two weeks after seeming to back the incumbent President, Mayor Byrne announced that she was throwing her support to Kennedy. Not long afterward, Neil Goldschmidt, the Secretary of Transportation in the Carter cabinet, was talking to reporters at a breakfast meeting in Washington. He said he had "lost confidence" in Mayor Byrne and indicated that he might withhold federal transit funds intended for Chicago.

Goldschmidt's remarks touched off a controversy. Kennedy supporters charged that Goldschmidt was playing politics with federal grant money. Three senators introduced legislation to take away the Secretary of Transportation's discretionary power to allocate $1.4 billion in mass transit funds. Goldschmidt denied that he had actually withheld any money from Chicago. But the mayor

Federalism and American Politics

Chicago's Mayor Jane Byrne and Senator Edward M. Kennedy

[28] As the system of senatorial courtesy has operated in recent years, the President has customarily notified both home-state senators of potential nominees, even when one or more senator does not belong to the President's party. However, in practice, only an objection by a member of the President's party is likely to affect a nomination.
[29] Eugene Kennedy, "Hard Times in Chicago," *The New York Times Magazine,* March 9, 1980, p. 20.

and the citizens of Chicago had received an interesting lesson in the workings of the federal system.

As the controversy illustrates, federalism affects party politics in the United States. National political parties are organized along federal lines. The United States has no national party system as, say, the British do. Rather, there is a federation of fifty state parties, precariously held together by a national committee between presidential nominating conventions.

The governors' chairs in the fifty states are political prizes. As a result, there are fifty centers of political power in the states competing with the locus of national power in Washington.

To a party out of power nationally, the existence of state political machinery takes on special importance. By building up state parties and demonstrating leadership ability on the same level, the "out" party may consolidate its position and prepare for the next national election. Often a strong governor or a former governor will emerge as a contender for the party's presidential nomination.

Although state political parties constitute basic political units in the United States, state political systems vary greatly. In some states, such as New York, there is lively competition between Democrats and Republicans. Other states have often been dominated by one party, as in the case of the Democrats in Alabama. The makeup of the electorate in the states may differ from that of the nation as a whole. For example, proportionately, there are fewer Democrats in Kansas and Nebraska than in the national electorate.

State governments also vary in what they do and in the quality of their performance. How good are the schools in a state? Does the state have effective programs in the fields of health services, penology, welfare, law enforcement, pollution control? As anyone who has driven across America knows, some states just look (and are) wealthier; they have better state roads, for example. Some have adopted innovative social programs that have led the way for other states and the federal government.

Policy Outcomes in the States. Since state governments do vary in quality, does the nature of a political system in a state affect the types of public policies that are adopted in the state? In other words, does the politics of a state make a difference in the lives of the people of that state?

Political scientists have done a good deal of research on this question, and their answers have varied. One analysis suggested that states with active two-party competition were more likely to enact broad social welfare programs because both parties would compete for the votes of a state's "have-nots."[30]

Later studies found that socioeconomic factors (whether a state was rich or poor in per capita income), rather than political factors, seemed to account for most of the differences in state welfare spending and for differences in spending, taxing, and services among the states generally.[31] But another study concluded that if taxing and spending in a state were measured in terms of their *redistributive* impact — who gets what and who pays for it — then the politics of

---

[30] V.O. Key, Jr., *Southern Politics in State and Nation* (New York: Knopf, 1949), p. 307.

[31] Richard E. Dawson and James A. Robinson, "Inter-Party Competition, Economic Variables and Welfare Policies in the American States," *Journal of Politics,* Vol. 25 (1963), pp. 265–89; Thomas R. Dye, *Politics, Economics, and the Public: Policy Outcomes in the American States* (Chicago: Rand McNally, 1966), p. 293; Thomas R. Dye, *Understanding Public Policy,* 2nd ed. (Englewood Cliffs, N.J.: Prentice-Hall, 1975), p. 304.

the state was considerably more important than its economics. Lower socio-economic groups did fare better, for example, in states with certain political characteristics, such as higher levels of political participation.[32]

Thus, at least some researchers have concluded that politics *does* make a difference in the quality and type of government provided by the states. In other words, the fact that America has a federal system directly affects people's lives because it affects the performance of the states in which they live. Not only the structure of government but the whole political process is federalized.

Federalism: 1980s Style

The *Budget of the United States Government, Fiscal Year 1981* is a white-covered volume almost the girth and weight of the Manhattan telephone book. It is 1174 pages long. To the nonexpert, it seems a bewildering mass of statistics and gobbledygook, filled with phrases like "object classification" and "unobligated balance lapsing."

Buried in the budget's somewhat mysterious statistics are figures that add up to a substantial total of federal aid to state and local governments. For 1981, the amount was estimated at $96.3 billion, or 15.6 percent of the total budget.[33] The following figures show the sharp increase in federal aid to state and local governments since 1950:

1950: $ 2.5 billion	1975: $49.8 billion
1960: $ 7.0 billion	1980 estimate: $88.9 billion
1970: $24.0 billion	1981 estimate: $96.3 billion

Despite these dollar increases, as a percentage of the total federal budget, federal aid to state and local governments has actually declined somewhat in recent years.

Any analysis of American government must take into account the huge sums of money flowing from people and corporations in the states to Washington in the form of taxes and back again in the form of federal aid. It is here that federalism moves from the realm of theory into practical meaning in terms of dollars and cents.

The federal government channels money to states and local communities in three ways:

Categorical grants, also known as *grants-in-aid,* are earmarked for specific purposes only, such as pollution control.

Block grants are for general use in a broad area, such as community development.

General *revenue-sharing* funds are distributed by formula with few or no strings attached about how the money is used.

By far the largest amount of federal aid (about 80 percent of the total) comes in the form of categorical grants. Block grants rank next, and then revenue sharing. (See Figure 3–1.) Because revenue sharing is the newest and most controversial of the three programs, it will be examined first.

---

[32] Brian R. Fry and Richard F. Winters, "The Politics of Redistribution," *American Political Science Review,* Vol. 64 (June 1970), pp. 508–22.

[33] "Special Analysis H," in *Special Analyses, Budget of the United States Government, Fiscal Year 1981* (Washington, D.C.: U.S. Government Printing Office, 1980), p. 254.

The Federal Aid Pipeline:
1980 Grants to States and Localities*

Figure 3–1

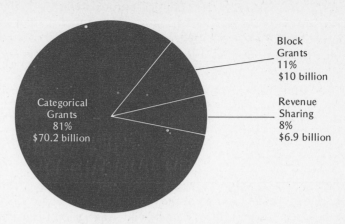

Block
Grants
11%
$10 billion

Revenue
Sharing
8%
$6.9 billion

Categorical
Grants
81%
$70.2 billion

* Dollar total does not include $1.8 billion in other general purpose grants.
Source: Adapted from Table H-8, "Special Analysis H," in *Special Analyses, Budget of the United States Government, Fiscal Year 1981* (Washington, D.C.: U.S. Government Printing Office, 1980), p. 257. Percentages are rounded; dollar figures are 1980 estimates.

Revenue Sharing

In 1980 the city of Anaheim, California, was building a new $12 million civic center. It had spruced up its street lights and purchased new materials for the library. Madison, Wisconsin, got a new fire station on the far west side and a pedestrian mall. Harrisburg, Pennsylvania, hired fifteen new police officers, bought several patrol cars, and funded a new Health Department. And the small city of Duncanville, Texas, finally got its new jail, installed lights at the local tennis courts, and acquired a street sweeper.[34]

What these communities of varying size, in four different regions of the country, had in common was that the money to finance these improvements and services came in part or entirely from the federal government's program of general revenue sharing. Under the program, first adopted in 1972, Washington has turned billions of dollars of federal tax monies back to state and local governments to spend as they wish.

In June 1960 economist Walter W. Heller proposed the basic idea of revenue sharing in a speech. Later, as a top economic adviser to Presidents Kennedy and Johnson, he restated his proposals. By the time Richard Nixon became President, the idea had gathered considerable momentum. In 1969, during his first year in office, Nixon proposed a "new federalism," with general revenue sharing as its keystone. The federal government, for the first time, would turn a share of its revenues back to the states "without federal strings."

In a message to Congress, Nixon contended that Americans no longer supported continued expansion of the federal government. People, he argued, were "turning away from the central government to their local and state governments to deal with their local and state problems." He added, "This proposal [revenue sharing] marks a turning point in federal-state relations, the beginning of decentralization of governmental power, the restoration of a rightful balance between the state capitals and the national capital."[35]

[34] Data from the National League of Cities, from its 1979 survey of revenue-sharing recipients.
[35] *New York Times,* August 14, 1969, p. 24.

During his first year in office, President Nixon outlined his concepts of new relationships within the federal system and proposed a program of revenue sharing, enacted by Congress in 1972:

After a third of a century of power flowing from the people and the states to Washington it is time for a New Federalism in which power, funds and responsibility will flow from Washington to the states and to the people. . . .

For a third of a century, power and responsibility have flowed toward Washington—and Washington has taken for its own the best sources of revenue.

We intend to reverse this tide, and to turn back to the states a greater measure of responsibility. . . . I shall propose to the Congress that a set portion of the revenues from federal income taxes be remitted directly to the states—with a minimum of federal restrictions on how those dollars are to be used. . . .

After nearly 40 years of moving power from the states to Washington, we begin in America a decade of decentralization, a shifting of power away from the center whenever it can be used better locally.

—President Nixon in a television address to the nation, August 8, 1969.

The administration faced formidable obstacles in pushing the revenue-sharing plan through Congress. Organized labor was opposed to placing money in the hands of traditionally conservative state legislatures. And some members of Congress were opposed to a program that would not enable them to take credit for specific projects that benefited their own districts.

Moreover, revenue sharing represented a departure from the way Congress was accustomed to appropriating money for the states and local communities. With some exceptions, federal funds up to that time were provided in the form of categorical grants, with the money earmarked for certain categories of spending—schools or hospitals, for example. If Congress gave out the money with virtually no strings, the chairmen of congressional committees concerned would lose some of their power; and some critics feared that local governments might use the money to build golf courses instead of health clinics.

Despite these political problems, Congress late in 1972 approved a six-year, $30.2 billion program of general revenue sharing for states and local governments. The law established a new trust fund and authorized payments from it of about $6 billion a year. Under the law, these billions of dollars were distributed according to a complex formula based on population and on each state's effort to raise its own tax revenues. The law required that one-third of the federal money go to the states and that two-thirds "pass through" to local governments.

In 1976 President Ford proposed that the program be increased and extended for almost another six years. The debate was intense. On one side, in favor of continuing the program without major changes, was a powerful coalition of revenue sharing's natural constituents—the state, county, and city officials whose areas benefited the most from the multibillion-dollar program. On the other side, pushing for reforms, was a coalition of civic groups, notably the League of Women Voters and civil rights and labor organizations. The reformers argued for changes that would channel more money into poor communities and disqualify communities that discriminated against minorities. Some reformers also complained that local communities were using revenue sharing to hold down taxes but were spending little on social programs.

Later in 1976, after several months of debate, Congress extended the revenue-sharing program, allocating $25.6 billion to states and localities over three and three-quarters years, until September 1980. Although the reformers failed to win a greater share of funds for poor persons, the new law did include stronger provisions against racial or other discrimination in any program financed by revenue sharing. And the law required greater citizen participation, including public hearings on how recipients planned to use the money.

But by 1979 revenue sharing was in trouble. Many members of Congress still objected to appropriating federal funds without controlling how the money was spent. Representative Jack Brooks, a Texas Democrat and chairman of the House committee with jurisdiction over the program, called revenue sharing a "snake."[36] There were published stories that President Carter would not seek to renew the program. The nation's governors and mayors lobbied hard for revenue sharing, however. In April 1980, a presidential election year, Carter proposed a five-year extension, through September 1985, at a level of about $5 billion a year on the average. But in a period of runaway inflation, there was increasing pressure on the President and Congress to cut the federal budget. Finally, late in 1980, Congress provided $4.6 billion a year in revenue-sharing funds for local governments through fiscal 1983 and authorized up to $2.3 billion a year for the states in 1982 and 1983—provided that Congress appropriates the money for those years. President Carter signed the revenue-sharing bill into law.

Underlying the political struggle over revenue sharing were philosophical differences about the program. Some conservatives, for example, supported revenue sharing on the grounds that more decisions should be made at the local level. But some liberals argued that *national* goals, such as a clean environment or decent medical care, can only be achieved if the federal government has more control over how the shared revenue is used.

Nevertheless, revenue sharing poured billions of dollars into the nation's states, cities, and towns, a fact of life that tended to overshadow specific objections to the program. For example, New Orleans Mayor Moon Landrieu (later Secretary of Housing and Urban Development), had no reservations. "General revenue sharing," he said, "has been the best thing since ice cream."[37]

What has revenue sharing meant to local governments? The first batch of checks mailed from Washington in December 1972 ranged from $100,847,538 to New York City—the largest amount—to $99 received by Anoka, Nebraska, and a few other small towns.[38] The federal government's reports of how states and localities were spending revenue-sharing money showed that in 1977, 73 percent was being spent on operating costs and the balance on construction and interest. The three highest categories of spending were, in order: public safety, education, and highways.[39] (Figure 3–2 shows how states and communities reported they spent their shared revenue.)

But various studies cautioned that the reports by state and local governments of how they spent their revenue-sharing funds might not give a realistic picture. One such study, by the Brookings Institution, suggested that state and local governments were using a substantial portion of shared revenues to hold

[36] *National Journal,* August 11, 1979, p. 1331.
[37] *National Journal,* August 9, 1975, p. 1142.
[38] *National Observer,* December 23, 1972, p. 4.
[39] "Expenditures of General Revenue Sharing and Antirecession Fiscal Assistance Funds: 1976–1977," Office of Revenue Sharing, Department of the Treasury (Washington, D.C.: U.S. Government Printing Office, 1979), p. 2.

Reported Use of the Revenue-Sharing Dollar, 1976–1977

Figure 3–2

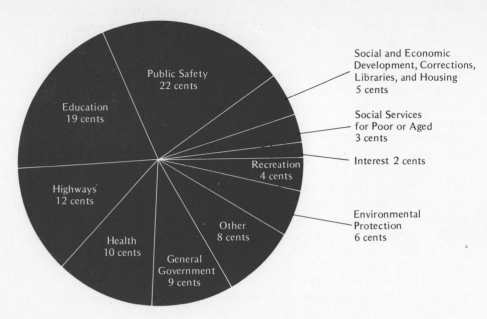

Source: Adapted from Office of Revenue Sharing, U.S. Department of the Treasury, "Expenditures of General Revenue Sharing and Antirecession Fiscal Assistance Funds: 1976–1977" (Washington, D.C.: U.S. Government Printing Office, 1979), p. 2.

down local taxes. Nevertheless, the study concluded this might be "defensible and even desirable" if it helped central cities facing fiscal problems.[40] A second Brookings study concluded that a major goal of some advocates of revenue sharing—increased decision making at the local level—had not happened in most communities. The program, the study reported, "has not decidedly changed the nature and type of participation in the political processes of recipient governments." Moreover, the study found that only county governments had used the money to start new programs. The Brookings study also concluded that "troubled central cities are not in any major way" helped by revenue sharing.[41]

Finally, some of the initial fears of opponents of revenue sharing were confirmed in practice. Since localities were free to spend the money as they wished, not all of it went for noble public purposes. Corpus Christi, Texas, spent $100,000 landscaping a golf course. Burlington, Vermont, spent $160,000 on an ice rink and $300,000 on bright new uniforms for the municipal band.[42]

In fiscal 1980, the $6.9 billion in shared revenue flowing to the states and local communities amounted to only about 8 percent of the total federal aid to these governments. The great bulk of federal aid came in the form of categorical

Categorical Grants

[40] Richard P. Nathan, Allen D. Manvel, Susannah E. Calkins, and associates, *Monitoring Revenue Sharing* (Washington, D.C.: The Brookings Institution, 1975), pp. 183, 233, 311.
[41] Richard P. Nathan, Charles F. Adams, Jr., and associates, *Revenue Sharing: The Second Round* (Washington, D.C.: The Brookings Institution, 1977), pp. 106, 164.
[42] *Washington Post,* June 18, 1973, p. A20.

grants-in-aid. A categorical grant is "money paid or furnished to state or local governments to be used for specific purposes"[43] in ways spelled out by law or administrative regulations. In 1980 there were 621 separate grant programs administered by federal agencies.[44] Not surprisingly, many state and local officials complained that the maze of federal grants-in-aid created a burdensome amount of paper work for them.

Typical categorical grants are in the fields of education, pollution control, highways, conservation, and recreation. The Medicaid and Food Stamp programs are examples of two very large categorical grants. As already noted, categorical grants in 1980 amounted to about 80 percent of all federal aid to states and localities. To be eligible for federal aid, the state and local governments must sometimes meet *matching requirements.* That is, Washington requires the recipients to put up some of their own funds in order to get the federal money. On the average, state and local governments in recent years have matched about $1 for every $3 received from the federal government.[45] And since 1976, state and local governments have been allowed to use revenue-sharing money to match federal funds.

When communities and states match federal money, they usually do so according to a formula that takes into account their ability to pay. Poor states pay less than rich states. This process is called *equalization.*

It is in the administration of federal grants that the gears of national, state, and local governments mesh or collide. Federal fiscal aid is the primary means by which local, state, and federal governments interrelate. In dealing with such programs as slum clearance, education, or welfare services, mayors, governors, and lesser officials communicate with one another and with officials in Washington. Because of these aid programs, the lines of the federal system crisscross, linking various levels of government that must cope with common problems, from pollution to poverty. The result is both cooperation and conflict. For example, cities and states collaborate in a wide range of programs such as law en-

[43] *Fiscal Balance in the American Federal System,* Vol. I, Advisory Commission on Intergovernmental Relations (Washington, D.C.: U.S. Government Printing Office, 1967), p. 137.
[44] Data provided by Office of Management and Budget.
[45] "Special Analysis H," in *Special Analyses, Budget of the United States Government, Fiscal Year 1981* (Washington, D.C.: Government Printing Office, 1980), p. 257.

"It's too bad you can't get federal matching funds, whatever they are."

Drawing by D. Fradon
© 1969 The New Yorker Magazine, Inc.

forcement and highway planning. But as a group, mayors tend to distrust state governments; they argue that the states are receiving too large a share of federal revenues at a time when the cities are desperate for funds.

In addition to general revenue sharing and categorical grants, since the 1960s, aid to the states and local communities has also flowed from Washington in the form of block grants. These grants are used "within a broad functional area largely at the recipient's discretion."[46]

Block Grants

The five major block grant programs in 1980 were:

Partnership for Health (enacted in 1966), which funded such activities as state public health services and research in cancer, mental retardation, neurological illnesses, tuberculosis, and other diseases.

Omnibus Crime Control and Safe Streets (1968), which provided federal funds to upgrade state and local police forces, improve riot control techniques, combat crime, and construct law enforcement facilities.

Comprehensive Employment and Training Act (CETA) (1973), which was designed to reduce unemployment by providing on-the-job and classroom train-

[46] *Summary and Concluding Observations: The Intergovernmental Grant System,* Advisory Commission on Intergovernmental Relations (Washington, D.C.: U.S. Government Printing Office, 1978), p. 3.

ing for unskilled workers, and summer jobs for disadvantaged youths. Critics charged the money was being used by local governments for other purposes.

Housing and Community Development (1974), which provided money for recreational lands, water and sewer facilities, slum clearance, model cities programs, and neighborhood centers.

Social Services (1974), which consolidated aid in the fields of child care, family planning, and special programs for the handicapped.

Where the Money Goes

How was the $88.9 billion total in federal aid spent in fiscal 1980? Federal budget estimates show that almost all of it was allocated to six categories: health, welfare, and income security; education and manpower; transportation; general revenue sharing; community development and housing; and natural resources and environment, in that order. (Figure 3–3 and Table 3–2 show where the money goes.)

Fiscal Headaches in the Federal System

As state and local authorities are quick to point out, state and local spending has been increasing about as fast as federal spending. For example, between 1970 and 1978, total federal spending rose from $197 billion to $479 billion, an increase of 143 percent. During the same period, state and local expenditures increased from $148 billion to $347 billion, an increase of 134 percent. Yet the federal government collects 59 percent of all revenues in the United States, while state governments collect only 23 percent and local governments 18 percent.

Federal Grants to State and Local Governments, 1971–1983

Figure 3–3

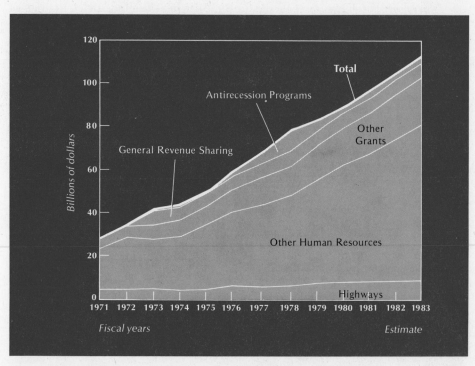

Source: "Special Analysis H," in *Special Analyses, Budget of the United States Government, Fiscal Year 1981* (Washington, D.C.: U.S. Government Printing Office, 1980), p. 240.

The American Democracy

Where the Money Goes: Federal Aid to State and Local Governments, by Function, 1980 (in billions of dollars)

Table 3–2

Percent	Category	Total	Major Items
38.9%	Health, welfare, and income security	$34.6	Welfare and medical assistance
24.6	Education and manpower	21.9	Aid to elementary and secondary schools
13.0	Transportation	11.5	Highways
7.8	General revenue sharing	6.9	Public safety, education, and transportation
6.5	Community development and housing	5.8	Housing and urban renewal
5.4	Natural resources and the environment	4.8	Pollution control
3.8	Other	3.4	
Total 100 %		$88.9	

Source: Adapted from Table H-3, "Special Analysis H," in *Special Analyses, Budget of the United States Government, Fiscal Year 1981* (Washington, D.C.: U.S. Government Printing Office, 1980), p. 251. Figures are rounded.

What is more, Washington collects 88 percent of the most important "growth" tax—the income tax.[47] Revenues from income taxes directly reflect economic growth, providing the federal government with increased tax receipts in an expanding economy. By contrast, local governments rely mainly on real estate taxes, and state governments on sales taxes; both sources of revenue tend to grow less rapidly than the economy as a whole. Although more states were taxing personal income, in 1978 there were still six states that did not.[48]

The Future of Federalism

Although revenue sharing became a reality during the Nixon administration, it did not receive universal acclaim. Caught in a cross fire of congressional criticism and anti-inflationary budget cutting, it survived under President Carter, but in modified form.

Yet the multibillion-dollar program of general revenue sharing was a major innovation in state-federal-local relationships, and there were other signs of change. The state of Minnesota, for example, has dramatically modified state and local fiscal relations. Minnesota revamped the system of school aid to ensure equal funds for students throughout the state, regardless of the wealth of the school districts where they lived. The reforms also guaranteed property tax relief to homeowners and businesses, and helped cities and counties by beginning a program of *state* revenue sharing for local governments.[49]

By 1977 twenty-nine states and the District of Columbia had adopted a

[47] U.S. Bureau of the Census, *Statistical Abstract of the United States, 1979*, pp. 254, 283; and the U.S. Bureau of the Census, *Governmental Finances in 1978–1979*, pp. 2, 4.

[48] U.S. Bureau of the Census, *Statistical Abstract of the United States, 1979*, p. 302.

[49] *State-Local Finances: Significant Features and Suggested Legislation.* Advisory Commission on Intergovernmental Relations (Washington, D.C.: U.S. Government Printing Office, 1972), pp. 6–8.

"circuit breaker" system of property tax relief for low-income homeowners and for the aged. Persons in these categories below certain income ceilings were guaranteed property tax reductions.[50]

The vast problems of urban areas provide one of the greatest challenges to the American federal system. Some efforts have been made at new approaches. For example, increasing attention is now being paid to solving problems on a metropolitan-area-wide basis. Many communities, especially in urban areas, have ignored traditional political jurisdictional lines to pool their efforts in attacking common problems (such as pollution) that respect no political boundaries, and in planning to take advantage of federal grants. Bills enacted by Congress such as the Mass Transportation Assistance Act of 1974 represent federal legislation designed to assist and encourage area-wide solutions to urban problems.

Other new ideas are being advanced. In 1980, for example, President Carter proposed a program of targeted fiscal assistance to cities and other areas with high unemployment and low growth rates. And Congress considered a plan, first tried out from 1976 to 1978, of countercyclical aid to communities in times of high unemployment.

Yet serious dislocations continue to plague the federal system. Many critics of the federal structure question whether states are willing or able to meet their responsibilities. By contrast, defenders of the states have noted that most of the successful programs of the New Deal "had been anticipated, by experiment and practice, on the state level or by private institutions."[51]

The states, some still caught in a fiscal squeeze, may find it difficult to play such an innovative role today. Some cities are in financial difficulty at the very time that more services are being demanded by the inner-city residents who are least able to pay for them.

"America's federal system," the Advisory Commission on Intergovernmental Relations has warned, "is on trial as never before in this century of crisis and change."[52] The problems that confront America in the 1980s raise the fundamental question of whether a federal system born in compromise almost two centuries ago can adapt itself to the needs of a technological, urban society in an age of onrushing change.

[50] Data provided by Advisory Commission on Intergovernmental Relations.
[51] Nelson A. Rockefeller, *The Future of Federalism* (Cambridge, Mass.: Harvard University Press, 1962), p. 15.
[52] *Ninth Annual Report,* Advisory Commission on Intergovernmental Relations (Washington, D.C.: U.S. Government Printing Office, 1968), p. 13.

Perspective

The United States has a federal system of government in which power is constitutionally shared by a national government and fifty state governments. Some countries have a unitary system in which policies are set by a single central government.

Advocates of a federal system argue that it permits diversity and that local officials may perform better than the federal bureaucracy since problems vary from one locality to another. Other arguments made for a federal system are that its many levels of government allow more points of access for citizens and that it protects individual rights, fosters experimentation, and is suited to a large country such as the United States.

A federal system also has disadvantages, however; it may make it harder to achieve national unity, local governments may frustrate national policies, or the system may serve as a mask for privilege and economic or racial discrimination. In addition, law enforcement and justice may be uneven, and local governments may lack skill and money and may be dominated by special interests.

The American federal system was created at the Constitutional Convention of 1787. The delegates reached a compromise: they would give up some of the states' independence in order to achieve enough unity to create a nation. Under the Constitution, the three branches of government are granted certain specifically enumerated powers. The Supreme Court has held that the national government also has broad implied powers, as well as inherent powers that it may exercise simply because it exists as a government. The federal government and the states also independently exercise concurrent powers.

The Supreme Court is the umpire of the federal system. The case of *McCulloch* v. *Maryland* (1819) established the key concepts of implied powers, broad construction of the Constitution, and supremacy of the national government. The *supremacy clause* of the Constitution makes it clear that the Constitution prevails over state laws. Under the federal system, local governments in the United States derive their powers from the states and are subject to the same constitutional restrictions as the states.

There have been sharp increases in federal aid to state and local governments since 1950, but as a percentage of the federal budget, aid has actually declined in recent years. There are three kinds of federal aid to the states: categorical grants, which are earmarked for specific purposes; block grants, which are for use in a broad general area; and general revenue sharing, under which the federal government turns a share of its revenues back to the states "without federal strings." Most of the federal aid to state and local governments falls into six categories: health, welfare, and income security; education and manpower; transportation; general revenue sharing; community development and housing; and natural resources and the environment. States and localities depend on federal aid in part because the federal government collects a major share of all taxes.

Suggested Reading

Davis, S. Rufus. *The Federal Principle* (University of California Press, 1978). An examination of the history of federalism from the Hellenic age through the twentieth century. Contains an interesting analysis of the American model of federalism created at the Constitutional Convention of 1787.

Derthick, Martha. *Between State and Nation: Regional Organizations of the United States** (The Brookings Institution, 1974). An analysis of the theory and actual operation of regional organizations in the American federal system. The Appalachian Regional Commission, the Tennessee Valley Authority, and the Delaware River Basin Commission are among the regional organizations discussed.

Elazar, Daniel J. *American Federalism: A View from the States,* 2nd edition* (Harper & Row, 1972). A good general treatment of American federalism. The book emphasizes some of the problems and areas of controversy in contemporary intergovernmental relationships, and traces the historical roots of cooperation and shared functions among the various layers of government in the federal system.

Glendening, Parris N., and Reeves, Mavis Mann. *Pragmatic Federalism* (Palisades Publishers, 1977). A useful analysis of the relationship among the national government, the states, and local governments. The authors maintain that the strength of the federal system lies in its ability to change and to work out solutions to citizen demands.

Grodzins, Morton. *The American System* (Rand McNally, 1966). A comprehensive analysis of American federalism by a leading authority on the subject.

MacMahon, Arthur W. *Administering Federalism in a Democracy* (Oxford University Press, 1972). A thoughtful examination of American federalism that emphasizes its administrative aspects. Analyzes federal grants-in-aid, the impact of Supreme Court decisions, and the role of state and local governments in administering federal programs.

Reagan, Michael D. *The New Federalism* (Oxford University Press, 1972). An excellent study of the pattern of federalism in the United States. The book questions traditional definitions of a federal system and examines the development of federal grants-in-aid, the limited ability of state governments to finance public services, and the dominant role of the federal government in the American federal system.

Riker, William H. *Federalism: Origin, Operation, Significance** (Little, Brown, 1964). A historical and comparative analysis of federalism. Riker examines with great clarity the conditions that give rise to federalism and maintain it. He is sharply critical of certain aspects of American federalism and argues that it has permitted the oppression of blacks.

Wheare, K. C. *Federal Government,* 4th edition* (Oxford University Press, 1963). A perceptive comparative analysis of federal governmental systems. Based primarily on a comprehensive examination of the workings of federalism in Australia, Canada, Switzerland, and the United States.

* Available in paperback edition

CIVIL LIBERTIES AND CITIZENSHIP

On March 9, 1979, in the city of Milwaukee, Wisconsin, federal district court judge Robert W. Warren issued an order restraining the *Progressive* magazine from publishing an article on how the hydrogen bomb works.

The United States government had gone into court to block publication of the article, which it claimed would help other countries to build thermonuclear bombs, bringing civilization "one step closer to its potential destruction in a nuclear holocaust." The Department of Justice submitted affidavits from various high officials, including the Secretary of State and the Secretary of Defense, to back up its arguments. The government warned that publication of the article would violate the Atomic Energy Act of 1954, which prohibits the disclosure of "restricted data" about nuclear weapons, no matter where the information is gathered. The article, the government contended, had been "born classified."

The magazine, a liberal monthly journal of opinion, countered that there were no secrets in the article. According to the magazine's editor, Erwin Knoll, the writer, Howard Morland, had been given no access to classified data and had pieced the story together by interviewing scientists and touring nuclear plants with the knowledge and permission of the government. The editor said the *Progressive* wished to publish the article to show that the government had cloaked its atomic weapons policy in excessive secrecy and to inform the public about an issue affecting the survival of the human race.

The First Amendment to the Constitution, on its face, might seem to prohibit the government from censoring an article in advance — even an article about

the hydrogen bomb. The amendment states that "Congress shall make no law . . . abridging the freedom . . . of the press." But the Supreme Court, the ultimate arbiter of what the Constitution means, has always balanced the First Amendment against other social needs and other parts of the Constitution. And so Judge Warren held that the First Amendment does not in all cases absolutely prohibit censorship in advance; he argued that a hydrogen bomb, if used, would not leave people alive to enjoy their rights under the First Amendment. "You can't speak freely when you're dead," he said.[1] Later in March, as he issued a preliminary injunction against the *Progressive,* he further argued that a mistaken ruling by the court "could pave the way for thermonuclear annihilation for us all." The battle lines were drawn; despite the First Amendment, a publication had been censored in advance by the government.

The strong tradition of a free press in the United States rests on the principle, rooted in English common law, that there must normally be no governmental "prior restraint" of the press. The Supreme Court had dealt with this issue almost half a century before, when it ruled that a Minneapolis weekly newspaper could not be suppressed because of articles attacking city officials as "corrupt" and "grafters."[2] The Court held that even "miscreant purveyors of scandal" were protected from prior restraint by the First Amendment. But the Court said that the press might be censored in advance by the government in "exceptional cases" relating to national security—and it gave as one example a news story that might report the sailing date of a troopship. Moreover, in 1971 the federal government, claiming that national security was endangered, had tried to stop the *New York Times* from continuing to publish a series based on a secret history of the Vietnam war—the so-called Pentagon Papers. For fifteen days, the federal courts restrained publication. Finally, the Supreme Court ruled 6–3 that the *Times* and the other newspapers that had been restrained were free to publish.[3] Justice Hugo Black, in the strongest of the opinions on the majority side, wrote: "The press was protected so that it could bare the secrets of government and inform the people."

Although the press had generally favored publication of the Pentagon Papers, many editors and reporters felt that the hydrogen bomb might not be a very good issue on which to test the First Amendment. And while the *Times* was the most prestigious newspaper in America, the *Progressive* was a relatively obscure monthly magazine.

[1] *New York Times,* March 10, 1979, p. 1.
[2] *Near* v. *Minnesota,* 283 U.S. 697 (1931).
[3] *New York Times Company* v. *United States,* 403 U.S. 713 (1971).

THE PROGRESSIVE

November 1979 $1.50

The H-bomb Secret

How we got it—why we're telling it

Gradually, however, additional facts began to emerge in the case. It developed that a number of documents detailing information about the hydrogen bomb had long been openly available in a government library. A government physicist, Theodore Postol, stated that the magazine article contained no information that could not be learned from the diagrams published by the *Encyclopedia Americana* to accompany an article by Dr. Edward Teller, a physicist known as the "father of the H-bomb."

The *Progressive* appealed its case to the federal court of appeals in Chicago. The United States Supreme Court declined to intervene. Finally, in September, a newspaper in Madison, Wisconsin, published a letter from an independent researcher in California containing many of the details about the hydrogen bomb that were in the still-censored Morland article. The next day, the government announced that it was dropping its suit against the *Progressive* because the newspaper article had published the very facts that the government was trying to suppress. In November, the *Progressive* finally published the Morland article.[4] But for six months, the federal government had succeeded in imposing prior restraint on the press. The government did not accept the argument of Erwin Knoll, editor of the *Progressive:* "If there is no First Amendment for the *Progressive,* there is no First Amendment for anyone."[5]

Despite the outcome in the *Progressive* case and in the Pentagon Papers case, the issues remain unresolved. The press is protected by the First Amendment, but how far that protection extends is not clear. The battle over the *Progressive* article illustrates one facet of the continuing struggle between the press and the government in the American democracy. The late Alexander Bickel suggested that this "pulling and hauling" in the "unruly contest between the press . . . and government" actually offers the best assurance of both a free flow of news to the public and protection of sensitive government information. Bickel added: "Madison knew the secrets of this disorderly system, indeed he invented it."[6]

Although the *Progressive,* in this instance, won its battle with the government, there was no assurance that the magazine would have prevailed had the case reached the Supreme Court for a decision on the issues. Indeed, many editors worried that the Court would have ruled against the press. As it happened, the *Progressive* case arose at a time when the Court, under Chief Justice Warren Burger, had issued a series of rulings against the press. By 1980, the Court had permitted the jailing of Myron Farber, a *New York Times* reporter, for

[4] Howard Morland, "The H-Bomb Secret: How We Got It—Why We're Telling It," *The Progressive,* November 1979, p. 14.

[5] Nat Hentoff, *The First Freedom: The Tumultuous History of Free Speech in America* (New York: Delacorte Press, 1980), pp. 221–22.

[6] Alexander M. Bickel, *The Morality of Consent* (New Haven: Yale University Press, 1975), pp. 86–87.

refusing to turn over his notes to the judge in a murder case; permitted police to search a newspaper office for photographs of demonstrators; made it much easier for individuals to sue the press for libel; and held that a former Central Intelligence Agency officer had to turn over to the government the income from a book that he had written criticizing the agency's record in Vietnam.

As these cases show, freedom of the press is a relative term, applied differently by the Supreme Court at different times. In the Pentagon Papers case, the Court protected the right of the press to publish important information that the government preferred to suppress. In a series of later decisions, the Court ruled that the press must yield to the needs of the process of criminal justice.

In deciding cases under the Bill of Rights, the Supreme Court often has the difficult task of attempting to balance the rights of the individual against those of society as a whole. The questions raised in this process are many and complex. Should freedom of the press and freedom of expression be absolute rights under the First Amendment? What if free speech conflicts with the rights of others? What does the law say now about government wiretapping and "bugging"? What are the legal rights of student demonstrators? Can police enter your home or residence without a search warrant? Is it against the law to be a member of the Communist party? What are your rights if you are arrested? Will the federal Bill of Rights be of any help to you if you are arrested by state or local police? These are some of the questions that will be explored in this chapter.

Individual Freedom and Society

The Supreme Court's decisions in the area of civil liberties and individual rights often illustrate the tension between liberty and order in a free society. Freedom is not absolute, for as Supreme Court Justice Oliver Wendell Holmes once said, "The right to swing my fist ends where the other man's nose begins." But the proper balance in a democracy between the rights of one individual and the rights of society as a whole can never be resolved to everyone's satisfaction.

The rights of the individual should not always be viewed as competing with those of the community; in a free society, the fullest freedom of expression for the individual may also serve the interests of society as a whole. As John F. Kennedy observed, "The rights of every man are diminished when the rights of one man are threatened."[7]

The nineteenth-century British philosopher John Stuart Mill advanced the classic argument for diversity of opinion in his treatise *On Liberty:* "Though

John Stuart Mill

[7] John F. Kennedy, "Radio and Television Report to the American People on Civil Rights," June 11, 1963, in *Public Papers of the Presidents, John F. Kennedy, 1963* (Washington, D.C.: U.S. Government Printing Office, 1964), p. 468.

THE REPORTER REFUSES AND IS SENT TO JAIL.

THE MORE CORRUPTION IN HIGH PLACES THE MORE REPORTERS SENT TO JAIL.

NO ONE WISHES TO ENCOURAGE CORRUPTION IN HIGH PLACES.

BUT IT'S EITHER THAT OR A FREE PRESS.

©1973 JULES FEIFFER

"The way they say it, it's as if there is liberty and justice, but there isn't."

Twelve-year-old Mary Frain, sitting pensively on a wooden rocker in her Jamaica, Queens, home, gave this explanation yesterday as one of her reasons for objecting to the daily Pledge of Allegiance to the flag in school.

The crank calls and angry letters have almost disappeared from the life of the introverted seventh grader who, with a classmate, Susan Keller, won a federal court decision on Dec. 10 permitting students in city schools to remain in their seats during the flag-saluting ceremony.

Because of the pressure, Susan Keller soon transferred to another school. But Mary still refuses to stand in the morning when most of the children in her honors class at Junior High School 217 at 85th Avenue and 148th Street stand to recite the pledge.

At home, following a quick lunch, the youngster discussed the impact of the court case on her life.

"Like when we walked along the halls, the kids used to call us commies. We had phone calls. One was obscene. Some just laughed or breathed when you picked it up. But it's dying down now. . . ."

Mary persisted, she said, because of strong objections to the wording of the pledge.

"Liberty and justice for all?" she said. "That's not true . . . for the blacks and poor whites. The poor have to live in cold miserable places. And it's obvious that blacks are oppressed."

The girl would compromise her position if the pledge were rephrased to be spoken as a "goal." "Like if when you say it you're making a vow to make it liberty and justice for all," she explained.

— *New York Times,* January 31, 1970.

the silenced opinion be an error, it may, and very commonly does, contain a portion of truth; and since the general or prevailing opinion on any subject is rarely or never the whole truth, it is only by the collision of adverse opinions that the remainder of the truth has any chance of being supplied."[8]

In American society, the Supreme Court is the mechanism called upon to resolve conflicts between liberty and order, between the rights of the individual and the rights of the many. In doing so, the Court operates within the framework of what James Monroe called that "polar star, and great support of American liberty," the Bill of Rights.

The Bill of Rights

The first ten amendments to the Constitution comprise the Bill of Rights.[9] These vital protections were omitted from the Constitution as drafted in 1787. (See Chapter 2.) The supporters of the Constitution, it will be recalled, promised to pass a Bill of Rights in part so that they might win the struggle over ratification.

While the Bill of Rights is the fundamental charter of American liberties, it is the Supreme Court that ultimately decides how those rights shall be defined and applied. It should be remembered that the Supreme Court does not operate in a vacuum. Its nine justices are human beings and actors in the drama of their time. As former Chief Justice Earl Warren once declared, "Our judges are not monks or scientists, but participants in the living stream of our national life."[10]

---

[8] John Stuart Mill, *On Liberty* (New York: Appleton-Century-Crofts, 1947), p. 52.

[9] As noted in Chapter 2, some scholars regard only the first eight or nine amendments as the Bill of Rights.

[10] Earl Warren, "The Law and the Future," *Fortune,* November 1955, p. 107.

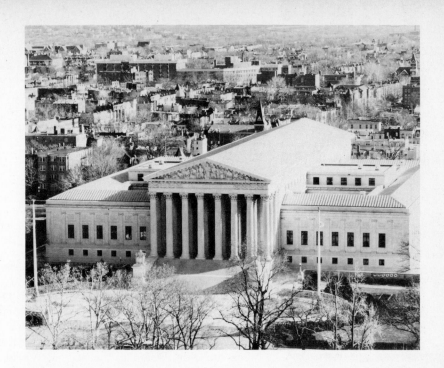

"... the Supreme Court does not operate in a vacuum."

Individual liberties may depend not only on what the Court says in particular cases but on what the political system will tolerate in any given era.

Although the Bill of Rights was passed to guard against abuses by the new federal government, the Supreme Court has ruled over the years, case by case, that virtually all the safeguards of the Bill of Rights apply as well to state and local governments and agencies.

Alpheus T. Mason, a leading constitutional scholar, has observed that the fundamental rights of a free society gained "no greater moral sanctity" by being written into the Constitution, "but individuals could thereafter look to courts for their protection. Rights formerly natural became civil."[11]

"Congress shall make no law respecting an establishment of religion, or prohibiting the free exercise thereof; or abridging the freedom of speech, or of the press; or the right of the people peaceably to assemble, and to petition the Government for a redress of grievances." **Freedom of Speech**

These forty-five words are the First Amendment of the Constitution. Along with "due process of law" and other constitutional protections, these words set forth basic American freedoms. As the late Justice Benjamin N. Cardozo once wrote, freedom of thought and of speech is "the matrix, the indispensable condition, of nearly every other form of freedom."[12] (Although the Constitution states that "Congress shall make no law" abridging First Amendment freedoms, the Supreme Court has interpreted this to mean that state and local authorities cannot do so, either.)

Yet, the courts have frequently placed limits on speech. Several types of

[11] Alpheus T. Mason, *The Supreme Court: Palladium of Freedom* (Ann Arbor, Mich.: University of Michigan Press, 1962), p. 58.
[12] *Palko* v. *Connecticut,* 302 U.S. 319 (1937).

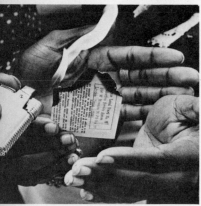

Justice Oliver Wendell
Holmes, Jr.

expression do not enjoy constitutional immunity from government regulation. These include fraudulent advertising, obscenity (which courts have had vast difficulty in defining), libel, and, in some cases, street oratory. The Supreme Court, for example, has ruled that police are justified in arresting a sidewalk speaker if he is too effective in stirring his audience.[13] Three decades earlier, Supreme Court Justice Oliver Wendell Holmes, Jr., had established the classic "clear and present danger" test to define the point at which speech loses the protection of the First Amendment:

> The character of every act depends upon the circumstances in which it is done.... The most stringent protection of free speech would not protect a man in falsely shouting fire in a theater and causing a panic. . . . The question in every case is whether the words used are used in such circumstances and are of such a nature as to create a clear and present danger that they will bring about the substantive evils that Congress has a right to prevent.[14]

Later, in the *Gitlow* case, the Court went even further, ruling that some speech could be prohibited if it threatened the overthrow of the government or in other ways injured the public welfare, a doctrine that came to be known as the "bad tendency" test.[15] The Court's free speech yardstick shifted again during the New Deal and the Second World War, then appeared to swing back to the "clear and present danger" test in the 1950s. Thus, even so fundamental a right as free speech, while broadly protected by the Constitution, has been limited by the Supreme Court according to the circumstances and the times.

In reconciling the requirement of free speech with other social rights and needs, the Supreme Court has often tried to draw a line between "expression" and "action." But that is not always an easy matter. In the principal "draft card burning" case in 1968, David P. O'Brien had argued that when he burned his card to protest the Vietnam war, his action was "symbolic speech," protected by the Constitution. But Chief Justice Warren declared: "We cannot accept the view that an apparently limitless variety of conduct can be labeled 'speech.'"[16]

On the other hand, in a 1974 case, the Supreme Court struck down a Massachusetts law under which Valarie Goguen had been arrested and sentenced to six months in jail for wearing an American flag patch on the seat of his blue jeans.[17] Although the Court majority based its conclusion on a finding that the law was unconstitutionally vague, Justice Byron R. White concurred in the decision on the grounds that the law restricted freedom of expression. The right of free expression by students and student demonstrators had been affirmed in 1969 when the Court ruled that a thirteen-year-old Iowa girl, Mary Beth Tinker, could not be suspended from her junior high school for wearing a black arm band to class in protest against the war in Vietnam. "In our system," the Court held, "state-operated schools may not be enclaves of totalitarianism. School officials do not possess absolute authority over their students."[18] In winning the fight for her constitutional rights, Mary Beth Tinker had made a

[13] *Feiner* v. *New York*, 340 U.S. 315 (1951).
[14] *Schenck* v. *United States*, 249 U.S. 47 (1919).
[15] *Gitlow* v. *New York*, 268 U.S. 652 (1925).
[16] *United States* v. *O'Brien*, 391 U.S. 367 (1968).
[17] *Smith* v. *Goguen*, 415 U.S. 566 (1974).
[18] *Tinker* v. *Des Moines School District et al.*, 393 U.S. 503 (1969).

Whatever theoretical merit there may be to the argument that there is a "right" to rebellion against dictatorial governments is without force where the existing structure of the government provides for peaceful and orderly change. . . .

Overthrow of the government by force and

violence is certainly a substantial enough interest for the government to limit speech. Indeed, this is the ultimate value of any society, for if a society cannot protect its very structure from armed internal attack, it must follow that no subordinate value can be protected.

—Chief Justice Fred M. Vinson, in *Dennis* v. *United States* (1951), upholding conviction of eleven leaders of the Communist party under the Smith Act.

Free speech has occupied an exalted position because of the high service it has given our society. Its protection is essential to the very existence of democracy. The airing of ideas releases pressures which otherwise might become destructive. When ideas compete in the market for acceptance, full and free discussion exposes the false and they gain few adherents.

. . . Some nations less resilient than the United States, where illiteracy is high and where democratic traditions are only budding, might have to take drastic steps and jail these men for merely speaking their creed. But in America they are miserable merchants of unwanted ideas; their wares remain unsold.

—Justice William O. Douglas, dissenting in *Dennis* v. *United States.*

much broader point for all students in America. For the Court concluded: "It can hardly be argued that either students or teachers shed their constitutional rights to freedom of speech or expression at the schoolhouse gate."

Preferred Freedoms and the Balancing Test. Different philosophies, often identified with particular justices, have emerged as the Supreme Court has struggled with problems of freedom of expression.

For example, Justices Hugo Black and William Douglas established themselves as advocates of the "absolute" position. Black argued that "there *are* 'absolutes' in our Bill of Rights"[19] that cannot be diluted by judicial decisions. He maintained, for instance, that obscenity and libel are forms of speech and therefore cannot be constitutionally limited. But a majority of the Court took the position that the rights of the First Amendment must be "balanced" against the competing needs of the community to preserve order and to preserve the state. This view was championed by Justice Felix Frankfurter and others. The balancing test was defined by Chief Justice Fred M. Vinson in a 1950 case. When the government regulates conduct "in the interest of public order" and thereby limits free speech, he said, "the duty of the courts is to determine which of these two conflicting interests demands the greater protection."[20]

In performing this delicate balancing act, however, some members of the Court have argued that the basic freedoms should take precedence over other

[19] Hugo L. Black, "The Bill of Rights," *New York University Law Review*, Vol. 35 (April 1960), p. 867.
[20] *American Communications Association* v. *Douds*, 339 U.S. 382 (1950), quoted in Thomas E. Emerson, *The System of Freedom of Expression* (New York: Random House, 1970), pp. 165–66.

Justice William O. Douglas

95

needs. Thus, Justice Harlan Fiske Stone argued that the Constitution had placed freedom of speech and religion "in a preferred position."[21]

Despite these mixed views, the Supreme Court, while reluctant to narrow the scope of basic liberties, has generally not hesitated to balance such freedoms against other constitutional requirements.

Freedom of the Press

Closely tied to free speech, and protected as well by the First Amendment, is freedom of the press. As the *Progressive* case illustrated, however, the courts do not always rule in favor of the press, despite the First Amendment.

The press plays a vital role in a democracy because it is the principal means by which the people learn about the activities of the government. A democracy rests on the consent of the governed, but in order to give their consent, the governed must be informed. For example, in developing political opinions or in choosing among candidates in an election campaign, most voters rely on the news media—newspapers, television, and magazines—for their information.

"In the First Amendment," Justice Black wrote in the Pentagon Papers case, "the Founding Fathers gave the free press the protection it must have to fulfill its essential role in our democracy. The press was to serve the governed, not the governors."[22]

As already noted, the Supreme Court has been reluctant to impose "prior restraint" on the press. And the Court has ruled unanimously that it is unconstitutional to compel a newspaper to provide free space for a political candidate to reply to editorial-page criticism.[23] The Court thereby rejected the argument that the First Amendment required citizen "access" to newspapers to present differing viewpoints.

While the Court has thus protected the press under the First Amendment, it has also placed limitations on freedom of the press in several other areas.

[21] *United States* v. *Carolene Products Co.,* 304 U.S. 144 (1938).
[22] *New York Times Company* v. *United States* (1971).
[23] *Miami Herald Publishing Co.* v. *Tornillo,* 418 U.S. 241 (1974).

Free Press and Fair Trial. When basic rights collide, the Supreme Court may be called upon to act as a referee. In recent years the Supreme Court has shown increasing concern over pretrial and courtroom publicity that may prejudice the fair trial of a defendant in a criminal case. The issue brings into direct conflict two basic principles of the Bill of Rights — the right of an accused person to have a fair trial and the right of freedom of the press.

The use of television has complicated the problem of a fair trial. In two cases the Supreme Court struck down convictions in which the defendants' televised confessions of murder were presumed to have influenced the jury.[24] In 1966 the Supreme Court reversed the conviction of Dr. Samuel H. Sheppard, a Cleveland, Ohio, osteopath found guilty in 1954 of bludgeoning his wife to death. The Court ruled that the defendant's constitutional rights had been prejudiced by the publicity that had surrounded the trial giving it the "atmosphere of a 'Roman holiday' for the news media."[25] The state of Ohio then retried Sheppard, and a jury acquitted him in November 1966. Similar excessive courtroom publicity influenced the 1966 decision of the Texas Court of Criminal Appeals to reverse the conviction of Jack Ruby for the murder of Lee Harvey Oswald, the accused assassin of President Kennedy. Before Ruby could be retried, he died of illness in January 1967.

It is entirely possible that some jurors are influenced for or against a defendant by news stories. However, in the television age, public figures in particular cannot avoid considerable pretrial publicity. And in 1981 the Supreme Court ruled that states could permit trials to be televised. But extensive coverage in the press does not necessarily result in a conviction.

In the mid-1970s the press was increasingly coming under judicial restraints in the form of "gag orders" issued by courts to restrict news gathering and publication. In 1976 the Supreme Court heard arguments in a Nebraska case that was viewed as a critical test of freedom of the press.

On October 18, 1975, in Sutherland, Nebraska (population 840), six members of the James Kellie family were found murdered, and a twenty-nine-year-old unemployed handyman, Erwin Charles Simants, who lived next door, was arrested and charged with murder in the course of a sexual assault. Details of the crime were considered so lurid that a local judge issued an order prohibiting the press from reporting a pretrial hearing. A coalition of news organizations in Nebraska took their case to the Supreme Court.

In June 1976 the Supreme Court unanimously ruled that the Nebraska gag order violated the First Amendment's provision for freedom of the press.[26] ". . . pretrial publicity — even pervasive, adverse publicity — does not inevitably lead to an unfair trial," Chief Justice Burger wrote. There were other steps that a judge might take to ensure a fair trial, he noted, such as delaying the trial, transferring it to another location, or sequestering the jury. Burger added that "prior restraints on speech and publication are the most serious and the least tolerable infringement on First Amendment rights. . . ." Three justices — but not a majority of the Court — ruled that such gag orders are never justified.

Although the Supreme Court had ruled that a gag order was unconstitutional in the Nebraska case, some judges soon found other ways to restrain

Dr. Samuel H. Sheppard talks to the press.

[24] *Irvin* v. *Dowd,* 366 U.S. 717 (1961); *Rideau* v. *Louisiana,* 373 U.S. 723 (1963).
[25] *Sheppard* v. *Maxwell,* 384 U.S. 333 (1966).
[26] *Nebraska Press Association* v. *Stuart,* 427 U.S. 539 (1976).

the press. In a number of instances, judges closed their courtrooms to the press in pretrial proceedings. In 1979, in the *Gannett* case, the Supreme Court upheld this practice. It ruled, 5–4, that the public and the press could be barred from pretrial hearings if a judge found a "reasonable probability" that publicity would harm a defendant's right to a fair trial. The Court held that "members of the public have no constitutional right under the Sixth and Fourteenth amendments to attend criminal trials."[27] Although the Sixth Amendment guarantees "the right to a speedy and public trial," Justice Potter Stewart, writing for the Court, said that a defendant could waive this right. If the judge agreed, the courtroom could be closed. The press and many members of the legal profession immediately protested the decision.

Following the *Gannett* case, the Supreme Court agreed to decide whether it is constitutional for a judge to conduct an *entire* trial in secret if he thinks publicity might impair a defendant's right to a fair trial. The case was brought by two Richmond, Virginia, newspapers who challenged the secret trial of a man accused of murdering a motel manager.

In 1980 the Supreme Court ruled in favor of the press in the *Richmond* case. In a 7–1 decision, the Court ruled that trials must be open to the public and the press except in the most unusual circumstances. "We hold that the right to attend criminal trials is implicit in the guarantees of the First Amendment," the Court declared.[28] While the Court thus appeared to be pulling back from the *Gannett* decision to some extent, *Gannett* was not overturned by the *Richmond* case, and *pretrial* proceedings can still be closed. Since a majority of cases are disposed of in such pretrial proceedings, the victory of the press was by no means total.

Thus, the issue of free press and fair trial remains unresolved and a subject of ongoing controversy. Students of the problem have suggested that one solution may lie in increased voluntary restraint by police, lawyers, and prosecutors in commenting on the past criminal records of defendants and other aspects of pending cases, and by the press itself.

Confidentiality: Shielding Reporters and Their Sources. The right to have a fair trial often conflicts with the First Amendment in another important area — that of confidentiality for reporters and their news sources.

Journalists argue that they must offer confidential sources complete anonymity, particularly in the case of investigative reporting, when disclosure of the name of a source might lead to reprisals against that person. (The importance of investigative reporting — which relies in part on confidentiality of sources — was dramatically illustrated during the Watergate affair, when reporters Bob Woodward and Carl Bernstein of the *Washington Post* uncovered many details of the cover-up by the Nixon administration.) But what if a news reporter has information vital to the defense in a criminal trial, or which the government needs to prove its case? Do reporters have the "privilege" under the First Amendment of refusing to surrender such evidence? The Supreme Court has said no.

In its 1972 decision in the *Caldwell* case, the Court explored the question of whether reporters have the constitutional right to protect their sources.

---

[27] *Gannett Co., Inc.* v. *De Pasquale,* 443 U.S. 368 (1979).
[28] *Richmond Newspapers, Inc.* v. *Virginia,* 100 S. Ct. 2814 (1980).

The issue in these cases is whether requiring newsmen to appear and testify before state or federal grand juries abridges the freedom of speech and press guaranteed by the First Amendment. We hold that it does not. . . .

Citizens generally are not constitutionally immune from grand jury subpoenas; and neither the First Amendment nor other constitutional provision protects the average citizen from disclosing to a grand jury information that he has received in confidence. . . .

We are asked . . . to grant newsmen a testimonial privilege that other citizens do not enjoy. This we decline to do.

—Justice Byron R. White in *Caldwell* v. *United States* (1972).

The Court's crabbed view of the First Amendment reflects a disturbing insensitivity to the critical role of an independent press in our society. . . . the Court in these cases holds that a newsman has no First Amendment right to protect his sources when called before a grand jury. The Court thus invites state and federal authorities to undermine the historic independence of the press by attempting to annex the journalistic profession as an investigative arm of government.

—Justice Potter Stewart, dissenting in *Caldwell* v. *United States.*

Specifically, the Court ruled that the First Amendment did not exempt news reporters from appearing and testifying before state and federal grand juries. The decision came in the case of Earl Caldwell, a reporter for the *New York Times,* and in two related cases.[29] Caldwell had declined to appear before a federal grand jury to testify about the Black Panthers in the San Francisco area. He argued that merely appearing would destroy his relationship of trust with his confidential news sources. But the Supreme Court said that the investigation of possible crimes by a grand jury was of greater importance to the public than the protection of news sources. The courts had generally taken this position even before the Supreme Court ruled. But some reporters have gone to jail rather than reveal their sources, and many members of the press feel that compelling reporters to testify abridges their First Amendment rights.[30]

New York Times reporter Earl Caldwell

The issue of reporters' sources arose again in 1978 during the dramatic murder trial of Dr. Mario Jascalevich, a New Jersey physician. Dr. Jascalevich had been indicted after a series of articles by Myron Farber of the *New York Times* suggested that a "Dr. X" had murdered patients at a small New Jersey hospital by injecting them with curare, a paralyzing drug used by South American Indians to poison their hunting arrows.

The defense demanded Farber's notes, and the judge ordered them turned over to the court for inspection. Farber refused, citing the First Amendment and New Jersey's press shield law, which was designed to protect reporters from revealing their sources. The court sent Farber to jail for contempt and fined the *Times.*

The jury acquitted Dr. Jascalevich after a long trial. But the Supreme Court

[29] *United States* v. *Caldwell,* 408 U.S. 665 (1972); *Branzburg* v. *Hayes,* 408 U.S. 665 (1972); *In the Matter of Paul Pappas,* 408 U.S. 665 (1972).

[30] Earl Caldwell did not go to jail because the term of the federal grand jury seeking his testimony had expired by the time the Supreme Court ruled.

Left: New York Times reporter Myron Farber goes to jail. *Right:* The defendant, Dr. Mario Jascalevich, is acquitted.

declined to overturn Farber's conviction.[31] The *Times* reporter spent a total of forty days in jail, but he never revealed his source. The newspaper was fined $285,000 and incurred an estimated $1 million in legal costs.[32]

By 1980, twenty-six states had passed shield laws for the news media. And Congress had made periodic efforts to enact a federal immunity law for journalists. But many journalists preferred no legislation, arguing that a shield law, even though well intentioned, would violate the First Amendment by defining—and thus limiting—reporters' rights.

Television and Radio: A Limited Freedom. Radio and television do not enjoy as much freedom as other segments of the press, because, unlike newspapers, broadcast stations are licensed by the Federal Communications Commission. The FCC does not directly regulate news broadcasts, but stations are required to observe general standards of "fairness" in presenting community issues and to serve the public interest. Otherwise the FCC may revoke their licenses, although the commission, in the past, has seldom exercised its power to do so. Potentially, the federal government has powerful leverage over the operations of the broadcasting industry.

Why is the government able to regulate broadcasters but not the written press? The reason advanced most often is that the broadcast spectrum has a limited number of spaces and that stations would overlap and interfere with each other if the government did not regulate them. As the Supreme Court has stated, "Unlike other modes of expression, radio [and television] is not available to all."[33] This *scarcity theory* has been criticized since, in fact, there are more broadcasting stations than newspapers in the United States. And new tech-

[31] *New York Times Company* v. *New Jersey,* 439 U.S. 997 (1978).
[32] *Washington Post,* October 25, 1978, p. 1.
[33] *National Broadcasting Co.* v. *United States,* 319 U.S. 190 (1943).

nology such as cable television and satellite broadcasts are opening up even more outlets to the public.[34]

The First Amendment clearly protects the written press. But the Founding Fathers did not foresee the invention of television. The result "is a major paradox: television news, which has the greatest impact on the public, is the most vulnerable and the least protected."[35]

In 1969 the Supreme Court specifically rejected the claim of the broadcasting industry that the free press provisions of the First Amendment protected it from government regulation of programs. The Court did so in upholding the FCC's "fairness doctrine," which requires radio and television broadcasters to present all sides of important public issues. Justice Byron White ruled for the Court that "it is the right of viewers and listeners, not the right of the broadcasters, which is paramount"; a licensed broadcaster has no First Amendment right to "monopolize a radio frequency to the exclusion of his fellow citizens."[36]

Two years later, however, the Court ruled in favor of a Philadelphia radio station that had been sued for libel by a distributor of nudist magazines after the station reported his arrest. The Court said the First Amendment protected freedom of broadcasters to report news events.[37] Here the Supreme Court was extending some constitutional protection to broadcasters, but just how much was by no means clear.

Then in 1978 the Supreme Court ruled in the "seven dirty words" case that the government has the right to prohibit the broadcasting of "patently offensive" language.[38] The case began at 2 P.M. one afternoon in New York City, when a station owned by the Pacifica Foundation broadcast a monologue by comedian George Carlin called "Filthy Words." In it, Carlin gave a detailed analysis of "the words you couldn't say on the public airwaves . . . the ones you definitely wouldn't say, ever." Soon after, a man wrote to the FCC complaining that he heard the broadcast while driving with his young son. The FCC reprimanded the station, but later indicated that it would permit such broadcasts at times of the day "when children most likely" would not be listening.

The Supreme Court, in upholding the FCC action, did not rest its decision on the scarcity theory. Perhaps recognizing that the new technology had eroded that concept, the Court instead argued that the broadcast media have established "a uniquely pervasive presence in the lives of all Americans" and that "indecent material presented over the airwaves confronts the citizen, not only in public, but also in the privacy of the home. . . ."[39]

Freedom of Information.   Freedom of the press is diminished if the news media are unable to obtain information from official agencies of government. Beginning in 1955, Congressman John E. Moss, a California Democrat, pushed for legislation to force the federal government to make more information available to the press and public. As a result, the "Freedom of Information Act" was signed into law by President Johnson in 1966. It requires federal executive

[34] See Norman Dorsen, Paul Bender, and Burt Neuborne, *Political and Civil Rights in the United States,* Vol. 1 (Boston: Little, Brown, 1976), pp. 774–77.
[35] David Wise, *The Politics of Lying: Government Deception, Secrecy, and Power* (New York: Random House, 1973), p. 273.
[36] *Red Lion Broadcasting Co., Inc.,* v. *Federal Communications Commission,* 395 U.S. 367 (1969).
[37] *Rosenbloom* v. *Metromedia,* 403 U.S. 29 (1971).
[38] *Federal Communications Commission* v. *Pacifica Foundation,* 438 U.S. 726 (1978).
[39] *Ibid.*

Frank W. Snepp III

branch and regulatory agencies to make information available to journalists and other persons unless it falls into one of several confidential categories. Exempted from disclosure, for example, are national security information, personnel files, investigatory records, and the "internal" documents of an agency. The law provides that individuals can go into federal district court to force compliance by the government. The Freedom of Information Act was strengthened in 1974 with a number of amendments. One permits federal courts to review whether documents withheld by the government on grounds of national security were properly classified in the first place; another provision requires the government to respond to requests under the law within ten days. The law has resulted in the release of considerable amounts of information to the public. Nonetheless, a House government information subcommittee noted that "foot dragging by the federal bureaucracy" had hindered the release of information under the act.[40] Often, federal agencies have refused to release meaningful information under the act unless citizens go into federal court and sue, an expensive and time-consuming process.

While encouraging a greater flow of government information to the public through the act, Congress has also responded to demands for tighter control over federal files on individuals. The Privacy Act of 1974 provides that the government may not make public its files about an individual, such as medical, financial, criminal, or employment records, without that person's written consent. The law also generally gives citizens the right of access to information in government files about them.

In the field of national security and foreign policy, government secrecy is supported by a formal *security classification* system. Under executive orders issued by every President since Truman in 1951, thousands of officials can stamp documents Top Secret, Secret, or Confidential, if, in their judgment, disclosure would jeopardize national security. Under this system, millions of government documents are classified every year. An order issued by President Carter in 1978 provided that some classified documents lose their secrecy labels after six years; others, however, are exempted from such automatic declassification.[41]

In 1980 the Supreme Court ruled that employees of the Central Intelligence Agency who sign secrecy agreements were not free to publish books about their experiences without prior approval of the CIA.[42] The Court ruled that Frank W. Snepp III, a former CIA officer in Vietnam, had to give the government the royalties earned from his book, *Decent Interval*, even though it contained no classified information. The Court declined to consider Snepp's argument that the agreement violated his First Amendment rights.

Obscenity

By the 1980s X-rated movie houses, showing endless varieties of sexual intercourse, in color, were commonplace in most large American cities and many smaller communities. Broadway audiences were attending the musical *Oh! Calcutta!* in which nude male and female dancers appeared, and which advertised itself as "New York's Funniest Sex Musical — For Mature Audiences

---

[40] U.S. Congress, House, Committee on Government Operations, *Administration of the Freedom of Information Act*, 92nd Cong., 2nd sess., Twenty-first Report (Washington, D.C.: U.S. Government Printing Office, 1972), p. 8.

[41] Executive Order 12065, *National Security Information*, June 29, 1978.

[42] *Snepp* v. *United States*, 444 U.S. 507 (1980).

Only." In books, films, even on television, human sexuality was described and depicted in explicit, often graphic terms.

All this seemed a far cry from only a few years earlier, when the books of Edgar Rice Burroughs were almost removed from a Downey, California, elementary school library because of persistent reports that Tarzan and Jane were unmarried. (When it was established that the jungle king and his mate were in fact husband and wife, the books were left on the shelves.)

Today, changing standards of public morality have resulted in freer acceptance of sex in art, literature, and motion pictures by some—but certainly not all—segments of the public. In 1957, in *Roth* v. *United States,* the Supreme Court held for the first time that "obscenity is not within the area of constitutionally protected speech or press."[43] Justice William Brennan, Jr., ruled for the Court that material that is "utterly without redeeming social importance" is not protected by the Constitution. Brennan went on to give his definition of obscene matter: "whether to the average person, applying contemporary community standards, the dominant theme of the material taken as a whole appeals to prurient interest."[44]

The Court, however, has had continued difficulty in defining obscenity. D. H. Lawrence, whose book *Lady Chatterley's Lover* was banned in the United

[43] *Roth* v. *United States* and *Alberts* v. *California,* 354 U.S. 476 (1957).
[44] *Webster's New International Dictionary* defines "prurient" as "itching; longing; uneasy with desire or longing; or persons, having itching, morbid, or lascivious longings; or desire, curiosity, or propensity, lewd."

"No one could claim that Judge Walker doesn't approach these obscenity hearings with an open mind."

Drawing by Stevenson
© 1969 The New Yorker Magazine, Inc.

States from 1928 until 1959, once said: "What is pornography to one man is the laughter of genius to another."[45]

Justice Potter Stewart, concurring in one Supreme Court decision, said he would not attempt to define "hard-core" pornography, "but I know it when I see it."[46] This somewhat subjective approach was further refined in the case of a book commonly known as *Fanny Hill* and first published in 1749. Justice Brennan, speaking for the Court, applied and expanded the Court's opinion in the *Roth* case in concluding that *Fanny Hill* was not obscene.[47]

The practical effect of these cases was to remove almost all restrictions on content of books and movies as long as the slightest "social value" could be demonstrated. Nevertheless, the Supreme Court affirmed the federal conviction of publisher Ralph Ginzburg, who went to prison for mailing obscene material. The divided Court based its 5–4 decision not on the material itself but on the way it had been advertised and exploited for "titillation" rather than "intellectual content."[48]

Then in 1973 came the landmark case of *Miller* v. *California*, which set new standards for defining obscenity.[49] Chief Justice Burger, who wrote the majority opinion in the 5–4 decision, explained that the case began when unsolicited mail arrived at a restaurant in Newport Beach, California. The envelope, "opened by the manager of the restaurant and his mother," included an advertising brochure for a book entitled *Sex Orgies Illustrated.*

The Court set three new guidelines for judging works dealing with sexual conduct:

1. Whether the average person, "applying contemporary community standards," would find that the work, taken as a whole, "appeals to prurient interest."
2. Whether the work depicts "in a patently offensive way" sexual conduct prohibited by state law.
3. Whether the work as a whole "lacks serious literary, artistic, political, or scientific value."

The Court ruled, in effect, that local communities should be permitted to set their own standards. Justice Burger wrote: "It is neither realistic nor constitutionally sound to read the First Amendment as requiring that the people of Maine or Mississippi accept public depiction of conduct found tolerable in Las Vegas or New York City."[50] The decision appeared to clear the way for state legislatures to pass laws giving local communities greater control over books, movies, magazines, and other materials.

In 1974, however, the Supreme Court made it clear that there were limits to the right of communities to ban material as obscene. The Court unanimously refused to uphold the conviction of a movie theater manager in Albany, Georgia, because the film *Carnal Knowledge* showed "a woman with a bare midriff." Justice William H. Rehnquist, who wrote the Court's opinion, declared that local juries did not have "unbridled discretion" under the *Miller* case to declare what was obscene.[51]

Publisher Ralph Ginzburg

[45] D. H. Lawrence, "Pornography and Obscenity," in Diana Trilling, ed., *The Portable D. H. Lawrence* (New York: Viking, 1947), p. 646.
[46] *Jacobellis* v. *Ohio*, 378 U.S. 184 (1964).
[47] *A Book Named "John Cleland's Memoirs of a Woman of Pleasure"* v. *Attorney General of Massachusetts*, 383 U.S. 413 (1966).
[48] *Ginzburg* v. *United States*, 383 U.S. 463 (1966).
[49] *Miller* v. *California*, 413 U.S. 15 (1973).
[50] *Ibid.*
[51] *Jenkins* v. *Georgia*, 418 U.S. 153 (1974).

The Supreme Court restricted censorship by local communities in other cases as well. In 1975 the Court ruled that the city of Jacksonville, Florida, could not prevent drive-in theaters from showing films including nudity.[52] And it found that the city of Chattanooga, Tennessee, had erred in banning the musical *Hair*.[53] On the other hand, the Court upheld the conviction of William Hamling, who had published an illustrated version of the report of the President's Commission on Obscenity and Pornography. The Court said a brochure used to advertise Hamling's book was hard-core pornography.[54] Hamling served four months in prison in 1976.

Libel

If a person is defamed by a newspaper or other publication, that person may be able to sue for libel and collect damages, for the First Amendment does not protect this form of "free speech." Libel is a published or broadcast report that exposes a person to public contempt or injures the person's reputation. For example, some years ago a New York newspaper suggested that one Stanislaus Zbyszko, a wrestler, was built along the general lines of a gorilla. It ran a picture nearby of a particularly hideous-looking anthropoid. The New York State courts held this to be libelous.[55]

Truth has always been an absolute defense in libel cases. That is, if a publication can show that a story is true, the person claiming to have been libeled cannot recover damages. More recently, under the *New York Times* rule, the Supreme Court has made it almost impossible to libel a public official, unless the statement is made with "actual malice" — that is, unless it is deliberately or recklessly false. Ruling against Alabama officials who had brought a libel suit against the *Times,* the Supreme Court held in 1964 that in a free society "debate on public issues should be uninhibited, robust and wide-open, and . . . may well include vehement . . . attacks on government officials."[56] Later Court decisions expanded the *New York Times* rule to include not only officials but "public figures" such as political candidates and persons involved in events of general or public interest.[57] But in the 1970s the Supreme Court greatly narrowed its definition of a public figure. It ruled that a lawyer who defended a youth accused of killing a police officer in Chicago was not a public figure; it upheld his lawsuit against a publication that had falsely accused him of being a "Communist-fronter."[58] Similarly, the Court ruled in favor of Mrs. Russell A. Firestone and against *Time* magazine, which inaccurately reported that her husband had been granted a divorce on grounds of adultery (although the judge did note that some of her reported but unsubstantiated extramarital escapades "would have made Dr. Freud's hair curl"). Despite the extensive publicity surrounding the divorce, the Court ruled that Mrs. Firestone was not a public figure. The two decisions left the press vulnerable to libel suits by persons who might — or might not — be considered public figures.[59]

The Supreme Court narrowed the definition of a public figure even further

Stanislaus Zbyszko

[52] *Erznoznik* v. *City of Jacksonville,* 422 U.S. 206 (1975).
[53] *Southeastern Promotions, Ltd.* v. *Conrad,* 420 U.S. 546 (1975).
[54] *Hamling* v. *United States,* 418 U.S. 87 (1974).
[55] Robert H. Phelps and E. Douglas Hamilton, *Libel* (New York: Macmillan, 1966), p. 62.
[56] *New York Times Co.* v. *Sullivan,* 376 U.S. 254 (1964).
[57] *Curtis Publishing Co.* v. *Butts* and *Associated Press* v. *Walker,* 388 U.S. 130 (1967); *Rosenbloom* v. *Metromedia* (1971).
[58] *Gertz* v. *Robert Welch, Inc.,* 418 U.S. 323 (1974).
[59] *Time* v. *Firestone,* 424 U.S. 448 (1976).

Senator William Proxmire

in 1979. Senator William Proxmire, a Wisconsin Democrat, gave one of his derisive "Golden Fleece" awards to a scientist who had received half a million dollars in federal funds to study aggression in monkeys. The purpose of the study was to help select crew members for submarines and spacecraft. Proxmire charged in a Senate speech and in news releases and newsletters that the scientist, Dr. Ronald R. Hutchinson, had "made a monkey out of the American taxpayer." Hutchinson sued the senator for libel. The Supreme Court said the scientist has not become a public figure by accepting federal funds, and it ruled that while the Constitution protected Proxmire's speeches in the Senate, his press release describing the monkey research was not immune.[60]

Similarly, the Court ruled that Ilya Wolston, a former State Department interpreter, did not become a public figure by pleading guilty to contempt of court after refusing to appear before a grand jury investigating Soviet espionage. Wolston had sued the *Reader's Digest* for publishing a book that included him in a list of "Soviet agents." ". . . a private individual is not automatically transformed into a public figure just by becoming involved in . . . a matter that attracts public attention," the Court held.[61]

Moreover, in 1979 the Supreme Court ruled 6–3 that journalists who are sued for libel could be forced to disclose their "state of mind"—their thoughts and motivations—in preparing a news story.[62] The information, the Court said, was needed by public figures attempting to prove that stories had been prepared with "actual malice." In the majority opinion, Justice Byron R. White said the Court could not require a libel plaintiff to prove malice, as it had done in the *New York Times* case, and then "erect an impenetrable barrier" to the collection of vital evidence. The case arose when a former Army officer, Colonel Anthony Herbert, sued a CBS television producer, Barry Lando, over a "60 Minutes" broadcast.

The same year, the Supreme Court permitted a libel award against a novelist.[63] The Court let stand a $75,000 judgment against the author of *Touching,* a novel about nude encounter groups. The suit had been brought by a California psychologist who said he was the recognizable model for one of the characters in the book.

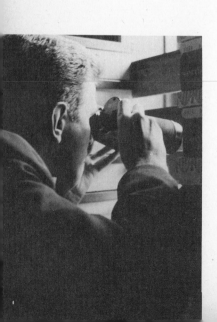

Privacy

Closely related to the issue of libel is the "right" to privacy. Although not specifically provided for in the Constitution, it has been recognized to a considerable extent by the courts. Justice Brandeis wrote that the makers of the Constitution sought to give Americans "the right to be let alone . . . the right most valued by civilized men."[64]

Today that right has been defined and protected by a series of Supreme Court decisions and by legislation. Nevertheless, in an era of computerized data banks and sophisticated surveillance techniques, the right of individuals to be free of intrusion into their privacy remains a subject of continuing concern and conflict. The government, corporations, credit firms, the press, insurance companies, schools, banks, and other institutions have all, to some degree, been accused of infringing on privacy.

[60] *Hutchinson* v. *Proxmire,* 443 U.S. 111 (1979).
[61] *Wolston* v. *Reader's Digest,* 443 U.S. 157 (1979).
[62] *Herbert* v. *Lando,* 441 U.S. 153 (1979).
[63] *Mitchell* v. *Bindrim* and *Doubleday* v. *Bindrim,* 444 U.S. 984 (1979).
[64] *Olmstead* v. *United States,* 277 U.S. 438 (1928).

Privacy: The Secret Zone

Generally speaking, the concept of a right to privacy attempts to draw a line between the individual and the collective, between self and society. It seeks to assure the individual a zone in which to be an individual, not a member of the community. In that zone he can think his own thoughts, have his own secrets, live his own life, reveal only what he wants to the outside world. The right of privacy, in short, establishes an area excluded from the collective life, not governed by the rules of collective living. It is based upon premises of individualism, that the society exists to promote the worth and the dignity of the individual. It is contrary to the theories of total commitment to the state, to society, or to any part thereof.

—Thomas I. Emerson, *The System of Freedom of Expression.*

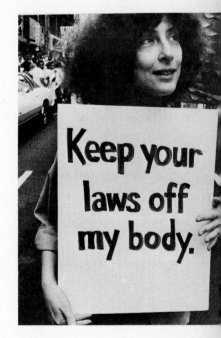

The concept of a right of privacy was first given expression by the Supreme Court in the 1965 case of *Griswold* v. *Connecticut.*[65] The head of the state's Planned Parenthood League and a physician who was also a professor at the Yale Medical School prescribed contraceptives and provided birth control information to married couples. They were convicted and fined under a state law. The Supreme Court, however, ruled that guarantees in the Bill of Rights cast "penumbras," or shadows, that may encompass other rights not specifically mentioned. "Various guarantees create zones of privacy," the Court said. The police must be kept out of the bedroom, the Court added, for marriage assumes "a right of privacy older than the Bill of Rights." In a 1972 case, the Court appeared to extend the legal right to use contraceptives to unmarried persons.[66]

In other cases, the Supreme Court has reiterated the right to privacy in very clear language. In *Roe* v. *Wade,* for example, the justices ruled that the concept of privacy included the right to a legal abortion. "The Constitution does not explicitly mention any right of privacy," the Court declared. But "the Court has recognized that a right of personal privacy, or a guarantee of certain areas or zones of privacy, does exist under the Constitution."[67]

And in yet another decision, the Court ruled that Robert Eli Stanley, a Georgia resident, had the right to watch pornographic movies in his own home.[68] The case arose when police with a warrant searched Stanley's home for evidence of bookmaking activity, found three reels of eight millimeter film, and viewed them on a projector in Stanley's living room.

What if the right of the press to report the news under the First Amendment conflicts with the individual's right to be left alone? Sometimes the Supreme Court has sided with the individual, sometimes with the press.

A landmark invasion of privacy case began in 1952, when James Hill and his family were held hostage by three escaped convicts for nineteen hours in their suburban Philadelphia home. Later a novel and a play, both called *The Desperate Hours,* appeared. *Life* magazine said the play was based on the Hills' experience. But in the play, the family was molested, while the Hills had not been harmed. The family sued the magazine. The Supreme Court ruled against

[65] *Griswold* v. *Connecticut,* 381 U.S. 479 (1965).
[66] *Eisenstadt* v. *Baird,* 405 U.S. 438 (1972).
[67] *Roe* v. *Wade,* 410 U.S. 113 (1973).
[68] *Stanley* v. *Georgia,* 394 U.S. 557 (1969).

the family, holding that the press could only be liable for "*calculated* falsehood" and not for inadvertent errors.[69] The lawyer who unsuccessfully argued the case for the Hills in the Supreme Court was Richard M. Nixon, later President.

In other cases, individuals have successfully defended their right to privacy against the news media. After a construction worker in West Virginia died in a bridge collapse, a Cleveland newspaper referred to his family as "hillbillies." The Court upheld a $60,000 judgment against the paper for invasion of privacy.[70] But in a Georgia case, the court ruled in favor of a television station that broadcast the name of a young woman who had been raped and killed by six teen-age boys. The victim's father sued the TV station, but the court said his privacy had not been invaded because the broadcaster had obtained his daughter's name from public court records.[71]

Congress has passed a series of laws in recent years relating to personal privacy. The Privacy Act of 1974, as already discussed, gives individuals a degree of control over government files maintained about them. The Fair Credit Reporting Act (1970) regulates credit agencies, department stores, and banks. And the Family Education Rights and Privacy Act (1974) gives parents or pupils the right to see school records and instructional material.

Freedom of Assembly

In addition to protecting free speech, the First Amendment protects "freedom of assembly." The Supreme Court has held this right to be "equally fundamental" to the right of free speech and free press.[72] It ruled in 1897 that a city can require a permit for the "use of public grounds."[73] But a city, in requiring licenses for parades, demonstrations, and sound trucks, must do so in the interest of controlling traffic and regulating the use of public streets and parks; it cannot — in theory — exercise its licensing power to suppress free speech.[74] The legitimate responsibility of public officials and police to control traffic or prevent a demonstration from growing into a riot is sometimes used as a device to suppress free speech because there is a thin, and not always readily distinguishable, line between crowd control and thought control.

In 1977 the heavily Jewish suburb of Skokie, Illinois, passed three local ordinances designed to prevent a march there by the American Nazi Party, an

[69] *Time* v. *Hill*, 385 U.S. 374 (1967).
[70] *Cantrell* v. *Forest City Publishing Co.*, 419 U.S. 245 (1974).
[71] *Cox Broadcasting Corp.* v. *Cohn*, 420 U.S. 469 (1975).
[72] *De Jonge* v. *Oregon*, 299 U.S. 353 (1937).
[73] *Davis* v. *Massachusetts*, 167 U.S. 43 (1897).
[74] *Hague* v. *C.I.O.*, 307 U.S. 496 (1939).

1980: American Nazis march in Cincinnati, Ohio

anti-Semitic group. The American Civil Liberties Union, although a liberal group opposed to the Nazis, went into court to defend the Nazi's right to march. Leaders of the Nazis ultimately called off plans to demonstrate in Skokie, the home of several thousand survivors of Hitler's Nazi regime. A few months later, in October 1978, the Supreme Court let stand a lower court ruling that Skokie's ordinances had violated the constitutional guarantees of free speech—possessed even by Nazis.[75]

President Jefferson wrote in 1802 that the freedom of religion clause of the First Amendment was designed to build "a wall of separation between Church and State." The wall still stands, but in several areas the Supreme Court has modified its contours.

Freedom of Religion

Many of the American colonies were settled by groups seeking religious freedom, but intolerant of religious dissent. Gradually, however, religious tolerance increased. When the Bill of Rights was passed, its first words were: "Congress shall make no law respecting an establishment of religion, or prohibiting the free exercise thereof."

The "Free Exercise" Clause. This clause of the First Amendment protects the right of individuals to worship or believe as they wish, or to hold no religious beliefs. It also means that people cannot be compelled by government to act contrary to their religious beliefs, unless religious conduct collides with valid laws. In that difficult area, the courts have had to try to resolve the conflict between the demands of religion and the demands of law.

For example, in a number of instances the Supreme Court has attempted to define the grounds that may be invoked by conscientious objectors to military service. Ever since the draft began during the Civil War, the law has provided some form of exemption for those whose religious beliefs would not permit them to serve in the armed forces. In 1965 the Supreme Court ruled that a "sincere and meaningful" objection to war on religious grounds did not require a belief in a Supreme Being.[76]

Then, in June 1970, with the war in Vietnam still in progress, the Court extended this protection to persons opposed to war for reasons of conscience. It ruled that Elliott Ashton Welsh II, a twenty-nine-year-old computer engineer from Los Angeles, could not be imprisoned for his refusal on ethical and moral grounds to serve in the armed forces. Welsh—and therefore other young Americans—the Court ruled, did not have to base his refusal on a belief in God or religious training. The government must exempt from military service, the Court declared, "all those whose consciences, spurred by deeply held moral, ethical, or religious beliefs, would give them no rest or peace if they allowed themselves to become part of an instrument of war."[77] The draft law, the Supreme Court ruled, did not exclude from draft exemption "those who hold strong beliefs about our domestic and foreign affairs or even those whose conscientious objection to participation in all wars is founded to a substantial extent upon consid-

Elliott Ashton Welsh II

[75] *Collin* v. *Smith*, 439 U.S. 916 (1978); see also *National Socialist Party* v. *Village of Skokie*, 432 U.S. 43 (1977).

[76] *United States* v. *Seeger*, 380 U.S. 163 (1965).

[77] *Welsh* v. *United States*, 398 U.S. 333 (1970).

erations of public policy."[78] But a year later the Court held that the Constitution did not permit conscientious objection to *particular* wars.[79]

In the *Flag Salute* cases, the Court initially ruled in 1940 that children of Jehovah's Witnesses could not be excused from saluting the American flag on religious grounds.[80] But three years later, the Court reversed itself and decided in favor of Walter Barnette, also a member of the Jehovah's Witnesses, whose seven children had been expelled from West Virginia schools for refusing to salute the flag.[81] Justice Robert H. Jackson, speaking for the Court, held that "the flag salute is a form of utterance" protected by the First Amendment. "If there is any fixed star in our constitutional constellation," Jackson said, "it is that no official, high or petty, can prescribe what shall be orthodox in politics, nationalism, religion or other matters of opinion." Because the Court's decision rested on the "free speech" clause, it protects anyone who refuses to salute the flag for whatever reason.

In 1962, a group of Navajo Indians were arrested in the California desert for using peyote in a religious ceremony. Peyote, a variety of cactus containing the hallucinogenic drug mescaline, is a narcotic under California law. But in 1964 the California Supreme Court ruled that the state could not prohibit the religious use of the drug by the Navajos.[82]

Not every religious practice is protected by the First Amendment, however. During the nineteenth century the Supreme Court outlawed polygamy.[83] In that case, although George Reynolds proved that as a Mormon he was *required* to have more than one wife, the Supreme Court sustained his conviction. The Court ruled that religious conduct could not violate the law, adding, rather gruesomely: "Suppose one believed that human sacrifices were a necessary part of religious worship?"

The "No Establishment" Clause. This clause of the First Amendment means, in the words of Justice Black, that "neither a state nor the federal government can set up a church. Neither can pass laws that aid one religion, aid all religions, or prefer one religion over another."[84]

Despite the constitutional separation between church and state, religion remains a significant factor in American life. Since 1865 the nation's coins have borne the motto "In God We Trust"; many major presidential speeches end with a reference to the Almighty; the pledge of allegiance contains the phrase "one nation under God"; public meetings often open with invocations and close with benedictions; a chaplain opens the daily sessions of the United States Senate; and so on.

Yet, hardly any subject generates more emotion than church-state relations. In 1962 the Supreme Court outlawed officially composed prayers in the public schools.[85] The initial school-prayer case arose after the Board of Regents of New York State composed a "nondenominational" prayer that it recommended local

[78] *Ibid.*
[79] *Gillette* v. *United States* and *Negre* v. *Larsen,* 401 U.S. 437 (1971).
[80] *Minersville School District* v. *Gobitis,* 310 U.S. 586 (1940).
[81] *West Virginia Board of Education* v. *Barnette,* 319 U.S. 624 (1943).
[82] William Cohen, Murray Schwartz, and DeAnne Sobul, *The Bill of Rights: A Source Book* (New York: Benziger Brothers, 1968), pp. 267–68.
[83] *Reynolds* v. *United States,* 98 U.S. 145 (1878); *Davis* v. *Beason,* 133 U.S. 333 (1890).
[84] *Everson* v. *Board of Education,* 330 U.S. 1 (1947).
[85] *Engel* v. *Vitale,* 370 U.S. 421 (1962).

school boards adopt.[86] The parents of ten children in New Hyde Park, New York, objected and went to court. In ruling the prayer unconstitutional, Justice Black, speaking for the Court, declared that the First Amendment means "that in this country it is no part of the business of government to compose official prayers for any group of the American people to recite as part of a religious program carried on by government."[87]

In 1963 the Court outlawed daily reading of the Bible and recitation of the Lord's Prayer in the public schools.[88] These decisions by the Court brought down a tremendous storm of protest upon its marble pillars. Ten years later, 10 percent of the nation's schools—and almost 28 percent in the South—were openly defying the Court's prayer ban, according to one study.[89] It was under the "no establishment" clause that the Court banned prayers in the public schools.

Some states had passed laws to permit voluntary prayers in the schools, but in Massachusetts a state court struck down such a law in 1980. About a dozen states have laws providing for a period of silent meditation in public schools, and these laws have generally not been challenged.

In 1967 Frederick Walz, a New York lawyer, purchased a small, weed-covered plot of land on Staten Island, taxed by the city at $5.24 a year. Walz then brought suit on the grounds that state tax exemption for churches raised his own tax bill and violated the constitutional barrier against "establishment of religion." But in 1970 the Supreme Court rejected his arguments.[90] The Court held that if church property were taxable, disputes would arise over assessments, and the result would be "excessive government entanglement" of church and state.

The main constitutional argument over church-state relations, however, centers on the question of whether, and to what extent, the government can aid

[86] "Almighty God, we acknowledge our dependence upon Thee, and we beg Thy blessings upon us, our parents, our teachers, and our country."

[87] *Engel* v. *Vitale* (1962).

[88] *Abington School District* v. *Schempp* and *Murray* v. *Curlett,* 374 U.S. 203 (1963).

[89] *New York Times,* April 20, 1980, "Spring Survey of Education," p. 3, quoting a survey by Professor Richard B. Dierenfield of Macalester College.

[90] *Walz* v. *Tax Commission of the City of New York,* 397 U.S. 664 (1970).

church-related schools. In 1979, for example, nearly 3.3 million students, about 7 percent of all schoolchildren, were enrolled in Roman Catholic schools.[91]

In 1947 the Supreme Court ruled as constitutional a New Jersey statute under which the parents of both public and parochial students were reimbursed by the local school district for the fares paid by their children to get to school on public buses.[92] This was the celebrated *Everson* case. The fare payments, the Court held, did no more than "help parents get their children, regardless of their religion" safely to and from school.

In 1960 John F. Kennedy became the first Roman Catholic to be elected President. Politically, it would have been awkward for him to propose federal aid to church-supported schools. In 1961 Kennedy submitted a bill to aid elementary and high schools that *omitted* aid to parochial schools "in accordance with the clear prohibition of the Constitution." President Kennedy relied on *Everson* in reaching this conclusion. He argued that the Supreme Court, in that instance, had permitted aid to the child, not to the school. The Catholic Church hierarchy attacked the bill, which went down to defeat in a tangle of religious controversy.

Congress in 1965, during the Johnson administration, passed the first general bill authorizing federal aid to elementary and secondary schools. It provided aid, through the states, to children in both public and church-supported schools. By emphasizing assistance to children in low-income areas it avoided much of the religious controversy that had surrounded previous attempts to pass an education bill.

Enrollments have dropped sharply in Roman Catholic and other church-affiliated schools in recent years, partly because of higher tuition fees imposed to meet greater operating costs. Hundreds of church schools have been forced to close. Since the *Everson* case in 1947, more than two-thirds of the states have enacted various kinds of aid to parochial schools, ranging from free lunches to driver education programs. Some of these programs have been upheld. For example, the Supreme Court has ruled that a state may lend textbooks to parochial school students.[93] It struck down a program of religious instruction in public schools by visiting teachers,[94] but upheld a "released time" program allowing public school students to attend religious classes outside of school.[95]

In 1971 the Supreme Court declared unconstitutional certain state programs of direct aid to parochial schools.[96] Although the Court ruled only on laws in Pennsylvania and Rhode Island, the effect was to severely limit state aid to church-affiliated schools throughout the nation. In 1973 the Supreme Court ruled that state programs of income tax credits and tuition reimbursements to parents of parochial school students violated the "no establishment" clause of the First Amendment. The Court struck down such programs in New York and Pennsylvania.[97] In 1975 the Court disapproved the direct loan to church-related

[91] Data provided by the National Center for Educational Statistics, Department of Education.
[92] *Everson* v. *Board of Education* (1947).
[93] *Board of Education* v. *Allen,* 392 U.S. 236 (1968).
[94] *Illinois ex rel. McCollum* v. *Board of Education,* 333 U.S. 203 (1948).
[95] *Zorach* v. *Clauson,* 343 U.S. 306 (1952).
[96] *Lemon* v. *Kurtzman,* the Pennsylvania case, and *Earley* v. *DiCenso* and *Robinson* v. *DiCenso,* the Rhode Island cases, all 403 U.S. 602 (1971). In all three decisions the Supreme Court relied on and expanded the "excessive government entanglement" standard it had cited in the *Walz* case.
[97] *Sloan* v. *Lemon,* 413 U.S. 825 (1973); *Committee for Public Education and Religious Liberty* v. *Nyquist,* 413 U.S. 756 (1973); and *Levitt* v. *Committee for Public Education and Religious Liberty,* 413 U.S. 472 (1973).

schools of materials such as films and laboratory equipment and the provision of other services, including counseling and testing.[98] Two years later, however, the Court upheld portions of an Ohio law that permitted counseling and diagnostic services off the school premises.[99]

Although the Supreme Court had curtailed state aid to church schools, it upheld a federal law providing construction funds for private colleges, including church-related colleges.[100] And in 1976 the Court for the first time approved state aid for general, nonreligious purposes to church-related colleges.[101]

Should those who would destroy the Bill of Rights enjoy its protection?

This dilemma is at the heart of a great public debate that began with the end of the Second World War. In this area two constitutional principles clash: the right to individual freedom of expression and the government's responsibility to protect national security.

The emergence of the Soviet Union as a rival power to the United States, the onset of the Cold War, and the division of the world during the 1950s into two armed nuclear camps created fear of communism at home and generated pressures to curb dissent and root Communists or "radicals" out of government posts.

Some political leaders, notably the late Senator Joseph R. McCarthy, a Wisconsin Republican, exploited public concern for political benefit. During the early 1950s McCarthy's freewheeling investigations of alleged Communists in the State Department and other agencies injured many innocent persons, destroyed careers, and created a widespread climate of fear in the federal government and in the nation. Few dared to raise their voices against him. When he attacked the Army in 1954, a series of public hearings exposed McCarthy's methods to the blinding light of television and led to his censure by the Senate later that year. After that, McCarthy lost influence. He died in 1957.

Against this background, two opposing views crystallized in the Court and within American society. One view was that a nation, like an individual, has the right to self-preservation; it must take action against internal enemies, and it need not wait until the threat is carried out, for that may be too late. The other view was that the First Amendment guarantees free speech for everyone; that if Americans have confidence in the democratic system they need not fear other ideologies or the clash of ideas.

The effort to suppress dissent did not begin with "McCarthyism." As early as 1798, the Alien and Sedition acts had provided a maximum fine of $2000 and two years in prison for "malicious writing" against the government of President John Adams. The first person to be convicted under the acts was Matthew Lyon, a Vermont congressman whose "crime" was to accuse President Adams of "a continual grasp for power . . . an unbounded thirst for ridiculous pomp, foolish adulation and selfish avarice." After Jefferson became President in 1801, the various Alien and Sedition acts were repealed or permitted to expire.

In 1940 Congress passed the Smith Act, which made it unlawful for any person to advocate overthrowing the government "by force or violence." In 1951 the Supreme Court upheld the constitutionality of the Smith Act and the

Loyalty
and Security

Senator Joseph R.
McCarthy

[98] *Meek* v. *Pittenger*, 421 U.S. 349 (1975).
[99] *Wolman* v. *Walter*, 433 U.S. 229 (1977).
[100] *Tilton* v. *Richardson*, 403 U.S. 672 (1971).
[101] *Roemer* v. *Maryland Public Works Board*, 426 U.S. 736 (1976).

conspiracy conviction of eleven leaders of the Communist party.[102] In later decisions, however, the Supreme Court severely restricted the use of the act.[103] Although the Court upheld the provision making it a crime to be a member of the Communist party,[104] it also ruled that only persons who held "active membership" and joined with "specific intent" of overthrowing the government could be convicted.[105]

After the outbreak of the Korean war, Congress passed the Internal Security Act of 1950, known as the McCarran Act. It required Communist "front" organizations to register with the Attorney General. The Supreme Court held that the Communist party could be compelled to register under the McCarran Act, but it was never actually forced to do so.[106] And the Court ruled that to require *individual* Communists to register would violate the Fifth Amendment.[107]

The vaguely worded Communist Control Act of 1954 was intended to outlaw the Communist party and deprive its candidates of a place on the ballot in local, state, or national elections. No political party had ever been outlawed in the United States and, as a practical matter, the 1954 act failed to accomplish this purpose. In 1980, as in some previous election years, a Communist party candidate for President appeared on the ballot in several states.

The anti-Communist actions of Congress had their parallel in the executive branch. In 1947 President Harry S. Truman issued an executive order establishing a federal loyalty program designed to screen out Communists and subversives from government service. The question of "security risks" in the government became a controversial political issue. The Supreme Court, however, limited the power of loyalty-security boards to dismiss federal employees and required that the government follow procedural "due process" of law in such cases.

As the postwar years have shown, however, freedom of expression has varied sharply with the political climate; even a "fixed star" may be viewed through a very different telescope in each decade.

Due Process of Law

"The history of liberty," Justice Felix Frankfurter once wrote, "is largely the history of the observance of procedural safeguards."[108] A nation may have an enlightened system of government, but if the rights of individuals are abused, then the system falls short of its goals.

In the United States, the Fifth and Fourteenth amendments to the Constitution provide for "due process of law," a phrase designed to protect the individual against the arbitrary power of the state. Sometimes, the distinction is made between *substantive due process* (laws must be reasonable) and *procedural due process* (laws must be administered in a fair manner). The Fourth Amendment also provides important protections against the government.

Searches and Seizures. Due process begins at home, for the right of individuals to "be secure in their persons, houses, papers and effects, against un-

[102] *Dennis* v. *United States,* 341 U.S. 494 (1951).
[103] *Yates* v. *United States,* 354 U.S. 298 (1957).
[104] *Scales* v. *United States,* 367 U.S. 203 (1961).
[105] *Noto* v. *United States,* 367 U.S. 290 (1961); *Elfbrandt* v. *Russell,* 384 U.S. 11 (1966).
[106] *Communist Party* v. *Subversive Activities Control Board,* 367 U.S. 1 (1961).
[107] *Albertson* v. *Subversive Activities Control Board,* 382 U.S. 70 (1965).
[108] *McNabb* v. *United States,* 318 U.S. 332 (1943).

Winthrop, Mass. — Fifteen burly policemen, carrying rifles and handguns, broke down two doors and poured into the home of the William Pine family last Tuesday. The men wore no uniforms, did not offer any identification and did not speak, Mrs. Pine said today in an interview, except for a few brusque orders followed by a rough shove to the living room couch. Bewildered, Mrs. Pine and her daughter screamed over and over:

"Please don't kill us, please don't kill us."

"Just don't move," came the only reply.

State and Federal agents and the narcotics squads of several communities had been surveying the house next to the Pine residence for the last two and a half months, where they believed a lucrative heroin factory was in operation. When the time came, they raided the wrong house.

"I thought they were all maniacs that had come to kill us," Mrs. Pine said. ". . . they never told us who they were or that they were police officers even after they left," she said. "I didn't know police operated like that in America. I'm ashamed that this could happen here."

—*New York Times,* January 15, 1973.

reasonable searches and seizures" is spelled out in the Fourth Amendment and marks a fundamental difference between a free and a totalitarian society.

In the United States, as a general principle police are not authorized to search a home without a search warrant signed by a judicial officer and issued on "probable cause" that the materials to be seized are in the place to be searched. Until 1980, police could lawfully enter a home without a warrant to make a valid arrest, and they could conduct a limited search at the same time. But in April of that year, the Supreme Court ruled that the Fourth Amendment prohibited police from entering a home without a warrant to make a routine arrest.[109] Police must obtain a warrant except in emergency circumstances, the Court held. The decision invalidated the laws of 23 states. The case arose from two arrests in New York City. In 1970 police believed that Theodore Payton had murdered the manager of a gas station. They went to his apartment without a warrant and used crowbars to break in. They did not find Payton but discovered a shell casing that helped to convict him of murder. Four years later, police were admitted to the home of Obie Riddick, an armed robbery suspect, by his three-year-old son. They had no warrant but arrested Riddick for two armed robberies. At the same time, police searched and turned up narcotics, leading to Riddick's indictment and conviction on drug charges.

In reversing these convictions, Justice John Paul Stevens ruled, in effect, that a family's home is its castle. "In terms that apply equally to seizures of property and to seizures of persons," he said, "the Fourth Amendment has drawn a firm line at the entrance to the house. Absent exigent circumstances, that threshold may not reasonably be crossed without a warrant."

Although the Constitution is designed to protect against unreasonable government intrusion, in actual practice constitutional principles are sometimes violated. Two innocent families in Collinsville, Illinois, found that out in April 1973 when federal narcotics agents kicked in the doors of their homes, terrorized them at gunpoint, and ransacked their houses in a drug raid based on false

[109] *Payton* v. *New York,* 445 U.S. 573 (1980).

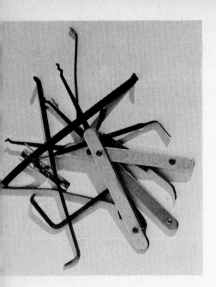

Lockpicks carried by one of the burglars at the Watergate

information. The agents had no search or arrest warrants. Subsequent investigations disclosed that dozens of other such raids, sometimes fatal to the victims, had been carried out by federal, state, and local narcotics agents.[110] During the Nixon administration, it was disclosed that agents employed by the White House had burglarized the office of a psychiatrist who had treated Daniel Ellsberg, the former government official who leaked the Pentagon Papers to the news media. This was in addition to the illegal entry into the Democrats' Watergate headquarters by burglars working for President Nixon's campaign. It was also disclosed that Nixon himself had approved for a time a plan that included "surreptitious entry" of the homes or offices of persons suspected by the government of being a threat to internal security—even though the President had been warned, in writing, that this was "clearly illegal" and "amounts to burglary." In 1975 the FBI admitted it had conducted hundreds of illegal break-ins against dissident groups and individuals, and a presidential commission found that the CIA had also engaged in illegal burglaries.[111]

In 1969 the Supreme Court ruled that police lacking a search warrant could not ransack a home in the course of making a lawful arrest but must confine their search to the suspect and his immediate surroundings.[112] The decision overturned the conviction of Ted Steven Chimel of California, who had been serving a five-year-to-life term for stealing rare coins—which police found after searching his home without a search warrant.

Under other Court rulings, police may search an automobile without a warrant if they have probable cause to believe it contains illegal articles.[113] Police who stop a car for a traffic violation may order the occupants to get out.[114] And they may "stop and frisk" a suspect on the street without a warrant if there is reasonable suspicion that the person is armed or dangerous.[115] A police officer may also "stop and frisk" a criminal suspect on the basis of an informant's tip that the officer considers to be reliable.[116] And police may arrest someone in a public place without a warrant on "probable cause" that the person has committed a crime.[117]

Cherished constitutional principles are usually established in cases involving criminals and people who are not pillars of the community. In 1957 Cleveland police, with no search warrant, barged into the house of a woman named Dollree Mapp. They did not find the fugitive or the betting slips they were after but seized some "lewd and lascivious books and pictures." She was tried and convicted for possession of these items. But the Supreme Court ruled that a state could not prosecute a person with unconstitutionally seized evidence, a decision that protected not only Dollree Mapp but every American.[118]

The Supreme Court had long held that the federal government could not use illegally seized evidence in court, a principle known as "the exclusionary

---

[110] *New York Times,* July 1, 1973, Section 4, p. 6.
[111] *New York Times,* September 26, 1975, p. 1, and *Report to the President by the Commission on CIA Activities Within the United States* (Washington, D.C.: U.S. Government Printing Office, 1975), pp. 167–68, 298. This report is generally known as the Rockefeller Report.
[112] *Chimel* v. *California,* 395 U.S. 752 (1969).
[113] *Carroll* v. *United States,* 267 U.S. 132 (1925); *Texas* v. *White,* 423 U.S. 67 (1976).
[114] *Pennsylvania* v. *Mimms,* 434 U.S. 106 (1977).
[115] *Terry* v. *Ohio,* 392 U.S. 1 (1968).
[116] *Adams* v. *Williams,* 407 U.S. 143 (1972).
[117] *United States* v. *Watson,* 423 U.S. 411 (1976).
[118] *Mapp* v. *Ohio,* 367 U.S. 643 (1961).

rule."[119] The *Mapp* case meant that the states, too, were subject to this rule.

But the Burger Court appeared to narrow the impact of the rule by holding in 1974 that a witness before a grand jury could not refuse to answer questions based on evidence seized unlawfully; and the following year, the Court seemed to move even farther away from the exclusionary rule, leading Justice William J. Brennan, Jr., to warn in a dissent that the rule faced "slow strangulation."[120] Then in 1976 the Court curtailed the power of federal courts to overturn state court convictions because of illegally seized evidence,[121] thereby further limiting the exclusionary rule. The trend has continued. Three years later, the Burger Court ruled that the courts could consider evidence seized by police in the course of an arrest—even when the law on which the police relied in "good faith" is later held to be unconstitutional.[122] And in 1980 the Supreme Court ruled that evidence illegally seized by the government could be used to discredit statements made by a defendant during cross-examination at his trial.[123]

In a controversial 1978 decision, the Supreme Court permitted police to search newspaper offices and seize evidence of a crime, even though the newspaper was an innocent "third party" not suspected of any wrongdoing.[124] The case arose in 1971 on the campus of Stanford University. A group of antiwar demonstrators at the university hospital attacked police, two of whom were seriously injured. The university newspaper, the *Stanford Daily,* published photographs of the incident. The next day, armed with a warrant, police swooped down on the paper's newsroom and searched its photo labs, filing cabinets, desks, and wastepaper baskets. The Supreme Court ruled that innocent third parties are not entitled to extra protection under the Fourth Amendment, and added that the First Amendment does not bar newsroom searches for criminal evidence. In a strong dissent, Justice Potter Stewart said unannounced searches of newsrooms would disrupt newspaper operations and possibly disclose confidential news sources to the police.

In the aftermath of the *Stanford* case, sheriff's deputies and other law enforcement officials raided a television station newsroom in Boise, Idaho, in 1980, searching for and seizing videotapes of a prison riot. The local prosecutor said he needed the tapes to identify the leaders of the riot. Reacting to these incidents, Congress later that year enacted a law barring most such newsroom searches. The law, the Privacy Protection Act of 1980, had been proposed by President Carter. It ordinarily requires federal, state, and local authorities to use subpoenas, rather than searches, in seeking evidence from journalists, authors, scholars, and others engaged in writing for publication.

The Uninvited Ear. In the technological age, the right of privacy has been threatened by highly sophisticated wiretapping and eavesdropping devices.

In Washington practically anyone of importance assumes, or at least jokes, that his telephone is tapped. (One leading columnist began his telephone conversations: "Hello, everybody.") As a Senate committee has demonstrated, even the olive in a martini may be an electronic bug. With infrared light, persons in

Sheriff's deputies search TV newsroom in Boise, Idaho.

[119] *Weeks* v. *United States,* 232 U.S. 383 (1914).
[120] *United States* v. *Calandra,* 414 U.S. 338 (1974); *United States* v. *Peltier,* 422 U.S. 531 (1975).
[121] *Stone* v. *Powell* and *Wolff* v. *Rice,* 44 USLW 5313 (1976).
[122] *Michigan* v. *DeFillippo,* 443 U.S. 31 (1979).
[123] *United States* v. *Havens,* 446 U.S. 620 (1980).
[124] *Zurcher* v. *Stanford Daily,* 436 U.S. 547 (1978).

117

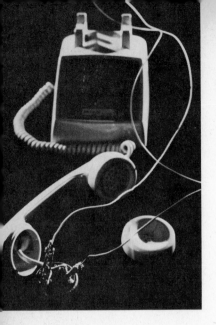

a room may be photographed through the wall of an adjoining room. Infrared light may also be used to pick up speech as far as *thirty-four miles* away. A person who swallows a "radio pill" becomes for a time a human broadcasting station, emitting signals that enable an investigator to follow the subject from some distance away.[125]

Modern technology has made possible a new form of government intrusion into the private lives of individuals, a threat that Justice Potter Stewart has called "the uninvited ear." Many prosecutors and law enforcement officials insist that wiretapping and electronic bugs are essential tools in cases involving espionage, kidnapping, and organized crime. Other observers feel that the use of such devices will inevitably be abused by government authorities and result in the violation of constitutional liberties.

Despite the denunciation of wiretapping by Justice Holmes as "dirty business," the Supreme Court for almost forty years (1928–1967) held that the practice did not violate the Fourth Amendment's protection against unreasonable search and seizure.[126] The Court did hold, however, that wiretap evidence could not be used in federal courts.[127] Finally, in 1967, the Court caught up with modern technology by ruling that a conversation was tangible and could be seized electronically, and that placing a bug or tap did not have to involve physical "trespass" to violate the Fourth Amendment. The Court also ruled that police could not eavesdrop without a court warrant. The case involved Charles Katz, a Los Angeles gambler who made interstate telephone calls to bookmakers from a public phone booth to bet on college basketball games. Unknown to Katz, the FBI had taped a microphone to the top of his favorite phone booth on Sunset Boulevard. Since the FBI had no warrant, the Supreme Court held that Katz's constitutional rights had been violated and threw out his conviction.[128]

When public concern over crime increases, so do pressures to employ wiretaps and electronic eavesdropping devices. In the late 1960s "law and order" became a growing political issue. In 1968 Congress passed the Omnibus Crime Control and Safe Streets Act permitting court-authorized wiretapping and bugging by federal, state, and local authorities in a wide variety of cases.

In 1969, when the Nixon administration came to power, Attorney General John N. Mitchell claimed that the Justice Department had power even *without* court approval to tap and bug domestic groups it considered to be a threat to internal security. In 1972, however, the Supreme Court ruled, in an 8–0 decision, that this highly controversial policy violated the Fourth Amendment of the Constitution.[129] In 1973 President Nixon confirmed that early in his first term, in an alleged effort to plug news "leaks" and protect "national security," he had authorized wiretaps of a total of seventeen White House aides, other officials, and news reporters. The Senate Intelligence Committee, formed after

The Constitution Protects Telephone Booths

The Fourth Amendment protects people, not places. . . . No less than an individual in a business office, in a friend's apartment, or in a taxicab, a person in a telephone booth may rely upon the protection of the Fourth Amendment.

One who occupies it, shuts the door behind him, and pays the toll that permits him to place a call, is surely entitled to assume that the words he utters into the mouthpiece will not be broadcast to the world.

—Justice Potter Stewart, in *Katz* v. *United States* (1967).

---

[125] Alan F. Westin, *Privacy and Freedom* (New York: Atheneum, 1967), pp. 70, 87.

[126] *Olmstead* v. *United States* (1928).

[127] *Nardone* v. *United States*, 302 U.S. 379 (1937); *Benanti* v. *United States*, 355 U.S. 96 (1957).

[128] *Katz* v. *United States*, 389 U.S. 347 (1967). *Katz* overruled the *Olmstead* decision. In a related case, *Berger* v. *New York*, 388 U.S. 41 (1967), the Supreme Court invalidated a New York State law that permitted police to engage in electronic surveillance with a court warrant; the Court held the state law was too broad in setting standards for electronic eavesdropping.

[129] *United States* v. *United States District Court for the Eastern District of Michigan*, 407 U.S. 297 (1972). In this case, sometimes also known as the *Keith* case, the Supreme Court did not address itself to the question of whether the President had power to order electronic surveillance against *foreign* intelligence activities or agents.

the Watergate scandal to investigate abuses by federal police agencies, reported that warrantless wiretapping and bugging had taken place under other Presidents as well, including Lyndon Johnson and John F. Kennedy.

In 1978 Congress passed the Foreign Intelligence Surveillance Act, which, for the first time, required a court order even for wiretapping and bugging in national security investigations. The law also established a special, seven-judge court to issue such warrants. The only exception in the law permits the government to eavesdrop on the communications of foreign powers without a warrant.

Since the 1968 Omnibus Crime Control Act required police to obtain court warrants to eavesdrop in domestic criminal investigations, the two laws, taken together, prohibit virtually all electronic surveillance without a warrant. But, in 1979 the Supreme Court held that a break-in by government agents to plant a court-authorized bug is constitutional; it said that Congress had not ruled out "covert entry" to carry out electronic surveillance.[130]

Rights of the Accused. "Due process of law" may mean little to average Americans—unless and until they are arrested. This is because most of the important procedural safeguards provided by the Constitution, as interpreted by the Supreme Court, concern the rights of accused persons.

Before anyone may be brought to trial for a serious federal crime, there must be a grand jury *indictment,* a finding that there is enough evidence to warrant a criminal trial. The Constitution does not require states to use grand juries, and in most state cases, in place of an indictment, a criminal *information* is filed with the court by the prosecutor in order to bring a defendant to trial. The Bill of Rights entitles suspects or defendants to be represented by a lawyer, to be informed of their legal rights and of the charges against them, to have a speedy and public trial by jury, to summon witnesses to testify in their behalf, to cross-examine prosecution witnesses, and to refuse to testify against themselves. In addition, they may not be held in excessive bail, or subjected to cruel and unusual punishment or to double jeopardy for the same offense. These rights are contained in the Fifth through Eighth amendments.

Under Chief Justice Earl Warren, the Supreme Court, in a series of split decisions in the mid-1960s, greatly strengthened the rights of accused persons, particularly in the period immediately following arrest. It is in the station-house stage that police traditionally attempt to extract a confession from suspects. It is also the very time at which accused persons may be most disoriented, frightened, and uncertain of their rights. The Court came under severe political attack for these decisions, which many law enforcement authorities argued would hamper their ability to fight crime. The Warren Court rulings came at a time of rising violence and unrest in America. Many citizens, worried about "law and order," focused their criticism on the Court and on the judicial system, which was often accused of "coddling criminals." Supporters of the Warren Court decisions and of civil liberties argued that there is no better test of a democracy than the procedural safeguards it erects to protect accused persons from the police power of the state.

A landmark case of the Warren era began in Chicago on the night of January 19, 1960. A man named Manuel Valtierra was shot in the back and killed. Police picked up his brother-in-law, Danny Escobedo, a laborer. He was ques-

[130] *Dalia* v. *United States,* 441 U.S. 238 (1979).

Drawing by Frascino
© 1970 The New Yorker Magazine, Inc.

"Quote. No person shall be held to answer for a capital, or otherwise infamous crime, unless on a presentment or indictment of a Grand Jury, except in cases arising in the land or naval forces, or in the Militia, when in actual service in time of War or public danger; nor shall any person be subject for the same offence to be twice put in jeopardy of life or limb; nor shall be compelled in any criminal case to be a witness against himself, nor be deprived of life, liberty, or property, without due process of law; nor shall private property be taken for public use, without just compensation. Unquote."

119

Ernesto Miranda after
his arrest on parole
violations

tioned, released, picked up ten days later, and interrogated again. He asked to see his lawyer, but the request was refused. During the long night at police headquarters, Danny Escobedo confessed. In 1964, by a vote of 5 to 4, the Supreme Court reversed his conviction, freeing him after four-and-a-half years in prison. Justice Arthur Goldberg ruled for the Court that under the Sixth Amendment, a suspect is entitled to counsel even during police interrogation once "the process shifts from investigatory to accusatory."[131] Nor can the government use incriminating statements made by a suspect to an informer imprisoned with him before a trial; the Supreme Court has ruled that use of such evidence deprives the suspect of the right to have an attorney present.[132]

As far back as 1957, the Court had laid down the *Mallory rule,* requiring that a suspect in a federal case be arraigned without unnecessary delay.[133] In 1966, in *Miranda* v. *Arizona,* the Supreme Court extended the protection it had granted to suspects with the *Escobedo* decision. Ernesto A. Miranda, an indigent twenty-three-year-old man, described by the Court as mentally disturbed, was arrested in March 1963, ten days after the kidnapping and rape of an eighteen-year-old woman near Phoenix. The woman picked Miranda out of a police lineup, and after two hours of interrogation—during which he was not told of his right to silence and a lawyer—he confessed. The Supreme Court struck down Miranda's conviction; in a controversial 5–4 decision, the Court ruled that the Fifth Amendment's protection against self-incrimination requires that suspects be clearly informed of their rights before they are asked any questions by police.

Chief Justice Warren declared for the narrow majority that statements made by an accused person may not be used against him in court unless strict procedures are followed: "Prior to any questioning, the person must be warned that he has a right to remain silent, that any statement he does make may be used against him, and that he has a right to the presence of an attorney, either retained or appointed."[134] Although a defendant may knowingly waive these rights, Warren ruled, he cannot be questioned further if at any point he asks to see a lawyer or indicates "in any manner" that he does not wish to be interrogated.

The Chief Justice, declaring that *Miranda* went to "the roots of our concepts of American criminal jurisprudence," argued eloquently that the "compelling atmosphere" of a "menacing police interrogation" was designed to intimidate the suspect, break his will, and lead to an involuntary confession in violation of the Fifth Amendment. That is why, he concluded, "procedural safeguards" must be observed in the police station. In a strong dissent Justice John Harlan said: "It's obviously going to mean a gradual disappearance of confessions as a legitimate tool of law enforcement." After the decision many police began carrying "Miranda cards" to read suspects their rights.

With the election of President Nixon, the era of the Warren Court came to an end. In 1969 Nixon named a new chief justice, Warren E. Burger. Within four years, Nixon had appointed three more Supreme Court justices who were, as a group, generally more conservative than their predecessors. Particularly in the area of criminal justice, the pendulum gradually began to swing back from the liberal philosophy of the Warren Court.

In 1971 the Burger Court handed down a decision that greatly narrowed

[131] *Escobedo* v. *Illinois,* 378 U.S. 478 (1964).
[132] *United States* v. *Henry,* 447 U.S. 264 (1980).
[133] *Mallory* v. *United States,* 354 U.S. 449 (1957).
[134] *Miranda* v. *Arizona,* 384 U.S. 436 (1966).

the scope of the *Miranda* ruling. The Court held that if a statement were made by a suspect without proper *Miranda* warnings, it could still be used to discredit his testimony at a trial.[135] In a further qualification of its *Miranda* decision, the Supreme Court ruled in 1972 that juries did not have to be convinced "beyond a reasonable doubt" in deciding whether a confession was voluntary and therefore admissible as evidence in court.[136] The Burger Court also upheld the admission of hearsay evidence to convict a defendant in a state court.[137] And in 1972 the Supreme Court diluted the Fifth Amendment's safeguard against self-incrimination; it upheld a law that diminished the immunity from prosecution granted to a witness compelled to testify.[138]

The Burger Court retreated even further from *Miranda* in three later decisions. In 1974 the Court ruled that evidence obtained by police after an incomplete warning of legal rights was given to a defendant could nevertheless be used against him.[139] In 1975 the Court additionally weakened *Miranda* by allowing prosecutors to use incriminating statements obtained by police after a defendant had demanded to see a lawyer.[140] And in another case, the Supreme Court ruled that even after suspects exercise the right to remain silent about one crime, they can still be questioned about another.[141]

Despite these decisions, in 1976 the Burger Court did reinforce the *Miranda* decision. Two men arrested for selling marijuana in Ohio were advised

---

[135] *Harris* v. *New York,* 401 U.S. 222 (1971). The defendant claimed at his trial that he had sold baking soda, not heroin, to an undercover narcotics agent. The prosecution then read a statement the defendant had made, without police warnings, just after his arrest, in which he admitted the sale and made no mention of baking soda.

[136] *Lego* v. *Twomey,* 404 U.S. 477 (1972).

[137] *Dutton* v. *Evans,* 400 U.S. 74 (1970).

[138] *Kastigar* v. *United States,* 406 U.S. 441 (1972).

[139] *Michigan* v. *Tucker,* 417 U.S. 433 (1974).

[140] *Oregon* v. *Hass,* 420 U.S. 714 (1975).

[141] *Michigan* v. *Mosley,* 423 U.S. 96 (1975).

Miranda Rights on Trial

In *Miranda* v. *Arizona* the Supreme Court in 1966 ruled that criminal suspects must be advised of their rights, including the right to have an attorney present.

On Christmas Eve two years later, a ten-year-old girl, Pamela Powers, was at the YMCA with her mother, watching her brother compete in a wrestling match. Pamela went to find a restroom. She was abducted, sexually molested, and murdered, her body thrown into a culvert along a country road, where animals nibbled at it.

A suspect, Robert Anthony Williams, turned himself in to police in Davenport, Iowa, on the advice of his attorney. Police read Williams his rights and promised his lawyer that he would not be questioned on the 160-mile drive back to Des Moines.

But during the ride, a Des Moines detective said to the suspect, "I feel that we could stop and locate the body, that the parents of this little girl should be entitled to a Christian burial for the little girl who was snatched away from them on Christmas Eve and murdered." Williams relented and directed the detectives to the body. At his trial, his actions and statements were used against him, and he was convicted and sentenced to life imprisonment.

The Supreme Court, in the case of *Brewer* v. *Williams,* held 5–4 in 1977 that Williams had been deprived of his constitutional rights. "Once adversary proceedings have commenced against an individual," Justice Potter Stewart wrote for the majority, "he has a right to legal representation when the government interrogates him." The Court reversed the conviction and ordered a new trial. A few months later, Robert Anthony Williams was retried, convicted, and again sentenced to life imprisonment.

—Adapted from *Washington Post,* October 4, 1976; and *New York Times,* October 4, 1976.

of their rights but later contended at their trial that they had been framed by an informer. The prosecutor emphasized that the defendants had not told that story at the time of their arrest. But the Court ruled that a suspect's silence after being advised of his *Miranda* rights could not later be used against him.[142] However, in 1980 the Supreme Court ruled that once a defendant took the stand at a trial, he could be questioned about his prearrest silence.[143]

In 1977 the Burger Court again upheld the *Miranda* decision in a grisly Iowa murder case[144] (see box, p. 121). The suspect, with no lawyer present, led police to the body after a detective drew him into conversation about the crime during a long automobile ride. The Supreme Court by a narrow 5–4 margin reversed the conviction. And in 1979 the Court ruled in a murder case that even when a suspect had been advised of his *Miranda* rights, incriminating admissions could not be used against him if police held him for questioning without valid grounds for arrest in the first place.[145]

On the other hand, the Court appeared to permit the use of subtle psychology on suspects unless police were aware that their actions or words were "reasonably likely" to make a suspect confess.[146] The case arose when Thomas Innis, a murder suspect, led police to a hidden weapon after officers remarked that there were "a lot of handicapped children running around in this area" and that it would be too bad if a child "would pick up the gun and maybe kill herself." The Court said that this was not the sort of "interrogation" forbidden by *Miranda*.

Ernesto Miranda was stabbed to death in a barroom quarrel in Phoenix, Arizona, on February 1, 1976. Fernando Rodriguez Zamora was arrested on a murder charge for allegedly handing the knife to the assailant, who fled. The police read Zamora his rights. They used a "Miranda card."

The right of an indigent defendant to have a lawyer in a state court might seem basic, but in fact it was not established by the Supreme Court until 1963 in the celebrated case of *Gideon* v. *Wainwright*.[147]

Clarence Earl Gideon

Clarence Earl Gideon petitioned the Supreme Court in 1962 from the Florida State Prison at Raiford, where he was serving a five-year term for breaking into a poolroom in Panama City, Florida, and allegedly stealing some beer, wine, and coins from a cigarette machine and a jukebox. A drifter, a man whose life had had more than the normal share of disasters, Gideon nevertheless had one idea fixed firmly in his mind—that the Constitution of the United States entitled him to a fair trial. And this, he insisted in his petition, he had not received. Clarence Earl Gideon had not been provided by the court with a lawyer. In 1942 the Supreme Court had ruled that the right of counsel was not a "fundamental right," essential to a fair trial in a state court and that it was not guaranteed by the "due process" clause of the Fourteenth Amendment.[148] But in *Gideon*, two decades later, the Supreme Court changed its mind. Justice Black declared for the majority: a person "who is too poor to hire a lawyer cannot be assured

[142] *Doyle* v. *Ohio* and *Wood* v. *Ohio*, 426 U.S. 610 (1976).
[143] *Jenkins* v. *Anderson*, 447 U.S. 231 (1980).
[144] *Brewer* v. *Williams*, 430 U.S. 387 (1977).
[145] *Dunaway* v. *New York*, 442 U.S. 200 (1979).
[146] *Rhode Island* v. *Innis*, 446 U.S. 291 (1980).
[147] *Gideon* v. *Wainwright*, 372 U.S. 335 (1963).
[148] *Betts* v. *Brady*, 316 U.S. 455 (1942).

*"You have a pretty good case, Mr. Pitkin.
How much justice can you afford?"*

Drawing by Handelsman
© 1973 The New Yorker Magazine, Inc.

a fair trial unless counsel is provided for him." A few months later, Gideon won a new trial and this time—with the help of a lawyer—he was acquitted.

The landmark *Gideon* decision left open a question of vital importance to millions of poor persons arrested each year for misdemeanors and so-called petty offenses, crimes carrying maximum penalties of six months in jail. Because Gideon had been convicted of a felony, the decision in his case did not clarify whether defendants accused of lesser offenses were also entitled to free counsel. Then in 1972 the Supreme Court overruled the conviction of Jon Richard Argersinger, a Tallahassee, Florida, gas station attendant who had not been offered an attorney when he pleaded guilty to carrying a concealed weapon, a misdemeanor.[149] The decision meant that no persons—unless they voluntarily give up their right to a lawyer—may be sentenced to jail for any offense, no matter how minor, unless they have been represented by an attorney at their trial.

The Bill of Rights was passed as a bulwark against the new *federal* government. It did not apply to the *states*. Congress, in fact, rejected a proposal by James Madison to prohibit the states from interfering with basic liberties.

Because America has a federal system of government, this created a paradox: the same constitutional rights established under the federal government were often meaningless within a state. It was as though the Bill of Rights were a ticket valid for travel on a high-speed train but no good for local commuting. Not until 1925 did the Supreme Court systematically begin to apply the Bill of Rights to the states. By 1970 the process was virtually complete. But even today, there is no *written* provision in the Constitution requiring the states to observe the Bill of Rights.

In 1833 the Supreme Court ruled in *Barron* v. *Baltimore* that the provisions of the Bill of Rights did not apply to the state governments and "this Court cannot so apply them."[150] Near the end of the Civil War, Congress passed the

An Expanding
Umbrella of Rights

[149] *Argersinger* v. *Hamlin,* 407 U.S. 25 (1972).
[150] Chief Justice John Marshall, in *Barron* v. *Baltimore,* 7 Peters 243 (1833).

Fourteenth Amendment, which for the first time provided that "No State shall . . . deprive any person of life, liberty, or property, without due process of law." Did Congress thereby mean to "incorporate" the entire Bill of Rights into the Fourteenth Amendment and apply the Bill of Rights to the states? The argument has never been settled, but the point—thanks to the decisions of the Supreme Court in this century—is rapidly becoming moot.

In the *Gitlow* case in 1925, the Court held that freedom of speech and press were among the "fundamental personal rights" protected by the Fourteenth Amendment from abridgment by the states.[151] The Court thus began a process of *selective incorporation* of the Bill of Rights. Two years later, the Court confirmed that freedom of speech was locked in under the Fourteenth Amendment.[152] In 1931 freedom of the press was specifically applied to the states.[153] In 1932, in the first of the *Scottsboro* cases, the Court partially incorporated the Sixth Amendment by requiring that a defendant in a capital case be represented by a lawyer.[154] Two years later, it applied freedom of religion to the states.[155] In 1937 freedom of assembly was held to apply to the states.[156]

Later that same year came the landmark incorporation decision of *Palko* v. *Connecticut*.[157] Frank Palko had been sentenced to life imprisonment for killing two policemen. Under an unusual Connecticut statute, the state could appeal and did; a new trial resulted in a death sentence. Palko appealed to the Supreme Court, contending that the second trial had placed him in double jeopardy, in violation of the Fifth Amendment. Justice Cardozo ruled that the Fourteenth Amendment *did* require the states to abide by the Bill of Rights where the rights at stake were so fundamental that "neither liberty nor justice would exist if they were sacrificed." But Cardozo added that while procedural rights such as the immunity against double jeopardy were important, "they are not of the very essence of a scheme of ordered liberty," and therefore not binding on the states. The distinction was not helpful to Frank Palko; he was executed.

In 1947 the *Everson* case incorporated the principle of separation of church and state, and in 1961 *Mapp* established that the Fourth Amendment applied to the states. In 1962 the Court carried the Eighth Amendment's protection against cruel and unusual punishment to the states; it further extended this protection in 1972 when it held that capital punishment as then administered constituted cruel and unusual punishment in violation of the Eighth Amendment.[158] In rapid succession, other rights were applied to the states: the Fifth Amendment's protection against self-incrimination,[159] and the Sixth Amendment's rights to counsel,[160] to a speedy trial,[161] to confrontation of an accused person by the witnesses against him,[162] to compulsory process for obtaining witnesses,[163] and to trial by jury in all serious criminal cases.[164]

[151] *Gitlow* v. *New York* (1925).
[152] *Fiske* v. *Kansas*, 274 U.S. 380 (1927).
[153] *Near* v. *Minnesota* (1931).
[154] *Powell* v. *Alabama*, 287 U.S. 45 (1932).
[155] *Hamilton* v. *Regents of the University of California*, 293 U.S. 245 (1934).
[156] *De Jonge* v. *Oregon* (1937).
[157] *Palko* v. *Connecticut* (1937).
[158] *Robinson* v. *California*, 370 U.S. 660 (1962); *Furman* v. *Georgia*, 408 U.S. 238 (1972).
[159] *Malloy* v. *Hogan*, 378 U.S. 1 (1964).
[160] *Gideon* v. *Wainwright* (1963); *Argersinger* v. *Hamlin* (1972).
[161] *Klopfer* v. *North Carolina*, 386 U.S. 213 (1967).
[162] *Pointer* v. *Texas*, 380 U.S. 400 (1965).
[163] *Washington* v. *Texas*, 388 U.S. 14 (1967).
[164] *Duncan* v. *Louisiana*, 391 U.S. 145 (1968).

In 1969, on Earl Warren's final day as Chief Justice, the Court, in *Benton* v. *Maryland*,[165] finally applied the Fifth Amendment's prohibition of double jeopardy to the states; it ruled that John Dalmer Benton should not have been tried twice for larceny. The Court thus overruled Justice Cardozo's decision in the *Palko* case.

The process of incorporation had in effect come full circle in the thirty-two years between *Palko* and *Benton*. Of the portions of the Bill of Rights that could apply to the states, almost every significant provision—with the exception of the Fifth Amendment's right to indictment by grand jury for major crimes—had been applied.[166] Thus, through the slow and shifting process of selective incorporation, the Supreme Court has brought the states almost entirely under the protective umbrella of the Bill of Rights.

At a time when democracy is under pressure, when the American political system is being tested to determine whether it can meet the problems of an urbanized, complex, and changing society, the Bill of Rights is more important than ever.

The Bill of Rights and the Supreme Court remain a buffer between popular emotion and constitutional principle. For it is precisely in times of stress and upheaval that fundamental liberties require the most protection. As Justice Jackson put it so eloquently, freedom to differ over "things that do not matter much" is a "mere shadow" of freedom. "The test of its substance is the right to differ as to things that touch the heart of the existing order."[167]

While the Supreme Court may at times be more zealous than other institutions in protecting civil liberties, it is by no means insensitive to public pressure. As John P. Frank has noted: "The dominant lesson of our history . . . is that courts love liberty most when it is under pressure least."[168] It is not enough, therefore, to leave the protection of fundamental liberties to the courts. Public support for civil liberties is a vital factor in the preservation of those liberties.

It is in the field of civil liberties and civil rights that some of the most sensitive demands and supports (inputs) are fed into the political system. For example, in weighing the rights of defendants versus the suppression of crime by society, the federal government is making some highly important allocations of values (outputs). And in Supreme Court decisions such as school desegregation, the rights of suspects, and school prayers, the public reaction (feedback) is formidable.

In applying the First Amendment and in balancing the claims of individual rights versus those of society, the Supreme Court generally moved during the 1960s in the direction of freer expression, reflecting the attitudes of a more permissive society.

However, the Warren Court's decisions on the rights of defendants col-

Balancing
Liberty and Order

"The Supreme Court generally moved during the 1960s in the direction of freer expression . . ."

[165] *Benton* v. *Maryland*, 395 U.S. 784 (1969).
[166] Four other provisions of the Bill of Rights have not been incorporated to apply to the states, but these provisions have seldom been tested in court cases. They are the right to a jury trial in civil cases where the amount in dispute exceeds $20 (Seventh Amendment); the ban on "excessive bail" and "fines" (Eighth Amendment); the right of the people "to keep and bear arms" (Second Amendment); and the ban on peacetime quartering of soldiers in private homes (Third Amendment). See Henry J. Abraham, *Freedom and the Court: Civil Rights and Liberties in the United States*, 3d ed. (New York, Oxford University Press, 1977), pp. 102–04.
[167] *West Virginia Board of Education* v. *Barnette* (1943).
[168] In Mason, *The Supreme Court: Palladium of Freedom*, p. 171n.

lided with a public alarmed over crime. In the 1970s, under Chief Justice Warren Burger, the Court appeared to shift away from the philosophy expressed in the *Miranda* case. But the Burger Court, although generally more conservative in tone, also defended civil liberties by expanding the right to counsel, forbidding government wiretapping of domestic groups without a warrant, and in other areas. It ruled, for example, that all charges must be dismissed against defendants who are denied their constitutional right to a speedy trial.[169] The decisions of the Burger Court could not in every instance be neatly categorized.

As always, the Court was charting new waters against a background of strong public sentiment. The delicate balance between liberty and order is constantly shifting, from issue to issue and from one decade to the next. Even with the Constitution as ballast, this will always be so.

Citizenship

Who Is a Citizen?

Although the Constitution as framed in 1787 uses the phrase "citizen of the United States," the term was not defined until the adoption of the Fourteenth Amendment in 1868. It provides that: "All persons born or naturalized in the United States . . . are citizens of the United States and of the State wherein they reside."

The amendment rests on the principle of *jus soli* (right of soil), which confers citizenship by place of birth. Congress by law has also adopted the principle of *jus sanguinis* (right of blood), under which the citizenship of a child is determined by that of the parents. All persons born in the United States, except for the children of high-ranking foreign diplomats, are citizens. But in addition, children born abroad of American parents, or even of one American parent, may become citizens if they and their parents meet the complex and varying legal requirements.

An immigrant who wishes to become a citizen may become "naturalized" after residing in the United States continuously for five years, or three years in the case of the spouse of a citizen. (Aliens who serve in the United States armed forces in peacetime for three years can then become citizens if they meet other provisions of law.) The oath of citizenship is administered by a federal judge, but the processing of applications for citizenship is handled by the Immigration and Naturalization Service of the Department of Justice. Children under eighteen of naturalized citizens normally derive their American citizenship from their parents. Generally speaking, naturalized citizens enjoy the same rights as native-born Americans, although no naturalized citizen may be elected President or Vice President.

Loss of Citizenship

It is sometimes believed that persons lose their citizenship if imprisoned for a year and a day, but this is not so; the laws of most of the fifty states deprive persons convicted of certain crimes of the right to vote, but no *state* may deprive Americans, native-born or naturalized, of their citizenship. In general, the Supreme Court has barred congressional attempts to deprive natural-born Americans of their citizenship as punishment for crimes. For example, in 1958 the Court ruled that desertion from the armed forces during wartime was not

---

[169] *Strunk* v. *United States,* 412 U.S. 434 (1973).

grounds for deprivation of citizenship because such a penalty would constitute "cruel and unusual punishment," forbidden by the Eighth Amendment.[170] In 1963 the Supreme Court struck down a law that provided automatic loss of citizenship for leaving the country in wartime to evade the draft.[171] As a result, the young men who went to live in Canada during the late 1960s to avoid military service in the Vietnam war did not lose their citizenship. In January 1977 President Carter granted a blanket pardon to most Vietnam draft evaders, although not to military deserters.

In 1964 the Supreme Court held that naturalized citizens enjoyed the same rights as native-born Americans.[172] It voided a law that had provided that naturalized persons lost their citizenship for living three years in their country of national origin.

In 1967, in the landmark case of *Afroyim* v. *Rusk*,[173] the Court ruled that Congress had no power to take away American citizenship unless it is freely renounced. An American, the Court said, had "a constitutional right to remain a citizen in a free country unless he voluntarily relinquishes that citizenship." Specifically, the Court held that Beys Afroyim, a naturalized citizen, could not be deprived of citizenship for voting in an election in Israel. In 1971, however, the Supreme Court ruled that the right of citizenship was not absolute for a child born abroad with one American parent. It held that Aldo Mario Bellei, who was born in Italy of an American mother, had lost his United States citizenship by failing to live here for five years continuously, as required by law.[174]

The McCarran-Walter Act, passed in 1952 over President Truman's veto, preserved the "national origins" system of immigration quotas first imposed by Congress in the 1920s to curb the wave of immigration that followed the First World War. Opponents of the national origins quota system argued that it was based on racial prejudice and designed to give preference to white, northern Europeans over immigrants from southern and eastern Europe. For example, in 1965, before the system was changed, the quota for all countries totaled 158,503. Of this, 108,931 (70 percent) was allotted to three countries—Great Britain, Ireland, and Germany. Italy, where thousands of young people desired to come to the United States, had a quota of 5666. India had a quota of 100, as did most of the Asian and African nations. (From 1917 until 1952 Chinese and all other Asians were completely excluded.)

A Nation of Immigrants

---

[170] *Trop* v. *Dulles*, 356 U.S. 86 (1958).
[171] *Kennedy* v. *Mendoza-Martinez*, 372 U.S. 144 (1963).
[172] *Schneider* v. *Rusk*, 377 U.S. 163 (1964).
[173] *Afroyim* v. *Rusk*, 387 U.S. 253 (1967).
[174] *Rogers* v. *Bellei*, 401 U.S. 815 (1971).

1890: Immigrants arrive by boat in New York

1980: Haitian refugees arrive by boat in Miami

Cuban refugee greeted
on arrival in Miami

The Immigration Act of 1965 abolished the national origins quota system and substituted a new annual ceiling of 120,000 immigrants from the Western Hemisphere and 170,000 from other nations, with a limit of 20,000 persons from any one nation. In 1977 Congress removed the hemispheric restrictions and permitted 290,000 immigrants per year worldwide. Then, in 1980 Congress lowered the ceiling to 270,000 a year but in addition permitted a minimum of 50,000 refugees to enter annually. The President, in consultation with Congress, was empowered to increase the refugee total, and in fiscal 1981 the ceiling for refugees was raised to more than 200,000. Thousands of Cuban and Haitian refugees who streamed into Florida by boat in 1980 were admitted outside any quotas and given special status. Vietnamese "boat people" who escaped from Vietnam during the same period were admitted to the United States under the parole authority of the Attorney General.

Change, Citizen Action, and Dissent

The Bill of Rights is really a list of promises by the government to the people. There is no similar list of constitutional obligations of the people to the government. Nevertheless, for a democracy to work, there must be concerned citizens who participate in the political process.

Students in the 1980s who work for a better environment or support political candidates are making tangible contributions to their society. When Americans speak out or organize on public issues, whether they dissent from established policy or support it, they are fulfilling an obligation of citizenship.

Voting in elections, active participation in political party activity and community programs, forming and expressing political opinions, either singly or through groups—all are necessary to the workings of a healthy democracy.

Yet, freedom to dissent is also an important aspect of a democracy. In fact, it may be argued that one of the responsibilities of citizenship is to exercise the rights protected by the Constitution, including those of free speech and dissent.

Many Americans lament that the system is not responsive enough to change, but sometimes those who feel this way fail to take as simple a step as registering to vote. Frequently it does seem that the political system is slow to respond to pressures for change and that there is no way for ordinary citizens to express themselves in ways that influence political leaders. Yet, at times, individual citizens have shown that it is not only possible to "fight City Hall" but, occasionally, it is possible to win.

In Los Angeles a few years ago, a social worker named John Serrano, the son of a Mexican shoemaker, was told by a principal to get his children out of the barrio of East Los Angeles and into a better school "if you want to give them a chance." Serrano took the advice and moved out to a suburb, but he did not forget the encounter. It seemed to him unjust that schools in a poor Mexican American neighborhood should be worse than those in wealthier neighborhoods. He joined forces with John E. Coons, a University of California law professor, who had been opposing inequalities in public school funding. Serrano, with the parents of a group of other Los Angeles schoolchildren, signed a complaint and went to court. On August 30, 1971, the Supreme Court of the state of California decided the case of *Serrano* v. *Priest*. It ruled that John Serrano was right, that a system of financing public schools through local property taxes "invidiously discriminates" against the poor because it makes the quality of a child's schooling depend on where he lives.

The implications of the California decision were dramatic. If extended elsewhere, it would mean a sweeping change in the way public schools are financed across America. Other states would have to find a way to equalize spending on education in all their school districts, since every state but Hawaii relied heavily on real estate taxes to pay for public schools.

Dozens of lawsuits were filed in other states to try to bring about just such a change. Then, in March 1973, the Supreme Court ruled on the issue in a similar case that arose in Texas.[175] The Court ruled 5 to 4 that the Texas system did not violate the Fourteenth Amendment "merely because the burdens or benefits . . . fall unevenly depending upon the relative wealth of the political subdivisions in which citizens live." The Court also noted that equal spending, in the view of some scholars, might actually result in a loss of money for some inner-city schools.

[175] *The San Antonio Independent School District* v. *Rodriguez,* 411 U.S. 1 (1973).

Despite the Supreme Court's decision, John Serrano's lawsuit had set in motion forces that might not be stopped. Many states were studying alternate methods of school financing as a result of the California decision, and by 1980, more than 25 states had modified their systems for financing public schools.[176] The United States Supreme Court's ruling had slowed down the momentum of change, but pressures for equality of school district financing continued. In California, and perhaps in America, John Serrano had demonstrated that one citizen can make a difference.

[176] Education Commission of the States, "School Finance Reform in the States: 1980," p. 1.

Perspective

In a democratic society, freedom is not absolute. The proper balance between the rights of one individual and the rights of society as a whole can never be resolved to everyone's satisfaction. In the American political system, the Supreme Court is the mechanism called upon to resolve conflicts between liberty and order and between the rights of the individual and the rights of society. The Court operates within the framework of the Bill of Rights, the fundamental charter of American liberty. The Bill of Rights is part of the Constitution, but it is the Supreme Court that decides how those rights will be defined and applied.

The First Amendment is designed to protect freedom of religion, speech, press, assembly, and petition. In interpreting the First Amendment, different Supreme Court justices have adopted different philosophies. For example, Justice Hugo Black argued that "there are 'absolutes' in our Bill of Rights" that cannot be diluted by judicial decisions. However, a majority of the Court has held that First Amendment rights must be "balanced" against the competing needs of the community to preserve order and to preserve the state.

In recent years, for example, the Court has shown increasing concern over pretrial and courtroom publicity. This is an issue that brings two principles of the Bill of Rights into conflict—the right of an accused person to have a fair trial and the right of freedom of the press. Although the Court has generally hesitated to impose prior restraint on the press, it has limited freedom of the press in other ways—requiring journalists to reveal sources, permitting individuals to sue the press for libel, recognizing the right of privacy, banning "obscene" publications, and supporting the right of the government to regulate radio and television.

The First Amendment contains two clauses protecting freedom of religion. The "free exercise" clause protects the right of individuals to worship or believe as they wish, or to hold no religious beliefs. The "no establishment" clause, in the words of Justice Hugo Black, means that "neither a state nor the federal government can set up a church. Neither can pass laws that aid one religion, aid all religions, or prefer one religion over another." In 1962 and 1963 the Supreme Court outlawed the daily reading of school prayer. On the other hand, the Court's decision in the *Everson* case (1947) allowed states to provide various kinds of aid to church-related schools for the purpose of helping the child. Since 1971, however, the Supreme Court has declared certain state programs of aid to parochial schools unconstitutional.

The Fourth Amendment protects the right of individuals to "be secure in their persons, houses, papers, and effects, against unreasonable searches and seizures." In the United States, as a general principle, police are not authorized to search a home without a search warrant signed by a judicial officer and issued on "probable cause" that the materials to be seized are in the place to be searched. Nor may police make routine arrests of persons in their homes without a warrant.

The right of privacy, or what Justice Brandeis called "the right to be let alone," has in the electronic age been threatened by sophisticated wiretapping and eavesdropping devices. But in 1968 and 1978 Congress passed laws requiring court warrants for electronic surveillance in domestic criminal cases and in national security cases.

The Bill of Rights entitles suspects or defendants to be represented by a lawyer, to be informed of their legal rights and of the charges against them, to have a speedy and public trial by jury, to summon witnesses to testify in their behalf, to cross-examine prosecution witnesses, and to refuse to testify against themselves. The Fifth through Eighth amendments also protect the accused from being held in excessive bail or subjected to cruel and unusual punishment or being tried twice for the same offense.

In the mid-1960s, the Warren Court strengthened the rights of the accused. In the *Escobedo* case (1964), the Court ruled that under the Sixth Amendment a suspect is entitled to counsel even during police interrogation once the process shifts from "investigatory to accusatory." In the *Miranda* case (1966), the Court held that suspects must be clearly informed of their rights—including the right to remain silent and have a lawyer present—before they are asked any questions by police. In the *Gideon* case (1963), the Court ruled that even poor defendants must be provided with a lawyer. In several cases dealing with the rights of criminal defendants, the Burger Court has retreated from the decisions of the Warren Court.

Under the Fourteenth Amendment, anyone born or naturalized in the United States is a citizen. The Supreme Court has held that Congress may not take away a person's citizenship unless it is freely renounced. As of 1980 Congress permitted 270,000 immigrants to enter the United States each year.

The Bill of Rights was passed as a safeguard against the new federal government. It did not apply to the states. But between 1925 and 1970, through the process of "selective incorporation," the Supreme Court brought the states and local governments almost entirely under the Bill of Rights.

Suggested Reading

Abraham, Henry J. *Freedom and the Court: Civil Rights and Liberties in the United States.* Fourth edition* (Oxford University Press, 1982). A detailed examination of the Bill of Rights. Analyzes how the Supreme Court, through decisions in specific cases, has gradually enlarged the area of constitutional freedom in the United States.

Berns, Walter. *Freedom, Virtue, and the First Amendment* (Louisiana State University Press, 1957). A provocative analysis that takes sharp issue with some of the major court decisions designed to protect freedom of expression in the United States.

Dorsen, Norman; Bender, Paul; and Neuborne, Burt. *Political and Civil Rights in the United States,* 4th edition (Little, Brown, 1976). A clear, comprehensive discussion of political and civil liberties in the United States, containing extensive excerpts of the Supreme Court's decisions in major constitutional cases. Published with biennial supplements covering the most recent Supreme Court decisions.

Hentoff, Nat. *The First Freedom: The Tumultuous History of Free Speech in America* (Delacorte, 1980). A lively, clearly written analysis of the history of the First Amendment. Contains a detailed discussion of leading Supreme Court cases involving free speech, freedom of the press, and freedom of religion.

Jackson, Robert H. *The Supreme Court in the American System of Government* (Harvard University Press, 1955). A very useful general discussion of the Supreme Court's role in the American political system. Jackson was an Associate Justice of the Supreme Court.

Lewis, Anthony. *Gideon's Trumpet* (Random House, 1964). A detailed and readable account of the Supreme Court case that established the right of a poor man to have a lawyer when charged with a serious criminal offense in a state court. Sheds light on the role of the Supreme Court in safeguarding the rights of defendants.

Mason, Alpheus T. *The Supreme Court: Palladium of Freedom* (University of Michigan Press, 1962). A concise discussion of the Supreme Court's place in the American political system by a distinguished scholar of constitutional law. Emphasizes the Bill of Rights and the Court's role in protecting minority views.

McCloskey, Robert G. *The Modern Supreme Court** (Harvard University Press, 1972). (Edited by Martin Shapiro.) This book, left partly unfinished at the time of Professor McCloskey's death, analyzes important periods in the recent history of the Supreme Court. Professor McCloskey had completed sections on the Stone (1940–1945) and Vinson (1946–1952) periods. For the years 1953–1969, the editor has reprinted some of the journal articles in which McCloskey analyzed aspects of the Warren Court.

Mill, John Stuart. *On Liberty** (Appleton-Century-Crofts, 1947). (Originally published in 1859.) A classic examination of the problem of balancing individual rights and the rights of the community.

Salisbury, Harrison E. *Without Fear or Favor* (Times Books, 1980). A useful and revealing study of the *New York Times* and its relationship to, and battles with, the federal government. Salisbury, a former foreign correspondent for the *New York Times,* analyzes the legal struggle over the publication of the Pentagon Papers and examines in detail the CIA's relationship with the *New York Times* and the news media in general.

*The Supreme Court and Individual Rights** (Congressional Quarterly, 1979). A useful survey of the impact of Supreme Court decisions on individual rights. Focuses on First Amendment rights and the guarantees of political participation, due process, and equal protection.

* Available in paperback edition

5

THE STRUGGLE
FOR EQUAL RIGHTS

The rights proclaimed in the Declaration of Independence and those set forth in the legal language of the Constitution are not enjoyed equally by all Americans. For many minority groups, the equality promised by these fundamental American charters has been an elusive goal rather than an achieved fact, a vision of a possible future rather than a description of the often bleak present.

For example, despite the civil rights laws enacted by Congress in the 1960s and the landmark decisions of the Supreme Court, even today many of the more than 26 million black Americans do not enjoy full social and economic equality. Almost one out of three blacks in the United States is poor—by official definition of the federal government—as opposed to one out of eleven whites.[1]

Blacks, it is true, have made some economic gains in recent years. For example, 36 percent of black families earn over $15,000 a year, a figure that, adjusted for inflation, has increased by about 4 percent since 1970.[2] But, at the same time, the gap in income levels and living standards has widened between the growing black middle class and the millions of blacks still below the poverty line. Economic gains registered by some blacks were little comfort in the 1980s

[1] Adapted from U.S. Bureau of the Census, *Current Population Reports,* Money Income and Poverty Status of Families and Persons in the United States: 1978, Series P–60, No. 120, November 1979, p. 4.

[2] *Ibid.,* p. 12.

to an unemployed black youth in an inner-city slum, a black worker frozen out of a construction job by a white union, or even to a middle-class black seeking to move into a hostile white suburb.

In America today, the infant mortality rate for black and other nonwhite children is almost twice as high as it is for whites. The percent of white adults who have completed college is more than twice that of blacks. Only 10 percent of blacks are members of professions, compared to 17 percent of whites. In 1980 the rate of black unemployment was double that of whites, and the percent of black families with income over $10,000 was less than two-thirds that of whites.[3]

This statistical portrait does not sketch in the daily indignities, the rebuffs, the humiliations and defeats that black Americans may face. Two decades ago, author James Baldwin declared: "The brutality with which Negroes are treated in this country simply cannot be overstated, however unwilling white men may be to hear it."[4]

And despite changes for the better since Baldwin wrote those words, the black citizen in many cases remains on the outside of American society, looking in. It is true that black income, education, and employment opportunities have increased since the civil rights movement of the 1960s. But the black American still has an excellent statistical chance of being born in a ghetto and of living in crowded, substandard housing. The black child's school may still be largely segregated if it is located in a black neighborhood, since the 1954 Supreme Court decision in the *Brown* case outlawed only official, government-backed segregation of public schools. And the school may also be old, overcrowded, and below the standards of public schools in white neighborhoods.

If the black youth does not succumb to rats, crime, heroin, and other soul-destroying forces of the ghetto, perhaps he or she will obtain work. But often the work will be menial and low-paying. Black families may have to buy shoddy merchandise at high credit rates from neighborhood merchants. The food at the local supermarket may be of poorer quality and priced higher than the same items at the chain's branches in white neighborhoods. If the black man or woman raises a family, their children may face the same bleak future, continuing the cycle of poverty and despair.

[3] Data provided by U.S. Department of Health and Human Services, National Center for Health Statistics; U.S. Bureau of the Census; and U.S. Department of Labor.
[4] James Baldwin, *The Fire Next Time* (New York: Dial Press, 1962), p. 82.

The earliest memory of my life is of an incident which occurred when I was three-and-a-half years old in Holly Springs, Mississippi. My father was registrar and professor of religion and philosophy at Rust College, a Negro Methodist institution there.

One hot summer day, my mother and I walked from the college campus to the town square, a distance of maybe half a mile. I remember it as clearly as though it were a few weeks ago. I held her finger tightly as we kicked up the red dust on the unpaved streets leading to the downtown area. When we reached the square she did her shopping and we headed for home. Like any other three-and-a-half-year-old on a hot day, I got thirsty.

"Mother," I said, "I want a Coke." She replied that we could not get Cokes there and I would have to wait until we got home where there was lots of Coke in the icebox.

"But I want my Coke now," I insisted. She was just as insistent that we could not get a Coke now.

"Do as I tell you," she said, "wait 'til we get home; you can have a Coke with plenty of ice."

"There's a little boy going into a store!" I exclaimed as I spied another child who was a little bigger than I. "I bet he's going to get a Coke." So I pulled my mother by the finger until we stood in front of what I recall as a drugstore looking through the closed screen doors. Surely enough, the other lad had climbed upon a stool at the counter and was already sipping a soft drink.

"But I told you you can't get a Coke in there," she said. "Why can't I?" I asked again. The answer was the same, "You just can't." I then inquired with complete puzzlement, "Well, why can *he?*" Her quiet answer thundered in my ears. "He's white."

We walked home in silence under the pitiless glare of the Mississippi sun. Once we were home she threw herself across the bed and wept. I walked out on the front porch and sat on the steps alone with my three-and-a-half-year-old thoughts.

—James Farmer, former National Director of CORE, in *Esquire*, May 1969.

Even if a black climbs out of the ghetto, gets a job as a skilled worker, or goes to college and enters a profession, his or her troubles are not necessarily over. On moving to a white neighborhood, black families may encounter social ostracism. Under the best of economic circumstances, black parents must still face the problem of explaining to their children the divisions in American society between white and black.

But it is not only blacks who are struggling for equal rights in the United States. For the more than one million American Indians, the rhetoric of equality has a particularly ironic sound. Often living in poverty, with an unemployment rate more than twice the national average, Indians are outcasts in a land that once was theirs.

The nation's Hispanic community, the fastest-growing segment of the population, is another large group that has been denied full equality in American society. The term "Hispanic" usually includes Mexican Americans — by far the largest group — as well as Puerto Ricans, Cubans, and persons of Central or South American or other Spanish origin. Although the 1980 census reported that there were 14.6 million Hispanics in the United States, unofficial estimates put the figure much higher, at 19 million, including perhaps 7.4 million illegal aliens. And some demographers have predicted that Hispanics will overtake blacks as the nation's largest minority group by 1985.[5]

According to a 1979 Census Bureau estimate, there were 7.3 million Mexican Americans in the United States — a figure that was expected to rise dramati-

[5] *New York Times,* February 24, 1981, pp. A1, A12; *Time,* October 16, 1978, p. 48; and *New York Times,* February 18, 1979, p. 1.

cally after the 1980 Census, in which the government made a special effort to count Hispanics. Although Mexican Americans make up a sizable population bloc in five Southwestern states, they are underrepresented politically. Many are migrant workers living in abysmal conditions.

Puerto Ricans are also American citizens and form another important segment of the Hispanic community. Yet many of the approximately 1.7 million Americans of Puerto Rican background who live on the mainland suffer discrimination and poverty and are locked in the *barrios,* or slums, of the great cities.

The Women's Liberation movement that emerged as an important social and political force during the 1970s reflected the growing awareness that women, although constituting a majority of the population, were another "minority group." Discrimination based on sex is built into many public and private institutions. Some indication of the problem may be seen in the gap in earnings between men and women. In 1978, for example, the median income of white men was $16,360 and of black men $12,530, while that of white women was $9732 and that of black women was $9020.[6]

Many other minorities have suffered discrimination. Jews have been widely accepted in many areas of American society but are still unwelcome in some private clubs, in the executive suites of some corporations, and in some residential areas. Prejudice against Catholics was a major issue as recently as John F. Kennedy's 1960 presidential campaign. Poles, Italians, Chinese, Japanese, Filipinos, and other groups are still victims of racial slurs and discrimination. And discrimination is not limited to ethnic or religious minorities. Children, the elderly, homosexuals, and handicapped persons have also sometimes been deprived of their rights.

All these inequalities cast a shadow over the future of America. Racial polarization in American society was reflected in the nation's politics; in 1980 President Carter and Ronald Reagan traded charges that each had injected "racism" into the presidential campaign. As blacks and other minority groups pressed demands for greater equality and opportunity, white blue-collar workers in many cases reacted with hostility. Many in this group held strong beliefs that "they," the blacks, were "asking too much," while "we had to make it on our own." Studies of the nation's ethnic patterns have noted, however, that other nationality groups, as members of the white majority, have been more easily assimilated into American society. Blacks and Hispanics migrating outward from the inner city frequently moved into white, ethnic neighborhoods. White factory or construction workers who had saved their money to buy modest houses in such neighborhoods often felt their housing investments, their schools — and perhaps their jobs — threatened by the newcomers. Social tension and racial protest put continuing pressure on American institutions.

Would the nation respond by mobilizing its energies to remove some of the causes of racial unrest — poverty, hunger, discrimination, slums, powerlessness, and unemployment? What is the history of the struggle for equal rights in America? How have government and private institutions contributed to discrimination? How did the civil rights movement of the postwar decades evolve? What steps has government taken to ensure the civil rights of minorities? Can

Puerto Rican festival, New York 1979

---

[6] U.S. Bureau of the Census, *Current Population Reports,* Consumer Income, Series P–60, No. 120, November 1979, pp. 18–19.

blacks and other minority groups achieve integration only at the cost of losing their ethnic and cultural identity? These are some of the problems we will explore in examining the continuing struggle for equality in America.

Some Groups in Profile

American Indians

Who is an Indian? Since there is no accepted demographic definition, an Indian is whoever tells the census taker he or she is one. According to the 1980 census, there were 1,400,000 Indians, Aleuts, and Eskimos in America. American Indians accounted for most of the total. This figure represented an increase since 1970, when the census counted 793,000 American Indians, of whom an estimated 649,000 lived on or near reservations. In addition, the 1970 census reported there were some 35,000 Aleuts and Eskimos in the United States.

Indians are American citizens (Congress conferred citizenship on all Indians in 1924), and there is no requirement that an Indian live on a reservation, an area of land "reserved" for Indian use and held in trust by the federal government. There are 267 reservations in the United States (excluding Alaska), varying in size from small settlements in California of only a few acres, to the 14-million-acre Navajo reservation spreading through Arizona, New Mexico, and Utah.

The federal government spends more than $900 million a year on aid to Indians. But the Bureau of Indian Affairs does not have responsibility for assisting Indians who are living off the reservation. Of American Indians dwelling in urban areas, approximately one-fourth are living in poverty.[7] And the plight of the reservation Indian is little better.

The average American born in 1970 could expect to live to seventy-one years; the life expectancy of the Indian is sixty-five. Few reservations can support their population; unemployment among Indians is extremely high on the poorest reservations and averages 11 percent nationally. Many Indians live in shacks, adobe huts, even abandoned automobiles. Incidence of illness and disease is significantly higher among Indians than among the white population; for example, in 1975 tuberculosis was nearly five times more prevalent among Indians than among other Americans. Unsanitary housing, unsafe water, and malnutrition all contribute to ill health among Indians. The drop-out rate for Indian schoolchildren is more than twice the national average, and Indians average less than ten years of school. (Other Americans average 12.1 years.)[8] The suicide rate among Indians is twice as high as that of all Americans, and among Indians aged fifteen to twenty-four, four times as high as the national average. The rate of deaths from alcoholism among Indians is about five times as high as the national average.[9]

The federal government has been deeply involved in the history of the white man's broken promises to the Indians. Until 1871 the government treated

[7] U.S. Bureau of the Census, *1970 Census of Population, Subject Report, American Indians,* p. 120.
[8] Data provided by U.S. Department of Health, Education, and Welfare, Indian Health Service; U.S. Commission on Civil Rights, *Social Indicators of Equality for Minorities and Women,* August 1978, p. 12; and U.S. Bureau of the Census, *1970 Census of Population, Subject Report, American Indians,* p. 18.
[9] U.S. Department of Health, Education, and Welfare, Indian Health Service, *Indian Health Trends and Services,* 1978 Edition, pp. 18–19.

Indian tribes as separate, sovereign nations. After that, the government stopped making treaties with the tribes and adopted a policy of breaking down the tribal structure. The Dawes Act of 1887 divided reservations into small allotments; but the land not distributed to individual Indians was put up for public sale. Between 1887 and 1934, some 90 million acres of land were removed from Indian hands in one way or another. When the Indian Reorganization Act of 1934 ended the practice of breaking up the reservations, the tribes regained some of their vitality.

In 1953 Congress adopted a policy declaration designed to end the special trustee relationship between the federal government and Indians. This policy of "forced termination" was almost unanimously opposed by the Indians, who feared that without federal protection their lands and cultural identity would vanish. Although the policy was curtailed in 1958, the congressional declaration stood. In a message to Congress in 1970, President Nixon called on Congress to renounce the termination policy and "explicitly affirm the integrity and right to continued existence of all Indian tribes and Alaska native governments."[10] Finally in 1974 Congress passed the Indian Self-Determination and Education Assistance Act, which ended the policy of forced termination and gave Indian tribes the right to control federal programs on their reservations.

In recent years, Indians have had some success in recovering lands taken by the government. In 1980, after a long court case, the state of Maine agreed to pay Indians there $81.5 million and return 300,000 acres. Later that year, 60,000 Sioux Indians were awarded $122.5 million by the United States Supreme Court in compensation for 7,000,000 acres that had been taken by Congress in the Black Hills region.[11]

Beset by poverty, disease, illiteracy, substandard housing, and the threat of forced cultural assimilation, Indians felt they had long overdue claims on the American political system. In the 1960s Indians added their voices to the protests of other minorities. In 1969 seventy-eight Indians invaded the abandoned federal prison on Alcatraz Island in San Francisco Bay and claimed it as their own. A group of Indians in the state of Washington closed off fifty miles of seashore reservation lands to protest littering of their beaches by whites.

In 1972 several hundred Indians came to Washington and occupied the Bureau of Indian Affairs. The Indians arrived in a caravan they called "The Trail of Broken Treaties." They pitched a twenty-foot-high tepee on the main lawn, flew the American flag upside down at half-mast, and for six days barricaded themselves inside the bureau to dramatize their demands. Even before the occupation of the building, much of the Indian militance had been directed at the BIA, which makes decisions affecting the lives of Indians but has traditionally been controlled by white executives.

In 1973, 200 armed supporters of the American Indian Movement (AIM) seized the tiny village of Wounded Knee on the Pine Ridge Indian Reservation in South Dakota. The militants had chosen their target carefully, and with a shrewd understanding of modern mass communications. For Wounded Knee was the site of the massacre of at least 153 Sioux Indians by the United States Army in 1890, and it was part of the title of a best-selling book.[12] The town's

[10] President Nixon's message to Congress on Indian affairs, *Congressional Record,* July 8, 1970, p. H6438.
[11] *United States* v. *Sioux Nation of Indians,* 100 S. Ct. 2716 (1980).
[12] Dee Brown, *Bury My Heart at Wounded Knee* (New York: Holt, Rinehart & Winston, 1971).

Indians set up a tepee on the Washington Monument grounds during 1978 protest.

1973: The Second Battle of Wounded Knee

occupation stirred national attention and network television coverage. For seventy days, U.S. marshals surrounded the village; although they were determined to avoid another massacre, two Indian supporters were killed in exchanges of gunfire, and one federal agent was paralyzed by a bullet.

In one sense, the occupation was a protest against poverty, federal policy toward Indians, and the paternalism of the Bureau of Indian Affairs. But the seizure also involved an internal political struggle among the Indians, a split between full-blood and mixed-blood Indians, and opposition by AIM to the elected chairman of the Oglala Sioux. After more than two months, the militants surrendered under a peace agreement. The Second Battle of Wounded Knee was over; but the broader problems faced by American Indians remained.

Mexican Americans

Like American Indians, Americans of Mexican origin must contend with the twin problems of discrimination and poverty.

The majority of the Mexican Americans in the United States live in five states of the Southwest, where they compose the largest single minority group. California has the largest Mexican American population, followed by Texas. Other Mexican Americans are concentrated in smaller numbers in Arizona, New Mexico, and Colorado.

According to one Census Bureau study, almost 19 percent of all Mexican American families were living in poverty—more than twice the national average. Unemployment was substantially higher than that of the rest of the population. Only about one-third of adult Mexican Americans had completed high school, lower than the rate for the nation as a whole.[13]

Between 1951 and 1964, hundreds of thousands of Mexican migrant laborers entered the United States temporarily as farm workers under the "bracero" program enacted by Congress. Millions of others have entered the country illegally to join the ranks of the migrants.

[13] Congressional Quarterly, *Weekly Report,* April 30, 1977, p. 822.

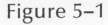

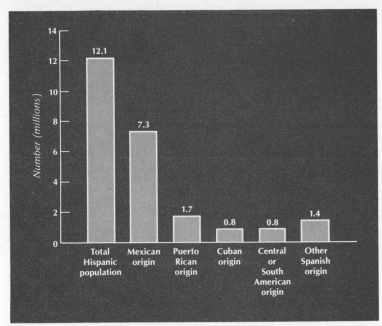

* The total for Hispanic Americans had increased to 14.6 million in the 1980 census.
Source: Adapted from U.S. Bureau of the Census, *Current Population Reports, Persons of Spanish Origin in the United States: March 1979 (Advance Report)*, Series P–20, No. 347, October 1979, Figure 1, p. 1; the *New York Times*, February 24, 1981, pp. A1, A12.

Many migrants, whether legal or not, live and work under the most difficult conditions. They perform backbreaking stoop labor in the fields under the hot sun, risking injury from insecticides used to protect the crops. Often, they must live in shacks without electricity or running water, their health endangered by open sewage and other unsanitary conditions. Migrant Mexican American

America the Beautiful

For a child born with brown skin in one of the southern tier of states, of farm-migrant parents who speak a different language from most Americans, the future is already charted.

The young Chicano—or Mexican American—migrant will move with his parents through the citrus groves of Florida or California, stoop over the beans and tomatoes in Texas, hoe sugarbeets in western Kansas, crawl through the potato fields of Idaho and Maine and pick cherries in Michigan, moving with the season and the harvests.

He will sleep, crowded with his family in shells of migrant housing without heat, refrigeration or sanitary facilities. He will splash barefoot through garbage-strewn mud infested with internal parasites and drink polluted water provided in old oil drums.

By the age of 12 he will have the face of an adult and his shoulders will form in a permanent stoop. He will acquire the rough dry skin and the pipestem arms and legs that indicate a lack of vitamins and proteins. He will be surrounded by children infected with diseases of the intestines, blood, mouth, eyes and ears and thus condemned to poor learning records at school—when they are able to attend school at all.

That was the picture of the Chicano's life painted at a Senate subcommittee hearing last week. Dr. Raymond M. Wheeler, a Southern physician who had served on a team studying health conditions of the migrants, told the Senators: "The children we saw have no future in our society. Malnutrition since birth has already impaired them physically, mentally and emotionally."

—*New York Times*, July 26, 1970.

In 1979 Cesar Chavez led a strike by his United Farm Workers against the lettuce growers of California. On February 9, in the Imperial Valley, Rufino Contreras, a young lettuce worker taking part in the strike, was shot to death during a clash between pickets and non-union workers. He left a widow and two young children. Two foremen and an equipment operator, all employees of the owner of the farm where Contreras died, were charged with murder, but the case was later dismissed.

Reporter Laurie Becklund of the *Los Angeles Times* attended the funeral and filed this account:

CALEXICO — Rufino Contreras, the 27-year-old lettuce picker who was shot to death on Saturday, was buried here Wednesday morning after an outdoor mariachi funeral mass in which he was mourned as a martyr by more than 7000 United Farm Workers of America members and their families.

"Rufino is not dead," UFW President Cesar Chavez said in his eulogy. "Wherever farm workers organize, stand up for their rights and strike for justice, Rufino Contreras is with them."

Sitting in . . . the front row of a flower-filled shrine where the Mass was celebrated was Rosa Contreras, the young man's widow. . . . Clutching her 5-year-old son to her, she seemed oblivious to the labor leader's words.

"Mis hijos," she said time after time, leaning her head back and moaning, tears running down her thin, youthful face. "My children, children of my heart. Where is their father; where are you, Fino?"

". . . What is the worth of a man?" Chavez asked during his eulogy. "Rufino and his father and his brother together gave the company 20 years of their labor . . ." The cries of Contreras's young widow could be heard throughout the eulogy. . . . She grabbed hold of [her son] and cried into his shoulder as if he were a man.

Her other child, Nancy Berenice, 4, smiled when she saw her mother. She did not know she was supposed to cry.

— *Los Angeles Times,* February 15, 1979.

Rosa Contreras and son Julio at funeral mass

workers have a life expectancy of forty-eight years. Their birth rate is double the national average, as is their infant mortality rate.

Farm workers are not covered by the National Labor Relations Act, and they have encountered great obstacles in organizing labor unions. More than a decade ago, Cesar Chavez and his United Farm Workers won a five-year strike against grape growers in central California. Chavez's effort, aided by a nation-wide boycott of table grapes by consumers in sympathy with the strike, helped to focus national attention on "La Causa," as the grape workers called their movement, and on "La Raza," the Mexican Americans themselves. In 1975 California passed legislation generally providing for farm workers the same rights held by union members in other industries. The landmark farm labor bill was a victory for Chavez. Chavez also sought to organize workers in the lettuce fields of California and in the early seventies led a boycott of iceberg lettuce that stirred national attention. In 1979 he began a long strike against the lettuce growers in the Imperial and Salinas valleys of California, and in Arizona.

During the 1960s, Chavez had emerged as an extraordinary figure, a quiet but determined man who became a symbol of the *Chicanos* (as many Mexican Americans proudly call themselves) while leading his union in the fight against the grape growers. Chavez's childhood reads like a passage in John Steinbeck's Depression-era novel, *The Grapes of Wrath.* His parents were Mexican migrant workers. Following the seasons, the family traveled back and forth between California's Imperial and San Joaquin valleys. By the time Chavez finished the eighth grade he had attended *thirty-seven* schools. Eventually the family settled in a slum neighborhood near San Jose called, appropriately, by its residents "Sal

Si Puedes" ("get out if you can"). Chavez began organizing his union in 1962; within six years, the United Farm Workers had 17,000 members.

Chavez's career has been closely linked to his cultural identity as a Mexican American. A biographer captured some of this when Chavez spoke to a group of Mexican American students:

> In the Union we're just beginning, and you're just beginning. Mexican American youth is just beginning to wake up. Five years ago we didn't have this feeling. Nobody wanted to be *chicanos,* they wanted to be anything *but chicanos*. But three months ago I went to San Jose State College and they had a beautiful play in which they let everybody know that they were *chicanos,* and that *chicanos* mean something and that they were proud of it.[14]

Cesar Chavez

The percentage of Mexican Americans in the general population is not reflected in the makeup of Congress. In California, for example, where Mexican Americans constitute about 16 percent of the population, only one of the forty-three members of Congress serving in 1980 — Edward R. Roybal — was a Mexican American.

The Chicanos have in recent years joined the ranks of other minority groups fighting for full equality in American society. Chavez was not the only example. In 1974 Jerry Apodaca was elected governor of New Mexico, the first governor of the state with a Spanish surname in more than half a century. Raul Castro, a naturalized American citizen born in Mexico, was elected governor of Arizona and later appointed as an ambassador by President Carter. Julian Nava, a California history professor who was of Mexican descent, was named Ambassador to Mexico by Carter. In Texas, leaders such as José Angel Gutiérrez attempted to weld Mexican American voters into a powerful political force. Gutiérrez organized "La Raza Unida" — the United People — to press Mexican American demands for higher wages, better housing, and integrated schools. Although by 1980 La Raza Unida was no longer a major political force in Texas, the party did enjoy a brief success in the mid-seventies, winning a number of local elections and running candidates for statewide office.

Mexican Americans have registered some political gains in the Southwest, electing members of the city councils in Houston, Dallas, and San Antonio, Texas, and members of the state legislatures in Texas, Arizona, and California. But many Mexican Americans, desiring to preserve their own identity, have not felt the need to participate in American politics. "We are another country," said Miguel Garcia of East Los Angeles. "We have our own culture, our own language. We feel different from the rest of America."[15]

Yet, when Mexican Americans have organized politically, they have often made their voices heard. In Parlier, California, a small town near Fresno, the local council refused to appoint a Chicano as chief of police. The Chicanos organized, defeated three members of the council, and elected Andrew Benitez, a twenty-two-year-old Mexican American, as mayor.[16]

Illegal Mexican Aliens. Although the precise number of illegal aliens in the United States is not known, it has been estimated by the federal government

---

[14] Peter Matthiessen, *Sal Si Puedes: Cesar Chavez and the New American Revolution* (New York: Random House, 1969), p. 109.
[15] *Washington Post,* March 29, 1978, p. A6.
[16] *New York Times,* April 21, 1978, p. 14.

Border patrol rounds up illegal Mexican aliens in California.

that the total is as high as 8 million.[17] The majority of the illegals are Mexicans or other Latin Americans. During the 1980 census the government made a major effort to count illegal aliens, but the task was difficult. Many illegals naturally tended to avoid census takers or did not trust the Census Bureau's promise that the information would remain confidential.

Some employers, particularly growers and farm owners in California and Texas, hire illegals as a source of cheap labor. But labor unions and some other groups argue that illegal aliens undermine minimum wage, health, and safety laws and other benefits of U.S. workers. The United States Supreme Court has ruled that states can bar the employment of illegal aliens.[18] But in Texas, a federal district court declared unconstitutional a state law barring the children of illegal aliens, most of them Mexicans, from attending public schools. The children were admitted to the schools in the fall of 1980, pending resolution of the dispute in the courts.

In 1977 the Immigration and Naturalization Service located more than one million deportable aliens, of whom 92 percent were Mexican nationals. That same year, President Carter proposed an amnesty for eligible aliens who have been in the U.S. since 1970 and a five-year temporary resident status for those who had come after January 1, 1977. As of 1980, however, Congress had not acted on these proposals.

Puerto Ricans

Puerto Rico has commonwealth status and Puerto Ricans are American citizens, with a nonvoting Resident Commissioner in the United States House of Representatives. As Americans, Puerto Ricans living on the island use U.S. currency, mails, and courts and may receive U.S. welfare benefits and food stamps. They pay no federal taxes unless they move to the mainland. Islanders cannot vote in U.S. elections, but in 1980, for the first time, they were able to vote in primaries to express their presidential preference and to select delegates to the Democratic and Republican national conventions. They sing their own national anthem, have their own flag, and are Spanish-speaking.

[17] U.S. Bureau of the Census, *Current Population Reports,* Persons of Spanish Origin in the United States: March 1978, Series P-20, No. 339, June 1979, pp. 6, 14.
[18] *DeCanas* v. *Bica,* 424 U.S. 351 (1976).

Yet many of the island's residents who come to the mainland seeking a better life encounter not only a language barrier but economic and racial discrimination as well. Puerto Ricans who migrate to the mainland frequently settle in cities. If the newcomers find employment at all, it is generally in unskilled, low-paying jobs in hotels, restaurants, and factories. Often forced to live in substandard housing, Puerto Ricans sometimes face hostility from inner-city blacks who regard them as an economic threat. The population of Puerto Rico was 3.4 million in 1978. In 1979 the U.S. Census Bureau reported that there were 1.7 million persons of Puerto Rican origin in the continental United States. Of this total, more than a million lived in New York City, and there were large Puerto Rican communities in Chicago, Philadelphia, Newark, and Bridgeport and Hartford, Connecticut. As in the case of many other minorities, the per capita income of Puerto Ricans on the mainland was much lower than that of other Americans, and the unemployment rate often twice as high.

On the island itself, there has been an ongoing debate over Puerto Rico's political status, which has focused on three choices: continuing as a commonwealth, statehood, or independence. The commonwealth status for Puerto Rico was established in 1952 under Luis Muñoz Marín's Popular Democratic party.

In 1976, however, the New Progressive party, which favored statehood, came to power when Carlos Romero-Barceló was elected governor. Just before President Gerald Ford left office in 1977, Ford endorsed statehood for Puerto Rico. President Carter, however, took a neutral stance, saying that the islanders should decide on their political status before Congress acts. In 1980 Romero-Barceló was re-elected, defeating the pro-commonwealth candidate in a very close race.

Few Puerto Ricans favor outright independence. One group that does, the Puerto Rican Armed Forces of National Liberation (FALN), has claimed responsibility for more than fifty bombings in New York City and elsewhere on the mainland, which have caused a number of deaths. In 1979 President Carter freed four Puerto Rican nationalists from jail. They had served long prison terms after attempting in 1950 to assassinate President Truman and firing shots at members of Congress on the floor of the U.S. House of Representatives. After their release, the nationalists threatened more violence to try to gain independence for the island. In 1967 voters in Puerto Rico voted 60 percent for commonwealth status, 39 percent for statehood, and less than 1 percent for independence.[19]

[19] Some supporters of independence boycotted the referendum, however.

Like other minority groups, Puerto Ricans in the United States have evidenced growing cultural pride and political awareness in recent years. In several cities, Puerto Rican citizen groups have organized to work for such goals as better education—particularly bilingual school programs—and employment. In 1970 Herman Badillo, a New Yorker born in Puerto Rico, was elected to the United States House of Representatives. In 1977 Badillo left Congress to become deputy mayor of New York City. His successor in Congress was Robert Garcia, also of Puerto Rican background.

Women

"Equality of rights under the law shall not be denied or abridged by the United States or by any state on account of sex." This proposed amendment to the Constitution, designed primarily to eliminate discrimination against women, had been introduced in the House every year since 1923, but it was not approved by both houses of Congress until 1972.

Congress provided that the amendment would become part of the Constitution (the Twenty-seventh Amendment) if ratified by legislatures of three-fourths of the states within seven years. With the 1979 deadline approaching and the amendment still not approved, supporters of the Equal Rights Amendment (ERA) succeeded in extending the date for ratification until June 30, 1982. If approved, the amendment would go into effect two years after its ratification.

In 1980 the amendment was still three states short of the necessary thirty-eight to win ratification. Regardless of the outcome, however, congressional approval of the ERA was a direct reflection of the growing movement in the 1970s to assure women equal rights and responsibilities in American society. Although the organized effort to end sex discrimination in American society was generally known as Women's Liberation, it encompassed many different groups. And it drew support from many people of both sexes who were not actively engaged in the Women's Liberation movement but agreed with the objectives of full equality for women.

Altering Rights

The New York State Division of Human Rights has announced that Macy's Department Store chain has agreed to end sex discrimination in its clothes alterations policy. From now on, women can get slacks altered free, as men have for years.

—*Civil Rights Update*, U.S. Commission on Civil Rights, August 1980.

The Equal Rights Amendment was aimed at state laws that discriminate against women in such areas as marriage, property ownership, and employment. For example, some state laws have excluded women from state universities, and others have required longer prison sentences for women than for men for the same offense. The Equal Rights Amendment, on the other hand, would also nullify certain laws favoring women. For instance, it would require that women generally assume equal responsibility for child support and alimony in divorce actions. And the amendment would make women legally subject to military service if there were a draft (although the extent and nature of such service remains unclear). Supporters of the ERA argued that women with children might be excused from military service, that women would not necessarily serve in all jobs in the armed forces, and that past practice deprived women of such veterans' benefits as education under the GI bill, loans, and life insurance.

In his 1980 State of the Union address, President Carter asked Congress to resume registration for the draft. He later asked for funds to register men under an existing 1948 law and for new authority to register women as well. However, Congress voted funds to register men only. Just before registration was to start, a three-judge federal court in Philadelphia ruled that the 1948 law empowering the President to register men only was unconstitutional. But Supreme Court Justice William J. Brennan stayed the lower court action until the

full Supreme Court could consider the case, and registration began on schedule in July of 1980.

Whether women, if called to military service, would be used in combat remains a subject of continuing debate. In 1980 more than half of the first women graduates of the United States Military Academy at West Point were assigned to combat branches at their own request. They were barred by law, however, from assignments likely to involve close combat.[20]

The Equal Rights Amendment would also nullify various state laws designed to protect women workers—statutes limiting the amount of weight that may be lifted by women, for example. But proponents of the constitutional amendment argued that many laws designed to protect women—such as those limiting the number of hours a woman may work—have, in fact, deprived women of economic benefits, including overtime pay.

In some states, opponents of the ERA argued that the amendment would mean "unisex" public toilets or other mingling of the sexes in public facilities. Charges of this kind frightened many voters, even though supporters of the amendment contended that the right of privacy, which has been recognized by the Supreme Court, would permit reasonable separation of sexes in public facilities. But perhaps the most effective argument used by opponents of the ERA was that the amendment somehow represented an attack on the sanctity of the home, and that it undermined the concept of the man as head of the household and the woman as homemaker, receiving special protection under the law. The battle over the ERA thus represented a philosophical conflict between the older, more traditional concept of the role of women and a newer view of women as both liberated and fully equal.

Whether or not ERA was ratified, the issue of equal rights for women was receiving increasing attention in state courts. By 1978, sixteen states had equal rights provisions in their constitutions. In Illinois, for example, a court ruled that a mother may not automatically be preferred over the father in awarding custody of children in a divorce. A court in the state of Washington ruled that it was unconstitutional under the state ERA to bar girls from playing football with boys.

The ERA, whether at the federal or state level, was designed to secure

---

[20] *New York Times,* January 25, 1980, p. 1.

The Earnings Gap: Why Women Complain

Figure 5-2

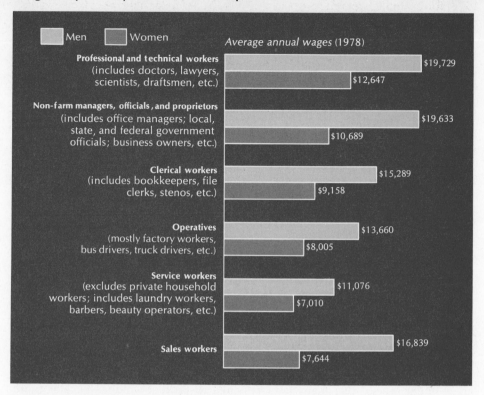

Men   Women   *Average annual wages* (1978)

Professional and technical workers
(includes doctors, lawyers,
scientists, draftsmen, etc.)
$19,729
$12,647

Non-farm managers, officials, and proprietors
(includes office managers; local,
state, and federal government
officials; business owners, etc.)
$19,633
$10,689

Clerical workers
(includes bookkeepers, file
clerks, stenos, etc.)
$15,289
$9,158

Operatives
(mostly factory workers,
bus drivers, truck drivers, etc.)
$13,660
$8,005

Service workers
(excludes private household
workers; includes laundry workers,
barbers, beauty operators, etc.)
$11,076
$7,010

Sales workers
$16,839
$7,644

Source: U.S. Bureau of the Census, *Current Population Reports,* Money Income and Poverty Status of Families and Persons in the United States: 1978, Series P-60, No. 120, November 1979, pp. 18–19.

equal *legal* rights for women. But the issue of women's rights was much broader than that.

American women still struggled for equality in the marketplace, for example. The stereotype of the female office worker as a secretary was all too real. In 1979, 43 million women workers in the United States composed just over 42 percent of the labor force. Yet women held 80 percent of all clerical jobs and earned only 59 percent of the median earnings of male workers. Only 37 percent of working women but 76 percent of working men earned $10,000 or more in 1977.[21] These statistics reflected the fact that many companies do not promote women to executive-level jobs. And even when women were hired in professional and executive positions, they earned considerably less than their male counterparts. (See Figure 5-2.) On the other hand, more women were entering the prestigious professions of law and medicine; during the 1970s, the number of women graduating from medical and law schools rose dramatically, from 1500 at the start of the decade to 12,000 in 1978.[22]

Although the last legal barriers to equal employment of women by the federal government were removed in 1962, the bureaucracy was not exempt

[21] Data provided by Women's Bureau and Bureau of Labor Statistics, U.S. Department of Labor.
[22] Data provided by U.S. Department of Education, National Center for Education Statistics.

from the bias against employment of women prevailing in private industry. In 1978, for example, women composed 37 percent of federal white-collar workers, but they held only 22 percent of the jobs that paid $16,255 and up.[23]

One of the most significant social developments of the past decade has been the dramatic increase in the number of employed women, who for the first time outnumber those at home. By 1980, 51 percent of adult American women held jobs outside the home. (By comparison, in 1970, 43 percent held jobs outside the home.)[24] (See Figure 5-3.)

Clearly, and despite the continuing barriers, American women are no longer limited to home, kitchen, and children (even though TV commercials persist in showing stereotyped women comparing laundry detergents and floor waxes). As Carol A. Whitehurst has suggested, "Women, today, seldom think in terms of career versus marriage, but instead believe that they can successfully combine the two. As an increased number of women enter the labor force and the time spent on motherhood shortens, careers become more attractive to women, and old negative images of women with careers begin to decline."[25]

In 1973 a Supreme Court decision gave dramatic evidence of the shifting social attitudes in America and the strength of the women's movement. In a 7–2 decision, the Court ruled that no state may interfere with a woman's right to

[23] *Ibid.*
[24] *Newsweek,* May 19, 1980, p. 72.
[25] Carol A. Whitehurst, *Women in America: The Oppressed Majority* (Santa Monica, Cal.: Goodyear Publishing Company, Inc., 1977), p. 69.

How Many Women Work: The Percentage
of Women Over 16 in the Labor Force

Figure 5–3

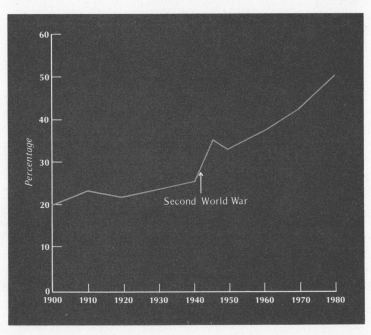

Source: Bureau of Labor Statistics: Bureau of the Census.

What goes largely unexamined, often even unacknowledged (yet is institutionalized nonetheless) in our social order, is the birthright priority whereby males rule females. Through this system a most ingenious form of "interior colonization" has been achieved. It is one which tends moreover to be sturdier than any form of segregation, and more rigorous than class stratification, more uniform, certainly more enduring. However muted its present appearance may be, sexual dominion obtains never-theless as perhaps the most pervasive ideology of our culture and provides its most fundamental concept of power.

This is so because our society, like all other historical civilizations, is a patriarchy. The fact is evident at once if one recalls that the military, industry, technology, universities, science, political office, and finance—in short, every avenue of power within the society, including the coercive force of the police, is entirely in male hands. As the essence of politics is power, such realization cannot fail to carry impact.

—Kate Millett, *Sexual Politics.*

have an abortion during the first three months of pregnancy.[26] The decision in effect struck down laws restricting abortion in forty-six states.

The Supreme Court's guidelines severely limited the power of a state government to regulate abortions. During the first three months, or trimester, the decision was up to the woman and her physician. During the last six months, the state could regulate abortion procedures, but only during the last ten weeks could a state ban abortions (except where necessary to preserve the life or health of the mother). The Court reasoned that a child born during the last ten weeks of normal pregnancy is presumed to be capable of survival. In the wake of the Supreme Court's decision, medical authorities have estimated, about 1.3 million American women a year have abortions to terminate unwanted pregnancies.

Abortion was now legal, but the Supreme Court's decision did not settle the question of who should pay for abortions. In 1977 the Court ruled that states did not have to spend Medicaid funds for elective abortions—those not "medically necessary" to preserve the health of the mother.[27] In the meantime, Congress in 1976 had passed a controversial amendment sponsored by Representative Henry J. Hyde, an Illinois Republican. The Hyde amendment banned federal Medicaid payments for abortions, even those medically necessary, except in cases of rape or incest or where the mother's life was "endangered." In 1980 the Supreme Court by a vote of 5–4 upheld the Hyde amendment.[28] The result was that poor women could no longer count on the government paying for abortions; Medicaid had been paying for an estimated 300,000 abortions a year.

Abortion is, of course, a politically volatile social issue on which Americans are sharply divided. Many women feel that state regulation of pregnancies violates their own right of privacy. "Pro-choice" groups, such as the Planned Parenthood Federation of America, argue that women have the right to control their reproductive systems.

Other Americans—including many women—strongly disagree. The Court's

[26] *Roe* v. *Wade,* 410 U.S. 113 (1973); *Doe* v. *Bolton,* 410 U.S. 179 (1973).
[27] *Maher* v. *Roe,* 432 U.S. 464 (1977).
[28] *Harris* v. *McRae,* 100 S. Ct. 2671 (1980).

1973 ruling legalizing abortion has been deplored by the Roman Catholic Church; many Americans feel abortions violate the rights of unborn children. Soon after 1973, the National Right to Life Committee was formed. This committee and other "pro-life" groups have worked to overturn the Supreme Court ruling by amending the Constitution to prohibit abortions. In 1980 nineteen of thirty-four states needed had passed resolutions calling for a constitutional convention to consider an anti-abortion amendment. The anti-abortion groups have become a powerful force in a number of political campaigns, where they have opposed candidates who favor abortion.

Rulings by the Supreme Court—even passage of an equal rights amendment—would not ensure immediate equality for women. "So widespread and pervasive are discriminatory practices against women, they have come to be regarded, more often than not, as normal," a presidential task force reported in 1970. "American women are increasingly aware and restive over the denial of equal opportunity, equal responsibility, even equal protection of the law. An abiding concern for home and children should not, in their view, cut them off from the freedom to choose the role in society to which their interest, education, and training entitle them."[29]

Two major groups represent women's rights, the National Women's Political Caucus and the National Organization for Women. The Caucus, with 45,000 members in fifty states, was founded in 1971. It helped to increase the number of women delegates to the national party conventions in 1972 and the total of women elected to public office that year. The Caucus emphasizes political goals, including the election and appointment of more women to public office and the improvement of social conditions for minorities and the poor through legislation. The organization has worked to defeat state legislators who voted against ratification of the Equal Rights Amendment.

Senator Nancy
Kassebaum of Kansas

The number of women holding public office has increased noticeably since the women's movement began. In 1981, for example, the Ninety-seventh Congress had 21 women, including 2 senators, Nancy Kassebaum of Kansas and Paula Hawkins of Florida. (In U.S. history, through 1980, 103 women had served in the Congress compared to 11,400 men.)

President Carter named three women to cabinet posts: Juanita Kreps to Commerce, Patricia Harris to HUD and later to Health and Human Services, and Shirley Hufstedler to Education. President Reagan named a woman, Jeane J. Kirkpatrick, as American ambassador to the United Nations. In 1980 there were two women governors and six women lieutenant governors. The number of women in state legislatures had more than doubled, from 305 (4.1 percent) in 1969 to 770 (10.3 percent) a decade later.

The National Organization for Women (NOW), founded in 1966, shares some of the political aims of the National Women's Political Caucus but places more emphasis on issues pertaining specifically to the status of women. NOW, with 110,000 members, has worked to improve equal employment opportunities for women, campaigned for the Equal Rights Amendment, defended the rights of lesbians, and supported the reform of laws dealing with women. NOW opposes all aspects of sex discrimination and is pledged to "take action to bring women into full participation in the mainstream of American society *now*, as-

Senator Paula Hawkins
of Florida

[29] *A Matter of Simple Justice.* The Report of the President's Task Force on Women's Rights and Responsibilities (Washington, D.C.: U.S. Government Printing Office, 1970), p. iii.

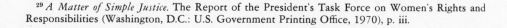

149

suming all the privileges and responsibilities . . . in fully equal partnership with men."

Gay Rights

In 1977 national attention was focused on Miami, where voters were asked to approve or repeal a law protecting homosexuals from discrimination in employment, housing, and public accommodations. The battle pitted the city's gay community against Anita Bryant, a television singer widely known for her commercials advertising Florida orange juice.

Miami homosexuals had persuaded the Dade County Commission to pass the law protecting their legal rights. Miss Bryant organized a "Save Our Children" campaign, warned at rallies that Miami would become "another Sodom and Gomorrah," and usually ended her appearances by singing "The Battle Hymn of the Republic." In San Francisco, homosexuals organized a "gaycott" of Florida orange juice in opposition to Miss Bryant.

In June, however, Miami area residents voted overwhelmingly, by 2 to 1, to repeal the law protecting gays. Similar laws protecting gay rights were later repealed in St. Paul, Minnesota; Wichita, Kansas; and Eugene, Oregon. Despite these votes, the battle in Miami and other cities had the effect of focusing increased public attention on the legal and civil rights of gays, who have gained greater political power in many areas of the nation in recent years.

According to the Kinsey Institute for Sex Research, 2 percent of American women and 4 percent of American men are exclusively homosexual, and 20 percent of women and 37 percent of men have had some homosexual experience during or after adolescence. Although no one knows the size of the gay population in the United States, "they are certainly in the millions."[30]

And, despite the vote in Miami and some other cities, a Gallup poll in 1977 indicated that 56 percent, or more than half of all Americans, favored equal job opportunities for homosexual men and women. At the same time, 65 percent of those polled did not approve of employing gay persons as teachers. But in a later poll, 66 percent of Americans said they would vote for a homosexual for President.[31]

Through a combination of court decisions, legislative action, and changing public perceptions of homosexuals, many jurisdictions have protected gay rights. By 1980, thirty-seven communities, including such major population centers as New York, San Francisco, Boston, Detroit, Los Angeles, and Washington, D.C., had passed local laws or taken executive action to protect gay rights in employment, housing, and other areas. Seven counties and two states—California and Pennsylvania—had taken similar action.

In addition, twenty states, including California, Illinois, Ohio, and Massachusetts, had removed criminal sanctions from private sex acts by consenting adults. Yet the laws concerning gays were uneven. In the state of Washington, a teacher who had not engaged in open homosexual conduct was fired when his homosexuality became known; the U.S. Supreme Court let the decision stand.[32] In Delaware he could not have been dismissed on those grounds. In seven Mid-

[30] Elizabeth Ogg, *Changing Views of Homosexuality* (New York: Public Affairs Committee, Inc., 1978), p. 3; and National Women's Political Caucus, *Gay Rights: A Position Paper.*
[31] *Gallup Opinion Index,* October 1977, Report No. 147, pp. 3–8; and Report No. 160, November 1978, p. 26.
[32] *Gaylord* v. *Tacoma,* 434 U.S. 879 (1977).

western states, public universities were under a court order in 1980 to permit students to use meeting rooms to discuss gay rights. In other states, universities could deny use of their facilities for this purpose.

Under the Civil Service Reform Act of 1978, most federal agencies could not discriminate against homosexuals in their hiring practices, although the Federal Bureau of Investigation, the Central Intelligence Agency, and other "sensitive" government agencies could dismiss or refuse to hire gay persons. The armed forces had the right to dismiss homosexuals, although a federal appeals court ruled in 1978 that the military could not dismiss homosexuals without "some reasoned explanation."[33]

But, federal law did permit the Immigration and Naturalization Service to bar gay persons from the United States. In 1980, however, the Justice Department ruled that homosexual aliens would not be barred unless they made a voluntary declaration of their homosexuality. And the Carter administration asked for repeal of the section of the law under which homosexuals had been excluded.

The law barring foreign homosexuals from entering the United States was passed three decades ago, long before the American Psychiatric Association, in 1973, removed homosexuality from its list of mental disorders and urged that gays be given the same legal protections as other citizens. Despite changing public views toward gays, however, a substantial number of Americans continued to regard homosexuality as offensive to their personal, community, or religious standards, as the vote in Miami attested.

On the other hand, in many states, political leaders could ignore gay power at their peril. In San Francisco, with its large gay population, Mayor Dianne Feinstein was forced into a runoff primary election in 1977 when a gay political activist received a substantial vote; and in Washington, D.C., in 1977 gay voters were credited with helping to elect Mayor Marion Barry. In California in 1978, voters rejected a proposition on the ballot that would have barred known homosexual teachers from teaching in the state's public schools. In 1979 Representative Ted Weiss, a New York Democrat, introduced legislation to extend the Civil Rights Act of 1964 to protect gays. Such legislation was supported by many gay organizations and by some 25,000 homosexuals who marched from the Capitol to the Washington Monument at the first national gay rights rally in October of 1979.

Black and White:
An American Dilemma

What is it like to be born with black skin in America? In his prophetic book *The Fire Next Time,* author James Baldwin tried to tell:

> Long before the Negro child perceives this difference, and even long before he understands it, he has begun to react to it, he has begun to be controlled by it. . . . He must be "good" not only in order to please his parents and not only to avoid being punished by them; behind their authority stands another, nameless and impersonal, infinitely harder to please, and bottomlessly cruel. And this filters into

[33] *New York Times,* December 8, 1978, p. 1.

the child's consciousness through his parents' tone of voice as he is being exhorted, punished, or loved; in the sudden, uncontrollable note of fear heard in his mother's or his father's voice when he has strayed beyond some particular boundary. He does not know what the boundary is, and he can get no explanation of it.[34]

Another writer, Ralph Ellison, explained that the black adult is unseen by the white world. "I am an invisible man," he wrote. "I am a man of substance, of flesh and bone, fiber and liquids—and I might even be said to possess a mind. I am invisible, understand, simply because people refuse to see me."[35]

Ellison wrote those words in 1952. If black men and women in America are visible today, it is because a revolution in civil rights has taken place since that time. Yet, black Americans still have not been able to reach the goal of full equality in American society.

It is paradoxical, and tragic as well, that a nation founded on the principle that all people are created equal should have "a race problem." It is this paradox that the Swedish sociologist Gunnar Myrdal termed the "American Dilemma" in his classic study more than a third of a century ago.[36] "The American Negro problem is a problem in the heart of the American," Myrdal wrote. "The American Dilemma . . . is the ever-raging conflict between, on the one hand, the valuations preserved on the general plane which we shall call the 'American Creed,' where the American thinks, talks, and acts under the influence of high national and Christian precepts, and on the other hand . . . group prejudice against particular persons or types of people."[37]

Author Charles E. Silberman has argued that in one sense "Myrdal was wrong. The tragedy of race relations in the United States is that there is no American Dilemma. White Americans are not torn and tortured by the conflict between their devotion to the American creed and their actual behavior. They are upset by the current state of race relations, to be sure. But what troubles them is not that justice is being denied but that their peace is being shattered and their business interrupted."[38]

The conflict between black and white Americans is not only a problem for the black citizen, who is still seeking his or her rightful place in American society, but a problem for all Americans, a moral contradiction that strikes at the roots of American democracy. Two decades after Myrdal had summarized his views, the "fire next time" that was predicted by James Baldwin visited American cities, in the form of racial disorders, and social conflict remained a continuing threat to the nation's future.

By the 1980s a substantial black middle class had emerged in the United States, and black incomes were growing. But the unprecedented migration of blacks from the South to Northern cities in the years after the Second World War had helped to create explosive ghetto conditions in those cities. And the poverty of the inner city continued to exist in the midst of an affluent society. Blacks in America, Silberman has noted, are "an economic as well as a racial minority." No matter how "assimilated" the black American is, because of his

[34] Baldwin, *The Fire Next Time,* p. 40.
[35] Ralph Ellison, *The Invisible Man* (New York: Random House, 1951), p. 3.
[36] Gunnar Myrdal, *An American Dilemma: The Negro Problem and Modern Democracy* (New York: Harper & Row, 1962). Originally published in 1944.
[37] *Ibid.,* p. lxxi.
[38] Charles E. Silberman, *Crisis in Black and White* (New York: Random House, 1964), p. 10.

skin color, "he cannot lose himself in the crowd. He remains . . . an alien in his own land."[39]

The Historical Background

"The Negro," Gunnar Myrdal observed, "was brought to America for the sake of the white man's profit. He was kept in slavery for generations in the same interest."[40]

Unlike most other immigrants, who came to these shores seeking freedom, blacks came in slavery. Theirs was a forced immigration. While the Irish American, the Italian American, or other Americans might regard their forebears' country of national origin with pride, until the 1960s few black Americans identified with African culture or the term Afro-American. In part this was because black Americans absorbed the whites' concept of Africa as a land of jungles and savages. It has been only in relatively recent years that substantial numbers of scholars have explored the history and culture of West Africa. According to one study: "Modern scholarship places the western Sudan among the important creative centers in the development of human culture."[41]

The Afro-American

It was here, south of the Sahara in the western Sudan, that the majority of the slaves brought to America were captured, to be transported across the sea under cruel conditions. The slaves, chained together and lying on their backs, were packed in layers between the decks in spaces that sometimes measured less than two feet. Often, only a third survived the voyage "and loss of half was not at all unusual."[42] It was not surprising that the slaves sometimes mutinied aboard ship.

No one knows how many slaves were brought to North and South America and the West Indies between the sixteenth and the mid-nineteenth centuries, but the figure has been estimated at 15 million. It may easily have been twice that.

In the 1950s a white or black child reading a textbook in American history would scarcely have realized that blacks were a significant part of the American past. Interest in the cultural heritage of Afro-Americans was accompanied in the 1960s and 1970s by new studies of the role of blacks in the nation's history.

A Black American Heritage

Perhaps the first person to fall in the American Revolution was a black man, Crispus Attucks. A twenty-seven-year-old runaway slave, he was the first of five men killed by British soldiers in the Boston Massacre of 1770, five years before the Revolutionary War began.[43] Black Americans took part in the battles of Lexington, Concord, and Bunker Hill; they were with Washington at Valley Forge. About 5000 blacks served in the Continental Army. And 186,000 blacks served in the Union ranks during the Civil War.

[39] *Ibid.,* pp. 43–44.
[40] Myrdal, *An American Dilemma: The Negro Problem and Modern Democracy,* p. lxxvi.
[41] August Meier and Elliott M. Rudwick, *From Plantation to Ghetto* (New York: Hill and Wang, 1966), p. 5.
[42] *Ibid.,* p. 33.
[43] John Hope Franklin, *From Slavery to Freedom* (New York: Knopf, 1967), p. 128.

Black explorers, soldiers, scientists, poets, writers, educators, public officials — the list of such men and women who made individual contributions is long and distinguished; moreover, black Americans as a group have contributed to the culture of America and participated in its historical development. Yet, from the start, the role of black people was overlooked or neglected.

"We hold these truths to be self-evident," the Declaration of Independence says, "that all men are created equal." But that soaring language was not meant to include the black American, who was recognized by the Founding Fathers at Philadelphia as only "three-fifths" of a person. The American Dilemma, even as the republic began, was engraved in the new nation's Constitution but had scarcely touched its conscience.

Dred Scott, Reconstruction, and "Jim Crow"

Citizens of a state automatically are "citizens of the United States" under the Constitution. But until after the Civil War, this in reality meant free white persons. The citizenship status of free blacks — there were almost 100,000 in the early 1800s — remained a subject of political dispute. The Supreme Court ruled on the question in the famous *Dred Scott* decision of 1857.

Dred Scott was a slave who had lived in the North for four years. Antislavery forces sought to bring Scott's case before the Supreme Court on the grounds that his residence on free soil had made him a free man. To sue for freedom, Scott first had to prove he was a citizen. But Chief Justice Roger B. Taney ruled that Dred Scott and black Americans "are not included, and were not intended to be included, under the word 'citizens' in the Constitution."[44]

It took a civil war and a constitutional amendment to reverse Taney's decision. In 1865, eight months after the surrender at Appomattox, the states ratified the Thirteenth Amendment, abolishing slavery. The Fourteenth Amendment, ratified in 1868, reversed the *Dred Scott* decision by making citizens of the freed slaves. The Fifteenth Amendment, ratified in 1870, was designed to give former slaves the right to vote.

During the Reconstruction era (1863–1877), Congress passed a series of civil rights measures, of which the last, the Civil Rights Act of 1875, was the strongest. The law was aimed at providing equal public accommodations for blacks. But this postwar trend toward equality for black Americans was short-lived. In the *Civil Rights Cases* of 1883, the Supreme Court struck down the 1875 Civil Rights Act, decreeing that the Fourteenth Amendment protected citizens from infringement of their rights by the *states* but not by *private individuals*. Discrimination by one citizen against another citizen was a private affair, the Court held.

Thus, less than two decades after the Civil War, the Supreme Court had seriously weakened the Fourteenth Amendment and neutralized the efforts of Congress to pass civil rights laws to protect black citizens. The Court decisions were also a sign of what was to come.

After 1883 the atmosphere was ripe for the rise of segregation and of "Jim Crow" laws designed to give legal recognition to discrimination.[45] Segregation, the separation of black and white Americans by law, became the new

Dred Scott

Chief Justice
Roger B. Taney

---

[44] *Dred Scott* v. *Sandford*, 19 Howard 393 (1857).

[45] In 1832 Thomas D. "Daddy" Rice, a blackface minstrel, had introduced a song and dance about a slave named Jim Crow (Weel a-bout and turn a-bout/And . . . jump Jim Crow"), and the term came to be applied to the antiblack laws of the 1890s.

way of life in the South. "Jim Crow" was accompanied by lynchings and terror for blacks.[46]

In 1896 the Supreme Court put its official seal of approval on racial segregation in America. The great constitutional test of legal discrimination began on a June day in 1892, when Homer Adolph Plessy bought a ticket in New Orleans, boarded an East Louisiana Railroad train, and took his seat—in a coach reserved for whites. He was asked to move, refused, and was arrested.

Plessy
v. Ferguson

Plessy was chosen for this test by opponents of the state's Jim Crow railroad law, which required equal but separate accommodations for white and black passengers. The Supreme Court ruled that the Louisiana statute did not violate the Fourteenth Amendment.

Yet, the case of *Plessy* v. *Ferguson* is remembered as well for the ringing dissent of a single justice, a former slaveholder from Kentucky, John Marshall Harlan. Shocked by the activities of the Ku Klux Klan, Harlan had become a champion of civil rights for blacks. And he declared: "Our Constitution is color-blind and neither knows or tolerates classes among citizens. . . . The thin disguise of 'equal' accommodations for passengers in railroad coaches will not mislead anyone nor atone for the wrong this day done."[47]

Despite Harlan's eloquent dissent, the doctrine of "separate but equal" remained the law of the land for fifty-eight years, until 1954, when the Supreme Court finally ruled that it had no place in American life.

In the city of Topeka, Kansas, more than half a century after *Plessy*, Oliver Brown, a black man and a welder by trade, was disturbed by the fact that his eight-year-old daughter, Linda Carol, attended an elementary school twenty-one blocks away from her home. The school was all black, for Topeka elementary schools were segregated by local option under state law. To go the twenty-one blocks to Monroe Elementary School, Linda Carol caught a school bus each morning at 7:40 A.M. The difficulty was that the bus arrived at the school at 8:30 A.M., but the doors of the school did not open until 9 A.M. Often, it meant that the children had to wait outside in the cold. To get home in the afternoon, she had to walk past the railroad tracks and cross a busy and dangerous intersection. Oliver Brown tried to enroll his children at Sumner Elementary School, which was only seven blocks from the Brown home. He was unable to do so. Sumner was a school for white children. With the help of the National Association for the Advancement of Colored People (NAACP), Oliver Brown took his case to court.

The Case of
Linda Carol Brown

On May 17, 1954, Chief Justice Earl Warren delivered the unanimous opinion of the Supreme Court in the case of *Brown* v. *Board of Education of Topeka, Kansas.*

The issue before the Supreme Court was very simple: the Fourteenth Amendment guarantees equal protection of the laws. The plaintiffs argued that

Brown
v. Board
of Education

[46] There were about 100 lynchings a year in the 1880s and 1890s; 161 lynchings took place in 1892.
[47] *Plessy* v. *Ferguson,* 163 U.S. 537 (1896).

From *Herblock's State of the Union* (Simon & Schuster, 1972).

"We are for speedy compliance, bearing in mind that there's been only fifteen years to desegregate these schools."

segregated schools were not and could never be equal, and were therefore unconstitutional.

Chief Justice Warren asked: "Does segregation of children in public schools solely on the basis of race, even though the physical facilities and other 'tangible' factors may be equal, deprive the children of the minority group of equal educational opportunities? We believe that it does." Such segregation of children, the Chief Justice added, "may affect their hearts and minds in a way unlikely ever to be undone. . . . We conclude that in the field of public education the doctrine 'separate but equal' has no place. Separate educational facilities are inherently unequal. Therefore, we hold that the plaintiffs . . . are, by reason of the segregation complained of, deprived of the equal protection of the laws guaranteed by the Fourteenth Amendment."[48]

The Supreme Court did not attempt in 1954 to enforce its decision. The Court, as Justice Robert Jackson pointed out, "is dependent upon the political branches for the execution of its mandates, for it has no physical force at its command."[49]

Much of the South reacted to the *Brown* decision by adopting a policy of massive resistance. How, then, would the Court's ruling be implemented? A year later, in May 1955 the Supreme Court itself faced the problem, unanimously ordering local school authorities to comply with the decision "with all deliberate speed."[50] But compliance was very slow, and in some instances there were direct armed confrontations between federal and state power.

Little Rock, Oxford, and Alabama

In September 1957 nine black children attempted to enter the previously all-white Central High School in Little Rock, Arkansas, under a federal court order. Governor Orval Faubus called out the National Guard to block integration of the school, but the troops were withdrawn by direction of the court. The black students braved a screaming mob of whites. President Eisenhower reluctantly dispatched federal paratroopers to Little Rock to quell the violence. Central High was (and is) integrated.

Violence continued to flare in the South during the Kennedy administration. When James Meredith, a black student, enrolled in the University of Mississippi at Oxford in 1962, two men were killed and several injured in the rioting that took place on the campus. President Kennedy dispatched federal marshals and ordered 16,000 troops to restore peace and protect Meredith. The following year, Alabama's Governor George Wallace attempted to block the enrollment of two black students at the University of Alabama at Tuscaloosa. Wallace backed down only after Kennedy federalized the Alabama National Guard.

The School Decision: Aftermath

Fifteen years after the *Brown* decision, only 20 percent of black students in the South attended integrated public schools (defined by the federal government as at least 50 percent white). Faced with continued defiance, the Supreme Court

[48] *Brown* v. *Board of Education of Topeka, Kansas,* 347 U.S. 483 (1954).

[49] In Robert H. Jackson, *The Supreme Court in the American System of Government* (Cambridge, Mass.: Harvard University Press, 1955), p. 11.

[50] *Brown* v. *Board of Education of Topeka, Kansas,* 349 U.S. 294 (1955). John Marshall Harlan, grandson of the justice who dissented in *Plessy* v. *Ferguson,* was by this time a member of the Supreme Court and participated in the second *Brown* decision.

ruled unanimously in October 1969 that school districts must end segregation "at once" and operate integrated systems "now and hereafter."[51] It was the first major Supreme Court decision presided over by the new Chief Justice, Warren Burger.

Through federal court rulings and the efforts of the federal government in working with local school boards, the pattern gradually changed. By 1972, 44 percent of black students in the eleven Southern states were attending integrated schools. In 1976 the Supreme Court ruled that private, nonreligious schools may not exclude black children because of their race.[52] By 1978, 40 percent of black and other minority children attended integrated schools in the United States.[53] Ironically, schools in the South were more integrated than those in the North. For example, 24 percent of black and other minority students in the South attended schools that were 90 to 100 percent minority — but in the Northeast 44 percent of black and minority pupils attended such schools.[54] Thus, the question of public school desegregation, in the North even more than in the South, remained a volatile issue.

And in Topeka, Kansas, where it had all begun, a federal judge in 1979 reopened the *Brown* case after a group of parents complained that, twenty-five years later, the city's schools were still segregated. "The wheel has turned all the way around," Charles Scott, Jr., attorney for the parents, said, "and nothing has changed."[55] Among the group of parents who filed the complaint was Linda Carol Brown, now the mother of two children in the Topeka public school system.

By the mid-seventies the familiar yellow school bus had become the symbol of a deeply divisive political and social issue in the United States. The *Brown* decision left many unanswered questions, among them whether the Constitution required busing of schoolchildren to achieve desegregation. In April 1971, the Supreme Court ruled unanimously that in some circumstances it did; the Court held that busing could be used "as one tool of desegregation."[56]

Busing:
The Controversy
Continues

That decision involved a busing plan for Charlotte, North Carolina. Since, at the time, 18 million public school children rode buses in the United States, the Court declared, there was no reason why busing could not be used to achieve school desegregation.

The Court has not upheld busing in every case, however. In 1973 it struck down a plan to bus children across city lines in Richmond, Virginia,[57] and the following year it overturned Detroit's cross-busing plan.[58]

Boston was the scene of prolonged violence over busing that began after a federal district judge ruled in 1974 that the city had knowingly imposed a systematic program of segregation in the schools. "Therefore the entire school system of Boston is unconstitutionally segregated," the court held. Under the plan the court ordered into effect, many black students were bused into the largely blue-collar, Irish Catholic neighborhoods of South Boston and Charles-

[51] *Alexander* v. *Holmes County Board of Education*, 396 U.S. 19 (1969).
[52] *Runyon* v. *McCrary*, 427 U.S. 160 (1976).
[53] Data provided by Department of Education, Office of Civil Rights.
[54] *New York Times*, May 17, 1979, p. B11.
[55] *Washington Post*, November 30, 1979, p. 1.
[56] *Swann* v. *Charlotte-Mecklenburg County Board of Education*, 402 U.S. 1 (1971).
[57] *School Board of the City of Richmond, Virginia* v. *State Board of Education*, 412 U.S. 92 (1973).
[58] *Milliken* v. *Bradley*, 418 U.S. 717 (1974).

Antibusing demonstrator, Louisville, Kentucky

town. Racial tension and intermittent violence by stone-throwing whites resulted.

Many parents, both white and black, have objected to busing to achieve desegregation. White parents have often opposed the busing of their children into largely black, inner-city schools. A number of parents, black and white, objected to long bus rides into unfamiliar neighborhoods for their children. Clearly, the busing of schoolchildren stirred up strong emotions.

In the cities of the North, school segregation often resulted not by law but because of *de facto* segregation—residential patterns that created black neighborhoods and, along with them, black schools. It was this kind of segregation that created one of the most difficult questions facing Americans. Millions of whites had moved to the suburbs, some at least partly in search of better schools; even those who did not consider themselves racists often reacted with hostility to the idea of busing their children back to the inner-city schools they had fled. On the other hand, to many black students trapped in ghetto schools, the school bus appeared to offer the only immediate means to quality education.

As the issue continued to trouble the nation, some black educators concluded that quality education did not depend on busing and desegregation. Wilson Riles, the superintendent of education in California, rejected the idea "that a black child can't learn unless he is sitting next to a white child," and political scientist Charles Hamilton called busing black children "a subtle way of maintaining black dependency on whites."[59]

Public opinion surveys indicated that busing was not an issue that clearly found whites on one side and blacks on the other. In 1975 Gallup and Harris polls showed about 75 percent of all whites were opposed to busing, but so were 47 percent of blacks.[60]

As in the case of school busing, the 1954 *Brown* decision did not deal with the issue of *de facto* segregation. But the question was involved in a case in Denver decided by the Supreme Court in 1973.[61] At stake was the future of the "neighborhood school" in Northern cities. Without directly deciding the issue of *de facto* segregation, the Court ruled that where a school board had intentionally segregated a "substantial portion" of students, a presumption is created that the school system as a whole is deliberately segregated. If that can be proved, local authorities must desegregate the entire school system. Denver, the Court made clear, would not be allowed to maintain a dual school system. In a separate opinion, Justice Lewis F. Powell, Jr., argued that there was no longer any validity to the distinction between *de jure* (official) and *de facto* segregation, and that "the evil of operating separate schools is no less in Denver than in Atlanta." The Supreme Court ruling warned the North that it could not operate deliberately segregated schools by manipulating school boundaries, any more than the South could. Denver began busing substantial numbers of students in 1974.

And the Supreme Court reaffirmed its Denver decision in 1979, when it approved sweeping cross-town busing plans in two Ohio cities, Dayton and Columbus. The Court concluded that its decision in the *Brown* case imposed a "continuing duty" on schools in the North and South alike to eliminate the

[59] Diane Ravitch, "Busing: The Solution That Has Failed to Solve," *New York Times,* December 21, 1975, Section 4, p. 3.
[60] *Ibid.*
[61] *Keyes* v. *School District No. 1,* 413 U.S. 189 (1973).

effects of official segregation.[62] It had become very clear in the years following the *Brown* decision that racial problems were not confined to any one section of the nation.

The Civil Rights Movement: Freedom Now

On the evening of December 1, 1955, Rosa Parks, a forty-three-year-old seamstress, boarded a bus in Montgomery, Alabama, as she did every working day to return home from her job at a downtown department store. When half a dozen whites got on at a bus stop, the driver asked black passengers near the front of the bus to give up their seats to the whites and move to the rear. Three other black passengers got up; Rosa Parks did not. She was arrested and fined $10, but her quiet refusal launched a boycott of the Montgomery bus line by a black population that had had enough. It was a remarkable year-long protest, and it catapulted to national fame the twenty-seven-year-old Baptist minister who led it. His name was Dr. Martin Luther King, Jr.

During the boycott King went to jail, and his home was bombed, but he won. The boycott ended in November 1956 as a result of a federal court injunction prohibiting segregation of buses in Montgomery. The victory set the pattern for other boycotts and for direct action throughout the South.

King, who led the civil rights movement and remained its symbolic head until his assassination in 1968, was an apostle of nonviolence, an eloquent man who attempted, with some success, to stir the American conscience. King grew up in comfortable middle-class surroundings in Atlanta, where his father was pastor of the Ebenezer Baptist Church. And it was in Atlanta in 1957, following the Montgomery boycott, that King formed the Southern Christian Leadership Conference (SCLC) as a vehicle for his philosophy of nonviolent change, in which he had been influenced by the teachings of Gandhi.

Until then, the principal black organization in the United States had been the NAACP, which stressed legal action in the courts as the road to progress. It was a lawyer's approach, and it had won many important struggles. King's battleground was the streets, rather than the courts, and he sought through nonviolent confrontation to dramatize the issue of civil rights for the nation and the world.

The civil rights movement came of age at a time when many blacks were growing impatient with the slow pace of "gradual" change. Their desire was for "freedom now"—rather than at some unspecified time in the future.

The Movement: The View from the Front of the Bus

As some civil rights workers have said, "What good is a seat in the front of the bus if you don't have the money for the fare?"

"We're in a new stage of the movement," Dr. King's widow, Coretta Scott King, said the other day, discussing civil rights developments over the last 10 years. "The issue now is jobs and money. In many ways, that's a harder nut to crack than the blatant discrimination that we were struggling against back in the old days."

—*New York Times,* April 2, 1978.

In February 1960 four black college students in Greensboro, North Carolina, sat down at a lunch counter at Woolworth's and asked politely for cups of coffee. They were refused service. They continued to sit for the rest of the morning.

[62] *Dayton Board of Education* v. *Brinkman,* 443 U.S. 526 (1979); and *Columbus Board of Education* v. *Penick,* 443 U.S. 449 (1979).

They came back the next day, and the next. Soon other students, white and black, joined them. They were spattered with mustard and ketchup and spat upon and cursed by whites. But at Greensboro the sit-in movement was born.

It spread to seven other states. The new tactics were a success. Within six months, not only the Woolworth's in Greensboro but hundreds of lunch counters throughout the South were serving blacks. In 1961 the sit-in technique was adapted to test segregation on interstate buses and in terminals. Black and white Freedom Riders rode into Alabama, where they were savagely beaten, slashed with chains, and stoned in attacks by whites. One bus was burned. But the Freedom Riders succeeded in publicizing the fact that segregation on interstate transportation, although outlawed by the Supreme Court, was then still a reality.[63]

Birmingham and the Dream

In the spring of 1963 Dr. King organized mass demonstrations against segregation in industrial Birmingham, Alabama. When arrests failed to stop the demonstrators, the authorities used high-pressure fire hoses, police dogs, and cattle prods. The demonstrators sang "We Shall Overcome" and continued to march. Photographs of the police dogs unleashed by Birmingham Police Commissioner Eugene "Bull" Connor went out on the news wires. Another photograph showed police kneeling on a black woman and pinning her to the sidewalk. The scenes outraged much of the nation and the world.

Late in August King led a massive, peaceful "March on Washington for Jobs and Freedom." Some 200,000 Americans, black and white, jammed the Mall between the Lincoln Memorial and the Washington Monument. The nationally televised, orderly demonstration had a powerful effect on the nation, but even more powerful were the words of Dr. King, who articulated the vision of what America could be and might become:

> I have a dream that one day this nation will rise up and live out the true meaning of its creed. . . .
>
> I have a dream . . . that my four little children will one day live in a nation where they will not be judged by the color of their skin but by the content of their character. . . .

The police dogs of Birmingham, 1963

[63] The Supreme Court had barred segregation on interstate transportation in a series of decisions; on buses in *Morgan* v. *Commonwealth of Virginia,* 328 U.S. 373 (1946); on trains in *Henderson* v. *United States,* 339 U.S. 816 (1950), which held that an interstate railroad could not segregate a dining car; and in other cases.

Dr. Martin Luther King, Jr., at the March on Washington, August 1963: "I have a dream. . . ."

So let freedom ring. . . . From every mountainside, let freedom ring . . . to speed up that day when all of God's children, black and white men, Jews and Gentiles, Protestants and Catholics, will be able to join hands and sing in the words of that old Negro spiritual, "Free at last! Free at last! Thank God Almighty, we are free at last!"[64]

In Birmingham, eighteen days later, a bomb was thrown into the Sixteenth Street Baptist Church on a Sunday morning. Four black girls attending Bible class died in the explosion. But from the agony of Birmingham that summer, from the impressive March on Washington, and from the powerful words of Dr. King, there emerged the strongest civil rights legislation since Reconstruction.

During the Eisenhower administration, Congress had passed the Civil Rights Act of 1957, the first such legislation since 1875. It created a United States Commission on Civil Rights and strengthened the civil rights section of the Justice Department. The Civil Rights Act of 1960 provided for federal voting referees to enroll voters where local officials denied them the right of suffrage. Both laws proved to be of limited value, however.

The Legislative Breakthrough

The Civil Rights Act of 1964. In 1963 President Kennedy proposed a comprehensive civil rights bill. After Kennedy's assassination that November, the House acted, but Southerners in the Senate staged a fifty-seven-day filibuster. In June the Senate invoked cloture to cut off debate — the first time it had ever done so on a civil rights bill — and passed the measure. On July 2 President Johnson signed the Civil Rights Act of 1964 into law. The principal provisions were designed to:

1. Prohibit racial or religious discrimination in public accommodations that affect interstate commerce, including hotels, motels, restaurants, cafeterias, lunch counters, gas stations, motion picture houses, theaters, and sports arenas.
2. Prohibit discrimination because of race, color, sex, religion, or national origin by employers or labor unions.
3. Bar voting registrars from adopting different standards for white and black applicants.
4. Permit the Attorney General to bring suit to enforce desegregation of public accommodations; and allow individuals to sue for their rights under the act.
5. Permit the executive branch of the federal government to halt the flow of funds to public or private programs that practice discrimination.
6. Extend the life of the Civil Rights Commission; create a Community Relations Service to conciliate racial disputes and an Equal Employment Opportunity Commission to enforce the fair employment section of the act.

The 1964 act did not cover violence directed at black Americans or at civil rights workers, white or black. Two days after President Johnson signed the bill into law, the bodies of three young civil rights workers — two of them from the North — were found in a shallow grave near Philadelphia, Mississippi.[65]

Martin Luther King's "Moral Theater"

When the anti-abortion mothers march around the Capitol, when the farmers jam the streets with their tractors, they are, consciously or otherwise, imitating the moral theater Martin Luther King staged for the mass audience of television. Sometimes it works, and often it doesn't, but a range of political strategies, now regarded as orthodox and acceptable, was considered outrageous [and] sometimes illegal when King introduced it.

—Washington Post,
April 2, 1978.

[64] *The Negro in American History*, Vol. 1, *Black Americans 1928–1968*, with an introduction by Saunders Redding (Chicago: Encyclopaedia Britannica Educational Corporation, 1969), pp. 175–76.

[65] In 1967 seven men were convicted of conspiracy against the slain civil rights workers under an 1870 federal statute. Because the murders of the rights workers did not constitute a federal crime, the conspiracy statute was the only weapon available to the Justice Department. The seven, including an Imperial Wizard of the Ku Klux Klan and the deputy sheriff of Neshoba County, were given prison sentences ranging from three to ten years.

In a civil rights act passed in 1968, Congress provided criminal penalties for injuring or interfering with civil rights workers or any persons exercising their civil rights; if the injury results in death, the maximum penalty is life imprisonment. The 1968 law also made it a federal offense to cross state lines with intent to incite a riot.

At the same time, Congress passed the Fair Housing Act, the first federal open housing law in the twentieth century. In 1970, when the law went fully into effect, it prohibited discrimination in the rental or sale of all privately owned single-family houses rented or sold through real estate agents or brokers. Private individuals who sold their houses without an agent were not subject to the law, but approximately 80 percent of all housing was covered. Even before the law went into effect, the Supreme Court, in a landmark case, outlawed discrimination in the sale of private housing.[66] It soon became clear, however, that the Department of Housing and Urban Development (HUD) had little power to punish violators of the 1968 housing act. In 1980, with strong backing from President Carter, Congress considered but did not pass amendments to the Fair Housing Act designed to empower HUD to enforce the law.

The Voting Rights Act of 1965.   During the Reconstruction era, state governments in the South were controlled by Northern radical Republicans. After the white South regained control over its governments, particularly in the 1890s and thereafter, blacks were systematically denied the right to vote. What the Ku Klux Klan could not accomplish by intimidation, a broad range of other obstacles did. Literacy tests rigged to keep black voters from the polls, the all-white primary (which rested on the theory, rejected by the Supreme Court in 1944, that political parties were private clubs), the poll tax, and gerrymandering of election districts were all deliberate attempts to keep black voters in the South from gaining political power and challenging or changing the existing order. In short, the Fifteenth Amendment was being systematically flouted.

Only 12 percent of black Americans of voting age were registered in the eleven Southern states in 1948. And, although the figure rose to 43.3 percent by November 1, 1964, it was still far below the 73.2 percent white registration in the same states.[67] (See Table 5–1.)

[66] *Jones* v. *Mayer,* 392 U.S. 409 (1968).
[67] Southern Regional Council data in *1965 Congressional Quarterly Almanac,* p. 537.

Voter Registration in the South Before and After the Voting Rights Act of 1965

Table 5–1

| | Percent of Voting-Age Population Registered | | |
	1964	1972	1976
Black	43.3%	56.6%	63.1%
White	73.2%	67.8%	67.9%

Sources: *1968 Congressional Quarterly Almanac,* pp. 772, 1055; Congressional Quarterly, *Revolution in Civil Rights,* p. 70; *The Voting Rights Act: Ten Years After,* Report of the U.S. Commission on Civil Rights (Washington, D.C.: U.S. Government Printing Office, 1975), p. 43; and Voter Education Project, Inc. data, in U.S. Bureau of the Census, *Statistical Abstract of the United States: 1979* (Washington, D.C.: U.S. Government Printing Office, 1979), p. 512.

March on Montgomery, Alabama, 1965

In Dallas County, Alabama, exactly 335 blacks out of a black population of 15,115 were registered to vote at the start of 1965. Martin Luther King chose Selma, the county seat, as the place where he would dramatize the voting rights issue. Dr. King called for a fifty-mile march from Selma to Montgomery, the state capital. But state troopers acting under orders of Governor Wallace used tear gas, whips, and night sticks to break up the march. President Johnson federalized the National Guard, and the march resumed under protection of the troops. Through the heat, the mud, and the rain, their ranks swelling in numbers and in pride, the marchers walked on until, joined by Dr. King, they reached the steps of the Alabama capitol building.

In the midst of the struggle in Selma, and before the marchers had finally reached Montgomery, President Johnson went on nationwide television to address a special joint session of Congress and to urge the passage of new legislation to assure black Americans the right to vote. Then, in a dramatic moment in that speech, the President from Texas invoked the song and the slogan of the civil rights movement. "And we shall overcome," he said slowly. Thunderous applause greeted the remark, and Congress responded to Johnson's appeal with a second landmark civil rights measure.

The Voting Rights Act of 1965, passed after the Senate once again imposed cloture to crush a filibuster, covered six Southern states, Alabama, Georgia, Louisiana, Mississippi, South Carolina, and Virginia as well as Alaska and parts of North Carolina, Arizona, and Idaho. Through an automatic "triggering" formula, the act suspended literacy tests in areas where less than half the voting-age population had registered for, or had actually voted in, the 1964 election. It gave the federal government power to appoint federal examiners to require enrollment of qualified voters in such areas. Even outside of such areas, the Attorney General could go into federal court to seek the appointment of examiners. The bill also provided penalties of up to five years in jail and a $5000 fine for intimidating voters or interfering with voting rights.

The effect of the Voting Rights Act was immediate. Within two years, black registration increased by more than 1,280,000 in the eleven states of the South. In Mississippi, black registration jumped from 6.7 percent of eligible voters to 59.8 percent.[68]

At the same time, however, in some Southern states, black registration

---

[68] United States Commission on Civil Rights, *Political Participation,* May 1968, pp. 171, 222.

The Struggle for Equal Rights

Increase of Black Voter Registration in the Seven Southern States Covered by the 1965 Voting Rights Act

Figure 5–4

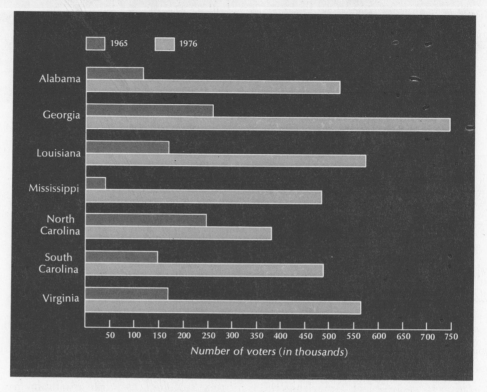

Source: Adapted from U.S. Bureau of the Census, *Current Population Reports,* Registration and Voting in November 1976—Jurisdictions Covered by the Voting Rights Act Amendments of 1965, Series P–23, No. 74, September 1978, pp. 3–11.

drives following passage of the Voting Rights Act also spurred new white registration. As a result, despite the percentage increase in black registration, in actual numbers, there were more new white voters in those states than new black voters.

In 1970 the Voting Rights Act (which would otherwise have expired that year) was extended to August 1975. At the same time, Congress acted to broaden its provisions. The "triggering" formula was amended to extend the law to areas of California, Oregon, four New England states, and parts of New York City. In addition, the use of literacy or "good character" tests was suspended in all states for five years. In 1975 Congress extended the act again, to August 1982, and broadened its basic provisions to protect language minorities—Spanish-speaking Americans, Indians, Asians, and Alaskan natives. The revised law required bilingual election materials for these voters and had the effect of extending the act to about a dozen more states. Literacy and character tests were permanently banned throughout the nation. (Other provisions to ease residence requirements for voters in presidential elections are discussed in Chapter 9.)

The Voting Rights Act encouraged blacks to run for office. In 1967, two years after passage of the act, approximately 1000 blacks sought party, state, and local offices in the South; nearly 250 were elected. However, the drive to expand black participation in the political process in the South received a setback in 1980 when the Supreme Court upheld the at-large system for electing city commissioners in Mobile, Alabama.[69] Black citizens in Mobile had challenged the system because no black had ever been elected to the commission, although the city is 35 percent black. If a system of electing commissioners from local wards were adopted, blacks argued, they would be able to elect some black candidates in areas where blacks predominated. The Court, however, held that the electoral system in Mobile was constitutional unless it could be shown that the *intent,* not only the result, was to exclude blacks.

Even as the major civil rights laws of the mid-1960s were taking effect, black protest in America entered a new phase. The great expectations aroused by the civil rights movement and legislative action by Congress had brought no visible change of status to the millions of black Americans in city slums. Frustration and poverty characterized the ghettos. Combined with summer heat and police incidents, the mixture proved volatile and tragic.

The Urban Riots

Los Angeles was sweltering in a heat wave on the night of August 11, 1965, when a highway patrolman stopped a young black driver for speeding and arrested him. A crowd gathered, more police arrived, and trouble flared. By the time the police had left, the residents of Watts, the city's black ghetto, were in an angry mood. Two days after the incident, arson, looting, and shooting broke out. The Watts riot had begun. Cries of "Burn, baby, burn!" filled the air. When it was all over, thirty-four persons were dead, hundreds had been injured, and $35 million in damages had been done.

The Watts explosion was the most dramatic event in a pattern of major violence that was to afflict dozens of American cities. Watts was followed by disorders in Chicago and Cleveland in 1966 and by even more destructive riots in Newark and Detroit in 1967. Outbreaks occurred in Washington and in more than one hundred other cities after the assassination of Martin Luther King in April 1968. A total of 13,600 federal troops were dispatched to Washington, where rioters had set fires only a few blocks from the White House. For twelve days, armed troops occupied the capital of the United States.

During the Detroit riot, President Johnson went on nationwide television to plead for calm and to announce the appointment of a National Advisory Commission on Civil Disorders. The commission reported in March 1968:

> Our nation is moving toward two societies, one black, one white—separate and unequal. . . . certain fundamental matters are clear. Of these the most fundamental is the racial attitude and behavior of white Americans toward black Americans. . . . Race prejudice has shaped our history decisively; it now threatens to affect our future. White racism is essentially responsible for the explosive mixture which has been accumulating in our cities since the end of World War II.[70]

To meet these problems, the commission recommended a massive national effort to eliminate racial barriers in employment, education, and housing,

"Race still divides us," said the Rev. Jesse Jackson . . . whose organization, PUSH, still confronts the issue with direct-action tactics. "Race still divides our churches, our communities, our schools, our jobs, our country."

—*Washington Post,* April 2, 1978.

[69] *City of Mobile, Alabama* v. *Bolden,* 446 U.S. 55 (1980).
[70] *Report of the National Advisory Commission on Civil Disorders* (New York: Bantam Books, 1968), pp. 1, 10.

A Florida National Guardsman during Miami riots, May 1980

and to create new jobs. The commission's findings were controversial—many Americans disagreed with the emphasis on white racism as the cause of the urban riots. Few could disagree, however, with the gravity of the problems underscored by the explosions in the cities.

During the 1970s there were noticeably fewer outbreaks of large-scale urban violence. But in May of 1980, a major racial disorder in Miami reminded Americans that the underlying problems remained. The rioting was touched off when a white jury acquitted four white police officers of murdering a black Miami man who had been beaten to death by police. For two nights, arson, looting, and sniper fire racked the black areas of downtown Miami. When it was over, 14 persons were dead, and more than 300 injured.

Black Power, Black Pride

During the late 1960s, advocates of direct, militant action had to a considerable extent drowned out the voices of more moderate black leaders. Black Power advocates and members of the militant Black Panthers often found it easier to capture the attention of the public and the press than did the moderates. And the assassination of Martin Luther King and other leaders committed to nonviolence weakened the position of the moderates.

Stokely Carmichael, a black leader who had popularized the phrase "Black Power," defined the term as "a call for black people in this country to unite, to recognize their heritage, to build a sense of community."[71] While there were various definitions of Black Power, a common theme was the need for black Americans to exercise political control of black communities, both in the urban ghettos and in rural areas of the South. Economically, the term was tied to the creation of independent, black-owned and black-operated businesses. Spiritually, it meant racial pride; it also gave rise to slogans such as "Black is Beautiful" and to the emphasis on "soul" and "soul brothers."

Black Panthers and local police were killed in a series of shootings in several cities. The most widely publicized case took place in 1969, when Chicago police raided an apartment before dawn, allegedly in a search for weapons, and shot to death Fred Hampton, chairman of the Illinois Black Panther party.[72]

[71] Stokely Carmichael and Charles V. Hamilton, *Black Power* (New York: Random House, 1967), p. 44.
[72] *New York Times,* May 23, 1970, p. 12.

Many Americans were dismayed by police excesses against Panthers, but deeply disturbed as well by the existence of armed militant groups and the use of violence to gain political objectives. A task force of the National Commission on the Causes and Prevention of Violence concluded that some black Americans had turned to violent action because peaceful efforts had failed to bring social change.[73]

Some of the black militants of the 1960s sought to draw a parallel between the successful revolt of blacks in Africa and of Asians against colonial powers and the struggle of American blacks. Some alienated blacks rejected integration or advocated an alliance of black Americans with "third world" liberation movements in other parts of the globe.

Although at the end of the sixties some black leaders were urging a new form of segregation or separation, most black Americans still preferred to seek equality as part of the larger United States society. A Gallup poll of black Americans showed that 74 percent of the blacks surveyed would prefer to live in an integrated neighborhood.[74]

By the early 1970s the voices of most of the black militants had become relatively quiet. The change was symbolized by Bobby Seale, the Black Panther leader. In 1973 Seale had put aside his black leather jacket and his black beret, substituted a shirt and tie and a business suit, and was running for mayor of Oakland. He lost, but the election campaign dramatized the effort of the Black Panthers in Oakland to achieve a new image, one that stressed health programs and community service rather than violence.

In sum, although militants had for a time commanded an audience, the majority of black Americans sought full social and economic equality and dignity *within* the American system rather than apart from it. Along with many white Americans, they still believed in Martin Luther King's dream.

Affirmative Action: The Supreme Court Rules

The civil rights movement and the legislation enacted in the sixties did not settle a larger constitutional question: Were government and private "affirmative action" programs—designed to favor minorities and remedy past discrimination—constitutional?

John F. Kennedy was the first President to call for affirmative action by the government in an executive order issued in 1961. The order prohibited discrimination by contractors who received federal money and instructed them to hire and promote members of minority groups.

The Civil Rights Act of 1964 barred discrimination by universities or others who received federal assistance. The act also outlawed discrimination by employers or unions. Many universities, employers, and unions went a step further and established affirmative action programs that gave *preference* in admissions or jobs to minorities. The programs were based on the theory that mem-

[73] Jerome H. Skolnick, *The Politics of Protest,* Staff Report to the National Commission on the Causes and Prevention of Violence (Washington, D.C.: U.S. Government Printing Office, 1969), p. 127.
[74] *Newsweek,* June 30, 1969, p. 20. Percentage of undecided omitted.

bers of these groups were disadvantaged as a result of past discrimination. Merely guaranteeing minorities equal opportunity, it was argued, would not solve the problem, because members of such groups would often be at a disadvantage when competing with whites who had not suffered discrimination. Advocates of affirmative action, therefore, pressed for positive steps to aid minorities in order to compensate for the past and bring about not only equality of opportunity but equality of results.

Bakke and Weber: The Battle Is Joined

Opponents of affirmative action programs argued that they were a form of "reverse discrimination" against whites. Since the Fourteenth Amendment to the Constitution extended equal protection of the laws to everyone, and the 1964 Civil Rights Act outlawed any form of discrimination, were programs unconstitutional and illegal if they favored a black or a Chicano over a white person?

As with many constitutional questions, these arguments and counterarguments ebbed and flowed and eventually focused on the case of one person — a white engineer who worked for the National Aeronautics and Space Administration named Allan Paul Bakke. Bakke, born in 1940, graduated from college in 1963 with an engineering degree and a 3.51 grade average. He joined the Marines, served in Vietnam, and later went to work on the moon program for NASA. But what he wanted most was to be a doctor. Nights and weekends, he was a hospital volunteer.

In 1973 and 1974 Bakke applied to the medical school of the University of California at Davis. He did not get in. Davis had a special admissions program which reserved 16 out of 100 places in the medical school each year for minorities. In both years, minority students were admitted with much lower scores than Bakke's. Bakke sued. He contended that he had been excluded on the basis of his race in violation of the Constitution and the 1964 act.

The California Supreme Court upheld Bakke and ordered him admitted to medical school. The University of California appealed. In an historic ruling in June 1978, the United States Supreme Court, by a vote of 5–4, ordered Bakke admitted to the medical school at Davis. At the same time, the Court upheld the right of universities to give special preference to blacks and other minorities as long as they do not use rigid racial "quotas" such as the one at Davis.

The majority based its decision not on the 1964 law, but on the Fourteenth Amendment's guarantee of equal protection of the laws. Associate Justice Lewis F. Powell, Jr., who provided the key, swing vote in the case, delivered the majority opinion: "Preferring members of any one group for no reason other than race or ethnic origin is discrimination for its own sake. This the Constitution forbids."

At the same time, Powell said that flexible admission programs, such as Harvard's, that "take race into account," but do not set a "fixed number of places" for minorities, were constitutional.[75]

In September, Bakke, by now thirty-eight, married, and the father of two young children, entered the medical school at Davis, California. The Supreme Court had interpreted the Constitution to protect the rights of an individual. Allan Bakke had won his case — but so had America's minorities, who could continue to be given some preference by colleges and universities under the standard defined by the Supreme Court.

Allan Paul Bakke

[75] *Regents of the University of California* v. *Allan Bakke,* 438 U.S. 265 (1978).

The *Bakke* decision left unsettled the question of affirmative action in employment. But a year later, the Supreme Court ruled in the case of Brian Weber, a blue-collar worker in a small town in Louisiana, who suddenly found himself in the vortex of a major constitutional test. Weber, a thirty-two-year-old white man, was employed as a lab technician for the Kaiser Aluminum and Chemical Corporation in Gramercy, Louisiana. He was also an officer of his local union and had helped to establish on-the-job training programs for workers at the plant. Workers selected for such training in a skilled craft could expect to earn as much as $15,000 a year or more.

Weber applied and was rejected for the training program, which set aside half the jobs for black workers. Several of the blacks selected had less seniority than Weber, who took his case to court and lost. The Supreme Court ruled 5–2 that the history of the 1964 Civil Rights Act showed that it was designed to help minorities and not to prohibit private affirmative action programs. The Court added: "It would be ironic indeed if a law triggered by a Nation's concern over centuries of racial injustice and intended to improve the lot of those who had been excluded from the American dream for so long . . . constituted the first legislative prohibition of all voluntary, private . . . efforts to abolish traditional patterns of racial segregation."[76] Then in 1980 the Supreme Court ruled that Congress could constitutionally require that 10 percent of federal public works contracts be awarded to minority-owned business firms in order to remedy past discrimination.[77]

Brian Weber

Equal Rights: A Balance Sheet for the 1980s

By 1981 there were 18 black members of the House of Representatives, and more than 4600 black elected officials throughout the nation. A black American served in the cabinet, and another sat on the Supreme Court. By that time, black mayors had been elected in 191 cities, including Los Angeles, Detroit, Atlanta, Newark, and Washington, D.C.[78] The American political system, in the civil rights legislation passed in the mid-1960s, had demonstrated its ability to respond to peaceful pressures for change. Black voters in the South, who began to come to the polls in increasing numbers, were better protected by federal law. Public accommodations were finally, by federal law, open to all Americans. And the nation had become aware that 26 million black Americans would no longer wait.

But these gains reflected only part of the picture. The ghettos of the nation still existed. Only 1 percent of all elected officials were black. In jobs, housing, education, and income, the black man or woman still sat, figuratively, in the back of the bus. A Census Bureau survey reported that median family income for blacks was $10,880 in 1978 compared to $18,370 for whites. Those figures alone told much of the story. Moreover, 32.6 percent of black Americans were

---

[76] *United Steelworkers of America* v. *Weber*, 443 U.S. 193 (1979).
[77] *Fullilove* v. *Klutznick*, 100 S. Ct. 2758 (1980).
[78] *National Roster of Black Elected Officials*, Vol. 9 (Washington, D.C.: Joint Center for Political Studies, 1979), pp. viii–xix.

below the poverty line compared to 8.7 percent of whites.[79] The unemployment rate for blacks was 12.6 percent in 1980 compared to 6.2 percent for whites. For black teenagers, traditionally a group acutely hit by unemployment, the rate was much higher — 37 percent in mid-1980, compared to 17 percent for whites of the same age.[80]

Still there were some economic gains registered by blacks by the 1970s. In 1965 only 25 percent of black families had incomes of $10,000 or more; the figure had risen to 54 percent in 1978. During the same period the percentage of white families with such incomes had increased at a slower rate from 59 to 79 percent. Despite these gains, the median income of black families in 1978 was only 59 percent of the median income for white families.[81] And in 1976 blacks composed less than 3 percent of the nation's physicians, lawyers, dentists, and engineers.[82] Because many blacks continued to be economically disadvantaged, there was increasing interest among traditional civil rights groups in economic issues.

Although racial prejudice existed among many groups in American society, it was often more strongly expressed among low-income whites, for it was this group that felt most immediately threatened by blacks, economically and socially. Belatedly, in the 1970s, more attention began to be focused both in and out of government on the problems of low-income whites and blue-collar workers.

For example, a study by a White House panel found that the purchasing power of blue-collar workers had remained almost static for five years. "These men are on a treadmill," the report said. It called blue-collar workers "the forgotten people." They live close to high-crime areas — but cannot afford to flee, the report said. They see welfare programs at close hand, yet their wages "are only a notch above the liberal states' welfare payments." To remedy these conditions, the study called for more job training programs, more adult education, and tax subsidies of day-care centers for children of working mothers.[83]

Although inequalities remained between whites and blacks, there were some signs of change. For example, more blacks had migrated to the suburbs. Between 1970 and 1978, the black suburban population grew by 1.3 million, a gain of 39 percent. Only 4.8 million blacks lived in suburbia, however, or about 20 percent of the total black population. By contrast, approximately 77 million whites, or 42 percent of all whites, lived in the suburbs. More than half of all blacks, 55 percent, lived in the central cities.[84]

Despite political and economic gains by blacks, serious racial divisions per-

[79] U.S. Bureau of the Census, *Current Population Reports*, Money Income in 1978 of Households in the United States, Series P-60, No. 121, February 1980, p. 2; and U.S. Bureau of the Census, *Current Population Reports*, Money Income and Poverty Status of Families and Persons in the United States: 1978, p. 4.

[80] U.S. Department of Labor press release, May 1980; U.S. Bureau of the Census, *Current Population Reports*, The Social and Economic Status of the Black Population in the United States: An Historical View, 1790–1978, Series P-23, No. 80, p. 209; and data provided by U.S. Bureau of Labor Statistics for August 1980.

[81] U.S. Bureau of the Census, *Current Population Reports*, Money Income and Poverty Status of Families and Persons in the United States: 1978 (Advance Report), p. 1.

[82] *New York Times*, May 31, 1976, p. 20.

[83] As cited in the *New York Times*, June 30, 1970, pp. 1, 20.

[84] Bureau of the Census, *Current Population Reports*, Population Profile of the United States: 1978, Series P-20, No. 336, April 1979, p. 34; Bureau of the Census, *Current Population Reports*, The Social and Economic Status of the Black Population in the United States: An Historical View, 1790–1978, p. 171.

sisted, and substantial numbers of blacks, Hispanics, Indians, and other minorities remained outside the mainstream of American affluence. More than a century after the Civil War, many Americans were still struggling for equality and justice. In 1963, in an address to the nation about civil rights for blacks, President Kennedy declared: "This is not a sectional issue. . . . We are confronted primarily with a moral issue. It is as old as the scriptures and is as clear as the American Constitution." America, he said, "will not be fully free until all its citizens are free."[85]

How America responded to this moral issue might well decide its future. The continued struggle for equality for all Americans remained a great domestic challenge, testing the nation's political system and the minds and hearts of the American people.

[85] "Radio and Television Report to the American People on Civil Rights," June 11, 1963, *Public Papers of the Presidents of the United States, John F. Kennedy 1963* (Washington, D.C.: U.S. Government Printing Office, 1964), p. 469.

Perspective

Despite the historic civil rights laws passed by Congress in the 1960s and despite landmark decisions of the Supreme Court, many minority groups in America still do not enjoy full social and economic equality. Almost one out of three blacks in the United States is poor, according to federal statistics, as opposed to one out of eleven whites.

American Indians are among the most disadvantaged of all minorities. Unemployment among Indians is high, life expectancy low. Many live in shacks, adobe huts, and abandoned automobiles.

Members of the nation's Hispanic community—Mexican Americans, Puerto Ricans, Cubans, and persons of Latin American or other Spanish origin—are the fastest-growing segment of the population. The Census Bureau estimated there were 14.6 million Hispanics in the United States in 1980, but if an estimated 7.4 million illegal aliens are included, the total is much higher. Hispanics comprise another group that has been denied full equality in American society.

The Women's Liberation movement that emerged in the 1970s reflected the awareness that women, although a majority of the population, were another group subject to discrimination. Bias based on sex is built into many public and private institutions. Women's salaries are often much lower than those of men performing the same work. The Equal Rights Amendment, designed primarily to eliminate discrimination against women, was approved by both houses of Congress in 1972. Although Congress later extended the deadline for ratification, in 1980 the amendment was still three states short of the needed thirty-eight. The Supreme Court has provided evidence of shifting social attitudes in America, and the strength of the women's movement. In 1973 the Court ruled that no state may interfere with a woman's right to have an abortion during the first three months of pregnancy.

Through a combination of court decisions, legislative action, and changing public perceptions, homosexuals have gained greater protection for their rights. By 1980, thirty-seven communities had passed local laws or taken executive action to protect gay rights in employment, housing, and other areas. The laws concerning gays are not uniform, however. Many other cities lack or have repealed laws protecting homosexuals. In 1977 national attention focused on Miami, where residents voted 2 to 1 to repeal a law protecting the rights of gay persons. In the state of Washington, a teacher who had not engaged in open homosexual conduct was fired when his homosexuality became known; the U.S. Supreme Court let the decision stand.

Unlike most other immigrants who came to these shores seeking freedom, blacks came as slaves. In the *Dred Scott* decision (1857), the Supreme Court ruled that blacks were not citizens under the Constitution. The decision was later reversed by the Fourteenth Amendment, which in 1868 made citizens of the freed slaves.

The Supreme Court ruled in *Plessy* v. *Ferguson*

The Struggle for Equal Rights

(1896) that a state law requiring equal but separate accommodations for white and black railroad passengers did not violate the Fourteenth Amendment. This doctrine of "separate but equal" remained the law of the land until 1954, when Chief Justice Earl Warren delivered the unanimous decision of the Supreme Court in the historic school desegregation case of *Brown* v. *Board of Education of Topeka, Kansas*. The justices ruled that school segregation violated the Fourteenth Amendment's requirement of equal protection of the law for individuals. Yet, more than twenty-five years later, public school segregation still exists in many cities of the North and South. School segregation in the North often resulted from patterns of residential segregation. In some instances, the Court has approved busing of students to achieve desegregation.

Dr. Martin Luther King, Jr., a black minister, led the civil rights movement that began in the 1950s. Largely in response to that movement, several important civil rights bills were enacted by Congress in the mid-1960s. The Civil Rights Act of 1964 prohibited racial or religious discrimination in public accommodations. The Voting Rights Act of 1965 suspended literacy tests in Southern counties in which blacks were being denied the right to vote. The 1965 law was later amended to apply to other minorities as well, and to states in the North and West. A 1968 law sought to prevent discrimination in housing and to protect persons exercising their civil rights.

In the wake of the civil rights movement, affirmative action programs were established to give preference in university admissions or jobs to minorities. The programs were based on the theory that members of these groups were entitled to special preference because they were disadvantaged as a result of past discrimination. Opponents of affirmative action argued that such programs were a form of reverse discrimination against whites. These arguments eventually focused on the case of Allan Bakke. In 1973 and 1974 Bakke applied to medical school at the University of California at Davis. He did not get in. But in both years, minority students were admitted with much lower scores than Bakke's.

Bakke sued and the case was finally decided by the Supreme Court in 1978. The Court ordered Bakke admitted to medical school, but upheld the right of universities to give preference to minorities as long as they do not use rigid "quotas," such as the one at the University of California at Davis. A year later, in the *Weber* case (1979), the Supreme Court upheld affirmative action in employment. And in 1980 the Court ruled that Congress could require that 10 percent of federal public works contracts be granted to minority businesses.

By 1981, 18 members of the House of Representatives, one cabinet member, and a Supreme Court Justice were black. As of 1978, the number of black families with incomes of $10,000 or more had risen to 54 percent. But the median income of black families was only 59 percent of that of white families. Moreover, in 1978 only 1 percent of all elected officials were black and 32.6 percent of black Americans were below the poverty level.

More than a century after the Civil War, many black and Hispanic Americans and members of other minority groups are still struggling for equality and justice.

Suggested Reading

Baldwin, James. *The Fire Next Time** (Dial Press, 1963). An examination of the status of blacks in America by a leading black writer. Baldwin argues for "total liberation" of blacks and maintains that blacks are the key to America's future.

Brown, Dee. *Bury My Heart at Wounded Knee** (Holt, Rinehart & Winston, 1971). A powerful, detailed, and highly readable account of how American Indians were driven from their villages and hunting grounds, often brutally, by white Americans as the frontier pushed westward. The book, which became a national best seller, contains excellent descriptions of major Indian chiefs and tribal leaders.

Carmichael, Stokely, and Hamilton, Charles V. *Black Power** (Random House, 1967). The political definition of Black Power. Carmichael, the black leader who popularized the term, and Hamilton, a political scientist, urged black Americans to seek community control and use other such political tools.

Ellison, Ralph. *The Invisible Man** (Random House, 1952). In this novel a black writer describes the identity problem of blacks in a white society. The "invisible man" cannot be seen, Ellison argued, because whites refuse to acknowledge his existence.

Franklin, John Hope. *From Slavery to Freedom,* 5th edition* (Knopf, 1978). A classic study of black history in America written by a distinguished black historian.

Freeman, Jo. *The Politics of Women's Liberation** (McKay,

1975). A lively analysis of the origins and development of the women's movement and its impact on public policy.

Garcia, F. Chris, and de la Garza, Rudolph O. *The Chicano Political Experience** (Duxbury Press, 1977). A comprehensive description of the Chicano culture and political movement. The authors argue that Mexican Americans have the potential to exert a much greater influence on the political process.

Jordan, Winthrop D. *White over Black: American Attitudes toward the Negro, 1550–1812** (University of North Carolina Press, 1968). A detailed examination of the attitudes of white people toward blacks during the first two centuries of slavery in North America. The book draws extensively on newspaper accounts, speeches, pamphlets, letters, and court records of the day.

Levitan, Sar A.; Johnston, William B.; and Taggart, Robert. *Still a Dream** (Harvard University Press, 1975). A comprehensive review of the changing social and economic status of black Americans, with emphasis on employment, education, family patterns, housing, and income.

Levitan, Sar A.; Johnston, William B.; and Taggart, Robert. *Minorities in the United States* (Public Affairs Press, 1976). An examination of the changes in the economic, political, and social status of minorities in the United States. Includes both government and privately published statistics on blacks, Mexican Americans, Puerto Ricans, and American Indians.

Meier, August, and Rudwick, Elliott M. *From Plantation to Ghetto*, 3rd edition* (Hill and Wang, 1976). A history of blacks in America with emphasis on black protest movements, particularly in the twentieth century. Includes a discussion of the African heritage of American blacks.

Myrdal, Gunnar. *An American Dilemma: The Negro Problem and Modern Democracy** (Harper and Row, 1962). (Originally published in 1944.) A classic study of race relations in the United States until the time of the Second World War. Traces the history of blacks in America and stresses the gap between the American creed of equality for all and the actual treatment black Americans have received. This book, by an eminent Swedish sociologist, has had a major influence on American thought about race relations.

Whitehurst, Carol A. *Women in America: The Oppressed Majority* (Goodyear, 1977). A comprehensive analysis of the role of women in American society. Explores the status of women in the world of work, education, politics, and the home.

Woodward, C. Vann. *The Strange Career of Jim Crow*, 3rd revised edition* (Oxford University Press, 1974). A classic study of the establishment and consequences of segregation laws in the South after the Civil War.

* Available in paperback edition

Part Two

POLITICS U.S.A.

PUBLIC OPINION AND INTEREST GROUPS

When Marie Antoinette, according to legend, responded to the bread shortage in France by remarking, "Let them eat cake," she was showing an unwise disregard for public opinion. In due course, her head was cut off on the guillotine.

After Lyndon Baines Johnson sent half a million men to fight in Vietnam, he discovered that public opinion had turned against him. In due course, he announced that he would not run again and retired to his ranch in Texas.

When his successor, Richard Nixon, became entangled in the Watergate scandal, his popularity dropped almost 40 points, the House Judiciary Committee voted to impeach him, and he was forced to resign.

When Jimmy Carter's Presidency foundered on the twin reefs of continued inflation and the seizure of the American hostages in Iran, the voters rejected him and put Ronald Reagan in the White House. Carter's popularity had dropped from 61 percent in December 1979 to 37 percent shortly before the 1980 election.[1]

All governments are based, to some extent, on public opinion. Even dictators must pay some attention to public opinion, if only in order to repress it.

---

[1] *The Gallup Opinion Index,* December 1979, Report No. 173, p. 3; and 1980 data provided by the Gallup poll.

In a democracy, public opinion is often described as a controlling force. "Public opinion stands out, in the United States," James Bryce wrote, "as the great source of power, the master of servants who tremble before it."[2]

But in fact, the role of public opinion in a democracy is extremely difficult to define. Who is the public? What is public opinion? Does a person's opinion matter? Do political candidates and leaders manipulate public opinion? Should government leaders try to follow public opinion or their own judgment? What influence should, or does, public opinion have on government? On policymaking? Who governs? These are questions that continue to divide philosophers, politicians, pollsters, and political scientists.

Public Opinion

Although people often speak about opinions held by "the public," the phrase is not very useful because there are few questions on which every citizen has an opinion. The concept of "special publics" was developed by political scientists "to describe those segments of the public with views about particular issues."[3] There are, in short, many publics.

What is opinion and when does it become public opinion? People have opinions on many subjects—music, fashions, and movies, for example. Sometimes, such views are loosely referred to as "public opinion." In a narrower context, however, only opinions about public matters constitute public opinion. Thus, public opinion may be defined as *the expression of attitudes about government and politics.*

Public opinion would mean little, however, if it had no effect. Many political scientists, therefore, talk about public opinion as a process of interaction between the people and the government. V. O. Key, Jr., for example, defined public opinion as "those opinions held by private persons which governments find it prudent to heed."[4] Floyd Allport conceived of public opinion in terms of enough people expressing themselves so strongly for or against something that

[2] James Bryce, *The American Commonwealth,* Vol. I (New York: Putnam, Capricorn Books, 1959), p. 296.
[3] V. O. Key, Jr., *Public Opinion and American Democracy* (New York: Knopf, 1961), p. 10.
[4] *Ibid.,* p. 14.

their views are likely to affect government action.[5] And W. Lance Bennett has suggested that public opinion is *situational,* because the people who hold and express opinions are constantly changing, as do the issues and conditions to which the public responds.[6] In the language of a political system (discussed in Chapter 1), public opinion can be thought of as one of the inputs of the system that may affect the outputs, or binding decisions, of the government.

Private opinions become public — provided they are expressed — when they relate to government and politics. Not all privately held opinions about government and politics are expressed publicly, however; because of pressures for conformity, a person may sometimes find it more prudent to keep his or her views private.[7] The phrase *political opinion* is sometimes used to refer to opinions on political issues — a choice among candidates or parties, for example.

How Public Opinion Is Formed

Walter Lippmann, in his classic study of public opinion, observed that each individual, in viewing distant events, tends to form a "picture inside his head of the world beyond his reach."[8] And, Lippmann noted, the mental snapshots do not always correspond with reality. How do individuals form their opinions about government and politics? As might be expected, the answer is as varied as the range of opinions people hold. The views of a sixty-year-old white Protestant dairy farmer in Wisconsin may vary sharply from those of a young, Hispanic college student in East Los Angeles. Why may their opinions differ? A person's political background, and such factors as the influence of family and schools, certainly play a part. So do such variables as age, social class, income, religion, sex, ethnic background, geography, group membership, and political party preference.

Political Socialization: The Family and the Schools. Over the years, a person acquires a set of political attitudes and forms opinions about social issues. In other words, a person undergoes *political socialization.*

The family plays a significant role in this process. In the view of Robert E. Lane, "The family incubates political man."[9] And the "crucial period" of a child's political, social, and psychological development is between the ages of nine and thirteen.[10]

Through watching television programs, and in various other ways, children acquire rudimentary ideas about politics at an early age. One study demonstrated that 63 percent of fourth-graders identified with a political party. Almost every one of the children interviewed thought of party affiliation as a family characteristic: "All I know is *we're* not Republicans."[11] Children may acquire not only party preferences by listening to their parents but "an orientation toward politics" and a set of "basic values and outlooks, which in turn may affect the individual's views on political issues long after he has left the family fold."[12]

[5] Floyd H. Allport, "Toward a Science of Public Opinion," *Public Opinion Quarterly,* Vol. 1, January 1937, p. 23.

[6] W. Lance Bennett, *Public Opinion in American Politics* (New York: Harcourt Brace Jovanovich, 1980), pp. 12–13.

[7] Allport, "Toward a Science of Public Opinion," p. 15.

[8] Walter Lippmann, *Public Opinion* (New York: Free Press, 1965), pp. 18–19. Originally published in 1922.

[9] Robert E. Lane, *Political Life* (New York: Free Press, 1959), p. 204.

[10] Fred I. Greenstein, *Children and Politics* (New Haven: Yale University Press, 1965), p. 1.

[11] *Ibid.,* pp. 71–73.

[12] Key, *Public Opinion and American Democracy,* pp. 301, 305.

How then to explain the students who protested the Vietnam war on college campuses in the 1970s, even though in some cases their parents may have supported the war? The answer is that children, obviously, do not always follow the political leanings of their parents and may even come to hold completely opposite views.

Some political scientists have questioned the long-established emphasis on the family as the primary political influence on children. After studying a national sample of high school seniors, M. Kent Jennings and Richard Niemi concluded that the political "similarity between students and their parents was often modest."[13] By late adolescence, in other words, many students had begun to hold political views that differed from those of their parents. The family, nevertheless, often remains an important influence on how opinions are formed.

Schools also have a part in the political socialization of children. Every country indoctrinates its schoolchildren with the basic values of its political system. American children salute the flag in school, sing patriotic songs, learn about George Washington's cherry tree (an invention of a literary charlatan named Parson Weems), and acquire some understanding of democracy and majority rule. In high school, they are required to take "civics" courses.

But the extent of the influence of schools on opinion formation has also been questioned. The same study that found a divergence in views between parents and older children also reported that in high school, "Students gravitated toward the opinions of their friends more so than toward those of their social studies teachers."[14]

The political socialization of students continues in college, and not only in the political science courses they may take. They also learn from the political environment on the campus. The high degree of political involvement, conflict, and controversy that characterized many American campuses in the 1960s and early 1970s, during the war in Vietnam, obviously had some influence on the political opinions of college students, whether or not they participated personally in the protest demonstrations.

While the gradual process of political socialization does have some general effect on the opinions people hold, a number of sociological and psychological factors may also have an influence on public opinion. Whether a person is young or old, rich or poor, farmer or city dweller, Westerner or Southerner may affect the opinions he or she holds. This can easily be measured by taking almost any controversial public issue and analyzing the findings of public opinion polls. For example, in February 1980, the Gallup poll asked people whether they favored or opposed resuming the military draft. Nationally, 59 percent of those sampled said yes, 36 percent were opposed, and 5 percent had no opinion. But the poll data also showed that more men (66 percent) than women (53 percent) favored a draft. And the poll disclosed that the draft was least popular among college-educated respondents, in the East, among persons 18–24, among political independents, and in urban areas. On any issue—from legalizing pot to school busing—opinions often vary with such factors. Which factors are more important than others varies with the individual, and their relative significance is difficult to measure with precision. But a number can be identified.

Social Class.   Differences in social class, occupation, and income do appear

[13] M. Kent Jennings and Richard G. Niemi, *The Political Character of Adolescence* (Princeton, N.J.: Princeton University Press, 1974), p. 319.
[14] *Ibid.,* p. 328.

to affect people's opinions on public matters. For example, one study indicates that people who identify with the working class are more likely to favor federal social welfare programs than are people who identify with the middle class.[15] Another survey found that community leaders are more tolerant of Communists, atheists, and nonconformists than are people of lower social and economic status.[16]

One study of political learning suggests that children brought up in homes of lower economic status are taught to accept authority more readily than children reared in upper-class homes. This study found that upper-class children are therefore more likely to criticize political authority, that they receive more political information from their parents, and that they are more likely to become politically active.[17]

Religion, Sex, and Ethnic Factors. Religion, sex, race, and ethnic background also may influence the opinions that people hold. To influence and attract voters from ethnic groups, political parties in New York and other large cities customarily run a "balanced ticket" — one that includes an Irish candidate, an Italian candidate, and a Jewish candidate. In the primary election for mayor of New York City in 1969, the victorious Democratic candidate, Mario Procaccino, repeatedly emphasized that he was once an immigrant boy from Bisacca, Italy. In a sentence that reached artistic perfection in its wide-ranging ethnic appeal, he told the crowds: "I couldn't get a job on Wall Street because my name was Procaccino and I was a Catholic, and my father was a shoemaker right in the heart of black Harlem."

Although Americans like to think that they form their opinions without reference to race, creed, sex, or color, studies of their political behavior have demonstrated that this has not been the case in years past. (See Table 6–1.) For example, no Catholic was elected President until 1960. But the poll data suggest that today Americans are much more willing to accept women or members of minority groups as political leaders.

A voter's religious or ethnic background may affect party preference or political leanings. In one survey, 65 percent of the Jews questioned and 63 percent of the Roman Catholics identified themselves as Democrats, compared to 45 percent of the Protestants.[18] Jewish and black voters questioned were more inclined to support government social welfare programs than were other groups.[19]

Religious affiliation may also affect public opinion on *specific* issues — Quakers may favor disarmament; Jews may support aid to Israel; and Catholics may oppose the use of federal funds for abortions for the poor. Similarly, ethnic identification may help to shape public opinion on certain issues — Americans of Italian descent may be offended by the depiction of fictional gangsters with Italian names on publicly licensed television stations; black Americans may favor stronger legislation aimed at preventing housing discrimination.

Geographic Factors. People's opinions are sometimes related to where

[15] Lloyd A. Free and Hadley Cantril, *The Political Beliefs of Americans* (New Brunswick, N.J.: Rutgers University Press, 1967), p. 216. See also extensive data of the Survey Research Center, University of Michigan, 1956, quoted in Key, *Public Opinion and American Democracy,* Chapter 6.

[16] Samuel A. Stouffer, *Communism, Conformity, and Civil Liberties* (Gloucester, Mass.: Peter Smith, 1963).

[17] Greenstein, *Children and Politics,* pp. 155–56.

[18] Free and Cantril, *The Political Beliefs of Americans,* p. 147.

[19] *Ibid.,* p. 148.

How Race, Religion, and Sex Influence Voter Attitudes

Table 6–1

Nationwide surveys taken by the Gallup poll have shown that voter prejudice against blacks, Jews, Catholics, and women in politics has declined dramatically in recent years.

Beginning in 1958, the Gallup poll asked voters whether they would vote for a black for President. Following are the answers received in selected years:

	Yes	No	No Opinion
1958	38%	53%	9%
1965	59%	34%	7%
1969	67%	23%	10%
1971	70%	23%	7%
1978	77%	18%	5%

Voters were also asked whether they would vote for a Jew for President. Following are the answers received in selected years:

	Yes	No	No Opinion
1937	46%	46%	8%
1958	62%	28%	10%
1969	86%	8%	6%
1978	82%	12%	6%

Voters were also asked whether they would vote for a Catholic for President. Following are the answers received in selected years:

	Yes	No	No Opinion
1937	64%	28%	8%
1958	68%	25%	7%
1969	88%	8%	4%
1978	91%	4%	5%

Voters were also asked whether they would vote for a woman for President. Following are the answers received in selected years:

	Yes	No	No Opinion
1937	34%	66%	—
1958	52%	43%	5%
1971	66%	29%	5%
1976	73%	23%	4%
1978	76%	19%	5%

Source: Adapted from *The Gallup Poll: Public Opinion 1935–1971*, Vols. I–III (New York: Random House, 1972), and *The Gallup Opinion Index*, March 1976, p. 20, and November 1978, p. 26.

they live. Democrats have traditionally been more numerous in the South and the big cities of the North; Republicans have been stronger in the Midwest and rural areas. Yet sectional and geographic differences among Americans are often exaggerated; on some broad questions of foreign policy, for example, sectional variations are likely to be minimal. And, on many issues, differences in outlook between the cities and suburbs have replaced the old sectional divisions. Whether people come from an urban or rural background may be more significant today than their geographic roots.

Group Influence. Although the shape of a person's opinions on public questions is initially influenced by the family, in later life other groups, friends,

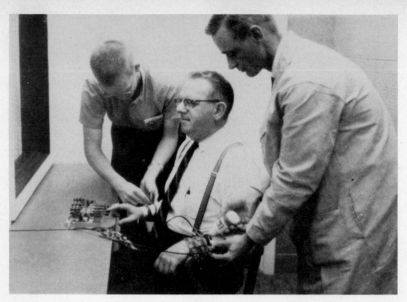

The Milgram experiment: preparing a "victim" for "electric shocks"

associates, and peers also influence individual views. In numerous experiments psychologists have discovered that people tend to "go along" with the decision of a group even when it contradicts accepted standards of morality and behavior. In a classic and controversial experiment at Yale University, Stanley Milgram placed subjects in groups of four, three of whom were secretly Milgram's assistants. The one unwitting subject was told to administer powerful electric shocks to the person serving as the "learner" in the experiment whenever the "learner" made an error in performing a laboratory task. In fact, no electricity was being administered, but the subject did not know that, and the "learner" shouted, moaned and screamed as the supposed voltage became higher. The results were surprising; egged on by their colleagues, 85 percent of the subjects administered shocks beyond 120 volts, and 17.5 percent went all the way to the maximum, a shock of 450 volts.[20]

On occasion group influence may even prevent the expression of opinion. Almost everyone has been in a situation at one time or another where he or she hesitates to express a political opinion because those listening might disagree or even be hostile. The author Mark Twain said he exposed to the world "only my trimmed and perfumed and carefully barbered public opinions and conceal carefully, cautiously, wisely, my private ones."[21] An individual who expresses an opinion is vulnerable, because "social groups can punish him for failing to toe the line."[22] If a view seems too risky to express, an individual may keep it private. But if public opinion changes, people may voice previously hidden feelings.[23]

[20] Stanley Milgram, "Group Pressure and Action Against a Person," *Journal of Abnormal and Social Psychology*, Vol. 69 (1964), pp. 137–43. In a somewhat similar experiment, Solomon Asch, a psychologist at Swarthmore College, placed subjects among groups of college students whose members, unknown to the subjects, deliberately responded incorrectly when they were asked to match up black lines of varying lengths on white cards. Influenced by the group's false judgments, the subjects gave incorrect answers 37 percent of the time. S. E. Asch, *Psychology Monograph*, Vol. 70, No. 416 (1956).

[21] Mark Twain, *The Autobiography of Mark Twain*, Charles Neider, ed. (New York: Harper and Row, 1959), p. 386.

[22] Elisabeth Noelle-Neumann, "The Spiral of Silence: A Theory of Public Opinion," *Journal of Communication*, Vol 24 (Spring 1974), p. 43.

[23] *Ibid.*, p. 45.

Various types of groups may influence people. A group whose views serve as guidelines to an individual's opinion is known as a *reference group*. There are two types of reference groups. Groups that people come into face-to-face contact with in everyday life—friends, office associates, and a local social club—are known as *primary groups,* since their influence is direct. *Secondary groups,* as the term implies, may be more remote. These are organizations or groups of people such as labor unions, or fraternal, professional, or religious groups.

Party Identification. In any campaign, voters are influenced by a candidate's personality and appearance, and by the nature of the issues that arise. But how they vote and what they think about public issues are also closely linked to their political party affiliation. Political scientists distinguish, therefore, among *candidate* orientation, *issue* orientation, and *party* identification.[24]

There is evidence that party ties are becoming somewhat less important; the number of Americans who consider themselves political independents has increased in recent years. Nevertheless, about two-thirds of all adult Americans identify with one of the two major parties. What is more, many voters maintain the same party allegiance for long periods of time. As we have noted, children often identify with their parents' political party by the time they have reached the fourth grade. Although children may later come to hold views very different from those of their parents, party loyalty tends to be passed on from one generation to the next. These factors will be discussed in more detail in the next three chapters.

Public opinion has identifiable *qualities.* Like pictures, public opinions may be sharp or fuzzy, general or detailed—and they may fade. In analyzing the qualities of opinions, political scientists speak of *direction, intensity,* and *stability.*

There was a time when political scientists would describe people as being "for" or "against" something. But after the Second World War, when public opinion polling evolved into a more exact science, pollsters and analysts discovered that simple "yes" or "no" answers sometimes masked wide gradations in

The Qualities of Public Opinion

[24] Angus Campbell, Philip E. Converse, Warren E. Miller, and Donald E. Stokes, Survey Research Center, University of Michigan, *The American Voter* (New York: Wiley, 1960).

"Grayson is a liberal in social matters, a conservative in economic matters, and a homicidal psychopath in political matters."

Drawing by Lorenz
© 1974 The New Yorker Magazine, Inc.

opinion on a given subject. In other words, it is possible to measure opinions in *direction* along a scale.[25] Thus, people speak of liberals and radicals as being to "the left," and conservatives to "the right," with moderates in "the center." If radical political opinions are thought of as being at one end of a line and conservative at the other end, the opinion of one individual may be located at a given point along the line. One person may favor government control of all medical programs; another may prefer federal health programs that are limited to the aged and needy; and a third person may favor wholly private health care.

Public opinion varies in *intensity* as well as direction. A person may have mild opinions or more deeply felt views. An automobile owner may be only mildly in sympathy with attempts to reduce gasoline consumption by lowering the speed limit. By contrast, a "right to life" anti-abortion activist may hold very strong opinions. Robert E. Lane and David O. Sears have suggested that there may be "something congenial" about extreme views and intensity of opinion "which suggests a mutual support."[26] That is, people well to the left or right may hold their political opinions more fiercely than others.

Another quality of public opinion is its degree of *stability*. Opinions change, sometimes slowly, sometimes rapidly and unpredictably, in response to new events or personalities. As noted earlier, public opinion concerning President Carter fluctuated greatly in the months before the 1980 presidential election. Carter had started out with an approval rating of 75 percent soon after his inauguration in 1977, but it plunged to 28 percent two years later. Then it climbed back up dramatically at the beginning of the crisis in Iran, only to drop again before the 1980 election.[27]

Public opinion may be measured and its qualities analyzed. The measuring tool is the political poll.

Political Polls

In the week before the 1980 election, most political observers and pollsters were terming the contest "too close to call." But during that final week, Ronald Reagan's campaign poll taker, Richard Wirthlin, assured the Republican nominee that he would defeat President Carter by 8 or 9 percentage points in the popular vote. As it turned out, Reagan won by 10 points.[28]

Four years earlier, in 1976, former Georgia Governor Jimmy Carter had seemed almost to come out of nowhere to win many of the important primary elections and to capture the Democratic party's presidential nomination. Carter appeared to have sensed the mood of the country. But Carter had professional advice in measuring the opinions of the electorate. He received it from Patrick J. Caddell, a twenty-six-year-old Harvard graduate who, even before the Carter campaign, had earned a reputation as one of the nation's most successful poll takers.

Caddell's influence continued during Carter's term as President. In the spring and summer of 1979, with Carter's popularity dropping and long gas lines forming across the nation, Caddell sent the President two memos, warning that his polls indicated that Americans had lost confidence in the future and suggesting that the President take dramatic action to change the direction of his admin-

Ronald Reagan's poll taker Richard Wirthlin

[25] Key, *Public Opinion and American Democracy,* p. 11.
[26] Robert E. Lane and David O. Sears, *Public Opinion* (Englewood Cliffs, N.J.: Prentice-Hall, 1964), p. 106.
[27] *Gallup Opinion Index,* August 1979, p. 2, and August 1980, p. 26.
[28] *Washington Post,* November 9, 1980, pp. A1, A2.

Election Eve, 1980: Carter Gets the News

When Jimmy Carter flew back to Washington on Sunday to handle the hostage crisis, he thought he was in good shape in the polls taken daily by his own expert, Pat Caddell. He had gone into the Cleveland debate one to two points ahead of Reagan by Caddell's soundings, and the trend was in his direction. "It looked good," said one of the President's aides. By Friday, however, the debate results seemed to be taking effect. Jody Powell spoke of a "pause in momentum." Carter had dropped about four points, to one or two behind. But he was still in striking distance. . . . He would have to campaign Monday, and so out he went.

The long day was nearly at an end when Carter's Air Force One dipped out of rainy skies into Seattle Monday night. Hamilton Jordan was on the phone from Washington with Powell. As the plane came in to land, the connection was broken. On the ground, Carter was rushed into the hangar packed with more than 1,000 cheering supporters and gave one of the best speeches of his campaign.

He was exhausted but exhilarated. It was over, and he felt a win was definitely possible. As he leaped off the stage to work the crowd, some junior staffers surprised him by putting on the public address system his 1976 campaign theme song. The tune had not been played since his last campaign. Carter started to choke with emotion when he heard it.

In the meantime, Powell was reconnected with Jordan. The President's chief political strategist had bad news. Caddell had just come over with his latest poll figures. Carter had dropped to ten points behind Reagan. The lead was insurmountable, Caddell had said. Jordan told Powell the election was lost. Powell was profoundly shocked. Carter was still inside shaking hands.

When the President bounded onto the plane for the long flight back to Georgia, Powell readied himself by pouring a stiff drink. He said he needed one to break that kind of news. But before he could collar the President, Carter was back in the staff cabin, talking with Domestic Affairs Adviser Stu Eizenstat and Rick Hertzberg, his chief speechwriter. They had been pleased with the day. The aides agreed that the last appearance had been great. . . .

Finally, after they were in the air more than an hour, and Carter had finished a double martini, Powell got the President alone [and] passed on Caddell's findings. Carter was devastated. He couldn't believe it. . . .

Rosalynn met her husband at the helipad when he arrived in Plains. When he told her the grim news, she was incredulous. She spent the rest of the morning fighting to maintain control . . . On the flight to Washington after voting in Plains, they were finally alone in their forward cabin. They broke down together and cried.

—Time, November 17, 1980.

Reagan's Pollster: "Getting Ready to Throw a Punch"

LOS ANGELES, Nov. 5 — Ronald Reagan won the Presidental election because he turned it into a referendum on President Carter's leadership, after first successfully combating public doubts about his own abilities, Mr. Reagan's campaign strategist and pollster said in a news conference here today.

. . . Richard Wirthlin opened the black vinyl notebook he carried throughout the campaign and produced poll figures that tracked a steady expansion of Mr. Reagan's support from a dead heat in early October to a lead of 5 percentage points in mid-month to an 11-point margin the day before the election.

Mr. Wirthlin cited the figures as a vindication of his strategy, which was sharply questioned by other Reagan advisors at critical points in the campaign. The strategy called for a patient effort to advertise Mr. Reagan's record as Governor of California before mounting a final assault on Mr. Carter's competence in the election's "peak week."

"It's like a boxer getting ready to throw a punch," said Mr. Wirthlin. "You've got to have source credibility before you can make your attack effective, and we just didn't have that base until the second week in October, and then we swung quickly and hit something."

—New York Times, November 6, 1980.

istration.[29] Carter cancelled a scheduled televised speech on energy and instead held a ten-day "domestic summit" at Camp David, where he met with leaders from many walks of life. On July 15, as the drama and suspense mounted, Carter went on television to announce "a crisis of confidence" in "the American spirit."[30] He then set forth a number of energy proposals, including a "massive" effort to develop synthetic and alternative fuel sources.

Wirthlin's role and Caddell's provided insight into the use of polls by presidential candidates and Presidents. But the data gathered by political polls are not always reliable.

In 1948 the Gallup and Roper polls wrongly predicted that Governor Thomas E. Dewey of New York, the Republican candidate, would defeat President Harry S Truman. Dewey lost. "I never paid any attention to polls myself," Mr. Truman later wrote in his typically direct style.[31]

The art of political polling has come a long way since 1948, and the margin of error has been greatly reduced. Even so, polls may still be wrong or in conflict with one another. In October 1978, Caddell and two other nationally known political pollsters, Peter D. Hart and Robert Teeter, each advised a client senator running for re-election. Each told his client—respectively, Thomas J. McIntyre of New Hampshire, Dick Clark of Iowa, and Edward W. Brooke of Massachusetts —that he held a substantial lead over his challenger. All three incumbents lost.[32]

Despite such well-publicized errors, political polls are substantially accurate more often than not, and frequently useful as a guide to voter sentiment. Politicians are convinced of their value.[33] Today, polls—before, during, and even

[29] Elizabeth Drew, "A Reporter at Large—Phase: In Search of a Definition," *The New Yorker,* August 27, 1979, pp. 45–60.

[30] *Weekly Compilation of Presidential Documents,* July 23, 1979, p. 1237.

[31] Harry S Truman, *Memoirs by Harry S Truman: Years of Trial and Hope.* Vol. II (Garden City, N.Y.: Doubleday, 1956), pp. 177, 221.

[32] "For Once, Some Polls Were Off, Way Off," *New York Times,* November 19, 1978, p. 4E.

[33] Louis Harris estimated in 1968, for example, that 80 percent of all candidates for the U.S. Senate used polls.

after Election Day—are a standard part of political campaigns. In a presidential election year, several million dollars are paid to the more than 200 polling organizations in the United States.[34]

How Polls Work. A political polling organization may question only 1500 people to measure public opinion on a given issue or to determine which candidate leads in a campaign.[35] Many people find it difficult to accept the idea that public opinion in an entire nation may be measured from such a small sample. Behind some of the skepticism is the belief that each individual is unique and that his or her opinions and thoughts cannot be so neatly categorized. If only 1500 Americans are polled in a population of 226,000,000, each person questioned is, in effect, "speaking for" 150,666 people. How, it may be asked, can the views of one individual represent the opinions of so many fellow citizens?

The answer lies in the mathematical law of *probability.* Toss a coin 1000 times and it will come up heads about 500 times. The same principle of probability is used by insurance companies in computing life expectancy. And it is used by poll takers in measuring opinion. Because the group to be measured, known as the *population* or the *universe,* is usually too large to be polled individually on every issue, the poll taker selects at random a sample of the population. The *random sample,* also called a *probability sample,* must be representative of the universe that is being polled. When the *Literary Digest* polled owners of automobiles and telephones in 1936—a time when many Americans had neither —it was not sampling a representative group of Americans. As a result, its prediction that Franklin Roosevelt would lose the presidential election proved incorrect. If the sample is of sufficient size and properly selected at random, the law of probability will operate, and the results will usually be accurate within a 4 percent margin of error.

One way to conceptualize the principles involved in polling is to think of a huge jar of white marbles to which a smaller number of yellow marbles are added. Suppose the jar is thoroughly shaken so that all the marbles are completely mixed together. If a scoop is then used to remove enough of the marbles, the sample should contain the same proportion of yellow to white marbles as exists in the entire jar.

Take another example. Suppose that one out of every four Americans has blue eyes. For the same reason that a flipped coin comes up heads half the time, or the same percent of yellow marbles can be scooped from the jar each time, the probability is that a random sample will catch in its net the same percentage of blue-eyed persons as exists in the whole population. Using this technique, we can estimate the number of blue-eyed Americans from a random sample. Similarly, we can estimate the number of Americans who support abortion or who oppose capital punishment.

But a true random sample of the entire United States would be very difficult (and very expensive) to take. A survey researcher would, in theory, have to have a list of everyone in the population and then select at random the names

---

[34] Major political polling organizations include the American Institute of Public Opinion (the Gallup poll) and Louis Harris & Associates, Inc. (the Harris survey), which publish their findings in newspapers and magazines. A number of pollsters also take private polls for political clients. In addition, there are many smaller regional polls as well as polls conducted by newspapers.

[35] The Gallup poll normally uses a national sample of 1500 persons. Louis Harris interviews 1600 people.

to be questioned. To simplify the task, most polling organizations use *cluster sampling*—interviewing several people from the same neighborhood. As long as the geographic areas are chosen at random, the clustering will not result in an unacceptable margin of error.[36] Poll takers often combine the cluster technique with the selection of geographic areas to be polled in a series of stages or steps, with each unit selected becoming successively smaller. For example, in pinpointing the location for an interview, the pollster might start by selecting regions of the country and then choose counties or other smaller areas at random within those regions. From there, still selecting at random, the researcher would scale down to a city, a neighborhood, a precinct, a block of houses, an apartment building, and then one apartment, where the actual interview would take place. The desirable size of the sample does not depend very much on the size of the population being measured, and beyond a certain point increasing the number of persons polled reduces the sampling error only slightly.

A less reliable method of polling is based on the *quota* sample. For example, an organization that wanted to test ethnic opinion would instruct its staff to interview blacks, Italians, Jews, Poles, Chicanos, and so on, in proportion to their percentage in the population as a whole. Under this method the interviewer has considerable discretion in the choice of persons selected to be questioned. The poll taker might select only well-dressed or cooperative individuals, thus skewing the results. Therefore, quota sampling is less useful than random sampling as a method of measuring political opinion.

The method of selecting the sample is not the only factor that may affect the reliability of a poll. The way in which questions are phrased, the personality of the interviewer, and the manner in which poll data are interpreted may all affect the result. Perhaps 10 to 20 percent of the people interviewed refuse to answer or answer only reluctantly. Gallup and Harris polls taken just before the 1980 election showed 3 to 4 percent "undecided"—a fairly normal percentage of persons in this flexible category. How this undecided vote is interpreted and allocated can drastically affect the accuracy of a political poll.

Political polls do not necessarily predict the outcome of an election. A poll only measures opinion at the moment the survey is taken. A poll taken four days before an election, for example, will not always match the vote on Election Day. In 1980 Dr. Gallup's final poll was taken from October 30 to November 1 and published on November 3, one day before the election; with the percent unde-

---

[36] Herbert F. Weisberg and Bruce D. Bowen, *An Introduction to Survey Research and Data Analysis* (San Francisco: Freeman, 1977), p. 24.

cided allocated evenly between the two major candidates, it gave Reagan 47 percent, Carter 44 percent, and John B. Anderson 8 percent. Reagan won the election by a greater margin than the polls had predicted. The actual vote was 51 percent for Reagan, 41 percent for Carter, and just under 7 percent for Anderson, the independent candidate.[37]

An intriguing question today is whether there is a danger that political polls themselves may create a "bandwagon effect" and influence the outcome of an election. Do some voters or convention delegates, out of a desire to be with the winner, jump on the bandwagon of the candidate who is leading in the polls?

Whether or not a "bandwagon effect" really exists has been debated by political scientists for some time. For example, Bernard Hennessy found "little evidence" of such an effect, arguing that indifferent voters would not care who won or even remember poll results, and concerned voters would not cast their ballot for a candidate simply because of a poll. Pollster Elmo Roper argued that if a bandwagon effect actually existed, polls would always underpredict the margin of victory, "since the whole theory of bandwagon is that more and more people jump on it." According to Roper, polls have overpredicted the margin of the winner at least as much as they have underpredicted it.[38]

But other scholars have suggested that there may indeed be a bandwagon effect. As already noted, people often compare their views to the dominant public opinion before speaking out. Elisabeth Noelle-Neumann argues that there exists a "spiral process which prompts . . . individuals to perceive the changes in opinion and to follow suit . . . ."[39]

It is also possible that polls may create other effects. If a candidate's polls seem low, supporters of that candidate may be more inclined to go to the polls. Conversely, if the candidate's rating in the polls is high, some potential supporters may become complacent and stay home on Election Day. Such theories, based on present evidence, are debatable, but the possible effect of polls on voting is a subject that merits further exploration.[40]

In any event, polls today are a permanent part of the political landscape and an important tool of the "new politics."

Drawing by Weber
© 1975 The New Yorker Magazine, Inc.

"That's the worst set of opinions I've heard in my entire life."

[37] *Washington Post,* November 3, 1980, p. A9; and *New York Times,* January 6, 1981, p. A14.

[38] Bernard Hennessy, *Essentials of Public Opinion* (North Scituate, Mass.: Duxbury Press, 1975), pp. 70–71.

[39] Elisabeth Noelle-Neumann, "Turbulences in the Climate of Opinion: Methodological Applications of the Spiral of Silence Theory," *Public Opinion Quarterly,* Vol. 41, No. 2 (Summer 1977), p. 144.

[40] For a pollster's view of the question, see Dr. George H. Gallup, "Polls and the Political Process," *Public Opinion Quarterly,* Vol. 29 (Winter 1965–1966), p. 546.

What Americans Believe

Do Americans agree on anything? Some people say that there is an underlying consensus in America, a basic agreement among its citizens on fundamental democratic values and processes, that permits democracy to flourish. But the supposed consensus often melts away and disappears upon closer examination. For example, Americans say they believe in fair play and justice, but they do not necessarily stick by those principles when their own interests are threatened. White homeowners may know that it is "fair" for a black family to buy the house next door, but they may oppose the sale if they believe that the value of their property would go down if the neighborhood becomes racially mixed.

On the whole, Americans seem to be pragmatic, approaching each issue as it comes up and judging it on its merits. Most Americans do not have a fixed, coherent set of political beliefs. People may have ideological preferences on specific issues, but often their convictions are not interrelated. A voter who is "liberal" on one issue may be "conservative" on another. For example, a majority of Americans have agreed that "the Federal Government should act to meet public needs" in such fields as education, medical care, public housing, urban renewal, unemployment, and poverty.[41] But when the same Americans are asked questions about their general concepts of the proper role of government, they are "pronouncedly conservative." Thus, a clear majority agreed with the statement: "We should rely much more on individual initiative and not so much on governmental welfare programs."[42] On some issues, in short, Americans seem to have a "split personality."

Why should Americans hold such seemingly contradictory opinions? One explanation may lie in the competing fundamental values of *individualism* and *equality* that observers such as Alexis de Tocqueville saw in America as far back as the early nineteenth century. The belief in "rugged individualism" may cause some Americans to complain about "welfare chiselers." The belief in equality may explain why the same individuals favor government social programs.[43]

Some political research has suggested that the pattern of beliefs in America is changing and that voters are becoming more aware of political issues and thinking about them more coherently. One study, *The Changing American Voter,* found "long-term tendencies of the public to move in one direction or another" on the issues.[44] Since the 1960s, the study found, voters have begun to evaluate candidates and parties more in terms of their issue positions, with this being reflected to some extent in how citizens vote.[45] "The role of the party has declined as a guide to the vote," the study reported. "And, as party has declined in importance, the role of issues appears to have risen."[46]

Political Participation

One way people can influence government is through the force of public opinion. An even more direct way that people can make their opinions felt is by voting. Yet, one of the more surprising facts about America is that almost half the people—and sometimes more than half—do not bother to vote.

[41] Free and Cantril, *The Political Beliefs of Americans,* p. 13.
[42] *Ibid.,* p. 30.
[43] See Bennett, *Public Opinion in American Politics,* pp. 141–50.
[44] Norman H. Nie, Sidney Verba, and John R. Petrocik, *The Changing American Voter* (Cambridge, Mass.: Harvard University Press, 1976), p. 348.
[45] *Ibid.*
[46] *Ibid.,* p. 156.

In 1980 the Census Bureau estimated that 160,491,000 citizens in the United States were old enough to vote. Of that total, approximately 105,000,000 registered to vote. Of these, about 86,000,000 actually cast their ballots for President on Election Day, November 4. That means that just under 54 percent of the population of voting age actually voted.

In off-year, nonpresidential elections, it is not unusual for less than half of the voting-age population to go to the polls to vote for senators and representatives. In 1970, for example, 43.8 percent cast their ballots for members of the House. In 1974 only 36.1 percent voted for members of the House. For 1978 the figure was down to 35.1 percent.[47]

These figures, not entirely uncommon for American elections, raise important questions about the nature of "government by the people." "Every regime lives on a body of dogma, self-justification, glorification and propaganda about itself," E. E. Schattschneider has written.

> In the United States, this body of dogma and tradition centers about democracy. The hero of the system is the voter who is commonly described as the ultimate source of all authority. The fact that something like forty million adult Americans are so unresponsive to the regime that they do not trouble to vote is the single most truly remarkable fact about it. . . . What kind of system is this in which only a little more than half of us participate? Is the system actually what we have been brought up to think it is?[48]

Some people do not vote because they may feel the system holds no benefits for them or because they feel there is no difference between the candidates. For some, therefore, nonvoting may be a form of protest. Others are nonvoters because they are apathetic about politics and political issues.

Americans not only fail to participate fully in the political system, it has been argued that they are often poorly informed about government and many public issues. One study found only 26 percent of the American public to be "well informed" on specific questions dealing with international affairs (such as the identity of four major world leaders).[49]

Public knowledge about many specific questions concerning domestic politics is equally limited. A Gallup poll reported that only 53 percent of the voters knew the name of their representative in Congress; only 62 percent knew the representative's party affiliation; and only 21 percent knew how he or she had voted on any major bill.[50] A nationwide survey of seventeen- and eighteen-year-olds conducted in 1978 found that only 45 percent knew who represented them in Congress; only 65 percent could name the three branches of the federal government; only 32 percent could name the Chief Justice of the United States; and only 67 percent knew that the Democrats controlled the House of Representatives.[51]

Drawing by H. Martin
© 1976 The New Yorker Magazine, Inc.

"In our view, the rapid pace of events on both the domestic and the international scene and the continuing uncertainty of the economic climate preclude any expression of voter preference at this particular time. I will say this, however. Both my husband and I will continue to monitor developments across the entire political spectrum, and we look forward confidently to rendering a fair and equitable judgment in November."

[47] U.S. Bureau of the Census, *Current Population Reports,* Population Estimates and Projections, Series P-25, No. 879, March 1980, p. 9.

[48] E. E. Schattschneider, *The Semisovereign People* (New York: Holt, Rinehart and Winston, 1960), p. 99. By 1980 the number of nonvoters totaled about 74 million.

[49] Free and Cantril, *The Political Beliefs of Americans,* p. 61.

[50] Quoted in David S. Broder, *The Party's Over: The Failure of Politics in America* (New York: Harper & Row, 1971), p. 184. It should be noted, however, that substantially more voters are able to identify and evaluate their representatives in Congress when presented with the names on a list. See Chapter 12, p. 443.

[51] Gallup poll, 1978, conducted for the National Municipal League. Data provided by the National Municipal League.

Schattschneider has concluded, "An amazingly large number of people do not seem to know very much about what is going on."[52] One effect of the lack of public knowledge is to give government officials wider latitude in making policy decisions—since they may assume that the public will neither know nor care very much about the results of those decisions.

Some scholars challenge the traditional assumption that many voters are politically ignorant. They suggest that the degree of information possessed by the public is "situational," that is, it may vary from one election to another. For example, when differences between candidates are sharper, the public seems to absorb more information. "Voters *can* take stands, perceive party differences, and vote on the basis of them. But whether they do or not depends heavily on the candidate and the parties."[53]

Violence

Democracy operates on the premise that at least a substantial number of citizens will participate peacefully in the political system. The "consent of the governed" implies that public opinion plays a role in the political process. But if the system fails to respond to the demands placed upon it, or if participation is slow to bring change, individuals or groups may vent their anger against the system in violent ways.

Sometimes the violence is viewed as a form of political or social protest, such as the rioting by blacks in Miami in 1980; that outbreak began after a jury acquitted four white police officers in the murder of a black man who had been beaten to death. At other times, organized groups, such as the radical Weather Underground in the 1960s or the Puerto Rican nationalists, have engaged in bombings for stated political ends. And all too often in American history, deranged assassins have struck at political leaders.

The United States has had a violent past, for Americans have not always sought to bring about political change through lawful or peaceful means. The American Revolution, the Civil War, the frontier, racial lynchings, and the Ku Klux Klan are some examples. Clearly, assassination and violence are not new forms of American political behavior. Four American Presidents have been assassinated—Lincoln, Garfield, McKinley, and Kennedy—and serious attempts have been made against the lives of five others—Andrew Jackson, Theodore Roosevelt, Franklin Roosevelt, Harry Truman, and Gerald Ford.

But political assassination and violence occurred with tragic frequency during the 1960s. The assassinations of President Kennedy in 1963, of his brother Robert Kennedy, a presidential candidate, in 1968, and of Dr. Martin Luther King, Jr., that same year—all had dramatic impact on the political process. So did the racial violence in the cities.

The Warren Commission, the presidential panel that studied President Kennedy's assassination, concluded that it had been carried out by Lee Harvey Oswald, who "acted alone," a finding that has been challenged by those who contend that Kennedy was the victim of a conspiracy. But most political assassinations in American history appear to have been the acts of unbalanced persons venting their rage and frustration on the national leader. Such purposeless acts

[52] Schattschneider, *The Semisovereign People*, p. 132.
[53] Richard G. Niemi and Herbert F. Weisberg, *Controversies in American Voting Behavior* (San Francisco: Freeman, 1976), p. 168. See also Bennett, *Public Opinion in American Politics*, pp. 27–30, 43–48, and 90–91.

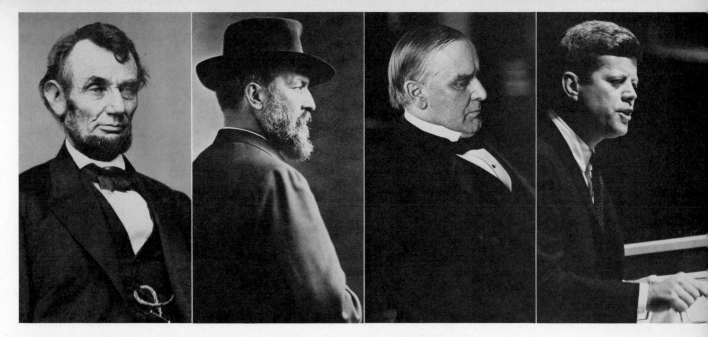

Four Presidents have been assassinated: Abraham Lincoln, James A. Garfield, William McKinley, John F. Kennedy

differ in motivation from the planned assassination of a political leader by conspirators or revolutionists. Planned assassinations may be viewed as an attempt to go *outside* the political system. They are not a form of "participation" in the political system but rather a rejection of that system. As a presidential study panel reported, "Assassination, especially when the victim is a President, strikes at the heart of the democratic process. It enables one man to nullify the will of the people in a single, savage act. It touches the lives of all the people of the nation."[54]

[54] "Assassination," *To Establish Justice, To Insure Domestic Tranquility,* Final Report of the National Commission on the Causes and Prevention of Violence (Washington, D.C.: U.S. Government Printing Office, 1969), p. 120.

November 22, 1963: President Kennedy is assassinated while riding in a motorcade in Dallas. Five years later, in 1968, similar violence claimed the lives of his brother Robert and Dr. Martin Luther King, Jr.

Drawing by Dana Fradon
© 1980 The New Yorker Magazine, Inc.

Suppose that the President of the United States could push a button every morning and receive, along with his scrambled eggs and coffee, a printout that would summarize the precise state of public opinion on a given spectrum of issues during the preceding twenty-four hours. And suppose that he tried to tailor his policies to this computerized intelligence. Would that be good or bad?

Good, one person might respond. After all, democracy is supposed to be government by the people, and if the President knows just what people are thinking, he can act in accordance with the popular will.

Bad, another might answer. The President is elected to exercise his best judgment and lead the nation, not to follow the shifting winds of public opinion. After all, if the people are not satisfied with a President's leadership and decisions, they may elect a new one every four years.

Both arguments have merit. A President or a member of Congress usually tries to lead public opinion and at the same time to follow it. No President can totally ignore public opinion during the four years between elections. But if our hypothetical President did try to rule according to his computer printouts, he would soon find there was no way to please everybody. He would also discover that if the policies suggested by his poll data failed to work, those policies—and he—would soon become highly unpopular.

Nevertheless, modern political candidates and leaders are highly attuned to techniques for measuring and influencing public opinion. Political polls, television spot commercials, and professional campaign managers are all part of the efforts at mass persuasion employed today. (These techniques are discussed in detail in Chapter 8.)

Political leaders often attempt to "manage" public opinion or to manipulate it in their favor by use of such techniques and by the conscious use of symbols. When a President addresses the nation on television in a military crisis, the dramatic format of the Oval Office of the White House and a nationwide TV address are impressive symbols of his power, designed to engender public support. When the President travels to a distant city to make a speech, the presidential seal goes with him, and an aide unobtrusively hangs it on the rostrum just before the Chief Executive appears to speak. Jimmy Carter's toothy smile, and his symbol—the peanut—helped voters identify with the Democratic candidate in 1976. By the 1980 campaign, the White House was his symbol.

Public officials, political candidates, professional campaign consultants, media advisers, and government information spokesmen customarily engage in political persuasion designed to influence or even manipulate the electorate. Indeed, as Dan Nimmo has suggested, "The political communicator not seeking to persuade others to his views is more rare than the whooping crane."[55]

Leaders may court public opinion, but it remains an elusive concept. The truth is that the role of public opinion in a democracy has never been satisfactorily defined. The people, Walter Lippmann has argued, "can elect the government. They can remove it. They can approve or disapprove its performance. But they cannot administer the government. They cannot themselves perform. . . . A mass cannot govern."[56]

Certainly the public does not possess nearly so much information as the President, who daily receives a massive flow of data from all over the globe to

[55] Dan Nimmo, *Political Communication and Public Opinion in America* (Santa Monica, Cal.: Goodyear, 1978), p. 98.
[56] Walter Lippmann, *Essays in the Public Philosophy* (Boston: Little, Brown, 1955), p. 14.

aid him in his decision making. On the other hand, as E. E. Schattschneider has pointed out, *"nobody knows enough to run the government*. Presidents, senators, governors, judges, professors, doctors of philosophy, editors and the like are only a little less ignorant than the rest of us."[57]

The unstated premise of opinion polls, Schattschneider adds, is that "the people really do decide what the government does on something like a day-to-day basis."[58] Obviously, that is rarely the case. It is reasonable to assume, however, that Presidents and legislators, because they hope to be re-elected, do take public opinion into consideration in reaching major policy decisions. In addition, they try to influence public opinion to win support for the decisions they have made.

Public opinion in a democracy, then, may be seen as a broad but flexible framework for policymaking, setting certain outer limits within which government may act. As Key has observed, "Unless mass views have some place in the shaping of policy, all the talk about democracy is nonsense."[59]

Mass Media and Public Opinion

In a modern society, the public forms its opinions largely on the basis of what the mass media — newspapers, television, radio, and magazines — present to it. Consequently, the quality of the mass media, the amount of time and space they devote to public affairs, their editorial stands, ownership patterns, and objectivity are all factors with potential influence on public opinion.

In recent years the American press has sometimes come under attack from government officials and others, and under government pressure. Some critics contend that the press is biased, unfair, or inaccurate in its reporting of public issues.[60] Much of this type of criticism stems from conservatives who feel the press is too "liberal."

Under President Nixon these attitudes were encouraged by various government actions and by attacks on the press by high administration officials. In a celebrated speech in November 1969, Vice President Spiro T. Agnew assailed "a small band of network commentators and self-appointed analysts" who had discussed a televised address to the nation by President Nixon. A week later, Agnew attacked the *Washington Post* and the *New York Times,* both Eastern newspapers often critical of the administration.

Possibly some of these government pressures on the press were designed to divert public attention from the question of the government's own truthfulness. At the same time, the pressures also seemed designed to persuade the news media to temper their criticism and present news about the government in a

Mass rally in support of equal rights for women, Washington, D.C., 1978

[57] Schattschneider, *The Semisovereign People,* p. 136.

[58] *Ibid.,* p. 133.

[59] Key, *Public Opinion and American Democracy,* p. 7.

[60] According to poll data, a majority of Americans do not share this view. For example, in a Gallup poll taken in May of 1979, 19 percent of those surveyed had "a great deal" of confidence in newspapers and 32 percent "quite a lot," for a total of 51 percent; 35 percent had "some" confidence, 12 percent had "very little," 1 percent had "none" and 1 percent had "no opinion." In another Gallup poll in January of 1980, 47 percent of the respondents said newspapers get "facts straight," 34 percent considered them "inaccurate," and 19 percent had no opinion. Sources: Gallup Opinion Index, May 1979, p. 6, and January 1980, p. 26.

Above: The Washington
Post newsroom

more favorable light. In this respect, the television networks are potentially in a vulnerable position, since they are composed of stations licensed by the federal government. Jeb Stuart Magruder, while an assistant to President Nixon, suggested in a memo that the administration could "get the media" by such tactics as threatening Internal Revenue Service investigations of news organizations. Another former White House official, Charles W. Colson, wrote a memo while counsel to Nixon noting that network officials were "very much afraid of us and are trying hard to prove they are 'good guys.' "[61]

The government's pressures on the press and the issue of press "fairness" stirred debate in the 1970s. During the Watergate investigation, however, there was wide recognition of the fact that the press, and particularly the *Washington Post,* had played a significant role in uncovering the massive abuse of power by the Nixon White House. The disclosures by the press were one factor among many leading to Nixon's resignation as President.

Government pressure on the press did not remain a major issue during Jimmy Carter's term as President. Although Carter occasionally criticized the news media, he was generally restrained, even during the flood of adverse publicity in 1980 about his brother Billy's payments from the government of Libya.

Television

With some 125 million television sets in American homes, the potential for creating an informed public through TV is vast. Entertainment is the economic heart of the television industry, however, and news and public affairs programs occupy only a small part of the broadcast day. The three major networks, CBS, NBC, and ABC, dominate the industry. In 1978, for example, 51 percent of all television revenues went to the three networks and their fifteen wholly owned TV stations. The networks sell popular packaged shows to affiliates across the

[61] *New York Times,* November 1, 1973, p. 7, and November 2, 1973, p. 24.

nation and charge large fees for airing sponsors' commercials during "prime time"—the after-dinner hours when millions of persons are tuned in to network programs. For example, on a typical weeknight during the prime time of 9 to 10 P.M., sponsors pay a total of about $2.7 million to the three networks for six minutes of advertising time on each network. For shows with top ratings, the cost of a minute of commercial time is $300,000.[62] Audience rating figures are the controlling statistics in the broadcast industry, and news programs may not be as profitable as popular, mass entertainment shows. Nevertheless, all three networks have evening television news programs that reach a combined, total audience of more than 32 million persons each night. Other news programs reach several million viewers by the newer cable and satellite systems.

In addition to news programs, Sunday panel shows like "Meet the Press" air political issues, and the networks and public television broadcast a wide range of news documentaries. The networks and many local stations maintain their own news staffs. Because television reaches millions of homes, news programs have a strong influence on public opinion. Certainly news reports of the fighting in Vietnam, by bringing that conflict into American living rooms night after night, were a major factor in swinging public opinion against the war. Similarly, the televised Senate Watergate hearings in 1973 played a major role in making the public aware of a scandal to which the voters had paid relatively little attention in the preceding presidential election. A year later millions of Americans were able to watch the debates of the House Judiciary Committee as it voted to impeach President Nixon. An estimated 100 million persons or more viewed the televised debate between Ronald Reagan and Jimmy Carter one week before the 1980 presidential election. Television coverage of hearings, political debates, and conventions conveys an immediacy and has an impact that no other medium can approach.

[62] *Broadcasting Yearbook,* 1980 edition (Washington, D.C.: Broadcasting Publications, Inc., 1980), p. A-2.

Dan Rather, CBS

Barbara Walters, ABC

John Chancellor, NBC

Newspapers

A farmer in Nebraska and an attorney in Manhattan may both read newspapers, but the treatment of news about government and politics may be very different in the pages they read. The attorney probably reads the *New York Times,* which places heavy emphasis on national and international news gathered by its own reporters. The farmer may read a small-town daily that concentrates on crop reports, wheat prices, and local events, and that relies on the wire services for sketchy reports about national and world events.

There are a number of excellent newspapers in the United States. A partial list would include the *New York Times,* the *Washington Post,* the *Los Angeles Times,* the *Wall Street Journal,* the *St. Louis Post-Dispatch,* the *Christian Science Monitor,* the *Chicago Tribune,* the *Chicago Sun-Times,* the *Baltimore Sun,* and the *Minneapolis Tribune.* But for most Americans, who live outside the circulation area of such publications, the outstanding fact about their newspaper is often not its excellence but how limited is its coverage of national and world news.

Moreover, daily newspapers have been disappearing. In 1909 there were 2600 dailies in the United States. By 1955 there were 1785, and by 1979, only 1763.

As a result, more and more cities have no competing newspapers—either there is only one newspaper or else all the papers are controlled by one owner. By 1980 there was no competition in almost 80 percent of cities with daily

Audiences Reached by Leading Media

Figure 6–1

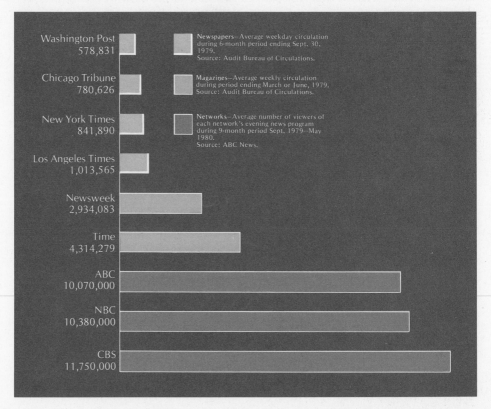

Source: *'80 Ayer Directory of Publications* (Bala Cynwyd, Pa.: Ayer Press, 1980), and ABC News.

papers. Because of a growing trend toward concentrated ownership of all media, there were dozens of communities in which one person or company owned or controlled all the local newspaper and television and radio outlets. As a result, the public often has less choice in selecting its sources of information. This has proved dramatically true in New York City, for example; it had eight major newspapers in 1948 and three in 1980. On the other hand, as the number of newspapers has declined, the number of electronic information sources has increased; there were 1013 television and 7726 radio stations in the United States in 1980, more than double the number two decades earlier.

Magazines

Citizens who feel that their local newspaper and broadcast outlets fail to provide them with enough news on public issues may, of course, subscribe to a weekly news magazine. Less than 5 percent of the population does so, however. The circulation of *Time* is 4,314,279; *Newsweek,* 2,934,083; and *U.S. News and World Report,* 2,067,321. By contrast, the circulation of the *Reader's Digest* is 18,094,192. Smaller magazines that comment on public affairs have relatively tiny circulations and are usually struggling to survive. For example, as of 1980, the *Atlantic* had a circulation of 332,649, the *New Republic*'s was 75,404, and *Harper's* was 300,103.[63]

The Press in a Democratic Society

In short, Americans do not read much about public affairs. According to one study of newspaper reading habits, 47 percent of the people interviewed said they only read the headlines; fully 20 percent said the part of the newspaper they were most interested in was the comic strips.[64]

Despite its shortcomings—the lack of quality newspapers in many communities, for example—a free press in the United States is essential to the functioning of democracy and a vital link between the public and the government. That is why the press is protected, in part, by the First Amendment. Public opinion is formed on the basis of what the news media present to the public. Democratic government rests broadly on public opinion and presupposes a fairly well-informed public. American Presidents have always had to worry about adverse public judgments on the quality of their performance in office. In the course of four years, opinions *are* formed about the merits of a President and his staff. (The role of the press in political campaigns is discussed in Chapter 8, and the relationship between the President and the press is discussed in Chapter 10.)

Aside from its role of informing the general public, the American press, particularly the quality newspapers, magazines, and television news programs, does an excellent job of informing those who are politically aware—politicians, opinion leaders, political scientists, lawyers, journalists, college students, and others who are attuned to politics.

Information about public affairs, in other words, is available to those who want it. There is nothing about democracy that guarantees an alert, educated public. Like voting and other forms of political participation, knowledge of public affairs—the basis of intelligent public opinion—is largely up to the individual.

[63] Magazine circulation figures from *'80 Ayer Directory of Publications* (Bala Cynwyd, Pa.: Ayer Press, 1980).

[64] Lane, *Political Life,* pp. 284–85.

Interest Groups in a Pluralist Society

Who governs in a democracy? Three different answers are possible. It can be said that "the people" govern through political leaders nominated as candidates of political parties and elected by the voters.

Another view is that a "power elite," a "power structure," or an "establishment" actually runs things. This was the view advanced more than two decades ago by sociologist C. Wright Mills in *The Power Elite*. Mills argued that a small group, "possessors of power, wealth and celebrity," occupies the key positions in American society.[65] This theory holds that *elites* rule, that power in America is held by the few, not by the masses of people. Many other social scientists have interpreted American society in terms of elite theory.[66] And "the establishment" is an expression that has come into everyday usage to describe elite power. Political writer Richard H. Rovere, in a semihumorous vein, described the "American Establishment" as a loose coalition of leaders of finance, business, the professions, and the universities who hold power and influence in the United States regardless of what administration occupies the White House.[67]

Although elites do exist in almost every field of human activity, many scholars reject the concept that a single economic and social elite wields ultimate political power. In his classic study of community power in New Haven in the late 1950s, Robert A. Dahl provided a third answer to the question of "Who governs?" He examined several specific public issues and traced the process by which decisions were made on those issues. He concluded that the city's economic and social "notables" did not run New Haven. Some individuals and groups were particularly influential in the making of one type of decision—educational policy, for example. But in other policy areas, very different individuals and groups often played the most important role. The city was dominated by many different sets of leaders: "It was, in short, a pluralist system."[68]

Other scholars have criticized Dahl's approach on the grounds that the wielders of power cannot always be identified by examining key decisions. For example, truly powerful persons might prevent certain issues from ever reaching the public arena.[69] On such issues, those favoring the status quo are the winners, because no decisions are made that might lead to change. In short, the power to set the *agenda*, to determine which public policy questions will be debated, or even considered, may prove at least as important as the power to decide on the issues themselves.

Nevertheless, the *pluralist* character of American democracy is widely, although not universally, recognized. Pluralism exists when many conflicting groups within the community have access to government officials and compete with one another in an effort to influence policy decisions. Pluralism supposes, of course, that individuals are active in many groups and associations to advance their interests and that these multiple interests and memberships overlap and, in many cases, conflict. For example, the same person who favors new school

[65] C. Wright Mills, *The Power Elite* (New York: Oxford University Press, 1959), pp. 8, 13.

[66] See, for example, Peter Bachrach, *The Theory of Democratic Elitism* (Boston: Little, Brown, 1966); G. William Domhoff, *Who Rules America?* (Englewood Cliffs, N.J.: Prentice-Hall, 1967), and *The Higher Circles* (New York: Vintage Books, 1970).

[67] Richard H. Rovere, *The American Establishment* (New York: Harcourt Brace Jovanovich, 1962), p. 6.

[68] Robert A. Dahl, *Who Governs?* (New Haven: Yale University Press, 1961), p. 86.

[69] See Peter Bachrach and Morton S. Baratz, "Two Faces of Power," *American Political Science Review,* Vol. 56, No. 4 (December 1962), pp. 947–52.

construction as a member of the PTA may oppose higher taxes as a member of a neighborhood association. As we shall see, however, many groups have been badly underrepresented or left out of the pluralist system.

It has been argued that pluralism really consists of competing groups of elites, so that even a pluralist system falls far short of the classic democratic model. Some scholars who contend that America is ruled by the few are critical of elite power and argue that the political system must be opened up to give more people access to it. Other scholars claim that only elites are dedicated to democratic principles and that the masses of voters have little allegiance to freedom, the right of dissent, First Amendment values, or equal opportunity. But this latter view diminishes the importance of the ordinary voter and citizen, and reflects little confidence in representative democracy.

To an extent, the debate over whether America is an elite or pluralist democracy may pose the question in terms that are too rigid. As with most things, there is a mix. Elites do exercise power in and out of government, but the voters retain the ultimate power of replacing elected leaders—from the school board member to the President of the United States.

Public opinion, as we have seen, is the expression of attitudes on public questions. When people organize to express attitudes held in common and to influence the government to respond to those attitudes, they become members of *interest groups.* When one group wins, another may lose. David B. Truman has pointed out that interest groups may make "certain claims upon other groups in the society" by acting through "the institutions of government."[70]

In the nineteenth century, political cartoonists were fond of drawing potbellied men in top hats and striped pants to represent Big Business. Muckrakers assailed oil, steel, and railroad barons as members of interest groups in league against the public welfare. Partly as a result of this muckraking tradition, many people tend to regard all interest groups as evil, business-dominated organizations that are plotting against the commonweal. But today many public interest groups champion consumers, the environment, or other causes that benefit the public as a whole.

Most political scientists now consider interest groups a normal and vital part of the political process, conveyors of the demands and supports that are fed into the political system. Whether such groups are called "interest groups," or "pressure groups," or "lobbies"—and there is some disagreement over which label is best—their purpose is much the same, to influence government policies and actions. These groups should not be confused with political parties, which also seek to influence government—but by electing candidates to office. As we noted in Chapter 1, the members of some interest groups—college students, for example—may not even be formally organized as a group.

The tendency of Americans to come together in groups was noticed in the early nineteenth century by Alexis de Tocqueville. "In no country of the world," he observed, "has the principle of association been more successfully used or applied to a greater multitude of objects than in America."[71]

Interest Groups: A Definition

Alexis de Tocqueville

Who Belongs?

---

[70] David B. Truman, *The Governmental Process* (New York: Knopf, 1951), p. 37.
[71] Alexis de Tocqueville, *Democracy in America*, Vol. I, Phillips Bradley, ed. (New York: Vintage Books, 1945), p. 198.

There are more than 100,000 clubs and associations in the United States. Not everyone belongs to a group, however. In America, "more than one-third of the population has no formal group association."[72] And nearly one-half of those who do belong to groups are affiliated with social, fraternal, or church-connected organizations that have little relation to politics.[73] Not all organizations are interested in influencing government, and so only a minority of Americans belong to interest groups. One survey reported that only 31 percent of the population belonged to groups that sometimes take a stand on housing, better government, school problems, or other public issues.[74] The fact that well over one-third of Americans belong to no groups at all raises basic questions about pluralist democracy that will be discussed later in this chapter.

Although interest groups vary tremendously in size, goals, budget, and scope of interest, they often employ the same techniques to accomplish their objectives. Some of these techniques are described below.

How They Operate

In 1977 the Senate was debating President Carter's energy package. The House had already passed a bill raising the price of natural gas but continuing government regulation of the industry. The big oil companies—which could raise the price of the natural gas they produced even higher if regulation ended—and their allies concentrated their campaign for deregulation in the Senate.

> When Congress returned, the lobbyists were waiting. In traditional fashion, some camped out in alcoves just off the Senate floor, where they propagandized senators with an array of computer studies and charts. So many executives of major firms swarmed to Washington to make personal pitches that an aide to Energy Czar James Schlesinger groused, "The sky was black with Learjets."[75]

The gas lobbyists and their friends were successful in the Senate, which voted to deregulate prices on new natural gas supplies. A year later Congress reached a compromise on the House and Senate versions; it agreed to end federal price controls on natural gas by 1985.

Lobbying. One of the most powerful techniques of interest groups is lobbying, *communication with legislators or other government officials to try to influence*

[72] Robert H. Salisbury, *Governing America: Public Choice and Political Action* (New York: Appleton-Century-Crofts, 1973), p. 90.
[73] *Ibid.*
[74] Lane, *Political Life*, p. 75.
[75] *Time*, October 17, 1977, p. 14.

Left: Lobbyists in the halls of Congress. *Right:* Representative Jack Kemp with labor lobbyists.

The life of a Washington lobbyist is not all fancy restaurants and high living, as this account by Marvin Caplan, a lobbyist for the AFL-CIO, demonstrates:

Tomorrow the House is scheduled to vote on a proposed anti-busing amendment to the Constitution (they can't vote today because of the congressional golf tournament) . . .

While the debate on the anti-busing amendment is going on, I and my fellow lobbyists are off the House floor, jammed into the narrow spaces marked for us on either side of the hall by brass stanchions and red velvet ropes. We compare notes, catch every unchecked or doubtful member who chances by and kibbitz. . . .

A bulletin from the front: Debate, scheduled for one hour, has been extended for one more. Four of

us go to the coffee shop in a basement tunnel of the House—our "Plastic Palace"—for a quick lunch of sandwiches, styrofoam bowls of bean soup and coffee. The debate's still on when we return. Now we just stand about waiting, sweltering in our cramped spot. Being a lobbyist sometimes has all the zing and glamor of guard duty in the Lincoln Tunnel.

At about 2:30 two bells ring. The doors to the House floor fling open. Several of us dash to the Republican side to greet members as they step off the elevators and urge "No" votes as they dash by. The sharp-eyed among us read the vote as it ticks off on the electronic scoreboard on the low wall around the spectators' gallery. The amendment doesn't come close to getting the two-thirds majority needed to pass. To a brief burst of handclapping in the House chamber, it is defeated, 216 to 209.

—*Washington Post,* August 12, 1979.

their decisions. Originally, the term "lobby-agent" was used to describe someone who waited in the lobbies of government buildings to buttonhole lawmakers. The term "lobbying" first came into use in the New York State capital at Albany and was being used in Washington by the early 1830s.

Although the term is often used to mean direct contact with lawmakers, in its broadest sense, lobbying is not confined to efforts to influence the legislative branch. Lobbyists also seek to influence officials of the executive branch, regulatory agencies, and sometimes even the courts.

One way that lobbyists influence officials is simple: they get to know them. By paying personal visits to members of Congress and government officials, by attending hearings of congressional committees, government agencies, and regulatory commissions, and by forming friendships with staff members and bureaucrats, lobbyists make their presence felt. Lester Milbrath found that more than half the Washington lobbyists thought the personal presentation of viewpoints was the most effective way of reaching members of Congress.[76] Senators and representatives are busy people—often the lobbyists' chief value is that they present carefully researched background material that may help a member of Congress decide how to vote on complex bills.

Money: The Lobbyist's Tool. In 1969 America's dairy industry wanted the price supports for milk raised. A Washington attorney for the largest of the milk cooperatives, the Associated Milk Producers, Inc. (AMPI), went to see an attorney for President Richard Nixon. After some negotiating, the dairymen agreed to contribute $100,000 to $250,000 in campaign funds to the President. In due

[76] Lester W. Milbrath, *The Washington Lobbyists* (Chicago: Rand McNally, 1963), pp. 212–13.

Seven Rules for the Successful Lobbyist

From extensive comments by lobbyists and their targets, Lester W. Milbrath drew up the following list of guidelines for Washington's lobbyists:

1. BE PLEASANT AND NON-OFFENSIVE
2. CONVINCE THE OFFICIAL THAT IT IS IMPORTANT FOR HIM TO LISTEN
3. BE WELL PREPARED AND WELL INFORMED
4. BE PERSONALLY CONVINCED
5. BE SUCCINCT, WELL ORGANIZED, AND DIRECT
6. USE THE SOFT SELL
7. LEAVE A SHORT WRITTEN SUMMARY OF THE CASE

—Lester W. Milbrath, *The Washington Lobbyists.*

course, the attorney for the milk producers delivered a little satchel containing $100,000 in cash to the President's lawyer. The milk producers later pledged to contribute $2 million to Nixon in the 1972 presidential campaign. Soon afterward, the President invited the dairy leaders to the White House, posed for pictures with them, and thanked them for their political support.

In the spring of 1970 the dairy industry won a large price increase. The following year, however, the Department of Agriculture ruled against any further price increase. The Secretary of Agriculture announced the unfavorable decision. The milk industry lobbied Congress furiously and generated thousands of letters to senators and representatives, urging legislation to boost milk prices. Secretary of the Treasury John Connally of Texas, a supporter of the dairy industry, warned the President that a veto of such legislation might cost him six farm states in the presidential election.[77] Nixon met with the dairy leaders again. He decided to increase milk prices—provided the milk producers kept their $2 million campaign pledge.

Less than two weeks after his original decision, the Secretary of Agriculture reversed himself and announced that milk prices would be increased, after all. With a satchel full of cash and a promise of $2 million, lobbyists for a powerful industry had influenced the President of the United States.[78]

The success of the dairy industry in winning price increases worth more than $300 million is a dramatic illustration of how lobbying by interest groups can affect—even reverse—public policy. In the policymaking process, interest groups play a key role.

As was demonstrated, money is often a useful tool for the lobbyist for an interest group. The public often thinks of the lobbyist as someone who hands out money to buy the votes of legislators. That may happen. A direct bribe,

[77] Connally was indicted by the federal government but acquitted in 1975 of charges that he had accepted a total of $10,000 from AMPI in return for urging Nixon to raise milk price supports.

[78] For more detailed accounts of the milk producers' lobbying, see Carol S. Greenwald, *Group Power* (New York: Praeger Publishers, 1977), pp. 3–8; and U.S. Senate, 93d Cong., 2d sess., *The Final Report of the Select Committee on Presidential Campaign Activities*, pp. 579–929.

The 116 Club: Lobbying over Lunch

An inconspicuous row house tucked away in a once-notorious alley on Capitol Hill has evolved into a headquarters of subterranean power, a place where Senators, Representatives and Federal officials do their lobbying.

The refurbished building houses the 116 Club, a name few Washingtonians have heard. It is the lunch and cocktail-hour watering hole where the city's most influential lobbyists present their employers' points of view to Government decision-makers away from the prying eyes of newsmen and the public.

"It's the sort of club where people in high places can be comfortable without feeling that they're in a fishbowl," explained a club member. "The membership is the innermost of the 'in' group."

Membership is about 200, including 116 "legislative relations specialists"—lobbyists—60 Government workers who are mostly staff aides to Con-

gressional committees and Federal regulatory agencies, and 30 nonresident members.

A few Senators and Representatives also belong, but their names, like those of other members, are closely guarded.

"I don't want to reveal any member's name," Robert H. Miller, the chairman of the club's board of governors, told a recent guest of the club. "This is a private club. . . ."

"Much of the major Congressional legislation affecting billions and billions of dollars is either written or influenced there," a club member said. . . .

Frequent visitors and the few members who were willing to discuss the club's affairs privately, insist that the most powerful men in Congress often lunch at the club. In keeping with the bipartisan attitude, the figures of both an elephant and a donkey decorate the mantelpiece of the club's dining room.

—*New York Times*, November 6, 1974.

however, is a violation of federal law. Under a 1962 statute, a person who bribes a member of Congress or a member of Congress who takes "anything of value" in exchange for a vote may be fined $20,000 and imprisoned up to fifteen years. The language of the statute is broad enough to cover any kind of valuable favor, not just money. Bribery is illegal and risky, and there are better, legal ways to channel money to legislators. For example, lobbyists are expected to purchase tickets or whole tables of tickets to fund-raising dinners for political parties and candidates. Lobbyists may take a senator to lunch at an expensive restaurant in Washington. They may arrange a weekend on a yacht or a free trip to a resort. Christmas may bring the legislator a ham, a case of Scotch, or a pair of gold cuff links.

But lunches and small favors are only minor props in the drama of influencing lawmakers. Many members of Congress are practicing lawyers, insurance agents, bankers, and business executives. For example, in 1980, 270 members of the Ninety-sixth Congress were lawyers. It is not difficult for interest groups with nationwide chapters and members to channel legal or insurance fees or bank loans to members of Congress. Unless such payments can be shown to be outright bribes, they are legal; in any event, they are difficult to trace.

For the most part, lobbyists for interest groups are able to exert influence by means of campaign contributions and fund raising. The American Medical Association, representing more than 200,000 physicians, is an example of a highly active interest group that has spent millions of dollars opposing national health insurance and other medical legislation. The American Medical Political Action Committee (AMPAC), the AMA's political arm, contributed $1.6 million to congressional candidates in the 1978 election, leading the list of big contributors, just as it had in 1974 and 1976.

Why does AMPAC contribute generously to Congress? In 1977 President Carter proposed a bill to hold down hospital costs, which the administration estimated could save consumers $27 billion over five years. The AMA opposed the bill. The measure was referred to a health subcommittee in the House. Its chairman, Representative Dan Rostenkowski, Democrat of Illinois, and ten other members had received contributions from the AMA. In 1978 the subcommittee voted to kill the Carter bill. The Ninety-fifth Congress took no action to contain hospital costs.[79]

Many large interest groups like the AMA are deeply involved in politics. They not only make campaign contributions to the candidates they favor; they publicly endorse and assist them as well. An example is the AFL-CIO Committee on Political Education (COPE). COPE contributes money to candidates, runs voter registration drives, publicly endorses candidates, publishes their voting records for union members, and often provides volunteers to assist in political campaigns. During 1978 COPE contributed $920,841 to candidates for Congress. Although ostensibly nonpartisan, COPE in fact has mainly aided Democrats, just as the AMA is Republican-oriented.

The popular image of a Washington lobbyist as a glamorous figure who entertains powerful senators and dines at the best places is not always accurate. As most lobbyists are quick to point out, much of their work consists of solid research, long hours of committee hearings, and conversations with lawmakers in their offices. Whatever their technique, lobbyists have a substantial influence on political decision making.

[79] "How Money Talks in Congress" (Washington, D.C.: Common Cause, 1979), pp. 12–13.

Campaign Contributions by Interest Groups to Members of Selected Congressional Committees, 1976

Figure 6–2

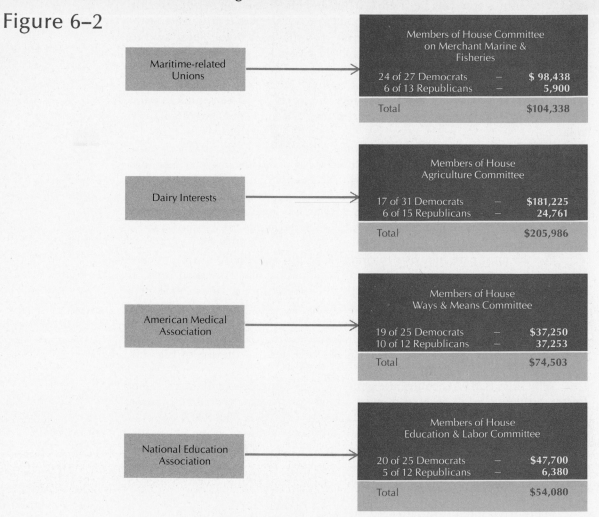

	Members of House Committee on Merchant Marine & Fisheries	
Maritime-related Unions	24 of 27 Democrats —	$ 98,438
	6 of 13 Republicans —	5,900
	Total	$104,338

	Members of House Agriculture Committee	
Dairy Interests	17 of 31 Democrats —	$181,225
	6 of 15 Republicans —	24,761
	Total	$205,986

	Members of House Ways & Means Committee	
American Medical Association	19 of 25 Democrats —	$37,250
	10 of 12 Republicans —	37,253
	Total	$74,503

	Members of House Education & Labor Committee	
National Education Association	20 of 25 Democrats —	$47,700
	5 of 12 Republicans —	6,380
	Total	$54,080

Source: Adapted from "How Money Talks in Congress" (Washington, D.C.: Common Cause, 1979), p. 15.

Mass Propaganda and Grass-Roots Pressure. One of the ways in which interest groups try to influence public opinion in order to influence government is through mass publicity campaigns. Using television, magazine, and newspaper advertising, and direct mailings to the general public and specialized audiences, interest groups seek to create a favorable climate for their goals. With the aid of a public relations firm, an interest group can utilize all the latest techniques of Madison Avenue. But it takes a great deal of money to influence public opinion enough to create a response from government, and only affluent interest groups can afford programs aimed at the manipulation of mass public opinion.[80]

[80] V. O. Key, Jr., *Politics, Parties, and Pressure Groups,* 5th edition (New York: Crowell, 1964), p. 130.

Grass-roots pressure: senior citizens meet with Senator Charles Percy of Illinois.

A classic example of an apparently successful campaign by an affluent group was the publicity campaign of the American Automobile Association in 1968 against a bill that would have allowed bigger trucks on the nation's roads. The AAA ran newspaper advertisements showing a triple-trailer truck with a huge boar's head devouring the highway as John Q. Motorist sat helplessly by, trapped in a monstrous traffic jam. The ad urged that the bill be defeated for reasons of safety and "because of the irreparable damage bigger trucks will do to our highways and bridges." With the public alarmed and the nation's bridges in apparent danger of imminent collapse, Congress abandoned the trucking bill. Presumably the AAA's publicity barrage influenced this outcome. But the AAA's victory was only temporary. In 1975 a bill became law permitting larger trucks on the roads.

In addition to such mass propaganda campaigns, many interest groups approach some members of the public directly, to try to create various forms of grass-roots pressure that will affect government. To influence senators, for example, an interest group might persuade powerful bankers in the senators' states to telephone them in Washington. Lobbyists may ask close personal friends of the senators to get in touch with them. Or lobbyists may try to get great numbers of legislators' constituents to write or wire them.

Both mass propaganda and grass-roots pressure were employed by highly organized evangelical Christian groups in the 1980 campaign. For example, the Reverend Jerry Falwell and his Moral Majority organization vigorously supported Ronald Reagan for President and several conservative candidates for Congress.

Today, many interest groups use computerized mailing lists to contact their members and supporters; the National Rifle Association, an aggressive group opposed to gun controls, reportedly can barrage Congress with a half a million letters on seventy-two hours' notice. But members of Congress are well aware that interest groups may be behind a sudden flood of postcards or letters on a pending bill. In addition, legislators know that, since most people do not write letters to their representatives in Congress, the mail they receive reflects the feelings of only a small percentage of their constituents. One study showed that only 17 percent of the general public writes letters to members of Congress.[81] Nevertheless, grass-roots pressure remains a popular form of trying to influence government, in part because interest groups, never certain which techniques are the most effective, tend to try them all.

The Reverend Jerry Falwell and members of his Moral Majority

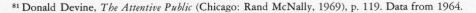

[81] Donald Devine, *The Attentive Public* (Chicago: Rand McNally, 1969), p. 119. Data from 1964.

The Washington
Lawyers:
Access
to the Powerful

Members of prestigious Washington law firms are among the capital's most effective lobbyists. Often, large corporations pay big fees to Washington lawyers, not only for their expert knowledge of how the bureaucracy works, but for their political access and friends inside the government and in Congress as well. On more than one occasion, Washington lawyers have been able to orchestrate the passage of legislation designed to help their clients: "The lawyer's historic role was that of advising clients how to *comply* with the law. The Washington lawyer's present role is that of advising clients how to *make* laws, and to make the most of them."[82]

One of the most renowned of Washington lawyers, Clark M. Clifford, served in the cabinet and as an adviser to Democratic Presidents. Aware of his stature, bureaucrats and members of Congress tended to return his telephone calls, giving Clifford the kind of political "clout" that corporate clients want—and pay large fees to obtain. President Kennedy, who received a good deal of free advice from Clifford, once joked: "All he asked in return was that we advertise his law firm on the backs of one-dollar bills."[83]

Public Interest
Groups

Corporate lawyers and lobbyists have increasingly faced a new kind of opponent in recent years. Beginning in the 1960s, *public interest* groups and public interest lawyers have also waged successful battles to influence public policy. In the fields of the environment, consumer protection, health, minority rights, and many other areas, these public interest groups have brought class action and other lawsuits, lobbied Congress, and through the powerful weapon of publicity, added new issues to the governmental agenda.

One such group is Common Cause, a national citizens' lobby with approximately 225,000 members. Common Cause received major credit for passage of the election reform laws of the 1970s.

The best-known public interest lobbyist, Ralph Nader, by 1980 headed a network of lawyers, lobbyists, and political analysts working in more than a dozen organizations. The Nader-affiliated public interest groups included Congress Watch, which concentrates on consumer affairs, the environment, transportation, congressional reform, and other legislation; the Center for Study of Responsive Law, a Nader clearinghouse for studies and reports by Nader task forces; the Freedom of Information Clearinghouse, which seeks to obtain government records under the Freedom of Information Act; the Health Research Group, which works to improve medical care, and food and drug safety; and the Citizen Action Group, which coordinates Public Interest Research Groups (PIRGs) in several states. These enlist students and other citizens in a variety of public interest and consumer projects.

In addition to lobbying and working for consumers, the Nader organizations have produced a number of studies and books, including profiles of each member of Congress and reports on antitrust enforcement, land use, the U.S. Department of Agriculture, chemical additives to food, air pollution, and many other subjects. Nader's activities are financed by foundations, income from the sale of these books, contributions from the public, and Nader's own funds, earned in lecturing and writing.

[82] Joseph C. Goulden, *The Superlawyers: The Small and Powerful World of the Great Washington Law Firms* (New York: Weybright & Talley, 1972), p. 6.
[83] *Ibid.*, p. 70.

Ralph Nader

Single-Issue Groups

In recent years, the "single-issue" interest group has become an increasingly significant phenomenon on the American political scene. These groups concentrate their efforts on lobbying for or against a particular issue, often with devastating effect.

The National Right to Life Committee and the National Rifle Association are examples of single-issue lobbies that have campaigned for such specific issues as ending legalized abortions and blocking gun control legislation. The anti-abortion and anti-gun control groups were credited in 1978 with a major role in the defeats of Senator Dick Clark, Democrat of Iowa, and Representative Donald M. Fraser, a Senate candidate in Minnesota, and with the election of Edward J. King as governor of Massachusetts.[84]

Former Senator Clark has shed light on how single-issue lobbying works in actual practice. Shortly before the election, he got a call from an official of the Machinists and Aerospace Workers Union which opposed the bill to deregulate natural gas. Clark planned to vote in favor of the bill. As Clark recalled it:

> He said to me, "OK, if that's the case, we won't support you." I responded, "Look at my voting record as a whole. Don't make a decision like this based on a single vote." His reply was: "We don't give a . . . about your overall voting record. We're interested in this bill—period."[85]

Political Action Committees

Often, single-issue lobbies work through political action committees (PACs, pronounced "packs")—which are sometimes independent organizations, but more often the political arms of corporations, labor unions, or interest groups—established to contribute to candidates or to work for general political goals.

In 1980 a powerful conservative political action committee based in Arlington, Virginia, distributed to voters in five states little cards that looked not unlike those that come in packages of bubble gum. But the cards did not contain pictures of baseball players; beneath the words, "Target '80," each had a photograph of one of five United States senators inside a red border.

On the backs of the cards appeared "ratings" of the senators by both conservative and liberal groups and notations such as:

[84] *New York Times,* November 14, 1978, p. 1.
[85] *Newsweek,* November 6, 1978, p. 48.

NCPAC
1500 Wilson Boulevard
Arlington, VA 22209
TARGET '80
GEORGE McGOVERN
Democrat, South Dakota

NCPAC
1500 Wilson Boulevard
Arlington, VA 22209
TARGET '80
BIRCH BAYH
Democrat, Indiana

NCPAC
1500 Wilson Boulevard
Arlington, VA 22209
TARGET '80
JOHN CULVER
Democrat, Iowa

NCPAC
1500 Wilson Boulevard
Arlington, VA 22209
TARGET '80
ALAN CRANSTON
Democrat, California

NCPAC
1500 Wilson Boulevard
Arlington, VA 22209
TARGET '80
FRANK CHURCH
Democrat, Idaho

Direct mail specialist
Richard Viguerie

"Favors sellout of Taiwan."

"Voted for New York City bailout."

The cards were directed against five "super-liberal" Democratic senators — Alan Cranston of California, George McGovern of South Dakota, Birch Bayh of Indiana, John Culver of Iowa, and Frank Church of Idaho. All five incumbents were the target of an intensive campaign to defeat them waged by the National Conservative Political Action Committee (NCPAC). And all but Cranston lost their seats in the 1980 Reagan sweep.

A key figure in the NCPAC campaign was Richard Viguerie, a direct-mail specialist, who with the aid of computerized mailing lists, has been extremely successful in raising money directly from the public for various conservative causes. By ElectionDay, 1980, NCPAC had spent $2.8 million nationwide.

Some of the money went for television commercials, such as one used in Indiana which opened with a picture of a large baloney on a cutting board. Suddenly, a meat cleaver sliced through the baloney and a voice intoned: "One very big piece of baloney is Birch Bayh telling us he's fighting inflation." A price tag reading $46 billion appeared on the baloney and the voice added: "That's how much deficit spending Bayh voted for last year alone." After a pause, the voice continued: "So, to stop inflation, you'll have to stop Bayh first. Because if Bayh wins, you lose."

The same commercial was used against Senator Cranston in California. NCPAC also used a radio commercial portraying a ubiquitous "Mrs. Smith":

In one version of the ad, used against Senator Cranston, Mrs. Verna Smith of Sacramento is asked how she thinks the National Taxpayers Union rates her Sena-

Politics by Mail

Richard A. Viguerie [is] called the "Godfather of the New Right" because of his leadership in raising money for conservative causes and candidates . . .

Viguerie is unrivaled as a direct-mail fund-raiser, a technique he has perfected to circumvent what he calls "the prevailing liberal power structure in the media." He founded his company (Richard A. Viguerie Co., Inc.) in January 1965 with $400, and has since built it into a private conglomerate with annual billings of $10 million or more. "You can get

into direct mail cheaply, bypass the monopoly the left has on communications in this country, tell people what the real issues are, ask them to write direct to their Congressmen, bypassing the media entirely. . . ."

He maintains lists with about five million names of "right of center" people and as many as 20 million others who might respond to a variety of conservative appeals.

— National Journal, January 21, 1978.

tor on the question of protecting her dollar. "One hundred percent!" she replies. "I'm sorry," the announcer replies, "You lose." The Senator's rating, he says, is a miserable 8 percent.

In another version, used against Senator Bayh, the same Mrs. Smith is living in Indianapolis. And she is as naive as ever. She loses all three guesses—on how her Indiana Senator stands on protecting her dollar, farm issues and national security. "That's three failing grades," Mrs. Smith says. "I never knew Birch Bayh voted like that." In Sacramento, she says the same thing about Senator Cranston.[86]

Several factors account for the rise of PACs. The Federal Election Campaign Act of 1974 permitted unions and corporations to establish political committees to contribute $5000 to each candidate in a primary or general election. The law was immediately challenged by Senator James Buckley of New York. In 1976 in the case of *Buckley* v. *Valeo,* the Supreme Court upheld many of the law's provisions. But the Court ruled unconstitutional the limits on "independent expenditures" made on behalf of candidates without their cooperation.[87]

The Supreme Court's decision—and a 1975 ruling of the Federal Election Commission allowing the Sun Oil Company to set up a PAC—opened the way for vastly increased expenditures by PACs in political campaigns. These may range all the way from bumper stickers and buttons to television spots endorsing a candidate. And, even though direct contributions by a PAC to a federal candidate are still limited to $5000 in each election, the number of committees has increased so greatly that PAC contributions totaled $35 million in 1978 and accounted for almost 25 percent of contributions to House races and more than 13 percent of contributions to Senate races.[88]

Later Supreme Court decisions have also encouraged corporate political activity. In 1978 the Court overturned a Massachusetts law which prohibited corporations from spending money to influence the outcome of public referenda. The Court ruled that the state law violated the corporation's First Amendment rights.[89] In 1980 the Supreme Court ruled that a public utility could insert with its monthly bills statements on controversial political issues.[90]

A Harvard University study prepared for Congress identified other reasons for the growth of PACs. The study gave as one reason the changes in the federal election laws that have made it more difficult to raise campaign funds from individuals. And the study suggested that the decline in the power of political parties has forced candidates to turn to interest groups for money.[91]

Undoubtedly the publicity given to PACs in recent years has encouraged the formation of even more such committees. Changes in the structure of Congress may have also contributed. In the 1970s Congress reduced the power of its committee chairmen; as a result, power became fragmented among hundreds of subcommittees, each of which is cultivated by various lobbyists.

[86] *The Wall Street Journal,* January 25, 1980, p. 40.
[87] *Buckley* v. *Valeo,* 424 U.S. 1 (1976). The federal campaign spending laws and the impact of Supreme Court decisions are discussed in detail in Chapter 8.
[88] Congressional Quarterly, *Weekly Report,* September 29, 1979, p. 2153, and June 2, 1979, p. 1043.
[89] *First National Bank of Boston* v. *Bellotti,* 435 U.S. 765 (1978).
[90] *Consolidated Edison* v. *Public Service Commission,* 447 U.S. 530 (1980).
[91] Institute of Politics, John F. Kennedy School of Government, Harvard University, "An Analysis of the Impact of the Federal Election Campaign Act, 1972–78," prepared for the Committee on House Administration, U.S. House of Representatives (Washington, D.C.: U.S. Government Printing Office, 1979), p. 4.

"A small group of zealots to see you, sir."

Drawing by Stan Hunt
© 1980 The New Yorker Magazine, Inc.

As the Harvard study noted, "PAC money is *interested* money."[92] That is, the committees often give contributions with specific legislative outcomes in mind. Fred Wertheimer, who analyzes political spending for Common Cause, has suggested that PAC contributions follow an "investment pattern," aimed at strengthening the group's influence with members of Congress. Otherwise, he contends, twenty-two House committee chairmen, "the most powerful group in the House and a relatively safe group of incumbents," would not have received 56 percent of their money in 1978 from PACs. When PACs give to safe incumbents, he notes, and the money is "not really needed for immediate re-election purposes, the contributions can only be considered a 'bonus' and of an investment nature."[93]

In 1974 there were 500 PACs. By 1980 there were approximately 2000. Beyond question, the explosive growth and influence of political action committees, often tied to single-issue lobbying, was having a significant and substantial influence on politics and policy in America.

Regulating
Interest Groups

Because the Constitution protects free speech and the right to petition the government, the efforts of interest groups to influence Congress are constitutionally protected. Nevertheless, public concern over lobbying abuses led Congress, beginning early in this century, to try to impose legal controls on interest groups. Not until 1946, however, did Congress pass a general bill that attempted to control lobbying.

The Federal Regulation of Lobbying Act of 1946 requires individuals and groups to register with the Clerk of the House and the Secretary of the Senate

[92] *Ibid.*
[93] Fred Wertheimer, "Of Mountains: The PAC Movement in American Politics" (Paper written for the Conference on Parties, Interest Groups and Campaign Finance Laws, Washington, D.C., September 1979), pp. 5–8.

if they solicit or collect money or any other thing of value "to be used principally to aid . . . the passage or defeat of any legislation by the Congress of the United States." In 1954 the Supreme Court narrowed the scope of the act by exempting grass-roots lobbying aimed at the public.[94] Because of this decision and the loose wording of the statute, many interest groups simply do not register on the grounds that lobbying is not their "principal purpose." Moreover, although the law contains penalties, it has no enforcement provision. As a result, there have been few prosecutions since its enactment in 1946.

In sum, the Lobbying Act does not effectively regulate lobbying of Congress. And, of course, it does not apply at all to lobbying of the executive branch or the independent regulatory commissions. In 1976 the Senate passed legislation to repeal the 1946 act and substitute much stricter regulations to control lobbying, including "grass-roots" lobbying. A Senate committee that considered the bill received testimony stating that as many as 10,000 people may be paid to lobby, but that only 2000 had bothered to register. Congress did not complete action on that bill or several subsequent bills to control lobbying, although both branches considered such legislation in 1980.

The view persists in American politics that interest groups are undemocratic and that they work for narrow goals against the general welfare. Some do. But an interest group like Common Cause represents no narrow economic interest; it works for its conception of the public welfare on a wide spectrum of issues. So have the organizations formed by consumer advocate Ralph Nader. It may be more realistic to view interest groups simply as one part of the total political process. Citizens have every right under the Constitution to organize to influence their government. Interest groups compete for the government's attention and action — but so do individual voters, political parties, and the press.

Interest Groups and the Policy Process

On many major issues, there are likely to be interest groups arrayed on opposite sides. Those who accept democratic pluralism and the politics of interest groups believe that out of these conflicting pressures some degree of balance may be achieved, at least much of the time.

Interest groups perform certain functions in the American political system that cannot be performed as well through the conventional structures of government, which are based largely on geographic representation.

The kind of *representation* that interest groups provide supplements the representation provided by Congress. They may also permit the *resolution of intergroup conflicts.* In collective bargaining, for example, differences between two powerful interest groups — management and labor — are resolved. Interest groups also perform a *watchdog* function; they can sound the alarm when new government policies threaten to injure the interests of their members. Finally, interest groups perform the function of *idea initiating,* that is, they generate new ideas that may become government programs. So important are these functions, Lester Milbrath has concluded, "if we had no lobby groups and lobbyists we would probably have to invent them."[95]

Some very serious criticisms can be leveled at interest groups, however.

[94] *United States* v. *Harriss,* 347 U.S. 612 (1954).
[95] Milbrath, *The Washington Lobbyists,* p. 358.

The poor are powerless because they are a minority of the population, are often difficult to organize, and are not even a homogeneous group with similar interests that could be organized into an effective pressure group. . . .

Although every citizen is urged to be active in the affairs of his community and nation, in actual practice participation is almost entirely limited to organized interest groups or lobbies who want something from government.

As a result, legislation tends to favor the interests of the organized: of businessmen, not consumers, even though the latter are a vast majority; of landlords, not tenants; doctors, not patients. . . . while the American political structure often satisfies the majority, it also creates *outvoted minorities* who can be tyrannized and repressed by majority rule, such as the poor and the black, students, migrant workers and many others.

—Herbert J. Gans, "We Won't End the Urban Crisis Until We End Majority Rule,"
New York Times Magazine, August 3, 1969.

Perhaps the most comprehensive criticism of interest group politics has been formulated by Theodore J. Lowi.[96] Lowi questions the assumption of many scholars and political leaders that the interest group process in a pluralist society provides a desirable, or satisfactory, way for the American governmental system to work. What are the effects of interest groups on public policy formation? Lowi argues that there is no assurance that the "pulling and hauling among competing interests" will result in policy decisions that are adequate to meet the social and political problems now facing the United States. In Lowi's view, interest group pluralism has not resulted in "strong, positive government" but in "impotent government" that can "neither plan nor achieve justice."[97]

As we have seen, most Americans do *not* belong to interest groups. Those who do, tend to come from the better-educated, middle- or upper-class backgrounds that produce citizens with a high degree of political motivation. "The flaw in the pluralist heaven," E. E. Schattschneider has observed, "is that the heavenly chorus sings with a strong upper-class accent. Probably about 90 percent of the people cannot get into the pressure system."[98]

Disadvantaged groups—the poor, blacks, Mexican Americans, slum dwellers, migrant workers—often have neither the knowledge nor the money to organize to advance their interests. Interest group politics, in other words, is biased against minorities and in favor of business organizations and other affluent groups.

The ordinary American consumer is not as well represented in interest group politics as are manufacturers. Americans who drive to work in a costly but possibly unsafe car, are assailed by noisy commercials, swim at a beach polluted by oil, inhale pesticides and smog-filled air, and eat food enhanced with dangerous additives may be forgiven if they wonder what interest group represents *them.*

In the 1980s there were hundreds of business groups represented in Washington but a much smaller number of consumer organizations. One reason is

[96] Theodore J. Lowi, *The End of Liberalism: Ideology, Policy, and the Crisis of Public Authority* (New York: Norton, 1969).
[97] *Ibid.,* p. x.
[98] Schattschneider, *The Semisovereign People,* p. 35.

that the interest of consumers is so general that it does not lend itself to organized expression as readily as the narrower interest of a special group, such as physicians or truckers. And as Mancur Olson, Jr., has pointed out, unless the number of individuals in a group is very small, or unless there is coercion or some special incentive to make individuals work together in their mutual interest, many people will not organize or act to achieve common or group interests through the political process.[99]

Even organized, active interest groups do not represent all they claim to represent. The leaders of an interest group tend to formulate policy positions for the group as a whole. Consequently, the public stance of an interest group often represents the views of an oligarchy rather than the views of the rank and file. The AMA, for example, is more conservative than are many of its 210,000 members. Moreover, at least 227,000 of the nation's physicians do not even belong to the AMA.

Despite all their flaws, interest groups do supplement formal channels of representation and allow for the expression of public opinion in an organized manner. But if American democracy is to become more responsive to the needs of its citizens, the nation's legislators must find new ways to heed the voice of the ordinary citizen, the consumer, the poor, the black and other minorities, and the powerless—groups that are much less likely to have a steel and glass office building and a team of registered lobbyists to speak for them in Washington.

[99] Mancur Olson, Jr., *The Logic of Collective Action: Public Goods and the Theory of Groups* (Cambridge, Mass.: Harvard University Press, 1965), p. 2.

Perspective

Public opinion is the expression of attitudes about government and politics. All governments are based, to some extent, on public opinion. In a democracy, public opinion is often described as a controlling force, but in fact its role is hard to define. Public opinion may be seen as a broad but flexible framework for policymaking, setting certain outer limits within which government may act.

Political socialization is the process by which a person acquires a set of political attitudes and forms opinions about social issues. The family and the school play a part in the political socialization of children. The "crucial period" of a child's political, social, and psychological development is between the ages of nine and thirteen.

Many other factors also influence the opinions people hold. Among the most important are: differences in social class, occupation, and income; religion, sex, race, and ethnic factors; sectional and geographic differences; and the views of reference groups (such as a political party) or primary groups (such as friends, office associates, or a local club). The qualities of public opinion, such as direction, intensity, and stability, may be measured.

Political polls, often useful as a guide to voter sentiment, are a standard part of political campaigns. They measure opinion by taking a random sample of a larger population, or universe. Because of the mathematical law of probability, the results of the poll usually reflect the opinions of the larger group. Although generally reliable, polls are sometimes wrong and do not necessarily predict the outcomes of elections.

In presidential elections, often only a little more than half of the voting-age population vote. In off-year, nonpresidential elections, it is not unusual for less than half of the voting-age population to vote for members of Congress.

Americans have not always sought to express their opinions or to bring about political change through lawful or peaceful means. If the political system fails to respond to the demands placed upon it, or if participation is slow to bring about change, individuals or groups may vent their anger against the system in violent ways.

In modern society, the public forms its opinions largely on the basis of what the mass media—newspapers, television, radio, and magazines—present to it. Consequently the quality of the mass media may have great influence on public opinion.

Who governs in the United States? One view is that the people govern through political leaders nominated as candidates of political parties and elected by the voters. Another view is that elites rule; power is held by the few rather than the masses of people. Another view emphasizes the pluralist character of American democracy; that is, conflicting groups within the community have access to government officials and compete with one another in an effort to influence policy decisions. But some issues may never reach the public agenda for debate.

When people organize to express attitudes held in common and to influence the government to respond to those attitudes, they become members of interest groups. Lobbying, mass propaganda, and grass-roots pressure are among the techniques employed by interest groups to achieve their objectives. One of the most powerful techniques is lobbying, communication with legislators or government officials to try to influence their decisions.

Single-issue lobbies often work through political action committees (PACs)—which are sometimes independent organizations, but more often the political arms of corporations, labor unions, or interest groups. Although PACs are limited in the amount they can contribute directly to a candidate's campaign, the Supreme Court has ruled that they may make unlimited "independent expenditures" on behalf of candidates.

Interest groups perform certain functions in the American political system that cannot be performed as well through the conventional structures of government. They provide a representation that supplements Congress. They may permit the resolution of intergroup conflicts, and they may perform watchdog and idea-initiating functions.

But most Americans do not belong to interest groups. Disadvantaged groups often have neither the knowledge nor the money to organize to advance their interests. And the ordinary American consumer is not as well represented in interest group politics as are business and industry.

Suggested Reading

Almond, Gabriel A., and Coleman, James S., eds. *The Politics of the Developing Areas** (Princeton University Press, 1960). An influential book that explores and develops, among other topics, the concept of "political socialization."

Armbruster, Frank, and Yokelson, Doris. *The Forgotten Americans: The Values, Beliefs and Concerns of the Majority* (Arlington House, 1972). An informative portrait of the social and political attitudes of the American public from the 1930s through 1971. Based on a review of hundreds of public opinion surveys covering a wide range of issues.

Berry, Jeffrey M. *Lobbying for the People** (Princeton University Press, 1977). A useful and readable analysis of the political and organizational behavior of public interest groups. Using case studies, Berry profiles the activities and strategies of two public interest lobbying organizations in considerable detail.

Cobb, Roger W., and Elder, Charles D. *Participation in American Politics** (Johns Hopkins University Press, 1975). A very useful introduction to the agenda-building process. Presents a variety of case studies to illustrate how issues get on the political agenda.

Dahl, Robert A. *Who Governs?** (Yale University Press, 1961). An influential and detailed exploration of the nature of political power, based on a study of political decision making in New Haven, Connecticut. Dahl maintains that there is a pluralism of power—rather than a single "power elite"—in the United States.

Graham, Hugh Davis, and Gurr, Ted Robert. *Violence in America: Historical and Comparative Perspectives** (Sage, 1979). An analysis by a study group of the National Commission on the Causes and Prevention of Violence that attempts to place violence in contemporary America in historical perspective, and to compare the level of violence in the United States with that of other countries.

Greenstein, Fred I. *Children and Politics*, revised edition* (Yale University Press, 1967). A study of the attitudes of young children toward politics and of how political attitudes are formed. Based on interviews with schoolchildren in New Haven, Connecticut.

Jennings, M. Kent, and Niemi, Richard G. *The Political Character of Adolescence** (Princeton University Press,

1974). An important study of political learning among high school students. The authors find that the divergence between the political attitudes of children and their parents increases as children grow older.

Key, V. O., Jr. *Public Opinion and American Democracy* (Philadelphia Book Co., 1961). A detailed analysis of public attitudes about government and politics and their relation to the way government operates.

Lane, Robert E. *Political Life** (Free Press, 1959). A comprehensive summary of political participation and public attitudes toward politics in the United States. Analyzes the factors that encourage and discourage political participation by the public.

Lippmann, Walter. *Public Opinion** (Free Press, 1965). (Originally published in 1922.) A basic work on how public opinion operates. As a distinguished political columnist, Lippmann helped to mold American public opinion for half a century.

Lowi, Theodore J. *The End of Liberalism: Ideology, Policy, and the Crisis of Public Authority** (Norton, 1979). A stimulating analysis of the theory and practice of interest group politics in the United States. Lowi is strongly critical of the consequences of the interest group bargaining process as it has developed since the New Deal.

Mills, C. Wright. *The Power Elite** (Oxford University Press, 1959). (Originally published in 1956.) One of the best-known statements of the view that there is a unified "power elite" in the United States. In Mills's view, wealth, prestige, and power in America are concentrated in the hands of a hierarchy of corporate, government, and military leaders.

Olson, Mancur, Jr. *The Logic of Collective Action: Public Goods and the Theory of Groups,* rev. edition* (Harvard University Press, 1971). An important analysis of the role of groups in the American political process. Based on an application of economic analysis to the relationships between individual self-interest and group membership and activity. Examines the consequences these relationships have for politics.

Truman, David B. *The Government Process,* 2nd edition* (Knopf, 1971). An influential study of interest groups in the United States. Develops and modifies a general theory of groups and applies it to American politics.

Weissberg, Robert. *Public Opinion and Popular Government** (Prentice-Hall, 1976). An interesting analysis of the role public opinion plays in determining which policies are adopted by government. Presents detailed results of polls conducted by Gallup, Harris, and other polling organizations on such topics as defense spending, health care, gun control, and racial integration.

*Available in paperback edition

POLITICAL PARTIES

7

When Ronald Reagan accepted his party's presidential nomination at the Republican National Convention in 1980, he surprised many among the millions watching him on television by quoting a Democratic President, Franklin D. Roosevelt: ". . . government—federal, state and local—costs too much . . . we must abolish useless offices. We must eliminate unnecessary functions of government."[1]

Aside from the fact that Roosevelt's words coincided with Reagan's own stand, the Republican candidate had good reason to invoke one of the most revered Democratic Presidents of this century. There are more persons in America who call themselves Democrats than who identify with any other group—either Republicans or independents. So mathematically, at least, a united Democratic party normally should have an advantage in a national election. Reagan understood that in order to win, he had to have the votes of millions of independents and Democrats. In November, he got them.

When Jimmy Carter, the incumbent Democrat, stood before the cheering delegates of the Democratic National Convention that renominated him that year, he warned that the Republican party lived in a "fantasy world" in which "inner-city people and farm workers and laborers do not exist. . . . Women, like children, are to be seen but not heard . . . The elderly do not need Medicare . . . .

[1] Congressional Quarterly, *Weekly Report,* July 19, 1980, p. 2066.

Workers do not require the guarantee of a healthy and a safe place to work."[2] Carter thus defended government social programs, many of which had been enacted under Democratic administrations.

The nature of the appeals by the two major-party presidential nominees told something about the topography of the political landscape in America in 1980 — the Republican candidate casting his net wide for Democratic voters, and the incumbent President appealing to his party's traditional coalition of blacks and other minorities, urban voters, and blue-collar workers.

On November 4, some 43.9 million persons cast their votes for Reagan and 35.5 million voted for Carter. The Republican nominee carried 44 states, won 489 electoral votes, and became President. Reagan won decisively. The size of his victory was all the more surprising because every advance indicator showed that many voters were discontented with both Carter and Reagan, the major-party nominees, and that the outcome would be close.

The drama of 1980 provided one set of answers to some recurring questions about American political parties: Have political parties declined in importance? Do they offer a genuine choice on the major issues facing the nation? Do they nominate the most able men and women to run the nation and its states and communities in the nuclear age? Are they truly responsive and responsible instruments of democracy? Or are they boss-controlled elitist organizations closed to outsiders? Are national conventions a circus and a farce, or useful tools of representative government? In discussing the role, history, organization, and performance of American political parties, we shall explore all these questions.

What Is a Party?

"As there are many roads to Rome and many ways to skin a cat," Frank J. Sorauf has written, "there are also many ways to look at a political party."[3] A political party is a group of men and women meeting in a small community in Connecticut to nominate a candidate for town council. It is a group of ward heelers turning out to cheer the mayor of Chicago at a political rally. It is congressional leaders having a private breakfast at the White House with the President to discuss the admin-

[2] Congressional Quarterly, *Weekly Report,* August 16, 1980, p. 2341.
[3] Frank J. Sorauf, *Political Parties in the American System* (Boston: Little, Brown, 1964), p. 1.

istration's legislative proposals. It is the delegates to a national political convention exploding in a frenzy of noise, emotion, confetti, and balloons after the name of their candidate for President is placed in nomination. It is the millions who vote on Election Day.

As Sorauf has concluded, the nature of a political party is somewhat in "the eye of the beholder."[4] Nevertheless, it is possible to identify some of the elements that make up a major political party. There are the *voters,* a majority of whom consider themselves Democrats or Republicans; the *party leaders outside of government,* who frequently control the party machinery and sometimes have important power bases; the *party activists,* who ring doorbells, serve as delegates to county, state, and national conventions, and perform the day-to-day, grassroots work of politics; and finally, the *party leaders in the government,* including the President, the leaders in Congress, and party leaders in state and local governments.

When someone speaks of "the Democratic party" or "the Republican party," that person may really mean any of these diverse elements—or all of them. Because a political party is like a big circus tent, encompassing so many different acts, it is as difficult to define in a shorthand way as it would be to define a circus. But, in very general terms, *a major political party is a broadly based coalition that attempts to gain control of the government by winning elections,* in order to exercise power and reward its members.

The Role
of Political Parties

The best way to look at political parties is not in terms of what they are but in terms of what they do. One of the major problems of government has been the management of the transfer of power. In totalitarian governments, power, once seized, is seldom peacefully relinquished. Usually the change comes unexpectedly. A democracy provides orderly institutional arrangements for the transfer of power.

In normal circumstances, in the United States, a President, running as the nominee of a political party, is elected every four years and serves one or two terms. American political parties thus perform "an essential function in the management of succession to power."[5] They serve as a vehicle for choice, offering the electorate competing candidates for public office, and, often, alternative policies. The element of choice is absolutely vital to democratic government. Where the voters cannot choose, there is no democracy. The parties operate the machinery of choice: nominations, campaigns, and elections.

Within the framework of a political system (the concept discussed in Chapter 1), political parties help to mobilize the demands and supports that are fed into the system and participate as well in the authoritative decision making, or outputs, of the government.

In a presidential election, the party in power traditionally defends its record, while the party out of power suggests that it is time for a change. For example, in 1980 President Carter defended the record of his administration, while Ronald Reagan successfully attacked it. By seeking to mobilize mass opinion behind their slogans and policies, political parties channel public support for, or against, the government. In so doing, they normally serve as an essential bridge between the people and the government. They provide a powerful means for the public's

[4] *Ibid.*
[5] V. O. Key, Jr., *Politics, Parties, and Pressure Groups,* 5th ed. (New York: Crowell, 1964), p. 9.

voice to be heard—and politicians must listen if they wish to survive in office. Parties thus help to hold officials accountable to the voters. They also help to recruit candidates for public office.

Because a political party consists of people expressing attitudes about government, it might seem to fit the definition of an interest group. But a political party runs candidates for public office. It is therefore much more comprehensive than an interest group. Instead of seeking only to *influence* government on a narrow range of issues, a major party attempts to win elections and *gain control* of the government.

The major political parties try to form "winning coalitions" by maneuvering "to create combinations powerful enough to govern."[6] In the process, they may serve to reconcile the interests of conflicting groups in society. The political party can fill the natural role of broker or mediator among interest groups, organized or not, because, in order to win elections, it usually tries to appeal broadly to many groups of voters.

Parties also play a key role in the governmental process. When the Reagan administration succeeded the Carter administration in January 1981, Washington real estate agents were happy; it meant that Democrats would be selling their houses and Republicans would be buying them. Following a presidential election, the White House staff, the cabinet, and the more important policymakers and officials of the various departments of the executive branch are for the most part appointed from the President's party. To the victors belong the White House limousines.

Political parties play a vital role in the legislative branch as well. The President appeals to party loyalty through the party's legislative leaders in order to get his programs through Congress (although he may face a Congress, or at least one house, controlled by the opposition party). Because political parties are involved in the governmental process, they serve to link different parts of the government: the President communicates with party leaders in Congress; the two houses of Congress communicate in part through party leaders; and relationships among local, state, and national governments depend to a considerable degree on ties among partisan officials and leaders.

In sum, political parties perform vital functions in the American political system. They (1) manage the transfer of power, (2) offer a choice of rival candidates and programs to the voters, (3) serve as a link between government and people by helping to hold elected officials accountable to the voters, (4) help to recruit candidates for office, (5) may serve to reconcile conflicting interests in society, (6) staff the government and help to run it, and (7) link various branches and levels of government.

The Development of American Political Parties

The framers of the Constitution created the delicately balanced machinery of the federal government and provided for regular elections of a President and Congress, but they said not a word about political parties. The reason was simple: in the modern sense, they did not exist.

[6] *Ibid.,* p. 167.

These political buttons for George Washington were intended to be sewn on clothing.

Yet, James Madison, the "father of the Constitution," foresaw that Americans would group together in factions. In *The Federalist* No. 10, he predicted that the task of regulating conflicting economic interests would involve "the spirit of party and faction in the necessary and ordinary operation of the government."

In his farewell address, George Washington warned against "the baneful effects of the spirit of party." His Vice President, John Adams, had declared: "There is nothing I dread so much as the division of the Republic into two great parties, each under its leader."[7] Yet, the American party system began to take just such a shape in the 1790s during Washington's administration.

Federalists and Democratic-Republicans

The Federalists, organized by Alexander Hamilton, Washington's Secretary of the Treasury, were the first national political party in the United States. The Federalists stood for strong central government, and their appeal was to banking, commercial, and financial interests.

Thomas Jefferson built a rival coalition that became known as the Republican party, or Democratic-Republicans.[8] It was primarily an agrarian party of small farmers, debtors, Southern planters, and frontiersmen. Being a practical politician, Jefferson sought to expand his coalition; in 1791 he made a famous trip to New York State, allegedly on a "butterfly hunting" expedition but actually to form an alliance with Aaron Burr and the Sons of Tammany, the political organization that was to dominate New York City. In the partnership of rural America and the cities, the Democratic party was born.

Jefferson's triumph in the election of 1800 inaugurated a twenty-eight-year period of ascendancy by the Jeffersonian Democratic-Republicans. In fact, the Federalists never again tried for the Presidency after 1816 when James Monroe, the Democratic-Republican candidate, was overwhelmingly elected. Monroe's victory launched the brief Era of Good Feelings, in which there was little partisan activity.

Democrats and Whigs

By 1824 the Democratic-Republicans had split into several factions and the first phase of party government in the United States came to an end. The election in 1828 of Andrew Jackson, the hero of the War of 1812, opened a new era of two-party rivalry, this time between Democrats and Whigs. Jacksonian democracy soon came to symbolize popular rule and the aspirations of the common man.

The rival Whigs, led by Henry Clay, William Henry Harrison, and Daniel Webster, were a coalition of bankers, merchants, and Southern planters held together precariously by their mutual distaste for Jacksonian democracy. The Whigs won two presidential elections between 1840 and 1854, and the two-party system flourished.[9] As Clinton Rossiter has noted, "Out of the conflict of Democrats and Whigs emerged the American political system—complete with such

---

[7] Wilfred E. Binkley, *American Political Parties* (New York: Knopf, 1963), p. 19.

[8] The name tends to be confusing to anyone attempting to trace the origins of the American party system. Today's Democratic party, the oldest political party in the world, claims the Jeffersonian Republican, or Democratic-Republican, party as its political and spiritual ancestor, a fact that Democratic orators remind us of endlessly and annually at Jefferson-Jackson Day dinners. Today's Republican party invokes Abraham Lincoln, not Jefferson.

[9] Four Whig Presidents occupied the White House. Only two were *elected*, however—William Henry Harrison in 1840 and General Zachary Taylor in 1848. Both died in office and were succeeded by their Vice Presidents, John Tyler and Millard Fillmore.

features as two major parties, a sprinkle of third parties, national nominating conventions, state and local bosses, patronage, popular campaigning, and the Presidency as the focus of politics."[10]

During the 1850s, the increasingly divisive issue of slavery caused the Democratic party to split between North and South. The Whigs, crushed by Democrat Franklin Pierce's landslide victory in 1852, were equally demoralized. The nation was about to be torn apart by civil war, and the major political parties, like the Union itself, were disintegrating.

The Republican party was born in 1854 as a party of protest against the extension of slavery into the territories. The Kansas-Nebraska Act, passed that year, permitted slavery to move westward with the frontier and aroused discontent in the North and West.

In February 1854, a group of Whigs, Free-Soilers, and antislavery Democrats gathered in a church at Ripon, Wisconsin, to recommend the creation of a new party to fight the further expansion of slavery.[11] The name "Republican party" was suggested at the meeting. The political organization that resulted from the meeting took the place of the Whigs as the rival party of the Democrats, but it was a new party and not merely the Whigs masquerading under another label.

The first Republican presidential candidate, John C. Frémont, the "Pathfinder of the Rockies," was unable to find the trail that led to the White House in the election of 1856. But in 1860 the Republicans nominated Abraham Lincoln. By that time, the Democratic party was so badly divided over the issue of slavery that its Northern and Southern wings each nominated separate candidates for President. A fourth candidate ran as the nominee of the Constitutional Union party. The four-way split enabled Lincoln to win with only 39.8 percent of the popular vote. His election was a rare fusion of the man and the times. Lincoln preserved the Union; in the process, he ensured the future of the Republican party. By rejecting slavery, the Republicans had automatically become a sec-

Democrats and Republicans

[10] Clinton Rossiter, *Parties and Politics in America* (Ithaca, N.Y.: Cornell University Press, 1960), pp. 73–74.

[11] The party birthplace is also claimed by Jackson, Michigan, where the Republicans held their first state convention five months later.

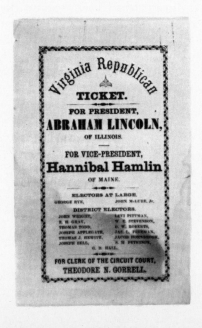

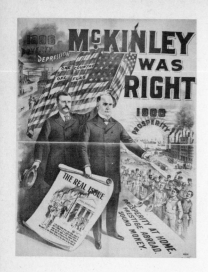

tional party, representing the North and West. And North and West meant Union, emancipation, and victory. The Democrats and the South meant slavery, secession, and defeat. Having been on the losing side of the bloody and tragic Civil War, the Democrats were a long time in recovering; the party was trapped and tangled in the folds of the Confederate flag.

For twenty-five years after 1860, the Republicans consolidated their strength and ruled America. But by 1876 the Democrats had recovered sufficiently to give the Republicans spirited two-party competition for two decades. Twice, in 1884 and 1892, the Democrats elected Grover Cleveland as President.

America was changing. After the Civil War, the nation gradually became industrialized; railroad tracks pushed westward, spanning the continent; immigrants from Europe poured in. As the rail and steel barons amassed great fortunes, small farmers found themselves squeezed economically and outnumbered by workingmen. Agrarian discontent was reflected in the rise of minor parties like the Grangers, the Greenbackers, and the Populists.

The Populists, or People's party, were a protest party of Western farmers. In 1892 their presidential candidate, James B. Weaver, showed surprising strength. By 1896 the spirit of Populism had captured the Democratic party, which nominated William Jennings Bryan for President. Bryan, running on a "free silver" platform, lost to Republican William McKinley, who defended the gold standard and conservative fiscal policies. The election resulted in a major realignment of the parties from which the Republicans emerged stronger than ever as a coalition of Eastern business interests, urban workers, Midwestern farmers, and New England Yankees.

Theodore Roosevelt held the coalition together while he was President from 1901 to 1909, but his attempt to move the Grand Old Party in a more progressive direction alarmed its conservative business wing. In 1912 the Republican party split apart. The conservative wing renominated William Howard Taft, who had been Roosevelt's handpicked successor. The Progressive ("Bull Moose") party nominated Roosevelt. The Republican split resulted in victory for Woodrow Wilson, the Democratic nominee.

Wilson's two terms proved to be a short Democratic interlude. A nation weary of the First World War chose to "return to normalcy" in the 1920s with the Republican administrations of Warren G. Harding and Calvin Coolidge, two of the less distinguished Presidents to occupy that office. Big Business dominated; it was the era of the Teapot Dome scandal, flappers, bathtub gin, and the Prohibition "speakeasy." In 1928 Republican Herbert Hoover defeated Al Smith, the first Roman Catholic nominee of a major party. A year later, the stock market crash and the onset of the Great Depression dealt the Republican party a blow comparable to the effect of the Civil War on the Democrats.

The result of these events was the election of Franklin D. Roosevelt in 1932, the New Deal, and twenty years of uninterrupted Democratic rule under

Roosevelt and his successor, Harry S Truman. Roosevelt put together a new, grand coalition composed of the South, the big cities of the North, labor, immigrants, blacks, and other minority groups.

In 1952, in the midst of the Korean war, the Republicans nominated General Dwight D. Eisenhower and recaptured the Presidency. But the Eisenhower magic could not be transferred to Richard Nixon, who narrowly lost the Presidency to John F. Kennedy in 1960. The "New Frontier" seemingly opened a new era of Democratic supremacy. But Kennedy was assassinated in 1963. In 1964 Barry Goldwater, a conservative from Arizona, captured control of the GOP from its long-dominant and more liberal Eastern, internationalist wing. The result was Republican disaster. Lyndon Johnson, who had succeeded to the Presidency after Kennedy's death, was elected in his own right with 61.1 percent of the total vote — the greatest share of the popular vote in history.

But American political parties have extraordinary resiliency: "Each one is a citadel that can withstand the impact of even the most disastrous national landslide and thus provide elements of obstinacy and stability in the two-party pattern."[12] The Republican party survived the Goldwater debacle. It regrouped around Richard Nixon, who accurately gauged the temper of the nation in 1968. Lyndon Johnson, unable to hold the Democratic coalition together in the face of war and urban riots, did not choose to run. With the Democrats divided into at least three camps, Nixon triumphed, restoring the Republican party to power and demonstrating anew the strength of the American two-party system. Nixon's landslide victory in 1972 was an even more dramatic illustration of the point, a triumph soon overshadowed by the scandal of Watergate, the resignation of Vice President Spiro Agnew, and Nixon's own resignation in 1974 on the brink of impeachment. Then in 1976 Jimmy Carter, starting from a very modest political base as the former governor of Georgia, captured the Democratic nomination, succeeded in reunifying the Democratic party, and went on to win the White House in a very close race against the incumbent, President Ford. The Democrats controlled both Congress, where they maintained their majority, and the executive branch. Only six years after Nixon's resignation, the Republican party surged back to power in 1980, capturing the White House under Ronald Reagan and gaining control of the Senate for the first time in more than a quarter of a century.

This ability of American political parties to survive adversity and rise again rests in part on the fact that many areas of the country and many congressional districts are dominated by one party; even when a party is defeated nationally, it will still have durable pockets of power across the nation. This remains true despite the spread of two-party politics to more states in recent years. For example, Reagan carried forty-four states in winning the Presidency in 1980, and his party took control of the Senate, but the Democrats retained twenty-seven of the state governorships and continued to control the House of Representatives.

The Two-Party System

Under the two-party system, to become the nominee of one of the two major parties is at least half the battle. In areas where one party dominates, it is equivalent to election. Throughout most of the nation's history, two major political

[12] Rossiter, *Parties and Politics in America*, p. 7.

parties have been arrayed against each other. The Democrats, in one guise or another, have endured. During successive eras they have been challenged by the Federalists, the Whigs, and the Republicans. Minor or third parties have joined the struggle, with greater or lesser effect, but the main battle has, historically, been a two-party affair. As Allan P. Sindler has observed, "From 1828 to the present with few exceptions the two parties together have persistently polled upward of 90 percent of the national popular vote — that is, there has been little multi-partyism."[13]

In 1968 George Wallace formed the American Independent party and ran for President outside the two-party framework. He received 13.5 percent of the popular vote. Although a substantial showing for a minor party candidate, it was nowhere near enough to win. In 1976 Eugene McCarthy, an independent candidate, received less than 1 percent of the popular vote. In 1980 Representative John B. Anderson, an Illinois Republican, won a place on the ballot in every state and waged a vigorous campaign for President. But he received only 6.6 percent of the popular vote and no electoral votes.

The Roots of Dualism

In the states and in many local communities, one party may dominate, as the Democrats did for decades in the Solid South and the Republicans did in Kansas and Vermont. But, on the whole, America has been a two-party nation. Why this should be so is a subject of mild dispute because there is no wholly satisfactory, simple answer. Among the explanations that have been offered are these:

Tradition and History. The debate over ratification of the Constitution split the country into two groups. Dualism, therefore, is as old as the nation itself. And, once established, human institutions tend to perpetuate their original form. To some extent, Americans accept the two-party system because it has almost always been there.

The Electoral System. Many features of the American political system appear compatible with the existence of two major parties. In the United States, the single-member district system prevails in federal elections. For example, only one member of Congress may be elected from a congressional district, no matter how many candidates run — it is a case of winner-take-all. The same is true of a presidential election; normally in each state the candidate who receives the most popular votes wins all of the state's electoral votes. Under such a system, minor parties lacking a strong geographical base have little chance of poaching on the two-party preserve; they tend to lose and, having lost, to disappear.[14] (By contrast, a system of proportional representation with multimember districts, as in Italy, encourages the existence of many parties by allotting seats to competing parties according to the percentage of votes that they win.)

Patterns of Belief. A majority of the American voters stand somewhere near the middle ground on many issues of American politics. Ideological differ-

[13] Allan P. Sindler, *Political Parties in the United States* (New York: St. Martin's Press, 1966), p. 15.

[14] The two parties need not be the same in all areas of the country, however. In some states, historically, minor parties have competed successfully with one of the two major national parties. For example, in Minnesota during the 1920s and 1930s, the Farmer-Labor party — not the Democratic party — was the chief competitor of the Republican party in state and congressional elections. Since a merger in 1944, the Democratic-Farmer-Labor party has been the principal rival to the Republicans in Minnesota.

ences among Americans have in the past normally not been strong enough to produce a broad range of established minor parties representing widely varying shades of political opinion, as is the case in many Western European nations.

As noted earlier, American presidential candidates generally try to make very broad-based appeals. Although there are more Democratic than Republican voters in America, neither party enjoys the support of a majority of the electorate, and both must therefore look outside their own ranks for victory. To put together a winning coalition, a presidential candidate usually appeals to the great mass of voters in the ideological center. As a result, in some elections it may appear that there is very little difference between the two major parties. Since both parties woo the same voters, it is not surprising that, to an extent, they look alike. But they have important differences as well.

A classic study of delegates to the 1956 national conventions found that the opinions of Democratic and Republican leaders diverged sharply on many important issues. What is more, these opinions were found to conform to party images: Republican leaders identified with "business, free enterprise, and economic conservatism in general," and Democrats were friendly "toward labor and toward government regulation of the economy." Differences of opinion among party leaders were found to be much sharper than the differences of opinion among ordinary members of the rank and file of the two parties.[15]

A more recent survey of party leaders, conducted in 1976, also found pronounced differences between the attitudes of Democratic and Republican leaders. Asked to rank current issues in their order of importance, the Republicans listed "reducing the role of government" as one of their two top priorities; Democrats put it at the very bottom of a list of ten.[16]

In one study of changes in American political parties, Everett Carll Ladd, Jr., and Charles D. Hadley suggested the emergence of a "two-tiered" party structure.[17] "There has been too much cultural change, too fast," they argued, with the result that middle-class white voters have tended to express their resistance to social change by voting for Republican presidential candidates but for Democrats for congressional and state offices. As the authors have expressed it, "in the two-tiered system . . . resistance to social and cultural change deemed excessive is expressed in balloting for its great national fulcrum, the Presidency; while general support for extending the managerial/welfare state is sustained by maintaining the Democratic majority at the subpresidential level. . . ."[18] Not every election conforms to this two-tiered model, however. In 1976 the voters elected a Democrat as President, and four years later the Republicans won the Senate as well as the Presidency.

The fading of party loyalties among many voters has been one of the most visible features of American politics in recent years. Beginning in 1974, about a third of the voters described themselves as independents. Only about two-thirds of the voters called themselves Republicans or Democrats.[19] As Ladd and Hadley have

Why France Has a Multi-Party System: One Explanation

How can one conceive of a one-party system in a country that has over 200 varieties of cheeses?

—Charles De Gaulle, *New York Times Magazine,* June 29, 1958.

Drawing by D. Fradon © 1969 The New Yorker Magazine, Inc.

"How would you like me to answer that question? As a member of my ethnic group, educational class, income group, or religious category?"

The Decline of Party Loyalties

noted, "All measures lead to the same conclusion. There has been a long-term decline of party allegiance, and a dramatic drop-off over the last decade."[20] And Austin Ranney has suggested that something approaching a "no-party system" has emerged in presidential politics.[21] The results of the 1980 election seemed to bear out this general movement away from party loyalties. The Republican candidate, President Reagan, won 51 percent of the vote even though less than one-quarter of the electorate described itself as identifying with the Republican party.

Various reasons have been suggested for the decline of party ties: a more educated electorate, less dependent on parties for guidance; an increase in "split-ticket" voting by persons who may, for example, vote for a Republican candidate for President and a Democrat for governor; the increasing importance of television and the news media generally; and the breaking up of the old loyalties and alignments within the major parties.[22]

Despite the fading of party loyalties, political parties in America have by no means become extinct. And even though the number of unaffiliated voters has been rising, there are still many more Americans who call themselves Democrats or Republicans than who term themselves independents.

The Democrats

A good way to perceive the differences between the two major parties is to examine their images. In the public's imagination, the "typical" Democrat lives in a big city in the North. He or she is a Catholic, a Jew, a black, a Pole, an Italian, a Mexican, a Puerto Rican, or a member of some other minority group. The imaginary Democrat drinks beer, belongs to a union, goes bowling, and has a fairly low income.

Genus Republican's habitat, by contrast, is the hedge-trimmed suburbs. He or she lives in a split-level house with a picture window, commutes to the city, and belongs to a country club that has no members from minority groups. The male of the species is almost certainly a white Protestant. He drinks martinis and eats white bread. His wife drives a station wagon. He owns his own company or works for a conglomerate. He golfs on weekends. He is rich, or at least comfortable, equally at home in the board room or the locker room. That, at any rate, is the popular image.

Like any caricature, these portraits are overdrawn. For example, one study of shifts in the American electorate concluded that the Democrats' base "has changed somewhat from the New Deal era ... they have lost ground among some of their old constituencies, such as trade unionists, big-city whites, and Southern whites; while they have made up for such losses with gains among the upper-middle-class. ...." The study suggested the Republicans have "lost their grip on the American establishment, most notably among young men and women of relative privilege."[23] Still, the image of each party and of individual Democrats and Republicans, at least to an extent, mirrors reality: studies have shown that the Democrats usually enjoy greater voter support from labor, Catholics,

[20] Ladd with Hadley, *Transformations of the American Party System: Political Coalitions from the New Deal to the 1970s,* p. 329.
[21] Austin Ranney, "The Political Parties: Reform and Decline," in Anthony King, ed., *The New American Political System* (Washington, D.C.: American Enterprise Institute for Public Policy Research, 1979), p. 245.
[22] Ladd with Hadley, *Transformations of the American Party System: Political Coalitions from the New Deal to the 1970s,* pp. 329–33.
[23] *Ibid.,* pp. 268, 258.

Jews, blacks, ethnic minorities, young people, and from persons who have not attended college, who have low incomes, and who live in the cities. Republicans are more likely to be Protestant, white, suburban, rural, wealthy, older, college educated, and professionals or business executives.

Since 1932, in presidential elections, the Democratic party has, in spirit, been the party of Franklin D. Roosevelt. The vast social welfare programs launched by the New Deal changed the face of America and gave the Democratic party an identity that has persisted for many years. Truman's "Fair Deal," Kennedy's "New Frontier," and Johnson's "Great Society" were all patterned on Roosevelt's New Deal. All sought to harness federal funds and federal energies to solve national problems.

Despite the success of Roosevelt's grand coalition, the Democratic party continues to display some of the characteristics of a bivalve, with two distinct halves. The Southern, rural, conservative wing of the party bears little resemblance to the Northern, urban, liberal wing. Thus, the Democrats are at once the party of Russell Long of Louisiana and of Edward Kennedy of Massachusetts. Normally, the overriding desire for power and electoral victory is the muscle that holds the two halves together. Sometimes the muscle fails. For example, in 1948 Southern Democrats walked out of the national convention over the civil rights issue.

For decades the Democrats could count on the eleven states of the Old Confederacy as a solid Democratic bloc. But the South is no longer a one-party Democratic enclave; it voted solidly for Nixon in 1972. And in the South in 1980 Carter carried only his home state of Georgia against his Republican opponent, Ronald Reagan. Since 1952, every Republican presidential candidate has won some Southern electoral votes. (See Table 7–1.)

In political campaigns, Republicans like to label the Democrats as "spenders." On the whole, Democrats have been more willing to appropriate federal funds for social action. As a result of this political reality, the Democratic party since 1933 has been the party of social security, TVA, Medicare, and federal aid to education. It has, in short, often been the party of social innovation.

In addition to differences of substance, the two parties show perceptible differences in style. "I don't belong to any organized party," the humorist Will Rogers once quipped. "I'm a Democrat."[24] Democrats do tend to be uninhibited and occasionally raucous, fighting among themselves; Republicans are normally more sedate.

Of course, these differences do not always hold true. In 1976 the Democrats gathered in unusual harmony as they nominated Jimmy Carter, the accepted front-runner; it was the Republican convention, split between Gerald Ford and Ronald Reagan, that provided the color and the excitement. Usually, however, it is the Democrats who brawl and squabble, as they did in 1980.

"A gathering of Democrats *is* more sweaty, disorderly, offhand, and rowdy than a gathering of Republicans . . ." Clinton Rossiter has noted. "A gathering of Republicans *is* more respectable, sober, purposeful, and businesslike than a gathering of Democrats . . ."[25] The Democratic donkey brays, snorts, kicks up its

Two delegates to the 1980 conventions

"Democrats . . . tend to be uninhibited . . ."

"Republicans are normally more sedate."

[24] Quoted in Andrew Hacker, "Is the Party Over?" *The New York Times Book Review,* November 26, 1978, p. 12.
[25] Rossiter, *Parties and Politics in America,* p. 117.

Republican Inroads in the South, 1950–1980

Table 7–1

Year	Number of Congressmen		Number of Senators		Number of Governors		Number of States Voting for Presidential Nominee	
	D	R	D	R	D	R	D	R
1950	103	2	22	0	11	0		
1952	100	6	22	0	11	0	7	4
1954	99	7	22	0	11	0		
1956	99	7	22	0	11	0	6	5
1958	99	7	22	0	11	0		
1960	99	7	22	0	11	0	7	3*
1962	95	11	21	1	11	0		
1964	89	17	21	1	11	0	6	5
1966	83	23	19	3	9	2		
1968	80	26	18	4	9	2	1	5†
1970	79	27	16 (1)‡	5	9	2		
1972	74	34	14 (1)‡	7	8	3	0	11
1974	81	27	15 (1)‡	6	8	3		
1976	82	26	16 (1)‡	5	9	2	10	1
1978	77	31	15 (1)‡	6	8	3		
1980	69	39	11 (1)‡	10	6	5	1	10

* The eight Mississippi electors voted for Harry Byrd.
† George Wallace won five states on the American Independent ticket.
‡ Harry Byrd, Jr., was elected in Virginia in 1970 and 1976 as an Independent.
  Source: House, Governor, and President figures in Congressional Quarterly, *Politics in America 1945–1966* (Washington, D.C.: Congressional Quarterly Service, 1967), pp. 101, 123, 117–21. Senate figures in Richard Scammon, *America Votes 7* (Washington, D.C.: Governmental Affairs Institute, 1968), pp. 12, 31, 74, 82, 147, 205, 289, 357, 371, 379, 404. Data since 1968 from Congressional Quarterly, *Weekly Reports* and *New York Times*.

heels, balks, fusses, and is a very different animal in appearance, substance, and temperament from the Republican elephant.

The Republicans   "Fundamentally," Theodore H. White once wrote, "the Republican Party is white, middle-class and Protestant. . . . Two moods color its thinking. One is the old Protestant-Puritan ethic of the small towns of America. . . . The other is the philosophy of private enterprise, the sense that the individual, as man or corporation, can build swifter and better for common good than big government. From middle-class America the Republicans get their votes; from the executive leadership and from the families of the great enterprises they get their funds."[26]

Despite its successes in 1968, 1972, and 1980, since the New Deal the Republican party has, in terms of party identification, enjoyed the support of only a minority of American voters; people who identify themselves as Democrats have, in recent decades, outnumbered people who say they are Republicans by 3 to 2, or more at times. In the face of such figures, the Republican party's constant task is to broaden its popular appeal and turn its minority into a majority, or at least a plurality. The Republican party won the Presidency in 1980 precisely because it was able to attract Democrats and independents.

[26] Theodore H. White, *The Making of the President 1968* (New York: Atheneum, 1969), p. 33.

The familiar Democratic charge that "the Republican party is the party of Big Business" is largely accurate, just as it is true that, nationally, the Democrats have traditionally been the party of organized labor. The preference of business for the Republican party may be measured by analyzing campaign contributions. For example, of the $9.8 million spent by corporate political action committees (PACs) in the 1978 elections, 62 percent went to Republicans. And by the start of the 1980 campaign, of the $8.9 million in large gifts contributed by corporate PACs up to that point, 56 percent went to Republicans and 42 percent to Democrats.[27]

During the Eisenhower years, federal regulatory agencies were markedly friendly to the broadcasting networks, airlines, and other businesses they were supposedly regulating. It can be argued that "it does make a difference to the television industry, the railroads, or the stock exchanges whether Democrats or Republicans have a majority in the independent commissions."[28]

Like the Democrats, the Republicans have a split personality. The scar left when Theodore Roosevelt bolted the party in 1912 has never entirely healed; in modern times the battle of Republican conservatives (the political heirs of William Howard Taft) against Republican liberal-moderates (the heirs of Theodore Roosevelt) continues as fiercely as ever.

The struggle broke out afresh in 1952 in the convention battle between Senator Robert A. Taft of Ohio (the son of William Howard Taft) and General Eisenhower, who was backed by the Eastern liberals. Then in 1964 Goldwater and the conservative wing won control of the party from the Eastern Establishment led by Nelson Rockefeller. In 1968 the ideological split was still highly visible, with liberals Rockefeller and George Romney on one side, Ronald Reagan of California at the conservative end of the spectrum, and Richard Nixon near the center. Again in 1976 the split was reflected in the battle between President Ford and Ronald Reagan for the party's presidential nomination, the most serious challenge to a Republican President within his own party since the revolt against William Howard Taft. It was doubtful that a cleavage that ran so deep would soon disappear. Despite Ford's nomination in 1976, the right wing of the Republican party remained a strong force within the GOP, ready to recapture the party, as it did in 1980. The Republican split was still visible that year, when Reagan was opposed in the primaries by three moderates, George Bush, John B. Anderson, and Howard H. Baker, Jr. This time, however, with Reagan as their standard-bearer, the conservative wing won the White House.

Minor Parties

Minor parties have been active throughout most of the nation's history, from the Anti-Masons of the 1830s and the Barnburners of the 1840s, to the Know-Nothings of the 1850s, the Greenbackers of the 1880s, the Populists of the 1890s, the Progressives of the 1920s, and the American Independents in 1968.

In 1968 the third-party movement of Alabama's George Wallace scared major-party supporters because of the possibility that Wallace would carry enough states to prevent either major-party candidate from gaining a majority of electoral votes. He would then be in a position to bargain with his electoral votes, or to throw the outcome into the House of Representatives. (The machinery of the electoral college is discussed on pp. 333–35.)

[27] *National Journal,* August 9, 1980, pp. 1305–06; and *Washington Post,* November 1, 1980, p. A9.
[28] Rossiter, *Parties and Politics in America,* p. 131.

Minor-Party and Independent Vote, 1880–1980*

Figure 7–1

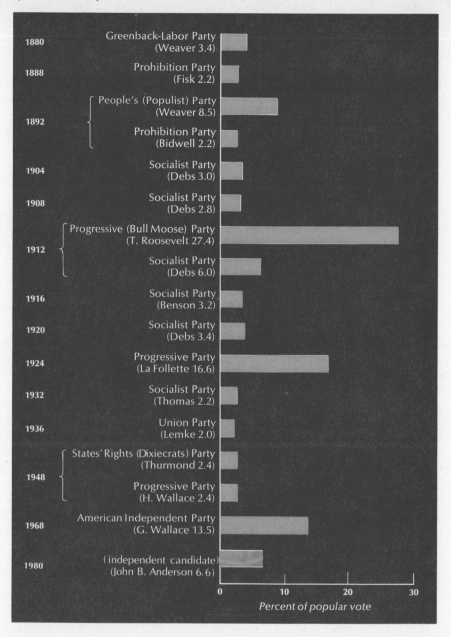

* Includes only those minor parties that polled 2 percent or more of the popular vote. In 1972 and 1976 no minor party received 2 percent.

Source: Neal R. Peirce, *The People's President* (New York: Simon and Schuster, 1968), pp. 305–07. Reprinted by permission of Simon and Schuster; Donald B. Cole, *Handbook of American History* (New York: Harcourt Brace Jovanovich, 1968), pp. 304–05; *Politics in America,* 4th ed. (Washington, D.C.: Congressional Quarterly, 1971), p. 91; and *New York Times,* January 6, 1981, p. A14.

Although Wallace appeared on the ballot in every state, usually as the candidate of the American Independent party, he carried only five Southern states; his 46 electoral votes were not enough to deadlock the presidential election. His 13.5 percent of the popular vote was considerably less than the 21.1 percent received by the Know-Nothings[29] in 1856, the 27.4 percent polled by Theodore Roosevelt's Bull Moose party in 1912, or the 16.6 percent received by Robert La Follette's Progressives in 1924. In 1980 independent candidate John B. Anderson carried no states. But with 6.6 percent of the popular vote, he did better than many others have, including Eugene McCarthy, who got less than 1 percent of the popular vote in 1976.

Ten minor parties ran candidates for President in 1980. Unlike Anderson, who was a serious factor in the 1980 campaign, the minor-party candidates had no hope of affecting the outcome. The best known of the 1980 minor-party candidates were Ed Clark of the Libertarian party and Barry Commoner of the Citizens' party. V. O. Key, Jr., has suggested that minor parties fall into two broad categories, "those formed to propagate a particular doctrine," and "transient third-party movements" that briefly appear on the American scene and then disappear. The Prohibition party and the Socialist party are examples of doctrinal parties that "have been kept alive over long periods by little bands of dedicated souls."[30] Among the transient third-party movements, Key perceived two types: parties of economic protest, such as the Populists, the Greenbackers, and the Progressives of 1924; and "secessionist parties" that have split off from one of the major parties, such as the Progressives in 1912 and the Dixiecrats in 1948.

Sometimes minor parties have a strong nativist streak. Just as the Wallace campaign played upon white fears of black Americans, more than a century ago the Know-Nothings, or Native American party, exploited fear of Irish immigrants and other "foreigners." The party platform in 1856, when Millard Fillmore ran as the Know-Nothing candidate, warned: "Americans must rule America."

In certain states minor parties have gained a powerful position. The Liberal party and the Conservative party in New York sometimes hold the balance of power in elections in that state. Nationally, however, minor parties have never consistently enjoyed much power or influence. On some occasions they have influenced the politics of the major parties—as when Populism captured the Democratic party in 1896.

"One of the persistent qualities of the American two-party system," Clinton Rossiter has concluded, "is the way in which one of the major parties moves almost instinctively to absorb (and thus be somewhat reshaped by) the most challenging third party of the time. In any case, it is a notable fact that no third party in America has ever risen to become a major party, and that no major party has ever fallen to become a third party."[31]

1980: Libertarian party presidential candidate Ed Clark

Party Structure

One could draw a neat organizational chart of a major political party, with the national chairman and national committee at the top of the pyramid, and state and local party machinery arrayed below. The chart would be technically correct but highly misleading. In fact, the national party exists more on paper than in reality, in theory more than in fact.

[29] The anti-Catholic, anti-Irish Native American party was so secret that its members pretended ignorance of party affairs; as a result editor Horace Greeley dubbed it the Know-Nothing party.
[30] Key, *Politics, Parties, and Pressure Groups,* p. 255.
[31] Rossiter, *Parties and Politics in America,* pp. 5–6.

American political parties are *decentralized* and only loosely organized. Rather than a pyramid, with all power flowing from the top down, party structure "may be more accurately described as a system of layers of organization. Each successive layer—county or city, state, national—has an independent concern about elections in its geographical jurisdiction."[32]

National
Political Parties

A national political party is somewhat like a sports trophy that a team may win and retain for a time but must return eventually so that it may be awarded to a new team. Thus, President Gerald R. Ford led the Republican party in 1976, but after his defeat, he was obliged to give up control of the party machinery. Four years later, it belonged to Ronald Reagan.

On paper, the party's quadrennial *national convention* is the source of all authority within the party. The convention nominates the party's candidates for President and Vice President; it writes a platform, settles disputes and writes rules, and elects the members of the national committee.

The *national chairman* is elected by the members of the national committee. In practice he or she is chosen or retained by the party's presidential nominee at the end of the national convention.

The *national committee* consists of one man and one woman from each state, the District of Columbia, Puerto Rico, and some of the territories, plus additional members chosen under party formulas based on population and party strength in the states. The Democratic National Committee includes representatives from Congress and the Democratic governors, for a total of 367 members. The Republican National Committee includes all GOP state party chairmen, plus one woman and one man from each state and the territories, for a total of 163 members. Within each state, members of the national committee are selected under state law by state party convention, by the state delegation to the national convention, by state committees, or in primary elections. The national convention formally "elects" the members of the national committee, but in fact it simply ratifies the choices of each state. An executive director of the Democratic National Committee once declared that the committee was composed of "people left over from the convention. They select a chairman, but there is a myth in the country that there is a national party structure."[33]

Both parties' national committees meet only twice a year. Beginning in 1974 the Democrats have held additional, midterm national conventions every four years to try to strengthen the party between presidential elections. In the past, national committees have sometimes been little more than the permanent offices in Washington that house the national chairman and the staff. But more recently, the national committees of both parties have become more active between presidential elections. Between elections, the chief functions of the staff of the national committee are public relations, patronage, research, and fund raising.

In 1980 the Republican party's gains in the states were partly credited to a vigorous drive by GOP Chairman Bill Brock aimed at cutting into Democratic strength at the state level. Brock committed $2 million to state legislative races in 1978 and $3 million in 1980. On Election Day, the Republicans picked up four

[32] Key, *Politics, Parties, and Pressure Groups*, p. 316.
[33] William Welsh, quoted in Congressional Quarterly, *Weekly Report*, March 18, 1972, p. 583.

governorships, increasing to twenty-three the number of Republican governors. In addition, the GOP increased from twelve to fourteen the number of states in which it controlled both houses of the state legislature. The gains were significant because the Republicans then had greater strength when the states redistricted the House of Representatives after the 1980 census. Brock also launched an aggressive direct-mail campaign to raise funds from small donors. Even before the campaign began, the Republican National Committee had raised $23.8 million. And it had received contributions from 600 "Eagles," persons who contributed amounts of $10,000 or more.[34]

As a rule, a presidential nominee either largely ignores the machinery of the national committee and builds a personal organization to run his campaign, or he takes over the national committee machinery and makes it his own. In theory, the national chairman's main job is to manage the presidential campaign; in practice, however, the candidate's real campaign manager is seldom the party chairman. In 1980, for example, William J. Casey, a sixty-seven-year-old New York lawyer, served as Ronald Reagan's campaign director. Although Bill Brock was the party chairman, Reagan relied on a tight-knit group of advisers—especially Edwin Meese III, who had been chief of staff when Reagan was governor of California—to run his campaign.

Independent of the national committees, and serving as further evidence of the decentralization of American party politics, are the *congressional leaders* of each party, elected by their colleagues, and the *congressional* and *senatorial campaign committees*. Both major parties have campaign committees in the House and Senate; their members are chosen by party members in each branch of Congress. The congressional committees channel money, speakers, advice, and assistance to party members who are up for election.

In both the Republican and Democratic parties, there is normally a good deal of conflict between the party leaders in Congress and the leaders of the more presidentially oriented national party organization, a built-in tension often reflected in rivalry and jealousy between the congressional campaign committees and the national committee.

Party organization and election laws vary tremendously in the states, with the result that one can find kaleidoscopic variety in almost any given phase of American politics below the national level. Just as the national party in power is controlled by the President, the state party is often dominated by the governor. In the case of some large Northern industrial states, the mayor of a large city may wield considerable influence. On the other hand, the state party may be led by a party chairman who is not obligated to, and was elected without the support of, the incumbent governor. And, of course, a state chairman may head a party that is out of power and does not control the governor's office.[35] Some state party organizations are the fiefdom of a single party boss—either an elected official or a party leader outside government. But this is less often the case today than in the past.

Republicans or Democrats may consistently dominate within a state; or

State and Local Parties

[34] *Washington Post*, November 6, 1980, p. A24; *National Journal*, November 8, 1980, p. 1893; and *Chairman's Report* (Washington, D.C.: Republican National Committee, January 1980).
[35] Robert J. Huckshorn, *Party Leadership in the States* (Boston: University of Massachusetts Press, 1976), pp. 69–95.

power may be divided between the two parties. But even within one party, there are great variations in party politics from state to state. The Democratic party in Alabama is very different from that in Michigan. In both parties, liberals may control one state, conservatives or moderates another. And these local differences tend to make American political parties decentralized, fragmented, and weak.

State politics often reflects geographic cleavages. In New York the Democratic party traditionally controls New York City, while Republicans dominate "upstate," the areas outside of the city. In Illinois the Democrats, strong in Chicago's Cook County, must contend with a heavy downstate Republican vote. In Michigan, Democrats are strong in Detroit, but Republicans dominate many other areas of the state.

The state parties are bound together within the national political party by a mutual desire to have a "winner" at the head of the national ticket. Often (although not always), a strong presidential candidate will sweep state and local candidates into office on his coattails. In 1980 Reagan's electoral sweep may have helped to defeat a number of well-known Senate and House Democratic liberals and to give the Republicans control of the Senate.

The layer of party organization below that of the national committees is the state committees. Like national committee members, members of the state committees are chosen in many different ways, including county conventions and direct primaries.

At the grass roots of each major political party is a third layer of party organization, consisting of the county committees, county chairmen, district leaders, precinct or ward captains, and party workers. The local party organization is held together in part by the paste of patronage—the rewarding of party faithfuls with government jobs. The old-style, big-city political machines depended almost entirely on patronage; even today a substantial portion of party workers may be found on town, city, and county payrolls.

Although big-city machines still exist, the cigar-chomping, derby-hatted political "boss" of the late nineteenth and early twentieth centuries has in most areas enjoyed his "last hurrah." At one time, Frank Hague, the Democratic boss of Jersey City, could blatantly declare: "I am the law." Edward J. Flynn, the boss of the Bronx, could rise to considerable power within the national Democratic party. Carmine De Sapio, the leader of Tammany Hall, was able to dominate New York City politics in the 1950s. But, Frank J. Sorauf has suggested, "The

The Old Politics—Machine Style

George Washington (Boss) Plunkitt, a political leader in New York City at the turn of the century, explained his philosophy for attracting votes:

What holds your grip on your district is to go right down among the poor families and help them in the different ways they need help. I've got a regular system for this. If there's a fire in Ninth, Tenth, or Eleventh Avenue, for example, any hour of the day or night, I'm usually there with some of my election district captains as soon as the fire engines.

If a family is burned out I don't ask whether they are Republicans or Democrats; and I don't refer them to the Charity Organization Society, which would investigate their case in a month or two and decide they were worthy of help about the time they are dead from starvation. I just get quarters for them, buy clothes for them if their clothes were burned up, and fix them up til they get things runnin' again. It's philanthropy, but it's politics, too—mighty good politics. Who can tell how many votes one of these fires brings me?

—Boss Plunkitt, in William L. Riordon, *Plunkitt of Tammany Hall.*

defeat of Carmine De Sapio and the Tammany tiger by the reformers in the fall of 1961 may stand as one of the great turning points in American politics."[36] Chicago's Mayor Richard J. Daley, long a power in national Democratic politics, drew substantial support from the city's business community. He gave them what they wanted, "a new downtown area, an expressway . . . confidence in the city's economic future," and in the process made it almost impossible for Republican candidates to find any support among business leaders.[37] Daley, often described as the last of the big-city bosses, died in 1976.

The urban machines drew their power from the vast waves of immigrants to America's cities. The machines offered all sorts of help to these newcomers— from food baskets to city jobs. In return, all the boss demanded was the newcomer's vote. Each ward captain knew precisely how many votes he could deliver—the captain who did not would soon find he was no longer a municipal inspector of sewers. Since the 1930s, social security, welfare payments, food stamps, unemployment benefits, and general prosperity have cut the ground out from under the city machines: the social services formerly provided by the party clubhouse now flow from the impersonal bureaucracy in Washington. And the establishment of the direct primary and internal party reforms have, in some cases, impaired the power of the bosses to control nominations.

However, the local party can still sometimes find a city job for a loyal worker, for "the power to hire is still an important power resource."[38] And urban machines can help the poor deal with complex city bureaucracies.[39] Or a city machine can award municipal construction contracts to party activists or financial contributors. But people participate in politics at the grass-roots level today for a variety of reasons, not only economic motives. The woman in Ohio who telephoned her neighbors and urged them to vote for Reagan in 1980 may have wanted to feel that she was personally participating in the election of a President. The volunteers ringing doorbells for a candidate in 1980 did so in many cases for the sheer excitement of being involved in a political campaign. The suburban man who serves as a precinct captain may be active in politics because he enjoys the added prestige he acquires in the eyes of his neighbors. (He is the person who can get a new street light installed or the potholes filled in.) He may even be a party worker because he likes to attend the party's national convention as a delegate every four years.

Increasingly, two new kinds of activists are taking part in American politics at various levels, including service as delegates to national conventions. These are the issue activists—persons committed to a particular issue, such as civil rights or women's rights—and activists who work in the organizations of political candidates. These new breeds are, to some extent at least, replacing the "ward heelers" and party regulars of yesteryear.

The number of political activists at any level is fairly small, however. Perhaps only 10 percent of the population could be classified as "politically involved." (See Table 7-2.) If we apply the percentages shown in the table for 1976

[36] Sorauf, *Political Parties in the American System*, p. 53.

[37] David Halberstam, "Daley of Chicago," in William J. Crotty, Donald M. Freeman, and Douglas S. Gatlin, *Political Parties and Political Behavior* (Boston: Allyn and Bacon, 1971), p. 286. Reprinted from *Harper's Magazine*, August 1968.

[38] Raymond E. Wolfinger, "Why Political Machines Have Not Withered Away and Other Revisionist Thoughts," *The Journal of Politics*, Vol. 34 (1972), p. 384.

[39] *Ibid.*, pp. 384–86.

Table 7-2

	1956	1960	1964	1968	1972	1976
Do you belong to any political club or organization?	3%	3%	4%	3%	NA*	NA*
Did you give any money or buy tickets or do anything to help the campaign for one of the parties or candidates?	10%	11%	11%	12%	10%	9% 8%**
Did you go to any political meetings, rallies, dinners, or things like that?	7%	8%	8%	14%	9%	6%
Did you do any other work for one of the parties or candidates?	3%	5%	5%	5%	5%	4%

* NA: Not Available.
** Percent mentioning a tax check-off contribution.
Source: Survey Research Center/Center for Political Studies, University of Michigan, in William H. Flanigan and Nancy H. Zingale, *Political Behavior of the American Electorate,* 4th ed. (Boston: Allyn and Bacon, 1979), p. 163. Reprinted with permission.

to the 1976 voting-age population of 146,548,000, we find that in round numbers 13.2 million Americans contributed to parties or candidates, 8.8 million attended political gatherings or functions, and 5.8 million did political work for parties or candidates. And only about 3.6 million Americans belonged to political clubs.[40]

The National Conventions

During the Republican National Convention in Detroit in 1980, millions of television viewers were treated to a rare spectacle. Walter Cronkite, then the senior anchor man for CBS News, interviewed former President Gerald Ford as rumors swept the convention of a "dream ticket" headed by Ronald Reagan, with Ford as his vice-presidential running mate.

Walter Cronkite
interviewing
former President Ford
at the 1980 Republican
National Convention

[40] Data for political clubs are for 1968.

It was the third day of the convention, and Reagan was about to be nominated for President by his party. Reagan and Ford had met twice to discuss the
possibility that the former President would join the ticket. In the interview with
Cronkite, Ford publicly laid down what seemed to be his demands for agreeing
to run for Vice President. Ford said he would have to play "a meaningful role."

"Something like a co-Presidency?" Cronkite asked.

"That is something Governor Reagan ought to consider," Ford replied.[41]

Within a few hours, the deal had fallen apart, apparently because the
Reagan camp felt that Ford was asking for too much authority. Reagan picked
George Bush for his running mate. But for a few moments, television viewers
had participated in a modern, electronic version of the old "smoke-filled room";
Walter Cronkite and the medium of television were directly involved in a politi-
cal negotiation.

Television has brought American politics into the living room. Perhaps
nowhere is this more apparent than in the drama of the presidential nominating
convention. Viewers at home have a better and closer view of a national convention than the delegates. Network television reporters, sprouting antennae and
electronic gear and looking like Martians, roam the convention floor interviewing
political leaders and generating excitement. In darkened rooms just off the convention floor, TV directors follow the action on glowing monitors. They bark
crisp orders; the camera cuts to Fred Graham of CBS or Judy Woodruff of NBC.
The latest gossip, the newest floor rumor, is fed back, in living color, to millions
of American homes.

True, the television viewer will miss some of the drama of the convention
hall, the actual feel of the crowd, the vast size of the amphitheater. On the other
hand, he or she can sit back in the comfort of home, beer in hand, and watch democracy in action as the Democrats and Republicans choose their candidates for
the most powerful office in the world.

Dan Rather interviews a
delegate at the
Republican National
Convention, 1980.

---

[41] *Washington Star,* July 18, 1980, p. A1. See also *New York Times,* July 18, 1980, p. A1, and
Congressional Quarterly, *Weekly Report,* July 19, 1980, pp. 1982–83.

The National Nominating Conventions:
Corn Pone and Apple Pie

The national nominating convention is something unknown to the Constitution and undreamed of by the founding fathers. It is an American invention, as native to the U.S.A. as corn pone or apple pie. A Democratic or a Republican national nominating convention, once it gets going, emits sounds and lights that never were on land or sea. . . . At different hours of the day or night, it has something of the painted and tinselled and tired gaiety of a four-ring circus, something of the juvenile inebriety and sympathetic fraternal sentiment of a class reunion, something of the tub-thumping frenzy of a backwoods camp meeting. . . . What goes on beneath the surface and behind locked doors is something both realistic and important. For it is here, unexposed to the public eye, that the deals and bargains, the necessary compromises are arranged — compromises designed to satisfy as well as possible all of the divergent elements within the party.

—Carl Becker, "The Will of the People," *Yale Review*, March 1945.

But is that really what the viewer is seeing? Are the delegates actually choosing the nominee, or are they merely ratifying what has been a foregone conclusion for weeks or months? Do the delegates have meaningful power and independent judgment, or are they robots legally bound to vote for the winner of their state's primary? Are some of them puppets taking orders from political bosses? Would it perhaps be better, after all, to watch a late movie? The answers to these questions depend entirely on what convention, what delegation, and which delegates one has in mind. Depending on the year and the circumstances, one can accurately answer "yes" or "no" to each question.

The national convention has been roundly denounced as a carnival and a bore, and vigorously defended as the most practical method of choosing political candidates in a democracy. It may be all three.

The national nominating convention evolved slowly in American politics. Until 1824 nominations for President were made by party caucus in Congress. As a presidential aspirant that year, Andrew Jackson knew he did not have enough strength in the congressional caucus to gain the nomination; so his supporters boycotted the caucus. The Tennessee legislature nominated Jackson, who received the most popular and electoral votes. But no candidate received a majority of the electoral votes, and the selection of a President fell to the House of Representatives. Jackson lost when the House chose John Quincy Adams. Jackson's efforts, however, successfully dethroned "King Caucus"; in the election of 1832, presidential candidates of all political parties were nominated by national conventions for the first time.

The early conventions provided no surprises, but in 1844, on the eighth ballot, the Democrats chose a "dark horse," James K. Polk, who won the election and proved an able President. Polk's nomination "marked the coming of age of the convention as an institution capable of creating as well as of ratifying consensus within the party."[42]

[42] Key, *Politics, Parties, and Pressure Groups,* p. 398.

Today, national party conventions normally take place over four days in July or August. The convention city is often hot and overcrowded; delegates spend long hours waiting for elevators and attempting to do such ordinarily simple things as ordering breakfast in a hotel coffee shop or getting through to someone on the telephone. Rival candidates set up headquarters in hotel suites. As the convention opens, rumors fly of deals and of switches by key delegations. There are press conferences, television interviews, parades, bands, and other forms of confusion and diversion.

Major decisions are often made outside the convention hall. Behind the scenes, presidential candidates and their lieutenants apply a combination of carrot and stick to party leaders and delegates, alternately pleading and pressuring for their support. The candidates know that state delegations seek to provide the winning margin of victory to a nominee, thereby earning his gratitude and, perhaps, future rewards. The psychological pressure on delegates is always the same: hop aboard this or that bandwagon before it is too late to matter.[43]

The convention, on its first day, normally hears the report of its credentials committee, the body that decides what delegates shall be seated. Often, rival delegations claim to represent the party in a state, or one faction may charge irregularities in the selection of delegates. The credentials committee must decide these disputes, subject always to the approval of the convention. In the evening the keynote speaker fills the air with the customary rhetoric. On the second day the party platform is debated and voted upon. The outcome of these struggles over credentials and the platform often signals which party faction has the votes to win the nomination for its candidate.

On the third day the nominations and balloting for presidential nominee usually begin. Traditionally, a candidate's name is not mentioned until the very end of the nominating speech. ("I give you the name of the next President of the United States, ———— ———— ————!") The name is a signal for a carefully planned "spontaneous" demonstration on the floor, often employing professional demonstrators and organized to the split second by experts armed with noisemakers, walkie-talkies, and stopwatches.

Despite time limits on oratory, the nominating and seconding speeches sometimes go on to the near limits of delegate endurance. Then the roll of states is called in alphabetical order for the balloting. In both parties, the candidate who wins a simple majority of the convention votes is nominated. Front-runners attempt to win on the first ballot. Lesser candidates and dark horses naturally hope that nobody wins on the first ballot; they may then have a chance of picking up increased delegate strength on the second, third, or subsequent ballots.

It is the traditional privilege of the presidential nominee to select the vice-presidential nominee.[44] The fourth day of the convention is devoted to the routine nomination of and balloting for the Vice President, the acceptance speeches of both candidates, and their climactic appearance with their families before the cheering delegates. This moment of high personal and political drama underscores the fact that a national convention also serves the function of a party pep

---

[43] Political candidates have a way of remembering who was for them when. Early backers enjoy a special status.

[44] In 1956 Adlai Stevenson, the nominee of the Democratic National Convention, threw open the choice of a vice-presidential candidate to the delegates. In the floor balloting, Senator Estes Kefauver of Tennessee narrowly defeated Senator John F. Kennedy to become Stevenson's running mate.

The Republican National
Convention, 1980

rally, generating enthusiasm for the ticket and, in effect, kicking off the presidential campaign.

Beneath the hoopla and the ballyhoo of a national party convention, serious business has taken place. Rival political leaders have clashed and fought, differences on issues within the party have been publicly aired, and a major political party has produced its nominees for the highest offices in the land.

The Delegates

Who are the few thousand men and women formally entitled to select the presidential nominees of the two major parties? In general, they represent a cross section of the party, but a generally affluent cross section, since the cost of travel to a convention city, of hotels and meals, mounts up to hundreds of dollars. The delegates usually include governors, senators, members of Congress, mayors, state legislators, state party officials, and activists and contributors at the grass-

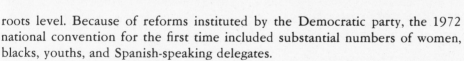

The Democratic
National Convention,
1980

Senator Edward M. Kennedy

roots level. Because of reforms instituted by the Democratic party, the 1972 national convention for the first time included substantial numbers of women, blacks, youths, and Spanish-speaking delegates.

Delegates to national party conventions are chosen by a variety of methods. In 1980 thirty-five states and the District of Columbia held presidential primaries in which voters in one or both parties expressed their preference for a presidential nominee and chose all or some convention delegates. In the remaining states, delegates were chosen by other methods—district conventions, state conventions, and, in a few cases, by state committees. In some instances, the results of the primaries were binding on the delegates; in others, the delegates went to the conventions unpledged to any particular candidate.

At the 1980 Democratic National Convention, President Carter's forces easily defeated a move by supporters of Senator Edward M. Kennedy for an "open convention." The Kennedy forces had sought to defeat a proposed rule

that would have bound all delegates to vote on the first ballot for the presidential candidate under whose banner they were elected. Since Carter had more than enough committed votes to win on the first ballot, Kennedy's attempt to free the delegates to vote as they pleased was his only hope of winning the nomination. He failed.

In 1976 the Democrats abandoned "winner-take-all" primaries, in which the presidential candidate who won a primary, no matter how slim the margin of victory, could win all of a state's convention delegates. Instead, the Democrats adopted a system of proportional representation, but with loopholes permitting a "winner-take-all" system at the district level in some states. In 1972 and previous years more delegates were chosen in the majority of states that did *not* hold presidential primaries. By 1980, however, 2267 regular delegates to the Democratic National Convention were elected in the primaries, while 1064 delegates were selected by the other methods.

These procedures have not always been democratic. For example, for many years, in some states, blacks, women, and young people were systematically excluded from Democratic party delegations to national conventions. After the divisive 1968 national convention, reform elements within the Democratic party sought means to democratize the delegate-selection process.

A Democratic reform commission reported in 1970 that in at least twenty states there had been no adequate rules for selection of delegates to the 1968

Delegates, by Selected Groups,
to the Democratic National Convention, 1968–1980

Table 7–3

	Women	Blacks	Youth*	Other†
1968	13%	5.5%	4%	NA
1972	38%	15%	21%	5%
1976	34%	9%	14.8%	NA
1980	49.9%	14.9%	NA	6%

* Eighteen to thirty years of age.
† Includes delegates of Spanish-speaking or Indian origin; not available for 1968 or 1976.
Source: *The Party Reformed, Final Report of the Commission on Party Structure and Delegate Selection* (Washington, D.C.: Democratic National Committee, July 7, 1972), pp. 7–8; *New York Times,* July 12, 1976, p. C5. 1980 data from Democratic National Committee.

convention, "leaving the entire process to the discretion of a handful of party leaders."[45] The commission issued a set of eighteen guidelines designed to eliminate such abuses, but it had no authority to enforce its recommendations on state and local party organizations. Somewhat to the surprise of everyone, even commission members, the panel's reform guidelines were followed by most state Democratic party organizations. As a result, the delegates to the 1972 national convention at Miami Beach were considerably different from their counterparts in 1968. Most of the delegates were attending a national convention for the first time, and a TV viewer could hardly fail to notice the substantial numbers of young delegates, women, and blacks. (See Table 7-3.)

Both major parties apportion delegates under complicated formulas based on population and party strength within each state. The Republican National Convention of 1980 had 994 regular delegates, each casting one vote, and an equal number of alternates. The Republicans allot a bonus of six delegates to each state that votes Republican in the preceding presidential, senatorial, or gubernatorial race. The Democrats base the size of state delegations on population, but also allot extra delegates to states according to the size of the Democratic vote in each state. Under the Democratic formula, the number of delegates at the 1980 national convention mushroomed to an unmanageable 5381 (3331 regular delegates and 2050 alternates).

Delegates who are chosen by state and local party organizations are sometimes under the control of party leaders. But the growth of binding primaries and caucuses that choose delegates pledged to vote for a particular candidate has greatly reduced the power of party leaders to control national conventions.

Until 1968 the Democrats permitted one form or another of the unit rule, which in some cases allowed the majority of a state delegation to cast the state's entire vote. The opponents of this system argued that it made boss rule easier. In 1968 the Democrats voted to drop the unit rule at all party levels for the 1972 convention. Thus, another tool of the "old politics" has fallen by the wayside.

Despite the tumult and the shouting, the results of many recent national conventions have been unsurprising. So the question remains: Are national conventions real arenas of democratic decision or mere rubber stamps?

Do Conventions
Decide?

[45] *Mandate for Reform, Report of the Commission on Party Structure and Delegate Selection to the Democratic National Convention* (Washington, D.C.: Democratic National Committee, 1970), pp. 10–11.

In 1960 the Brookings Institution, an independent research organization, published a study of national nominating conventions. Analyzing sixty-five conventions from 1832 to 1960, the study identified five types of nominations:[46]

1. *Confirmation.* An existing President or party titular leader is confirmed as the party's choice.
2. *Inheritance.* A political understudy or previous leader inherits the party mantle.
3. *Inner group selection.* Dominant party leaders get together and agree on the nominee.
4. *Compromise in stalemate.* A deadlocked convention turns to a dark horse or unexpected candidate.
5. *Factional victory.* One of several competing factions within the party succeeds in nominating its candidate.

Although twenty-two conventions during this period were "confirming," fully nineteen, the second highest number, fell into the category of "factional victory," evidence that genuine competition had characterized national nominating conventions a substantial share of the time. Only three of the nineteen conventions—those nominating McKinley in 1896, Dewey in 1944, and Kennedy in 1960—had outcomes that were generally anticipated in advance of the convention.[47]

The struggle for nomination at a convention can, of course, take many different shapes. The phrase "smoke-filled room," often used to describe the selection of a candidate by political bosses operating in secret, grew out of the 1920 GOP convention. There, a group of Republican leaders met in a room of Chicago's Blackstone Hotel and ended a convention stalemate by selecting Warren G. Harding of Marion, Ohio, who *looked* like a President but was otherwise a mediocre Chief Executive. The Democrats set a record at their 1924 convention in New York, the longest ever held. The weary delegates finally chose John W. Davis, a New York corporation lawyer and former congressman from West Virginia, on the 103rd ballot; but the voters preferred the Republican candidate, Calvin Coolidge. Franklin D. Roosevelt led the field at the Democratic National Convention in 1932, but he was not nominated until the fourth ballot. In 1940, with the galleries chanting "We want Willkie," the Republicans nominated Wendell L. Willkie, Wall Street lawyer and a true dark horse. The Taft-Eisenhower convention battle in 1952 reflected the greatest split in the Republican party since 1912.

Since 1960, however, national conventions have filled more of a *ratifying* than a selecting function. For example, George McGovern's delegate strength going into the 1972 Democratic Convention was sufficiently great to make his nomination reasonably certain. In 1976 Gerald Ford had to fight for the Republican nomination against Ronald Reagan, but shortly before the convention, it appeared that Ford had enough delegates to win. Carter's nomination in 1976 was preordained after his primary victories. The 1980 Republican National Convention merely ratified Ronald Reagan as the party's choice. And it was clear that year, even before the convention met, that the Democrats would renominate Jimmy Carter, the incumbent President.

This "ratifying" trend since 1960 does not mean that conventions have lost

[46] Paul T. David, Ralph M. Goldman, and Richard C. Bain, *The Politics of National Party Conventions,* Kathleen Sproul, ed. (New York: Vintage Books, 1964), pp. 127–38. A paperback condensation of the study originally published by the Brookings Institution.
[47] *Ibid.,* p. 286.

all power to decide or that vigorous battles will not take place in the future. But two factors have combined to diminish the decisional role of the convention in recent years.

First, preconvention campaigns by presidential hopefuls have gained in intensity and length. Reagan, who triumphed in November 1980, had announced his candidacy on November 13, 1979, almost a year earlier. Even before then, he had begun building his organization and making speeches around the country. And in 1980 he campaigned in virtually all the primaries, beginning in the snows of New Hampshire in February.

Second, extensive coverage by television and other media has focused national attention on these preconvention campaigns and increased their importance. Consequently, they have become, to some extent, elimination races. In 1980, for example, Carter's victories over Senator Edward M. Kennedy in a series of primaries all but removed Kennedy from the race.

As a result of the intense press coverage now given to presidential primaries and to preconvention campaigning, one or another candidate has tended to gain a clear lead before the convention in the public mind, in the political polls, and often, within the rank and file of the party. William R. Keech, in a study made public in 1972, concluded that the front-runners within each party usually receive the nomination. With one exception, the candidate ranking highest in support among the party rank and file, as measured by the last Gallup poll before the national convention, had emerged as the nominee in major party nominations since 1936.[48] Nevertheless, as long as the institution of the national convention remains, the potential exists for a sharply contested battle for the nomination if two or more candidates enter the arena with roughly equal support and resources.

National conventions nominate candidates for President who go before the voters every four years. But many Americans do not participate in selecting the convention delegates who make this crucial choice. In 1980, for example, more than 32 million people voted in the primaries, the method by which most delegates were selected. But this total primary turnout was still less than a quarter of the number of Americans of voting age. And Austin Ranney has concluded that those who do vote in the presidential primaries are "quite unrepresentative" of the party identifiers who do not participate.[49] Even fewer people choose the delegates who are selected in other ways. Most people, for example, have never attended a district or state party convention where delegates are chosen.

From time to time various proposals have been made to revamp the national nominating convention or even replace it with some presumably more representative or more dignified procedure. One of the recurrent proposals is for a *national presidential primary,* in which the voters could directly choose the presidential candidates of the major parties. Those who advocate a national primary

The Future of the Convention System

[48] William R. Keech, "Presidential Nominating Politics: Problems of Popular Choice," paper prepared for the 1972 annual meeting of the American Political Science Association (Washington, D.C.: American Political Science Association, 1972), pp. 1–3. The exception was Senator Estes Kefauver, who led in the poll in 1952 but lost the nomination to Adlai Stevenson.

[49] Austin Ranney, "Turnout and Representation in Presidential Primary Elections," *American Political Science Review,* Vol. 66 (March 1972), p. 27. The number of Americans who voted in the 1980 primaries was 32,146,906. Congressional Quarterly, *Weekly Report,* May 31, 1980, p. 1469; and Congressional Quarterly, *Weekly Report,* June 7, 1980, p. 1547.

argue that it would be more democratic because it would reflect the choice of more voters.

The plan has some possible drawbacks, however: there is no assurance that voters in a national primary would be typical of nonvoting party rank-and-file members. Critics have also argued that if too many candidates entered the primary, the candidate who polled the most votes might be one who enjoyed intense but limited support, and who could not, therefore, win a general election. Or, no single candidate might receive a majority of the votes. In such a case, if a runoff were held, the candidate who initially led the field in the primary might lose.[50] Moreover, a national presidential primary might work against lesser known candidates — John B. Anderson of Illinois, for example, in 1980. Such candidates benefit from a nominating process that is spread out over several months, allowing them to gain greater public recognition. And, it has been suggested, a national primary would further weaken American political parties by bypassing party organizations, while increasing the power of the news media to influence the electoral process.[51]

In any event the convention system, having survived since 1832, is not likely to disappear in the television age, at a time when it has grown into a sort of political Super Bowl. Nor is it at all clear that the national convention should be replaced. The Brookings Institution study concluded, "The continuing contributions made by the conventions to the survival and stability of the American political order are unique, indispensable, and, granted our form of Constitution, probably irreplaceable. . . . The services of the convention as a general conclave for the selection and recognition of top leadership in each party, and for its replacement when necessary, could be abandoned only at serious national peril."[52]

Political Parties and Democratic Government

At best, Americans have always had a somewhat ambivalent attitude toward politics and politicians. "Politics," Clinton Rossiter has noted, "is sin, and politicians, if not sinners, are pretty suspicious fellows."[53]

In 1952 General Eisenhower enjoyed the support of many voters who felt he was "above politics" or "not a politician." The same was true of Ronald Reagan when he ran for governor of California for the first time in 1966, in a campaign that emphasized his nonprofessional political status. Among many voters, the image of the politician as an unprincipled opportunist persists. The initial reaction of many Americans to the Watergate scandal was not shock at the illegal acts committed by the Nixon administration but the view that "they all do it."

Since political parties are vital to the functioning of American democracy, it is somewhat paradoxical that politics and politicians — especially with their access

---

[50] For a discussion of the pros and cons of a national presidential primary, see Judith H. Parris, *The Convention Problem* (Washington, D.C.: The Brookings Institution, 1972), pp. 172–77.

[51] Austin Ranney, *The Federalization of Presidential Primaries* (Washington, D.C.: American Enterprise Institute for Public Policy Research, 1978), pp. 33–38.

[52] David, Goldman, and Bain, *The Politics of National Party Conventions*, p. 339.

[53] Rossiter, *Parties and Politics in America*, p. 34.

to the image-making resources of Madison Avenue—do not enjoy greater prestige.

The truth about politics and its practitioners may lie somewhere between Aristotle's view that "the good of man" is the object of politics and the classic statement of Simon Cameron, the Republican boss of Pennsylvania, that "an honest politician is one who, when he is bought, will stay bought."

Possibly Americans would have a more generous view of the craft of politics if it were more widely understood that parties and democracy are mutually dependent. Competition among political parties is the essence of democracy. Political parties in America, as we have seen, provide a vehicle of political choice, manage the transfer of power, help to hold politicians accountable to the voters, recruit candidates, staff and link branches of the government, and may sometimes resolve social conflict.

The rest of the world also has a vital stake in the politics of American democracy; certainly the party nominee chosen by the electorate to be President has greater power than any other leader in history. How an American President uses that power, including the nuclear weapons under his control, is of direct concern to all other nations, as well as to the voters at home.

The "brokerage" role of political parties in mediating among interest groups (whether such groups are organized or not), and in resolving social conflict, is of tremendous importance in a democracy under pressure. Both major political parties try to form a broad base by appealing to diverse groups in society. As a result, when one party loses power and another wins the Presidency, the change tends to be accepted, or at least tolerated, by the voters. At the same time, the party out of power plays a valuable role as the opposition party, offering alternative programs in Congress and serving as a rallying point for its followers. The "out" party keeps alive the possibility of change for another four years. In these ways parties help to keep conflict manageable, for if substantial numbers of voters violently opposed the election results, the political system could not work.

In his classic complaint about the similarity of American political parties, James Bryce concluded that "neither party has any principles, any distinctive tenets." The similarities of American parties are often lamented, but, as noted earlier, there are significant differences as well.

A Choice, Not an Echo?

Some of these differences can be measured by comparing contrasting party platforms in presidential elections. Although the conventional view is that platforms are "meaningless," Gerald M. Pomper has concluded that platforms in fact "are reasonably meaningful indications of the party's intentions" and serve to commit the parties to "particular policies."[54]

Moreover—as surprising as it might be to many people—in a majority of cases, Pomper concluded, political parties actually carry out the promises contained in their platforms. Analyzing 1400 platform pledges over two decades (1944–1964), Pomper concluded that 72 percent of these promises were fulfilled.[55]

While it is true that American parties are not sharply ideological, it is also

[54] Gerald M. Pomper, *Elections in America: Control and Influence in Democratic Politics* (New York: Dodd, Mead, 1971), p. 178.
[55] *Ibid.,* p. 186. See also Paul T. David, "Party Platforms as National Plans," in *Public Administration Review.* Vol. XXXI, No. 3 (May/June 1971), pp. 303–15.

true that many American voters have not been sharply ideological. The argument is often made that major parties should offer a more pronounced choice on issues, not merely a choice between candidates; but it is by no means clear that extreme polarization of the parties on issues that divide American society is desirable. "The difference between Democrats and Republicans," Max Lerner has observed, "while it is more than the difference between Tweedledum and Tweedledee, is not such as to split the society itself or invite civil conflict. . . . The choices between the two are usually substantial choices but not desperate ones."[56]

Are Parties Accountable to the Voters?

When Americans go to the polls, they do not elect parties; they elect officials who usually run as the candidates of political parties. By its very nature, the American political system holds these officials accountable to the voters while holding the parties only indirectly accountable.

The most frequent criticism of the American party system is that the parties are not "responsible" to the electorate, that there is no way to make them keep the promises outlined in their platforms, and that, in any event, they lack the internal discipline to whip their programs through Congress.[57] One difficulty is that party platforms "are written for use in *presidential* campaigns, yet they consist mainly of proposals for legislation that will be meaningless unless there is congressional action."[58] Yet, as Gerald Pomper has noted, political parties often do carry out platform pledges.

In a parliamentary system of government, such as that in Great Britain, political parties are more closely linked to the popular will because the voters choose a majority party that is responsible for the conduct of both the executive and legislative branches of government. Since few critics of the American party system advocate parliamentary government for the United States, party accountability in America is likely to remain a matter of degree.

Many political scientists do not agree on the need for or desirability of greater party responsibility. For example, party cohesion strong enough to pass programs in Congress could only be achieved by reducing the importance and independence of individual legislators. But advocates of strong, responsible parties point to several ways that party responsibility can be strengthened, short of adopting the British system of parliamentary government: attempting to achieve greater discipline within parties by rewarding cooperative members with campaign funds, and electing the chairmen of congressional committees on the basis of party loyalty rather than seniority.

To an extent, however, a measure of party responsibility already exists. When American parties embark on courses of action that displease large numbers of voters, the voters may retaliate. In 1964 Barry Goldwater, the Republican candidate, was the "hawk" who advocated "total victory" over communism. President Johnson, on the other hand, presented himself as a "dove," promising: "We are not about to send American boys nine or ten thousand miles away from home

[56] Max Lerner, *America as a Civilization.* Vol. 1 (New York: Simon and Schuster, 1967), pp. 389–90.
[57] See, for example, Report of the Committee on Political Parties of the American Political Science Association, *Toward a More Responsible Two-Party System* (New York: Holt, Rinehart and Winston, 1950).
[58] David, Goldman, and Bain, *The Politics of National Party Conventions,* p. 344.

to do what Asian boys ought to be doing for themselves."[59] In less than a year, however, Johnson was sending combat troops to Vietnam. Many of his supporters felt misled; it turned out that they had voted for a "dove" and elected a "hawk." But in the election of 1968, Johnson found it prudent not to run again, and the nation sent a Republican to the White House. Jimmy Carter's rejection in 1980 by an electorate angry and frustrated over the state of the nation under his Presidency is further evidence that a measure of accountability is not wholly lacking in American politics.

Attempting to predict the future of American political parties is a perilous business. Like life itself, politics is often unpredictable; those who forecasted the eclipse of the Republican party in 1964 were required to watch the elephant ride into the White House in 1968 and again in 1972. Although similar predictions of Republican doom were heard after Nixon's resignation over the Watergate scandal in 1974, six years later, the GOP had again recaptured the White House.

A Look Ahead

One fact seems clear. Over a period of time, political parties must respond to the pressures for, or against, change, or pay the price of defeat. And it seems likely that in times of substantial social stress in America, minor parties of the right and left will continue to arise. Possibly, more "non-party" candidates will seek the Presidency as did Eugene McCarthy in 1976 and John B. Anderson in 1980. Yet, in one form or another, the two-party system has flourished since the beginning of the republic and will probably survive.

The increased importance of television and of preconvention campaigns probably makes the last-minute selection of an unknown candidate by a national convention less likely than in the past. Candidates will probably continue to rely more on television, which can reach millions of people, than on old-fashioned stump campaigning. Political commercials and professional campaign managers skilled in media techniques now play a major role in campaigns. So do political polls.

Political parties mirror the society in which they function. If government can be made more responsive to the public, political parties may play a vital part in that process, for they are uniquely situated to translate the hopes of the American people into action by the American government.

[59] Public Papers of the Presidents. *Lyndon B. Johnson 1963–64,* Book II (Washington, D.C.: U.S. Government Printing Office, 1965), p. 1391.

Perspective

A major political party is a broadly based coalition that attempts to gain control of the government by winning elections. Political parties perform vital functions in the American political system. They manage the transfer of power, offer a choice of rival candidates and programs to the voters, and serve as a link between government and people by helping to hold elected officials accountable to the voters. In addition, they may reconcile conflicting interests in society, they staff the government and help to run it, and they link various branches and levels of government.

The elements that make up a major political party include the voters; the party activists, people who serve as delegates to political conventions and perform the day-to-day, grass-roots work of politics; the party leaders outside of government, who frequently control the party machinery; and finally, the party leaders in the government, including the President, the leaders in Congress, and the party leaders in state and local governments.

Throughout most of the nation's history, two major political parties have been arrayed against each other. The Democrats, in one guise or another, have endured. During successive eras they have been challenged by the Federalists, the Whigs, and the Republicans. Minor or third parties have joined the struggle, with greater or lesser effect; but the main battle, historically, has been a two-party affair. Democrats usually enjoy greater voter support than Republicans from labor, Catholics, Jews, blacks, ethnic minorities, young people, and from persons who have not attended college, who have low incomes, and who live in the cities. Republicans often receive greater support among voters who are Protestant, white, suburban, rural, wealthy, older, college educated, and professionals or business executives. But about one-third of the voters identify with no political party and consider themselves independents. The decline of party loyalties among many American voters has been pronounced in recent years.

Several explanations have been offered for the existence of the two-party system. The debate over ratification of the Constitution split the country into two groups. Dualism, therefore, is as old as the nation itself. In the United States, a single-member district system prevails in federal elections. Under such a system, minor parties lacking a strong geographical base have little chance of poaching on the two-party preserve. And, ideological differences among Americans have in the past normally not been strong enough to produce established minor parties representing widely varying shades of political opinion, as in many Western European nations.

Yet, minor parties have been active throughout most of the nation's history, from the Anti-Masons of the 1830s to the American Independents in 1968. Ten minor parties ran candidates for President in 1980, in addition to the independent candidacy of John B. Anderson of Illinois. In certain states, such as New York, minor parties have gained a powerful position. Nationally, however, minor parties have never consistently enjoyed much power or influence.

A party's quadrennial national convention is theoretically the source of all authority within the party. The convention nominates the party's candidates for President and Vice President. In recent years, however, conventions have tended to select the candidate who is already the front-runner. The party convention also writes a platform, settles disputes and writes rules, and elects the members of the national committee. The national chairman is formally elected by the members of the national committee, although in practice he or she is chosen or retained by the party presidential nominee at the end of the national convention. Between elections, the chief functions of the staff of the national committee are public relations, patronage, research, and fund raising.

Independent of the national committees are the congressional leaders of each party, elected by their colleagues, and the congressional and senatorial campaign committees. The congressional committees channel money, speakers, advice, and assistance to party members who are up for election.

Political parties are vital to the functioning of American democracy. There are significant differences among parties that are evident from their campaign platforms. Furthermore, platform promises are often carried out. There is, in addition, evidence that parties are, in some measure, responsible to the voters. Over a period of time, political parties must respond to the pressures for, or against, change, or pay the price of defeat.

Suggested Reading

American Political Science Association, Committee on Political Parties. *Toward a More Responsible Two-Party System: A Report** (Johnson Reprint Corporation, 1970). (Originally published in 1950.) Statement of the case for stronger, more disciplined, and more centralized political parties in the United States. This report, by sixteen authorities on political parties, initiated a lively debate among political scientists over the nature of American political parties.

Binkley, Wilfred E. *American Political Parties,* 4th edition (Knopf, 1963). A comprehensive treatment of the historical development of the American party system. Emphasizes the building of coalitions by American political parties.

Costikyan, Edward N. *Behind Closed Doors: Politics in the Public Interest** (Harcourt Brace Jovanovich, 1968). (Originally published in 1966.) An inside examination of the workings of politics in New York City by a reform Democrat and former party leader. Includes detailed explanations of primaries, conventions, campaigns, and the job of local political leaders.

Crotty, William J. *Decision for the Democrats: Reforming the Party Structure* (Johns Hopkins University Press, 1978). A detailed study of the reform movement within the Democratic party in the years following the 1968 Democratic Convention. Traces the major changes that were made in party structure and procedures, and summarizes their consequences.

Crotty, William J., and Jacobson, Gary C. *American Parties in Decline** (Little, Brown, 1980). A revealing analysis of the declining influence and significance of political parties in the United States. Discusses the weakened role of party in the electorate, in election campaigns, and in Congress.

David, Paul T.; Goldman, Ralph M.; and Bain, Richard C. *The Politics of National Party Conventions* (The Brookings Institution, 1960). A detailed examination of the historical development of national party conventions. Stresses the functions that the national conventions perform in the American party system.

Duverger, Maurice. *Political Parties: Their Organization and Activity in the Modern State,* 3rd edition** (Methuen, 1969). An influential comparative analysis of political parties in a number of countries. Among other topics, Duverger, a French political scientist, examines the nature of party organization in different types of parties and explores the relationship between the electoral system in a country and the type of party system that flourishes there.

Epstein, Leon D. *Political Parties in Western Democracies** (Transaction Books, 1979). A useful comparative study of political parties in various countries, with special stress on those in Great Britain and the United States. Examines the historical development of parties, recruitment of party leaders, and the contribution of the parties to governing.

Keech, William R., and Matthews, Donald R. *The Party's Choice** (The Brookings Institution, 1977). An analysis of the process by which presidential candidates were nominated between 1936 and 1976.

Key, V. O., Jr. *Politics, Parties, and Pressure Groups,* 5th edition (Crowell, 1964). A comprehensive analysis of political parties and interest groups. The extensive footnotes serve as a useful guide to much of the scholarly work on political parties and interest groups up to 1963. Examines the nature of the American party system, party structure and procedures, the relations between parties and the voters, and the impact of parties on government.

Ladd, Everett Carll, Jr., with Hadley, Charles D. *Transformations of the American Party System: Political Coalitions from the New Deal to the 1970s,* 2nd edition** (Norton, 1978). An interesting analysis of the changes in the American party system that have taken place since the New Deal. Emphasizes the changing makeup of the Democratic and the Republican electoral coalitions.

Mazmanian, Daniel A. *Third Parties in Presidential Elections** (The Brookings Institution, 1974). A comprehensive examination of American third parties: the conditions that cause them to arise, the factors that impede their success, and their role in the American party system.

Parris, Judith H. *The Convention Problem: Issues in Reform of Presidential Nominating Procedures** (The Brookings Institution, 1972). A comprehensive examination of the rules and procedures of national conventions, and the methods of choosing convention delegates.

Ranney, Austin. *Curing the Mischiefs of Faction: Party Reform in America** (University of California Press, 1975). A thoughtful analysis of the theory and practice of party reform in the United States. Emphasizes three main periods when major changes were made in American party institutions: 1820–1840; 1890–1920; and 1956–1974.

Sorauf, Frank J. *Party Politics in America,* 4th edition (Little, Brown, 1980). A comprehensive analysis of political parties in the United States. Examines political party organization, the behavior of party supporters in the mass electorate, the role of parties in contesting elections, and the impact of parties on government.

* Available in paperback edition

POLITICAL CAMPAIGNS AND CANDIDATES

Americans watching television one night in 1980 saw an interesting one-minute commercial. It was not the typical advertisement for a detergent, a dentrifrice, or a floor wax. Rather, it sought to sell the voters the Republican candidate for President of the United States. Television commercials have become an important aspect of modern political campaigns; candidates at the presidential level and below routinely advertise their qualifications on TV. The 1980 commercial began like this:

VIDEO	AUDIO
Reagan taking oath of office as Governor of California Zoom in to Reagan Cut to motorcade to state capitol Cut to Reagan shaking hands in crowd	This is a man whose time has come. A strong leader with a proven record. In 1966, answering the call of his party, Ronald Reagan was elected governor of California . . . next to President, the biggest job in the nation . . . What the new governor inherited was a state of crisis. California was faced with a $194-million-dollar deficit and was spending a million dollars a day more than it was taking in. The state was on the brink of bankruptcy.

| Cut to Reagan signing bill | Governor Reagan became the greatest tax reformer in the state's history. When Governor Reagan left office, the $194-million-dollar deficit had been transformed into a $550-million-dollar surplus. |

| Cut to capitol dome and super of *San Francisco Chronicle* | The *San Francisco Chronicle* said Governor Reagan has saved the state from bankruptcy. |

| Cut to Reagan for President | The time is now for strong leadership. Reagan for President. |

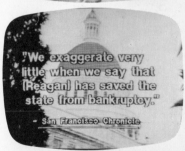

For an instant, through the medium of television, the consciousness of millions of viewers had been touched by a political message. It should not be surprising in the television age that candidates for political office try to sell themselves on TV. Once nominated, candidates must appeal to the voters. The campaign is often concentrated in a period of no more than nine weeks, and television offers the surest means of reaching the largest number of voters.

As a result, television has dramatically changed American political campaigns since 1948. The day is long past when a William McKinley could campaign from his front porch in Canton, Ohio. Today's candidates hire an advertising agency to prepare one- to five-minute commercial "spots." They may debate their opponents on television, as the two major presidential rivals did in 1960, 1976, and in 1980, or appear in carefully staged, televised question-and-answer sessions designed to display their warm personalities and firm grasp of the issues. Or, they may buy an expensive half-hour of prime TV time for a sincere talk to the American people. Television, in short, is an integral part of a modern political campaign.

For every candidate, between nomination and election, there stands the campaign. In American politics, the campaign is the battleground of power. Victory may depend on how well the battle is fought, for a third or more of the voters decide how to vote during the campaign. Mostly because of the wide use of television, campaigns are expensive: in 1976 candidates at all levels spent $540 million.[1] But political candidates do not always have equal financial and

[1] Herbert E. Alexander, *Financing Politics: Money, Elections and Political Reform,* 2nd ed. (Washington, D.C.: Congressional Quarterly Press, 1980), p. 7.

creative resources. In the era of electronic mass media, disturbing questions have arisen. Will the candidate with the best "image"—the most attractive appearance, the cleverest television advisers, the smoothest packaging—win the election? Do Americans vote for the carefully sanitized "image" of the candidate, rather than the person? Does the candidate with the most money always win? Should one candidate enjoy a financial advantage over another in a democracy? If not, what can be done about it? Above all, amid the hoopla, the oratory, and the television commercials, can the voters make a reasonable choice for themselves and for the nation?

These questions have no easy answers. And yet, however imperfect campaigns may be, however raucous and divisive, they are a vital part of the American political system. Campaigns, in the words of the historian Henry Adams, are "the dance of democracy."

How Campaigns Are Organized

Campaigns are organized chaos. On a national level, large numbers of people, professionals and volunteers, are thrown together for a relatively short period of time to mount an incredibly complex effort to elect a President. The candidate is rather like someone in the eye of a hurricane; as he jets around the country—stumping, speechmaking, and handshaking—the crowds and camera crews, the press and the voters, local politicians and aides swirl around him. He may arise at 5 A.M. and not get to sleep until 2 A.M. the next morning, with a dozen cities and thousands of miles traversed in between. Physically exhausted, his hands cut and bruised from the crowds, he is expected to keep smiling throughout his ordeal and to remain alert, ready to respond instantly to any new issue or crisis. In some remote cornfield of Iowa, he may be asked to comment on a sudden and complicated development in Moscow or Peking. He worries that an inappropriate word

Left: Ronald Reagan, campaigning for President, 1980. *Right:* Candidate Reagan conferring with campaign advisers.

or phrase might cost him the election. An assassin may lurk in the hotel kitchen. In the jet age, the pressures on the candidate are constant and cruel.

The candidate, jetting about the country at 500 miles an hour, obviously must have an elaborate campaign organization behind him with a headquarters staff to plan and coordinate the total effort. His ultimate success may depend on many variables — his charisma, his TV makeup, his advertising agency, his experience, the issues, the number of registered Democrats and Republicans, a sudden foreign policy crisis, an ill-advised remark, the weather on Election Day — but not the least of these factors is the quality of his campaign organization.

The Republican party's 1980 manuals for campaign workers tell a good deal about the work of politics. The titles and subheadings of the volumes suggest the wide range of problems faced in organizing a campaign: "How to Recruit Party Candidates," "Precinct Organization," "Blockworkers," "Get to Know Your Precinct," "Fund Raising Drives," "Voter Registration," "Boiler Room Telephoning," "Volunteers," "Volunteer Recruitment Pitch," "Public Relations," "Radio and TV Exposure," "Media Kits," and "The Advance Team."[2]

A presidential candidate must have a campaign manager and a small group of top-level aides to give overall direction to the campaign. He must have someone in charge of fund raising, for a national campaign costs millions of dollars. He needs a media team to handle advertising and television, a press secretary, representatives to handle advance details of his personal appearances, speechwriters, regional and state coordinators, and citizens' groups to enlist volunteer support. He must attempt to coordinate the work of national, state, and local party organizations.

In 1980 Ronald Reagan's successful campaign for President was managed by a close-knit group of advisers with varied professional backgrounds and experience. The campaign director was William J. Casey, a wealthy New York lawyer and former supporter of President Nixon. (Nixon had appointed Casey chairman of the Securities and Exchange Commission.) There were seven deputy directors: Edwin Meese III, issues and research; William E. Timmons, political operations; Richard B. Wirthlin, polling and strategy; Peter Dailey, media; Franklyn (Lyn)

Reagan's 1980 Campaign Manager William J. Casey, later Director of the CIA

[2] 1980 Republican party campaign manuals (Washington, D.C.: Republican National Committee, 1980).

The following are excerpts from publications of the Republican National Committee:

Telephone Boiler Room. The best method for making phone calls is the "boiler room" system. Volunteers are brought to one central location, the "boiler room," to place their calls. This may be a specially installed phone bank or donated business office space with 5 to 20 phones that can be used after normal business hours.

Door-to-Door Canvassing. Personal contact with a potential voter will always be the most effective political tool in having him register Republican. . . . The "BLITZ" technique is most effective for door-to-door canvassing. The concept is simple: Hundreds of volunteers literally blanket the targeted precincts, walk their assigned streets, gather data, identify unregistered Republicans, and return to the central headquarters all within two or three hours.

News Relations. For a successful campaign, candidates need the goodwill and respect . . . of news media. Candidates need reporters and, as a rule, reporters do not need candidates. This is a point that should always be foremost in the minds of candidates and staff. One reckless or rude remark to a reporter is probably among the worst of public relations blunders.

News Releases. Publicity should always contain some news value. News releases sometimes come out fast and furiously from campaign headquarters and reporters often groan over the lack of real news in them. . . . Too often the releases are "filed" in the nearest trash can.

Volunteer Recruitment Pitch.

Hello,
Mr. Miss Mrs. Ms. _____,
This is _____ calling from Republican Headquarters. This is a crucial year for Republican candidates, and we need your help. . . . Would you be willing to give us a couple of hours of your time . . . as a telephone interviewer? . . .
If Yes: May we sign you up for a 3-hour shift [suggest a day and time]? [Secure agreement.] . . .
If No: That's fine. We really need your vote. Thank you very much for all your time. [Hang up, but only after they have hung up first.]

Boxes. Lots and lots of boxes . . . . "in" boxes, "out" boxes, "pending" boxes, "correspondence" boxes . . .

The more boxes you have on your desk, the busier you look . . . and a scheduler must look busy or he is derelict in his duty. Heaven forbid! And occasionally pitch something new in each box so it looks like you really know what you're doing.

Telephones. At least two! It impresses the person who is calling in to check on an invitation if you can pick up the other phone and talk to two people at once. Again, it makes you sound important, not to mention busy! And we know how important it is to sound busy! . . . And make sure that any caller is put on hold for at least 60 seconds before you speak to them, even if you're doing nothing but reading the [newspaper], because we must always give the impression of busy, busy, busy.

Factory Visits. Factory visits are a favorite type of street campaigning, and they can be very effective. Republicans often fall into a trap, however, by making the tour escorted by the company president or plant manager. Remember, most of the workers don't like that guy, and our Party is constantly fighting its "big business" image. Get the union shop steward to take you around if he will, and if he won't, get an ordinary worker who's on our side.

Schools. College campuses contain many voters and a candidate who can appeal to them will find a good source of volunteers as well. In recent years, campus visits have been fraught with peril for Republicans, but the age of mass demonstrations seems to have passed. Nonetheless, any campus visit should be carefully planned so as to avoid confrontations which demean the candidate. (Of course, there are times when such confrontations may be sought.) Also to be avoided, however, are elitist visits. The campus paper will take you to task if you whisk in and out of a YR meeting without at least giving the general student body a chance to see the candidate. More important . . . than that, the candidate will have missed an opportunity. If he isn't competent to handle students, don't send him to the campus at all.

Evening Hangouts. A troublesome question for many schedulers is what to do in the evening. The candidate shouldn't be making speeches every night . . . The answer is a trip to some local evening hangouts. The people in the bars and bowling alleys are not used to candidates and, if they are not too tipsy, are often particularly responsive. Buying a round for the house is as sure a way as I know of winning friends.

—Republican National Committee campaign manuals, 1980.

Nofziger, press and communications; Verne Orr, administration; and Drew Lewis, policy and planning. Other advisers also played important roles: Richard V. Allen, foreign policy and national security; Martin Anderson, domestic policy; Michael K. Deaver, chief aide for the campaign tour; Peter Hannaford, speechwriting; and Tom C. Korologos and Stuart Spencer, political specialists.[3] (Spencer managed Reagan's 1966 gubernatorial campaign.) James A. Baker III, the Houston attorney who directed George Bush's campaign for the Republican

[3] *National Journal,* July 26, 1980, p. 1224.

How to Win an Election: Democratic Version

The following are excerpts from the official instruction manuals for Democratic party workers:

Volunteer Recruitment. The biggest reason more people don't get involved in political action is THAT THEY ARE NEVER ASKED. . . . First, identify friendly voters, and second, make sure they are asked to help.

Acquire Voter Lists. There are computer service companies who own the master phone number list for your area. For a fee, they will take your voter tape and "pass" it against their phone number tape, automatically marking your print-out with the phone numbers for each voter. This can cost from $20 per thousand to $30 per thousand. A good program can identify phone numbers for approximately 70 percent of your voters.

Telephone Canvassing. Class practice is essential to the training process. A typical method is to have ten toy phones placed on a table in front of the room. Ten people are selected at random to fill the positions in the "phone bank." Response cards . . . are handed out to people in the audience – coded only by a phone number. These response cards should be . . . written to show typical situations. One at a time, each phoner calls out a number. The person in the audience with that number stands up to answer the call. The interview follows.

Voter Registration. Free media is a valuable tool in promoting your voter registration drive. . . . Don't expect the media outlets to do much work, though. You'll have to spoon-feed them by providing press kits, feature stories, photographs, regular releases and audio and video tapes of public service announcements (PSAs).

Door-to-Door Canvassing. Bird dogs are advance people for door-to-door registrars. They scout the territory, uncovering unregistered Democrats and directing the registrar to them. . . .

The call of the canvasser should be followed as closely as possible by a call from the registrar. A good system is for Bird Dogs working on a single street to use colored cards, pinning them to the door of a prospect with tape or thumbtack. The registrar, working ten or fifteen minutes behind the Bird Dogs, simply goes to the doors where the colored card has been posted.

Target on Young People. In places dominated by a large university, politicians often fear wholesale student registration, which could tilt the political balance of power dramatically. This dictates discretion in approaching local officials. Curb the wild-eyed look. Try to get Democratic candidates and party officials to back up your request. Remember: the goal is to get registrars on campus.

Candidate Activity. Although the personal needs of each candidate vary, everyone needs some time and has a particular method for recharging one's batteries. Included in "down-time" are the periods for study and thinking on the issues, presentation methods and general campaign strategies. Determine your candidate's need for rest, meditation and study and plan to accommodate these needs in the schedule.

Fund Raising. Focus on Motivations. Few people are going to contribute money to you simply because you ask them to. To loosen their pursestrings, you have to appeal to basic human motivations for giving. Include Altruism . . . Idealism . . . Compassion . . . A Sense of Obligation . . . Ego Gratification . . . and Gratitude. . . .

Communicating the Message. A voter is persuaded only when touched in some personally meaningful and fully believable way by the candidate and campaign. . . . Touching voters in a personalized way is quite a simple process. Voters do not get enough personal attention to satisfy them. A phone call, a visit, a personal letter will do wonders.

—Democratic National Committee campaign manuals, 1980.

From left to right: Edwin Meese III. William E. Timmons. Lyn Nofziger.
Martin Anderson

Robert S. Strauss

nomination, joined the Reagan campaign after the convention as a senior adviser.
He was named White House chief of staff by Reagan after the election.

Some of these advisers, like Timmons and Korologos, were experienced
Washington operatives who had served in the White House under Nixon.
Others, like Meese, had worked with Reagan in California when he served as
governor. In addition to these key advisers, more than 100 working groups developed high-priority issues during the campaign for Reagan to consider after
his election.

Despite the normal advantages enjoyed by an incumbent President, Jimmy
Carter's campaign organization in 1980 experienced some initial difficulties.
There were two campaign directors at first, and some confusion about who was
in charge until Hamilton Jordan resigned as Carter's senior White House assistant to become campaign director. Robert S. Strauss, who had been Carter's
special representative for trade negotiations, became chairman of the Carter
re-election effort. Despite the outcome of the election, most observers agreed
that Carter had a well-run campaign organization. With the elaborate communications available to a President aboard *Air Force One* and everywhere else he
moves, and with a huge White House staff to support his campaign, Carter probably enjoyed logistical advantages over his rival. But in the end, he lost, the
second President in a row to be voted out of office.

Campaign Strategy

Aiming
for the Undecided

Studies have shown that many voters are committed to one candidate or another
in advance of the campaign. For example, in 1976 more than half of a sample of
voters reported they had made up their minds *before* the campaign got underway.
But a very large group of voters—45 percent—decided during the campaign.
(See Table 8–1.)

Presidential Elections: When the Voter Decides*

Table 8-1

Decided how to vote	1960	1964	1968	1972	1976
Before conventions	30%	40%	33%	43%	33%
During conventions	30	25	22	17	20
During the campaign	36	33	38	35	45
Don't remember, not ascertained	4	3	7	4	2

* Figures are rounded.

Source: University of Michigan Survey Research Center/Center for Political Studies data in William H. Flanigan and Nancy H. Zingale, *Political Behavior of the American Electorate*, 4th ed. (Boston: Allyn and Bacon, 1979), p. 171.

Nelson Polsby and Aaron Wildavsky have contended that, for the majority of citizens in America, "campaigns do not function so much to change minds as to reinforce previous convictions."[4] Nevertheless, when 35 percent or more of the people *do* make up their minds during a campaign, their votes may well determine the outcome. If 86 million votes are cast in a presidential election, 35 percent, 30.1 million votes, is a sizable bloc by any standards. The undecided voters hold the key to victory in close elections.

Since about two-thirds of all American voters identify with one of the two major parties, political candidates try to preserve their party base — to hold on to their natural constituency — while winning over voters from the other party, the independents, and the undecided.

While some poll data suggest that political campaigns do not influence the choice of a majority of voters, political analysts have concluded that campaigns may influence "a small but crucial proportion of the electorate.... Clearly, professional politicians drive themselves and their organizations to influence every remaining undecided voter in the hope and expectation that they are providing or maintaining a winning margin."[5]

And a number of scholars have disagreed with the view that campaigns have minimal influence on voters. Dan Nimmo and Robert L. Savage have argued that "there is a close relationship between candidate images and voting behavior."[6] They have concluded that while candidates' images usually emerge early in a campaign and remain about the same, those images can and do change during campaigns; as examples they cite John F. Kennedy in 1960 and Hubert Humphrey in 1968, whose images improved as the campaign progressed.[7] In arguing that "campaigns make a difference," Nimmo and Savage emphasize that this is particularly true for independent voters, who are more likely than other voters to shift their impressions of the candidates during campaigns.[8]

[4] Nelson W. Polsby and Aaron B. Wildavsky, *Presidential Elections*, 5th ed. (New York: Scribner's, 1980), p. 157.

[5] William H. Flanigan and Nancy H. Zingale, *Political Behavior of the American Electorate*, 4th ed. (Boston: Allyn and Bacon, 1979), p. 170.

[6] Dan Nimmo and Robert L. Savage, *Candidates and Their Images: Concepts, Methods, and Findings* (Pacific Palisades, Cal.: Goodyear, 1976), p. 208.

[7] *Ibid.*, pp. 136–37.

[8] *Ibid.*, p. 143.

Hubert Humphrey: the image improved

"I'm going to do a flip-flop on Africa. Can you make it look good?"

Drawing by Weber
© 1976 The New Yorker Magazine, Inc.

"Voters . . . arrive at a decision by interpreting the symbols offered to them."

Nimmo and others view political campaigns as "a process of communication," in which voters do not respond automatically on the basis of their socio-economic backgrounds or party loyalties. Rather, Nimmo contends, voters tend to "construct" their own individual view of the campaign; they arrive at a decision by interpreting the symbols offered to them, often by drawing upon their own experience.[9]

Norman Nie, Sidney Verba, and John Petrocik in *The Changing American Voter* have argued that campaigns may affect voting because "the public responds to the political stimuli offered it." The behavior of voters, they concluded, is influenced not only by psychological and sociological factors, "but also by the issues of the day and by the way in which candidates present those issues."[10]

Similarly, Walter DeVries and V. Lance Tarrance have emphasized that in many elections the outcome is determined by "ticket-splitters." They defined the term as a voter likely "to be basically a Republican or Democrat, but one who occasionally splits off to vote for a candidate of another party."[11] To convince the ticket-splitters, DeVries and Tarrance contend, candidates must use campaigns to communicate their views on the issues.[12]

Which Road to the White House?

Long before they can get into a general election campaign, aspiring presidential candidates must decide whether to enter the bruising arena of the primaries. In 1980 Ronald Reagan's victories in New Hampshire and later in South Carolina and Illinois were important to his successful drive for the Republican nomination. Conversely, former President Gerald R. Ford's decision not to enter the primaries in 1980 may have been the decisive factor in his failure

[9] Dan Nimmo, *Political Communication and Public Opinion in America* (Santa Monica, Cal.: Goodyear, 1978), pp. 361–72. See also David L. Swanson, "Political Communication: A Revisionist View Emerges," in *The Quarterly Journal of Speech,* Vol. 64 (1978), pp. 211–22.

[10] Norman H. Nie, Sidney Verba, and John R. Petrocik, *The Changing American Voter,* Enlarged Edition, A Twentieth Century Fund Study (Cambridge, Mass.: Harvard University Press, 1979), p. 319.

[11] Walter DeVries and V. Lance Tarrance, *The Ticket-Splitter: A New Force in American Politics* (Grand Rapids, Mich.: William B. Eerdmans, 1972), p. 37.

[12] *Ibid.,* p. 111.

Before the campaign can begin, there must be a candidate. And that job is not easy, as the following excerpt from a Republican party manual suggests:

The person who cannot answer virtually all of the following questions in the affirmative should not be running.

1. Does your family fully support your candidacy? Are they prepared to assume much more responsibility at home and put in extra time campaigning? Can they tolerate the verbal abuse you may receive and long hours you will spend away from home? Will your children accept and understand your frequent absence from home?

2. Can you afford to run? Can you expect enough contributions to keep out of serious personal debt? Is your business in good hands while you campaign? If you are employed, do you have a job to go back to in the event you lose?

3. Can your personal background stand intensive scrutiny? Are you fully prepared to have the public know about your debts, personal and organizational associations, past relationships with members of the opposite sex, family background, sources of income, health history, partners, etc.?

4. Are you strong enough physically and emotionally to stand up to the rigors of a tough campaign? Can your health tolerate long hours, poor food, erratic rest, continuing pressure, rejection and frustration? Most important, could your ego tolerate a loss if it should come?

—*Candidate Recruitment,* Republican National Committee campaign manual, 1980.

to win the Republican nomination. And that same year, Carter's defeat of Senator Edward M. Kennedy in key primaries ensured Carter's renomination as his party's presidential candidate.

For relatively unknown political candidates, the primary route may prove an attractive means of demonstrating their strength and gaining nationwide exposure in the media. For example, Jimmy Carter was a relative unknown in 1976, and his primary election victories that year were essential to his successful campaign for the Democratic presidential nomination; Carter's triumphs throughout the spring proved that he was a viable candidate and, of course, won him many convention delegates. In 1980 George Bush lost several key primaries to Ronald Reagan. But the fact that Bush also won some may have helped to persuade Reagan to select him as his vice-presidential running mate. Even for a presidential aspirant who is far out in front, entering the primaries may be

Senator Edward M. Kennedy

Left: "Jimmy Carter was a relative unknown in 1976." *Right:* George Bush lost several primaries but won the Vice Presidency.

necessary in order to win the nomination. Each candidate attempts to calculate the potential advantages and disadvantages of taking the primary route.

With preconvention campaigns growing in importance, a candidate may find it necessary to have a well-financed campaign organization already in operation long before the national convention. In 1980, for example, the preconvention campaign organizations of Jimmy Carter and, on the Republican side, Ronald Reagan, were hardly distinguishable in size from those of major-party nominees in a general election.

Where and How to Campaign

Once nominated, candidates must decide how and where their precious time (and money) can most profitably be spent. In 1960 Richard Nixon pledged to become the first candidate to take his presidential campaign to all fifty states. He did, but at great physical and political cost. By contrast, in 1968 Nixon moved at a relatively serene pace that preserved his physical energies. He concentrated on ten populous "battleground states," on those states in the South that might be captured from George Wallace, and on the border states.[13] This time, he won.

In general, presidential candidates of both parties have tended to spend more time stumping in the pivotal big states with a large number of electoral votes, such as California, New York, Pennsylvania, Illinois, Ohio, Texas, and Michigan.

And television has, of course, influenced the pattern of political campaigning. Aside from the advantages offered by television in reaching large numbers of voters, it also can reduce the risk to the safety of the candidate. In the light of the assassinations of President Kennedy and Robert Kennedy, the attempt on the life of George Wallace, and the two attempts against President Ford, precautions would seem sensible; yet candidates are under great pressure to mingle with the voters and to show themselves in person: "Rightly or wrongly, presidential candidates judge that they must be personally seen by audiences throughout the country, through such rituals as motorcades, shopping center rallies and whistle-stop campaigns."[14]

Political candidates also worry about timing in a campaign. Generally speaking, candidates attempt to gear their campaign to a climactic windup in the

[13] Theodore H. White, *The Making of the President 1968* (New York: Atheneum, 1969), pp. 326–33.

[14] "Assassination," in *To Establish Justice, To Insure Domestic Tranquility,* Final Report of the National Commission on the Causes and Prevention of Violence (Washington, D.C.: U.S. Government Printing Office, 1969), p. 132.

President Theodore Roosevelt campaigning

last two weeks. In the final two weeks of the 1980 presidential campaign, for example, the airwaves were saturated with a "media blitz" of Reagan television commercials. There were many commercials for Carter, as well.

Political campaigns help to weld political parties together; for instance, campaign rallies generate enthusiasm among partisan workers and volunteers. Candidates are concerned about maintaining their momentum and a certain level of excitement, not only with the voters, but for the sake of their own party organization as well.

Although two incumbent Presidents, Ford and Carter, were defeated in the elections of 1976 and 1980, an incumbent starts out with a great potential advantage over an opponent in a presidential campaign. Not only do the prestige and power of the office follow the President on the hustings, but all the visible trappings go along as well: *Air Force One,* the gleaming presidential jet, lands for an airport rally, the band plays "Hail to the Chief," and the voters are enveloped by the aura and mystique of the Presidency. Just before a President speaks, an aide hangs a portable presidential seal on the lectern. Aside from prestige, an incumbent President already has a huge organized staff and all the advantages of White House communications and facilities, including advance men and established press arrangements. He may be able to dominate the news by taking actions as President that are carefully timed for maximum political advantage. For example, in presidential election years, federal grants may flow in large amounts to states in which key primaries will take place.

An incumbent President may be in such a strong position that he will decide to restrict his campaigning, allow the dignity of his office to work for him, and, in effect, campaign from the White House. He may adopt "the lofty, nonpartisan pose."[15] In 1976 President Ford attempted for a time to campaign from the White House, but when Carter accused him of trying to "hide in the Rose Garden," he soon took to the campaign trail. Yet Carter himself stayed close to the Rose Garden during the early primaries in 1980, claiming that the hostage crisis in Iran required his full attention to presidential duties in the White House.

Until 1968 the President-as-candidate enjoyed another advantage: he alone had the Secret Service to plan his movements and provide security. Candidates other than a President (or Vice President) had to move through the crowds unprotected, or at best with a private, and often amateur, bodyguard or a few local police. After Robert Kennedy was fatally shot during the preconvention cam-

The President as Candidate

[15] V. O. Key, Jr., *Politics, Parties, and Pressure Groups,* 5th ed. (New York: Crowell, 1964), p. 471.

Left: Robert F. Kennedy campaigning in Detroit, 1968. *Right:* Ronald Reagan, surrounded by Secret Service men, campaigning in Illinois, 1980.

paign of 1968, however, President Johnson assigned Secret Service agents to all the candidates, a practice that Congress speedily made law.[16]

The Issues

Political candidates in most cases develop a central theme for their campaign. Sometimes it emerges as the battle progresses; often it is well thought out in advance. Candidates attempt to choose their terrain, staking out certain issues that they believe will give them the advantage over their opponents.

But to a great extent the campaign theme is shaped by the candidate's status — incumbent President, political heir to an incumbent, or candidate of the "out" party. For example, in 1976 Carter was able to attack the record of eight years of Republican rule in the White House. He won the Presidency. But in 1980 it was Reagan's turn to attack Carter's record, and this time, Reagan emerged as the winner.

As Polsby and Wildavsky have noted, "One of the most difficult positions for a candidate is to try to succeed a President of his own party. . . . No matter how hard he tries to avoid it he is stuck with the record made by the President of his own party."[17] There is evidence that some incumbent Presidents are a bit reluctant to expend their prestige on behalf of the heir apparent — who may not always want help. In 1968, for example, President Johnson's attitude toward Vice President Hubert Humphrey, the Democratic nominee, seemed ambivalent at first, although in the end he publicly supported him. But Humphrey lost the election.

President Johnson and Hubert Humphrey

Bread and Butter Issues

Peace and pocketbook issues have tended to dominate presidential campaigns. On domestic issues the Democrats can point to a wide range of social legislation passed during Democratic administrations. Not all of these programs have

---

[16] The law authorizes Secret Service protection, unless declined, for "major presidential or vice-presidential candidates." The Secretary of the Treasury, after consultation with an advisory committee that includes leaders of Congress, decides who qualifies as a candidate under this definition. The law does not specifically provide protection for preconvention candidates, but the precedent was set in 1968 when the Secret Service guarded a total of twelve candidates: six presidential candidates before the conventions and six party nominees (for President and Vice President).

[17] Polsby and Wildavsky, *Presidential Elections,* 2nd ed. (New York: Scribner's, 1968), p. 129.

worked equally well, and some, such as the welfare program, have been widely criticized. Nevertheless, Democratic candidates since the New Deal have been able to campaign on the party's efforts toward achieving social progress at home. And, perhaps remembering the Great Depression that began in 1929 under a Republican President, voters have, in some years, tended to associate prosperity with Democrats. (See Figure 8-1.)

Bread and butter issues do not always work for the Democrats, however. In 1980, for example, double-digit inflation and continued high unemployment made the economy one domestic issue that President Carter preferred not to emphasize; it proved, in fact, one of the weakest issues for the Democratic incumbent.

In the area of foreign affairs, the Republicans often have an advantage. (See Figure 8-2.) Because the Democrats were in power during the First World War, the Second World War, Korea, and Vietnam, the Republicans have been able to tag the Democrats, fairly or not, as the "war party." Richard Nixon in 1968 was able to promise new leadership to bring an end to the war in Vietnam. Although Nixon did not succeed in ending the American combat role in the Vietnam war until more than two months after his re-election in 1972, his trips to Peking and Moscow earlier that year, and the appearance of progress toward a Vietnam peace agreement during the campaign, once again provided the Republican candidate with an advantage in the area of foreign policy. In 1976 Gerald Ford repeatedly stressed the fact that America was at peace under his Republican administration. **Foreign Policy Issues**

Yet it is also true that foreign policy issues are not always the Republicans' strongest ground. For example, in 1980, even though President Carter lost the election, most observers felt that he had effectively emphasized the "war or peace" issue, by suggesting that Reagan might be more likely than he to involve the country in a military action. Even so, Reagan undoubtedly benefited from the prolonged hostage crisis in Iran and the flurry of attention focused on that issue just forty-eight hours before the election.

A sudden foreign policy crisis, a personal scandal, a chance remark—these are among the many imponderables that may affect voter attitudes in political campaigns. **The Imponderables**

In 1884, when Grover Cleveland was the Democratic nominee, his Republican opponents chanted: "Ma, Ma, where's my Pa? Gone to the White House, Ha, ha, ha." The slogan was a gleeful reference to the illegitimate child that Cleveland was accused of fathering.[18] It was soon overshadowed, however, by another slogan. A few days before the election, a Protestant minister supporting James G. Blaine, the Republican candidate, referred to the Democrats

[18] The story broke during the campaign in a Buffalo newspaper, under the headline: "A Terrible Tale—A Dark Chapter in a Public Man's History." Ten years earlier, Maria Crofts Halpin, an attractive widow, had given birth to a son, whom she named Oscar Folsom Cleveland, charging Cleveland with its paternity. Cleveland said he was not certain he was the father, but he had assumed full responsibility for supporting the child; when the scandal broke, he telegraphed his friends in Buffalo: "Tell the truth." Because of his open attitude, Cleveland managed to minimize the damage to his presidential campaign. After Cleveland's election, the Democrats celebrated their first presidential victory in twenty-eight years by singing: "Hurrah for Maria, Hurrah for the kid, We voted for Grover, And we're damned glad we did!"

Political Party Rated Best for Prosperity

Figure 8–1

Question: "Looking ahead for the next few years, which political party—the Republican or Democratic—do you think will do the best job of keeping the country prosperous?"

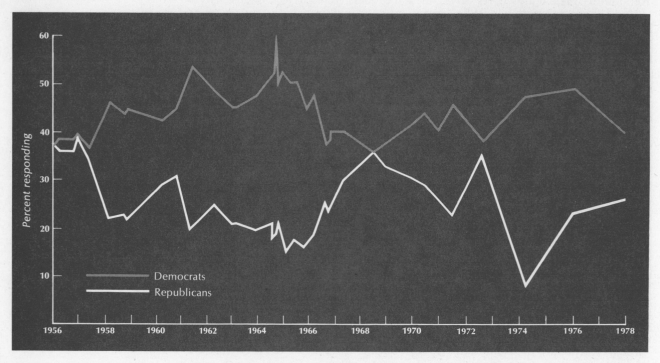

Source: *Gallup Opinion Index,* Report No. 106 (April 1974), p. 21; Report No. 135 (October 1976), p. 5; and Report No. 159 (October 1978), p. 21.

as the party of "rum, Romanism, and rebellion." The insult to Roman Catholics may have cost Blaine New York State and thereby the election.

In 1948 Dewey's campaign train, the *Victory Special,* lurched backward into the crowd while the Republican nominee was orating at Beaucoup, Illinois. "Well, that's the first lunatic I've had for an engineer," snapped Dewey. The remark was widely publicized and did not sit well with the railroad unions. Over-

1952: Richard M. Nixon delivers his "Checkers" speech on television.

Question: "Which political party do you think would be more likely to keep the United States out of World War III — the Republican party or the Democratic party?"

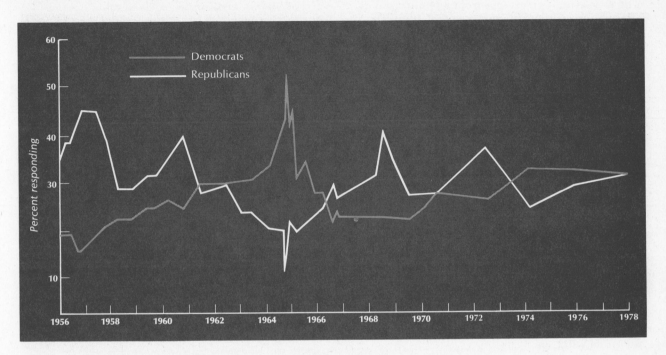

Source: *Gallup Opinion Index,* Report No. 106 (April 1974), p. 19; Report No. 135 (October 1976), p. 6; and Report No. 159 (October 1978), p. 22.

night, "Lunatic Engineers for Truman" and similar groups sprang up to plague the Republican candidate along the right-of-way of the *Victory Special.*

In 1952 Richard Nixon's place as the vice-presidential candidate on the Republican ticket was endangered when newspapers reported the existence of the "Nixon fund," some $18,000 contributed by a group of California business-men to meet Nixon's political expenses as a United States senator. Nixon went on nationwide television and, in his famed "Checkers" speech, defended his use of the $18,000 fund, listed his personal finances, noted that his wife, Pat, wore a "respectable Republican cloth coat," and announced that, come what may, his family intended to keep a black-and-white cocker spaniel named Checkers, which had been given to his two children.[19] Although the speech was a patently emotional appeal for which Nixon was often assailed by later critics, it turned the tide of public opinion and impressed General Eisenhower, the Republican presidential nominee. Nixon stayed on the ticket.

[19] Checkers died in September 1964, and is buried at Westhampton, Long Island. He was not the first canine to gain fame in a presidential campaign. Running for a fourth term in 1944, Franklin D. Roosevelt ridiculed the Republicans for charging that he had sent a destroyer to fetch his dog: "The Republican leaders have not been content to make personal attacks upon me — or my wife — or my sons — they now include my little dog, Fala. . . . I am accustomed to hearing malicious falsehoods about myself but I think I have a right to object to libelous statements about my dog." See Robert E. Sherwood, *Roosevelt and Hopkins* (New York: Harper & Row, 1948), p. 821.

269

Political Campaigns and Candidates

The following is an excerpt from a publication of the Republican National Committee that advises GOP candidates on campaign techniques.

Researching Scandals in the Democratic Party

With proper research and publicity, exposure of scandals can serve as a public service and as a source of votes. . . . Most scandals evolve from "tips," usually coming from newsmen, victims of the "scandal," public reports such as those of the State Auditor, or abused factions within or on the fringes of the wrongdoer's organization. . . .

Publicizing the Scandal. A "believable" springboard from which to break the scandal must be found. A newsman, a disenchanted insider, or a local prosecutor are possible means for breaking the scandal to the public.

Once the public has been informed that a scandal in fact does exist, it must be kept continually aware that its trust has been violated. . . . Question the principals of the opposition at every opportunity—at public gatherings as well as in the press. In other words, take advantage of every possible form of publicity—and be sure to cry, SCANDAL!

—Republican National Committee, *Research Techniques for Republican Campaigns* (1969).

Ronald Ziegler on Watergate

White House spokesman Ronald L. Ziegler told reporters in Florida with the President that he would not comment on "a third-rate burglary attempt." In addition, Ziegler said that "certain elements may try to stretch this beyond what it is."

—*Washington Post,* June 20, 1972.

The Watergate buildings

Mudslinging and charges of corruption are common in campaigns. Under the unwritten rules of the seamier side of American politics, a candidate may attempt to "get something" on an opponent. (The information might not be publicized, however, if the other side possesses equally damaging information, or if it is felt that the opponent can successfully cry "smear.") Because mudslinging, rumors, and scandals presumably influence some voters, their use in political campaigns persists. It is often near the end of a campaign that a candidate's supporters try to leak such stories to the newspapers to damage a rival.

Perhaps the most startling and disturbing surprise development of any modern presidential campaign occurred in June 1972, when five men, wearing surgical rubber gloves and carrying electronic eavesdropping equipment, were arrested inside the Washington headquarters of the Democratic National Committee in the Watergate building. One of the men, James W. McCord, Jr., a former CIA agent, turned out to be director of security for President Nixon's campaign organization. Three weeks before the election, a federal grand jury in Washington indicted the five men plus two former White House aides, E. Howard Hunt, Jr., and G. Gordon Liddy, on charges of burglary, illegal wiretapping, and bugging.

The case immediately raised a host of questions about who had sent the men on their espionage mission to Democratic headquarters. The White House and President Nixon repeatedly denied involvement. But one of the Watergate defendants, it developed, had $89,000 in his bank account that had been delivered to the Republican campaign committee and "laundered" through Mexico to disguise its origin.

The charges of espionage and financial irregularities seemed to have little impact on the voters in the 1972 election.[20] The Watergate case and the issue of

[20] A Gallup poll published in October showed that 52 percent of the voters had heard of the Watergate scandal, but only about a third were able to recite the key facts of the situation. Eight out of ten persons who knew about the incident said it was not a strong reason for voting for Nixon's Democratic opponent, Senator George McGovern. Source: Gallup poll, *Washington Post,* October 8, 1972, p. A5.

political espionage began to grow into a major scandal only well *after* the presidential election campaign. Early in 1973, five of the defendants pleaded guilty, and two others were convicted by a federal jury. Within months, the scandal had reached the President; several of his top aides resigned and some went to prison. A year later Nixon, facing impeachment, resigned in disgrace, his Presidency shattered less than two years after his re-election by a landslide.

World crises that erupt suddenly during a campaign are still another category of imponderables that may affect voter decisions. In general, foreign policy crises tend to help the party in power because of voter reluctance to "change horses in midstream." The Tonkin Gulf crisis of 1964, many details of which are disputed, created an atmosphere of wartime tension that, in the short run, may have benefited the election campaign of President Johnson. On the other hand, a foreign crisis that leads to a war, as in Korea or Vietnam, or that damages the prestige of the country, such as the seizure of American hostages in Iran, may, in the long run, erode the strength of the party in power and lead to retribution at the polls.

President Nixon announcing his resignation

Campaign Techniques

The little girl in the television commercial stood in a field of daisies, plucking the petals and counting, as birds chirped in the background. Then, as the little girl reached number ten, a doomsday voice began a countdown. When the voice reached zero, there was a rumbling explosion and a huge mushroom cloud filled the screen. As it billowed upward, President Lyndon Johnson's voice boomed

Television and Politics

"Ten, nine, eight, seven . . .

six, five, four, three . . .

two, one . . .

These are the stakes. To make a world in which all of God's children can live . . .

or to go into the dark. We must either love each other or we must die . . .

VOTE FOR PRESIDENT JOHNSON ON NOVEMBER 3.

The stakes are too high for you to stay home."

out: "These are the stakes. To make a world in which all of God's children can live or to go into the dark. We must either love each other or we must die." A message was then flashed on the screen, reading: "Vote for President Johnson on November 3."

Millions of Americans saw the famous "Daisy Girl" commercial during the 1964 campaign. To many it seemed to suggest that Barry Goldwater, the Republican candidate, might lead the nation into nuclear war. As Theodore White has noted, "The film mentioned neither Goldwater nor the Republicans specifically—but the shriek of Republican indignation fastened the bomb message on them more tightly than any calculation could have expected."[21]

The marriage of television and politics took place in 1948, the first year in which substantial numbers of Americans viewed parts of the national nominating conventions on TV.[22] Since less than 200,000 homes had television sets in 1948, however, the real impact of television was not felt until the 1952 and 1956 Eisenhower-Stevenson campaigns. By 1956 almost 35 million homes had TV sets. In 1960, of America's 53 million households, 46.6 million, or 88 percent, had sets. By this time, television was playing a central role in presidential campaigns.

The Kennedy-Nixon Debates. It was in 1960 that the major-party candidates were first able to reach vast audiences in a series of televised debates. Congress made the debates possible. Under Section 315 of the Federal Communications Act, broadcasters are required to provide "equal time" to all legally qualified candidates. The television networks argued that this provision forced them to give time to minor-party candidates. Congress in 1960 suspended the "equal time" provision, clearing the way for the four "great debates" between Senator John F. Kennedy and Vice President Richard Nixon, his Republican opponent. Most observers believed that the debates helped Kennedy to win the election, in part because Nixon looked pale and haggard in the first debate and wore "Lazy Shave" powder as makeup. By contrast, Kennedy, looking tanned and vigorous, presented a much more telegenic image to the public.

[21] Theodore H. White, *The Making of the President 1964* (New York: Atheneum, 1965), p. 322. Because of protests, the film was shown only once.
[22] 1948 was not the first year in which the national conventions were televised. But because very few people owned TV sets in the 1940s, less than 100,000 persons saw television broadcasts of the 1940 and 1944 conventions.

1960: John F. Kennedy and Richard M. Nixon in television debate

1976: Jimmy Carter and Gerald
Ford debate on television.

The millions of voters watching the first debate may have remembered little of what the candidates said, but they noticed that Nixon did not *look* as pleasing as Kennedy. As White put it, "Probably no picture in American politics tells a better story . . . than that famous shot of the camera on the Vice President as he half slouched, his 'Lazy Shave' powder faintly streaked with sweat, his eyes exaggerated hollows of blackness, his jaw, jowls, and face drooping with strain."[23]

The Carter-Ford Debates.   In 1976, for the first time since the presidential campaign of 1960, the major-party candidates reached millions of viewers in a series of televised debates. The debates were credited by some analysts with providing Jimmy Carter with his narrow margin of victory over President Ford, the Republican incumbent. Although Congress in 1976 did not suspend the "equal time" provision again, the debates were made possible by a 1975 FCC ruling that debates could be broadcast as long as they were not sponsored by the television networks or held in a TV studio, and were telecast in their entirety. The nonpartisan League of Women Voters sponsored three Carter-Ford presidential debates and a debate between the vice-presidential candidates, Senator Walter F. Mondale, Democrat, of Minnesota, and Senator Robert Dole, Republican, of Kansas.

As President, Ford was better known than Carter at the start of the 1976 campaign, and thus in theory would have had more to lose by debating his opponent. Normally, an incumbent President, or the better known of two candidates, has little incentive to debate an opponent; the television exposure only serves to help his rival become better known to the public. But after the mid-July Democratic National Convention that nominated Carter, Ford was behind by 33 points in the polls.[24] He sought to regain the initiative by challenging his opponent to debate, and Carter accepted.

A Gallup poll reported that Ford won the first debate, which was on domestic issues, 38 to 25 percent.[25] Carter made a comeback in the second de-

---

[23] Theodore H. White, *The Making of the President 1960* (New York: Atheneum, 1961), p. 289.

[24] The Democrats nominated Carter on July 14. The Gallup poll of July 16–26 showed Carter leading Ford, 62 to 29 percent, with 9 percent undecided. Source: *Gallup Opinion Index,* Report No. 134 (September 1976), p. 8.

[25] *Newsweek,* October 4, 1976, p. 27. Twenty-nine percent thought neither candidate won and 8 percent were "not sure."

1980: President Carter
debates . . .

bate, which dealt with foreign affairs. He was more aggressive in attacking the Ford administration, demonstrated a grasp of foreign policy issues—and benefited from Ford's pronouncement that the Soviet Union did not dominate Eastern Europe. This time, the Gallup poll indicated that Carter won the debate, 50 to 27 percent.[26]

The third and final debate of the presidential candidates was probably the most interesting, since it covered a wide range of substantive issues. According to the Gallup poll, 32 percent of those who saw the final debate thought Carter had won, and 27 percent believed Ford had won.[27] More than a third of the registered voters interviewed—35 percent—thought the debates had been "fairly helpful" in making a choice between the candidates.[28] And since the poll data indicated that more people thought Carter, rather than Ford, had won the second and third debates, on balance, it appeared that these encounters helped Carter to win the Presidency. Despite complaints by some viewers that the debates were "dull," they drew tremendous audiences and became the central drama of the election campaign.

The 1980 Debates. Again in 1980 voters were able to watch the major candidates debate, although all three—Reagan, Carter, and Anderson—did not come together in a single televised appearance.

Two debates took place, both sponsored by the League of Women Voters and televised nationally. In the first, in Baltimore on September 21, Ronald Reagan, the Republican nominee, debated independent John Anderson. President Carter refused to take part, arguing that it would be unfair for him to debate two Republicans. (Many observers, however, felt that Carter was reluctant to elevate Anderson's status as a candidate by appearing with him.) Reagan and Anderson covered a wide range of issues, from the economy and taxes, to defense and energy. For many viewers, it was the first opportunity to see Anderson

[26] *Newsweek,* October 18, 1976, p. 22. Fifteen percent thought neither candidate won and 8 percent were "not sure."

[27] *Newsweek,* November 1, 1976, p. 20. Twenty-one percent thought neither candidate had won and 20 percent were "not sure."

[28] *Ibid.*

Televised debate between independent candidate John B. Anderson and Ronald Reagan in 1980

in action. A Louis Harris poll reported that 36 percent of the voters watching thought Anderson had won, compared to 30 percent who thought Reagan had won.[29]

Ronald Reagan

In Cleveland on October 28, just one week before the election, the main debate of the 1980 presidential campaign took place between Reagan and Carter. Both candidates performed well, but many observers thought that Reagan had gained ground by displaying an affable, apparently relaxed manner, thereby offsetting Carter's previous warnings that the Republican nominee might be likely to lead the country into a military adventure. Carter appealed to the Democrats' traditional constituency, emphasizing social security and other social welfare programs. But Reagan hammered away at the economy. Near the end of the ninety-minute debate, he urged voters to ask themselves: "Are you better off than you were four years ago? Is it easier for you to go and buy things in the stores than it was four years ago?"[30]

A Gallup poll for *Newsweek* magazine showed that a national sample of registered voters thought Reagan had won the debate, 34 to 26 percent.[31] And the poll indicated that the debate made more voters lean toward voting against Carter than toward voting for him.[32]

In one sense, it may be unfair to both candidates and voters to have so much depend on the impression two office seekers make in one ninety-minute, televised debate. Both candidates misstated some facts, which many viewers at home probably did not realize.[33] On the other hand, the pre-election debate of 1980 gave millions of voters an opportunity they would not otherwise have had to watch the candidates in action, to hear and contrast their views on a wide range of domestic and foreign policy issues, and to make judgments about the candidates' style and character.

Studies of the effect of televised debates on elections have reached varying conclusions. To an extent, some studies suggest, viewers see what they wish to see; that is, their perception of the candidates and issues hews close to their "original voting preference."[34] But other studies suggest that debates may have "a measurable direct influence on the outcome of the election."[35]

Madison Avenue: The Packaging of the President. By 1977 there were 113.2 million television sets in about 71.2 million homes in America; 93.9 percent of all homes with electricity in the United States had TV sets — more than had bathtubs or telephones. The ability of political candidates to reach increased numbers of voters through television was reflected in a dramatic rise in campaign spending for TV broadcasts. In 1972 almost $60 million was spent for political broadcasts, $10.8 million at the presidential and vice-presidential levels. In 1976, even with their budgets limited under the new federal elections law, the two major candidates spent $16.9 million on television advertising.[36]

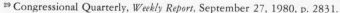

[29] Congressional Quarterly, *Weekly Report*, September 27, 1980, p. 2831.
[30] *New York Times*, October 30, 1980, p. B19.
[31] *Newsweek*, November 10, 1980, p. 37.
[32] *Ibid.* According to the Gallup/*Newsweek* poll, 33 percent of the respondents said the debate made them more likely to vote against Carter; 29 percent said the debate made them more likely to vote for Carter.
[33] For details of misstatements by the candidates, see Adam Clymer, "Contradictions in the Debate: Record Shows 2 Rivals Misstated Some Facts," *New York Times*, October 30, 1980, p. 1.
[34] Sidney Kraus and Dennis Davis, *The Effects of Mass Communication on Political Behavior* (University Park, Pa.: The Pennsylvania State University Press, 1976), p. 59.
[35] *Ibid.*
[36] Alexander, *Financing Politics: Money, Elections and Political Reform*, p. 10.

Reagan's media adviser
Peter Dailey

"Reagan had a
professional actor's
advantage over his
opponent."

Carter commercial: the
light burned late

The increasing use of television and Madison Avenue techniques has, of course, raised the question of whether political candidates can be merchandised and packaged like toothpaste. To some extent the answer must be yes; certainly many of the advertising men who handle political "accounts" think in just those terms.

In 1980, for example, Ronald Reagan hired as his media adviser Peter Dailey, head of Dailey & Associates, the largest advertising agency in the western United States, with headquarters in Los Angeles and branches in several overseas capitals. "We will focus on his record and on the man," Dailey said. "He is an open, warm, flexible and pragmatic leader, who took over a state which was predominantly Democratic and in eight years achieved a record of major accomplishments."[37]

And that is exactly how Reagan was presented in the commercials that Dailey prepared. Viewers were presented with television spots that emphasized the candidate's personal qualities, while extolling his record as governor of California. The *Washington Post* gave this account of the Reagan commercials in 1980:

> . . . near the beginning of a five-minute version of a commercial called "Peace," devoted to national security, Reagan says: "It's impossible to capture in words the feelings we [he and Nancy Reagan] have about peace in the world, and how desperately we want it for our children and our children's children . . ."
>
> In these commercials Reagan avoids specifics . . . Dailey's ads end with the voice of actor Robert Stack . . . repeating Reagan's campaign slogan: "The time is now for Reagan—Reagan for President."
>
> Reagan's skill as a performer strengthens these commercials. Dailey is particularly pleased with the "Peace" spot, in which Reagan speaks with great sincerity and intimacy into the camera. Dailey has used film, not videotape, to make the candidate look "softer."[38]

As a professional actor for most of his adult life, Reagan enjoyed an added advantage on television. "Reagan," the *Washington Post* reported, ". . . calls upon his actor's training to get misty on cue, near the end of his talks. . . . His Sunday night closer was an anecdote . . . about looking into the faces of young people in Kansas City and feeling all warm and lumpy about it."[39]

But if Reagan had a professional actor's advantage over his Democratic opponent, Jimmy Carter had the Presidency, and he did not hesitate to use it in his television commercials. One of Carter's most effective commercials portrayed him working late at the White House while a narrator lauded his accomplishments in office. In the commercial, Carter mounted the stairs of the White House and disappeared inside. Viewers could then see a light flick on in the window as Carter presumably toiled far into the night, working for the energy program, peace, and a strong America.

Another Carter commercial evoked Abraham Lincoln and showed Carter walking at Camp David with Anwar Sadat of Egypt and Menachem Begin of Israel. The commercial ended: "President Jimmy Carter—peacemaker."[40]

Besides praising the candidate, television commercials often jab at opponents. In 1980, for example, Carter ran spots of ordinary-looking Californians on

[37] *National Journal,* July 26, 1980, p. 1227.
[38] *Washington Post,* September 9, 1980, p. A2.
[39] *Washington Post,* October 21, 1980, p. B4.
[40] *Washington Post,* March 18, 1980, p. A3.

the street talking about their former governor, Ronald Reagan. "Reducing government? He didn't do a very good job of reducing government in California," said one citizen. A woman added: "What he did to the mental hospitals was a crime." And another person said, "I think he would have gotten us into war by now."[41]

What is the impact of television in a political campaign? Thomas E. Patterson and Robert D. McClure have argued that nightly news broadcasts on the major networks provide less information to voters than do political commercials. In a study highly critical of the networks, they wrote: "The nightly network newscasts of ABC, CBS, and NBC present a distorted picture of a presidential election campaign. These newscasts pay only limited attention to major election issues. These newscasts almost entirely avoid discussion of the candidates' qualifications for the Presidency. Instead . . . [they] devote most of their election coverage to the trivia of political campaigning that make for flashy pictures. Hecklers, crowds, motorcades, balloons, rallies, and gossip—these are the regular subjects of network campaign stories."[42] Patterson and McClure contend that viewers of the nightly news broadcasts therefore "learn almost nothing of importance about a presidential election." By contrast, "presidential ads contain substantially more issue content than network newscasts."[43]

In a study of the impact of television on voters in Summit County, Ohio, Harold Mendelsohn and Garrett J. O'Keefe found that persons who made up their minds late in a campaign were more likely than others to be influenced by television commercials. Similarly, they reported that "switchers," those who changed their mind during the course of a campaign, were more likely to be influenced by commercials.[44]

The impact of television on American politics since 1952 should not be underestimated, but it is easy to exaggerate the influence of Madison Avenue and "the tube." The idea that a few advertising executives in New York can manipulate the mass of voters ignores other important factors—such as party identification or the voters' personal economic circumstances—that affect how voters cast their ballots.

With the increased importance of television, however, there is at least a danger that a candidate with more money or more skilled media advisers or a better television style will enjoy an unfair advantage in resources over a rival. (Under federal election laws the two major presidential candidates in 1980 accepted public funding and were held to equal spending levels, but that was not true in congressional and state campaigns.) Moreover, with access to an audience of millions of voters through the electronic media, a political candidate may be tempted to display an "image" that masks the real person, to present the issues in capsulized, simplistic form, and to become a performer rather than a leader. But the candidate who goes too far in this direction takes the risk that the voters may "see through" the slickness and, in effect, switch channels—by voting for the opposing candidate. And even the cleverest media advisers must work within the existing political framework; their advertising campaigns are limited by the

[41] *New York Times,* October 8, 1980, p. B8.
[42] Thomas E. Patterson and Robert D. McClure, *The Unseeing Eye: The Myth of Television Power in National Politics* (New York: G. P. Putnam's Sons, 1976), pp. 22–23.
[43] *Ibid.*
[44] Harold Mendelsohn and Garrett J. O'Keefe, *The People Choose a President: Influences on Voter Decision Making* (New York: Praeger, 1976), p. 171.

The sign next to the American flag in the assembly room at the Mount Carmel center said "Benvenuto Vice President Mondale," and the mouth-watering odor of baked ziti filled the hall.

Mr. Mondale told the crowd of elderly persons awaiting lunch that the Carter Administration had saved the Social Security system from bankruptcy.

"That Social Security check should be just as sure as the sun coming up in the morning," he said, and they applauded.

Representative Mario Biaggi escorted the Vice President past food stores in the Italian section [of the Bronx] on crowded Arthur Avenue.

For Joseph Lucciola of Cosenza's fish store, Mr. Mondale posed holding bacala, a dried codfish.

At the Two Brothers From Italy fruit store, he accepted a bag of tangerines and lemons from Vincenzo Vitale. "We ought to come back here more often," Mr. Mondale said with a grin.

Then, standing on the platform of a red, white and blue bus parked near the Arthur Avenue Poultry Market, he spoke into a hand microphone, laughingly telling the street crowd that if they voted for President Carter, "you'll get old Walter Mondali, too."

— *New York Times*, March 13, 1980.

issues that seem important to the voters, by campaign spending laws, and by the strengths and weaknesses of their client, the candidate. There are, in short, limits to the ability of Madison Avenue to package and sell a candidate.

Professional Campaign Managers

When Representative John B. Anderson of Illinois decided to run for President in 1980, he hired David Garth. Although Garth's name might not be known to the mass of voters, it was well known in the political world. He was a professional campaign manager with a reputation for a high degree of success.

A colorful, cigar-smoking New Yorker, Garth at one point scribbled a note on a sign-up sheet at Anderson headquarters in Washington. The sheet encouraged campaign workers to enter an upcoming softball game. "We don't have time for softball," Garth wrote. "We're playing hardball."[45]

Garth, who had previously managed the successful campaigns of the mayor of New York and the governors of New York, New Jersey, and Connecticut, was quick to defend his craft against critics who argue that professional campaign managers manipulate the voters. "What is *not* manipulation?" he asked. "One of the great stupidities is that somehow what we do is manipulation, which it is, and that nothing else is. Ted Kennedy gave a great speech at the convention. Didn't someone write that speech? When Roosevelt sat down to discuss his next fireside chat did they say 'You go ahead and say just what you think is right?' What I'm trying to say is, what happens behind the scenes hasn't changed in politics."[46]

Increasingly, at all levels of politics, candidates have turned to professional campaign managers and consultants. The firms earn large fees for their varied services, which include advertising, public relations, research on issues, public opinion sampling, fund raising, telephone solicitations, computer analysis, and speechwriting.

In the spring of 1965, when Ronald Reagan was thinking about running for

David Garth

45 *New York Times*, September 19, 1980, p. B1.
46 *Ibid.*

278

Politics U.S.A.

governor of California, he approached the Spencer-Roberts political management firm to see whether it would handle his campaign. Such was the reputation of the California firm that aspirants for political office sought out Spencer-Roberts rather than vice versa. George Christopher, the former mayor of San Francisco (who eventually opposed Reagan in the primary), had also approached Spencer-Roberts. After meeting with Reagan, the political management firm "accepted" him, rather than Christopher, as a client.[47]

Spencer-Roberts managed Reagan's successful campaign against incumbent Governor Edmund "Pat" Brown, providing a wide range of public relations and other professional services. For example, because Reagan was an actor, some voters felt he was simply playing the part of a candidate and memorizing his speeches. Spencer-Roberts advised Reagan to hold question-and-answer periods after each of his speeches, to demonstrate to the voters that he had a real grasp of the issues. The firm's advice helped elect Reagan governor. (As noted earlier, Stuart Spencer was an important adviser to Reagan again in the 1980 presidential campaign.)

From its beginnings in California in the 1930s, campaign management has rapidly grown to the status of being a profitable nationwide industry. Two major California firms, Whitaker and Baxter and Spencer-Roberts, handle only Republican candidates. Many other firms, such as Joseph Napolitan Associates, Inc., of Washington, specialize in managing Democrats. Almost inevitably, public relations firms that have branched out into campaign management have evolved from technicians giving advice on press releases to strategists helping candidates make major campaign policy decisions. As Stanley Kelley, Jr., has observed: "It is hard to see why the same trends which have brought the public relations man into political life will not also push him upward in political decisionmaking. His services are valuable because effective use of the mass media is one of the roads to power in contemporary society, and it is difficult clearly to separate strategic and tactical considerations in that use."[48]

One political scientist, Dan Nimmo, has contended that the use of professional campaign managers raises disturbing questions about American politics. The campaign consultants, he has observed, tend to approach elections as "contests of personalities" rather than choices between political parties or principles. And, he warns, the professional image makers "can make a candidate appear to be what he is not. . . ."[49]

After Ronald Reagan was elected President in 1980, it was revealed that during his campaign he had relied extensively on a highly sophisticated, computerized system of poll data known as the Political Information System (PINS). The system was developed for the Republican candidate by his chief poll taker, Richard Wirthlin. In the words of Wirthlin's assistant, Richard S. Beal, PINS allowed Reagan "to use polling data, not just to satisfy the information needs of the campaign, but to help the campaign decision-makers with their strategic judgments."[50]

The Polls

Richard Wirthlin

[47] James M. Perry, *The New Politics* (New York: Clarkson N. Potter, 1968), pp. 25–26.

[48] Stanley Kelley, Jr., *Professional Public Relations and Political Power* (Baltimore: Johns Hopkins Press, 1956), p. 212.

[49] Dan Nimmo, *The Political Persuaders* (Englewood Cliffs, N.J.: Prentice-Hall, 1970), pp. 197–98.

[50] David S. Broder, "How They Rehearsed the Election," *Washington Post,* November 16, 1980, p. L7.

Patrick J. Caddell

According to David S. Broder, the senior political correspondent of the *Washington Post*, PINS combined current polling data with historic voting patterns and subjective judgments on political trends. As a result, the data presented on computer terminal screens could provide possible answers to specific questions, such as: "If the unions scare half their members about Reagan's labor record, should he step up his attacks on Carter or try to rebut their specific claims?"[51]

With fresh data flowing in constantly from national-sample interviews and surveys in 20 states, Reagan's poll taker was able to track shifts in opinion among the electorate, and to take action based on the information. As Wirthlin described it, "Tracking allows you to watch a campaign almost the same way you watch a movie."[52] When Carter's strength suddenly improved in Oregon and Washington in mid-October, for example, Reagan was able within two days to begin "a stepped-up advertising effort to counteract it."[53] Carter, too, received detailed poll data throughout the campaign from his personal poll taker and adviser, Patrick J. Caddell.

Public opinion polls, as Chapter 6 pointed out, are widely used in political campaigns. Political candidates are always concerned over their standing in the polls published by the press, but the use of public opinion surveys has become much more sophisticated than a simple comparison of the relative standing of competing candidates. Politicians may order a confidential poll to be taken well before a campaign in order to gauge their potential strength; they may decide whether to run on the basis of the findings. Once candidates are committed to running in a primary or running in a general election campaign, they may commission private polls to test voter sentiment, as Reagan and Carter did in 1980; these assist them in identifying the issues and planning their campaign strategy. After the campaign is underway, additional private polls are taken to measure the success of the candidate's personal appeal and handling of the issues; both the candidate's style and positions on the issues may be adjusted accordingly. If elected, officials may rely on polls to measure voter reaction to their performance in office.

There is a close interrelationship among the various tools and techniques of "the new politics." The images candidates try to project on television may be tailored to the advice provided by professional campaign managers, who in turn rely on polls they have taken or commissioned. Many of these expensive, interlocking, and highly professionalized services were relatively new in the campaigns of the 1960s; today they are taken for granted.

The Press

"You won't have Nixon to kick around any more . . ."

After he lost the governor's race in California in 1962, Richard Nixon held a famous news conference in which he declared: "You won't have Nixon to kick around any more, because, gentlemen, this is my last press conference. . . ." The press, Nixon added, should recognize "that they have a right and a responsibility, if they're against a candidate, to give him the shaft, but also recognize if they give him the shaft, put one lonely reporter on the campaign who will report what the candidate says now and then."[54]

[51] *Ibid.*
[52] *Time,* September 15, 1980.
[53] Broder, "How They Rehearsed the Election," p. L7.
[54] Earl Mazo and Stephen Hess, *Nixon, A Political Portrait* (New York: Harper & Row, 1968), p. 282.

The Campaign: "Some Kind of a Cross-Country Race"

Reporters and candidates live at a breakneck pace during presidential campaigns. A sense of the hectic nature of life on the campaign trail was captured by author Timothy Crouse in a conversation with reporter James Doyle of the *Washington Star:*

Doyle was slouching in an armchair by the picture window of his bedroom, dead tired from a week on the road. . . . He took a gulp of beer and looked out the window at the sun setting on the river.

"A lot of people," he said, "look at this coverage as if it were some kind of a cross-country race—you gotta get two paragraphs in when he stops at Indianapolis and two more when he stops at

Newark. If you do it that way, without making any meaning out of it, it *is* going to come out like some crazy disjointed trip across the country.

"The problem is, if you try to write every day, you get caught up in sheer exhaustion. It's as simple as that. You do it by rote, because that's all you've got the energy for. It's the lack of sleep, the keeping up with deadlines, the disorientation from all this flying around—your mind just goes blank after a while. When it comes time to write the story, all you can do is just kind of a level job of stumbling through the day's events. I don't think I know how to cover a campaign."

—Timothy Crouse, *The Boys on the Bus.*

Nixon was exhausted and upset when he made these remarks, but his comments reflected his feelings after the 1960 presidential campaign and the 1962 California contest that he had been treated unfairly by the press. The complaint was not a new one; in 1807 President Jefferson had lamented "the falsehoods of a licentious press."

Modern candidates for political office can ill afford to ignore the press. In 1960 a mutual hostility developed between the press and Nixon, who allowed himself to be interviewed only by a few, favored correspondents. By contrast, Kennedy and his staff cultivated the friendship of the reporters assigned to his campaign, and a friendly atmosphere prevailed on his press plane. Determined not to repeat his mistake, Nixon in 1968 paid great personal attention to the creature comforts of the reporters traveling with him; his staff was available to the press and conspicuously affable.[55]

Until 1964, when many normally Republican publishers failed to back Barry Goldwater, most newspapers endorsed Republican candidates in their editorials. "Democratic candidates probably have to work a little harder at cultivating good relations [with the press] in order to help counteract the editorial slant of most papers. But Republicans have to work a little harder to win the sympathies of reporters of liberal tendency who dominate the national press corps."[56] However, the personal politics of news reporters may not be reflected in their stories, since many news reporters attempt to adhere to professional standards of fairness in covering the candidates. For example, despite charges by the Nixon administration that reporters have a Democratic and liberal bias, it was the intense coverage of Senator Thomas F. Eagleton's medical history—perhaps more than any other factor—that forced him to resign from the Democratic ticket in 1972. The highly publicized Eagleton story was very damaging to George McGovern's campaign for President.

National political correspondents and columnists play an influential role

"Candidates . . . can ill afford to ignore the press."

[55] See White, *The Making of the President 1960,* pp. 336–38, and *The Making of the President 1968,* p. 327.

[56] Polsby and Wildavsky, *Presidential Elections,* 5th ed., p. 181.

Political Division of Daily Newspapers
in Presidential Elections, 1932–1980*

Table 8–2

Year	Republican	Democratic	Independent or Neutral
1932	55.5%	38.7%	5.8%
1936	60.4	34.5	5.1
1940	66.3	20.1	13.6
1944	60.1	22.0	17.9
1948	65.2	15.4	19.4
1952	67.3	14.5	18.2
1956	59.0	17.0	24.0
1960	54.0	15.0	31.0
1964	34.7	42.4	22.9
1968†	60.8	14.0	24.0
1972	71.4	5.3	23.3
1976	62.0	12.0	26.0
1980‡	42.2	12.0	42.0

* Figures represent percentages of total number of papers replying to questionnaires. The number responding varied from year to year.
†Wallace had the support of 1.2 percent.
‡ Anderson had the support of 3.8 percent.
Source: Data for 1932–1960 from William B. Dickinson, Jr., "Politicians and the Press," in Richard M. Boeckel, ed., *Editorial Research Reports,* Vol. 2, No. 2 (September 2, 1964), p. 659. Data for 1964–1980 from *Editor & Publisher,* October 31, 1964, November 2, 1968, November 4, 1972, October 30, 1976, and November 1, 1980.

in interpreting political developments and even in recruiting candidates. Speculation in the press about who may or may not become a candidate and published stories analyzing the relative strengths and abilities of rival contenders may affect what happens at the conventions and on Election Day.

In contrast, editorial support of political candidates by newspapers has a less demonstrable effect on the outcome of presidential campaigns. (See Table 8-2.) During the New Deal years, Roosevelt was consistently opposed by one-half to two-thirds of the nation's daily newspapers; Harry Truman in 1948 and John Kennedy in 1960 were endorsed by only 15 percent of the daily papers, but both won. So did Jimmy Carter in 1976 with endorsements from only 12 percent of the daily papers.

Despite the emphasis on television in politics there are some 62.2 million daily newspaper readers in the United States, and the impressions they receive in political campaigns are formed in part by what they read. As a result, candidates must include the written press in their calculations of campaign techniques and strategy, even if they rely on television for direct mass appeal to the electorate.

Campaign Finance

When Abraham Lincoln ran for Congress in 1846, it cost him 75 cents: "I made the canvass on my own horse; my entertainment, being at the houses of friends, cost me nothing; and my only outlay was 75¢ for a barrel of cider, which some farm-hands insisted I should treat to."[57]

Clearly, times have changed. The immense cost of American political campaigns can be seen at a glance from these figures, which represent total spending at all levels in presidential years since 1960:[58]

$175 million in 1960	$425 million in 1972
$200 million in 1964	$540 million in 1976
$300 million in 1968	$1 billion in 1980 (est.)

By the presidential election of 1976, the nature of political spending in the United States had been completely reshaped by Watergate, Congress, and the Supreme Court. For the first time, under the Federal Election Campaign Act of 1974 and its 1976 amendments, both major candidates, Jimmy Carter and Gerald Ford, financed their election campaigns with federal funds; each candidate spent the approximately $22 million allotted to him under law. In 1980 Carter and Reagan, the major-party candidates, each accepted $29.4 million in public funds, and John Anderson received $4.2 million, for a total of $63 million.

The presidential election of 1976 was the first in which the law provided effective limits on the size of contributions to candidates. In 1972 Max Palvesky, a California millionaire, gave almost $320,000 to George McGovern, the Democratic candidate. In 1976 he could give only $1000 to Jimmy Carter. The conclusion that might logically be drawn is that a candidate who receives a $1000 contribution will feel less obligated to the donor than one who receives $320,000. And that result is precisely what the new law was designed to achieve.

Money is a subject cloaked by a good deal of secrecy, and a vast amount of confusion. Over the years Congress has attempted to control the sources, amounts, and reporting of campaign expenditures, but until 1974 the overlapping and largely ineffective legislation on the subject resulted in more loophole than law.

In the past, at least, no politician or political scientist accepted the officially reported campaign spending figures as fully reflective of actual political campaign costs. Of the iceberg that is campaign finance, very little showed above the surface. Partly as a result, an atmosphere of public cynicism and mistrust has tended to surround the subject of money and politics. Voter attitudes on the subject are reflected in such knowing statements as: "Money wins elections," "Politicians can be bought," or "Politics is a rich man's game."

Widespread financial abuses in President Nixon's 1972 campaign, revealed by the Senate Watergate committee and by the press, increased broad-gauge sentiment for public financing of elections and related reforms. The result was the Federal Election Campaign Act of 1974. (Provisions of the act are summarized on p. 285.)

Money *is* important. It did not, however, win the Democratic nomination for Averell Harriman in 1956, nor did it put Nelson Rockefeller in the White House in 1960, 1964, or 1968—and neither man lacked money. Since the Second World War, the Republicans have generally spent more than the Demo-

1980: Reagan's campaign manager happily accepts $29.4 million federal check to finance campaign.

"There are limits to the influence of money": Nelson Rockefeller campaigns in 1968.

[57] Carl Sandburg, *Abraham Lincoln: The Prairie Years,* Vol. I (New York: Harcourt Brace Jovanovich, 1926), p. 344.

[58] Herbert E. Alexander, *Financing Politics: Money, Elections and Political Reform,* p. 9; and 1980 data from Citizens' Research Foundation.

crats on national campaigns. Therefore, if money *alone* had determined the result of presidential elections, the Democrats could not have won. There are, in other words, some limits to the influence of money in elections.

A series of laws enacted in the 1970s have strengthened the regulation of campaign spending in federal elections. The previous patchwork of federal legislation had also sought to require disclosure of gifts and expenditures, and to limit amounts spent, but the laws had fallen far short of achieving these goals. Most states have campaign financial reporting laws, but they vary greatly and few are stringent.

The Federal Election Campaign Act of 1971 required disclosure of the names of all persons giving more than $100 to a federal campaign. The law also placed limits on what candidates or their families could spend on their own campaigns. Other provisions limited spending for advertising. The 1971 law repealed the Corrupt Practices Act of 1925, which had failed to limit political spending and did not apply to primary elections. In addition, the law repealed certain provisions of the Hatch Act of 1940 which sought to limit political contributions and spending in federal elections. These provisions had been evaded by various subterfuges.

As far back as 1907 Congress prohibited corporations from contributing to candidates for office in federal elections. The Taft-Hartley Act of 1947 bars gifts by labor unions or corporations to federal election campaigns, but the law did not stop unions or corporations from financing political campaigns; they simply set up separate political arms to make campaign contributions, such as the AFL-CIO Committee on Political Education (COPE), and BIPAC, the Business-Industrial Political Action Committee.

In 1971 Congress for the first time let individuals take a limited federal income tax credit for political contributions. In addition, Congress provided that, starting in 1973, taxpayers could specify that $1 of each person's federal income taxes go into a campaign fund to be distributed among the candidates in the next presidential election. The checkoff law was designed to provide public financing of presidential campaigns, in order to free political parties of dependence on private contributions. Beginning in 1974, this option was included in the standard income tax forms to make it more convenient for taxpayers.

Form **1040** Department of the Treasury—Internal Revenue Service **U.S. Individual Income Tax Return** 19**78**		
For Privacy Act Notice, see page 3 of Instructions	For the year January 1–December 31, 1978, or other tax year beginning	1978, ending 19

Use IRS label. Other-wise, please print or type.	Your first name and initial (if joint return, also give spouse's name and initial) James E. and Rosalynn	Last name Carter	Your social security number 259 20 7368
	Present home address (Number and street, including apartment number, or rural route) The White House		Spouse's social security no. 257 62 4042
	City, town or post office, State and ZIP code Washington, D.C. 20500		Your occupation President
▶	Do you want $1 to go to the Presidential Election Campaign Fund? X Yes No	If joint return, does your spouse want $1 to go to this fund? . . X Yes No Note: Checking Yes will not increase your tax or reduce your refund.	Spouse's occupation

Filing Status   1 ☐ Single
                    2 ☐ Married filing joint return (even if only one had income)

The New Rules. As already noted, the Federal Election Campaign Act of 1974 rewrote the laws of campaign finance in the United States. The law was modified by the Supreme Court in an important ruling in January 1976.[59] Amendments enacted later that year and in 1979 made further changes. The law as of 1980 provided as follows:

Contribution limits. Individuals may give up to $1000 to each candidate in each federal election or primary; up to $5000 per year to a political action committee, such as those sponsored by corporations or labor unions; and $20,000 per year to a national political party committee. Total contributions by one person are limited to $25,000 a year. Political action committees that qualify may contribute $5000 to a candidate in each election.

Public financing. Presidential—but not Senate or House—candidates have the option of accepting federal money to pay for general elections or primaries, as did both major-party candidates in 1980. To qualify for public funds in the primaries, a candidate must raise $5000 in each of twenty states in contributions of $250 or less, for an overall total of $100,000. In addition, public funds may be used to help each major political party to finance its national convention.

Spending limits. Presidential candidates who accept federal funds are limited to a spending ceiling, set at $29.4 million each for Reagan and Carter in 1980, and in the general election they can accept no private contributions.[60] For each candidate in the presidential primaries who accepted federal funds, the spending limit in 1980 was $14.7 million, in both private contributions and federal matching funds.[61]

Disclosure. Candidates must file periodic reports with the government disclosing the names and addresses of all donors of more than $100 and listing all expenditures of more than $100.

Federal Election Commission. The law created a new, bipartisan six-member Federal Election Commission (reconstituted after the Supreme Court decision) to enforce the campaign finance laws and administer the public financing machinery.

The 1974 law had sought to limit campaign expenditures in all federal elections and to restrict individual spending by candidates or their families. But the Supreme Court, ruling that these limits, in general, restricted freedom of expression, struck them down—except for presidential candidates who accept public financing. The Court upheld the limits on contributions, ruling that this imposed less of a burden on free expression.

In many districts it costs more than $100,000 to run for Congress; nine House candidates reported spending more than $500,000 in 1978. One House candidate in 1978, Carter Burden of New York, spent more than $1 million, and

How Much Does It Cost?

[59] *Buckley* v. *Valeo,* 424 U.S. 1 (1976).

[60] John B. Anderson was eligible for $4.2 million in public funds in 1980. In order to qualify for public funds, he had to poll 5 percent or more of the vote, which he did. Because Anderson, under the law, received his funds only *after* the election, he could also accept private contributions.

[61] The Federal Election Campaign Act of 1974 set the limits for each presidential candidate at $10 million in the primaries and $20 million in the general elections. But the 1976 amendments contained an escalator clause keyed to the cost of living index; that is why the dollar totals were higher in 1980.

Senator Jesse Helms

lost. The mean expenditure for House campaigns that year was $108,829.[62] And in 1980 one Republican incumbent in the House, Representative Robert K. Dornan of California, spent $1.5 million to win re-election.[63]

To run for the United States Senate, a candidate may spend several million dollars. All told, House and Senate candidates of both parties spent more than $300 million in 1980.[64] In 1976 H. John Heinz III of Pennsylvania, heir to the catsup and pickle fortune, spent more than $2 million to win election to the United States Senate, more than any other Senate candidate that year. His opponent, Representative William J. Green, was able to raise less than half the amount spent by Heinz, and lost. But even Heinz's record was broken in 1978 by Senator Jesse Helms, a Republican of North Carolina, who spent $7.5 million to win re-election, and by Senator John Tower of Texas, who spent $4.3 million and also won re-election.[65] The mean expenditure for Senate races in 1978 was $951,390.[66]

Gubernatorial races also often prove to be very expensive. In 1980 Jay Rockefeller, a member of one of America's wealthiest families and heir to the Standard Oil fortune, spent about $12 million in winning re-election as governor of West Virginia. Almost all of the money was his own.[67]

The Rockefeller campaign was a dramatic example of the enormous financial resources that may be enjoyed by a wealthy candidate. As already noted, the 1974 campaign finance act sought to limit such personal spending, but those provisions were invalidated by the Supreme Court except for presidential (and vice-presidential) candidates who accept public funds.

Running for President is vastly more expensive than running for Congress: in 1980, according to one analysis, the Reagan campaign, including public funds, spending by independent committees and state and local Republican parties, cost $62 million. For Carter, the figure was $56.1 million, and for Anderson, $12.5 million.[68] Thus, spending by the major candidates in the 1980 presidential election totaled approximately $130.6 million. The preconvention campaigns and the national conventions brought the cost of nominating and electing a President in 1980 to about $250 million.[69] Of this total, about $104.8 million was spent in *public* funds: $63.4 million for the general election campaign, $30.6 million for the primaries, and $8.8 million for the two national conventions.[70] The cost of the 1980 presidential election was the highest in history, despite the ceiling on the use of public funds. (See Figure 8-3.)

Alexander Heard, author of an authoritative study of campaign finance, has concluded that money is particularly important in "the shadow land of our politics" where it is decided who shall be a nominee of a political party: "Cash is far more significant in the nominating process than in determining the outcome of elections."[71]

[62] John F. Bibby, Thomas E. Mann, Norman J. Ornstein, *Vital Statistics on Congress, 1980* (Washington, D.C.: American Enterprise Institute for Public Policy Research, 1980), p. 26.
[63] *Washington Post,* November 8, 1980, p. A4.
[64] *New York Times,* November 23, 1980, p. B3.
[65] Congressional Quarterly, *Weekly Report,* September 29, 1979, p. 2152.
[66] Bibby, Mann, and Ornstein, *Vital Statistics on Congress, 1980,* p. 28.
[67] *Washington Post,* November 30, 1980, p. A1.
[68] *New York Times,* November 23, 1980, p. B3.
[69] *Ibid.*
[70] Data provided by Federal Election Commission.
[71] Alexander Heard, *The Costs of Democracy* (Chapel Hill, N.C.: University of North Carolina Press, 1960), pp. 14, 35.

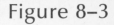

Major-Party Campaign Spending in Presidential Elections, 1956–1980*

Figure 8–3

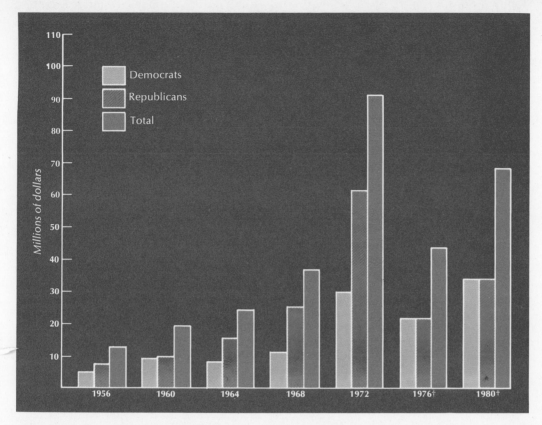

* Figures are for the postconvention campaigns.

†Both major-party presidential candidates accepted public funding in 1976 and 1980. Lower totals for those years reflect limits set for such candidates by the Federal Election Campaign Act of 1974.

Source: Herbert E. Alexander, *Financing Politics: Money, Elections and Political Reform,* 2nd ed. (Washington, D.C.: Congressional Quarterly Press, 1980), p. 5; data for 1980 provided by Federal Election Commission; totals include the full $4.6 million maximum allotted to major-party committees.

Today, radio and television costs are by far the biggest single item in campaign spending. In 1976 almost $17 million, or more than a third of all presidential campaign expenditures, was spent on political broadcasting.[72] Political committees also spend money on other forms of publicity and advertising. They must pay for polls and data processing, printing costs, telephone bills, headquarters costs, and salaries of party workers. A great deal of money is spent on Election Day to pay poll workers, to provide transportation to get the voters to the polls—and, sometimes, illicitly, to pay voters, Alexander Heard has estimated that Election Day spending accounts for "as much as one-eighth of the total election bill in the United States."[73]

Where Does the Money Go?

[72] Alexander, *Financing Politics: Money, Elections and Political Reform,* p. 10.
[73] Heard, *The Costs of Democracy,* p. 394.

By the 1980 election, *political action committees* (PACs) had become a powerful and controversial source of campaign money. PACs are independent organizations, or more often, political arms of corporations, unions, or interest groups. (See Chapter 6 for a detailed discussion of PACs and single-issue groups.)

The best known of these organizations, the National Conservative Political Action Committee, spent $1.7 million on the presidential race, $940,000 in five Senate races, and $176,000 on 112 other candidates.[74] Even before the 1980 campaign was underway, one study showed, corporate PACs had already contributed $10.7 million and union PACs $6.6 million to more than 1000 congressional candidates.[75] All told, PAC spending in all 1980 campaigns had reached more than $61 million by mid-year. And the figure had grown to more than $127 million by November.[76]

As noted in Chapter 6, by 1980 the number of PACs had quadrupled in six years to some 2000. The growth of PACs was due, in part, to the 1976 Supreme Court decision permitting "independent expenditures" in political campaigns by groups not formally connected with a candidate.[77] PACs often contribute to political campaigns because they hope a candidate will support legislation that will benefit a specific industry, union, or interest group.

The reasons why people give money to campaigns vary widely. Some contributors simply believe in a party or a candidate and wish to express their support. Others give because they do expect some tangible benefit or reward from the winning candidate. Others hope to buy access to a public official; for some who long for social recognition, an invitation to a White House dinner may be reward enough.[78]

Some of America's wealthiest families have contributed heavily to political campaigns. The bulk of the contributions from these families—whose wealth is rooted in the oil, steel, auto, railroad, and other large industries—went to the Republican party. While the contribution limits in the 1974 act have reduced the

---

[74] Data provided by the National Conservative Political Action Committee.
[75] *Washington Post*, November 1, 1980, p. A9.
[76] Federal Election Commission press release, September 25, 1980, and January 13, 1981.
[77] *Buckley* v. *Valeo* (1976).
[78] For a discussion of the complex motives for campaign giving, see Heard, *The Costs of Democracy*, Chapter 4.

"Senator, according to this report, you've been marked for defeat by the A.D.A., the National Rifle Association, the A.F.L.-C.I.O., the N.A.M., the Sierra Club, Planned Parenthood, the World Student Christian Federation, the Clamshell Alliance . . ."

Drawing by Dana Fradon
©1980 The New Yorker Magazine, Inc.

influence of individual donors, wealthy individuals and families can still contribute substantially to congressional and presidential candidates, since the law permits an aggregate contribution of $25,000 a year by each person. And the federal law does not apply in state or local elections, where wealthy individuals can make their presence felt.

Both major parties rely on a variety of sources to raise money: PAC contributions, individual contributions from the public, $100-a-plate and even $1000-a-plate dinners, direct mail solicitation, televised appeals, contributions from members of labor unions and corporation executives, and corporate advertising in convention programs and political booklets.

An unadvertised source of campaign funds is the underworld. In some communities close ties exist between organized crime and politics; elected officials may take graft to protect criminal operations, and sometimes the payoffs take the form of campaign contributions. Heard has guessed that perhaps "15 percent of political campaign expenditures at state and local levels" comes from the underworld.[79]

Democratic fund-raising dinner

The reforms in the election laws during the 1970s sought to limit contributions, to provide meaningful public disclosure of campaign gifts and spending (in place of laws that invited evasion), to broaden the base of campaign giving through tax incentives, and to provide government subsidies. These reforms were based on the belief that candidates should not have to depend on big contributors to whom they might become obligated and that roughly equal resources should be available to candidates for public office.

Campaigns, Money, and Democracy

The case for reform was compelling, since inadequate controls only served to reinforce voter cynicism about politics. Despite the partial success of the new law in the 1976 and 1980 presidential and congressional elections, there were pressures for further change.

Many analysts felt that special-interest money from PACs had, by 1980, achieved undue influence in the electoral process. It was this concern that led President Carter, in his farewell address to the nation, to warn that "single-issue groups and special-interest organizations" had become "a disturbing factor in American political life."[80] In 1980 millions of dollars in special-interest money that might have gone into presidential campaigns was funneled into the congressional campaigns instead, through political action committees. The growth and power of the PACs threatened to undermine the reforms of the federal election laws.

Most observers felt the federal money allotted to each presidential candidate in 1980 was insufficient—leaving little left over for bumper stickers, buttons, and volunteer programs. Herbert E. Alexander and other experts on campaign finance suggested in the wake of the 1980 campaign that the amount of public funds allocated to presidential candidates be increased to reflect higher costs, particularly the increased cost of television time for commercials. In addition, Alexander and others proposed that the $1000 limit on individual gifts per candidate be raised to $2500 or $5000.[81] Some analysts have also suggested

[79] Heard, *The Costs of Democracy,* p. 163.
[80] *New York Times,* January 15, 1981, p. B10.
[81] *New York Times,* November 23, 1980, p. E3.

that public financing of presidential campaigns be extended to congressional campaigns.

Many problems remain. The fact that some candidates have unequal financial resources, for example, tends to undermine public confidence in the American political process. And campaigns are a vital part of that process, for, within limits, they give the voters a chance to decide who shall govern.

Perspective

Studies have shown that a majority of voters are committed to one candidate in advance of the campaign. But a third or more of the electorate decide during the campaign, and their votes may well determine the outcome of the election. Campaigns, therefore, are an important part of the political process.

For a relatively unknown presidential candidate, entering the primaries may prove an attractive way to demonstrate strength and gain nationwide exposure in the media. An incumbent President may lose the election, but he starts out with a potential advantage over an opponent in a presidential campaign. Not only do the prestige and power of the office follow the President on the hustings, but all the visible trappings go along as well. Aside from prestige, an incumbent President already has a large, highly organized staff and all the advantages of White House communications and facilities. He may be able to dominate the news by taking actions as President that are timed for maximum political advantage.

Peace and pocketbook issues are usually of major importance in presidential campaigns. Democratic candidates since the New Deal have campaigned on the party's efforts to achieve social progress at home. In the area of foreign affairs, the Republicans often have an advantage. However, a sudden foreign policy crisis, a personal scandal, a chance remark—these and other imponderables—may affect voter attitudes in political campaigns.

The ability of political candidates to reach increased numbers of voters through television commercials has been reflected in a dramatic rise in campaign spending for TV broadcasts. In 1980, as in other recent elections, the major candidates relied on large numbers of television commercials to get their message to the voters.

With the increased importance of television, there is at least a danger that a candidate with more money or more skilled media advisers or a better television style will enjoy an unfair advance in resources over a rival. Moreover, with access to an audience of millions of voters through the electronic media, a political candidate may be tempted to display an "image" that masks the real person. A candidate may present the issues in capsulized, simplistic form, and become a performer rather than a leader.

In 1960, for the first time, the major-party candidates were able to reach vast audiences in a series of televised debates. In 1980 voters were able to watch the major candidates debate, although all three candidates—Reagan, Carter, and Anderson—did not come together in a single televised appearance.

Increasingly, at all levels of politics, candidates have turned to professional campaign managers and consultants. The firms provide a variety of services. These include advertising, public relations, research on issues, public opinion sampling, fund raising, telephone solicitations, computer analysis, and speechwriting. The images candidates try to project on television or in the newspapers may be tailored to the advice given them by professional campaign managers. Those managers in turn often rely on polls they have taken or commissioned.

By the presidential election of 1976, the nature of political spending in the United States had been completely reshaped by Watergate, Congress, and the Supreme Court. For the first time, under the Federal Election Campaign Act of 1974 and its 1976 amendments, both major candidates, Jimmy Carter and Gerald Ford, financed their election campaigns with federal funds.

The Federal Election Campaign Act of 1974 revamped the laws governing campaign finance in the United States. As of 1980, after various modifications, the law provided: (1) Individuals could give up to $1000 to each candidate in each federal election or primary; (2) Total contributions by one person were limited to $25,000 per year; (3) Presidential candidates had the option of accepting federal money to pay for general elections or primaries; (4) Candidates who accepted federal funds were then limited to a spending ceiling and could accept no private contributions for the general election; (5) Candidates were required to file periodic reports with the government disclosing the names and addresses of all donors of more than $100 and listing all expenditures of more than $100.

By the 1980 election, political action committees (PACs) had become a powerful and controversial source of campaign money. PACs are either independent organizations or, more often, political arms of corporations, unions, or interest groups. PACs often contribute to political campaigns because they hope a candidate will support legislation that will benefit a specific interest.

Suggested Reading

Alexander, Herbert E. *Financing Politics: Money, Elections, and Political Reform,* 2nd edition* (Congressional Quarterly Press, 1980). A comprehensive analysis of how campaign money is raised, spent, and regulated. Examines campaign financing in the 1976 and 1978 national elections, traces the impact of election law reforms, and speculates on the role of money in politics during the 1980s.

Barber, James David, ed. *Race for the Presidency: The Media and the Nominating Process** (Prentice-Hall, 1978). An interesting analysis, written by four political scientists, of the role that journalists play in the presidential nominating process. Examines the relationship between candidates and reporters and discusses the enlarged role of the news media in providing information to the public about political campaigns.

Heard, Alexander. *The Costs of Democracy** (University of North Carolina Press, 1960). A comprehensive and useful analysis of the relationships between money and politics. Examines the motives for campaign contributions, who contributes, techniques for raising money, efforts to regulate campaign financing, and some of the political consequences of various campaign financing practices. Makes specific policy recommendations.

Kelley, Stanley, Jr. *Professional Public Relations and Political Power** (Johns Hopkins Press, 1956). An influential early analysis of the use of public relations techniques on behalf of candidates for public office and in campaigns focused on specific political issues. Kelley traces the rise of professional public relations firms that are involved in politics, examines the political role of public relations specialists, and assesses the consequences for American politics.

McGinniss, Joe. *The Selling of the President, 1968** (Trident Press, 1969). A critical, behind-the-scenes description of Richard Nixon's use of television in the 1968 presidential campaign by a writer who had extensive access to the advertising, television, and political advisers of the Republican candidate.

Mendelsohn, Harold, and O'Keefe, Garrett J. *The People Choose a President: Influence on Voter Decision Making* (Praeger, 1976). A detailed study of the impact of television on voters in the 1972 presidential election. The authors found that the voters who made their decision late in the campaign were more likely than other voters to be influenced by televised political commercials.

Nimmo, Dan. *The Political Persuaders: The Techniques of Modern Election Campaigns** (Prentice-Hall, 1970). A valuable survey of campaign techniques in the television age. Includes discussions of campaign management, political polls and statistical analysis of the electorate, and the use of mass media to try to influence voters.

Nimmo, Dan. *Political Communication and Public Opinion in America** (Goodyear, 1978). A useful examination of the interplay between political communications and public opinion. Nimmo argues that voters tend to construct their own individual views of campaigns, and that voters arrive at their decisions by interpreting the symbols offered to them.

Nimmo, Dan, and Savage, Robert L. *Candidates and Their Images: Concepts, Methods, and Findings** (Goodyear, 1976). An interesting analysis of modern campaign techniques. Argues that in recent years election campaigns have had an increasingly important effect on how voters view candidates and how voters decide.

Patterson, Thomas E., and McClure, Robert D. *The Unseeing Eye: The Myth of Television Power in National Politics* (Putnam's, 1976). An interesting study of television's impact on campaigns and the discussion of political issues. The authors argue that nightly news programs on television networks provide less information to voters than do paid political advertisements.

Polsby, Nelson W., and Wildavsky, Aaron B. *Presidential Elections,* 5th edition* (Scribner's, 1980). An excellent, concise analysis of the basic strategic considerations affecting the conduct of presidential election campaigns.

Wayne, Stephen J. *The Road to the White House** (St. Martin's Press, 1980). A useful guide to the politics of presidential election campaigns, from the primaries to Election Day. Includes an analysis of the provisions and consequences of legislation regulating campaign finance.

White, Theodore H. *The Making of the President 1972* (Atheneum, 1973); *The Making of the President 1968* (Atheneum, 1969); *The Making of the President 1964** (Atheneum, 1965); *The Making of the President 1960** (Atheneum, 1961). Colorful, detailed accounts of American presidential campaigns, set against the background of the social and cultural forces at work in American society. White is a leading political analyst who has access to many of the political figures he writes about.

* Available in paperback edition

VOTING BEHAVIOR AND ELECTIONS

There comes a moment in every campaign when the bands are silent and the cheering stops. The candidate has given the last speech, made the last promise, answered the last question in the election-eve telethon, smiled at the red light on the TV camera for the last time. There is nothing left to do but to board the campaign plane and fly home to await the verdict of the voters.

There is a certain majesty and mystery in this moment, for until the votes are counted, no one—not the candidates, the voters, the poll takers, the news reporters, not even the computers blinking and buzzing in the control centers of the television networks—knows what the precise outcome will be.

In a democracy, the people choose who shall govern, and that choice is expressed in the voting booth. Although the right to vote is basic to the American political system, it is not as common elsewhere as might be thought. Only about 25 percent of the world's countries hold regular, free elections in which the people may choose among rival candidates.

Chapter 1 examined the reciprocal nature of power in a democracy: government makes authoritative, binding decisions about who gets what in society, but derives its power from the people. People may influence government in a number of ways—by taking part in political activity, by the opinions they hold, by belonging to interest groups, by direct action. But a fundamental way that people influence government is through the ballot box; voting is a very powerful

"input" in the political system. As 1980 demonstrated anew, one of the most potent weapons of popular control in a democracy is the ability of the electorate to remove a party from power.

In the federal system that exists in the United States, the voters choose at all levels of government. In a presidential year, for instance, the voters select many of the more than 500,000 local, state, and federal elected officials, including the President and Vice President, 435 members of the House, one-third of the Senate, and about 13 state governors.

American voters normally may choose among two or more *competing* candidates for the same office. In a democracy, voting is an act of choice among alternative candidates, parties, and, depending on the election, alternative policies.

Under a democratic form of government, then, the voter is theoretically supreme. Yet, as we have seen, there is often a gap between democratic theory and practice. For example, candidates for public office—at least below the presidential level—may compete with vastly unequal financial resources. TV commercials may attempt to manipulate the voters and create "images" of candidates, rather than informing the electorate. What the voters perceive may sometimes be distorted if one side or the other engages in unethical campaign practices or "dirty tricks." Some voters may be unenthusiastic about the nominees of *both* major parties and may believe that their choice is between the lesser of two evils. They may easily come to feel that, for them, voting is a waste of time.

In this chapter we shall examine some central questions about voting in a democratic society: Do enough people vote? Why do large numbers of people fail to vote? How do voters make up their minds? What do elections mean in a democracy—do voters speak in a voice that can be understood by those whom they elect? Do their votes influence government policies?

Who Votes?

The voter may have the final say in the United States—but how many people vote? To those who hold an idealized view of representative democracy, the statistics are bound to be disappointing. In some elections there are as many nonvoters as voters.

Carter: . . . there is a disturbing pattern in the attitude of Governor Reagan. He has never supported any of those arms control agreements—the limited test ban, SALT I, nor the Antiballistic Missile Treaty, nor the Vladivostok Treaty . . . and now he wants to throw into the wastebasket a treaty to control nuclear weapons on a balanced and equal basis between ourselves and the Soviet Union, negotiated over a seven-year period, by myself and my two Republican predecessors.

Carter: We have demanded that the American people sacrifice, and they have done very well. As a matter of fact, we're importing today about one-third less oil from overseas than we did just a year ago. We've had a 25% reduction since the first year I was in office. At the same time, as I have said earlier, we have added about nine million net new jobs in that period of time—a record never before achieved.

Carter: We have made good progress, and there is no doubt in my mind that the commitment to unemployment compensation, the minimum wage, welfare, national health insurance, those kinds of commitments that have typified the Democratic party since ancient history in this country's political life are a very important element of the future. In all those elements, Governor Reagan has repeatedly spoken out against them, which, to me, shows a very great insensitivity to giving deprived families a better chance in life. This, to me, is a very important difference between him and me in this election, and I believe the American people will judge accordingly.

Reagan: I am not talking of scrapping. I am talking of taking the treaty back, and going back into negotiations. And I would say to the Soviet Union, we will sit and negotiate with you as long as it takes, to have not only legitimate arms limitation, but to have a reduction of these nuclear weapons to the point that neither one of us represents a threat to the other. That is hardly throwing away a treaty and being opposed to arms limitation.

Reagan: President Carter also has spoken of the new jobs created. Well, we always, with the normal growth in our country and increase in population, increase the number of jobs. But that can't hide the fact that there are eight million men and women out of work in America today . . . We don't have inflation because the people are living too well. We have inflation because the Government is living too well.

Reagan: Next Tuesday is Election Day. Next Tuesday all of you will go to the polls, will stand there in the polling place and make a decision. I think when you make that decision, it might be well if you would ask yourself, are you better off than you were four years ago? Is it easier for you to go and buy things in the stores than it was four years ago? Is there more or less unemployment in the country than there was four years ago? Is America as respected throughout the world as it was? Do you feel . . . that we're as strong as we were four years ago? And if you answer all of those questions yes, why then, I think your choice is very obvious as to whom you will vote for. If you don't agree . . . then I could suggest another choice that you have.

—Excerpts from the televised Reagan-Carter debate, October 28, 1980.

"And now with a rebuttal . . ."

Drawing by Richter
© 1979 The New Yorker Magazine, Inc.

More than half of Americans of voting age have voted for President in each election since 1928. But in nonpresidential election years, considerably less than half have bothered to vote for members of Congress. In the seven presidential elections between 1956 and 1980, an average of 58.3 percent cast their ballots for President (although the turnout dropped to 53.9 percent in 1980). In the six off-year congressional elections during the same period, an average of only 41.6 percent voted for the House of Representatives. And the turnouts both in 1974 and 1978 were well below 40 percent.[1] (See Figure 9-1.)

The Voter

Although twentieth-century Americans have made great technological progress, their forebears in the horse-and-buggy era scored much higher in voting participation. A much larger proportion of voters took part in presidential elections in the 1890s than in 1980. In the election of 1896, for example, almost 80 percent of all of the eligible voters cast their ballots. The drop in turnout is often attributed to the fact that the adoption of women's suffrage in 1920 brought into the electorate a large new group unaccustomed to voting. But the decline in voter participation had begun well before then. After voter turnout dipped to a

[1] *Statistical Abstract of the United States: 1979* (Washington, D.C.: Government Printing Office, 1979), p. 517; U.S. Bureau of the Census, *Current Population Reports,* Population Estimates and Projections, Series P-25, No. 879, March 1980, p. 2; *New York Times,* January 6, 1981, p. A14; and Congressional Quarterly, *Weekly Report,* November 8, 1980, pp. 3338–45.

Voter Participation in Presidential and House Elections, 1956–1980

Figure 9–1

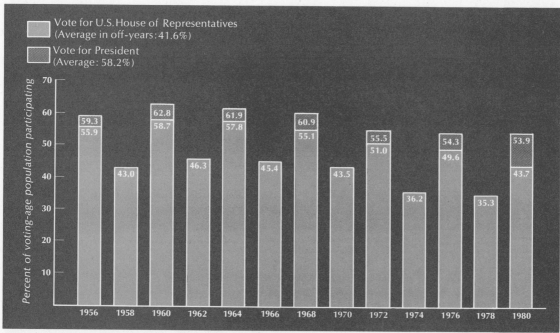

Source: *Statistical Abstract of the United States: 1979* (Washington, D.C.: Government Printing Office, 1979), p. 517; U.S. Bureau of the Census, *Current Population Reports,* Population Estimates and Projections, Series P-25, No. 879, March 1980, p. 2; *New York Times,* January 6, 1981, p. A14; and Congressional Quarterly, *Weekly Report,* November 8, 1980, pp. 3338–45.

Voter Participation in Presidential Elections, 1880–1980

Figure 9–2

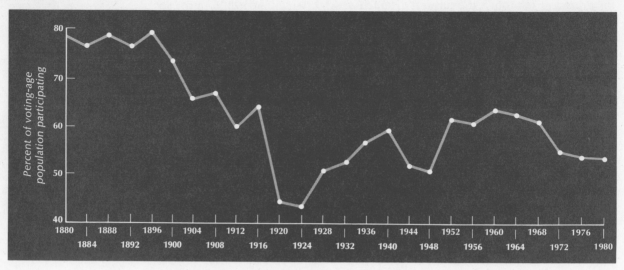

Sources: Figures for 1880 to 1916 in Robert E. Lane, *Political Life* (New York: The Free Press, 1965), p. 20. Reprinted with permission of Macmillan Publishing Co., Inc., from *Political Life* by Robert E. Lane. Copyright © 1959 by The Free Press. Figures for 1920 to 1948 in the U.S. Bureau of the Census, *Statistical Abstract of the United States 1969*, p. 368. Data for 1952 to 1972 in the U.S. Bureau of the Census, *Current Population Reports,* Population Estimates and Projections, Series P–25, No. 626, May 1976, p. 11. Data for 1976 from the *New York Times,* December 13, 1976, p. 65. Data for 1980 from the *New York Times,* January 6, 1981, p. A14.

low point in the early 1920s, it moved to generally higher levels in 1928 and in subsequent elections. (See Figure 9-2.) Despite this trend, voting participation in the United States is substantially lower than it is in many other countries of the world, including Great Britain, West Germany, France, and Canada. (See Table

Voter Participation in Other Countries

Table 9–1

Nation	Election Date	Turnout
Australia*	1980	94%
Canada	1980	70%
France	1978	85%
Great Britain	1979	76%
Ireland	1977	74%
Italy†	1980	88%
Netherlands	1977	88%
New Zealand‡	1978	69%
Sweden	1979	91%
West Germany	1980	89%

* Compulsory registration and voting
† Compulsory voting
‡ Compulsory registration
 Source: Data provided by the Australian Electoral Office, and the embassies of the other listed countries, Washington, D.C.

9-1.) Because other nations calculate voter turnout in varying ways, however, the comparison with the United States is not precise.

Socioeconomic Factors.   It is clear that who votes varies with factors of geography, age, sex, education, ethnic background, religion, income, social class, and occupation. This does not mean that people vote or do not vote *because* of such social, demographic, and economic factors; it merely means that these factors often coincide with higher or lower voting participation.[2] For example, regional differences in voter participation may be associated with social and economic factors in those areas, the degree of two-party competition, and, in some cases, differences in the election laws governing registration and voting.

Middle-aged people vote more than the young or the very old. Although some college students and young people take an active part in election campaigns, poll data indicate that about 50 percent of Americans between the ages of eighteen and twenty-nine did not register to vote in 1980.[3] In general, studies have shown that voting and political participation increase slowly with age, peak in the mid-forties and fifties, and decline after age sixty.[4]

During the first several decades after the women's suffrage amendment was ratified in 1920, men voted more than women. By 1976, however, the percent of women who turned out to vote was almost as high as that of men.[5] Because there are more women than men in the U.S. population, in absolute numbers there are likely to be more women than men voters in future elections. Sandra Baxter and Marjorie Lansing concluded in a recent study, "A major shift has occurred in the voting balance in the last decade: more women than men have gone to the polls to vote for president."[6]

College graduates vote substantially more than people with high school or grade school educations. One survey found that 79.8 percent of college-educated Americans reported that they voted in the 1976 presidential election; but only 59.4 percent of those with four years of high school and 51.4 percent of those with grade school educations said they voted.[7] Education seems to cause the greatest variation in voter turnout of all the factors.[8]

Income, education, social class, and occupation are closely related; the higher the level in all these categories, the more likely a person is to vote. (See Table 9-2.)

Jews vote more than Catholics, and Catholics vote more than Protestants. Churchgoers are more likely to vote than nonchurchgoers, a phenomenon perhaps associated with the willingness of the churchgoer to participate in organized activity and the inclination of some religious groups to get involved in politics. Blacks vote less than whites—but historically black voters in the South were often prevented from voting by legal subterfuge, violence, or intimidation. As

Drawing by Stevenson
© 1980 The New Yorker Magazine, Inc.

"Before I tell you who I'm for, perhaps you'd be interested to hear a little something about how my political thinking has evolved over the years."

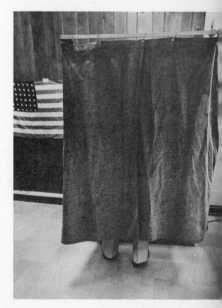

---

[2] See Lester W. Milbrath and M. L. Goel, *Political Participation,* 2nd ed. (Chicago: Rand McNally, 1977), for detailed citations of studies of political participation.

[3] *Gallup Opinion Index,* Report No. 180, August 1980, p. 27.

[4] Milbrath and Goel, *Political Participation,* p. 114; and Raymond E. Wolfinger and Steven J. Rosenstone, *Who Votes?* (New Haven: Yale University Press, 1980), pp. 37–38. However, Wolfinger and Rosenstone add that "The decline in turnout among people over sixty . . . is explained not by their greater age but by differences in education, marital status, and sex." (p. 47)

[5] Sandra Baxter and Marjorie Lansing, *Women and Politics: The Invisible Majority* (Ann Arbor, Mich.: University of Michigan Press, 1980), p. 181.

[6] *Ibid.,* p. 1.

[7] Data provided by U.S. Bureau of the Census.

[8] For a discussion of the "very strong relationship between rates of voting and years of education," see Wolfinger and Rosenstone, *Who Votes?,* pp. 17–20 and 34–36.

Voter Turnout by Group and Region, 1976

Table 9–2

Voting Groups	Percent Voting
College education	79.8%
White collar	72.1
$10,000 and above	69.3
Farm workers	62.5
Nonagricultural industrial workers	62.1
North and West	61.2
White	60.9
Male	59.6
High school education	59.4
Metropolitan area	59.2
Nonmetropolitan area	59.1
Female	58.8
65 years and above	56.5
South	54.9
Service workers	52.8
Grade school education	51.4
Black	48.7
21–24 years	45.6
Below $5,000	45.6
18–20 years	38.0

Source: Data for 1976 presidential election, provided by the U.S. Bureau of the Census. Preliminary data for 1980 show a similar pattern.

Drawing by Ed Arno
© 1976 The New Yorker
Magazine, Inc.

"If the election were held today, who would you like to take a punch at?"

was noted in Chapter 5, the number of black registered voters in the South increased dramatically after passage of the Voting Rights Act of 1965.

Voter Attitudes. Voter turnout does vary with demographic and social differences, but other research has identified additional factors that seem to influence participation at the polls. This research has focused on voter *attitudes.*

For example, a strong Democrat or a rock-ribbed Republican is more likely to get out and vote than a citizen whose party loyalties are casual. The higher the *intensity of partisan preference,* therefore, the more likely it is that the person will vote. Similarly, the *degree of interest* people have in the campaign and their *concern over the election outcome* appear to be related to whether they vote. If people think the election is close, they are more likely to vote, because they may feel their votes will count. And, if people think they can understand and influence politics, they are more likely to vote than are those who regard politics and government as distant and complicated. The greater a person's *sense of political effectiveness,* in other words, the greater the chance that he or she will vote. Americans, moreover, are indoctrinated with the importance of voting, long before they are old enough to do so. Thus the voter's *sense of civic duty* also bears on whether he or she goes to the polls.[9]

The Nonvoter

Some 35 to 45 percent or more of Americans do not vote in presidential elections. Who are they? Why don't they vote?

[9] Angus Campbell, Philip E. Converse, Warren E. Miller, and Donald E. Stokes, *The American Voter* (New York: Wiley, 1960), pp. 96–101. Our discussion of voter attitudes is based in part on Chapter 5 of this landmark study of voting conducted at the Survey Research Center, University of Michigan.

The preceding section indicated that the nonvoter is more likely to be less educated, rural, nonwhite, Southern, very young or very old, a person "whose emotional investment in politics . . . is on the average much less than that of the voter."[10] Although a rough portrait of the nonvoter can be sketched in these terms, the picture does not answer the question of *why* he or she does not vote.

As noted earlier, and in Chapter 6, about 54 percent of the voting age population—or more than 86 million people—voted in the 1980 election. But another 74 million Americans of voting age did not. After the 1980 election the Gallup poll released the following breakdown of "eligible" nonvoters and the reasons they gave for not voting (with the percentages from the sample projected into numbers of people):

31 million were not registered
12.5 million did not like the candidates
6 million were ill or disabled
4 million were not interested in politics
4 million were not American citizens
3 million were new residents of their community and had not met the residence requirements
2 million were traveling and away from home
2 million said they could not leave their jobs
740,000 had no way to get to the polls
370,000 had not obtained an absentee ballot
1.5 million mentioned a variety of other reasons[11]

Even taking into account the fact that some people had good reasons for not voting, a nation with some 74 million persons who do not turn out in a presidential election would seem to fall somewhat short of the idealized model of popular democracy. But some political scientists believe that what might work in a simple, agrarian society does not apply in a modern, highly industrialized society like the United States today.[12] The harassed parent with five young children may well find it difficult to get to the polls on Election Day. Most people spend more time worrying about money, sex, illness, crime, the high cost of living, automobile repairs, and a host of other things than they do worrying about politics.

So if we ask whether enough people vote in the United States, we must also ask: "How much is enough?" A turnout of some 50 to 60 percent in a presidential election may not meet the classic standards of democracy, but it may be the best that can be expected in the United States today. In any event, it is reality; it is what we have.

One overall pattern that emerges from all these data about the voter and the nonvoter in the United States is that those who are more advantageously situated in the social system vote more than the "have-nots," or less advantaged. If members of all social groups in the United States voted in equal proportions, candidates might have to offer programs that appealed more to the disadvantaged groups that do not now come to the polls. In short, if everybody voted, the candidates and policies of the American political system might be somewhat different from what they are today.

[10] *Ibid.,* p. 111.
[11] Adapted from the Gallup poll, press release, December 7. 1980. An additional 7.4 million gave "no particular reason" for not voting.
[12] Milbrath and Goel, *Political Participation,* p. 143.

How the Voter Decides

We have an idea who votes and who does not. The next question is: Why do people vote the way they do? How people make up their minds to vote for one candidate instead of another is obviously of great interest to politicians, campaign managers, advertising executives, and pollsters. But the question also has much broader implications for all citizens and for democratic government; the kind of society in which we live depends in part on whether voters flip a coin in the voting booth or choose on a somewhat more rational basis — satisfaction or dissatisfaction with the incumbent administration, for example.

Although American voters have been extensively analyzed, we still do not know *precisely* why they behave the way they do. We do not know which of many factors ultimately causes a person to stay home or to vote for one candidate or party instead of another. To say, for example, that many Catholics are Democrats does not mean a person is a Democrat *because* he or she is a Catholic. And, although party loyalty appears to be related to voting habits, we do not know, for example, that a Vermont farmer votes Republican *because* he identifies with the Republican party. Psychologists know that it is extremely difficult to judge people's motives from their behavior; even asking voters to explain their actions may not produce satisfactory answers.

So there are limits to the ability of political science to interpret the behavior of voters. Even allowing for these limits, however, a great deal has been learned about voting habits in recent decades.

Two basic approaches have been followed in studying how the voters decide:

1. *Sociological.* This method focuses on the social and economic background of the voters — their income, class, ethnic group, education, and similar factors — and attempts to relate these factors to how they vote.
2. *Psychological.* This method attempts to go beyond socioeconomic factors and find out what is going on inside the minds of the voters, to measure their *perceptions* of parties, candidates, and issues. This second approach is based on the premise that how the voter responds depends less on *static* factors, such as social class, than on *dynamic* changing factors of issues and politics. In short, voting behavior may change as the issues and candidates change.

The difference between these two approaches is not as great as it might seem at first glance: how the voters currently perceive the issues may well be shaped by their social and economic backgrounds. The social psychologists who followed the second approach beginning in the 1950s built on the foundations laid by the political sociologists in the 1940s.

The Sociological Factors

The first of two classic voter studies was conducted in 1940 by Paul F. Lazarsfeld and his associates.[13] They chose a sample of 600 residents of Erie County, Ohio. The Ohio county was chosen because it was small and because, until then, it had reflected national voting trends in every presidential election in this century.

[13] Paul F. Lazarsfeld, Bernard Berelson, and Hazel Gaudet, *The People's Choice* (New York: Columbia University Press, 1968). Originally published in 1944.

The researchers' method was new; instead of tabulating results after an election, they attempted to probe "votes in the making." Grouping the 600 Ohio residents by socioeconomic status, the study found that: "The wealthier people, the people with more and better possessions, the people with business interests—these people were usually Republicans. The poorer people, the people whose homes and clothes were of lower quality, the self-acknowledged laboring class—they voted Democratic. Different social characteristics, different votes."[14] But the voter is a member of several groups simultaneously. Sometimes the claims of one group conflict with those of another. For example, the study concluded that rich people are more likely to vote Republican, Catholics are more likely to vote Democratic. What of wealthy Catholics? Such persons are said to be "cross-pressured" because their social affiliations are pulling them in opposite directions. The study found that these voters were more likely than others to delay their decision and change their minds during a campaign.

In 1948 the same research method was used in a study of how 1000 voters in Elmira, New York, made up their minds during the Truman-Dewey campaign.[15] This more detailed study also concluded that social class influenced voting behavior. It also found that voters who liked a candidate tended to think that the candidate's stand matched their own. Moreover, only about one-third of the voters were accurate in their understanding of where the candidates stood on the issues.[16]

From these and many other studies, it is possible to draw a picture of the American voter in terms of his or her social class and other sociological factors. (A breakdown of how different groups have voted in presidential elections is summarized in Table 9-3.)

Social Class, Income, and Occupation. Upper-class and middle-class voters are more likely to vote Republican than are lower-class voters, who tend to be Democrats.

Professional and business people are more apt to support Republicans than Democrats. For example, with the exception of 1964—when Republicans in droves deserted Goldwater for Johnson—business and professional people voted heavily Republican in the seven elections between 1956 and 1980. (See Table 9-3.) Among persons in the highest income brackets, Republican candidates usually draw more votes than do Democrats. Manual workers tend to vote Democratic, and 60 percent of a national sample of persons with incomes of under $5000 identified themselves as Democrats.[17] These sociological factors in voting represent trends as measured in many past elections. That does not mean that they hold true in a given election. A business executive from Atlanta who voted Republican in many past years may have voted for Jimmy Carter, a fellow Georgian, in 1980.

Education. In the past, at least, college graduates have tended to vote for Republicans rather than for Democrats. College-educated voters were solidly in

[14] *Ibid.,* p. 21.

[15] Bernard R. Berelson, Paul F. Lazarsfeld, and William N. McPhee, *Voting* (Chicago: University of Chicago Press, 1966). Originally published in 1954.

[16] *Ibid.,* Chapter 10.

[17] *Gallup Opinion Index,* Report No. 180, August 1980, p. 31; and *Gallup Opinion Index.* Report No. 137, December 1976, p. 17.

Votes by Groups in Presidential Elections, 1956–1980

Table 9–3

	1956 Dem.	1956 Rep.	1960 Dem.	1960 Rep.	1964 Dem.	1964 Rep.
National	42.2%	57.8%	50.1%	49.9%	61.3%	38.7%
Men	45	55	52	48	60	40
Women	39	61	49	51	62	38
White	41	59	49	51	59	41
Nonwhite	61	39	68	32	94	6
College education	31	69	39	61	52	48
High school education	42	58	52	48	62	38
Grade school education	50	50	55	45	66	34
Professional and business people	32	68	42	58	54	46
White-collar workers	37	63	48	52	57	43
Manual workers	50	50	60	40	71	29
Union members	57	43	65	35	73	27
Farmers	46	54	48	52	53	47
Under 30	43	57	54	46	64	36
30–49 years	45	55	54	46	63	37
Over 49	39	61	46	54	59	41
Protestants	37	63	38	62	55	45
Catholics	51	49	78	22	76	24
Republicans	4	96	5	95	20	80
Democrats	85	15	84	16	87	13
Independents	30	70	43	57	56	44

Source: Gallup poll, published November 1968, December 1968, December 1972, and December 1976. Data for 1980 provided by the Gallup poll.

the ranks of the GOP during the elections of Eisenhower, Kennedy, and Nixon. Although Nixon averaged 43.4 percent of the popular vote in 1968, he received 54 percent of the votes of college graduates; by contrast, only 33 percent of voters with a grade school education voted for Nixon. In 1980 differences in voting preference by educational level were less pronounced than in the 1960s. But the Democratic candidate, Jimmy Carter, made his best showing among voters with a grade school education. (See Table 9-3.)

Religion and Ethnic Background. In a 1980 survey, 65 percent of Jews, 53 percent of Catholics, but only 45 percent of Protestants said they considered themselves Democrats.[18] In 1960 Jews, Catholics, and Protestants voted 81, 78, and 38 percent, respectively, for Kennedy. Because Kennedy was the first Roman Catholic to be elected President, the 1960 election was carefully analyzed

[18] The question was phrased: "In politics, as of today, do you consider yourself a Republican, Democrat, or Independent?" *Gallup Opinion Index,* Report No. 180, August 1980, p. 31.

| 1968 | | | 1972 | | 1976* | | | 1980 | | | |
Dem.	Rep.	Wallace	Dem.	Rep.	Dem.	Rep.	McCarthy	Dem.	Rep.	Anderson	Other
43%	43.4%	13.6%	38%	62%	50%	48%	1%	41%	50.8%	6.6%	1.4%
41	43	16	37	63	53	45	1	38	53	7	2
45	43	12	38	62	48	51	†	44	49	6	1
38	47	15	32	68	46	52	1	36	56	7	1
85	12	3	87	13	85	15	†	86	10	2	2
37	54	9	37	63	42	55	2	35	53	10	2
42	43	15	34	66	54	46	†	43	51	5	1
52	33	15	49	51	58	41	1	54	42	3	1
34	56	10	31	69	42	56	1	33	55	10	2
41	47	12	36	64	50	48	2	NA‡	NA‡	NA‡	NA‡
50	35	15	43	57	58	41	1	48	46	5	1
56	29	15	46	54	63	36	1	50	43	5	2
29	51	20	NA‡	NA‡	NA‡	NA‡	NA‡	31	61	7	1
47	38	15	48	52	53	45	1	47	41	11	1
44	41	15	33	67	48	49	2	38	52	8	2
41	47	12	36	64	52	48	†	41	54	4	1
35	49	16	30	70	46	53	†	39	54	6	1
59	33	8	48	52	57	42	1	46	47	6	1
9	86	5	5	95	9	91	†	8	86	5	1
74	12	14	67	33	82	18	†	69	26	4	1
31	44	25	31	69	38	57	4	29	55	14	2

* Figures for some groups do not add to 100% because of the vote for other minor-party candidates.

† Less than 1 percent

‡ Not available

to assess the effect of his religion on the result. The Michigan Survey Research Center concluded that Kennedy won a "bonus" from Catholics of 4.3 percent of the two-party vote (2.9 million votes) but lost 6.5 percent (4.4 million votes) from Protestant Democrats and independents. His religion cost him a net loss of 2.2 percent, or 1.5 million popular votes.[19] On the other hand, the heavy Catholic vote in big Northern industrial states probably helped him win the electoral college.[20] It cannot be demonstrated, however, that Kennedy won *because* he was a Catholic.

Various studies have shown that voters of Irish, Italian, Polish, Eastern European, and Slavic descent often favor Democrats, although President Reagan

[19] Angus Campbell, Philip E. Converse, Warren E. Miller, and Donald E. Stokes, "Stability and Change in 1960: A Reinstating Election," *American Political Science Review*, Vol. 55, No. 2 (June 1961), pp. 269–80. Actual votes were obtained by applying percentages to the 1960 total two-party vote.

[20] See Ithiel de Sola Pool, Robert P. Abelson, and Samuel L. Popkin, *Candidates, Issues, and Strategies* (Cambridge, Mass.: Massachusetts Institute of Technology Press, 1964), pp. 68, 117–18.

made strong gains among several of these groups in 1980. Black Americans, who generally had voted Republican until the New Deal, shifted away from the party of Lincoln to give approximately 94 percent of their votes to the Democrats in 1964, 85 percent in 1968, 87 percent in 1972, 85 percent in 1976, and 86 percent in 1980. (See Table 9-3.)

Primary Groups. In addition to conventional social groups, voters are influenced by personal contacts with much smaller "primary" groups, such as families, co-workers, and friends. Sometimes these influences may change a voter's mind. However, because people of similar social background tend to associate with one another, primary groups often merely reinforce the political views that are already held by the voter.

Geography. In general, the Democrats still draw their strength from the big cities of the North and East. Outside the South, voters in rural areas are more likely to be Republicans. But the Democrats can no longer count on the South in presidential contests. In 1972, for example, President Nixon polled 71 percent of the popular vote in the South; and for the first time since Reconstruction, the Republican presidential ticket carried all eleven states of the former Confederacy. In 1976 the Democratic candidate, Jimmy Carter, was a former governor of the Deep South state of Georgia, and he carried every Southern state except Virginia. But in 1980 Ronald Reagan, the Republican candidate, polled 51 percent of the popular vote in the South. Although Carter ran more strongly in the Deep South than in most other regions of the country, Reagan carried every Southern state except Carter's Georgia.[21]

The suburbs, originally Republican strongholds after the Second World War, are today more a mixture of Democrats and Republicans. Democratic strength has grown in suburbia as lower-class and middle-class whites and an increasing number of blacks have left the cities, but Republicans still dominate many suburbs.

Sex. Until 1980, in most presidential elections, whether voters were men or women did not seem to have a significant influence on how they voted.[22] In 1980, however, it was different. The election that year provided the most striking example of a difference in voting behavior between men and women since voter polls began in the 1930s. In 1980 men voted for Ronald Reagan over Jimmy Carter by a dramatic margin of 15 percentage points or more. By contrast, women — perhaps because they perceived Reagan as being more likely to engage in a military adventure than Carter — split their votes more evenly between the two candidates.[23] (Virtually all surveys on the subject have shown that women

[21] Congressional Quarterly, *Weekly Report,* February 10, 1973, p. 308; Congressional Quarterly, *Weekly Report,* November 6, 1976, p. 3118; and the *New York Times,* January 6, 1981, p. A14. Vote totals are for the eleven states of the Old Confederacy: Alabama, Arkansas, Florida, Georgia, Louisiana, Mississippi, North Carolina, South Carolina, Tennessee, Texas, and Virginia.

[22] For a comparison of voting between men and women in the Eisenhower era, see Campbell, Converse, Miller, and Stokes, *The American Voter,* p. 493.

[23] The Gallup poll data, which are presented in Table 9-3, indicated that Reagan ran 15 percentage points ahead of Carter among men. The ABC News exit poll, based on interviews of 9341 voters leaving voting precincts on Election Day, reported that Reagan's margin over Carter was 19 percentage points among men. Both the Gallup poll and the ABC News exit poll found that among women who were interviewed, Reagan ran 5 percentage points ahead of Carter.

are substantially less likely than men to favor military action.)[24] The voting pattern suggested that if women had been the only voters in 1980, the outcome of the presidential contest would have been fairly close.[25] But the 1980 election also suggested that men and women may vote differently—when the images and issue positions of the candidates coincide with differences in political attitudes between men and women.

Age. Younger voters are more likely to vote Democratic than Republican. Older voters seem to find the GOP attractive. In presidential elections from 1956 to 1980, the Democrats consistently received a higher proportion of the vote from voters under age thirty than from those fifty and over. Voters under thirty were the one major age group that gave Carter a slight edge over Reagan in 1980. (See Table 9-3.)

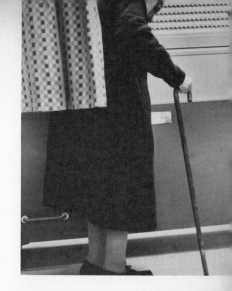

It would be wrong to give too much weight to sociological factors in determining how voters behave. To do so would be to ignore the very important question of people's changing attitudes toward politics. After the Second World War, a group of scholars at the University of Michigan conducted new studies of voting behavior, concentrating on the psychology of voting—on how individuals perceive and evaluate politics.

The Psychological Factors

The Michigan researchers noted that social characteristics of the population change only slowly over a period of time. The percentage of Catholics or Jews in the United States does not change overnight, for example. Yet the electorate may behave very differently from one election to the next. Long-term factors such as social class did not seem adequate to explain such sudden shifts; candidates and issues, which change in the short term, provided a more likely explanation: "It seemed clear that the key to the finer dynamics of political behavior lay in the reactions of the electorate to these changes in the political scene."[26]

In measuring voter attitudes, the Michigan electoral analysts identified three powerful factors: *party identification, candidates,* and *issues.*

Party Identification. Many Americans display persistent loyalties to the Democratic or Republican parties. Voters may form an attachment to one party or the other and often do not change. Most national elections have taken place within the framework of this basic division in the electorate.

Since the late 1930s there have been substantially more Democrats than Republicans in the United States. (See Table 9-4.) In fact, in 1964, 1976, and 1980, Democrats outnumbered Republicans by *more* than 2 to 1. Political analysts watched to see if a durable shift toward the GOP followed Reagan's election.

Although party identification remains a key factor in American politics, there are signs that it may be growing somewhat less important. In the 1972 presidential election, according to the University of Michigan election analysts, "issues were at least equally as important as party identification" as an explanation

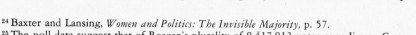

[24] Baxter and Lansing, *Women and Politics: The Invisible Majority,* p. 57.

[25] The poll data suggest that of Reagan's plurality of 8,417,813 votes over Jimmy Carter, roughly 2,000,000 of that margin was provided by women voters. Reagan probably ran more than 6,000,000 votes ahead of Carter among men. Source for Reagan's plurality: *New York Times,* January 6, 1981, p. A14.

[26] Campbell, Converse, Miller, and Stokes, *The American Voter,* p. 17.

Party Identification Among the American Electorate, 1940–1980

Table 9–4

| Year | Percentage of Voters Identifying Themselves as: | | |
	Democrats	Republicans	Independents
1940	42%	38%	20%
1950	45	33	22
1960	47	30	23
1964	53	25	22
1966	48	27	25
1968	46	27	27
1970	45	29	26
1972	43	28	29
1974	44	23	33
1976	46	22	32
1980	47	23	30

Source: *Gallup Opinion Index*, Report No. 131, June 1976, p. 11; and *Gallup Opinion Index*, Report No. 180, August 1980, p. 31.

of the vote.[27] Moreover, as shown in Table 9-4, the number of people who identified with either of the two major parties dropped from 80 percent in 1940 to 70 percent in 1980, as the number of independents rose from 20 to 30 percent. And in most elections since the Second World War, there has also been extensive ticket splitting by many voters. For example, a person may vote for a Republican presidential candidate and a Democratic senator or representative. In 1980 Reagan won by a large margin despite the heavy Democratic advantage in party identification.

The Candidates. Between 1952 and 1980 the GOP won five of the eight presidential elections that were held. How was this possible, given the much higher percentage of those who identify with the Democratic party?

The answer is that although people may identify with a party, and frequently vote for its candidates, they do not always vote that way. Short-term factors, such as changes in candidates or issues, may cause enough voters to switch from the party they normally favor to have a decisive impact on the outcome of the election. In 1952 and 1956 Dwight Eisenhower, the Republican candidate, easily defeated Adlai Stevenson, a Democrat. Eisenhower's personal appeal, his smile, his image as an outstanding military hero of the Second World War, and—in the second election—his popularity as President all helped to offset normal party loyalties.

Clearly, the personal impression that a candidate makes on the voters may influence the election returns. Thus, dour Calvin Coolidge looked like he had been "weaned on a pickle." Thomas E. Dewey, in the classic phrase of Mrs. Alice Roosevelt Longworth, resembled "the bridegroom on a wedding cake." Nixon in 1968 remained "Tricky Dick" to many strong Democratic partisans. Humphrey

[27] Arthur H. Miller, Warren E. Miller, Alden S. Raine, and Thad A. Brown, "A Majority Party in Disarray: Policy Polarization in the 1972 Election," *American Political Science Review*, Vol. 70, No. 3 (September 1976), p. 770.

"talked too much." Ford struck many voters as "well-meaning but dull." Carter was often seen as "decent but ineffective." And Ronald Reagan was "just a movie actor" to some voters, but was an "affable leader who inspired confidence" for many others. Appearance, personality, and popularity of the candidates obviously bear some relation to the number of votes they receive.

The Issues. Two central questions should be asked about the role that issues play in a political campaign: Do voters vote according to their opinions about public issues? If so, do their policy preferences later affect the direction of the government? Both points will be discussed later in this chapter. For now, it is enough to note that a voter must be aware of the existence of an issue and must have an opinion about it if he or she is to be directly motivated by it.[28]

If an issue is to have a direct effect on an individual's voting behavior, a voter must not only recognize the issue and have a minimum degree of feeling about it, he or she must also come to think that one candidate or the other is closer to his or her own position. Research shows, however, that human beings are sometimes highly selective in accepting political messages. If they do not happen to be tuned in to the proper "wavelength," the messages may be received only as so much noise. Increasing the volume may only make the voter flick the "off" switch. Like mechanisms that control the body's blood pressure and temperature, this mental fuse "seems to protect the individual citizen from too strenuous an overload of incoming information."[29] In some elections, even among voters who do hold opinions on public issues, only 40 to 60 percent can perceive differences between the parties on those issues.[30]

On certain *major* issues, or on issues that affect them directly, the voters do seem to "tune in" and form definite party preferences. It was noted in Chapter 8 that in most elections before 1980 many people thought the Democrats were more likely to preserve prosperity and the Republicans were more likely to keep the peace.

When one group of voters is directly affected by a political issue, its members may listen carefully to the political debate. For example, in 1964 Barry Goldwater voted against the first major civil rights bill since Reconstruction. Partly because black voters seemed to know in general where Goldwater stood on civil rights, they turned out in unprecedented numbers to vote for Johnson.

Moreover, issues may be more important in some elections than in others. Research by Norman Nie, Sidney Verba, and John Petrocik suggests that substantial "issue voting" took place during the elections of 1964, 1968, and 1972. Issues such as the Vietnam war, race, and several controversial social issues sharply divided the voters during those election years.[31] Arthur H. Miller also found widespread issue voting in the 1972 election, ranking it as a more important influence that year than party identification on the voters' attitudes toward the candidates. But in 1976 the relative importance of issues declined. The data

"YOU CALL THAT A CHOICE?"

© 1980 by Herblock from *Herblock on All Fronts* (New American Library, 1980)

---

[28] Issues may also have an *indirect* effect on voters. For example, if a candidate takes a position pleasing to labor union leaders, the union leaders may work enthusiastically on a voter registration drive. That in turn may result in more votes for the candidate.

[29] Campbell, Converse, Miller, and Stokes, *The American Voter*, pp. 171–72.

[30] *Ibid.*, p. 180.

[31] Norman H. Nie, Sidney Verba, and John R. Petrocik, *The Changing American Voter*, Enlarged Edition (Cambridge, Mass.: Harvard University Press, 1979), pp. 96–109, 156–73.

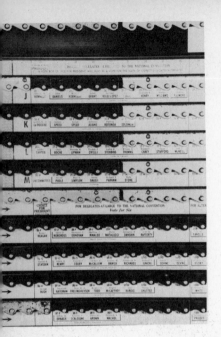

Voting Patterns

Although the act of voting represents an individual decision, the result of an election is a group decision. On Election Day as the sun moves west across the continent's four time zones, the tides and patterns of electoral choice are already beginning to form. The polls have closed in the East as voters in California and elsewhere along the Pacific coast are still casting their ballots.[33] The results from first precincts in New England trickle in, then more, and in time, the decision takes shape much as a photograph gains definition in the developing trays of a darkroom.

Sometimes the resulting picture is sharp, quickly seen, and its meaning clear; other times it is as blurred as an impressionist painting. Yet the trained eye analyzing the result of American elections can detect patterns and trends, interrelationships, currents, sectional nuances, and sometimes national meaning.

Control

For national political parties, the prize is control of the Presidency. But party success or failure is measured in terms of states won or lost. Broad voting patterns on the national level can easily be seen by comparing political maps in presidential years, such as those in Figure 9-3. Some political results are geographically dramatic—for example, Franklin D. Roosevelt's 1936 landslide, in which the map is solidly Democratic except for Maine and Vermont, and Nixon's 1972 landslide, in which the map is solidly Republican except for Massachusetts and the District of Columbia. In 1980 Ronald Reagan's strong electoral victory also covered nearly all parts of the map; the Democrats that year carried only six widely scattered states and the District of Columbia.

Bedrock GOP strength in the Midwest is illustrated by the maps of the elections of 1940, 1944, and 1948; in each case the Plains states are a Republican island in a Democratic sea. Or look for a moment at the maps of Republican victories in 1928 and 1952; they bear a strong resemblance to each other because in each case the losing Democratic candidates, Smith and Stevenson, carried a hard core of Southern states. Then look at the 1964 map; it looks a good deal like the other two, but this one charts a Republican defeat. In this election it was Goldwater, the Republican candidate, who carried five states of the Old Confederacy.

The landslides of popular votes in the Roosevelt, Eisenhower, Johnson, Reagan, and the 1972 Nixon victories swept nearly all before them, leaving behind a rather homogeneous map. But the "checkerboard" effect of 1960 and 1968 reflects the fact that the nation was narrowly divided in those elections.

[32] Arthur H. Miller, "Partisanship Reinstated? A Comparison of the 1972 and 1976 U.S. Presidential Elections," *British Journal of Political Science,* Vol. 8, Part 2 (April 1978), p. 152.

[33] Sometimes the major television networks project the winner of a presidential race before the polls have closed in the West. In 1980 President Carter conceded while the polls were still open in California, Oregon, the state of Washington, Alaska, and Hawaii.

The election of 1976 was also close; but the concentration in the South and the Northeast of most of the states carried by Carter underscores the regional bases from which Carter assembled his victory.

The broad outline of the national vote can be shown on a map, but much that is politically significant is less visible. Electoral victories are built not merely on simple geographic foundations; they are also formed by alliances of segments of the electorate, of interest groups, and unorganized masses of voters who coalesce behind the winner. Politicians and political scientists are interested, therefore, in *coalitions* of voters.

Coalitions

Roosevelt's New Deal brought together a coalition of the South, the urban North, minority groups, and labor unions. Nixon's winning coalition in 1968 included part of the South, most of the Midwest, the West, whites, Protestants, businessmen, and white-collar workers. Long-term trends in American politics can be traced by analyzing the makeup of winning and losing coalitions.

In analyzing these alignments, however, congressional as well as presidential voting patterns should be considered. Although, as will be shown, the two are often linked, in most presidential elections since the New Deal days, the Democratic party has been stronger in congressional elections than in contests for the Presidency. In the period from 1932 to 1980, Republican presidential nominees were elected to five four-year terms in the White House. Yet, during that same period the Republicans won full control of Congress for a total of only four years (1947–1948 and 1953–1954). In presidential election years since the 1940s, the Democratic presidential nominee has received fewer votes than the total vote polled by Democratic candidates for the House of Representatives in every presidential election except 1964.

Congress

The entire House of Representatives and a third of the Senate are elected every two years. In a presidential election year, the vote for President frequently affects the vote for Congress and may have a powerful effect on state and local offices, although there are signs that in recent years the impact of the presidential vote on contests for other offices may be lessening.

Coattails

The interrelationship between the vote for President and for members of the House is illustrated in Figure 9-4. Some individual members of Congress are strong enough to withstand the tides of presidential voting, but a President has often carried into office with him a majority of his own party in the House.

The fortunes of presidential and senatorial candidates are also frequently linked, especially in the more competitive two-party states. In this century, however, two Presidents have been elected along with a Congress controlled by the opposition party in both wings of the Capitol—Eisenhower in 1956 and Nixon in 1968 and 1972. And when President Reagan was elected in 1980, the Democratic party retained control of the House but lost the Senate. (See Table 9-5.)

As Table 9-6 shows, the President's party generally loses strength in midterm congressional elections. In off-year elections since 1920, the party in power

Presidential Elections, 1928–1980

Figure 9–3

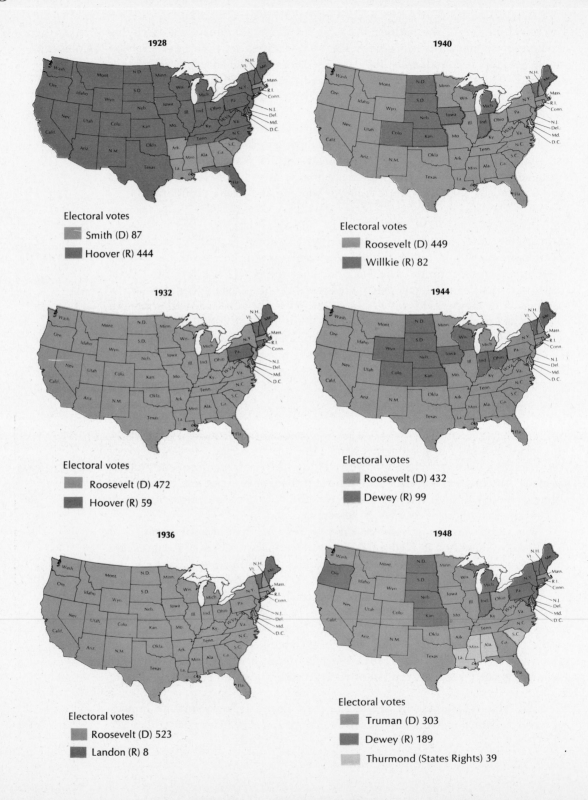

1928

Electoral votes
Smith (D) 87
Hoover (R) 444

1940

Electoral votes
Roosevelt (D) 449
Willkie (R) 82

1932

Electoral votes
Roosevelt (D) 472
Hoover (R) 59

1944

Electoral votes
Roosevelt (D) 432
Dewey (R) 99

1936

Electoral votes
Roosevelt (D) 523
Landon (R) 8

1948

Electoral votes
Truman (D) 303
Dewey (R) 189
Thurmond (States Rights) 39

1952

Electoral votes

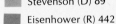 Stevenson (D) 89

Eisenhower (R) 442

1956

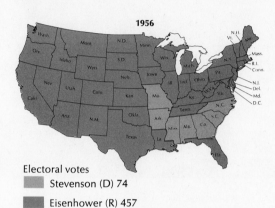

Electoral votes

Stevenson (D) 74

Eisenhower (R) 457

1960

Electoral votes

Kennedy (D) 303

Nixon (R) 219

Byrd (D) 15

1964

Electoral votes

Johnson (D) 486

Goldwater (R) 52

1968

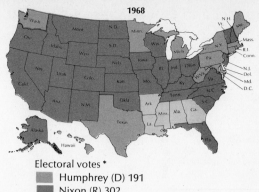

Electoral votes *

Humphrey (D) 191

Nixon (R) 302

Wallace
(American Independent) 45

*A North Carolina Republican elector cast his vote for George Wallace, making the official count: Nixon, 301; Humphrey, 191; Wallace, 46.

1972

Electoral votes†

McGovern (D) 17

Nixon (R) 521

†A Virginia Republican elector cast his vote for Libertarian party candidate John Hospers, making the official count: Nixon, 520; McGovern, 17; Hospers, 1.

1976

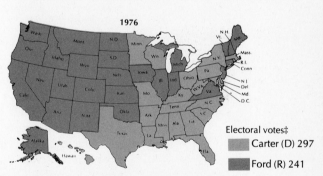

Electoral votes‡

Carter (D) 297

Ford (R) 241

‡A Republican elector from the state of Washington cast his vote for Ronald Reagan, making the official count: Carter, 297; Ford, 240; Reagan, 1.

1980

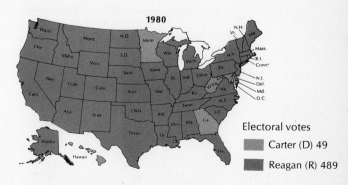

Electoral votes

Carter (D) 49

Reagan (R) 489

Presidential and House Vote, 1928–1980

Figure 9–4

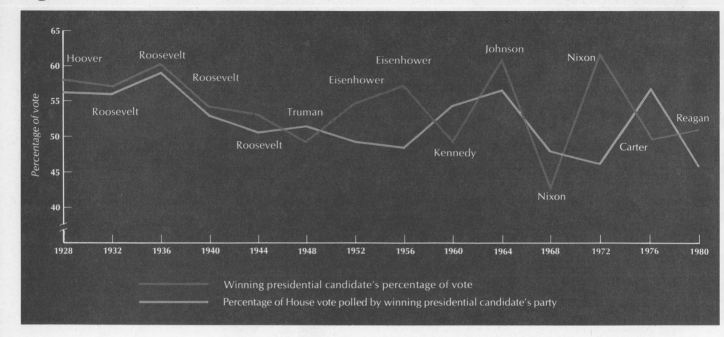

Winning presidential candidate's percentage of vote

Percentage of House vote polled by winning presidential candidate's party

Source: Congressional Quarterly, *Politics in America* (Washington, D.C.: Congressional Quarterly Service, May 1969), p. 41. Reprinted with permission; 1972 data from Congressional Quarterly, *Weekly Report*, February 10, 1973, p. 308, and *Statistics of the Presidential and Congressional Election of November 7, 1972* (Washington, D.C.: U.S. Government Printing Office, 1973), p. 55; 1976 data from Congressional Quarterly, *Weekly Report*, November 6, 1976, pp. 3147–54; and 1980 data from Congressional Quarterly, *Weekly Report*, November 8, 1980, pp. 3338–45.

has lost an average of thirty-four seats in the House; in some of these election years, the party's losses were well above average, as in 1922 and 1938. In unusual circumstances, the party in power may actually gain a few seats, as in 1934, or suffer only minor losses, as in 1962.

Why the voters normally reduce the strength of the party of the President they elected two years earlier has been the subject of considerable scholarly research. It is clear that many fewer voters turn out in off years. (See Figure 9-1.) Angus Campbell has suggested that in presidential elections that stimulate a high degree of public interest, the normally "less involved peripheral voters" tend to turn out and vote for the winner, as do many independents and people who switch from the opposing party. In the midterm elections, the peripheral voters tend to "drop out," and many independents and party switchers move back to their usual positions. The result is a decline in the proportion of the vote for the President's party.[34] Barbara Hinckley, in an analysis of midterm House results from 1954 through 1966, found that the "midterm loss was concentrated" in marginal House districts where the President ran ahead of his party's

[34] Angus Campbell, "Surge and Decline: A Study of Electoral Change," in Angus Campbell, Philip E. Converse, Warren E. Miller, and Donald E. Stokes, *Elections and the Political Order* (New York: Wiley, 1966), pp. 44–45, 59, 61–62.

Major-Party Lineup: President and Congress, 1932–1980*

Table 9–5

Election Year†	President and Party		Congress	House D R	Senate D R	President's Popular Vote Percentage
1932	Roosevelt	D	D	313–117	59–36	57.4%
1934	Roosevelt	D	D	322–103	69–25	
1936	Roosevelt	D	D	333– 89	75–17	60.8
1938	Roosevelt	D	D	262–169	69–23	
1940	Roosevelt	D	D	267–162	66–28	54.7
1942	Roosevelt	D	D	222–209	57–38	
1944	Roosevelt	D	D	243–190	57–38	53.4
1946	Truman	D	R	188–246	45–51	
1948	Truman	D	D	263–171	54–42	49.6
1950	Truman	D	D	234–199	48–47	
1952	Eisenhower	R	R	213–221	47–48	55.1
1954	Eisenhower	R	D	232–203	48–47	
1956	Eisenhower	R	D	234–201	49–47	57.4
1958	Eisenhower	R	D	283–154	66–34	
1960	Kennedy	D	D	263–174	64–36	49.5
1962	Kennedy	D	D	259–176	68–32	
1964	Johnson	D	D	295–140	67–33	61.1
1966	Johnson	D	D	248–187	64–36	
1968	Nixon	R	D	243–192	58–42	43.4
1970	Nixon	R	D	255–180	54–44§	
1972	Nixon	R	D	243–192	56–42	60.7
1974	Ford	R	D	291–144	60–37‡	
1976	Carter	D	D	292–143	61–38	50.0
1978	Carter	D	D	277–158	58–41	
1980	Reagan	R	D/R	243–192	46–53	50.8

* Does not include independents and minor parties.

† Presidential years appear in boldface.

§ In 1970 Harry Byrd, Jr., of Virginia was elected as an Independent and is therefore not included in this and subsequent totals. However, he received committee assignments as a Democrat. Also in 1970 James Buckley was elected as a Conservative from New York. He generally voted Republican but is not included in this table. In 1976 he was defeated.

‡ The total became Democrats 61, Republicans 37, after a disputed Senate contest in New Hampshire was won by the Democratic candidate in a new, special election in September 1975.

Source: Adapted from Congressional Quarterly, *Politics in America* (Washington, D.C.: Congressional Quarterly Service, 1979), pp.120–21; and 1980 data from *National Journal,* November 8, 1980, pp. 1875, 1879, and 1886, and the *New York Times,* January 6, 1981, p. A14.

winning congressional candidate in the preceding election.[35] In the ensuing off-year election, when the party's presidential nominee was not heading the ticket, these members of Congress were particularly vulnerable to defeat.

But why are the midterm losses of the President's party sometimes very large, and sometimes quite small? Edward R. Tufte has suggested that such variations are related to two factors, which can vary greatly from one midterm election year to another—voters' evaluations of how well the President is handling his job as President, and the general state of the economy shortly before the midterm election. Tufte concluded: ". . . the vote cast in midterm congres-

[35] Barbara Hinckley, "Interpreting House Midterm Elections: Toward a Measurement of the In-Party's 'Expected' Loss of Seats," *American Political Science Review,* Vol. 61, No. 3 (September 1967), p. 699.

Midterm Loss in House of Representatives of Party in Control of Presidency, 1922–1978

Table 9–6

Size of Loss (Average loss: 34 seats)	Net Number of Seats Lost or Gained Since Previous Election	Year	Incumbent President
Massive	−75	1922	Harding
	−71	1938	Roosevelt
	−55	1946	Truman
	−49	1930	Hoover
Above average	−48*	1974	Ford
	−47	1958	Eisenhower
	−47	1966	Johnson
	−45	1942	Roosevelt
	−29	1950	Truman
	−18	1954	Eisenhower
	−12†	1970	Nixon
Below average	−12	1978	Carter
	−10	1926	Coolidge
	− 4	1962	Kennedy
	+ 9	1934	Roosevelt

* Republicans lost five House seats in special elections in 1974; their net loss on Election Day in 1974 was forty-three seats.

† Republicans lost three House seats in special elections in 1969; their net loss on Election Day in 1970 was nine seats.

Source: Adapted from Congressional Quarterly, *Weekly Report,* November 6, 1970, p. 2779; Congressional Quarterly, *Weekly Report,* November 9, 1974, p. 3065; and Congressional Quarterly, *Weekly Report,* November 11, 1978, p. 3243.

Party Control of Governorships

Table 9–7

Following Elections of*	Democrats	Republicans
1946	23	25
1948	30	18
1950	23	25
1952	18	30
1954	27	21
1956	28	20
1958	35	14
1960	34	16
1962	34	16
1964	33	17
1966	25	25
1968	19	31
1970	29	21
1972	31	19
1974	36	13†
1976	37	12†
1978	32	18
1980	27	23

* Presidential years appear in boldface.

† There was also one independent governor, in Maine, after the 1974 and 1976 elections.

Source: Congressional Quarterly, *Politics in America* (Washington, D.C.: Congressional Quarterly Service, 1969), p. 69; and Congressional Quarterly, *Weekly Reports.*

"Callahan, get off my coattails!"

Drawing by Stevenson
© 1974 The New Yorker Magazine, Inc.

sional elections is a referendum on the performance of the President and his administration's management of the economy." The size of the midterm loss, Tufte added, "is substantially smaller if the President has a high level of approval, or if the economy is performing well, or both."[36]

Although the "coattail" effect in presidential voting exists, it can be overstated. In 1972, for example, the Republicans made a net gain of only thirteen seats in the House of Representatives and actually lost strength in the Senate—despite a Nixon landslide in the presidential voting. And in most elections, many candidates of the party that loses nationally are able to survive. This is because voters are selective: some do not vote for all candidates on the ballot; others pick and choose and split their tickets. Sometimes the coattail effect may work in reverse, as when a local candidate runs ahead of the national ticket.[37]

Sometimes, candidates for governor may ride into the statehouse on a sufficiently long presidential coattail, for there is a relationship between national and state election results in presidential election years. "The great tides of presidential politics," V. O. Key, Jr., observes, "tend to engulf the affairs of states and often to determine the results of state elections."[38]

One reason for the relationship between presidential and gubernatorial voting is that many voters find it convenient to vote a straight party ticket by making a single mark or pulling a single lever (in the states where they are permitted to do so). Even so, ticket splitting between candidates for President and governor is common, particularly in states where there is strong two-party rivalry.

A growing number of states have scheduled gubernatorial elections in off years to insulate themselves from the tides of national presidential politics. In 1980, a presidential year, thirteen governors were elected; but in 1982, an off

[36] Edward R. Tufte, "Determinants of the Outcomes of Midterm Congressional Elections," *American Political Science Review,* Vol. 69, No. 3 (September 1975), p. 824.

[37] For an additional discussion of the coattail phenomenon, see Warren E. Miller, "Presidential Coattails: A Study in Political Myth and Methodology," *Public Opinion Quarterly,* Vol. 19, No. 1 (Spring 1955), pp. 353–68.

[38] V. O. Key, Jr., *Politics, Parties, and Pressure Groups,* 5th ed. (New York: Crowell, 1964), p. 304.

How the Governors Are Elected (through 1982)

Table 9–8

Four-year Term	
Election in presidential years	9
Election in even-numbered years at midterm	34
Election in odd-numbered years	3
Total, four-year terms	46
Two-year Term	
Election in even-numbered years	4
Total, all states	50

Source: Adapted from Congressional Quarterly, *Weekly Report,* November 6, 1976, p. 3134; *National Journal,* November 6, 1976, p. 1605; and data provided by the National Governors Association.

year, thirty-eight governors' races were scheduled. (See Table 9-8.) This separation of gubernatorial and presidential elections often helps the candidates of the party that is out of power nationally.[39]

Presidential '80: A Case Study

The 1980 presidential election—in sharp contrast to the close Carter-Ford race of 1976—resulted in a decisive victory for Ronald Reagan, the Republican nominee, over Jimmy Carter, the incumbent Democrat, and John B. Anderson, an independent. Reagan carried 44 of the 50 states; and for the second time in a row, an incumbent President went down to defeat. The 1980 results were:

	Popular Vote	*Electoral Vote*	*Popular Vote Percentage*
Ronald Reagan (R)	43,899,248	489	50.8
Jimmy Carter (D)	35,481,435	49	41.0
John Anderson (ind.)	5,719,437	—	6.6
Others[40]	1,395,558	—	1.6
	86,495,678	538	100.0%

[39] In 1942 only ten states with four-year gubernatorial terms scheduled their election for governor midway through the President's term. By 1962 the number of such states stood at twenty; for 1982 it was thirty-four. Adapted from Congressional Quarterly, *Politics in America* (Washington, D.C.: Congressional Quarterly Service, May 1969), pp. 148–55; and Congressional Quarterly, *Weekly Reports.*

[40] Among the other candidates were: Ed Clark, Libertarian, 920,859; Barry Commoner, Citizens, 230,377; Gus Hall, Communist, 43,871; John Rarick, American Independent, 41,172; Clifton DeBerry, Socialist Workers', 40,105; Ellen McCormack, Right-to-Life, 32,319; Margaret Smith, Peace and Freedom, 18,117; Deirdre Griswold, Workers' World, 13,211; Benjamin Bubar, National Statesman, 7,100; David McReynolds, Socialist, 6,720; Percy Greaves, American, 6,539; Andrew Pulley, Socialist Workers', 6,032; Richard Congress, Socialist Workers', 4,029; Kurt Lynen, Middle Class Candidate, 3,694; Bill Gahres, Down With Lawyers, 1,718; Frank Shelton, American, 1,555; Martin Wendelken, independent, 923; Harley McLain, National People's League, 296; and write-ins, 16,921. Source: *New York Times,* January 6, 1981, p. A14.

More than a year before the election, it was apparent that the Democratic party would have serious problems in its attempt to retain control of the White House. Unemployment, although down somewhat from 1976, was still substantial; OPEC oil prices had almost doubled during Carter's years in office; and Americans in many walks of life were feeling the effects of one of the highest inflation rates since the Second World War—13.3 percent in 1979. (See Table 9-9.) In addition, by 1979 there was widespread criticism, both inside and outside the Democratic party, of President Carter's leadership.

The Democratic Race

These political problems for the Carter administration were reflected in the public opinion polls. Carter enjoyed generally high ratings for his performance as President during his first year in office. But in 1979 the President's ratings began to drop sharply. By mid-summer only 28 percent of the American

Annual Rates of Inflation and
Unemployment in the United States,
1976–1980

Table 9–9

Inflation		Unemployment	
1976	4.8%	1976	7.7%
1977	6.8	1977	7.0
1978	9.0	1978	6.0
1979	13.3	1979	5.8
1980*	10.4	1980*	7.1

* 1980 figures are the annualized rate for the first ten months of the year.
Source: U.S. Bureau of Labor Statistics.

President Carter's Job Rating, 1977–1980*

Table 9–10

Date of Interviews	Approve	Disapprove	No Opinion
Carter Inaugurated, January 20, 1977			
February 4–7, 1977	66%	8%	26%
March 18–21, 1977	75	9	16
June 17–20, 1977	63	18	19
Bert Lance's Resignation Accepted, September 21, 1977			
November 18–21, 1977	56	30	14
February 10–13, 1978	47	34	19
Production of Neutron Bomb Deferred, April 7, 1978			
April 14–17, 1978	40	44	16
Panama Canal Treaty Ratified, April 18, 1978			
April 28–May 1, 1978	41	42	17
August 4–7, 1978	39	44	17
Camp David Peace Agreements Concluded, September 17, 1978			
September 22–25, 1978	48	34	18
January 5–8, 1979	50	36	14
March 2–5, 1979	39	48	13
June 29–July 2, 1979	28	59	13
Cabinet Reshuffled, July 17–20, 1979; Kennedy Decides to Run			
November 2–5, 1979	32	55	13
Iran Seizes American Hostages, November 4, 1979			
December 5–6, 1979	61	30	9
USSR Invades Afghanistan, December 27, 1979			
January 4–7, 1980	56	33	11
March 7–10, 1980	43	45	12
April 11–14, 1980	39	50	11
Hostage Rescue Attempt Fails, April 24, 1980			
May 2–5, 1980	43	47	10
June 13–16, 1980	32	56	12
July 14–25, 1980	21	63	16
Democratic Convention Meets, August 11–14, 1980			
August 15–18, 1980	32	55	13

* Responses to the question: "Do you approve or disapprove of the way Carter is handling his job as President?"
Source: *Gallup Opinion Index*, Report No. 180, August 1980, p. 26.

public approved of the way Carter was "handling his job as President." Fifty-nine percent disapproved. (See Table 9-10.) In similar circumstances, two earlier Democratic Presidents had chosen not to run.[41]

Many Democrats became alarmed that their party might lose not only the Presidency but also the control of Congress, which they had enjoyed since 1954. And many of those same Democrats urged Senator Edward Kennedy of Massachusetts to oppose Carter for the Democratic nomination. Three times—in 1968, 1972, and 1976—Kennedy had turned down earlier suggestions that he run for President. By the end of the summer of 1979, however, it seemed clear that this time he was going to seek the Democratic nomination. Shortly before Kennedy formally announced that he would run, the polls indicated that Democratic voters favored Kennedy over the President by a margin of two to one. (See Table 9-11.)

On November 4, 1979, however, just two days before Kennedy's announcement, an event took place that was to have an enormous impact on the 1980 presidential campaign. Iranian demonstrators stormed the American embassy in Teheran and seized a group of American hostages. In the days that

Senator Edward M. Kennedy

[41] In February 1952 Harry Truman had received a favorable job rating from only 25 percent of the American people. The following month, Truman announced that he would not seek re-election in 1952. In March 1968 another Democratic President, Lyndon Johnson, received a low favorable job rating of 36 percent. Within a few days, Johnson also bowed out of the race. Sources: George H. Gallup, *The Gallup Poll: Public Opinion 1935–1971*, Vol. II, 1949–1958 (New York: Random House, 1972), p. 1051; George H. Gallup, *The Gallup Poll: Public Opinion, 1935–1971*, Vol. III, 1959–1971 (New York: Random House, 1972), p. 2113.

Carter Versus Kennedy: The Gallup Poll's "Test Election" Results Among Democratic Voters Between March 1978 and August 1980*

Table 9–11

Date of Interviews	For Carter	For Kennedy	Undecided
March/April 1978	40%	53%	7%
June 1978	31	55	14
February 23–26, 1979	28	60	12
August 17–20, 1979	25	63	12
October 12–15, 1979	30	60	10
Iran Seizes American Hostages, November 4, 1979			
November 16–19, 1979	36	55	9
December 7–10, 1979	46	42	12
January 4–7, 1980	51	37	12
January 25–28, 1980	63	24	13
February 1–4, 1980	61	32	7
July 11–14, 1980	60	34	6
August 1–3, 1980	47	43	10

* During 1980 the question respondents were asked was phrased as follows: "Suppose the choice for President in the Democratic Convention this year narrows down to Jimmy Carter and Edward Kennedy. Which one would you prefer to have the Democratic Convention select?" Similar wordings, but with references to the 1980 Democratic Convention that lay ahead, were used in 1978 and 1979.

Source: *Gallup Opinion Index*, Report No. 173, December 1979, p. 4; *Gallup Opinion Index*, Report No. 175, February 1980, p. 18; and Gallup poll, news release, August 5, 1980.

Left: 1980: President Carter campaigns for re-election. *Right:* Senator Edward M. Kennedy, who challenged President Carter in the primaries.

followed, American television viewers watched Iranian leaders and street mobs assail Carter and the United States. For a while, Carter became a rallying point for millions of Americans who wished to express their anger against Iran.

Almost immediately, Carter's approval rating in the polls began to rise dramatically. From early November to early December, it went from 32 percent to 61 percent—the largest one-month increase in the history of the Gallup poll. Then, in late December, the Soviets invaded Afghanistan, another factor that temporarily rallied the American people behind their President.

While Carter's popularity was going up in the polls, support for Kennedy was declining. The same day that American hostages were seized in Iran, CBS televised an interview with the senator by Roger Mudd. Kennedy was asked a number of probing questions about his personal life, about why he wanted to be President, and about the accident on Chappaquiddick Island in 1969 when a young Kennedy campaign worker, Mary Jo Kopechne, had drowned inside a car the senator had driven off a bridge at night.[42] Many viewers felt that Kennedy fielded the questions badly; the Kennedy campaign had suffered an important setback even before it began. All these events combined to bring about a startling reversal in the relative standing of Carter and Kennedy in the polls. By the first week in February 1980, Carter led Kennedy by 61 percent to 32 percent. (See Table 9-11.)

In January Carter won Iowa's Democratic caucus by a decisive margin. He also won most of the early primaries, beginning in New Hampshire on February 26. (Carter aides persuaded several Southern states to hold their primary elections on an earlier date in order to help the President get off to a fast start.)[43] By March 18, when Carter swept the important Illinois primary, it appeared that Kennedy's drive for the nomination was lost.

By this time, however, Carter's job rating had begun to slip again. (See Table 9-10.) And on March 25, Kennedy won the Democratic primaries in New York and Connecticut. As a result, Kennedy continued his campaign, and the struggle for the support of Democratic delegates lasted until the party's convention in August. A week and a half before the Democratic National Convention opened in New York City on August 11, the pledged delegates were divided roughly 60–40 for Carter over Kennedy.[44]

Senator Edward M. Kennedy and President Carter at the 1980 Democratic National Convention

[42] Richard Harwood, ed., *The Pursuit of the Presidency 1980* (New York: Berkley Books, 1980), p. 41.

[43] *Ibid.,* pp. 92–93.

[44] Congressional Quarterly, *Weekly Report,* August 2, 1980, p. 2169.

The Democrats thus went into their convention as a sharply divided party, with an unpopular incumbent President who was determined to seek re-election. Less than a month before the convention, Carter's job rating in the Gallup poll dropped to 21 percent favorable — the lowest ever received by an American President in more than four decades of public opinion surveys by the Gallup poll. (See Table 9-10.) After three months of standing relatively well in the polls, following the onset of the crisis in Iran, Carter was right back where he had been during the summer of 1979. The convention nevertheless renominated Carter and Vice President Mondale.

The Republican Race

While the Democrats fought over their party's nomination for nine months, the major question facing the Republicans was whether the GOP would choose a candidate who could take advantage of the Democrats' difficulties. The early front-runner, and the choice of many of the party's conservatives, was the former governor of California, Ronald Reagan. But more than a half dozen other Republicans, representing a considerable range of views on the issues, also announced that they would seek the GOP nomination in the primaries. Former President Gerald R. Ford, perhaps hoping a deadlocked convention would turn to him, indicated that he did not plan to enter the primaries. Ford's decision may have been an important turning point in the fight for the Republican nomination. A Gallup poll taken three weeks before the first primary showed Ford virtually even with Reagan as the choice of Republicans for their party's nomination. When Ford's name was removed as a possible choice in the poll, Reagan had a large lead for the nomination.[45] Had Ford chosen to fight actively for the nomination, the battle might well have been close.

Ronald Reagan: the early front-runner

The candidacy of George Bush of Texas received a lift in January when Bush was the victor in the Iowa caucus. But in late February, Reagan won the first primary, in New Hampshire. After that, Reagan was never behind again.

Other Republican candidates now began to drop out of the race. Senator Howard Baker of Tennessee, John Connally of Texas, and Senator Robert Dole of Kansas withdrew in March. In response to the sudden momentum toward Reagan, Ford again considered whether he should become an active candidate. But on March 15, Ford once more declared that he would not actively seek the nomination.

For a while in March there was a boomlet within the Republican party for John Anderson, who ran a close second in several primaries. But when Anderson lost his own state of Illinois to Reagan on March 18, it seemed clear that Anderson, too, would be unable to win the GOP nomination. On April 24, Anderson announced that he would run for President as an independent. At the peak of his popularity, in June, Anderson was the presidential choice of 24 percent of the American electorate.

Bush alone continued the contest with Reagan through April and May. But although Bush won some major primaries, including Pennsylvania in late April and Michigan in May, he withdrew on May 26. The Republican National Convention met in Detroit in July and nominated Ronald Reagan and George Bush, whom Reagan had selected as his vice-presidential running mate.

[45] *Gallup Opinion Index,* Report No. 175, February 1980, p. 20.

John B. Anderson, who ran as an independent candidate

The General Election

As the general election campaign approached, Carter was trailing in the polls. Earlier, at the beginning of 1980, shortly after the dramatic events in Iran and Afghanistan, Carter had been far ahead of Reagan in the polls. But then Carter's position began to weaken. The initial support of the President after the hostages were seized seemed to give way to frustration over the lack of progress in obtaining their release. Problems with the economy continued. In April an American attempt to rescue the hostages by military force ended in humiliating failure. By late June, Reagan had moved into a clear lead over the President. At the beginning of August, after the Republican Convention (and following much unfavorable publicity for Carter over his brother's involvement with the government of Libya), Reagan was ahead of Carter by 16 percentage points. (See Table 9-12.)

Carter and his advisers, knowing they were behind, began to press for a series of television debates with Reagan. (Incumbent Presidents who are ahead usually try to avoid debates since such television confrontations publicize their opponents.) However, the Carter camp apparently feared that Anderson would siphon more votes from the Democratic ticket than from the Republican ticket. As a result, Carter sought to avoid a three-way debate that would include John

Reagan Versus Carter Versus Anderson: The Gallup Poll's "Test Election" Results Among Registered Voters Between March and Election Eve, 1980

Table 9–12

Date of Interviews	For Reagan	For Carter	For Anderson	For Others or Undecided
March 28–31	34%	40%	21%	5%
April 11–14	34	42	18	6
Hostage Rescue Attempt Fails, April 24, 1980				
May 2–5	33	38	21	8
May 30–June 2	32	39	21	8
June 13–16	33	35	24	8
June 27–30	37	32	22	9
July 11–14	37	34	21	8
Republican Convention Meets, July 14–17, 1980				
August 1–4	45	29	14	12
Democratic Convention Meets, August 11–14, 1980				
August 15–18	38	39	13	10
September 12–14	40	38	15	7
Reagan-Anderson Television Debate, September 21, 1980				
October 10–12	45	42	8	5
October 24–26	42	45	9	4
Reagan-Carter Television Debate, October 28, 1980				
October 30–November 1	47	44	8	1
Actual Election Results	51	41	7	1

Source: Gallup poll, news release, September 16, 1980; *Washington Post*, October 28, 1980, p. A1; and *Washington Post*, November 3, 1980, p. A9.

Anderson. When the League of Women Voters, the sponsors of the proposed debate, invited all three candidates to appear in Baltimore on September 21, Carter refused to participate. The debate took place between Reagan and Anderson. When it was over, Anderson had lost ground against Reagan, but Reagan remained ahead of Carter. (See Table 9-12.) Soon afterward, the Reagan advisers indicated that their candidate would not engage in any more televised debates.

Then in October the rhythm of the campaign seemed to change. Carter moved sharply to the attack, charging that a Reagan Presidency would increase the risk that the United States might become involved in a war. Carter's charges underscored the extent to which 1980 differed from most other recent presidential elections. The "economic issue," usually a factor working in favor of the Democrats, was being heavily emphasized by the Republicans in 1980. But by mid-October, the "war-peace issue," a concern that had often benefited the Republicans in earlier elections, was the theme being stressed by Carter.

Carter began to gain on Reagan; the Gallup poll and some other polls reported that the President was ahead; and the Reagan camp said that they now wanted a two-person debate with President Carter. The place and the date selected were Cleveland, Ohio, on October 28 — just one week before Election Day.

The debate was watched by an enormous television audience of more than 100 million people. In the debate, both candidates stressed the major themes of their campaigns. Polls taken after the debate indicated that more Americans felt Reagan had won the debate than thought Carter was the winner. (See Table 9-13.) And some observers felt that Reagan had achieved another objective during the ninety-minute television appearance of the two candidates. To many voters, Reagan had appeared relaxed and reassuring; he may have allayed fears among some voters that he was a man who might recklessly lead the country into war.

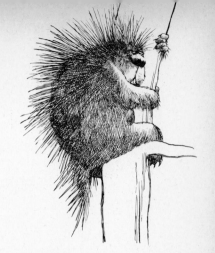

"The Untouchable Incumbent. Incumbents . . . evolved in the manner of the porcupine: They grew longer and longer quills."

Source: Drawing by Jeff MacNelly from *A Political Bestiary* by Eugene J. McCarthy and James J. Kilpatrick, McGraw-Hill Book Company, 1979

Carter and Reagan: the televised debate, 1980

Which Candidate "Won" the 1980 Reagan-Carter Television Debate — The Voter's Response

Table 9–13

The Gallup Poll	
Reagan	**34%**
Carter	26
Neither	31
Not Sure/Don't Know	9
New York Times/CBS News Poll	
Reagan	**44%**
Carter	36
Tie/Don't Know	20
ABC News/Harris Survey	
Reagan	**44%**
Carter	26
Not Sure/Don't Know	30

Source: For the Gallup poll, *Newsweek*, November 10, 1980, p. 37; for the *New York Times*/CBS News poll, *New York Times*, October 30, 1980, p. A1; for the ABC/Harris Survey, *Newsweek*, November 10, 1980, p. 34. Numbers in boldface indicate candidate with the larger percentage.

During the final week of the campaign, most national polls indicated that there was a substantial movement of voters to Reagan. Another element of drama was added to the campaign when, just two days before the election, the Iranian Parliament approved a set of conditions under which Iranian leaders said they would release the American hostages. The final poll of the Gallup Organization, which one week earlier had put Carter 3 percentage points ahead of Reagan, now reported that Reagan led by 3 points. Gallup said: "Never in the 45-year history of presidential election surveys has the Gallup poll found such volatility and uncertainty."[46] The final Harris poll had Reagan 5 percentage points ahead; and Harris declared Reagan would be the winner.[47] All of the major published polls understated the magnitude of Reagan's final margin of victory — 10 percentage points and a popular vote plurality of more than 8 million.

Several noteworthy features marked the voting patterns in 1980:

1. More than 86 million voters, the largest number ever to vote in a presidential election, went to the polls. But the voter turnout of 53.9 percent was lower than in any of the seven previous presidential elections, continuing the downward slide that has prevailed in every presidential election after 1960.

2. The Reagan sweep extended across almost every portion of the country, even Massachusetts, a state that had not voted for a Republican presidential candidate since 1956. But beneath the Reagan tide there was a pronounced sectional pattern in the vote. The ten states in which Reagan did best — winning with 60 percent or more — were all to the west of the Mississippi River.

3. By contrast, the region in which Carter remained relatively strongest was the South, despite the fact that the only Southern state Carter was able to carry was his home state of Georgia. Carter lost three states on the rim of the South — Virginia, Florida, and Texas — by decisive margins. Elsewhere in the South, however, the race was close. Had Carter polled just over one percent more of the major-party vote, he would have carried North Carolina, South Carolina, Alabama, Mississippi, Arkansas, and Tennessee.

4. During the summer and the fall campaign, support for John Anderson's independent candidacy dropped sharply. In the middle of June, 24 percent of the nation's registered voters said they planned to vote for Anderson. In November, he polled 6.6 percent of the vote. Even so, except for George Wallace's 1968 third-party showing, Anderson polled the highest percentage of the vote given to a third-party or independent presidential candidate since 1924.

5. Like the vote for Reagan and for Carter, the Anderson vote showed a clear-cut sectional pattern, with New England his best region. Throughout the country, the five states that turned in the highest Anderson percentages were, in order, Massachusetts, Vermont, Rhode Island, New Hampshire, and Connecticut.

6. Contrary to some earlier expectations, the Anderson vote could not have changed the outcome in the contest between Carter and Reagan. Polls during the fall campaign indicated that Anderson was drawing significant support from voters who might otherwise have voted for Reagan, as well as from poten-

[46] *Washington Post,* November 3, 1980, p. A9.
[47] The results of the final Harris Survey, based on interviews taken on October 31 and November 1, were as follows: Reagan, 45%; Carter, 40%; Anderson, 10%; others, 1%; and undecided, 4%. *Washington Star,* November 4, 1980, p. A-4.

tial Carter voters. But even if every Anderson vote had gone to Carter, Reagan still would have won the popular vote tally by more than 2.5 million votes. And Reagan also would have won in the electoral college, 330 votes to 208. However, Anderson's candidacy may have damaged Carter in other less measurable ways. For example, Carter's refusal to debate Anderson and Reagan together may have cost Carter support among some voters.

7. As noted earlier, there was a marked difference in the way women and men voted in the 1980 presidential race. Among women voters, Reagan ran 5 percentage points ahead of Carter. Among the men who voted, Reagan led by a much larger margin of 15 points or more.

8. Carter suffered heavy losses among a number of groups that in the past had frequently given strong support to Democratic presidential candidates. For the first time since 1924, Jewish voters gave a Democratic presidential nominee less than 50 percent of their vote.[48] Carter's support among Catholics was also under 50 percent, and was well below the vote that Catholics had given to most recent Democratic presidential nominees. Among major voting groups that have often been part of the Democratic electoral coalition, only blacks gave Carter an overwhelming share of their votes. Gallup poll figures indicated that 86 percent of all black voters supported Carter.

9. The Democratic party also suffered substantial losses in contests for the state legislature, governor, and the House of Representatives. And the Democrats suffered a massive loss of twelve seats in the Senate, thereby losing control of that body for the first time in twenty-six years.

10. Part of the heavy Republican gains in the Senate reflected a major shift of Senate strength in the South. Going into the 1980 election, the Republican party controlled only six of the South's twenty-two Senate seats. After the election, ten of the twenty-two Southern Senate seats were occupied by Republicans; and for the first time since Reconstruction, Republican Senate strength in the South almost equaled that of the Democrats.

11. Much of the large Republican gain in the Senate also stemmed from the GOP's unusual success in winning the close races. There were ten Senate contests in 1980 where a shift of just one percent of the vote to the loser would have changed the outcome. Of these ten very close Senate races, the Republicans won eight.

12. Despite these major Republican gains, the Democrats, as in every postwar presidential election year except 1964, were substantially stronger in congressional and state races than in the presidential race. Democrats polled slightly over 50 percent of all votes cast for House candidates in 1980, while Carter received only 41 percent of the vote for President.

The broad pattern of the election returns made it clear that the coalition that had produced many Democratic electoral victories since 1932 had shattered in 1980. But still left open were the answers to two questions: Would the Republican triumph of 1980 be followed by a series of GOP victories, such as those

[48] ABC exit poll of 9,341 people who voted on Election Day, in the *Washington Post,* November 6, 1980, p. A24. According to the ABC poll, 42 percent of the Jewish voters who were interviewed said they had voted for Carter. Data on earlier voting trends for President among Jews can be found in a wide variety of national and state polls for the years 1956 through 1976. For the elections from 1924 to 1952, see Lawrence H. Fuchs, *The Political Behavior of American Jews* (Glencoe, Ill.: The Free Press, 1956).

The Washington Post

FINAL

Weather
Today—Becoming partly cloudy, high 55-60, low tonight 30-35. The chance of rain is near zero through tonight. Thursday — Sunny. High 52-56. Yesterday —3 p.m. AQI 25; temperature range 59-83. Details are on Page B12.

84 Pages — 5 Sections
Amusements E11 Financial D 7
Classified C 2 Metro B 1
Comics E14 Obituaries B 6
Crossword E16 Sports D 1
Editorials A14 Style E 1
Fed. Diary B 2 TV-Radio E10

103rd Year · · · · No. 336 · ·   ©1980 Washington Post Co.   WEDNESDAY, NOVEMBER 5, 1980   Subscription Rates See Box on A3   20¢

Reagan Sweeps to a Landslide Victory; Magnuson, McGovern, Bayh, Culver Lose

GOP Narrows Gap in Senate

By Helen Dewar
Washington Post Staff Writer

Republicans knocked off Sens. George McGovern (S.D.), Warren G. Magnuson (Wash.), John C. Culver (Iowa) and Birch Bayh (Ind.) last night and threatened enough other liberal Democrats to take control of the Senate for the first time in 26 years.

Democrats currently control 59 of the 100 Senate seats, and Republicans were winning or leading in races for seats now held by 8 Democrats, including 7 where incumbents were seeking reelection.

A loss of nine seats would create a tie that could be broken by Republican Vice President-elect George Bush, who will preside over the Senate. Also Sen. Harry F. Byrd Jr. (Ind.-Va.), who has caucused with the Democrats but supported Ronald Reagan, could switch to the GOP.

In a major victory for conservative Republicans, Rep. James Abdnor beat McGovern, the Democratic presidential nominee in 1972, and Rep. Dan Quayle trounced Bayh, and Rep. Dan Quayle state Attorney General Slade Gorton, a moderate, unseated Magnuson, the senior Democrat in the next Senate and its president pro tempore as well as chairman of the Appropriations

Carter blinks back tears during an early-morning address at a rally in Plains, Ga.
By Jerome McClendon — Associated Press

The Reagans salute supporters at a victory celebration in a Los Angeles hotel.
By John McDonnell — The Washington Post

Carter Yields Early in Night

By David S. Broder
Washington Post Staff Writer

Ronald Wilson Reagan, the 69-year-old former governor of California who transferred his acting talents and conservative views from the sound stages of Hollywood to the halls of government, yesterday won a sweeping victory as the 40th president of the United States and immediately pledged to "seize the historic opportunity to change things."

Nominated by the Republicans who had twice earlier rejected his bid to head their ticket, Reagan defeated President Carter by a landslide margin in electoral votes, with independent contender John B. Anderson far behind and winning no states.

Reagan appeared before his supporters in Los Angeles at midnight EST and promised to "do my utmost to justify your faith." As he had done so often in the long campaign, he promised that "we're going to put America back to work again."

In ratifying Reagan's claim that the Carter administration had damaged America's economy and international standing, the voters also turned thumbs down on a half-dozen leading liberal Democratic senators and elected the most conservative Congress in a generation. Their action strengthened the

---

the Democrats enjoyed after they captured the White House in 1932? Or would 1980 be more like 1952, the last time that the Republican party elected a President and made substantial gains in the Congress? In the six presidential and midterm elections that followed 1952, the Republican party lost five times.

The Electoral System

The act of choice performed by the American voter on Election Day takes place within a legal and structural framework that strongly influences the result. The electoral system in the United States is not neutral—it affects the dynamics of voting all along the way. Before voters can step into the voting booths, they must meet a number of legal requirements. The candidates whose names appear on the ballot must have qualified under state law. The form of the ballot may influence voters' decisions—if they are allowed to pull a single lever, for example, they are more likely to vote a straight party ticket than if they must pull many levers to vote that way. How their votes count in a presidential election is controlled by custom, state law, and the Constitution, for all three affect the workings of the electoral college. In short, the structure, details, and workings of the electoral system affect the people's choice.

Suffrage

The Constitution provides for popular election of members of the House of Representatives, a provision extended to the election of senators by the Seventeenth Amendment, ratified in 1913. In electing a President, the voters in each state actually choose electors, who meet in December of election year and cast their ballots for a Chief Executive. (See pp. 333–35.)

Voting is a basic right provided for by the Constitution. Under the Fourteenth Amendment, it is one of the privileges and immunities of national citizenship that the states may not abridge and that Congress has the power to protect by federal legislation. For example, in 1970 Congress limited state residence requirements for voting in presidential elections. The states, however, set many requirements for voting. State laws in part govern the machinery of choice—residence and other voting requirements, registration, primaries, and the form of the ballot. And state laws regulate political parties.

Until the age of Jackson, voting was generally restricted to men who owned property and paid taxes. Since then, suffrage has gradually been broadened. Most states lifted property requirements in the early nineteenth century. In 1869 Wyoming became the first state to enact women's suffrage, and three other Western states did so in the 1890s. In 1917 the suffragettes began marching in front of the White House; they were arrested and jailed. In 1919 Congress passed the Nineteenth Amendment, making it unconstitutional to deny any citizen the right to vote on account of sex. The amendment was ratified by the states in time for women to vote in the presidential election of 1920.

Exercise your right to vote. BE A VOTER

The long struggle of black Americans for the right to vote is described in Chapter 5. As we have seen, even though the Fifteenth Amendment specifically gave black citizens the right to vote, it was circumvented when the South regained political control of its state governments following Reconstruction. Poll taxes, all-white primaries, phony literacy tests, intimidation, and violence were all effective in disenfranchising blacks in the South. In 1964 the Twenty-fourth Amendment eliminated the last vestiges of the poll tax in federal elections.[49] But blacks still faced many of the other barriers to voting; only 44 percent of voting-age black citizens in the South voted in the 1964 presidential election. The Voting Rights Act of 1965, which was modified and extended in 1970 and 1975, sought to throw the mantle of federal protection around these voters. It was followed by a dramatic increase in blacks voting in the South: 51.6 percent of the black voting-age population took part in the election of 1968. In 1972 and 1976, however, voting turnout among both blacks and whites in the South dropped several percentage points from the 1968 levels. (See Table 9-14.)

Residence Requirements. When Congress extended the Voting Rights Act in 1970, it included a provision permitting voters in every state to vote in presidential elections after living in the state for thirty days. This uniform federal standard was designed to override state residence requirements, some of which had prevented millions of persons from voting for President. The Voting Rights Act also required states to permit absentee registration and voting. Subsequently, the Supreme Court ruled that states may not require residence of more than thirty days to vote in federal, state, and local elections,[50] although in 1973 the Court modified this standard to permit a state residency requirement of fifty days, at least in state and local elections.[51] But neither case changed the thirty-day maximum residence requirements for voting in *presidential* elections.

[49] Only five Southern states still imposed a poll tax as a requirement for voting in federal elections when the Twenty-fourth Amendment went into effect on January 23, 1964. Under the Voting Rights Act of 1965, the United States Attorney General filed lawsuits against four of the twenty-seven states still imposing poll taxes in state and local elections. In 1966 the United States Supreme Court ruled in *Harper* v. *Virginia State Board of Elections*, 383 U.S. 633, that any state poll tax violated the Fourteenth Amendment. The decision outlawed the use of poll taxes at any level of election.
[50] *Dunn* v. *Blumstein*, 405 U.S. 330 (1972).
[51] *Marston* v. *Mandt*, 410 U.S. 679 (1973); *Burns* v. *Fortson*, 410 U.S. 686 (1973).

The Voting Rights Act of 1965

Table 9–14

	Percentage of Voting-Age Population in the South Who Reported Voting Before and After Passage of the Act			
	1964	1968	1972	1976
Black*	44.0%	51.6%	47.8%	45.7%
White	59.5	61.9	57.0	57.1

* The comparison between 1964 and later figures is not exact because the Census Bureau took the percentage of "Negro" voters in 1968 and 1972, and of "nonwhite" voters in 1964; the latter is a broader category including American Indians and Asians. However, the difference in 1968 between reported voters in the two categories was only two-tenths of 1 percent.

Source: Adapted from U.S. Bureau of the Census, *Current Population Reports*, Population Characteristics, Series P–20, No. 172, May 3, 1968, p. 3; No. 244, December 1972, p. 1; and No. 322, March 1978, p. 20.

Literacy and Character Tests. Historically, literacy tests were used to keep recent immigrants and blacks from voting. The Voting Rights Act of 1965 suspended literacy tests in the six Southern states and all or part of four other states where less than half the voting-age population had registered or voted in the 1964 election. The law also suspended in those areas tests requiring voters to prove "good moral character."

Later amendments to the Voting Rights Act extended the ban against literacy and character tests to all states. Prior to passage of the law, twelve states — including California and New York — still listed literacy as a requirement for voting. Two states, Idaho and Connecticut, had "good character" tests. Under Idaho law, prostitutes, their customers, madams, bigamists, persons of Chinese or Mongolian descent, and persons who "lewdly or lasciviously cohabit together"[52] were banned from voting. And Connecticut had a law on its books requiring that voters be of "good moral character."

Although these anachronistic character tests were suspended along with literacy tests by the 1970 amendments to the Voting Rights Act, a number of states retained other odd barriers to voting on the statute books. The laws of nine states, for example, disqualified paupers, and Louisiana law disqualified parents of illegitimate children. The laws of seven states disqualified persons engaging in duels. Such oddities were not affected by the Voting Rights Act or its extension, but they were generally not enforced by the states anyway.

Most states bar mentally incompetent persons and inmates of prisons from voting. Persons convicted of certain types of crimes lose the right to vote under the laws of forty-six states. Some states restore the right to vote on release from prison, or after a set number of years of imprisonment, or by executive or legislative clemency.

Age. In the late 1960s, with young Americans fighting and dying in Vietnam — but denied the right to vote — pressure to lower the voting age to eighteen built up rapidly. After November 1970 eight states had their legal voting age below twenty-one. In all other states the minimum voting age was twenty-one years.

[52] Elizabeth Yadlosky, *Election Laws of the Fifty States and the District of Columbia*, Legislative Reference Service of The Library of Congress, June 5, 1968, p. 305.

Efforts to amend the Constitution to allow people to vote at age eighteen had failed to pass Congress in the 1950s and 1960s. In 1970 Congress, by statute, lowered the voting age to eighteen in all elections, but later that year the Supreme Court ruled that Congress had power to do so only in *federal* elections.[53] The result was confusion. In 1971 Congress passed, and the necessary three-fourths of the states ratified, a constitutional amendment lowering the voting age to eighteen in all elections.

The new Twenty-sixth Amendment enfranchised approximately 10.5 million persons between the ages of eighteen and twenty-one in time to vote in the 1972 presidential election. Many political observers reasoned that the addition of so large a group of young voters could have an impact on the political system. But the lower voting age did not result in dramatic political change, in part because younger voters have traditionally had a low rate of turnout. In fact, in the first election in which all persons from eighteen through twenty could vote (1972), less than half (48 percent) voted.[54]

Citizenship. Only United States citizens can vote. This was not always the case, however. In the nineteenth century twenty-two states and territories gave aliens the right to vote; the last state to abolish alien voting was Arkansas, in 1926. As a result, the presidential election of 1928 was the first in which only United States citizens could vote. About 4 million United States residents could not vote in 1980 because they were not American citizens.

Voting requirements restrict the number of people who can step into the voting booth. The nominating process restricts choice, since the voter is effectively limited to those candidates nominated by parties or running as independents and placed on the ballot. (Write-in votes, where permitted, seldom elect anyone.)

The Nominating Process: Primaries and Conventions

State laws govern the nominating process and the selection of party leaders. Although the Constitution provides for election of members of Congress and the President, it makes no direct mention of how they shall be nominated and placed on the ballot. In the nineteenth century, candidates for public office were chosen by backroom caucuses of politicians or by local or state conventions. The abuses of that manner of selection led to demands for reform. By 1915 two-thirds of the states had some kind of law providing for primary elections to choose candidates for the general elections. Today every state has provisions for primary elections to choose some candidates who run in statewide contests. Party officials may also be chosen in primaries.

Currently most states hold direct primaries to nominate candidates for the House and Senate. In a handful of other states, nominations are by convention, party committee, or by a combination of methods. In states using primaries, the most common form is the closed primary, in which only registered members of a party or persons declaring their affiliation with a party can vote. Several states use the open primary, in which any voter may participate and vote for a slate of candidates of one political party. Two states, Washington and Alaska, use the blanket or jungle primary, in which voters can pick and choose among two or

---

[53] *Oregon* v. *Mitchell*, 400 U.S. 112 (1970).
[54] U.S. Bureau of the Census, *Current Population Reports,* Population Characteristics, Series P–20, No. 244, December 1972, p. 3.

more political party slates, crossing back and forth to select nominees for each office.

Political parties still hold conventions to nominate candidates for President and Vice President. As noted in Chapter 7, thirty-five states and the District of Columbia held presidential preference primaries in 1980 in which most of their convention delegates were selected. Other states chose delegates to national nominating conventions by different methods, including selection by state conventions and party committees. But because most of the large states used a presidential primary in 1980, close to three-fourths of the national convention delegates were selected in presidential primary states in that year.

Voter Registration

The old Tammany Hall slogan, "Vote Early and Vote Often," still brings nostalgic smiles to the faces of some political leaders in New York. But the use of "repeaters" to vote more than once, and of "tombstone" voters (using the names of deceased voters), and similar devices is made much more difficult—although by no means impossible—by modern systems of voter registration.

Before voters can vote, they must register. Under state laws, when voters register, their names are entered on a list of people qualified to vote. They may, if they wish, declare their party affiliation when they register. On Election Day, the registration list may be checked for each voter who comes to the poll to ensure that he or she is qualified to cast his or her ballot.

Permanent registration, under which the voter registers only once in his or her district, prevails in all but a few states. *Periodic* registration, under which the voter must register every year or at other stated intervals, is used in a very small number of states. North Dakota requires no registration.

Like other forms of election machinery, registration procedures can affect the political result. For example, in Idaho roving canvassers remind people to register to vote, and the turnout has consistently been higher than the national average. No doubt other factors are at work in Idaho, but, as a presidential commission concluded: "The average American is far more likely to vote if few barriers stand between him and registration."[55]

A basic factor affecting registration and voting in the United States is that an American who wishes to register must usually take the initiative and appear in person at the local registration office. (In Great Britain and a number of Western European countries, the government takes the initiative in attempting to register eligible voters.) In 1976 the House passed a bill that would allow registration by postcard in federal elections, but the Senate did not pass the bill.

Ballots

The secret, so-called Australian, ballot was not adopted by every state in the United States until 1950. Early in American history the voter often orally announced his vote at the polling place. After the Civil War, this method was replaced by ballots printed by each political party; since the ballots were often of different colors, it was easy to tell how someone voted. Concern over voter intimidation and fraud led to pressure for secret ballots printed by public authorities. By 1900 a substantial number of states had adopted the secret ballot. This ballot has two chief forms:

[55] *Report of the President's Commission on Registration and Voting Participation*, p. 32.

1. The *party-column ballot,* or Indiana ballot, used in a majority of states, lists the candidates of each party in a row or column, beside or under the party emblem. In most cases, the voter can make one mark at the top of the column, or pull one lever, and thus vote for all the party's candidates for various offices. This ballot encourages straight-ticket voting.
2. The *office-column ballot,* or Massachusetts ballot, groups candidates according to the office for which they are running—all the presidential candidates of all the parties appear in one column or row, for example.

Research has demonstrated that the form of the ballot may influence the vote. Among independent voters, one study found that a party-column ballot increased straight-ticket voting by 60 percent.[56] (Examples are shown on p. 332.)

The first voting machine was used in 1892 by the city of Lockport, New York. By 1980 more than half the states used machines statewide or in most areas.

Counting the Votes

On election night the results in each state are tabulated by state and local election officials and reported to the nation through the News Election Service, a cooperative pool of the three major television networks and the Associated Press and United Press International, the two major wire services.

The drama of election night is in a sense entirely artificial. As the night wears on, one candidate may appear to lead, then fall behind, and perhaps forge ahead again. Actually, once the polls close, the popular vote result is already recorded inside the ballot boxes and voting machines.

In recent years the nation has no longer had to wait until the votes were actually counted to know the results of some elections, because the television networks have developed systems of *projecting* the vote with the aid of electronic computers. In 1980 NBC predicted a victory for Ronald Reagan at 8:15 P.M. EST, when most of the actual vote was still to be counted.[57] In 1976, however, the election was so close that neither the computers nor the commentators were willing to make any predictions for many hours. Jimmy Carter was not declared the winner, by NBC, until 3:30 A.M. EST. In some instances the computers have predicted the wrong winners in state contests.

The computerized vote-projection systems are based on analysis of key precincts in selected areas. Past election data about the sample precincts are

[56] Campbell, Converse, Miller, and Stokes, *The American Voter,* p. 285.
[57] Harwood, ed., *The Pursuit of the Presidency 1980,* p. 320.

Winning Votes—Machine Style

I know every man, woman, and child in the Fifteenth District, except them that's been born this summer—and I know some of them, too. I know what they like and what they don't like, what they are strong at and what they are weak in, and I reach them by approachin' at the right side.

For instance, here's how I gather in the young men. I hear of a young feller that's proud of his voice, thinks that he can sing fine. I ask him to come around to Washington Hall and join our Glee Club. He comes and sings, and he's a follower of Plunkitt for life. Another young feller gains a reputation as a baseball player in a vacant lot. I bring him into our baseball club. That fixes him. You'll find him workin' for my ticket at the polls next election day. . . . I don't trouble them with political arguments. I just study human nature and act accordin'.

—Boss Plunkitt, in William L. Riordon, *Plunkitt of Tammany Hall.*

NAME OF PARTY	1 Presidential Electors (For President and Vice President)	2 United States Senator	3 Governor	4 Lieutenant Governor	5 Attorney General	6 Superintendent of Public Instruction	7 Reporter of Supreme Court and Court of Appeals	8 Representative in Congress 4th District	9 State Senator 16th District	10 State Representative 15th District	11 (Vote for Three Only)	12	13 County Treasurer	14 County Coroner	15 County Surveyor	16 County Commissioner 1st District	17 County Council-at-Large	18 (Vote for Three Only)	19
Republican Ticket	1A RONALD REAGAN / GEORGE BUSH	2A DAN QUAYLE	3A BOB ORR	4A JOHN M. MUTZ	5A LINLEY E. PEARSON	6A HAROLD H. NEGLEY	7A MARILOU WERTZLER	8A DAN R. COATS	9A JOHN R. SINKS	10A THOMAS K. FRUECHTENICHT	11A PHYLLIS J. POND	12A RICHARD L. WORDEN	13A LINDA K. BLOOM	14A ROLAND C. AHLBRAND	15A WILLIAM L. SWEET	16A RICHARD M. ELLENWOOD	17A JACK C. McCOMB	18A RICHARD L. SUMMERS	19A THOMAS J. WYSS
Democratic Ticket	1B JIMMY CARTER / WALTER F. MONDALE	2B BIRCH BAYH	3B JOHN HILLENBRAND, II	4B ROBERT E. PETERSON	5B BOB WEBSTER	6B JOHN LOUGHLIN	7B PHYLLIS SENEGAL	8B JOHN D. WALDA	9B	10B SAMUEL J. LETO, JR.	11B DON McCLAIN	12B GEORGE C. WOMAK, JR.	13B THERESE I. MILLER	14B ERNEST ANDERSON, JR.	15B	16B CHARLES L. MONTGOMERY	17B JOSEPH M. HILGER	18B KIMBERLY B. PONTIUS	19B CHRISTIAN H. SCHULTZ
American Party of Indiana Ticket	1C PERCY L. GREAVES, JR. / FRANK VARNUM	2C	3C CLETUS R. ARTIST	4C SHIRLEY M. GEPHART	5C	6C LINDA KAY PATTERSON	7C	8C	9C	10C LARRY E. DAVIS	11C BENJAMIN J. DIXON	12C KENNETH LEE MANIFOLD	13C	14C	15C	16C	17C	18C	19C
Libertarian Party Ticket	1D EDWARD E. CLARK / DAVID H. KOCH	2D	3D	4D	5D	6D	7D	8D	9D	10D	11D	12D	13D	14D	15D	16D	17D	18D	19D
Communist Party U.S.A. Ticket	1E GUS HALL / ANGELA Y. DAVIS	2E	3E	4E	5E	6E	7E	8E	9E	10E	11E	12E	13E	14E	15E	16E	17E	18E	19E
Socialist Workers Party Ticket	1F CLIFTON DeBERRY / MATILDE ZIMMERMAN	2F	3F	4F	5F	6F	7F	8F	9F	10F	11F	12F	13F	14F	15F	16F	17F	18F	19F
Independent Ticket	1G JOHN ANDERSON / PATRICK LUCEY	2G	3G	4G	5G	6G	7G	8G	9G	10G	11G	12G	13G	14G	15G	16G	17G	18G	19G
The Citizens Party Ticket	1H BARRY COMMONER / LaDONNA HARRIS	2H	3H	4H	5H	6H	7H	8H	9H	10H	11H	12H	13H	14H	15H	16H	17H	18H	19H

Sample Ballots

Figure 9–5

Above: The party-column, or Indiana ballot, used in most states, lists candidates alongside the party emblem. Usually, the arrangement allows a person to vote a straight ticket by pulling a single lever—in this case the large handle at left. The illustration is a sample of the face of an Indiana voting machine in 1980.

Below: The office-column, or Massachusetts ballot, groups candidates by office, making straight-ticket voting more difficult. Shown is a paper ballot used in Massachusetts in the 1976 election.

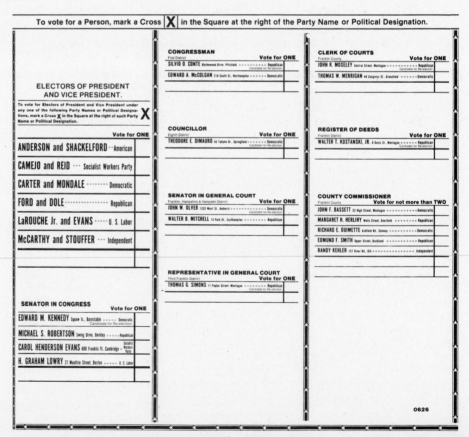

Left: November 4, 1980: Carter concedes. *Right:* Reagan and Bush are elected.

coded and stored in the computers and compared with actual returns as they come in on election night. As the computer processes the data flowing in, it is able to make a statistical forecast of the probable outcome. In 1980 a number of Western Democratic candidates as well as other political leaders complained sharply when the television networks declared Reagan the projected winner early in the evening, and President Carter conceded at 8:50 P.M. EST. These events, coming while the polls were still open on the West Coast, they argued, discouraged many potential voters from voting.

With so much at stake on election night, it is not surprising that from time to time there are charges of voting fraud, even in presidential elections.

Fraud

In 1960, after John Kennedy's narrow popular-vote victory over Richard Nixon, some Republicans charged that there had been election frauds in Cook County, Illinois, and in Texas. If Kennedy had failed to carry these two states, Nixon would have won in the electoral college. Kennedy carried Illinois by a mere 8858 votes, but his margin in Texas was much larger, 46,257 votes. Nixon considered but decided not to ask for an investigation or a recount.[58]

It may well be that in the age of the computer, some form of electronic voting system will be developed so that votes can be recorded and tallied quickly with a minimum possibility of tampering.

The Constitution does not provide for the popular election of the President. Instead, it provides that each state "shall appoint, in such manner as the legislature thereof may direct," electors equal in number to the representatives and senators that each state has in Congress. Instead of voting directly for President, an American in casting his or her ballot votes for a slate of electors that is normally pledged to the presidential candidate of the voter's choice. Many voters are unaware that they are voting for electors because their names do not even

The Electoral College

[58] Richard M. Nixon, *Six Crises* (New York: Doubleday, 1962), p. 413.

appear on the ballot in about two-thirds of the states. The slate that receives the most votes meets in the state capital in December of a presidential election year and casts its ballots. Each state sends the results to Washington, where the electoral votes are officially counted in a joint session of Congress early in January. The candidate with a majority of the electoral votes is elected President. If no one receives a majority, the House of Representatives must choose the President from among the three candidates with the largest number of electoral votes, with each state delegation in the House having one vote. If there is no majority vote for Vice President, the Senate makes the choice.[59]

Custom, not the Constitution, is the reason that electors are chosen in each state by popular vote. In the first four presidential elections, state legislatures chose the electors in most cases. South Carolina was the last state to switch to popular election, in 1860. Although there is hardly any possibility that a state would discontinue popular election of electors, legally, a state may select them any way it wishes.[60]

The framers of the Constitution had great difficulty in agreeing on the best way to elect the President. Some favored direct election, but others thought this would give an advantage to the more populous states. The provision for presidential electors represented a compromise between the big and little states. For, "only a few delegates to the Constitutional Convention felt that American democracy had matured sufficiently for the choice of the President to be entrusted directly to the people."[61]

Over the decades, the electoral college has been severely criticized as an old-fashioned device standing between the people and their choice of a President. The criticism may be summarized as follows:

1. The "winner-take-all" feature of the electoral college means that if a candidate carries a state by even one popular vote, he wins *all* of the state's electoral votes, distorting the will of the voters because the minority votes cast within a state count for nothing. As a result, a President may be elected who has lost the total popular vote. This actually happened in the elections of John Quincy Adams in 1824, Rutherford B. Hayes in 1876, and Benjamin Harrison in 1888.
2. The system, with its winner-take-all feature, gives an advantage to the populous states that have many electoral votes, and to the members of minority groups that constitute powerful voting blocs within those states. At the same time, very small states are overrepresented because every state has a minimum of three electoral votes.
3. Electors are not constitutionally bound to vote for the candidate to whom they are pledged. In 1976 Mike Padden, a Republican from Spokane, Washington, voted for Ronald Reagan instead of for Gerald Ford, the Republican party's

[59] The House chose the President twice, after the election of 1800, when it elected Jefferson, and following the election of 1824, when it elected John Quincy Adams. The Senate chose the Vice President only once, when it elected Richard M. Johnson of Kentucky to that office in 1837. In the case of a tie in the presidential balloting in the House that is not resolved by Inauguration Day, January 20, the Vice-President-elect becomes acting President. Since the Senate chooses the Vice President in the event of an electoral vote deadlock, the Senate, in effect, would select the new President. On Inauguration Day, if no President or Vice President is qualified, the Presidency would go to the Speaker of the House, or next to the President pro tempore of the Senate, or down through all the cabinet posts under the Presidential Succession Act.

[60] In fact, in 1969 Maine changed its system of choosing presidential electors; under a new state law, two electors are chosen at large and two are chosen from Maine's two congressional districts. Previously, all states elected electors on a statewide basis.

[61] Neal R. Peirce, *The People's President* (New York: Simon and Schuster, 1968), p. 41.

presidential nominee. He did so even though Ford had carried the state of Washington. Since the nation began, ten other electors have defected in similar fashion.

In 1968 major-party supporters feared that George Wallace would receive enough electoral votes to deprive Nixon or Humphrey of a majority; the third-party candidate might then be in a position to win concessions in return for his electoral votes, or force the election into the House of Representatives, where he might strike further bargains.

The closeness of the 1960 election, the Wallace campaign in 1968, and other factors, all combined to create new pressures for electoral college reform. Past debates had centered on plans to choose presidential electors by district (as members of Congress are chosen), or to award each candidate electoral votes in proportion to his share of the popular vote within each state. In the 1960s, however, the idea of *direct election* of the President gained in popularity. It seemed closest to the principle of "one person, one vote," enunciated by the Supreme Court.

In September 1969 the House passed a proposed constitutional amendment to abolish the electoral college and substitute direct election of the President and Vice President. Under the amendment, if no candidate received 40 percent of the popular vote, a runoff election would be held between the top two presidential candidates. Congress was authorized to set the date for the election and for any runoff. The states would continue to run the election machinery, but Congress reserved the right to set uniform nationwide residence requirements for voting in presidential elections. Although the states would still set the qualifications for candidates to appear on the ballot, Congress for the first time would have the power to override and change the relevant state laws. This provision was included to ensure that candidates of major parties would appear on the ballot in every state — if only to avoid the threat of intervention by Congress. As under the present system, however, minor parties could find it difficult to qualify for the ballot in many states.

In 1970 a filibuster by opponents of direct election prevented the Senate from voting on the proposal. Interest in direct election of the President waned for a time after the proposed amendment died in the Senate. One reason such an amendment did not pass in 1970 was a widespread reluctance, in and out of Congress, to change a fundamental aspect of the American political system. There were also a number of specific objections. Critics argued that it would encourage the growth of splinter parties. The result, they warned, could be fragmentation of American politics and destruction of the two-party system.[62] And the two-party system, these critics have contended, is a vital instrument in resolving social conflict and managing the transfer of power.

Those opposed to direct election also argued that the electoral college is compatible with the federal system and that direct election would (1) increase the temptation for fraud in vote counting, leading to prolonged recounts and

Direct Election of the President

---

[62] See, for example, Irving Kristol and Paul Weaver, "A Bad Idea Whose Time Has Come," *New York Times Magazine,* November 23, 1969.

chaos, (2) rob minority groups of their influence in big electoral-vote states, and (3) tempt states to ease voter qualification standards in order to fatten the voter rolls.

During the 1960s the Supreme Court ruled in a series of *reapportionment* decisions that each person's vote should be worth as much as another's. Yet, the decisions were controversial, for they upset the balance of political power between urban and rural areas in the United States. The result was a concerted but unsuccessful effort in Congress and the states to amend the Constitution to overturn the Supreme Court rulings.

One Person, One Vote

The State Legislatures. All votes are equal when each member of a legislative body represents the same number of people. In the United States, however, successive waves of immigration and the subsequent growth of the cities resulted in glaring inequalities in the population of urban and rural state legislative districts by the turn of the century. The 1920 census showed that for the first time more Americans lived in urban than in rural areas. The rural state legislators, representing sparsely populated districts, passed state laws to maintain their advantage over the cities. By 1960, in every state, the largest legislative district was at least twice as populous as the smallest district.

In Tennessee that year, the smallest district in the lower house had a population of 3400 and the largest 79,000. Obviously, the people in the biggest district were not equally represented with the voters in the smallest. Because the legislature had refused to do anything about it, a group of urban residents, including a county judge named Charles W. Baker, sued Joe C. Carr, Tennessee's secretary of state. The case went to the United States Supreme Court, which in 1946 had refused to consider a case involving malapportionment in Illinois (*Colgrove* v. *Green*). Justice Felix Frankfurter, in that earlier opinion, ruled that the Supreme Court "ought not to enter this political thicket."[63]

But in 1962, in *Baker* v. *Carr,* the Supreme Court ruled in favor of the voters who had challenged the established order in Tennessee.[64] In 1964, in *Reynolds* v. *Sims,* the Supreme Court made it clear that the Fourteenth Amendment required that seats in *both* houses of a state legislature be based on population. Second, the Court ruled that although legislative districts might not be drawn with "mathematical exactness or precision," they must be based "substantially" on population.[65] The Court had laid down the principle of "one person, one vote."

The reapportionment decisions had an immediate effect on the political map of America. The legislature of Oregon had reapportioned on the basis of population in 1961; between the *Baker* v. *Carr* ruling in 1962 and 1970, the other forty-nine states took similar steps.

Conservative and rural forces reacted strongly to the Supreme Court rulings. In 1965 and 1966 the late Senator Everett M. Dirksen proposed a constitutional amendment to allow a state to apportion one house of its legislature on a basis other than population. Although the "Dirksen amendment" received majority support in the Senate both years, it fell short of the needed two-thirds

[63] *Colgrove* v. *Green,* 328 U.S. 549 (1946).
[64] *Baker* v. *Carr,* 369 U.S. 186 (1962).
[65] *Reynolds* v. *Sims,* 377 U.S. 533 (1964).

majority. Undaunted, Dirksen and his backers encouraged the states to petition Congress for a constitutional convention, an alternate method of amending the Constitution that has never been used (see Chapter 2). On April 30, 1969, Iowa became the thirty-third state to pass a resolution requesting a constitutional convention, one short of the necessary two-thirds of the states. But even before the Iowa resolution, some states had moved to rescind their petitions; and the possibility of a constitutional convention to consider the Dirksen amendment appeared to have ended.

Congressional Districts. It was not just the state legislatures that were malapportioned prior to the mid-1960s. Although the *average* congressional House district had a population of 410,000 in the 1960s, the actual population of these districts varied greatly. For example, in Georgia, one rural district had 272,000 people, but the Fifth Congressional District (Atlanta and its suburbs) numbered 823,000 people. In 1964, in the case of *Wesberry* v. *Sanders,*[66] the Supreme Court ruled that this disparity in the size of Georgia congressional districts violated the Constitution. Within two years, twenty-seven states with a total of 258 congressional districts had redistricted to conform to the Court ruling.

The Supreme Court's reapportionment decisions left open the question of how much the population of state legislative and congressional districts might vary from one another without violating the principle of "one person, one vote." In a series of decisions the Court shifted ground as it grappled with this difficult question, eventually ruling that deviations as high as 10 percent in state legislative districts were too small to merit attention by the courts.[67]

Under the Constitution and federal law, Congress determines the total *size* of the House of Representatives, which grew from 65 members in 1790 to 435 in 1912. Congress has kept the House membership at 435 since then, although it could change that semipermanent figure.[68] After each ten-year census, federal law requires that the *number of representatives for each state* be reapportioned on the basis of population. If a state gains or loses members of Congress, the state legislature *redistricts* by drawing new boundary lines for its House districts.[69] In 1972, for example, California gained a total of five seats as a result of the 1970 census, making its House delegation the largest in the nation. Previously New York's was the largest. Again, after the 1980 census, California, Florida, and Texas gained seats, and New York, Pennsylvania, Ohio, and Illinois lost seats. The average population of House districts had risen to about 520,000 by the time of the 1980 elections.

As a result of the reapportionment revolution of the 1960s, rural areas had been expected to lose power to the cities. But because of the population exodus from the cities, the *suburbs* have proven to be the areas that gained the most from reapportionment of state legislatures and congressional districts. As far back as 1965 an official of the National Municipal League noted that almost half of the big cities in the United States had less population than their suburbs: "No center city contains the necessary 50 percent of the people to dominate the

---

[66] *Wesberry* v. *Sanders,* 376 U.S. 1 (1964).

[67] *Kirkpatrick* v. *Preisler,* 394 U.S. 526 (1969); *Mahon* v. *Howell, City of Virginia Beach* v. *Howell, Weinberg* v. *Prichard,* 410 U.S. 315 (1973); *Gaffney* v. *Cummings,* 412 U.S. 735 (1973); and *White* v. *Regester,* 412 U.S. 755 (1973).

[68] The membership of the House increased only briefly, to 436 in early 1959 and to 437 from late 1959 through 1962, as a result of the admission to statehood of Hawaii and Alaska.

[69] In a few instances the new lines have been drawn by federal courts.

Population Trends in Rural, City, and Suburban Areas

Figure 9–6

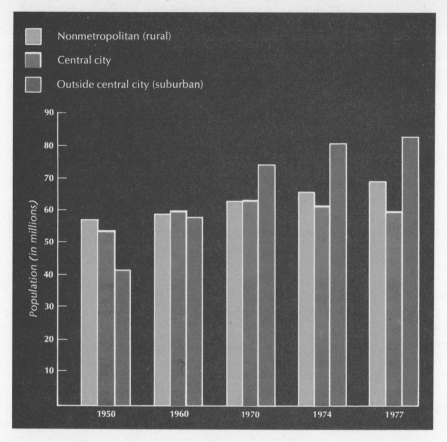

Source: Adapted from U.S. Bureau of the Census, *Statistical Abstract of the United States 1972*, p. 16; U.S. Bureau of the Census, *Current Population Reports*, Social and Economic Characteristics of the Metropolitan and Nonmetropolitan Population: 1974 and 1970, Series P–23, No. 55, p. 5; and U.S. Bureau of the Census. *Current Population Reports*, Social and Economic Characteristics of the Metropolitan and Nonmetropolitan Population: 1977 and 1970, Series P–23, No. 75, p. 4.

Suburban, Central City, and Rural Congressional Districts in the United States House of Representatives, 1962–1974

Table 9–15

	1962	1966	1974
Metropolitan Districts	254	264	305
Central City	106	110	109
Suburban	92	98	132
Mixed Metropolitan	56	56	64
Rural Districts	181	171	130
Total	435	435	435

Source: Richard Lehne, "Suburban Foundations of the New Congress," *Annals of the American Academy of Political and Social Science*, November 1975, p. 143.

state. . . . The U.S. is an urban nation, but it is not a big-city nation. The suburbs own the future."[70]

Because the suburbs have grown much faster than the nation as a whole, in the 1970s, for the first time, there were more members of the House of Representatives from the suburbs than from the cities. (See Table 9-15.) As the political battle shifts to the suburbs, Gerald Pomper has predicted, "Suburban power will influence the way both politics and government are conducted."[71]

Elections and Democratic Government

Who won the election? In the United States, with its federal system, the question must be asked on all levels—national (the Presidency, Congress), state (statehouses and state legislatures), and local (county and city governments). Since candidates of both major parties win these offices, the outcome of American elections is mixed. Which party won or lost is not always as simple as it might appear. In 1972, for example, Nixon, a Republican, won by a landslide in the presidential election, but the Republican party made only modest gains in the House and suffered a net loss of two seats in the Senate. Yet there are differences in elections; the voice of the voter speaks more clearly in some years than in others.

V. O. Key, Jr., has suggested three broad types of presidential elections.[72] A *landslide* for the out-party "expresses clearly a lack of confidence in those who have been in charge of affairs." Some observers felt that the decisive defeat of President Carter in 1980 was fundamentally an election of this type. In other election years, however, the voters may approve an incumbent administration in a vote of confidence that amounts to a *reaffirmation* of support. A third type of election, a *realignment,* may return a party to power, but with the support of a new coalition of voters. (There may also be a major realignment when the President's party loses control of the White House.) When the realignment within the electorate is "both sharp and durable," Key suggests that a "critical" election has taken place, one that results in "profound readjustments" in political power.[73] The extensive Republican gains in 1980 triggered some speculation about whether that election reflected a basic realignment and the emergence of a new Republican majority.

Angus Campbell and his associates have classified presidential elections in somewhat similar fashion: they relate the election returns to the basic pattern of party identification. They speak of *maintaining elections,* which reflect the standing party identification of the voters; of *deviating elections,* in which the majority party (according to party identification) is defeated in a temporary reversal; and of *realigning elections,* which may lead to a basic shift in the party identification of the electorate.[74]

Types
of Elections

[70] William J. D. Boyd, in Congressional Quarterly, *Weekly Report,* November 21, 1969, p. 2342.
[71] Gerald M. Pomper, "Census '70: Power to the Suburbs," *Washington Monthly,* May 1970, p. 23.
[72] Key, *Politics, Parties, and Pressure Groups,* pp. 520–36.
[73] V. O. Key, Jr., "A Theory of Critical Elections," *Journal of Politics,* Vol. 17 (February 1955), pp. 3–18.
[74] Campbell, Converse, Miller, and Stokes, *The American Voter,* pp. 531–38.

The Meaning of Elections

Much of the discussion in this chapter has focused on the wide variety of reasons, sociological and psychological, that may cause different voters to vote for the same political candidate. Regardless of these individual reasons, the overall election verdicts have broad meaning for the political system as a whole.

First of all, elections decide which individuals shall govern. Who wins can make a difference — in the political philosophy and caliber of those appointed to the Supreme Court by the President and approved by Congress, to take but one example.

Second, elections can have important consequences for the broad direction of public policy. Naturally, many specific questions are not settled by elections, but 1936 was rather clearly a broad approval of the New Deal, just as 1964 was a repudiation of conservative Republicanism in that year. The series of four Democratic presidential victories from 1936 to 1948 ("maintaining elections" in Angus Campbell's terminology, "reaffirmations of support" in Key's classification) served to ensure that most of the policy innovations of the New Deal would become established public programs.

The voice of the people is not always so clear. The meaning of a particular election, the "mandate" of the people to the President on specific issues, may be subject to varying interpretations. As we have noted, many different people vote for the same candidate for different reasons; this candidate, once elected, may make decisions that cause some of his voters to feel misled. For example, in 1964 Americans voted for a President who seemed to promise, among other things, to avoid an Asian war, but did not.[75] In the presidential election of 1968 some voters retaliated by voting Republican.

It is also true that issues may be warped and facts concealed from the public in campaign debate, so that people may cast their votes on the basis of inadequate information. For example, during the 1972 campaign President

[75] See Chapter 7, pp. 250–51. At the start of the 1964 campaign there were 16,000 American troops in Vietnam as "advisers." Three months after his election, President Johnson ordered the bombing of North Vietnam. By June 1965 U.S. troops were admittedly fighting, not advising. By 1968 more than 500,000 American troops were in Vietnam. The last U.S. forces were pulled out by President Nixon in March 1973.

Nixon, his press secretary, and spokesmen for the President's election committee all repeatedly denied responsibility for the burglary and bugging of the Democrats' Watergate headquarters. In the summer of 1973 Senate hearings disclosed in great detail the involvement of high government officials in the incident and in subsequent attempts to cover it up. But in the 1976 presidential election, Watergate, which had occurred during a Republican administration, worked to Gerald Ford's disadvantage.[76]

To summarize, elections leave elected officials with a great deal of flexibility in governing. Yet, elections also often set broad guidelines within which decision makers must stay—or risk reprisal by the voters.

It is true that most American elections have tended to be fundamentally centrist, or middle-of-the-road in character. Parties and candidates have competed for the center ground in American politics because that is where the parties believed that the biggest bloc of voters were.[77] For this reason candidates do not as a rule endorse radical programs of social change. Yet the New Deal marked a considerable departure in government's approach to America's problems. Since 1932 government has intervened in the social and economic order to an unprecedented extent. Its role as economic regulator has been approved by many voters in elections over four decades. Elections do at times set broad parameters for change.

Continuity and Change

"The people," Key has observed, "may not be able to govern themselves but they can, through an electoral uprising, throw the old crowd out and demand a new order, without necessarily being capable of specifying exactly what it shall be. An election of this type may amount, if not to revolution, to its functional equivalent."[78]

Besides establishing a framework for change, elections also provide continuity and a sense of political community, for they are links in a chain that bind one generation of voters to the next. Every four years the voters come together in an act of decision that is influenced by the past and present, but designed to shape the future.

[76] On Election Day 1976, CBS News interviewed 14,836 persons as they left the polls. Those who voted for Jimmy Carter were given a list of ten possible issues and asked to check as many as three that "led you to vote for Jimmy Carter." By far the largest group—49 percent—checked "Restoring trust in government." One in five checked "Watergate and the pardon." Source: *National Journal,* November 6, 1976, p. 1588.

[77] For a detailed statement of the view that elections are won and lost "in the center," see Richard M. Scammon and Ben J. Wattenberg, *The Real Majority* (New York: Coward-McCann, 1971).

[78] Key, *Politics, Parties, and Pressure Groups,* pp. 522–23.

Perspective

Voting is a fundamental way by which people influence government. In the federal system that exists in the United States, the voters choose public officials at all levels of government. In a presidential year, for instance, voters select the President and Vice President, 435 members of the House, one-third of the Senate, about 13 state governors, and numerous other state and local officials. In a democracy, voting is an act of choice among alternative candidates, parties, and—depending on the election—alternative policies.

More than half of Americans of voting age have

voted for President in each election since 1928. But in nonpresidential election years, considerably less than half have bothered to vote for members of Congress.

Two basic approaches have been followed in studying how the voters decide. The sociological method focuses on the social and economic background of the voters — their income, social class, ethnic group, education, and similar factors — and attempts to relate these factors to how they vote. The psychological method attempts to go beyond socioeconomic factors and find out what is going on in the minds of the voters, to measure their perceptions of parties, candidates, and issues.

Voter studies of sociological factors, for example, have found that upper-class and middle-class voters are more likely to vote Republican than are lower-class voters, who tend to be Democrats. Professional, business people, and college graduates are more likely to vote for Republicans than Democrats. Manual workers, Jews, and Catholics have tended to vote Democratic. In general, the Democrats still draw their strength from the big cities of the North and East, and they usually receive a strong vote from black Americans.

In measuring voter attitudes, three important factors have been identified: party identification, candidates, and issues. Voters may form an attachment to one party or the other and often do not change. However, the personal impressions that a candidate makes on the voters may also influence the election results. And, on certain major issues, or on issues that affect them directly, the voters seem to "tune in" and form definite issue-based preferences.

In a presidential election year, the vote for President can affect the vote for Congress and for state and local offices. In the congressional races, for example, a President has sometimes helped to carry a majority of his own party into office with him through the "coattail" effect.

The 1980 presidential election — in sharp contrast to the close Carter-Ford contest in 1976 — resulted in a decisive victory for Ronald Reagan, the Republican nominee, over Jimmy Carter, the incumbent Democrat, and John B. Anderson, independent. Reagan carried forty-four of the fifty states, and for the second time in a row, an incumbent President went down to defeat.

The Democratic party also suffered substantial losses in contests for state legislature, governor, and the House of Representatives. In addition, the Democrats suffered a massive loss of twelve seats in the Senate, thereby losing control of that body for the first time in twenty-six years. The broad pattern of the election returns made it clear that the coalition that had produced many Democratic electoral victories since 1932 had shattered in 1980.

The electoral system in the United States is not neutral. It affects the dynamics of voting all along the way. Before voters can step into the voting booths, they must meet a number of legal requirements. The candidates whose names appear on the ballot must have qualified under state law. The form of the ballot may influence voters' decisions. In short, the structure, details, and workings of the electoral system affect the people's choice.

Voting is a basic right provided for by the Constitution. Under the Fourteenth Amendment, it is one of the privileges and immunities of national citizenship that the states may not abridge. It is also a right that Congress has the power to protect by federal legislation. Until the age of Jackson, voting was generally restricted to men who owned property and paid taxes. Since then, suffrage has gradually been broadened, particularly by the Fifteenth Amendment which enfranchised black men, the Nineteenth Amendment which enfranchised women, and the Twenty-sixth Amendment which lowered the voting age to eighteen in all elections.

The Constitution does not provide for the popular election of the President. Instead, it provides that each state shall select electors equal in number to the representatives and senators it has in Congress. Instead of voting directly for President, an American voter casts his or her ballot for a slate of electors that normally is pledged to the presidential candidate of the voter's choice. The candidate who wins a majority of the electoral votes is elected President.

During the 1960s the Supreme Court ruled in a series of reapportionment decisions that each person's vote should be worth as much as another's.

The overall verdicts of elections have broad meaning for the political system as a whole. Elections decide which individuals shall govern. Elections can have important consequences for the direction of public policy. And elections often set broad guidelines within which decision makers must stay — or risk reprisal by the voters.

Berelson, Bernard R.; Lazarsfeld, Paul F.; and McPhee, William N. *Voting: A Study of Opinion Formation in a Presidential Campaign** (University of Chicago Press, 1954). An influential study of how voters decide for whom they will vote. Based on a series of interviews with about 1000 residents of Elmira, New York, during the Truman-Dewey presidential contest of 1948.

Campbell, Angus; Converse, Philip E.; Miller, Warren E.; and Stokes, Donald E. *The American Voter* (University of Chicago Press, 1976). (Originally published in 1960; an abridged paperback edition was published in 1964.) A landmark study of voting behavior, based on interviews with national samples of the American electorate conducted by the Survey Research Center of the University of Michigan.

Harwood, Richard, ed. *The Pursuit of the Presidency 1980** (Berkley Books, 1980). An interesting and informative general account of the 1980 presidential election. Written by journalists who covered the campaign for the *Washington Post.*

Flanigan, William H., and Zingale, Nancy. *Political Behavior of the American Electorate,* 4th edition* (Allyn and Bacon, 1979). Useful, concise analysis and summary of research on how and why Americans vote.

Key, V. O., Jr. *The Responsible Electorate* (The Belknap Press of Harvard University Press, 1966). An examination of American voting behavior in presidential elections, based primarily on analyses of Gallup poll data from 1936 to 1960. Key argues that the voters' views on issues and government policy are quite closely related to how they vote in such elections.

Key, V. O., Jr. *Southern Politics in State and Nation* (Knopf, 1949). A classic study of the politics of the South. Analyzes why the Democratic party dominated that region for nearly three generations after the Civil War, and what the political consequences were.

Lazarsfeld, Paul F.; Berelson, Bernard; and Gaudet, Hazel. *The People's Choice: How the Voter Makes Up His Mind in a Presidential Campaign** (Columbia University Press, 1968). (Originally published in 1944.) A classic in the study of voting behavior, based on a series of interviews with potential voters in Erie County, Ohio, during the Roosevelt-Willkie presidential contest of 1940. The book stresses the relationship between the voters' socio-economic status and how they voted.

Mann, Thomas E. *Unsafe at Any Margin: Interpreting Congressional Elections** (American Enterprise Institute for Public Policy Research, 1978). A revealing analysis of the influence that local candidates and local events have in congressional elections. The author argues that members of the House are growing more independent of their party and the President, and that individual House candidates are becoming increasingly responsible for their own margins of victory or defeat.

Milbrath, Lester W., and Goel, M. L. *Political Participation: How and Why Do People Get Involved in Politics,* 2nd edition (Rand McNally, 1977). A comprehensive, general analysis of who participates in politics and why.

Nie, Norman H.; Verba, Sidney; and Petrocik, John R. *The Changing American Voter,* Enlarged Edition* (Harvard University Press, 1979). An important sequel to the classic 1960 study, *The American Voter,* based primarily on public opinion polls from 1956 to 1973. The authors concluded that, compared with the 1950s, issues were more visible and had a greater effect on voting, in the elections from 1964 through 1972.

Page, Benjamin I. *Choices and Echoes in Presidential Elections: Rational Man and Electoral Democracy** (University of Chicago Press, 1978). An important and perceptive analysis of American voting behavior. Focuses on the policy stands that are taken by presidential candidates, as well as on the voters' response to the choices that are presented to them.

Peirce, Neal R. *The People's President** (Simon and Schuster, 1968). A detailed study of the history of the electoral college and its effect in past presidential elections. Presents the case for abolishing the electoral college and electing the President directly by popular vote.

Scammon, Richard M., and Wattenberg, Ben J. *The Real Majority** (Coward-McCann, 1971). A lively analysis of political attitudes and voting patterns in America. Argues that the majority of American voters are "unyoung, unpoor, and unblack," and contends that candidates who take moderate positions on issues—close to the "political center"—are more likely to be elected than candidates who take more extreme positions.

Sundquist, James L. *Dynamics of the Party System: Alignment and Realignment of Political Parties in the United States** (The Brookings Institution, 1973). A comprehensive historical analysis of the relative electoral strength of America's political parties over a 140-year period. Includes a discussion of the probable voting strength of the Republican and Democratic parties in the future.

* Available in paperback edition

Part Three

THE
POLICYMAKERS

10

THE PRESIDENT

"The imperial Presidency": a formal reception at the White House

The American Presidency is a place of paradox. It is an office of enormous contrasts, of great power — and great limits. By the time Ronald Reagan took office in 1981, a number of factors and events had altered the public's perception of the Presidency. President Kennedy had been assassinated in 1963, and his four successors had left office under adverse circumstances. President Johnson, criticized over the war in Vietnam, chose not to run; President Nixon was forced to resign; Presidents Ford and Carter were defeated.

Why had presidential power apparently become so fragile? Perhaps one reason was that many of the problems faced by Presidents had become more difficult to manage. The economy was one example; it worked against Carter in the election of 1980. As Ben W. Heineman, Jr., has noted, economic problems do not easily yield to a President's policies: "Fifteen years ago, the economy was a strong ally of presidential power. It appeared to respond magically to executive will, providing on a lavish scale the resources needed for a long agenda of social reforms. Today the economy is an adversary of presidential power — perhaps the greatest adversary. It appears to mock all executive ministrations, provides insufficient resources for a host of governmental objectives and vexes Presidents with choices between politically unacceptable evils."[1]

[1] Ben W. Heineman, Jr., and Curtis A. Hessler, *Memorandum for the President: A Strategic Approach to Domestic Affairs in the 1980s* (New York: Random House, 1980), p. 56.

WELCOME
ABOARD
Air Force One

Against this background, some observers asked whether the Presidency had become an arena for failure and whether any Chief Executive, however able, could govern. And a number of scholars were exploring the question of how the Presidency might be made more effective.

Only a decade earlier, many commentators and some voters had been concerned with a different problem. They worried about the expansion of presidential power and the emergence of what Arthur M. Schlesinger, Jr., termed "the imperial Presidency."[2] Particularly in the area of foreign and military policy, Schlesinger and others contended, the Presidency had exceeded constitutional bounds and usurped congressional war-making power.

The growth of the power of the Presidency, many scholars noted, was accompanied by excessive reverence for the person of the President, a phenomenon that Louis Koenig called "the Sun King complex."[3] In Schlesinger's view, "the age of the imperial Presidency had in time produced the idea that run-of-the-mill politicians, brought by fortuity to the White House, must be treated thereafter as if they had become superior and perhaps godlike beings."[4] Similarly, Thomas E. Cronin criticized the "textbook Presidency," the creation, he argued, of political scientists, journalists, and others who endow the Chief Executive with a "halo." Cronin perceived a "cult of the Presidency," in which

"The Sun King complex": President Nixon decreed that these ceremonial uniforms be worn by White House guards; the uniforms were quickly abandoned as a result of public derision.

[2] Arthur M. Schlesinger, Jr., *The Imperial Presidency* (Boston: Houghton Mifflin, 1973).
[3] Louis W. Koenig, *The Chief Executive,* 3rd ed. (New York: Harcourt Brace Jovanovich, 1975), p. 3.
[4] Schlesinger, *The Imperial Presidency,* p. 410.

"The Reverence Due a Monarch"

The life of the White House is the life of the court. It is a structure designed for one purpose and one purpose only—to serve the material needs and the desires of a single man. It is felt that this man is grappling with problems of such tremendous consequence that every effort must be made to relieve him of the irritations that vex the average citizen. His mind, it is held, must be absolutely free of petty annoyances so that he can concentrate his faculties upon the "great issues" of the day.

To achieve this end, every conceivable facility is made available, from the very latest and most luxurious jet aircraft to a masseur constantly in attendance to soothe raw presidential nerves. Even more important, however, he is treated with all of the reverence due a monarch. No one interrupts presidential contemplation for anything less than a major catastrophe somewhere on the globe. No one speaks to him unless spoken to first. No one ever invites him to "go soak your head" when his demands become petulant and unreasonable.

—George E. Reedy, *The Twilight of the Presidency.*

One bright morning last May, the President of the United States strode briskly from the Oval Office into the White House Rose Garden and seated himself at a little table where, surrounded by smiling members of Congress, he signed into law a bill authorizing millions of dollars in emergency funds for farmers caught in the dust of an extended drought.

"This legislation will provide immediate relief," he said as he happily scribbled "Jimmy Carter" across the bottom of the bulky document, finishing with a confident flourish.

Now, nearly eight weeks later, as the drought continues and deepens, not a single penny of the Federal money authorized in that law has reached a single American farmer. And Mr. Carter, who was inaugurated six months ago, has learned another lesson in his continuing education on the limitations of his office. . . .

The lethargic movement of the drought-relief money through the Federal pipeline underscores what several of his aides have said may be the most important lesson of his White House experience, his discovery that there are limits to his power.

— *New York Times*, July 25, 1977.

the occupant of the White House becomes "benevolent, omnipotent, omniscient."[5]

Even as the Presidency was being criticized for an excess of power, however, it was simultaneously perceived as weakened by Vietnam and Watergate. Both of those traumatic events diminished public trust in the institution of the Presidency, and — some analysts believed — diminished the actual power of that office as well.

The paradox of the Presidency was vividly demonstrated by the Watergate drama and its central figure, Richard Nixon. A year after his triumphant re-election in 1972, Nixon was a beleaguered Chief Executive, the subject of an investigation in the House of Representatives, his ability to govern seriously impaired. Less than two years after his re-election, Nixon had resigned in disgrace. Had he not been pardoned by his successor, Gerald Ford, Nixon might have faced criminal prosecution and prison.

Any discussion of the modern Presidency is inevitably colored by Watergate. To some extent, that massive scandal may have resulted from political and institutional factors, among them the growth of presidential power in the twentieth century, increasing government secrecy, a lack of government credibility, a burgeoning national security bureaucracy, and the use of intelligence agencies and techniques in domestic politics. At the same time, Watergate was a result of the policies and actions of a particular Chief Executive and his aides. Institutional factors may contribute to government corruption, but they do not absolve individual guilt; Watergate was in this sense the responsibility of one President and one administration.

In the wake of Vietnam and Watergate, Congress in the early 1970s moved to reassert its power within the political system. It enacted the War Powers Resolution in an effort to curb presidential military adventures; it imposed other restrictions on the President in the foreign policy and military fields; and it created a new structure to deal with the federal budget — an action designed to

[5] Thomas E. Cronin, *The State of the Presidency,* 2nd ed. (Boston: Little, Brown, 1980), pp. 76, 90.

permit Congress to share power with the President over the budget process and the establishment of national priorities.

This effort to reassert congressional power coincided to some extent with the administration of President Ford. Most analysts regarded the Ford period as one of a weak Presidency. However, Ford was an unelected President, the first to take office under the provisions of the Twenty-fifth Amendment; and he served only two and a half years. But his successor, Jimmy Carter, did not prove to be a strong Chief Executive either. Beset by foreign policy problems and a lagging economy, he was decisively defeated by Ronald Reagan in 1980. Nor did Carter fare very well with Congress; although Democrats controlled both the House and Senate during Carter's Presidency, major parts of his legislative program were not enacted. The history of Carter and other recent Presidents led the columnist Joseph Kraft to conclude that Arthur Schlesinger's "imperial Presidency" had, by 1980, become the "post-imperial Presidency."[6]

The opposing perceptions of the Presidency—either as an office grown too powerful, or one in danger of being weakened by a reassertive Congress—leave unresolved the question of how the Presidency can be controlled without so reducing its powers that the President cannot manage national problems and lead the nation. "The American democracy," Schlesinger has suggested, "must discover a middle ground between making the President a czar and making him a puppet. . . . we need a strong Presidency—but a strong Presidency *within the Constitution*."[7]

In the light of the nation's experience over the past two decades, a number of questions may be asked about the American Presidency. Has the office grown too powerful? Are there enough checks on presidential power? Or is the Presidency too weak? Does a President have enough control over the bureaucracy and policy formation, and enough influence with Congress, to solve the problems that come to him? Can the Presidency be made more effective? Or will the President's impact always be marginal? Can any President govern? In exploring these questions, it might be useful to begin by examining the Presidency as it appeared to two men who held that office.

[6] Joseph Kraft, "The Post-Imperial Presidency," *The New York Times Magazine,* November 2, 1980, p. 31.
[7] Schlesinger, *The Imperial Presidency,* p. x.

The Oval Office

The American Presidency

The day before he took the oath of office as thirty-fifth President of the United States, John F. Kennedy called upon President Eisenhower at the White House. "There are no easy matters that will ever come to you as President," Eisenhower told the younger man. "If they are easy, they will be settled at a lower level."

The accuracy of this parting advice had come home to President Kennedy when he told the story almost two years later during an interview over the three major television networks.[8] Kennedy's conversation with three newsmen in his Oval Office provided an unusual insight into the dimensions and perspectives of the American Presidency. When asked how the job had matched his conception of it, Kennedy replied: "Well, I think in the first place the problems are more difficult than I had imagined they were. Secondly, there is a limitation upon the ability of the United States to solve these problems."

Although Kennedy was speaking of world problems, the same tone was apparent in his remarks about the President's domestic power. "The fact is," he said, "I think the Congress looks more powerful sitting here than it did when I was there in the Congress. . . . When you are in Congress you are one of a hundred in the Senate or one of 435 in the House, so that the power is so divided. But here I look at a Congress, and I look at the collective power of the Congress . . . and it is a substantial power."

In addition, Kennedy, an activist President, impatient to get things done, fumed at the bureaucracy: "You know, after I met Mr. Kruschchev [the Soviet Premier] in Vienna and they gave us an *aide-mémoire,* it took me many weeks to get our answer out through the State Department. . . . This is a constant problem in various departments. . . . You can wait while the world collapses."

As Kennedy was well aware, an American President bears enormous responsibility in the nuclear age. In the event of an atomic war, Kennedy observed in the interview, "this is the end, because you are talking about Western Europe, the Soviet Union, the United States, of 150 million fatalities in the first 18 hours. . . . One mistake can make this whole thing blow up."

This candid discussion of the Presidency illuminated both the power and limits of the office. It pointed up the fact that the President is not merely the symbolic and actual leader of more than 226 million Americans, sworn to "preserve, protect and defend" the Constitution — but also a world leader, whose decisions may affect the future of 4.6 billion inhabitants of the globe.

[8] Television and Radio Interview: "After Two Years — a Conversation With the President," December 17, 1962, in *Public Papers of the Presidents of the United States, John F. Kennedy, 1962* (Washington, D.C.: U.S. Government Printing Office, 1963), pp. 889–904.

"There are no easy matters that will ever come to you as President. . . ." President Kennedy (left) is visited by former President Eisenhower at Camp David, Maryland.

A President Looks to the Future

It is not by any means the sole task of the Presidency to think about the present. One of the chief obligations of the Presidency is to think about the future. We have been, in our one hundred and fifty years of constitutional existence, a wasteful nation, a nation that has wasted its natural resources and, very often, wasted its human resources.

One reason why a President of the United States ought to travel throughout the country and become familiar with every State is that he has a great obligation to think about the days when he will no longer be President, to think about the next generation and the generation after that.

—Franklin D. Roosevelt,
in Arthur Bernon Tourtellot, *The Presidents on the Presidency.*

Kennedy's sense of his power and its limits illustrates the paradox of the modern Presidency, discussed at the start of this chapter. The core of the dilemma is that the technology of the nuclear age and the growth of government in a modern, industrial society have combined to concentrate great power in the hands of a Chief Executive in some policy areas while restricting his options in others. For example, the President's power to use military force without a declaration of war by Congress was demonstrated during the 1960s in Southeast Asia. In 1973, over President Nixon's veto, Congress enacted a law designed to recapture its war powers, but whether the legislation would effectively limit presidential war power had not been clearly demonstrated by the time President Reagan took office in 1981. Although, as President, Nixon was able to continue the war in Vietnam for five years and invade and bomb Cambodia with American forces, in the domestic sphere he could not get Congress to pass his plan to reform the welfare system.

A President was able to bring the nation to the brink of nuclear disaster, as in the Cuban missile crisis of 1962, or involve America in war, as in Southeast Asia, almost entirely by his own decisions and actions. Despite the war powers legislation and the new assertiveness of Congress in this area, the President's sheer military power, which he exercises as Commander in Chief of the armed forces, remains formidable. Yet the President may not be able to get an energy bill through Congress, reduce poverty, or cope with a lagging economy.

The Presidency is both an institution and a person. The *institution* is the office created by the Constitution, custom, cumulative federal law since 1789, and the gradual growth of formal and informal tools of presidential power. The *person* is a human being, powerful yet vulnerable, compassionate or vain, ordinary or extraordinary. To the institution, the President brings the imprint of his personality and style. Under the Twenty-second Amendment, the incumbent must normally change at least once every eight years. The Presidency is, then, both highly institutionalized and highly personal.

The Institution,
the Person

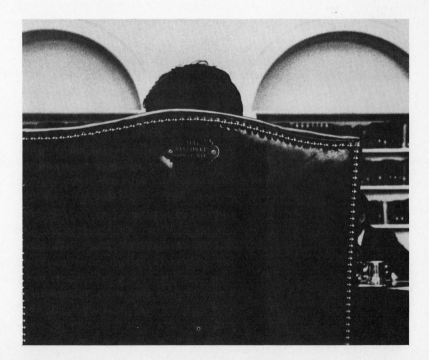

"The Presidency is both an institution
and a person . . ."

I can't make a damn thing out of this tax problem. I listen to one side and they seem right, and then God! I talk to the other side and they seem just as right, and there I am where I started. I know somewhere there is a book that would give me the truth, but hell, I couldn't read the book. . . . God, what a job!

—Warren G. Harding, in Richard F. Fenno, Jr., *The President's Cabinet.*

"We Never Once Thought of a King"

George Washington assumed the office feeling not unlike "a culprit who is going to the place of his execution." William Howard Taft thought it "the loneliest place in the world." Harry Truman declared that "being a President is like riding a tiger. A man has to keep on riding or be swallowed." Warren Harding thought the White House "a prison." Lyndon Johnson spoke of "the awesome power, and the immense fragility of executive authority," both of which he experienced. Jimmy Carter called it "the most difficult job, maybe, on earth."

The strands of power have come together in the person and the institution of the modern Presidency. When the President speaks to the nation, millions listen. His words are instantly transmitted around the globe by satellite and high-speed communications. When he pulls his beagle's ears, as Lyndon Johnson did, the bark of dog lovers is heard round the world. If he cancels a subscription to a newspaper, as John Kennedy did, a thousand thunderous editorials denounce him. Is his wife spending too much on her clothes? His kitten ill? His chef disloyal? Does he carry his own garment bag aboard the plane? Does he dye his hair? No detail in the life of a modern President (and these are real examples) escapes the eyes of the media, which provide such information to a public apparently hungry for more.

Public disclosure of intimate details of a President's life is not limited to the press, or to the literary endeavors of White House cooks, seamstresses, and bottle-washers. His own distinguished, high-level staff assistants may be secret diarists, scribbling away nights for the sake of posterity and the best seller lists. Indeed, Presidents themselves write books, not only for money but to give their own version of events and, they hope, to secure their place in history. Truman, Eisenhower, Johnson, Nixon, and Ford all published memoirs after they left the White House (in Nixon's case reportedly for a fee in excess of $2 million).

The intense public interest in the person and office of the President is a reflection of how the job of Chief Executive has become magnified in the twentieth century. The immense pressures on the human being who occupies the office of President have intensified because the institution of the Presidency has evolved and grown with the nation.

The Expanding Presidency

The framers of the Constitution who met at Philadelphia toiled in the greatest secrecy. No television cameras invaded their privacy in 1787. Yet even in that pre-electronic age, the Founding Fathers felt it necessary to issue a press release (their only one) to counteract rumors that were circulating around the country. The statement was leaked to the *Pennsylvania Herald* in August: "Tho' we cannot, affirmatively, tell you what we are doing; we can, negatively, tell you what we are not doing—we never once thought of a king."[9]

The men who made the American Revolution were, perhaps understandably, prejudiced against kings. At the same time, the difficulties encountered

---

[9] Carl Van Doren, *The Great Rehearsal* (New York: Viking Press, 1948), p. 145. Alexander Hamilton, however, did propose a virtual monarchy in the form of a lifetime Chief Executive, but his plan won no support.

under the Articles of Confederation had exposed the shortcomings of legislative government and demonstrated the need for a strong executive. But how strong?

James Wilson and Gouverneur Morris championed a single, powerful Chief Executive, and James Madison eventually adopted that view. Many of the framers considered legislatures to be dangerously radical; the blessings of liberty could best be enjoyed, they felt, if popular government was checked by a strong executive branch that could protect wealth, private property, and business. Support for a powerful, single President was by no means unanimous, however; some of the framers had specifically proposed a plural executive, and some wanted the President to be chosen by Congress.

Out of the debates emerged the basic structure of the Presidency as we know it today: a single President who headed one of three separate branches of government and was elected independently for a four-year term. The great authority given to the President by the framers was limited by the separation of powers among three branches of government, by the checks and balances engraved in the Constitution, by the federal system, and, in time, by other, informal controls generally unforeseen in 1787 — the rise of political parties and mass media, for example.

"I prefer to supervise the whole operations of the government myself . . . and this makes my duties very great," President James Polk wrote in his diary in 1848.[10]

So great had those duties become in the twentieth century that by fiscal 1981 the President presided over a federal budget of more than $615 billion and a bureaucracy of 2.9 million civilians and 2 million members of the armed forces. He would not have dreamed of attempting to "supervise the whole operations of the government" by himself.

Great crises and great Presidents have contributed to the growth of the Presidency since 1789. George Washington, Andrew Jackson, Abraham Lincoln, Theodore Roosevelt, Woodrow Wilson, and Franklin Roosevelt all placed their personal stamp on the Presidency. When a President strengthens and reshapes the institution, the change may endure even after he leaves. The modern Presidency, for example, is rooted in the style and approach of Franklin D. Roosevelt.

Although Presidents and events have played a decisive role in the development of the Presidency, several broad historical factors, discussed below, have combined to create a powerful Chief Executive today.

The Nuclear Age. The United States and the Soviet Union each possess nuclear missiles that could destroy the other country in half an hour; given the time factor, the President, rather than Congress, has of necessity become the one who must decide whether to use such hideous, and ultimately irrational, weapons. (As Clinton Rossiter noted, the next wartime President "may well be our last."[11]) The constitutional power of Congress to declare war has become eroded in the twentieth century by the power of the President to use nuclear weapons, to commit United States forces to meet sudden crises, and to fight so-called limited

The Growth
of the American Presidency

Franklin D. Roosevelt
influenced the modern
Presidency more than any
other Chief Executive.

[10] In Richard F. Fenno, Jr., *The President's Cabinet* (Cambridge, Mass.: Harvard University Press, 1959), p. 217.
[11] Clinton Rossiter, *The American Presidency,* rev. ed. (New York: Harcourt Brace Jovanovich, 1960), p. 25.

Of course I miss it. . . . President Nixon said to me, "How did you feel when you weren't President any more?" And I said, "I don't know whether you'll understand this now or not, but you certainly will later. I sat there on that platform and waited for you to stand up and raise your right hand and take the oath of office, and I think the most pleasant words . . . that ever came into my ears were 'So help me God' that you repeated after that oath. Because at that time I no longer had the fear that I was the man that could make the mistake of involving the world in war, that I was no longer the man that would have to carry the terrifying responsibility of protecting the lives of this country and maybe the entire world, unleashing the horrors of some of our great power if I felt that that was required. But that now I could ride back down that avenue, being concerned about what happened, being alarmed about what might happen, but just really knowing that I wasn't going to be the cause of it." . . . The real horror was to be sleeping soundly about three-thirty or four or five o'clock in the morning and have the telephone ring and the operator say, "Sorry to wake you, Mr. President," . . . there's just a second between the time the operator got me on the line until she could get . . . Mr. Bundy in the Situation Room, or maybe . . . Secretary McNamara. . . . And we went through the horrors of hell that thirty seconds or minute or two minutes. Had we hit a Russian ship? Had an accident occurred? We have another *Pueblo?* Someone made a mistake—were we at war? Well, those experiences are gone.

—Lyndon B. Johnson, Excerpts from a CBS Television News Special, "LBJ: Why I Chose Not to Run," December 27, 1969.

---

wars. As already noted, Congress sought to regain some of its control over the use of American military power and passed a war powers law in 1973. (See pp. 361–63 and Chapter 14.) But the President remains the dominant figure in responding to crisis with military force.

Foreign Affairs. The President, under the Constitution, has the prime responsibility for conducting the foreign affairs of the United States. From its isolationism before the Second World War, the United States emerged in the postwar period as one of the two major world powers. During the Eisenhower administration, when John Foster Dulles exercised a powerful influence as Secretary of State, the United States adhered to the principle of collective security to

"The question is, do we want to emphasize foreign policy to take the people's minds off domestic policy, or emphasize domestic policy to take the people's minds off foreign policy?"

Drawing by Dana Fradon
© 1979 The New Yorker Magazine, Inc.

"contain" communism and entered into a series of military alliances with other nations for this purpose. The wisdom of the role of the United States as a "world policeman" was seriously questioned in the 1960s and 1970s, when the United States became bogged down in the Vietnam war. By 1980, following the hostage crisis in Iran and Soviet intervention in Afghanistan, some of the post-Vietnam emphasis on détente and disarmament had given way to a greater concern over national security and military strength. And in that year the voters in the presidential election chose Ronald Reagan, who favored higher defense spending. Because the United States remains one of the two most powerful nations in the world, the President is inevitably a world leader as well as a national leader.

Domestic Affairs. The great increase in presidential power in recent decades has taken place in the domestic field as much as in foreign affairs. Roosevelt's New Deal, as Edward S. Corwin has pointed out, brought "social acceptance of the idea that government should be active and reformist, rather than simply protective of the established order of things."[12]

With the tremendous growth of government as manager, the President directs a huge bureaucracy. Modern government is expected to "solve" social problems, from racial discrimination to health care, and the President has become the chief problem solver. Although President Nixon cut back and dismantled some federal programs, stressed the role of individual self-help, and sought to channel more power to local communities, the federal budget increased substantially during his Presidency. President Ford attacked the federal bureaucracy during the 1976 campaign; but the budget and the number of persons on the federal payroll also went up during his period in office. Ronald Reagan promised in 1980 to reduce the role of the federal government and cut non-military spending. But any President's domestic responsibilities remain enormous, whatever his political philosophy about the role of the federal government.

The Mass Media. Television and the other news media have helped to magnify the person and the institution of the Presidency. All the major networks, newspapers, magazines, and wire services have correspondents assigned full time to covering the President. These "White House regulars" accompany the Chief Executive wherever he travels, sending out a steady flow of news about his activities.

When a President wants to talk to the people, the networks (whose stations are licensed by the federal government) customarily make available free prime time. Presidential news conferences are often televised live. People identify with a President they see so often on television; his style and personality help to shape the times and the national mood.

The Impossible Burden:
The Many Roles of the Chief Executive

During Ronald Reagan's first week in office, he conferred with congressional leaders, met several times with his cabinet, held a meeting of the National Security Council, telephoned the heads of state of six allied nations and talked

[12] Edward S. Corwin, *The President, Office and Powers 1787–1957* (New York: New York University Press, 1957), p. 311.

"Okay, bring in the new guy . . ."

Cartoon by Auth
© 1976 *The Philadelphia Inquirer*

with each, greeted the freed American hostages, who were newly returned from Iran. Even before his inauguration, he had crossed the border to meet with the President of Mexico.

The President is one individual but he fills many separate roles: Chief of State, Chief Executive, Commander in Chief, Chief Diplomat, and Chief Legislator. All these are required of him by the Constitution; in addition, as one scholar of the Presidency suggested, he is expected to be Chief of Party, Voice of the People, Protector of the Peace, Manager of Prosperity, and World Leader.[13] A modern President is expected to be all these things and more. But, of course, no human being can live up to such exalted expectations.

Moreover, it would be simplistic and misleading to think of the President as rapidly "changing hats" as he goes about filling these varied roles. Many of the presidential roles blend and overlap; some of the roles may collide with others. Being a vigorous party leader, for example, will often conflict with playing the role of Chief of State, of being President of all the people. For a President's roles, as Cronin has noted, "are not compartmentalized, unrelated functions, but rather a dynamic, seamless assortment of tasks and responsibilities."[14]

For purposes of analysis, however, it is convenient to separate out the principal roles of the President. When we do so, we see that the "awesome burden" has identifiable parts.

Chief of State

President Eisenhower
with Queen Elizabeth II

The President of the United States is the ceremonial and symbolic head of *state,* as well as head of *government.* In many countries, the two jobs are distinct; a figurehead King, Queen, or President is head of state, but the Premier or Prime Minister is head of government and exercises the real power. It is because the two functions are combined in the person of the American President that he finds himself declaring National Codfish Week or toasting the Grand Duchess of Luxembourg at a state dinner on the same day that he makes a vital foreign policy decision or vetoes a major bill sent to him by Congress.

The distinction between head of state and head of government may seem

---

[13] Rossiter, *The American Presidency,* pp. 16–41.
[14] Cronin, *The State of the Presidency,* p. 156.

trivial — of interest only to protocol officers and society columnists — but it is not. Much of the awe and mystery, the power and dignity that have surrounded the institution of the Presidency are due precisely to the fact that the President *is* more than a Prime Minister; he is a symbol of nationhood as well as a custodian of the people's power. In Theodore Roosevelt's famous phrase, he is almost both "a king and a prime minister."[15]

As noted earlier in this chapter, some critics of presidential power have argued that Presidents lose their perspective and their ability to make sound judgments because they are treated too much like monarchs and are isolated from the problems faced by ordinary citizens. In part, this may happen because a President is surrounded by the trappings of power — large staffs, private aircraft, and the Secret Service.

Because the Chief Executive is such a symbolic and familiar figure, when a President dies in office, people often react as though they have suffered a great personal loss. Even the radio announcers wept as they told of Franklin Roosevelt's death. After President Kennedy's assassination, the nation went through a period of mourning; 250,000 people braved cold weather to line up to pass his bier in the Capitol rotunda; 100,000,000 people watched the funeral on television. Social scientists studying the effect of the assassination on children and

[15] Letter to Lady Delamere, March 7, 1911.

As the train bearing the body of Franklin D. Roosevelt left Warm Springs, Chief Petty Officer Graham Jackson played "Going Home."

November 1963: President John F. Kennedy lies in state in the Capitol rotunda.

adults found definite physical and psychological effects.[16] The nation again experienced a sense of loss when two former Presidents, Harry Truman and Lyndon Johnson, died within a month of each other in December 1972 and January 1973.

Chief Executive

"The executive Power shall be vested in a President of the United States of America." So reads Article II of the Constitution, which also states: "he shall take Care that the Laws be faithfully executed."

Under this simply worded but powerful grant of executive authority, the President runs the executive branch of the government. As of fiscal 1981, the President headed a federal establishment with a total payroll of $72 billion. No executive in private industry has responsibilities that match the President's. The President receives $200,000 a year plus $50,000 in expenses (both taxable) and up to $100,000 in travel expenses (tax-free) as well as handsome retirement benefits, including a lifetime pension of $63,000 a year. There are few legal qualifications for the office; the Constitution requires only that the President be a "natural-born" citizen, at least thirty-five, and fourteen years a resident of the United States.[17]

Obviously, there would be more than enough work in the President's in-basket to keep him busy if he did nothing else but administer the government. And, in fact, Presidents do find themselves bogged down under a mountain of paper. Most Presidents work at night to try to keep up; the sight of Franklin Roosevelt, a polio victim, being wheeled to his office at night, preceded by wire baskets full of paper work, was a familiar one to White House aides during the New Deal era. President Eisenhower tried to solve the paper-work problem by ordering his staff to prepare memos no more than one page long. Lyndon Johnson took a swim and nap each afternoon, then began a second working day at 4 P.M., often summoning weary aides for conferences at the end of *their* working day.

Because administering the government is only one of six major presidential roles, the President cannot spend all of his time running the executive branch. He has a White House staff, other agencies in the Executive Office of the President, and his cabinet to help him. He tries to confine himself to *presidential* decisions, such as resolving major conflicts within the bureaucracy, or among his own advisers, and initiating and approving major programs and policies.

Beneath the President in the executive branch are the thirteen cabinet departments (as of January 1981) and about sixty major independent agencies, boards, and commissions. (See Figure 11-3, pp. 410–11.) These agencies are of two main types: *executive agencies* and *regulatory agencies*. The independent executive agencies are units of government under the President within the executive branch, but not part of a cabinet department. They are, therefore, "independent"

[16] For example, among adults, one study found that "the assassination generally evoked feelings similar to those felt at the death of a close friend or relative." Of a sample of the adult population, 43 percent said they did not feel like eating, 29 percent smoked more than usual, 53 percent cried, 48 percent had trouble sleeping, and 68 percent felt nervous and tense. Source: Paul B. Sheatsley and Jacob J. Feldman, "A National Survey on Public Reactions and Behavior," in Bradley S. Greenberg and Edwin B. Parker, eds., *The Kennedy Assassination and the American Public* (Stanford, Cal.: Stanford University Press, 1965), pp. 158, 168.

[17] A citizen born abroad of American parents might well be regarded as "natural-born." The question arose in 1968 because George Romney, a Republican hopeful, had been born in Mexico. The requirement of fourteen years' residence apparently does not mean that a President must have resided in the United States for fourteen successive years immediately prior to the election, since Herbert Hoover had not.

The Case of the White House Mouse

Little problems, like the White House mice, have proved as intractable as big ones. When a couple of mice scampered across the President's study one evening last spring, an alarm went out to the General Services Administration, housekeeper of Federal buildings. Some weeks later, another mouse climbed up inside a wall of the Oval Office and died. The President's office was bathed in the odor of dead mouse as Carter prepared to greet visiting Latin American dignitaries. An emergency call went out to G.S.A. But it refused to touch the matter. Officials insisted that they had exterminated all the "inside" mice in the White House and this errant mouse must have come from outside, and therefore was the responsibility of the Interior Department. Interior demurred, saying that the dead mouse was now inside the White House. President Carter summoned officials from both agencies to his desk and exploded: "I can't even get a damn mouse out of my office." Ultimately, it took an interagency task force to get rid of the mouse.

—*New York Times,* January 8, 1978.

---

of the departments, not of the President. The members of the major independent regulatory agencies are appointed by the President from both major parties to staggered, fixed terms but do not report to him. The regulatory agencies, which exercise quasi-judicial and quasi-legislative powers, are administratively independent of both the President and Congress (although politically independent of neither).

The neat organizational charts do not show the overlapping and intricate real-life relationships among the three branches of government. Nor do they give any hint of the difficulties a President faces in controlling his own executive branch and in making the bureaucracy carry out his decisions.

President Truman understood the problems that Eisenhower would have as an army general elected President: "He'll sit here," Truman would remark (tapping his desk for emphasis), "and he'll say, 'Do this! Do that!' *And nothing will happen.* Poor Ike—it won't be a bit like the army. He'll find it very frustrating."[18]

Despite his vast constitutional and extraconstitutional powers, the President is sometimes as much a victim of bureaucratic inertia as anyone else. "I sit here all day," Truman said, "trying to persuade people to do the things they ought to have sense enough to do without my persuading them.... That's all the powers of the President amount to."[19]

Richard Neustadt agrees with Truman that "Presidential *power* is the power to persuade."[20] In persuading people, however, the President can draw upon formidable resources, not the least of which is his power to appoint and remove officials. Under the Constitution, the President, "with the advice and consent of the Senate," appoints ambassadors, Supreme Court judges, and a total, under present law, of about 2500 upper-level federal officials. (The great bulk of the 2.9 million federal civilian employees are appointed by department heads through the civil service system.)

The Constitution does not specifically give the President the power to re-

A President Views His Power

Power? The only power I've got is nuclear—and I can't use that.

—Lyndon Johnson, quoted in Hugh Sidey, *A Very Personal Presidency.*

---

[18] In Richard E. Neustadt, *Presidential Power* (New York: Wiley, 1960), p. 9. (A second edition was published in 1976.)
[19] *Ibid.,* pp. 9–10.
[20] *Ibid.,* p. 10.

President Ford signing pardon of Richard Nixon

move government officials, but the Supreme Court has ruled that Congress cannot interfere with the President's right to fire officials whom he has appointed with Senate approval.[21] During Franklin Roosevelt's administration, the Court held that the President did *not* have the right to remove officials serving in administratively independent "quasi-legislative or quasi-judicial agencies."[22] Even though commissioners of regulatory agencies are thus theoretically immune from removal by presidential power, in practice, they may not be. When a scandal touched the chairman of the FCC in 1960, the incident embarrassed President Eisenhower; within a week the official resigned.

To the task of bureaucrat-in-chief, therefore, the President brings powers of persuasion that go beyond his formal, constitutional, and legal authority. By the nature of his job, he is the final decision maker in the executive branch. As the sign on Harry Truman's desk said: "The buck stops here."

The President also has the power to grant "reprieves and pardons for offenses against the United States," a power that seemed relatively unimportant in modern times until President Ford granted a pardon to his predecessor, Richard Nixon (who had appointed Ford Vice President). Ford noted that in the Watergate affair, the former President had "become liable to possible indictment and trial for offenses against the United States." Ford said such a trial would divide the country, and he pardoned Nixon for all crimes that he "has committed or may have committed" as President. Ford later testified under oath that, prior to taking office, he had not entered into any arrangement with Nixon to grant the pardon.

Commander in Chief

The "black box": during a visit to England by President Carter, his naval aide carried the locked briefcase containing the coded orders for nuclear war.

When President Kennedy died at Parkland Hospital in Dallas on November 22, 1963, an army warrant officer named Ira D. Gearhart, armed but dressed in civilian clothes, picked up a locked briefcase known as the "football," or "black box," and walked down a hospital corridor to a small room where President Lyndon Johnson was being guarded by Secret Service agents. The man who carries the "football" must be near whoever is the President. He guards "a national security portfolio of cryptographic orders the President would send his military chiefs to authorize the launching of nuclear missiles. The orders can be dispatched by telephone, teletype, or microwave radio."[23]

In effect, the warrant officer has custody of the "nuclear button," which is not a button, but a set of coded orders. That such a person and such machinery exist is a reminder of the fact that, regardless of his other duties, the President is at all times Commander in Chief of the armed forces of the United States.

Although a President normally delegates most of this authority to his generals and admirals, he is not required to do so. During the Whiskey Rebellion of 1794, President Washington personally led his troops into Pennsylvania. During the Civil War, Lincoln often visited the Army of the Potomac to instruct his generals. Franklin Roosevelt and Prime Minister Winston Churchill conferred on the major strategic decisions of the Second World War. Truman made the decisions to drop the atomic bomb on Japan in 1945 and to intervene in Korea

[21] *Myers* v. *United States,* 272 U.S. 52 (1926).
[22] *Humphrey's Executor* v. *United States.* 295 U.S. 602 (1935).
[23] Bob Horton, Associated Press Staff Writer, "The Job of Guarding the President's Code Box," *Washington Star,* November 21, 1965. See also William Manchester, *The Death of a President* (New York: Harper & Row, 1967), pp. 62, 321.

The Policymakers

in 1950. Kennedy authorized the Bay of Pigs invasion of Cuba by Cuban exiles armed and trained by the Central Intelligence Agency. Johnson personally approved bombing targets in Vietnam. President Nixon made the decision to send American troops into Cambodia in 1970, to bomb North Vietnam, and to bomb Cambodia in 1973.

The principle of *civilian supremacy* over the military is embodied in the clear constitutional power of the President as supreme commander of the armed forces. The principle was put to a severe test during the Korean war when General Douglas MacArthur repeatedly defied President Truman's orders. The hero of the Pacific theater during the Second World War, MacArthur enjoyed personal prestige to rival the President's and had a substantial political following of his own. Truman finally dismissed MacArthur in April 1951. In the most dramatic conflict in modern times between the military and the President, the President prevailed.

The Constitution declares that "Congress shall have Power . . . To declare War," but Congress has not done so since December 1941, when it declared war against Japan and Germany following the Japanese attack on Pearl Harbor.[24] In the intervening years the President has made the decision to go to war. By 1970, however, Congress was trying to regain some of its control over the war power. Congress repealed the Tonkin Gulf Resolution, which it had passed in 1964 to support President Johnson's Vietnam policy, and it restricted President Nixon's future use of American troops in Cambodia. Sentiment continued to grow in Congress to curb the President's power to wage undeclared war. In August 1973 Congress cut off funds for the bombing of Cambodia; it was the first time in the long war in Indochina that Congress had used its power of the purse to prevent military action by the President.

Later in 1973 Congress passed legislation to limit presidential war-making power. President Nixon vetoed the measure as an unconstitutional restraint on his power as Commander in Chief. But Congress overrode the President's veto, and the War Powers Resolution became law. The measure provided:

October 1950: President Truman meets General MacArthur on Wake Island.

[24] Congress has declared war five times: in the War of 1812, the Mexican War, the Spanish-American War, the First World War, and the Second World War. It did not declare war in Korea or Vietnam.

1. Within 48 hours after committing armed forces to combat abroad, the President must report to Congress in writing, explaining the circumstances and scope of his actions.

2. Use of American forces in combat would have to end in 60 days unless Congress authorized a longer period, but the deadline could be extended for another 30 days if the President certified that the time was necessary for the safe withdrawal of the forces.

3. Within the 60- or 90-day period, Congress could order an immediate withdrawal of American forces by adopting a concurrent resolution — which is not subject to a presidential veto.

Some members of Congress and other persons who were against the expansion of presidential war power opposed the bill. They argued that the measure actually increased the President's power to make war by giving congressional authorization for "60-day wars." But the vote to override Nixon's veto indicated that most members of the House and Senate disagreed; for them, the moment had come to attempt to reassert congressional authority over the combat use of American military power. In addition, Congress in 1974 required the CIA to report to it about covert operations, and in 1976 Congress enacted a law that gave it the right to veto arms sales by the executive branch of $7 million or more.

Up to the beginning of the Reagan administration, however, the War Powers Resolution had not clearly succeeded in restricting presidential military power. President Nixon did not report to Congress under the War Powers Resolution when twenty-two U.S. helicopters were sent to rescue Americans from Cyprus during disorders on the island in July 1974. In 1975 President Ford used U.S. troops on three occasions to evacuate Americans and others from Cambodia and South Vietnam, and he sent in the Marines to recapture the American merchant ship *Mayagüez* in the Gulf of Siam. Ford reported to Congress in each case, but said he had acted under his constitutional powers as President and Commander in Chief. He thus clearly implied that the War Powers Resolution did not apply in each of the cases and that his reports to Congress were a matter of courtesy rather than a legal requirement.

Ford did not report to Congress when a U.S. task force was stationed near Lebanon in 1976 and unarmed American military personnel twice went ashore to rescue Americans and others.[25] President Carter authorized an airlift of other nations' troops to Shaba province in Zaire during fighting in that African nation in 1977, but he did not report to Congress.[26] In 1980 Carter did report to Congress the ill-fated attempt to rescue the American hostages in Iran. But he, too, maintained he had acted within his powers as President. And Carter implied he was not required to make the report.[27] Thus, during the Nixon, Ford, and Carter administrations, Presidents reported a total of five times out of nine instances in which some type of American military intervention had taken place.

The "military-industrial complex" — the term often used to describe the ties between the military establishment and the defense-aerospace industry — is another limit on the President's power as Commander in Chief. For example, a

[25] Pat M. Holt, *The War Powers Resolution: The Role of Congress in U.S. Armed Intervention* (Washington, D.C.: American Enterprise Institute for Public Policy Research, 1978), pp. 19–20.

[26] Thomas M. Franck and Edward Weisband, *Foreign Policy by Congress* (New York: Oxford University Press, 1979), pp. 71–72.

[27] *Weekly Compilation of Presidential Documents*, May 5, 1980, pp. 777–79.

President Ford on the War Powers Resolution

President Ford, soon after leaving office, revealed his genuine disdain of the resolution. Ford told a University of Kentucky audience on April 11, 1977: "The United States was involved in six military crises during my presidency: The evacuation of U. S. citizens and refugees from DaNang, Phnom Penh, and Saigon in the Spring of 1975, the rescue of the *Mayagüez* in May 1975, and the two evacuation operations in Lebanon in June 1976. In none of those instances did I believe the War Powers Resolution applied. . . . I did not concede that the resolution itself was legally binding on the President on constitutional grounds."

—*Inquiry*, June 26, 1978.

"I knew from the start," Johnson told me in 1970, describing the early weeks of 1965, "that I was bound to be crucified either way I moved. If I left the woman I really loved—the Great Society—in order to get involved with that bitch of a war on the other side of the world, then I would lose everything at home. All my programs. All my hopes to feed the hungry and shelter the homeless. All my dreams to provide education and medical care to the browns and blacks and the lame and the poor. But if I left that war and let the Communists take over South Vietnam, then I would be seen as a coward and my nation would be seen as an appeaser and we would find it impossible to accomplish anything for anybody anywhere on the entire globe.

"Oh, I could see it coming all right. History provided too many cases where the sound of the bugle put an immediate end to the hopes and dreams of the best reformers."

—Lyndon Johnson, quoted in Doris Kearns, *Lyndon Johnson and the American Dream.*

President may find it difficult to cancel production of a fighter plane, a bomber, an aircraft carrier, or some other weapons system that enjoys the strong support of the Joint Chiefs of Staff, Congress, and private industry.

Despite these limits, Presidents have claimed and exercised formidable war powers during emergencies. In the ten weeks after the fall of Fort Sumter in April 1861, Lincoln called out the militia, spent $2 million without authorization by Congress, blockaded Southern ports, and suspended the writ of habeas corpus in certain areas. Lincoln declared: "I felt that measures otherwise unconstitutional might become lawful by becoming indispensable to the preservation of the Constitution through the preservation of the nation. Right or wrong, I assumed this ground and now avow it."[28]

During the Second World War, Franklin Roosevelt exercised extraordinary powers over food rationing and the economy, only partly with congressional authorization. And in 1942, with the consent of Congress, he permitted the forced removal of 112,000 persons of Japanese descent—most of them native-born citizens of the United States—from California and other Western states to camps called "relocation centers" in the interior of the country.

During the Korean war, Truman seized the steel mills in the face of a strike threat, but the Supreme Court ruled he had no constitutional right to do so, even as Commander in Chief.[29] President Johnson expanded American forces in Vietnam after Congress passed the Tonkin Gulf Resolution, empowering the President to take "all necessary measures" in Southeast Asia. The President contended, however, that he did not need congressional approval to fight the war in Vietnam.

"I make American foreign policy," President Truman declared in 1948. By and large, Presidents do make foreign policy; that is, they direct the relations of the United States with the other nations of the world. The Constitution does not

Chief Diplomat

[28] In Arthur Bernon Tourtellot, *The Presidents on the Presidency* (Garden City, N. Y.: Doubleday, 1964), p. 311.
[29] *Youngstown Sheet and Tube Co.* v. *Sawyer,* 343 U.S. 579 (1952).

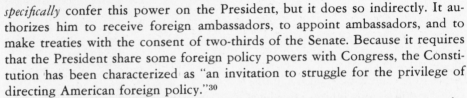

"Presidents do make foreign policy."
British Prime Minister Winston
Churchill, President Truman, and
Soviet Premier Stalin at Potsdam, 1945

specifically confer this power on the President, but it does so indirectly. It authorizes him to receive foreign ambassadors, to appoint ambassadors, and to make treaties with the consent of two-thirds of the Senate. Because it requires that the President share some foreign policy powers with Congress, the Constitution has been characterized as "an invitation to struggle for the privilege of directing American foreign policy."[30]

In this struggle the President usually enjoys the advantage. Because the State Department, the Pentagon, and the CIA report to him as part of the executive branch, the President—or so it is often assumed—has more information about foreign affairs available to him than do members of Congress. But senators and representatives also have sources of information—official briefings, background memoranda from the Library of Congress, data from the Congressional Budget Office, unofficial "leaks" from within the bureaucracy, and friends in the press and the universities. A President, therefore, does not have a monopoly of information. Much of the information he does receive is conflicting, because it represents different viewpoints within the bureaucracy; and even with the best intelligence reports, a President may make decisions that prove to be misguided. Nevertheless, the information that flows in daily is a substantial source of power for the President.

Those who lack the information that the President has, or is presumed to have, including senators and representatives, find it difficult to challenge the President's actions. Often, at least in the short run, a foreign policy crisis may increase the public's support of the President's actions. This was true, for example, for President Carter after Iranian militants seized American hostages. (See Figure 10-1.) Over a period of time, however, public opinion can change and Congress can chip away at a President's power in foreign affairs. In the mid-1960s, for example, during the height of the Vietnam war, the Senate Foreign Relations Committee under Chairman J. William Fulbright strongly criticized Johnson's war policies. The committee held a series of televised hearings that aired the Vietnam issue and may have helped to turn the tide of public opinion against the war.

The President has sole power to negotiate and sign treaties. The Senate may block a treaty by refusing to approve it, but it seldom does so. In 1920,

"The information that flows in daily is a substantial source of power for the President."

[30] Corwin, *The President, Office and Powers 1787–1957,* p. 171.

364

The Policymakers

The Iranian Crisis and President Carter's Popularity Rating

Figure 10–1

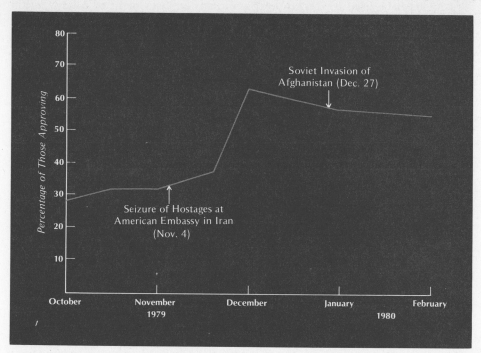

When the American hostages were seized in Iran, President Carter's popularity rose 29 points from 32 to 61—the largest increase since the Gallup poll began measuring presidential popularity.
Source: The Gallup poll in Congressional Quarterly, *Weekly Report,* March 15, 1980, p. 726.

however, it did refuse to ratify the Treaty of Versailles and its provision for United States membership in the League of Nations. Sometimes a President does not submit a treaty to the Senate because he knows it will not be approved; or he may modify the treaty to meet Senate opposition. In 1977 President Carter submitted two treaties to the Senate turning over the Panama Canal to Panama in the year 2000. The Senate finally approved the treaties in 1978, but only after months of controversy.

Since 1900 *executive agreements,* which do not require Senate approval, have been employed by the President in the conduct of foreign affairs more often than treaties. Some executive agreements are made by the President with the prior approval of Congress. For example, in the Trade Act of 1974, Congress restored the President's power to negotiate tariff agreements with other countries. And sometimes, to gain political support, a President will submit an executive agreement to Congress after it is signed, although he is not legally required to do so.

Because a President can sign an executive agreement with another nation without the constitutional necessity of going to the Senate, the use of this device has increased enormously. This has been particularly true since the Second World War, as the United States' role in international affairs has expanded. Today, in a single year, a President may sign several hundred executive agreements.

The President also has sole power to recognize or not recognize foreign governments. The United States did not recognize the Soviet Union until No-

President Reagan with Prime Minister Thatcher of England, 1981

365

The President

vember 1933, sixteen years after the Russian Revolution. Since Wilson's day, Presidents have used diplomatic recognition as an instrument of American foreign policy. President Nixon's historic journey to Peking early in 1972 marked the start of diplomatic contacts between the United States and the People's Republic of China. President Carter recognized China in 1979, and the two countries opened full diplomatic relations.

In acting as Chief Diplomat, the President, as Commander in Chief, can back up his diplomacy with military power. Both the arrows and the olive branch depicted in the presidential seal are available to him, a good example of how presidential roles overlap.

Chief Legislator

"He shall from time to time give to the Congress Information of the State of the Union, and recommend to their Consideration such Measures as he shall judge necessary and expedient." With this statement in Article II, "the Constitution puts the President right square into the legislative business," as President Eisenhower observed at a 1959 press conference.

Today, Presidents often use their televised State of the Union address, delivered to a joint session of Congress in January, as a public platform to unveil their annual legislative program. The details of proposed legislation are then filled in through a series of special presidential messages sent to Capitol Hill in the months that follow.

This was not always the case. Active presidential participation in the legislative process is a twentieth-century phenomenon, and the practice of Presidents sending a comprehensive legislative package to Congress developed only after the Second World War during the Truman administration.[31]

The success of the President's role as Chief Legislator depends on the cooperation of Congress. A Republican President faced with a Democratic House (as in Reagan's case when he took office in 1981), or a Democratic President blocked by a coalition of Republicans and Southern Democrats (as in Kennedy's case), may find his role as Chief Legislator frustrating. As President Kennedy observed ruefully: "It is very easy to defeat a bill in the Congress. It is much more difficult to pass one. . . . They are two separate offices and two separate powers, the Congress and the Presidency. There is bound to be conflict."[32]

The conflict at times revolves around the doctrine of *executive privilege.* This doctrine is nowhere explicitly stated in the Constitution but rests on the separation of powers of the three branches of the federal government. By invoking executive privilege, Presidents have claimed the inherent right to withhold information from Congress and the judiciary. Congress in turn has argued that its legislative powers include the right to make inquiries and investigations of the executive branch and to obtain all necessary information from the President and his administration. Usually conflicts over executive privilege arise when a congressional committee demands documents from, or testimony by, presidential assistants.

As the Watergate scandal unfolded during the Nixon administration, the

[31] Richard E. Neustadt, "Presidency and Legislation: Planning the President's Program," *American Political Science Review,* Vol. 49 (December 1955), p. 981.
[32] "After Two Years—a Conversation With the President," p. 894.

President was accused by his former counsel of participating in an illegal plot to cover up the bugging of the Democratic party's headquarters. Nixon's tapes of his own conversations became the crucial evidence. Both a Senate committee and the Watergate special prosecutor, Archibald Cox, went into federal court in an effort to force the President to give up certain tapes. Nixon refused at first, and even fired Cox. But then he reversed course and agreed to turn over some of the tapes to a federal court. It soon developed, however, that two subpoenaed tapes could not be produced, and an eighteen-and-a-half-minute segment of a third had apparently been erased. Eventually, the new Watergate special prosecutor, Leon Jaworski, demanded the tapes of sixty-four White House conversations for use in the Watergate cover-up trial, and the issue went to the United States Supreme Court. In ruling 8–0 that Nixon must surrender his tapes, the Court for the first time recognized the doctrine of executive privilege—but declared that the right of the President to keep some matters confidential must yield to the need for evidence in a criminal trial.[33]

The President is also chief legislator . . .

Every President has staff assistants in charge of legislative liaison. Their job is to pressure Congress to pass the President's program. The senator or representative who wants the administration to approve a new federal building, or dam, or public works project in his state or district may discover that the price is his vote on a bill that the President wants passed. There are other, more subtle pressures. When a senator opposes a President's foreign policies, he may find he is no longer being invited to White House social functions. Often, on an important measure, the President himself takes charge of the "arm twisting"—telephoning members of Congress in their offices or inviting them to the White House for a chat about the merits of his program.

On the other hand, George C. Edwards III has argued, "while legislative skills may at times gain support for presidential policies, this is not typical." Examining the various resources available to a President, Edwards concluded that a Chief Executive "has relatively little influence to wield over Congress."[34]

As Chief Legislator, however, the President is not limited entirely to the arts of persuasion. He has an important constitutional weapon in the *veto*. The President, if he approves a bill, may sign it—often in front of news photographers and with much fanfare and handing out of pens. If he disapproves, however, he may veto the bill and return it with his objections to the branch of Congress in which it originated. By a vote of two-thirds of each house, Congress may pass the bill over the President's veto. If the President does not sign or veto a bill within ten working days after he receives it, the measure becomes law without his signature. If Congress adjourns during this ten-day period, the President can exercise his *pocket veto* and kill the bill by taking no action. But the Constitution was unclear on whether a President could pocket veto a bill anytime Congress was in recess. During the 1970s, Senator Edward M. Kennedy successfully challenged in court three pocket vetoes by Presidents Nixon and Ford. The court rulings suggested that a President may not pocket veto legislation when Congress is in recess but only when it adjourns for good at the end of the second session of a Congress. Except for joint resolutions, which are the same as bills,

---

[33] *United States* v. *Nixon,* 418 U.S. 683 (1974).
[34] George C. Edwards III, *Presidential Influence in Congress* (San Francisco: W. H. Freeman, 1980), pp. 10, 205.

Presidential Vetoes, 1789–1980

Table 10–1

	Regular Vetoes	Pocket Vetoes	Total Vetoes	Vetoes Overridden
Washington	2	—	2	—
Madison	5	2	7	—
Monroe	1	—	1	—
Jackson	5	7	12	—
Tyler	6	3	9	1
Polk	2	1	3	—
Pierce	9	—	9	5
Buchanan	4	3	7	—
Lincoln	2	4	6	—
A. Johnson	21	8	29	15
Grant	45	49	94	4
Hayes	12	1	13	1
Arthur	4	8	12	1
Cleveland	304	109	413	2
Harrison	19	25	44	1
Cleveland	43	127	170	5
McKinley	6	36	42	—
T. Roosevelt	42	40	82	1
Taft	30	9	39	1
Wilson	33	11	44	6
Harding	5	1	6	—
Coolidge	20	30	50	4
Hoover	21	16	37	3
F. Roosevelt	372	261	633	9
Truman	180	70	250	12
Eisenhower	73	108	181	2
Kennedy	12	9	21	—
L. Johnson	16	14	30	—
Nixon	24	19	43	5
Ford	44	22	66	12
Carter	13	18	31	2
Total	1375	1011	2386	92

Source: Senate Library, *Presidential Vetoes* (U.S. Government Printing Office, 1969), p. 199. Data for L. Johnson from *Congressional Quarterly Almanac, 1968* (Washington, D.C.: Congressional Quarterly Service, 1968), p. 23. Data for Nixon, Ford, and Carter from the White House Records Office.

resolutions of Congress do not require presidential action since they are expressions of sentiment, not law.[35]

Because Congress normally finds it difficult to override a presidential veto, merely the threat of a veto is often enough to force Congress to tailor a bill to conform to administration wishes. Only about 4 percent of presidential vetoes have been overriden by Congress. (See Table 10-1.)

The presidential veto power is limited by the fact that unlike the governors of most states, the President does not possess the *item veto*, the power to disapprove particular parts of a bill. As a result, Congress is encouraged to pass *riders*, provisions tacked on to a piece of legislation that are not relevant to the bill. Sponsors of riders know that the President must swallow the legislation whole or veto the entire bill—he cannot veto just the rider.

[35] The War Powers Resolution of 1973 is an example of a law enacted in the form of a joint resolution.

Since the 1920s, until Congress legislated against the practice in 1974, modern Presidents at times employed another weapon in dealing with Congress: *impoundment* of funds. The Constitution provides that Congress shall appropriate funds to run the government, but it does not specifically say that the President must spend them. And Presidents have periodically refused to spend money for programs they have opposed. In the Congressional Budget Act of 1974, however, Congress required the President to spend appropriated funds.

As Chief Legislator, the President may call Congress back into session. He may also adjourn Congress if the House and the Senate should disagree about when to adjourn, although no President has exercised this constitutional power.

The Supreme Court has held that Congress may not delegate legislative authority to the President, but Congress has in some cases passed legislation setting broad guidelines within which the President may act. For example, under such laws the President may be authorized to reduce tariffs. And since 1939 Congress has periodically passed a series of Reorganization Acts that permit the President to restructure federal agencies under plans that he must submit to Congress. Unless Congress *disapproves* the plans within sixty days, they go into effect. In 1980 presidential reorganization authority was renewed again through April of 1981.

The President's real ability to persuade Congress often rests on his personal popularity rather than on his formal or informal powers. The veto, arm twisting, threats to withhold a public works project, and social ostracism of a representative or senator are, over the long run, less important than the ability of a President to enlist public support for his programs and the extent of his prestige with both Congress and the electorate.

Chief of Party

"No President, it seems to me, can escape politics," John Kennedy said in 1960 when he sought the Presidency. "He has not only been chosen by the Nation—he has been chosen by his party."[36]

Not every President has filled the role of party chief with the same enthusiasm that Kennedy brought to it. President Eisenhower, a career army officer for most of his life, displayed a reluctance to engage in the rough and tumble of politics. As he told a press conference in 1955: "In the general derogatory sense . . . I do not like politics . . . the word 'politics' as you use it, I think the answer to that one, would be, no. I have no great liking for that."[37]

For many months in 1980, President Carter declined to campaign actively for re-election, claiming that the hostage crisis in Iran took precedence over his political duties and made it necessary for him to remain in the White House. "I am not going to resume business as usual as a partisan campaigner out on the campaign trail until our hostages are back here, free and at home," Carter declared.[38] Carter thus attempted to adopt a presidential, "above politics" stance. But when, on April 30, Carter announced that the country's foreign and domestic problems "are manageable enough now for me to leave the White House," his statement brought hoots of disbelief from his critics.[39]

The President is chief of his political party.

[36] *Congressional Record,* January 18, 1960, pp. 710–12.
[37] Neustadt, *Presidential Power,* p. 166.
[38] *Weekly Compilation of Presidential Documents,* February 13, 1980, p. 310.
[39] See Dom Bonafede, "Who's He Trying to Kid?" *National Journal,* May 10, 1980, p. 781.

Whether or not a President enjoys his partisan role, he is the chief of his party. The machinery of the national committee reports to him; he can install his own choice as national chairman; he can usually demand his party's renomination and stage-manage the convention that acclaims him. Since his success as Chief Legislator depends to a considerable degree on the political makeup of Congress, he may find it to his advantage to campaign for congressional candidates in off-year elections.

Given the decentralized nature of American political parties, a President's influence may not extend to state and local party organizations in every case. Nor does it prevail at all times with members of his party in Congress. In fact, his own leaders in Congress may not always bow to his political wisdom or his policy wishes. A dramatic example occurred in 1973, when Hugh Scott of Pennsylvania, the Senate Republican leader, voted for the Senate bill limiting presidential war powers, even though President Nixon had threatened to veto the measure and did.

When a President makes decisions, he is, in the broadest sense, engaging in politics. A successful President must lead and gauge public opinion, he must be sensitive to change, and he must have a sure sense of the limits of the possible. All of these are *political* skills. As Chief of Party, the President is also the nation's Number 1 professional politician. And, as Neustadt has suggested, "The Presidency is no place for amateurs."[40]

The President, it must be emphasized again, fills all of these various presidential roles at once. The powers and duties of his office are not divisible. The roles conflict and overlap; and in performing one role, the President may incur political costs that make it more difficult for him to perform another. In short, the Presidency is a balancing act.

In addition to these basic roles, Americans expect the President to take on many other roles. In the event of a major civil disturbance, he is expected to act as a policeman and restore domestic tranquility. As the manager of the economy, he is expected to prevent a recession, ensure prosperity, and hold down the cost of butter and eggs. He is expected to set an example in his personal life — and woe unto the President who drives too fast or is photographed too often with a highball glass in his hand. He is expected to be a teacher, to educate the people about great public issues. In some mysterious way, the President is expected to speak for all the people and to give voice to their deepest aspirations and ideals. "The Presidency," Franklin Roosevelt said, "is not merely an administrative office. That is the least of it. It is pre-eminently a place of moral leadership."[41]

The Tools of Presidential Power

In the exercise of power, the President of the United States has available to him a formidable array of tools, money, and manpower. In ever widening circles, this last category includes the White House staff (his own secretaries and advisers), the Executive Office of the President (a conglomerate of presidential substaffs), the Vice President, the cabinet, the thirteen cabinet departments, the many other

[40] Neustadt, *Presidential Power,* p. 180.
[41] Rossiter, *The American Presidency,* p. 148.

agencies of the executive branch, and the 4.9 million employees of the federal bureaucracy and the military.

He has almost unlimited personal resources as well. When President Johnson had reviewed the Marines in California on one occasion and was walking back to a helicopter, he was stopped by an officer who pointed to another helicopter and said, "That's your helicopter over there, sir." Johnson replied, "Son, they are all my helicopters."[42]

When the President travels, he has at his disposal not only helicopters, but a fleet of jets; aboard *Air Force One,* he can communicate with his aides or with the military anywhere in the world. If he flies to Kansas City to deliver a speech, a special switchboard, manned by a Pentagon communication unit that travels with the President, connects him with the White House.

In addition to the formal machinery of government at the President's command, he has other, informal resources—his reputation, his personality and style, his ability to arouse public opinion, his political party, and his informal advisers and friends.

As one leading presidential scholar has warned, however, listing the President's cabinet and all the other panels, staffs, and informal advisers that serve him might create the impression that a President "must have just about all the inside information and good advice anyone could want." One might even conclude that a President "can both set and shape the directions of public policy and can see to it that these policies *work as intended.*"[43] Yet, that is often not the case. As we have already seen, there are limitations on presidential power at almost every turn. Indeed, one of the measures of his power is how well he can use the tools at his command.

President Reagan confers with members of his White House staff.

The President, the Vice President, and the officials who run the executive departments of the government constitute the cabinet. The Constitution speaks of "the principal Officer in each of the executive Departments" and of "Heads of Departments." The Twenty-fifth Amendment, ratified in 1967, allows for the possibility of the department heads acting as a group in case of presidential disability. But the cabinet as an organized body is nowhere specifically provided for by law or in the Constitution.

The President, Richard F. Fenno points out, "is not required by law to form a Cabinet or to keep one," and the cabinet has become "institutionalized by usage

The Cabinet

---

[42] Hugh Sidey, *A Very Personal Presidency* (New York: Atheneum, 1968), p. 98.
[43] Cronin, *The State of the Presidency,* p. 80.

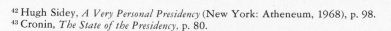

President Reagan meets with members of his cabinet.

Cabinet meetings are normally secret, but in 1978 the *Nation* magazine somehow obtained and printed excerpts from the minutes of several cabinet meetings held during the Carter administration. The secret minutes suggested that the President and other members of the Carter cabinet often commented on press reports about themselves:

April 25, 1977: The President said that he regretted missing Dr. Schlesinger on *Face the Nation* yesterday, but he had watched the energy industry representatives on *Meet the Press*.

June 13: The President described a recent television show by Bill Moyers on CIA operations. . . .

July 11: Dr. Brzezinski noted a good editorial in Sunday's *New York Times* on U.S./Soviet relations. . . .

August 1: The President expressed his concern about recent leaks to the press regarding specific discussions at Cabinet meetings. He urged Cabinet members and White House staff *not* to characterize to the press what he and others say during the Cabinet meetings. . . .

August 1: The President said that some weekly summaries submitted by Cabinet members are superb, while others contain unnecessary information about travel plans, speeches and related items. . . . He noted that he will not complain about the brevity of reports. . . .

August 29: Mr. Blumenthal asked whether press reports that the new leadership in China is focusing more on economic development than on ideology were true. Mr. Vance said that it is true. . . . The President said that he is pleased that three Cabinet members appeared on Sunday television talk shows.

March 6: The President noted that there was a good article today in the *New York Times* on the Middle East. . . . Mr. Blumenthal said that today's *New York Times* editorial on the loan to New York City is also excellent.

— *The Nation*, September 30, 1978.

alone."[44] Perhaps because the cabinet is entirely a creature of custom, it is a relatively weak institution. The weakness of the cabinet under a strong President is often illustrated by the story of how Lincoln counted when the entire cabinet was opposed to him: "Seven nays, one aye — the ayes have it."

In any case, a cabinet member may not be competent to discuss problems of a general nature, for "beyond his immediate bailiwick, he may not be capable of adding anything to the group conference."[45] For this reason, President Kennedy thought that cabinet meetings were "a waste of time."[46]

Modern Presidents have made varied use of the cabinet. Lyndon Johnson met regularly with his cabinet, but the conduct of the war in Vietnam was normally discussed not in the cabinet, but at regular Tuesday luncheon meetings of the President and selected officials. Nixon sought, only briefly, to revitalize the cabinet as a formal advisory body but seldom held cabinet meetings in his second term. President Ford tried to restore the cabinet to greater influence and held frequent cabinet meetings. Carter met with his cabinet more frequently than any President since Eisenhower. However, in one tumultuous week in 1979, he fired or accepted the resignations of five cabinet members. The shakeup brought considerable criticism of the President. When Ronald Reagan moved into the White House in 1981, there was much speculation that he would attempt to make even greater formal use of the cabinet.

Although the cabinet is often considered to be a device to assist the Presi-

[44] Fenno, *The President's Cabinet*, p. 19.
[45] *Ibid.*, p. 137.
[46] "Conversation Between President Kennedy and NBC Correspondent Ray Scherer," broadcast over NBC television network, April 11, 1961, Stenographic Transcript, p. 17.

The President's Cabinet

Table 10–2

The Executive Departments in Order of Formation*	
State	1789
Treasury	1789
Interior	1849
Justice†	1870
Agriculture‡	1889
Commerce§	1913
Labor§	1913
Defense‖	1947
Housing and Urban Development	1965
Transportation	1966
Energy	1977
Education	1979
Health and Human Services¶	1979

* As of January 1981. The office of Postmaster General, created in 1789, received cabinet rank in 1829 and was made a cabinet department in 1872. In 1970 Congress abolished the Post Office as a cabinet department and replaced it with the United States Postal Service, an independent federal agency.

† The office of Attorney General, created in 1789, became the Department of Justice in 1870.

‡ Originally created in 1862 and elevated to a cabinet department in 1889.

§ The Department of Commerce and Labor, created in 1903, was divided into two separate departments in 1913.

‖ The Department of War (the Army), created in 1789, and the Department of the Navy, created in 1798, were consolidated along with the air force under the Department of Defense in 1949.

¶ Originally created as the Department of Health, Education, and Welfare in 1953, it was divided into two separate cabinet departments in 1979.

dent, it also limits his power to some extent. "The members of the Cabinet," Vice President Charles G. Dawes said, "are a President's natural enemies."[47] In part, this is because cabinet members after a time tend to adopt the parochial view of their own departments. They may become narrow advocates of the programs and needs of their bureaucracies, competing with other cabinet members for bigger budgets and presidential favor. As Fenno has noted, a cabinet member's "formal responsibilities extend both upward toward the President and downward toward his own department."[48]

Immediately after the 1980 election, Ronald Reagan appointed James A. Baker III, chief of staff at the White House and Edwin Meese III, counselor to the President with cabinet rank. The announcements signaled to official Washington that Baker and Meese would probably become two of the most powerful individuals in the capital during the Reagan administration.

Modern Presidents depend upon large staffs. And great power is often wielded by those who surround the President, some of whom rise from relative obscurity to great influence. Wilson had his Colonel House, Franklin Roosevelt

The White House Staff

Edwin Meese III and
James A. Baker III

[47] Neustadt, *Presidential Power*, p. 39.
[48] Fenno, *The President's Cabinet*, p. 218.

his Harry Hopkins, Eisenhower his Sherman Adams, Johnson his Bill Moyers, and Richard Nixon his H. R. (Bob) Haldeman and John D. Ehrlichman—both of whom went to jail in the Watergate scandal. Jimmy Carter's aide, Hamilton Jordan, became a powerful figure in the White House. All modern Presidents have come to rely on their advisers, and in every case, some aides have emerged as more influential than others.

The power of the President's assistants, however, flows from their position as extensions of the President. Seldom possessing any political prestige or constituency of their own, they depend entirely on staying in the President's good graces for their survival. Their power is derivative, though nonetheless real—it is not uncommon in the White House to see a cabinet member waiting to confer with a member of the President's staff.

In recent administrations, the President's assistant for national security affairs has often taken a central role in foreign policy formation and crisis management. With access to the President and the White House "Situation Room," the downstairs office into which all military, intelligence, and diplomatic information flows, the "man in the basement" may emerge as a powerful rival to the Secretary of State. Henry A. Kissinger took the post in the Nixon administration and quickly emerged as the most powerful White House adviser in the field of foreign affairs, overshadowing Secretary of State William P. Rogers. Eventually, Kissinger himself was named Secretary of State by Nixon.[49] President Ford retained Kissinger as Secretary of State but required him to relinquish the White House post. President Carter named Zbigniew Brzezinski of Columbia University as White House national security adviser. Brzezinski, too, overshadowed Cyrus Vance and Edmund Muskie, both of whom served under Carter as Secretary of State.

The members of the President's staff fill a variety of functions that are essential to presidential decision making. Some act as gatekeepers and guardians of the President's time. Others deal almost exclusively with Congress. Still others serve as links with the executive departments and agencies, channeling problems and conflicts among the departments to the President. Some advise the President on political questions, patronage, and appointments. Others may write his speeches. The press secretary issues presidential announcements on matters large and small and fences with correspondents at twice-daily press briefings.

Presidents use their staffs differently. Eisenhower had a tight, formal system, with Adams, as chief of staff, screening all problems and deciding what the President should see. Kennedy favored a less structured arrangement, regarding his staff as "a wheel and a series of spokes" with himself in the center.[50]

The Office of Personnel Management in fiscal 1981 listed 404 persons under "The White House Office," with a budget of $20.5 million. Of these presidential staff members, perhaps fewer than a dozen occupied top-ranking positions of policy influence. Inevitably, the Chief Executive's vision, to a degree, is filtered through the eyes of his assistants. An Eisenhower or a Nixon, with a rigid staff system, may become isolated in the White House. A Lyndon Johnson, with an overpowering, demanding personality, may surround himself with deferential yes-men. In short, the President's staff may not let him hear enough, or it may tell him only what he wants to hear.

"Presidents use their staffs differently."

[49] In a new departure, Nixon also permitted Kissinger to keep his title as assistant to the President for national security.

[50] "Conversation Between President Kennedy and NBC Correspondent Ray Scherer," p. 3.

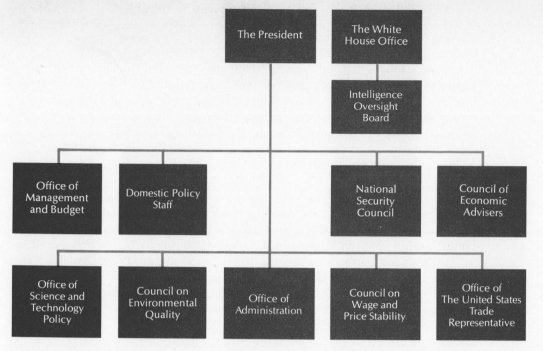

Executive Office of the President, 1980

Figure 10–2

Source: *United States Government Manual: 1980–1981* (Washington, D.C.: U.S. Government Printing Office, 1980). President Reagan took steps to dismantle the Council on Wage and Price Stability in 1981.

The White House staff is only a small part of the huge presidential establishment that has burgeoned since Franklin D. Roosevelt's day. Under the umbrella of the Executive Office of the President, there are more than half a dozen key agencies serving the President directly, with a combined budget in fiscal 1981 of $105 million and a total staff of 1900. (See Figure 10-2.) Many of these employees have offices in the Executive Office Building just west of the White House.

The Executive Office of the President

President Roosevelt established the Executive Office of the President in 1939, by executive order, after a committee of scholars had reported to him: "The President needs help." Since that time, the office has grown substantially. President Reagan planned to make some changes in the organization of the White House staff and the Executive Office of the President. But as that office existed in 1981 at the start of the Reagan administration, its major components included:

National Security Council. When the United States emerged as a major world power after the Second World War, no central machinery existed to advise the President and help him coordinate American military and foreign policy. The National Security Council (NSC) was created under the National Security Act of 1947 to fill this gap. Its members are the President, the Vice President, and the Secretaries of State and Defense. The President's assistant for national security directs the NSC staff.

Like the cabinet, the NSC has been put to vastly different use by different Presidents. Eisenhower used the NSC extensively, and during his administration a substructure of boards and committees mushroomed beneath it. During the Cuban missile crisis in 1962, Kennedy established an informal body known as the Executive Committee of the National Security Council. Much larger than the statutory membership of the NSC, it consisted of some sixteen top officials and advisers in the foreign policy, military, and intelligence fields whom the President felt it appropriate to consult. Nixon, an NSC member during the Eisenhower administration, sought as President to restore the NSC and its staff to its former place in the White House policy machinery. During the Nixon administration the NSC under Kissinger generated a steady flow of voluminous memoranda on foreign policy problems, all of which helped to increase Kissinger's great influence and power in foreign affairs. President Reagan named Richard V. Allen, his foreign policy adviser in the campaign, as his assistant for national security.

Domestic Policy Staff. All recent Presidents have had a staff to assist them in formulating domestic policy. Creation of a formal staff for this purpose began under Lyndon Johnson in the 1960s. Nixon established a Domestic Council in 1970. President Carter renamed the panel the Domestic Policy Staff and appointed a key campaign aide, Stuart E. Eizenstat, as its director. Eizenstat had several assistants who specialized in such policy fields as energy and natural resources, economics and taxes, human resources, and civil rights. To shape domestic policies, President Reagan named Martin Anderson, an economist, as assistant to the President for domestic policy development.

Office of Management and Budget. The Office of Management and Budget (OMB) was created by President Nixon in 1970 under the same reorganization plan that established the Domestic Council. A successor agency to what had been called the Bureau of the Budget, OMB was designed to tighten presidential control over the federal bureaucracy and improve its performance.

The OMB has two overlapping functions: preparing the federal budget and serving as a management tool for the Chief Executive. The director of the office advises the President on the allocation of federal funds, and he attempts to resolve the competing claims of the departments and agencies for a larger share of the federal budget. The task of preparing and administering the annual budget gives OMB enormous power within the government. At the same time, because of OMB's monitoring of federal spending, it serves as a valuable instrument of presidential control over the executive branch. Subject to congressional action, of course, OMB helps the President control the purse strings. It thus can serve as an important managerial tool for the President. OMB also has responsibility for evaluating the performance of federal agencies.

Council of Economic Advisers. Since the Great Depression of the thirties, the President has been expected to manage the nation's efforts to achieve prosperity. Because few Presidents are economic experts, Presidents since 1946 have relied on a Council of Economic Advisers to assist them in the formation of national economic policy.

The three members, one of whom is designated chairman by the President, are subject to Senate confirmation. The council is expected to give impartial, professional advice, but since its members are also part of the President's administration, they perform a difficult task. Before an election, for example, the council

David Stockman,
Director of the Office
of Management and
Budget

may express optimism about the economy even though the cost of living and unemployment are rising. As in the case of other presidential advisers, the council operates within a political framework.

The Vice President

"I am Vice President," said John Adams. "In this I am nothing, but I may be everything."[51]

The remark remains apt today. Under the Constitution, the Vice President's only formal duties are to preside over the Senate, to vote in that body in case of a tie, and (under the Twenty-fifth Amendment) to help decide whether the President is disabled, and, if so, to serve as Acting President.

If the President dies, resigns, or is removed from office, however, the Vice President becomes President. Through 1980 this had occurred nine times as the result of the death or resignation of a President. In four of those cases, the President had been assassinated.

Traditionally, the candidate for Vice President is chosen by the presidential nominee to "balance the ticket," to add geographic or other strength to the campaign. Thus, in 1980 Reagan, a sixty-nine-year-old conservative, chose George Bush, a fifty-six-year-old Republican moderate, to give the ticket a somewhat younger look and solidify Reagan's ties to the Eastern, internationalist wing of the party. Similarly, in 1968 Nixon chose Spiro Agnew of Maryland, a relatively obscure governor, in an effort to strengthen the national ticket's appeal in Southern and border states.

Agnew quickly emerged as a controversial political figure. He attacked leaders of the protest against the Vietnam war and assailed network news commentators who had been critical of the President. It appeared that Nixon had found in his Vice President a useful political instrument to woo Southern and conservative voters. In the midst of the Watergate crisis, however, at a time when Nixon was battling for his own political survival, it was disclosed that the Vice

[51] Donald Young, *American Roulette: The History and Dilemma of the Vice Presidency* (New York: Holt, Rinehart and Winston, 1965), p. 10.

Vice President
George Bush

Some Vice Presidents View Their Office

JOHN ADAMS
My country has in its wisdom contrived for me the most insignificant office that ever the invention of man contrived or his imagination conceived.

THOMAS JEFFERSON
The second office of this Government is honorable and easy, the first is but a splendid misery.

JOHN NANCE GARNER
The vice presidency isn't worth a pitcher of warm spit.

HARRY TRUMAN
Look at all the Vice Presidents in history. Where are they? They were about as useful as a cow's fifth teat.

THOMAS R. MARSHALL
Like a man in a cataleptic state [the Vice President] cannot speak; he cannot move; he suffers no pain; and yet he is perfectly conscious of everything that is going on about him.

SPIRO AGNEW
Now I know what a turkey feels like before Thanksgiving.

WALTER MONDALE
They know who Amy is, but they don't know me.

— In Donald Young, *American Roulette;* Spiro Agnew quoted in the *Los Angeles Times West Magazine,* June 22, 1969; Walter Mondale quoted in the *Los Angeles Times,* January 13, 1978.

Spiro Agnew after resigning as Vice President and receiving a sentence of three years' probation, and a $10,000 fine, for tax evasion

President was under investigation by a federal prosecutor in Baltimore for possible violation of criminal laws dealing with extortion, bribery, tax evasion, and conspiracy. Agnew resigned, pleaded no contest to income tax evasion, received a $10,000 fine, and was placed on probation for three years. Nixon then nominated House Republican leader Gerald R. Ford of Michigan to replace Agnew. Ford was confirmed by Congress and became Vice President in December 1973. When Nixon resigned in 1974, Ford became President.

In the twentieth century, through 1980, five Vice Presidents had succeeded to the Presidency through the death or resignation of an incumbent President.[52] These statistics and the Agnew case would seem to recommend that Vice Presidents be carefully selected on merit rather than solely for political considerations.

Presidential Commissions

From time to time, Presidents appoint *ad hoc* "blue ribbon" commissions of prominent citizens to study special problems. Such panels can be helpful to a President by dealing with a major crisis, by providing influential support for his programs, or by deflecting political pressure from the White House. But they may also cause him headaches by criticizing his administration, by proposing remedies he does not favor, or in other ways. For example, in 1976 President Ford named the Rockefeller Commission to study published reports of spying within the United States by the CIA. But the commission also gathered information about CIA plots to assassinate foreign leaders, causing Ford political embarrassment.

After President Kennedy's assassination, the nation was torn by doubt and speculation over the facts of his death. President Johnson convinced the prestigious Chief Justice Earl Warren to head an investigating commission. The Warren Commission concluded that Lee Harvey Oswald shot the President and had "acted alone." At first this conclusion seemed to reassure much of the public that no conspiracy existed, but later the Warren Commission's conclusions were widely attacked by many critics who refused to accept the shooting as the act of one person.

The Informal Tools of Power

Many factors affect a President's ability to achieve his objectives. The President is the chief actor on the Washington stage. He is carefully watched by bureaucrats, members of Congress, party leaders, and the press. The decisions he makes affect his professional reputation among these groups. In turn, his effectiveness as President depends on this professional reputation.[53]

In the exercise of presidential power, the President has available to him not only the formal tools of the office, but a broad range of *informal techniques*. Many Presidents since Andrew Jackson have had a "kitchen cabinet" of informal advisers who hold no official position on the White House staff. Theodore Roosevelt had his "tennis cabinet," Warren Harding his "poker cabinet," and Herbert Hoover, who liked exercise, his "medicine ball cabinet." More recently, President Johnson often called on friends such as Washington attorneys Abe Fortas, James H. Rowe, Jr., and Clark Clifford for advice. Ronald Reagan, too, had a "kitchen cabinet" of old friends who were for the most part California businessmen.

[52] The Vice Presidents who succeeded to the Presidency in the twentieth century were Theodore Roosevelt, Calvin Coolidge, Harry S Truman, Lyndon B. Johnson, and Gerald R. Ford.
[53] Neustadt, *Presidential Power,* Chapter 4.

With the development of electronic mass media, Presidents can make direct appeals to the people. Roosevelt began the practice with his famous "Fireside Chats" over radio. Today, the President may schedule a live televised speech or press conference to publicize his policies. He may call a White House Conference to dramatize a major issue. He may flatter key members of Congress by inviting them to cruise down the Potomac on the presidential yacht. He bargains with congressional leaders at weekly White House breakfasts, an informal institution that pays presidential homage to the importance of the leaders and incidentally allows them to make statements for the television cameras as they emerge from the executive mansion.

The President and the Press

After his election, President Reagan named James S. Brady, a campaign official and public relations man, as his press secretary. Although it was not a cabinet appointment, Reagan's choice was one of the most important early decisions that he made. A modern President relies on a press secretary to speak for him in day-to-day dealings with the news media. In recent years, most presidential press secretaries have held daily briefings for the White House press corps. The press secretary becomes a familiar personality to the public—but not always to the President's advantage. When the Watergate affair surfaced, President Nixon's press spokesman, Ronald L. Ziegler, repeatedly denied White House involvement and dismissed the break-in at Democratic headquarters as a "third-rate burglary attempt." After the truth began to emerge in April 1973, Ziegler announced that all previous White House denials were "inoperative," an explanation that did little to restore confidence in the administration's veracity—or Ziegler's. The White House had lied to the people, and the President found confidence in his administration shattered. (After Nixon left the White House, he told television interviewer David Frost: "I want to say right here and now, I said things that were not true."[54])

Administrations normally believe it to be in their self-interest to suppress embarrassing information. Mistakes, errors in judgment, poorly conceived or badly executed policies are seldom brought to light unless discovered by the press or congressional investigators. Even then, White House spokesmen try to minimize unfavorable events. In describing military or intelligence operations, in particular, government sometimes tends to conceal or distort. If the truth later becomes known, public confidence may be undermined.

Presidential Press Secretary James S. Brady

[54] *New York Times*, May 5, 1977, p. 33.

The President Versus the Press

Every President, when he first enters the White House promises an "open Administration." He swears he likes reporters, will cooperate with them, will treat them as first-class citizens. The charade goes on for a few weeks or months, or even a couple of years. All the while, the President is struggling to suppress an overwhelming conviction that the press is trying to undermine his Administration, if not the Republic. He is fighting a maddening urge to control, bully, vilify, prosecute, or litigate against every free-thinking reporter and editor in sight. Then, sooner or later, he blows. Teddy Roosevelt sued newspapers. Franklin Roosevelt expressed his displeasure over a certain article by presenting its author with an Iron Cross. Lyndon Johnson . . . but there is no sense singling out a few. Every President from Washington on came to recognize the press as a natural enemy, and eventually tried to manipulate it and muzzle it.

—Timothy Crouse, *The Boys on the Bus.*

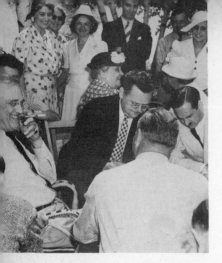

"Roosevelt played the press like a virtuoso."

Most Presidents grant private interviews with a few syndicated columnists and influential Washington correspondents. They hope in that way to gain support for their views in the press and among readers. But the presidential press conference is a more direct device used by the Chief Executive to reach the public. Wilson began the practice by inviting reporters into his office. Harding, Coolidge, and Hoover accepted only written questions, and their press conferences were generally dull. Roosevelt held regular news conferences, cancelled the requirement for written questions, and played the press like a virtuoso. Truman moved the press conference from his office to the Executive Office Building, establishing a more formal atmosphere.

Since Wilson's day, reporters could not quote the President directly without permission, but Eisenhower changed this, allowing his news conferences to be filmed and released to television after editing. Kennedy instituted "live," unedited TV press conferences in the modern auditorium of the State Department, and he dazzled the press with his skill in fielding questions. Johnson had some full-dress press conferences but often preferred to answer questions from reporters while loping rapidly around the White House South Lawn. Nixon reverted to formal, televised press conferences, usually in the White House East Room. In his first term, however, Nixon held fewer press conferences than any modern President, averaging about seven per year. (See Table 10-3.) To an extent that exceeded any modern predecessors, the Nixon-Agnew administration considered the press a political target. President Ford's amiable personality helped him to maintain fairly good relations with the press. During much of his Presidency, Carter had reasonably good relations with the press, although political cartoonists had a field day, invariably caricaturing him with thick "blubber lips."

President Reagan, initially, at least, enjoyed the traditional "honeymoon" from intense press criticism normally afforded to any new Chief Executive. But as Fred I. Greenstein has noted, it does not take the press very long to begin criticizing a President: "Media coverage of the President-elect and the first few months of an administration tends to emphasize the endearing personal touches — Ford's preparation of his own English muffins, Carter's fireside chat in informal garb. No wonder both of these Presidents enjoyed high poll ratings during their initial months in office. But the trend can only go downward . . . after idealizing Presidents, the media quickly search out their warts."[55]

[55] Fred I. Greenstein, "Change and Continuity in the Modern Presidency," in Anthony King, ed., *The New American Political System* (Washington, D.C.: American Enterprise Institute for Public Policy Research, 1978), pp. 74-75.

Presidential Press Conferences

Table 10-3

President	Number	Years in Office*	Average Per Year*
Roosevelt	998	12	83
Truman	322	8	40
Eisenhower	193	8	24
Kennedy	64	3	21
Johnson	126	5	25
Nixon	37	5½	7
Ford	39	2½	16
Carter	59	4	15

* Figures rounded.

Watergate: A Case Study

It had begun shortly after 1 A.M. on the morning of June 17, 1972, when Frank Wills, a twenty-four-year-old, $80-a-week security guard at the Watergate office building, had pulled a piece of masking tape from the edge of a garage-level door. The tape had presumably been placed there to keep the door from latching shut. He left, but returned in a few minutes. To his astonishment, he found the door had been taped again—apparently by a persistent but foolish burglar. He called the police.

When Frank Wills pulled the tape off the door of the Watergate, it was as though one tiny strand of thread had unraveled a whole skein of corruption and criminal activity planned and condoned in what—until then—had seemed the least likely of places, the White House.

At first, however, the press treated the break-in as little more than a routine crime story. Five men had been arrested inside the headquarters of the Democratic National Committee in the Watergate office building, part of a high-rise complex along the Potomac River. But one of the men turned out to be James W. McCord, Jr., director of security for the Committee for the Re-election of the President (CREEP). Later two other suspects were arrested, E. Howard Hunt, Jr., and G. Gordon Liddy, both former White House aides. Liddy, like McCord, was an official of CREEP.

Several of the burglars had worked for the CIA—both Hunt and McCord were twenty-year veterans of the CIA—and it soon developed that the break-in team had been financed by money contributed to President Nixon's 1972 election campaign. Two young reporters on the *Washington Post,* Bob Woodward and Carl Bernstein, pursued the story.

As the scandal unfolded, it was disclosed that the burglars had "bugged" the Democratic headquarters and that telephone conversations of Democratic party officials had been broadcast by a concealed transmitter to a room across the street at a Howard Johnson's motel. Reports of these conversations had been delivered to the President's re-election committee.

"You Could Get a Million Dollars"

On March 21, 1973, President Nixon, White House counsel John Dean, and H. R. Haldeman, Nixon's chief of staff, met in the Oval Office to discuss payoffs to buy the silence of the Watergate burglars. Their conversation, recorded by the President's secret taping system, became a crucial part of the evidence in the House Judiciary Committee's impeachment investigation of President Nixon. Following are excerpts from the March 21 conversation:

Nixon: How much money do you need?
Dean: I would say these people are going to cost a million dollars over the next two years.
Nixon: We could get that. . . . You could get a million dollars. You could get it in cash. I know

where it could be gotten. It is not easy, but it could be done. But the question is who the hell would handle it? Any ideas on that?
Haldeman: . . . we thought Mitchell ought to be able to know how to find somebody who would know how to do all that sort of thing, because none of us know how to.
Dean: That's right. You have to wash the money. You can get $100,000 out of a bank, and it all comes in serialized bills.
Nixon: I understand.
Dean: And that means you have to go to Vegas with it or a bookmaker in New York City. I have learned all these things after the fact. I will be in great shape for the next time around.
Haldeman: (Expletive deleted).

—From the White House transcripts, released April 30, 1974.

John W. Dean III

John N. Mitchell

H. R. Haldeman

John D. Ehrlichman

But the President denied any knowledge of the break-in, and within the White House, his advisers took steps to cover up the links between the burglars and the President's campaign. Nixon was overwhelmingly re-elected in November. Watergate seemed to have been "contained."

In January 1973 five of the defendants pleaded guilty and two others who chose to stand trial were convicted by a federal jury. In March, McCord, facing a long prison term from federal judge John J. Sirica, suggested that White House and other officials had advance knowledge of the Watergate bugging. As public pressure mounted, President Nixon again denied prior knowledge of the Watergate bugging or the subsequent official cover-up. He accepted the resignations of his two principal aides, H. R. Haldeman and John Ehrlichman, and of his Attorney General, Richard Kleindienst, and reshuffled the cabinet and the White House staff. But the storm did not abate.

Nixon admitted that he had established a special investigative unit in the White House, known as "the Plumbers," to find the source of national security news leaks. The Plumbers had been headed by none other than Howard Hunt and Gordon Liddy.

The daily headlines brought one startling disclosure after another:

• In 1971 some of the same Watergate burglars, equipped by the Central Intelligence Agency—which by law has no internal police powers—had, on White House orders, traveled to Los Angeles and broken into the office of Dr. Lewis Fielding, a psychiatrist. They were ordered to search for and photograph the medical records of his patient, Daniel Ellsberg, the man who leaked the Pentagon Papers to the press.

• In 1970 President Nixon approved a plan for burglary, secret opening of first-class mail, and electronic surveillance of persons suspected of endangering national security, although he was warned, in writing, that burglary was "clearly illegal." The President said that he rescinded the plan after five days.

• From 1969 to 1971 the President ordered the secret wiretapping of seventeen persons, including a number of his own assistants and several journalists.

• The President's personal attorney, Herbert W. Kalmbach, raised and secretly distributed $220,000 to the Watergate burglars and their attorneys.

• The acting director of the Federal Bureau of Investigation destroyed vital Watergate evidence—he burned the documents with his Christmas trash—and testified he had done so at the instigation of two of the President's top assistants.

• The President concealed secret microphones in his offices in the White House to record conversations on tape, in most cases without the knowledge of the persons being recorded.

• The President's assistants compiled an "enemies list" and requested tax audits of political opponents.

• The Attorney General of the United States, John Mitchell, was present during a discussion of proposals for bugging the headquarters of the opposition political party, kidnapping American citizens and taking them to Mexico, and establishing a bordello on a yacht to gather political information by blackmail.

• The White House ordered the CIA to attempt to persuade the FBI to limit its investigation of the Watergate burglary.

In May 1973 a Senate select committee under chairman Sam J. Ervin, Jr., a North Carolina Democrat, began holding televised hearings into Watergate and the 1972 campaign. Within a few months, all seven of the Watergate burglars had been given jail sentences by Judge Sirica. Several other high administration officials pleaded guilty to crimes. In October Nixon dismissed the Watergate special prosecutor, but was forced by the tremendous public outcry to appoint another. The House of Representatives began its impeachment investigation. Nixon agreed to surrender some of the tapes of his conversations about Watergate.

Then came the climactic events of the summer of 1974. The Supreme Court ordered Nixon to surrender more tapes to the new Watergate special prosecutor, and the House Judiciary Committee voted to impeach the President. In addition, one of the newly released tapes showed that Nixon had lied when he denied he had participated in the cover-up of the Watergate burglary. On June 23, 1972, the tapes revealed, Nixon had ordered the CIA to try to confine the FBI investigation of the break-in, and he now admitted he knew he would gain political advantage from that order.

Nixon's support in Congress within his own Republican party crumbled almost totally. A delegation of Republican leaders from the House and Senate called on the President and told him the blunt truth: he did not have enough votes in Congress to avoid impeachment and removal from office.

Richard Nixon resigned on August 9, 1974, the first President in the na-

Senator Sam J. Ervin, Jr., presides over Senate Watergate hearings in 1973.

President Nixon speaks to the nation about Watergate.

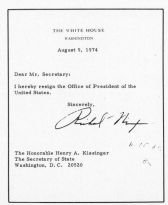

tion's history ever to do so. A month later, he accepted a pardon from his successor, President Ford, and thus could not be prosecuted for acts committed while President. Many of Nixon's higher advisers were less fortunate. In 1975 John Ehrlichman, H. R. Haldeman, and John Mitchell were convicted of covering up the Watergate break-in. All three went to prison.

A total of nineteen persons were convicted or pleaded guilty in connection with Watergate-related crimes, including ten Nixon aides and three CREEP officials. All nineteen served prison sentences.

Presidential Impeachment, Disability, and Succession

Impeachment

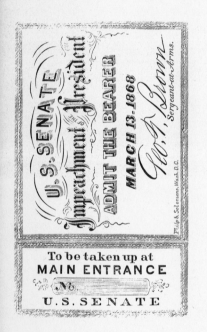

Despite the enormous power of the President, under the Constitution he may be impeached by Congress and, if convicted of "Treason, Bribery or other high Crimes and Misdemeanors," removed from office.[56] Only the House can bring impeachment proceedings against a President, by majority vote. He is tried by the Senate with the Chief Justice presiding. A two-thirds vote of the Senate is required to convict a President and remove him from office, a fate that Andrew Johnson escaped by one vote in 1868.

The unsuccessful attempt to remove Johnson from office grew out of the turmoil of the Civil War. The President hoped to carry out Lincoln's conciliatory Reconstruction policies toward the South after the war. This placed him in direct conflict with the Radical Republicans in Congress, who favored much harsher policies. When Johnson dismissed his Secretary of War, the House charged he had violated the Tenure of Office Act and brought impeachment proceedings. The trial and balloting in the Senate went on for more than two months.

Historically, Congress has hesitated to impeach and remove a President, for several reasons. First, there has been an understandable reluctance to act against the highest official in the land, who—unless he succeeds to his office—is elected by all the people. Second, there has been a fear that impeachment, as a political remedy, might become a partisan weapon to remove a President whenever he displeased a Congress controlled by the opposition political party or by political opponents in his own party.

Third, the language of the Constitution dealing with impeachment, scattered in four places, leaves many unanswered questions. For example, can officials be indicted before they are impeached, or in place of impeachment? Many legal scholars believe the answer is yes, for judges and officials up to and including the Vice President. But they also contend that a President must first be impeached and removed before prosecution. Otherwise the country might find itself in the untenable position of having its national leader behind bars while still holding office.

[56] Not only the President, but the Vice President and other federal officials and federal judges— as the Constitution puts it, all "civil officers of the United States"—are subject to impeachment. Members of Congress are subject to discipline and expulsion by their respective houses, but it is not clear whether they are "civil officers" subject to impeachment. At least some scholars believe that members of Congress are not exempt from removal by impeachment. See, for example, Raoul Berger, *Impeachment: The Constitutional Problems* (Cambridge, Mass.: Harvard University Press, 1973), pp. 214–23.

Yet another difficult problem is whether the "high crimes and misdemeanors" required as grounds for an impeachment conviction must literally be crimes in the legal sense—the breaking of specific laws—or whether that constitutional language encompasses serious abuses of the office of the President that might fall short of actual, indictable crimes.

Before 1973 it seemed most unlikely that any modern President could be impeached, but the Watergate scandal changed all that. A resolution to impeach President Nixon was introduced in the House on July 31 by the Rev. Robert F. Drinan, a Massachusetts Democrat. Some of those who might otherwise have favored such a course were dismayed at the prospect of the succession of Vice President Agnew to the Presidency in the event of Nixon's removal from office. But Agnew resigned in October and that same month the House Judiciary Committee began an inquiry into the possible impeachment of President Nixon. It was the first time since 1868 that Congress had taken steps to consider whether a President of the United States should be impeached.

The formal proceedings of the committee, under chairman Peter W. Rodino, Jr., began in February 1974. A large staff under special counsel John Doar amassed thirty-eight volumes of evidence, dealing with the Watergate break-in, Nixon's wiretapping of seventeen aides and news reporters, the White House "enemies list," and other abuses. The committee members, earphones clamped to their heads, listened for hours to the White House tapes. They heard presentations by the President's attorney, James D. St. Clair, and by John Doar. They heard witnesses in closed session and then on July 24 began six historic days of public deliberation. The sessions were televised and watched by millions of Americans.

The Judiciary Committee voted three articles of impeachment. Article I accused Nixon of obstruction of justice by "using the powers of his high office" to "delay, impede, and obstruct" the investigation of the break-in at Democratic headquarters. The article specifically charged that Nixon had made false public statements "for the purpose of deceiving the people of the United States" into believing that the investigation had been thorough and that the President's campaign organization had not been involved. Article II accused the President of violating the constitutional rights of citizens by misusing the FBI, the CIA, the IRS, and other agencies, and by establishing a secret investigative unit, "the Plumbers," in the White House itself. Article III charged Nixon had defied the committee by failing to produce subpoenaed tapes and documents.

The full House had no opportunity to vote on these articles nor was there a Senate trial, as occurred in the case of Andrew Johnson. On August 9, 1974, ten days after the last of the articles had been approved by the Judiciary Committee, Nixon resigned.

Chairman Peter W. Rodino, Jr., Chairman of the House Judiciary Committee, after panel voted to impeach President Nixon

Twice in American history, Presidents were incapacitated for long periods. Garfield lived for eighty days after he was shot in 1881. Wilson never fully recovered from the illness that struck him in September 1919; yet he remained in office until March 1921. To a considerable extent, Mrs. Wilson was President. President Eisenhower suffered three serious illnesses, including a heart attack in 1955 that incapacitated him for four days and curtailed his workload for sixteen weeks. Sherman Adams and Press Secretary James Hagerty ran the executive branch machinery during this period.

Disability
and Succession

We arrived at Love Field in Dallas, as I remember, just shortly after 11:30 A.M. . . .

. . . The President and Mrs. Kennedy walked along the fence, shaking hands with people in the crowd that had assembled. . . .

Mrs. Johnson, Senator Ralph Yarborough, and I then entered the car which had been provided for us in the motorcade. . . . We were the second car behind the President's automobile. . . .

After we had proceeded a short way down Elm Street, I heard a sharp report. . . .

I was startled by the sharp report or explosion, but I had no time to speculate as to its origin because Agent Youngblood . . . shouted to all of us in the back seat to get down . . . he vaulted over the back seat and sat on me. I was bent over under the weight of Agent Youngblood's body. . . .

When we arrived at the hospital, Agent Youngblood told me to get out of the car, go into the building, not to stop, and to stay close to him and the other agents. . . .

In the hospital room to which Mrs. Johnson and I were taken, the shades were drawn—I think by Agent Youngblood. . . .

It was Ken O'Donnell who, at about 1:20 P.M., told us that the President had died. I think his precise words were "He's gone." . . .

I found it hard to believe that this had happened. The whole thing seemed unreal—unbelievable. A few hours earlier, I had breakfast with John Kennedy; he was alive, strong, vigorous. I could not believe now that he was dead. I was shocked and sickened.

—Statement of President Lyndon B. Johnson to the Warren Commission, July 10, 1964.

Dallas, November 22, 1963: President Johnson takes the oath of office.

President Eisenhower recovering from his 1955 heart attack

Eisenhower's heart attack in 1955 raised anew the question of presidential disability. The Constitution was exceedingly vague on the subject. It spoke of presidential "inability" and "disability," but left it up to Congress to define those terms and to decide when and how the Vice President would take over when a President was unable to exercise his powers and duties. If a President became physically or mentally ill, or disappeared, or was captured in a military operation, or was under anesthesia in the hospital, what was the Vice President's proper role? Did he become President or only assume the "powers and duties" of the office? And for how long? Eisenhower and Nixon sought to cover these contingencies with an unofficial written agreement, a practice followed by Kennedy and Johnson, and Johnson and Humphrey.

But suppose a President was unable or unwilling to declare that he was disabled? Who would then decide whether he was disabled or when he might resume his duties? Could a scheming Vice President, with the help of psychiatrists, somehow have a perhaps temporarily unstable President permanently removed from office?

The Twenty-fifth Amendment, ratified in 1967, sought to settle these questions. It provides that the Vice President becomes *Acting President* if the President informs Congress in writing that he is unable to perform his duties. Or, the Vice President may become Acting President if the Vice President and a majority of the cabinet, or of some "other body" created by Congress, decide that the President is disabled. The President can reclaim his office at any time unless the Vice President and a majority of the cabinet or other body contend that he has not recovered. Congress would then decide the issue. But it would take a two-thirds vote of both houses within three weeks to support the Vice President; anything less and the President would resume office.

Until the Twenty-fifth Amendment was ratified, there was no constitutional provision for replacing a Vice President when that office became vacant.[57] So the amendment also provided that the President shall nominate a Vice President, subject to the approval of a majority of both houses of Congress, whenever that office becomes vacant. The provision reduces the possibility of presidential succession by the House Speaker or the Senate President pro tempore, or by cabinet members, unless the President and Vice President die simultaneously, or unless a President dies, resigns, or is impeached while the Vice Presidency is vacant and before Congress has acted to approve a new Vice President.

The Twenty-fifth Amendment was used for the first time in October 1973 when President Nixon nominated Gerald R. Ford to succeed Agnew. Congress approved his choice, 92 to 3 in the Senate and 387 to 35 in the House. Until Ford was sworn in that December, the office of Vice President had remained vacant for fifty-seven days. During that period, if Nixon had ceased to be President, his successor would have been House Speaker Carl Albert.

The Twenty-fifth Amendment was used for the second time to fill a vice-presidential vacancy after Nixon resigned and Ford succeeded him as President. In August 1974 Ford nominated former New York governor Nelson A. Rockefeller to be Vice President. After lengthy hearings and approval by the House and Senate, Rockefeller took the oath of office in December.[58]

The Splendid Misery: Personality and Style in the White House

Thomas Jefferson conceived of the Presidency as "a splendid misery." Others, like Franklin Roosevelt and Kennedy, brought great vigor and vitality to the job; they seemed to *enjoy* being President. The personality, style, and concept of the office that each President brings with him to the White House affect the nature of his Presidency. William Howard Taft expressed the classic, restrictive view of the Presidency: "The President can exercise no power which cannot be fairly and reasonably traced to some specific grant of power."[59] Theodore Roosevelt adhered to the "stewardship" theory. He saw the Chief Executive as "a steward of the people" and believed that "it was not only his right but his duty to do anything that the needs of the Nation demanded unless such action was forbidden by the Constitution or by the laws."[60] Lincoln and Franklin Roosevelt went even further, contending that in great emergencies the President could exercise almost unlimited power to preserve the nation.

Louis W. Koenig has classified Presidents as "literalist" (Madison, Buchanan, Taft, and, to a degree, Eisenhower) and "strong" (Washington, Jackson, Lincoln, Wilson, and the Roosevelts), adding that many Chief Executives fall somewhere in the middle. A literalist President, as defined by Koenig, closely

[57] As of 1980 the nation had been without a Vice President eighteen times for a total of thirty-seven years. Below the level of Vice President, the order in which other officials might succeed to the Presidency is spelled out in the Presidential Succession Act of 1947.

[58] Because of the extraordinary circumstances of a President and a Vice President resigning during the same term, the United States had four Vice Presidents in a period of less than four years from 1973 to 1977: Spiro T. Agnew, Gerald R. Ford, Nelson A. Rockefeller, and Walter F. Mondale.

[59] Tourtellot, *The Presidents on the Presidency,* p. 426.

[60] *Ibid.,* pp. 55–56.

Left: Ronald Reagan rides the range. *Center:* Lyndon Johnson issues orders to a doubtful steer on his Texas ranch. *Right:* William Howard Taft, who weighed 332 pounds, displays a graceful follow-through.

Theodore Roosevelt in a typically exuberant pose

obeys the letter of the Constitution; a strong President, who generally flourishes in times of crisis and change, interprets his constitutional powers as liberally as possible.[61]

A President's personality and approach to the office may leave a more lasting impression than his substantive accomplishments or failures. We think of Teddy Roosevelt shouting "Bully!"; Wilson, austere and idealistic, in the end shattered by events; Franklin D. Roosevelt in a wheelchair, cigarette holder tilted at a jaunty angle, conquering paralysis with élan. We think of Eisenhower's golf, Kennedy's glamour, Johnson's cowpuncher image, Nixon's isolation—all say something about how they occupied the office of President.

James David Barber has attempted to systematize the study of presidential behavior by analyzing how childhood and other experiences may have molded a President's character and style. He has proposed four broad, general character types into which Presidents may be grouped, and has suggested that from such an analysis it might ultimately be possible to theorize about future presidential behavior.[62] Thus, Barber has contended that Eisenhower reluctantly ran for President because he was "a sucker for duty" as a result of his background; that Johnson ruled through "manipulative maneuvering"; and that Nixon "isolated himself."[63]

[61] Koenig, *The Chief Executive,* pp. 14–17.
[62] James David Barber, *The Presidential Character: Predicting Performance in the White House* (Englewood Cliffs, N. J.: Prentice-Hall, 1972). The four types that Barber identified are active-positive, active-negative, passive-positive, and passive-negative.
[63] *Ibid.,* pp. 94, 159, 423–24, 441.

In an accurate prediction of Watergate and Nixon's downfall, Barber warned in 1972 that Nixon's character "could lead the President on to disaster. . . . The danger is that crisis will be transformed into tragedy. . . . The loss of power to forces beyond his control would constitute a severe threat. That would be a time to go down, if go down one must, in flames."[64]

Some observers contend that because of the many variables affecting human behavior, Presidents may not act in ways that psychological analysis of their lives might suggest.[65] But because of the work of Barber and others, this approach has gained increasing attention.

The American Presidency: Triumph and Tragedy

Running for President in 1980, Ronald Reagan said he wanted to "bring our government back under control and make it acceptable to the people."[66] He would, he declared, eliminate "extravagance and fat in government."[67]

Twenty years earlier, President Kennedy, seeking the Presidency in 1960, viewed it as "the vital center of action in our whole scheme of government." The problems of America, he said, "demand a vigorous proponent of the national interest—not a passive broker for conflicting private interests," a President who will "place himself in the very thick of the fight."[68]

Whether a President takes an activist approach, like Kennedy, or a more conservative approach, like Reagan, the voters tend to look to the White House for solutions to major problems. Yet the President may *not* be able to solve the

[64] *Ibid.,* pp. 441–42.

[65] It is interesting to note in this connection that before President Kennedy met in Vienna in 1961 with Soviet Premier Khrushchev, he had access to an assessment of Khrushchev's character prepared for the CIA by a panel of psychiatrists and psychologists. See Bryant Wedge, "Khrushchev at a Distance—A Study of Public Personality," *Trans-Action,* October 1968.

[66] Congressional Quarterly, *Weekly Report,* July 19, 1980, p. 2064.

[67] Congressional Quarterly, *Weekly Report,* November 1, 1980, p. 3282.

[68] *Congressional Record,* January 18, 1960, p. 711.

Lyndon B. Johnson

"Hi! We're the Clark family, from Paducah, Kentucky, and we thought we'd just drop in and see the President to tell him what we're thinking."

Drawing by Dana Fradon
© 1979 The New Yorker Magazine, Inc.

After the Watergate scandal, a Senate intelligence committee under Senator Frank Church, Democrat, of Idaho, investigated abuses by the FBI, CIA, and other federal intelligence and police agencies. Former President Nixon, responding to written questions from the committee, attempted to argue that a President was in some way above the law: "It is quite obvious," he said, "that there are certain inherently governmental actions which if undertaken by the sovereign in protection of the interest of the nation's security are lawful but which if undertaken by private persons are not." The committee emphatically rejected this concept of the President as "sovereign," and noted in its final report: "There is no inherent constitutional authority for the President or any intelligence agency to violate the law."

—Excerpts from the final report of the Senate Select Committee on Intelligence, Book IV, 1976.

worst national problems that confront him. He cannot singlehandedly end the energy crisis, environmental pollution, inflation, or high unemployment. Nor can he easily use the nation's nuclear power in foreign policy crises—to prevent the seizure of American hostages, for example. Koenig has suggested the concept of "the imagined Presidency," which is "vested in our minds with more power than the Presidency really has."[69] The difference between the real and the imagined Presidency, he contends, may lead to public frustration over presidential performance.

Although the great power of the Presidency tends to overshadow its limitations, we have seen how, in many spheres, that power is circumscribed. As Chief Executive, the President faces an often intractable bureaucracy. As Chief Legislator, under the constitutional separation of powers, he faces an independent and often hostile Congress. As military and foreign policy leader, his powers are enormous, but he must, at least to some extent, consider sentiment in Congress and the bureaucracy. The Twenty-second Amendment limits the President to two terms and thereby weakens his power in the second term (since everyone knows he will not be President again). Federal law may restrict his options. The Supreme Court may strike down his programs. The press may expose corruption in the bureaucracy or in the White House itself. Public opinion may turn against him. The necessities of politics may occasionally force him to weigh his actions in terms of their effect on his party. Finally, he may be impeached and removed from office.

Whether the Presidency is too powerful, or not powerful enough, depends, then, to some extent not only on how a President uses his power but also on what he hopes to accomplish. Presidents have different goals. Most recent Democratic Presidents have tried to press forward with energetic programs of social reform. Other Presidents, such as Eisenhower and Ford, have tried to act with restraint.

The answer to the question of whether Presidents have too much power depends ultimately on what one expects of the office and of the American po-

[69] Koenig, *The Chief Executive,* p. 11.

litical system. In the domestic arena, those who regard the Presidency as an essential instrument to meet the social challenges and problems of the nation today do not necessarily tend to regard that office as too powerful. Others, alarmed at the size of the federal bureaucracy and opposed to social welfare programs, may take a different view.

In any event, presidential power fluctuates, depending in part on the situation in which it is being exercised. Franklin Roosevelt was able to wield enormous economic powers during the early years of the New Deal because the nation was in the throes of an acute depression. By 1938 he was encountering substantial domestic opposition. When the Second World War came along, he was able to exercise great powers once more—people expected it.

The power a President exercises not only depends on the times and the circumstances but also on the policy area involved. A strong argument can be made that—until the War Powers Resolution of 1973—for several decades there had been relatively few serious attempts to curb the President's power to commit American military forces abroad. In the field of domestic legislation, however, presidential powers may not be strong enough. For example, both Nixon and Carter were unable to get Congress to approve their welfare reform programs.

The President (along with the Vice President) is the only official of the American government elected by all the people. The Presidency, therefore, would seem to be the branch of government best situated to view and act on national problems in the interest of a national constituency. In a diverse democracy of conflicting interests and competing groups, the President is the one official who represents all the people, and who can symbolize their aspirations. He is the custodian of the future. Despite the limits on his powers, he can be the greatest force for national unity—or disunity. He can recognize the demands of minorities for social justice, or he can repress or ignore their rights. He can protect constitutional liberties or turn loose federal police power to wiretap, eavesdrop, and burglarize. He can lead the nation into war or preserve the peace. Such is his power that he leaves his indelible mark on the times, with the result that the triumph or tragedy of each Presidency is, in some measure at least, also our own.

Perspective

The Presidency is a place of paradox. At times, the office may be viewed as too powerful, and at other times, as not powerful enough. And a modern President may have great power in some policy areas, but limited options in others.

The Presidency is both an institution and a person. The institution is the office created by the Constitution, custom, federal laws since 1789, and the gradual growth of various tools of presidential power. The person is a human being who brings the imprint of a particular personality and style to the White House. The Presidency, then, is both highly institutionalized and highly personal.

Several broad historical factors have combined to create a powerful Chief Executive today. The United States remains one of the two most powerful nations in the world; the President is a world leader, as well as a national leader. With the tremendous growth of the government's managerial role, the President directs a huge bureaucracy. Finally, television and other news media have helped to magnify the person and the institution of the Presidency.

The President is the ceremonial and symbolic head of state, as well as the head of government. Under the authority granted by the Constitution, the President runs the executive branch of government with the aid of a White House staff, the cabinet, and various agencies in the Executive Office of the President.

The President is Commander in Chief of the armed forces of the United States. The Constitution declares that "Congress shall have Power . . . To declare War," but Congress has not done so since 1941. In the intervening years the President has made the decision to go to war. In 1973, however, Congress passed the War Powers Resolution to attempt to limit presidential war-making power.

Presidents make foreign policy; they direct the relations of the United States with other nations of the world. The Constitution does not specifically confer this power on the President, but it does so indirectly. It authorizes the President to receive foreign ambassadors, to appoint ambassadors, and to make treaties with the consent of two-thirds of the Senate. The President can also sign executive agreements with other nations.

Active presidential participation in the legislative process is a twentieth-century phenomenon. The President has many formal and informal powers at his disposal in his role as Chief Legislator, among them the veto and "arm twisting." But the success of the President's legislative efforts depends on the cooperation of Congress and the support of the electorate.

The President is also chief of his party. The director and staff of the national committee report to him; he can install his own choice as national chairman; he can usually demand renomination by his party and stage-manage the convention that acclaims him. Given the decentralized nature of American political parties, a President's influence may not extend to state and local party organizations in every case. Nor does it prevail at all times with members of the President's own party in Congress.

The President, the Vice President, and the officials who head the executive departments of the government are members of the cabinet. The cabinet as an organized body is not specifically provided for by law or in the Constitution. The cabinet has been a relatively weak institution.

A huge presidential establishment has burgeoned since Franklin D. Roosevelt took office in 1933. At its center is the White House staff, which guards the President's time, serves as a link with Congress and the executive departments, advises the President on political affairs, deals with the press, and performs various other functions. The White House staff is part of the Executive Office of the President, which includes more than a half dozen key agencies that serve the President directly.

Under the Constitution, the Vice President's only formal duties are to preside over the Senate, to vote in that body in case of a tie, and (under the Twenty-fifth Amendment) to help decide whether the President is disabled, and, if so, to serve as Acting President. However, if the President dies, resigns, or is removed from office, the Vice President becomes President.

Despite the enormous power of the President, under the Constitution he may be impeached by Congress and removed from office if convicted of "Treason, Bribery, or other High Crimes and Misdemeanors." Only the House can bring impeachment proceedings, by majority vote. The President is then tried by the Senate with the Chief Justice of the United States presiding. A two-thirds vote of the Senate is required to convict a President and remove him from office.

Barber, James David. *The Presidential Character: Predicting Performance in the White House,* 2nd edition* (Prentice-Hall, 1977). An important analysis of why Presidents act as they do. Based on research on Presidents from Taft to Carter, Barber's study explores the relationships between each President's personality type and his performance in office.

Burns, James MacGregor. *Roosevelt: The Lion and the Fox** (Harcourt Brace Jovanovich, 1956). A political biography of Franklin D. Roosevelt, one of the foremost practitioners of the art of presidential leadership. Focuses primarily on Roosevelt's first two terms in office.

Corwin, Edward S. *The President, Office and Powers 1787–1957,* 4th revised edition* (New York University Press, 1974). A classic analysis of the American Presidency. Stresses the historical development and the legal powers of the office.

Cronin, Thomas E. *The State of the Presidency,* 2nd edition* (Little, Brown, 1980). A comprehensive analysis of both the promise and limitations of the American Presidency, based on interviews with White House staff members, cabinet officials, and department advisers. Includes discussions of presidential leadership, policymaking, and accountability; and explores the President's relations with Congress and the bureaucracy.

Donovan, Robert J. *Conflict and Crisis: The Presidency of Harry S Truman, 1945–1948** (Norton, 1977). A thorough review and analysis of the first three years of the Truman Presidency, written by a respected Washington journalist and author. Draws upon newly opened documents and diaries from Truman's term in the White House. A second volume is planned to cover the last four years of the Truman era.

Edwards, George C. III *Presidential Influence in Congress** (Freeman, 1980). A detailed examination of the sources and weaknesses of presidential power in Congress. The author argues that the President has little influence over Congress, and that party affiliation, presidential prestige, and legislative skills have only a limited effect in enlisting support for presidential policies.

Fenno, Richard F., Jr. *The President's Cabinet: An Analysis in the Period from Wilson to Eisenhower* (Harvard University Press, 1959). A thoughtful study of the development of the cabinet and its role as a distinct political institution. Examines the dual role of cabinet members as presidential advisers and department heads and the place of the cabinet in the larger political system.

Heineman, Ben W., Jr., and Hessler, Curtis A. *Memorandum for the President: A Strategic Approach to Domestic Affairs in the 1980s* (Random House, 1980). An assessment, by two authors who held appointive positions in the Carter administration, of some of the difficulties that modern Presidents confront. Suggests ways to make the executive branch more effective in the area of domestic policy.

Hodgson, Godfrey. *All Things to All Men: The False Promise of the Modern American Presidency* (Simon and Schuster, 1980). A provocative analysis of the declining power of the modern American Presidency. Hodgson argues that the President is increasingly isolated, due to the thicket of bureaucracies and presidential staffs and the decline of traditional parties. Contains several specific proposals for reform.

Kearns, Doris. *Lyndon Johnson and the American Dream** (Harper and Row, 1976). A revealing examination of the character and behavior of Lyndon Johnson. Assesses his public and private life, his early career, his years in the Senate, and his Presidency.

Koenig, Louis W. *The Chief Executive,* 3rd edition* (Harcourt Brace Jovanovich, 1975). An excellent, readable, and comprehensive study of the many facets of the Presidency.

Nathan, Richard P. *The Plot That Failed: Nixon and the Administrative Presidency** (Wiley, 1975). A lively account of President Nixon's attempts in 1972 and 1973 to control the administration of domestic affairs in order to achieve his major policy objectives.

National Journal (Government Research Corporation). A very useful weekly report on American politics and government. Provides comprehensive, detailed reports about current policy issues in many areas, and analyzes how Congress, the executive branch, and various interest groups interact on these issues.

Neustadt, Richard E. *Presidential Power: The Politics of Leadership from FDR to Carter** (Wiley, 1979). (Originally published in 1960.) A knowledgeable exploration of the problems faced by a modern President in seeking to exercise his power. The first edition of this book was influential in the Kennedy administration, in which its author served for a time as a special consultant.

Rossiter, Clinton. *The American Presidency,* rev. edition* (Harcourt Brace Jovanovich, 1960). A short, lucid analysis of the American Presidency. Develops the concept of a varied, overlapping set of presidential roles and views the Presidency as the central political force in the American system.

Schlesinger, Arthur M., Jr. *A Thousand Days** (Houghton Mifflin, 1965). A well-written, detailed account of the Kennedy years by a scholar and former presidential aide. Although Schlesinger was not at the center of power in the Kennedy White House, he had the advantage of viewing events with the eye of a trained historian.

Wise, David. *The Politics of Lying: Government Deception, Secrecy, and Power** (Random House, 1973). An analysis, with detailed examples from recent presidential administrations, of how government deception and official secrecy led to an erosion of confidence in the government during the late 1960s and early 1970s. Explores the relationship between the government and the press.

* Available in paperback edition

THE BUREAUCRACY

During the 1980 presidential campaign, the victorious Republican nominee, Ronald Reagan, frequently lambasted the bureaucrats in Washington. For example, Reagan in attacking the bureaucracy, said he would abolish "several thousand . . . unnecessary regulations" of the federal government that he said were hampering the U.S. auto industry. "Regulations," Reagan told Chrysler employees in Detroit, "have caused your problem." Repeatedly, Reagan promised "to take government off the backs of the people."

But Jimmy Carter, as the incumbent President defending his record, found it necessary to praise the achievements of the federal bureaucracy. The record of his administration, after all, was largely the result of what bureaucrats had accomplished. "The social security system has been stabilized and put back on a sound basis," Carter said. "We also have . . . completely reversed the despair that existed among our older cities. . . . we've improved the structure of our defense establishment."

Only four years earlier, it was Carter who had hammered away at the "confused and overlapping and wasteful federal bureaucracy." Attacking the bureaucracy in Washington was, in fact, a major theme of his campaign. Carter's stance as an outsider who would reform and control the bureaucracy once the people sent him to Washington helped him to win the election in 1976.

As these presidential campaigns illustrate, bureaucracy—and bureaucrats—are handy political targets to blame for society's ills. By one dictionary defini-

tion, "bureaucrat" is a neutral word—it simply means an administrator—but its connotations are far from complimentary. "Bureaucrat" and "bureaucracy" are words that, to some people, conjure up an image of self-important but inefficient petty officials wallowing in red tape. It has been wryly suggested, and is widely believed, that, once established, bureaucracies tend to mushroom under "Parkinson's Law": "Work expands so as to fill the time available for its completion."[1] Hannah Arendt has described bureaucracy as "rule by Nobody," that is, "an intricate system of bureaus in which no men, neither one nor the best, neither the few nor the many, can be held responsible."[2]

Yet government at every level, federal, state, and local, could not function without people to run it. Many government programs are highly complex and require experts and professional people to administer them. *Public administration* is the term preferred by most political scientists to describe the bureaucratic process—the business of making government work—and bureaucrats are *public administrators*. The same bureaucrats who are blamed for red tape have also accomplished some remarkable tasks; NASA put men on the moon, and the TVA brought about the greening of a large area of America.

Today, Americans frequently turn to the federal government to solve or alleviate problems of unemployment and the economy, of the cities, of mass transportation, of poverty, pollution, and energy. In all of these fields, public

[1] C. Northcote Parkinson, *Parkinson's Law* (Boston: Houghton Mifflin, 1957), p. 2.
[2] Hannah Arendt, *Crises of the Republic* (New York: Harcourt Brace Jovanovich, 1972), p. 137.

Editorial cartoon by Paul Conrad
Copyright © 1978, *Los Angeles Times*
Reprinted with permission

"99,999 bucks! I've been working here in Washington for 30 years, and I only make 72,000!"

Donald Duck Goes to Washington

WASHINGTON—The General Accounting Office disclosed Thursday that it put Donald Duck's name on the payroll of the Department of Housing and Urban Development, and gave him a salary of $99,999 a year—without being challenged.

The department's computer, which is supposed to head off such shenanigans, not only failed to detect the "hiring" of the cartoon character, it raised no objections to a salary more than twice the legal limit, $47,500, for civil service pay.

It was not revealed what, if any, task the loquacious duck was supposed to perform at HUD, where 16,000 employees are charged with "providing for sound development of the nation's communities and metropolitan areas."

Officials of the GAO, Congress' watchdog over federal spending, disclosed the incident in testimony before the subcommittee on compensation and employee benefits of the House Post Office and Civil Service Committee. The subcommittee is looking into abuses of federal overtime pay.

—*Los Angeles Times*, October 27, 1978.

"I'm sorry, dear, but you knew I was a
bureaucrat when you married me."

Drawing by Weber
© 1980 The New Yorker Magazine, Inc.

administrators—bureaucrats—make important decisions and bear great responsibilities.

The millions of persons who receive social security checks every month
would not be getting them unless the Social Security Administration were part
of the federal bureaucracy. The same "faceless bureaucrats" who are attacked
in political campaigns process the social security checks. There *is* waste and red
tape and inefficiency in the federal government, but as in any large organization
outside government, there are also thousands of honest, competent people.

Americans tend to be against "Big Government" in the abstract, but to
demand all kinds of government services. The "bureaucracy in Washington" did
not grow overnight, but developed gradually, largely in response to public needs.
Most government departments and agencies have been created as a result of

The Uses of "Big Government"

Sometimes the government steps in and nobody
minds.

When tropical storm Agnes hit eastern Pennsylvania in June 1972, the property damage came to
$2 billion. In money terms, it was the worst natural
disaster in the nation's history, and it called forth
an unprecedented response from Federal, state and
local governments. Among the details:

• More than 12,000 mobile homes were imported
to the area to help house 20,000 people displaced
by the flood.

• The Small Business Administration granted
loans totaling $725 million to 81,000 homeowners
and 9,000 businessmen.

• $108 million was spent to repair roads and
bridges.

• Five devastated libraries, which lost 300,000
books, were almost fully restocked.

• About $550 million was allocated for urban
renewal, with state bonds committed to pay $140
million of the total.

"Our work wasn't perfect, but I think we did a
helluva job," says Jerome E. Parker, director of the
U.S. Department of Housing and Urban Development's Office of Disaster Housing Management in
Wilkes-Barre. "Big government does provide some
use, there's no question about it."

—*Newsweek*, December 15, 1975.

pressure from some segment of the population. And the same citizens who complain about "the bureaucracy" may protest the loudest if Washington proposes to close a defense installation that provides jobs in their local community.

Criticism of bureaucracy is not limited to attacks on the government in Washington. The student in the "multiversity" may feel crushed by an impersonal bureaucracy. So may an employee of a large corporation. The growth of computers and the tendency to assign numbers to individuals (credit cards, bank accounts, social security) has made many people feel that they are mere cogs in a vast bureaucratic machine.

Some of the sentiment directed against the federal bureaucracy can be traced to the social welfare programs of the New Deal, which vastly expanded the role of government in the lives of individual citizens. For three decades much of the criticism of the bureaucracy came from Republicans and conservatives opposed to the welfare state and the concentration of power in Washington. (Yet during eight years of Republican rule under President Eisenhower, the federal government increased in size.) In the late 1960s Democratic liberals began to voice similar thoughts. Ideological disenchantment with the federal bureaucracy had come full circle; conservatives and liberals joined in an antibureaucratic alliance of sorts.

Some critics, such as Peter F. Drucker, have gone so far as to conclude that "modern government has become ungovernable." Drucker contends that because of bureaucratic inertia and "administrative incompetence" government is unable to perform the tasks assigned to it. He adds, "There is no government today that can still claim control of its bureaucracy and of its various agencies. Government agencies are all becoming autonomous, ends in themselves, and directed by their own desire for power, their own rationale, their own narrow vision rather than by national policy."[3]

Even if such criticisms are overstated, they raise important, valid questions about the role of bureaucracy in modern society. But, as long as people demand more and more services from their government—social security, Medicare, aid to education, housing, and the like—some form of bureaucracy is inevitable.

The classic concept of the bureaucracy was developed by the pioneering German sociologist Max Weber, who saw it as a strict hierarchy, with authority flowing from the top down, within a fixed framework of rigid rules and regulations. In Weber's view, the bureaucracy draws its power from its expertise. Political rulers are in no position to argue with the technical knowledge of the trained bureaucrat: "The absolute monarch is powerless opposite the superior knowledge of the bureaucratic expert."[4] Even the Russian czar of old, Weber noted, could seldom act against the wishes of his bureaucracy.

In the nineteenth century, elected officials in the United States customarily rewarded their supporters with government jobs. Selection of bureaucrats on the basis of merit rather than politics was the goal of the civil service reform movement of the late nineteenth century.

One result was that in the first third of the twentieth century, classic theories of public administration emerged that were rooted in the civil service reform movement. As Dwight Waldo has noted, early theorists in the field of public administration concluded that "politics and administration are distinct"

"Among the most familiar creatures of the political seas is the Bloated Bureaucracy . . . it cannot be hurried; it swims at its own pace."

Source: Drawing by Jeff MacNelly from *A Political Bestiary* by Eugene J. McCarthy and James J. Kilpatrick, McGraw-Hill Book Company, 1979

[3] Peter F. Drucker, *The Age of Discontinuity* (New York: Harper & Row, 1969), p. 220.
[4] In H. H. Gerth and C. Wright Mills, *From Max Weber: Essays in Sociology* (New York: Oxford University Press, 1953), p. 234.

and that "politics in any 'bad' sense ought not to intrude upon administration."[5] Today, however, political scientists recognize that politics and bureaucracy are inseparable, and that bureaucratic decision making involves political as well as policy choices.

Since bureaucrats have great discretion in the decisions they make, a central problem is how to make bureaucracy accountable to popular control.[6] In short, how to reconcile bureaucracy and democracy.

Because civil servants are not elected and are free of direct control by the voters, the bureaucracy is semipermanent in character and, at times, an independent center of power. Can the President or Congress control it? In a democracy this is a serious question, for democratic institutions should be *responsive* to the people. But it is also important to ask, *to whom* is the bureaucracy responsive? A government agency may yield to pressure from an interest group or from some narrow segment of society rather than responding to broader public interests.

There is another danger, too. The executive branch may abuse its power and seek to misuse the bureaucracy—particularly police and intelligence agencies—against its political opponents. So, at the same time that it is responsive, bureaucracy, particularly in its law enforcement and regulatory functions, must also, in some degree, be *independent*. If it is *too* responsive, it may yield to improper political pressures.

The bureaucracy must also be *effective* if government is to solve the social problems that face it. A poverty program that creates jobs for bureaucrats but fails to meet the needs of the poor, and a pollution program that issues regulations but fails to eliminate smog add to the taxpayers' burden without alleviating social ills. Today, many students of public administration contend that bureaucracy should be designed to serve people and to be sensitive to human needs and social inequality. They argue that the first goal of bureaucracy should not be efficiency and economy, but influencing and carrying out public policies "which more generally improve the quality of life for all."[7]

A number of complex questions are raised in assessing the role of public administration in a democratic political system. Can government really be too "big" when people demand increased services? Should the federal bureaucracy be broken up, decentralized? Is greater community control the answer? Closely tied to these questions is the important issue of whether the bureaucracy has been captured by industry or other interest groups, whether government regulators are tools of the regulated. Is the bureaucracy a responsive democratic institution, or does it make public policy solely by its own decisions?

Bureaucracy and the Policy Process

In theory, bureaucrats are simply public servants who administer policy decisions made by the accountable officials of the government—the President, his principal appointees, and Congress. In fact, government administrators by their actions—

[5] Dwight Waldo, "Public Administration," *Journal of Politics,* Vol. 30, No. 2 (May 1968), p. 448.
[6] Wallace Sayre, "Premises of Public Administration: Past and Emerging," *Public Administration Review,* Vol. 18, No. 2 (Spring 1958), p. 105.
[7] H. George Frederickson, "Toward a New Public Administration," in Frank Marini, ed., *Toward a New Public Administration: The Minnowbrook Perspective* (Scranton, Pa.: Chandler, 1971), p. 314.

or inaction—often make policy. That is, they play an important role in choosing among alternative goals and selecting the programs to achieve those goals. As Francis E. Rourke has noted, "Bureaucrats themselves have now become a central factor in the policy process: in the initiation of proposals, the weighing of alternatives, and the resolution of conflict."[8]

Moreover, there is no single bureaucracy in America, and the term is not limited to the federal government: bureaucrats administer programs at every level, down to the smallest units of state and local government. Public administration in the United States is fragmented by the system of federalism. And at each level of government there are hundreds of bureaus and divisions.

Bureaucrats have great *discretionary powers;* what they decide to do, or not to do, constitutes a policy output of the political system. A bureaucrat has discretion when the power he exercises leaves him "free to make a choice among possible courses of action or inaction."[9]

Bureaucracy and Client Groups

The American bureaucracy is deeply involved in politics as well as policy. As in the case of the President and members of Congress, government agencies have *constituencies.* These are interest groups, or client groups, either directly regulated by the bureaucracy or vitally affected by its decisions.

Sometimes, through close political and personal association between a government agency and its client group, the regulating agency becomes a captive of the industry it is supposed to regulate. "In its most developed form," Rourke observes, "the relationship between an interest group and an administrative agency is so close that it is difficult to know where the group leaves off and the agency begins."[10] One reason for this close relationship is that a bureaucracy is often able to increase its political strength by building a constituency. As Rourke notes: "The groups an agency provides tangible benefits to are the most natural basis of . . . political support, and it is with these interest groups that agencies ordinarily establish the firmest alliances. Such groups have often been responsible for the establishment of the agency in the first place. Thereafter the agency and the group are bound together by deeply rooted ties that may be economic, political, or social in character."[11]

Viewed in this light, the behavior of the bureaucracy becomes somewhat predictable. Thus, the Agriculture Department is a natural spokesman for farmers; the Commerce Department is friendly toward business; the Food and Drug Administration may be sympathetic to the drug industry; and the Pentagon is allied with defense contractors. The close relationship, at times, between the Federal Communications Commission and the broadcasting industry also illustrates how some government agencies have mobilized the support of client groups.

Client groups do not always dominate, however. Although a government bureau may be influenced by its clients, it may at the same time be sensitive to, and responsive to, pressures from the public, Congress, and other actors in the political system. For example, often bureaucrats are particularly sensitive to

THE LEFT HAND AND THE RIGHT HAND

Warning: Smoking Is Dangerous To Your Health

SPENDING ON TOBACCO PROGRAMS

U.S. GOVT.

© 1977 by Herblock
in *The Washington Post*

[8] Francis E. Rourke, ed., *Bureaucratic Power in National Politics* (Boston: Little, Brown, 1965), p. vii.
[9] Kenneth Culp Davis, *Discretionary Justice* (Baton Rouge, La.: Louisiana State University Press, 1969), p. 4.
[10] Francis E. Rourke, *Bureaucracy, Politics, and Public Policy,* 2nd ed. (Boston: Little, Brown, 1976), p. 46.
[11] *Ibid.*

wishes of the congressional committees that monitor their activities and control their appropriations.

The bureaucracy acts and reacts in a political way. It responds to a variety of pressures because it is at once accountable to several groups—its clients, the public at large, the press, Congress, and the President. Public administrators, in short, play a major role in the American political system, and their decisions are of crucial importance to government and society as a whole.

Bureaucracy and Congress

Senator John Stennis, Democrat, of Mississippi

Senator John Tower, Chairman of the Senate Armed Services Committee

In addition to client groups, another source of bureaucratic power stems from the political support that an agency may enjoy in Congress, particularly among influential committee chairmen. For many years, the military services were able to count on the friendly support of powerful Democrats who chaired the House and Senate Armed Services committees—men like John Stennis of Mississippi, chairman of the Senate committee. His Republican successor, John Tower of Texas, was no less friendly to the military. Similarly, the FBI and the CIA have enjoyed the protection of a small group of influential representatives and senators.

Agencies that do not enjoy cordial relations with important members of the legislative branch may find their power diminished. For years, the late Representative John J. Rooney, a Brooklyn Democrat, was the nemesis of the State Department, whose appropriations were handled by his House subcommittee. Rooney's hostility to "striped-pants cookie pushers" in the foreign service was legendary, and State Department officials dreaded their annual ordeal of testifying before his subcommittee.

The United States Corps of Engineers is a classic example of a federal agency that has won virtually independent status by mobilizing political support in the legislative branch. Its rivers-and-harbors, navigation, and flood-control projects bring important benefits to local communities—and to members of Congress in those districts.[12]

Government agencies exert considerable effort to maintain cordial diplomatic relations with Capitol Hill. The cabinet departments employ hundreds of persons to engage in liaison with Congress. Liaison officers watch over legislation concerning their agencies; they also field requests made by members of Congress on behalf of constituents who have business pending before their agency. The large number of liaison officers, therefore, reflects congressional demands as well as an effort by government agencies to win support on Capitol Hill. At the same time, the growth of legislative staff in Congress in recent years reflects, in part, efforts of Congress to oversee the agencies.

Morris P. Fiorina has formulated an intriguing theory about the symbiotic relationship between Congress and the bureaucracy. He suggests that "the Washington System" follows a cycle: first, members of Congress earn credit from their constituents by establishing federal programs. Second, the legislation is drafted in very general terms, so that some government agency must create rules and regulations, which means "the trampling of numerous toes. At the next stage, aggrieved and/or hopeful constituents petition their congressmen to intervene in the complex (or at least obscure) decision processes of the bureaucracy.

[12] See Arthur Maass, *Muddy Waters* (Cambridge, Mass.: Harvard University Press, 1951); and "Congress and Water Resources," in Rourke, ed., *Bureaucratic Power in National Politics.*

The cycle closes when the congressman lends a sympathetic ear, piously denounces the evils of bureaucracy, intervenes in the latter's decisions, and rides a grateful electorate to ever more impressive electoral showings. Congressmen take credit coming and going. They are the alpha and the omega."

As long as the bureaucracy responds to and accommodates members of Congress, Fiorina adds, Congress "will oblige with ever larger budgets and grants of authority. Congress does not just react to big government—it creates it."[13]

Of course, in the relationship between Congress and the bureaucracy, the bureaucracy is not without powerful resources. Members of Congress, for example, are particularly sensitive to any plans by the Defense Department to close military bases in their districts. And when some members of Congress talked about reducing the subsidies for rail lines, Amtrak countered by revealing plans for reduced operations. "Just coincidentally, lines to be eliminated seemed to run through the districts of critical members of the Appropriations and Commerce committees."[14]

The bureaucracy, interest groups, and congressional committees interact. In some areas, such as agriculture and defense, the relationship among the three actors is so close, that it is often referred to as a *triangle,* an *iron triangle,* or a *subgovernment.* Although the terms may vary, they refer essentially to the same phenomenon: a powerful alliance of mutual benefit among an agency or unit of the government, an interest group, and a committee or subcommittee of Congress.

Bureaucracy, Triangles, and Subgovernments

The Veterans' Affairs "Triangle"

Figure 11–1

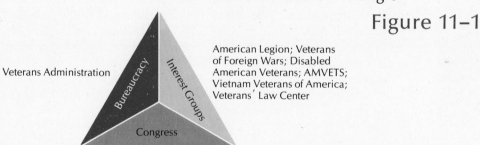

Veterans Administration

Bureaucracy

Interest Groups

American Legion; Veterans of Foreign Wars; Disabled American Veterans; AMVETS; Vietnam Veterans of America; Veterans' Law Center

Congress

House Veterans' Affairs Committee; Senate Veterans' Affairs Committee

As Robert L. Lineberry has suggested, in such a situation, policymaking is a result of "close cooperation and interaction among these triads of power." Lineberry adds: "When a group becomes strong enough, it gets a part of the government, its own piece of the action. The measure of an interest group's strength is how many 'shares' of the government it controls. 'Little' interests, such as the fisheries or tobacco growers, may have only an agency or two within

[13] Morris P. Fiorina, *Congress: Keystone of the Washington Establishment* (New Haven: Yale University Press, 1977), pp. 48, 49.
[14] *Ibid.,* p. 78.

General Alexander M.
Haig, Jr., as NATO
Commander . . . and later
as defense contractor

a cabinet department and only a subcommittee of Congress. 'Big' interests, such as business and labor, have whole cabinet departments . . ."[15]

Douglass Cater, who has used the term "subgovernments" to define the triangle relationship, cites the case of sugar as an example. For many years, until the system was changed in 1974, the price that Americans paid for the sugar on their breakfast table was governed by a system of import quotas and price subsidies to protect domestic producers. As Cater noted, political power within the sugar subgovernment was shared by the chairman of the House Agriculture Committee, who worked out the quotas; the director of the Sugar Division of the U.S. Department of Agriculture; and Washington lobbyists for the domestic sugar industry and foreign producers.[16]

There are numerous other examples of such triangles or subgovernments. In many cases the movement of people among the three corners of the triangle is also an important element; a Pentagon general may, after a required waiting period, end up as a lobbyist for a missile manufacturer, or a staff member of the House Armed Services Committee may go to work for a defense contractor. Typically, in such triangles, many of the participants know one another and play "musical chairs" in changing jobs within the triangle.

The existence of such triangles or subgovernments raises questions about the nature of the pluralist system. Instead of competing with one another, some analysts argue, interest groups merely capture a segment of the bureaucracy and call it their own.[17]

The Politics of Bureaucracy

A new cabinet secretary in Washington often discovers that a title does not assure actual authority over his or her department. "I was like a sea captain who finds himself on the deck of a ship that he has never seen before," wrote one. "I did not know the mechanism of my ship; I did not know my officers—even by sight—and I had no acquaintance with the crew."[18]

As the cabinet member had quickly realized, the bureaucracy has its own sources of power that enable it to resist political authority. Cabinet secretaries come and go; the civil service remains. The expert technician in charge of a bureau within a department may have carved out considerable independence over the years and may resent the effort of a political appointee to take control of the bureau.

In his study of the politics of bureaucracy, Francis Rourke has developed three central themes: the bureaucracy exercises an *impact on policy;* it does so by *mobilizing political support* and *applying its expertise.*[19] As Rourke points out, the growth of the civil service and the removal of much of the appointment power

---

[15] Robert L. Lineberry, *American Public Policy: What Government Does and What Difference It Makes* (New York: Harper & Row, 1977), p. 55.

[16] Douglass Cater, *Power in Washington* (New York: Random House, 1964), p. 18.

[17] See Theodore J. Lowi, *The End of Liberalism: Ideology, Policy, and the Crisis of Public Authority* (New York: Norton, 1969), Chapter 3.

[18] In Richard F. Fenno, Jr., *The President's Cabinet* (Cambridge, Mass.: Harvard University Press, 1959), p. 225. The cabinet secretary who voiced this nautical complaint was William Gibbs McAdoo, Wilson's Secretary of the Treasury.

[19] Rourke, *Bureaucracy, Politics, and Public Policy*, Chapter 3.

The State Department instructed me to survey Prague staffing needs, following the Communist seizure of the country, at which time the American staff, which I inherited, numbered 80. Six months after my recommendation, approved by the State Department, that personnel be reduced to 40, I had managed to get rid of two persons—two only . . .

Today, a decade and a half later, it exhausts me to remember the struggle with Washington required to obtain that reduction from 80 to 78 persons. If I had started to dig the projected Nicaraguan Canal with a teaspoon, those 6 months might have shown a more impressive achievement . . .

"Go cut the heads off somebody else's dandelions," was the gist of successive representations lodged in Foggy Bottom.

It was at that point that the Communists got into the act. Far as I know, they had no idea of the personnel war I was fighting—and losing—with Washington. They possibly thought they were dealing the American Ambassador the most painful blow imaginable when they suddenly declared five-sixths of my staff persona non grata. They gave the Embassy 2 weeks to get 66 American employees and all their families over the border.

For 30 months thereafter, I ran the American Embassy in Prague with 12 individuals—13, counting the Ambassador. No propaganda establishment. No country team. No Peace Corps. No Minister Counselor of Embassy for Administration.

The staff . . . included a deputy who acted as chargé d'affaires in the absence of the Ambassador, an extremely competent man who used to drive the Communists crazy by talking Eskimo over the telephone on a tapped line . . .

It was the most efficient Embassy I ever had.

—Former Ambassador Ellis O. Briggs, testimony to Senate Subcommittee on National Security Staffing and Operations in *Administration of National Security.*

---

from politics does not mean that politics has been removed from the bureaucracy. Quite the contrary; federal departments and bureaus are extremely sensitive to the winds of politics. A request or inquiry from a member of Congress usually brings speedy action by a government agency—the officials in that agency know where appropriations come from.

Furthermore, in mobilizing support, the bureaucracy practices politics, often in expert fashion. The bureaucracy draws support from three areas—the public, Congress, and the executive branch.[20]

A government agency that enjoys wide public support has an advantage over agencies that do not. The President and Congress are both sensitive to public opinion, and a popular, prestigious agency may receive more appropriations and achieve greater independence than others. In the 1970s it was disclosed that the FBI under J. Edgar Hoover had committed burglaries and in other ways had violated the constitutional rights of Americans.[21] But for more than four decades, the FBI had managed to build such a favorable image with the general public that, until Hoover's death in 1972, both the bureau and its chief enjoyed a status of virtual independence.

During the 1960s the National Aeronautics and Space Administration (NASA) and its Apollo astronauts captured the public imagination. To enable it to place men on the moon in 1969, NASA received massive appropriations,

Bureaucracy and Public Opinion

---

[20] *Ibid.*
[21] Frank J. Donner, *The Age of Surveillance: The Aims and Methods of America's Political Intelligence System* (New York: Knopf, 1980).

at a time when some Americans were demanding a reordering of national priorities to meet social needs on earth.

To improve their "image" and enlist public support for their programs, many federal agencies employ substantial numbers of public relations people and information officials. These information specialists issue news releases and answer questions from members of the press and the general public. The federal government some years back estimated that the executive branch employed 6144 people in public relations at a cost of $161 million a year.[22] In 1978 the Pentagon *alone* listed 1823 civilian and military public relations officials at a cost of $25.3 million. And the actual cost and number of people performing public relations activities in the federal government are probably much higher than the "official" figures.

Bureaucracy and the President

The image of the department head as a sea captain aboard a strange ship with an unknown crew may be applied as well to a President seeking control over the bureaucracy. President Kennedy was particularly exasperated by vacillation and delay in the foreign policy bureaucracy. "The State Department is a bowl of jelly," he once declared. "It's got all those people over there who are constantly smiling. I think we need to smile less and be tougher."[23]

Other Presidents have voiced similar complaints. Franklin Roosevelt complained that it was "almost impossible" to get results from the Treasury Department.

> But the Treasury is not to be compared with the State Department. You should go through the experience of trying to get any changes in the thinking, policy, and action of the career diplomats. . . . But the Treasury and the State Department put together are nothing compared with the Na-a-vy. The admirals are really something to cope with—and I should know. To change anything in the Na-a-vy is like punching a feather bed. You punch it with your right and you punch it with your left until you are finally exhausted, and then you find the damn bed just as it was before you started punching.[24]

Often, Presidents attempt to gain tighter control of the bureaucracy by reorganizing its structure. Postwar efforts toward administrative reform led in

[22] David Wise, *The Politics of Lying: Government Deception, Secrecy, and Power* (New York: Random House, 1973), pp. 200, 210. Data for 1970.
[23] Arthur M. Schlesinger, Jr., *A Thousand Days* (Boston: Houghton Mifflin, 1965), p. 406.
[24] Richard E. Neustadt, *Presidential Power* (New York: Wiley, 1960), p. 42.

Franklin Delano Roosevelt: "But the Treasury and the State Department . . . are nothing compared with the Na-a-vy."

Kennedy . . . was determined to . . . recover presidential control over the sprawling feudalism of government. This became a central theme of his administration and, in some respects, a central frustration. The presidential government, coming to Washington aglow with new ideas and a euphoric sense that it could not go wrong, promptly collided with the feudal barons of the permanent government, entrenched in their domains and fortified by their sense of proprietorship; and the permanent government, confronted by this invasion, began almost to function . . . as a resistance movement, scattering to the *maquis* in order to pick off the intruders. This was especially true in foreign affairs.

—Arthur M. Schlesinger, Jr., *A Thousand Days*.

1947 to creation of the first of two Hoover Commissions. Formally entitled the Commission on Organization of the Executive Branch of the Government, the study panel was headed by former President Herbert Hoover. It first reported in 1949, and of its nearly 300 recommendations for streamlining the federal government, about half were adopted. Most of the commission's proposals emphasized centralization of authority and the need to simplify the organization of government.[25]

Since 1918 Congress has from time to time given Presidents the right to restructure the executive branch. Presidents have made extensive use of this power under a series of Reorganization acts passed since 1939; this power was increased by the Reorganization Act of 1949. Under the law, reorganization plans prepared by the executive branch took effect in sixty days unless vetoed by Congress. From 1949 through 1972, seventy-two out of the ninety-one reorganization plans submitted by five Presidents went into effect. The President's authority to submit such plans expired in 1973, but in 1977 and again in 1980 Congress granted reorganization power to the President.

The creation in 1970 of the Office of Management and Budget (OMB) was designed to shift to the President and his budget officials tighter control over management of the federal bureaucracy. OMB is a unit of the Executive Office of the President (see Chapter 10, pp. 375–77). The budget process, which OMB manages, can be a major tool of presidential control over the executive branch. The federal government runs on a fiscal year that starts October 1 and ends the following September 30. Each spring, agencies and departments begin planning their requests for the fiscal year starting seventeen months later. Matching these requests against economic forecasts and revenue estimates from his advisers, the President establishes budget guidelines; within this framework individual agency requests are studied by OMB and presented to the President for decision. The budget then goes to Congress in January.

The in-fighting and competition among government agencies for a slice of the budget pie give the President, through OMB, an important lever for bureau-

[25] Commission on Organization of the Executive Branch of the Government, *Reports to Congress* and *Task Force Reports* (Washington, D.C.: U.S. Government Printing Office, 1949). The second Hoover Commission was established in 1953 and reported in 1955. Because it urged that the government eliminate many activities that competed with private enterprise, its proposals were more politically controversial. The second Hoover Commission report had little impact. See Commission on Organization of the Executive Branch of the Government, *Reports to Congress* and *Task Force Reports* (Washington, D.C.: U.S. Government Printing Office, 1955).

cratic control. Indeed, as Aaron Wildavsky observed, "the budget lies at the heart of the political process."[26] Moreover, the bureaucrat "whose requests are continually turned down in Congress finds that he tends to be rejected in the Budget Bureau and in his own department as well. . . . The Bureau finds itself treating agencies it dislikes much better than those it may like better but who cannot help themselves nearly as much in Congress."[27]

Bureaucracy and Policymaking

In theory, Presidents make policy and bureaucrats carry it out. In fact, officials often play a major role in policy formation. In large part, this is because Presidents rely on bureaucratic *expertise* in making their policy decisions. Frederick C. Mosher has noted the tendency of professionals with "specialized knowledge, science, and rationality" to dominate many areas of the bureaucracy.[28]

But Presidents who rely too much on such expertise may get into trouble. For example, in April of 1980, President Carter ordered a military force to attempt to rescue the American hostages being held in the U.S. embassy in Iran. Although the Secretary of Defense, Harold Brown, and the Joint Chiefs of Staff had apparently assured the President the mission would have a reasonable chance of success, it failed. It also cost the lives of eight American servicemen who died when a helicopter and a transport plane crashed into each other on the ground in a remote desert staging area. Of course, Carter was not only relying on his military experts. He undoubtedly felt that a successful rescue mission would be of enormous political benefit to him in an election year.

Previous administrations have suffered similar setbacks. In 1961 President Kennedy approved a CIA plan to invade Cuba and topple Premier Fidel Castro. After the invasion of the Bay of Pigs proved a disaster, Kennedy publicly took responsibility for the mess, although privately he complained: "All my life I've known better than to depend on the experts. How could I have been so stupid, to let them go ahead?"[29] Of the Joint Chiefs of Staff, who had approved the CIA plan, Kennedy bitterly told a visitor: "They don't know any more about it than anyone else."[30]

Just as federal officials can promote policies that get the nation into trouble, they can also be instrumental in changing those policies. In 1968 several high-level Pentagon officials privately urged Clark M. Clifford, the Secretary of

[26] Aaron Wildavsky, *The Politics of the Budgetary Process* (Boston: Little, Brown, 1964), p. 5.
[27] *Ibid.,* pp. 41–42.
[28] Frederick C. Mosher, *Democracy and the Public Service* (New York: Oxford University Press, 1968), pp. 21, 109.
[29] Theodore C. Sorensen, *Kennedy* (New York: Harper & Row, 1965), p. 309.
[30] In David Wise and Thomas B. Ross, *The Invisible Government* (New York: Random House, 1964), p. 185.

Iran rescue mission, 1980:
The advisers . . .

The result

Defense, to try to bring about a reversal of President Johnson's Vietnam policy. As Clifford studied administration policy in Vietnam—and a request by the military for 206,000 more troops—he gradually became convinced of the folly of further escalation. Although his warm friendship with the President "grew suddenly formal and cool," Clifford and an advisory group of prestigious civilians were apparently instrumental in persuading the President to reverse his policies.[31]

A Profile of the American Bureaucracy

Who Are the Administrators?

In 1792 the federal government had 780 employees. Today there are approximately 2,900,000 civilian employees of the federal government.[32] A study of this total reveals some surprising facts. In the first place, "the bureaucracy in Washington" is not in Washington—at least most of it is not. One recent statistical breakdown, for example, showed that only 361,058 government employees—slightly more than 12 percent of the federal total—worked in the metropolitan Washington area. The rest were scattered throughout the fifty states and overseas. California alone had 290,052 federal workers, and some 125,200 employees worked overseas.[33]

In addition to workers on the federal payroll, however, there are an esti-

[31] Townsend Hoopes, *The Limits of Intervention* (New York: David McKay, 1969), p. 181, Chapters 8–10. No President likes to think that he is manipulated by the bureaucracy. After he left the White House, President Johnson went to great lengths to counter the widely held image of himself as a beleaguered Chief Executive persuaded by his advisers to reverse his Vietnam policy. He insisted that he himself had ordered a major policy review and that the suggestion to stop the bombing had come from Secretary Rusk, not Clifford. See "LBJ: The Decision to Halt the Bombing," CBS Television News Special, February 6, 1970, Transcript, pp. 18–24.

[32] U.S. Bureau of the Census, *Public Employment in 1979*, Series GE79, No. 1, June 1980, p. 7.

[33] Data provided by U.S. Office of Personnel Management, as of February 1980.

Drawing by Ziegler
© 1979 The New Yorker Magazine, Inc.

mated 6 to 10 million persons working *indirectly* for the federal government.[34] These are people working for defense contractors, as outside consultants, or in other programs funded by the government. According to one estimate, the federal government spent $9.3 billion in 1979 on 13,848 contracts with outside consultants.[35] Some of this outside consulting work has been criticized as wasteful or as a way of expanding the bureaucracy without seeming to do so.

In 1980 one-third of the full-time civilian employees of the federal government worked for the Department of Defense. The 964,500 workers in the Pentagon and other military installations, added to the 659,500 employees of the Postal Service, and the 235,700 in the Veterans Administration, comprised approximately 65 percent of the entire full-time federal bureaucracy. In other words, almost two-thirds of all federal employees worked in these three agencies. In contrast, the State Department employed only 23,700 persons.

The federal civilian bureaucracy of some 2,900,000 persons is unquestionably large compared to private industry; General Motors, the biggest corporation in America, had 700,000 employees in 1979. Yet federal workers comprise only 18.9 percent of total (federal, state, and local) government employment in the United States. More than four times as many people work for state and local governments as for the federal government. By 1980 local governments had some 9,403,000 employees (including 4,200,000 teachers and other school employees) and state governments employed 3,700,000 persons.[36] And state and local governments have been growing in size, while the number of federal employees has remained fairly level in recent years. A comparison of federal, state, and local bureaucracies is shown in Figure 11–2.

A rough portrait can be drawn of the "average" man or woman in the federal service: he or she is 42.5 years old, has worked for the government for 14.8 years, and earns an annual salary of $19,372.[37] The President receives $200,000 a year, the Vice President $79,125, and members of the cabinet $69,630. About two-thirds of the bureaucracy are members of the career civil service, with their salaries in many cases fixed on a General Schedule that ranges from a starting salary of $7210 for clerks (GS-1) to $50,112 for a relative handful of top civil servants (GS-18).[38]

[34] James Q. Wilson, "Round and Round with Consultants," *Washington Post,* July 11, 1980, p. A13; and *National Journal,* May 5, 1979, p. 730.
[35] *Washington Post,* June 22, 1980, p. 1.
[36] U.S. Bureau of the Census, *Public Employment in 1979,* p. 1.
[37] Data provided by the U.S. Office of Personnel Management, as of November 1979.
[38] Salaries as of 1980.

Government Employment— Federal, State, and Local

Figure 11–2

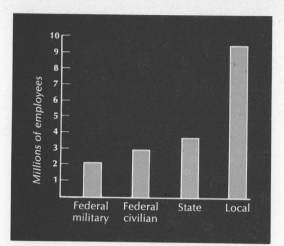

Source: U.S. Bureau of the Census, *Public Employment in 1979;* Department of Defense, Office of the Assistant Secretary for Public Affairs, data for 1980; and U.S. Office of Personnel Management, *Monthly Release,* April 1980.

What kinds of workers make up the bureaucracy? Although almost half a million fit the conventional image of bureaucrats—general administrative and clerical employees—the government also employs 154,200 engineers and architects, 125,800 accountants and budget specialists, 123,100 doctors and health specialists, 58,200 social scientists, psychologists, and welfare workers, 9800 librarians and archivists, and 3200 veterinarians. Among federal white-collar workers, 746,600, or 38 percent, are women.[39]

As noted in Chapter 10, the federal bureaucracy consists of three basic types of agencies: the cabinet departments, the independent executive agencies, and the independent regulatory commissions. Figure 11–3 shows the *major* executive branch agencies as of 1980, but there were approximately one hundred smaller independent units of government in existence, some even too small to warrant a line in the *United States Government Organization Manual.*

The Structure of the Bureaucracy

As Richard E. Neustadt has emphasized, the executive branch is not a monolith: "Like our governmental structure as a whole, the executive establishment consists of separated institutions sharing powers. The President heads one of these; cabinet officers, agency administrators, and military commanders head others. Below the departmental level, virtually independent bureau chiefs head many more."[40]

A President attempts to control the bureaucracy through his White House staff and other units of the Executive Office of the President—particularly the Office of Management and Budget—and through his department heads. Because

---

[39] Data provided by U.S. Office of Personnel Management, as of October 1979. Figures rounded.
[40] Neustadt, *Presidential Power,* p. 39.

Executive Branch of the Government

Figure 11–3

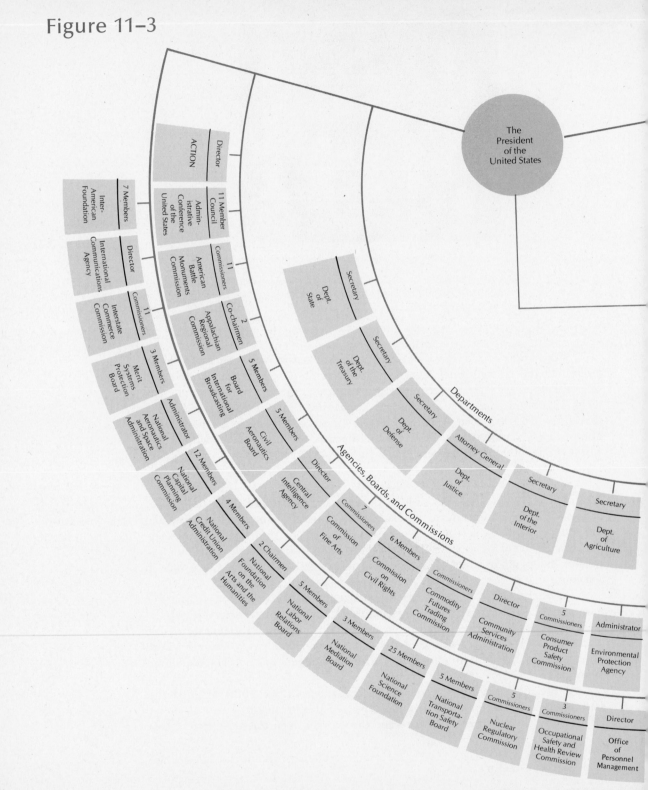

The Policymakers

Source: Adapted from *The United States Government Manual, 1980–1981* (Washington, D.C.: U.S. Government Printing Office, 1980).

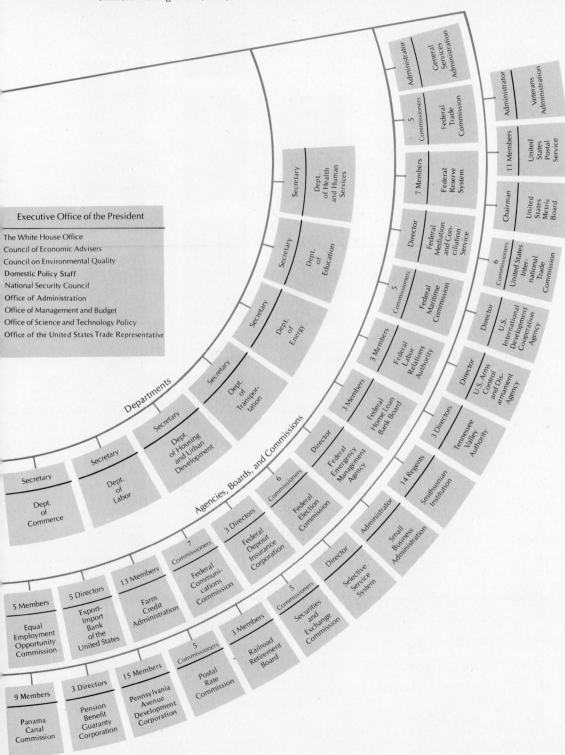

Executive Office of the President

The White House Office
Council of Economic Advisers
Council on Environmental Quality
Domestic Policy Staff
National Security Council
Office of Administration
Office of Management and Budget
Office of Science and Technology Policy
Office of the United States Trade Representative

Departments

Agencies, Boards, and Commissions

Administrator / General Services Administration

Secretary / Dept. of Health and Human Services

Secretary / Dept. of Education

Secretary / Dept. of Energy

Secretary / Dept. of Transportation

Secretary / Dept. of Housing and Urban Development

Secretary / Dept. of Labor

Secretary / Dept. of Commerce

5 Commissioners / Federal Trade Commission

7 Members / Federal Reserve System

Director / Federal Mediation and Conciliation Service

5 Commissioners / Federal Maritime Commission

3 Members / Federal Labor Relations Authority

3 Members / Federal Home Loan Bank Board

Director / Federal Emergency Management Agency

6 Commissioners / Federal Election Commission

3 Directors / Federal Deposit Insurance Corporation

7 Commissioners / Federal Communications Commission

13 Members / Farm Credit Administration

5 Directors / Export-Import Bank of the United States

5 Members / Equal Employment Opportunity Commission

9 Members / Panama Canal Commission

3 Directors / Pension Benefit Guaranty Corporation

15 Members / Pennsylvania Avenue Development Corporation

5 Commissioners / Postal Rate Commission

3 Members / Railroad Retirement Board

5 Commissioners / Securities and Exchange Commission

Director / Selective Service System

Administrator / Small Business Administration

14 Regents / Smithsonian Institution

3 Directors / Tennessee Valley Authority

Director / U.S. Arms Control and Disarmament Agency

Director / U.S. International Development Cooperation Agency

6 Commissioners / United States International Trade Commission

Chairman / United States Metric Board

11 Members / United States Postal Service

Administrator / Veterans Administration

Department of Transportation

Figure 11-4

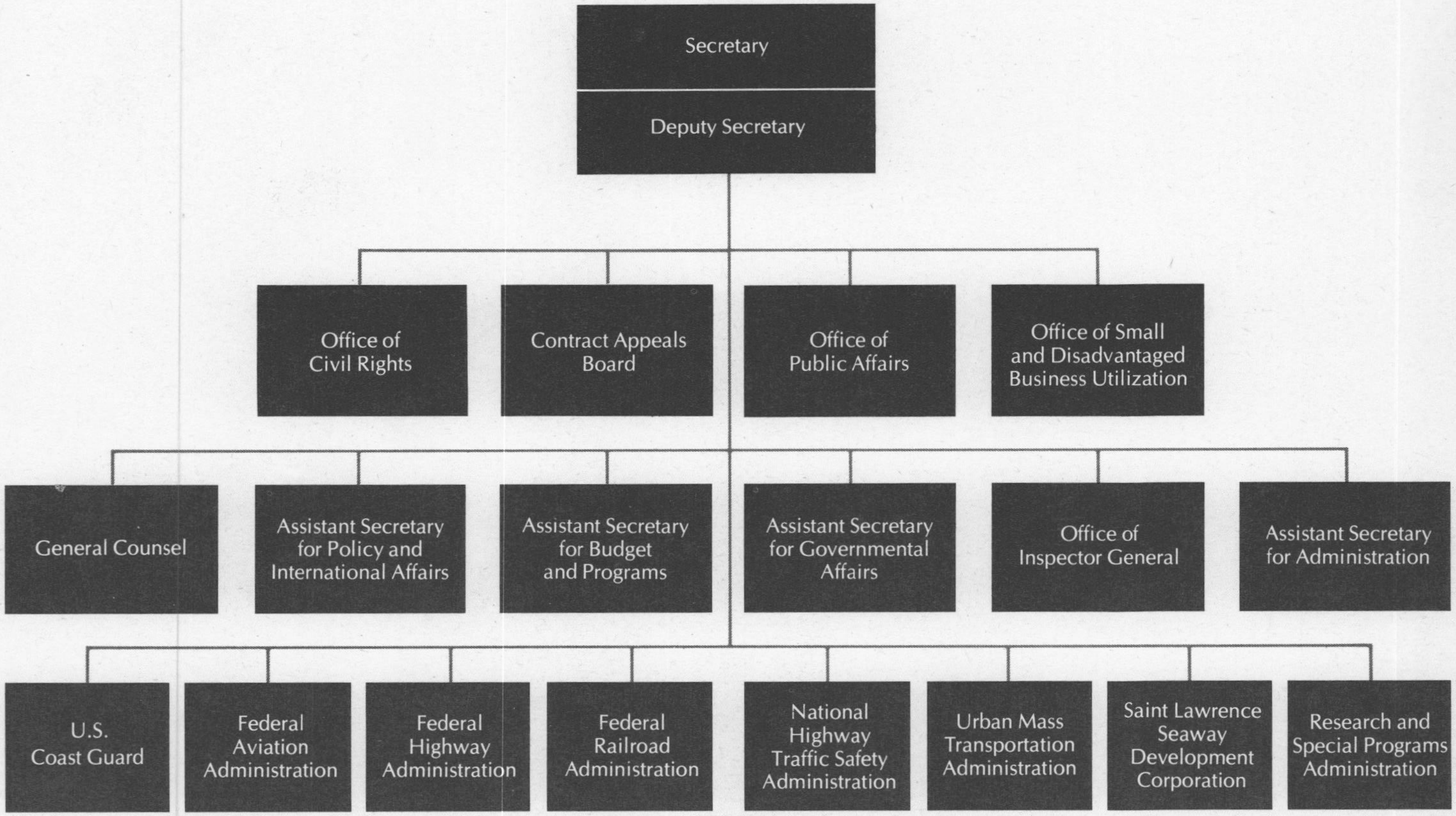

Source: Department of Transportation, 1980.

of the sheer size of the federal government, however, no President can really hope to supervise all the activities of the administrators. And the effort to control the bureaucracy has led to the growth of the White House staff—creating a new bureaucracy at the presidential level.

The Cabinet Departments. The thirteen cabinet departments are major components of the federal bureaucracy. Some idea of the structure of the executive branch and the problem of presidential control can be grasped by studying the organization chart of a cabinet department. At first glance, it might appear to be a tightly organized agency, with lines of authority flowing upward to the secretary, who in turn reports to the President. In fact, the chart masks entrenched bureaus and key civil servants, some of whom enjoy close outside ties with interest groups and congressional committees, relationships that give them power independent of the cabinet secretary and the President. The sheer size of most departments would seem to defy presidential control. To take one example, the Department of Transportation, formed in 1966, had some 72,900 employees in 1980. As shown in Figure 11–4, the department was headed by a secretary, a deputy secretary, and four assistant secretaries, each of whom had responsibility for several offices down the line.

In addition, several major agencies—with sometimes competitive client groups—were loosely grouped under the Department of Transportation, including the United States Coast Guard, the Federal Aviation Administration (FAA), the Federal Railroad Administration, the Urban Mass Transportation Administration, and the Federal Highway Administration. Although the organization chart does not show it, the Department of Transportation, like the other cabinet departments, is dispersed geographically. The air traffic controllers of the FAA operate airport towers across the United States; the Coast Guard and the Federal Highway Administration have field offices in several cities.

The creation of the cabinet departments parallels the growth of the American nation. Only three departments—State, War, and Treasury—were created in 1789. But new areas of concern have required the establishment of executive departments to meet new problems. This fact is reflected in the names of the departments created in recent decades—Housing and Urban Development in 1965, Transportation in 1966, Energy in 1977, Education in 1979, and Health and Human Services also in 1979.[41]

The Executive Agencies. The *independent executive agencies* report to the President in the same manner as departments, even though they are not part of any cabinet department. They are not, therefore, independent of the President. Their heads are appointed by the President and may be dismissed by him. The fact that these agencies are independent of the departments does not necessarily mean that they are small. The Veterans Administration (VA), for example, with more than 235,700 employees, is the third biggest agency of the government, ranking just after Defense and the United States Postal Service. And the executive agencies include several powerful units of the bureaucracy: the National Aeronautics and Space Administration, the Central Intelligence Agency, and the Selective Service System, to name a few.

[41] The Department of Education and the Department of Health and Human Services replaced the Department of Health, Education, and Welfare that had been created in 1953.

Drawing by Gerberg
© 1980 The New Yorker Magazine, Inc.

Grouped with the executive agencies but somewhat different in status are *government corporations*. At one time these were semiautonomous, but through legislation since 1945 they have been placed under presidential control. In 1970 Congress abolished the Post Office as a cabinet department and established the U.S. Postal Service as an independent, government-owned corporation. The President appoints nine of the eleven members of the Board of Governors of the Postal Service, who in turn select a Postmaster General and a Deputy. The hope was to increase efficiency, remove postal employees from politics, and give the new service power to raise rates to meet expenses. But new forms of organization do not automatically solve bureaucratic problems. Many citizens complained that under the new system postal rates increased but the mail seemed slower than ever in reaching its destination. Some other examples of government corporations are the Federal Savings and Loan Insurance Corporation, which protects savings bank deposits, and the Tennessee Valley Authority, which has built dams and provided hydroelectric power and other economic benefits to an area covering eight states.

The Regulatory Commissions. The *independent regulatory commissions* occupy a special status in the bureaucracy, for they are administratively independent of all three branches of the government. In fact, however, as has been made abundantly clear over the years, the regulatory commissions and agencies are sometimes susceptible to pressures from the White House, Congress, and the industries they regulate. The regulatory agencies decide such questions as who shall receive a license to operate a television station or build a natural gas pipeline to serve a large city. These licenses and franchises are worth millions of dollars, and the competition for them is fierce. As a result, the regulatory agencies are the target of intense pressures, including, at times, approaches by skillful and well-paid Washington lawyers who go in the "back door" to argue their clients' cases in private meetings with agency officials. Such *ex parte* (one-sided) contacts are becoming less frequent, however; the Government-in-the-Sunshine Act

(1976) opened up most agency meetings to the public and also prohibited secret contacts. In addition, a 1977 federal appeals court ruling in a case dealing with pay-cable television barred secret contacts with regulatory commission members when they were engaged in rule making.

The agencies were created because of the need for rule making and regulation in highly complex, technical areas involving the interests of the public. In awarding licenses, they also exercise a quasi-judicial function. Despite the separation of powers provided for in the Constitution, regulatory agencies combine aspects of all three branches of government—legislative, executive, and judicial.

Commission members are appointed by the President with the consent of the Senate, but, unlike cabinet members, they do not report to the President. Although members of the regulatory commissions cannot, by law, all be drawn from the same political party, the President designates the chairman. Through his appointive powers a President may in time gain political control of the commissions.

More than two decades ago, a House inquiry into regulatory agencies demonstrated during a dramatic series of hearings that the agencies had, in many cases, become servants of industry instead of regulating in the interest of the larger public. The hearings, and subsequent disclosures, revealed a pattern of fraternization by commissioners and regulated industries. Some commission members have accepted free transportation, lecture fees, hotel rooms, and gifts from businesses subject to their authority.[42] Others have left the commissions for well-paying jobs in the regulated industry. Many have seemed more concerned with protecting pipeline companies, airlines, railroads, and television networks than with making sure the industries are serving the public satisfactorily. On the other hand, at times, the regulatory agencies have been defenders of the public interest; for example, the Securities and Exchange Commission has protected investors from stock frauds, and the Federal Trade Commission has attempted to curtail false television advertising.

The major regulatory agencies, in order of their creation, are:

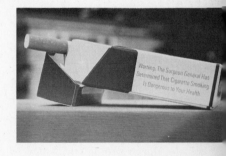

1. *The Interstate Commerce Commission* (1887): eleven members, seven-year terms; regulates and fixes rates for railroads, trucking companies, bus lines, freight forwarders, oil pipelines, express agencies.
2. *The Federal Trade Commission* (1914): five members, seven-year terms; regulates industry; responsible for preventing unfair competition, price fixing, deceptive advertising, mislabeling of textile and fur products, false packaging, and similar abuses.
3. *The Federal Communications Commission* (1934): seven members, seven-year terms; licenses and regulates all television and radio stations in the United States; regulates frequencies used by police, aviation, taxicabs, citizens' band and "ham" operators, and others; fixes rates for telephone and telegraph companies in interstate commerce.
4. *The Securities and Exchange Commission* (1934): five members, five-year terms; created to protect the public from investing in securities on the basis of false or misleading claims; requires companies offering securities for sale to file an accurate registration statement and prospectus; registers brokers; regulates stock exchanges.
5. *The Civil Aeronautics Board* (1938): five members, six-year terms; grants do-

---

[42] Bernard Schwartz, *The Professor and the Commissions* (New York: Knopf, 1959), p. 48.

mestic airline routes and sets air fares; grants overseas routes subject to presidential approval; passes upon airline mergers.

6. *The Federal Energy Regulatory Commission* (1978): five members, four-year terms; although within the Department of Energy, is an independent regulatory commission; fixes rates and has jurisdiction over natural gas companies, electric utilities, and interstate oil pipelines.

Paper shredder,
Washington, D.C.

Many other agencies of the government have regulatory functions in whole or in part. For example, the Federal Maritime Commission regulates shipping, the National Labor Relations Board prohibits unfair labor practices, and the Board of Governors of the Federal Reserve System regulates the money supply, interest rates, and the banking industry. Many units of the regular cabinet departments also have regulatory functions. Examples include the Food and Drug Administration (FDA) in the Department of Health and Human Services; the Occupational Safety and Health Administration (OSHA) in the Labor Department; and the Antitrust Division of the Justice Department.

Deregulation: The Pattern Changes. "One of my administration's major goals is to free the American people from the burden of overregulation," President Carter said in 1977. "Whenever it seems likely that the free market would better serve the public, we will eliminate government regulation."[43] Specifically, Carter as President called for deregulation of airlines, banking, trucking, railroads, and telecommunications.

Even before Carter took office in 1977, Congress had begun exploring deregulation of the airline and other industries. The rising tide of sentiment in Congress reflected complaints by business of excessive and costly government regulation, red tape, delay, and paper work. In 1978 Congress enacted the Airline Deregulation Act, which ordered the Civil Aeronautics Board (CAB) to emphasize competition and simplify its procedures. The CAB's powers were

[43] Congressional Quarterly, *Federal Regulatory Directory 1979–80*, p. 51.

The Paper Chase

The sheer volume of paper generated by the federal bureaucracy has long been the target of criticism. A few years ago, Congress, responding to public complaints about the amount of paperwork demanded by the government, established the Commission on Federal Paperwork. The task of the commission was to reduce the flood of official paper.

The commission acquired a staff of some three dozen people and issued 36 reports and 770 recommendations before it went out of business in 1977. Its major recommendation was that a new cabinet-level Department of Administration be created to manage federal paperwork.

Congress was less than enthusiastic over the idea of creating yet another bureaucracy to manage the bureaucracy. Representative Peter H. Kostmayer,

a Pennsylvania Democrat, declared: "We can encourage each department to tighten up its operations without hiring thousands of more bureaucrats who, as we know, have an unsurpassed ability to produce paperwork." Congress did not establish the new department.

President Carter also attempted to cope with the paperwork problem. He ordered his bureaucrats to write government regulations in "simple and clear" language. Despite these efforts, the federal government still imposed a formidable paperwork burden on the public. In one year, according to the government's own figures, it took Americans 913 million hours to fill out 4900 different kinds of government forms.

—Adapted from Congressional Quarterly, *Weekly Report,* December 10, 1977; and *New York Times,* December 1, 1979.

to be phased out by the law; it could grant routes until 1982 and set rates until 1983 and then was to go out of business on January 1, 1985.

In 1980 Congress passed the Motor Carrier Act to deregulate the trucking industry. The law promoted competition among truckers, made it easier for new companies to enter the business, and reduced the powers of the Interstate Commerce Commission (ICC) over trucking. Also in 1980, Congress passed the Staggers Rail Act substantially deregulating the railroads. The new law gave the railroads much more freedom to set the prices they charge their customers and reduced regulation by the ICC. And that same year, Congress voted to continue to fund the Federal Trade Commission (FTC), but with a two-chamber veto by Congress over the FTC's regulations. The law was the first to permit Congress to overrule the actions of an independent regulatory agency. And in January 1981 President Reagan took office after an election campaign in which he frequently promised to reduce government regulation.

The Commission on Federal Paperwork views forty-five feet of official forms required to process aid to one dependent child.

Those at the Top

The *New York Times* once posed this question for its readers: "What's a new administration anyhow?" The newspaper went on to say that officially, at least, it was "one President, [13] cabinet appointees, 300 sub-cabinet officials and agency heads, 124 ambassadors and 1700 aides, assistants and confidential secretaries."[44] Most of the nearly 2,900,000 federal workers are civil servants, not "the President's men" or women. They are not appointed by him to the key policy jobs in the bureaucracy.

In presidential election years, the House or Senate Post Office and Civil Service Committee has obligingly published something known affectionately in Washington as "the plum book" (as in "political plum"), a listing of the non-civil service jobs that the incoming President may fill.[45] For White House aides assigned to screen patronage appointees for the new administration, the plum book is an indispensable reference guide. Job seekers in the Reagan administration who studied the new edition published after the 1980 presidential election found about 2500 positions listed in the 161-page book—beginning with the White House staff.

Usually, an incoming President makes approximately 2000 key appointments, for the most part exempt from civil service requirements. Of this total, perhaps 500 are important policy-advisory posts.

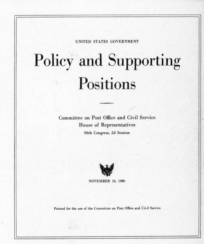

UNITED STATES GOVERNMENT

Policy and Supporting Positions

Committee on Post Office and Civil Service
House of Representatives
96th Congress, 2d Session

NOVEMBER 18, 1980

Printed for the use of the Committee on Post Office and Civil Service

"The plum book"

The Civil Service

Today the vast majority of government jobs are filled through the competitive civil service system. Yet Presidents have always rewarded their political supporters and friends with government jobs. (In many cases, of course, Presidents appoint persons recommended by powerful senators or House members.) Although George Washington declared that he appointed officials on the basis of "fitness of character," he favored members of his own party, the Federalists. Jefferson dismissed hundreds of Federalists from the government when he became President, replacing them with members of his own party.

---

[44] Max Frankel, "Priorities for the Nixon Team," *New York Times,* November 15, 1968, p. 32.

[45] U.S. Congress, House, Committee on Post Office and Civil Service, *United States Government Policy and Supporting Positions,* 96th Cong., 2nd sess. (Washington, D.C.: U.S. Government Printing Office, 1980).

The Spoils System.   After Andrew Jackson was elected in 1828, he dismissed more than a third of the 612 presidentially appointed officeholders and 10 to 20 percent of the 10,000 lesser government officials. Although Jackson thereby continued a practice started by Jefferson, he is generally credited with introducing the "spoils system" to the national government. (Jackson preferred to call it "rotation in office.") In 1832 Senator William Learned Marcy of New York, defending a Jackson ambassadorial appointment, declared: "To the victor belong the spoils." The phrase became a classic statement of the right of victorious politicians to reward their followers with jobs. Political workers expected such rewards; when Lincoln became President, office seekers prowled the White House stairways and hallways.

The Road to Reform.   Inefficiency and corruption in the federal government led to the first efforts at reform in the 1850s. After the Civil War the reform movement gathered momentum. Although President Grant's administration was riddled by corruption, it was Grant who persuaded Congress in 1871 to set up the first Civil Service Commission. But the reform efforts had faltered by 1875, partly because Congress declined to appropriate new funds for the commission.

In 1880 the Republican party was divided into two factions, for and against civil service reform. James A. Garfield, the Republican presidential candidate, ran on a reform platform. To appease the "Stalwarts," or antireform faction, Chester A. Arthur was chosen for Vice President.

After Garfield's election, Charles J. Guiteau, an eccentric evangelist and lawyer, decided he deserved the post of ambassador to Austria or at least the job of Paris consul. In 1881 it was easy to get into the White House, and Guiteau actually had an unsuccessful interview with President Garfield. Brooding over his failure to join the diplomatic service, Guiteau purchased a revolver. On July 2, he approached Garfield at the railroad station in Washington and shot him in the back, crying: "I am a Stalwart and now Arthur is President!" Garfield died eighty days later and his assassin was hanged.

To the dismay of his political cronies, Chester Arthur became a champion of civil service reform. In the wake of public indignation over the assassination, Congress passed the Civil Service Reform Act of 1883 (the Pendleton Act). It established a bipartisan Civil Service Commission under which about 10 percent of federal employees were chosen through competitive examinations. (Under President Carter, Congress enacted the Civil Service Reform Act of 1978, which replaced the commission with the Office of Personnel Management and two other agencies.)

The basic purpose of the 1883 act was to transfer the power of appoint-

President Chester A. Arthur

ment from politicians to a bipartisan commission that would select federal employees on merit. In this century Congress has placed more and more government workers under the protective umbrella of civil service. Today 85 percent of the federal bureaucracy is appointed under the merit system.

To a degree, the removal of civil service appointments from politics has done the President a favor. No matter who a President selects for a government post, he may antagonize others. William Howard Taft complained that every time he made an appointment he created "nine enemies and one ingrate."[46]

In 1980 just over one million government jobs were exempt from the civil service system. But many of these were in agencies such as the U.S. Postal Service, the Foreign Service of the Department of State, and the Federal Bureau of Investigation, which have their own merit systems.

Recruiting the Bureaucrats. The Office of Personnel Management (OPM) acts as a recruiting agency for the bureaucracy. It does so through Federal Job Information Centers located in many states. In some cases, examinations for various kinds of positions are held by civil service boards located in major population areas. When a job opens up in a federal agency, OPM may refer a list of names of eligible persons to the agency, which then selects the applicant from among the three names at the top of the list. Or, the agency may fill the job itself, from its own resources and lists. Under a system of "veteran preference," disabled veterans and certain members of their families receive up to ten extra points on their examination scores; most other honorably discharged veterans receive five points.

Before being accepted for government employment, applicants are told that an investigation will be made of their reputation, character, and loyalty to the United States. OPM conducts most of these investigations, but if the job is in the national security area, in which the applicant has access to classified material, the FBI usually conducts the background check. New government employees must swear or affirm that they will support and defend the Constitution. Employees must also swear that they will not participate in a strike against the government or any agency of the government. Within that framework, they are free to join one of the numerous unions and employee organizations that represent federal workers. Unions of government workers at the federal, state, and local level have in recent years advocated a national law to give full collective bargaining rights to their members. But in a number of cases, the courts have ruled against the position favored by the unions, most notably in 1976 when the U.S. Supreme Court struck down a federal law that extended the minimum wage provisions to employees of state and local governments.[47] The Court held that Congress had unconstitutionally infringed states' rights.

Government workers receive annual vacations that increase from two to five weeks with length of service, and liberal sick leave and fringe benefits. Under the merit system, they will almost certainly be promoted if they remain in the career service. Federal employees may express political opinions, contribute to political parties, vote, badger their representatives in Congress, wear a campaign button, display a bumper sticker on their cars, and attend political rallies, but under the Hatch Act they may not take an *active* part in party politics or cam-

Civil service reform: applicants taking exams for government jobs at the New York City Customs House

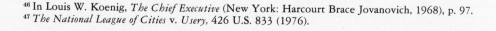

[46] In Louis W. Koenig, *The Chief Executive* (New York: Harcourt Brace Jovanovich, 1968), p. 97.
[47] *The National League of Cities* v. *Usery,* 426 U.S. 833 (1976).

An official explains the number of steps necessary to fire a federal employee.

paigns, or run for political office. Many federal workers consider the law a violation of their rights of free speech. In 1973, however, the Supreme Court upheld the constitutionality of the Hatch Act; the Court noted that Congress had passed the law because of the danger that a political party might use federal workers in campaigns and that promotions and job security might depend on party loyalty.[48]

There is no mandatory retirement age for federal employees, but they can voluntarily retire with a pension, on reaching the age of fifty-five to sixty-two, depending on length of service. Retired government workers drawing a pension may receive about half pay for the rest of their lives, in the case of employees with many years of service.

For most of the bureaucracy below the level of political appointees, a government career has offered a relatively high degree of security. It is true that federal employees may be fired for cause (such as misconduct or inefficiency),

[48] *Civil Service Commission* v. *National Association of Letter Carriers, AFL-CIO,* 413 U.S. 548 (1973).

How to Fire a Bureaucrat in 21 Months

What has 21 feet and 85 boxes and makes you want to pull your hair out?

Answer: A chart of the procedure for dismissing one Government clerk for being late or absent from work all the time.

Looking like a diagram of the circuitry for an intercontinental ballistic missile, its 21 feet (one foot for each month the process took) of boxes, triangles and zigzagging lines chronicle the memos, warnings, suspensions and conferences needed to dismiss one lowly Federal employee. . . .

The 21-foot chart represented the case of a clerk-typist in an unnamed agency. In Government par-

lance, he or she was a GS-4, near the bottom of the [15]-grade Federal pay scale. A GS-4 starts at $8,902 a year.

According to a report accompanying the diagram, the process demonstrates "why so many supervisors would rather put up with a marginal employee than subject themselves to the discomforts of the firing process . . ."

But all the streamlined procedures in the world will not make it easier to dismiss high-level workers. "If a GS-4 cannot type, that's pretty clear," said Howard M. Messner of the budget office. "But if a GS-15 cannot think, what can you do?"

—*New York Times,* February 22, 1978.

or if they are adjudged a security risk. Or employees may be given little to do, or dull work, or be transferred to the bureaucratic equivalent of Siberia, if they offend a superior. But, by and large, they are protected from arbitrary dismissal. Firing most career federal workers is difficult because it still entails a complex and lengthy series of hearings and appeals. On the other hand, Congress may end a government program or cut the appropriation, resulting in a "reduction in force" in the bureaucracy. Workers who are thus "riffed" may be transferred to another job in their agency or to some other government unit, or they may be fired. About 25 percent of federal employees leave or retire each year, representing a turnover of more than 700,000 employees annually.[49]

"We want a government that can be trusted," President Carter said in a speech in 1978, ". . . that will be efficient, not mired in its own red tape."

The Carter Reforms

Carter went on to propose major changes in the civil service system, designed, he said, to reward merit and penalize incompetence. Before the year was out, Congress had passed, and the President had signed, the Civil Service Reform Act of 1978, redeeming a campaign promise made by Carter two years earlier.

The new law, the first major overhaul of the government civil service system in almost a century, established three new agencies: the Office of Personnel Management, to act as the President's personnel arm, handling recruitment, examinations, pay policy, job classification and retirement; the Merit Systems Protection Board, to hear appeals and conduct investigations, including inquiries into complaints by "whistle-blowers" about corruption and waste; and the Federal Labor Relations Authority, to oversee labor-management relations and arbitrate labor disputes between federal agencies and employee unions.

Under the law, federal officials were given somewhat more flexibility in firing employees for incompetence, although not nearly as much as Carter had requested. The appeals process still gave employees substantial job protection. For the first time, a system of merit pay increases, rather than entirely automatic raises, was established at the upper-middle levels of the bureaucracy.

The Senior Executive Service (SES). Perhaps the most important feature of the reform act was the establishment of the Senior Executive Service, a corps of about 8000 high-level administrators and managers at the top of the government bureaucracy. Those senior executives who chose to join SES knew they would have less job tenure and could be transferred more easily within an agency or to another agency. At the same time, they became eligible for substantial cash bonuses for merit. Well over 90 percent of eligible government executives joined SES.

The idea behind the creation of SES was to establish a nucleus of top executives in the government in a way that would balance career risk-taking against rewards for high performance, and at the same time would emphasize mobility, managerial discretion in assignments, and accountability.[50]

[49] Data for 1979 provided by Work Force Analysis and Statistics Branch, Office of Personnel Management.

[50] James P. McGrath, *Civil Service Reform Act: Implementation* (Washington, D.C.: The Library of Congress, Congressional Research Service, 1980), p. 9.

President Carter is abolishing 176 more federal advisory committees because they have outlived their usefulness, a White House spokesman said yesterday.

The latest order, coupled with the reductions announced May 25, will result in elimination of 480 advisory panels at an estimated savings of $15 million.

Most of the committees targeted for elimination are not widely known. They include such panels as the Board of Tea Experts, the Advisory Board on Hog Cholera Eradication, the Underwater Sound Advisory Committee and the Lyndon B. Johnson National Grasslands Advisory Board.

— *San Francisco Chronicle*, August 25, 1977.

Bureaucracy and Society

During his first campaign for President in 1976, Jimmy Carter promised to reorganize the federal bureaucracy if elected. Carter had revamped the state government in Georgia and claimed as his biggest accomplishment as governor the consolidation of some 300 state offices into 22 agencies. Repeatedly, as a candidate, Carter promised to bring about the same sort of reorganization in Washington. He pledged that he would cut the federal bureaucracy from 1900 agencies to 200.[51] However, once Carter was in the White House, the goal of reducing the number of federal agencies to 200 was quickly abandoned and little was heard about the campaign promise.[52]

President Carter scaled down the scope of his plans to reorganize the government. He did propose and achieve reorganization of the civil service system, as already discussed. And Congress at his request established the Department of Energy and created the Department of Education and the Department of Health and Human Services, largely from the old Department of Health, Education, and Welfare. The Carter administration also reorganized some other parts of the bureaucracy, including agencies dealing with civil rights, civil defense, and international communications.

Rational
Decision Making

One of the criticisms of bureaucracy is that its decision making tends to be "incremental"—that is, what was decided yesterday limits the scope of choice today. New policies, instead of replacing old ones, tend to be "added on" to existing programs, because government officials are usually wary of sweeping change or policy innovations.

Peter Drucker has suggested: "Certain things are inherently difficult for government. Being by design a protective institution, it is not good at innova-

[51] Jules Witcover, *Marathon: The Pursuit of the Presidency, 1972–1976* (New York: Viking, 1977), p. 207.

[52] Ironically, however, depending on how one counts, the number of federal departments and agencies was well below 200 all along. According to a *Fact Book* issued by the Office of Management and Budget in 1977, there were 2018 federal agencies, but of those, 1185 were advisory panels, 129 were interagency committees, and 332 were subagencies—divisions of cabinet departments. Counting the President, the cabinet departments, the independent executive agencies, and the regulatory commissions, there were only about 100 operating departments and agencies in the government. Source: *New York Times*, April 7, 1977, p. A17.

tion. It cannot really abandon anything. The moment government undertakes anything it becomes entrenched and permanent."[53]

Because of the obstacles to innovation, bureaucracy may overlook problems that do not fit into established forms. In 1967, for example, the Surgeon General of the United States, Dr. William H. Stewart, told a Senate subcommittee on poverty that the federal government did not know the extent of hunger and malnutrition in America. "We just don't know," he said. "It hasn't been anybody's job."

Often, when government is confronted with a new task, a new agency is established to handle it. For example, during the Kennedy administration, the Peace Corps was made independent of the State Department, and during the Johnson administration, the poverty program was created as a separate agency. The tendency to start new agencies for new programs to some extent reflects resistance to change on the part of old-line, existing agencies.

In an attempt to break through traditional forms of bureaucratic decision making, the federal government tried to apply new techniques of management technology to policy problems. The goal of the "rationalists," as advocates of the new techniques were sometimes called, was to arrive at decisions on the basis of systematic analysis, rather than on the basis of guesswork or custom.

The new methods often utilized electronic computers to analyze masses of data. One of the new management tools, known as "cost effectiveness," or "systems analysis," was inaugurated at the Pentagon in 1961 by Defense Secretary Robert S. McNamara, who said that the technique helped to measure the benefits of alternative policies against their dollar costs. In 1965 President Johnson ordered that these techniques be applied throughout most of the bureaucracy. He established a planning-programming budgeting system (PPBS) within the executive branch. Federal departments were required to define their goals precisely and measure the costs and benefits of alternative programs to achieve those goals.[54]

In 1971 the system was abolished by the Nixon administration and a program of management by objective (MBO) was created. Federal agencies were required to make periodic checks to be sure they were achieving their objectives. In modified form, the system continued under President Ford. President Carter substituted a system of Zero-Base Budgeting (ZBB). A principal goal of ZBB was to "examine the need for . . . existing programs as if they were being proposed for the first time."[55]

Efforts to apply the tools and techniques of rational decision making to reform the management of the executive branch have been both praised and criticized. The system works best in areas in which goals can be "quantified"— expressed in dollar amounts. Thus the Pentagon can use this technique to measure the relative merits and cost of weapons systems and military hardware. But in areas like welfare, education, and foreign policy, correct choices cannot so easily be arrived at by measuring benefits against costs. The long-range benefits to American society from an improved educational system, for example, cannot be evaluated wholly by a computer.

---

[53] Drucker, *The Age of Discontinuity,* p. 226.

[54] For an analysis of the abandonment of PPBS by the federal government, see Allen Schick, "A Death in the Bureaucracy: The Demise of Federal PPB," in *Public Administration Review,* Vol. 33, No. 2 (March-April 1973), pp. 146–56.

[55] Office of Management and Budget, memo to heads of executive departments, "Zero-Base Budgeting," May 5, 1978.

The overriding concern with institutions should be how we as individuals can tell our institutions that they are not going to have a momentum of their own . . . that they are going to reflect individual inputs . . . that the individual in these large institutions, whether they are companies or government agencies or other organizations, must reassert his rights . . . and that every person who is part of a large organization must have that line drawn for himself beyond which he will no longer subserve himself to the dictates of the organization, beyond which he will say . . . my loyalty to mankind, to my society, to my fellow citizen, overrides my loyalty to my organization and that is where I must place my commitment and knowledge. Unless every individual somewhere in his mind draws that line when he will no longer simply take orders . . . unless every individual has that line drawn for himself, he will have within him a potential slice of the Nuremberg problem.

—Ralph Nader, commencement address at Franklin Pierce College, 1970.

Checks on Bureaucratic Power

Bureaucracy is big, and powerful. There are, however, some visible checks on that power. First, government agencies must share power with other elites in the political system, not only competing agencies in the executive branch, but also Congress, the courts, and groups and leaders outside the government. When government agencies mobilize political support among private industry or other "client" groups, they give up some of their independence and power in the process. In addition to sharing power with other parts of government and with interest groups, officials are held in check to some degree by the press. Fear of adverse publicity is a powerful factor in decision making in Washington, as well as in state and local government. Moreover, in recent years some government employees have become "whistle-blowers"; that is, they have publicly exposed evidence of waste or corruption that they learned about in the course of their duties.

A. Ernest Fitzgerald, cost-minded Pentagon employee

Whistle-Blowers. Whistle-blowing can sometimes turn out to be a significant factor within the bureaucracy. For example, in 1968, A. Ernest Fitzgerald, a Pentagon official, exposed a $2 billion cost overrun in the C-5A aircraft program. After this, Fitzgerald was forced out of his $32,000-a-year job; he was not reinstated until 1973. (His reinstatement followed the disclosure in Senate Watergate testimony that a White House aide had complained about Fitzgerald's revelations in a memo that said, "only a basic no-goodnik would take his official

Newly disclosed transcripts of White House tape recordings show that former president Richard Nixon personally ordered the 1970 firing of A. Ernest Fitzgerald, the Pentagon financial analyst who exposed the $2 billion cost overrun in the production of the C5A cargo plane.

"This guy that was fired," Nixon remarked in a Jan. 31, 1973, conversation with presidential aide Charles W. Colson, "I'd marked it in the news summary. That's how that happened. I said get rid of that son of a b. . . ."

In another conversation the same day, Nixon told presidential aide John D. Ehrlichman, "Yeah, well, the point was not that he was complaining about the overruns, but that he was doing it in public."

"That's the point," Ehrlichman replied, "and cutting up his superiors."

—*Washington Post,* March 7, 1979.

business grievances so far from normal channels." Later it was revealed that President Nixon had personally ordered Fitzgerald fired.)

And whistle-blowers often pay a high price for their actions. Although Fitzgerald was reinstated, he was never reassigned to the same level of work as he had done before his dismissal. Other whistle-blowers, less well known, have also been fired.

Consider, for example, the case of Dr. J. Anthony Morris, a government virologist. In 1976 a soldier at Fort Dix, New Jersey, died of swine flu. Fearing a nationwide epidemic, the director of the federal Center for Disease Control called for a national program of immunization. Two weeks later, President Ford told the nation he was asking for $135 million to launch a massive inoculation program.[56] Alone within the government, Dr. Morris opposed the program; he had been questioning the value of flu shots for several years. Vigorously, he protested that there was no evidence that the swine flu would cause an epidemic like the one that had occurred in 1918. And, he warned, the vaccine was dangerous. At age fifty-eight, Dr. Morris was fired from his $32,000 research job by the head of the Food and Drug Administration, who found him guilty of "insubordination and inefficiency."[57]

Dr. J. Anthony Morris opposed the government's swine flu program.

Inoculations started in October 1976, were suspended for a time, and then cut off entirely in February 1977. Some 50 million Americans were given swine flu vaccine, but the program was halted after several persons became seriously ill with Guillain-Barré syndrome, a rare paralytic disease. By March 1980, 38,000 claims totaling $3.5 billion had been filed against the government by persons who claimed they were injured by the vaccine. The lawsuits also claimed that 360 deaths and more than 700 cases of Guillain-Barré disease had resulted from the flu shots. The government had already paid out $10 million and the litigation was expected to go on for years.[58] Although whistle-blowers may pay a high price, the possibility of such exposure from within the bureaucracy may act to curb potential abuses.

Other Checks on Bureaucracy. In addition, there are certain "inner checks" on the bureaucracy. To some extent at least, bureaucrats may be inhibited from abusing their power by the social and political system in which they operate. Like other citizens, bureaucrats have been politically socialized, and in many cases they may tend to adhere to standards of fair play and respect for individual rights. But relying on human nature and individual conscience is a rather uncertain means of controlling public servants, and the search continues for institutionalized methods of control. The device of the *ombudsman,* for example, has proved popular in Sweden and in some other countries. The *ombudsman* is an official complaint taker; he tries to help citizens who have been wronged by the actions of government agencies.

The courts and the legal system also play a role in controlling bureaucracy. Ten officials of the Nixon administration were convicted and jailed in the Watergate scandal. And, in the fall of 1980, two former high FBI officials were tried in federal court on charges of violating the constitutional rights of citizens

[56] See Richard E. Neustadt and Harvey V. Fineberg, M.D., *The Swine Flu Affair* (Washington, D.C.: U.S. Department of Health, Education, and Welfare, 1978).

[57] Helen Dudar, "The Price of Blowing the Whistle," *New York Times Magazine,* October 30, 1977, pp. 48–49.

[58] Data provided by Torts Division, Department of Justice; and *New York Times,* June 10, 1979, p. 1.

by authorizing FBI break-ins in the search for radical fugitives in the early 1970s. They were convicted, but said they would appeal.

As long as government has responsibility for allocating things of value, for deciding who gets what in American society, there will be bureaucrats to help make and carry out those decisions. The problem of controlling bureaucracy and making it serve the people is a continuing challenge to the American system.

Perspective

Bureaucracy—and bureaucrats—are handy political targets to blame for society's ills. Yet government at every level—federal, state, and local—could not function without bureaucrats, or public administrators, to run it.

In theory, bureaucrats are simply public servants who administer policy decisions made by the accountable officials of the government, including the President and Congress. In fact, government administrators have discretionary powers; what they decide to do, or not to do, constitutes a major policy output of the political system.

The American bureaucracy is deeply involved in politics. Bureaucrats have constituencies; these are interest groups, or client groups, either directly regulated by the bureaucracy or vitally affected by its decisions. Sometimes, through close political and personal association between a government agency and its client group, the agency becomes a captive of the industry it is supposed to regulate.

Another source of bureaucratic power stems from the political support an agency may enjoy in Congress, particularly among influential committee chairmen. Agencies that do not enjoy cordial relations with important members of the legislative branch may find their power diminished.

The bureaucracy, interest groups, and congressional committees interact, sometimes forming an especially powerful alliance of mutual benefit, known as a "triangle."

A government agency that enjoys wide public support has an advantage over agencies that do not. The President and Congress are both sensitive to public opinion, and a popular, prestigious agency may receive more appropriations and achieve greater independence than others. To improve their "image" and enlist public support for their programs, many federal agencies employ public relations and information specialists.

Often, Presidents attempt to gain tighter control of the bureaucracy by reorganizing its structure. Since 1918, Congress has from time to time given Presidents the right to restructure the executive branch. The creation in 1970 of the Office of Management and Budget (OMB) gave the President an important lever for bureaucratic control.

Today there are approximately 2.9 million civilian employees of the federal government. Yet, more than four times as many people work for state and local governments as for the federal government.

The federal bureaucracy consists of three basic types of agencies: cabinet departments, independent executive agencies, and independent regulatory commissions. In 1980 there were thirteen cabinet departments. In theory, a department is a tightly organized agency, with lines of authority flowing upward to the secretary, a presidential appointee who in turn reports to the President. In reality, each department has entrenched bureaus and key civil servants, some of whom enjoy close outside ties with interest groups and congressional committees and have power independent of the secretary and the President.

Independent executive agencies report to the President in the same manner as departments, but are separate from the cabinet departments. Their heads are appointed by the President and may be dismissed by him.

Independent regulatory commissions occupy a special status in the bureaucracy, for they are administratively independent of all three branches of government. In fact, however, they are susceptible to pressures from the White House, Congress, and the industries they regulate. These agencies were created because of the need for rule making and regulation in highly complex technical areas involving the interests of the public. But more recently, Congress has begun to deregulate some industries; it has reduced government control over the airline, trucking, and railroad industries, for example. The rising tide of deregulation sentiment reflected complaints by business of excessive and costly government regulations, red tape, delay, and paper work.

Presidents have always rewarded their political supporters and friends with government jobs. But the vast majority of government jobs are filled through the competitive civil service system, which was reorganized under President Carter in 1978. The Office of Personnel Management (OPM) acts as a recruiting agency for the bureaucracy. The Senior Executive Service (SES) offers top-level federal officials cash incentives for high performance, but less job security.

Although the bureaucracy is powerful, there are external checks on that power. Government agencies must share power with other elites in the political system, including Congress, the courts, and interest groups. Officials are also held in check to some degree by the press. In recent years some government employees, acting as "whistle-blowers," have publicly exposed evidence of waste or corruption in government. There are also inner checks on the bureaucracy. Like other citizens, bureaucrats have been politically socialized and may tend to adhere to standards of fair play and respect for individual rights. And bureaucrats who break the law may be punished by the courts. But controlling the bureaucracy remains a continuing challenge.

Suggested Reading

Altshuler, Alan A., and Thomas, Norman C. eds. *The Politics of the Federal Bureaucracy** (Harper & Row, 1976). A useful examination of the role of the federal bureaucracy in the political system. Stresses the political dynamics of how the bureaucracy operates.

Heclo, Hugh. *A Government of Strangers** (The Brookings Institution, 1977). An important analysis of the relations between political leaders and the bureaucracy. Heclo identifies weaknesses in the nation's political structure and suggests reforms to bring about more effective executive leadership.

Kaufman, Herbert. *Are Government Organizations Immortal?** (The Brookings Institution, 1976). An interesting and thought-provoking exploration of the factors that work for or against the survival of governmental agencies once they have been established.

Mosher, Frederick C. *Democracy and the Public Service** (Oxford University Press, 1968). An excellent and readable discussion of various trends in the public service, including professionalization, unionization, and the merit system. Discusses their implications for democratic government.

Rourke, Francis E. *Bureaucracy, Politics, and Public Policy,* 2nd edition* (Little, Brown, 1976). A concise and valuable general introduction to the role of the bureaucracy in the making of public policy. Among other topics, the book analyzes the sources of power of government bureaucracies, and new approaches to policymaking in bureaucratic agencies.

Seidman, Harold. *Politics, Position, and Power: The Dynamics of Federal Organization,* 2nd edition* (Oxford University Press, 1975). An enlightening discussion of the operations of government agencies and the political realities affecting proposals for their reorganization.

Simon, Herbert A. *Administrative Behavior: A Study of Decision-Making Processes in Administrative Organizations** (Free Press, 1976). A classic theoretical and empirical analysis of decision making in government bureaucracies. This book, first published in 1947, has influenced modern scholarly work on bureaucratic organizations.

White, Leonard D. *The Federalists* (Greenwood, 1978) (Originally published in 1948); *The Jeffersonians, 1801–1829* (Macmillan, 1951); *The Jacksonians, 1829–1861* (Macmillan, 1954); and *The Republican Era, 1869–1901* (Macmillan, 1958). A notable and detailed study, in four volumes, of the historical development of the American public service from 1789 to the turn of the twentieth century.

Wildavsky, Aaron. *The Politics of the Budgetary Process,* 3rd edition* (Little, Brown, 1979). A revealing analysis of the nature of the federal budgetary process and its relationship to the making of public policy.

Wilson, James Q. *The Politics of Regulation* (Basic, 1980). A valuable collection of nine case studies on public policymaking and the relationship between the public and private sectors in Washington regulatory agencies. Includes a discussion of the political and historical origins of a wide range of agencies — from state public utility commissions to the Federal Trade Commission.

12

THE CONGRESS

Chairman Peter W. Rodino, Jr., of the House Judiciary Committee, presiding over hearings on the impeachment of President Nixon, July 1974

On the evening of July 24, 1974, under the bright television lights, Congressman Peter W. Rodino, Jr., the silver-haired chairman of the House Committee on the Judiciary, slowly began reading a statement as the nation watched. An American flag and the oil portraits of Rodino's predecessors on the wall formed a backdrop in the dark-panelled committee room on Capitol Hill.

"Almost two centuries ago," he said, "the Founding Fathers of the United States reaffirmed . . . that here all men are under the law, and it is only the people who are sovereign. So speaks our Constitution, and it is under our Constitution, the supreme law of the land, that we proceed through the sole power of impeachment. We have reached the moment when we are ready to debate . . . whether or not the Committee on the Judiciary should recommend that the House of Representatives adopt articles calling for the impeachment of Richard M. Nixon.

"Make no mistake about it. This is a turning point, whatever we decide. Our judgment is not concerned with an individual but with a system of constitutional government. . . . Let us leave the Constitution as unimpaired for our children as our predecessors left it to us."

For six days the thirty-eight members of the committee debated the question of the impeachment of the President. Although the committee was deeply divided, the debate was conducted with dignity and, at times, with great eloquence. Some citizens might hold Congress in low esteem, but on this occasion the committee and its chairman earned the nation's respect.

Three articles of impeachment were adopted by the committee. The articles accused President Nixon of covering up the burglary of the Democratic headquarters in the Watergate office building, of abuse of power by using the FBI, the CIA, the Internal Revenue Service, and other federal agencies in an illegal manner, and of failing to surrender tapes and documents subpoenaed by the committee. Within ten days of the final vote of the committee, Richard Nixon had resigned his office.

In 1978 Tongsun Park, who described himself as a "businessman" but had close ties to the government of South Korea and the Korean Central Intelligence Agency, testified that he had paid $850,000 to members of Congress over several years, mostly in cash. Congressional investigations of the free-spending Korean revealed that Park had been using the money to buy influence in Congress to ensure military and economic aid to the Korean government. Tongsun Park was the key figure in a network of Korean agents in Washington. Over six years, Seoul spent millions of dollars on operations with code names such as "White Snow" and "Ice Mountain" to influence members of Congress and other Americans on behalf of South Korea.

As a result of these revelations, former Representative Richard T. Hanna, a California Democrat, pleaded guilty to conspiring with Park to defraud the government. He went to prison. The congressional investigations disclosed that thirty-six members and former members of Congress—thirty representatives and six senators—had received money from the Koreans.[1]

South Korean lobbyist
Tongsun Park

[1] *Washington Post,* April 4, 1978, p. 1; *New York Times,* April 25, 1978, p. 22, and May 22, 1978, p. 15.

Representative Michael
O. Myers, Democrat, of
Pennsylvania . . .

is shown on FBI video-
tape taking $50,000 in
cash during Abscam case.

Then, in February 1980, Washington was stunned by news stories revealing that the Federal Bureau of Investigation, in an operation called "Abscam," had ensnared several members of Congress on alleged bribery charges. Undercover agents, posing as wealthy Arab sheiks, had videotaped the lawmakers accepting payments as high as $50,000 from the "Arabs." The members of Congress had allegedly promised to help the "Arabs" gain permanent residence in the United States or to assist them in business deals. The news reports named seven representatives and one senator, two of whom were widely respected committee chairmen. Although all eight denied any wrongdoing, seven were indicted and six convicted within a year.

Representative Michael O. Myers of Pennsylvania, a Democrat and a former South Philadelphia longshoreman, was convicted after jurors watched a videotape of the congressman taking an envelope containing $50,000 in cash from an undercover FBI man in an airport motel. Boasting of his "inside connections," Myers told the supposed Arab sheik's representative: "Money talks in this business and bull . . . walks. And it works the same way down in Washington."[2] In October 1980, the House voted 376–30 to expel Myers, the first time in history that a member had been expelled for official corruption. Soon afterward, the United States Supreme Court released the videotapes to the news media, and they were shown to the public on network news broadcasts. That same month, a second Abscam defendant, John W. Jenrette, Jr., a South Carolina Democrat, was also found guilty of bribery and conspiracy. By February 1981, in addition to Myers and Jenrette, four other representatives had been convicted—Raymond F. Lederer of Pennsylvania, Frank Thompson, Jr., of New Jersey, John M. Murphy of New York, and Richard Kelly of Florida. All except Lederer were defeated in 1980.

The FBI's methods in the Abscam operation brought some public criticism, including suggestions that the bureau had been guilty of entrapment. But many other Americans were dismayed by the scandal, and by the reported corruption of members of Congress, rather than by the question of whether government agents should offer bribes to representatives and senators.[3]

The performance of the House Judiciary Committee during the impeachment inquiry and the behavior of some lawmakers in the "Koreagate" and "Abscam" cases tell something both about Congress and public perceptions of Congress. In the impeachment debate, the House committee acted in a manner worthy of a great deliberative body. In the bribery scandals, Congress was dragged through the mud by the actions of a few of its members. The contrast in these episodes is reflected in the public's varying views of Congress.

Fundamental questions may be asked about the performance of Congress in the American political system. Are too many members of Congress insensitive to ethical standards? Can Congress meet the social needs of the American people in the twentieth century? Or is it a hopelessly outmoded institution, hobbled by powerful special interests and by internal procedures that are undemocratic? How well does Congress represent the voters, and should it lead or follow them? What is the role of Congress in the American political system as a whole? How well does it perform that role?

Congress is a much-criticized institution. At the outset, therefore, we shall

[2] *Washington Post,* August 14, 1980, p. 1.
[3] *Washington Post,* February 3, 1980, p. 1; *New York Times,* June 19, 1980, p. 1.

discuss Congress within the framework of the controversy that swirls around it. We shall examine in some detail the case for and the case against Congress.

Congress: Conflict and Controversy

For more than twenty years, until the enactment of Medicare in 1965, Congress declined to pass health care legislation for the elderly. Yet the need for such help was clear enough: in March 1965, a few months before passage of Medicare, the median income of Americans aged sixty-five and over was $1355 a year.[4] Obviously, on such incomes, most older Americans were unable to afford adequate health care in the face of rising medical costs. What is more, the public supported such legislation; a Gallup poll in 1962 showed 69 percent in favor of Medicare.[5] By 1940 every Western European country had some form of government health insurance. Yet the United States, the richest country in the world, had failed to act. A powerful interest group, the American Medical Association, fought Medicare as "socialized medicine," and for two decades Congress would not be moved.

The Case Against Congress

   Nor was Medicare an isolated example. President Kennedy was killed by gunfire in 1963, his brother Robert in 1968, and Martin Luther King that same year. While campaigning for the Democratic presidential nomination, Alabama Governor George Wallace was shot and severely wounded in 1972. Despite the hue and cry for gun control after each tragedy, America in 1980 had no broadly effective federal gun control legislation. Congress, under pressure by the gun lobby, passed only limited legislation to deal with this major national problem.

   Representative Richard Bolling, a Missouri Democrat and congressional reformer, has put the question bluntly: "Is the Congress to continue as the least

[4] U.S. Bureau of the Census, *Statistical Abstract of the United States, 1969,* p. 279.
[5] Peter A. Corning, *The Evolution of Medicare,* U.S. Department of Health, Education, and Welfare (Washington, D.C.: U.S. Government Printing Office, 1969), p. 93.

The Guns of March

345 in U.S. Killed by Guns in One Week

   In one week this month, 345 men, women and children in the United States were shot to death. Some were the victims of armed robbers, some were policemen killed in the line of duty, some were shot during family quarrels.

   Other gun deaths were more bizarre: a bartender machine gunned as he sat in his car at a Boston intersection, a teen-aged couple executed as they kneeled by a sleeping bag in the Arizona desert.

   The 345 deaths, counted in an Associated Press survey the week of March 4–11, represented a 40 percent increase over those counted in the last similar survey four years ago. . . . In the latest survey, 236 deaths were classified as homicides, 89 as suicides, and 20 as accidents. . . .

   —*Washington Post,* March 30, 1973.

From *The Herblock Gallery* (Simon & Schuster, 1968)

responsible organ of Government, acting, if at all, ten and twenty and thirty years late?"[6] Although Congress has reformed and modernized its procedures in recent years and has opened up most of its committee meetings, it is still sometimes criticized for placing too much power in the hands of the leadership and in certain influential committee and subcommittee chairmen in both houses. These criticisms have focused attention on two conflicting aspects of Congress: the legislative branch, usually characterized as the most "democratic" because it is considered to be the closest to the people, has an internal structure that is, in part, undemocratic. The resulting inner tension permeates the institution. Yet today it is also argued that reforms have diluted the power of the leadership and the committee chairmen and left Congress fragmented and undirected.

Until the mid-1970s, under the workings of the seniority system, those members of Congress with longest continuous service on a committee automatically became committee chairmen. That is no longer true, but the procedure for selecting chairmen, its critics argue—even with significant reforms adopted in the 1970s—still tends to reward age (and sometimes senility) rather than competence.

Congress has sometimes been assailed in the past, although less frequently today, for rules and procedures designed to block rather than facilitate the passage of legislation. In the Senate, the filibuster is the traditional weapon of obstruction and delay. In the House, until 1961 and even beyond, the Rules Committee exercised rigid control over what bills were brought to the floor for debate.

And many of the norms and customs of the House and Senate have tended to reward conformity. Although it is much less true today than in the past, to some extent the newcomer to Congress is expected to be seen and not heard. The paternalistic atmosphere was best summarized by Speaker Sam Rayburn's advice to his colleagues in the House: "If you want to *get* along, *go* along."[7]

In the field of foreign affairs, Congress was long criticized for yielding too much power to the President. Under the Kennedy, Johnson, and Nixon administrations, the United States engaged in a major, divisive military conflict in Vietnam, although Congress never declared war. The War Powers Resolution, passed in 1973, was an important attempt by Congress to reassert its authority.

[6] Richard Bolling, *Power in the House* (New York: Dutton, 1968), p. 269.
[7] In Roger H. Davidson, *The Role of the Congressman* (New York: Pegasus, 1969), p. 180. The slogan was often heard in the Senate as well.

"*Perhaps the witness would care to reconsider his answer to the last question?*"

Drawing by Stevenson
© 1979 The New Yorker Magazine, Inc.

And as congressional investigations in the mid-1970s revealed, Congress (and the executive branch) failed to exercise proper control over the activities of the federal intelligence agencies.

In the domestic field, many critics have asserted, Congress has largely approved or disapproved programs proposed by the Chief Executive but has not initiated or innovated very much. In the twentieth century, there has been a discernible loss of power by legislatures and parliaments to Presidents and Prime Ministers, and the United States has not been exempt from this "shift of initiative toward the executive."[8]

And, as already noted, Congress has been tarnished by scandal and by the questionable ethics and activities of some of its members. Some members of Congress travel abroad on "junkets" for dubious legislative purposes. Some have relatives on their office payroll. Many accept speaking fees from lobbyists.

Nor have criminal cases against members of Congress been limited to the Korean and "Abscam" episodes. Since 1970, an astonishing twenty-seven members of Congress have been the subject of criminal charges.[9] Among them were two influential members, Representative Daniel J. Flood, a Pennsylvania Democrat, and Representative Charles C. Diggs, Jr., a Democrat of Michigan. Flood, the chairman of a powerful appropriations subcommittee, was a colorful figure — a former Shakespearean actor with a pointed, waxed mustache who dressed flamboyantly. He was accused in a federal indictment of taking bribes of $60,000 in return for using his influence to contact federal agencies on behalf of various businessmen. He pleaded guilty to a misdemeanor in 1980 and was given a year's probation. Diggs, chairman of the House Committee on the District of Columbia, was convicted of taking more than $60,000 in kickbacks from his congressional staff; he went to prison in 1980. And many other members were prosecuted on charges that often involved using their influence as legislators in return for bribes.

Drawing by Mulligan
© 1979 The New Yorker Magazine, Inc.

"I'm sorry, sir. Congressman Clayborne isn't in at the moment. He's doing two to five for mail fraud."

Many political scientists who have studied the operation of Congress closely have concluded that Congress does a fairly good job on the whole. Those who defend Congress argue that it is a generally representative assembly that broadly mirrors the desires of the people. If it fails to act "fast enough" to meet social needs, perhaps it is because the people do not want it to act any faster. And one may ask: "How fast is fast enough?"

To some extent, at least, Congress mirrors the diversity of American society. And often, when Congress is divided on an issue and fails to act, it is because the country is divided on that issue. Ralph K. Huitt, a leading authority on the congressional process, notes that in the past much criticism of Congress as being "obstructive" has come from liberals. As Presidents encountered obstacles to liberal programs, he argues, the critics urged reform of the structure and procedures of Congress to make it more responsive to the President. But Huitt also suggests that "elections do count and representation does work." For example, in 1965, "in the first session of the Eighty-ninth Congress, with a top-heavy Democratic majority that included some seventy generally liberal fresh-

The Case for Congress

---

[8] David B. Truman, *The Congressional Party* (New York: Wiley, 1959), p. 7.
[9] Congressional Quarterly, *Weekly Report*, February 9, 1980, pp. 340–42.

men, President Johnson got approval of a massive domestic legislative program that might normally have taken twenty years."[10]

It may be argued that, to some degree, an internal system that places great power in the hands of individual committee and subcommittee chairmen is necessary in Congress so that it can function at all. Richard F. Fenno, Jr., studying the House of Representatives, noted that "a body of 435 men must process a workload that is enormous, enormously complicated and enormously consequential. . . . To meet the more general problems, the House has developed a division of labor—a system of standing committees."[11] And the workload of Congress, measured by hours in session and the number of committee meetings, has increased dramatically since Fenno's study.[12]

Fenno concluded that the House enjoys stability as a result of "internal processes which have served to keep the institution from tearing itself apart while engaged in the business of decision making." For example, it is generally assumed that members will not "pursue internal conflicts to the point where the effectiveness of the House is impaired."[13]

In short, the House operates under a set of rules that may be necessary for *system maintenance*—that is, to keep a diverse, unwieldy institution functioning. From this basic premise has flowed the defense of such congressional procedures as seniority (now modified), the committee system, and the tradition of elaborate courtesy that senators normally, although not always, display in addressing one another on the floor.

A case may also be made for some of the other procedures of Congress that are often condemned. Much criticism of Congress has originated with liberals and activists who are impatient for the national legislature to get on with the business of meeting social needs. And certainly the filibuster was used by Southern senators to impede major civil rights legislation. Yet in the 1970s, Northern liberals discovered that they, too, were able to use the filibuster to oppose legislation. Moreover, congressional procedures sometimes protect the country against hasty or misguided action in a crisis that could result from bowing to popular emotion.

In reply to the charge that Congress is run by an elite group of leaders, many scholars emphasize the pluralistic nature of Congress. They dispute the importance or even the existence of a ruling elite, such as the "Senate establishment," denounced on the floor two decades ago by Senator Joseph S. Clark of Pennsylvania, or journalist William S. White's "Inner Club."[14] But, whatever the power of the Senate elite twenty years ago, the picture has changed substantially today. Lyndon Johnson, Robert S. Kerr, Richard B. Russell, and the other Senate grandees are gone; in their place has emerged a younger breed, many of whom have become highly visible as freshmen senators. Yet no one who has spent any amount of time watching the United States Senate in action can doubt that some senators are a good deal more influential than others. As Nelson

[10] Ralph K. Huitt, "Congress, The Durable Partner," in Ralph K. Huitt and Robert L. Peabody, eds., *Congress: Two Decades of Analysis* (New York: Harper & Row, 1969), p. 219.

[11] Richard F. Fenno, Jr., "The Internal Distribution of Influence: The House," in David B. Truman, ed., *The Congress and America's Future,* prepared for the American Assembly, Columbia University (Englewood Cliffs, N.J.: Prentice-Hall, 1965), p. 53.

[12] Samuel C. Patterson, "The Semi-Sovereign Congress," in Anthony King, ed., *The New American Political System* (Washington, D.C.: American Enterprise Institute for Public Policy Research, 1978), pp. 158–59.

[13] Fenno, "The Internal Distribution of Influence: The House," p. 70.

[14] William S. White, *Citadel* (New York: Harper & Row, 1957), p. 84.

Polsby has noted, however, each United States senator "enjoys high social status, great visibility, a large staff, and substantial powers in his own right."[15]

Some of the institutional factors that have distorted the representative nature of Congress have changed dramatically. In particular, the seniority system has been modified and made less rigid (see pp. 459–60). As will be discussed, Congress in recent years has also made other important internal reforms. The abuses of malapportionment in the makeup of the House have been declared unconstitutional by the Supreme Court. As a result, the ideal of equal representation in terms of population is coming closer to being a reality. (Even though congressional districts must now be nearly equal, the problem remains of how the district lines should be drawn. Where these lines are drawn by state legislatures for political advantage, in order to favor one party or group over another, the district is said to be *gerrymandered*.)

To the charge that Congress no longer effectively legislates and has become a "rubber stamp" for the Chief Executive, one can reply that this was certainly not President Carter's view as he struggled to pass his energy program. Nor could it have been Richard Nixon's view. Congress rejected two of his nominees for the Supreme Court and passed the War Powers Resolution over his veto. And in 1974 it was the threat of impeachment by Congress that forced Nixon to resign—the first President ever to do so.

The War Powers Resolution is discussed in detail on pp. 361–62. That measure requires the President to report to and, where possible, consult with Congress when committing American combat troops overseas. The resolution has not proved as effective as its sponsors had hoped. Nevertheless, it represented a significant step by Congress toward exercising more authority over foreign policy.

Certainly Congress does not confine itself to saying "yes" or "no" to presidential programs. To an extent that is perhaps underemphasized, Congress innovates and initiates, sometimes on matters of great importance. And since the passage of the Congressional Budget and Impoundment Control Act of 1974, Congress has taken a greater role in the entire budget process—the way in which the government decides how its money is spent.

Finally, those who view Congress in a more favorable light argue that scandal and dishonesty among its members are the exception and not the rule, and that the vast majority of senators and representatives are both hard-working and honest. Not every lawmaker junkets to the French Riviera at the taxpayers' expense, and if the Senate produced Warren Harding and Thomas Dodd, who was censured for misuse of campaign funds, it also produced Robert Taft, Hubert H. Humphrey, and John F. Kennedy. In fact, four out of five Presidents elected between 1948 and 1972, and every presidential nominee of a major party between 1960 and 1972, had served in the United States Senate.

Congress plays a central and crucial role in the political system by making laws—the general rules that govern American society. It is called upon to deal with all of the major issues confronting the nation in the 1980s—energy, inflation, unemployment, the economy, and many other problems. No less than the President, Congress, by legislating, makes and implements national policy.

The Varied Roles of Congress

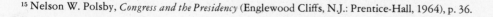

[15] Nelson W. Polsby, *Congress and the Presidency* (Englewood Cliffs, N.J.: Prentice-Hall, 1964), p. 36.

"Did you ever have one of those days when you didn't know whether to advise or consent?"

Cartoon by Mischa Richter. © 1967 by Saturday Review Co. First appeared in *Saturday Review* June 3, 1967. Used with permission.

Most of the controversy over how well or how badly Congress performs focuses on this lawmaking function. But Congress plays other important roles. It has several nonlegislative functions: it proposes amendments to the Constitution; it may declare war; it can impeach and try the President or other civil officers of the United States, including judges; it may rule on presidential disability; it regulates the conduct of its members, and can punish, censure, or expel them; and it has power to decide whether a prospective member has been properly elected or should be seated. The House may choose the President in the event of electoral deadlock. The Senate approves or rejects treaties and presidential appointments, and, through the unwritten custom of *senatorial courtesy,* individual senators who belong to the same political party as the President exercise an informal veto power over presidential appointments in their states.

In addition, Congress oversees and supervises the operations of the executive branch and the independent regulatory agencies. For example, when bureaucrats are closely questioned at appropriations hearings, Congress is exercising its supervisory powers. The power of the purse, which the Constitution grants to Congress, carries with it the power to monitor how well the money is spent. For this purpose Congress conducts investigations and holds hearings. These are ostensibly tied to a legislative purpose, but often they serve a broader function of focusing public attention on specific social problems. During the early 1950s, Senator Joseph R. McCarthy achieved formidable personal political power by using the Senate's investigatory function to conduct "witch hunts" in search of alleged Communists in government. McCarthy succeeded in creating an atmosphere of fear in which the rights of witnesses were frequently violated. But congressional investigations have also been used to publicize the risks of birth control pills, the problems of American policy in Southeast Asia, the tragedy of hunger in the midst of plenty, the political corruption of Watergate, and the violation of individual rights by government intelligence agencies.

Perhaps even more important than some of these formal roles is the function of Congress in "legitimizing" the outputs of the political system. People are more likely to accept the policy decisions of a political system if major decisions are made by representative institutions. Congress, therefore, at times plays a key role in the *resolution of conflict* in American society. As in the case of all political institutions, Congress is subject to external pressures by organized interest groups, unorganized public opinion, the press, and individual constituents. Not every problem can be solved by passing a law. But in responding to social needs with legislation, Congress can at least help to ease the friction points.

In thus managing conflict (or making conflict manageable), Congress helps to *integrate* various groups and interests within the community by acting, to some extent, as a referee. However, as was noted in Chapter 6, not all groups in a

Congressional investigation by House committee

Senator John C. Culver of Iowa was one of five liberal Democrats in the Senate targeted in 1980 by the National Conservative Political Action Committee (NCPAC), a conservative interest group. He was defeated for re-election. Before the election, he offered these thoughts on interest group pressures:

The interest group that is against something is disciplined, marshalled, mobilized, informed, and organized, with computerized mailings and propaganda and newsletters and visitations and all the rest, and is obsessed with that one issue. And, of course, that fact is not lost sight of by anybody up here, no matter what the issue is. It happens on gun control, abortion—you name it. And on the other side of the ledger is that amorphous constituency that wants you to do "the right thing . . ."

Strident and self-righteous groups of voters are proliferating in number and narrowing in focus . . . for each narrow, self-defined lobby . . . the worth of every public servant is measured by a single litmus test of ideological purity. Taken together, the tests are virtually impossible for any officeholder who hopes to keep both his conscience and his constituency.

—Senator John C. Culver of Iowa, quoted in Elizabeth Drew, *Senator.*

---

pluralistic society have equal power. And highly organized, well-financed, single-issue lobbies may exercise an influence out of proportion to their number of supporters. Disadvantaged groups—the poor and the blacks, for example— may find it more difficult to influence Congress than does the oil industry. Consequently, in resolving conflict, Congress may still leave many groups unsatisfied. Yet Congress does provide one of several points of access to the political system for many individuals and groups. The inputs, in the form of demands and supports by segments of the community, are transformed by Congress through the legislative process into policy outputs and binding decisions for all of society.

But Congress is more than just a machine for making decisions. It is also a group of 535 men and women, and who they are is worth examining in some detail, for it may affect what they do.

The Legislators

When the Ninety-seventh Congress convened in January 1981, the average age of its members was 49.2 years.[16] A total of 72 House members, or 17 percent, were between the ages of sixty and eighty.[17] Members of Congress were, on the average, 6.2 years older than other adult Americans.

Portrait
of a Lawmaker

In part, the age level of Congress is slightly higher because of constitutional restrictions: a member of the House must be at least twenty-five (and a citizen for seven years) and a senator must be at least thirty (and a citizen for nine years). In part, of course, it is explained by the fact that senators and representatives usually do not achieve their office without considerable prior experience in politics or other fields.

[16] Congressional Quarterly, *Weekly Report,* January 24, 1981, p. 200.
[17] Congressional Quarterly, *Weekly Report,* January 10, 1981, pp. 95–102.

A legislator's work is never done, as seen in this series of photographs of Representative Ed Markey, Democrat, of Massachusetts.

A member of Congress must visit with constituents . . .

Respond to their problems . . .

Hurry to . . .

More than half the nation's population are women, but the Ninety-seventh Congress had only twenty-one women members. All but two, Senator Nancy Landon Kassebaum, a Kansas Republican, and Senator Paula Hawkins, a Florida Republican, served in the House. Only eighteen blacks served in the Ninety-seventh Congress, all in the House.

In many other respects, the socioeconomic makeup of Congress is not representative of the general population. For example, almost half of the Ninety-seventh Congress, or 253 out of 535 members, were lawyers. In the population as a whole, lawyers compose half a percent of the labor force. Other major occupational groups of members of Congress were: business or banking, 162; education, 69; agriculture, 37; and journalism, 28.[18] As Roger Davidson has suggested, representatives "are recruited almost wholly from the same relatively high-status occupations."[19]

Although today America is a highly urbanized society, Congress historically has been predominantly Main Street and rural. Donald Matthews reported in a study some years ago that a majority of senators were born in towns of 2500 to 5000 people.[20] Congress is also mostly Protestant; for example, in the Ninety-seventh Congress there were 336 Protestants, 136 Catholics, and 33 Jews. (Protestants made up 63 percent of Congress and about 46 percent of the adult population.)

If one were to draw a portrait of a typical member of Congress, that person might turn out to be about fifty, male, white, Protestant, and a lawyer.

How significant is it that in many ways Congress is not literally a cross section of America? Obviously, Congress does not have to be an exact model of the population in order to represent its constituents. Nor is it entirely surprising that lawyers are overrepresented in a body that makes laws. Yet it is not hard to see how blacks, other minorities, women, white blue-collar workers, the poor, and members of underrepresented socioeconomic groups in general may feel "left out" of a system that produces a predominantly white, male, Protestant, and upper-middle-class national legislature.

The Life of a Legislator

"It is true that we just don't have much time to legislate around here."[21] The complaint was voiced by a Republican congressman who participated in a series of round-table discussions about life on Capitol Hill. It could easily have come from almost any one of the 435 members of the House or the 100 senators. There are so many demands on members of Congress that lawmakers soon discover they cannot possibly do all that is expected of them. One House member attempted some years ago to list all the aspects of his job. Only a sample is quoted here: "a Congressman has become an expanded messenger boy, an employment

[18] Occupational breakdown from Congressional Quarterly, *Weekly Report*, January 10, 1981, p. 93, and January 24, 1981, p. 199.
[19] Davidson, *The Role of the Congressman*, p. 69.
[20] Donald R. Matthews, *U.S. Senators and Their World* (Chapel Hill, N.C.: University of North Carolina Press, 1960), p. 16.
[21] Charles L. Clapp, *The Congressman: His Work as He Sees It* (Washington, D.C.: The Brookings Institution, 1963), p. 61.

Committee meetings . . .

Answer the mail . . .

And the phones . . .

Campaign . . .

Vigorously . . .

And love children.

agency . . . wardheeler . . . kisser of babies, recoverer of lost baggage . . . contributor to good causes—cornerstone layer . . . bridge dedicator, ship christener."[22]

Although members of Congress differ in how they choose to allocate their time, it is constituents who elect legislators, and most of those elected spend a fair portion of their day trying to take care of their constituents' problems. Many lawmakers bounce back and forth between Washington and their districts like ping-pong balls.

As of 1980 members of the House and Senate received salaries of $60,660 a year, plus funds to hire a staff (senators from populous states are permitted to hire more assistants), and certain other allowances for office supplies, telephone calls, and travel, as well as the franking privilege for their official mail. Although the basic salary and benefits are considerable, members of Congress also have substantial expenses—many maintain residences both in Washington and their hometowns, for example.

The mail pours in from constituents, and it must, somehow, be answered. Because the volume of mail is so great, many lawmakers use robotypers, machines that type personalized form letters. Few senators and representatives dare to reply to abusive letters as Congressman John Steven McGroarty of California did. He wrote to a constituent: "One of the countless drawbacks of being in Congress is that I am compelled to receive impertinent letters from a jackass like you in which you say I promised to have the Sierra Madre mountains reforested and I have been in Congress two months and haven't done it. Will you please take two running jumps and go to hell."[23]

On a typical day, a member of Congress may spend an hour reading mail, making calls, dictating memos, then rush off to a 10 A.M. committee meeting, eat lunch (if there is time), dash to the floor for a vote, and then after that, return to a committee hearing. Perhaps late in the afternoon the member manages to get back to the office, where a group of constituents are waiting. A powerful interest group (a labor union or business association, for example) has invited the member to one or more cocktail receptions, and he or she must dutifully put in an appearance, have a drink, and chew on a rubbery shrimp before getting home for dinner—that is, on the nights not spent at a dinner in some hotel banquet hall. And some evenings members must remain on Capitol Hill; for the past several

[22] Luther Patrick, "What Is a Congressman?" *Congressional Record,* May 13, 1963, p. A2978.
[23] In John F. Kennedy, *Profiles in Courage* (New York: Harper & Row, 1956), p. 30.

years, the House has held legislative sessions on Wednesday nights. Members spend many weekends in their home state or district, flying there to march in the Veterans Day parade or listen to constituents' woes. All of this can be difficult for the family of a representative or senator.

Although members of Congress do spend a great deal of time handling problems of constituents, 77 percent of House members questioned in one study listed legislative work as their most time-consuming job; only 16 percent listed "Errand Boy; lawyer for constituents."[24] Members of Congress must choose among alternative roles open to them—whether, for example, to concentrate on working for the interests of their districts, on seeking to become party leaders, on running for higher office, on specializing in a committee, or on seizing an issue that may bring them national recognition.

The Image of the Legislator

Congress and its individual members enjoy a somewhat mixed public image. Voter attitudes toward Congress fluctuate markedly. For example, in 1965, after Congress passed landmark Great Society legislation, 64 percent of the public rated its performance "Excellent to pretty good."[25] However, the percentage of those approving of congressional performance dropped much lower over the next several years. (See Table 12-1.)

Public Attitudes Toward Congress, 1967–1978

Table 12-1

	Positive	Negative	Not Sure
1965	64%	26%	10%
1967	38	55	7
1968	46	46	8
1969	34	54	12
1970	34	54	12
1971	26	63	11
1974	38	54	8
1978	34	63	3

Source: Louis Harris, "Congress Gets Poor Ratings," *Washington Post*, March 1, 1971, p. A13; "Congress Rating Improves," *Washington Post*, September 23, 1974, p. 4; and "Job Rating for Congress Is Higher Than Carter's," *Washington Post*, August 28, 1978, p. A3.

Representation: The Legislators and Their Constituents

Should members of Congress lead or follow the opinion of their constituents? The question poses the classic dilemma of legislators, mixing as it does problems of the proper nature of representation in a democracy with practical considerations of the lawmaker's self-interest and desire for re-election.

One answer was provided by Edmund Burke, the eighteenth-century

[24] Davidson, *The Role of the Congressman,* pp. 98–99.
[25] Louis Harris, "Public Gives Congress Mixed Rating for Year's Work," *Philadelphia Inquirer,* January 13, 1969. Respondents were asked: "How would you rate the job Congress did this past year... —excellent, pretty good, only fair, or poor?"

British statesman, in his famous speech to the voters of Bristol, who had just sent him to Parliament. As Burke defined the relationship of a representative to his constituents, "Their wishes ought to have great weight with him; their opinion high respect. . . . But his unbiased opinion, his mature judgment, his enlightened conscience, he ought not to sacrifice to you. . . . Your representative owes you, not his industry only, but his judgment."[26] Parliament, Burke contended, was an assembly of one nation, and local interests must bow to the general, national interest.

The Burkean concept of the legislator as *trustee* for the people clashes with the concept of the representative as *instructed delegate,* who automatically mirrors the will of the majority of his constituents. (Burke encountered political difficulties with his own constituents; six years after his speech, he withdrew as the member from Bristol.) On the other hand, members of Congress who attempted faithfully to follow opinion in their districts would soon discover that it was very difficult to measure opinion accurately. They would find that on some issues many voters had no strong opinions. Even when opinions could be discerned and measured, they would also find that a constituency is made up of competing interests and is really several constituencies. Often, they could please one group only at the expense of offending another.

A large proportion of House and Senate members, therefore, reject the role solely of trustee or that of instructed delegate. Instead they try to combine the two by exercising their own judgment *and* representing constituency views. As Roger Davidson has suggested, "Many congressmen observe that their problem is one of balancing the one role against the other."[27] In interviews with eighty-seven members of the House of Representatives, Davidson found that almost half, by far the largest group of respondents, were "politico" types who sought to blend the trustee and delegate conceptions.[28]

Sometimes a member of Congress faces the dilemma of local versus national interest. Constituents may feel foreign aid is a waste of money, but the legislator may decide it is in the best interests of the United States and vote accordingly. Often, however, local interests are put first—that is where the voters are. And some members of Congress feel that their first obligation is to the constituency that elected them.

Political scientists have studied the process of how legislators make up their minds on an issue. David R. Mayhew has suggested that the "electoral connection," the relationship between members of Congress and their constituents, profoundly influences congressional behavior. "United States congressmen are interested in getting re-elected," Mayhew emphasizes, and that basic fact, he adds, influences the kinds of activities congressmen find it "electorally useful to engage in."[29] And Richard F. Fenno, Jr., has emphasized that the re-election prospects of members of Congress depend greatly on their "home style"—the way they present themselves to constituents back in the district.[30]

Aage R. Clausen has concluded that members of Congress generally vote according to their previously stated policy positions and display substantial

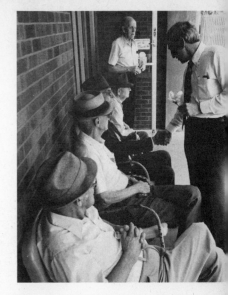

Representative Romano L. Mazzoli, Democrat, of Kentucky chats with senior citizens.

[26] Edmund Burke, *The Works of the Right Honourable Edmund Burke,* Vol. II (London: Oxford University Press, 1930), pp. 164–65.
[27] Davidson, *The Role of the Congressman,* p. 119.
[28] *Ibid.,* pp. 117–19.
[29] David R. Mayhew, *The Electoral Connection* (New Haven: Yale University Press, 1974), pp. 13, 49.
[30] Richard F. Fenno, Jr., *Home Style: House Members in Their Districts* (Boston: Little, Brown, 1978).

stability and continuity in their voting patterns.[31] Donald R. Matthews and James A. Stimson have reported that when members of Congress must cast a vote on a complex issue about which their knowledge is limited, they search "for cues provided by trusted colleagues" who may possess more information about the legislation in question.[32]

To an extent the dilemma faced by the members of Congress may be artificial. One major study of constituent influence discovered that average voters know little about their representative's activities—a finding that contrasted with the view of most members of Congress, who regard their voting record as important to their re-election.[33] Approximately half the voters surveyed in one House election year had heard *nothing* about either the incumbent or the opposing candidate. The study, based on interviews with both members of Congress and voters, also indicated that, while legislators tend to think that the views of their constituents match their own, there is often a gap between the actual opinions of constituents and the member's *perception* of their views.[34]

Polling Constituents. Even if members of Congress want to sample opinion among their constituents to help them in making up their minds on an issue, they face the practical problem of how to go about it. To gauge the thinking back home, members of Congress rely on conversations with friends, party leaders and journalists in their states or districts, the mail (particularly personal letters), local newspapers, and political polls published in their states. In recent years increasing numbers of lawmakers have been using questionnaires mailed to the voters, or have turned to professional polling organizations for help. Without professional assistance congressional polls are likely to be amateurish and the results distorted. In fact, such polls may be taken not so much to gauge constituency thinking as to promote legislators by flattering their constituents with a questionnaire.[35]

The House

Although Congress is one branch of the federal government, the House and Senate are distinct institutions, each with its own rules and traditions and each jealous of its own powers and prerogatives.

One basic difference, of course, was established by the Constitution, which provided two-year terms for members of the House and staggered, six-year terms for senators. The result is that all members of the House, but only one-third of the Senate, must face voters every other year.

Because the House has 435 members compared to 100 in the Senate, the House is a more formal institution with stricter rules and procedures. For example, the Senate permits unlimited debate most of the time, but representatives in the House may be limited to speaking for five minutes or less during debate.

[31] Aage R. Clausen, *How Congressmen Decide: A Policy Focus* (New York: St. Martin's Press, 1973), pp. 9, 53.

[32] Donald R. Matthews and James A. Stimson, *Yeas and Nays: Normal Decision-Making in the U.S. House of Representatives* (New York: Wiley, 1975), p. 45.

[33] Warren E. Miller and Donald E. Stokes, "Constituency Influence in Congress," *American Political Science Review*, Vol. 57 (March 1963), pp. 53–54.

[34] *Ibid.*

[35] V. O. Key, Jr., *Public Opinion and American Democracy* (New York: Knopf, 1961), pp. 492–93.

And because there are so many representatives, they generally enjoy less prestige than senators. At Washington dinner parties where protocol is observed, House members sit below the salt, ranking three places down the table from their Senate colleagues. (House members are outranked not only by senators, but by governors and former Vice Presidents.)[36] In the television age, some senators, especially those who are presidential aspirants, have become celebrities, instantly recognizable to the spectators in the galleries. By contrast, visitors in the House galleries find it difficult to pick out their own representative, let alone any other.

In one survey, only 46 percent of adult Americans were able to name their representative.[37] While the figure is low, it does not give the whole picture. Al-

Major Differences Between the House and Senate

Table 12–2

House	Senate
Larger (435 members)	Smaller (100 members)
Shorter term of office (2 years)	Longer term of office (6 years)
Less flexible rules	More flexible rules
Narrower constituency	Broader, more varied, constituency
Policy specialists	Policy generalists
Power less evenly distributed	Power more evenly distributed
Less prestige	More prestige
More expeditious in floor debate	Less expeditious in floor debate
Less reliance on staff	More reliance on staff
Less press and media coverage, but floor proceedings televised	More press and media coverage

Source: Adapted from Walter J. Oleszek, *Congressional Procedures and the Policy Process* (Washington, D.C.: Congressional Quarterly Press, 1978), p. 24.

though many voters cannot *remember* the name of their own representative, a much higher percentage can *recognize* the name from those on a list. In a selected group of congressional districts, "virtually all voters recognized the name of the incumbent when they heard it," and "most had a positive or negative response."[38]

Despite its size, the House has achieved a stability of tenure and a role never envisioned by the Founding Fathers. The men who framed the Constitution distrusted unchecked popular rule, and provided an indirectly elected Senate to restrain the more egalitarian House of Representatives (the Seventeenth Amendment in 1913 provided for the direct election of the Senate). As Gouverneur Morris put it: "The second branch [the Senate] ought to be a check on the first [the House]. . . . The first branch, originating from the people, will ever be subject to precipitancy, changeability, and excess. . . . The second branch ought to be composed of men of great and established property—an aristocracy. . . . Such an aristocratic body will keep down the turbulency of democracy."[39]

[36] Virginia F. Depew, ed., *The Social List of Washington, D.C., and Social Precedence in Washington* (Kensington, Md.: Jean Shaw Murray, 1980).

[37] Louis Harris survey in *Newsweek*, December 10, 1973, p. 48.

[38] Thomas E. Mann, *Unsafe at Any Margin: Interpreting Congressional Elections* (Washington, D.C.: American Enterprise Institute for Public Policy Research, 1978), p. 30.

[39] In Robert A. Dahl, *Pluralist Democracy in the United States: Conflict and Consent* (Chicago: Rand McNally, 1967), p. 35.

Ironically, the House and Senate have on some issues exchanged places in terms of these expectations of the framers. One reason is that House seats are safer; in recent decades the turnover in the House of Representatives has been relatively small. A commonly cited standard for a "safe" congressional district is one in which the winner receives 55 percent of the vote or more. Less than that is considered "marginal." According to a study by the Congressional Quarterly, between 1952 and 1968 only 20.1 percent of House races were won with less than 55 percent of the vote.[40] And recent House elections have shown a pattern of what David Mayhew has called "vanishing marginals."[41] That is, the number of unsafe, marginal districts appears to be declining even further. In 1976 only 78 of the 435 members of the House, or 17.9 percent, were elected with less than 55 percent of the vote.[42] In 1978 only 66 House members, or 15.2 percent, were elected from such districts.[43] And in 1980, 73 members of the House, or 16.8 percent, were elected from marginal districts.[44]

Morris P. Fiorina has suggested one possible explanation for these "vanishing marginals." He contends that "the Washington system" (discussed in Chapter 11) may be responsible. Under it, members of Congress create new bureaucracies in the executive branch and then gain credit by helping constituents deal with the complex rules issued by the new agencies. As this system has developed, Fiorina concludes, representatives from marginal districts have increasingly found it possible to base their re-election on such casework for constituents and on "procuring the pork."[45]

Senate seats are less safe. In 1976, for example, eleven members, or 33.3 percent of those running, were elected with less than 55 percent of the vote. In 1978 nine senators, or 27.3 percent, were elected from marginal districts. In 1980 the number doubled; eighteen senators, or 54.5 percent, were elected with less than 55 percent of the vote. Because Senate races tend to be close, there is a greater possibility of dramatic shifts in party strength in the Senate, such as occurred in 1980.[46]

Because members of the House are more likely to come from safe districts than their colleagues in the Senate, the House is often *less* responsive than the Senate to pressures for change in the status quo. Senators have state-wide constituencies that are frequently dominated by urban areas with powerful labor and minority group vote blocs; as a result, the Senate at times has proved to be the *more* "liberal" branch of Congress.[47] In 1981, however, in the wake of Reagan's victory, the Republicans took control of the Senate, and several strongly conservative members became chairmen of important committees.

Another result of the greater stability of House seats has been the "institutionalization" of that body. For many representatives, being a member of the

---

[40] Congessional Quarterly, *Weekly Report,* February, 20, 1970, p. 451.
[41] David R. Mayhew, "Congressional Elections: The Case of the Vanishing Marginals," *Polity,* Vol. 6 (Spring 1974), pp. 295–317.
[42] Based on data in Congressional Quarterly, *Weekly Report,* November 6, 1976, pp. 314–54.
[43] Congressional Quarterly, *Weekly Report,* November 11, 1978, pp. 3283–91.
[44] Congressional Quarterly, *Weekly Report,* November 8, 1980, pp. 3338–45.
[45] Morris P. Fiorina, *Congress: Keystone of the Washington Establishment* (New Haven: Yale University Press, 1977), p. 50.
[46] *1974 Congressional Quarterly Almanac,* pp. 857–64; *National Journal,* November 6, 1976, p. 1599; Congressional Quarterly, *Weekly Report,* November 11, 1978, pp. 3283–91; and Congressional Quarterly, *Weekly Report,* November 8, 1980, pp. 3338–45.
[47] Lewis A. Froman, Jr., *Congressmen and Their Constituencies* (Chicago: Rand McNally, 1963), pp. 69–84.

House has become a career, with predictable steps up the ladder. Because the House is decentralized, a number of rewards, such as committee and subcommittee chairmanships, usually await career members; and as an institution, the House can gain the loyalty of its members.[48]

On the other hand, despite the relative safety of House seats, there has been a dramatic turnover in the membership of the House over the past decade. Some members, tired of constituent pressures and election campaigns every two years, have quit. Others, of course, have been defeated. As of 1981, 273 members of the House, well over half, were first elected in 1974 or later. (In the Senate, 62 members had arrived in or since 1974.)

In the House, the Speaker is the most powerful member. But the Speaker must contend with the chairmen of the twenty-two standing committees of the House, many of whom are powerful in their own right.

The Speaker exercised great power until 1910 when the rules were revised to strip the Speaker of much of his formal power, including the right to appoint members to committees of the House. But a Speaker with a strong personality and great legislative skill can still exert great influence in the House, as Sam Rayburn of Texas demonstrated during his seventeen-year tenure between 1940 and 1961. Over bourbon and branch water in a small room in the Capitol, Rayburn and his intimates would plan strategy for the House and swap political stories in an informal institution known as the "Board of Education."[49] Despite the loss of some *formal* powers since 1910, the Speaker remains a key figure. Thomas P. "Tip" O'Neill, Jr., of Massachusetts became Speaker in 1977. O'Neill, a huge, barrel-chested man with a thatch of shaggy white hair and a booming, easy laugh, proved to be a colorful Speaker. He looked exactly like what he was—an old-time Irish politician from Boston. (He had succeeded John F. Kennedy in the House.) As Speaker, O'Neill played a key role in the decision to hold the impeachment hearings that became an important factor in Nixon's

Power in the House: The Leadership

House Speaker Thomas P. "Tip" O'Neill, Jr.

[48] Nelson W. Polsby, "The Institutionalization of the U.S. House of Representatives," *American Political Science Review*, Vol. 62 (March 1968), pp. 144–68.

[49] Neil MacNeil, *Forge of Democracy: The House of Representatives* (New York: David McKay, 1964), pp. 82–83.

Drawing by Stan Hunt.
© 1977 The New Yorker
Magazine, Inc.

"There are days, Hank, when I don't know who's President, what state I'm from, or even if I'm a Democrat or a Republican, but, by God, I still know how to bottle up a piece of legislation in committee."

decision to resign as President in 1974. And during the Carter administration, O'Neill proved to be an accomplished legislative leader, shepherding several controversial bills through the House with great skill.[50]

The position of Speaker is provided for in the Constitution ("The House of Representatives shall chuse their Speaker and other Officers."). The Speaker has a number of official powers: to preside over the House, to recognize or ignore members who wish to speak, to appoint members of special or select committees that conduct special investigations (but not standing committees), and to exercise other procedural controls. Much of the Speaker's real power, however, stems from the combination of these formal duties with that of *political leader* of the majority party in the House. Technically, the Speaker is elected by the House, with each party offering a candidate. In practice, the Speaker is chosen at the start of each Congress by a caucus, or meeting, of the majority party. Since in the past, at least, the formal voting in the House has been strictly along party lines, the majority party's candidate for Speaker has automatically won.

The Speaker has two chief assistants, the majority leader, chosen by the party caucus, and the majority whip (appointed by the Democratic majority leader, elected in the case of the Republicans). The majority leader is the party's floor leader and a key strategist. Together with the Speaker and the members of the House Rules Committee, the majority leader schedules debate and negotiates with committee chairmen and party members on procedural matters. The majority whip, along with a number of deputy whips, is responsible for rounding up party members for important votes and counting noses. (The term "whip" comes from "whipper-in," the person assigned in English fox hunts to keep the hounds from straying.) The minority party also elects a minority leader and elects or appoints a minority whip. Republican members of the House receive committee assignments from a Committee on Committees. Democratic members receive their committee assignments from the Democratic Steering and Policy Committee, which is usually dominated by the Speaker (when Democrats control the House) and by the other majority party leaders.

In recent years House Democratic liberals, led by such members as Richard Bolling of Missouri and Morris Udall of Arizona, have sought within the party caucus to challenge the Democratic establishment. A number of the liberals banded together in 1959 in an informal organization known as the Democratic Study Group. In 1973 House reformers, led by members of the Democratic Study Group, succeeded in achieving a number of changes in Democratic party rules in the House. These included modification of the seniority system; opening up more bills to floor amendment; and the new provisions to limit committee secrecy.

Then early in 1975 the House and Senate made a number of significant internal reforms. In the House, Democrats, finally departing from the seniority system, ousted three committee chairmen and granted more power to subcommittees and increased their staffs. The Senate changed its rules to make it easier to end debate; and Senate Democrats, too, modified the seniority system for the selection of committee chairmen. There were other changes and reforms that, taken together, modernized and liberalized the more restrictive procedures of both houses.

[50] Michael Barone, Grant Ujifusa, and Douglas Matthews, *The Almanac of American Politics 1980* (New York: E. P. Dutton, 1979), pp. 406–08.

In the past, the House Committee on Rules had considerable control over what bills could be brought to the floor for debate. In the early 1970s, however, the committee's power was restricted. In one important change, House Democrats empowered the Speaker of the House to nominate all Democratic members of the Rules Committee. Even so, most major legislation cannot be debated without a "rule" from the Rules Committee, which sets the terms of the debate, the time to be allowed for floor discussion, and the extent to which the bill may be amended on the floor.[51]

The Rules Committee

In 1961 President Kennedy and Speaker Sam Rayburn barely won a fight to enlarge the House Rules Committee and thus curb the power of its conservative chairman. Democrats at that time controlled the House, but a coalition of Southern Democrats and Republicans frequently succeeded in blocking passage of liberal legislation. In the 1961 change, the committee's size was increased, and the new members often supported the administration on controversial bills. At the same time, the basic jurisdiction of the Rules Committee was not altered.[52] During the 1970s, however, the Rules Committee was not usually a bottleneck to legislation and often operated as an arm of the House Democratic leadership.

The basic power structure of the House, then, consists of the Speaker, the floor leaders and whips of the two major parties, the Rules Committee, and the chairmen of the twenty-one other standing committees. How these individuals and committees interact powerfully affects the fate of legislation. But the business of making laws is also governed by a complicated, even byzantine, set of rules and procedures. Although most citizens are not familiar with them, these procedures can affect policy outcomes. Whether a bill is successfully steered through the legislative labyrinth or gets lost along the way, often depends on how the rules and procedures are applied.

The Legislative Labyrinth: The House in Action

Less than 4 percent of all bills introduced in Congress become public laws. In the Ninety-sixth Congress in 1979–1980, 14,594 bills were introduced but only 535 became public laws.[53]

After a bill is introduced by a House member, it is referred to a committee by the Speaker. Often his choice is limited by the jurisdictions of the standing committees, but when jurisdictions overlap or when new kinds of legislation are introduced, the Speaker may have considerable discretion in deciding where to assign a bill.

Only about 6 percent of bills get out of committee in the House. The committee chairman may assign the measure to one of the 146 subcommittees of the standing committees.[54] If the bill is reported out of committee, it is placed

"Less than 4 percent of all bills introduced in Congress become public laws."

---

[51] For a detailed study of the complex rules and procedures of the House and Senate, see Walter J. Oleszek, *Congressional Procedures and the Policy Process* (Washington, D.C.: Congressional Quarterly Press, 1978); and text of the Legislative Reorganization Act of 1970.

[52] Milton C. Cummings, Jr., and Robert L. Peabody, "The Decision to Enlarge the Committee on Rules: An Analysis of the 1961 Vote," in Robert L. Peabody and Nelson W. Polsby, eds., *New Perspectives on the House of Representatives* (Chicago: Rand McNally, 1963), p. 193.

[53] Congressional Quarterly, *Weekly Report,* December 20, 1980, p. 3595; and *1979 Congressional Quarterly Almanac,* p. 4. It should be noted that many of the bills introduced were either *private* bills for the benefit of individuals or duplicated another bill. A *public* law applies to whole classes of citizens.

[54] Data as of April 1, 1980. In addition there were eight select subcommittees in the House, for a total of 154. Source: U.S. Congress, House of Representatives, Select Committee on Committees, *Final Report,* 96th Cong., 2nd sess. (Washington, D.C.: Government Printing Office, 1980), p. 321.

Table 12–3

Consent	For noncontroversial bills. Bills on the Consent Calendar are normally called on the first and third Mondays of each month, but debate may be blocked by the objection of any member. The second time a bill is called in this manner, three members must object to block consideration.
Discharge	Motions to force a bill out of committee are placed on the Discharge Calendar when they receive the necessary 218 signatures from House members.
House	Bills that do not appropriate money or raise revenue go on the House Calendar.
Private	Bills that affect specific individuals and deal with private matters, such as claims against the government, immigration, or land titles, are placed on the Private Calendar and can be called on the first and third Tuesdays of each month.
Union	Bills that directly or indirectly appropriate money or raise revenue are placed on the Union Calendar.

on one of five *calendars,* or lists of business pending before the House. The various House calendars and the kinds of bills referred to them are shown in Table 12–3.

Certain bills from the Appropriations Committee may be taken on the floor without going through the Rules Committee. On specified days, bills on the Consent Calendar and Private Calendar may be called up directly for House action. And if two-thirds of the members who are voting agree, any bill may be debated under a procedure permitted four times a month called "suspension of the rules."

A quorum consisting of a majority of the House, 218 members, is required for general debate. When the House is considering legislation sent to it by the Rules Committee, however, it sits as a Committee of the Whole, a device that allows the House to conduct its business with less formality (and a quorum of only one hundred members).

One kind of vote in the Committee of the Whole is a "teller vote," in which members file down the aisle and are counted. This was much more common before 1970. As a result, a representative's vote was secret unless reported by a watching journalist—no easy feat since members filed down the aisle *away* from the press gallery, with their backs to the news reporters. Under this practice, as old as the Congress itself, constituents usually had no way of knowing how their representative had voted. Growing pressures for reform led the House in 1970 to provide for recorded votes, if enough representatives demand it. Under this procedure, members vote electronically, or sometimes drop green or red cards into a ballot box to vote "yes" or "no."

When debate is concluded in the Committee of the Whole, the House may send the bill back to its committee of origin (thereby killing it permanently or temporarily), or it may vote final passage. The new system of electronic voting was installed in the House in 1973. Under it, when an electronic vote is taken, members insert a plastic identification card in one of forty-four voting stations on the floor and press one of three buttons. If the member votes "yes," a green light appears on a display board over the Speaker's head; for "no," a red light

Representatives Charles B. Rangel, Democrat, of New York and William L. Clay, Democrat, of Missouri discuss a bill in committee.

WASHINGTON, Jan. 23—Like a roomful of children with a new mechanical toy, the members of the House of Representatives used their new electronic voting system for the first time today.

There was no legislation on the calendar, so the representatives tried out the computerized system, amid much merriment, on the daily quorum call.

The quorum procedure, which used to take from thirty to forty-five minutes as a clerk read twice through the roll of 435 names, took only fifteen minutes this afternoon.

By the time it was finished, 331 members had come into the chamber, placed their personalized plastic vote card into one of forty-four recording stations on the backs of seats throughout the chamber and watched an amber light appear next to their names on the display panel on the south wall above the Speaker's desk.

According to House officials, the system worked without a flaw.

— *New York Times,* January 24, 1973.

---

appears, and for "present," an amber light. The use of electronic voting has greatly reduced the time needed for roll-call votes; under the old system, the clerk called the roll and each member present had to answer by name. The changes in voting procedure in the Committee of the Whole and the inauguration of electronic voting in the House itself have, taken together, greatly increased the number of on-the-record votes by representatives. Record votes in the Committee of the Whole and the House increased from 266 in 1970 to 706 in 1977.[55]

Supporters or opponents of a bill sometimes request roll-call votes as a delaying tactic, to gain time to round up their forces. Often, however, such votes are demanded to place members on the spot. Representatives know that in a roll-call vote their position must become a matter of public record. Some interest groups regularly rate the records of members on the basis of their roll-call votes. Constituents may not pay much attention to how representatives vote, but opponents in an election campaign may use the legislators' roll-call votes on a key issue against them.

Televising the House

In March 1979, amid much controversy, the House began live color television and radio broadcasts of floor debate. The broadcasts are carried gavel-to-gavel by a network of about 700 cable television systems in all 50 states, with a potential audience of 5.5 million homes. In addition, excerpts are sometimes carried by local stations and the major networks. The stations and networks are permitted to carry up to two minutes a day of debate.

When the television coverage began, there were dire predictions that publicity-seeking members would engage in ham-acting and long-winded oratory. Although some members did play to the cameras, a majority of House members —65 percent—reported they were satisfied with the results. But the opportunity to posture for audiences at home has lengthened House sessions. "There

---

[55] Oleszek, *Congressional Procedures and the Policy Process,* p. 124.

are an awful lot of added speeches that we wouldn't have without television," Speaker O'Neill complained.[56]

Not all members of the public have been impressed by watching the House in action on television. "The results of government in action are disgusting enough without having to have it aired," a woman in Winston-Salem, North Carolina, wrote to the House. But a man in Chelsea, Massachusetts, wrote: "This has given me much more knowledge of the manner in which the laws of this great nation are devised, debated, amended and finally resolved."[57]

Many viewers do not know, however, that television in the House operates under restrictions. The cameras are operated by employees of the House, not by the cable networks. And the cameras are not permitted to pan around the floor and show members sleeping, fidgeting, or walking around.

The Senate does not permit televising of floor debate. However, Senate committee meetings, particularly important investigations that attract widespread public interest, are often televised.

The Senate

The Senate may not be "the most exclusive club in the world" nor a "rich man's club," although it has been called both. (In 1978 there were seventeen millionaires in the Senate.[58]) It may not have an "Inner Club." But it certainly has both the atmosphere and appearance of a club. Its membership is relatively small; its quarters are ornate and gilded; its ways are slow.

But the folkways and customs of the Senate have changed markedly since the days, more than two decades ago, when William S. White, then Senate correspondent of the *New York Times,* wrote of the "Inner Club" run by Southerners.[59] Around the same period, Donald Matthews, a political scientist, described the Senate's "unwritten rules of the game, its norms of conduct." The freshman senator, Matthews wrote, was expected to serve a silent apprenticeship, to be one of the Senate "work horses" rather than one of the "show horses," to develop a legislative specialty, pay homage to the institution, and observe its folkways.[60] These include the elaborate courtesy with which senators, even bitter enemies, customarily address each other on the floor.

A decade later, Nelson Polsby argued that "the role of the Senate in the political system has changed over the last 20 years," decreasing the importance of Senate norms. He contended that television, with its ability to publicize individual senators, had made the Senate "an incubator of presidential hopefuls" and eroded the significance of its rules of behavior.[61] And Ralph Huitt observed that the Senate has always had a place for "mavericks" and "independents."[62]

Robert L. Peabody, Norman J. Ornstein, and David W. Rohde have ana-

[56] Congressional Quarterly, *Weekly Report,* March 15, 1980, p. 735.
[57] Boris Weintraub, "TV in Congress—Measuring the Impact," *Washington Star,* March 19, 1980, p. C5.
[58] *New York Times,* May 20, 1978, p. 1.
[59] White, *Citadel,* pp. 2, 82–84.
[60] Matthews, *U.S. Senators and Their World,* pp. 92–117.
[61] Nelson W. Polsby, "Goodbye to the Inner Club," *Washington Monthly,* August 1969, pp. 30–34.
[62] Ralph K. Huitt, "The Outsider in the Senate: An Alternative Role," in Huitt and Peabody, *Congress: Two Decades of Analysis,* pp. 159–78.

lyzed the decline of folkways and norms in the Senate. The emergence of the Senate as "a major breeding ground for presidential candidates," they suggest, has affected the behavior of "a wider circle of senators." For example, when Senator John F. Kennedy set his sights on the presidency, he spoke out on a variety of subjects "beyond the jurisdictions of his original committee assignments." Kennedy was contributing to the decline of the silent apprenticeship as a Senate norm. Soon other senators with presidential ambitions began to speak out, adding to "the breakdown of apprenticeship."[63]

As more senators run for President, they can be expected to ignore the norm of "legislative work," the authors argue. Partisan infighting has even modified the "traditional civilities" of Senate debate, which at times has become quite rancorous. And the tradition that senators should specialize in certain subjects has been weakened by the need for presidential contenders to be generalists, with a wide knowledge of public policy questions.[64]

Just as the Speaker is elected by the House, the Senate elects a President pro tempore, who presides in the absence of the Vice President. Although the office is provided for in the Constitution, it has little formal power.

The closest parallel to the Speaker is the Senate majority leader. He is the most powerful elected leader of the Senate, although, as in most political offices, a great deal depends on the person and political circumstances.

Lyndon Johnson, the Democratic Senate leader from 1953 to 1960, was widely regarded as an extraordinarily skillful and powerful floor leader. Johnson's power to persuade was formidable. A big man, he towered over most other senators as, on occasion, he subjected them to "The Treatment"—a prolonged exercise in face-to-face persuasion that combined elements of a police "third degree" with Johnson's flair for dramatic acting.

In addition to his powerful personality, Johnson had several tangible tools at his disposal. He could assist a senator in getting legislation passed; he controlled committee assignments; and, above all, he built an intelligence system known as "the Johnson Network." At its heart was Bobby Baker, "a country boy from Pickens, South Carolina, who had come to Washington as a teen-aged Senate page" and whom Johnson made his top assistant.[65] Baker knew how to count noses; because Johnson was well informed of sentiment in the Senate, he was able to anticipate the outcome of close votes. The effect was cumulative, for after a while "it was taken for granted that 'Lyndon's got the votes.'"[66] Through his network, Johnson came to know the strengths and weaknesses of each senator, and he used that knowledge to further his goals; his was a highly personal leadership.

In contrast, Johnson's successor as majority leader, soft-spoken Mike

Power
in the Senate:
The Leadership

[63] Robert L. Peabody, Norman J. Ornstein, and David W. Rohde, "The United States Senate as Presidential Incubator: Many Are Called but Few Are Chosen," *Political Science Quarterly*, Vol. 91, No. 2 (Summer 1976), pp. 252–53.

[64] *Ibid.*, pp. 253–56.

[65] Rowland Evans and Robert Novak, *Lyndon B. Johnson: The Exercise of Power* (New York: New American Library, 1966), pp. 68, 99. When it later developed that Bobby Baker had used his Senate position to amass a personal fortune, the scandal became an issue in the 1964 presidential election campaign and embarrassed Lyndon Johnson, who by then was President.

[66] Ralph K. Huitt, "Democratic Party Leadership in the Senate," in Huitt and Peabody, *Congress: Two Decades of Analysis*, p. 147.

Senate Minority Leader
Robert C. Byrd

Senate Majority Leader
Howard H. Baker, Jr.

Mansfield of Montana, did not attempt to exercise power in the way that Johnson had. When Mansfield was accused of not providing sufficient leadership for the Senate, he declared: "I am neither a circus ringmaster, the master of ceremonies of a Senate nightclub, a tamer of Senate lions, or a wheeler and dealer."[67] When Mansfield retired from the Senate in January 1977, Robert C. Byrd of West Virginia was elected as the majority leader. In 1981, after the Democrats lost control of the Senate in the 1980 election, Byrd became the minority leader.

Byrd, who rose from rural poverty in the hills of West Virginia, earned a law degree in night school after working as a butcher, a welder, and a grocer and after joining, for a time, the Ku Klux Klan. He played country music on his fiddle for the voters and even released a record album. Extremely hard-working, Byrd, when he served as majority leader, concentrated more on making the Senate work than on influencing legislation ideologically.[68]

There has been a parallel on the Republican side to these changes in Senate leadership style. Senator Everett McKinley Dirksen, the Senate minority leader from 1959 to his death in 1969, was a flamboyant, theatrical personality who wielded considerable power. Howard H. Baker, Jr., of Tennessee, who became Senate minority leader in 1977 and majority leader in 1981, had a quieter style.

Baker, who married Dirksen's daughter, Joy, was born into a prosperous political family in eastern Tennessee. Elected to the Senate in 1966, he gained national attention during the televised Senate Watergate hearings in 1973, repeatedly asking about President Nixon: "What did the President know and when did he know it?" As minority leader, Baker opposed many of President Carter's policies, but supported him on the Panama Canal treaty. He tried to win the Republican presidential nomination in 1980 but lost to Ronald Reagan.[69]

The Senate majority and minority leaders represent their party in the Senate. But they may not represent majority sentiment in their party nationally. While the Senate majority or minority leaders are nominally responsible for steering their party's program through the Senate, they may oppose parts of it.

Senate Democrats and Republicans are organized along party lines for both political and legislative purposes:

The *floor whips.* As in the House, the leader of each party is assisted by a whip, and assistant whips, to round up senators for key votes.

The *party conference.* The conference, or caucus, of each party consists of all the senators who are members of that party. The Republican Conference meets regularly, often weekly. The Democratic Conference, although supposedly the highest Democratic party body in Congress, seldom meets more than a few times a year. Both party conferences elect leaders, who assume the title of majority or minority leader, depending on which party controls the Senate.

The *policy committee.* The policy committee of each party provides a forum for discussion of party positions on legislative issues.

The *assignment committee.* The Republican Committee on Committees appoints Republicans to the fifteen standing committees of the Senate. The Democratic counterpart is known as the Democratic Steering Committee.

[67] *Congressional Record,* November 27, 1963, p. 22862.
[68] Mark Green, with Michael Calabrese et al. and Ralph Nader Congress Watch, *Who Runs Congress,* 3d ed. (New York: Bantam Books, 1979), pp. 100–01.
[69] *Ibid.,* pp. 102–04.

Although the organization of each party appears to be much the same, there are important differences in how the machinery operates. The Democratic party leadership tends to be centralized in the hands of the floor leader. The Republicans tend to spread the party posts around. For example, in the Ninety-sixth Congress, Senator Byrd was majority leader and chairman of the Democratic Conference, the Policy Committee, and the Senate Steering Committee; on the Republican side, the corresponding posts were held by four senators.

Unlike the House, with its complex procedures, five calendars, and tight restrictions on debate, the Senate is relaxed, informal, and less attentive to the rules. Senate bills appear on only one legislative calendar, and they are usually called up by *unanimous consent.* Since a single senator may object to this procedure, the majority leader, in conducting floor business, consults with the minority leader across the aisle on most major matters to avoid objections.

The Senate
in Action

The Filibuster. Most of the time, the Senate allows unlimited debate. Because of this, a single senator, or a group of senators, may stage a *filibuster* to talk a bill to death.[70] Usually, the filibuster is employed to defeat a bill by tying up the Senate so long that the measure will never come to a vote. But a number of factors, including the 1975 rule change making it easier to cut off debate, have combined to diminish the importance of the filibuster as a weapon to block legislation.

To filibuster, all that senators must do is remain on their feet and keep talking. For the first three hours, their comments must relate to the subject of the debate, but after that, they may, if they wish, read the telephone book. The record for such marathon performances by a single senator was set by Senator Strom Thurmond of South Carolina, who spoke against the Civil Rights Act of 1957 for twenty-four hours and eighteen minutes. A group filibuster may go on for many days or even months. When one senator tires, he or she merely "yields" to a fresher colleague, who takes over. To counter these tactics, the Senate may

[70] The word "filibuster" originally meant a privateer or pirate, and its origin in American politics is not certain. See William Safire, *The New Language of Politics* (New York: Random House, 1968), p. 143.

Night of the Filibuster

For nine days in September of 1977, Senators James Abourezk of South Dakota and Howard M. Metzenbaum of Ohio staged a filibuster against a gas deregulation bill that was part of President Carter's energy package. The filibuster included an all night session, described in this newspaper account:

The usually decorous Senate chamber was not very dignified early Wednesday morning as senators jumped up from folding cots every half hour or so to answer yet another roll-call vote demanded by Metzenbaum and Abourezk.

Under normal circumstances, senators wear ties and jackets on the Senate floor, but Wednesday some removed their ties and left their shirt-tails hanging out over their trousers. Sen. Ernest F. Hollings (D-S.C.) showed up in a jogging costume.

Shoeless, Sen. Barry Goldwater (R-Ariz.) padded onto the floor in his socks and asked, "Isn't it time to go home?"

Sen. Robert J. Dole (R-Kan.) said the Senate was looking ridiculous and quoted a tourist who had remarked to him Wednesday, "I'm so happy the Senate is open because the zoo is closed."

—*Los Angeles Times,* September 29, 1977.

meet round-the-clock, in the hope of wearing down the filibusterers. But the senators conducting the filibuster may retaliate by suggesting the absence of a quorum (fifty-one senators). Such a demand voiced at, say, 4 A.M. is inconvenient for other senators. So, senators attempting to break the filibuster set up cots in the halls and straggle in to answer the roll; then they try to go back to sleep.

Under Rule XXII of the Senate, a filibuster may be ended if sixteen members petition, and three-fifths of the entire Senate (sixty members) vote, for *cloture.* Until 1959 the vote of two-thirds of the entire Senate was required to impose cloture. In 1959 the cloture rule was eased to require only two-thirds of those present and voting. As a result, liberal forces were able to vote cloture to cut off the debate of Southern senators on civil rights legislation in 1964, 1965, 1968, and 1972. Then in 1975 the rule was eased even further, to require only sixty senators to end debate.[71] Even with the less restrictive rule, cloture is difficult to impose. From 1917, when the rule passed, through 1980, cloture was voted only fifty times in 157 attempts.

Although filibusters are often used by Southern conservatives, Northerners and liberals have used them, too. For example, Northern liberals filibustered in the early 1970s against funds for the supersonic transport plane (SST), extension of the military draft, a government loan to the Lockheed Aircraft Corporation, and funds for the Vietnam war. In 1972 Northern Democrats and Republican liberals defeated three attempts by *Southern* senators and their allies to impose cloture to end debate on a strong antibusing bill. As a result, the bill was defeated.

In 1976 Senator James Allen of Alabama used a loophole in the filibuster rules to stage a new kind of post-cloture filibuster. Under the then-existing rules, once cloture was invoked, debate was limited to 100 hours, one for each senator. But quorum calls, roll-call votes, and other procedural devices did not count against a senator's hour. Allen, with the help of forty roll calls, managed to delay action on a civil rights bill for two weeks. Then in 1977 Senators Abourezk and Metzenbaum staged their post-cloture filibuster against the natural gas bill, tying the Senate up into a pretzel and forcing the first all-night session in thirteen years. As a result, in February of 1979, the Senate voted a ceiling of 100 hours on all post-cloture debate, including roll calls and other parliamentary maneuvers. Thus, any post-cloture filibuster is now limited to 100 hours.

The Committee System

Committees and subcommittees are where Congress does most of its work. It is here that policies are shaped, interest groups heard, and legislation hammered out.

Long before Woodrow Wilson became President, he described what he called "government by the chairmen of the Standing Committees of Congress." Wilson saw congressional committees as "little legislatures," and added that the House sat "not for serious discussion, but to sanction the conclusions of its

COMMITTEE ROOM ·

---

[71] To cut off debate on changes in Senate rules, a vote of two-thirds of the senators present is still required.

Committees as rapidly as possible." "Congress in its committee-rooms," Wilson concluded, "is Congress at work."[72]

The growth of the modern Presidency has modified the Wilsonian view of the power of Congress and its committees. The committees are, nevertheless, vital centers of congressional activity. (The thirty-seven standing committees of Congress are listed in Table 12-4.)

[72] Woodrow Wilson, *Congressional Government* (New York: World, Meridan Books, 1956), pp. 69, 82–83. Originally published in 1885.

Standing Committees of the Ninety-seventh Congress

Table 12–4

Senate Committees	Chairman	State	Age*
Agriculture, Nutrition, and Forestry	Jesse A. Helms	N.C.	59
Appropriations	Mark O. Hatfield	Ore.	58
Armed Services	John G. Tower	Tex.	55
Banking, Housing, and Urban Affairs	Jake Garn	Utah	48
Budget	Pete V. Domenici	N.M.	48
Commerce, Science, and Transportation	Bob Packwood	Ore.	58
Energy and Natural Resources	James A. McClure	Ida.	56
Environment and Public Works	Robert T. Stafford	Vt.	67
Finance	Robert Dole	Kan.	57
Foreign Relations	Charles H. Percy	Ill.	61
Governmental Affairs	William V. Roth, Jr.	Del.	59
Judiciary	Strom Thurmond	S.C.	78
Labor and Human Resources	Orrin G. Hatch	Utah	46
Rules and Administration	Charles McC. Mathias, Jr.	Md.	58
Veterans' Affairs	Alan K. Simpson	Wyo.	49

House Committees	Chairman	State	Age*
Agriculture	E(Kika) de la Garza	Tex.	54
Appropriations	Jamie L. Whitten	Miss.	70
Armed Services	Melvin Price	Ill.	76
Banking, Finance, and Urban Affairs	Fernand J. St. Germain	R.I.	53
Budget	James R. Jones	Okla.	41
District of Columbia	Ronald V. Dellums	Cal.	45
Education and Labor	Carl D. Perkins	Ky.	68
Energy and Commerce	John D. Dingell	Mich.	54
Foreign Affairs	Clement J. Zablocki	Wis.	68
Government Operations	Jack Brooks	Tex.	58
House Administration	Augustus Hawkins	Cal.	73
Interior and Insular Affairs	Morris K. Udall	Ariz.	58
Judiciary	Peter W. Rodino, Jr.	N.J.	71
Merchant Marine and Fisheries	Walter B. Jones	N.C.	67
Post Office and Civil Service	William D. Ford	Mich.	53
Public Works and Transportation	James J. Howard	N.J.	53
Rules	Richard Bolling	Mo.	64
Science and Technology	Don Fuqua	Fla.	47
Small Business	Parren J. Mitchell	Md.	58
Standards of Official Conduct	Louis Stokes	Ohio	56
Veterans' Affairs	Gillespie V. Montgomery	Miss.	61
Ways and Means	Dan Rostenkowski	Ill.	61

* Names and ages of chairmen as of January 15, 1981.

The Subcommittees and Decentralization

The thirty-seven chairmen of the standing committees of the House and Senate still wield substantial power. Yet, here, too, Congress is changing. As Anthony King has observed, "by the late 1970s, committee chairmen, although still very influential people, had lost much of their former power. They felt bound to defer to the other members of the committee; much of the committees' work had been devolved onto subcommittees, often chaired by junior, even freshman, congressmen and senators."[73]

As a result of these changes, Congress has become substantially *decentralized.* "The most striking feature of congressional organization is decentralization," Samuel C. Patterson has observed, "and congressional government by subcommittee has grown in the 1970s."[74] The proliferation of subcommittees is, in fact, one of the most dramatic changes in the structure of Congress over the past decade.

Representative David R. Obey of Wisconsin, who has studied the organization of the House, observed that a few years ago, that body was run by its committee chairmen, "a few old bulls" who held on to their power because of seniority.[75] The reforms of the 1970s stripped the chairmen of some of their power and dispersed it to the subcommittees, each with its own chairperson. The heads of the subcommittees enjoyed their new-found power and liked the system of divided authority. Under this system, Obey pointed out, every interest group has "a port of entry into Congress, but the bulwark of strong central leadership is lacking."[76]

The subcommittee explosion can be clearly traced by studying the subcommittee totals in the House over the past two decades. In 1951 there were only 69 subcommittees in the House; by 1971 the number had climbed to 109, and by 1980 it had reached 146—an increase since 1951 of 111 percent.[77] The Senate had at least 90 subcommittees.[78]

All of this made Congress a place of "buzzing confusion," confronting outside groups with "a bewildering array of access points."[79] Where lobbies or executive branch agencies could once deal with a handful of members of Congress, "large numbers of legislators must now be contacted."[80]

The Committees at Work

Committees perform the valuable functions of division of labor and specialization in Congress. No member of the House or Senate could hope to know the details of all of the 14,594 bills introduced, for example, in the Ninety-sixth Congress. For that reason, senators and representatives tend to rely on the expert knowledge that members of committees may acquire. If a committee has

[73] Anthony King, Introduction, in Anthony King, ed., *The New American Political System,* p. 2.
[74] Samuel C. Patterson, "The Semi-Sovereign Congress," p. 160.
[75] *New York Times,* November 13, 1978, p. B9.
[76] *Ibid.*
[77] U.S. Congress, House of Representatives, Select Committee on Committees, *Final Report,* p. 321.
[78] *1979 Congressional Quarterly Almanac,* pp. 48–89. In addition, there were 10 select subcommittees in the Senate, for a total of 100 Senate subcommittees. There were 5 joint House and Senate subcommittees. When added to the total of 154 House subcommittees (146 standing, 8 select), the grand total of subcommittees in both houses was 259. But no one knew the precise total, since the number of subcommittees changed frequently.
[79] Roger H. Davidson, "Subcommittee Government: New Channels of Policy Making," in Thomas E. Mann and Norman J. Ornstein, eds., *The New Congress* (Washington, D.C.: American Enterprise Institute for Public Policy Research, 1981).
[80] *Ibid.*

approved a bill, other members generally assume that the committee has considered the legislation carefully, applied its expertise, and made the right decision. That is why Congress, for the most part, approves the decisions of its committees.

As a result of the committee system, members of Congress specialize in various fields. Sometimes they become more knowledgeable in their areas than the bureaucrats in the executive branch. Finally, many scholars argue that a legislative body should have some forum where members of competing parties can resolve their differences. Committees serve this purpose; they are natural arenas for political bargaining and legislative compromise.

The standing committees constitute the heart of the committee system. At times, Congress also creates *special* or *select committees* to conduct special investigations. In addition, the Ninety-sixth Congress had four *joint committees* of the House and Senate dealing with such subjects as the economy and taxes.

Not all committees are alike. Richard F. Fenno, Jr., has identified a number of factors that may affect a committee's degree of independence, influence in Congress, and success in managing legislation. Fenno found five key variables in committee behavior: *Member goals* reflect the benefits desired by each committee member; for instance, members of the Post Office Committee are primarily interested in improving their own chances of re-election by getting new post offices for their districts, but members of the House Education and Labor Committee are oriented more toward making public policy for the nation as a whole. *Environmental constraints* are the outside influences that affect a committee—primarily the other members of the House, the executive branch, client groups, and the two major political parties. *Strategic premises* are the basic rules of the game for a committee—the Appropriations Committee often tries to reduce presidential budget requests, for example, and thus appears more responsible with taxpayers' money, but other committees may find it more to their advantage to agree to the President's requests. *Decision-making processes* are the internal rules for each committee. Finally, *decisions* of committees vary; the Appropriations Committee, for example, generally does cut the President's budget, but the Foreign Affairs Committee tends to respond to the President's wishes.[81]

Although committees basically process legislation, they perform other tasks, such as educating the public on important issues through hearings and investigations. In 1973 the Senate Select Committee on Presidential Campaign Activities began its far-reaching inquiries into the Watergate affair. These hearings revealed that President Nixon had tape-recorded his White House conversations, a disclosure that precipitated the legal confrontation between the President and the courts over access to the tapes.

More than anything that had gone before, the Watergate hearings revealed the inside workings of the executive branch at that time. The hearings demonstrated the tremendous power of a congressional investigation, particularly a televised Senate investigation, to focus the nation's attention on its political process. Within little more than a year, the hearings were followed by the House Judiciary Committee's impeachment investigation and Nixon's resignation.

Congressional Investigations

[81] Richard F. Fenno, Jr., *Congressmen in Committees* (Boston: Little, Brown, 1973).

A hearing of the Senate Watergate investigating committee. The committee members are at left; the witness sits at the table facing them.

Some congressional investigations, such as those conducted by Senator Joseph R. McCarthy, have trampled on individual rights. But a series of Supreme Court decisions, starting in 1957, have attempted to give some protection to witnesses before committees. For example, the Supreme Court has ruled that Congress has no power "to expose for the sake of exposure" and that questions asked by a congressional investigating committee must be relevant to its legislative purpose.[82] On the other hand, the Supreme Court has ruled that witnesses cannot refuse under the First Amendment to answer questions about their political beliefs if the questions are pertinent to the committee's legislative purpose.[83] Of course, witnesses before a committee can invoke the Fifth Amendment on the grounds that their answers might tend to incriminate them. But many people infer that witnesses who invoke this constitutional privilege are guilty of something, and the witnesses may lose their jobs or suffer other social penalties as a result.

[82] *Watkins* v. *United States,* 354 U.S. 178 (1957).
[83] *Barenblatt* v. *United States,* 360 U.S. 109 (1959).

The House Judiciary Committee after voting to recommend the impeachment of Richard Nixon

The party that controls the House or Senate selects the chairmen and that party's members of the standing committees for that house. Although the system has been modified in recent years, in practice, most committee chairmen still achieve their power and position by the unwritten rule of *seniority*. Today, however, in both the House and Senate, members can no longer count on length of service to promote them automatically to committee chairmen. Until 1973, unless representatives or senators died, resigned, or were defeated, they could eventually move up the seniority ladder and become chairmen, if their party controlled the house of Congress in which they served. Until 1971, if they were not members of the majority party, they could automatically become *ranking minority members* of the various committees.

But in 1971 House Republicans agreed to vote by secret ballot to select the highest ranking Republican on each House committee. The Republican move placed increasing pressure on the Democrats to modify their seniority system. In 1973 House Democrats approved a new rule, under which 20 percent of the party members could, and did, demand a secret vote to elect each chairman. As a result, the House Democrats voted for all committee chairmen for the first time, by secret ballot.

Having adopted these procedural reforms, the House Democrats proceeded to award all committee chairmanships to the same colleagues who would have received them through the normal workings of seniority. Starting in 1975, the House Democrats agreed that each committee chairman would always be elected by secret ballot. And in an historic and unprecedented action, the Caucus voted to replace three veteran committee chairmen—Representatives Wright Patman of Texas (the Banking Committee), F. Edward Hébert of Louisiana (the Armed Services Committee), and W. R. Poage of Texas (the Agriculture Committee). In the Senate, the Democrats voted to select committee chairmen by secret ballot whenever 20 percent of the Democrats requested it. When the Republicans control the Senate, they follow the same procedure to elect chairmen.

Until these reforms were adopted, no aspect of Congress had been criticized more often than the seniority system (sometimes assailed as "the senility system"). The system has not been abandoned, merely modified. In January 1981 the average age of the chairmen of the standing committees of Congress was fifty-eight. (See Table 12–4 for the ages of the individual chairmen.)

The chief argument against seniority has been that it bestows power not necessarily on the most qualified, but on the longest-lived; that the power of committee chairmen dilutes party responsibility and congressional support for presidential programs; and that committee chairmen returned by "safe" constituencies tend to be more conservative than the nation as a whole.

Criticism of the seniority system used to focus on the number of older, conservative Southern Democrats who had been re-elected from safe districts and who had eventually become committee chairmen. By 1981, however, the Senate was Republican controlled. And in the House, the percent of Democrats from the South actually exceeded the percent of committee chairmen who were Southerners. Five out of twenty-two chairmen, or 23 percent, were from the South although Southerners made up 28 percent of House Democrats.[84]

The same seniority system that historically has benefited Southerners also has rewarded those Northerners and liberals who are regularly returned to

[84] Adapted from Congressional Quarterly, *Weekly Report*, November 8, 1980, pp. 3315, 3325–26.

Representative Augustus F. Hawkins, Chairman of the House Administration Committee

Capitol Hill. By 1981, for example, Representative Ronald V. Dellums, a liberal black congressman from California, was chairman of the House Committee on the District of Columbia, a post held for many years by a conservative from North Carolina. Two other House committees had black chairmen—Representative Augustus F. Hawkins of California headed the House Administration Committee and Representative Parren J. Mitchell of Maryland chaired the Small Business Committee.

Members of the House and Senate are assigned to committees by the party machinery discussed earlier in this chapter. House members are generally limited to serving on one minor and one major standing committee, and senators may serve on two but not more than three.[85] By tradition, each party is usually allotted seats on committees roughly in proportion to its strength in each house of Congress.

Members are assigned to committees partly on the basis of seniority, but other factors are taken into account, including the party standing of members, willingness to vote with the leadership, geographical balance, the number of available vacancies, the interests of the legislators' districts, and whether the assignment will help their re-election. Certain committees are more important than others. In the House, members compete for places on Appropriations, Rules, and Ways and Means. In the Senate, particularly desirable committees include Appropriations, Finance, Foreign Relations, and Armed Services.

Committee chairmen still wield considerable influence. They schedule meetings, decide what bills will be taken up, and usually control the hiring and firing of the majority committee staff. In some cases a committee chairman can pigeonhole a bill simply by refusing to hold hearings.

In recent years, however, there has been a trend toward greater democracy within some of the committees. Rules have been adopted by some committees giving rank-and-file members a greater voice in committee operations and providing for regularly scheduled meetings. In the House, a majority of members can file a *discharge* petition to dislodge a bill from any committee, including Rules, but the device is little used and seldom successful.[86]

Congressional Staffs

Senator Nancy Kassebaum, Republican, of Kansas confers with staff aide.

Congress is becoming a bureaucracy. In recent years, the number of people on the congressional payroll has increased enormously. By 1980 Congress employed more than 38,000 persons, including clerical help and Library of Congress employees, and had a budget of more than a billion dollars.

In addition to staff members on their office payrolls, senators and representatives have large committee and subcommittee staffs to serve them. Office staffs are likely to concentrate on legislative and constituent services, while on the committees, staff members draft and analyze bills, coordinate with officials in the executive branch, and prepare for hearings. In 1957 congressional staffs totaled 4489. By 1977 the figure had more than tripled, to 13,894.[87]

Although congressional staff members have been criticized for having too much influence, one study concluded that members of the staff "do much of the

[85] In the House, members of either the Appropriations or the Ways and Means committee may not serve on any other committee.

[86] The Senate, too, has a discharge procedure, but it is almost never invoked.

[87] Adapted from Harrison W. Fox, Jr., and Susan Webb Hammond, *Congressional Staffs* (New York: Free Press, 1977), p. 171.

congressional work and . . . in many instances, this work could not be done without staff."[88] The staffs have grown because of "a greater congressional workload" and the desire of senators and representatives to have "the assistance of skilled experts."[89]

Before Congress passed the Congressional Budget and Impoundment Control Act of 1974, it was hard for members to keep track of the dollar total of the various appropriations bills it passed. The new law required Congress to adopt *budget resolutions* each year setting target figures for total spending. The act also created a House Budget Committee, a Senate Budget Committee, and a Congressional Budget Office within Congress to provide the experts, the computers, and the data needed by the members. Moreover, the law established a timetable for Congress and its committees to act on spending bills. This schedule was an attempt to give Congress time to evaluate the President's budget and to choose among competing programs.

Congress and the Budget

The President begins preparing his budget in March. In January, he submits it to Congress. Two months later, by March 15, the various congressional committees must report on the budget to the budget committees. The budget timetable sets May 15 as the date for Congress to complete action on the first concurrent resolution containing budget targets for spending and taxes. After further congressional review, the schedule calls for a second concurrent resolution to be passed by September 15. On October 1, the federal fiscal year begins, running until the following September 30.

The 1974 act also provided that if a President "impounds" or refuses to spend money that Congress has appropriated, either house can pass a resolution to force him to release the money. This provision was included because President Nixon had withheld billions of dollars appropriated by Congress.

As part of the overall budget process, Congress, as in the past, also *authorizes* spending programs. In separate legislation, it then enacts *appropriations* to pay for them.

Many members of Congress have complained that the procedural demands of the budget act have proved burdensome. On the other hand, the new process has "helped Congress overcome its image of fiscal irresponsibility."[90] And the creation of the Congressional Budget Office meant that Congress no longer had to rely on the executive branch for fiscal facts and figures.

A Bill Is Passed

All of these institutions, people, and procedures—the formal organization of Congress, the party leadership, the floor maneuvering, the committee system, staff work—bear some relationship to whether a bill will make its way into law. To do so, it must cross hurdles every step of the way.

The formal route that a bill must follow is shown in Figure 12-1. Any member may drop a bill in the "hopper." (Some legislation is introduced as a

[88] *Ibid.*, p. 2.
[89] *Ibid.*, p. 27.
[90] Joel Havemann, *Congress and the Budget* (Bloomington, Ind.: Indiana University Press, 1978), p. 205.

How a Bill Becomes Law

Figure 12–1   This illustration shows the most typical way in which proposed legislation is enacted into law. There are more complicated, as well as simpler, routes. Most bills fall by the wayside and never become law.

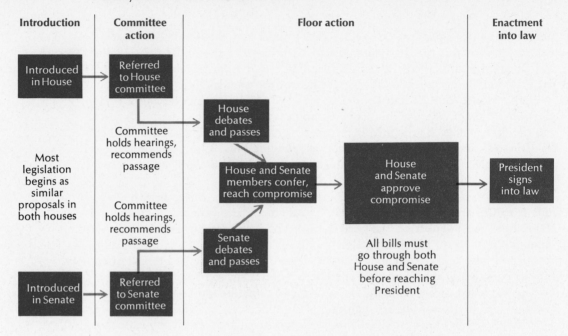

Source: Adapted from 1979 *Congressional Quarterly Almanac*, p. xxv. Reprinted with permission.

"Joint Resolution," which becomes law in the same manner as a bill.) After a bill is introduced in either the House or the Senate, or both, it is referred to a committee, which may hold hearings or assign the bill to a subcommittee. Hearings may be open to the public or closed. After receiving the subcommittee's recommendations, the full committee meets in executive session to decide what action to take on the bill. It may do nothing, or it may rewrite the bill completely, or it may report out the original bill to the House or Senate, with or without amendments. A written report, and often a minority report, accompanies the bill from committee.[91] The bill is placed on one of the House calendars or the Senate calendar. If it clears the Rules Committee, it will be debated in the House. The Senate may also debate the bill.

If a bill is passed by one house, it is sent to the other chamber, which may pass the bill as is, send it to committee, or ignore it and continue to press its own version of the legislation. If there are major differences in the final bill passed by each house, one house may ask for a *conference.* The presiding officer of each house names a conference committee usually composed of senior members of the standing committees or subcommittees that have managed the bill. The se-

[91] A minority report sets forth the views of those opposed to the majority recommendation of the committee. Typically, but not always, a minority report is signed primarily by members of the committee who belong to the minority party in that house of Congress.

lection of members to serve on the conference committee may influence whether any legislation emerges or the nature of the legislation that is reported out. The conferees attempt to iron out disagreements and reconcile the two versions. Usually, they reach some form of agreement and report back to their respective houses. But agreement is not always reached, or it may be reached only after important changes in the legislation are made. Each house then approves or rejects the conference report. If both houses approve, the final version is signed by the Speaker and the President of the Senate and is sent to the President, who may sign the bill into law, let it become law without his signature, or veto or pocket veto the bill, as described in Chapter 10. If Congress overrides a presidential veto by a two-thirds vote in both houses, the bill becomes law without the President's signature.

Increasingly in recent years, Congress has enacted laws containing a "legislative veto" over acts of the executive branch. Presidents have consistently opposed such provisions as being unconstitutional. By one count, Congress had approved at least 167 laws with one or more congressional veto provisions by February 1980.[92] President Carter several times informed Congress that he would not feel legally bound to comply when Congress vetoed actions taken by his administration. The most dramatic example came in May 1980, when Congress passed a law giving it veto powers over rules and regulations issued by the Federal Trade Commission, an independent regulatory agency. The Supreme Court will probably be called upon to decide whether such provisions are constitutional.

Legislative Vetoes

Congress and the American Political System

Congress is a major battleground of American democracy. But in attempting to manage the external demands placed on it, it is caught among the crosscurrents of a restless and rapidly changing society. And, as we have seen, it is subject as well to an "inner tension" between its assigned role as the democratic representative of the people and its own rigid and sometimes undemocratic internal structures.

Its decentralized pattern of organization, with power allocated among various committees and subcommittees, may work against innovative leadership on Capitol Hill. Moreover, programs enacted by Congress may not fit together as a coherent whole. This policy fragmentation is particularly visible in the House, where bills on major subjects such as energy and health are sometimes referred to well over a dozen committees and subcommittees. In recent years, the House has formed temporary, ad hoc committees to deal with energy and welfare reform. These temporary arrangements are symptoms of "the difficulties the House has in attempting to come to grips with major policy questions that cut across the dispersive power structure of subcommittee governments."[93]

[92] Congressional Quarterly, *Weekly Report,* March 8, 1980, p. 662.
[93] Patterson, "The Semi-Sovereign Congress," p. 163.

Senate Foreign Relations
Committee Chairman
Charles Percy

On the other hand, the Congressional Budget and Impoundment Control Act of 1974 represented a major effort by Congress to adopt a more coherent approach to federal spending. "Most important, budget reform forced Congress to confront the budgetary consequences of its own actions."[94]

For many years, Congress failed to exercise a leadership role in the field of foreign policy; it tended to defer to the President in the exercise of its war powers. One result was Vietnam: the longest war in American history, fought without a declaration of war by Congress. But starting in 1973, Congress began to reassert its power in the field of foreign policy. It ended the bombing of Cambodia, enacted the War Powers Resolution, and ordered the Central Intelligence Agency to report to Congress on covert operations. Congress had suddenly become revitalized. As Thomas M. Franck and Edward Weisband observed, "It had, indeed, become an independent, militant force in formulating foreign policy."[95]

Some scholars have argued that the American political system is not designed to cope with change, that the checks and balances embedded in the Constitution, combined with differences between the President and Congress, make the legislative branch unable to act. Others have criticized the procedures of Congress itself.

Certainly there is still room for reform in Congress. The behavior of some members who violate ethical standards casts a cloud over all members. For many years Congress showed little desire to institute reforms. Its prevailing attitude was reflected by the late Senator Everett Dirksen, who, when asked about prospects for a reform measure, replied: "Ha, ha, ha; and I might add, ho, ho, ho."

In the wake of scandals, however, both the House and Senate established ethics committees, and in 1968 both houses adopted weak codes of conduct for their members. In 1977 the House strengthened its ethics code, requiring broad financial disclosure by members and limiting outside earned income. The Senate also adopted a stricter code of ethics in 1977. Like the House code, it required annual financial disclosure reports and restricted outside earned income, a provision that takes effect January 1, 1983.

In the 1970s, both the Democrats and the Republicans modified the seniority system and adopted many other important reforms. The changes in the seniority system—such as the election of committee chairmen by the majority party caucus—have altered power relationships by making chairmen more responsive to the majority sentiment in their party and more representative of the country as a whole. The impact of these changes has already been felt; committee chairmen now have to seek the support of their colleagues to ensure their re-election as chairmen—a major departure from the autocratic ways of the past.

In addition, as we have seen, Congress does more than approve legislation. At times, it does innovate and initiate, and it serves to give a measure of legitimacy to the process of rule making for society. Many of the innovative measures that a President finally adopts as his own have first been proposed by individual legislators.

There are times when Congress seems to be still operating in the nineteenth century. But at other times it is perhaps slow to act because the consensus that

---

[94] Havemann, *Congress and the Budget*, p. 205.
[95] Thomas M. Franck and Edward Weisband, *Foreign Policy by Congress* (New York: Oxford University Press, 1979), p. 23.

it *needs* to act and to innovate is slow to develop. To a great extent, Congress reflects the decentralization and pluralism that characterize the American political system as a whole. A powerful argument can be made that Congress does act when the people demand it, their voice is clear, and the need unmistakable. E. E. Schattschneider has described American government as a political system "in which the struggle for democracy is still going on."[96] Viewed in that context, Congress is neither ideal nor obsolete, but rather an enduring arena for political conflict and a crucible for democratic change.

[96] E. E. Schattschneider, *The Semisovereign People* (New York: Holt, Rinehart and Winston, 1960), p. 102.

Perspective

Congress plays a central role in the political system by making laws. In doing so, it makes and implements national policy. Congress has nonlegislative functions as well, such as proposing amendments to the Constitution, declaring war, and ruling on presidential disability. It oversees and supervises the operations of the executive branch and the independent regulatory agencies. Congress provides one of several points of access to the political system for individuals and groups, and it plays a key role in resolving conflict among groups.

In recent years, Congress has been tarnished by scandal and by the questionable ethics and activities of some of its members. Since 1970, twenty-seven members of Congress have been the subject of criminal charges.

Congress has instituted a number of procedural reforms in recent years. For example, in response to criticism that it has rewarded age rather than competence, it has modified the seniority system, so that members with the longest service no longer automatically chair committees. Congress was also long criticized for failure to exercise power over foreign affairs. In response, Congress in 1973 passed the War Powers Resolution and has taken a greater role in the conduct of foreign policy.

The socioeconomic makeup of Congress is not representative of the general population. In the Ninety-seventh Congress, convened in 1981, there were only twenty-one women (including two women senators), and eighteen blacks. The typical member of Congress is about fifty years old, male, white, Protestant, and a lawyer.

The classic dilemma of legislators is whether they should lead or follow the opinion of their constituents. Should they follow their own judgment and serve as trustees for the people? Or should they act as instructed delegates who automatically mirror the will of the majority of constituents? Most House and Senate members try to combine the two roles by exercising their own judgment and representing constituency views as well.

The 435 members of the House of Representatives serve two-year terms. Because of its larger size, the House is a more formal institution than the Senate, with stricter rules and procedures. In the House, the Speaker is the most powerful member. The Speaker's formal duties include the power to preside over the House and to recognize or ignore members who wish to speak. Much of the Speaker's power comes from the combination of his official duties with his position as political leader of the majority party in the House, although he must share his power with committee chairmen. The Speaker has two chief assistants, the majority leader and the majority whip. Most legislation in the House must be cleared by the Rules Committee before it can be debated on the floor.

The Senate has 100 members who serve six-year terms. The closest parallel in the Senate to the Speaker of the House is the Senate majority leader, the most powerful elected leader of the Senate. The minority party in the Senate is headed by an elected minority leader. As in the House, each leader is assisted by a whip and assistant whips.

Most of the time, the Senate allows unlimited debate. Because of this, a single senator or group of senators may stage a filibuster, which may be ended only if sixteen members petition and three-fifths of the entire Senate (sixty members) vote for cloture. Once cloture is invoked, debate, including roll calls and other parliamentary maneuvers, is limited to 100 hours, one for each senator.

The norms and rules—for example, silent apprenticeship, specialization—that once characterized the Senate have been weakened as more senators have emerged as presidential candidates.

Committees and subcommittees are where Congress does most of its work. Committees perform the valuable roles of division of labor and specialization in Congress. It is here that policies are shaped, interest groups heard, and legislation hammered out. The standing committees are the heart of the committee system. At times, Congress may create special or select committees to conduct special investigations.

The thirty-seven chairmen of the standing committees of the House and Senate wield substantial power. But power in Congress has become substantially decentralized. Much committee work is now dispersed to subcommittees, each with its own chairperson. The proliferation of subcommittees is one of the most dramatic changes in the structure of Congress over the past decade. During the same period, the size of the congressional staff has also increased greatly.

In 1974 Congress passed the Congressional Budget and Impoundment Control Act. The new law made it easier for members to keep track of the dollar totals of the various appropriations bills it passed. The act required Congress to adopt budget resolutions each year setting target figures for total spending. The act also created a House Budget Committee, a Senate Budget Committee, and a Congressional Budget Office. The law established a timetable for Congress and its committees to act on spending bills. This schedule was an attempt to give Congress time to evaluate the President's budget and to choose among competing programs.

House and Senate members may introduce legislation by placing a bill in the "hopper." The bill is then referred to a committee that decides what action to take. It may do nothing with the bill, rewrite the bill completely, or report out the original bill with or without amendments. If a bill is passed by one house, it is sent to the other chamber. If both houses pass different versions of the bill, the differences may be resolved by a conference committee composed of senior members of the committees that originally handled the bill in each house. If agreement is reached, and both houses approve the conference report, the bill is sent to the President. The President may sign the bill into law, let it become law without his signature, or veto or pocket veto the bill. If Congress overrides a presidential veto by a two-thirds vote in both houses, the bill becomes law without the President's signature.

Suggested Reading

Barone, Michael; Ujifusa, Grant; and Matthews, Douglas. *The Almanac of American Politics 1980,* published biennially (E. P. Dutton, 1979). An extremely useful, comprehensive guide to political leaders at the local, state, and national levels. Includes political profiles of the governors, senators, and representatives, their districts, voting records on major issues, and ratings from various interest groups.

Clausen, Aage R. *How Congressmen Decide: A Policy Focus* (St. Martin's Press, 1973). An examination of how members of Congress vote on specific policy issues. Based on a detailed analysis of congressional roll-call votes in the years 1953–1964 and 1969–1970.

Congressional Quarterly, *Weekly Report* and annual *Almanac* (Congressional Quarterly, Inc.). A comprehensive and very useful report on American politics, with special emphasis on Congress and current legislation. Published weekly, with an annual almanac that contains much of the material from the weekly reports.

Davidson, Roger H., and Oleszek, Walter J. *Congress Against Itself* (Indiana University Press, 1977). A comprehensive study of committee reform in the House of Representatives. Focuses on the people, pressures, and events that led to the adoption of several major committee system changes in October of 1974.

Drew, Elizabeth. *Senator* (Simon and Schuster, 1978). A lively account of the daily activities of the then United States senator from Iowa, John Culver. Offers insight into the pressures and procedures of the Senate and the personalities of its members.

Fenno, Richard F., Jr. *Congressmen in Committees* (Little, Brown, 1973). A revealing and important comparative analysis of how congressional committees make decisions. Based on a detailed examination of six different committees in the House of Representatives, and their six Senate counterparts.

Fenno, Richard F., Jr. *Home Style* (Little, Brown, 1978). A thoughtful analysis of a very important aspect of the political behavior of House members — their relationships with the constituents in their home district.

Fiorina, Morris P. *Congress: Keystone of the Washington Establishment** (Yale, 1977). A lively and interesting discussion of how Congress creates new bureaucracies in Washington and then gains credit at home by helping voters to deal with those agencies. The author argues that House seats are safer as a result.

Fox, Harrison W., Jr., and Hammond, Susan Webb. *Congressional Staffs** (Free Press, 1977). A detailed and informative analysis of the professional, nonelected men and women who work for Congress. Focuses on their backgrounds, personalities, and work-related roles, and assesses the impact of staffs on Capitol Hill.

Franck, Thomas M., and Weisband, Edward. *Foreign Policy by Congress* (Oxford University Press, 1979). An illuminating study of the expanded role of Congress in the making of foreign policy. Includes analyses of the 1973 War Powers Resolution, foreign policy lobby groups, and the growth of congressional staff expertise in the field of foreign affairs.

Huitt, Ralph K., and Peabody, Robert L., eds. *Congress: Two Decades of Analysis** (Greenwood, 1979). (Originally published in 1969.) Peabody presents an excellent summary and analysis of research on Congress from the mid-1940s to the mid-1960s, and Huitt offers a series of perceptive and influential articles on congressional behavior. Contains a useful bibliography of books and articles on Congress.

Matthews, Donald R. *U.S. Senators and Their World** (Norton, 1973). (Originally published in 1960.) A readable and revealing analysis of the United States Senate as of 1960. Examines the senators' geographical and occupational origins, their activities in the Senate, and the nature of the environment in which they worked.

Mayhew, David R. *The Electoral Connection** (Yale University Press, 1974). A stimulating and thoughtful analysis of congressional behavior. Argues that a member of Congress' basic motivation is to win re-election, and traces the effects this has on a member's legislative behavior and the way Congress makes policy.

Oleszek, Walter J. *Congressional Procedures and the Policy Process** (Congressional Quarterly Press, 1978). An extremely useful, clearly written examination of the rules and procedures in the Senate and the House of Representatives. Describes the congressional legislative process in detail, from the introduction of a bill to final presidential action.

Peabody, Robert L. *Leadership in Congress** (Little, Brown, 1976). An important study of party leadership in Congress. Examines the personalities, activities, and recruitment of House and Senate leaders through a series of case studies of leadership contests from 1955 to 1974.

Peabody, Robert L., and Polsby, Nelson W., eds. *New Perspectives on the House of Representatives,* 3rd edition* (Rand McNally, 1977). A useful series of articles on various aspects of the House, including specific congressional committees, leadership contests, and legislative-executive relations.

Polsby, Nelson W. *Congress and the Presidency,* 3rd edition* (Prentice-Hall, 1976). A concise, readable analysis of the legislative and executive branches of government. Polsby makes useful observations on the Senate and House of Representatives as distinct political institutions, and traces the budgetary process in the executive branch and Congress.

Wilson, Woodrow. *Congressional Government: A Study in American Politics* (Peter Smith, 1958). (Originally published in 1885.) A classic study of congressional government in the late nineteenth century by a scholar who later became President of the United States. Stresses the separation of powers in the American political system, the importance of congressional committees and committee chairmen, and what Wilson viewed as the predominance of congressional power over that of the President in that era.

* Available in paperback edition

JUSTICE

In the high-ceilinged marble chamber of the Supreme Court, on July 2, 1980, the Marshal of the Court rapped his gavel on a wooden block and cried: "The honorable, the Chief Justice and the Associate Justices of the Supreme Court of the United States. Oyez, oyez, oyez. All persons having business before the honorable, the Supreme Court of the United States, are admonished to draw near."

As the Marshal spoke, Chief Justice Warren E. Burger and the Associate Justices, wearing their black robes, filed in through the red velvet curtains behind the bench. It was the last day of the Court's term before the summer adjournment, and decisions were announced in two important cases. The Court ruled, 7–1, that the First Amendment to the Constitution gave the public and the press the right to attend criminal trials.[1] "We are bound to conclude," Chief Justice Burger said, "that a presumption of openness inheres in the very nature of a criminal trial under our system of justice." In another landmark case handed down the same day, the Burger Court upheld as constitutional a federal public works program in which 10 percent of the money spent was reserved for blacks and other minorities.[2] Both of these decisions, one guaranteeing the press access to criminal trials, the other extending the reach of "affirmative action" programs, were hailed by liberals.

[1] *Richmond Newspapers Inc.* v. *Virginia,* 100 S. Ct. 2814 (1980).
[2] *Fullilove* v. *Klutznick,* 100 S. Ct. 2758 (1980).

But other decisions during the 1980 term pleased conservatives. The Court, 5–4, upheld the Hyde Amendment, a federal law cutting off Medicaid funds for most abortions for the poor.[3] It permitted evidence seized illegally by the government from one person to be used in the trial of another.[4] And it held that a former CIA agent who had signed a secrecy agreement had to give the government all his profits from a book he wrote that criticized the intelligence agency's activities in Vietnam.[5]

The Court under Burger was often closely divided, and thus unpredictable. Yet, well before 1980, the Supreme Court had gradually become distinctly recognizable as the "Burger Court." It had, in previous years, upheld the death sentence in certain circumstances, narrowed the reach of the Fourth Amendment's protections against unreasonable search and seizure, and limited the rights of criminal defendants.

More than a decade earlier, in 1969, Chief Justice Earl Warren had retired, and Chief Justice Burger had been named by President Nixon to succeed him. Over the next three years, Nixon had appointed three more justices to the Court, and in 1975 President Ford chose one justice. Thus by 1976 a majority of the nine-member Court had been appointed since Earl Warren's retirement.

By no means did all of the Burger Court's decisions narrow and restrict the interpretations of the Warren Court. In some areas, such as desegregation and privacy, the Burger Court extended and even broadened the decisions of the Warren Court. Nevertheless, it was clear that the Supreme Court, under Chief Justice Burger, was moving in a somewhat different path than it had under Chief Justice Warren.

During Earl Warren's sixteen years as Chief Justice, the Supreme Court had a profound impact on politics and government in America. The Warren Court was an extraordinarily activist, innovative tribunal that wrought far-reaching change in the meaning of the Constitution. Among its major decisions, the Warren Court outlawed official racial segregation in public schools, set strict national standards to protect the rights of criminal defendants, required the equal apportionment of state legislatures and the House of Representatives, and ruled that prayers and Bible-reading in the public schools were unconstitutional. And it handed down other dramatic decisions that won it both high praise and sharp criticism—and engulfed it in great controversy.

Chief Justice Earl Warren

[3] *Harris* v. *McRae,* 100 S. Ct. 2671 (1980).
[4] *U.S.* v. *Payner,* 447 U.S. 727 (1980).
[5] *Snepp* v. *U.S.,* 444 U.S. 507 (1980).

The Court is and always will be a storm center of controversial issues. For to it come most of the troublesome, contentious problems of each age, problems that mirror the tensions, fears and aggressiveness of the people. It will be denounced by some group, whatever it does.

— William O. Douglas,
The Court Years: 1939–1975.

Chief Justice Warren E. Burger flanked by George Bush and Ronald Reagan

Riding the crest of the tidal wave of social change that swept through America in the 1950s and 1960s, the Court became a natural target of those who felt that it was moving too fast and too far. The political reaction to its bold decisions was symbolized by automobile bumper stickers that read "Impeach Earl Warren."

During the 1968 presidential campaign, Nixon promised to appoint to the Supreme Court "strict constructionists who saw their duty as interpreting law and not making law. They would see themselves as caretakers of the Constitution and servants of the people, not super-legislators with a free hand to impose their social and political viewpoints upon the American people."[6]

Nixon's campaign comments clearly reflected one side of the historical argument over the "proper" role of the Supreme Court. Although the argument was as old as the republic itself, it had, by 1968, taken on new political meaning; for the Warren Court had become linked in the minds of many voters with black militancy, urban riots, rising crime, and the volatile issue of "law and order" and justice in America. By contrast, others viewed the Warren Court as a humanitarian force that had revitalized American democracy.

In Chief Justice Burger, Nixon made it clear, he believed he had found a "strict constructionist" who would fit his political and philosophical requirements. After appointing Burger, Nixon sought to change the political balance on the Court further by nominating a conservative federal appeals court judge, Clement F. Haynsworth, Jr., of South Carolina, to be an Associate Justice. When the Senate rejected Haynsworth in 1969 after a prolonged battle centering on conflict-of-interest charges, Nixon in 1970 nominated another conservative Southerner, G. Harrold Carswell, a federal appeals court judge in Florida. Carswell, too, was rejected after another dramatic fight in the Senate over charges that Carswell had shown racial bias and was a mediocre jurist. Finally, Nixon nominated Harry Andrew Blackmun, a Minnesota Republican and federal appeals court judge. Blackmun, a moderate, was confirmed. In 1971 Nixon nominated two more Supreme Court justices whom he said shared his "conservative" philosophy. They were Lewis F. Powell, Jr., a prominent Richmond attorney, and Assistant Attorney General William H. Rehnquist. Both were confirmed, giving President Nixon four appointees on the highest court. Since Byron R. White, a Kennedy appointee, and Potter Stewart, an Eisenhower appointee, voted in a number of important cases with the four new justices, from that point forward, in some decisions at least, Nixon had an effective majority in the highest tribunal. In 1975 Justice William O. Douglas, an outspoken champion of individual liberties, retired after more than thirty-six years on the Court when a stroke left him unable to carry on. President Ford chose as his replacement a moderate, John Paul Stevens, a federal appeals court judge from Chicago. The appointment meant that of the nine members of the Court, seven had been appointed by Republican Presidents. In the space of only a few years, the members and political philosophy of one of the three branches of the federal government had changed measurably. And, given the advanced ages of many of the justices, in the 1980s there would be further change. By the 1980 presidential election, five of the nine justices of the Supreme Court were more than 70 years old. As a result, the victor in that presidential contest might be able to shape the

[6] Campaign speech, November 2, 1968, quoted in Congressional Quarterly, *Weekly Report,* May 23, 1969, p. 798.

character of the Court for years to come—an argument that was used during the campaign by supporters of both President Carter and his successful Republican challenger, Ronald Reagan.

The System of Justice

The Supreme Court stands at the pinnacle of the American judiciary, but it is only one part of the fragmented, decentralized system of justice in America, a system that encompasses a network of federal courts, state and local courts and prosecutors, the United States Department of Justice, state and local police, the FBI, prisons and jails, probation and parole officers, and parole boards.

During a time of political activism, as in the 1960s and early 1970s, the police and the courts became the cutting edge and the enforcement arm of the "Establishment" in the eyes of dissident groups. To the mass of Americans, however, the police and courts represent the forces of "law and order."

In recent years, the quality of justice in America, the crime rate, and the actions of the police have in themselves become political issues. Events during the Vietnam war focused widespread public attention on the American system of justice and raised important questions about its operations, adequacy, and fairness. For example, in prosecuting antiwar protesters, the government sometimes relied on informers who encouraged or committed the same acts for which their associates were later tried. During the same period, federal grand juries were used to gather intelligence against the peace movement and to suppress political dissent. The Federal Bureau of Investigation conducted its counterintelligence program (COINTELPRO), in which the FBI secretly harassed American citizens and in some cases even endangered lives.

In 1973 the extraordinary developments in the Watergate scandal led to the appointment of a special prosecutor, Archibald Cox, operating outside regular Justice Department channels, to handle the case. The appointment symbolized public skepticism over whether the normal machinery of justice could be relied on in a case involving the highest officials of the government. When Nixon fired Cox for demanding presidential tapes, the strong public reaction forced him to name another special prosecutor. For months, Nixon and his attorneys resisted the courts; Nixon yielded his tapes only after the Supreme Court had ruled 8–0 that he was required to produce them, and then only in the face of the growing sentiment for his impeachment in the House of Representatives.[7] In time, the President's two principal aides, Attorney General John Mitchell, and several other high officials of the White House and of the President's campaign organization went to prison. The President himself was named by a federal grand jury as an unindicted co-conspirator in the cover-up of the Watergate burglary and eventually resigned and received a presidential pardon. It was clear that the President and his aides had tried to block the investigation of a crime. The Watergate controversy intensified the doubts already raised about the system of justice in America. Against this background, a number of questions may be asked about the courts and the law.

What is the "proper" role of the Supreme Court in the American political

Former Attorney General John Mitchell enters prison.

---

[7] *United States* v. *Nixon,* 418 U.S. 683 (1974).

system? Since the Constitution created three separate branches of the federal government, can the Supreme Court, as head of the judicial branch, overrule the other two branches—the President and Congress? Since its members are appointed and not accountable to the voters, should the Supreme Court "legislate" and make social policy? What has been the political impact of the Court's decisions? How is the system of criminal justice supposed to operate? How does it really operate? Is it stacked against blacks and other minorities? Do the rich have a better chance under the system than the poor?

The Law

In a political sense, law is the body of rules made by government for society, interpreted by the courts, and backed by the power of the state. While this is a simple, dictionary-type definition, there are conflicting theories of law and little agreement on how it should be defined.

If law were limited to what can be established and enforced by the state, then Louis XIV would have been correct in saying, "It is legal because I wish it." The men who founded the American nation were influenced by another tradition, rooted in the philosophy of John Locke and in the principle of natural rights. This was the theory that human beings, living in a state of nature, possessed certain fundamental rights that they brought with them into organized society. The tradition of natural rights was used by the American revolutionaries of 1776 to justify their revolt against England and, more recently, by Dr. Martin Luther King, Jr., the civil rights leader, and others who practiced "civil disobedience" against laws they believed to be unjust, unconstitutional, or immoral.

Still another approach to law is sociological. In this view, law is seen as the gradual growth of rules and customs that reconcile conflict among people in societies; it is as much a product of culture, religion, and morality as of politics. There is always a problem of incorporating majority morality into criminal law; if enough people decide to break a law, it becomes difficult to enforce. One example was Prohibition, which was widely ignored and finally repealed; more recently, there have been pressures to legalize marijuana.

Much American law is based on English *common law*. In twelfth-century, medieval England, judges began to dispense law, and their cumulative body of decisions, often based on custom and precedent, came to be called common law, or judge-made law (as opposed to written law made by legislatures). In deciding cases, judges have often relied on the principle of *stare decisis,* the Latin phrase meaning "stand by past decisions." In other words, judges generally attempt to find a *precedent* for a decision in an earlier case involving similar principles. Most law that governs the actions of Americans is *statutory law* enacted by Congress, or by state legislatures or local legislative bodies; but many statutes embody principles of English common law.

Laws do not always ensure fairness. If a man discovers that his apple trees are gradually being cut down by a neighbor, he can sue for damages, but by the time the case is decided the trees may all be felled. Instead, he may, under the legal principle of *equity,* seek an immediate injunction to prevent any further tree chopping. Equity, or fair dealing, may provide preventive measures and legal remedies unavailable under ancient principles of common law.

Cases considered by federal and state courts are either *civil* or *criminal*. Civil cases concern relations between individuals or organizations, such as a divorce action, or a suit for damages arising from an automobile accident or for violation of a business contract. The government is often party to a civil action—when the Justice Department files a civil antitrust suit against a corporation, for example. Criminal cases concern crimes committed against the public order. Most crimes are defined by local, state, and federal statutes, which set forth a range of penalties as well.

A growing body of cases in federal courts concerns questions of *administrative law,* the rules and regulations made and applied by federal regulatory agencies and commissions. Corporations and individuals can go into federal court to challenge the rulings of these agencies.

Supreme Court Justice Robert Jackson once observed that people are governed either by the will of one person, or group of persons, or by law. He added, "Law, as the expression of the ultimate will and wisdom of a people, has so far proven the safest guardian of liberty yet devised."[8]

The Supreme Court

The Supreme Court is a *political institution* that makes both policy and law. Although insulated by tradition and judicial tenure from the turmoil of everyday politics, the Supreme Court lies at the heart of the ongoing struggle in the American political system. "We are very quiet there," said Justice Oliver Wendell Holmes, Jr., "but it is the quiet of a storm centre."

In giving the Constitution contemporary meaning, the Supreme Court inevitably makes political and policy choices. "To consider the Supreme Court of the United States strictly as a legal institution," Robert A. Dahl has suggested, "is to underestimate its significance in the American political system. For it is also a political institution, an institution, that is to say, for arriving at decisions on controversial questions of national policy."[9]

A basic reason for the political controversy surrounding the Supreme Court is that its precise role in the American political system was left ambiguous by the framers of the Constitution. The Supreme Court is at the apex of one of the three independent, constitutionally coequal branches of the federal government. But does it have the constitutional right to resolve conflicts among the three branches? As Robert G. McCloskey noted, "The fact that the Constitution is supreme does not settle the question of who decides what the Constitution means."[10] This was dramatically illustrated during the 1974 court battle over the tape recordings that President Nixon secretly made of his White House conversa-

The Supreme Court:
Politics, Policy,
and Public Opinion

[8] Robert H. Jackson, *The Supreme Court in the American System of Government* (Cambridge, Mass.: Harvard University Press, 1955), p. 27.
[9] Robert A. Dahl, "Decision-Making in a Democracy: The Role of the Supreme Court as a National Policy-Maker," in Raymond E. Wolfinger, ed., *Readings in American Political Behavior* (Englewood Cliffs, N.J.: Prentice-Hall, 1966), p. 166.
[10] Robert G. McCloskey, *The American Supreme Court* (Chicago: University of Chicago Press, 1960), p. 8.

tions. When the special Watergate prosecutor subpoenaed certain presidential tapes, the White House announced that the President would comply only with a "definitive" Supreme Court ruling, a term that was not explained. The President cited the doctrine of separation of powers and claimed executive privilege; he argued that because the Constitution established three independent branches of government, the Supreme Court could not compel the President to release the tapes. The Court held otherwise; it recognized the existence of executive privilege, but ruled that the President could not hold back evidence needed for the criminal trial of his subordinates.[11] Despite his threats of possible defiance, Nixon yielded to the Supreme Court.

Judicial Review. Since Chief Justice John Marshall's day, the Supreme Court has exercised the right of *judicial review,* the power to declare acts of Congress or actions by the executive — or laws and actions at any level of local, state, and federal government — unconstitutional. Lower federal courts and state courts may exercise the same power, but the Supreme Court normally has the last word in deciding constitutional questions. "We are under a Constitution," Charles Evans Hughes declared, "but the Constitution is what the judges say it is."[12]

Yet why, it is often asked, should nine justices who are appointed for life and not elected by the people, have the power in a democratic system to strike down the laws and decisions of popularly elected legislatures and leaders? The question is asked most often by people who disapprove of what the Supreme Court is doing at a particular time. Those who approve of the philosophy of a given Court seldom complain that it is overstepping its power.

One view of the Supreme Court holds that, because the justices are not popularly elected, the Court should move cautiously and interpret the Constitution "strictly." Popular democracy and the principle of majority rule are more consistent, in this view, with legislative supremacy. An opposite view holds that the Court is the cornerstone of a system of checks and balances and *restraints* on majority rule provided by the Constitution. In this view, the Supreme Court may often be the *only* place in the political system where minorities are protected from the majority.

The debate over the role of the Supreme Court in the American system is sharpened by the fact that the Constitution is written in broad and sometimes ambiguous language. As a result, the Supreme Court has interpreted the meaning of the Constitution very differently at different times.

Justice Felix Frankfurter once observed:

The meaning of "due process" and the content of terms like "liberty" are not revealed by the Constitution. It is the Justices who make the meaning. They read into the neutral language of the Constitution their own economic and social views. . . . Let us face the fact that five Justices of the Supreme Court are the molders of policy rather than the impersonal vehicles of revealed truth.[13]

---

[11] *United States* v. *Nixon* (1974).

[12] Alpheus T. Mason, *The Supreme Court: Palladium of Freedom* (Ann Arbor, Mich.: University of Michigan Press, 1962), p. 143. Hughes, later Chief Justice of the United States Supreme Court, made this comment in 1907 as governor of New York.

[13] Felix Frankfurter, "The Supreme Court and the Public," *Forum,* Vol. 83 (June 1930), pp. 332–34.

The Supreme Court must, however, operate within the bounds of public opinion, and, in the long run, within the political mainstream of the times. The Court possesses no armies, and it must finally rely on the executive branch to enforce many of its rulings. It was this truth that supposedly led President Andrew Jackson to declare of his Chief Justice, "John Marshall has made his decision— *now let him enforce it.*"[14] The Court cannot completely ignore the reactions to its decisions in Congress and in the nation, because, ultimately, as a political institution its power rests on public opinion.

The Constitution gives the Supreme Court power to consider "all Cases . . . arising under this Constitution." The principle of judicial review traces back to English common law, although the Constitution nowhere *explicitly* gives this power to the Court. The question of the framers' intent is still debated, but in 1788 Alexander Hamilton argued in *The Federalist* that the judicial branch did in fact have the right to judge whether laws passed by Congress were constitutional.[15] James Madison made the same point during the debate in Congress over the Bill of Rights. Later, so did James Wilson, another influential framer of the Constitution. And, according to Henry J. Abraham, "a vast majority" of the delegates to the constitutional convention favored the idea of judicial review.[16]

The Road to Judicial Review

During the colonial period, the British Privy Council in London exercised judicial review over laws passed by the colonial legislatures. And during the first decade of the new nation's existence, the Supreme Court, in a few cases, considered whether federal laws were constitutional and at least twice struck down minor state laws.[17]

Despite this history, the power of judicial review was not firmly enunciated and established by the Supreme Court until 1803 in the case of *Marbury* v. *Madison*.[18] When Jefferson became President in 1801 he was angered to find that his Federalist predecessor, John Adams, had appointed a number of federal judges just before leaving office, among them one William Marbury as a Justice of the Peace in the District of Columbia. When Jefferson discovered that Marbury's commission had not actually been delivered to him, he ordered Secretary of State James Madison to hold it up. Under a provision of the Judiciary Act of 1789, Marbury sued in the Supreme Court for a writ of mandamus compelling the delivery of his commission. The Supreme Court under Chief Justice John Marshall dismissed the case, saying it lacked jurisdiction to issue such a writ. The Court held that the section of the Judiciary Act under which Marbury had sued was unconstitutional, since the Constitution did not empower the Court to issue a writ of mandamus, as the act provided. The ruling thus avoided an open political confrontation with the executive branch over Marbury's commission but at the same time established the power of the Court to void acts of Congress. "The Constitution is superior to any ordinary act of the legislature," Marshall wrote, and "a law repugnant to the Constitution is void."[19]

---

[14] Quoted in Robert H. Jackson, *The Supreme Court in the American System of Government*, p. 11.

[15] Edward Mead Earle, ed., *The Federalist*, No. 78 (New York: The Modern Library), p. 506.

[16] Henry J. Abraham, *The Judicial Process*, 4th ed. (New York: Oxford University Press, 1980), p. 322.

[17] *Ibid.*, pp. 324–36.

[18] *Marbury* v. *Madison*, 1 Cranch 137 (1803).

[19] *Ibid.*

Felix Frankfurter

Although the Court's power of judicial review was thus established, the question of *how* the Court should apply its great power has remained a subject of controversy up to the present day. The debate has centered on whether the Court should practice *judicial activism* or *judicial restraint*.

As one scholar has posed the central questions: "Should the Court play an active, creative role in shaping our destiny, equally with the executive and legislative branches? Or should it be characterized by self-restraint, deferring to the legislative branch whenever there is room for policy judgment and leaving new departures to the initiative of others?"[20]

The philosophy of judicial restraint is associated with Justices Felix Frankfurter, Louis D. Brandeis, and Oliver Wendell Holmes, Jr. Briefly stated, that philosophy requires the Court to avoid constitutional questions where possible and to uphold acts of Congress unless they clearly violate a specific section of the Constitution. Frankfurter held that the Court should avoid deciding "political questions" that could involve it in conflicts with other branches of the federal government.

The philosophy of judicial activism was embraced on many issues by a majority of the members of the Warren Court, which boldly applied the Constitution to social and political questions. For example, in protecting the rights of criminal defendants and in its reapportionment decisions, the Court moved into controversial areas that earlier Supreme Court justices had avoided.

The Changing Role of the Supreme Court

Although John Marshall had set forth the right of judicial review in 1803, the Supreme Court did not declare another act of Congress unconstitutional until the *Dred Scott* case in 1857. Under Marshall's successor, Roger B. Taney (1836–1864), the Court protected states' rights and stressed the power of the states over that of the federal government.

After the Civil War, the Court refused to apply the Fourteenth Amendment to protect the rights of black Americans, even though Congress had passed the amendment for this specific purpose (see Chapter 5). Instead, the Court used the amendment's "due process" clause to protect business from state regulation. The Fourteenth Amendment provides that no state shall "deprive any person of life, liberty, or property, without due process of law." The Court accepted the argument that a corporation was a "person" within the meaning of the amendment. In a series of cases, it used the Fourteenth and Fifth amendments to protect industry, banking, and public utilities from social regulation. In the 1890s the Supreme Court struck down the federal income tax and emasculated the federal antitrust laws. In general, the Court during this era served as a powerful guardian of the "robber barons"—the businessmen who amassed great fortunes in the late nineteenth century—as well as a champion of *laissez-faire* capitalism, a philosophy that government should interfere as little as possible in the affairs of business.

The Court continued to expound a conservative philosophy under Chief Justice William Howard Taft in the 1920s. The election of Franklin D. Roosevelt in 1932 was followed by vast social change in America; but a majority of the Supreme Court was not in sympathy with the programs of the New Deal. Between 1933 and 1937 the Court struck down one after another of Roosevelt's programs.

[20] Archibald Cox, *The Warren Court* (Cambridge, Mass.: Harvard University Press, 1968), p. 2.

Louis D. Brandeis

The Policymakers

In 1936 the average age of members of the Court was seventy-one, and the justices were dubbed the "nine old men."[21] Re-elected by a landslide that year, Roosevelt risked his prestige in 1937 when he proposed his famous "court-packing" plan. His objective was to put younger justices on the Court who would be more sympathetic to the New Deal. Roosevelt's plan to bring the Supreme Court out of what he termed "the horse and buggy age" provided that whenever a justice refused to retire at age seventy, the President could appoint an additional justice. Under the plan, the Court could have been expanded to a maximum of fifteen members.

The debate raged in and out of Congress all that spring, but in less than six months the proposal was dead. Although Roosevelt's plan failed, by the time the Court recessed that summer it had already begun to shift to a liberal position and to uphold New Deal programs. As a result, 1937 is regarded as a watershed year in the history of the Supreme Court. From that date on, the Court gradually emerged as the protector, not of big business but, in many cases, of the individual.

The Chief Justices of the United States

John Jay (1789–1795)
John Rutledge (1795)
Oliver Ellsworth (1796–1800)
John Marshall (1801–1835)
Roger B. Taney (1836–1864)
Salmon P. Chase (1864–1873)
Morrison R. Waite (1874–1888)
Melville W. Fuller (1888–1910)
Edward D. White (1910–1921)
William Howard Taft (1921–1930)
Charles Evans Hughes (1930–1941)
Harlan F. Stone (1941–1946)
Fred M. Vinson (1946–1953)
Earl Warren (1954–1969)
Warren E. Burger (1969–   )

The Warren Court

Before he retired as Chief Justice, Earl Warren was asked to name the most important decisions of the Warren Court.[22] He singled out those dealing with reapportionment, school desegregation, and the right to counsel, in that order.[23] Each of these cases symbolized one of three broad fields in which the Warren Court brought about far-reaching changes in America: the political process itself, civil rights, and the rights of the accused.

In its reapportionment decisions, the Warren Court required that each citizen's vote count as much as another's. If the quality of a democracy can be gauged, certainly the individual's vote is a basic unit of measurement. Until the reapportionment revolution of the Warren Court, voters were often powerless to correct basic distortions in the system of representation itself.

The *Brown* decision has not eliminated racial segregation in American schools or American society. But by striking down the officially enforced dual school system in the South, the Court implied "that all racial discrimination sponsored, supported, or encouraged by government is unconstitutional."[24] Thus the decision foreshadowed a social upheaval. The civil rights movement, the civil rights legislation of the 1960s, and the continuing controversy over the busing of public school children all followed in the Supreme Court's wake.

By the 1980s, "integration" in itself appeared to be less important to many black Americans than freedom, dignity, and a full share of the economic opportunities of American society. Nevertheless, the *Brown* decision remains a judicial milestone; by its action at a time when much of white America was complacent and satisfied with the existing social order, the Supreme Court provided moral as well as political leadership — it reminded the nation that the Constitution applies to *all* Americans.

The third broad area of decision by the Warren Court — the protection of the rights of criminal defendants — was discussed in Chapter 4. In a series of con-

---

[21] A phrase popularized by columnists Drew Pearson and Robert S. Allen. See William Safire, *The New Language of Politics* (New York: Random House, 1968), p. 286.

[22] *1968 Congressional Quarterly Almanac*, p. 539.

[23] *Baker* v. *Carr*, 369 U.S. 186 (1962); *Brown* v. *Board of Education of Topeka, Kansas,* 347 U.S. 483 (1954); *Gideon* v. *Wainwright,* 372 U.S. 335 (1963).

[24] Robert L. Carter, "The Warren Court and Desegregation," *Michigan Law Review,* Vol. 67, No. 2 (December 1968), p. 246.

troversial decisions, including *Miranda, Escobedo, Gideon,* and *Mapp,* the Court bit by bit threw the mantle of the Bill of Rights around persons accused of crimes by state authorities. In so doing, the Court collided directly with the electorate's rising fear of crime; it was accused of "coddling criminals" and "handcuffing the police." Under the Burger Court the pendulum has swung back somewhat, in favor of the police and prosecutors.

The Warren Court moved aggressively in several other areas as well—banning prayers in the public schools, curbing the anti-Communist legislation of the 1950s, and easing the laws dealing with "obscenity." All this activity provided ample ammunition to the Warren Court's conservative critics: the Court, they charged, had tinkered with legislative apportionment, forced school integration, overprotected the rights of criminals, banished prayer from the classroom, tolerated Communists, and encouraged pornography. Moreover, as many of the Court's critics frequently pointed out, it decided many important cases by a narrow 5–4 margin. The Burger Court moved more cautiously in the 1970s and 1980s and narrowed the sweep of some of the Warren Court's decisions, particularly in the fields of criminal justice and pornography. Yet one leading scholar concluded that

> the doctrines of equality, freedom, and respect for human dignity laid down in the numerous decisions of the Warren Court cannot be warped back to their original dimensions. . . . Generations hence it may well appear that what is supposedly the most conservative of American political institutions, the Supreme Court, was the institution that did the most to help the nation adjust to the needs and demands of a free society.[25]

The Burger Court   As noted at the outset of this chapter, even before the 1980s it had become clear that the Burger Court was moving in a different direction than the Warren Court. In decisions involving the rights of criminal defendants, for example, the Burger Court usually sought to strengthen the hand of the police and prosecu-

[25] William M. Beaney, "The Warren Court and the Political Process," *Michigan Law Review,* Vol. 67, No. 2 (December 1968), p. 352.

The Supreme Court, 1980

Table 13–1

Justices	Appointed by	Date
William J. Brennan, Jr.	Eisenhower	1957
Potter Stewart	Eisenhower	1959
Byron R. White	Kennedy	1962
Thurgood Marshall	Johnson	1967
Warren E. Burger*	Nixon	1969
Harry A. Blackmun	Nixon	1970
Lewis F. Powell, Jr.	Nixon	1971
William H. Rehnquist	Nixon	1971
John Paul Stevens	Ford	1975

* Chief Justice of the United States

The Supreme Court in 1980. From left: John Paul Stevens, Lewis F. Powell, Jr., Harry A. Blackmun, William H. Rehnquist, Thurgood Marshall, William J. Brennan, Jr., Chief Justice Warren E. Burger, Potter Stewart, and Byron R. White

tors. The Court restricted the landmark *Miranda* decision, narrowed the Fifth Amendment's protection against self-incrimination, made it easier for police to stop and frisk suspects, and handed down a number of other decisions more favorable to police than to defendants. Thus, one of the Burger Court's most significant actions was to chip away at the "exclusionary rule" in a series of decisions making it easier for state and local prosecutors to use illegally seized evidence to convict defendants. And, of course, as previously noted, the Burger Court restored the death penalty. In addition, the Court ruled that journalists had no First Amendment privilege to protect confidential sources and that journalists must answer questions about what they were thinking when they prepared reports resulting in libel suits. Many observers concluded that the Burger Court was more conservative than its predecessor and could be characterized as being to the right of center.

On a number of important issues this was certainly true, but it was not the whole picture. In some policy areas, the Burger Court gave little comfort to conservatives: it legalized abortion, declined to stop the publication of the Pentagon Papers, extended the right to counsel to poor defendants even in misdemeanor cases, outlawed wiretapping of domestic groups without a court warrant, greatly enlarged the rights of prisoners, limited the power of local communities to ban pornography, and ruled that even the President must yield evidence to the courts. In the field of civil rights, the Burger Court banned racial discrimination in private schools, declared that federal courts can require low-cost public housing for blacks in the white suburbs, ordered busing to desegregate schools in several cities, and upheld affirmative action in education, jobs, and in federal contracts.

Thus, even as the Supreme Court shifted to the right, many of its decisions still protected individual liberties and minority groups. But, clearly, the Burger Court had developed its own style and philosophy, as it carried out its task of interpreting the Constitution.

Historically, Presidents have picked Supreme Court justices for their politics more than for their judicial talents. By nominating justices whose political views appear compatible with their own, they try to gain political control of the Supreme Court.

When Franklin Roosevelt unsuccessfully attempted to "pack" the Supreme Court, he was aiming not so much at the age of its members as at their political views. As Justice Hugo Black put it, "Presidents have always appointed people who believed a great deal in the same things that the President who appoints them believes in."[26]

This practice is not necessarily bad if it does not lead to the appointment of mediocre judges. In fact, it is one important way in which the Supreme Court is at least *indirectly* responsive to the electorate. Along with the power of public opinion and the power of the Senate to confirm or reject the President's nominee, the presidential appointment power to some degree links the Court to the voters and the rest of the political system.

Approximately 90 percent of all Supreme Court justices in American history have belonged to the appointing President's political party; some have been selected from the President's inner circle of political advisers. In 1965, for example, President Johnson named Washington attorney Abe Fortas — a Democrat who had been his lawyer and political confidant for many years — to the Supreme Court.[27] The requirement that a majority of the Senate approve a Supreme Court nominee restricts the President's ability to shape the Court completely to his political liking. Up to 1980 the Senate had failed to approve 28, or more than 20 percent, of the 132 Supreme Court nominations sent to it.

Nor do justices always act as Presidents expect. Supreme Court justices have a way of becoming surprisingly independent once they are on the bench; more than one President has been disappointed to find that he misjudged his appointee. As governor of California, Earl Warren helped to elect President Eisenhower. There was nothing in Warren's background as a moderate Republican to make the President think his Chief Justice would preside over a social upheaval. Later, Eisenhower reportedly called the Warren appointment "the biggest damn-fool mistake I ever made."[28] And President Nixon was bitterly disappointed when Chief Justice Burger, joined by two other Nixon appointees, voted with the rest of the Court to require the President to yield his crucial tape recordings.[29]

As Supreme Court Justice Jackson once suggested, conflict among the branches of the federal government is always latent, "ready to break out again whenever the provocation becomes sufficient."[30] The Supreme Court, in deciding cases, must worry not only about public opinion, but about how Congress may react.

[26] "Justice Black and the Bill of Rights," interview broadcast over CBS television network, December 3, 1968; transcript in Congressional Quarterly, *Weekly Report,* January 3, 1969, p. 9.

[27] In 1968 the Senate declined to approve Johnson's elevation of Fortas to be Chief Justice. In 1969 Fortas resigned from the Court when it developed that three years earlier he had accepted a $20,000-a-year retainer from a foundation controlled by Louis E. Wolfson, a financier who went to prison for his stock dealings shortly before the Fortas resignation.

[28] In Joseph W. Bishop, Jr., "The Warren Court Is Not Likely to Be Overruled," *New York Times Magazine,* September 7, 1969, p. 31.

[29] J. Anthony Lukas, *Nightmare: The Underside of the Nixon Years* (New York: Viking, 1976), p. 518. Associate Justice William H. Rehnquist disqualified himself and did not participate in the tapes decision, since he had served in the Justice Department under Nixon.

[30] Jackson, *The Supreme Court in the American System of Government,* p. 9.

Walter F. Murphy has suggested that the Court's conflicts with Congress ebb and flow in a three-step pattern: First, the Court makes decisions on important aspects of public policy. Second, the Court receives severe criticism coupled with threats of remedial or retaliatory action by Congress. The third step, according to Murphy, has generally been "judicial retreat."[31]

Robert A. Dahl has concluded that the dominant policy views of the Court "are never for long out of line" with the dominant views of the legislative majority.[32] Or, as humorist Finley Peter Dunne's "Mr. Dooley" put it, "the Supreme Court follows the election returns."

Under the Constitution, Congress can control the *appellate jurisdiction* of the Supreme Court as well as its *size.* In its early history the Court had five, six, seven, and ten justices. Congress did not fix the number at nine until 1869.

After the Civil War, Congress blocked the Court from reviewing Reconstruction laws. During the late 1950s, a coalition in Congress of Southern Democrats and conservative Republicans mounted a legislative assault to curb the power of the Supreme Court and limit its jurisdiction. That effort failed, but the threat of congressional retaliation is always present.

Congress (in conjunction with the states) also possesses the power to overturn Supreme Court decisions by amending the Constitution.[33] Senator Dirksen's attempts to nullify the reapportionment decisions of the 1960s by this means provide one example. The Sixteenth Amendment, establishing the federal income tax, passed by Congress in 1909 and ratified in 1913, was adopted as a direct result of a Supreme Court decision; in 1895 the Court had ruled unconstitutional an attempt by Congress to levy a national income tax.[34] And the Twenty-sixth Amendment, giving persons eighteen and over the right to vote in all elections, was passed by Congress in 1971 and ratified that year because the Supreme Court had ruled that Congress could lower the voting age only in federal, not in state and local, elections. More recently, "pro-life" groups have tried to get Congress to propose a constitutional amendment to overturn the Supreme Court's decision legalizing abortion.

Finally, Congress may attempt to overturn specific Supreme Court rulings by legislation. For example, Title II of the Omnibus Crime bill of 1968 sought to overturn three major decisions of the Warren Court dealing with the rights of accused persons.[35] Police continued to be guided by the Court rulings, however.

Unlike Congress and the Presidency, institutions that are the subject of continual scrutiny by the press, the Supreme Court has usually operated in secrecy. Its internal workings and deliberations have, until recently, gone largely unreported, although oral arguments and decisions in major cases are given wide publicity.

Some of this traditional secrecy was stripped away in 1979 with the publication of *The Brethren,* a controversial book about the operations of the Su-

The Supreme Court in Action

---

[31] Walter F. Murphy, *Congress and the Court* (Chicago: University of Chicago Press, 1962), pp. 246–47.

[32] Dahl, "Decision-Making in a Democracy: The Role of the Supreme Court as a National Policy-Maker," pp. 171, 180.

[33] The Eleventh, Fourteenth, Sixteenth, and Twenty-sixth amendments to the Constitution reversed specific Supreme Court rulings.

[34] *Pollock* v. *Farmers' Loan and Trust Co.,* 158 U.S. 601 (1895).

[35] *Miranda* v. *Arizona,* 384 U.S. 436 (1966); *Mallory* v. *United States,* 354 U.S. 449 (1957); *United States* v. *Wade,* 388 U.S. 218 (1967).

Chief Justice
Warren E. Burger

preme Court by two investigative reporters.[36] The book, which covered the years 1969 through 1975, published internal memoranda of the justices and reported in great detail on the private weekly conferences in which justices discuss pending cases. A number of scholars criticized the book because its material was unsourced, and some lawyers and judges argued that the judicial process was not served by exposing the Court's internal deliberations.

Nevertheless, in one area, *The Brethren* seemed persuasive — it revealed a degree of conflict and intense competition among the justices that had previously been guessed at but not reported in detail. As already noted, the Supreme Court is a political institution. According to *The Brethren,* the justices engage in trade-offs and deals, and form shifting alliances, much as do political participants in the executive and legislative branches.

Nor should it have been surprising that in the period 1969 to 1975 there was sharp conflict and controversy inside the Court. It was precisely during those years that a Republican President was appointing justices with a very different philosophy from that of the Supreme Court's liberals, some of whom had been on the Court since the administration of Franklin D. Roosevelt.

The Brethren was particularly harsh on Chief Justice Warren Burger, whom it portrayed as a jurist of distinguished bearing, but a man of personal pomposity and shallow intellect. It quoted Justice William J. Brennan, Jr., as calling Burger a "dummy," and quoted Justice Lewis F. Powell, Jr., as saying of Burger's draft in a busing case: "If an associate in my law firm had done this . . . I'd fire him."[37]

The book's gossipy style and its emphasis on personalities are of less value to the scholar and student than the light it sheds on the ways that justices determine which cases reach the Court's docket and how those cases are decided. In choosing even whether to consider a case, the Supreme Court makes law (because, usually, the Supreme Court's refusal to take a case means that a lower court decision stands).

How Cases Reach the Court. Most cases never get to the Supreme Court. Those that do usually reach the Court in one of three ways. Under the Constitution the Court has *original jurisdiction* to hear certain kinds of cases directly. These include cases involving foreign diplomats or cases in which one of the fifty states is a party. But the Court rarely exercises original jurisdiction; many more cases reach the Supreme Court under its *appellate jurisdiction.* That is, they are appealed on the grounds that they concern violations of constitutional rights. But the Court, which theoretically is obliged to hear such cases, can in practice dismiss them if it decides that no substantial federal question is involved. The overwhelming majority of cases presented to the Court come in the form of petitions for a writ of *certiorari* (a Latin term meaning "made more certain"). The Court can choose which of the cases it wants to hear by denying or granting certiorari. The votes of four justices are needed to grant "cert." Between 85 and 90 percent of all such applications are denied.[38]

Cases may reach the Supreme Court for review either from *state* or *federal* courts. The cases come from a state court of last resort (usually a state supreme court), or from federal courts of appeals, U.S. district courts, or special purpose federal courts.

[36] Bob Woodward and Scott Armstrong, *The Brethren: Inside the Supreme Court* (New York: Simon and Schuster, 1979).

[37] *Ibid.,* p. 284.

[38] Abraham, *The Judicial Process,* p. 187.

Of the more than 10 million cases tried annually in American courts, only some 4700 are taken to the Supreme Court. Of this total, the Court customarily hears argument on fewer than 200. In the 1979 term the Supreme Court disposed of a total of 4781 cases. But the Court heard oral arguments in only 156. It handed down signed opinions in 143 of these.[39] The rest of the cases on the Court's docket were dismissed, affirmed, or reversed by written "memorandum orders."

Court Tradition. The Court normally sits from October through June. The Court building on Capitol Hill is a majestic structure of white marble, built in 1935 and modeled after the Greek Temple of Diana at Ephesus, one of the seven wonders of the ancient world. The great bronze doors weigh six and a half tons each; the courtroom seats 300 and has a ceiling 44 feet high. Tradition is observed; federal government lawyers appearing for oral argument still wear morning clothes—a formal cutaway coat with tails and striped pants—as do a few private attorneys. The rather grandiose setting of the building and the formal atmosphere are designed to preserve the dignity of the nation's highest tribunal, but they also provide some comfort to its critics, particularly political cartoonists, who find it easy to lampoon the Court's elaborate Grecian setting.

Lawyers arguing before the Court usually have one-half hour to make their case. Five minutes before their time expires a white light comes on; when a red light flashes on they must stop. But the justices often use up some of the precious time by interrupting to question the attorneys, a procedure that can be totally unnerving for lawyers making their initial appearance before the Supreme Court.

[39] U.S. Supreme Court, Statistical Sheet No. 29, July 2, 1980.

The Death Penalty: The Supreme Court Deliberates

In 1972 the Supreme Court, by a vote of 5–4, struck down the death penalty as then administered in the United States. (Four years later, the Court approved new, more carefully drawn capital punishment laws.) The following is an account of the conference at which the justices reached their 1972 decision:

Marshall was opposed to the death penalty in any form. . . . It almost seemed a penalty designed for poor minorities and the undereducated. The rich and well-educated were rarely sentenced to death. They hired fancy lawyers. With his experience in the South, and a year spent during the Korean War investigating the cases of black GIs sentenced to death, Marshall knew very well how the system worked. The death penalty was the ultimate form of racial discrimination. . . .

The conference met on the death cases on January 21, 1972. . . . The Chief began. He observed that if he were a legislator, he would vote against the death penalty, but he was not. He would uphold. Clearly the penalty was constitutional.

Douglas and Brennan argued to strike the death penalty as Marshall had expected.

Then, there was a surprise. . . . Stewart indicated that he was inclined to vote to strike the current capital punishment laws. He would not go along with a sweeping Eighth Amendment abolition of the death penalty. But the randomness and arbitrariness of the sentencing decisions made the laws "cruel and unusual."

Marshall was pleased. He now had four votes. But White and the three Nixon appointees had not spoken.

Then came another surprise. White said that he too was troubled by the infrequency [of the death penalty's use]. It had changed his perspective. Infrequency nullified the state interest in deterrence. He too was inclined to vote to strike.

Blackmun and Powell voted tentatively to uphold the laws. Rehnquist voted firmly to uphold. . . .

"Boys, it is a surprise to me, but the death cases seem to be coming out 5 to 4 against the death penalty," Brennan told his clerks after conference.

—Bob Woodward and Scott Armstrong, *The Brethren: Inside the Supreme Court.*

On Fridays when the Court is sitting, the justices meet in *conference* to discuss and vote on pending cases and applications for certiorari. The justices, by a tradition established in 1888, shake hands as they file into the oak-paneled conference room. The meetings are secret and presided over by the Chief Justice. Beneath a portrait of Chief Justice John Marshall, which hangs over the marble fireplace, the members of the Court gather around a conference table. In the era of the Burger Court, the Chief Justice sits at the east end of the table, with the Associate Justices seated clockwise by seniority. Behind each justice is a cart on which law clerks have placed all the legal documents the justices may need to expound their positions on the various cases. During these deliberations, no one other than the nine justices is allowed in the conference room, not even a clerk. The Chief Justice himself takes notes to record the actions of the Court.

The Chief Justice.   Although theoretically equal to the other eight justices, "the Chief" has four important tools available to him: prestige, the power to influence the Court's selection of cases through his position of leadership, the power to chair the conference, and the power to assign the writing of opinions by the justices. The Chief Justice, therefore, may play a very important role as "Court unifier."[40] Or, as *The Brethren* suggests, the Chief Justice may be a source of disunity.

Leadership styles among Chief Justices differ. Charles Evans Hughes, Chief Justice during the 1930s, was popular among the justices on the Court even though he ran the conference with a firm hand. His successor, Harlan Fiske Stone, was much less reserved, and delighted in joining in the debate. " 'Jackson,' he would say, 'that's damned nonsense,' 'Douglas, *you* know better than that.' "[41]

The Chief Justice, if in the majority, decides who will write the Court's opinion; otherwise, the ranking justice among the majority assigns the writing of the opinion. According to *The Brethren,* Chief Justice Burger often maneuvered in conference to assign opinions (and thus perhaps influence their content) even when he was not in the majority on a case. In one such instance, the authors

---

[40] David J. Danelski, "The Influence of the Chief Justice in the Decisional Process," in Walter F. Murphy and C. Herman Pritchett, eds., *Courts, Judges and Politics: An Introduction to the Judicial Process,* 3d ed. (New York: Random House, 1979), pp. 695–703.

[41] In Danelski, "The Influence of the Chief Justice in the Decisional Process," p. 698.

reported, Justice William O. Douglas complained in a 1972 memo that Burger should not have assigned a group of major abortion cases to Justice Harry A. Blackmun:

> When . . . the minority seeks to control the assignment, there is a destructive force at work in the Court. When a Chief Justice tries to bend the Court to his will by manipulating assignments, the integrity of the institution is imperilled.
>
> Historically, this institution has been composed of fiercely independent men with fiercely opposed views. . . . But up to now the Conference, though deeply disagreeing on legal and constitutional issues, has been a group marked by good-will. . . . Perhaps the purpose of the Chief Justice, a member of the minority in the *Abortion Cases,* in assigning the opinions was to try to keep control of the merits. If that was the aim, he was unsuccessful.[42]

According to *The Brethren,* Douglas eventually withdrew his threat to publish the explosive memo.

Dissenting Opinions.   Once an opinion is assigned, justices are free to write dissenting opinions if they disagree with the majority, or concurring opinions if they reach the same conclusion as the majority, often for different reasons. Important bargaining takes place backstage among the justices as the opinions are written and circulated informally; and justices may trade their votes to influence the shape of an opinion. Some legal experts believe that dissents, because they publicly reveal disunity, weaken the prestige of the Court—the large number of 5–4 decisions by the Warren Court, for example, provided fuel for its enemies. But many of the most eloquent arguments of the Supreme Court have been voiced in dissents by justices such as John Marshall Harlan, Sr., Holmes, Brandeis, Cardozo, Stone, Black, and Douglas. Today's dissent may become tomorrow's majority opinion when the Court, as it has frequently done, overrules past decisions to meet new problems.

When it is in session, the Court, by custom, has handed down its opinions each week on "Decision Monday," and, in more recent years, on other days of the week as well. The justices read or summarize their opinions in the courtroom, sometimes adding informal comments. The words that echo through the marble chamber, often with enormous consequences for society, become the law of the land and renew the meaning of constitutional government.

The American Court System

Because the United States encompasses both a federal government and fifty state governments, it has a *dual* court system. "In effect, this means that there exist, side by side, two major court systems—one could even say fifty-one—which are wholly distinct. . . ."[43]

At the top of the system is the United States Supreme Court. But as we have seen, relatively few cases get there. The average citizen has neither the time nor the money to fight a case all the way to the highest tribunal. In any event the

[42] Woodward and Armstrong, *The Brethren,* pp. 187–88.
[43] Abraham, *The Judicial Process,* p. 146.

Court only considers cases involving a substantial federal question or constitutional issue, and normally after all remedies in the state courts have been exhausted.

The Federal Courts

The bulk of the cases that come before the judicial branch of the federal government are handled in the "inferior" courts created by Congress under the Constitution. Immediately below the Supreme Court are the United States *courts of appeals*. The nation is divided geographically into twelve judicial circuits, each with a court of appeals. Every state and territory falls within the jurisdiction of one of these circuit courts. Each court of appeals has from four to twenty-six judges, but usually three judges hear a case. The circuit courts hear appeals from lower federal courts and review the decisions of federal regulatory agencies. In 1980 there were a total of 132 circuit court judges. Each year about 20,000 cases reach the circuit courts.

Below the circuit courts are the *federal district courts.* In 1980 there were eighty-nine district courts in the fifty states, plus one each for the District of Columbia, Puerto Rico, Canal Zone, Virgin Islands, Guam, and the Mariana Islands, making a total of 95. Each district has from one to twenty-seven judges, making a total of 516 district judgeships. More than half of the federal judicial districts coincide with state lines, but some populous states, such as New York, are divided into as many as four districts. The federal district courts are trial courts; they handle cases involving disputes between citizens of different states and violations of federal law—for example, of civil rights, patent and copyright, bankruptcy, immigration, counterfeiting, antitrust, and postal laws. In 1979, 187,354 cases were commenced in the federal district courts, of which 32,688 were criminal and the rest civil.[44]

Special Federal Courts

Congress has created special purpose courts to deal with certain kinds of cases. These include the United States Court of Claims, which has jurisdiction over such cases as claims against government appropriation of property, claims for income tax refunds, or claims by government workers for back pay; the United States Customs Court, which hears civil actions arising under the tariff laws; the United States Court of Customs and Patent Appeals, which hears tariff appeals and trademark and patent cases; and the United States Court of Military Appeals, often termed "the G.I. Supreme Court."

The Court of Military Appeals, whose three judges are civilians, is the final appellate tribunal in court-martial convictions. It was established by Congress in 1950, along with a Uniform Code of Military Justice. The code represented the first major overhaul of the system of military justice since the early nineteenth century.

The Vietnam war focused new attention on the process of military justice. The most controversial case growing out of that war was the murder conviction of First Lieutenant William L. Calley, Jr. In 1968 American soldiers swept through the South Vietnamese hamlet of My Lai and killed somewhere between 102 and 347 men, women, and children, all civilians. The tragedy was covered up for

[44] *Annual Report of the Director of the Administrative Office of the United States Courts, 1979,* pp. 358, 410.

486

The Policymakers

more than a year, until journalist Seymour M. Hersh publicized the story, for which he won a Pulitzer Prize. The government brought charges in connection with the massacre and the cover-up against twenty-five officers and enlisted men, including the general who commanded the division at the time of the murders. But only Lieutenant Calley, who led his platoon through My Lai, was convicted. In 1971 an army court found Calley guilty of the premeditated murder of at least twenty-two South Vietnamese civilians at My Lai. He was sentenced to life imprisonment, but the army later reduced the sentence to ten years. Calley was paroled by the Army after he had served one-third of his sentence.

The cases occurring in Vietnam dramatized the fact that many Americans — some 2 million by 1980 — were subject to military justice and therefore were at least temporarily outside the civilian system of justice as it has evolved under the Constitution. Moreover, there is always the danger that justice in military trials will be swayed by command influence; that is, that the decisions of prosecutors and officers who serve on military juries may be affected by the views of their commanding officers. In recent years, however, the Supreme Court has afforded certain protections to military defendants. Although there is no direct appeal from decisions of the Court of Military Appeals, the Supreme Court has asserted a limited right to review certain types of military cases.[45] In 1969 the Supreme Court ruled that servicemen must be tried in civilian courts for crimes not connected with the service and committed in peacetime while on leave or off duty.[46] Moreover, in the past several years, the Court of Military Appeals itself has moved to broaden the legal rights of servicemen and women — insisting, for example, that military defendants be brought to trial speedily. As far back as 1967, the Court of Military Appeals held that the Supreme Court's *Miranda* decision, ruling out involuntary confessions, must also apply in military cases.[47] Protections against self-incrimination for military defendants, however, are even broader than those provided by the Fifth Amendment.

Lt. William Calley, Jr.

In 1974 the Supreme Court upheld the controversial Article 134, the "general article" of the Uniform Code of Military Justice, which permitted the military to impose criminal penalties for any offense that imperiled "good order and discipline" in the armed forces. In the first of two cases, the Court ruled that the article did not deny servicemen their constitutional rights.[48] That case involved Captain Howard Levy, who refused to train Green Beret troops during the Vietnam war; he was court-martialed and served more than two years in a federal prison. Three justices dissented strongly, arguing that, as Justice Stewart put it, the article permitted prosecutions "for practically any conduct that may offend the sensibilities of a military commander."

In the second case, a marine corps private, Mark Avrech, had been convicted for attempting to publish a statement against the war in Vietnam while stationed there. The Court upheld his court-martial.[49] Although the Supreme Court thus declined to do away with the "general article," reforms were gradually taking place in the system of military justice. And in 1980 President Carter ordered that the rules of evidence used in federal criminal trials must also apply to military courts-martial.

---

[45] *Burns* v. *Wilson*, 346 U.S. 137 (1953).
[46] *O'Callahan* v. *Parker*, 395 U.S. 258 (1969).
[47] *United States* v. *Tempia*, 16 USCMA 629 (1967).
[48] *Parker* v. *Levy*, 417 U.S. 733 (1974).
[49] *Secretary of the Navy* v. *Avrech*, 418 U.S. 676 (1974).

**The State
Court System**

State and local courts, not the federal courts, handle most cases in the United States. The quality and structure of the court system in the states vary tremendously with each state, but most states have several layers of courts:

1. *Magistrates' courts* are courts in which justices of the peace, or magistrates, handle minor offenses (misdemeanors), such as speeding, and perform civil marriages. Most "J.P.'s" do not have law degrees, but what they may lack in legal training they make up for in their well-known zeal for convictions, which average 80 percent in criminal cases.[50]
2. *Municipal courts* are known variously as police courts, city courts, traffic courts, and night courts. These courts, generally one step up from the magistrates' courts, usually hear civil cases involving $500 to $1000, and lesser criminal offenses.
3. *County courts,* also called superior courts, try serious criminal offenses (felonies) and major civil cases. At this level, jury trials are held in some cases.
4. *Special jurisdiction courts* are sometimes created at the county level to handle domestic relations, juveniles, probate of wills and estates, and other specialized tasks.
5. *Intermediate courts of appeals,* or appellate divisions, exist in some states to hear appeals from the county and municipal courts.
6. *Courts of appeals,* often called state supreme courts, are the final judicial tribunals in the states.

The Judges

Federal Court Judges. All federal court judges are appointed by the President, subject to Senate approval. Historically, federal judges have been selected under a Senate patronage system that has often drawn criticism. The system changed somewhat under Carter, but traditionally it has worked this way: senators present the President with the names of candidates for federal judgeships; the Justice Department and the FBI check their backgrounds; the American Bar Association files a report; and the names are submitted to the Senate for confirmation.

During the 1976 presidential campaign, however, Jimmy Carter promised to appoint all federal judges "strictly on the basis of merit without any consideration of political aspect or influence." As President, Carter in 1978 issued two executive orders, one creating merit commissions to recommend circuit court judges, and another encouraging the creation of such commissions in the states to recommend candidates for federal district courts. The change was important because that same year Congress created 152 new federal judgeships.

Commissions were established in about half the states. Despite the loose, partly voluntary nature of the merit system, Carter's orders had an impact. And, more women and minorities were appointed to the federal bench. Early in 1981, the Reagan administration moved to modify President Carter's system for selecting federal judges.

President Reagan, like Carter, was publicly committed to the "merit selection" of judges. As governor of California, he supported a constitutional amendment to institutionalize merit selection of the judiciary, but it was defeated by the legislature. Reagan might be expected to select conservative jurists; the 1980 Republican platform called for appointment of judges who believed in shifting federal power to state and local governments and "who respect traditional family

Drawing by Whitney Darrow
© 1975 The New Yorker Magazine, Inc.

"God forbid some poor wretch should throw himself on the mercy of the court today."

[50] Abraham, *The Judicial Process,* p. 148.

values and the sanctity of innocent human life"—language that indicated a preference for judges who are against abortion.[51] And, as already noted, Reagan might have a chance to select several members, perhaps even a majority, of the United States Supreme Court.

State and Local Judges. A majority of the roughly 14,000 state and local judges in the United States are elected. In a few states, judges are appointed, in some cases by special commissions. More than twenty states now employ the merit system for the selection of judges, patterned after the "Missouri plan." The basic elements of that plan, which went into effect in Missouri in 1940, are as follows:

1. Nomination of the judges by a nonpartisan commission made up of lawyers, a judge, and citizens.
2. Appointment by the governor.
3. Approval by the voters after an initial term on the bench.

Despite the efforts to bring about judicial reform, in most cases "it is the politicians who select the judges. The voters only ratify their choices."[52] Political parties sometimes do not run competing candidates for the judiciary; rather, political leaders of both major parties get together and carve up the available judgeships. The nominees then run with the endorsement of *both* parties. In the process, political hacks are sometimes elevated to the bench.

In 1967 a citizens' commission named by President Johnson issued a massive study, with nine supplementary task force reports, on problems of crime and justice in America. The commission emphasized the importance of the judicial selection process, declaring: "The quality of the judiciary in large measure determines the quality of justice."[53] Bad judges do more than administer bad law; in the process they erode public respect for the entire system of criminal justice and the political system of which it is a vital part.

Criminal Justice in America

A high-level presidential commission has observed, ". . . the poor—like the rich—can go to court. Whether they find satisfaction there is another matter. . . . Too frequently courts . . . serve the poor less well than their creditors. . . . The poor are discouraged from initiating civil actions against their exploiters. Litigation is expensive; so are experienced lawyers."[54]

The commission that issued this critical report included a mixture of liberals, moderates, and conservatives. The report went on to criticize the na-

---

[51] Congressional Quarterly, *Weekly Report,* July 19, 1980, p. 2046.

[52] Glenn R. Winters and Robert E. Allard, "Judicial Selection and Tenure in the United States," in Harry W. Jones, ed., *The Courts, the Public, and the Law Explosion,* prepared for the American Assembly, Columbia University (Englewood Cliffs, N.J.: Prentice-Hall, 1965), p. 157.

[53] *The Challenge of Crime in a Free Society.* A Report by the President's Commission on Law Enforcement and Administration of Justice (Washington, D.C.: U.S. Government Printing Office, 1967), p. 146.

[54] "Violence and Law Enforcement," in *To Establish Justice, To Insure Domestic Tranquility,* Final Report of the National Commission on the Causes and Prevention of Violence (Washington, D.C.: U.S. Government Printing Office, December 1969), pp. 143–44.

Half of all major crimes are never reported to police.

Of those which are, less than 25 percent are solved by arrests.

Half of these arrests result in dismissal of charges.

90 percent of the rest are resolved by a plea of guilty.

The fraction of cases that do go to trial represent less than 1 percent of all crimes committed.

About 25 percent of those convicted are sent to prison; the rest are released on probation.

Nearly everyone who goes to prison is eventually released.

Between half and two-thirds of those released are arrested and convicted again; they become repeat criminals known as recidivists.

— Adapted from *To Establish Justice, To Insure Domestic Tranquility,*
Final Report of the National Commission on the Causes and Prevention of Violence.

tion's criminal justice system in words that were often harsh. In fact, the commission said, there is no real *system* of criminal justice.

> There is, instead, a reasonably well-defined criminal *process* . . . through which each accused offender may pass: from the hands of the police, to the jurisdiction of the courts, behind the walls of a prison, then back onto the street. . . . criminal courts themselves are often poorly managed and . . . seriously backlogged. . . . prisons . . . are . . . schools in crime. . . . the typical prison experience is degrading . . . and the outlook of most ex-convicts is bleak.[55]

Most criticism of the administration of justice in the United States is directed not at the principles of the system—the presumption that a defendant is innocent until proven guilty and the protections of the Bill of Rights—but at the failure of the system to work the way it is supposed to work.

Americans, Edward L. Barrett, Jr., has noted, tend to think that the procedure of the criminal courts protects the dignity of the individual against the power of the government.

> Such is the general image we have of the administration of criminal justice. But if one enters the courthouse in any sizeable city and walks from courtroom to court-

[55] *Ibid.,* pp. 149–52, 155.

room, what does he see? One judge, in a single morning, is accepting pleas of guilty from and sentencing a hundred or more persons charged with drunkenness. Another judge is adjusting traffic cases with an average time of no more than a minute per case. A third is disposing of a hundred or more other misdemeanor offenses in a morning. . . .

Suddenly it becomes clear that for most defendants in the criminal process, there is scant regard for them as individuals. They are numbers on dockets, faceless ones to be processed and sent on their way. The gap between the theory and the reality is enormous.[56]

In 1979 there were almost 12.1 million serious crimes reported to law enforcement agencies in the United States, of which 1,178,540, or 9.6 percent, fell into the category of violent crimes that people fear the most—murder, rape, robbery, and assault. (See Table 13-2.) In the United States in 1979, 21,460 persons were murdered. There were more than 3.2 million burglaries reported, 64 percent of these in homes. Just over one million cars were stolen. Put another way, on the average a violent crime was committed every twenty-seven seconds, a murder every twenty-four minutes, a rape every seven minutes, a robbery every sixty-eight seconds, and a car stolen every twenty-nine seconds.[57] (See Figure 13-1.)

A Profile of Crime in America

But these figures, compiled annually by the FBI from reports received by law enforcement agencies, do not reflect the full magnitude of crime in the United States. A presidential commission estimated that, based on population sampling, the actual amount of crime committed is "several times" greater than the amount of crime reported to the authorities.[58] People fail to report crime for

[56] Edward L. Barrett, Jr., "Criminal Justice: The Problem of Mass Production," in Jones, *The Courts, the Public, and the Law Explosion,* pp. 86–87.
[57] *Crime in the United States,* Uniform Crime Reports—1979, Federal Bureau of Investigation (Washington, D.C.: U.S. Government Printing Office, 1980), p. 5.
[58] *The Challenge of Crime in a Free Society,* pp. 21–22.

Crime in the United States, 1979

Table 13–2

Crime Offenses	Estimated Number of Crimes	Rate per 100,000 Inhabitants
Total	12,152,700	5,521.5
Violent	1,178,540	535.5
Property	10,974,200	4,986.0
Murder	21,460	9.7
Forcible rape	75,990	34.5
Robbery	466,880	212.1
Aggravated assault	614,210	279.1
Burglary	3,299,500	1,499.1
Larceny	6,577,500	2,988.4
Auto theft	1,097,200	498.5

Source: Adapted from *Crime in the United States,* Uniform Crime Reports—1979, Federal Bureau of Investigation (Washington, D.C.: U.S. Government Printing Office, 1980), p. 37.

Crime Clocks—1979

Figure 13–1

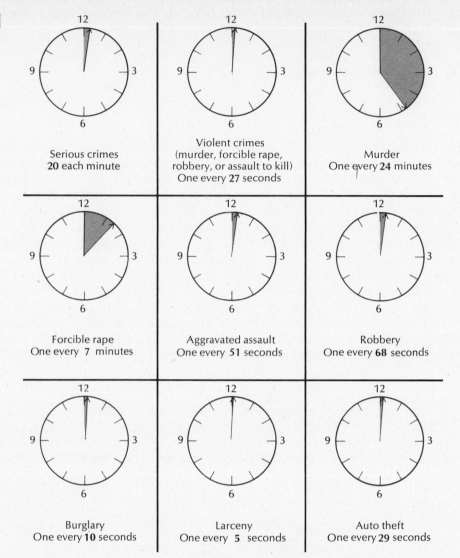

Serious crimes
20 each minute

Violent crimes
(murder, forcible rape,
robbery, or assault to kill)
One every **27** seconds

Murder
One every **24** minutes

Forcible rape
One every **7** minutes

Aggravated assault
One every **51** seconds

Robbery
One every **68** seconds

Burglary
One every **10** seconds

Larceny
One every **5** seconds

Auto theft
One every **29** seconds

Source: Adapted from *Crime in the United States,* Uniform Crime Reports—1979, Federal Bureau of Investigation (Washington, D.C.: U.S. Government Printing Office, 1980), p. 5.

a variety of reasons, including a reluctance to "get involved," or doubt that police can do anything about it, or fear of reprisal by the criminal.[59]

There are some popular misconceptions about crime. As the President's commission noted, "the risks of personal harm are spread very unevenly. The actual risk for slum dwellers is considerably more; for most Americans it is considerably less."[60] Richard Harris has observed: "By far the greatest number of

[59] *Task Force Report: Crime and Its Impact—An Assessment,* The President's Commission on Law Enforcement and Administration of Justice (Washington, D.C.: U.S. Government Printing Office, 1967), pp. 93–94.
[60] *The Challenge of Crime in a Free Society,* p. 19.

Among all age groups, close to ninety percent of those arrested for violating the laws on addictive drugs had criminal records, and seventeen percent of them were armed, presumably to enable them to commit crimes to support their habit.

It is an exceedingly expensive one. A heroin addict—the principal user involved—needs between fifty and sixty dollars a day to keep himself supplied. Since an addict is rarely able to hold down an ordinary job, let alone a job paying that kind of money, he must steal money or else merchandise that can easily be converted into money. As a rule, stolen goods bring about ten percent of their value in cash, so, theoretically, the country's sixty-three thousand known addicts must steal three and a half million dollars a day in cash or thirty-five million dollars a day in merchandise, or a combination of the two, in order to survive. In trying to raise funds, the addict most often relies on muggings, holdups, or burglaries, and in the course of committing them he not infrequently assaults or murders his victims.

—Richard Harris, *Justice: The Crisis of Law, Order, and Freedom in America.*

all crimes reported were committed by slum-dwellers upon slum-dwellers. For a resident of the black slums of Chicago, for instance, the chance of being physically assaulted, on the basis of reported crimes, was one in seventy-seven, whereas for the white resident of a nearby suburb the chance was one in ten thousand."[61]

Crime by youths accounts for a substantial share of all crime. In 1979, for example, 38.8 percent of the arrests for violent and serious crimes were of persons under eighteen. Narcotics addiction is another source of crime. Estimates vary greatly as to how much crime is committed by heroin addicts in order to get money to support their habit. Some estimates attribute as much as three-quarters of all serious crime in New York City and Washington, D.C., to drug addicts.[62]

There is considerable dispute among criminologists and law enforcement authorities over the *rate* at which crime has increased in America in recent years; in part this controversy is due to inadequate systems of crime reporting prior to 1958. But that the crime rate has gone up is generally acknowledged; between 1975 and 1979, it is estimated, the rate of violent crime increased 15 percent. Even if the crime rate had remained level, there would be more crime, because the population has increased.

The Prisons

In 1980 there were 314,000 persons in prison in the United States in federal, state, and local institutions, plus tens of thousands more in jail awaiting trial and in juvenile detention facilities. Of the total, about 26,000 persons were inmates of federal prisons.[63] The bulk of prisoners were in the state prison systems, where uprisings and the seizure of hostages have become increasingly frequent in recent years.

The nation's prisons, instead of rehabilitating offenders, may contribute to the crime rate by serving in many instances as "human warehouses" for the custody of convicts. At least half the felons released from prison commit new crimes.

[61] Richard Harris, *Justice: The Crisis of Law, Order, and Freedom in America* (New York: Dutton, 1970), pp. 27–28.
[62] *Ibid.,* p. 44.
[63] U.S. Department of Justice, *National Prisoner Statistics Bulletin,* May 1980.

We Americans have made our prisons disappear from sight as if by an act of will. We locate them mostly in places remote from view, and far removed from the homes of the inmates; we emphasize security almost to the exclusion of rehabilitation; and we manage to forget inmates and custodians alike by pretending that the prisoners will not return to our cities and our villages and our farms. . . .

The Atticas of this country have become lethal crucibles in which the most explosive social forces of our society are mixed with the pettiness and degradation of prison life, under intense pressure of maintaining "security." . . .

There was no escape within the walls from the growing mistrust between white middle America and the residents of urban ghettos. Indeed, at Attica racial polarity and mistrust were magnified by the constant reminder that the keepers were white and the kept were largely black and Spanish-speaking.

—Attica: The Official Report of the New York State Special Commission on Attica, 1972.

In many cases little is done to prepare prisoners for their return to the outside world. More than half of all state prisons have no vocational training programs. A presidential study commission concluded that "for a great many offenders . . . corrections does not correct."[64] Moreover, state and federal parole systems are badly overburdened. As a result, the decision on when to release prisoners is often arbitrary and unfair, creating further bitterness among those who must remain behind bars.

[64] *The Challenge of Crime in a Free Society*, p. 159.

Frequently, the tensions in America's prisons run so high that they explode in prison riots, in which guards or other hostages are seized and inmates demand better conditions. One of the most dramatic and tragic outbreaks occurred in 1971 at Attica, a maximum-security state prison in New York State. The dismal conditions at Attica were typical of many state prison systems: old and over-crowded buildings, with guards who are often poorly trained and sometimes brutal. Racial tensions ran high at Attica, as at other prisons where many inmates are black and most of the guards usually white.

For four days, convicts took control of the courtyard of a cell block and held hostages. Governor Nelson Rockefeller ordered 200 state troopers to storm the prison. Thirty-two inmates and eleven hostages died. Almost all of them had been killed in the hail of troopers' bullets. A special New York State commission that investigated the bloodshed at Attica concluded that the conditions that sparked the revolt were, in a sense, universal: "Attica is every prison; and every prison is Attica."[65]

"He is the most important American. . . . He works in a highly flammable environment. A spark can cause an explosion. . . . If he overacts, he can cause a riot. If he underacts, he can permit a riot. He is a man on a tightrope."[66] An Attorney General of the United States used these words to describe the typical police officer. Police are indeed on a tightrope; often underpaid, with inadequate train-

The Police

[65] *Attica: The Official Report of the New York State Special Commission on Attica* (New York: Bantam Books, 1972), p. xii.

[66] Attorney General Ramsey Clark, quoted in Harris, *Justice: The Crisis of Law, Order, and Freedom in America*, pp. 76–77.

ing, manpower, and resources, they are expected to fight rising crime, enforce the law, keep the peace, and provide a wide variety of social and community services.

Police must spend much of their time performing such community services —from directing traffic to rescuing stray cats. These duties greatly reduce the amount of time police can spend fighting crime. As the armed embodiment of the law, police are caught between the established order and dissident or minority groups seeking change. Mutual hostility between police and militant minorities or political protesters has erupted in tragic violence and bloodshed. And police face violence in fighting crime. From 1970 through 1979, 1143 police officers in the United States were killed in the line of duty.[67]

"The policeman," in the words of a task force report to a presidential commission, "lives on the grinding edge of social conflict, without a well-defined, well-understood notion of what he is supposed to be doing there."[68] Differences in social and cultural background of police and minorities or dissidents may contribute to tension between them. The task force report argued that "police in the United States are for the most part white, upwardly mobile lower-middle-class, conservative in ideology and resistant to change. . . . They tend to share the attitudes, biases and prejudices of the larger community."[69]

Many Americans—perhaps a majority—strongly support and defend the police. Even when police employed violence against young antiwar demonstrators at the 1968 Democratic National Convention in Chicago, 56 percent of the public approved of the way the police had acted.[70] Later, a staff study of a

---

[67] *Crime in the United States,* Uniform Crime Reports—1979, p. 309.

[68] James S. Campbell, Joseph R. Sahid, and David P. Stang, *Law and Order Reconsidered,* Report of the Task Force on Law and Law Enforcement to the National Commission on the Causes and Prevention of Violence (Washington, D.C.: U.S. Government Printing Office, 1969), p. 290.

[69] *Ibid.,* p. 291.

[70] Gallup poll, September 17, 1968. The question asked of 1507 persons was, "Do you approve or disapprove of the way the Chicago police dealt with the young people who were registering their protest against the Vietnam war at the time of the Chicago convention?" The nationwide findings were:

Approve	*Disapprove*	*No Opinion*
56%	31%	13%

presidential commission adjudged the events at Chicago "a police riot."[71] But in times of turmoil and fear of violence, many Americans appear to regard "law and order" as a requirement that takes precedence over all other considerations, including the constitutional right of peaceful dissent.[72]

The controversy over the role of the police in responding to social protest has to some extent tended to obscure the conventional role of the police officer in the system of criminal justice. Police officers are, after all, highly visible and important public officials. As "the cop on the beat" dealing with everyday social conflict and crime, they exercise great discretionary powers.[73] Should a fight be broken up, a speeding car stopped, a street-corner crowd dispersed? The police officer must decide. To a great extent, law enforcement policy is made by the police.

Police do not capture most lawbreakers, however. There is a huge gap between the number of crimes reported and the number of criminals arrested. In

[71] Daniel Walker, *Rights in Conflict,* Report of the Chicago Study Team to the National Commission on the Causes and Prevention of Violence (New York: Bantam Books, 1968), p. 5.

[72] For example, 76 percent of the people questioned in a telephone survey by the Columbia Broadcasting System said extremist groups should not be allowed to "organize protests" against the government; 55 percent said news media should not report stories that the government considers harmful to the national interest; and 58 percent thought that a suspect in a serious crime should be held in jail by police until they can get enough evidence to charge him with the crime. (*The CBS News poll,* Survey Operations Department, CBS News Election Unit, March 20, 1970, pp. 1–6.)

[73] See, for example, James Q. Wilson, *Varieties of Police Behavior* (Cambridge, Mass.: Harvard University Press, 1968), pp. 7, 278.

Crime and Law Enforcement

Figure 13–2

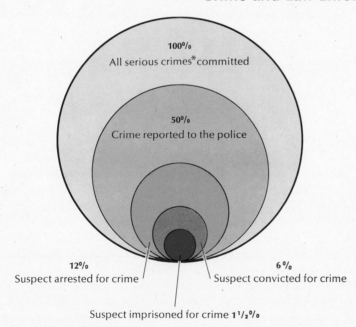

100%
All serious crimes* committed

50%
Crime reported to the police

12%
Suspect arrested for crime

6%
Suspect convicted for crime

Suspect imprisoned for crime 1 1/2%

* Homicide, forcible rape, robbery, aggravated assault, burglary, larceny over $50, auto theft. Based on estimates.

Source: *To Establish Justice, To Insure Domestic Tranquility,* Final Report of the National Commission on the Causes and Prevention of Violence (Washington, D.C.: U.S. Government Printing Office, December 1969), p. xviii.

1979, for example, only 20 percent of known serious offenses were "cleared" from police record books by arrests (although for certain crimes, such as murder, 73 percent were cleared by arrests).[74] Crime can be viewed as a series of concentric circles, in which the smallest, innermost circle represents persons actually convicted and sent to prison. (See Figure 13–2.)

The Department
of Justice

Archibald Cox

Leon Jaworski

Although criminal justice and law enforcement are primarily the responsibility of state and local authorities, the federal government wields substantial power in this field. The Department of Justice in recent years has emerged as a major policymaking agency in relation to a broad range of political, legal, and social issues. The department is headed by the Attorney General, who is both a cabinet officer and the President's chief legal adviser.

One of the Justice Department's basic responsibilities is to conduct criminal prosecutions in the federal courts. This means that the Attorney General has tremendous power to make political decisions about who will be prosecuted and who will not. As noted earlier, during the Watergate inquiries, there was deep public suspicion about the willingness of the Justice Department to prosecute high officials of the Nixon administration who had participated in wrongdoing or helped to cover it up.

Against this background, a special prosecutor, Harvard law professor Archibald Cox, was named to pursue the Watergate and related cases. When Cox sought presidential tape recordings to learn whether Nixon himself had participated in covering up the burglary of Democratic headquarters and in obstructing justice, Nixon dismissed the special prosecutor. Attorney General Elliot L. Richardson then resigned, along with the Deputy Attorney General.[75] But many members of Congress and the public were dismayed that the Watergate investigation had been removed from the hands of the special prosecutor. How could the President's Justice Department investigate the President? There were immediate demands for the appointment of a new special prosecutor. Responding to these pressures, Nixon named Texas attorney Leon Jaworski to the post. The appointment, dismissal, and replacement of the special Watergate prosecutor was a dramatic illustration of the politically sensitive nature of the Justice Department.

An Attorney General might publicly disclaim any suggestion that the decisions of that office were political. But, as a cabinet officer responsible to the President, the Attorney General's political viewpoint is normally an important factor weighed by the President in selecting an individual for that post. In exercising discretion about whom to prosecute, the Attorney General may also reflect personal ideology and outlook. Should an antitrust suit be brought against ITT? Should the Vice President of the United States be brought to trial on criminal charges? Should the department crack down on organized crime? The Attorney General may decide.

In 1980, for example, Attorney General Benjamin Civiletti was widely criticized when he admitted that he had privately advised President Carter that his brother, Billy, would not be prosecuted by the Justice Department if he registered as a foreign agent. Before making his admission, Civiletti had denied that he had ever discussed the case with the President.

[74] *Crime in the United States,* Uniform Crime Reports—1979, p. 177.
[75] A separate confrontation over Nixon's tapes in 1974 resulted in the Supreme Court ruling requiring him to surrender additional tape recordings.

The Justice Department prosecutes persons accused of federal crimes through its United States attorneys in each of the federal judicial districts. Although United States attorneys are appointed by the President, subject to Senate approval, they serve under the Attorney General. There were 94 United States attorneys and 1818 assistant United States attorneys in 1980. Under the supervision of the department's criminal division, the United States attorney in each district initiates investigations and decides whether to prosecute or to seek a grand jury indictment in criminal cases.

Separate divisions of the Justice Department deal with criminal, civil, antitrust, tax, civil rights, and natural resources cases. A special unit in the criminal division handles cases involving organized crime. The Justice Department also includes the Immigration and Naturalization Service, the Drug Enforcement Administration, the Law Enforcement Assistance Administration—created in 1968 to distribute federal funds through the states to local police—and the Bureau of Prisons, which is in charge of federal prisons and youth centers.

1980: Attorney General Benjamin Civiletti explaining his role in the Billy Carter case.

The FBI

Best known of all the arms of the Justice Department is the Federal Bureau of Investigation. In 1980 the FBI had a budget of $615 million and employed 19,300 people (almost 35 percent of all the Justice Department's employees). About 7800 of the total were FBI agents; most of the rest were laboratory experts, clerks, and secretaries. The FBI is the investigative arm of the Justice Department, and its jurisdiction is limited to suspected violations of *federal* law. It has fifty-nine field offices and twelve offices abroad for liaison with foreign police and intelligence services. In its files are the fingerprints of 65 million people.[76]

Senate and House investigations of the FBI in the wake of the Watergate scandal revealed that for years—while the FBI enjoyed a highly favorable public image—the bureau had systematically engaged in illegal activities that violated the constitutional rights of American citizens. FBI agents, for example, engaged in hundreds of burglaries of individuals and groups to plant microphones or photograph documents. From 1956 to 1971, the bureau, through its counterintelligence program (COINTELPRO), harassed American citizens and disrupted their organizations through a wide variety of clandestine techniques, some of which broke up marriages or endangered lives. Moreover, since the administration of Franklin D. Roosevelt, the FBI has gathered intelligence on domestic groups and individuals with only the shakiest legal authority to do so. The bureau has compiled various indexes or lists of politically unreliable persons to be rounded up in an emergency. And as the congressional investigations also disclosed, the FBI opened first-class mail in violation of the law.[77] All of these disclosures of FBI abuses surfaced several years after the death of the bureau's long-time chief, J. Edgar Hoover, but many of the illegal practices had taken place under his leadership.

For forty-eight years, until his death in 1972 at the age of seventy-seven, Hoover was director of the FBI. Under eight Presidents, Hoover and the FBI acquired an unprecedented degree of power and independence. One major

© 1977 by Herblock
from *Herblock on All Fronts*
(New American Library, 1980)

"Except for those of us who are above it."

[76] *The Budget of the United States Government, Fiscal Year 1981,* p. 471; and *99 Facts About the FBI: Questions and Answers,* 6th ed. (Washington, D.C.: U.S. Government Printing Office, 1979), pp. 4, 23.

[77] For details of these and other abuses by the intelligence agencies, see U.S. Congress, Senate, Select Committee to Study Governmental Operations with Respect to Intelligence Activities, *Intelligence Activities and the Rights of Americans, Book II,* 94th Cong., 2nd sess., Final Report (Washington, D.C.: U.S. Government Printing Office, 1976).

J. Edgar Hoover

L. Patrick Gray

William Webster

source of Hoover's power was the secret dossiers and files of the FBI. A member of Congress who had a drinking problem, or who had accepted a campaign contribution from someone rumored to have connections with organized crime, or who was having an extramarital affair, might have good reason to fear the contents of the FBI's file on him.

Even Presidents respected Hoover's power, and under his reign, the FBI, although an arm of the Justice Department, became largely independent of the Attorney General. With a masterful gift for publicity, Hoover invented the "Ten Most Wanted" list and helped to project the image of the "G-man" as square-jawed, clean-cut, and infallible. Through movies, a television serial, and guided tours of its headquarters for the millions of tourists who visit Washington each year, the FBI became the most publicized agency of the federal government. During Hoover's years, it was able to obtain almost anything it wanted from Congress, including a new $126 million headquarters building that opened in 1975.

Even before Hoover's death, the FBI had become controversial. The majority of Americans traditionally thought of it in favorable terms, as an agency adept at catching bank robbers and spies.[78] But other Americans worried about the concentration of power in the hands of the FBI, and they feared that its wiretaps and dossiers might be used for political ends, or to enhance the power of the director. Because Hoover's political views were generally conservative, liberals feared that the FBI was more concerned about pursuing domestic radicals than organized crime.

The FBI's reputation suffered after President Nixon named an old political associate, L. Patrick Gray, as acting director to succeed Hoover. According to evidence published by congressional investigating committees, Gray—at Nixon's request, relayed through the Central Intelligence Agency—slowed down and restricted the FBI investigation of the Watergate burglary. In 1973 Gray's nomination to be permanent FBI director ran into trouble in the Senate, and he asked that his name be withdrawn. Later, Gray admitted that he had burned key files in the Watergate case.

After Gray, Nixon appointed Clarence M. Kelley, the police chief of Kansas City, Missouri, as FBI director, and he was confirmed by the Senate. But Kelley retained many of Hoover's former aides, and he soon found himself in difficulty. The Justice Department began an investigation of FBI burglaries and alleged financial irregularities in the bureau. In 1976 Congress enacted a law that limits the director of the FBI to one ten-year term of office. In 1978 President Carter named a federal judge, William Webster of Missouri, as FBI director.

The FBI's entanglement in the Watergate case had raised a question exactly the opposite of that posed by Hoover's independence. Gray's actions had illustrated the danger of an FBI chief who was *too* responsive to political control. More recently, some critics questioned whether the FBI had improperly entrapped members of Congress in its "Abscam" investigation, in which eight law-

[78] The Gallup poll in 1965 asked a cross section of the American public: "If you had a son who decided to become an FBI agent, would you be pleased or displeased?" Of those questioned, 77 percent said they would be pleased. (Congressional Quarterly, *Weekly Report,* December 26, 1969, p. 2697.) But the disclosures of FBI lawbreaking and other abuses were followed by a decline in public esteem for the bureau. The Gallup poll reported in 1979 that the number of persons who gave a "highly favorable" rating to the FBI had dropped from 84 percent in 1965 to 37 percent. Even so, 81 percent of the public gave the FBI a generally positive rating. Source: *The Gallup Opinion Index,* Report No. 172 (November 1979), p. 24.

makers were alleged to have taken bribes from agents posing as wealthy Arabs. Six members of the House had been convicted by early 1981. Clearly the role and power of a secret police agency raises disturbing problems in a democracy.

Americans who have never had a brush with the law may tend to think of the system of criminal justice in terms of "due process of law," trial by jury, and the right of counsel—in short, the *adversary system* of justice, in which the power of the state is balanced by the defendant's constitutional rights and by the presumption, not specifically written in the Constitution, but deeply rooted in Anglo-Saxon law, that a person is innocent until proven guilty beyond a reasonable doubt.[79]

The Criminal Courts

Plea Bargaining. These protections may prevail *when* a case goes to trial. But in fact, the great majority of cases never *go* to trial. According to one report, "Most defendants who are convicted—as many as 90 percent in some jurisdictions—are not tried. They plead guilty, often as the result of negotiations about the charge or the sentence."[80] In other words, the machinery of the adversary system of justice exists—but it may not be used. Most guilty pleas are the result of backstage discussions between the prosecutor and defense counsel. The practice is commonly known as "plea bargaining," or, less elegantly, as "copping a plea."

The practice sometimes serves everyone's needs but the defendant's. The government is saved the time and expense of a public prosecution; the defense attorney can collect a fee and move on to the next client; the judge can keep the business of the court moving along. But the guilt or innocence of the accused person is not proven.

Usually, the plea bargaining process works this way: a defendant agrees to plead guilty to a less serious charge than might be proven at a trial; in return the prosecutor agrees to reduce the charges or recommend leniency. Often, the accused person will get a lighter sentence this way than if the case went to trial and resulted in a conviction. There is no guarantee, however, that the judge will act as the prosecutor has promised. And, an innocent person may be persuaded to plead guilty to a crime he or she did not commit.

In 1970 the Supreme Court upheld the practice of plea bargaining.[81] The Court ruled that a guilty plea, entered voluntarily and intelligently with the advice of counsel, was constitutional.

Court Delay. American courts do not have enough judges to handle the volume of cases that come before them. In a single year the courts may dispose of more than 3 million cases.[82]

The high caseload, the lack of judges, and poor administration of the courts all result in major delays in the criminal process. The courts are badly back-

Drawing by Henry Martins
© 1978 The New Yorker Magazine, Inc.

"In a concerted effort to get home for the holidays, we find the defendant guilty, as charged."

---

[79] The Supreme Court has held that the "due process clause" of the Constitution requires the presumption that a criminal defendant is innocent until proven guilty beyond a reasonable doubt. *Davis* v. *United States*, 160 U.S. 469 (1895); *Coffin* v. *United States*, 156 U.S. 432 (1895); *In the Matter of Samuel Winship*, 396 U.S. 885 (1970).

[80] *The Challenge of Crime in a Free Society*, p. 134.

[81] *Brady* v. *United States*, 396 U.S. 809 (1970).

[82] *Attica: The Official Report of the New York State Special Commission on Attica*, p. xiii.

The courts in the [New York] metropolitan area, as nearly everyone connected with them readily admits, are overcrowded, understaffed and months behind in their work.

In Brooklyn's dilapidated Criminal Court, some sessions are held in judges' robing rooms, where, before the sessions begin, guards look in the closets for defendants who may have escaped.

In the Bronx, because there is no air-conditioning in the Criminal Court, windows are left open in the summer—even though the elevated trains next door are so noisy that, as one judge said, "you can't hear yourself, much less the defendant; it's impossible to try a case." . . .

A number of judges and lawyers have also pointed out problems common to most, if not all, the courts: judges so harried they often spend whole days doing no more than adjourning the cases on the day's calendars; correction facilities so overcrowded that some judges say they hesitate to sentence the people they convict. . . .

The pressures are so great on all concerned that one day recently Criminal Court Judge Milton Shalleck, after arraigning scores of people at an average speed of 2 minutes 2½ seconds per defendant, finally blurted out: "There is no justice here. I'm not dispensing justice."

—Lesley Oelsner, "The Creaky Courts: Overhaul Needed to End Delays,"
New York Times, April 7, 1970.

---

logged; in many large cities the average delay between arrest and trial is close to a year. In Great Britain the period from arrest to final appeal frequently takes four months, but the same process in many states in America averages ten to eighteen months.

Bail Reform. During the long wait for their trials, accused persons may be free on bail or detained. Bail is a system designed to ensure that defendants will appear in court when their cases are called; typically, arrested persons go before a judge or magistrate who fixes an amount of money to be "posted" with the court as security in exchange for the defendant's freedom. If defendants do not have the money, a bondsman may post bail for them, but the defendants must pay the bondsman a premium of 5 to 20 percent. If the accused persons cannot raise bail either way, they may have to remain in jail until their case comes up. If they go free on bail but fail to appear for their trial, the bail is forfeited.

The rights of the individual and the community conflict during the pretrial period. The accused person may have a job and a family to support; and he or she needs to be free in order to prepare a defense. The community demands that the accused appear for trial and not endanger society by committing a crime in the meantime; that is the rationale of the bail system.

Such a system obviously discriminates against the poor, who may not be able to buy their way out of jail. "Millions of men and women are, through the American bail system, held each year in 'ransom' in American jails, committed to prison cells often for prolonged periods before trial," Ronald Goldfarb has written. "Because they are poor or friendless, they may spend days, weeks, or months in confinement, often to be acquitted of wrongdoing in the end."[83]

Until the Bail Reform Act of 1966 federal judges had often deliberately set a high bail for defendants they considered dangerous, in the hope that the

---

[83] Ronald Goldfarb, *Ransom* (New York: Harper & Row, 1965), p. 1.

bail could not be paid; the practice was an illegal but widespread system of pre-trial detention. Under the 1966 act this subterfuge was no longer possible. *Federal* judges were required to release defendants before trial except in capital cases — in which death was the possible punishment — and unless there were good reasons to believe that the defendant would flee if released. A federal judge might still set bail, but defendants could no longer be held because they did not have the money. The reform legislation does not apply to *state* or *local* courts, however, where the amount of bail remains up to the judge. And in those courts, many defendants are still imprisoned because they lack bail money.

Capital Punishment. On July 2, 1976, there were 611 men and women in death row cells in the United States awaiting execution. On that day the United States Supreme Court ruled 7–2 that the death penalty was constitutional.[84] The majority specifically held that capital punishment, if administered under adequate guidelines, did not violate the Eighth Amendment's prohibition against "cruel and unusual punishments." Approximately half of the inmates on death row faced possible execution as a result of the Court's decision. They were imprisoned either in the three states whose laws were upheld or in states with similar statutes.

The Supreme Court held that judges and juries could impose the death sentence as long as they had sufficient information to determine whether the sentence was appropriate in each case. The Court upheld state laws providing for capital punishment in Georgia, Florida, and Texas, but it struck down two other state statutes requiring automatic death sentences for murder.[85]

"We now hold that the punishment of death does not invariably violate the Constitution," the Supreme Court declared. And it noted that the framers of the Constitution accepted capital punishment: "At the time the Eighth Amendment was ratified, capital punishment was a common sanction in every state. Indeed, the first Congress of the United States enacted legislation providing death as the penalty for specified crimes."

In 1972, four years earlier, the Supreme Court had ruled out executions under any law then in effect. In a 5–4 decision that year, the Court held that capital punishment, as then administered, was unconstitutional.[86] At that time, thirty-eight states, the federal government, and the District of Columbia had laws authorizing the death penalty for various crimes. But no one had been executed in the United States since 1967.

By the time the Supreme Court faced the constitutional issue in 1972, thirty-seven nations had abolished the death penalty in peacetime. In Western Europe, for example, only France and Spain retained capital punishment. After the 1972 decision, thirty-five states and the federal government passed new laws providing for capital punishment and designed to satisfy the standards set forth by the Supreme Court. (The new federal law provided the death penalty for air hijacking resulting in death.) Most of the new state laws prescribed death sentences for such crimes as mass murder, killing a police office, fire fighter, or prison guard, and murder while committing rape, kidnapping, arson, or hijacking.

Since the federal government began keeping statistics on executions in

[84] *Gregg* v. *Georgia,* 428 U.S. 153 (1976).
[85] *Woodson* v. *North Carolina,* 428 U.S. 280 (1976); and *Roberts* v. *Louisiana,* 428 U.S. 325 (1976).
[86] *Furman* v. *Georgia,* 408 U.S. 238 (1972).

"Of course everybody is looking at you accusingly. You are, after all, the accused."

Drawing by Ross
© 1976 The New Yorker Magazine, Inc.

1930, 3859 persons had been executed by civil authority in the United States prior to the Supreme Court's ruling in 1972. Increasingly, however, the death penalty came under attack for moral and legal reasons. Nevertheless, in upholding capital punishment in 1976, the Court concluded: "It is an extreme sanction, suitable to the most extreme of crimes." In 1977 Gary Gilmore, a convicted killer who had demanded to die, was shot by a Utah firing squad in the first execution in America in a decade. On May 25, 1979, as demonstrators outside the Florida State Prison chanted "Death Row Must Go," John Arthur Spenkelink, a thirty-year-old drifter and convicted murderer, became the second person to be executed in America since 1967.

The Trial. Under the Fifth Amendment, a person charged with a serious *federal* crime must first be accused in an *indictment* by a grand jury. The Supreme Court has not applied this requirement to the states, where defendants are more often brought to trial on an *information* issued by a judge. The grand jury, so named because it is larger than the trial jury, does not determine guilt or innocence. It does seek to establish whether there is enough evidence to justify a criminal trial.

Within the states, although procedures vary in different jurisdictions, in general, arrested persons are brought before a magistrate for a preliminary hearing at which they are either held or released on bail. They may be assigned counsel if they cannot afford a private attorney. The district attorney or prosecutor may seek a grand jury indictment or may present the case to a judge who may issue an information. Now formally accused, defendants are arraigned—which means that the formal charges in the indictment or information are read to them —and they plead guilty or not guilty. (In some cases they may plead "no contest" and put themselves at the mercy of the court.) At every critical stage, a criminal suspect is entitled to have the advice of a lawyer, and defendants too poor to hire one must be offered or assigned counsel in all criminal cases where conviction might mean imprisonment.

Jury trials are required in *federal* courts in all criminal cases and in all common law civil suits where the sum involved is larger than $20. Under a 1968

Supreme Court decision, *states* must also provide jury trials in "serious" criminal cases,[87] which the Supreme Court defined in 1970 as all cases in which the penalty for conviction could exceed six months.[88] However, in 1971 the Supreme Court held 6–3 that juveniles do not have a constitutional right to a trial by jury in state courts.[89] (In a federal court, if a defendant wishes to waive the right of a jury trial, it is usually possible, but many states do not permit this practice.)

Federal juries must render a unanimous verdict in criminal and civil cases, but more than half of the states permit a less-than-unanimous verdict (usually by three-fourths of the jurors) in civil cases. In 1972 the Supreme Court ruled that unanimous jury verdicts were not required for convictions even in state criminal cases.[90] At the time, five states—Oregon, Louisiana, Idaho, Montana, and Oklahoma—permitted split jury decisions in certain types of criminal cases. Today, some states still permit split verdicts in criminal cases that do not carry a possible death penalty.

In a number of states, juries may consist of fewer than the traditional number of twelve persons. The Supreme Court in 1970 upheld the constitutionality of juries with fewer than twelve members.[91] Federal criminal juries contain twelve members. But federal civil cases may be tried with juries of six persons.[92] This is now the practice in 85 percent of the federal district courts.[93]

Although courtroom procedures vary on the federal, state, and local levels, in general the pattern is the same. First, the jury is chosen, with the prosecution and the defense each having the right to challenge and replace prospective jurors. Then the prosecution presents its case, and the defense cross-examines the witnesses for the prosecution. After that, the defense presents its own witnesses, who are cross-examined in turn by the prosecutor. A defendant does not have to take the stand to testify on his or her own behalf. A trial may be over in a few hours or drag on for months. Finally, the judge delivers a charge to the jury, explaining the law and emphasizing that the defendant's guilt must be proven beyond a reasonable doubt. The jury deliberates, and renders its verdict.

[87] *Duncan* v. *Louisiana*, 391 U.S. 145 (1968).
[88] *Baldwin* v. *New York*, 399 U.S. 66 (1970).
[89] *McKeiver* v. *Pennsylvania*, 403 U.S. 528 (1971).
[90] *Johnson* v. *Louisiana*, 406 U.S. 356 (1972); and *Apodaca* v. *Oregon*, 406 U.S. 404 (1972).
[91] *Williams* v. *Florida*, 399 U.S. 78 (1970).
[92] *Colgrove* v. *Battin*, 413 U.S. 149 (1973).
[93] Data provided by Administrative Office of the United States Courts.

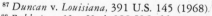

"The jury will disregard the witness's last remarks."

Drawing by Lorenz
© 1977 The New Yorker Magazine, Inc.

Organized Crime

From time to time an event occurs that reveals to the public the power of organized crime in America. Such was the case in 1970, when a flurry of federal indictments, along with tape recordings of "bugged" conversations made public by the FBI, suggested that mobsters virtually dominated the government of Newark, New Jersey. Much of the power in Newark, at least according to these documents, was wielded not by the elected mayor, Hugh Addonizio, but by the local crime chieftain, Anthony ("Tony Boy") Boiardo, heir to a crime empire built by his father, Ruggiero ("Richie the Boot") Boiardo.[94]

The FBI transcripts included these conversations between Angelo ("Gyp") De Carlo, identified as "Ray," and an associate named "Joe":

> *Joe:* You know . . . it's going to take three weeks but we'll own this Hughie [Addonizio]. This guy here. I'll guarantee we'll own him. I'll use that term — in three or four weeks. . . .
> *Ray:* Hughie [Addonizio] helped us along. He give us the city.[95]

According to another tape-recorded conversation, "Tony Boy" and DeCarlo discussed an important question — who should be appointed police director of Newark. "Tony Boy" said the decision was up to De Carlo.[96] Summoned before a federal grand jury, the mayor of Newark invoked his constitutional immunity and declined to answer any questions about his alleged ties with the mob. In July, after losing the mayoralty race to Kenneth Gibson (who became the first black mayor of Newark), Addonizio, along with four codefendants, was convicted of extorting money from a contractor doing work for the city. Addonizio was sentenced to ten years in prison and fined $25,000.

There is still argument over whether organized crime in America should be called the Mafia, the mob, or the syndicate, but there is little doubt that it exists

---

[94] Fred J. Cook, "The People v. the Mob; Or, Who Rules New Jersey?" *New York Times Magazine*, February 1, 1970.
[95] *New York Times,* January 7, 1970, p. 28.
[96] Cook, "The People v. the Mob; Or, Who Rules New Jersey?" p. 36.

The Cost of Corruption

Narcotics dealers, gamblers and businessmen make illicit payments of millions of dollars a year to policemen of New York, according to policemen, law-enforcement experts and New Yorkers who make such payments themselves. . . .

A detective with many years of experience in the narcotics division said one of his colleagues had arranged payoffs to the police from major heroin dealers of up to $50,000, in return for such favors as the destruction of evidence gathered on secret wiretaps. . . .

A report by the Joint Legislative Committee on Crime . . . charged that gambling in the slums of New York "could not function without official tolerance induced by corruption . . . ghetto residents are perfectly aware of the corrupt relationship between racketeers and certain elements in the Police Department, and, for this reason, have a deep cynicism concerning the integrity of the police in maintaining law and order in the community."

Putting an exact price tag on corruption is impossible . . . however, . . . the city's 10,000 small Puerto Rican grocery stores were estimated to give the police $6.2 million a year . . . Numbers operators, according to federal and state agencies and private researchers' estimates, make payoffs between $7 million and $15 million a year.

—David Burnham, "Graft Paid to Police Here Said to Run Into Millions," *New York Times,* April 25, 1970.

A rare glimpse inside the world of organized crime was offered in 1980 by Aladena (Jimmy the Weasel) Fratianno, a government witness in a federal court trial:

The witness . . . described . . . a secret organization that was divided into "families" that conducted criminal activities in major cities throughout the country. In his testimony last week, he said he became a member of the Los Angeles group in 1948.

Recalling the initiation ceremony, he said: "They took me in a room by myself. There was a long table where all of the members were; most of the members were sitting. There was a gun and a sword crossing one another in the middle of the table."

"They all stood up," he continued. "We held hands; the boss said something in Italian. It lasts about two or three minutes.

"Then they prick your finger with a needle or a sword until blood draws. Then you go around and meet each member of the family. You kiss them on the cheek and you're a member."

Mr. Fratianno testified that the organization operated in 20 cities, with one family in each city except New York, which had five.

Each family is headed by a boss elected by all of its members, the witness said. He added that the boss appointed an underboss and a consiglieri, or counselor, to assist him and that capos, or captains, supervised the members, called soldiers.

There is also a "national commission" composed of the five New York City bosses and the Chicago boss, he said, adding that "they more or less handle disputes with other families." . . .

The prosecutor questioned him about the requirements for becoming a member . . . "You are more or less proposed by somebody," he answered. "Sometimes you do something significant. Sometimes you have a brother or a father in it."

He said one of its main rules was "never divulge anything about the organization." If you violate the rules, he said, "they kill you."

— *New York Times,* November 2, 1980.

---

on a major scale. (Some Italian American groups have objected to the term "Mafia" on the grounds that it reflects unfairly on the majority of law-abiding Italian Americans.) Organized crime controls nonlegal gambling, loan sharking, narcotics, and other unlawful activities. It also owns legitimate businesses and infiltrates labor unions. In some instances it corrupts public officials by paying them to permit the mob to operate.

A presidential commission has estimated that the mob operates in 80 percent of all cities of more than one million residents.[97] One White House statement declared, "Investigations of the national crime syndicate . . . show its membership at some 5000 divided into twenty-four 'families' around the nation."[98] According to the presidential commission, each "family" is organized to resemble the structure of the Mafia that has operated for more than a century in Sicily: a "boss" at the top; an underboss; a counselor; several lieutenants; beneath them, the "soldiers" or "button men"; an "enforcer" whose job is "the maiming and killing of recalcitrant members"; and a "corrupter" who buys off public officials. "The highest ruling body of the twenty-four families is the 'commission,'" a combination supreme court and board of directors composed of nine to twelve of the most powerful bosses.[99]

"All available data indicate that organized crime flourishes only where it has

[97] *The Challenge of Crime in a Free Society,* p. 191.
[98] President Nixon's message to Congress on organized crime, *New York Times,* April 24, 1969, p. 30.
[99] *The Challenge of Crime in a Free Society,* pp. 193–94.

corrupted local officials," the presidential commission has emphasized.[100] Donald R. Cressey, a sociologist and an expert on organized crime, reports that in one instance a United States congressman resigned when ordered to do so by a crime boss. In this district, the crime syndicate "also 'owns' both judges and the officials who assign criminal cases to judges. About 90 percent of the organized crime defendants appear before the same few judges."[101]

The Justice Department's Organized Crime and Racketeering Section is the government unit in charge of attempts to curb the power of the crime syndicate. In 1979 the Justice Department convicted 531 organized crime figures.[102] But no one in Washington claimed that the federal government had succeeded in controlling the problem.

Organized crime could not thrive if the public did not demand the services it provides, and if law enforcement and elected officials refused to be bought. Corruption of the political system is the most disturbing threat posed by the mob. "The extraordinary thing about organized crime," the presidential commission concluded, "is that America has tolerated it for so long."[103]

Justice and the American Political System

Although the Supreme Court and the Constitution may seem remote from the lives of most citizens, the decisions of the Court—the ultimate outputs of the system of justice—have direct, immediate relevance for the individuals involved and much broader meaning for the political system as a whole. As Chief Justice Earl Warren noted in his last words from the bench, ". . . the Court develops the eternal principles of our Constitution in accordance with the problems of the day."[104]

In 1980, for example, the power of the Supreme Court meant that Joline Thiboutot could sue the state of Maine for denying her children social welfare benefits. It meant that Thomas Cornwell, a factory worker in Marion, Ohio, could not be forced to perform dangerous work that had already claimed the life of a fellow employee. And it meant that Robert Franklin Godfrey, a convicted murderer, could not be executed by the state of Georgia.

The list is much longer. Although each case might affect only one person directly, the Supreme Court's decisions had wider implications for the nation. The victory for the Thiboutot family in Maine, for example, meant that citizens could now sue state or local officials for denying them rights guaranteed by any federal law. The ruling made it a little bit easier for Americans to "fight City Hall." And the Court's decision affected society as a whole.

The decisions of the Supreme Court have great *political* significance. In the field of civil rights, for example, the Warren Court was well ahead of the executive branch or Congress. Because its power rests on public opinion, the Court

[100] *Ibid.,* p. 191.

[101] Donald R. Cressey, *Theft of the Nation* (New York: Harper & Row, 1969), pp. 252–53.

[102] Data provided by Organized Crime and Racketeering Section, Criminal Division, U.S. Department of Justice.

[103] *The Challenge of Crime in a Free Society,* p. 209.

[104] Woodward and Armstrong, *The Brethren: Inside the Supreme Court,* p. 26.

cannot get too far ahead of the country, but it can, in the words of Archibald Cox, attempt to respond to the "dominant needs of the time."[105] And it can also serve as the conscience of the nation and a guardian of minorities, the poor, and the forgotten.[106]

There are serious inequalities and flaws in the American system of justice, as we have seen—backlogged criminal courts and a bail system that often penalizes poor defendants; plea bargaining in the place of trial by jury; some judges and officials who are puppets of organized crime; prisons that do not rehabilitate. Some of these problems can, of course, be solved by specific reforms—bringing defendants to trial more rapidly by appointing more judges, strengthening law enforcement, improving facilities for handling juvenile offenders, and so forth. At the same time, a presidential commission has concluded: "The most significant action that can be taken against crime is action designed to eliminate slums and ghettos, to improve education, to provide jobs. . . . We will not have dealt effectively with crime until we have alleviated the conditions that stimulate it."[107]

Ultimately, as Justice Robert Jackson observed, the third branch of government, the judiciary, maintains "the great system of balances upon which our free government is based"—the balances among the various parts of the federal system, between authority and liberty, and between the rule of the majority and the rights of the individual.[108] Chief Justice Earl Warren confessed on the day he retired that performing this task is extremely difficult, "because we have no constituency. . . . We serve only the public interest as we see it, guided only by the Constitution and our own conscience."[109]

The resolution of conflict in American society through law, rather than through force, depends on public confidence in the courts and in the process of justice. And confidence in the system of justice requires that the words "Equal Justice Under Law," carved in marble over the entrance to the Supreme Court, be translated into reality at every level of the system.

[105] Cox, *The Warren Court*, p. 5.
[106] See, for example, Justice Black's opinion in *Chambers* v. *Florida*, 309 U.S. 227 (1940).
[107] *The Challenge of Crime in a Free Society*, p. 15.
[108] Jackson, *The Supreme Court in the American System of Government*, p. 61.
[109] *New York Times*, June 24, 1969, p. C24.

Perspective

Law is the body of rules made by government for society, interpreted by the courts, and backed by the power of the state. Law, in addition, can be seen as the gradual growth of rules and customs that reconcile conflict among people. In applying the law and deciding cases, judges often rely on *stare decisis*, or precedent. Most American law is statutory law enacted by Congress, or by state or local legislative bodies; but many statutes are based on English common law.

The United States has a dual court system, consisting of federal courts and the courts in the fifty states. At the top of the system is the United States Supreme Court. Most federal cases are handled by the inferior courts created by Congress under the Constitution—federal courts of appeals, federal district courts, and special purpose courts, such as the Court of Military Appeals, that deal with specific kinds of cases. The states also have several layers of courts, including magistrates' courts, municipal courts, county courts, special jurisdiction courts, intermediate appellate divisions, and courts of appeals.

The United States Supreme Court is a political

institution that makes both policy and law. Although insulated from everyday politics, the Supreme Court lies at the heart of the ongoing struggle in the American political system.

Much of the Supreme Court's power stems from its exercise of judicial review: the power to declare acts of Congress or actions by the executive—or laws and actions at any level of local, state, and federal government—unconstitutional. Most cases never reach the Supreme Court. Those that do usually reach the Court through original jurisdiction, appellate jurisdiction, or through the granting of a writ of certiorari.

How the Supreme Court should apply its power has always been a subject of controversy. Should the Court practice judicial activism by boldly applying the Constitution to social and political questions, or should the Court practice judicial restraint by avoiding constitutional questions when possible and by upholding acts of Congress unless they clearly violate a specific section of the Constitution?

All federal court judges are appointed by the President, subject to Senate approval. A majority of state and local judges are elected. Although traditional politics plays a major role in the selection of federal judges, since 1978 merit commissions have been established in about half the states. And more women and minorities have been appointed to the federal bench.

Much of the burden of law enforcement in the United States falls on local police. Police are caught between the established order and dissident or minority groups seeking change. Often underpaid, with inadequate training, manpower and resources, they are expected to fight rising crime, enforce the law, keep the peace, and provide a wide variety of community and social services.

The federal Department of Justice has major responsibility for criminal justice and law enforcement. In recent years, the Justice Department has emerged as a major policymaking agency for a broad range of political, legal, and social issues. The department is headed by the Attorney General. The Justice Department conducts criminal prosecutions in the federal courts. Separate divisions of the department deal with criminal, civil, antitrust, tax, civil rights, and natural resources cases. A special unit in the criminal division handles cases involving organized crime. The Federal Bureau of Investigation is the investigative arm of the Justice Department.

In processing criminal cases, the machinery of the adversary system of justice is available, but it may not be used. Instead, plea bargaining is more often used to avoid a trial. Widespread court delays and a discriminatory bail system are other flaws in the system.

The Supreme Court's decisions affect not only the individuals involved in specific cases, but also society as a whole. The resolution of conflict in American society through law depends on public confidence in the courts and in the legal process.

Suggested Reading

Abraham, Henry J. *The Judicial Process,* 4th edition* (Oxford University Press, 1980). A very useful general introduction to the American judicial process. Explains the operations of local, state, and federal courts and the legal system, and compares the United States judicial system with that of other countries.

Berger, Raoul. *Government by Judiciary* (Harvard University Press, 1977). An interesting, historical study of the Fourteenth Amendment and the intentions of its framers. Berger argues that the original meaning attached to the amendment must still be binding on the Court.

Bickel, Alexander. *The Supreme Court and the Idea of Progress* (Yale University Press, 1978). (Originally published in 1970.) A critical and detailed assessment of some of the major areas of judicial decision making by the Warren Court. Argues that the Court went further than was prudent in a number of decisions that had controversial public-policy consequences.

Clark, Ramsey. *Crime in America: Observations on Its Nature, Causes, Prevention, and Control* (Simon and Schuster, 1971). A broad indictment of the system of criminal justice in the United States, especially the police departments, the courts, and the prisons. The author, a former Attorney General in the Johnson administration, stresses the social roots of crime.

Cressey, Donald R. *Theft of the Nation* (Harper and Row, 1969). A comprehensive study of organized crime in the United States by a sociologist who served as consultant to the President's Crime Commission. Describes the corruption of law enforcement and government by organized crime.

McCloskey, Robert G. *The American Supreme Court* (University of Chicago Press, 1960). A lucid and penetrating analysis of the role of the Supreme Court in the American system of government.

Murphy, Walter F. *Elements of Judicial Strategy* (University of Chicago Press, 1973). An informative study of the nature of judicial decision making and its consequences for public policy. Analyzes the Supreme Court's role as a major decision maker in the political system.

Murphy, Walter F., and Pritchett, C. Herman, eds. *Courts, Judges, and Politics,* 3rd edition (Random House, 1979). A comprehensive collection of cases, documents, and essays on the role of judges and the courts in the policy-making process.

Schubert, Glendon. *Judicial Policy-Making,* revised edition* (Scott Foresman, 1974). An introduction to the role the judiciary plays in the making of public policy. Applies systems theory to the activities of the courts.

The Supreme Court, Justice and the Law, 2d edition* (Congressional Quarterly, 1977). A useful study of the Supreme Court and federal judiciary from 1969 to 1977. Includes summaries of the Court's major decisions and biographical sketches of the justices who served on the Court during those nine years.

Ungar, Sanford J. *FBI** (Atlantic-Little, Brown, 1976). A detailed analysis of the Federal Bureau of Investigation — its history and development, and its personnel, procedures, and power. Examines J. Edgar Hoover's forty-eight-year reign as director, as well as events since his death, including the Watergate investigation.

Wise, David. *The American Police State** (Random House, 1976). Details and summarizes the abuse of power and violation of constitutional rights of individuals by the federal intelligence agencies, including the FBI, CIA, and others. Includes the major findings of the Senate and House select committees on intelligence, and additional case studies.

Woodward, Bob, and Armstrong, Scott. *The Brethren** (Simon and Schuster, 1979). An account by two Washington journalists of the internal workings of the Supreme Court from 1969 to 1976. Examines the Court's step-by-step decision-making process, from preliminary votes to the final drafts of written opinions.

* Available in paperback edition

Part Four

GOVERNMENT IN OPERATION

14

FOREIGN POLICY AND NATIONAL SECURITY

On January 27, 1981, one week after President Reagan's inauguration, yellow ribbons sprouted like spring flowers all over Washington. Half a million people lined the streets to cheer the fifty-two Americans freed from captivity in Iran, as their motorcade wound its way to the White House. President Reagan greeted the former hostages in a ceremony on the South Lawn, and that night the sky above the Washington Monument sparkled with showers of fireworks in celebration. The hostages had come home.

Thus ended one of the longest and most painful experiences for the American government, and the American people, in the history of United States foreign policy. The crisis had begun on November 4, 1979, when Iranian militants forced their way into the American embassy in Teheran and seized more than sixty Americans as hostages. The militants demanded that the deposed Shah of Iran, then in New York, be returned to Iran by the United States in exchange for the hostages. Their demands were backed by the Ayatollah Khomeini, leader of Iran's Islamic revolution. While shouting, chanting Iranian demonstrators gathered daily outside the embassy gates, the fate of the hostages hung in the balance.

Although it was President Carter who had to deal with the Iranian crisis, its roots reached back two decades. In 1953, with the aid of the CIA, the Shah had been restored to his shaky throne after a short time in exile. Although he had pursued ambitious plans to modernize his country, he headed an authoritarian political system, a military dictatorship that imprisoned and sometimes tortured

January 27, 1981: the Americans released from Iran are greeted by cheering crowds in Washington.

its opponents. By the time the Shah decided to leave Iran for an "extended vacation" in January 1979, the country was in turmoil, in the midst of the revolution that brought to power an Islamic government.

In response to the seizure of the hostages, President Carter brought economic, diplomatic, and military pressure to bear on Iran. He froze Iranian assets in the United States and cut off imports of oil from Iran. Carter had permitted the Shah to come to the United States for medical treatment; and he declined to return the exiled ruler to Iran.[1]

In April 1980 Carter approved a military rescue mission to Iran that turned into a disaster in the desert, leaving eight American servicemen dead and the hostages still imprisoned. Secretary of State Cyrus Vance, who had opposed the military action, resigned his post.

The seizure of the hostages was a major issue in the 1980 presidential election campaign. As Election Day approached, there were recurrent reports that the hostages would be released. Iran, by now locked in a war with Iraq, badly needed American military supplies and appeared to be willing to trade the fifty-two remaining American hostages for weapons.[2]

Forty-eight hours before the election, the Iranian parliament agreed to re-

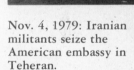

Nov. 4, 1979: Iranian militants seize the American embassy in Teheran.

---

[1] The Shah died in July 1980 in Egypt, but the hostages were not freed at that time.
[2] Soon after the seizure of the embassy, thirteen hostages, eight black men and five women, were released. In July 1980 another embassy official was released because of illness.

Left: the Ayatollah Khomeini. *Right:* the Shah at the height of his power.

Soviet tanks in Afghanistan, 1979

Moslem students shouting anti-American slogans

lease the hostages if Washington met certain conditions, which President Carter said offered a "positive basis" for resolving the crisis. But any hope on the part of Carter and his supporters that the hostages might be released before the election was dashed. Election Day—the first anniversary of the seizure of the Americans—came and went with the hostages still in Iran. Carter lost to Reagan. Negotiations between the United States and Iran continued, with Algeria now serving as intermediary. The United States agreed to unfreeze several billion dollars in Iranian assets. Then came the final drama on Inauguration Day. Only moments after Ronald Reagan had taken the oath of office, all fifty-two hostages flew out of Iran to Algeria and then to Wiesbaden, West Germany, where they were met by former President Carter. Then it was on to West Point, New York, where they were reunited with their families. Finally, the freed Americans flew to Washington for a personal meeting with President Reagan.

About a month after the hostages had been seized in Iran, another major international incident occurred. Late in December 1979, Soviet troops invaded Afghanistan. Amid heavy street fighting, the President of Afghanistan was ousted and executed, and the Soviets installed their own leader. Carter denounced the Soviet action and in retaliation embargoed U.S. grain sales to the Soviets, postponed further consideration of the SALT II agreement, and succeeded in blocking American participation in the 1980 Olympic games in Moscow. In addition, Carter asked Congress to resume draft registration, which began in the summer of 1980.

The crises in Iran and Afghanistan had enormous impact. They created new tensions and caused a general reassessment of foreign policy, not only in Washington, but in many other capitals of the world. They altered America's perception of the world, opened up an argument at home over the adequacy of U.S. military strength, strongly influenced the course of political events in a presidential election year, and brought a chill to the period of détente, or relaxed tensions, between the United States and the Soviet Union. As 1980 came to a close, tension between Washington and Moscow increased over the political unrest in Poland. President Carter warned that Soviet military intervention in Poland "would have the most negative consequences for East-West relations in general and U.S.-Soviet relations in particular."[3]

During the presidential campaign in 1980, Ronald Reagan had argued that the seizure of the hostages demonstrated American weakness and that defense spending had declined and must be increased. Carter in turn emphasized the "war and peace" issue and sought to portray the Republican candidate as

[3] *New York Times,* December 4, 1980, p. A10.

In November 1979, just before the Soviet invasion of Afghanistan, the Center for Defense Information, a nonprofit research organization in Washington, published a survey of armed conflicts then taking place around the globe. It counted 37 major and minor wars, involving more than 8 million soldiers and paramilitary fighters. "The total loss of lives in these conflicts is unknown," the center reported, "but rough estimates run between 1 and 5 million killed." The following were rated as the eight most violent wars:

Conflict	Number of Deaths	Year Started
1. Cambodia	500,000 to 4 million	1970
2. Afghanistan	100,000 to 250,000	1978
3. East Timor	100,000 or more	1975
4. Lebanon	50,000 or more	1975
5. Sino-Vietnamese war	30,000 or more	1979
6. Philippine guerrilla wars	30,000 or more	1972
7. Guatemala	22,000 or more	1967
8. Rhodesia	20,000 or more	1972

—*Washington Post,* January 27, 1980.

---

a man likely to lead the nation into a dangerous military adventure. In particular, Carter sought to picture Reagan as naive about the dangers of atomic weapons, someone who could push America closer to a "nuclear precipice."[4]

The events in Iran, and Afghanistan, and the 1980 presidential election, underscored the fact that American foreign policy and national security are closely related to, and interwoven with, domestic politics. The long and tragic war in Vietnam also had far-reaching influence on the nation's domestic politics.

The Vietnam war demonstrated the overriding importance of American foreign policy, not only to Americans, but to the world in which the United

[4] *New York Times,* October 20, 1980, p. 1.

Don Wright, *The Miami News.*

"Thanks a lot."

Vietnam peace accords are signed in Paris, January 1973.

The most ominous change that marked our period was the transformation in the nature of power. Until the beginning of the nuclear age it would have been inconceivable that a country could possess too much military strength for effective political use; every addition of power was—at least theoretically—politically useful. The nuclear age destroyed this traditional measure. A country might be strong enough to destroy an adversary and yet no longer be able to protect its own population against attack. By an irony of history a gargantuan increase in power had eroded the relationship of power to policy. Henceforth, the major nuclear powers would be able to devastate one another. But they would also have great difficulty in bringing their power to bear on the issues most likely to arise. They might be able to deter direct challenges to their own survival; they could not necessarily use this power to impose their will. The capacity to destroy proved difficult to translate into a plausible threat even against countries with no capacity for retaliation. The margin of the superpowers over non-nuclear states had been widening; yet the awesomeness of their power had increased their inhibitions. As power had grown more awesome, it had also turned abstract, intangible, elusive.

—Henry Kissinger, *White House Years.*

States plays so powerful a role. Vietnam also illustrated the central role of the President in the conduct of foreign relations. The Constitution gives Congress the power to declare war, but Congress never did so in the case of Vietnam. A President made the decision to go to war.

In the 1980s the American President faced a complex mix of foreign policy problems. Despite congressional actions to reassert the authority of the legislative branch in the conduct of foreign policy, much of the time, although certainly not always, the President remained the dominant figure in foreign and military matters. The great power of the President over foreign policy has disturbed many Americans because of the new and terrifying dimension added to the conduct of international relations since the Second World War. For the first time in human history, nations possess the technological power to destroy each other. The threat of nuclear annihilation overshadows all other foreign policy considerations; for small wars now carry the potential of growing out of control into nuclear war. Although political candidates and leaders debate about America's military strength and the best way to ensure "national security," it is also possible to ask whether nations and people can really achieve security in the atomic era.

Against this background, we may ask: What is foreign policy? Who makes it? What role should the President play? the Congress? And how, in a democratic society, can people make their views felt and influence foreign policy? What should America's objectives be in its relations with the rest of the world? How much of the nation's resources should go into military spending? What dangers are posed to U.S. institutions by a multibillion-dollar defense budget?

The United States and World Affairs

American
Foreign Policy

Foreign policy is the sum of the goals, decisions, and actions that govern a nation's relations with the rest of the world. But the world changes, and so does foreign policy. A President may adopt one policy only to discard it later; a new

518

"The world changes, and so does foreign policy." President Carter with Soviet leader Leonid Brezhnev . . . and Chinese Deputy Premier Deng Xiaoping

President may reverse the policies of his predecessor. Alliances shift; the Soviet Union, America's ally against Nazi Germany in the Second World War, became its principal adversary in the "Cold War" that began soon afterward. Japan, which had been America's wartime enemy, became its peacetime ally, as did West Germany.

So "foreign policy" is a changing and elusive concept. Roger Hilsman, a former Assistant Secretary of State, has suggested that the problem of foreign policy is not so much one of relating decisions to a single set of goals as it is "precisely one of choosing goals" in the midst of onrushing events and crises, and of reconciling the advocates of competing goals and policies. "The making of foreign policy," he concluded, "is a political process."[5]

The preservation of national security is a basic consideration in the formulation of foreign policy. But "national security" is so broad and vague a term that it can be used to justify almost any action that a nation or a President takes. President Nixon, for example, invoked it to attempt to justify a broad range of abuses of power that eventually led to his resignation. Since the Second World War, there have been two approaches to the question of national security and American foreign policy. One view emphasizes threats to the United States security posed by the power of Communist or unfriendly nations. Another regards the security of the United States as dependent on some form of world order "compatible with our values and interests."[6] This second view of American foreign policy holds that there can be no real security for the United States without world peace and security for all people.

Yet security is a relative term in the thermonuclear age. During the Cuban missile crisis of 1962, President Kennedy's advisers knew that their decisions, if wrong, "could mean the destruction of the human race."[7] So any description

COMMUNISM IS THE GREATES ENEMY OF MANKIN

[5] Roger Hilsman, *To Move a Nation* (Garden City, N. Y.: Doubleday, 1967), pp. 12–13, 541.
[6] Paul H. Nitze, "The Secretary and the Execution of Foreign Policy," in Don K. Price, ed., *The Secretary of State*, prepared for the American Assembly, Columbia University (Englewood Cliffs, N. J.: Prentice-Hall, 1960), pp. 6–7.
[7] Robert F. Kennedy, *Thirteen Days* (New York: Norton, 1969), p. 44.

Drawing by Handelsman
© 1976 The New Yorker
Magazine, Inc.

"My principals in Washington wish to know, Excellency, whether you would prefer to be propped up overtly or covertly."

Coca Cola shipment bound for Canton, China

of national security and foreign policy must take into account the changed nature of the world since the beginning of the atomic age.

Since the Second World War, the United States and the Soviet Union have dominated the world stage. The two superpowers have confronted each other and sometimes clashed in Europe, the Middle East, Africa, Cuba, and other parts of the world. And twice since 1945, in Korea and Vietnam, the United States has fought a protracted war against Communist power in Asia. Faced with often hostile, armed Communist nations, the United States has sought to maintain a high level of military strength. American policymakers have argued that this costly arms burden must be borne to protect the national security, American liberties at home, and the freedom of other nations. Only the shield of American power, they have contended, has prevented Communist expansion to a degree that would threaten American security.

Critics of this view maintain that the United States has often used its vast power to support military governments in Asia, Latin America, and elsewhere in the world, including some that violate human rights and civil liberties. Some of these critics argue that the United States already has enough nuclear weapons to destroy any adversary several times over and therefore does not need to continue such a high level of defense spending.

Marxist economists and others contend that America has become a modern imperial power, intervening on the world stage to protect its own political and economic interests. For example, one socialist scholar, Harry Magdoff, argues that "there is a close parallel between, on the one hand, the aggressive United States foreign policy aimed at controlling . . . as much of the globe as possible, and on the other hand, an energetic international expansionist policy of U.S. business."[8] In Magdoff's view American foreign policy is designed to keep areas of the world open for investment and to make certain that underdeveloped countries provide the raw materials needed by American industry.

But this point of view is sharply challenged by other scholars, who argue that the radical economists have failed to show that governments conduct foreign policy to serve corporate interests. Business interests may influence governments, Benjamin J. Cohen has suggested, but "economics cannot account for everything."[9] The United States' "traditional support of Israel against the Arab states runs in diametric opposition to the interests of major U.S. oil companies," Cohen argued. And he cited the lengthy war in Southeast Asia as another example. "Can United States policy in Vietnam possibly be explained in terms of concern for the economic advantages of American business?"[10]

Increasingly, scholars and political leaders today have turned their attention to another phenomenon on the international stage—the powerful multinational corporations, many of them based in the United States, whose activities cut across national borders. Richard J. Barnet and Ronald E. Müller argue that these giant corporations are primarily concerned with profits, ignoring the social or environmental effects of their activities. They ask: ". . . by what right do a self-selected group of druggists, biscuit makers, and computer designers become the architects of the new world?" And they add that "the managers of

---

[8] Harry Magdoff, *The Age of Imperialism: The Economics of U.S. Foreign Policy* (New York: Modern Reader Paperbacks, 1969), p. 12.

[9] Benjamin J. Cohen, *The Question of Imperialism: The Political Economy of Dominance and Dependence* (New York: Basic Books, 1973), p. 130.

[10] *Ibid.*, p. 126.

the global corporations are neither elected by the people nor subject to popular scrutiny or even popular pressure, despite the fact that in the course of their daily business they make decisions with more impact on the lives of ordinary people than most generals and politicians."[11]

Within the United States, the continuing high degree of military spending has created several paradoxes. America faces the problem of how to balance its military needs against social needs at home. Billions of dollars that might, in part at least, have been used for education, housing, transportation, and similar programs have been siphoned off into arms. A "military-industrial complex" spawned to protect American security has created numerous problems for American society.

The creation of a "garrison state" has at times threatened liberties at home. During the Watergate scandal, President Nixon argued that the wiretapping of his own aides and of journalists, the creation of a special White House investigative unit known as "the Plumbers" to plug news leaks, and a plan to open first-class mail and burglarize the homes or offices of suspected persons were all justified by "national security."

Some critics of American foreign policy have focused on what former Senator J. William Fulbright has called an "excessive moralism."[12] Especially in the 1950s, when John Foster Dulles served as Secretary of State under President Eisenhower, the rhetoric and sometimes the reality of American foreign policy took on the aspect of a missionary crusade against communism.

In recent years, however, many of these concepts and attitudes have been changing. During the 1960s American policymakers came to recognize that communism was not a monolith, but contained many variations and rivalries — particularly in the case of the Soviet Union and mainland China. President Nixon was able to open doors to Moscow and Peking because, in both America and the Soviet Union, there was gradual recognition that the arms race not only threatened the survival of humanity, but also was distorting the economies of both nations, and diverting energies and resources into military hardware that might better be used to serve people. The Vietnam war illustrated the limits of American world power, and in its wake much of the crusading zeal that had marked the nation's foreign policy had given way to a more cautious, pragmatic approach. By the start of the 1980s, however, after the crises in Iran and Afghanistan, the American electorate responded to Ronald Reagan's promises to strengthen the nation's diplomacy and its military power.

John Foster Dulles

1972: President Nixon visits the Great Wall of China.

It would be impossible to review the entire history of United States foreign policy in these pages, but some recurring strands and major themes that are relevant to today's world may be sketched.

One deeply rooted historical characteristic of American foreign policy was that of *isolationism.* President George Washington declared that it was the nation's policy "to steer clear of permanent alliance," and Jefferson said that America wanted peace with all nations, "entangling alliances with none."

During the nineteenth century, the diplomats of Europe maneuvered to preserve the "balance of power" in the Old World; America, protected by the

The Historical Setting

[11] Richard J. Barnet and Ronald E. Müller, *Global Reach: The Power of the Multinational Corporations* (New York: Simon and Schuster, 1974), pp. 25, 214.
[12] J. W. Fulbright, *Old Myths and New Realities* (New York: Random House, 1964), p. 45.

A Cold War symbol:
the Berlin Wall

President Truman and
Secretary of State
George C. Marshall

broad Atlantic, could afford to remain relatively aloof from the problems of Europe. In 1823 the Monroe Doctrine warned European powers to keep out of the Western Hemisphere and pledged that the United States would not intervene in the internal affairs of Europe. American isolation, of course, was only relative. The United States fought a war with Great Britain in 1812; it acquired Texas in a war with Mexico in 1846; and it took possession of Puerto Rico, Guam, and the Philippines under the treaty ending the Spanish-American War in 1898. (The Philippines gained independence in 1946.) However, the United States did not become a major colonial power, with vast overseas territories, on a scale comparable with Great Britain or some of the nations of Europe.

By the end of the nineteenth century, an opposite strand of American foreign policy, that of *interventionism,* was visible. In the early twentieth century, the United States practiced "gunboat diplomacy," intervening militarily in Mexico, the Caribbean, and Latin America. The First World War brought major United States military involvement in Europe for the first time. After the war, however, the United States declined to join with other countries in the League of Nations. Woodrow Wilson's dream of world order was shattered, and America retreated "back to normalcy" and isolationism.

But during the Second World War, the United States and its allies defeated Nazi Germany and Japan, and America emerged in the position of a great world power. The United States traded its former position of isolationism for one of *internationalism.*

A world weary of war and destruction centered its hopes for peace on the United Nations, created in 1945. It quickly became clear, however, that the future of the postwar world would be shaped not in the UN but in the relations between the two major powers, the United States and the Soviet Union. In a speech at Fulton, Missouri, in March 1946, Winston Churchill declared that from the Baltic to the Adriatic seas, "an iron curtain has descended across the continent." In retrospect, it became clear that a Cold War had begun.

During this period, the United States adopted a policy of *containment* of the Soviet Union, first elaborated in the quarterly *Foreign Affairs* by George F. Kennan, a senior American diplomat who later became ambassador to Russia. Kennan, who was a State Department official in 1947 when the article was published, signed his name "X" to preserve his anonymity. The article set forth a doctrine that became "the Bible of Western foreign policy in the mid-twentieth century."[13] Kennan argued that the Soviet Union would expand its power wherever it could to challenge Western institutions. He advocated that United States policy toward the Soviet Union be one of "firm and vigilant containment of Russian expansive tendencies."[14]

In the immediate aftermath of the Second World War, the United States moved to counterbalance Soviet power. Under the "Truman Doctrine," Washington began a program of military aid to Greece, which was fighting Communist guerrillas, and Turkey, which was under pressure to cede military bases to the Soviet Union. As enunciated by President Truman, the doctrine declared that American security and world peace depended on United States protection for the "free peoples of the world."[15]

[13] H. Bradford Westerfield, *The Instruments of America's Foreign Policy* (New York: Crowell, 1963), p. 165.
[14] Mr. X, "The Sources of Soviet Conduct," *Foreign Affairs,* July 1947, pp. 566–82.
[15] Harry S. Truman, *Memoirs by Harry S. Truman,* Vol. II, *Years of Trial and Hope* (Garden City, N. Y.: Doubleday, 1958), p. 106.

In the summer of 1947, the United States launched the Marshall Plan (named for its creator, Secretary of State George C. Marshall) and poured more than $13 billion in four years into Western Europe to speed its postwar economic and social recovery. The Soviet Union and other Eastern European nations declined to join the Marshall Plan.

In 1949 the United States and many of the nations of Western Europe formed the North Atlantic Treaty Organization (NATO), whose members were pledged to defend each other against attack. NATO was the first and most important of a series of postwar collective security pacts signed by the United States. These arrangements were greatly expanded during the Eisenhower administration. In 1980 the United States was pledged under security pacts to defend forty nations. (See Figure 14-1.)

Although America was preoccupied with European recovery and collective security, and with containing Soviet expansion, it was in the Pacific that a new war broke out only five years after the end of the Second World War. During the Korean war (1950–1953), the United States became involved for the first time in a land war in Asia.

New forces, sometimes obscured by the rhetoric of the Cold War, were loose in the world. The United States, the sole nuclear power at the end of the Second World War, lost that advantage when the Soviet Union acquired atomic weapons in 1949. About the same time, however, world Communist unity began to come apart. As early as 1948, Yugoslavia's President Tito had broken with the Soviet Union. In 1956 Soviet tanks crushed a revolt against Communist rule in Hungary. By 1962 Russia and its former ally, Communist China, were open and bitter adversaries. In 1968 Soviet and Warsaw Pact troops invaded Czechoslovakia in order to put down a movement toward democratic reforms in that country.

During the same postwar period, a rising tide of *nationalism* brought independence to various nations in Africa, Asia, and the Middle East and stirred political currents in Latin America. In 1947 India and Pakistan gained their independence from Britain, and in 1949 Indonesia became free of Dutch control. The 1960s saw a second wave of nationalism, in Africa. As European powers withdrew from what remained of their nineteenth-century colonial empires, the "Third World" became a new battleground in which the United States, the Soviet Union, and Communist China competed for influence and power. In the 1970s the United States and the Soviet Union vied for power in the Middle East and Africa. In many of these areas of the globe, poverty, hunger, disease, illiteracy, and political instability were combined in a volatile mixture.

Not all relationships that cut across national boundaries are controlled by governments. Modern scholars have also focused on *transnationalism,* which includes such global activities as trade, personal contacts, and business relationships. Transnational relations may be defined as "contacts, coalitions, and interactions across state boundaries that are not controlled by the central foreign policy organs of governments."[16]

In addition, foreign policy analysts today often speak of *interdependence,* or mutual dependence, among nations. Sometimes, this mutual dependence is cooperative, as when several nations agree to combat an environmental problem. Or it can be involuntary, as in the case of the United States and the Soviet

[16] Joseph S. Nye, Jr., and Robert O. Keohane, eds., *Transnational Relations and World Politics* (Cambridge, Mass.: Harvard University Press, 1972), pp. x–xi.

United States Security Pacts

Figure 14–1

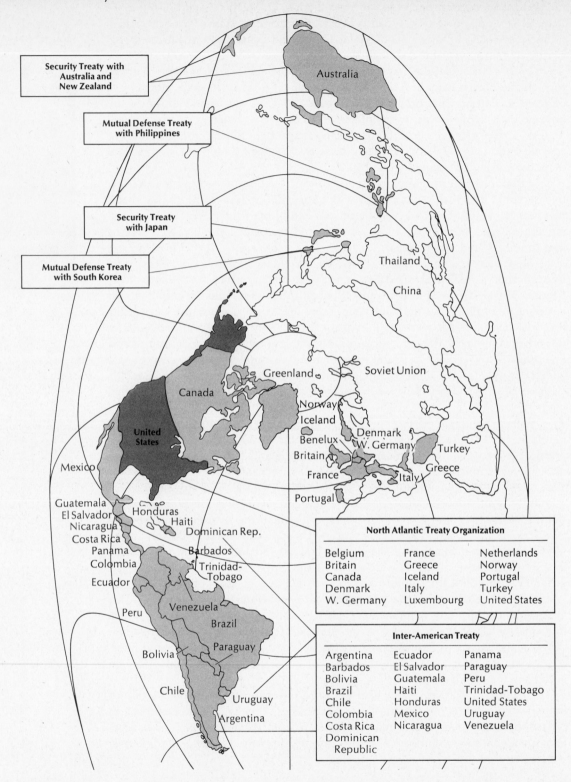

Security Treaty with Australia and New Zealand

Mutual Defense Treaty with Philippines

Security Treaty with Japan

Mutual Defense Treaty with South Korea

Australia

Thailand

China

Greenland

Soviet Union

Canada

Norway

Iceland

United States

Denmark
W. Germany

Benelux

Turkey

Britain

France

Italy

Greece

Mexico

Portugal

Guatemala
El Salvador
Nicaragua
Costa Rica
Panama
Colombia
Ecuador

Honduras
Haiti
Dominican Rep.

Barbados

Trinidad-Tobago

Peru

Venezuela

Brazil

Bolivia

Paraguay

Chile

Uruguay

Argentina

North Atlantic Treaty Organization

Belgium	France	Netherlands
Britain	Greece	Norway
Canada	Iceland	Portugal
Denmark	Italy	Turkey
W. Germany	Luxembourg	United States

Inter-American Treaty

Argentina	Ecuador	Panama
Barbados	El Salvador	Paraguay
Bolivia	Guatemala	Peru
Brazil	Haiti	Trinidad-Tobago
Chile	Honduras	United States
Colombia	Mexico	Uruguay
Costa Rica	Nicaragua	Venezuela
Dominican Republic		

Source: Department of State, Bureau of Public Affairs. Data as of 1980.

Government in Operation

Union, whose "strategic interdependence . . . derives from the mutual threat of nuclear destruction."[17]

In Vietnam, the United States gradually moved into the power vacuum created when the French withdrew from Indochina following their defeat in 1954 by Ho Chi Minh. Presidents Eisenhower and Kennedy supported the government of South Vietnam, and Kennedy sent 16,000 troops there as "advisers." But it was President Johnson who, in 1965, committed the United States to a full-scale war against Communist North Vietnam and the National Liberation Front, or Vietcong. Eventually, Johnson sent more than 500,000 combat troops to Vietnam. The war proved divisive and increasingly unpopular at home, and it was a major factor in Johnson's decision to announce, in March 1968, that he would not seek the Presidency again.[18]

Vietnam and Its Aftermath

Richard Nixon's promise to end the war helped to bring about his election in November 1968. Yet it took Nixon four years to redeem his pledge. By the time the peace agreement was signed in Paris in January 1973, more than 47,000 Americans had died in combat in eight years and more than 303,000 had been wounded. Perhaps a million Vietnamese soldiers, North and South, were killed. At least 415,000 civilians died in South Vietnam. The United States dropped more than 7 million tons of bombs in Southeast Asia in eight years, three times the total bomb tonnage dropped in the Second World War. In money, even excluding billions in veterans' benefits, the cost of the war was more than $140 billion.

For almost a decade the Vietnam issue divided the nation and cast a shadow

[17] Robert O. Keohane and Joseph S. Nye, *Power and Interdependence: World Politics in Transition* (Boston: Little, Brown, 1977), p. 9.

[18] Polls indicated that a majority of Americans considered the United States' involvement in Vietnam to have been an error. For example, a Gallup poll of June 1970 reported that 56 percent of the public considered that the United States had made "a mistake" in sending troops to Vietnam. The percentage of people who answered "yes" when asked "Do you think the United States made a mistake sending troops to fight in Vietnam?" rose above 50 percent for the first time in August 1968 and remained above 50 percent thereafter.

Left: Vietnam: the costs were high. *Right:* 1975: the last Americans leave Vietnam.

Henry A. Kissinger

over the quality of American life. The lengthy war caused many Americans to become disillusioned with the workings of the political system itself. For that reason alone, the cost of the Vietnam war may be felt for many years to come.

Even before the United States had disengaged from Vietnam, a period of détente between the two superpowers had begun in May 1972, when President Richard Nixon held a summit meeting in Moscow with Soviet party chief Leonid Brezhnev. The meeting followed Nixon's historic trip to China, the first by an American President. In Moscow, Nixon signed the SALT agreement placing a measure of control over nuclear weapons.

Secretary of State Henry A. Kissinger was the architect of the new policy of détente. To officials in Washington the policy was one of attempting to involve the Soviets in a continuing series of agreements, toning down the rhetoric on both sides. But in 1973 the Soviet Union became involved in the war in the Middle East and later in the political turmoil in Portugal and the conflict in Angola. These Soviet actions gave critics an opportunity to argue that détente had failed to restrain Moscow. Thus the concept of détente had eroded even before the Soviet invasion of Afghanistan in 1979.

One of the legacies of Vietnam was a reluctance on the part of many Americans and their political leaders to undertake another foreign venture that might embroil the United States in a war. This period of "disillusionment with American involvement in the Vietnam conflict and of ensuing diplomatic retrenchment lasted until the late 1970s."[19] By 1980, however, there was a new mood of frustration over the limits of American power, triggered to a great extent by the events in Iran and Afghanistan. As a result, "the Carter administration encountered severe criticism inside and outside the United States for its failure or inability to use American power decisively. . . ."[20]

The war that broke out between Iran and Iraq in September of 1980 was another reminder that the Middle East remained a volatile trouble spot. The United States depended on the oil fields along the Persian Gulf to fuel its economy, and in 1980 President Carter declared that the United States would use "military force" if necessary to repel any attack on the Persian Gulf region. The warning was aimed at the Soviet Union.

[19] Cecil V. Crabb, Jr., and Pat M. Holt, *Invitation to Struggle: Congress, the President and Foreign Policy* (Washington, D.C.: Congressional Quarterly Press, 1980), p. 55.
[20] *Ibid.,* p. 56.

Iranian refinery in Abadan burning after Iraqi attack

The Camp David accords: Israel's
Prime Minister Begin embraces an old
foe, President Sadat of Egypt, after
reaching agreement on a peace treaty.

But Carter also achieved a major foreign policy breakthrough in the Middle East. In March of 1979, he brought about the signing of a peace treaty between Israel and Egypt after a generation of hostility between those two nations. The agreement followed a summit meeting between the leaders of Egypt and Israel that had taken place six months earlier at Camp David, the presidential retreat near Washington. The treaty provided for the withdrawal of Israeli troops from the Sinai Peninsula and for talks on autonomy for Palestinians on the West Bank of the Jordan River and in the Gaza Strip.

Also in 1979, the United States under President Carter entered into full diplomatic relations with the People's Republic of China and ended diplomatic relations with the Republic of China (Taiwan). In 1980 the United States ended its defense treaty with Taiwan.

How Foreign Policy Is Made

In the field of foreign affairs, as President Kennedy once remarked, "the President bears the burden of the responsibility. . . . The advisers may move on to new advice."[21]

**The President
and Foreign Policy**

In Chapter 10 we noted that the President is both chief diplomat and Commander in Chief. Particularly in the twentieth century, the two roles overlap. National security, foreign policy, and domestic programs are closely related because the President must decide how much money to allocate for each area within the overall framework of his annual budget. A large defense budget means less money for meeting priorities at home; and the level of defense expenditures affects the economy. As a Senate subcommittee headed by Senator Henry M. Jackson put it: "The boundary between foreign and domestic policy has almost been erased."[22]

[21] Television and Radio Interview: "After Two Years—a Conversation With the President," December 17, 1962, in *Public Papers of the Presidents of the United States. John F. Kennedy, 1962* (Washington, D.C.: U.S. Government Printing Office, 1963), p. 889.
[22] "Basic Issues," Subcommittee on National Security Staffing and Operations, Committee on Government Operations, United States Senate, in *Administration of National Security* (Washington, D.C.: U.S. Government Printing Office, 1965), p. 7.

What kind of peace do I mean? What kind of peace do we seek? Not a Pax Americana enforced on the world by American weapons of war. . . . I am talking about genuine peace, the kind of peace that makes life on earth worth living, the kind that enables men and nations to grow and to hope and to build a better life for their children — not merely peace for Americans but peace for all men and women — not merely peace in our time but peace for all time. . . . Total war makes no sense . . . in an age when the deadly poisons produced by a nuclear exchange would be carried by wind and water and soil and seed to the far corners of the globe and to generations yet unborn. . . .

First: Let us examine our attitude toward peace itself. Too many of us think it is impossible. . . .

We need not accept that view. Our problems are manmade — therefore, they can be solved by man. . . . No problem of human destiny is beyond human beings. . . . And if we cannot end now our differences, at least we can help make the world safe for diversity. For, in the final analysis, our . . . common link is that we all inhabit this small planet. We all breathe the same air. We all cherish our children's future. And we are all mortal.

—John F. Kennedy, Commencement Address at The American University in Washington, June 10, 1963.

The President has the responsibility of deciding whether to use nuclear weapons. In Richard Neustadt's words, the President "lives daily with the knowledge that at any time he, personally, may have to make a human judgment . . . which puts half the world in jeopardy."[23] The vast power of the President in the realm of foreign policy carries with it great risks — risks that a President will exercise his judgment unwisely or that he will act without public or congressional support.

In conducting the nation's foreign and military policies, the President must often choose among conflicting advice as he makes his decisions. "The State Department wants to solve everything with words, and the generals, with guns," President Johnson was quoted as saying.[24] A President's background, experience, and beliefs may strongly influence his attitude toward foreign affairs. President Nixon, for example, had long been identified with international affairs as Vice President; as President he put great emphasis on foreign policy and negotiations. In time, however, a domestic event — Watergate — beclouded his diplomatic initiatives and ended his Presidency.

[23] Richard E. Neustadt, testimony to Subcommittee on National Security Staffing and Operations, Committee on Government Operations, United States Senate, March 25, 1963, in *Administration of National Security*, p. 76.

[24] Eric F. Goldman, *The Tragedy of Lyndon Johnson* (New York: Knopf, 1969), p. 383.

Under the Constitution, power to conduct foreign and military affairs is divided between Congress and the President. While the Constitution gave the President power to appoint ambassadors and command the armed forces, Congress was given power to declare war, raise and support armies, and appropriate money for defense; and the Senate was granted power to approve or disapprove treaties and ambassadorial nominations made by the President.

But the Constitution does not spell out the boundaries of the power that each branch shall exercise. The result has been intermittent conflict between the President and Congress over foreign policy. For example, it took months of controversy before Congress, in 1978, finally agreed with President Carter and ratified two treaties turning over the Panama Canal to Panama in the year 2000. Congress' action ended an era that had begun 75 years before when President Theodore Roosevelt acquired the land to build the waterway. The Senate voted to approve the two treaties only after adding a "reservation" specifying that the United States could intervene militarily to keep the canal open.

In the struggle between Congress and the President over foreign policy, at various times in history one branch has dominated. After the Second World War, Congress lost to the President much of its war power and control over foreign policy. In the late 1960s and early 1970s, as a result of the increasing unpopularity of the war in Vietnam, a movement began in Congress to try to restore some of the war power to the legislative branch. (These efforts are traced in Chapter 10, on pp. 361–63.)

It was not until 1973 that Congress succeeded in placing any significant restrictions on presidential power to wage war. The first congressional victory was a bill barring any combat in, or bombing of, Cambodia after August 15, 1973. That same year, Congress passed the War Powers Resolution, designed to limit to sixty or ninety days the President's ability to commit American troops to combat without congressional authorization. The bill became law over President Nixon's veto. In an amendment to the foreign aid appropriation in 1974, Congress provided that the Central Intelligence Agency could not spend money on covert operations without reporting them to six (later eight) congressional committees "in timely fashion." In 1980 Congress reduced to two the number of committess to which the CIA must report, but required "prior notice" of most secret operations and directed the President to furnish any intelligence information requested by the House or Senate intelligence committees.

Between 1950 and 1970, five American Presidents committed United States troops to foreign soil (in Korea, Lebanon, the Dominican Republic, Viet-

Congress
and Foreign Policy

Together we shall save our planet, or together we shall perish in its flames.

—John F. Kennedy, address to the General Assembly of the United Nations, September 25, 1961.

American troops in Santo Domingo, 1965

nam, and Cambodia) without any declaration of war by Congress. In no case did the President do so with clear, specific, prior congressional approval, although in four instances Congress had passed resolutions broadly supporting presidential action in various geographic areas: the Formosa Resolution (1954); the Middle East Resolution (1957); the Cuba Resolution (1962); and the Tonkin Gulf Resolution (1964), in which Congress said the President might "take all necessary steps, including the use of armed force" in Southeast Asia.

Congress passed the Tonkin Gulf Resolution after President Johnson announced on nationwide television on August 4, 1964, that two United States destroyers, the *Maddox* and the *Turner Joy,* had been attacked in the Gulf of Tonkin off Vietnam. Secretary of Defense Robert S. McNamara declared that the two ships had been under "continuous torpedo attack." Up to this point 163 Americans had died in Vietnam and there were 16,000 troops there as "advisers." After passage of the Tonkin Gulf Resolution, President Johnson — beginning early in 1965 — vastly expanded the war.

It developed, however, that reports of the attack in the Tonkin Gulf had been considerably exaggerated. For example, the captain of the *Maddox,* Commander Herbert L. Ogier, later said he thought that two torpedos were fired but that subsequent reports of torpedos were actually sonar readings caused by the destroyer's own propellers.[25] Indeed, the task force commander warned Washington that, "Freak weather effects and over-eager sonarmen may have accounted for many reports."[26] At a Senate hearing four years later, Senator Albert Gore, Democrat, of Tennessee, told Secretary McNamara to his face: "I feel that I have been misled, and that the American people have been misled."[27]

One major reason Congress lost so much of its power over foreign affairs to the President prior to 1973 is that diplomatic, military, and intelligence information flows directly to the President. As a result, Congress and the public

[25] David Wise, "Remember the Maddox!" *Esquire,* April 1968, p. 126. See also, Joseph C. Goulden, *Truth Is the First Casualty* (New York: Rand McNally, 1969).

[26] U.S. Congress, Senate, Committee on Foreign Relations, *The Gulf of Tonkin, The 1964 Incidents,* Hearings, 90th Cong., 2nd sess. (Washington, D.C.: U.S. Government Printing Office, 1968), p. 54.

[27] *Ibid.,* p. 91.

"Refresh my memory. Just what is it we're supposed to be assuring them of here?"

Drawing by Stevenson
© 1977 The New Yorker Magazine, Inc.

have tended to assume that the President "has the facts" and is acting on the basis of expert advice. Second, foreign policy decisions are often made in crisis situations, in "an atmosphere of real or contrived urgency."[28] This, too, puts pressure on Congress to defer to presumed presidential wisdom. More recently, however, there has been an increasing realization that the extensive flow of information to the President does not guarantee that his foreign policy decisions will necessarily prove correct or wise.

Today the President of the United States has powerful tools available to him for the conduct of foreign policy, including his personal staff and that of the National Security Council, the State Department, the Pentagon, the CIA, and other agencies. (The existence of this machinery does not mean, however, that the United States can always influence, let alone control, the course of international events. American policymakers may not be able to affect the price of OPEC oil or to prevent the seizure of American diplomats by Islamic revolutionaries.) Until 1947 no formal centralized machinery existed to aid the President in his foreign policy tasks. In that year, Congress attempted to give the President the tools to match his responsibilities.

The Machinery

The National Security Council. The National Security Act of 1947 created the National Security Council (NSC) to advise the President on the integration of "domestic, foreign, and military policies relating to the national security." In one sense the act, amended and expanded in 1949, was an effort to institutionalize the power that had been wielded over military-diplomatic affairs by President Roosevelt in the Second World War. It was also an effort to provide continuity from one administration to the next in the conduct of national security affairs. The NSC, however, has been used very differently by a succession of Presidents.

Eisenhower made frequent use of the NSC. But by the time President Kennedy was inaugurated in 1961, the NSC had spawned such a formidable growth of subcommittees and coordinating groups that paper work was begin-

---

[28] U.S. Congress, Senate, Committee on Foreign Relations, *National Commitments.* 90th Cong., 1st sess., Report (Washington, D.C.: U.S. Government Printing Office, 1967), p. 14.

Richard V. Allen

ning to overwhelm policy formation. President Kennedy's national security adviser, McGeorge Bundy, "promptly slaughtered committees right and left."[29] Kennedy used the NSC infrequently and informally, and some critics contended that the result was a lack of foreign policy coordination. During both the Kennedy and Johnson administrations, the NSC was occasionally used for "window-dressing," to give the appearance during a crisis of somber decisions being made by the President with his highest national security advisers. Real decisions were sometimes reached in less formal meetings. But even Kennedy and Johnson promulgated major national security decisions *within* the administration in the form of NSC directives.

President Nixon directed that the NSC "be reestablished as the principal forum for Presidential consideration of foreign policy issues."[30] Various interagency groups, special panels, and review committees began to flourish once again under Nixon and his adviser for national security, Henry A. Kissinger. The basic structure Kissinger had established remained in effect under President Ford, Nixon's successor. President Carter named Columbia University professor Zbigniew Brzezinski as his national security adviser. Brzezinski said he did not envision his job as a policymaking position but rather as that of a staff adviser to assist the President in decision making. But all of his predecessors, whatever their original intentions, had soon become deeply involved in policymaking. And so did Brzezinski. President Reagan named Richard V. Allen, formerly of Stanford University's Hoover Institution, as his national security adviser.

The State Department. George F. Kennan has described the American State Department in a less turbulent era: "The Department of State . . . in the 1920s when I entered it, was a quaint old place, with its law-office atmosphere, its cool dark corridors, its swinging doors, its brass cuspidors, its black leather rocking chairs, and the grandfather's clock in the Secretary of State's office."[31]

Today the State Department is huge; it occupies a large, antiseptically modern building that houses more than half of its 23,700 employees. Department couriers hand-carry diplomatic documents 10,000,000 miles a year in travels between Washington and its 143 embassies abroad.[32] High-speed coded communications link the Secretary of State to American embassies overseas, handling more than 300,000 words daily. In an Operations Center on the seventh floor, behind a locked door that is opened by a buzzer, the Secretary can monitor a developing crisis. A device called a Telecon flashes incoming cables on a screen, and the center can communicate with any United States post abroad in two minutes.

Despite all this, the State Department's level of efficiency has been the target of periodic criticism. As the United States became a world power, the size of the department increased vastly; bureaus and Assistant Secretaries proliferated. One reason that the State Department is slow to form policy is the "clearance factor" — the tendency of each branch of the department to check and clear matters with other branches and bureaus and other agencies of government. The department's snail-like replies to President Kennedy's requests were a constant source of frustration in the White House. According to Arthur M. Schlesinger,

[29] Arthur M. Schlesinger, Jr., *A Thousand Days* (Boston: Houghton Mifflin, 1965), p. 210.
[30] Congressional Quarterly, *Weekly Report,* February 20, 1970, p. 518.
[31] George F. Kennan, *American Diplomacy* (Chicago: University of Chicago Press, 1951), pp. 91–92.
[32] Data provided by Office of Media Services, Bureau of Public Affairs, Department of State.

Left: "Henry Kissinger was far more powerful than Secretary of State William P. Rogers . . ." *Right:* "There were further policy clashes . . .": Secretary of State Edmund P. Muskie and Zbigniew Brzezinski with President Carter.

Jr., Kennedy "would say, 'Damn it, Bundy and I get more done in one day in the White House than they do in six months at the State Department. . . . They never have any ideas over there,' he complained, 'never come up with anything new.'"[33]

The role of the Secretary of State varies greatly according to his personal relationship with the President. The Secretary's role is further complicated by the fact that while he is in theory principal foreign policy adviser and the ranking officer of the cabinet, he may be overshadowed by the President's national security assistant and the Secretary of Defense, or even by prestigious subordinates. As national security adviser, Henry Kissinger was far more powerful than Secretary of State William P. Rogers during the first Nixon administration. Later Nixon designated Kissinger as Secretary of State, as well as national security assistant. Ford retained Kissinger as Secretary of State but required him to give up his other hat as a presidential assistant.

Carter also followed tradition and kept the two posts separate, naming Cyrus Vance as Secretary of State and Brzezinski as national security adviser. Vance was at least partially overshadowed by Brzezinski and resigned in protest when, against his advice, President Carter dispatched a military mission that failed in an attempt to rescue the American hostages in Iran. There were further policy clashes between Vance's successor, Edmund P. Muskie, and Brzezinski. Ronald Reagan's Secretary of State, former Army General Alexander M. Haig, had been Nixon's chief of staff during the Watergate scandal. Haig moved quickly to try to consolidate his power in foreign affairs. Reagan also received foreign policy advice from his national security adviser, Richard Allen.

State Department Iranian Crisis Center created after the seizure of American hostages

To help administer the department and its annual budget of about $2.2 billion, the Secretary of State has an Executive Secretariat, which controls the flow of paper work and tries to keep the Secretary from being drowned in a sea of words. There are five geographic bureaus: African Affairs; European Affairs; East Asian and Pacific Affairs; Inter-American Affairs; and Near Eastern and South Asian Affairs. Within the geographic bureaus are more than a hundred country desks. In addition, there are functional bureaus for security and consular affairs; congressional relations; public affairs; human rights; education and cultural affairs; economic and business affairs; intelligence; politico-military

[33] Schlesinger, *A Thousand Days*, p. 406.

Secretary of State
Alexander M. Haig, Jr.

American embassy in
London

affairs; oceans and international environmental and scientific affairs; protocol; administration; and international organization (the bureau that manages United States policy at the United Nations).

The United States Foreign Service consists of the professional diplomats who represent the United States overseas and staff key policy posts in the State Department in Washington. Most foreign service officers are stationed abroad as ambassadors, ministers, and political and consular officials. Posts are normally rotated, and members of the foreign service periodically return to Washington between tours of duty overseas. In 1980 the foreign service numbered more than 9600 men and women, of whom 3021 were foreign service "officers" — the professional diplomats.

Overseas, the ambassador is the President's personal representative to the Chief of State and government to which he or she is accredited. Appointed by the President and subject to Senate confirmation, the ambassador is formally in charge of the entire United States mission in a foreign capital. The mission may include representatives of the Agency for International Development (AID), the International Communication Agency (ICA), the military service attachés, military assistance advisory groups, and agents of the CIA, all of whom make up the so-called "country team." Often it is a team in name only, however, with each element reporting back to its own headquarters in Washington and some officials working at cross-purposes to the ambassador. "To a degree," a Senate subcommittee concluded, "the primacy of the ambassador is a polite fiction."[34]

In addition to problems of coordination with other agencies of government, the State Department also faces competition from those agencies. In the past it has competed for the President's attention, not only with the White House national security adviser but with other agencies involved in foreign policy — the Office of International Security Affairs in the Defense Department, for example, and the CIA. To some extent the State Department must even compete with outside sources of advice in foreign policy — defense research firms, the universities, presidential task forces, private organizations interested in foreign policy, and former government officials who may be called in and consulted by the President.

Intelligence and Foreign Policy: The CIA. During the 1970s Senate and House investigating committees disclosed a series of startling actions by the Central Intelligence Agency: the CIA had hired two underworld figures, Sam

[34] "Basic Issues," in *Administration of National Security,* p. 16.

"You idiot! Wrong dart gun!"

Don Wright, *The Miami News*

Giancana and Johnny Rosselli (both of whom were later murdered), to assassinate Cuban Premier Fidel Castro with poison. During four presidential administrations, the CIA had also plotted the assassination of, or coups against, seven other foreign leaders.[35] The congressional committees also disclosed abuses by the FBI and other branches of the intelligence community.

The congressional inquiries were launched after Seymour M. Hersh, an investigative reporter for the *New York Times,* revealed that for several years, beginning in the late 1960s, the CIA had, in violation of its charter, spied on American citizens at home and infiltrated antiwar and other dissident groups.[36] These charges were later documented in a report of a presidential commission headed by Vice President Nelson A. Rockefeller, which found that some of the CIA's actions were "plainly unlawful."[37]

The Rockefeller Report and the congressional committees disclosed that the CIA had photographed and followed American citizens; engaged in break-ins, wiretapping, and bugging; and for twenty years had opened, read, and photographed first-class mail in violation of federal law. The agency had also experimented with mind-altering drugs; one subject, an Army civilian researcher, committed suicide several days after the CIA had laced his after-dinner drink with LSD. He was not told about the drug until twenty minutes after it was administered.

Activities of this sort were not mentioned in the law passed by Congress in 1947 establishing the CIA. The law said that the agency was to advise the National Security Council and to acquire and analyze political, military, and economic knowledge about other countries on which the President could base his foreign policy decisions. But, in addition to collecting intelligence, the CIA

---

[35] U.S. Congress, Senate, Select Committee to Study Governmental Operations with Respect to Intelligence Activities, *Alleged Assassination Plots Involving Foreign Leaders,* 94th Cong., 1st sess., Interim Report (Washington, D.C.: U.S. Government Printing Office, 1975). The report also details CIA plots against Patrice Lumumba of the Congo; Rafael Trujillo of the Dominican Republic; President Salvador Allende and General René Schneider of Chile; President Ngo Dinh Diem of South Vietnam; President François Duvalier of Haiti; and President Achmed Sukarno of Indonesia.

[36] *New York Times,* December 22, 1974, p. 1.

[37] *Report to the President by the Commission on CIA Activities within the United States* (Washington, D.C.: U.S. Government Printing Office, 1975), p. 10.

The Central Intelligence Agency, Langley, Virginia

CIA: Don't Talk About Assassinations

. . . the difficulty with this kind of thing, as you gentlemen are all painfully aware, is that nobody wants to embarrass a President of the United States discussing the assassination of foreign leaders in his presence. This is something that has got to be dealt with in some other fashion. Even though you use euphemisms you've still got a problem. . . . I think any of us would have found it very difficult to discuss assassinations with a President of the United States. I just think we all had the feeling that we were hired to keep those things out of the Oval Office.

—Richard M. Helms, former CIA director, testifying to Senate Intelligence Committee, June 13, 1975.

535

The SR-71, an American spy plane

has engaged in covert operations—secret political action within other countries. The law establishing the CIA makes no specific reference to such covert operations abroad, although the statute does permit the CIA to perform such "other functions and duties" as the National Security Council may direct. But the Senate Intelligence Committee concluded, "Authority for covert action cannot be found in the National Security Act."[38] Yet, the committee reported that the CIA had carried out 900 major covert operations between 1961 and 1975. And it found that the CIA's widespread domestic spying, to which it gave the code name Operation CHAOS, violated the provisions of the 1947 act designed to prohibit the agency from acting as a domestic police force.

Prior to the Japanese attack on Pearl Harbor in 1941, the United States had no central intelligence-gathering agency. After Pearl Harbor, President Roosevelt created the Office of Strategic Services (OSS) to gather intelligence and conduct secret political warfare and sabotage operations behind enemy lines during the Second World War. The CIA was the direct descendant of the wartime OSS. The director of the CIA wears one hat as head of that agency. But the director is simultaneously chairman of the National Foreign Intelligence Board and, as such, is responsible for coordinating the work of the other government intelligence agencies, including the National Security Agency (NSA), the codemaking and code-breaking arm of the Pentagon; the Defense Intelligence Agency (DIA), the military rival to the CIA; the FBI; and the State Department's Bureau of Intelligence and Research (INR). (Together, these agencies spend more than $12 billion a year.)

The CIA has two principal divisions. An *Intelligence Directorate* engages in overt collection, research, and analysis of foreign intelligence. Most of the criticism of the CIA has been directed at its *Operations Directorate,* which engages in the secret collection of intelligence (espionage) and in secret political warfare. On occasion this directorate has helped to overthrow governments—in Iran in 1953 and Guatemala in 1954, for example. It was this clandestine arm of the CIA that plotted the assassination of such leaders as Cuba's Fidel Castro and Patrice Lumumba in the Congo, launched the invasion of Cuba at the Bay of Pigs in 1961, and supported a 30,000-man secret army in Laos.

Although, unlike the FBI, the CIA has no police power within the United States, in 1967 it was disclosed that the agency was subsidizing the National Student Association and dozens of foundations and private groups *within* this country. President Johnson ordered that most of the secret funding be ended.

In 1972 the CIA again became enmeshed in domestic activities. Most of the burglars caught in the Watergate break-in had CIA backgrounds, and one was on the intelligence agency's payroll at the time of the break-in. A year earlier, at the request of the White House, the CIA had secretly assisted E. Howard Hunt, Jr., a former CIA operative and White House "plumber" and one of the men eventually convicted in the Watergate burglary. And President Nixon tried to use the CIA to block the FBI from probing the burglary of Democratic headquarters.

The CIA's size and budget are secret, but it has been unofficially estimated that the agency spends more than $1 billion a year and employs well over 15,000 people. The CIA has its headquarters in a secluded, wooded area of Langley, Virginia, just across the Potomac River from Washington.

[38] U.S. Congress, Senate, Select Committee to Study Governmental Operations with Respect to Intelligence Activities, *Foreign and Military Intelligence,* 94th Cong., 2nd sess., Final Report (Washington, D.C.: U.S. Government Printing Office, 1976), Book 1, p. 128.

During the 1950s, under its director, Allen W. Dulles, the CIA toiled largely out of the limelight. The loss of a U-2, a CIA spy plane, on a flight over the Soviet Union in 1960 and the disaster at the Bay of Pigs in 1961 thrust the CIA into the headlines and focused attention on its activities. By 1964 critics charged that the CIA stood at the center of what had become "an invisible government."[39] Former Assistant Secretary of State Roger Hilsman wrote: "The root fear was that the CIA represented . . . a state within a state, and certainly the basis for fear was there."[40]

On the other hand, because the CIA is a secret agency, and usually does not make any public comment, it is sometimes blamed for things it does not do. Defenders of the CIA argue that it already operates under sufficient control. For example, Allen Dulles wrote that the CIA has never carried out any covert operations abroad "without appropriate approval at a high political level in our government *outside the CIA*."[41] Dulles was referring to the interagency board, designated the Special Coordination Committee by President Carter, and known in the past under various other names, which has responsibility for authorizing covert operations. However, the Senate Intelligence Committee (formerly known as the Church Committee for its then chairman, Senator Frank Church, Democrat, of Idaho) reported that the group seldom met. And former CIA director Richard Helms conceded in testimony to the committee that the panel acted as a "circuit breaker" to insulate the President from responsibility for covert CIA operations.[42]

The CIA's defenders have argued that despite the agency's mistakes, it is an essential arm of the government. Allen Dulles wrote, for example, that the United States "is being challenged by a hostile group of nations," and that only the CIA could learn the defense secrets of the Soviet Union and China. "The special techniques which are unique to secret intelligence operations are needed to penetrate the security barriers of the Communist Bloc," he wrote, adding that an intelligence service "is the best insurance we can take out against surprise." As for covert CIA operations inside other countries, Dulles contended

CIA dart gun

[39] David Wise and Thomas B. Ross, *The Invisible Government* (New York: Random House, 1964), p. 3.
[40] Hilsman, *To Move a Nation*, pp. 64–65.
[41] Allen Dulles, *The Craft of Intelligence* (New York: Harper & Row, 1963), p. 189.
[42] U.S. Congress, Senate, Select Committee to Study Governmental Operations with Respect to Intelligence Activities, *Foreign and Military Intelligence*, p. 46.

"Intelligence Agencies Must Be Made Subject to the Rule of Law."

The Committee's fundamental conclusion is that intelligence activities have undermined the constitutional rights of citizens. . . . we do not question the need for lawful domestic intelligence. We recognize that certain intelligence activities serve perfectly proper and clearly necessary ends of government. Surely, catching spies and stopping crime, including acts of terrorism, is essential to insure "domestic tranquility" and to "provide for the common defense." . . .

[But] we must be wary about the drift toward "big brother government." . . . Through a vast network of informants, and through the uncontrolled or illegal use of intrusive techniques— ranging from simple theft to sophisticated electronic surveillance—the Government has collected, and then used improperly, huge amounts of information about the private lives, political beliefs and associations of numerous Americans. . . . intelligence agencies must be made subject to the rule of law.

—Final report of the Senate Intelligence Committee, 1976.

"We don't consider ours to be an underdeveloped country so much as we think of yours as an overdeveloped country."

Cartoon by John A. Ruge. © 1970 The Saturday Review Co. First appeared in *Saturday Review* January 10, 1970. Used with permission

U.S. aid shipment in Chad, Africa

that the United States could not limit its activities "to those cases where we are invited in."[43]

In the wake of the various investigations of the CIA and the FBI, Congress finally moved to strengthen its control over the intelligence establishment. The Senate and the House each created a permanent Select Committee on Intelligence with authority over the CIA and the other intelligence agencies. By 1980, however, following the crises in Iran and Afghanistan, the CIA's supporters charged that the various investigations had weakened the intelligence agency. In the new, more militant atmosphere, Congress declined to enact detailed reform bills to control the intelligence agencies. Instead, in 1980 it passed a more limited bill requiring the President to furnish information to the intelligence committees and to notify them in advance of covert operations in most circumstances. At the same time, Congress reduced from eight to two the number of committees that the executive branch must notify of such operations.

However necessary it may be to protect American security, the existence of a clandestine intelligence and espionage establishment creates special problems in a free society. The operations of the CIA and the other United States intelligence agencies pose the continuing dilemma of how secret intelligence machinery can be made compatible with democratic government.[44]

Other Instruments: AID, ICA, the Peace Corps, and the Arms Control and Disarmament Agency. Today the State Department must compete in the foreign policy field not only with the President's NSC staff, the CIA, and the Pentagon, but with many other agencies and units of the federal government.

One of the agencies with foreign policy responsibilities both in Washington and in the field is the *Agency for International Development* (AID). AID, as its initials imply, is responsible for carrying out programs of financial and technical assistance to less economically developed nations. AID is an arm of the International Development Cooperation Agency, an umbrella agency formed in 1979 to advise the President and coordinate the foreign assistance programs of the government.

Since the initiation of the Marshall plan, the United States has spent more than $175 billion on foreign aid, contributions to international organizations, and military assistance. For fiscal 1981, for example, the President's budget request for economic aid totaled $6.2 billion, and included economic assistance for some sixty countries in Latin America, Asia, and Africa. Although foreign aid appropriations have declined in recent years, the United States has placed greater emphasis on channeling aid through multilateral financial institutions, and it has increased its participation in the International Bank for Reconstruction and Development (World Bank), which makes loans to and promotes foreign investments in underdeveloped nations.

AID is politically unpopular because many Americans regard it as a "giveaway" program with little visible benefit to the taxpayers. But the aid program can be defended both on humanitarian grounds and, more narrowly, on political grounds. As the richest nation in the world, the United States has felt a moral obligation to try to alleviate poverty, disease, and malnutrition in other nations. At the same time, supporters of the aid program contend, peace and stability are

[43] Dulles, *The Craft of Intelligence,* pp. 48–51, 235–36.
[44] See David Wise, *The American Police State* (New York: Random House, 1976).

unlikely to be achieved for the United States or the world as a whole as long as such conditions exist in the poorer nations.

Despite some popular misconceptions, most foreign aid is not given to other countries in the form of cash. Most AID dollars are spent in the United States to buy commodities and to hire technical experts for projects overseas. AID provides technical assistance by sending abroad specialists in such fields as health, education, and agriculture. Through development loans, repayable in dollars, AID offers other countries long-term, low-interest financing for such projects as highways, dams, schools, and hospitals. In addition, the United States donates and sells agricultural commodities at low cost under the Food for Peace Program.

The *International Communication Agency* (ICA), according to an official description, helps to achieve the objectives of United States foreign policy by "telling the world about the society and policies of the United States."[45] The ICA is, in short, the official foreign propaganda agency of the United States government. It was created in 1978 as the successor to the United States Information Agency.

Wary that such an agency might be used by a President to influence domestic opinion, Congress has generally restricted the ICA to operations overseas. The agency has about 8800 employees and branches in 125 countries. Its libraries and information centers in foreign countries are sometimes visible and popular targets of anti-American mob violence. Through the Voice of America, the ICA each week beams abroad 847 hours of news broadcasts, music, and feature programs in thirty-eight languages. As a government radio station, it operates under policy restrictions and guidelines set by the State Department.

The *Peace Corps* was created under President Kennedy in 1961 to provide a trained corps of highly motivated American volunteers, many of them young, to help people in developing nations. More than a decade later, the Peace Corps was administered by ACTION, an umbrella agency that runs both overseas and domestic volunteer programs, such as Volunteers in Service to America (VISTA).

In 1980 almost 6000 Peace Corps volunteers were in training or serving abroad in sixty-two countries as teachers, agricultural aides, doctors, and in many

[45] *United States Government Organization Manual, 1980–81* (Washington, D.C.: U.S. Government Printing Office, 1980), p. 597.

Peace Corps volunteers in Venezuela

other capacities. The volunteers, who must be U.S. citizens and at least eighteen, serve abroad for two years and receive $125 per month, plus allowances for food, clothing, housing, and other living expenses. By 1980, 80,000 persons had served in the Peace Corps.

The *Arms Control and Disarmament Agency* was established in 1961 during the Kennedy administration. Although technically not a division of the State Department, the director is an adviser to the Secretary of State and the President. The agency prepares and manages United States participation in international arms control and disarmament negotiations, but it also has important responsibilities in conducting long-range research on techniques of arms control. The agency played an active role in negotiations leading to a United States–Soviet agreement in 1971 to reduce the danger of accidental nuclear war, and to an eighty-five-nation pact, ratified by the Senate in 1972, to prohibit implanting of nuclear weapons on the ocean floor. In addition, the agency participated in talks that resulted in the 1972 SALT agreement on nuclear arms. It also took part in separate negotiations that led to the signing by the United States in 1972 of an international convention to ban germ warfare.

AID, the ICA, the Peace Corps, and the disarmament agency all receive policy guidance from the State Department. The State Department itself must share the foreign policy field with dozens of other agencies of the federal government involved in various aspects of foreign affairs. These include the departments of Defense, Agriculture, Labor, Commerce, Justice, and Transportation.

The United Nations

The United Nations was founded in San Francisco in 1945 to fulfill the dream of a community of nations, a world body that could take collective action to keep the peace and work for the betterment of humanity. The opening words of the UN charter declare its principal goal: "We the peoples of the United Nations determined to save succeeding generations from the scourge of war, which twice in our lifetime has brought untold sorrow to mankind. . . ."

The United Nations, however, has generally been unable to keep the peace on issues that divide the major world powers. Decisions affecting world peace are made in Washington, Moscow, Peking, and other capitals, but less often at UN headquarters in New York City. In part, this was predictable from the structure of the UN and the nature of international relations. The Security Council, with fifteen members, cannot act over the veto of any of the five permanent members—as of 1980, the United States, the Soviet Union, Britain,

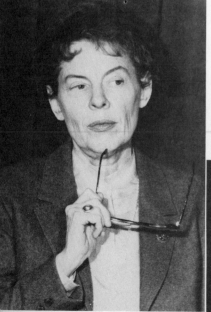

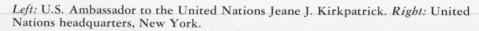

Left: U.S. Ambassador to the United Nations Jeane J. Kirkpatrick. *Right:* United Nations headquarters, New York.

1978: UN peacekeeping force in Lebanon

France, and the People's Republic of China. Because the Soviet Union has frequently exercised a veto in the Security Council, UN members sought a way to circumvent the Council. In November 1950 the General Assembly decided that it could act to meet threats to peace when the Security Council failed to do so because the permanent members lacked unanimity. There is no veto power in the General Assembly, to which all member nations belong. Although the General Assembly has thus increased somewhat in importance, it, too, has proved unable to cope with many major conflicts.

The UN has acted with varying success in several world crises: in Korea in 1950, Suez in 1956, the Congo in 1961, Cyprus in 1964. And in the Arab-Israeli war of October 1973, the UN played a significant role in reducing tensions and avoiding a military confrontation between the United States and the Soviet Union. At the height of the 1973 Mideast crisis, the UN Security Council passed a resolution to send a multinational peacekeeping force to the war zone. Ultimately, two UN peacekeeping forces were dispatched to the Middle East, one to the Sinai Peninsula and, later, a second to the Golan Heights at the time of the disengagement of Israeli and Syrian troops in 1974. In its actions following the 1973 war, the UN provided an alternative to direct intervention by the big powers. But the UN was not able to end the tragic war in Nigeria or the fighting in Vietnam; and it had scant success in the Middle East during the Arab-Israeli Six-Day War in 1967.

The United States, which provides one-quarter of the UN's budget, lost much of its influence in that organization in the 1960s as the UN shifted from a pro-Western to a neutralist stand. As many of the former colonial territories of Africa and Asia gained independence, they joined the UN, and the United States could no longer count on winning its political battles in that body. In 1980 the Secretary General was Kurt Waldheim of Austria, an officially neutral nation.

By 1980 the UN had expanded from its original 50 to 152 members. The United States is represented by an ambassador who heads a United States mission in New York. Although the UN has had somewhat limited success as a peacekeeping agency, it has served several other constructive purposes. It provides a forum for discussion, a place where new and small nations can be heard. It sometimes helps to defuse world crises by allowing nations to talk instead of fight. And its economic, social, and health agencies have made significant contributions in improving the lives of millions of people all over the world. In the 1980s, the UN was also having some success in dealing with such international

A UN Ambassador Speaks Out

Am I embarrassed to speak for a less than perfect democracy? Not one bit. Find me a better one. Do I suppose there are societies which are free of sin? No, I don't. Do I think ours is on balance incomparably the most hopeful set of human relations the world has? (I mean by ours those two-dozen-odd democracies of the world.) Yes, I do. Have we done obscene things? Yes, we have. How did our people learn about them? They learned about them on television, in the newspapers.

—Daniel P. Moynihan, then U.S. Ambassador to the United Nations, quoted in *Time*, January 26, 1976.

Daniel P. Moynihan while UN Ambassador

environmental problems as the peaceful use of outer space and seabeds, pollution of the oceans, and overpopulation. Finally, the UN, for all its inadequacies, still remains a symbol of hope, the tangible embodiment of humanity's fragile dream of peace.

The Politics of Foreign Policymaking

Over a period of time, widespread or intense domestic reaction to foreign policy may have an impact on government. During the late 1960s, there was domestic protest against the war in Vietnam by students, professors, and many other citizens. Some Americans reacted against the protesters, but others were undoubtedly favorably influenced by the peace movement. Eventually, a majority of Americans felt the war was a mistake, and a climate developed in which President Johnson felt it prudent to leave the White House. The growing opposition to the war provided the political backdrop for President Nixon's decision in 1969 to begin the withdrawal of American troops and for the lengthy peace negotiations, conducted initially in secret, that finally brought an end to United States participation in the war in 1973.

The Role of the Public. Despite public awareness of highly publicized issues like Vietnam or the seizure of American diplomats in Iran, some political scientists have argued that on most foreign policy issues, the public is both uninterested and uninformed. Gabriel Almond has observed that "Americans tend to exhaust their emotional and intellectual energies in private pursuits." While members of the public may develop well-defined views on domestic questions that affect them directly, he has argued, on questions of foreign policy they tend to react in changeable, "formless and plastic moods."[46] Almond has suggested that relatively small leadership groups play the major role in the making of most specific foreign policy decisions, and that the public's role is largely confined to the expression of mass attitudes that provide a framework within which officials may work.[47]

James N. Rosenau has also differentiated between public response to domestic issues and foreign policy issues, but he emphasizes that when a foreign policy question becomes so big that it involves "a society's resources and relationships" it quickly turns into a domestic political issue—and he cites the war in Vietnam as an example.[48]

Nevertheless, a President has wide latitude in conducting foreign policy. Kenneth N. Waltz has suggested that as a rule, "The first effect of an international crisis is to increase the President's popular standing." But, Waltz points out, a President sometimes risks political unpopularity in a foreign policy crisis no matter what he does.[49] And a President who responds too readily to public opinion may be pushed into dangerous choices if public sentiment is running high for quick or simple solutions. Just as the public may demand peace, at other times it may demand retaliation that risks war.

[46] Gabriel A. Almond, *The American People and Foreign Policy* (New York: Praeger, 1960), p. 53.
[47] *Ibid.,* pp. 4–6.
[48] James N. Rosenau, "Foreign Policy as an Issue-Area," in James N. Rosenau, ed., *Domestic Sources of Foreign Policy* (New York: Free Press, 1967), p. 49.
[49] Kenneth N. Waltz, "Electoral Punishment and Foreign Policy Crises," in Rosenau, ed., *Domestic Sources of Foreign Policy,* pp. 273, 283.

Domestic influence on foreign policy is not limited to mass public opinion, as reflected in polls, letters, or protest demonstrations. Congress, individual legislators or committee chairmen, interest groups, private organizations concerned with foreign policy, opinion leaders, the press, TV commentators, and proximity to an election may all have some effect on policy outcomes. Some foreign policy questions are of special importance to particular groups. A President who is interested in carrying New York, California, and Illinois, for example, may frame United States policy toward Israel with at least some thought to the likely reaction among the many Jewish voters in those states. On Polish patriotic days, members of Congress from heavily Polish areas such as Buffalo or Chicago rise in the House and Senate and carefully pay homage to the contribution of Polish heroes to the nation's heritage.

Presidential Credibility. A President's conduct of foreign policy depends in large measure on whether he is able to carry the public along with him on big decisions. Without public trust in his leadership, he may fail. President Johnson suffered from a "credibility gap" that seriously hampered his Presidency. The Tonkin Gulf episode, already discussed, was one example of an event that took on a far different coloration after the fact.

Other Presidents have encountered credibility problems. Since the Second World War, the government has on more than one occasion told official lies designed to protect secret intelligence operations. Under President Eisenhower, for example, the administration claimed at first that the U-2 spy plane shot down 1200 miles inside the Soviet Union was a "weather research" aircraft that had strayed off course. Under President Kennedy, the government initially denied, but later admitted, that it was responsible for the CIA-backed invasion of Cuba at the Bay of Pigs. During the Watergate scandal, President Nixon claimed he had concealed certain information for "national security" reasons, but he later admitted political motivation as well; "national security" had been used as a pretext to cover up a crime.[50] Official statements about foreign policy and national security, in short, have contributed to an erosion of public confidence in government honesty.

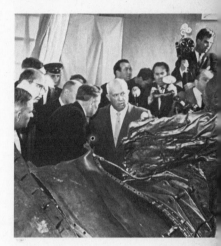

Soviet Premier Khrushchev inspects wreckage of U-2 spy plane in 1960.

Political Parties, Campaigns, and Foreign Policy. The two-party system tends to push both major parties toward the center on foreign policy issues. Kenneth N. Waltz explains that "failure to do so will give a third party the chance to wedge itself in between its two larger competitors. . . . The policy positions of two competing parties begin to approach one another, and the candidates even begin to look and talk very much alike."[51]

Nevertheless, foreign policy issues are often important factors in elections. In the 1980 campaign, for example, President Carter, the incumbent, charged that his Republican opponent, Ronald Reagan, might lead the nation into war.

Advocates of *bipartisanship* in foreign policy contend that both major political parties should broadly support the President, and that foreign policy issues should not be sharply debated in political campaigns. They argue that it is in the

[50] "President Nixon's August 5, 1974 Statement," and "The June 23, 1972 Nixon-Haldeman Transcripts," in New York Times, *The End of a Presidency* (New York: Bantam Books, 1974), pp. 324–53.

[51] Kenneth N. Waltz, *Foreign Policy and Democratic Politics* (Boston: Little, Brown, 1967), p. 86.

nation's interest to appear united to the rest of the world. Opponents of bipartisanship have argued that foreign policy issues must be discussed in political campaigns precisely *because* those issues are so important. Bipartisanship flourished particularly in the period shortly after the Second World War. It was symbolized by the phrase, "Politics stops at the water's edge," a concept popularized in 1950 by Senator Arthur H. Vandenberg, a Michigan Republican who had served as chairman of the Senate Foreign Relations Committee under a Democratic President, Harry Truman.

The Defense Establishment

Near Great Falls, Montana, Aberdeen Angus cattle graze placidly on a grassy hillside. Some fifty feet below, two officers of the Strategic Air Command (SAC) control ten Minuteman missiles, each tipped with a hydrogen bomb. Within thirty seconds after receiving an order, the two officers could fire the missiles. The Third World War would have begun.

This was the setting described to readers of the *New York Times* when the Department of Defense permitted a reporter to visit the Minuteman launch control center at Malmstrom Air Force Base. The story explained:

> No one here knows the targets. Each missile's destination is determined by the . . . Strategic Air Command. The target is put on magnetic tape, which is fed into the guidance system of each rocket. . . . "The purpose of the ball game is to throw a warhead," said Col. Rex Dowtin, the missile wing commander. . . . A statement made by Captain Johnson . . . illustrated the [missilemen's] language. "When a launch is voted anywhere in the system of 50 missiles, a bell rings," he said ringing it manually to show how the trump of doom would sound in that small room. "We can go to inhibit launch. We have 205 seconds to signal inhibit." . . . The young officers wear pistols—to use on each other to prevent a take-over of control of a missile firing center. Further, the two [launching] keys must be turned simultaneously, and in locks about 10 feet apart. "Murder to get control would be useless," said Captain Crislip.[52]

Although the dialogue might have come from the satiric motion picture *Dr. Strangelove,* it was real. Across the Arctic Circle, the Soviet equivalent of the

[52] Wallace Turner, "Minuteman Missile Squads Are Poised on Montana Hillsides Ready to Launch Hydrogen Bombs," *New York Times,* February 28, 1965, p. 90.

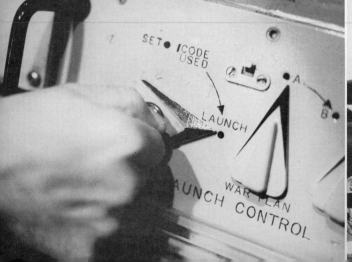

"*All those in favor of declaring the military budget sacrosanct raise their right hand.*"

Drawing by Dana Fradon
© 1979 The New Yorker Magazine, Inc.

SAC officers sat in *their* missile silos ready to launch huge SS-18 ICBMs at the United States. A study by the federal government estimated in 1980 that in a nuclear exchange as many as 260 million American and Soviet citizens would be killed.[53]

Since the Second World War the United States has spent more than $1 trillion on national defense; in fiscal 1981 the Defense Department's budget request was $147 billion. Because of expanding technology, however, some weapons systems become obsolete even as they are deployed. And because of the nuclear threat, a strong argument can be made that, as spending for armaments has increased, national security has actually diminished. Aside from this paradox, the existence of a multibillion-dollar military machine has created numerous problems for American society. Within the "military-industrial complex," whole industries depend on government defense contracts; aerospace industry lobbyists attempt to guard their clients' interests in Washington; and some universities compete for classified military research contracts. A society that devotes some 30 percent of its total national budget to defense-related spending cannot allocate as much as it otherwise might to eliminate slums and poverty or improve health, schools, and the natural environment. The "cost" of a defense economy cannot be measured simply in terms of the size of the annual Pentagon budget.

Thus far, America's nuclear weapons have remained in their underground silos and beneath the sea in submarines. But since the Second World War, the United States has fought a series of costly, so-called limited or conventional wars in Korea and in Southeast Asia. Despite its vast weaponry, manpower, and technology, the United States learned in Vietnam that superior size and resources were of little advantage against an elusive and politically dedicated enemy skilled in guerrilla warfare.

The United States could not employ nuclear weapons against a smaller nation without being morally condemned by most of the rest of the world as well as by millions of citizens at home. And the use of tactical or strategic nuclear weapons in a conventional "limited war" carries with it the threat of escalation into a big war, some argue, for it might bring the Soviet Union or Communist China into the conflict. To a great extent, therefore, the "usable power" of

[53] Adapted from Congress of the United States, Office of Technology Assessment, "The Effects of Nuclear War," Summary, April 1980, p. 18.

Drawing by Mike Peters
for the *Dayton Daily News*

the United States has been limited. Recent experience has taught that its vast military force cannot be applied very effectively in view of the risks of an ultimate holocaust. Furthermore, domestic opposition to the United States involvement in Southeast Asia demonstrated the additional *political* risks and limitations for American leaders pursuing military solutions to foreign policy problems. For example, there were political risks for the Carter administration in 1980, a presidential election year, when 4 million 18- and 19-year-old men registered for a possible military draft. In response to events in Iran and Afghanistan, President Carter had asked Congress in January to resume draft registration. Congress passed legislation in June, and the registration at 34,000 post offices began in July. The Selective Service System did not issue draft cards or classify those who registered. There could be no actual draft unless Congress approved a call-up. Although Carter had asked for authority to register both men and women, Congress refused to approve draft registration for women. In December 1980 the Supreme Court said it would consider whether draft registration for men only was constitutional. (See pp. 512–13.)

Foreign policy and defense policy are intimately linked. Ideally, as Burton Sapin notes, "Foreign policy establishes the broad outlines within which the defense establishment must do its work."[54] A modern President must contend with the problems of controlling a huge, powerful military establishment with its friends and protectors in Congress and its clients in private industry. The President must see that the generals serve his foreign policy goals, rather than the other way around.

The Department of Defense

The principle of civilian control over the American military establishment is deeply rooted in the Constitution and the nation's tradition. The President is Commander in Chief of all the armed forces, and the Secretary of Defense, by law, must be a civilian. Yet the effectiveness of civilian control of the military has sometimes been open to question.

Across the Potomac River from Washington, in Arlington, Virginia, lies the Pentagon. Completed in 1943 at a cost of $83 million, the Pentagon houses some 22,700 civilian and military employees. In its concourse is a shopping center large enough for most suburban cities. The Pentagon has its own bank, post office, barber shop, department stores, florist—even an optometrist and medical and dental clinics. The Secretary of Defense is the Western world's big-

[54] Burton M. Sapin, *The Making of United States Foreign Policy* (New York: Praeger, for the Brookings Institution, 1966), p. 136.

The Pentagon. *Left:* aerial view. *Right:* the War Room.

gest employer, in charge of more than 1,000,000 civilians and 2,050,000 members of the armed forces as of 1979. (Indirectly, the Pentagon is also the biggest private employer in America; by 1980, for example, the Defense Department's contracts were running at a level of $63 billion a year.)[55]

The National Security Act of 1947, as amended in 1949, unified the armed forces under the control of a single Secretary of Defense. The army, navy, and air force continue to exist as separate entities within the Defense Department, each with its own Secretary. The Secretaries of the armed services do not control their military operations, however; that is the responsibility of the President, acting through the Secretary of Defense and the Joint Chiefs of Staff. The Pentagon has its own "little State Department," the Office of International Security Affairs (ISA), which serves both as the Defense Department's link with the State Department and as a competing source of foreign policy formulation. The Pentagon also has its own intelligence organization, the Defense Intelligence Agency (DIA), created in 1961, as well as the supersecret National Security Agency (NSA), which intercepts the codes of other nations and conducts electronic espionage.

Secretary of Defense
Caspar Weinberger

The members of the Joint Chiefs of Staff are the chairman, the chiefs of staff of the three armed services, and, when marine corps matters are under consideration, the Commandant of the marines. By law they advise the President and the Secretary of Defense and are the chiefs of their respective military services.

**The Joint
Chiefs of Staff**

The chairman and other members of the Joint Chiefs are appointed by the President. Sometimes the President may skip over senior officers to appoint a more dynamic, younger service chief. The chairman of the Joint Chiefs outranks his colleagues. Together, the Joint Chiefs are responsible for day-to-day conduct of military operations as well as long-range strategic planning. They are assisted by a Joint Staff of not more than 400 officers selected about equally from the three services. Although the President relies on the Joint Chiefs for military advice, he may choose to disregard their views. The President has the responsibility to weigh military risks against the nation's total foreign policy objectives.

Robert Kennedy has related that during the Cuban missile crisis in 1962, one member of the Joint Chiefs advocated the use of nuclear weapons. "I thought, as I listened, of the many times that I had heard the military take posi-

[55] U.S. Department of Defense, *100 Companies*, Fiscal Year 1979, p. 1.

The Joint Chiefs of Staff, 1980: General Edward C. Meyer, Army; Admiral Thomas B. Hayward, Navy; General David C. Jones, Chairman, Air Force; General Lew Allen, Jr., Air Force; General Robert H. Barrow, Marine Corps

tions which, if wrong, had the advantage that no one would be around at the end to know."[56]

But not every military officer is a "hawk." A whole series of leading military figures in recent decades, generals like George Marshall, Omar Bradley, Matthew Ridgway, James Gavin, and Maxwell Taylor, proved themselves capable of viewing foreign policy in its broadest context — not merely in narrow, military terms. Another career military man, General Eisenhower, successfully resisted the advice of some of his military advisers and refused, for example, to intervene in Southeast Asia in 1954. And some high-ranking military officers and ex-officers criticized the war in Vietnam.

Strategic Arms: The Balance of Terror

Since the 1950s, the world has lived with the knowledge that it is less than thirty minutes away from nuclear disaster. The American nuclear monopoly was broken when the Soviet Union exploded an atomic bomb in 1949. In 1957 the Soviet Union launched the first Sputnik, or earth satellite. The military implications were clear; if Russia possessed the technology to boost a satellite into outer space, it had long-range missiles that could be targeted on American cities. In October 1964 Communist China exploded its first nuclear bomb, and the "nuclear club" then had five members — the United States, the Soviet Union, Britain, France, and China. India became the sixth member when it exploded a nuclear device in May 1974. Israel is also widely believed to possess nuclear weapons.

Since the Second World War, the United States has adopted a policy of *strategic deterrence.* The theory of deterrence, developed in the Pentagon, with the assistance of defense "think tanks" such as the Rand Corporation and the Institute of Defense Analyses (IDA), involved deploying enough nuclear weapons so that an enemy would not, in theory, attack the United States, for fear of being attacked in retaliation.

[56] Kennedy, *Thirteen Days,* p. 48.

Waiting for Armageddon

In underground silos in Minot, North Dakota, United States Air Force officers stand by at the controls of a group of Minuteman Intercontinental Ballistic Missiles (ICBMs). According to a published account, this is how they would receive an order from the President of the United States to launch their missiles:

The two crew members decode the message, which includes an "enabling" code, then turn to a small red metal box located above the assistant's console. The box is secured by two combination locks (each crew member knows only his lock's combination).

Inside the box are two keys and authentication documents that enable the crew to prove that the go-to-war order is real.

The two men sit in front of their consoles and feed the "enabling" code into their computer (in effect, arming the missiles).

An alarm bell rings. The men insert their keys — the keyholes are 12 feet from each other so that one man cannot insert both.

The commander starts his countdown:

"Five . . . four . . . three . . . two . . . one . . . Key turn."

The two men turn their keys simultaneously and hold them in the launch position for a five-second count by the commander:

"One . . . two . . . three . . . four . . . five . . . Release."

The light on the console panel that says "Missile Away" lights up. It is all over — unrecallable and quite final.

—*Los Angeles Times,* January 1, 1978.

Potential Destruction from Nuclear Weapons

Figure 14–2

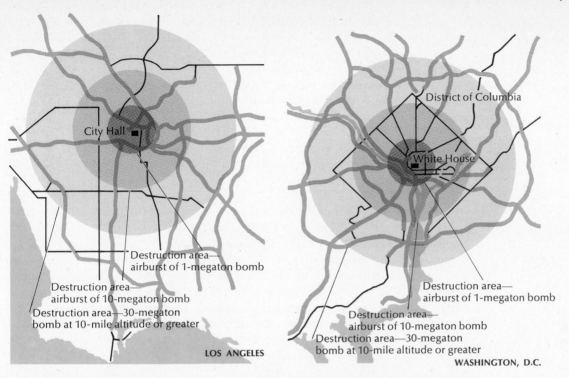

City Hall

Destruction area—
airburst of 1-megaton bomb

Destruction area—
airburst of 10-megaton bomb

Destruction area—30-megaton
bomb at 10-mile altitude or greater

LOS ANGELES

District of Columbia

White House

Destruction area—
airburst of 1-megaton bomb

Destruction area—
airburst of 10-megaton bomb

Destruction area—30-megaton
bomb at 10-mile altitude or greater

WASHINGTON, D.C.

Source: Abram Chayes and Jerome B. Wiesner, eds., *ABM: An Evaluation of the Decision to Deploy an Antiballistic Missile System* (New York: Signet Books, 1969), pp. 274–75. Originally published by Harper & Row.

But how, if it relied on nuclear arms alone, could the United States respond to nonnuclear military challenges? President Kennedy believed it was necessary for the United States to supplement its nuclear power by expanding its capacity to fight "conventional" wars. During the 1960s, the policy of massive nuclear retaliation changed to one of "limited" or "flexible" response; and the Pentagon trained its Special Forces in guerrilla warfare and "counterinsurgency." In Vietnam, at least, the new theory and techniques did not prove to be very successful.

Henry A. Kissinger, who became President Nixon's national security adviser in 1969 and later Secretary of State, argued in 1957 that the United States must be able to fight a "limited nuclear war,"[57] a position from which he later retreated.[58]

Some defense intellectuals shocked many people by their attempts at rational analysis of an essentially irrational process—thermonuclear war. For example, Herman Kahn wrote in 1961 that a nuclear war "would not preclude normal and happy lives for the majority of survivors and their descendants."[59] The picture of nuclear survivors living happy lives amid the debris did not convince everyone. Other analysts, such as Ralph E. Lapp, argued that the nation's arsenal of weapons had grown into "a monstrous stockpile which could not only kill, but overkill, any possible enemy."[60]

The strategy of deterrence has a language all its own. Military theorists speak of "first strike capability" and "second strike capability," "stable deterrent," or "counterforce." By the late 1960s the jargon included ominous new acronyms: MIRV (Multiple Independently Targetable Reentry Vehicle), MAD (Mutually Assured Destruction), and ABM (antiballistic missile). Whatever parity had been achieved in the "balance of terror" was threatened by new technology—the simultaneous development of the ABM as a defense against ballistic missiles, and the MIRV, designed to overwhelm the ABM system by firing from one missile a cluster of real and dummy warheads to confuse radar defenses.

The spiraling arms race, in short, threatened to go out of control. The history of United States development of the ABM illustrates the problem: in 1967 the Johnson administration disclosed that the Soviet Union had deployed an antiballistic missile system around Moscow. The administration opposed deployment of the ABM by the United States, arguing that Soviet countermeasures would leave both countries with no net increase in security.

But the Joint Chiefs of Staff and powerful members of Congress favored an ABM program. In June Communist China exploded its first hydrogen bomb. Soon after, the Johnson administration reversed course and proposed that the United States build a "thin" ABM defense against Communist China. Johnson's critics suggested that the decision was essentially political, designed to show a firm Democratic defense posture in advance of the 1968 election. Columnist James Reston characterized it as "an anti-Republican missile defense."[61] Al-

[57] Henry A. Kissinger, *Nuclear Weapons and Foreign Policy* (New York: Harper & Row, 1957), pp. 174–202. Published for the Council on Foreign Relations.

[58] Henry A. Kissinger, *The Necessity for Choice* (New York: Harper & Row, 1961), p. 81.

[59] Herman Kahn, *On Thermonuclear War* (Princeton, N. J.: Princeton University Press, 1961), p. 21.

[60] Ralph E. Lapp, *Kill and Overkill* (New York: Basic Books, 1962), p. 10.

[61] James Reston in the *New York Times*, September 22, 1967, p. 46.

though President Nixon modified Johnson's plan, the United States in 1969 embarked on a round of strategic spending for the Safeguard ABM system that would cost the taxpayers many billions of dollars.

On October 1, 1975, the enormous complex of radars, missiles, and computers, located in the wheat fields near Grand Forks, North Dakota, was completed, at a cost of $5.7 billion. The Pentagon announced that Safeguard was fully operational. By an irony of history, the next day, the House of Representatives voted to dismantle the project. The Senate concurred and the missile facilities were shut down. Even before its completion, the ABM had become obsolete when the Soviets developed MIRV, multiple, independently targetable warheads that could overwhelm the antimissile defense system.[62] This was precisely the argument that the original critics of the ABM had used during the Senate debate over the ABM in 1968.

The 1972 SALT agreement limited ABM deployment by the United States and the Soviet Union and included a five-year freeze on production of offensive nuclear weapons. At the time of the agreement, however, the United States had 1054 intercontinental ballistic missiles (ICBMs) and 656 submarine-launched missiles; the Soviet Union had 1618 ICBMs and 650 submarine-launched missiles.[63] Both sides, in other words, continued to possess immense destructive power despite the agreement and a later accord signed at Vladivostok, in the Soviet Union, in 1974.

[62] *Washington Post,* November 20, 1975, p. 1; *New York Times,* November 25, 1975, p. 1.
[63] *New York Times,* May 27, 1972, p. 1.

Close encounter between U.S. and Soviet aircraft over Iceland

B-52 bombers

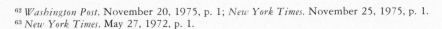

In 1977 President Carter cancelled full production of the controversial neutron bomb, which kills people but spares buildings. A year later, however, he ordered the Department of Energy to begin building components of the neutron, or Enhanced Radiation (ER), bomb. Then in 1979 Carter announced plans for a $33 billion system of 200 mobile MX intercontinental nuclear missiles, to be deployed in the Utah-Nevada area. The covered mobile missiles, each containing ten warheads, would shuttle on giant launchers among 4600 underground shelters along roads shaped in loops, like racetracks. The theory behind MX was that with so many shelters, the Soviets could not know which shelters contained the missiles. At the same time, the shelters could be uncovered, when necessary, to permit Moscow to verify with photography satellites that the United States was not hiding missiles beyond the limits contained in the SALT treaty. American strategic planners argued that the enormously expensive missile system was necessary because Minuteman ICBMs were becoming vulnerable in their underground, "hardened" sites.

American strategic deterrence has long rested on a "triad" of nuclear weapons—land-based missiles, nuclear missile-firing submarines, and the Strategic Air Command's bombers. But the theories of how these deadly weapons should be used have changed over the years. In August 1980, for example, President Carter signed Presidential Directive 59, which adopted a new nuclear strategy. The new strategy placed greater emphasis on destroying Soviet military forces and missiles, rather than cities.[64]

Arms Control and Disarmament

The arms race and the strategy of deterrence, however "logical," could lead to disaster. One obvious but elusive alternative is arms control and disarmament, the subject of intermittent negotiations between Moscow and Washington since the Second World War.

In recent years, "nuclear proliferation," the spread of atomic weapons to more countries, has complicated the picture. In 1963 the United States and the Soviet Union reached agreement on a nuclear test ban treaty. The treaty, banning tests in the air, under water, and in outer space—but not underground—was signed in Moscow and ratified by the United States Senate. More than one hundred nations signed the treaty, but two atomic powers—France and Communist China—refused to do so.

In 1968 the United Nations General Assembly voted approval of a draft treaty banning the spread of nuclear weapons to states not already possessing them. The United States, the Soviet Union, and sixty other nations signed, and the Senate ratified the Nonproliferation Treaty in March 1969. But Israel, India, and Japan, all potential nuclear powers at the time, did not sign, nor did France or Communist China.

In 1969 President Nixon announced that the United States was renouncing germ warfare and would no longer stockpile *biological* weapons. But he said the United States would continue to engage in "defensive research" in biological weapons. At that time the United States did not renounce *chemical* warfare, including the production of deadly nerve gases like GB, or Sarin, a tiny drop of which kills instantly. But in 1970 President Nixon submitted to the Senate the Geneva Protocol outlawing chemical and biological warfare among nations. The

[64] *Washington Post*, August 6, 1980, p. 10.

United States had signed the treaty in 1925, but the Senate had never ratified it. It finally did so in 1974. In 1972 the United States, the Soviet Union, and some seventy other nations signed an international agreement to outlaw biological weapons. This treaty, too, was ratified by the Senate in 1974. Thus, today, the United States is formally pledged not to use chemical or biological weapons.

In 1980, however, Congress approved $3 million to build a plant at Pine Bluffs, Arkansas, that could produce a new generation of deadly nerve gas weapons. Congress voted funds only for construction of the plant, not for production of nerve gas. Actual production would require a presidential directive. In that event, the plant could turn out binary nerve gas shells for the army — devices in which two harmless chemicals are kept separate inside a projectile but then mixed during flight to create the lethal gas.

Despite the various arms control agreements, the major problem, reduction and control of nuclear weapons by the two superpowers, has remained. Late in 1969 the United States and the Soviet Union opened SALT (Strategic Arms Limitation Talks) discussions. These negotiations were successfully completed in May 1972, when President Nixon flew to Moscow and signed two historic arms agreements. The first limited each country to two ABM sites, one to defend the capital and one to defend strategic missiles. (The United States ordered the construction of only the one ABM site, at Grand Forks, North Dakota, to protect ICBM silos; but as already noted, it was completed only to be shut down as obsolete.) The second agreement was an interim five-year accord to freeze land-based and submarine-based missiles at the level then in operation or under construction. Both countries agreed to conduct further talks to limit or reduce offensive arms; these SALT II talks began later in 1972.

In November 1974 President Ford met Soviet leader Leonid Brezhnev in Vladivostok and signed an agreement, to run through 1985, limiting each country to 2400 strategic nuclear weapons systems, excluding tactical aircraft and medium bombers. Since the Vladivostok accords left open many questions, the SALT II talks between Washington and Moscow continued.

In Vienna's Hofburg Palace during the summer of 1979, President Carter and Brezhnev signed leather-bound copies of the SALT II arms limitation agreement between the United States and the Soviet Union. SALT II, if ratified by the U.S. Senate, would set a ceiling of 2250 strategic missiles or bombers for both sides by the end of 1981. The agreement also limited the number of missiles that could have multiple warheads and the number of warheads per missile.

1974: President Ford and Soviet leader Leonid Brezhnev in Vladivostok

The Soviet Backfire bomber was not included in the treaty, although Moscow agreed to limit production of the aircraft.

Opponents of the treaty, who tended to be political conservatives, argued that it would diminish U.S. security and that it would be impossible for the United States to verify Soviet compliance. Even before the events in Iran and Afghanistan, SALT II faced a difficult fight in the Senate. In the wake of these foreign policy crises, President Carter early in 1980 asked Congress to postpone action on the treaty. During the election campaign Carter promised, if re-elected, to seek Senate approval of the treaty in 1981. Ronald Reagan called the pact flawed and said that he would seek to negotiate a "SALT III" treaty if elected. Although the Republicans won control of the Senate in 1980, President Reagan would still have to win the support of two-thirds of the Senate for any new SALT treaty.

President Eisenhower warning against the "military-industrial complex"

The Military-Industrial Complex

In his final speech to the nation, President Eisenhower warned against what he called "unwarranted influence" by the "military-industrial complex."[65] Eisenhower thus focused attention on the consequences for America of a vast military establishment linked to a huge arms industry. In the years after Eisenhower's 1961 warning, the concept of the "military-industrial complex" was expanded to encompass universities conducting defense research, scientists, laboratories, aerospace industry contractors, and research firms.

Government defense contracts totaled $63 billion in 1979. Entire communities in some areas were dependent on defense industries or military installations. In fiscal 1979 the General Dynamics Corporation received $3.5 billion in defense contracts from the government, heading the list of the hundred largest defense contractors in the United States.[66] The top ten defense contractors in America are shown in Table 14–1.

[65] Dwight D. Eisenhower, *The White House Years, Waging Peace 1956–1961* (New York: Doubleday, 1965), p. 616.
[66] U.S. Department of Defense, *100 Companies,* Fiscal Year 1979, p. 3.

Top Ten Defense Contractors in Fiscal 1979

Table 14–1

Rank	Company*	Amount of Defense Contracts (in billions)
1	General Dynamics Corp.	$3.5
2	McDonnell Douglas Corp.	3.2
3	United Technologies Corp.	2.6
4	General Electric Co.	2.0
5	Lockheed Corp.	1.8
6	Hughes Aircraft Co.	1.6
7	Boeing Co.	1.5
8	Grumman Corp.	1.4
9	Raytheon Co.	1.2
10	Tenneco, Inc.	1.1

* Includes subsidiaries.
Source: U.S. Department of Defense, *100 Companies,* Fiscal Year 1979, p. 3.

The B-1 bomber

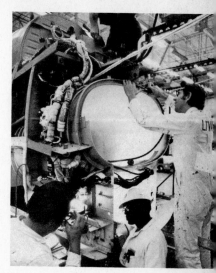

Defense spending fattens the congressional "pork barrel." Powerful individual legislators can, and do, obtain multimillion-dollar contracts for their states and districts. Another example of the interrelationships within the military-industrial complex is the fact that retired military officers are frequently hired by aerospace industry contractors.

The effect of the military-industrial complex is pervasive, and difficult to measure. But with many billions of dollars at stake, the scramble for contracts, the pressure on Congress and the Pentagon, and the political and economic rewards involved have given some Americans a substantial interest in an economy geared to defense production.

The debate over the controversial B-1 bomber provided an example of the enormous economic stakes in a new weapons system. For years the air force had pushed for production of the supersonic, missile-firing bomber, proposing to build 244 planes at a total cost of almost $22 billion. Each bomber would therefore cost about $88 million. In 1976 Congress, at President Ford's urging, approved funds to build three prototype models. As the Democratic presidential nominee, Jimmy Carter announced that he opposed the program as "wasteful." As President, therefore, Carter had to decide what to do about the B-1 bomber program. Six months after taking office, Carter announced that he had

Eisenhower's Warning: The Military-Industrial Complex

This conjunction of an immense military establishment and a large arms industry is new in the American experience. The total influence—economic, political, even spiritual—is felt in every city, every statehouse, every office of the federal government. We recognize the imperative need for this development. Yet we must not fail to comprehend its grave implications. Our toil, resources, and livelihood are all involved; so is the very structure of our society.

In the councils of government, we must guard against the acquisition of unwarranted influence, whether sought or unsought, by the military-industrial complex. The potential for the disastrous rise of misplaced power exists and will persist.

We must never let the weight of this combination endanger our liberties or democratic processes. We should take nothing for granted. Only an alert and knowledgeable citizenry can compel the proper meshing of the huge industrial and military machinery of defense with our peaceful methods and goals, so that security and liberty may prosper together.

—Dwight David Eisenhower
—Farewell Radio and Televison Address to the American People, January 17, 1961.

decided not to proceed with production of the B-1 bomber. He said he believed it was too expensive and unnecessary because of the development of the cruise missile. Carter had succeeded in halting a major weapons system, but he had also opened himself to criticism of his defense policies.

One result of the military-industrial complex is that the United States has become arms merchant to the world. About half the United States arms sales abroad represent direct sales by the Pentagon to other countries. In addition, the United States ships war materiel, ranging from rifles to jet planes, to other nations under a military assistance program that totaled $751 million in fiscal 1981.

The military-industrial complex has also had social and political effects. Demographically, it has been partly responsible for increased population in states such as California, Texas, and Florida with large defense or aerospace industries. This, in turn, has increased the political power of those states. Influential committee chairmen in Congress have channeled huge defense expenditures to their states, bringing economic benefits to those states and political benefits to the legislators.

America's World Role in the 1980s

Despite some progress in the field of arms control, in the 1980s the United States — and the world — still lived under the shadow of nuclear disaster. But in the aftermath of the war in Vietnam and the crises in Iran and Afghanistan, new currents were discernible in American foreign policy. Congress, in an effort to avoid more Vietnams, had restricted the power of the President to wage war without its approval. And in the 1980s, foreign policy issues were arising in new forms. They tended, perhaps even more than in the past, to involve economic issues — oil reserves and prices, the threat of oil embargoes, the multinational corporations, world trade, raw materials; the international environment — the ocean bed, hunger, and overpopulation; and nuclear proliferation. Yet the old tensions among nations continued to exist, in addition to these newer concerns.

The United States emerged from the Second World War as a major power, and it cannot wish away its power and global responsibility. But former Undersecretary of State George W. Ball has suggested that America can honestly redefine its foreign policy goals. Ball argued that while proclaiming itself in exag-

This Endangered Planet

The scale of modern technology is overflowing every political boundary. Whether it is a matter of radioactive fallout, carbon monoxide, or other poison effluents, multinational corporations, computer technology, satellite broadcasting, or air and space travel, we constantly witness a drive toward operations on a planetary scale. And yet most political behavior continues to be dominated by the territorial state. States compete with one another for power, wealth, and prestige, and jealously guard their sovereign prerogatives. This competitive pattern generates conflict, waste, and distrust. Huge amounts of resources are devoted to national defense, collective violence is persistent and pervasive, and wars occur at many points of the planet. . . . Governments at all levels have not demonstrated a great capacity to solve the most urgent problems of human society. Violence and misery persist in most national societies of the world.

— Richard A. Falk, *This Endangered Planet.*

Ronald Reagan and President José
Lopez Portillo of Mexico

gerated rhetoric as the champion of freedom, the United States in the two
decades after the Second World War was in reality pursuing the more modest
goal of maintaining a balance of power with the Soviet Union and mainland
China. "But while practicing balance-of-power politics, we felt compelled to
disavow it. . . . Thus we have gone steadily forward talking one game while
playing another."[67]

By the 1980s, despite the continuing tensions in the Middle East, rapid
changes were taking place in the relations among nations. American forces had
come back from Vietnam, an American President had opened the door to the
People's Republic of China, Congress was reasserting its voice in the conduct
of foreign policy, and the United States and the Soviet Union had moved part
of the way down the road to limiting nuclear armaments.

In the immediate aftermath of United States involvement in Southeast
Asia, the conviction grew among many Americans that the nation should exercise great caution in intervening in armed conflicts beyond its borders. Yet in
the wake of Afghanistan and the seizure of American hostages in Iran, a new
concern arose in the debate over foreign policy—whether the United States
was sufficiently strong militarily to protect its interests in the Persian Gulf and
elsewhere around the globe. At the same time, economic and other domestic
problems increased the pressures on the policymakers to weigh the legitimate
concerns of American national security against needs at home. Nevertheless,
America in the last quarter of the twentieth century was a major international
power, its relations with the rest of the world both broad-ranging and highly
complex. And the formation of American foreign policy continued to be a
major challenge to the nation's political leadership.

President Carter and
former Indian Prime
Minister Morarji Desai

[67] George W. Ball, "Foreign Policy Is Camouflaged," *Washington Post,* May 10, 1970, p. B2.

Perspective

Foreign policy is the sum of the goals, decisions,
and actions that govern a nation's relations with the
rest of the world. The preservation of national security is a basic consideration in the formulation of
foreign policy. Since the Second World War, there

have been two approaches in America to the question of national security. One view emphasizes
threats to the security of the United States posed by
the power of Communist or unfriendly nations. Another view holds that there can be no real security

for the United States without world peace and security for all people.

Under the Constitution, the President is Commander in Chief of the armed forces and chief diplomat. However, the power to conduct foreign and military affairs is divided between Congress and the President. While the Constitution gives the President power to appoint ambassadors and command the armed forces, Congress is given power to declare war, raise and support armies, and appropriate money for defense. The Senate also has the power to approve or disapprove treaties and ambassadorial nominations made by the President.

Between 1950 and 1970, five American Presidents committed United States troops to foreign soil without any declaration of war by Congress. In the late 1960s and early 1970s, as a result of the unpopular war in Vietnam, Congress began to try to restore some of the war power to the legislative branch. One result was the 1973 War Powers Resolution, designed to limit to sixty or ninety days the President's ability to commit American troops to combat without congressional authorization.

Today, the President has powerful tools available to him for the conduct of foreign policy, including his personal staff and that of the National Security Council, the State Department, the Pentagon, the CIA, and other agencies. The existence of this machinery does not mean, however, that the United States can always influence, let alone control, the course of international events. Nor has the United Nations been able to keep the peace on issues that divide the major world powers.

Since the Second World War, the United States has spent more than $1 trillion on national defense. In fiscal 1981 the Defense Department's budget request was $147 billion. Because of expanding technology, however, some weapons systems become obsolete even as they are deployed. And because of the nuclear threat, a strong argument can be made that, as spending for armaments has increased, national security has actually diminished. Moreover, the military-industrial complex has had far-reaching economic, social, and political effects on American society.

The National Security Act of 1947, as amended in 1949, unified the armed forces under the control of a single Secretary of Defense. Today, the Secretary of Defense is the Western world's biggest employer, in charge of more than one million civilians and more than two million members of the armed forces.

Since the 1950s, the United States has lived with the knowledge that it is less than thirty minutes away from nuclear disaster. Against this background, it has adopted a policy of strategic deterrence. The theory of deterrence involves deploying enough nuclear weapons so that an enemy would not attack the United States for fear of being attacked in retaliation. But the arms race and the strategy of deterrence, however "logical," could lead to a nuclear war.

One obvious but elusive alternative is arms control and disarmament. In 1963 the United States and the Soviet Union agreed to a treaty banning nuclear tests in the air, under water, and in outer space (but not underground). In 1972 the two nations signed the historic SALT arms limitation agreements. In 1974 American and Soviet leaders signed another arms control pact in Vladivostok. In 1970 Washington and Moscow signed the SALT II agreement to limit strategic weapons, but it had not been approved by the Senate when President Reagan took office two years later.

By the 1980s, despite some progress in the field of arms control, the United States — and the world — still lived under the shadow of a potential nuclear disaster. And foreign policy issues tended, perhaps even more than in the past, to involve economic issues, the international environment, and nuclear proliferation.

Suggested Reading

Almond, Gabriel A. *The American People and Foreign Policy*, 2nd edition (Greenwood, 1977). (Originally published in 1950.) An influential and valuable study of public opinion on foreign policy questions and how it relates to the formulation and conduct of American policy overseas.

Barnet, Richard J., and Müller, Ronald E. *Global Reach: The Power of the Multinational Corporations* (Simon and Schuster, 1975). A lively analysis of the role of the new multinational corporations whose enormous power transcends national borders. The authors argue that the corporations' drive to maximize profits threatens the

Government in Operation

environment, undermines the ability of governments to manage their own economies, and ignores the adverse social and economic effects of turning the world into a "global shopping center."

Bauer, Raymond A.; Pool, Ithiel de Sola; and Dexter, Lewis Anthony. *American Business and Public Policy: The Politics of Foreign Trade,* 2nd edition* (Aldine, 1972). A detailed analytical study of the varied factors affecting the development of American trade policy. Provides a useful assessment of the activities and influence of interest groups in this policy area.

Falk, Richard. *This Endangered Planet** (Random House, 1972). A thought-provoking analysis of the interrelated dangers facing the earth's inhabitants. The author warns that nuclear war, population pressures, depletion of natural resources, and environmental damage, all threaten the stability of international relations and future life on this planet.

Halberstam, David. *The Best and the Brightest** (Random House, 1972). A detailed account of the men and the policies that led the United States into the costly war in Vietnam. Written in a highly readable, anecdotal style by a leading journalist who was one of the first to challenge the optimistic official reports on the progress of the war.

Hersh, Seymour M. *My Lai 4: A Report on the Massacre and Its Aftermath** (Random House, 1970). An account of the massacre of South Vietnamese civilians by American troops in the village of My Lai 4, and of the subsequent effort by the army to cover up what happened. Seymour Hersh is a journalist who won the Pulitzer Prize for his reporting of the My Lai affair.

Kennedy, Robert F. *Thirteen Days** (Norton, 1971). (Originally published in 1969.) A short, fascinating account of the Cuban missile crisis of 1962, as it appeared to a key participant in the crucial decisions made by the Kennedy administration. Reflects the great tension during the world's first nuclear confrontation.

Kissinger, Henry. *White House Years* (Little, Brown, 1979). An important, personal account of foreign policy during the first four years of the Nixon administration. Kissinger, who served as assistant to the President for national security affairs from 1969 to 1973, covers the first SALT negotiations, the Vietnam peace talks, diplomacy in the Middle East, and the historic summit meetings in Peking and Moscow.

Rosenau, James N., ed. *Domestic Sources of Foreign Policy* (Free Press, 1967). A useful series of essays on the interrelations between domestic politics and American foreign policy, written by a number of specialists in the field.

Rostow, Eugene V. *Peace in the Balance: The Future of U.S. Foreign Policy* (Simon and Schuster, 1972). A spirited defense of American foreign policy—including American involvement in the Vietnam war—during President Johnson's administration. Includes an analysis and critique of major works by revisionist critics of American foreign policy during the late 1960s.

Schlesinger, Arthur M., Jr. *A Thousand Days** (Fawcett, 1977). (Originally published in 1965.) This account of the Kennedy Presidency, by an historian and former White House aide, contains useful insights into Kennedy's relations with the State Department and the administration's response to specific foreign policy crises.

Waltz, Kenneth N. *Foreign Policy and Democratic Politics: The American and British Experience* (Little, Brown, 1967). A thoughtful analysis of the problems faced by democratic states in making foreign policy. Contains useful comparative data on Great Britain and the United States.

* Available in paperback edition

559

PROMOTING
THE GENERAL WELFARE

When Ronald Reagan ran for President in 1980, he advocated turning back to the states certain federal programs, chief among them education and housing.

"We should transfer general federal education funding programs back to the state and local school districts, along with the tax resources to pay for them," the Republican candidate said. "In addition, we should abolish the Department of Education and end unnecessary federal intervention in education." Similarly, Reagan advocated turning over to states and localities those housing programs "which can be more effectively managed there."[1] And he opposed national health insurance.[2]

In contrast, President Carter hewed to the Democratic party's traditional position in support of the federal government's social programs. "In the next four years," he told labor leaders at a White House picnic, "we'll continue our urban policy, which has reversed the decline of many of our cities. And I want to enact new welfare reform proposals, as well as to expand our youth employment programs, and I stand ready with you to fully implement a national health insurance program for the people of the United States."[3]

[1] "Ronald Reagan on the Issues" (Arlington, Va.: Reagan-Bush Committee, 1980), pp. 3–4.
[2] Congressional Quarterly, *Weekly Report,* March 8, 1980, p. 659.
[3] "Labor Day Remarks at a White House Picnic for Representatives of Organized Labor, September 1, 1980," in *Weekly Compilation of Presidential Documents,* September 8, 1980 (Washington, D.C.: U.S. Government Printing Office, 1980), p. 1605.

Reagan's view was very different from that of Carter, and their clash over the best approach to social and economic issues was never far below the surface as the campaign wore on. The 1980 presidential contest raised basic questions about the role of government. Beneath the campaign rhetoric the questions were both moral and pragmatic: whether one segment of society should pay for the needs of another, and beyond that, whether even with the best of intentions, federal social programs can achieve their objectives.

By the 1980s, it was not only conservatives such as President Reagan who criticized government social welfare programs and "Big Government." Some liberals, too, wondered whether federal social welfare programs inevitably created so much regulation and so many controls that they failed to help the people they were designed to help.

The large social programs begun by President Franklin D. Roosevelt during the New Deal and expanded by John F. Kennedy and Lyndon B. Johnson were coming under increasing scrutiny. Among liberals and conservatives alike, there was growing debate over the effectiveness and cost of government solutions to social problems. One observer, Anthony King, pointed to what he called "the decline of the ideas of the New Deal as the principal organizing themes of American political life. The central idea of the New Deal was a simple one: that the federal government could, and should, solve the country's economic and social problems."[4]

Although views about the proper role of government vary greatly, the responsibility of the national government to make *social policy* was recognized at the beginning of the American nation, for the Constitution was established, among other purposes, to "promote the general welfare."

To take one example of the need for federal intervention, it would be very difficult, if not impossible, for people, or even for groups, to compel American industry to reduce pollution of the environment. But government, supported by public opinion and public demands, possesses the power to accomplish that task.

E. E. Schattschneider has suggested that "the struggle for power is largely a confrontation of two major power systems, government and business." The function of democracy, he argued, has been "to provide the public with a second power system, an alternative power system, which can be used to counterbalance the economic power."[5]

[4] Anthony King, "The American Polity in the Late 1970s: Building Coalitions in the Sand," in Anthony King, ed., *The New American Political System* (Washington, D.C.: American Enterprise Institute for Public Policy Research, 1978), p. 371.
[5] E. E. Schattschneider, *The Semisovereign People* (New York: Holt, Rinehart and Winston, 1960), pp. 118, 121.

To "promote the general welfare," the federal government fills several major roles. It is regulator, promoter, manager, and protector. It performs these roles in a wide variety of ways. It regulates business and labor. But it also promotes business and labor. It assists farmers. It runs such agencies as the Food and Drug Administration and the Tennessee Valley Authority. It tries to manage the economy through fiscal and monetary policies and, at times, wage and price controls. It acts, to some extent, as protector in consumer affairs, health, education, welfare, science, poverty, hunger, and the environment.

The government does not necessarily perform all of these roles well. The high food prices in the supermarket in the early 1980s, the losing battle against inflation, and the high level of unemployment might have led the average family to take a rather dim view of the ability of the government to manage the economy. As noted throughout this book, there are many areas in which American government and society have failed to live up to American expectations. So in discussing government in operation, a careful distinction must be made between the various roles of the government and its actual performance.

A government like that of the United States, which exercises responsibility for the welfare of its citizens in such areas as social security, housing, and education, is sometimes described as a "welfare state." The term is often used as one of criticism. But the responsibility of the federal government to make social policy has been well established in this century, particularly since the days of the New Deal. As one study suggested, "social welfare programs substantially improve the well-being of most beneficiaries and . . . retrenchment does have serious repercussions . . . there is no reason to abandon the aim of providing a minimal level of support for all who remain in need."[6]

Today, the terms of the argument usually concern the proper *extent* of government intervention in domestic problems, as well as *how* government should respond to national needs. Government services require government spending, and the size of government programs is directly related to the level of taxes. The level of government taxing and spending for welfare and social programs is a volatile *political* issue, directly affecting votes. That is why the question of how much the government should spend on such programs is often an important issue in presidential campaigns. Substantial numbers of Americans are persuaded that welfare "chiselers" are "getting something for nothing." But many poor people, and other citizens as well, believe government welfare programs are inadequate. Each group tends to vote for political leaders who appeal to its view. Where people stand on social welfare issues may be related to their economic, social, and political background. The homeowner in a comfortable suburb may have less sympathy for federal welfare-assistance programs than the mother of four children living in a rat-infested Harlem tenement.

How and to what extent should the federal government "promote the general welfare"? How well does it do so? How efficiently does government regulate corporate power on behalf of the consumer? How does government attempt to manage the economy? How well has it performed in the field of social welfare, in eliminating poverty and hunger, in coping with rising medical costs and educational needs, in protecting the environment?

[6] Sar A. Levitan and Robert Taggart, *The Promise of Greatness* (Cambridge, Mass.: Harvard University Press, 1976), pp. 283, 293.

Government as Regulator and Promoter

The Constitution, as Justice Oliver Wendell Holmes, Jr., once wrote, "is not intended to embody a particular economic theory."[7] But the Supreme Court, which interprets the meaning of the Constitution, has often embodied the particular economic theory of its time. For half a century, from the late 1880s until 1937, during Franklin Roosevelt's New Deal, the Court generally interpreted the Constitution in such a way as to prevent government from regulating industry. It adopted the prevailing laissez-faire philosophy, which held that government should intervene as little as possible in economic affairs.

During the late nineteenth century, economic power was concentrated in the "trusts" and in the hands of the "robber barons." But a rising tide of populism created public demands that led to the passage of state and federal laws regulating industry. Nevertheless, the Supreme Court, as was noted in Chapter 13, interpreted the Fourteenth Amendment to protect business from social regulation by the states and by Congress.

Justice Holmes made the comment quoted at the beginning of this section in his famous dissent in the *Lochner* case. In that 1905 decision the majority of the Supreme Court struck down a New York State law that had limited bakery employment to "sixty hours in any one week" and "ten hours in any one day." Today it might seem incredible that the Supreme Court would permit a bakery owner to work his employees more than sixty hours a week. But in 1905 the Supreme Court refused to approve the use of the power of the state to regulate private property—in this case a bakery.

The Great Depression and the New Deal brought about a reversal of Supreme Court thinking. Since 1937 the Court has upheld laws policing business; and the right of government to regulate wages, hours, and working conditions of employees is now firmly established. Indeed, some of the regulations of the Occupational Safety and Health Administration (OSHA) have been so detailed and stringent that they have brought a storm of protests from business and industry.

Regulating Business: Antitrust Policy. In 1890 Congress passed the Sherman Antitrust Act, which was designed to encourage competition in business and prevent the growth of monopolies. The Supreme Court severely limited the scope of the act, however, by ruling that it was up to the states to control industrial monopolies. Then in 1914 Congress passed the Clayton Act, which sought to put teeth into the federal antitrust law by defining illegal business practices and by providing the remedy of court injunctions and giving the Federal Trade Commission power to issue cease and desist orders. The same measure exempted labor unions from antitrust actions.

Subsequent legislation has strengthened the antitrust laws, and both the antitrust division of the Justice Department and the Federal Trade Commission have blocked many large corporate mergers. In a famous case in 1957, the Supreme Court, under the Clayton Act, forced du Pont to divest itself of 23 percent of the stock of General Motors.[8] But the degree of enforcement of the antitrust laws varies with the attitudes of the administration in power in Washington.

[7] *Lochner* v. *New York*, 198 U.S. 45 (1905).
[8] *United States* v. *E. I. du Pont de Nemours and Co.*, 353 U.S. 586 (1957).

In 1971 the Nixon administration agreed to an antitrust settlement favorable to International Telephone and Telegraph, the giant multinational conglomerate. ITT was forced to give up ownership of two smaller companies but was permitted to retain the huge Hartford Fire Insurance Company. Early in 1972, however, a memo was leaked to the press suggesting that ITT had been allowed to keep the Hartford company in return for a pledge of $400,000 to the Republican National Convention that year.[9] Attorney General Richard Kleindienst denied that anyone in the White House had influenced his handling of the antitrust case. But he later admitted that President Nixon had given him instructions to drop the government's court appeal in the case. Kleindienst pleaded guilty to a charge of failing to give accurate testimony to the Senate and was given a small fine and a thirty-day suspended jail sentence.

Although government regulation has had some success at blocking *monopoly,* control of a market by a single company, it has not been able to prevent *oligopoly,* the concentration of economic power in the hands of a relatively few large companies. Economist John Kenneth Galbraith has noted that "in the characteristic market of the industrial system, there are only a handful of sellers."[10]

The 500 largest corporations in the United States control more than two-thirds of all manufacturing assets. In 1979 the revenues of Exxon were almost seven times those of the state of Ohio. The ten largest corporations in the United States are shown in Table 15-1.

Despite government regulation, American corporations are increasing in both size and diversity. Nothing illustrates the trend better than the rise in recent years of giant *conglomerates;* multi-interest, and often multinational, corporations may, under one corporate roof, manufacture products ranging from missiles to baby bottles.

[9] *New York Times,* March 12, 1972, Section 4, p. 2.
[10] John Kenneth Galbraith, *The New Industrial State* (Boston: Houghton Mifflin, 1967), p. 179.

The Ten Largest Industrial Corporations in the United States, 1979

Table 15-1

Rank (by sales volume)	Company	Employees	Sales (in billions)	Assets (in billions)
1	Exxon	169,096	$79.1	$49.5
2	General Motors	835,000	$66.3	$32.2
3	Mobil	213,500	$44.7	$27.5
4	Ford Motor	494,579	$43.5	$23.5
5	Texaco	65,814	$38.3	$23.0
6	Standard Oil of California	39,676	$29.9	$18.1
7	Gulf Oil	57,600	$23.9	$17.3
8	International Business Machines	337,119	$22.9	$24.5
9	General Electric	405,000	$22.5	$16.6
10	Standard Oil of Indiana	52,282	$18.6	$17.1

Source: *Fortune* Magazine, May 5, 1980, p. 276.

Because conglomerates are formed by mergers of companies in unrelated fields, they have long been considered exempt from most antitrust regulation. And conglomerate mergers are increasing rapidly. Between 1951 and 1977, there were 1669 such mergers, involving combined assets of $84 billion. The government contested only 2 percent of these cases.[11] Congress has periodically weighed various proposals to ban or restrict mergers, at least among giant conglomerates.

The ordinary consumer cannot keep up with the complexities of corporate ownership in what Galbraith has called "the new industrial state." As ownership of industry becomes more and more impersonal and remote, it is increasingly difficult for the private citizen to fix responsibility for corporate actions. In some instances, individuals have turned to the courtroom.

In 1978 the Ford Motor Company recalled 1.5 million Pintos to improve the safety of their fuel tanks. That same year, three young women died after their Pinto caught on fire when hit by a van. The owners of the car destroyed in the accident had not received a recall notice. In 1980 the state of Indiana prosecuted Ford for reckless homicide in the deaths. The case was brought under a state law making corporations liable for the safety of their products. Ford spent a million dollars on its defense and was acquitted.

Ford Pinto in which three young women died in 1978: the auto company was acquitted.

But the issue of corporate responsibility extends beyond the individual to the larger question of the responsibility of corporations toward society as a whole. The consumer movement, public concern over pollution by industry, and similar pressures have led a number of corporations to take steps to improve their public image in the area of corporate responsibility. Several large companies, for example, have participated in efforts to solve urban ills through such organizations as the Urban Coalition. In the wake of well-publicized pressure by minority stockholders for the appointment of directors to serve "in the public interest," the General Motors Corporation beginning in 1970 designated six directors to serve on a Public Policy Committee to monitor "all phases" of GM operations that affect the community at large. Ralph Nader's crusade for auto safety brought federal legislation and prodded the automobile industry to produce safer cars and to recall those with suspected defects. Increasing awareness of the issue of corporate responsibility has led in recent years to the emergence of *public interest law firms* composed of young law school graduates. Instead of joining traditional, old-line law firms representing large corporations, they have offered their skills to protect consumers, minorities, and the poor.

The Regulatory Agencies. Although the Justice Department has responsibility for fostering competition through the antitrust laws, much of the day-to-day contact between government and industry is carried on through federal regulatory agencies, including the six major commissions discussed in Chapter 11. Thus, the Securities and Exchange Commission (SEC) has responsibility for regulating the stock market; the Federal Communications Commission (FCC), the broadcast industry; the Interstate Commerce Commission (ICC), the transportation industry; the Federal Energy Regulatory Commission (FERC), power companies and pipelines; the Civil Aeronautics Board (CAB), airlines (until 1985 when the CAB is scheduled to go out of business); and the Federal

[11] Lawrence Mosher, "Conglomerate Mergers—A Threat or a Blessing?" *National Journal,* March 24, 1979, pp. 480–84.

Trade Commission (FTC), industry as a whole. Other federal agencies, such as the Food and Drug Administration and the Consumer Product Safety Commission, have played an important role in regulating business.

As Chapter 11 pointed out, many of these commissions have to varying degrees become captives of their client industries. Nor has regulation always been successful. A case in point is the railroad industry, which has long asserted that its passenger operations lose money while its freight operations make money. The great increase in air and highway travel in the past few decades was a major factor in reducing railroad revenues. Poor management by some railroads was certainly another factor. But some would argue that the government also bears part of the responsibility for the deterioration of the railroads. The ICC, although responsible for regulating the railroads in the public interest, permitted passenger service to decline to a point approaching extinction. Americans visiting Japan or Europe will find better rail service in cleaner, more modern trains than is the case in many parts of their own country. On the other hand, the railroads have complained that government regulation forced the railways to continue service on unwanted passenger routes and in other ways made it difficult for them to compete with the airlines.

In 1970 Congress passed legislation to establish a federally subsidized national rail network of passenger trains. The law created a government-sponsored corporation to run many of the nation's intercity passenger trains (but not commuter lines). The National Railroad Passenger Corporation, better known as Amtrak, lost money. But the corporation expanded its Metroliner service between Washington, New York, and New Haven, providing comfortable high-speed train service at frequent intervals. Because the Metroliner was well run and competitive with the airlines in the heavily traveled northeast corridor, the Metroliner initially made a profit, even though Amtrak as a whole did not. Congress later enacted legislation increasing Amtrak's authority, independence, and budget. Amtrak's future was controversial, and the likely subject of more battles in Congress.

In 1973 Congress established a new federal agency to reorganize the Penn Central and the six other bankrupt lines; it also provided for Conrail, a new, federally financed corporation to run the reorganized railroads. But the fact that the government found itself in the railroad business was at least partially a result of the failure of previous government policies. In 1980, as part of a general trend toward deregulation, Congress passed the Staggers Rail Act, which substantially deregulated the nation's railroads, giving them more freedom to set rates and drop unwanted routes.

Aiding Business. Related to the concept of government as regulator is that of government as promoter. Government promotes commerce by providing services and direct and indirect subsidies to producers and farmers. Many business firms and farmers benefit from government aid.

Appropriations for highways are indirect subsidies to truckers, bus lines, and automobile manufacturers and users. The federal government pays the airlines and the railroads to carry the mail; it helps support the merchant marine through subsidies to shipbuilders and ship operators; and it finances airport construction.

In the "alphabet soup" of government agencies in Washington there are several service agencies for industry—the Commerce Department and the Small

Business Administration (SBA), for example—as well as the Agriculture Department, which serves farmers.

At times the government has even extended direct aid to large corporations in financial trouble. In 1971, for example, Congress approved $250 million in federal loan guarantees to the Lockheed Corporation, a major manufacturer of aircraft for the Pentagon. Then, in 1979, Congress authorized a massive $3.5 billion aid package, including $1.5 billion in federal loan guarantees, for the ailing Chrysler Corporation, the nation's third largest automobile manufacturer. Chrysler had miscalculated the extent of consumer demand for small cars that would use less gasoline and started building them too late; by 1979 the company's losses had mounted to $1.1 billion for the year. Congress acted, and President Carter signed the bill, because of growing concern over the impact on the economy if the government permitted the huge auto manufacturer to go under.

In addition to subsidies and services, the federal government assists industry through its *trade and tariff* policies. In the United States a tariff is a federal tax on imports. A high tariff discourages other nations from sending goods to United States markets and is therefore "protective" of American manufacturers. But a tariff wall can work two ways; other countries have retaliated by raising their tariffs on imports from the United States. Pressure from American industry seeking foreign markets for its products, and from consumers wanting lower prices, has resulted in a gradual reduction of United States tariff barriers since the 1930s. In 1947 the United States and twenty-two other nations signed the General Agreement on Tariffs and Trade (GATT), which provided a formal framework for international tariff reductions. The Trade Expansion Act of 1962 gave President Kennedy broad tariff-cutting authority, and more trade barriers fell during the 1960s after the Kennedy round of trade talks in Geneva.

During the same period, however, industry in Japan and the growth of the Common Market in Western Europe threatened the competitive advantage previously enjoyed at home by American business. Protectionist sentiment succeeded in placing many restrictions on tariff reductions—for example, by imposing quotas on certain categories of imports. The President's authority to reduce tariffs lapsed in 1967, and for several years Congress, responding to protectionist pressures, did not move to renew the tariff-making authority of the executive branch. But in 1974 this presidential authority was restored by Congress so that the United States could participate in a new round of world trade negotiations. These discussions, which were held in Tokyo, culminated in another broad tariff agreement signed by major trading nations in Geneva in 1979. Later that year, Congress passed a new trade bill, carrying out changes agreed to in Geneva and extending the President's tariff-making authority until January of 1988.

Aiding Agriculture. Since the New Deal administration of Franklin D. Roosevelt, the federal government has attempted to stabilize farm prices. It has done so through a three-pronged program of price supports, acreage controls, and buying and storing of surplus crops. Under the price support program, when farm prices fall below certain minimums, known as "target prices," the government steps in and pays the farmer the difference. The government has also required farmers to hold acreage out of production. And over the years the government has also bought up huge farm surpluses. In the early 1970s, however, market

Chrysler chairman
Lee Iacocca with federally guaranteed check

567

Farmers demonstrate in Washington for higher prices.

prices for agricultural products were so high that for several years the government did not have to intervene. One reason for the high price levels was the 1972 wheat deal with the Soviet Union, in which the Russians bought 19 million tons of grain from the United States for more than $1 billion.

Early in 1980, however, after the Soviet invasion of Afghanistan, President Carter announced an embargo on the 17 million tons of grain, mostly feed corn, that American firms had planned to sell to the Soviet Union. Although the administration budgeted almost $3 billion to support grain prices to make up for the embargo, the move dismayed most farmers in the Corn Belt in a presidential election year. Two weeks before the election, the United States signed an agreement to sell up to 32 million tons of grain to China over four years. Both the embargo and the timing of the sale to Peking were reminders that the government's actions as promoter and regulator often have political implications.

Government and Labor

As in the case of business, labor is both regulated and assisted by the federal government. Today organized labor wields great economic and political power in the United States. This was not always the case; the history of the labor movement in America is one of long struggle, intermittent violence, and only gradual recognition.

The industrialization of the nineteenth century brought American laborers job opportunities in factories but scant bargaining power with employers. As a result they worked long hours, at low wages, and under hazardous working conditions. In 1881 Samuel Gompers, a London-born cigarmaker, founded what became the American Federation of Labor (AFL). The Federation fought for "bread-and-butter" improvements—the eight-hour day, higher pay, fringe benefits, and restrictions on child labor. The AFL was largely a federation of craft unions—groups of skilled workers organized by trades: construction, printing, mining, clothing manufacturing, and others.

The Great Depression, which threw millions of people out of work, and the liberal policies of the New Deal created a favorable climate for the labor movement. In the mid-1930s a group of labor leaders within the AFL began to organize industrial unions in the mass production industries, thus bringing unskilled workers into a labor movement dominated until then by craft unions. Led by John L. Lewis, head of the United Mine Workers, the dissidents formed a new labor organization that became known in 1938 as the Congress of Industrial Organizations (CIO). The CIO rapidly won recognition from the automotive, steel, rubber, and other industries. In 1955 the AFL merged with the CIO. By 1980 there were more than 21 million union members in the United States, of which almost 14 million belonged to unions in the AFL-CIO.

In its early years the labor movement was unable to gain protection in the courts, so in the 1920s it turned to Congress for help. As early as 1926, the Railway Labor Act stated labor's right to organize and established a National Mediation Board to assist in settling rail strikes. The Norris-LaGuardia Act of 1932 sharply restricted the power of the courts to issue injunctions in labor disputes. Up to that time employers were frequently able to break strikes by obtaining court injunctions against the unions. The National Labor Relations Act of 1935 was labor's great milestone. Sponsored by Senator Robert F. Wagner, Democrat, of New York, it established labor's right to collective bargaining and barred employers from setting up "company unions" (unions controlled by the employer) or discriminating against any worker for union activity or membership. The act also established the National Labor Relations Board (NLRB), an independent regulatory agency that supervises union elections and determines unfair labor practices. The Fair Labor Standards Act of 1938 established a minimum wage for American workers, a maximum forty-hour workweek, and time-and-a-half for overtime. It also outlawed child labor. Over the years, the minimum wage law has been amended by Congress and its coverage expanded. By 1981 the minimum wage was $3.35 per hour, and the law covered 60 million workers.

The power gained by labor during the New Deal inevitably brought a political reaction. The National Labor Relations Act had placed restrictions on employers but none on unions. In 1947 Congress passed the Taft-Hartley Act, which sought to shift some of labor's newly won power back to management. The act prohibited the "closed shop," under which only union members may be hired, but it did permit the "union shop," under which any person may be hired provided he or she joins the union within a specified time. Under Section 14B of the Taft-Hartley Act, twenty states (ten in the South) passed state "right to work" legislation to outlaw the union shop. The act also defined and prohibited unfair labor practices by unions; expanded the membership of the NLRB, an agency that employers had considered too favorable to labor; barred labor unions from making political contributions; and outlawed strikes by government employees. Finally, the law provided that in strikes creating a national emergency, the President can seek a court injunction against a union during an eighty-day "cooling off period."

Big labor unions continued to prosper and grow, despite the restrictions of the Taft-Hartley Act. And the legislation had one result that its Republican sponsors had not intended; because passage of the law demonstrated to labor that legislation aimed at unions could win support in Congress, it had the effect of increasing the political activity of labor unions. Often, although not always, that labor support went to Democrats.

In the late 1950s a Senate committee held a series of hearings to investigate labor racketeering. Two successive Teamsters' Union presidents, Dave Beck and James R. Hoffa, eventually went to jail after the disclosures, and the AFL-CIO expelled the Teamsters. The televised hearings brought national recognition to the Senate committee's chief counsel, Robert F. Kennedy. It also led to demands for reform legislation.

The Labor Reform Act of 1959 (Landrum-Griffin Act) grew out of the hearings. The act (1) required unions to file elaborate financial reports, constitutions, and bylaws with the Secretary of Labor; (2) granted union members the right to elect officers by secret ballot; (3) barred ex-convicts from holding union office; and (4) tightened Taft-Hartley provisions against secondary boycotts, organizational picketing, and other labor practices that employers felt gave unions an unfair advantage.

Despite provisions for injunctions that sometimes avert or delay major strikes, the public is often unprotected against walkouts that may inconvenience millions of people—airline, rail, and garbage strikes, for example. Compulsory arbitration to settle major labor disputes has not won wide acceptance, and the problem of disruptive strikes in an industrial society remains.

Because unions have concentrated on bread-and-butter gains through collective bargaining, organized labor has made great economic progress in the United States. The extent of labor's *political* power is less clear. Unlike many industrial nations, the United States has never had a major, enduring "labor party." Rather than run its own candidates for political office, labor has usually worked through the two-party system. Since the New Deal era, labor has usually supported the national Democratic party, but it carefully watches the records of members of Congress in both parties and supports those whom it considers friendly to labor.

Although labor support is vital to many political candidates, the concept of a deliverable "labor vote" is dubious since union members are also Republicans and Democrats as well as members of other groups. In the 1972 presidential campaign, for example, the organization's executive council failed to support the Democratic nominee and instead voted to remain neutral in the presidential race. That November, union members voted 54 percent for Nixon to 46 percent for McGovern.[12] But in 1976, after the worst recession since the Great Depression of the 1930s, organized labor returned to the Democratic camp and supported Jimmy Carter, as most unions did again in 1980.

The Department of Labor, which achieved cabinet status in 1913, administers and enforces laws relating to the welfare of wage earners in the United States. Its responsibilities include manpower and job training programs, administering the wages and hours law, and enforcing the safety and health standards for workers set by various federal laws.

Managing the Economy

In the fall of 1980 the United States was in the grip of serious inflation. Steadily rising consumer prices and high unemployment threatened the nation's economic health. In the election campaign, President Carter and Ronald Reagan

[12] Gallup poll, *Washington Post*, December 14, 1972, p. A4.

argued over what kind of tax cuts or other government action was needed to improve the economy.

At the very start of the campaign, President Carter unveiled an "economic blueprint for the 80s," calling for $27.6 billion in tax cuts, an expanded jobs program, extension of unemployment benefits, and creation of an Economic Revitalization Board to promote cooperation between government and the private sector.

Carter's plan called for tax credits to encourage industry to invest more in new plants and equipment. Like many other political leaders and economists, Carter was concerned with the declining productivity of American industry and labor. In effect, he endorsed the concept of "reindustrialization," a term that had come to mean a form of partnership between government and industry to increase production.

Ronald Reagan, the Republican candidate, criticized Carter's plan and continued to press for his own solution, an immediate 10 percent tax cut. This was to be the first stage in a 30 percent cut in personal income taxes over three years, a plan endorsed by Reagan earlier and first proposed by two Republican members of Congress, Representative Jack Kemp of New York and Senator William Roth of Delaware. Recession, unemployment, and inflation kept the economic issue central to the 1980 campaign.

Few Americans expressed concern that a nation priding itself on a system of "free enterprise" should look to the government in Washington to provide a solution to the country's economic problems. Today most people expect the federal government to exercise a major responsibility for the health, stability, and growth of the national economy.

The federal government took a major role in economic affairs with the coming of Franklin D. Roosevelt's New Deal. When Roosevelt was inaugurated in 1933, at the height of the Great Depression, 13 million people — 25 percent of the labor force — were unemployed. And unemployment remained high until the rapid recovery of the economy during the Second World War. National growth with full employment became a major goal in the postwar world.

The Employment Act of 1946 spelled out in law the responsibility of the federal government for the economy and required it "to promote maximum employment, production, and purchasing power." The law directed the President to submit an annual economic report to Congress; it created a three-man Council of Economic Advisers to assist the President; and it established a Joint Economic Committee, made up of members of the House and Senate, to study the President's report and the economy.

In making economic policy, the President has a number of tools and advisers available to him — the Council of Economic Advisers, the Office of Management and Budget, the Secretary of the Treasury, the Department of Labor, and the economists and experts who staff these government agencies. He can invoke his powers to delay major strikes under the Taft-Hartley Act. Various Presidents have had power to negotiate and alter U.S. tariffs. Through his appointment power, the President can influence the makeup of the Federal Reserve Board. And, of course, the President is free to consult outside economists and experts in the private sector, including the universities. The President can also impose economic controls or voluntary guidelines on prices and wages. He may call upon all of these resources in shaping the fiscal and monetary policies of the federal government. (See pp. 573–77.)

Yet Presidents in recent years have been remarkably unsuccessful in con-

Drawing by Sack for the
Fort Wayne Journal-Gazette

trolling inflation, recession, or high unemployment. In part, this may be due to world economic conditions—factors that are beyond any President's control. But it may also stem from the nature of the American economic system, in which there are limits on the government's ability to manage the economy.

The United States operates predominantly under an economic system of free enterprise, or capitalism. Under capitalism, there is private ownership of the means of production. In such a system, in its purest form, there is little room for government; people own private property, either directly or as shareholders; and as consumers they participate in a free marketplace that responds to the laws of supply and demand. In practice, however, the United States has a *mixed,* or modified, free enterprise system in which both private industry and government play important roles.

The individual's economic freedom is sharply limited by federal, state, and local economic policies. To begin with, the higher the federal, state, and local taxes a person pays, the less money he or she will have to spend on consumer goods. If government fails to prevent a recession, the person may be out of work. If government fails to prevent inflation, the dollar buys less; and retired people living on pensions and savings may find their fixed incomes inadequate.

In general, Democrats have favored a larger role for government in regulating the welfare of society and the individual, and Republicans generally have favored less government intervention. But the basic responsibility of government for economic policy is now well established.

Economic Controls

During the 1980 presidential primaries, President Carter's economic policies were severely criticized by Senator Edward M. Kennedy of Massachusetts, his opponent for the Democratic nomination. To combat inflation, Kennedy called for a freeze on wages and prices followed by a period of mandatory economic controls. Carter rejected mandatory wage and price controls, which he said caused "distortions" in the economy. He continued to rely on the voluntary wage and price guidelines set in October 1978 by his Council on Wage and Price Stability, a unit dismantled by his successor, President Reagan.

Most Presidents have been reluctant to take the drastic step of imposing compulsory controls on the economy, although President Nixon did so. In 1971 Nixon announced a program of sweeping new economic controls. His economic policy amounted to a sharp reversal of traditional Republican philosophy and of his own previous statements.

Nixon announced a ninety-day freeze of all wages, prices, rents, and salaries. The freeze was Phase One of what became a long-range, four-phase administration program of economic controls. Nixon was able to impose such controls by executive order alone because Congress granted the President the authority in the Economic Stabilization Act of 1970. There was precedent for Nixon's actions; economic controls were imposed during the First World War, the Second World War, and the Korean war. There was also some peacetime precedent, since for a time controls were kept on prices and rents during the Truman administration.

The economic stabilization measures imposed by President Nixon were extraordinary rules issued to meet an inflationary crisis. Usually, the federal government has attempted to influence the total shape of the economy through two sets of tools: *fiscal policy* and *monetary policy.* The fiscal tools of the government are primarily spending and taxation. The monetary tools are control of the supply of money and control of the supply of credit through the Federal Reserve System.

Since the New Deal, many government economists have been influenced by the thinking of the British economist John Maynard Keynes. Keynes argued that when people did not consume and invest enough to maintain national income at full employment levels, government must step in and regulate the economy through *fiscal policy*—by cutting taxes or increasing spending in the public sector, or both. Keynesian economists and their modern successors place major emphasis on fiscal policy to guide the economy, although they recognize the role of monetary policy.

Fiscal Policy

The Budget. The federal budget reflects an allocation of resources by the national government. But the budget is also an important tool of fiscal policy. During a time of inflation, the President may cut spending and ask for higher taxes to cool down the economy. Or in a recession he may propose a bigger budget, more public works spending, and lower taxes. By planning a budget surplus or deficit, the federal government attempts to pump money into or out of the economy, to stimulate it or slow it down.

But the President must share with Congress his fiscal control over the economy. Only Congress can vote to spend federal funds. It does so in a three-step process. First, it passes *budget resolutions* to set overall spending targets. Second, it passes *authorizations* to spend federal money. Third, it passes *appropriations* bills to pay for the spending it has authorized. Under this system legislative committees deal with the substance of programs and, by authorizing funds, set forth their view of what *ought* to be spent. Within that framework, the appropriations committees decide what *actually* may be spent. The idea behind this system is that appropriations committees have an overview of expenditures by Congress—which legislative or "program" committees do not have—and are therefore in a better position to allocate funds. Since an authorization without an appropriation is meaningless, the system places great power in the hands of the House and Senate appropriations committees and subcommittees. Congress may increase or cut the President's appropriations requests. The Congressional Budget and Impoundment Act of 1974 established the budget committees in the House and Senate and created a new framework for Congress to deal with the President's budget. (See also Chapter 12.)

During the Nixon administration the issue of *impoundment* emerged as an especially controversial source of tension between the President and the Congress regarding fiscal policy. The President refused to spend billions appropriated by Congress. But the administration lost all but about five of some thirty federal court cases challenging the President's right to withhold appropriated funds. In enacting budget reform legislation in 1974, Congress included provisions to deal with impoundment. Under the law, the President can propose to cut a program by means of a permanent impoundment, but unless Congress rescinds the appropriation within 45 days, the money must be spent. Congress need take no action, in other words, to force the funds to be used. If, however, the President merely postpones spending, either house can pass a resolution to force the release of the funds. Once money is appropriated, Congress has its own accountant to check up on how it is spent—the Comptroller General of the United States, who heads the General Accounting Office (GAO).

Taxes. "The Congress shall have Power to lay and collect Taxes." And Congress, as every taxpayer knows, exercises this constitutional authority. Under the budget for fiscal 1981 the federal government planned to spend $615.8 billion, all but a small fraction of it to be raised from taxes. Of every dollar the government took in during fiscal 1981, 46 cents came from individual income taxes, 12 cents from corporation income taxes, 31 cents from social insurance taxes, 7 cents from excise taxes (taxes on commodities), and 4 cents from other revenue sources.[13] Estimated tax receipts for 1981 appear in Table 15-2.

The Federal Budget: Where the Money Comes From

Table 15–2

Source	1981 Estimate (in billions)	Percent
Individual income taxes	$274.4	46%
Corporation income taxes	71.6	12
Social insurance taxes and contributions	187.4	31
Excise taxes	40.2	7
All other receipts	26.4	4
Total budget receipts:	$600.0	100%

Source: Adapted from *The Budget of the United States Government, Fiscal Year 1981*, pp. 60, 61.

As these figures show, individual income taxes are the federal government's largest single source of revenue. The federal income tax is graduated, on the theory that persons with higher incomes should be taxed at a higher rate. But

[13] Adapted from estimates for fiscal 1981, in *The Budget of the United States Government, Fiscal Year 1981*, pp. 60, 61.

"*Now let's be absolutely certain I have this all straight. Your taxes, regardless of circumstances, are not—I repeat not—to be used for waging war, manufacturing munitions, financing espionage, or for any other activity designed to subvert the legitimate democratic aspirations of peoples at home or abroad. Rather, these moneys will be spent to reduce poverty, advance education, fight pollution, and, in short, to do whatever is necessary to improve the human lot and make this planet a viable habitat for mankind once again.*"

Drawing by Mulligan
© 1973 The New Yorker Magazine, Inc.

taxpayers at all levels grumble about the tax squeeze; not many people enjoy paying their taxes or consider them low.

Until this century the Constitution required the federal government to collect income taxes in proportion to state population. The Sixteenth Amendment, ratified in 1913, permitted the government to levy a general income tax. Since that time, however, various interest groups have lobbied Congress and won special tax advantages. Until 1975 the major oil producers had their "depletion allowance." Business executives enjoy liberal "expense account" deductions. People who sell property or stock pay a lower "capital gains" tax than most ordinary wage earners pay on income. There are many other "loopholes" in the tax law. A rich person can afford to hire a high-priced tax attorney to find them. People in high income brackets may set up foundations, invest in tax-free municipal bonds or various types of "tax shelters," or take business losses that enable them to avoid high taxes.

By the end of the 1960s growing public awareness of inequalities in the federal tax laws led to talk of "a taxpayers' revolt." Congress responded by passing the Tax Reform Act of 1969, which, among its many provisions, raised personal exemptions and social security benefits, exempted several million low-income taxpayers from paying any tax at all, established a minimum income tax on some kinds of formerly tax-free income, and tightened the tax laws applying to foundations. The Tax Reform Act's provision for a minimum income tax meant that more wealthy individuals had to pay taxes, but a few millionaires still managed to pay no income tax at all.[14]

In 1975 Congress, seeking to aid a lagging economy, passed the largest tax-cut bill in history, totaling $22.8 billion. Then in 1976 Congress enacted an omnibus tax revision act containing the most significant changes in the tax laws since the Tax Reform Act of 1969. The new law restricted tax shelters for the wealthy to some extent, made it more difficult to use the lower capital gains tax, and increased the minimum income tax. In 1978 Congress passed an $18.7 billion tax cut.

The politics of taxation results in intense pressures on Congress from interest groups when changes in the structure of the tax laws are under consideration. And Congress and the President often fight political battles over how tax policy should be used as a fiscal tool to slow down or stimulate the economy. The use of fiscal policy to control the economy depends, in theory, on delicate timing; but Congress tends to move very slowly in passing tax legislation.

Borrowing. When the federal government spends more than it earns, it has to borrow. The national debt stood at $16.2 billion in 1930, or almost 18 percent of the nation's Gross National Product (GNP), the total national output of goods and services; by fiscal 1981 the national debt was $939 billion, or 34 percent of the GNP. The government borrows by selling federal securities to individuals, corporations, and other institutions. In 1917 Congress passed a statutory debt limit, or ceiling, on government borrowing, but the limit has been revised upward many times. Borrowing costs money; in fiscal 1981 the government expected to spend $67.2 billion, almost 11 percent of the federal budget, on interest payments.

"The Gross National Product . . . Its favorite drink is oil . . ."

Source: Drawing by Jeff MacNelly from *A Political Bestiary* by Eugene J. McCarthy and James J. Kilpatrick, McGraw-Hill Book Company, 1979

[14] *New York Times*, March 27, 1972, p. 23; see also Philip M. Stern, *The Rape of the Taxpayer* (New York: Random House, 1973), p. 14.

Government also attempts to regulate the economy by *monetary policy*—controlling the supply of money and the cost and availability of credit. It does this through the operations of the Federal Reserve System. "The Fed," as the system is often called, was established in 1913. Prior to that time, the United States had no way in which to expand and contract the money supply according to the needs of the economy. To provide such an elastic system, Congress created the Federal Reserve.

The Fed is headed by the Board of Governors of the Federal Reserve System. Although the board's seven members are appointed by the President with the approval of the Senate, they serve overlapping fourteen-year terms and are largely independent of both Congress and the White House. The chairman, appointed by the President for a term of four years, can, and sometimes does, oppose the policies of the administration. The Fed is the central banking system of the United States; it operates through twelve Federal Reserve Banks and twenty-five branches across the nation. All national banks and about 10 percent of state banks are members of the system.

When individuals or corporations need money, they normally borrow from a bank. When banks need money, they may borrow from the Federal Reserve System. The Federal Reserve is, therefore, a banker's bank. When it lends to the banks, it can, in effect, create new money.

Through its control of the flow of money and credit within the United States, the Fed attempts to pump more money into the economy when a recession threatens. In a time of rising prices and excessive spending, the Fed normally tries to tighten the supply of money and credit so that people will have less to spend. As one chairman remarked, the Fed tries "to lean against the prevailing economic winds." It does so chiefly in four ways:

1. Open Market Operations. Banks lend money to people in relation to the amount of reserves the banks have on deposit with the Federal Reserve. When the Fed sells government bonds on the open market, the effect is to reduce bank reserves and tighten credit; banks then have less money to lend to people. Or, the Federal Reserve can buy government securities and expand credit.
2. The Fed can raise or lower the "rediscount rate" that it charges member banks for loans. This affects interest rates in the economy generally.
3. It can raise or lower the size of the reserves that member banks must keep in the Federal Reserve banks against their deposits and thus tighten or expand credit.
4. It can raise or lower the "margin requirements" for persons buying securities. The margin requirement defines how much money people can borrow to purchase stocks.

In recent years, the "Chicago school" of economists, led by Milton Friedman of the University of Chicago, has suggested that the money supply—the quantity of money in circulation—is the key to government regulation of the economy. Friedman has argued that interest rates, which are one aspect of monetary policy, and fiscal policy—taxes and spending—have little impact or importance. He also has argued that the money supply should be increased at a constant rate. Friedman received the Nobel Prize in 1976. His views have won increasing, but by no means universal, acceptance in the United States and abroad.

Most United States economists believe that a stock market crash and a depression as severe as that which began in 1929 are unlikely to happen again because there are more built-in economic stabilizers today. But there is wide disagreement among economists and politicians over the best way to maintain price stability, full employment, and economic growth. Some measures are politically safer to take than others; for example, it is easier for government to spend money on public works to combat recession than it is to impose wage-price controls to fight inflation. Whatever steps an administration takes carry great political risks if they fail. Prosperity and "bread-and-butter" concerns are often key election issues, as they were in 1980, and both the President and Congress try to steer a safe course between the twin reefs of recession and inflation.

Government as Protector

During the major televised debate of the 1980 presidential campaign, President Carter charged that Ronald Reagan had proposed making social security "voluntary." Reagan said he had suggested certain voluntary features "many years ago," but he denied it was his position as a candidate. The exchange was of intense personal interest to millions of viewers who were drawing social security retirement benefits.

In the past four decades the national government has enacted multibillion-dollar social welfare programs—ranging from school breakfasts for the young to social security for the aged. By the late 1970s, however, a degree of disillusionment had set in among liberals and conservatives alike about the ability of government to solve social problems with government programs. Even so, while many Americans might criticize specific programs—the welfare system, for example—by and large people expect the government to act as protector of the general welfare. Proposing to tamper with or modify established social programs that enjoy broad public support carries a high political risk. In the rest of this chapter, we shall explore some of the important aspects of government as protector.

Today, most Americans would agree that government has a responsibility to protect ordinary consumers from the perils of the marketplace. Two decades ago few citizens were aware of consumer issues. That the picture changed dramatically was, to a considerable extent, the work of a single crusader for consumer protection, attorney Ralph Nader.

Government and the Consumer

In his book, *Unsafe at Any Speed,* published in 1965, Nader charged that the automobile industry bore partial responsibility for many highway accidents and deaths by making cars that emphasized style over safety.[15] Nader was then investigated by private detectives hired by attorneys for the General Motors Corporation. A Senate subcommittee disclosed that the private detectives had put Nader under surveillance and had even checked into his sex life. As a result of the Senate investigation, James M. Roche, the president of GM, found it prudent to apologize publicly to Nader at a committee hearing.[16]

[15] Ralph Nader, *Unsafe at Any Speed* (New York: Grossman, 1965).
[16] In 1970, four years after the Senate hearings, GM paid Nader $425,000 in an out-of-court settlement of his invasion of privacy suit. See *New York Times,* August 14, 1970, p. 1.

In 1965, Ralph Nader, then a thirty-one-year-old Connecticut attorney, criticized the safety of American automobiles, particularly the General Motors Corvair, in his book *Unsafe at Any Speed.* General Motors, through an attorney in Washington, hired a "private eye" to investigate Nader. Senate investigators found that the New York detective agency, Vincent Gillen Associates, Inc., had issued the following instructions to its "gumshoes":

[Nader] apparently is a freelance writer and attorney. Recently he published a book *Unsafe at Any Speed,* highly critical of the automotive industry's interest in safety. Since then our clients' client apparently made some cursory inquiries into Nader to ascertain his expertise, his interest, his background, his backers, etc. They have found out relatively little about him, and that little is detailed below. Our job is to check his life and current activities to determine "what makes him tick," such as his real interest in safety, his supporters, if any, his politics, his marital status, his friends, his women, boys, etc., drinking, dope, jobs—in fact all facets of his life. This may entail surveillance which will be undertaken only upon the OK of Vince Gillen as transmitted by him to the personnel of Vincent Gillen Associates, Inc.

—Hearings before the Subcommittee on Executive Reorganization, Committee on Government Operations, United States Senate, *Federal Role in Traffic Safety,* March 22, 1966.

The congressional investigation of GM's flagrant action against a private citizen made Nader a national figure overnight. In the years that followed, he played a vital role in the passage of five major federal consumer laws. GM removed the Corvair from production after Nader charged that the car was hazardous to drive under certain conditions. Today, major auto companies routinely recall cars from consumers to correct safety defects. Ralph Nader's crusades found a response among the public, the press, Congress, and the executive branch.

The basic demand of the consumer movement is that government step in to protect buyers from hazardous products, shoddy merchandise, mislabeling, fraudulent sales techniques, consumer credit abuses, and other deceptive or dangerous practices. "Consumerism" holds that when business will not police itself, government must act.

The woman who must return her coffeepot to the repair shop three times before it is fixed properly; the child playing with an inflammable toy; the ghetto resident talked into buying an overpriced bedroom suite for "only $599"; the family injured in an auto crash because of defective tires—all are victims of consumer abuses. Many products that Americans buy seem to have "built-in" obsolescence—that is, they are designed to wear out after a certain amount of time.

Consumer frauds victimize the most those who can afford it the least. Various studies have shown that "the poor pay more." Residents of urban ghettos often buy low quality merchandise at high prices. Why? One reason is that neighborhood merchants extend "easy" credit terms to poor people who may not be able to buy on credit in major department stores. And, as David Caplovitz has noted in his study of poverty areas in Manhattan, "neighborhood merchants . . . compensate for extending credit to poor risks by high markups."[17] The result is that poor families often end up paying higher prices for appliances such as tele-

[17] David Caplovitz, *The Poor Pay More* (New York: Free Press of Glencoe, 1963), p. 85.

"Granted the public has a right to know what's in a hot dog, but does the public really *want* to know what's in a hot dog?"

Drawing by Richter
© 1978 The New Yorker Magazine, Inc.

vision sets, phonographs, and washing machines than do more affluent families.[18] To deal with customers who cannot keep up the payments, the merchant can use the weapons of repossession and salary garnishment, backed by the power of the law.

During the 1960s and 1970s, legislation was passed to deal with consumer problems, and limited machinery to deal with those problems was established within the executive branch. Presidents Kennedy, Johnson, Nixon, Ford, and Carter all appointed staff assistants for consumer affairs. Several federal agencies are involved in consumer matters, but the principal responsibility is in the hands of the Federal Trade Commission. Consumer issues are also monitored by the Office of Consumer Affairs, a unit of the Department of Health and Human Services. In 1976 Congress considered but did not pass legislation to create a single Consumer Protection Agency in the executive branch to act as an advocate and protector of consumers. Two years later, another bill to establish a separate consumer agency was rejected in the House. But Congress had already acted in a number of important consumer areas.

[18] *Ibid.,* p. 84.

Accelerating Problems of the Consumer

The gas gauge was nearing "empty" so the University of Arizona co-ed pulled off the freeway into the nearest service station. All went routinely enough until suddenly she noticed white smoke billowing out from under the open hood. The attendant, standing over it with a properly concerned expression, informed her that the car needed "a new accelerator in its generator" and that if she tried to drive out of the station without having it fixed, the car would be ruined.

One tank of gas and $119 later the student was back on the freeway, heading for the university campus. To confirm her growing suspicion, she took the car to her regular mechanic for a recheck. His verdict: Potassium powder had been used to simulate smoke, and she had been "conned" (a generator does not have an accelerator).

The case is not as exceptional as one might think. Despite stepped-up efforts by law-enforcement agencies and more widespread and vehement complaining on the part of car owners, deceptive auto-repair practices persist as a major consumer problem.

—*Christian Science Monitor,* January 29, 1970.

The principal consumer laws include:

1. *Auto safety* (1966). One law required manufacturers to meet federal standards for automobile and tire safety, and another required each state to establish federally approved highway safety programs or lose 10 percent of federal highway construction funds.
2. *Truth-in-packaging* (1966). To help shoppers make price comparisons, a law was passed requiring manufacturers to label their products more clearly. But it did not require standard package sizes, which would have aided shoppers in threading their way through the supermarket jungle of "jumbo," "family," and "large economy" sizes.
3. *Meat and poultry inspection* (1967 and 1968). Two laws were designed to tighten consumer protection against poor quality meat and poultry. Prior to this legislation these products were subject to federal inspection when shipped between states, but products consumed within a state were subject only to state inspection. And, seven states had *no* meat inspection at all.
4. *Truth-in-lending* (1968). This legislation requires merchants and lenders to provide full, honest, and understandable information about credit terms. For example, a customer who agrees to pay "only 3 percent per month" must now be told that the *annual* interest rate is actually 36 percent.
5. *Product safety* (1972). The law established an independent five-member Consumer Product Safety Commission. The commission was given broad power to act against hazardous products that caused an estimated 30 million consumer injuries each year.

In almost every case, industry has lobbied against consumer bills and has often succeeded in weakening the final versions. There is some danger, therefore, that the passage of consumer legislation will create the appearance of government regulation without the reality. Consumer advocates in the 1980s were increasingly focusing their attention on how consumer laws are put into effect and on their real impact once enacted. At the same time, the power of the consumer movement had diminished as Congress and the electorate became preoccupied with inflation and related issues.

The General Welfare

In fiscal 1981 about 36 million Americans—retired or disabled workers and their dependents—received about $135 billion in social security payments. Another 10.3 million people received public assistance (welfare) payments of almost $10.7 billion, of which the federal government paid about half (with state and local governments paying the rest). Another $6.9 billion a year in federal benefits went to 4.2 million persons under the Supplemental Security Income program. In addition, during 1981, it was estimated that 11.8 million jobless workers would collect almost $19 billion in unemployment insurance.[19]

Yet, prior to 1935 these programs did not exist. The hardships of old age, ill health, poverty, unemployment, blindness, or disability were problems for individuals, their families, private charity, states, and local communities.

The Depression of the 1930s changed all that. Millions lost their jobs, and a blight of hunger and poverty descended on the land. "Brother, can you spare a dime?" was a popular song of 1932. America realized that individuals needed help from the national government to maintain their income in hard times. In the

[19] Estimates in *The Budget of the United States Government, Fiscal Year 1981*, pp. 261, 263, 268; and data provided by the U.S. Department of Labor.

midst of the Great Depression, Franklin D. Roosevelt proposed, and Congress passed, the landmark Social Security Act of 1935. Although to some Americans it seemed a revolutionary step at the time, the United States was the last major industrial nation in the world to adopt a general system of social security.

There are two kinds of social welfare programs in operation, both designed to guarantee personal economic security to individuals. One is called *social insurance.* The social security program is, in effect, a compulsory national insurance program, in theory self-financed by taxes on employers and employees. The other kind of program, *public assistance,* has no pay-as-you-go features; it simply distributes public funds to people who are poor. (Recipients are usually said to be on "relief" or on "welfare.") The distinction is important, because each approach has significant political consequences.

Social insurance is widely accepted because it is "earned." People assume they have a "right" to retirement income after a lifetime of work. But "welfare" programs do not enjoy the same acceptance by the public. Many Americans who receive welfare payments, and many others who do not, believe society has a responsibility to care for those who are less fortunate. However, as Gilbert Steiner points out, some Americans:

> resent supporting those who can't make their own way. . . . The idea of "toughening up" is forever popular. Toughening up, it is argued, will drive the cheaters out, the slackers to work, the unwed mothers into chastity; and it will save money. It is this clash between the ideas of public aid as a right and public aid as a matter of sufferance, to be granted with suspicion, with strings, and with restraints, that is reflected in public policy debates and political action.[20]

Social Security. The Social Security Act of 1935 and its later amendments provide for *both* social insurance and public assistance programs. The insurance aspects fall into four categories: old-age and survivors insurance, disability insurance, Medicare, and unemployment insurance.

When people talk about receiving "social security," they generally mean the monthly cash payments received by retired, older people. A man or woman who reaches the age of sixty-two may draw social security payments if he or she has worked enough years to qualify—about seven years in 1980, increasing gradually to ten years by 1991.[21] The payments depend on a person's average earnings over a period of years. In 1980 the *average* monthly benefit for a retired worker was $330. (Examples of social security payments are shown in Table 15-3.)

As originally passed, social security provided only retirement benefits. In 1939 the program was expanded to provide payments to dependents and survivors of workers covered by the system. And in 1956 it was expanded to include disabled workers. By fiscal 1981, 35.9 million retired or disabled workers and their dependents and survivors were receiving $135 billion in social security benefits.

Over the years, Congress has extended social security coverage to virtually all types of workers outside the federal government. The system is financed by a

---

[20] Gilbert Y. Steiner, *Social Insecurity: The Politics of Welfare* (Chicago: Rand McNally, 1966), pp. 7–8.

[21] Men and women who have worked long enough to qualify may receive social security at a higher rate beginning at age sixty-five.

Social security: a program in difficulty

Examples of Monthly Cash Payments Under Social Security

Table 15–3

	Average Yearly Earnings Since 1950	
	$4000	$10,000
Retired worker at 65	$325.60	$587.70*
Retired worker at 62	260.50	470.20
Wife or husband at 65	162.80	293.90
Wife or husband at 62	122.10	220.50
Wife under 65 and one child in her care	230.80	440.80
Maximum family payment	556.40	1028.40

* The actual maximum benefit for a sixty-five-year-old retired worker in 1980 was $572 a month; the higher payment shown is the amount that would be reached by workers retiring in future years, when average annual earnings covered by social security will be higher.

Source: "Your Social Security," U.S. Department of Health and Human Services, Social Security Administration (Washington, D.C.: U.S. Government Printing Office, 1980), p. 19. Data as of 1980.

social security tax levied equally on employers and employees. Self-employed persons also must pay a social security tax. In 1981 employers and employees each paid 6.65 percent of an employee's income up to a ceiling of $29,700 (earnings beyond this amount were not taxed for social security purposes); self-employed persons paid 8.1 percent. Inflation hits hardest at persons living on fixed incomes, such as retired workers who depend on social security payments. Because of this, Congress has linked social security benefits to the cost of living; increases in the amounts paid out under the program are now automatic.

The expansion of the social security system, coupled with continuing inflation, has created enormous financial strain on the system. To put it simply, social security has been running out of money. Social security taxes go into trust funds so that the program can be self-sustaining. But payments to recipients have been outpacing the growth of the system's reserves. Part of the problem is demographic: compared to when the program started there are, proportionately, fewer people of working age to pay taxes and more people of retirement age to draw benefits, and this trend can be expected to continue. Despite steep social security tax increases passed by Congress in 1977, the program is still in difficulty.

Medicare. In 1965 Congress added health insurance for persons sixty-five and over to the social security program.[22] Medicare helps to pay hospital bills, and for those who choose to pay an extra amount ($8.70 a month in 1980), it also pays part of doctor bills. In 1981, of the estimated 26.7 million people on Medicare, all but 200,000 had also enrolled in the voluntary insurance program for doctor bills.

The program cost $37 billion in 1981 and will undoubtedly cost more in the future, even if it is merged into a general program of national health insurance. Some of the proposed bills to create a national health insurance system would keep Medicare; others would absorb Medicare into a general plan covering all persons.

[22] In 1980 Medicare also covered 3 million disabled persons *under* age sixty-five.

Unemployment Insurance. The social security benefits discussed above are paid directly by the federal government. But the Social Security Act of 1935 also virtually forced the *states* to set up unemployment insurance programs to pay benefits to people out of work. The program is financed by federal and state taxes on employers (and on employees in three states). Every state has an unemployment insurance program, but the size of benefits and the amount of time they are granted vary greatly. In 1979, 87 million workers were covered but 16 million were not. Most states paid unemployment benefits for twenty-six weeks (up to thirty-nine weeks in areas with high unemployment), but a weekly payment of $90—the national average—was scarcely enough to support a jobless worker with a family.

Unemployment line, Springfield, Mass.

Welfare: Politics and Programs. The Social Security Act of 1935 created three public assistance, or "welfare" programs: old-age assistance, aid to the blind, and the largest program, known later as Aid to Families with Dependent Children (AFDC). In 1950 a fourth program was added—aid to the permanently and totally disabled. Then in 1974 the Supplemental Security Income program (SSI) was established to provide uniform federal benefits to needy aged, blind, or disabled persons.

The federal government provides most of the money for the welfare system in the form of grants to the states. In some states, local governments also assume part of the cost. State and local welfare agencies run the programs.

The welfare system has come under attack on several grounds. First, it does not cover all the poor. Moreover, because the states control the programs, benefits vary sharply. Southern states pay lower welfare benefits than do the big industrial states of the North.

For many years, more than one-third of the states had some kind of rule barring welfare payments to families in which there was a "man in the house" who was not married to the mother. Welfare recipients objected strongly to this attempt by the states to regulate moral behavior. The United States Supreme Court has ruled that states may no longer restrict welfare payments to dependent children just because there is a "man in the house," unless it can be shown that he is actually contributing some of his income to the support of the children.[23]

The welfare system has frequently been criticized on the grounds that it degrades those whom it is attempting to help. Welfare agencies regularly investi-

[23]*King* v. *Smith*, 392 U.S. 309 (1968); *Lewis* v. *Martin*, 397 U.S. 552 (1970).

Welfare: Waiting for the 90 Cents

Ain't no lazy people on Welfare. . . . But every time you want something extra from them, it's a whole nuisance. Like carfare. Sometimes I got to spend ninety cents for carfare for me and the kids to go off to Bellevue, because, as I told you, you can't leave them alone if you got to go there for some reason. And when I come back from Bellevue clinic, I got to rush over here to 28th Street for that carfare money or else I'm going to run short on food. Well, even so, they don't just give you your money like that. Sometimes they want proof. Sometimes they say they will owe it to you. You got to be careful about the ones who say that. I learned you got to insist right then and there you want that carfare or else you don't get it. So you just got to sit there and wait for the man until he gives it to you. You think they care? Sometimes I spend half my life waiting somewhere for ninety cents.

—Barbara Dugan, quoted in Richard M. Elman, *The Poorhouse State.*

gate those on relief, and poor people often regard welfare workers as unwelcome detectives. Behind all this is the public suspicion that many welfare recipients are "loafers" and "chiselers."

The welfare program that emerged from the New Deal has been criticized on the basis that it "creates a class of dependent persons and then sustains them in their dependency."[24] During the 1960s an alternative approach evolved, sometimes called a "guaranteed annual income," or a "negative income tax." This concept, if put into action, would guarantee everyone a minimum income, making the existing welfare system unnecessary.

In modified form this approach was adopted by President Nixon when he submitted his welfare reforms to Congress in 1969. Nixon's program, called the Family Assistance Plan, would have provided poor families with a federal cash payment. If a father or mother worked, the welfare payment would be gradually reduced. But up to a cutoff point, the recipients could keep both their earnings and some welfare money, thus providing an incentive to work. Congress did not approve Nixon's plan, however.

The concept of a guaranteed annual income remained under consideration in and out of Congress. And in 1972, although rejecting the Family Assistance Plan, Congress established the first guaranteed minimum income program, which began in 1974. This Supplemental Security Income program (SSI) replaced a web of state and local programs to provide uniform federal payments to the needy aged, blind, or disabled. SSI supplemented but did not replace social security payments to such persons.

In 1977 President Carter proposed a sweeping welfare reform package that included 1.4 million public service jobs for those who need work, but which also required persons receiving benefits to take jobs if they had no children at home under the age of fourteen. The Carter plan also included expanded tax credits for the poor. Congress did not enact his proposals.

[24] Daniel P. Moynihan, "One Step We Must Take," *Saturday Review of Literature,* May 23, 1970, p. 22.

Shirley Chisholm on Aiding Minorities

I hope I have been wrong about Ronald Reagan. I hope I have been totally wrong about his new conservative economic policies. And I hope that the president . . . is right when he says that his ideas will finally, and permanently, cure the plague of structural unemployment afflicting millions of able-bodied minority men and women in America.

The Reagan approach runs contrary to the Democratic Party doctrines I have advocated during my entire career. . . . The reality remains, however, that years of federal efforts and billions of federal dollars have not brought prosperity and full employment to minority communities. . . .

The best-intentioned CETA programs disappointed those of us who created and funded them, and frustrated those who expected meaningful employment skills and well-paying jobs. On thou-

sands of city street corners, unemployed CETA graduates mingle with thousands of other jobless young men and women. Their training turned out to be irrelevant or inadequate for local employers who advertise in vain for the craftsmen they need.

I freely admit that Democratic Party solutions have been less than successful in bringing the structurally unemployed into this country's economic mainstream. The major challenge to the Reagan administration is to demonstrate quickly and conclusively that its proposals will succeed where others have failed.

. . . for now, I will not stand in their way. If President Reagan succeeds in really putting all of America back to work, he will have my sincere admiration and support.

—Representative Shirley Chisholm, Democrat, of New York, "Giving Reagan a Chance," *Washington Post,* December 12, 1980.

"This administration," President Lyndon B. Johnson declared in his first State of the Union message, "today here and now declares unconditional war on poverty in America."[25]

When President Johnson spoke these words in January 1964, many Americans might have wondered what he was talking about. Through the picture window of split-level suburbia, the poor could not be seen. Yet they were there, millions of people living in poverty in the mountains of Appalachia and the slums of the great cities. When the black urban ghettos exploded in flames during the second half of the decade, the poor became more visible.

The federal antipoverty program resulted in part from the publication in 1962 of Michael Harrington's *The Other America,* a book that described in forceful language the extent of poverty in the United States and had a substantial impact among segments of the public and within the federal government. The poor, he noted, were "across the tracks," out of view of more comfortable Americans.[26] The poor lived, in Ben Bagdikian's words, "in the midst of plenty," occupying "a world inside our society in which the American dream is dying." Yet, poor people "are not made so differently from their fellow Americans."[27]

Who are the poor?

The federal government answers the question in terms of how many people have incomes below a certain "poverty" level. But to some extent poverty is a relative term; people may feel poor if they have a good deal less than most other people have. And, with affluence no farther away than the commercials shown on television, the poor in American society are constantly reminded of their poverty.

In statistical terms the Census Bureau estimated that in 1978 there were 24.5 million poor people in the United States. The government defined poverty in that year as an income of $6662 or less for a nonfarm family of four. The profile of the poor included these facts:

1. There were more than twice as many poor white people as poor blacks — 16.3 million as compared with 7.6 million. But a higher percentage of black Americans were poor — almost one out of every three blacks as opposed to one out of every eleven whites.
2. About 11 percent of the nation's population was poor.[28]

In response to President Johnson's "war on poverty," Congress in 1964 passed legislation creating the Office of Economic Opportunity (OEO). Community action programs became a highly controversial aspect of the antipoverty program. They were designed to give federal grants to a wide range of programs organized and administered by local public or private groups "with maximum feasible participation" of the poor. While successful in some areas, the community action programs led in some other cases to what one critic, Daniel P. Moynihan, has termed a "maximum feasible misunderstanding."[29]

The political struggle that erupted over the poverty program in the mid-1960s had its roots in the early 1960s, when a group of government officials and academics joined to propose the idea of community action. They argued that

Job retraining program in North Carolina, part of President Johnson's War on Poverty program

[25] *1964 Congressional Quarterly Almanac,* p. 862.
[26] Michael Harrington, *The Other America* (New York: Macmillan, 1962), p. 4.
[27] Ben H. Bagdikian, *In the Midst of Plenty* (Boston: Beacon Press, 1964), pp. 6–7.
[28] U.S. Bureau of the Census, *Current Population Reports,* Money Income and Poverty Status of Families and Persons in the United States: 1978, Series P–60, No. 120, November 1979, pp. 1, 4.
[29] Daniel P. Moynihan, *Maximum Feasible Misunderstanding: Community Action in the War on Poverty* (New York: Free Press, 1969).

through community action the poor could be organized *politically* to express their grievances to the "power structure." But in some cases the strategy led to widely publicized confrontations between the poor and established political leaders.

Soon big-city mayors and other critics of OEO charged that the federal government was financing rebellion, funding community action groups to march on City Hall and challenge the entrenched power of local political organizations. Such conflict was inevitable. For, as James L. Sundquist has suggested, "can a national government maintain, for long, a program that sets minorities against majorities in communities throughout the land? Clearly it cannot, even if it should. The affluent majority will not be persuaded that tranquility is not also an objective of society—and one superior, if a choice must be made, to the eradication of poverty itself."[30] Perhaps one of the problems as well was that President Johnson, by promising, in effect, to end poverty in the United States, had created public expectations that exceeded the ability of that particular program to achieve its goal.

President Nixon did not look with enthusiasm on the poverty program that had been started by his predecessor. Soon after he took office in 1969 he moved to break up OEO and disperse its functions to other government units. In 1971, by executive order, Nixon created ACTION, an umbrella agency for various volunteer programs. ACTION took over VISTA, a part of the poverty program that trained people to work in poor areas. It also acquired the Peace Corps and a number of other volunteer programs, including some that used the talents of older Americans. Early in 1975, what was left of OEO was shifted to a new Community Services Administration, an independent agency. CSA funded the 878 community action programs still in operation in 1980.

The Politics of Hunger

Figures on the extent of hunger in America vary, but a little more than a decade ago it was estimated that as many as 15 million people had incomes so low that they could not afford proper nutrition.[31] By 1980 that picture had been substantially improved by a massive federal food stamp program. Hunger has been reduced, although not eliminated. America was largely unaware of the hunger problem until a Senate subcommittee toured the Mississippi delta in April 1967. Citizen groups, the CBS television documentary *Hunger in America,* and hearings conducted by Senator George McGovern spurred congressional and public response to the problem over the next few years.

Although pressures to alleviate hunger in America gained momentum in the late 1960s, influential Southern chairmen of key congressional committees succeeded in blocking or restricting proposals for increased federal spending on food programs.

In 1961 President Kennedy, by executive order, initiated the food stamp program to increase the buying power of low-income families. Congress established a food stamp system by law in 1964. Most recipients of food stamps have incomes well below the national poverty level. Under the program, a poor family could purchase stamps worth much more than their actual cost in dollars when presented in a store for food; the federal government reimbursed the grocer for

---

[30] James L. Sundquist, *Politics and Policy* (Washington, D.C.: The Brookings Institution, 1968), p. 152.
[31] Nick Kotz, *Let Them Eat Promises* (Englewood Cliffs, N.J.: Prentice-Hall, 1969), p. 23.

the full cost of the food. But critics charged that the stamps were still too expensive for many poor people to buy. In 1977 Congress eliminated the requirement that recipients of food stamps—technically known as Food Coupons—pay a portion of their value. But in 1981, as part of a plan for wide-ranging cuts in social programs, President Reagan asked Congress to reduce spending for food stamps.

From its modest beginnings, the food stamp program rapidly spiraled into one of the federal government's largest welfare programs. For the fiscal year 1981, $9.6 billion was budgeted for food stamps for more than 20 million low-income people each month.[32] In addition to food stamps, the federal government distributed surplus food crops to the poor through local welfare agencies, and it financed a school lunch program and a special milk program for children.

In fiscal 1981 the federal government planned to spend about $62 billion, or more than 10 percent of the national budget, for health services.[33] The funds were allocated for research, training and education, hospital construction, Medicare and Medicaid, and prevention of disease.

Health

The *Medicare* program, discussed earlier in the chapter, provides hospital and medical services to older persons through the social security program. *Medicaid,* also established in 1965, is a public assistance program to help pay hospital, doctor, and medical bills for persons with low incomes. It is financed through general federal, state, and local taxes. Under a formula, Washington pays from 50 to 78 percent of the cost of state programs established under Medicaid. In 1981 it was estimated that Medicaid would pay out $15.9 billion in federal dollars to aid 23 million people. Annual federal and state Medicaid costs had reached a combined total of more than $22 billion.[34]

While federal programs have assisted the aged and the needy, they have not helped the majority of Americans to obtain adequate health care at a reason-

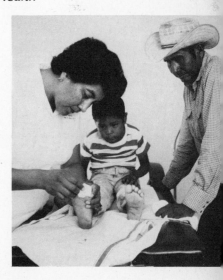

[32] *The Budget of the United States Government, Fiscal Year 1981,* p. 271.
[33] *Ibid.,* p. 79.
[34] *Ibid.,* p. 245.

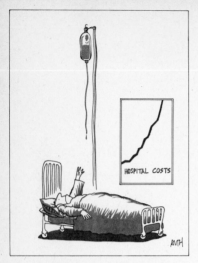

able cost. The cost of hospital rooms, physicians' care, and other health services has increased at an alarming rate. Major illness could easily wipe out the financial resources of the average American family, and private insurance plans often fail to cover the cost of prolonged hospitalization or medical treatment. In 1979 Americans spent more than $212 billion on health care.

As a result of skyrocketing health costs, by 1980 pressure for a general federal program of health insurance was growing. The proposal had a long history. In 1935 a report to President Franklin D. Roosevelt that formed the basis for the social security program also recommended compulsory national health insurance. President Truman recommended such a plan, financed through social security, in 1945. In 1970 Senator Edward M. Kennedy and others introduced legislation to establish national health insurance financed through social security taxes and general revenues. By 1976, opinion polls indicated that the public favored comprehensive national health insurance by a heavy majority.[35] Carter sent a health plan to Congress in 1979. The plan, combining public and private coverage, would have allowed people to purchase individual or group health insurance, but no family would have paid more than $2500 for health care in any one year. In addition, most poor people would have been given all necessary medical care at public expense. Carter estimated the plan would cost $18 billion a year. Congress did not pass his program.

Much of the argument over national health insurance centered on the question of who would pay for such a multibillion-dollar program—for an estimated 15 million operations and 1 billion prescriptions a year. In general, liberals wanted the government to finance health insurance, while their opponents favored placing most of the cost on employers and workers, except for those too poor to pay for health care.

Education

At the start of the 1979–1980 school year, almost 58 million students were enrolled in the nation's schools and colleges. Of the total, 9.9 million were enrolled in colleges, 15.1 million in high schools, 27.8 million in elementary schools, and 4.8 million in kindergarten and nursery schools.[36]

In fiscal 1981 the federal government budgeted $14.4 billion for various kinds of direct aid to education. (See Table 15-4.) This aid was channeled in two ways: to *educational institutions* and to *individuals*.

As far back as 1862, Congress had passed the Morrill Act to establish "land-grant" colleges. And millions of veterans of the Second World War went to college under the federally financed GI Bill of Rights. In 1958, after the Soviet Union launched its Sputnik earth satellite, Congress enacted the National Defense Education Act to provide loans for college students in the fields of science, engineering, mathematics, and foreign languages. In 1963 Congress began appropriating funds for the construction of college classrooms.

Not until 1965, however, did Congress pass a law providing for general federal aid to education. In that year, the high-water mark of President Johnson's

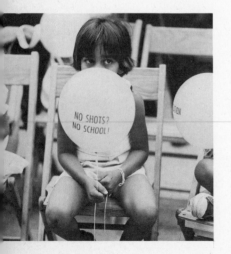

[35] For example, in answer to the question, "Do you favor a comprehensive national health bill?" 61 percent of those surveyed answered "yes," and 23 percent "no." The poll was conducted in August 1976 by the research firm of Yankelovich, Skelly and White, Inc. Source: *Time*, September 6, 1976, p. 12.

[36] U.S. Bureau of the Census, *Current Population Reports*, "School Enrollment—Social and Economic Characteristics of Students: October 1979," Series P–20, No. 355, August 1980, p. 3.

Federal Outlays for Education, 1964–1981
(in billions of dollars)

Table 15–4

	1964	1968	1972	1976	1979	1981 (est.)
Elementary and secondary education	$0.6	$3.2	$ 5.4	$4.7	$ 5.9	$ 6.9
Higher education	1.7	4.4	4.9	2.6	4.5	5.2
Adult and other education	.8	1.2	1.6	.8	2.0	2.3
Total	$3.1	$8.8	$11.9	$8.1	$12.4	$14.4

Source: Adapted from *Budget of the United States Government,* for fiscal years 1964–1981.

"Great Society," it enacted the Elementary and Secondary Education Act and the Higher Education Act. Until 1965 the church-state controversy had blocked passage of a general aid to education bill. (See Chapter 4, p. 112.) The Elementary and Secondary Education Act bypassed that dispute by providing aid to children on the basis of economic need in both public and private (including religious-affiliated) schools. Although most counties in the nation were eligible, the bulk of the money was concentrated in urban and rural areas with a high percentage of children from poor families. Under the law, the federal government also provided general purpose grants plus money for textbooks, library books, special programs for handicapped children, and teacher training. Congress later extended the act through 1983.

The Higher Education Act of 1965 for the first time provided federal scholarships ("educational opportunity grants") for college undergraduates. The law also provided federally insured loans for college students, federal subsidies to pay the interest on student loans from private lenders, and a work-study program to help the colleges pay the wages of students with part-time jobs obtained through the schools. It channeled money to colleges to buy library books and created a program of fellowships for graduate students. It also established a Teacher Corps to aid schools in city slums and poor rural areas. By 1981 the federal government was spending $4 billion a year to support 3.5 million college undergraduate and graduate students. In 1980 Congress extended the program of aid to higher education, including student loans, through 1985; it authorized a total of $48.4 billion, but increased interest on Guaranteed Student Loans to 9 percent.

But federal spending has failed to avert a growing crisis in the nation's public schools. Political battles continue over school desegregation and busing. The quality of education in many big-city public school systems has deteriorated. As large numbers of middle-class residents have moved to the suburbs, big cities have found their tax dollars dwindling; one result is that schools are often poorest where their services are needed most—in low-income, inner-city communities.

In 1979 Congress created a new Department of Education at the cabinet level. The department, which was given responsibility for the entire federal educational effort, absorbed the education branches of the old Department of Health, Education, and Welfare, as well as units concerned with education in

589

several other government departments. The department had long been advocated by the National Education Association, the influential teachers' lobby, which supported President Carter in both 1976 and 1980 because of his backing for an education department. As already noted, Ronald Reagan, Carter's 1980 opponent, opposed the new department, and during the campaign he called for its abolition. However, as President, Reagan in 1981 appointed a Secretary of Education to his cabinet; any move to abolish the department required the cooperation of Congress and could not be accomplished solely by the President.

Science

In an age of science and technology some people have come to feel that, more and more, decisions affecting their lives are being made not by elected political leaders, but by "faceless technocrats in long, white coats."[37]

Should American astronauts try to land on Mars? Should a new weapons system be developed? Can the United States depend on its spy satellites to police an international agreement to reduce nuclear arms? For the answers to such questions, the President must turn to scientists. Government today has become far too complicated for political leaders to know all the scientific data they need to make policy decisions.

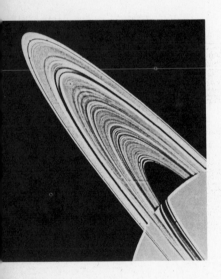

The federal government spends billions of dollars every year on scientific research and development. In fiscal 1981, $35.6 billion was budgeted for this purpose. Of the total, $15 billion went to military programs. The National Aeronautics and Space Administration accounted for $5.3 billion. About $4.2 billion was spent on research in colleges and universities. This level of spending has raised questions about the relationship of science and government. For instance, what is the proper role of science within the political system? Today, some critics regard science as "something very close to an *establishment* . . . a set of institutions supported by tax funds, but largely on faith, and without direct responsibility to political control."[38] Another question is whether universities can accept government funds for research without restricting or losing their academic independence.

The President has a science adviser within the White House. The adviser heads the Office of Science and Technology Policy, which has broad responsibility for advising the President on scientific affairs. In addition, the National Science Foundation, a government agency established in 1950, supports basic and applied research.

In the years after 1957 the federal science effort in large part was geared to responding to Soviet space accomplishments, particularly the launching of Sputnik, the world's first earth satellite. American scientists were called on to solve scientific, military, and technological problems, and America soon surpassed the Soviet Union in outer space. In 1969 the Apollo 11 astronauts landed on the moon. In 1976 America's Viking robot spacecraft landed on Mars and transmitted photographs back to earth. And in 1980, Voyager I photographed the rings of Saturn almost a billion miles away in outer space. In the 1980s many problems involving science — such as the development of nuclear power plants — have been linked to social, environmental, and political factors.

[37] Senator E. L. Bartlett, D., Alaska, in Don K. Price, *The Scientific Estate* (Cambridge, Mass.: Belknap Press of Harvard University Press, 1965), p. 57.
[38] Price, *The Scientific Estate,* p. 12.

Drawing by Keefe for the *Denver Post*

In October 1976 a federal judge, Robert R. Merhige of the United States District Court in Richmond, Virginia, fined a chemical company $13.2 million for secretly dumping Kepone, a dangerous pesticide, into the James River. The poisonous chemical, discharged by the Allied Chemical Corporation and a smaller company, polluted the river and the Chesapeake Bay into which it flows. The poison caused tremors or other neurological disturbances in some eighty workers at the smaller plant. Traces of Kepone were found in bluefish hundreds of miles away in Atlantic coastal waters.

It was the largest fine ever imposed in a water pollution case, and Judge Merhige made it plain that he wanted to deliver a warning to every corporation in America: "I hope, after this sentence, that every corporate employee who has any reason to believe that pollution is going on will say to himself, 'I'd better do something about this if I want to keep my company, if I want to keep my job.'" He added: "I hate to use clichés, but the environment belongs to every citizen in this country from the lowest to the highest. . . . Today is really the first day of our environment for the rest of our lives."[39]

Two decades ago, words and phrases like pollution, the environment, and energy crisis were unfamiliar. By the 1970s, however, Americans were acutely aware of the danger to the environment posed by technology. At the same time, they wanted to enjoy the benefits of that technology.

[39] *Washington Post*, October 6, 1976, p. 1.

Protecting the Environment

The Polluted Land

Those of us who were born after 1900, or even after 1920, inherited a land that was generally pleasant, livable, and lovely to look at. To be sure, there were slums and tenements and soft coal soot, and quite a lot of mud mixed with the horse manure, but the quality of life, as measured in clean air, clean water, and verdant hills, was something to remember with wonder—and with dismay.

For the generations of this century have squandered that inheritance. Never was so great a trust so grossly violated. We turned our valleys into dust bowls and our rivers into sewers, killed the lakes, fouled the air, choked the cities. With the brute efficiency of systematic vandals, we combined stupidity and greed. Now we measure the quality of our life by the tons of litter we leave behind. The hallmark of our society is stamped on 10 million roadside bottles: No deposit, no return.

—James J. Kilpatrick, *Washington Star,* January 8, 1970.

Americans wanted clean air and water—but they were also aware that cars that met clean air standards would cost more money. They were concerned about oil spills polluting their beaches—but they were also worried about possible new gasoline shortages. There was a conflict, in other words, between the environment and energy.

In the winter of 1973–1974 the nation found itself facing a major energy crisis. The President appointed an "energy czar" to allocate oil supplies; gasoline stations were closed down on Sundays; speed limits were lowered; the federal government ordered cutbacks in deliveries of heating oil to homes and offices; and airlines laid off thousands of pilots, flight attendants, and other employees as a shortage of jet fuel forced the cancellation of many flights. Other industries that depended on oil were adversely affected. The immediate shortages were the result of a cutoff of oil shipments by the Arab states after the Arab-Israeli war in October 1973. But the crisis forced the nation to reassess its entire approach to the use of energy; the long lines of cars at gas stations left little choice.

A few years earlier, as the decade began, Americans in large numbers had begun to understand that humanity in the technological age was slowly destroying nature and the earth itself—and endangering its own survival. Scientists warned that economic growth combined with overpopulation might end in disaster for the world.

In the United States, cities had become enveloped in smog, rivers clogged with human and industrial waste, sea birds and shorelines ravaged by oil spills. Alarmed and concerned, the public focused on the science of ecology, which deals with the relationship of living organisms and their environment.

The upsurge of interest in the quality of the natural environment was soon reflected in the political environment. Political leaders of both major parties scrambled to stake out a position. Public pressure for a cleanup led rapidly to major legislation. First, the Clean Air Act amendments of 1970 set federal air quality standards to control automobile and industrial pollution. Legislation to clean up the nation's waterways followed two years later. A new government unit, the Environmental Protection Agency, began operating in 1970.

Pollution is a result of industrialization and increased consumption, combined with population growth. The close relationship between pollution and "the population bomb" has been emphasized by Barry Commoner, a leading ecologist (and a minor-party presidential candidate in 1980). He has predicted that the present population of the earth, over 4 billion people, will grow by the year 2000 to between 6 and 8 billion. Somewhere near that population level is what Commoner has called "the crash point," at which, he argues, the air, water, and earth can no longer support human life.

As with most major national problems, progress toward restoring the environment requires cooperation by individuals, corporations, and institutions—but it also requires coercion in the form of government legislation and enforcement. For that reason, many organizations and individuals who supported environmental causes were concerned when the Reagan administration came to power. They feared that protection of the environment would be given a lower priority than either the search for new energy sources or the effort to reduce government regulation of business.

The dollar cost of a cleaner environment, the personal inconvenience caused by new laws and regulations, and the competing pressures for development of energy sources have combined to create many conflicts. Despite counter-pressures, the environmental movement has become firmly rooted in only a few years, with some visible results. In 1971, for example, Congress cancelled plans to build an American supersonic jet transport (SST) in part because of the danger that the plane's exhaust would deplete the ozone layer in the stratosphere. The ozone layer filters out ultraviolet sunlight, and some studies concluded that the SST exhaust might thus lead to an increase in skin cancer in humans. The environmentalists do not always win, however; in 1976 the Secretary of Transportation permitted the British Concorde, a supersonic plane, to fly into Washington, D.C., and New York for a limited test period. Four years later, the British and French Concordes were flying regular routes into both cities.

With the competing pressures in American society, environmentalists will inevitably lose some battles. Energy needs will often prevail over environmental concerns. Nevertheless, the political power of the environmental supporters is tangible. Millions of persons belong to an estimated 2000 to 3000 environmental organizations across the country. Public interest in the environment has been followed by legislation and expansion of the government's role as environmental regulator. Clean air, clean water, land use, and other similar issues are significant factors in political campaigns. And a major new concern has been added to the government's policy agenda.

The Environmental Protection Agency. The federal government's efforts to protect the environment are the responsibility of the Environmental Protection Agency, an independent unit of the executive branch established in 1970. The creation of EPA pulled together under one roof various regulatory powers that had been scattered through a dozen bureaus and agencies. EPA's administrator is often called on to make hard and controversial decisions — whether to grant the auto industry more time to manufacture cars with cleaner engines, for example.

In recent years Congress has passed major legislation dealing with the environment:

Air Pollution. The Clean Air Act amendments of 1970, steered through the Senate by Edmund Muskie of Maine, set strict federal air quality standards governing major forms of pollution by industry, including automobile emissions. The law provides heavy fines for violators. Under the 1970 act, auto manufacturers were required by 1975 to reduce by 90 percent the levels of carbon monoxide, hydrocarbons, and nitrogen oxides in engine exhaust. When the big auto companies in Detroit claimed they needed more time to comply, Congress and the administrator of EPA granted extensions. The act was amended again in 1977, under President Carter; the auto emission deadlines were extended through 1979 but tightened beginning in 1980 and 1981. The act also required cities to meet national clean air standards by 1982, except for cities with severe pollution problems, which were given until 1987. The law authorized the courts to impose fines of up to $25,000 a day on violators.

Water Pollution. By the start of the decade of the 1970s, all across America, rivers, lakes, and streams were getting dirtier. Cities and towns were dumping their waste into rivers. Industrial plants pumped chemical wastes and toxic compounds into once clear waters. The result: fouled drinking water, polluted beaches unfit for swimming, dead fish, and algae-clogged streams.

Congress responded by passing the Water Pollution Control Act of 1972, which has as its goal the complete elimination of discharges of pollutants into the nation's waterways by 1985. The law allotted $18 billion to the states to build the waste treatment plants they needed to clean up the water. By 1977 pollution was beginning to diminish in at least some of the nation's waterways. According to one federal report, of twelve major rivers studied, five, including the Colorado and the Ohio, showed significant reductions in bacterial counts.[40] The law was amended in 1977, with both environmentalists and industry making some gains. Certain deadlines for compliance were extended. At the same time, the law tightened the Environmental Protection Agency's control over toxic substances, such as chemicals from plants that manufacture plastics, which have become a major source of pollution. In 1980 Congress enacted a scaled-down version of a "superfund" bill, providing approximately $1.5 billion to clean up toxic wastes and chemical spills.

Oil spills from drilling rigs or tankers, which have fouled the nation's beaches and endangered wildlife, are also a major form of pollution. One major oil spill occurred off Santa Barbara, California, in 1969. In 1976 an oil tanker, the *S.S. Argo Merchant,* ran aground off Nantucket, Massachusetts, spilling 7.5 million gallons of thick, gummy oil and threatening New England beaches, birds, and marine life. And in 1979, 140 million gallons of oil spilled into the Gulf of Mexico after a blowout on a Mexican oil rig.

Environmental Impact. The National Environmental Policy Act of 1969 required the government to assess the impact on the environment of all new projects involving the federal government. The provision is important because it has since been adopted by many states and communities; in addition, it has provided the basis for environmental lawsuits. The 1969 act also established a three-member Council on Environmental Quality to advise the President, and required the President to submit an annual "state of the environment" report to Congress.

The battle over the tiny snail darter, a rare fish in the Little Tennessee River, symbolized the clash between energy and the environment. In 1973 David Etnier, a University of Tennessee zoologist, discovered the three-inch fish in an area where the Tennessee Valley Authority planned to build the Tellico Dam. The fish was placed on a list under the Endangered Species Act, entitling it to protection from actions of the government. Opponents of the dam took their case to the United States Supreme Court and won a ruling in 1978 requiring the TVA to halt the project. A special board created by Congress studied the problem and also sided with the fish. But in 1979 Congress voted to finish construction of the dam, including it in a $10.8 billion energy and water development bill. The measure also allowed exemptions to the Endangered Species Act in the future. Reluctantly, President Carter signed the bill. The snail darter had lost.[41]

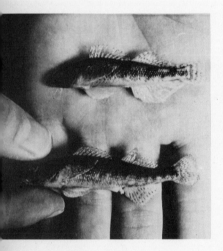

The snail darter

Energy
Policy

Three months after he took office, President Jimmy Carter went on national television to talk to the American people about the energy crisis, "the greatest challenge our country will face during our lifetimes . . . the moral equivalent of

[40] *Seventh Annual Report,* Council on Environmental Quality (Washington, D.C.: U.S. Government Printing Office, 1976), p. 272.

[41] In 1976, 710 snail darters were transplanted to a tributary of the Little Tennessee, 10 miles downstream from the dam, and the species was thriving there. Then, in 1980, fourteen baby snail darters were unexpectedly discovered 80 miles below the dam in the South Chickamauga Creek. See *Washington Post,* November 8, 1980, p. A1.

A revealing memorandum to President Carter from his chief adviser on domestic policy fell into the hands of the press. The following are excerpts:

June 28, 1979

MEMORANDUM FOR:
    THE PRESIDENT
FROM:
    STU EIZENSTAT
SUBJECT:
    Energy

Since you left for Japan, the domestic energy problem has continued to worsen:

• Gas lines are growing throughout the Northeast and are spreading to the Midwest . . .
• The latest CPI [Consumer Price Index] figures have demonstrated how substantially energy is affecting inflation—gasoline prices have risen 55% since January.
• Congress is growing more nervous by the day over the energy problem . . .

I do not need to detail for you the political damage we are suffering from all of this. It is perhaps sufficient to say that nothing which has occurred in the administration to date—not the Soviet agreement on the Middle East, not the Lance matter, not the Panama Canal treaties, not the defeat of several major domestic legislative proposals, not the sparring with Kennedy, and not even double-digit inflation—have added so much water to our ship. Nothing else has so frustrated, confused, angered the American people—or so targeted their distress at you personally, as opposed to your advisers, or Congress or outside interests . . .

In many respects, this would appear to be the worst of times. But I honestly believe we can change this to a time of opportunity. We have a better opportunity than ever before to assert leadership over an apparently insolvable problem, to shift the cause for inflation and energy problems to OPEC, to gain credibility with the American people, to offer hope of an eventual solution, to regain our political losses . . .

With strong steps we can mobilize the nation around a real crisis and with a clear enemy—OPEC.

—*New York Times,* July 7, 1979.

war." Two days later, in another televised speech to Congress, Carter unveiled his energy program. The struggle in Congress over that program marked one of the major and continuing battles of his Presidency.

The energy crisis hit home in America during the winter of 1973–1974 when long gas lines formed across the nation, and again in the summer of 1979 when the shortage recurred in many areas. Its reminders were everywhere: in the steadily rising gasoline prices at the pump, in the higher costs faced by con-

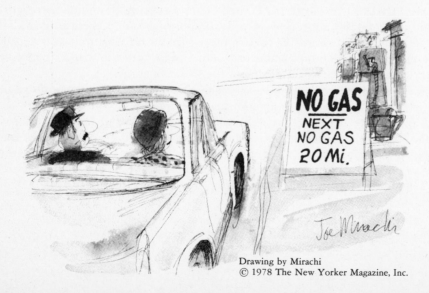

Drawing by Mirachi
© 1978 The New Yorker Magazine, Inc.

sumers to heat their homes in winter or cool them in summer, in the soaring profits of the oil companies and the seemingly continual announcements of price increases by the Organization of Petroleum Exporting Countries (OPEC). In the fall of 1980 conflict between Iraq and Iran in the Middle East again threatened to reduce oil supplies to the West; even Americans who normally paid little attention to foreign policy were aware that their ability to take the family out for a Sunday drive might well depend on what happened 6000 miles away in the Persian Gulf.

Nevertheless, for the ordinary citizen, the energy crisis was difficult to understand. Some argued that there had been no shortage at all, that gas lines and the crisis were artificial, created by the actions of "Big Oil." Many Americans were reluctant to adjust their affluent life styles to the energy crisis—to commute to work in car pools or turn down their thermostats in winter. Energy legislation was extremely complex and detailed, and even concerned citizens were bewildered by the array of facts, figures, and explanations.

Some of the basic facts were not all that complicated, however. The United States has abundant petroleum deposits in Texas, Louisiana, Oklahoma, California, and offshore in the oceans and the Gulf of Mexico. Before the Second World War, domestic fields supplied about 95 percent of the oil used in this country. By 1980, however, the United States was using 18 million barrels of oil a day, and domestic sources were providing only about 60 percent of the total. The other 40 percent was imported, mostly from OPEC nations in the Middle East. Although the United States had only 6 percent of the world's population, it consumed more than 30 percent of the world's energy.[42]

The dependence on foreign oil created all kinds of problems at home. Rising fuel prices contributed to inflation and unemployment. The billions of dollars paid annually to import oil accounted for a major share of the U.S. trade and balance-of-payments deficit, which in turn weakened the dollar in relation to foreign currencies. And the energy crisis was directly linked to the nation's foreign policy. In 1980, for example, President Carter proclaimed in his State of the Union address that the United States would use "any means . . . including force" to repel an attack on the Persian Gulf.

[42] *Energy Policy* (Washington, D.C.: Congressional Quarterly, Inc., 1979), p. 59.

Carter's approach to the energy crisis incorporated several basic ideas: to force oil and gas prices up so that people would use less; to encourage conservation in various other ways as well; to stimulate the use of alternative energy sources, such as synthetic fuels (called *synfuels*) and solar power; to tax some of the profits reaped by the oil companies because of the higher prices; and to ensure that the companies retained enough of the increased profits to be able to produce more and to develop new reserves.

Specifically, in 1977 Carter proposed to: raise domestic oil prices to the world level; require federal price controls on all natural gas, even if sold within the state where it was produced; impose a "gas guzzler" tax on the purchase of cars that did not meet federal fuel efficiency standards; and levy a five-cents-a-gallon gasoline tax if consumption rose above target levels.

Congress shredded Carter's proposals almost beyond recognition, reshaping and making substantial changes in virtually every facet of the administration's plan. After eighteen months, Congress in October 1978 approved a natural gas bill that decontrolled prices in 1985; it also enacted a coal conversion bill requiring that new power plants use coal or fuel other than oil or gas. And homeowners and businesses were given tax credits for installing energy-saving equipment, such as insulation, or solar, wind, or geothermal energy systems.

In 1979 President Carter again appealed to the nation and proposed additional energy measures. He announced that he would use his executive authority to decontrol oil prices and asked Congress to enact a stiff windfall profits tax to recoup the "huge and undeserved windfall profits" that the oil companies would reap from his action. He also announced mandatory thermostat settings for winter and summer in nonresidential buildings. He asked for import quotas and establishment of a federal program to encourage production of synfuels, such as liquids from coal, oil from shale, and alcohol from grain. He also asked for standby power to ration gasoline, and he made numerous other proposals.

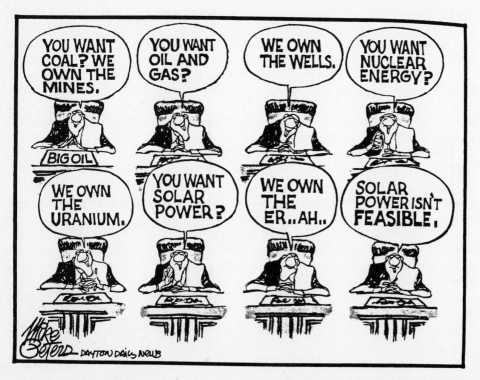

Drawing by Mike Peters for the *Dayton Daily News*

Three Mile Island: a frightening accident

Again, Congress responded only in part to the President's program. In 1980 it created a Synthetic Fuels Corporation, which could spend $20 billion to promote the production of synfuels from such materials as coal, vegetation, and garbage. It approved a windfall profits tax of from 30 to 70 percent of new oil company profits after decontrol. And it passed legislation requiring the President to submit a standby gasoline rationing plan to Congress.

One of Carter's requests did go through Congress substantially intact. In 1977 he asked for and got a new cabinet-level Department of Energy. The creation by Congress of the new department underscored the importance of a problem that the nation had been slow to recognize, but which would doubtless continue to have an enormous impact on the political system and the lives of individual Americans. (President Reagan, as a candidate in 1980, said that he would abolish the Department of Energy; but he appointed a cabinet member in 1981 to head the department.)

Nuclear Power: Three Mile Island.   March 28, 1979 was a routine night in the control room of the nuclear power plant on Three Mile Island, in the Susquehanna River, eleven miles southeast of Harrisburg, Pennsylvania. Inside the control room, a horseshoe-shaped panel stretched forty feet along three walls. It was lined with dials, gauges, and 1200 red and green warning lights.

Suddenly, at 4 A.M., a klaxon sounded. A voice on a loudspeaker intoned: "Turbine trip in Unit 2." It was the beginning of the worst accident in the history of nuclear power production in the United States.

A valve had failed in the nuclear reactor's cooling system, and the nuclear core of the reactor was rapidly overheating, raising the possibility of a "meltdown." If that happened, the nuclear core would burn through steel and concrete walls and would release lethal levels of radioactivity into the atmosphere. What opponents of nuclear power had always warned against — a nuclear disaster in a populated urban area — seemed close at hand.

The governor of Pennsylvania closed nearby schools and advised pregnant women and preschool children within five miles of the site to leave and people within ten miles to stay indoors. An evacuation of up to 300,000 people was planned, but not ordered. Many residents left on their own.

It took seven days before technicians and government experts were able to bring the danger under control. Although the feared "meltdown" did not take place, some radiation was released. There were no reported injuries to the public, but the incident sowed fear and confusion among residents of the area and alerted millions of Americans to the dangers of nuclear power.

President Carter appointed a presidential commission to study the accident. The panel released its report in October 1979. Among its recommendations were the replacement of the Nuclear Regulatory Commission with a new agency headed by a single administrator and the construction of new nuclear plants in areas remote from population centers.

Despite the dangers dramatized by the accident at Three Mile Island, there were 72 nuclear power plants operating across the nation by 1979 and almost 100 more under construction. Advocates of nuclear power argued that nuclear plants were an important element in the nation's energy supply. Opponents maintained that the disaster averted at Three Mile Island would surely come, sooner or later. In September 1980 voters in Maine had a chance to be heard directly on the issue. They voted 3 to 2 against shutting down the "Maine

Yankee" nuclear power plant in that state. But the controversy over nuclear power remained a major national political issue.

Can Government Meet the Challenge?

This discussion of government in operation has examined a number of crucial areas in which government—and therefore American society—has attempted to solve urgent social and economic problems. The results have varied.

In some policy areas, the government has had only limited success. Complex fiscal and monetary policies—even direct economic controls—have not consistently avoided the evils of recession or inflation. Government has been slow to respond to the energy crisis and to develop new and alternative sources of energy to meet the nation's needs in the future. In many cases, regulatory agencies have served corporate power and have failed to protect the public. Inequities in the tax structure remain a target of widespread criticism.

In the field of social welfare, the federal government has promised much and delivered less. President Johnson declared his "war on poverty" in 1964, but two decades later some 25 million Americans were still poor. The public assistance program has helped millions of people, but has been widely criticized. President Carter proposed reform of the welfare system, but Congress did not act during his Presidency. And President Reagan proposed deep cuts in many social programs.

On the other hand, Congress had renewed the multibillion-dollar program of revenue sharing, under which many local communities have achieved a larger voice in how federal taxes are spent. Environmental legislation and new federal agencies dealing with the environment are an example of government responding to public demands and societal needs. And the social security program was providing benefits to nearly 36 million Americans.

Achieving desirable social and economic ends requires money, however, and not all Americans want or can afford to pay the price in higher taxes and other costs. For example, as previously noted, if America really wants a better environment, it will have to pay for it, both in terms of expanded government programs and in higher prices as the cost of pollution control is passed on to the consumer.

How to deal with the complex social and economic problems confronting America is by no means clear. Not every problem may have an answer. But massive programs at any level of government may mean hard choices, high taxes, and other sacrifices. In the area of social policy, the real dilemma facing Americans today is whether they are willing to pay the costs of "promoting the general welfare" and attempting to build a better society.

Is Government the Problem?

Ten years ago a review of major economic and social problems would have concentrated on asking how government might best deal with them. In today's climate of public opinion, the same kind of review must begin by asking whether government is capable of dealing with them. Ten years ago, government was widely viewed as an instrument to solve problems; today government itself is widely viewed as the problem.

—Charles Schultze and Henry Owen, *Setting National Priorities: The Next Ten Years.*

Perspective

The Constitution was established, in part, to "promote the general welfare." In promoting the general welfare, the federal government exercises many responsibilities, with varied results. It regulates and promotes business and labor, manages the armed forces and the civilian bureaucracy, and tries to guide the economy through the use of fiscal and monetary policies. And government acts as protector in the areas of consumer affairs, health, education, welfare, science, poverty, hunger, and the environment.

From the late 1880s until 1937, the Supreme Court adopted a laissez-faire philosophy; it held that government should intervene as little as possible in economic affairs. But the Great Depression and Franklin D. Roosevelt's New Deal brought a change in the Court's thinking. Since 1937 the Supreme Court has upheld the right of government to regulate wages, hours, and working conditions and to police business.

In regulating business, the government has several tools available to it. For example, the antitrust laws are designed to encourage competition in business and to prevent the growth of monopolies. The Justice Department and the Federal Trade Commission have responsibility for carrying out antitrust policy. Although the government has had some success in preventing monopoly, it has not been able to prevent oligopoly. American corporations are increasing in both size and diversity, with economic power concentrated in the hands of a relatively few large companies. The 500 largest corporations in the United States control more than two-thirds of all manufacturing assets.

Government aids business by providing services and direct and indirect subsidies to producers and farmers. At times the government has even given direct aid to large corporations in financial trouble, such as the Chrysler Corporation. American industry receives indirect aid from federal trade and tariff policies as well.

The federal government also regulates and assists organized labor. The National Labor Relations Act of 1935 established labor's right to collective bargaining and barred employers from setting up company unions or discriminating against union workers. Congress has enacted a minimum wage, a maximum forty-hour workweek, and time-and-a-half pay for overtime. It also outlawed child labor. The Taft-Hartley Act of 1947 sought to curb some of labor's power and shift it back to management. The act defined and prohibited unfair labor practices by unions and provided for an eighty-day "cooling off period" in strikes creating a national emergency.

Today, the federal government is expected to exercise a major responsibility for the health, stability, and growth of the national economy. The President has a number of tools for shaping economic policy, but in recent years Presidents have not been able to control inflation, recession, or high unemployment.

One reason may be world economic conditions, a factor beyond the control of any President. Another may be the nature of America's modified free enterprise system, in which there are limits on the government's power to manage the economy.

The government tries to guide the economy through fiscal policy and monetary policy. The President and Congress exercise fiscal policy by cutting taxes or increasing government spending, or both. The government exercises monetary policy by controlling the supply of money and the cost and availability of credit. The Federal Reserve System can pump more money into the economy when a recession threatens, or it can tighten the supply of money and credit in a time of rising prices and excessive spending.

During the Great Depression, Franklin D. Roosevelt proposed, and Congress passed, the landmark Social Security Act of 1935. This was the beginning for two types of social welfare programs: social insurance and public assistance. The social security program is a compulsory national insurance program, in theory self-financed by taxes on employers and employees. In contrast, public assistance programs have no pay-as-you-go features; they simply distribute funds to people who are poor. The costs of these programs and the number of people receiving such payments have increased greatly.

Today, most Americans agree that government has a responsibility to protect consumers from the perils of the marketplace. The work of consumer advocate Ralph Nader and his associates contributed to the passage of a wide range of consumer laws during the 1960s and the 1970s.

Over the past two decades, Americans have become concerned about the environment. Reflecting this concern, Congress in 1970 created the Environmental Protection Agency and has passed several additional laws to protect the air and water.

The dependence of the United States on foreign oil has created many problems at home. Rising fuel prices have contributed to inflation and unemployment. The billions of dollars paid annually to import oil accounts for a major share of the U.S. trade and balance-of-payments deficit, which in turn has weakened the dollar in relation to foreign currencies. As President, Carter appealed to the nation and proposed several energy measures. Congress responded only in part to the President's proposals. It created a Synthetic Fuels Corporation, approved a windfall profits tax, and mandated a standby gasoline rationing plan. President Carter also asked for and got a new Department of Energy in 1977. The problem of energy resources will undoubtedly continue to have an enormous impact on the political system and on the lives of individual Americans.

Suggested Reading

Davies, Barbara S., and Davies, J. Clarence III. *The Politics of Pollution,* 2nd edition* (Pegasus, 1975). A useful analysis of pollution as a political issue, covering federal antipollution legislation, the role of Congress, public opinion, and interest groups. The authors emphasize that improvement of the environment depends upon public pressure on the executive branch and on Congress.

Derthick, Martha. *Policymaking for Social Security* (The Brookings Institution, 1979). A comprehensive study of policymaking for social security. Examines the basic policies that have shaped the program, the small group of people who influence decisions, and the future of the social security system.

Donovan, John C. *The Politics of Poverty,* 2nd edition* (Pegasus, 1973). A comprehensive examination of attempts by government to alleviate poverty in the United States. Discusses the various political forces that affect policymaking in this area.

Dubos, René J. *Reason Awake: Science for Man* (Columbia University Press, 1970). A collection of essays by a distinguished microbiologist focusing on the threat to people and the environment caused by the technological and population explosions. Analyzes a whole range of problems—from nuclear weapons to urban sprawl—that have resulted from a constantly expanding technology.

*Energy Policy** (Congressional Quarterly, Inc., 1979). A useful examination of the responses by the President and Congress to the nation's energy crisis in the 1970s. Contains a complete chronology of major energy-related legislation and a selected bibliography on energy policy.

Harrington, Michael. *The Other America** (Penguin, 1971). (Originally published in 1962.) One of the most widely read introductory surveys of the nature and extent of poverty in the United States in the early 1960s.

Levitan, Sar A., and Taggart, Robert. *The Promise of Greatness* (Harvard University Press, 1976). A careful, detailed examination of recent social welfare programs, including Medicare and Medicaid, CETA, and Aid to Families with Dependent Children. The authors argue that the federal programs and policies of the 1960s moved the nation toward a better, more equitable society and urge renewed government efforts to achieve social reform.

Moynihan, Daniel Patrick. *Maximum Feasible Misunderstanding: Community Action in the War on Poverty** (Free Press, 1969). A readable account of the origins of the Johnson administration's "War on Poverty" and some of the political problems encountered in attempting to stimulate "maximum feasible participation" of the poor in the development and administration of community action programs.

Nader, Ralph; Green, Mark; and Seligman, Joel. *Taming the Giant Corporation** (Norton, 1977). A critical analysis of the political, economic, and social consequences of large corporations. Argues that big corporations should be chartered by the federal government and made to reveal far more information about their activities to the public.

Price, Don K. *The Scientific Estate* (Belknap Press of Harvard University Press, 1965). A thoughtful and perceptive analysis of science and scientists, and their relation to public policymaking in the United States.

Schlesinger, Arthur M., Jr. *The Coming of the New Deal* (Houghton Mifflin, 1959). A revealing and highly readable historical account of the inauguration of Franklin Roosevelt's New Deal, which established the basis for much of the nation's current economic welfare legislation. Part of a multivolume historical study by Schlesinger of Roosevelt and New Deal politics.

Steiner, Gilbert Y. *The State of Welfare** (The Brookings Institution, 1971). A detailed analysis of major government welfare programs in the United States. Includes a discussion of proposed changes in federal welfare policies and considers the political factors affecting welfare reform.

Sundquist, James L. *Politics and Policy: The Eisenhower, Kennedy, and Johnson Years** (The Brookings Institution, 1968). An informative and valuable study of the battles in Congress and in the country to pass what became the new domestic social welfare programs of the Johnson administration.

* Available in paperback edition

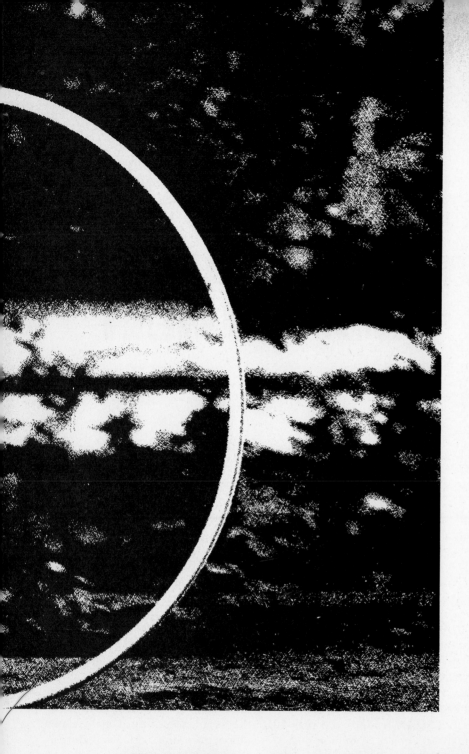

Part Five

THE AMERICAN
COMMUNITY

16

STATE AND LOCAL GOVERNMENT

In the Washington suburb of Suitland, Maryland, five miles southeast of the Capitol dome and far from the familiar paths trod by the tourists, a complex of federal buildings houses a group of men and women whose business, in part, is to peer into the future.

The building is the headquarters of the United States Bureau of the Census, a division of the Commerce Department. By using electronic computers, and calculating birth and death rates and other factors, the Census Bureau is able to make population projections for the future. It cannot do so with precision, because there is a wide margin for error in such tabulations. Nevertheless, the Census Bureau is able to guess that the population of the United States, which was more than 226 million after the 1980 census, will, by the year 2000, stand somewhere between 246 million and 283 million.

Even taking the lower figure, an increase of about 20 million people in twenty years would be like adding the populations of Sweden and Portugal to the United States. And, by the year 2015, the population of the United States will range between 253 million and 335 million, according to Census Bureau estimates.[1] In other words, there is a possibility that the 1980 population of 226 million will increase by more than 100 million in less than forty years.

Today American society is burdened with multifold, interlocking problems

[1] U.S. Bureau of the Census, *Current Population Reports,* Projections of the Population of the United States — 1977 to 2050, Series P–25, No. 704, July 1977, p. 3; figures rounded.

—inflation, unemployment, energy shortages, racial tensions, pollution, poverty, and urban crime. If, as seems possible, the population increases substantially in less than four decades, will the American political system and American society be able to cope with these problems? To take a random example—and assuming there is enough gasoline or other fuel to go around—would anyone care to visualize what it might be like driving along the San Bernardino Freeway during the morning rush hour in the year 2000? It is bad enough now, as Los Angeles commuters can attest.

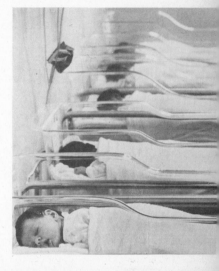

Not only the size of the population but its geographic distribution affects the nature of a society. In the United States, almost 70 percent of the people are crowded into just over 10 percent of the land area. More than half of the population of the United States lives in just nine states.[2] Since 1920 the popu-

[2] California, New York, Texas, Pennsylvania, Illinois, Ohio, Florida, Michigan, and New Jersey. Together these large states, ranked above in order of population in 1980, comprise 51.2 percent of the population. Source: Adapted from the *New York Times,* January 1, 1981, p. A6.

Where the People Are*

Figure 16–1

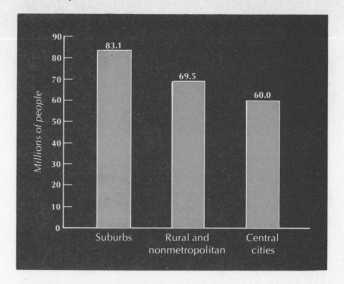

* Data for 1978.
Source: U.S. Bureau of the Census, *Current Population Reports,* Social and Economic Characteristics of the Metropolitan and Nonmetropolitan Population: 1977 and 1970, Series P–23, No. 75, November 1978, p. 4.

lation of the United States has been more urban than rural. In 1977, when the population stood at almost 213 million, 143 million Americans, or 67 percent, lived in metropolitan areas. Of this total, 60 million lived in central cities and about 83 million outside the cities, mostly in the suburbs. About 70 million lived in rural or other nonmetropolitan areas.[3]

In 1977 there were 82 million Americans living in metropolitan areas of more than one million.[4] As America has become urbanized, many of the nation's difficult problems have developed in their most acute form in urban areas — in the central "core" cities and the surrounding suburbs. Obviously, the decisions and actions of state, city, and other local governments have a direct impact on the quality of American life.

Much of this book has focused on the national government and national politics, but at last count there were, in addition to the government in Washington, 79,912 units of state and local government in the United States.[5] The performance of these governments is often criticized for failure to keep pace with the complex problems they face — transportation, housing, slum clearance, pollution, welfare services, schools, crime, narcotics — to name some of the major

[3] U.S. Bureau of the Census, *Current Population Reports,* Social and Economic Characteristics of the Metropolitan and Nonmetropolitan Population: 1977 and 1970, Series P–23, No. 75, November 1978, p. 4. The terms urban, rural, metropolitan, and suburban are subject to varying definitions. The federal government has divided the nation into Standard Metropolitan Statistical Areas (SMSAs), each of which contains at least one central city of 50,000 persons or twin cities with a total population of 50,000. The data above are based on population inside SMSAs. Not all the 83 million people living outside cities but within the Census Bureau definition of a metropolitan area lived in suburbia; suburban population obviously depends on how one defines a "suburb."

[4] *Ibid.*

[5] U.S. Bureau of the Census, *Census of Governments,* Governmental Organization, Vol. 1, No. 1, 1977, p. 1.

ones. This inability to keep pace is not always the fault of the state or community; many of the problems that exist have been compounded by urbanization and patterns of population migration in recent decades. These factors have interacted to place a serious strain on the federal system.

Since the Second World War, for a variety of reasons, large numbers of low-income blacks and whites have migrated from rural areas to big cities. At the same time, many middle-class families and business firms have moved out to the suburbs, taking the city tax base with them. The newcomers to the inner city have required costly government services—schools, welfare, police and fire protection, for example—but have not had sufficient taxable incomes and property to finance these services.

By the early 1970s the flow of black migrants to the cities had declined sharply.[6] And by that time, blacks were also migrating to the suburbs. Nevertheless, in 1978 only about 6 percent of suburban residents were black. Some of the outward migration by blacks represented a spilling over of city neighborhoods into adjoining suburbs. Moreover, many black Americans in the suburbs continued to live in highly segregated neighborhoods. More than half of black Americans still lived in the cities, and the percentage of blacks living in the central cities was more than twice that of whites.[7]

For the most part, cities rely on the property tax to finance the bulk of municipal services. Suburban governments now collect the taxes on the property of families and industries that have left the cities—and suburban residents have little desire to "bail out" City Hall. Big-city mayors look to Washington and the statehouses for relief. But, the mayors maintain, what limited federal funds are available have been siphoned off in part by the states for use in the suburbs and in rural areas.

[6] Karl E. Taeuber, "Racial Segregation: The Persisting Dilemma," *Annals of the American Academy of Political and Social Science*, November 1975, p. 93.

[7] U.S. Bureau of the Census, U.S. Bureau of Labor Statistics, *The Social and Economic Status of the Black Population in the United States: An Historical View, 1790–1978*, Series P–23, No. 80, 1979, p. 171.

A "mismatch" exists not only between urgent problems and state and local financial resources, but between the magnitude of the problems and the performance of state and local governments. Two overriding conclusions may be drawn from many of the studies of state and local problems:

1. *Many of the problems are larger than the boundaries of the governmental units that are attempting to deal with them.* Smog, for example, respects no city lines, and the issue of commuter transportation in a metropolitan area may involve two dozen local communities.
2. *The solutions frequently cost more than the governmental units have available or are willing to spend.* A suburban area cannot possibly afford, for example, to build a mass transit line to carry its residents to downtown offices, nor can the central cities raise the tax revenues to provide adequate social services for those inner-city residents who need them most.

Against this background, we may ask: How well are state and local governments meeting their responsibilities? How are state and local governments organized? What is the relationship among federal, state, and local governments? What are the major problems of the cities and the suburbs? Given the politics and existing structure of state and local governments, can they hope to solve problems that are larger than their geographic boundaries and financial resources? What are the implications of these problems for America's future?

The States

America is a nation of states. The political institutions of the thirteen colonies foreshadowed the shape of the federal system created under the Constitution. The states, in short, were here *before* the American nation. They grew in number as the frontier was pushed westward to the Pacific. They are not mere administrative or geographic units established for the convenience of the central government. Rather, the states are key political institutions rooted in the nation's historical development, sharing power under the federal system with the national government in Washington.

But the federal system was constructed when the United States was a small, rural nation. In today's predominantly urban America, a nation of congested cities, black ghettos, and sprawling suburbs, are the states any longer relevant? Can they meet the new demands placed on them by urbanization?

Many critics of state government feel that the states are not doing as much as they should, particularly in the crucial area of urban problems. However, the states have been making an effort to meet their responsibilities. For example, during the 1970s state and local expenditures increased about as fast as federal spending. (See Chapter 3, p. 84.) And state taxes have increased at a faster rate than federal taxes. In addition, in recent years, the staffs of the bureaucracies that run the state governments have become more professional.

The states and localities do not, of course, spend as much as the federal government, but their level of spending often actually exceeds that of federal spending on domestic needs. In 1978, for example, the federal government was spending at the rate of $451 billion a year. But if the $116 billion contained in that year's budget for defense, international affairs, space, and science is subtracted from this total, federal domestic expenditures were running at about

$335 billion annually, or less than the $415 billion a year being spent by state and local governments.[8]

But often a serious imbalance, or income gap, has existed between the demands on state and local governments and the revenues they raise through taxes. One reason for this is that state and local governments rely heavily on property and consumer taxes, which do not reflect the general growth of the economy as rapidly as the income tax does. At present, the federal government collects more than half of all taxes; the states and communities divide the remainder.

During the late 1960s and early 1970s, in an effort to find new sources of revenue, states raised taxes and imposed new taxes on a massive scale, although the trend did not continue for long. During 1979, for example, about forty-five states made either major or minor reductions in taxes of various kinds.[9]

By that time, however, there had been a significant tax revolt in several states, most notably in California. In 1978 California voters approved by 2–1 a constitutional amendment that appeared on the ballot as Proposition 13. It limited real estate taxes in the state to 1 percent of previous property values and was approved by the electorate despite warnings that it would result in cuts in government services. Proposition 13 transformed its chief sponsor, 74-year-old Howard A. Jarvis, into an instant, national celebrity. In Washington, and across the nation, political leaders read the returns as a general "taxpayers' revolt" and a demand for lower taxes.

The impact of Proposition 13 was cushioned by a $5 billion state surplus that had accumulated in California. But two years later, in 1980, the atmosphere in California had changed. Jarvis, a long-time crusader against high taxes, sponsored Proposition 9, which would have cut the state's income tax in half. The initiative was defeated by a margin of 5–3.

In 1980 nine states still had no personal income tax, however, and many that did taxed incomes at relatively low rates.[10] States are cautious in taxing in part because they must compete with one another. They "must be wary of increasing taxes or redistributing income in a way that will enable neighboring states to attract away industry."[11]

The federal government provides some financial help. In 1981 federal aid to the states was budgeted at $96.3 billion, or 15.6 percent of the federal budget. Between 1972 and 1980, Congress allocated more than $55 billion in general revenue-sharing money to states and local communities. In 1980 Congress renewed but modified the program. The new law provided $4.6 billion a year in revenue-sharing funds for local governments through fiscal 1983, and authorized up to $2.3 billion a year for state governments during the last two years of this period, provided that Congress appropriated the money. State and local governments were free to use the money largely as they wished.

What do the states do? They have major responsibilities in the fields of

[8] Federal, state, and local expenditures as of fiscal 1978, in *Budget of the United States Government, Fiscal Year 1980*, p. 85; and U.S. Bureau of the Census, *Government Finances in 1977–78* (Washington, D.C.: U.S. Government Printing Office, 1980), p. 5.
[9] *Book of the States, 1980–1981* (Lexington, Ky.: Council of State Governments, 1980), p. 22.
[10] The nine states without a general income tax were Connecticut, Florida, Nevada, New Hampshire, South Dakota, Tennessee, Texas, Washington, and Wyoming. Data from Advisory Commission on Intergovernmental Relations.
[11] James Q. Wilson, "Urban Problems in Perspective," in James Q. Wilson, ed., *The Metropolitan Enigma* (Washington, D.C.: U.S. Chamber of Commerce, 1967), p. 395.

Howard A. Jarvis

Drawing by Henry Martins
© 1977 The New Yorker
Magazine, Inc.

"Im afraid I must concur with Dr. Hamilton and Dr. Movin. The cause of death was taxes."

Major Expenditures of State and Local Governments, 1977–1978 (in millions of dollars)

Figure 16–2

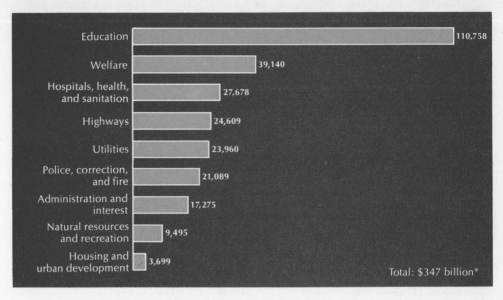

Education	110,758
Welfare	39,140
Hospitals, health, and sanitation	27,678
Highways	24,609
Utilities	23,960
Police, correction, and fire	21,089
Administration and interest	17,275
Natural resources and recreation	9,495
Housing and urban development	3,699

Total: $347 billion*

* Total is for all state and local expenditures, including items not shown.
Source: Adapted from U.S. Bureau of the Census, *Governmental Finances in 1977–78*, p. 16.

education, welfare, transportation, the administration of justice, the prisons, agriculture, public health, and the environment. (See Figure 16-2.) States share with local governments responsibility for the delivery of these and many other vital public services. And this responsibility is the source of many of the difficulties faced by the states, as well as by local governments. To provide these services, state and local governments employ more people than does the federal government—with all of the accompanying problems of unionization, strikes, and control of the bureaucracy. Even though states are spending more money on public services, they have not proved very innovative in attacking the urban problems they now face. There is a wide variation in the performance and effectiveness of the fifty states, just as there are substantial differences in state politics and state political institutions.

Beyond providing services, states have a major impact on people's lives. It is the states, not the federal government, that regulate marriage, divorce, child custody, drivers' licenses, auto inspection, transfer of property, wills and estates, and many other matters. And it is the states, as well as the federal government, that determine the penalty for possession of marijuana, or whether capital punishment shall be applied for certain crimes. The federal courts may eventually review state cases, but initially at least, the states decide.

The State Constitutions

State constitutions spell out the basic structure of each state government. Every state constitution provides for an executive, legislative, and judicial branch. Although each includes a bill of rights, some state constitutions are more liberal than others. For example, the constitutions of the newest states, Alaska and Hawaii, have strong civil rights provisions.

State constitutions tend to be lists of what the state cannot do; they limit the power of the governor and of the legislature—to levy taxes and borrow money, for example. As a result, state constitutions are often condemned as restrictive, negative documents that impede the ability of states to meet modern problems.

In the late 1960s and early 1970s, many states streamlined their constitutions. But modernizing state constitutions does not in itself improve governmental performance; there also must be changes in the political climate in which those governments operate. In many areas there is political resistance to massive, costly undertakings by governments to solve urban problems. For example, New Jersey has one of the most modern state constitutions, but it has not surpassed other states in responding to urban problems.

The state constitutions, as Duane Lockard pointed out, "have been amended more than 3000 times and in some instances it is necessary to read the constitution backwards like a Chinese newspaper, in order to see what the last word is on an original provision."[12] Lockard also found a number of oddities; the California constitution, for example, limited the power of the legislature to regulate the length of wrestling matches, and the Georgia constitution provided a $250,000 reward for the first person to strike oil within the borders of the Peach State.[13]

The most common means of amending state constitutions is by a two-thirds vote of the legislature and approval of a majority of the voters at the next election. But seventeen states permit the *initiative*.[14] Under this method, proposed constitutional amendments can be placed on the ballot if enough signatures are obtained on a petition. California's Proposition 13 was an example of a constitutional amendment approved by the voters in this fashion. All states also permit the rewriting of constitutions at conventions convened with the approval of the voters. In a number of states, changes may be proposed by constitutional commissions.

The Governors

At first glance, it might appear as though the fifty states are federal governments in miniature. Each has the familiar three branches with checks and balances. The governors are usually reasonably prestigious figures, at least within their states; like the President, they head an executive branch. And, like the President, they have armed forces under their command in the form of the state police and the National Guard. Appearances are deceptive, however, for the position of governor in some states is much less powerful than is popularly imagined.

In the first place, the states have come to occupy a less prominent position within the federal system than they enjoyed in years past. The actions of a governor, and of other state officials, and the laws passed by state legislatures cannot conflict with federal law and are subject to judicial review by the United States Supreme Court. At Little Rock and elsewhere in the South, federal power has prevailed over that of state governors in confrontations over public school desegregation.

[12] Duane Lockard, *The Politics of State and Local Government*, 2nd ed. (New York: Macmillan, 1969), p. 85.
[13] *Ibid.*
[14] *Book of the States, 1980–81*, p. 18.

611

Beyond this, the position of governor has been weakened by historical and political factors. During the colonial period, the royal governors clashed with the elected legislatures. The state constitutions written at the time of the American Revolution reflected the prevailing distrust of executive power; in most states, the legislature chose the governor. During the nineteenth century, popular election of governors spread through the states, but the power of the governors remained relatively weak. Not until the twentieth century were state governments reorganized and executive power increased in some states. But even today, the office of governor is weak in many states.

Variations in the power of state governors were shown in a study published by a federal commission. In only ten states was the governor said to be "very strong."[15] Another study by Thad L. Beyle, a political scientist, found that more than two-thirds of the governors felt that inadequate appointive power was a principal weakness in their ability to govern.[16] Since these studies were published, a number of states have taken steps to strengthen the power of the governor. For example, in Georgia and South Carolina the power of the governor can no longer be listed as "weak." In more than a dozen states, the governor now has power to reorganize the executive branch by executive order, subject to veto by the legislature. Several governors have been given broader power to appoint department heads and other state officials.[17]

In most states, the governor shares executive power with at least one other popularly elected official. Typically, the officials elected by the voters along with the governor may include the lieutenant governor, attorney general, secretary of state, treasurer, auditor, and superintendent of education. The governor's difficulties are increased if one or more of these elected executive branch officials belong to the opposing political party. The power of governors to appoint important officials (in states where they are not elected independently) varies from state to state; in some cases their choices are subject to approval by the state senate.

All states except North Carolina grant their governors the power to veto state legislation. The veto is one of the few areas in which governors actually have more power than the equivalent power of the President. Governors in forty-three states can exercise an *item veto* over single parts of appropriations bills. The President can only veto entire bills (see Chapter 10, pp. 367–68).

Almost half the states limit the term of office of the governor, restricting the governor either to two four-year or two two-year terms, or to one four-year term. But more than half of the states now have four-year terms with unlimited succession, and the trend is toward increasing the governor's term and powers. In 1980 only four states had two-year terms for governor.[18] In general, a governor's power, and ability to develop long-range policies, are greater if the term in office is four years and he or she is permitted to seek re-election. Otherwise, to some extent, the governor becomes a "lame duck" as soon as the inauguration takes place. The governor's control over the state budget is another index of power. In all but a few states, the governor prepares an executive budget and

[15] *Fiscal Balance in the American System,* Vol. I, Advisory Commission on Intergovernmental Relations (Washington, D.C.: U.S. Government Printing Office, October 1967), pp. 233–34.
[16] Thad L. Beyle, "The Governor's Formal Powers: A View from the Governor's Chair," *Public Administration Review,* Vol. XXVIII, No. 6 (November/December 1968), pp. 540–45.
[17] Data provided by National Governors Association.
[18] *Book of the States, 1980–1981,* pp. 184–85.

submits it to the legislature. While this usually serves to increase the governor's strength, much still depends on the skill a governor shows in managing the state bureaucracy and on other fiscal and political practices within the state. Since federal grants provide a substantial share of state revenues, the power of governors also varies with the degree of control they have over state participation in federal programs.

When the American nation began, state legislatures were powerful and prestigious political institutions. Today, they are sometimes described in unflattering terms. During the nineteenth century, in the era of Jacksonian democracy and again after the Civil War, voters in many states wrote various restrictions on legislative power into the state constitutions, limiting state expenditures and borrowing power, for example. Many of these curbs are still in effect.

The Legislatures

Public respect for state legislators and legislatures has also been eroded by occasional disclosures of bribes and corruption among the lawmakers. One result has been a suspicion that some state legislators manage to use their position for private gain. Closely tied to this assumption is the belief that lobbyists and special interest groups can work their will at the statehouse more easily than in Washington. Certainly, an industry, utility, or labor union that exercises great power within a state capital often achieves its legislative aims more easily at the state level than in Congress, where its power may be diffused and it must compete with many other interest groups.

Finally, until the Supreme Court's reapportionment decisions of the 1960s, overrepresentation of rural areas in the state legislatures diminished legislative prestige in urban areas. City dwellers grumbled about state legislatures controlled by "appleknockers" and "farmers" who primarily served rural interests.

There have been some signs of improvement, however. By the 1970s, a number of state legislatures had begun modernizing both their procedures and facilities—for example, strengthening their committee system, installing computers, and initiating other reforms.

Every state has a two-house legislature except Nebraska, which has a unicameral legislature. The 7482 state lawmakers serve in legislatures that range in

The State Legislatures

Table 16–1

	Senate	Length of Term	House	Length of Term	Years Sessions Are Held	Salary*
Alabama	35	4	105	4	annual	$ 10 (d)
Alaska	20	4	40	2	annual	11,750
Arizona	30	2	60	2	annual	6,000
Arkansas	35	4	100	2	odd	7,500
California	40	4	80	2	even	25,555
Colorado	35	4	65	2	annual	12,000
Connecticut	36	2	151	2	annual	6,500
Delaware	21	4	41	2	annual	9,360
Florida	40	4	120	2	annual	12,000
Georgia	56	2	180	2	annual	7,200
Hawaii	25	4	51	2	annual	12,000
Idaho	35	2	70	2	annual	4,200
Illinois	59	—‡	177	2	annual	28,000
Indiana	50	4	100	2	annual	6,000
Iowa	50	4	100	2	annual	12,000
Kansas	40	4	125	2	annual	35 (d)
Kentucky	38	4	100	2	even	50 (d)
Louisiana	39	4	105	4	annual	50 (d)
Maine	33	2	151	2	even	2,500
Maryland	47	4	141	4	annual	16,750
Massachusetts	40	2	160	2	annual	20,334
Michigan	38	4	110	2	annual	27,000
Minnesota	67	4	134	2	odd	18,500
Mississippi	52	4	122	4	annual	8,100
Missouri	34	4	163	2	annual	15,000
Montana	50	—‡	100	2	odd	33.50 (d)
Nebraska†	49	4	—	—	annual	4,800
Nevada	20	4	40	2	odd	80 (d)
New Hampshire	24	2	400	2	odd	100
New Jersey	40	4	80	2	annual	18,000
New Mexico	42	4	70	2	annual	40 (d)
New York	60	2	150	2	annual	23,500
North Carolina	50	2	120	2	odd	6,000
North Dakota	50	4	100	2	odd	5 (d)
Ohio	33	4	99	2	annual	22,500
Oklahoma	48	4	101	2	annual	12,948
Oregon	30	4	60	2	odd	7,848
Pennsylvania	50	4	203	2	annual	25,000
Rhode Island	50	2	100	2	annual	5 (d)
South Carolina	46	4	124	2	annual	250 (d)
South Dakota	35	2	70	2	annual	2,400
Tennessee	33	4	99	2	odd	8,308
Texas	31	4	150	2	odd	7,200
Utah	29	4	75	2	annual	25 (d)
Vermont	30	2	150	2	odd	2,000§
Virginia	40	4	100	2	annual	8,000
Washington	49	4	98	2	annual	9,800
West Virginia	34	4	100	2	annual	5,136
Wisconsin	33	4	99	2	annual	19,767
Wyoming	30	4	62	2	annual	30 (d)

* Salaries annual unless otherwise noted as (d), per day.
† Unicameral legislature.
‡ Terms vary from two to four years.
§ Salary up to this amount depending on length of session.
Source: Adapted from *Book of the States, 1980–81* (Lexington, Ky.: Council of State Governments, 1980), pp. 85, 90–91, 108–09.

size from 60 in Nevada and Alaska to 424 in New Hampshire.[19] Typically, the upper house has about forty members and the lower house about one hundred members. Most state senators serve four-year terms; most state representatives in the lower house serve for two years.

In thirty-six states the legislature meets annually.[20] In the remainder, the legislatures meet regularly only every two years, normally in January. This fact alone tells something of the status and power of state legislatures.

For the majority of state legislators, public service is only a part-time job. In almost two-thirds of the states the length of regular legislative sessions is constitutionally limited, often to sixty days. Even then, the legislators may spend only a few days in the capital each week, often ending the session with a great flurry of last-minute legislation. Sometimes the clock is literally stopped to permit the passage of bills within the time limit.

In 1980 Illinois legislators were paid $28,000 a year, the highest state legislative salaries in the nation. Although some big states — California, New York, Ohio, Pennsylvania, Massachusetts, and Michigan — paid legislators $20,000 or more annually, twelve states paid only a per diem rate. The median pay of state legislators is about $12,000.

Who are the legislators? State lawmakers tend to come from a higher-than-average social and economic background. As Thomas R. Dye has noted:

> More than three-quarters of the nation's state legislators have been exposed to a college education, a striking contrast to the educational level of the total population. Legislators are also concentrated in prestigious occupations. A great majority of legislators are either engaged in the professions, or are proprietors, managers, or officials of businesses. . . . lawyers are the largest single occupational group.[21]

Perhaps the most important aspect of state legislatures today is their changing nature as a result of the "reapportionment revolution" discussed in Chapter 9 (pp. 336–39). In *Baker* v. *Carr* in 1962, the Supreme Court held that the voters of Tennessee did have the right to challenge unequal representation in the state's legislature.[22] And in *Reynolds* v. *Sims* in 1964, it ruled that apportionment of both houses of state legislatures must be based closely on population and the principle of "equal representation for equal numbers of people."[23]

The Court's decisions did not, despite popular expectations, shift the base of state political power from rural areas to the central cities. Instead, the main beneficiary has proved to be the suburbs. And suburban legislators have often proved to be just as conservative on many social welfare and urban issues as lawmakers from the state's rural areas.

The Judges

Most Americans never see the inside of the United States Supreme Court, or even of a federal district court. But many have been to state and local courts — for example, traffic court to pay a fine, or divorce court — where most criminal

[19] *Ibid.,* p. 85.

[20] *Ibid.,* pp. 108–09. The constitutions of thirty-six states required such annual meetings.

[21] Thomas R. Dye, "State Legislative Politics," in Herbert Jacob and Kenneth N. Vines, eds., *Politics in the American States,* 2nd ed. (Boston: Little, Brown, 1971), pp. 178–79.

[22] *Baker* v. *Carr,* 369 U.S. 186 (1962).

[23] *Reynolds* v. *Sims,* 377 U.S. 533 (1964).

and civil cases are handled. The quality of justice in America, therefore, depends to a great extent on the quality of justice in the states and communities. These courts, rather than federal courts, are most visible to the average citizen.

As in the case of the Supreme Court, state courts often strike down state laws as conflicting with their state constitutions. But the decisions of state and local courts must conform to the United States Constitution as interpreted by the Supreme Court.

State and local judgeships are important political prizes. Young lawyers who "go into politics" may serve in the legislature or in a state or municipal administration. But often their hope is to be appointed a judge, as their safe, prestigious, and ultimate political reward.

The structure of the state and local judiciary and the problems of the nation's criminal justice system are discussed in detail in Chapter 13.

Politics and Parties

In Chapter 7 we examined the structure of state political party organizations, their relation to national parties, the geographic cleavage that exists between "upstate" and "downstate" urban-rural areas in many states, and the decline of big-city political machines. In Chapter 9 we mentioned the various national in-

Party Competition in the States

Figure 16–3

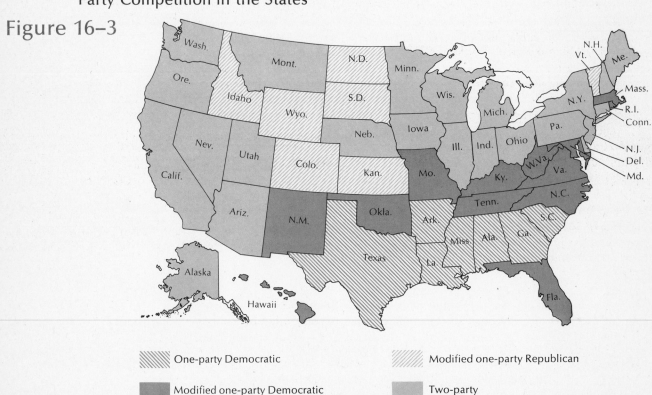

One-party Democratic
Modified one-party Republican
Modified one-party Democratic
Two-party

Source: From Austin Ranney, "Parties in State Politics," in Herbert Jacob and Kenneth N. Vines, eds., *Politics in the American States,* 3rd ed., p. 62. Copyright © 1976, 1971, 1965 by Little, Brown and Company, Inc. Reprinted by permission.

fluences on state politics and the increasing effort of states to isolate themselves from the tides of presidential politics by scheduling elections for governor in the off-years. In the American federal system, state politics and state political parties cannot be separated from any discussion of politics and government at the national level.

In 1980 a former governor, Ronald Reagan, was elected President. Fourteen other Presidents had served as governors.

The states are the building blocks of the national political parties. But among the states, the pattern of party competition differs widely. For example, for many years in the one-party states of the deep South competition was largely *within* the Democratic party. The real battles were fought for the Democratic nomination; the winner of the nomination was virtually assured victory over a Republican opponent in the general election.

The emergence of Alabama governor George Wallace's third party in the 1960s, combined with major Republican inroads in the "Solid South," changed the face of Southern politics. In 1968 President Nixon carried five Southern states, and in 1972 he won the entire South. Four years later a Southerner, Jimmy Carter, headed the Democratic ticket and carried all but one Southern state. But in 1980 the Republican candidate, Ronald Reagan, accomplished exactly the reverse, carrying the entire South except for Carter's home state of Georgia.

Some states have vigorous two-party competition. Other states have modified two-party competition—one party is on the average stronger than the other. But in both types of states, control of the statehouse and the legislature can swing back and forth. In a study measuring party competition for state offices from 1962 to 1973, Austin Ranney characterized seven states as one-party Democratic, thirteen as modified one-party Democratic, twenty-three as two-party, and seven (including once staunchly Republican Vermont) as modified one-party Republican.[24] (See Figure 16–3.) Since then, the pattern has changed in some states, but not in most.

Within the states, political parties show considerable ideological variation. A Democrat from rural Florida may be much closer to a Republican in ideological hue than he or she is to a Wisconsin Democrat. The Republican party in Mississippi bears little resemblance to the Republican party in Massachusetts.

The rise of the direct primary for state political nominations (discussed in Chapter 9) has weakened control of state political machines by party leaders. The primary has at least partially shifted control over nominations to the voters, in those states where they care to exercise that power.

Ronald Reagan while governor of California

Local Governments

The cartoon in the *New Yorker* showed a woman sitting at a table on her apartment terrace, calling to her husband, "Hurry, dear, your soup is getting dirty." For most city dwellers, air pollution is no joke. And a city's laws and regulations affect the battle for cleaner air. Whether one lives in a skyscraper, a ghetto, or a small town,

[24] Austin Ranney, "Parties in State Politics," in Herbert Jacob and Kenneth N. Vines, eds. *Politics in the American States,* 3rd ed. (Boston: Little, Brown, 1976), pp. 60–62.

the quality of local government is likely to have immediate impact on a person's life. In this sense, local government is "closer" to the citizen, even though the federal government may have a greater effect on one's life in the long run.

New York City is a case in point. In recent years its residents have lived through financial crises and strikes by sanitation workers, transit workers, and teachers. One way or another, these inconveniences involved the city government. If New Yorkers watch noxious trash piling up on the sidewalks, if they must walk several miles to work, or if they cannot send their children to school, they have ample reason to be aware of the impact of local government on their lives.

Although the connection is not always well understood, local governments are in actuality legal creatures of the states. The state constitutions vest power in the state governments; local governments only exercise the power that the state gives to them.

Cities

Cities are municipal corporations chartered by the states. The charters define the municipal powers. About half the states have widely varying provisions for local *home rule.* As the term implies, home rule empowers municipalities to modify their charters and run their affairs without approval by the legislature, subject to the constitution and laws of the state. While home rule may give municipalities more freedom in choosing their *form* of government, in most states their freedom is not much greater than that of other localities in such fields as education, police power, and other substantive areas. Home rule, in other words, may not help cities solve problems. At a time when so many urban problems cut across the boundaries of local government units, many urban specialists believe there is a need for greater interdependence and cooperation among local governments, not greater autonomy and independence.

There are three basic forms of city government:

The Mayor-Council Plan. Today, most of the nation's cities of half a million people or more employ a strong mayor-council form of government. Under it, the mayor has substantial formal power over the executive agencies of government and in dealings with an elected city council. In some cities, however, a weak mayor-council form is still in use. Under it, the mayor is merely a figurehead and must share administrative power with the council and other elected officials. Some cities employ a mixture of the two systems. About half the cities of more than 5000 people use the mayor-council plan.

New York City
Council meeting

The Council-Manager Plan. The council-manager form of government was first adopted before the First World War by the communities of Staunton, Virginia, and Sumter, South Carolina. Under this system a council, usually elected on a nonpartisan ticket, hires a professional city manager, who runs the city government and has power to hire and fire city officials. The council in turn has power to fire the city manager (although the council is not supposed to interfere in the day-to-day administration of city affairs). City managers often bring trained, professional skills to the business of running a city and may frequently receive high salaries. Although city managers are nominally "nonpolitical," they may be dismissed as a result of a political battle within the community. More than one-third of all cities under 500,000 have city managers. The plan is employed all across the nation, from Portland, Maine, to San José, California, but is particularly popular in California and other Western states.

The Commission Plan. When a hurricane and high waves smashed Galveston, Texas, in 1900, more than 5000 people were killed and property damage was estimated to be in the millions. In the emergency, while the city government was paralyzed, the Texas state legislature appointed a commission of five local businessmen to run Galveston.

The plan caught on and for a time, at least, was extremely popular in American cities. Under it, a board of city commissioners, usually five, is popularly elected (on a nonpartisan ballot in a majority of cities that use the system). The commissioners make policy as a city council, but they also run the city departments as administrators. One commissioner is usually designated mayor, but often has no extra power. In time, the commission plan proved disappointing to reformers. Responsibility was diffused under the system, and commissioners frequently lacked the skills needed to administer city departments. Some 210 cities of more than 2500 people still use this form of local government. But the number of cities using the commission plan is declining. In 1960 it was abandoned by Galveston, which turned to the council-manager plan.

Counties

In rural areas the county is the most important geographic unit of local government. There are more than 3000 counties in the United States. Their size and power vary, but typically, the elected officials include the sheriff, county prosecutor, coroner, clerk, and treasurer. These officials share governing power with elected county boards, most frequently called a "board of commissioners" or a "board of supervisors." Some large counties elect a county executive to act as a chief administrator. The county courthouse is usually the local center of political power, the gathering place of those local officials, political leaders, and hangers-on referred to in some counties as "the courthouse gang." But county governments are changing. By 1980, about 147 counties with a total of 45 million people were governed by elected county executives. A much larger group of almost 500 counties, with nearly 70 million people, was run by professional county administrators. These administrators are appointed, much like city managers.

Towns and Townships

The New England town meeting has long stood as a symbol of direct, participatory democracy. These meetings are still held in many New England towns: the townspeople come together for an annual meeting in the spring, at which they elect a board of selectmen and settle local policy questions. But today, urbanization and a vastly increased population have sapped the town meeting of much of its former strength.

In New England and New York, the "town" includes the village and the surrounding countryside. In the Middle Atlantic states and the Midwest, counties are often subdivided into townships. By order of Congress, many Midwest townships were laid out early in the nation's history in six-by-six-mile checkerboard fashion. For this reason, many townships today are thirty-six square miles in area. Rural townships are declining in importance and number. But in a number of urban areas, townships perform the function of cities.

Special Districts

Special districts are established within states to deal with problems that cut across the boundary lines of local units of government or to spread the tax burden over a geographic area larger than that of the pre-existing local units. They are created for such purposes as fire protection, sewage, water, schools, and parks. The number of special districts has been growing at a rapid rate.

The existence of so many different kinds and layers of local government results in fragmentation and overlapping, contributing to the inability of local governments to respond effectively to their problems. For example, the existence in so many states of a separate system of government control for schools often makes it difficult for local governments to coordinate education with other programs. Special districts often mean that problems will be dealt with by experts and specialists. But such districts may also mean that local governments give up control over those programs.

Cities and Suburbs: The Metropolitan Dilemma

For more than a decade, the suburbs, by Census Bureau estimates, have formed the largest segment of the American population.[25] One political result can be measured in the increase in suburban representation in Congress and in state legislatures. Another result has been to sharpen the conflict between the suburbs and the cities on issues where their interests differ. Even before the suburbs had outgrown the cities in population, the urban-suburban rift was clearly visible. In state after state, suburban legislators, sometimes in alliance with rural forces, defeated legislation to aid central cities.

[25] As noted in footnote 3 of this chapter, suburbia is defined here as persons living outside central cities but within the Census Bureau description of a metropolitan area.

More than half a century ago, George Washington Plunkitt, the Tammany district leader, complained that rural legislators had imposed an unfair tax burden on New York City:

> This city is ruled entirely by the hayseed legislators at Albany. . . . In England . . . they make a pretense of givin' the Irish some self-government. In this state, the Republican government makes no pretense at all. It says right out in the open: "New York City is a nice big fat goose. Come along with your carvin' knives and have a slice." They don't pretend to ask the Goose's consent.[26]

Today, the white suburban resident has largely replaced the "hayseeds" of yesteryear as the adversary of the city dweller. If Boss Plunkitt were around today, he would probably be complaining about the "commuters" in New York City's suburban Nassau and Westchester counties.

The picture of conflict between cities and suburbs might be even bleaker but for two emerging factors. First, the pattern of metropolitan growth has created an *interdependence* among all governments in the area, especially in such fields as air pollution, mass transit, and land use, where no single government's boundaries conform to the size of the problem. Suburbs and cities can, and have, cooperated on problems in which their mutual benefit is at stake. Second, many of the problems of the cities—crime, overcrowding, welfare rolls, traffic, housing— have begun to appear in the suburbs as their population has increased. Suburban residents are discovering that, to some extent, they "took the city with them."

As a result, more and more suburbs and cities may come to realize that, on certain issues at least, they are in the same boat. This happened in Georgia; urban and suburban legislators, formerly political enemies, joined in an "Urban Caucus"—in part because the area around Atlanta, including Cobb County, began experiencing many of the same problems afflicting the core city. With the

[26] In William L. Riordon, *Plunkitt of Tammany Hall* (New York: Dutton, 1963), p. 21.

population shift to suburbia, the "urban crisis" in America has become the "urban-suburban crisis," or, more accurately, a "metropolitan crisis."

The Problems of the Cities

In Greece, more than 2000 years ago, planners dreamed of a new city-state called Megalopolis. *Polis* was the Greek word for city-state (from which "politics" is derived), and "mega" comes from the word for "large," so Megalopolis meant a very large city. In 1961 Jean Gottmann used the word to describe "the unique cluster of metropolitan areas of the northeastern seaboard of the United States."[27] Stretching 600 miles through eleven states in a band thirty to one hundred miles wide, this region in 1979 contained a total of 54 million people and included the cities of Boston, New York, Philadelphia, Baltimore, and Washington.[28] Driving through the area, it seemed almost one continuous community. Some urban experts foresee the time when the United States will have three megalopolises, "Boswash," "Chipitts" (a strip from Chicago to Pittsburgh), and "San-San" (San Francisco to San Diego) along the West Coast.

But is this how people were meant to live? Since the beginning of civilization, people have clustered together in cities, which have served as magnets of communication, commerce, and culture. But critics of megalopolis have deplored the effect of the modern city on the quality of life. Lewis Mumford has asked: "Will the whole planet turn into a vast urban hive?"[29] Mumford argued that the modern metropolis has grown in "a continuous shapeless mass," that its residents are subject to constant frustration and harassment in their daily lives; at the same time they have become increasingly removed from nature.[30]

On the other hand, Edward C. Banfield has argued that most city dwellers "live more comfortably and conveniently than ever before." In Banfield's view, many urban problems—congestion, for example—are overstated: "people come to the city . . . precisely *because* it is congested. If it were not congested, it would not be worth coming to." In defending the city, Banfield adds: "To a large extent, then, our urban problems are just like the mechanical rabbit at the racetrack, which is set to keep just ahead of the dogs no matter how fast they may run. Our performance is better and better, but because we set our standards and expectations to keep ahead of performance, the problems are never any nearer to solution."[31] Despite Banfield's defense of urban life, a more general view is that the nation's cities *are* in difficulty and that problems such as race, slums, crime, housing, and transportation are not being solved fast enough in the world's richest society.

Part of the problem is that cities are no longer performing the same role they performed in the past. In the nineteenth and early twentieth centuries, America's cities were great socializing engines, taking unskilled immigrants from Europe and, in a generation or two, turning many of them into middle-class or even affluent Americans. But to some extent, that process has stopped. The migrants to the cities in recent decades have been black Americans. And, historically, blacks have not been integrated into American society in the same way

[27] Jean Gottmann, *Megalopolis* (New York: Twentieth Century Fund, 1961), p. 4.
[28] U.S. Bureau of the Census, *Current Population Reports,* Population Profile of the United States: 1979, Series P-20, No. 350. May 1980, p. 28.
[29] Lewis Mumford, *The City in History: Its Origins, Its Transformations, and Its Prospects* (New York: Harcourt Brace Jovanovich, 1961), p. 3.
[30] *Ibid.,* pp. 543–48.
[31] Edward C. Banfield, *The Unheavenly City* (Boston: Little, Brown, 1970), p. 5.

as the Irish, Italians, Jews, Poles, and other groups; blacks have faced greater and more persistent discrimination.

Who will pay for the cost of providing schools, housing, and other social services for residents of the inner city? That remains the core of the dilemma; the cities say they cannot, and many residents of the suburbs either have little desire to do so or feel they cannot afford higher taxes. City mayors complain that the federal government has simply not allocated enough money to bridge the gap. And many taxpayers—81 percent in one survey—either do not want an increase in services that would require higher taxes, or they favor a decrease in taxes and services.[32]

"The deterioration of urban life in the United States is one of the most complex and deeply rooted problems of our age," President Carter declared.[33] Some cities have attempted to reverse the trend by building attractive new commercial or residential complexes in the downtown area. Detroit's Renaissance Center, a multimillion-dollar office, shopping, and hotel development, is one example. Baltimore's impressive Harborplace complex opened in 1980, and similar projects have been developed in Boston and Philadelphia. But some critics have argued that expensive downtown centers, catering mainly to business executives and visitors, may only serve to mask the continuing and serious problems of the cities.

"Help!"   From *The Herblock Gallery* (Simon & Schuster, 1968)

Population Trends. Census Bureau figures tell much of the story of the "sorting out" of city and suburban population. During the decade of the 1960s the white population of the central cities *declined* by about 600,000 persons, but the white population of the suburbs *increased* by 15.5 million. During the same period, the black population of the central cities *increased* by 3.2 million persons. By 1978, 55 percent of all black Americans lived in central cities, and only 20 percent lived in suburbs surrounding the cities. By contrast, only 24 percent of

---

[32] Opinion poll conducted by the Advisory Commission on Intergovernmental Relations, March 1976, and quoted in *National Journal,* September 18, 1976, p. 1322. The poll showed that 51 percent of respondents wanted governments to "keep taxes and services about where they are," while 30 percent favored a decrease, for a total of 81 percent.

[33] *Urban America: Policies and Problems* (Washington, D.C.: Congressional Quarterly Inc., 1978), p. 1.

Left: Renaissance Center, Detroit. *Right:* Harborplace, Baltimore.

Distribution of White and Black Population: 1978

Figure 16–4

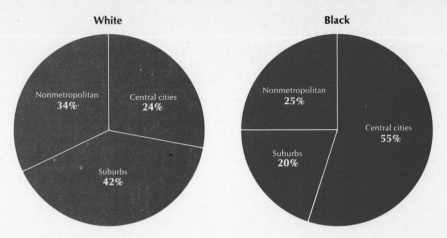

White

- Nonmetropolitan 34%
- Central cities 24%
- Suburbs 42%

Black

- Nonmetropolitan 25%
- Central cities 55%
- Suburbs 20%

Source: Adapted from U.S. Bureau of the Census, *The Social and Economic Status of the Black Population in the United States: An Historical View, 1790–1978,* Series P–23, No. 80, 1979, p. 171. Percentages are rounded.

the white population lived in central cities, and 41 percent lived in suburbia. (See Figure 16-4.)

As noted earlier in this chapter (and in Chapter 5, p. 170), more black Americans were migrating to the suburbs. Between 1960 and 1980, according to a Census Bureau survey, in round numbers the black suburban population jumped from 2.8 to 4.8 million people, an increase of about 71 percent. During the same period, white suburbia grew from 56.3 to 76.9 million people, an increase of 36 percent. But the percentage of whites who lived in the suburbs was twice that of blacks.

Despite the popular image of poor whites and blacks pouring into the cities to go on relief rolls, one study of urban migration indicates that people come to the cities for jobs, not social services, and that, compared to the nonwhite population already living in the cities, the average nonwhite who comes to the city has a higher occupational and educational background.[34] But the newcomers face job and housing discrimination; they are not in the same position as whites moving to a pleasant suburban neighborhood. As one observer put it, "the Welcome Wagon rarely calls in the ghetto."[35]

Housing, HUD, and Community Development. Officials of the federal government and others who have studied urban problems differ widely on how to break the circle of poverty in the inner city. Where should government begin in attempting to eliminate poverty and slums? With housing? Schools? Jobs? All of those things at once? Nobody really knows the answer.

The difficulties of making progress in attacking the overall problem can be illustrated by a close look at just one aspect of urban needs: housing. Substandard housing exists in rural as well as urban areas. Nevertheless, inner-city slums were and are a highly visible, urgent social problem.

[34] Charles Tilly, "Race and Migration to the American City," in Wilson, *The Metropolitan Enigma,* pp. 129–31.
[35] *Ibid.,* p. 142.

Left: St. Louis: Pruitt-Igoe housing project is dynamited. *Right:* New York City: the South Bronx.

How well has the United States coped with that problem? In the Housing Act of 1949, Congress proclaimed the goal of "a decent home and a suitable living environment for every American family." That goal, the law states, shall be met "as soon as feasible." Yet in 1960 there were 8.5 million dwellings listed as substandard in the United States. And ten years later there were still 4.7 million.[36]

Not long ago, a New York family that asked for an apartment in a public housing project became No. 130,801 on the waiting list. At the existing rate of construction, the family could expect to move into a project *in fifty-one years.*[37] The government has spent billions on housing, yet the federal effort has nowhere near kept pace with the need for better housing. And many public housing projects tend to be institutional-looking, sterile places plagued by crime and vandalism. In St. Louis, the government blew up the Pruitt-Igoe housing project, which had been built with federal support, because vandals and the high crime rate had led to the abandonment of most of the apartments.

In many cities, and most notably in St. Louis, and the South Bronx, in New York, whole neighborhoods have become wastelands of rubble-strewn streets,

[36] Data for "households," provided by U.S. Bureau of the Census.
[37] David K. Shipler, "The Changing City: Housing Paralysis," in *The Changing City* (New York: New York Times, 1969), p. 25.

The Myth of Money

There is a wistful myth that if only we had enough money to spend—the figure is usually put at a hundred billion dollars—we could wipe out all our slums in ten years, reverse decay in the great, dull, gray belts that were yesterday's and day-before-yesterday's suburbs, anchor the wandering middle class and its wandering tax money, and perhaps even solve the traffic problem.

But look what we have built with the first several billions: Low-income projects that become worse centers of delinquency, vandalism, and general social hopelessness than the slums they were supposed to replace. Middle-income housing projects which are truly marvels of dullness and regimentation, sealed against any buoyancy or vitality of city life. Luxury housing projects that mitigate their inanity, or try to, with a vapid vulgarity. Cultural centers that are unable to support a good bookstore. Civic centers that are avoided by everyone but bums, who have fewer choices of loitering place than others. Commercial centers that are lackluster imitations of standardized suburban chainstore shopping. Promenades that go from no place to nowhere and have no promenaders. Expressways that eviscerate great cities. This is not the rebuilding of cities. This is the sacking of cities.

—Jane Jacobs, *The Death and Life of Great American Cities.*

Four-year-old Carmen had fallen from the fifth-floor tenement window and the congressman walked up the stairs to pay his respects. He could have used the elevator, but its floor was covered with urine.

The light fixtures on each landing were ripped out, there were huge gaping holes in the sheet-rocked hallways, the walls were covered with the foulest graffiti, and it was necessary for Rep. Robert Garcia, who represents this South Bronx district, to sidestep the feces in the hallway.

The mother was not at home; she was with her child, who was in critical condition at the hospital. But kids "from somewhere" had already burglarized the apartment.

Welcome to Jose de Diego-Beekman housing project, where upwards of 6,000 people live in the largest government-subsidized effort at rehabilitated housing in the country.

. . . the security man says the addicts come to this neighborhood from all over New York: "It's every-where, every street corner. How are we gonna keep them out? The elevators don't work because the junkies rob the copper from the motors to sell for a fix. They steal anything. They live anywhere. The hallway is their living room and bathroom. We try, but it's a bigger job than I have men to deal with."

— *Los Angeles Times,* August 8, 1978.

boarded-up and abandoned buildings, vacant lots, and stripped automobiles. "Tens of thousands of deteriorated but structurally sound housing units have been abandoned," the *New York Times* reported in a national survey in 1978.[38]

Sometimes federal programs appear to have conflicting goals. More than 800 communities and practically every large city in America participated in the federal urban renewal program that began in 1949. Under the program, the federal government defrayed two-thirds to three-fourths of the cost of local slum-clearance projects. In many cases, however, urban renewal has *added* to inner-city tensions by forcing poor people from their homes to make way for middle- or upper-income housing and commercial centers. Fannie Lou Hamer, an outspoken black civil rights leader in Mississippi, made this observation on the subject of urban renewal: "We're already living nowhere, and now they're going to move us out of that."[39]

The responsibility of the federal government for housing was given recognition at the cabinet level in 1965 when Congress established the Department of Housing and Urban Development (HUD). The same year, Congress passed a comprehensive housing bill, including for the first time a program of rent supplements for low-income families.

In 1966 Congress approved a major new Model Cities program under the direction of HUD. The goal of the Model Cities program was to rebuild entire poverty neighborhoods in selected cities, particularly in black urban ghettos, and to attack social problems as well as the physical problem of decaying buildings. Model Cities was one of the major legislative programs passed under President Johnson's "Great Society." Over a period of several years Congress provided almost $4 billion for Model Cities in 150 communities, but the program became embroiled in controversy. Even friends of the Model Cities program were disappointed in its record. In Atlanta, Representative Charles L. Weltner had high

[38] *New York Times,* February 26, 1978, p. 28.
[39] Speech, Robert F. Kennedy Memorial Journalism Awards dinner, Washington, D.C., June 19, 1969.

hopes for that city's $32 million project. But in 1978 Weltner reported that the number of housing units in the Atlanta program had actually decreased and the percentage of families on welfare had gone up. "For the most part," he said, "things . . . are about the same, except maybe a little worse."[40]

In 1973 President Nixon curtailed or ended a number of federal housing programs, including Model Cities, public housing, and urban renewal, and proposed to consolidate these and other programs into one large community development package. Nixon argued that federally aided public housing had often failed. "All across America, the federal government has become the biggest slumlord in history," Nixon said.[41]

In 1974 Congress approved a program of block grants, absorbing Model Cities into a new, $11.1 billion housing package. In addition to the block grants for urban development, the new Housing and Community Development Act provided for rent supplements and various forms of housing rehabilitation, apartment subsidies, and mortgage interest subsidies. Finally, in 1976, Congress revived public housing construction on a limited scale, ending a three-year moratorium that had been imposed by Nixon. And the following year it enacted a program of Urban Development Action Grants to aid the most distressed cities through joint public and private developments.

Some middle-class voters have opposed spending tax money for low-income housing for the poor. Yet, middle-income and more affluent homeowners receive what amounts to a huge federal housing subsidy because they can deduct the interest they pay on their mortgage loans in figuring their federal income taxes. Low- and middle-income homeowners benefit as well from the fact that the Federal Housing Administration (FHA) insures the mortgages of many homes.

Federal housing policy is closely related to civil rights issues; in 1976 the Supreme Court ruled that under certain circumstances, the federal government might be required to finance federal housing projects in white suburban neighborhoods—not just in black areas within cities.[42] But in 1977 the Supreme Court held that suburban communities could not be compelled to change their zoning to permit low- and middle-income housing unless the "intent" of the zoning was to keep out blacks or other minorities.[43] The net result of these two decisions was that suburbs had considerable power to exclude public housing. "For large numbers of suburbanites," Michael N. Danielson has observed, "subsidized housing is a threat, the incarnation of everything in urban society they have sought to insulate themselves from in politically autonomous communities."[44] Danielson suggests that racial prejudice is an important factor in such suburban resistance to housing projects, but he argues that many suburbanites are also concerned about the socioeconomic impact in their communities of low-income families; they fear lower property values, crime, and higher taxes for social services.[45]

By fiscal 1981 the federal government had budgeted $11.7 billion for

[40] William Raspberry, "Model Cities: Learning from Their Failure," *Washington Post,* January 9, 1978, p. A23.

[41] President Nixon's message to Congress on community development, September 19, 1973, quoted in Congressional Quarterly, *Weekly Report,* September 22, 1973, p. 2522.

[42] *Hills* v. *Gautreaux,* 425 U.S. 284 (1976).

[43] *Village of Arlington Heights* v. *Metropolitan Development Corporation,* 429 U.S. 252 (1977).

[44] Michael N. Danielson, *The Politics of Exclusion* (New York: Columbia University Press, 1976), p. 83.

[45] *Ibid.,* pp. 83–92.

housing programs. There were 1.1 million units of occupied public housing, and about 900,000 families were assisted under "Section 8" of the 1974 housing act and its amendments. Under this program, low-income families paid up to one-quarter of their rent for private housing, and the federal government paid the rest directly to the landlord.

Taken as a whole, however, the federal housing program illustrates the difficulties confronting the nation in meeting the urban crisis. Only 8 percent of eligible families were receiving housing aid.[46] And, although housing has finally been recognized as a cabinet-level problem, the nation's need for decent housing for all Americans remains a goal rather than a reality.

Urban Transportation. The man in the traffic helicopter seldom broadcasts good news; getting in and out of the nation's cities during morning and evening rush hours, or getting to work within the city limits, is often an ordeal. Americans spend a substantial part of their lives commuting to and from their jobs; and time spent in a crowded subway, as Lewis Mumford has suggested, takes its toll: "Emerson said that life was a matter of having good days, but it is a matter of having good minutes too. Who shall say what compensations are not necessary to the metropolitan worker to make up for the strain and depression of the twenty, forty, sixty, or more minutes he spends each night and morning passing through these metropolitan man-sewers?"[47]

Metropolitan transportation in the United States has been dominated by the automobile and the highway. Commuter railroads and other forms of mass transit were permitted to decline during the 1950s and 1960s. Federal policy has to some extent influenced the dominance of highways over rails. The federal government pays 90 percent of the cost of the huge interstate highway program, a massive incentive for states and cities to build roads rather than transit lines. The federal funds come from highway user taxes on trucks and buses, tires, and

---

[46] *National Journal,* March 1, 1980, p. 363. Data as of 1978.
[47] Mumford, *The City in History: Its Origins, Its Transformations, and Its Prospects,* pp. 549–50.

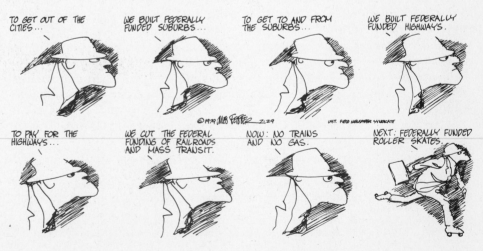

© 1979 Jules Feiffer

gasoline; the program, passed by Congress in 1956, was designed to link the nation's cities with 41,000 miles of superhighways, almost all of them four lane. Powerful interest groups have major stakes in highway politics. But the nation has not developed an overall transportation policy, one that would balance highways and rapid transit, and ease congestion in metropolitan centers. The nation's dependence on the automobile became painfully obvious when Americans were confronted in 1973 and 1979 with a shortage of oil and gasoline.

The Urban Mass Transportation Act of 1970 authorized a ten-year, $12 billion program to enable cities to build or improve rapid rail, subway, and bus commuter lines. Congress in 1973 raised the federal share of urban mass transit funds to 80 percent, and for the first time approved the use of millions of dollars in the Highway Trust Fund for urban transit needs; the law provided up to $800 million a year from the trust fund for buses, railways, and subways. In the Mass Transportation Assistance Act of 1974, Congress provided another $11.9 billion over six years for the nation's urban mass transit systems. The law for the first time authorized federal money — almost $4 billion — to pay the operating costs of transit systems. Under President Carter, Congress enacted the Highway and Public Transportation Act of 1978, which provided $54 billion for highways and mass transit through 1982.

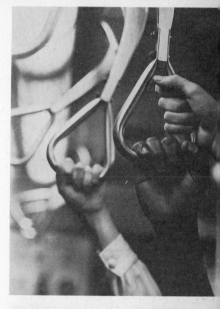

"I'm supposed to be in the new U.S. Department of Transportation — if I can get to it."

From *The Herblock Gallery* (Simon & Schuster, 1968)

629

State and Local Government

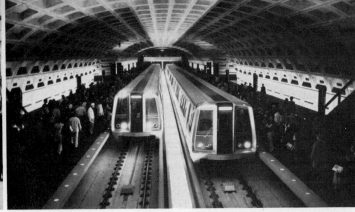

Left: BART, San Francisco. *Right:* METRO, Washington, D.C.

San Francisco's gleaming BART subway system, Washington, D.C.'s subway, and Atlanta's MARTA are examples of both the benefits and limitations of mass transit. BART has provided modern transportation for many residents of the San Francisco Bay area, but it has not—as its sponsors hoped—substantially reduced traffic jams on the highways. The commuters who now use BART instead of cars to get to work appear to have been replaced by other drivers. And the system has been running at a huge deficit.[48] The first segment of Washington's Metro opened in 1976 and provided fast, comfortable, and esthetically pleasing downtown transportation for the nation's capital. But Metro construction costs were expected to soar to $8 billion by the project's scheduled completion date in 1990, and the system has been losing money.[49] Atlanta's MARTA opened in 1979 and was expected to cost $3.3 billion; but it will be years, perhaps a decade or longer, before it extends far enough out to serve the city's northside commuters.

Problems interlock. The dominance of the automobile and the highway is directly related both to the energy crisis and to the problem of pollution, since automobiles produce at least 60 percent of total air pollution in the United States (electric power plants and industry account for most of the rest).

Poverty. Poverty remains a pervasive problem in American cities, overshadowing or underlying almost all other problems. In 1978 almost 62 percent of all poor persons lived in metropolitan areas. Of these, about one-quarter of the poor white families lived in the central cities, but for blacks the total was 60 percent.[50]

This does not mean that urban and racial problems are synonymous. However, the black, Mexican American, or Puerto Rican child in the inner-city ghetto is caught up in a circle of poverty from which there is often no exit. Education may be one key to eliminating poverty, but inner-city schools often occupy the oldest buildings and have the least experienced teachers, since many teachers with seniority shun assignments to ghetto classrooms. Blacks and other minorities face discrimination in employment and housing as well. Un-

[48] See Robert Lindsey, "Mass Transit, Little Mass," *New York Times Magazine,* October 19, 1975, p. 17.

[49] *National Journal,* August 7, 1976, p. 1110.

[50] U.S. Bureau of the Census, *Current Population Reports,* Characteristics of the Population Below the Poverty Level: 1978, Series P-60, No. 124, July 1980, pp. 2–7.

like such physical problems as transportation or air pollution, racial bias involves social attitudes that work against certain minority groups. Many of the problems of the nation's cities, therefore, are bound up with the larger problem of ensuring full equality for all Americans.

On a bleak day in October 1975, New York City stood literally only two hours away from financial default. The proud Eastern city, which considers itself America's cultural and business leader, the city that is the home of Wall Street and the great television networks, stood on the brink of insolvency. It was unable to meet its fiscal obligations to its bondholders.

Urban Fiscal Problems: The Case of New York City

At that perilous moment, Albert Shanker, the leader of the city's teachers' union, came forward and saved New York from default by investing $150 million in union pension funds in the bonds of the Municipal Assistance Corporation, known colloquially as "Big Mac."

There was, in that fall of 1975, widespread fear that if New York went under, other cities facing similar financial problems might find it impossible to sell their bonds to investors. Default by New York and other cities, it was believed by some experts, might have serious effects on the already troubled United States economy. And, like New York, other major cities had found it necessary to cut back city services, freeze wages, or lay off municipal workers while attempting to cope with inadequate tax revenues and increasing costs.

The crisis faced by New York City and its mayor, Abraham Beame, had historical roots. For many years, the city, which has a liberal political tradition, spent billions for social services and welfare programs. At the same time, its expenditures were rising much faster than its revenues — three times as fast in the decade prior to 1975.[51] Increasingly, the city turned to short-term borrowing to raise money.

By 1975 mounting city deficits — despite heavy borrowing — had shaken the municipal bond market. Put simply, the city found that no one wanted its bonds. New York State moved to help the city, and the legislature assisted MAC, a special borrowing agency for the city. The legislature also established an emergency financial control board to monitor city spending, which meant that Governor Hugh Carey and a state-dominated board, rather than Mayor Beame, were now in control of the city's finances.[52]

President Ford, sensing a profitable political issue, campaigned for a time against New York City. "I am prepared to veto any bill that has as its purpose a federal bailout of New York City to prevent a default," he said.[53] By November the hostility toward New York had given way to fear; bankers, economists, and politicians worried that the snowballing effect of default by the city might cause a more general financial crisis. Ford reversed course and proposed a $2.3 billion package of aid to New York City, which Congress approved. The immediate crisis was over, but the city continued to face severe financial difficulties; in 1978, under the Carter administration, Congress approved a long-range program of $1.65 billion in federal loan guarantees for the city.

Donald H. Haider has suggested that New York's fiscal problems follow a

[51] Donald H. Haider, "Fiscal Scarcity: A New Urban Perspective," in Louis H. Masotti and Robert L. Lineberry, *The New Urban Politics* (Cambridge, Mass.: Ballinger Publishing, 1976), p. 187.
[52] *Ibid.,* p. 202.
[53] *Ibid.,* p. 204.

"You should have been here in the old days, before the budget cutbacks.... There were cops and fire engines and planes buzzing around ..."

Mike Peters for the *Dayton Daily News*

pattern; he has concluded that higher taxes were usually imposed in the city in the one year in four in which there was no city, state, or national election. The mayor, the governor, the state legislature, and the city labor unions all bargained for advantage within this "election-tax cycle." In Haider's view, "The city has an insufficient tax base to carry out the range of services and redistributive programs it gradually became wedded to."[54] The precarious situation of the nation's largest city and its more than 7 million residents was a dramatic reminder of the serious nature of the problems faced by America's cities.

Urban Politics: Governing the Cities

The term "power structure" is often heard today. It was popularized three decades ago by Floyd Hunter, a sociologist who studied community leadership in Atlanta, Georgia.[55] Hunter concluded that a group of about forty people, mostly top businessmen, determined policy in Atlanta and used the machinery of government to attain their own goals.

But in a study of New Haven, Connecticut, Robert Dahl concluded that the city was not run by a power elite of economic or social notables, and that policy decisions were made by changing coalitions of leaders drawn from different segments of the community.[56] As we noted in Chapter 6, scholars have provided diverse answers to the question of "Who governs?" Some scholars argue that power elites make public policy, but other political scientists see American society as pluralistic, with many—although not all—groups sharing in the decision making.

Edward C. Banfield and James Q. Wilson have contended that, regardless of how decisions are made in various American cities, all cities have one thing in common: "Persons not elected to office play very considerable parts in the making of many important decisions."[57] Banfield and Wilson have suggested the term "influentials" for these powerful citizens who hold no official position.

When most people think of city government, however, they usually think of decisions being made by officials elected to political office by the voters. As on the national and state levels, parties, politics, and the ballot box play a central role in the decisions made at the city level that affect people's lives.

Thomas Bradley, Mayor of Los Angeles

[54] *Ibid.*, pp. 186–200.

[55] Floyd Hunter, *Community Power Structure* (Chapel Hill, N.C.: University of North Carolina Press, 1953).

[56] Robert A. Dahl, *Who Governs?* (New Haven, Conn.: Yale University Press, 1961).

[57] Edward C. Banfield and James Q. Wilson, *City Politics* (Cambridge, Mass.: Harvard University Press, 1963), pp. 244–45.

Left: Coleman Young, Mayor of Detroit. *Center:* Maynard Jackson, Mayor of Atlanta. *Right:* Marion Barry, Mayor of Washington, D.C.

One result of the migration of many whites to the suburbs has been that more cities with a large black electorate have chosen black officials. In 1980, for example, Los Angeles; Detroit; Atlanta; Gary, Indiana; Newark, New Jersey; and Washington, D.C., all had black mayors; in several of these cities the black population exceeded the white population. By 1979, 191 American cities had black mayors.

Historically, the big-city political machine has characterized urban politics. The political machines traded jobs and social services for the votes of immigrants. But with the changing nature of American society, urban political machines have declined. The power of Tammany Hall was broken in New York City in the early 1960s by a Democratic reform movement. In Chicago the reign of Chicago's powerful political leader, Mayor Richard J. Daley, often described as the last of the big-city bosses, ended with his death in 1976.

As the tightly structured, old-style political machines have faded away,

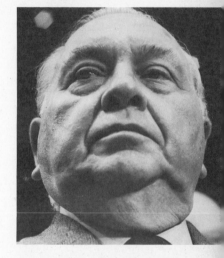

The late Mayor Richard J. Daley of Chicago

"Honest Graft": Boss Plunkitt's Philosophy

Nobody thinks of drawin' the distinction between honest graft and dishonest graft. There's all the difference in the world between the two. . . . My party's in power in the city, and it's goin' to undertake a lot of public improvements. Well, I'm tipped off, say, that they're going to lay out a new park at a certain place.

I see my opportunity and I take it. I go to that place and I buy up all the land I can in the neighborhood. Then the board of this or that makes its plan public, and there is a rush to get my land, which nobody cared particular for before.

Ain't it perfectly honest to charge a good price and make a profit on my investment and foresight? Of course, it is. Well, that's honest graft.

— Boss Plunkitt, quoted in William L. Riordon, *Plunkitt of Tammany Hall.*

mayors of large cities have found it more difficult to govern. Their power has become diffused. One reason for this is the growth of "functional fiefdoms," specialized government agencies that operate specific programs, such as urban renewal or highway construction.[58] As these agencies have increased in number, they have often made independent decisions, bypassing the power of mayors and city councils.

Just as public administrators exercise great power in the federal government, bureaucracies on the local level influence and limit the power of a big-city mayor—as do other factors. One study of urban politics noted that the mayor of New York must share his power with party leaders, appointed and elected public officials, the bureaucracy, nongovernmental associations and the media, and officials and agencies of governments outside New York City. Since no one group dominates, decisions are actually the result of "mutual accommodation."[59] In short, the business of governing a metropolis usually means that mayors are constantly striving to build and maintain workable coalitions of interest groups; their power is limited and they are handy targets when things go wrong. Another study of how mayors govern found at least five distinct mayoral styles and concluded that no one approach was necessarily the "best." And the study noted that mayors, because of the difficulties and frustrations of their jobs, may not ever achieve any higher political office.[60]

The Face
of the Suburbs

The 1980 census figures confirmed the existence of a trend that urban specialists had begun to suspect—some suburbs closest to central cities had actually begun to lose population. The only suburban growth occurring in the New York City region, for example, was found in the far outer edges of the metropolitan region.

"This is a national phenomenon," Dr. George Sternlieb of Rutgers University said. "It is a pattern that is occurring within every large metropolitan area." Blue- and white-collar workers, he said, are "leapfrogging" farther out into "exurbia" to find housing they can afford.[61]

The changing population pattern in the suburbs in the 1980s was in marked contrast to the massive migration to the closer-in suburbs after the Second World War. One of the phenomena of that migration was the construction of whole new communities by a single builder. In 1958 Herbert Gans, a young sociologist, moved with his family into one such instant suburb, Levittown, New Jersey. His purpose was to study the community as a participant and observer. In recording the quality of social life in this suburb of Philadelphia, Gans quoted one woman describing her next-door neighbor: "We see eye to eye on things, about raising kids, doing things together with your husband, living the same way; we have practically the same identical background."[62]

Although most suburbs are not modeled on Levittown, the quote summarizes both sides of the argument about suburbia. In an impersonal society, where people toil on assembly lines or in beehive offices of large corporations, many Americans long for a sense of identity and belonging. In part, people have

[58] John J. Harrigan, *Political Change in the Metropolis* (Boston: Little, Brown, 1976), pp. 139–46.
[59] Wallace S. Sayre and Herbert Kaufman, *Governing New York City: Politics in the Metropolis* (New York: Norton, 1965), pp. 710–12.
[60] John P. Kotter and Paul R. Lawrence, *Mayors in Action: Five Approaches to Urban Governance* (New York: Wiley, 1974).
[61] *New York Times,* October 7, 1980, p. 1.
[62] Herbert J. Gans, *The Levittowners* (New York: Pantheon Books, 1967), p. 155.

moved to the suburbs in "a search for community." To some extent, the migration to the suburbs may be seen as a turning back to the grass roots, a yearning for the small-town America celebrated by Booth Tarkington and Mark Twain. On the other hand, the suburbs have been assailed as centers of conformity and homogeneity, in which community pressures tend to produce narrow social and political attitudes among suburbanites and massive unconcern for urban and national problems.

Why do people move to the suburbs in the first place? According to Peter Rossi, they are both "pushed" and "pulled."[63] The "push" reasons are often emphasized: crime in the cities, fear of crime, bad schools, deteriorating housing. But the "pull" reasons are also highly important: the desire for more space and to "own our own home" and the attraction of suburban schools, for example. The automobile and FHA mortgage guarantees, allowing lower- and middle-income families to purchase their own homes, have been powerful factors as well.

The move to suburbia has brought change to the center of America's cities. Despite the efforts of a number of cities to revitalize their downtown districts, in many metropolitan areas not only people, but jobs and industry, have moved to the suburbs. Suburban residents no longer need to go to the city to shop; the department stores have moved to suburban shopping centers to be near *them*. There is still a need for downtown business areas, but often less as centers of retail trade than as places for the conduct of businesses that require face-to-face contact — banking, finance, and communications, for example.

Not all suburbs are alike. Some of the older, more affluent suburbs have been able to preserve their residential character. But the newer suburbs have mammoth retail shopping centers, office buildings, industrial parks, and other hallmarks of cities. Thus, as Louis H. Masotti has noted, suburbia is "becoming increasingly less *sub*urban and more urban."[64]

In the popular image, however, life in the suburbs tends to be centered around home and family. And the stereotype of the suburban father happily barbecuing steaks on his outdoor grill or fussing with his lawn sometimes reflects the reality. But what about his less fortunate fellow citizens back in the city? Gans suggests that the Levittowners "deceive themselves into thinking that the community, or rather the home, is the single most influential unit in their lives. . . . the real problem is that the Levittowners have not yet become aware of how much they are a part of the national society and economy."[65]

[63] Peter H. Rossi, *Why Families Move* (New York: Free Press of Glencoe, 1955).
[64] Louis H. Masotti and Jeffrey K. Hadden, eds., *The Urbanization of the Suburbs* (Beverly Hills, Cal.: Sage Publications, 1973), p. 17.
[65] Gans, *The Levittowners*, p. 418.

Today, however, the suburbs face many of the same problems that are faced by cities. The suburbanites who take pride in their shrubs, homes, and communities are also part of a larger American community with many unpleasant problems that cannot be wished away. Particularly the older suburbs, closest to the central cities, are facing difficult problems, including rising welfare costs and physical deterioration. Sooner or later—and it may be happening sooner—the quality of life in the nation as a whole will be reflected in the suburbs.

Although social problems such as inferior education, poor housing, crime, and inadequate health care have greatest impact in the cities, "they are not unknown to the suburbs and are increasingly being found there. . . . more and more suburban communities have city-like characteristics and all the problems associated with those characteristics."[66] There is, in short, no place to hide from the problems faced by American society as a whole.

The Politics of Suburbia

The fact that more Americans—in excess of 83 million now—live in what could be termed "the suburbs" might be expected to have some impact on the political system. A closely related question is whether people who live in the suburbs really hold different political views from residents of other areas, or whether the suburbs are merely experiencing the first stages of urbanization—growing into cities, as it were.

One way to measure the political impact of the population shift to suburbia is to study the reflection of that growth in the Congress. Richard Lehne has noted that in 1974, following the redistricting in Congress after the 1970 census, for the first time representatives from suburban areas composed the largest single group in Congress. There were 132 suburban legislators, 130 from rural districts, 109 from the central cities, and 64 from mixed metropolitan areas.[67]

"The election of large and increasing numbers of suburban representatives to Congress means that, today and in the future, Congress must come to grips with the policy positions and reform preferences of suburbanites," Lehne suggested.[68] Analyzing ratings of representatives by interest groups, Lehne concluded that central-city legislators take liberal policy positions, rural representatives favor conservative policies, and men and women who represent suburban constituents "strike a moderate balance between the other two groups."[69]

But Lehne also discovered that members of Congress from older, established suburbs tend to take more liberal positions on most issues than representatives from the newer suburbs. These findings, Lehne concluded, support those who contend that the process of urbanization has extended to the suburbs. The members of Congress from older suburbs tended to vote much like their city cousins.[70]

Another study of emerging suburban political power, by Thomas P. Murphy and John Rehfuss, found great diversity among the suburbs and their representa-

[66] Alan K. Campbell and Donna E. Shalala, "Problems Unsolved, Solutions Untried: The Urban Crisis," in Alan K. Campbell, ed., *The States and the Urban Crisis* (Englewood Cliffs, N.J.: Prentice-Hall, 1970), p. 21.

[67] Richard Lehne, "Suburban Foundations of the New Congress," in *Annals of the American Academy of Political and Social Science,* November 1975, p. 143.

[68] *Ibid.,* p. 142.

[69] *Ibid.,* p. 144.

[70] *Ibid.,* p. 150.

636

The American Community

tives in Congress. "Despite the increase in the number of congressmen representing suburban districts," the authors said, "a strong suburban bloc has not emerged."[71] One reason they cite is that "different types of suburbs have different needs." The study concluded: " 'Suburban power' remains a paper tiger, but it has the potential to exert great influence."[72]

Exploding Metropolis and America's Future

If metropolitan problems are larger than the boundary lines of local governments, why not create larger political units to solve these problems? The approach might seem logical, but there are many obstacles to metropolitan government. Not the least of these is the reluctance of suburban areas to give up their political independence and to pay for services for residents of the central cities. And black residents of the cities, having finally achieved greater political power, electing black mayors in several cases, are equally reluctant to lose that hard-won power to a metropolitan government.

Metropolitan Solutions

Some efforts at "metro" solutions are being made, however, including the creation of special districts to handle specific functions, interstate compacts, area-wide planning agencies, consolidated school and library systems, and various informal intergovernmental arrangements. Annexation of outlying areas by the central city and the consolidation of cities and surrounding counties have all been tried; in many cases, they have been found wanting. Another approach has been the plan adopted in Los Angeles, under which the county has assumed responsibility for many area-wide functions, but local communities have retained their political autonomy.

Some urban experts have advocated metropolitan federalism as the best solution. Toronto, Canada, and its suburbs have operated under this system since 1953. Mass transit, planning, highways, and many other functions are run by a council made up of elected officials from the central city and surrounding suburbs. London also has a federated system encompassing the thirty-two boroughs of Greater London.

In Florida, Miami and Dade County narrowly opted for "Metro" government in 1957. Under the plan, Miami and twenty-seven suburban cities retain control of local functions, but have ceded to "Metro" area-wide functions such as fire and police protection and transportation. Political control is vested in an elected board of commissioners, which appoints a county manager.

Varying degrees of area-wide consolidation have been established in Nashville, Tennessee; Jacksonville, Florida; Baton Rouge, Louisiana; Seattle, Washington; Portland, Oregon; Indianapolis, Indiana; Columbus, Georgia; and Lexington, Kentucky. In all, there have been sixteen such consolidations since 1949.

Despite steps toward consolidation and metropolitan government in many areas of the country, some scholars have strongly disputed the "reformist"

[71] Thomas P. Murphy and John Rehfuss, *Urban Politics in the Suburban Era* (Homewood, Ill.: The Dorsey Press, 1976), p. 42.
[72] *Ibid.*, pp. 29, 40.

belief that a single metropolitan government, by eliminating overlapping jurisdictions, will promote greater efficiency. For example, one study has concluded that since individuals have different preferences in government services, "a system of government composed of many different units will be more responsive to the interests of citizens than a single government for any one urban region."[73]

As urban growth continues, however, old concepts of metropolitan areas may change. The cities of the industrial northeast, for example, may indeed come closer to the concept of "Boswash"—a single, giant city stretching along the eastern seaboard. One scholar has suggested that tomorrow's metropolis may look less like a fried egg, with a clearly defined center and outer ring, and more like "a thin layer of scrambled eggs over much of the platter."[74]

Intergovernmental Relations

Although this chapter has focused on state and local problems, any real solution to metropolitan ills depends in large measure on the relationship among federal, state, and local governments.

State and local governments frequently do not have enough revenues to meet the social demands of both urban and rural areas. The confused, overlapping programs of federal grants have been widely criticized. At the same time, state and local revenues have often lagged behind national economic growth. The federal system, insofar as intergovernmental fiscal relations are concerned, has become rather creaky at the joints.

One possible solution is revenue sharing, the multibillion-dollar experiment initiated by Congress in 1972. (Revenue sharing is discussed in detail in Chapter 3.) Under this system, the federal government, instead of channeling funds to state and local governments through highly structured federal programs, has simply given states and localities money to spend largely as they wish. The money is distributed under complex formulas based on population, per capita income, and each state and local government's effort to raise its own revenues. Under the extension passed by Congress in 1980, as in the past, the $4.6 billion a year in revenue-sharing funds for localities was to be paid directly to the communities. Such direct payments to localities, rather than channeling aid through the governors, is vital to any revenue-sharing plan, since city mayors do not trust state governors to pass on enough money to the cities voluntarily.

The American Challenge

The problems discussed in this chapter involve the question of what kind of nation America wants to be. How people live in their local communities reflects the quality of American life.

Do Americans have a sense of national community? Will comfortable or affluent Americans be willing to pay for better schools and for other social services for the poor? There is no constitutional requirement that an affluent majority take such steps on behalf of a less affluent minority. But the future of the nation's democratic institutions may be affected by the answer. John Gardner, a former cabinet member, has suggested:

[73] Robert L. Bish and Vincent Ostrom, *Understanding Urban Government: Metropolitan Reform Reconsidered* (Washington, D.C.: American Enterprise Institute for Public Policy Research, 1973), p. 73.

[74] York Willbern, *The Withering Away of the City* (Tuscaloosa, Ala.: University of Alabama Press, 1964), p. 33.

If Americans continue on their present path their epitaph might well be that they were a potentially great people—a marvelously dynamic people—who forgot their obligations to one another, who forgot how much they owed one another.

A further question is whether political institutions created when America was a rural nation can respond to, and cope with, the demands and problems of a highly urbanized, changing society. American democracy is under pressure; its institutions are being tested. Yet, the problems of American society—inflation, unemployment, the energy crisis, crime, pollution, racial discrimination, poverty, political corruption, and all the rest—are not necessarily beyond solution if Americans, acting through the political process, insist on change. To a great extent, the America of tomorrow can be what we try to make it.

More than one hundred years ago, the English philosopher John Stuart Mill voiced much the same thought in his essay, *On Liberty:* "The worth of a State, in the long run, is the worth of the individuals composing it."

Perspective

Since 1920 the population of the United States has been more urban than rural. By 1977 two-thirds of all Americans lived in metropolitan areas. And many of the nation's problems have developed in their most acute form in urban areas.

Today, the states have major responsibilities in the fields of education, welfare, transportation, the administration of justice, prisons, agriculture, public health, and the environment. States share with local governments responsibility for the delivery of these and many other vital public services. Each state has a constitution that provides for an executive, legislative, and judicial branch. A governor heads the executive branch.

There are three basic forms of city government: the mayor-council plan, the commission plan, and the council-manager plan. Other units of local government are counties, towns, townships, and special districts—created for such purposes as schools or fire protection—that extend beyond the boundary lines of local jurisdictions.

The nation's cities face a number of serious problems, among them race relations, slums, crime, housing, and transportation. The question remains: Who will pay the cost of providing social services for residents of the inner city?

The responsibility of the federal government for housing was given recognition at the cabinet level in 1965 when Congress established the Department of Housing and Urban Development. Federal housing policy is often related to civil rights issues. Although in fiscal 1981 the federal government had budgeted

$11.7 billion for its various housing programs, the need for decent housing is still unmet for millions of Americans.

The federal government has paid 90 percent of the cost of the interstate highway program, but it permitted mass transit to decline during the 1950s and 1960s. Until recently, there has been little interest in developing a national transportation policy that would balance highways and rapid transit, and ease congestion in metropolitan centers.

Many cities have been facing serious financial difficulties. In part, this is because many middle-class residents and businesses have moved out to the suburbs, taking the city tax base with them. At the same time, newcomers to the city have required costly government services. In the past, big-city political machines provided some of these services, but as these machines have declined, mayors of large cities have found it more difficult to govern.

Today, the suburbs are becoming increasingly urbanized and subject to many of the same social and economic problems faced by the cities—from education to high crime rates.

Two conclusions emerge from the numerous studies that have been made of state and local problems. First, many of the problems are larger than the boundaries of the governmental units that are attempting to deal with them. And second, the solutions frequently cost more money than the governmental units have available or are willing to spend.

Suggested Reading

Banfield, Edward C., and Wilson, James Q. *City Politics** (Harvard University Press, 1963). A comprehensive examination of politics in American cities.

Beyle, Thad, and Williams, J. Oliver, eds. *The American Governor in Behavioral Perspective* (Harper & Row, 1972). A valuable collection of essays that explore the political roles of the American governor. Examines specific policy areas within the states, including health care, crime, and education.

Danielson, Michael N. *The Politics of Exclusion** (Columbia University Press, 1976). An examination of the development and impact of exclusionary policies in the nation's suburbs. Analyzes the economic, social, and racial isolation of individual communities and discusses the role of suburban politics in perpetuating that isolation.

Gottmann, Jean. *Megalopolis** (M.I.T. Press, 1964). (Originally published in 1961.) A pioneering study of the geographical, economic, social, and cultural characteristics of America's northeastern urban corridor.

Harrigan, John J. *Political Change in the Metropolis** (Little, Brown, 1976). A detailed assessment of political change in urban America. Harrigan focuses on the decline of the old-style political machine and on the growth of specialized government agencies that operate specific programs and often bypass the power of elected officials.

Jacob, Herbert, and Vines, Kenneth N., eds. *Politics in the American States: A Comparative Analysis,* 3rd edition (Little, Brown, 1976). A useful collection of essays on various aspects of the political systems in the states, written by a number of leading authorities in the field.

Kotter, John P., and Lawrence, Paul R. *Mayors in Action: Five Approaches to Urban Governance* (Wiley, 1974). An informative study of how mayors govern in urban areas. The authors found at least five distinct types of mayoral styles; they concluded that no one approach to the job is necessarily the best.

Lockard, Duane. *The Politics of State and Local Government,* 2nd edition (Macmillan, 1969). A comprehensive analysis of the politics of U.S. state and local governments.

Meltsner, Arnold J. *The Politics of City Revenue** (University of California Press, 1971). A useful study emphasizing the political factors that make it difficult to raise money to pay for urban public services.

Murphy, Thomas P., and Rehfuss, John. *Urban Politics in the Suburban Era** (The Dorsey Press, 1976). A comprehensive and valuable study of the growth of suburban political power. Murphy and Rehfuss found great diversity among American suburbs in their purpose, size, politics, and representation in Congress. The authors concluded that despite increases in the number of suburban district representatives in Congress, a strong suburban bloc has not yet emerged.

Peirce, Neal R. *The Megastates of America* (Norton, 1972); *The Pacific States of America* (Norton, 1972); *The Mountain States of America* (Norton, 1972); *The Great Plains States of America* (Norton, 1973); *The Deep South States of America* (Norton, 1974); *The Border South States* (Norton, 1975); *The New England States* (Norton, 1976); *The Mid-Atlantic States of America* (Norton, 1977); and *The Great Lake States of America* (Norton, 1980). An unusually comprehensive and richly detailed sociopolitical guide to America, state by state.

Urban America: Policies and Problems* (Congressional Quarterly, Inc., 1978). A useful survey of the major urban issues in the United States. Examines various urban policy areas—from housing to mass transit—and summarizes the major urban legislation that was passed during the years 1973–1977.

Wilson, James Q. *Thinking About Crime** (Basic Books, 1975). A discussion of the problems of crime and law enforcement that are faced by many urban and suburban areas. Includes an analysis of the ways local communities attempt to deal with crime and offers some suggestions for improving public policies in this area.

* Available in paperback edition

THE CONSTITUTION OF THE UNITED STATES OF AMERICA*

We the people of the United States, in Order to form a more perfect Union, establish Justice, insure domestic Tranquility, provide for the common defence, promote the general Welfare, and secure the Blessings of Liberty to ourselves and our Posterity, do ordain and establish this Constitution for the United States of America.

ARTICLE I

Section 1. All legislative Powers herein granted shall be vested in a Congress of the United States, which shall consist of a Senate and House of Representatives.

Section 2. The House of Representatives shall be composed of Members chosen every second Year by the People of the several States, and the Electors in each State shall have the Qualifications requisite for Electors of the most numerous Branch of the State Legislature.

No Person shall be a Representative who shall not have attained to the Age of twenty-five Years, and been seven Years a Citizen of the United States, and who shall not, when elected, be an Inhabitant of that state in which he shall be chosen.

[Representatives and direct Taxes shall be apportioned among the several States which may be included within this Union, according to their respective Numbers, which shall be determined by adding to the whole Number of free Persons, including those bound to Service for a Term of Years, and excluding Indians not taxed, three fifths of all other Persons.] [1] The actual Enumeration shall be made within three Years after the first Meeting of the Congress of the United States, and within every subsequent Term of ten Years, in such Manner as they shall by Law direct. The Number of Representatives shall not exceed one for every thirty Thousand, but each State shall have at Least one Representative; and until such enumeration shall be made, the State of New Hampshire shall be entitled to chuse three, Massachusetts eight, Rhode-Island and Providence Plantations one, Connecticut five, New-York six, New Jersey four, Pennsylvania eight, Delaware one, Maryland six, Virginia ten, North Carolina five, South Carolina five, and Georgia three.

When vacancies happen in the Representation from any State, the Executive Authority thereof shall issue Writs of Election to fill such Vacancies.

The House of Representatives shall chuse their Speaker and other Officers; and shall have the sole Power of Impeachment.

Section 3. The Senate of the United States shall be composed of two Senators from each State, [chosen by the Legislature thereof,] [2] for six Years; and each Senator shall have one Vote.

Immediately after they shall be assembled in Consequence of the first Election, they shall be divided as equally as may be into three Classes. The Seats of the Senators of the first Class shall be vacated at the Expiration of the second Year, of the second Class at the Expiration of the fourth Year, and of the third Class at the Expiration of the sixth Year, so that one-third may be chosen every second Year; [and if Vacancies happen by Resignation, or otherwise, during the Recess of the Legislature of any State, the Executive thereof may make temporary Appointments until the next Meeting of the Legislature, which shall then fill such Vacancies].[3]

No Person shall be a Senator who shall not have attained to the Age of thirty Years, and been nine

---

* The Constitution and all amendments are shown in their original form. Parts that have been amended or superseded are bracketed and explained in the footnotes.
[1] Modified by the Fourteenth and Sixteenth amendments.

[2] Superseded by the Seventeenth Amendment.
[3] Modified by the Seventeenth Amendment.

Years a Citizen of the United States, and who shall not, when elected, be an Inhabitant of that State in which he shall be chosen.

The Vice-President of the United States shall be President of the Senate, but shall have no vote, unless they be equally divided.

The Senate shall chuse their other Officers, and also a President pro tempore, in the absence of the Vice-President, or when he shall exercise the Office of the President of the United States.

The Senate shall have the sole Power to try all Impeachments. When sitting for that purpose, they shall be on Oath or Affirmation. When the President of the United States is tried, the Chief Justice shall preside: And no person shall be convicted without the Concurrence of two thirds of the Members present.

Judgment in Cases of Impeachment shall not extend further than to removal from Office, and disqualification to hold and enjoy any Office of honor, Trust, or Profit under the United States: but the Party convicted shall nevertheless be liable and subject to Indictment, Trial, Judgment, and Punishment, according to Law.

Section 4. The Times, Places and Manner of holding Elections for Senators and Representatives, shall be prescribed in each state by the Legislature thereof; but the Congress may at any time by Law make or alter such Regulations, except as to the Places of Chusing Senators.

The Congress shall assemble at least once in every Year, and such Meeting shall [be on the first Monday in December,] [4] unless they shall by Law appoint a different Day.

Section 5. Each House shall be the Judge of the Elections, Returns and Qualifications of its own Members, and a Majority of each shall constitute a Quorum to do Business; but a smaller number may adjourn from day to day, and may be authorized to compel the Attendance of absent Members, in such Manner, and under such Penalties, as each House may provide.

Each House may determine the Rules of its Proceedings, punish its Members for disorderly Behavior, and, with the Concurrence of two thirds, expel a Member.

Each House shall keep a Journal of its Proceedings, and from time to time publish the same, excepting such Parts as may in their Judgment require Secrecy; and the Yeas and Nays of the Members of either House on any question shall, at the Desire of one fifth of those Present, be entered on the Journal.

Neither House, during the Session of Congress, shall, without the Consent of the other, adjourn for more than three days, nor to any other Place than that in which the two Houses shall be sitting.

Section 6. The Senators and Representatives shall receive a Compensation for their Services, to be ascertained by Law, and paid out of the Treasury of

the United States. They shall in all Cases, except Treason, Felony, and Breach of the Peace, be privileged from Arrest during their Attendance at the Session of their respective Houses, and in going to and returning from the same; and for any Speech or Debate in either House, they shall not be questioned in any other Place.

No Senator or Representative shall, during the Time for which he was elected, be appointed to any civil Office under the Authority of the United States, which shall have been created, or the Emoluments whereof shall have been increased, during such time; and no Person holding any Office under the United States shall be a Member of either House during his continuance in Office.

Section 7. All Bills for raising Revenue shall originate in the House of Representatives; but the Senate may propose or concur with Amendments as on other bills.

Every Bill which shall have passed the House of Representatives and the Senate, shall, before it become a Law, be presented to the President of the United States; If he approve he shall sign it, but if not he shall return it, with his Objections, to that House in which it shall have originated, who shall enter the Objections at large on their Journal, and proceed to reconsider it. If after such Reconsideration two thirds of that House shall agree to pass the bill, it shall be sent, together with the objections, to the other House, by which it shall likewise be reconsidered, and if approved by two thirds of that House, it shall become a Law. But in all such Cases the Votes of both Houses shall be determined by Yeas and Nays, and the Names of the Persons voting for and against the Bill shall be entered on the Journal of each House respectively. If any Bill shall not be returned by the President within ten Days (Sundays excepted) after it shall have been presented to him, the Same shall be a Law, in like Manner as if he had signed it, unless the Congress by their Adjournment prevent its Return, in which Case it shall not be a Law.

Every Order, Resolution, or Vote to which the Concurrence of the Senate and House of Representatives may be necessary (except on a question of Adjournment) shall be presented to the President of the United States; and before the Same shall take Effect, shall be approved by him, or being disapproved by him, shall be repassed by two thirds of the Senate and House of Representatives, according to the Rules and Limitations prescribed in the Case of a Bill.

Section 8. The Congress shall have Power To lay and collect Taxes, Duties, Imposts and Excises, to pay the Debts and provide for the common Defence and general Welfare of the United States; but all Duties, Imposts and Excises shall be uniform throughout the United States;

To borrow money on the credit of the United States;

To regulate Commerce with foreign Nations, and among the several States, and with the Indian Tribes;

To establish an uniform Rule of Naturalization,

---

[4] Superseded by the Twentieth Amendment.

and uniform Laws on the subject of Bankruptcies throughout the United States;

To coin Money, regulate the Value thereof, and of foreign Coin, and fix the Standard of Weights and Measures;

To provide for the Punishment of counterfeiting the Securities and current Coin of the United States;

To establish Post Offices and post Roads;

To promote the Progress of Science and useful Arts, by securing for limited Times to Authors and Inventors the exclusive Right to their respective Writings and Discoveries;

To constitute Tribunals inferior to the Supreme Court;

To define and punish Piracies and Felonies committed on the high Seas, and Offenses against the Law of Nations;

To declare War, grant Letters of Marque and Reprisal, and make Rules concerning Captures on Land and Water;

To raise and support Armies, but no Appropriation of Money to tnat Use shall be for a longer Term than two Years;

To provide and maintain a Navy;

To make Rules for the Government and Regulation of the land and naval forces;

To provide for calling forth the Militia to execute the Laws of the Union, suppress Insurrections and repel Invasions;

To provide for organizing, arming, and disciplining the Militia, and for governing such Part of them as may be employed in the Service of the United States, reserving to the States respectively, the Appointment of the Officers, and the Authority of training the Militia according to the discipline prescribed by Congress;

To exercise exclusive Legislation in all Cases whatsoever, over such District (not exceeding ten Miles square) as may, by Cession of particular States, and the acceptance of Congress, become the Seat of the Government of the United States, and to exercise like Authority over all Places purchased by the Consent of the Legislature of the State in which the Same shall be, for the Erection of Forts, Magazines, Arsenals, dock-Yards, and other needful Buildings; —And

To make all Laws which shall be necessary and proper for carrying into Execution the foregoing Powers, and all other Powers vested by this Constitution in the Government of the United States, or in any Department or Officer thereof.

Section 9. The Migration or Importation of such Persons as any of the States now existing shall think proper to admit shall not be prohibited by the Congress prior to the Year one thousand eight hundred and eight, but a tax or duty may be imposed on such Importation, not exceeding ten dollars for each Person.

The privilege of the Writ of Habeas Corpus shall not be suspended, unless when in Cases of Rebellion or Invasion the public Safety may require it.

No Bill of Attainder or ex post facto Law shall be passed.

[No capitation, or other direct, Tax shall be laid unless in Proportion to the Census or Enumeration herein before directed to be taken.] [5]

No Tax or Duty shall be laid on Articles exported from any State.

No Preference shall be given by any Regulation of Revenue to the Ports of one State over those of another: nor shall Vessels bound to, or from, one State, be obliged to enter, clear, or pay Duties in another.

No Money shall be drawn from the Treasury, but in Consequence of Appropriations made by Law; and a regular Statement and Account of the Receipts and Expenditures of all public Money shall be published from time to time.

No Title of Nobility shall be granted by the United States: And no Person holding any Office of Profit or Trust under them, shall, without the Consent of the Congress, accept of any present, Emolument, Office, or Title, of any kind whatever, from any King, Prince, or foreign State.

Section 10. No State shall enter into any Treaty, Alliance, or Confederation; grant Letters of Marque and Reprisal; coin Money; emit Bills of Credit; make any Thing but gold and silver Coin a Tender in Payment of Debts; pass any Bill of Attainder, ex post facto Law, or Law impairing the Obligation of Contracts, or grant any Title of Nobility.

No State shall, without the Consent of the Congress, lay any Imposts or Duties on Imports or Exports, except what may be absolutely necessary for executing its inspection Laws: and the net Produce of all Duties and Imposts, laid by any State on Imports or Exports, shall be for the Use of the Treasury of the United States; and all such Laws shall be subject to the Revision and Control of the Congress.

No State shall, without the Consent of Congress, lay any duty of Tonnage, keep Troops, or Ships of War in time of Peace, enter into any Agreement or Compact with another State, or with a foreign Power, or engage in War, unless actually invaded, or in such imminent Danger as will not admit of delay.

ARTICLE II

Section 1. The executive Power shall be vested in a President of the United States of America. He shall hold his Office during the Term of four years, and, together with the Vice-President, chosen for the same Term, be elected, as follows:

Each State shall appoint, in such Manner as the Legislature thereof may direct, a Number of Electors, equal to the whole Number of Senators and Representatives to which the State may be entitled in the Congress: but no Senator or Representative; or Person holding an Office of Trust or Profit under the United States, shall be appointed an Elector.

[The Electors shall meet in their respective States, and vote by Ballot for two persons, of whom one at least shall not be an Inhabitant of the same State with themselves. And they shall make a List of all the Persons voted for, and of the Number of Votes for each; which List they shall sign and certify, and

[5] Modified by the Sixteenth Amendment.

transmit sealed to the Seat of the Government of the United States, directed to the President of the Senate. The President of the Senate shall, in the Presence of the Senate and House of Representatives, open all the Certificates, and the Votes shall then be counted. The Person having the greatest Number of Votes shall be the President, if such Number be a Majority of the whole Number of Electors appointed; and if there be more than one who have such Majority, and have an equal Number of Votes, then the House of Representatives shall immediately chuse by Ballot one of them for President; and if no Person have a Majority, then from the five highest on the List the said House shall in like Manner chuse the President. But in chusing the President, the Votes shall be taken by States, the Representation from each State having one Vote; a quorum for this Purpose shall consist of a Member or Members from two-thirds of the States, and a Majority of all the States shall be necessary to a Choice. In every Case, after the Choice of the President, the Person having the greatest Number of Votes of the Electors shall be the Vice-President. But if there should remain two or more who have equal votes, the Senate shall chuse from them by Ballot the Vice-President.] [6]

The Congress may determine the Time of chusing the Electors, and the Day on which they shall give their Votes; which Day shall be the same throughout the United States.

No person except a natural-born Citizen, or a Citizen of the United States, at the time of the Adoption of this Constitution, shall be eligible to the Office of President; neither shall any Person be eligible to that Office who shall not have attained to the Age of thirty-five years, and been fourteen Years a Resident within the United States.

[In Case of the Removal of the President from Office, or of his Death, Resignation, or Inability to discharge the Powers and Duties of the said Office, the same shall devolve on the Vice-President, and the Congress may by Law provide for the Case of Removal, Death, Resignation, or Inability, both of the President and Vice-President, declaring what Officer shall then act as President, and such Officer shall act accordingly, until the disability be removed, or a President shall be elected.] [7]

The President shall, at stated Times, receive for his Services a Compensation, which shall neither be increased nor diminished during the Period for which he shall have been elected, and he shall not receive within that Period any other Emolument from the United States, or any of them.

Before he enter on the execution of his Office, he shall take the following Oath or Affirmation:—"I do solemnly swear (or affirm) that I will faithfully execute the Office of President of the United States, and will, to the best of my Ability, preserve, protect, and defend the Constitution of the United States."

Section 2. The President shall be Commander in Chief of the Army and Navy of the United States, and of the Militia of the several States, when called into the actual Service of the United States; he may require the Opinion, in writing, of the principal Officer in each of the executive Departments, upon any subject relating to the Duties of their respective Offices, and he shall have Power to Grant Reprieves and Pardons for Offenses against the United States, except in Cases of Impeachment.

He shall have Power, by and with the Advice and Consent of the Senate, to make Treaties, provided two thirds of the Senators present concur; and he shall nominate, and by and with the Advice and Consent of the Senate, shall appoint Ambassadors, other public Ministers and Consuls, Judges of the supreme Court, and all other Officers of the United States, whose Appointments are not herein otherwise provided for, and which shall be established by Law: but the Congress may by Law vest the Appointment of such inferior Officers, as they think proper, in the President alone, in the Courts of Law, or in the Heads of Departments.

The President shall have Power to fill up all Vacancies that may happen during the Recess of the Senate, by granting Commissions which shall expire at the End of their next Session.

Section 3. He shall from time to time give to the Congress Information of the State of the Union, and recommend to their Consideration such Measures as he shall judge necessary and expedient; he may, on extraordinary occasions, convene both Houses, or either of them, and in Case of Disagreement between them, with respect to the Time of Adjournment, he may adjourn them to such Time as he shall think proper; he shall receive Ambassadors and other public Ministers; he shall take Care that the Laws be faithfully executed, and shall Commission all the Officers of the United States.

Section 4. The President, Vice-President and all civil Officers of the United States, shall be removed from Office on Impeachment for, and Conviction of, Treason, Bribery, or other high Crimes and Misdemeanors.

ARTICLE III

Section 1. The judicial Power of the United States, shall be vested in one supreme Court, and in such inferior Courts as the Congress may from time to time ordain and establish. The Judges, both of the supreme and inferior Courts, shall hold their Offices during good Behaviour, and shall, at stated Times, receive for their Services, a Compensation, which shall not be diminished during their Continuance in Office.

Section 2. The judicial Power shall extend to all Cases, in Law and Equity, arising under this Constitution, the Laws of the United States, and treaties made, or which shall be made, under their Authority;—to all Cases affecting ambassadors, other public ministers and consuls;—to all cases of admiralty and maritime Jurisdiction;—to Controversies to which the United States shall be a Party;—to Controversies between two or more States;—[between a

---

[6] Superseded by the Twelfth Amendment.
[7] Modified by the Twenty-fifth Amendment.

State and Citizens of another State;] [8]—between Citizens of different States,—between Citizens of the same State claiming Lands under Grants of different States, and between a State, or the Citizens thereof, and foreign States, Citizens or Subjects.

In all Cases affecting Ambassadors, other public Ministers and Consuls, and those in which a State shall be Party, the supreme Court shall have original Jurisdiction. In all the other Cases before mentioned, the supreme Court shall have appellate Jurisdiction, both as to Law and Fact, with such Exceptions, and under such Regulations as the Congress shall make.

The trial of all Crimes, except in Cases of Impeachment, shall be by Jury; and such Trial shall be held in the State where the said Crimes shall have been committed; but when not committed within any State, the Trial shall be at such Place or Places as the Congress may by Law have directed.

Section 3. Treason against the United States, shall consist only in levying War against them, or in adhering to their Enemies, giving them Aid and Comfort. No Person shall be convicted of Treason unless on the Testimony of two Witnesses to the same overt Act, or on Confession in open Court.

The Congress shall have power to declare the Punishment of Treason, but no Attainder of Treason shall work Corruption of Blood, or Forfeiture except during the Life of the Person attainted.

ARTICLE IV

Section 1. Full Faith and Credit shall be given in each State to the public Acts, Records, and judicial Proceedings of every other State. And the Congress may by general Laws prescribe the Manner in which such Acts, Records and Proceedings shall be proved, and the Effect thereof.

Section 2. The Citizens of each State shall be entitled to all Privileges and Immunities of Citizens in the several States.

A Person charged in any State with Treason, Felony, or other Crime, who shall flee from Justice, and be found in another State, shall on demand of the executive Authority of the State from which he fled, be delivered up, to be removed to the State having Jurisdiction of the crime.

[No Person held to Service or Labour in one State, under the Laws thereof, escaping into another, shall, in Consequence of any Law or Regulation therein, be discharged from such Service or Labour, but shall be delivered up on Claim of the Party to whom such Service or Labour may be due.] [9]

Section 3. New States may be admitted by the Congress into this Union; but no new State shall be formed or erected within the Jurisdiction of any other State; nor any State be formed by the Junction of two or more States, or parts of States, without the Consent of the Legislatures of the States concerned as well as of the Congress.

The Congress shall have Power to dispose of and make all needful Rules and Regulations respecting the Territory or other Property belonging to the United States; and nothing in this Constitution shall be so construed as to Prejudice any Claims of the United States, or of any particular State.

Section 4. The United States shall guarantee to every State in this Union a Republican Form of Government, and shall protect each of them against Invasion; and on Application of the Legislature, or of the Executive (when the Legislature cannot be convened) against domestic Violence.

ARTICLE V

The Congress, whenever two-thirds of both Houses shall deem it necessary, shall propose Amendments to this Constitution, or, on the Application of the Legislatures of two-thirds of the several States, shall call a Convention for proposing Amendments, which, in either Case, shall be valid to all Intents and Purposes, as part of this Constitution, when ratified by the Legislatures of three-fourths of the several States, or by Conventions in three-fourths thereof, as the one or the other Mode of Ratification may be proposed by the Congress; Provided that no Amendment which may be made prior to the Year One thousand eight hundred and eight shall in any Manner affect the first and fourth Clauses in the Ninth Section of the first Article; and that no State, without its Consent, shall be deprived of its equal Suffrage in the Senate.

ARTICLE VI

All Debts contracted and Engagements entered into, before the Adoption of this Constitution, shall be as valid against the United States under this Constitution, as under the Confederation.

This Constitution, and the Laws of the United States which shall be made in Pursuance thereof; and all Treaties made, or which shall be made, under the Authority of the United States, shall be the supreme Law of the Land; and the Judges in every State shall be bound thereby, any Thing in the Constitution or Laws of any State to the Contrary notwithstanding.

The Senators and Representatives before mentioned, and the Members of the several State Legislatures, and all executive and judicial Officers, both of the United States and of the several States, shall be bound by Oath or Affirmation to support this Constitution; but no religious Test shall ever be required as a qualification to any Office or public Trust under the United States.

ARTICLE VII

The Ratification of the Conventions of nine States shall be sufficient for the Establishment of this Constitution between the States so ratifying the same.

Done in Convention by the Unanimous Consent of the States present the Seventeenth Day of September in the Year of our Lord one thousand seven hundred and Eighty seven, and of the Independence of the United States of America the Twelfth. In

---

[8] Modified by the Eleventh Amendment.
[9] Superseded by the Thirteenth Amendment.

Witness whereof We have hereunto subscribed our Names.

Articles in Addition to, and Amendment of, the Constitution of the United States of America, Proposed by Congress, and Ratified by the Legislatures of the Several States, Pursuant to the Fifth Article of the Original Constitution.

AMENDMENT I [10]

Congress shall make no law respecting an establishment of religion, or prohibiting the free exercise thereof; or abridging the freedom of speech, or of the press; or the right of the people peaceably to assemble, and to petition the Government for a redress of grievances.

AMENDMENT II

A well regulated Militia, being necessary to the security of a free State, the right of the people to keep and bear Arms shall not be infringed.

AMENDMENT III

No Soldier shall, in time of peace, be quartered in any house, without the consent of the Owner, nor in time of war, but in a manner to be prescribed by law.

AMENDMENT IV

The right of the people to be secure in their persons, houses, papers, and effects, against unreasonable searches and seizures, shall not be violated, and no Warrants shall issue, but upon probable cause, supported by Oath or affirmation, and particularly describing the place to be searched, and the persons or things to be seized.

AMENDMENT V

No person shall be held to answer for a capital or otherwise infamous crime, unless on a presentment or indictment of a Grand Jury, except in cases arising in the land or naval forces, or in the Militia, when in actual service in time of War or public danger; nor shall ar y person be subject for the same offence to be twice put in jeopardy of life or limb; nor shall be compelled in any criminal case to be a witness against himself, nor be deprived of life, liberty, or property, without due process of law; nor shall private property be taken for public use, without just compensation.

AMENDMENT VI

In all criminal prosecutions, the accused shall enjoy the right to a speedy and public trial, by an impartial jury of the State and district wherein the crime shall have been committed, which district shall have been previously ascertained by law, and to be informed of the nature and cause of the accusation; to be confronted with the witnesses against him; to have compulsory process for obtaining witnesses in his favor, and to have the Assistance of Counsel for his defence.

AMENDMENT VII

In suits at common law, where the value in controversy shall exceed twenty dollars, the right of trial by jury shall be preserved, and no fact tried by a jury, shall be otherwise reexamined in any Court of the United States, than according to the rules of the common law.

AMENDMENT VIII

Excessive bail shall not be required, nor excessive fines imposed, nor cruel and unusual punishments inflicted.

AMENDMENT IX

The enumeration in the Constitution, of certain rights, shall not be construed to deny or disparage others retained by the people.

AMENDMENT X

The powers not delegated to the United States by the Constitution, nor prohibited by it to the States, are reserved to the States respectively, or to the people.

AMENDMENT XI (1795) [11]

The Judicial power of the United States shall not be construed to extend to any suit in law or equity, commenced or prosecuted against one of the United States by Citizens of another State, or by Citizens or Subjects of any Foreign State.

AMENDMENT XII (1804)

The Electors shall meet in their respective States and vote by ballot for President and Vice-President, one of whom, at least, shall not be an inhabitant of the same State with themselves; they shall name in their ballots the person voted for as President, and in distinct ballots the person voted for as Vice-President, and they shall make distinct lists of all persons voted for as President, and of all persons voted for as Vice-President, and of the number of votes for each, which lists they shall sign and certify, and transmit sealed to the seat of the government of the United States, directed to the President of the Senate;—The President of the Senate shall, in the presence of the Senate and House of Representatives, open all the certificates and the votes shall then be counted;—The person having the greatest number of votes for President, shall be the President, if such number be a majority of the whole number of Electors appointed; and if no person have such majority, then from the persons having the highest numbers not exceeding three on the list of those voted for as President, the House of Representatives shall choose immediately, by ballot, the President. But in choosing the President, the votes shall be taken by states, the representation from each state

[10] The first ten amendments were passed by Congress September 25, 1789. They were ratified by three-fourths of the states December 15, 1791.

[11] Date of ratification.

having one vote; a quorum for this purpose shall consist of a member or members from two-thirds of the states, and a majority of all the states shall be necessary to a choice. [And if the House of Representatives shall not choose a President whenever the right of choice shall devolve upon them, before the fourth day of March next following, then the Vice-President shall act as President, as in the case of the death or other constitutional disability of the President.] [12]—The person having the greatest number of votes as Vice-President, shall be the Vice-President, if such number be a majority of the whole number of Electors appointed, and if no person have a majority, then from the two highest numbers on the list, the Senate shall choose the Vice-President; a quorum for the purpose shall consist of two-thirds of the whole number of Senators, and a majority of the whole number shall be necessary to a choice. But no person constitutionally ineligible to the office of President shall be eligible to that of Vice-President of the United States.

AMENDMENT XIII (1865)

Section 1. Neither slavery nor involuntary servitude, except as a punishment for crime whereof the party shall have been duly convicted, shall exist within the United States, or any place subject to their jurisdiction.

Section 2. Congress shall have power to enforce this article by appropriate legislation.

AMENDMENT XIV (1868)

Section 1. All persons born or naturalized in the United States, and subject to the jurisdiction thereof, are citizens of the United States and of the State wherein they reside. No State shall make or enforce any law which shall abridge the privileges or immunities of citizens of the United States; nor shall any State deprive any person of life, liberty, or property, without due process of law; nor deny to any person within its jurisdiction the equal protection of the laws.

Section 2. Representatives shall be apportioned among the several States according to their respective numbers, counting the whole number of persons in each State, excluding Indians not taxed. But when the right to vote at any election for the choice of electors for President and Vice-President of the United States, Representatives in Congress, the Executive and Judicial officers of a State, or the members of the Legislature thereof, is denied to any of the male inhabitants of such State, being twenty-one years of age, and citizens of the United States, or in any way abridged, except for participation in rebellion, or other crime, the basis of representation therein shall be reduced in the proportion which the number of such male citizens shall bear to the whole number of male citizens twenty-one years of age in such State.

Section 3. No person shall be a Senator or Representative in Congress, or elector of President and Vice-President, or hold any office, civil or military, under the United States, or under any State, who, having previously taken an oath, as a member of Congress, or as an officer of the United States, or as a member of any State legislature, or as an executive or judicial officer of any State, to support the Constitution of the United States, shall have engaged in insurrection or rebellion against the same, or given aid or comfort to the enemies thereof. But Congress may by a vote of two-thirds of each House, remove such disability.

Section 4. The validity of the public debt of the United States, authorized by law, including debts incurred for payment of pensions and bounties for services in suppressing insurrection or rebellion, shall not be questioned. But neither the United States nor any State shall assume or pay any debt or obligation incurred in aid of insurrection or rebellion against the United States, or any claim for the loss or emancipation of any slave; but all such debts, obligations, and claims shall be held illegal and void.

Section 5. The Congress shall have the power to enforce, by appropriate legislation, the provisions of this article.

AMENDMENT XV (1870)

Section 1. The right of citizens of the United States to vote shall not be denied or abridged by the United States or by any State on account of race, color, or previous condition of servitude—

Section 2. The Congress shall have power to enforce this article by appropriate legislation.

AMENDMENT XVI (1913)

The Congress shall have power to lay and collect taxes on incomes, from whatever source derived, without apportionment among the several States, and without regard to any census or enumeration.

AMENDMENT XVII (1913)

The Senate of the United States shall be composed of two Senators from each State, elected by the people thereof, for six years; and each Senator shall have one vote. The electors in each State shall have the qualifications requisite for electors of the most numerous branch of the State legislatures.

When vacancies happen in the representation of any State in the Senate, the executive authority of such State shall issue writs of election to fill such vacancies: *Provided*, That the legislature of any State may empower the executive thereof to make temporary appointments until the people fill the vacancies by election as the legislature may direct.

This amendment shall not be so construed as to affect the election or term of any Senator chosen before it becomes valid as part of the Constitution.

AMENDMENT XVIII (1919) [13]

Section 1. After one year from the ratification of this article the manufacture, sale, or transportation of intoxicating liquors within, the importation

---

[12] Superseded by the Twentieth Amendment.

[13] Repealed by the Twenty-first Amendment.

thereof into, or the exportation thereof from the United States and all territory subject to the jurisdiction thereof for beverage purposes is hereby prohibited.

Section 2. The Congress and the several States shall have concurrent power to enforce this article by appropriate legislation.

Section 3. This article shall be inoperative unless it shall have been ratified as an amendment to the Constitution by the legislatures of the several States, as provided in the Constitution, within seven years from the date of the submission hereof to the States by the Congress.

AMENDMENT XIX (1920)

The right of citizens of the United States to vote shall not be denied or abridged by the United States or by any State on account of sex.

Congress shall have power to enforce this article by appropriate legislation.

AMENDMENT XX (1933)

Section 1. The terms of the President and Vice-President shall end at noon on the 20th day of January, and the terms of Senators and Representatives at noon on the 3d day of January, of the years in which such terms would have ended if this article had not been ratified; and the terms of their successors shall then begin.

Section 2. The Congress shall assemble at least once in every year, and such meeting shall begin at noon on the 3d day of January, unless they shall by law appoint a different day.

Section 3. If, at the time fixed for the beginning of the term of the President, the President elect shall have died, the Vice-President elect shall become President. If a President shall not have been chosen before the time fixed for the beginning of his term, or if the President elect shall have failed to qualify, then the Vice-President elect shall act as President until a President shall have qualified; and the Congress may by law provide for the case wherein neither a President elect nor a Vice-President elect shall have qualified, declaring who shall then act as President, or the manner in which one who is to act shall be selected, and such person shall act accordingly until a President or Vice-President shall have qualified.

Section 4. The Congress may by law provide for the case of the death of any of the persons from whom the House of Representatives may choose a President whenever the right of choice shall have devolved upon them, and for the case of the death of any of the persons from whom the Senate may choose a Vice-President whenever the right of choice shall have devolved upon them.

Section 5. Sections 1 and 2 shall take effect on the 15th day of October following the ratification of this article.

Section 6. This article shall be inoperative unless it shall have been ratified as an amendment to the Constitution by the legislatures of three-fourths of the several States within seven years from the date of its submission.

AMENDMENT XXI (1933)

Section 1. The eighteenth article of amendment to the Constitution of the United States is hereby repealed.

Section 2. The transportation or importation into any State, Territory, or possession of the United States for delivery or use therein of intoxicating liquors, in violation of the laws thereof, is hereby prohibited.

Section 3. This article shall be inoperative unless it shall have been ratified as an amendment to the Constitution by conventions in the several States, as provided in the Constitution, within seven years from the date of the submission hereof to the States by the Congress.

AMENDMENT XXII (1951)

No person shall be elected to the office of the President more than twice, and no person who has held the office of President, or acted as President, for more than two years of a term to which some other person was elected President shall be elected to the office of the President more than once.

But this Article shall not apply to any person holding the office of President when this Article was proposed by the Congress, and shall not prevent any person who may be holding the office of President, or acting as President, during the term within which this Article becomes operative from holding the office of President or acting as President during the remainder of such term.

AMENDMENT XXIII (1961)

Section 1. The District constituting the seat of Government of the United States shall appoint in such manner as the Congress may direct:

A number of electors of President and Vice-President equal to the whole number of Senators and Representatives in Congress to which the District would be entitled if it were a State, but in no event more than the least populous State; they shall be in addition to those appointed by the States, but they shall be considered, for the purposes of the election of President and Vice-President, to be electors appointed by the State; and they shall meet in the District and perform such duties as provided by the twelfth article of amendment.

Section 2. The Congress shall have power to enforce this article by appropriate legislation.

AMENDMENT XXIV (1964)

Section 1. The right of citizens of the United States to vote in any primary or other election for President or Vice-President, for electors for President or Vice-President, or for Senator or Representative in Congress, shall not be denied or abridged by the United States or any State by reason of failure to pay any poll tax or other tax.

Section 2. The Congress shall have power to enforce this article by appropriate legislation.

AMENDMENT XXV (1967)

Section 1. In case of the removal of the President from office or of his death or resignation, the Vice-President shall become President.

Section 2. Whenever there is a vacancy in the office of the Vice-President, the President shall nominate a Vice-President who shall take office upon confirmation by a majority vote of both Houses of Congress.

Section 3. Whenever the President transmits to the President pro tempore of the Senate and the Speaker of the House of Representatives his written declaration that he is unable to discharge the powers and duties of his office, and until he transmits to them a written declaration to the contrary, such powers and duties shall be discharged by the Vice-President as Acting President.

Section 4. Whenever the Vice-President and a majority of either the principal officers of the executive department or of such other body as Congress may by law provide, transmit to the President pro tempore of the Senate and the Speaker of the House of Representatives their written declaration that the President is unable to discharge the powers and duties of his office, the Vice-President shall immediately assume the powers and duties of the office as Acting President.

Thereafter, when the President transmits to the President pro tempore of the Senate and the Speaker of the House of Representatives his written declaration that no inability exists, he shall resume the powers and duties of his office unless the Vice-President and a majority of either the principal officers of the executive department or of such other body as Congress may by law provide, transmit within four days to the President pro tempore of the Senate and the Speaker of the House of Representatives their written declaration that the President is unable to discharge the powers and duties of his office. Thereupon Congress shall decide the issue, assembling within forty-eight hours for that purpose if not in session. If the Congress, within twenty-one days after receipt of the latter written declaration, or, if Congress is not in session, within twenty-one days after Congress is required to assemble, determines by two-thirds vote of both Houses that the President is unable to discharge the powers and duties of his office, the Vice-President shall continue to discharge the same as Acting President; otherwise, the President shall resume the powers and duties of his office.

AMENDMENT XXVI (1971)

Section 1. The right of citizens of the United States, who are eighteen years of age or older, to vote shall not be denied or abridged by the United States or by any State on account of age.

Section 2. The Congress shall have power to enforce this article by appropriate legislation.

PRESIDENTS OF THE UNITED STATES

Year	President	Party	Vote	Electoral Vote	Percentage of Popular Vote
1789	George Washington	no designation		69	
1792	George Washington	no designation		132	
1796	John Adams	Federalist		71	
1800	Thomas Jefferson	Democratic-Republican		73	
1804	Thomas Jefferson	Democratic-Republican		162	
1808	James Madison	Democratic-Republican		122	
1812	James Madison	Democratic-Republican		128	
1816	James Monroe	Democratic-Republican		183	
1820	James Monroe	Democratic-Republican		231	
1824	John Quincy Adams	Democratic-Republican	108,740	84	30.5
1828	Andrew Jackson	Democratic	647,286	178	56.0
1832	Andrew Jackson	Democratic	687,502	219	55.0
1836	Martin Van Buren	Democratic	765,483	170	50.9
1840	William H. Harrison	Whig	1,274,624	234	53.1
1841	John Tyler*	Whig			
1844	James K. Polk	Democratic	1,338,464	170	49.6
1848	Zachary Taylor	Whig	1,360,967	163	47.4
1850	Millard Fillmore*	Whig			
1852	Franklin Pierce	Democratic	1,601,117	254	50.9
1856	James Buchanan	Democratic	1,832,955	174	45.3
1860	Abraham Lincoln	Republican	1,865,593	180	39.8
1864	Abraham Lincoln	Republican	2,206,938	212	55.0
1865	Andrew Johnson*	Democratic			
1868	Ulysses S. Grant	Republican	3,013,421	214	52.7
1872	Ulysses S. Grant	Republican	3,596,745	286	55.6
1876	Rutherford B. Hayes	Republican	4,036,572	185	48.0
1880	James A. Garfield	Republican	4,453,295	214	48.5
1881	Chester A. Arthur*	Republican			
1884	Grover Cleveland	Democratic	4,879,507	219	48.5
1888	Benjamin Harrison	Republican	5,447,129	233	47.9
1892	Grover Cleveland	Democratic	5,555,426	277	46.1
1896	William McKinley	Republican	7,102,246	271	51.1
1900	William McKinley	Republican	7,218,491	292	51.7
1901	Theodore Roosevelt*	Republican			
1904	Theodore Roosevelt	Republican	7,628,461	336	57.4
1908	William H. Taft	Republican	7,675,320	321	51.6
1912	Woodrow Wilson	Democratic	6,296,547	435	41.9
1916	Woodrow Wilson	Democratic	9,127,695	277	49.4
1920	Warren G. Harding	Republican	16,143,407	404	60.4
1923	Calvin Coolidge*	Republican			
1924	Calvin Coolidge	Republican	15,718,211	382	54.0
1928	Herbert C. Hoover	Republican	21,391,993	444	58.2
1932	Franklin D. Roosevelt	Democratic	22,809,638	472	57.4
1936	Franklin D. Roosevelt	Democratic	27,752,869	523	60.8
1940	Franklin D. Roosevelt	Democratic	27,307,819	449	54.8
1944	Franklin D. Roosevelt	Democratic	25,606,585	432	53.5
1945	Harry S. Truman*	Democratic			
1948	Harry S. Truman	Democratic	24,105,812	303	49.5
1952	Dwight D. Eisenhower	Republican	33,936,234	442	55.1
1956	Dwight D. Eisenhower	Republican	35,590,472	457	57.6
1960	John F. Kennedy	Democratic	34,227,096	303	49.9
1963	Lyndon B. Johnson*	Democratic			
1964	Lyndon B. Johnson	Democratic	43,126,506	486	61.1
1968	Richard M. Nixon	Republican	31,785,480	301	43.4
1972	Richard M. Nixon	Republican	47,169,905	520	60.7
1974	Gerald R. Ford**	Republican			
1976	Jimmy Carter	Democratic	40,827,394	297	50.0
1980	Ronald Reagan	Republican	43,899,248	489	50.8

*Succeeded to Presidency upon death of the incumbent.
**Succeeded to Presidency upon resignation of the incumbent.

Random House, Inc. For excerpt from *The System of Freedom of Expression* by Thomas I. Emerson (Random House, 1971). Also for excerpts from *The Boys on the Bus* by Timothy Crouse (Random House, 1973). Also for excerpt from *This Endangered Planet* by Richard A. Falk (Random House, 1972). Also for excerpt from *The Court Years: 1939–1975* by William O. Douglas (Random House, 1980).

Reprint House International. For excerpt from William Allen White, *Masks in a Pageant* (1928), quoted in Richard F. Fenno, Jr., *The President's Cabinet* (Harvard University Press, 1959).

Simon & Schuster, Inc. For excerpt from *Senator*. Copyright © 1979 by Elizabeth Drew. Also for excerpt from *The Brethren: Inside the Supreme Court*. Copyright © 1979 by Bob Woodward and Scott Armstrong. Also for excerpt from *All Things to All Men: The False Promise of the Modern American Presidency*. Copyright © 1980 by Godfrey Hodgson. Reprinted by permission of Simon & Schuster, a Division of Gulf and Western Corp.

Time Magazine. Reprinted by permission from *Time*, The Weekly Newsmagazine; Copyright Time Inc., 1980.

The *Washington Post*. For excerpts from stories in The *Washington Post* by Bob Woodward and E. J. Bachinski, June 20, 1972; William Greider, April 2, 1978; Kenneth Bredemeier, March 7, 1979; Marvin Caplan, "Company Town," August 12, 1979; Shirley Chisholm, December 12, 1980. © The *Washington Post*. Reprinted by permission. Also for excerpt titled "A World at War" in The *Washington Post*, January 27, 1980; statistics from the Center for Defense Information reprinted by permission.

Washington Star Syndicate, Inc. For excerpt from column by James J. Kilpatrick in the *Washington Evening Star*, January 8, 1970.

Illustrations

Part I   Martin Gonzales/DPI
Part II   Fred Ward/Black Star
Part III   Sepp Seitz/Woodfin Camp & Associates
Part IV   Susan Greenwood/Liaison
Part V   Rafael Maldonado, *Santa Barbara News-Press*

Chapter 1   Page 4, UPI; p. 5, (top) Wide World, (bottom) David C. Conklin; p. 6, (top) Simon Nathan/NYT Pictures, (center) J. Giannini/Sygma, (bottom left) Sipa Press/Black Star, (bottom right) David C. Conklin; p. 7, D. Simon/Gamma-Liaison; p. 8, (top left) *Miami Herald*/Black Star, (top center) Donald McCullin/Magnum, (top right) Dennis Brack/Black Star, (bottom) Warren Ballard/DPI; p. 9, Brown Brothers; p. 10, John Olson, Life Picture Service, © Time, Inc.; p. 11, Tom Ebenhoh/Black Star; p. 12, M. Norcia/Sygma; p. 14, Culver Pictures; p. 15, (left) Ivan Massar/Black Star, (center) Bob Fitch/Black Star, (right) Black Star; p. 18, (top) Fred Anderson/Black Star, (bottom) Wide World; p. 19, (top) Chester Higgins, Jr./NYT Pictures, (bottom) Dave Repp/DPI; p. 21, Katrina Thomas/Photo Researchers, Inc.; p. 22, (top) Susan Greenwood/Liaison, (bottom) Owen Franken/Sygma; p. 23, (top left) Wide World, (top center) Martin Levick/Black Star, (top right) Harvey Stein, (bottom) Arthur Grace/Sygma; p. 24, Paul S. Conklin.

Chapter 2   Page 27, (left) engraving by Chappell/Brown Brothers, (center) National Archives, (right) Paul S. Conklin; p. 28, (top) Fred Ward/Black Star, (bottom) UPI; p. 29, (left) UPI, (center) Wide World, (right) Margaret Thomas, *The Washington Post;* p. 30, (left) detail of portrait by Rembrandt Peale/New-York Historical Society, (right) The Smithsonian Institution; p. 31, detail of portrait attributed to Michael Dahl/National Portrait Gallery, London; p. 33, Brown Brothers; p. 34, (top) The Smithsonian Institution, (center and bottom) Historical Pictures Service; p. 35, (top) Library of Congress, (center) Historical Pictures Service, (bottom) portrait by C. W. Peale/Independence National Historical Park; p. 36, (top) Culver Pictures, (bottom) Brown Brothers; p. 37, (top) detail of portrait by John Trumbull/Courtesy Museum of Fine Arts, Boston, Robert C. Winthrop Fund; (bottom) Culver Pictures; p. 38, (left) detail of engraving by A. B. Durand from portrait by Trumbull/Brown Brothers, (center and right) Culver Pictures; p. 39, (top) Historical Pictures Service, (bottom) Virginia State Library; p. 43, The Bettmann Archive; p. 46, Brown Brothers; p. 51, (left) Frank Johnston, *The Washington Post*, (right) George Tames/NYT

Pictures; p. 52, (top) The Smithsonian Institution, Ralph E. Becker Collection, (bottom) drawing by St. Mémin/New-York Historical Society; p. 55, Brown Brothers; p. 57, (left) UPI, (center) Margaret Thomas, *The Washington Post*, (right) Dino Pellegrino/Black Star.

Chapter 3   Page 61, (left) Marion Bernstein, (right) UPI; p. 65, (top) New York News, Inc., (center and bottom) UPI; p. 66, UPI; p. 69, Boston Atheneum; p. 72, Uniphoto; p. 73, Robert D. Randolph/Uniphoto; p. 74, Hiroyuki Matsumoto/Black Star; p. 75, UPI; p. 77, UPI; p. 82, Charles Moore/Black Star; p. 83, Richard A. Bloom.

Chapter 4   Page 89, (top left) Leonard Freed/Magnum, (top center) Fred Ward/Black Star, (top right) Andy Levin/Black Star; p. 91, Culver Pictures; p. 92, Vince Compagnone/Jeroboam; p. 93, A. Pierce Bounds/Uniphoto; p. 94, (top) Culver Pictures, (center) Martin Levick/Black Star, (bottom) Mark Godfrey/Magnum; p. 95, Paul S. Conklin; p. 96, Dennis Brack/Black Star; p. 97, Schaefer and Seawell/Black Star; p. 98, (bottom) Jean Shapiro/Black Star; p. 99, Wide World; p. 100, (left and right) Wide World; p. 102, (top) Fred Ward/Black Star, (bottom) UPI; p. 103, Bill Powers/Criminal Justice Publications; p. 104, (top) Dennis Brack/Black Star, (bottom) Edward Klamm/Black Star; p. 105, Wide World; p. 106, (top) Dennis Brack/Black Star, (bottom) Bob Adelman/Magnum; p. 107, Martin Levick/Black Star; p. 108, (top) Dennis Brack/Black Star, (bottom) T. Simon/Liaison; p. 109, UPI; p. 111, (top) Eileen Christelow/Jeroboam, (bottom) Arnold Zann/Black Star; p. 113, Robert Phillips/Black Star; p. 116, (top) *The New York Times*, (bottom) Christina Thomson/Woodfin Camp & Associates; p. 117, (top) David R. Frazier/Black Star, (center) cartoon by Ployardt. Reproduced by permission of *The Reporter*, © 1953 by Fortnightly Publishing Co., Inc., (bottom) UPI; p. 118, Dennis Brack/Black Star; p. 120, (top) *The Arizona Republic*, (bottom) Police Department, The City of New York; p. 122, Flip Schulke/Black Star; p. 125, Gilbert Uzan/Gamma-Liaison; p, 127, (left) Museum of the City of New York, (right) Bill Frakes, *Miami Herald*/Black Star; p. 128, (top) *Miami Herald*/Black Star, (bottom left) Winston Vargas/Photo Researchers, Inc., (bottom center) David Margolin/Black Star, (bottom right) Michael D. Sullivan; p. 129, George W. Gardner.

Chapter 5   Page 133, (top left) Andy Levin/Black Star, (top right) Bob Adelman/Magnum, (center) Bruce Davidson/Magnum, (bottom) Paul S. Conklin; p. 135, Evelyn Collazo/Black Star; p. 136, (top) Dan Budnik/Woodfin Camp & Associates, (bottom)

651

Paul S. Conklin; p. 137, Frank Johnston, *The Washington Post;* p. 138 (top) UPI, (bottom) Paul S. Conklin; p. 140, Robert Lachman, *The Los Angeles Times;* p. 141, (top) Curt Gunther/Camera 5; (bottom) HBJ photo; p. 142, (left) Robert Burroughs/Jeroboam, (right) Alex Webb/Magnum; p. 143, (left) Fred R. Conrad/NYT Pictures, (right) Sygma; p. 144, (top) Brown Brothers, (bottom) Harvey Stein; p. 145, (top left) Harvey Stein, (top right) UPI, (bottom) Leif Skoogfors/Woodfin Camp & Associates; p. 148, (top) Mark Antman, (bottom) Paul S. Conklin; p. 149, (top) Paul S. Conklin, (bottom) Thomas A. Shine/Black Star; p. 150, Harvey Stein; p. 151, Judy Rolfe/Uniphoto; p. 154, (top) National Archives, (bottom) Library of Congress; p. 157, Craig Herndon, *The Washington Post;* p. 158, Wide World; p. 160, (top) Wide World, (bottom) *Ebony Magazine*, Johnson Publishing Co.; p. 163, (top) James Karales/DPI, (bottom) Dan Budnik/Woodfin Camp & Associates; p. 166, (top) Wide World, (bottom) Harvey Stein; p. 168, UPI; p. 169, Harris/Liaison.

Chapter 6   Page 177, (top left) Paul S. Conklin, (center) Charles Gatewood/Stock, Boston, (right) Jeff Albertson/Stock, Boston; p. 178, (top) Martin Levick/Black Star, (bottom) Richard Stack/Black Star; p. 182, Stanley Milgram; p. 184, (top) Jean-Claude Lejeune/Black Star, (bottom) Wide World; p. 186, UPI; p. 188, (top) Jeff Albertson/Stock, Boston, (bottom) Paul S. Conklin; p. 193, (top, left to right) Library of Congress, Library of Congress, The Smithsonian Institution, United Nations photo, (bottom) UPI; p. 194, Wide World; p. 195, Arthur Grace/Sygma; p. 196, (left) Dennis Brack/Black Star, (right) Paul S. Conklin; p. 197, (top) Diego Goldberg/Sygma, (margin, top to bottom) Wide World, Ken Regan/Camera 5, Chip Hires/Liaison; p. 198, Donald Dietz/Stock, Boston; p. 199, (top) Paul Fortin/Stock, Boston; (bottom) Yvonne Steiner Gerin; p. 201, Picture Collection, The New York Public Library; p. 202, (top) Moore/Uniphoto, (bottom left) Dennis Brack/Black Star, (bottom right) Paul S. Conklin; p. 207, (top) Paul S. Conklin, (top) Paul S. Conklin, (bottom) William E. Sauro/NYT Pictures; p. 208, (top) Sylvia Johnson/Woodfin Camp & Associates, (bottom) Franklin Wing/Stock, Boston; p. 209, Patricia Gross/Stock, Boston; p. 210, Dennis Brack/Black Star.

Chapter 7   Page 219, (top) Dennis Brack/Black Star, (margin) Collection of Stephen Fisher; p. 221, University of Hartford; p. 222, The Hermitage; p. 223, (top, bottom left, bottom center) The Smithsonian Institution, (center, bottom right) New-York Historical Society; p. 224, (top) The Smithsonian Institution, (bottom left and right) The Smithsonian Institution, Ralph E. Becker Collection, (bottom center) Culver Pictures; p. 229, (top) Bob McNeely/Camera 5, (bottom) Steve Kagan/Photo Researchers, Inc.; p. 231, *The Washington Post;* p. 233, (top) Lester Sloan, *Newsweek,* (bottom) Collection of Stephen Fisher; p. 238, (left) David Kennerly/Contact, (right) Wide World; p. 239, Steve Kagan/Photo Researchers, Inc.; p. 241, Sygma; p. 242, (top) UPI, (bottom left) Paul S. Conklin, (bottom right) Richard A. Bloom; p. 243 (all) Sygma; p. 244, (top, left to right) Ken Regan/Camera 5, UPI, Jim Colburn/Photoreporters, Diego Goldberg/Sygma, Diego Goldberg/Sygma, (bottom) Sygma; p. 245, (top, left to right) *The Washington Star,* Sygma, Philippot/Sygma, Mary Ellen Mark/Magnum, *The Washington Star,* (bottom) Philip Griffiths/Magnum; p. 246, (top) The Smithsonian Institution, Ralph E. Becker Collection; p. 247, Richard A. Bloom.

Chapter 8   Page 255, (top left) Jeff Albertson/Stock, Boston, (top center) Roger Sandler/Black Star, (top right) Dennis Brack/Black Star; pp. 254–55, (margins) Richard A. Bloom, p. 256, Cornell Capa/Magnum; p. 257, (top left and right) Michael Evans/Sygma, (bottom) Tony Korody/Sygma; p. 260, (top, left to right) Richard A. Bloom, Dennis Brack/Black Star, Richard Kalvar/Magnum, Roger Sandler/Black Star, (bottom) UPI; p. 261, Leif Skoogfors/Woodfin Camp & Associates; p. 262, Michael Evans/Sygma; p. 263, (top) UPI, (bottom left) Eddie Adams/Contact, (bottom right) Ric Ferro/Black Star; p. 264, (top) UPI, (bottom left) Library of Congress, (bottom center) Harvard University Library, Theodore

Roosevelt Collection, (bottom right) Wide World; p. 265, (top) Alain Keler/Sygma, (bottom left) Brown Brothers, (bottom center) Harvard University Library, Theodore Roosevelt Collection, (bottom right) Brown Brothers; p. 266, (top left) Andy Sacks/Black Star, (top right) David Burnett/Contact, (bottom) Wide World; p. 268, UPI; p. 270, UPI; 271, (top) UPI, (bottom, all) With the permission of Doyle Dane Bernbach, Inc. Photos courtesy of *The New York Times;* p. 272, CBS photo; p. 273, NBC photo; p. 274, (top) Arthur Grace/Sygma; p. 276, (top) Dirck Halstead/Liaison, (center) Michael Evans/Sygma, (bottom) Richard A. Bloom; p. 277, (top) Jan Lukas/Photo Researchers, Inc., (bottom) Jeff Albertson/Stock, Boston; p. 278, UPI; p. 279, Michael Evans/Sygma; p. 280, (top) Owen Franken/Stock, Boston, (bottom) UPI; p. 281, (top) Michael Evans/Contact, (bottom) Dennis Brack/Black Star; p. 283, (top) UPI, (bottom) Gene Daniels/Black Star; p. 286, David Burnett/Contact; p. 289, Owen Franken/Stock, Boston.

Chapter 9   Page 293, (top left) Kenneth Siegel, (top center) Leo Choplin/Black Star, (top right) Penny Coleman/NYT Pictures; p. 295, Michael D. Sullivan; p. 297, Martin Levick/Black Star; p. 305, John Alexandrowicz/Black Star; p. 308, Andy Levin/Black Star; p. 317, (left) Republican National Committee, (right) Democratic National Committee; p. 319, J. P. Laffont/Sygma; p. 320, (top left) John Ficara/Woodfin Camp & Associates, (top right) Tom Zimberoff/Sygma, (center) Harvey Stein, (bottom) Wide World; p. 321, (top) Ken Love/Photoreporters, (center) Steve Kagan/Photo Researchers, Inc.; p. 323, Wally MacNamee, *Newsweek;* p. 326, © 1980 *The Washington Post*. Reprinted with permission; p. 327, Owen Franken/Stock, Boston; p. 330, Dan Miller/DPI; p. 333, (left) Owen Franken/Sygma, (right) Michael Evans/Sygma; p. 336, Edward Hausner/NYT Pictures; p. 340, Peeter Vilms/Jeroboam.

Chapter 10   Page 346, Fred Ward/Black Star; p. 347, (top left) Fred Ward/Black Star, (top center) David Kennerly/Black Star, (top right) Fred Ward/Black Star, (bottom) UPI; p. 348, (top) Robert Burroughs/Jeroboam, (bottom) Fred Ward/Black Star; p. 349, (top) Arthur Grace/Sygma, (bottom) Dennis Brack/Black Star; p. 350, George Tames/NYT Pictures; p. 351, (top) Dennis Brack/Black Star, (bottom) Cornell Capa/Magnum; p. 352, UPI; p. 353, Wide World; p. 355, David Burnett/Contact; p. 356, (top) White House photo, (bottom) UPI; p. 357, (top) Edward Clark, *Life Magazine* © 1945 Time, Inc., (bottom) White House photo; p. 360, (top) Fred Ward/Black Star, (center) Wide World, (bottom) Sipa Press/Black Star; p. 361, (top left) Library of Congress, (top right) UPI, (bottom) The Bettmann Archive; p. 364, (top) UPI, (bottom) Arthur Grace/Sygma; p. 365, Paul S. Conklin; p. 366, Dennis Brack/Black Star; p. 367, Wide World; p. 369, Michael Evans/Sygma; p. 371, (top) Michael Evans/Sygma, (bottom) UPI; p. 373, Wide World; p. 374, Lyndon Baines Johnson Library, Austin, Texas; p. 376, (top) Paul S. Conklin, (bottom) Roger Sandler/Black Star; p. 377, UPI; p. 378, Wide World; p. 379, Dennis Brack/Black Star; p. 380, (top) Wide World, (bottom) Paul S. Conklin; p. 381, (top) UPI, (bottom) Mark Godfrey/Magnum; p. 382, (top, left and right) J. P. Laffont/Sygma, (center and bottom) NBC photos; p. 383, (center) J. P. Laffont/Sygma, (bottom left) Wide World, (bottom center) National Archives, (bottom right) Alex Webb/Magnum; p. 384, Library of Congress; p. 385, (top) UPI, (bottom) Dennis Brack/Black Star; p. 386, (top) UPI, (bottom) Wide World; p. 388, (top left) Michael Evans/Contact, (top center) Wide World, (top right, bottom) Brown Brothers; p. 389, UPI; p. 391, (left) Arthur Grace/Sygma, (right) Michael Evans/Sygma.

Chapter 11   Page 395, (top left) Dennis Brack/Black Star, (top center) George W. Gardner, (top right) courtesy Pfizer, Inc.; p. 400, (top) Dennis Brack/Black Star, (bottom) George Tames/NYT Pictures; p. 401, UPI; p. 402, (top) Black Star, (bottom) Dennis Brack/Black Star; p. 404, (top) NASA, (bottom) Culver Pictures; p. 406, (left) UPI, (right) Jean-Louis Atlan/Sygma; p. 407, Mike Mazzaschi/Stock, Boston; p. 408, Dennis Brack/Black Star; p. 413, Henri Cartier-Bresson/Magnum; p. 414, (top) Wide World, (bottom) Arthur Grace/Sygma; p. 415, George W. Gardner; p.

Acknowledgments and Copyrights

416, Fred Ward/Black Star; p. 417, *The New York Times;* p. 418, (top) Picture Collection, The New York Public Library, (bottom) Culver Pictures; p. 419, Culver Pictures; p. 420, Dennis Brack/ Black Star; p. 424, UPI; p. 425, (top) George Tames/NYT Pictures, (bottom) UPI.

Chapter 12 Page 428, J. P. Laffont/Sygma; p. 429, (top) Rodney Mims/Sygma, (bottom) Penelope Breese/Liaison; p. 430, (top) George Tames/NYT Pictures, (bottom) Wide World; p. 434, (top to bottom) Wolf von dem Bussche, Wolf von dem Bussche, George Tames/NYT Pictures, Wolf von dem Bussche, Wolf von dem Bussche; p. 435, Wolf von dem Bussche; p. 436, Paul S. Conklin; p. 438, Paul S. Conklin; p. 439, (top left, top center, bottom) Paul S. Conklin, (top right, center) Markey for Congress Committee; p. 441, Paul S. Conklin; p. 442, (top) Sepp Seitz/ Woodfin Camp & Associates, (bottom) Jerome Hirsch; p. 443, Paul S. Conklin; p. 445, (top) Dennis Brack/Black Star, (bottom) Richard A. Bloom; p. 447, Sepp Seitz/Woodfin Camp & Associates; p. 448, Paul S. Conklin; p. 450, Paul S. Conklin; p. 452, (top) Dennis Brack/Black Star, (bottom) Richard A. Bloom; p. 454, Dennis Brack/Black Star; p. 457, (top) Debra Jennings, Courtesy Congressional Quarterly, (bottom) Alex Webb/Magnum; p. 458, (top) Christopher Little, (bottom) J. P. Laffont/Sygma; p. 460, (top) Wide World, (bottom) Paul S. Conklin; p. 463, George Tames/ NYT Pictures; p. 464, Paul S. Conklin.

Chapter 13 Page 469, (top left) Okamoto/Photo Researchers, Inc., (top right, bottom) Fred Ward/Black Star; p. 470, Teresa Zabala/NYT Pictures; p. 471, (top) Paul S. Conklin, (bottom) UPI; p. 472, Wolf von dem Bussche; p. 473, Declan Haun/Black Star; p. 476, (top) UPI, (bottom) Library of Congress; p. 478, Fred Ward/ Black Star; p. 479, Okamoto/Photo Researchers, Inc.; p. 481, Leif Skoogfors/Woodfin Camp & Associates; p. 482, Dennis Brack/ Black Star; p. 484, Fred Ward/Black Star; p. 486, © Fred Lombardi 1981; p. 487, UPI; p. 490, (top) Matt Herron/Black Star, (bottom left and center) Charles Gatewood/Magnum, (bottom right) Harvey Stein; p. 492, J. B. Cuny-Panicker/Photoreporters; p. 493, Bill Powers, *Corrections Magazine;* p. 494, (left) Shelly Katz/ Black Star, (right) Cornell Capa/Magnum; p. 495, (top) John Launois/Black Star, (bottom left) Martin J. Dain/Magnum, (bottom center) Alon Reininger/Woodfin Camp & Associates, (bottom right) Marc & Evelyne Bernheim/Woodfin Camp & Associates; p. 496, (top) Marilyn K. Yee/NYT Pictures, (bottom) © Fred Lombardi 1981; p. 498, (top) Dennis Brack/Black Star, (bottom) UPI; p. 499, Wide World; p. 500, (top) Okamoto/Photo Researchers, Inc., (center) Steve Northup/Camera 5, (bottom) Dennis Brack/ Black Star; p. 504, (center) Alex Webb/Magnum, (bottom) Eve Arnold/Magnum; p. 505, (top) Mary Ellen Mark/Magnum, (center) John T. Urban/Stock, Boston; p. 509, Harvey Stein.

Chapter 14 Page 514, Paul S. Conklin; p. 515, (top left) UPI, (top center) Cornell Capa/Magnum, (top right) Stanley Tretick/ Sygma, (center) Sipa Press/Black Star, (bottom left) UPI, (bottom right) Marilyn Silverstone/Magnum; p. 516, (top) Henri Bureau/ Sygma, (center) Sipa Press/Black Star; p. 517, (right) Wide World; p. 519, (top left) UPI, (top right) Arthur Grace/Sygma, (bottom) F.P.G.; p. 520, (bottom) UPI; p. 521, (top) Photoworld, F.P.G., (bottom) ABC photo; p. 522, (top) Dan Budnik/Woodfin Camp & Associates, (bottom) U.S. Army photo; p. 523, Leif Skoogfors/ Woodfin Camp & Associates; p. 525, (top) © Richard Brummett 1981, (bottom left) Bill Strode/Woodfin Camp & Associates, (bottom right) UPI; p. 526, (top) Mark Godfrey/Magnum, (bottom) Henri Bureau/Sygma; p. 527, Wide World; p. 528, (top) Rhoda Galyn/Photo Researchers, Inc., (bottom left) Ellis Herwig/Stock, Boston, (bottom right) Jim Anderson/Woodfin Camp & Associates; p. 529, (bottom) UPI; p. 532, Wide World; p. 533, (top left) UPI, (top right) Alon Reininger/Contact, (bottom) David Burnett/ Contact; p. 534, (top) UPI, (center) Harry W. Rinehart; p. 535, (left) J. P. Laffont/Sygma, (right) Stanley Tretick/Sygma; p. 536, (top) J. P. Laffont/Sygma, (bottom) UPI; p. 537, (top) UPI; p. 538, (bottom) Alain Nogues/Sygma; p. 539, Donald Patterson/Stock,

Boston; p. 540, (top) UPI, (bottom) David Burnett/Contact; p. 541, (top) Karel/Sygma, (bottom) UPI; p. 542, (top) Burt Glinn/ Magnum, (bottom) George W. Gardner; p. 543, (top) Tony Korody/Sygma, (bottom) Semyon Raskin/Magnum; p. 544, (top) F. W. Owen/Black Star, (center, bottom left and right) Herman Kokojan/Black Star; p. 545, George Cohen/Liaison; p. 546, (center) U.S. Army photo, (bottom left and right) Roger Malloch/ Magnum; p. 547, (top) David Kennerly/Contact, (bottom) Jim Moore/Gamma-Liaison; p. 549, Rick Meyer/*Los Angeles Times* photo; p. 550, (left) Sygma, (right) Edward Thompson/F.P.G.; p. 551, (top left) Regis Bossu/Sygma, (top right) Peeter Vilms/Stock, Boston, (center) R. Diaz/Gamma-Liaison, (bottom) Paul Hosefros/ NYT Pictures; p. 552, Regis Bossu/Sygma; p. 553, David Kennerly/Photoworld, F.P.G.; p. 554, UPI; p. 555, (top) Uniphoto, (bottom) Cary Wolinski/Stock, Boston; p. 557, (top) Sipa Press/ Black Star. (bottom) Dilip Mehta/Contact.

Chapter 15 Page 561, (left) Harvey Stein, (right) Jeff Albertson/Stock, Boston; p. 562, (top) Nik Kleinberg/NYT Pictures, (center) Cary Wolinski/Stock, Boston, (bottom) Peter Southwick/ Stock, Boston; p. 565, Wide World; p. 566, (bottom) Daniel S. Brody/Stock, Boston; p. 567, (top) UPI, (bottom) Eric Smith/ Liaison; p. 568, (left) Teresa Zabala/NYT Pictures, (right) Paul S. Conklin; p. 570, (both) Owen Franken/Stock, Boston; p. 571, (bottom) Russell Abraham/Stock, Boston; p. 572, (top) Paul S. Conklin, (bottom) Christopher Springmann/Black Star; p. 575, (top) IRS photo, p. 580, Dorothea Lange/Culver Pictures; p. 581, (top) Dorothea Lange, F.S.A./Franklin Delano Roosevelt Library, Hyde Park, N.Y., (bottom) Arthur Grace/Stock, Boston; p. 583, (top) Alex Webb/Magnum, (bottom) Hap Stewart/Jeroboam; p. 585, (top) Harvey Stein, (bottom) Paul S. Conklin; p. 586, Bernard Gotfryd, *Newsweek;* p. 587, (top) Mark Antman, (bottom) Paul S. Conklin; p. 588, (top) Neal Boenzi/NYT Pictures; p. 589, © Marjorie Pickens 1981; p. 590, UPI; p. 591, (top right) Michael D. Sullivan, (bottom) David M. Grossman; p. 592, Syeus Mottel/ Nancy Palmer Photo Agency, (bottom) Robin Forbes; p. 593, Wide World; p. 594, Wide World; p. 596, (bottom) Paul S. Conklin; p. 598, (top) Gamma-Liaison, (center) Martin Levick/ Black Star, (bottom) Wide World.

Chapter 16 Page 604, Martin Levick/Black Star; p. 605, (top left) Marion Bernstein, (top center) Andy Levin/Black Star, (top right) Kent Reno/Jeroboam, (center) Martin Levick/Black Star, (bottom) Photoworld, F.P.G.; p. 607, Bob Combs/Photo Researchers, Inc.; p. 608, Ellis Herwig/Stock, Boston; p. 609, (top) UPI, (center) Christopher Springmann/Black Star; p. 613, (top) Alan Carey, (bottom) Geoffrey Clifford/Black Star; p. 615, Mimi Forsyth/Monkmeyer Press Photo Service; p. 617, (top) UPI, (bottom) George W. Gardner; p. 618, (top left) Aero Service Division, Geophysical Co. of America, (top right) George W. Gardner, (bottom) UPI; p. 619, (top) Jim Anderson/Woodfin Camp & Associates, (bottom) Cary Wolinski/Stock, Boston; p. 621, (left) © Marjorie Pickens 1981, (right) Mark Antman; p. 622, Wide World; p. 623, (bottom left) Ellis Herwig/Stock, Boston, (bottom right) Kerwin B. Roche/Photoworld, F.P.G.; p. 624, Leo Choplin/Black Star; p. 625, (left) Wide World, (right) Mark Antman; p. 627, Marion Bernstein; p. 628, (left) Christopher Springmann/Black Star; p. 629, (top left) Wide World, (top right) Donald Dietz/ Stock, Boston, (center) Neal Boenzi/NYT Pictures, (bottom) Sepp Seitz/Woodfin Camp & Associates; p. 630, (top left) UPI, (top right) Dennis Brack/Black Star, (bottom) George W. Gardner/ Stock, Boston; p. 631, (top) Tim Eagan/Woodfin Camp & Associates; p. 632, (bottom) Tony Korody/Black Star; p. 633, (top left) UPI, (top center) Wide World, (top right) Paul S. Conklin, (bottom) Dennis Brack/Black Star; p. 635, (left) George W. Gardner, (right) Cary Wolinski/Stock, Boston; p. 637, © Marjorie Pickens 1981; p. 639, (top left) Peter Gerba/Jeroboam, (top center) Elliott Erwitt/Magnum, (top right) Cary Wolinski/Stock, Boston, (center) Barbara Klutinis/Jeroboam.

GLOSSARY

administrative law The rules and regulations made and applied by federal regulatory agencies and commissions.

adversary system of justice A judicial system in which the power of the state is balanced by the defendant's constitutional rights and by the presumption that a person is innocent until proven guilty beyond a reasonable doubt.

affirmative action programs Programs of government, universities, and businesses that are designed to favor minorities and remedy past discrimination.

agenda setting The power to determine which public policy questions will be debated or considered.

Antifederalists Those Americans who opposed ratification of the Constitution.

appellate jurisdiction The right of the Supreme Court to hear cases that are appealed from lower state or federal courts on the grounds that they concern violations of constitutional rights.

appropriations bills Bills passed by Congress to pay for the spending it has authorized.

arraignment The proceeding before a judge in which the formal charges of an indictment or information are read to an accused person, who may plead guilty or not guilty.

Articles of Confederation (1781–1789) The written framework for the government of the original thirteen states before the Constitution was adopted. Under the Articles of Confederation, the national government was weak and dominated by the states. There was a unicameral legislature, but no national executive or judiciary.

bail An amount of money "posted" with the courts as security in exchange for a defendant's freedom until the case comes to trial.

balancing test The view of the majority of the Supreme Court that First Amendment rights must be weighed against the competing needs of the community to preserve order.

bandwagon effect The possible tendency of some voters or convention delegates to support the candidate who is leading in the polls and seems likely to win.

bicameral legislature A two-house legislature.

bill of attainder A law aimed at a particular individual.

Bill of Rights The first ten amendments to the Constitution (sometimes defined as only the first eight or nine amendments), which set forth basic protections for individuals.

binding rule Requires all delegates to national conventions to vote, on the first ballot, for the presidential candidate under whose banner they were elected.

bipartisanship A view that both major political parties should broadly support the President on foreign policy issues.

block grants Federal grants to state and local communities that are for general use in a broad area, such as community development.

Brown* v. *Board of Education of Topeka, Kansas Ruling by the Supreme Court in 1954 that racial segregation in public schools violated the Fourteenth Amendment's requirement of equal protection of the law for individuals.

budget resolutions Overall spending targets set by the Congress.

bureaucrats Public administrators.

cabinet The President, the Vice President, and the officials who run the executive departments of the government. (At times, other officials are included in the cabinet.)

capitalism An economic system of free enterprise with private ownership of the means of production.

caucus A group or a meeting of a group of a political party or organization in which such matters as selection of candidates, leaders, or positions on issues are decided.

***certiorari,* writ of** A writ which, if granted by the Supreme Court, means that it agrees to hear a case.

charter colonies Colonies in which freely elected legislatures chose the governors, and laws could not be vetoed by the king.

checks and balances The provisions of the Constitution that divide power among three constitutionally equal and independent branches of government—legislative, executive, and judicial—in the hope of preventing any single branch from becoming too powerful.

civil cases Court cases that concern relations between individuals and organizations, such as a divorce action or a suit for damages arising from an automobile accident or for violation of a business contract.

civil disobedience The conscious refusal to obey laws that are believed to be unjust, unconstitutional, or immoral.

civil liberties The fundamental rights of a free society that are protected by the Bill of Rights against the power of the government, such as freedom of speech, religion, press, and assembly.

civil rights The constitutional rights of all individuals, and especially of blacks and other minorities, to enjoy full equality and equal protection of the laws.

civil service The civilian employees of the government and the administrative system in which they work.

clear and present danger test A test established by Supreme Court Justice Oliver Wendell Holmes in 1919 to define the point at which speech loses the protection of the First Amendment.

closed primary A form of primary election in which only registered members of a political party or persons declaring their affiliation with a party can vote.

closed shop A place of work in which only union members may be hired.

cloture A Senate procedure to cut off a filibuster by a vote of three-fifths (sixty members) of the entire Senate.

cluster sampling A technique used by polling organizations in which several people from the same neighborhood are interviewed.

coalitions Alliances of segments of the electorate, interest groups, and unorganized masses of voters who coalesce behind a political candidate or party.

coattail effect The ability of a major candidate, such as a presidential or gubernatorial candidate, to help carry into office lesser candidates from the same party who are also on the ballot.

COINTELPRO The "counterintelligence program" of the FBI that harassed American citizens and disrupted their organizations through a wide variety of clandestine techniques.

collective security A principle embraced by the United States during the Truman and Eisenhower administrations, under which the nation attempted to "contain" communism and entered into a series of military alliances with other countries for this purpose.

commission plan A form of city government under which a board of city commissioners is popularly elected (often on a nonpartisan ballot). The commissioners make policy as a city council, but they also run city departments as administrators.

Committee of the Whole A device used by the House of Representatives when it considers legislation sent to it by the Rules Committee. When the House sits as a Committee of the Whole, it is able to conduct business with less formality, and with a quorum of only 100 members.

Committees of Correspondence A political communications network established in 1772 by Samuel Adams to unite the colonists in their fight against British rule.

common law The cumulative body of law as expressed in judicial decisions and custom rather than by statute.

concurrent powers Powers of government exercised independently by both the federal and state governments, such as the power to tax.

conference committee A committee composed of senior members of the House and Senate that tries to reconcile disagreements between the two branches of Congress over differing versions of a bill.

conglomerates Multi-interest and often multinational corporations that, under one corporate roof, may manufacture a wide variety of products.

Connecticut Compromise The plan adopted during the Constitutional Convention of 1787 providing for a House of Representatives based on population and a Senate with two members from each state. (Also known as the Great Compromise.)

constituencies Voters in a political district; interest groups or client groups either directly regulated by the bureaucracy or vitally affected by its decisions.

Constitution The written framework for the United States government that established a strong national government of three branches—legislative, executive, and judicial—and provided for the control and operation of that government.

constitutional amendment A change to the Constitution proposed by a two-thirds vote of both houses of Congress or a constitutional convention, and ratified by legislatures or ratifying conventions in three-fourths of the states.

containment The foreign policy of the United States during the Cold War, designed to contain the expansion of Soviet power.

cooperative federalism A view that the various levels of government in America are related parts of a single governmental system, characterized by cooperation and shared functions.

council-manager plan A form of city government under which a council, usually elected on a nonpartisan ticket, hires a professional city manager, who runs the city government and has power to hire and fire officials.

court-packing plan A plan proposed by President Franklin D. Roosevelt in 1937, which Congress rejected, to add younger justices to the Supreme Court who would be more sympathetic to the New Deal.

covert operations Secret political action within other countries.

creative federalism A term coined by President Lyndon B. Johnson to describe his own view of the relationship between Washington and the states.

credentials committee The body of a political convention that decides which delegates should be seated, subject to approval of the entire convention.

criminal cases Court cases that concern crimes committed against the public order.

delegates The men and women formally entitled to select the presidential nominees of the two major parties at their party's presidential nominating convention.

demands What people and groups want from the political system.

democracy Rule by the people.

deregulation The elimination or reduction of government regulation of industry.

desegregation The process of ending separation of persons by race.

détente A relaxation of international tensions.

deviating elections Elections in which the majority party (according to party identification) is defeated in a temporary reversal.

direct mail fund raising A technique to raise money

directly from the public with the aid of computerized mailing lists.

discharge petition A petition which can be filed by a majority of House members in order to dislodge a bill from any House committee.

distributive policy A public policy that benefits everyone.

double jeopardy More than one prosecution for the same offense. Prohibited by the Constitution.

Dred Scott **decision** A ruling by the Supreme Court in 1857 — reversed by the Fourteenth Amendment in 1868 — that black Americans were not citizens under the Constitution.

dual federalism The concept — accepted until 1937 — of the federal government and the states as competing power centers, with the Supreme Court as referee.

due process of law A phrase, contained in the Fifth and Fourteenth amendments, that protects the individual against the arbitrary power of the state. *Substantive due process* means that laws must be reasonable. *Procedural due process* means that laws must be administered in a fair manner.

elastic clause Article I, Section 8 of the Constitution, which allows Congress to make all laws that are "necessary and proper" to carry out the powers of the Constitution.

elections The procedure by which voters choose, usually among competing candidates, to determine who shall hold public office. *See also* deviating elections, maintaining elections, and realigning elections.

electoral college The body composed of electors from the fifty states, who formally have the power to elect the President and Vice President of the United States. Each state has a number of electors equal to its number of senators and representatives in Congress.

elite theory The political view that power in America is held by the few, not by the masses of people.

enabling act A congressional act that allows the people of a territory desiring statehood to frame a state constitution.

enumerated powers Powers of government that are specifically granted to the three branches of the federal government under the Constitution.

equal protection clause The provision of the Fourteenth Amendment that seeks to guarantee equal treatment for individuals.

Equal Rights Amendment (ERA) A proposed amendment to the Constitution, aimed at ending discrimination against women, that states: "Equality of rights under the law shall not be denied or abridged by the United States or by any state on account of sex."

equal time provision A provision of the Federal Communications Act that requires broadcasters to provide "equal time" to all legally qualified candidates.

equality A concept that all people are of equal worth, even if not of equal ability.

equalization A formula for federal matching requirements that takes into account the state's or community's ability to pay.

equity A legal principle of fair dealing, which may provide preventive measures and legal remedies that are unavailable under ancient principles of common law.

exclusionary rule A doctrine established by the Supreme Court that bars the federal government from using illegally seized evidence in court.

executive agencies Units of government under the President, within the executive branch, that are not part of a cabinet department.

executive agreements Agreements made by the President in the conduct of foreign affairs, that, unlike treaties, do not require Senate approval.

executive privilege A doctrine under which Presidents have claimed the right to withhold information from Congress and the judiciary.

ex parte **contacts** One-sided contacts, such as an approach to a regulatory agency by a lawyer representing one side in a case.

ex post facto **laws** Laws that punish an act that was not illegal at the time it was committed.

extradition A constitutional provision allowing a state to request another state to return fugitives.

fairness doctrine A requirement by the Federal Communications Commission that radio and television broadcasters present all sides of important public issues.

Federal Election Campaign Act of 1974 An act to regulate campaign finance by providing for public funding of presidential elections and by placing limits on campaign contributions.

Federal Election Commission A six-member commission created in 1974 to enforce campaign finance laws and administer public financing of presidential elections.

federalism A system of government characterized by a constitutional sharing of power between a national government and regional units of government.

Federalist papers, The A series of letters published in the late 1780s by Alexander Hamilton, James Madison, and John Jay to explain and help bring about ratification of the Constitution.

Federalists Those who supported the Constitution during the struggle over its ratification following the Constitutional Convention of 1787.

feedback The response of the rest of society to decisions made by the authorities of a political system.

felony A major crime, such as murder, arson, or rape.

filibuster The process by which a single senator, or a group of senators, can sometimes talk a bill to death and prevent it from coming to a vote.

fiscal policy Government regulation of the economy through its control over rates of taxation and government spending.

flexible construction The principle, established by Chief Justice Marshall in 1819 in the case of *McCulloch* v. *Maryland,* that the Constitution must be interpreted flexibly to meet changing conditions.

foreign policy The sum of the goals, decisions, and actions that govern a nation's relations with the rest of the world.

Freedom of Information Act A law passed in 1966 which requires federal executive branch and regulatory agencies to make information available to journalists and the public unless it falls into one of several confidential categories.

free exercise clause The First Amendment provision that Congress shall make no law "prohibiting the free exercise" of religion.

full faith and credit A clause in Article IV of the Constitution, requiring that each state respect the laws, records, and court decisions of another state.

gerrymandering The drawing of the lines of congressional districts, or of any other political district, in order to favor one political party over another.

government The individuals, institutions, and processes that make the rules for society and possess the power to enforce them.

government corporations Agencies that were at one time semiautonomous, but that through legislation have been placed under presidential control since 1945.

grants-in-aid Federal aid to states and localities that is earmarked for specific purposes only. Also known as categorical grants.

Gross National Product The total national output of goods and services.

guaranteed annual income A proposed alternate approach to welfare that would guarantee everyone a minimum income, making the existing welfare system unnecessary.

Hatch Act A federal law that prevents federal employees from taking an active part in party politics or campaigns, or from running for political office.

Hispanic A term used in the United States to include persons of Mexican American, Puerto Rican, Cuban, Central or South American, or other Spanish origin.

home rule The power of some municipalities to modify their charters and run their affairs without approval by the state legislature.

impact The consequences of a policy, both in its immediate policy area and in other areas.

impeachment Under the Constitution, the formal proceedings against the President or other federal officials, who may be removed from office if convicted of "Treason, Bribery or other high Crimes and Misdemeanors."

implementation The action, or actions, taken by government to carry out a policy.

implied powers Powers of the national government that flow from its enumerated powers and the "elastic clause" of the Constitution.

impoundment The practice, curtailed in 1974, whereby a President refused to spend funds appropriated by Congress.

independent executive agencies Agencies that report to the President in the same manner as departments, even though they are not part of any cabinet department.

independent expenditures The spending of money on behalf of candidates but without their cooperation.

independent regulatory commissions *See* regulatory agencies.

Indiana ballot Also known as the party-column ballot. Used in a majority of states, it lists the candidates of each party in a row or column, beside or under the party emblem. Allows for and encourages straight-ticket voting.

indictment A finding by a grand jury that there is enough evidence against an individual to warrant a criminal trial.

inherent powers Powers of government that the national government may exercise simply because it exists as a government, such as the right to conduct foreign relations.

initiative A method of amending state constitutions, used in seventeen states, under which proposed constitutional amendments can be placed on the ballot if enough signatures are obtained on a petition.

injunction An order from a court to require or prevent an action.

instructed delegate A legislator who automatically mirrors the will of the majority of his constituents.

interest groups Private groups that attempt to influence the government to respond to the shared attitudes of their members.

interstate compacts Agreements between or among states made with the approval of Congress.

interventionism A strand of American foreign policy that was visible by the end of the nineteenth century; it included "gunboat diplomacy" and other forms of military involvement in various parts of the world.

isolationism A policy of avoiding foreign entanglements.

item veto The power of most governors to disapprove particular parts of appropriations bills.

Jim Crow laws Laws that were designed to segregate black and white Americans.

Joint Chiefs of Staff The chairman, the chiefs of staff of the three armed services, and, when marine corps matters are under consideration, the Commandant of the marines. By law, the Joint Chiefs of Staff advise the President and the Secretary of Defense and are the chiefs of their respective military services.

joint committees Committees composed of both representatives and senators.

judicial activism A philosophy, often embraced by a majority of the members of the Warren Court, that boldly applies the Constitution to social and political questions.

judicial restraint A philosophy often associated with Justices Frankfurter, Brandeis, and Holmes, that requires the Supreme Court to avoid constitutional questions when possible, and to uphold acts of Congress unless they clearly violate a specific section of the Constitution.

judicial review The power of the Supreme Court to declare acts of Congress or actions by the executive—or laws and actions at any level of local, state, and federal government—unconstitutional.

jungle primary A form of primary election, also known as a blanket primary, in which voters can pick and choose among two or more political party slates, crossing back and forth to select nominees for each office.

jus sanguinis Right of blood. Under this principle, the citizenship of a child is determined by that of the parents.

jus soli Right of soil. Under this principle, citizenship is conferred by place of birth.

kitchen cabinet   Informal advisers to the President who hold no official position on the White House staff.

laissez faire   The philosophy that government should intervene as little as possible in economic affairs.

"lame duck"   A legislator or other official whose term of office extends beyond an election at which he or she has been defeated.

legislative veto   A law in which Congress asserts the power to nullify actions of the executive branch. As of 1980, the Supreme Court had not ruled whether the "legislative veto" was constitutional.

liaison officers   Employees of government agencies whose job is to maintain good relations with Congress.

literacy tests   Tests of a voter's ability to read and write, which were often used to keep recent immigrants and blacks from voting.

lobbying   Communication with legislators or other government officials to try to influence their decisions.

magistrates' courts   Courts in which justices of the peace, or magistrates, handle minor offenses (misdemeanors), such as speeding, and perform civil marriages.

Magna Carta   An historic British document, signed by King John in 1215, in which the nobles confirmed that the power of the king was not absolute.

maintaining elections   Elections that reflect the basic party identification of the voters.

majority leader   A leader elected by the majority party in a legislative house.

majority rule   A concept of government by the people under which everyone is free to vote, but normally whoever gets the most votes wins the election and represents all the people (including those who voted for the losing candidate).

Mallory rule   A rule established by the Supreme Court in *Mallory* v. *United States* (1957) requiring that a suspect in a federal case be arraigned without unnecessary delay.

management by objective (MBO)   A program for managing the executive branch that required federal agencies to make periodic checks to be sure they were achieving their objectives.

Marbury v. *Madison*   The 1803 case in which the Supreme Court first exercised the power of judicial review, declaring an act of Congress unconstitutional on the basis that the Constitution is superior to an act of Congress.

marginal district   A congressional district in which the winning candidate receives less than 55 percent of the vote.

Massachusetts ballot   Also known as the office-column ballot. This ballot groups candidates according to the office for which they are running.

matching requirements   The federal government's requirement that state or local governments put up some of their own funds in order to be eligible for federal aid for a program.

mayor-council plan   A form of city government under which power is divided between a mayor and an elected city council.

McCulloch v. *Maryland*   An important decision of the Supreme Court in 1819 that established the key concepts of implied powers, broad construction of the Constitution, and supremacy of the national government.

Medicaid   A public assistance program established in 1965 to help pay hospital, doctor, and medical bills for persons with low incomes. It is financed through general federal, state, and local taxes.

Medicare   A federal program established in 1965 that provides hospital and medical services to older persons through the social security program.

megalopolis   By definition, a very large city. The term has also been used to describe the cluster of metropolitan areas of the Northeastern seaboard of the United States.

merit commissions   Commissions set up to recommend candidates for federal district and circuit courts on the basis of merit.

military-industrial complex   A term often used to describe the ties between the military establishment and the defense-aerospace industry.

minority leader   A leader elected by the minority party in a legislative house.

Miranda warnings   Warnings that police must give suspects to advise them of their constitutional rights. Under the Supreme Court decision in *Miranda* v. *Arizona* (1966), before suspects are questioned, they must be warned that they have the right to remain silent, that any statements they make may be used against them, and that they have the right to a lawyer.

misdemeanor   A minor offense.

mixed (or modified) free enterprise system   An economic system, such as that of the United States, in which both private industry and government play important roles.

Model Cities   A controversial program approved by Congress in 1966 that sought to rebuild entire poverty neighborhoods in selected cities.

monetary policy   Government regulation of the economy through its control over the supply of money and the cost and availability of credit.

money supply   The quantity of money in circulation.

monopoly   Control of a market by a single company.

national chairman   The head of a national political party.

national committee   Between conventions, the governing body of a major political party whose members are chosen in the states and formally elected by the party's national convention.

national convention   The formal source of all authority in each major political party. It nominates the party candidates for President and Vice President, writes a platform, settles disputes, writes rules, and elects the members of the national committee.

national presidential primary   A proposed new form of primary in which voters could directly choose the presidential candidates of the major parties.

National Security Council   A White House council created in 1947 to help the President coordinate American military and foreign policy.

neutron bomb   A controversial bomb that kills people but spares buildings.

new federalism   President Richard Nixon's effort to return federal tax money to state and local governments through such programs as general revenue sharing.

New Jersey Plan   A plan offered at the Constitutional Convention of 1787 by William Paterson of New Jersey, and favored by the small states, which called for one vote for each state in the legislature, an executive of more than one person to be elected by Congress, and a Supreme Court to be appointed by the executive.

New York Times rule   A rule established by the Supreme Court in the case of *New York Times Company* v. *Sullivan* (1964), which makes it almost impossible to libel a public official unless the statement is made with "actual malice"—that is, unless it is deliberately or recklessly false.

no establishment clause   The First Amendment provision that "Congress shall make no law respecting an establishment of religion."

nuclear proliferation   The spread of atomic weapons to more countries.

oligopoly   The concentration of economic power in the hands of a relatively few large companies.

ombudsman   An official complaint taker who tries to help citizens who have been wronged by the actions of government agencies.

open primary   A form of primary election in which any voter may participate and vote for a slate of candidates of one political party.

original jurisdiction   The right of the Supreme Court, under the Constitution, to hear certain kinds of cases directly, such as cases involving foreign diplomats.

out party   A major political party that functions as an opposition party because it does not control the Presidency.

outputs   The binding decisions that a political system makes, whether in the form of laws, regulations, or judicial decisions.

party activists   People who ring doorbells or serve as delegates to political conventions. They perform the day-to-day, grass-roots work of politics.

party identification   Attachment to one political party by a voter.

Pentagon Papers   A forty-seven volume study of the Vietnam war compiled by the Defense Department and leaked to the press by a former Pentagon official in 1971.

periodic registration   A system of voter registration in which the voter must register every year or at other stated intervals.

permanent registration   A system of voter registration in which the voter registers only once in his or her district.

planning-programming budgeting system (PPBS)   A management tool that required federal departments to define their goals precisely and measure the costs and benefits of alternative programs to achieve those goals.

plea bargaining   A bargain in which a defendant in a criminal case agrees to plead guilty to a less serious charge than might be proven at a trial. In return, the prosecutor agrees to reduce the charges or recommend leniency.

plum book   A listing of the non-civil service jobs that an incoming President may fill.

pluralism   A system in which many conflicting groups within the community have access to government officials and compete with one another in an effort to influence policy decisions.

pocket veto   A power of the President to kill a bill by taking no action (if Congress adjourns at the end of a second session during the ten-day period after the President receives the bill).

policy   A course of action decided upon by a government—or by any organization, group, or individual—that usually involves a choice among competing alternatives.

political action committees (PACs)   Independent organizations, but more often the political arms of corporations, labor unions, or interest groups, established to contribute to candidates or to work for general political goals.

political opinion   Opinions on political issues, such as a choice among candidates or parties.

political participation   The involvement of citizens in the political process of a nation.

political party, major   A broadly based coalition that attempts to gain control of the government by winning elections, in order to exercise power and reward its members.

political socialization   The process through which an individual acquires a set of political attitudes and forms opinions about social issues.

poll tax   A tax on voting repealed by the Twenty-fourth Amendment in 1964, long used by Southern states to keep blacks (and, in some cases, poor whites) from participating in elections.

power   The possession of control over others.

power structure   A term popularized by sociologist Floyd Hunter to describe the community leaders who determined policy in Atlanta, Georgia. More broadly, the term is used to describe "power elites" generally.

precedent   An earlier court case that serves as a justification for a decision in a later case. Also known as *stare decisis.*

presidential primary   Method used by more than two-thirds of the states in which voters in one or both parties express their preference for a presidential nominee and choose all or some convention delegates.

press secretary, presidential   The White House official who speaks for the President in day-to-day meetings with the news media.

primary group   A group that a person comes into face-to-face contact with in everyday life; for example, friends, office associates, or a local social club.

prior restraint   The censoring of printed material by the government prior to publication.

proportional representation   A system of multimember election districts that encourages the existence of many parties by allotting legislative seats to competing parties according to the percentage of votes that they win.

Proposition 13   A constitutional amendment approved by California voters in 1978 that limited real estate taxes in the state to one percent of previous property values.

proprietary colonies Colonies in which the proprietors (who had obtained their patents from the king) named the governors, subject to the king's approval.

psychological method An approach in studying how voters decide that attempts to find out what is going on inside the minds of the voters and to measure their perceptions of parties, candidates, and issues.

public administration The term preferred by political scientists to describe the bureaucratic process — the business of making government work.

public assistance A welfare program that distributes public funds to people who are poor.

public interest law firms Law firms, often staffed by young lawyers, that represent consumers, minorities, and the poor.

public opinion The expression of attitudes about government and politics.

public policy A course of action chosen by government officials.

quota sample A method of polling, considered less reliable than a random sample, in which members of a particular group are interviewed in proportion to their percentage in the population as a whole.

random sample A group, chosen by poll takers, that is representative of the universe that is being polled.

realigning elections Elections which may lead to a basic shift in the party identification of the electorate.

reapportionment The drawing of new boundary lines for legislative districts based on the results of a census of the population.

redistributive policy A public policy that takes something away from one person and gives it to someone else.

reference group A group whose views serve as guidelines to an individual's opinion.

regulatory agencies Government agencies that exercise quasi-judicial and quasi-legislative powers. They are administratively independent of both the President and Congress (although politically independent of neither).

representative democracy A democracy in which leaders are elected to speak for and represent the people.

revenue sharing, general Federal grants to state and local communities, distributed by formula with few or no strings about how the money is to be used.

riders Provisions tacked on to a piece of legislation that are not relevant to the bill.

right to work laws State legislation designed to outlaw the union shop, passed by twenty states acting under Section 14B of the federal Taft-Hartley Act.

roll-call vote A method of voting in a legislature in which all members present at a session must vote, and their positions become a matter of public record.

royal colonies Colonies controlled by the British king through governors appointed by him and through the king's veto power over colonial laws.

rule A measure from the House Rules Committee, which sets the terms of the debate for a bill, the time to be allowed for discussion on the floor of the House, and the extent to which the bill may be amended on the floor.

safe congressional district As usually defined, a district in which the winner receives 55 percent or more of the vote.

secondary group An organization or group of people, such as a labor union, or a fraternal, professional, or religious group, that may influence an individual's opinion.

Secret Service The government agency that guards the President, the Vice-President, the major presidential and vice-presidential candidates, and their spouses.

segregation The separation of persons by race.

select committees *See* special committees.

senatorial courtesy An unwritten custom by which individual senators who belong to the same political party as the President exercise an informal veto power over presidential appointments in their states.

Senior Executive Service (SES) A corps of about 8000 high-level administrators and managers at the top of the government bureaucracy who have less job security but who are eligible for substantial cash bonuses for merit.

seniority system A system, until modified and reformed in the 1970s, that automatically resulted in those members of the majority party in a house of Congress with the longest continuous service on a committee becoming committee chairmen.

separate but equal A doctrine established by the Supreme Court in 1896 under which "Jim Crow" segregation laws were held to be constitutional.

separation of powers The principle that each of the three branches of government is constitutionally equal to and independent of the others.

shared powers The fusing or overlapping of powers and functions among the separate branches of government.

shield laws Laws passed by state legislatures that are designed to protect reporters from being forced to reveal their news sources.

smoke-filled room A phrase that grew out of the 1920 Republican Convention in Chicago, symbolizing the selection of a candidate by political bosses operating in secret.

social security A compulsory national insurance program, financed by taxes on employers and employees. The insurance falls into four categories: old-age and survivors insurance, disability insurance, Medicare, and unemployment insurance.

sociological method An approach in studying how the voters decide that focuses on the social and economic background of the voters, their income, social class, ethnic group, education, and similar factors.

Speaker of the House The presiding officer and most powerful member of the House of Representatives. He is technically elected by the full House but in practice is chosen by the majority party.

special committees Committees created by Congress to conduct special investigations.

special publics A concept developed by political scientists to describe those segments of the public with views about particular issues.

spoils system A practice under which victorious politicians reward their followers with jobs.

standing committees The permanent committees of a legislature that consider bills and conduct hearings and investigations.

stare decisis A Latin phrase meaning "stand by past decisions," that is often, but not always, used by judges in deciding cases.

statutory law Law enacted by Congress, or by state legislatures or local legislative bodies.

steering committee A committee appointing senators to standing committees. Also known as assignment committee.

Strategic Arms Limitation Talks (SALT) Negotiations between the United States and the Soviet Union that resulted in the signing of two arms agreements in 1972, and the SALT II agreement in 1979. As of 1980, SALT II had not been ratified by the Senate.

strategic deterrence A policy followed by the United States since the Second World War that assumes that if enough nuclear weapons are deployed by the United States, an enemy would not attack for fear of being destroyed by a retaliatory blow.

subcommittees Small committees formed from the members of a larger committee.

subpoena A written document issued by a court that orders a person to appear in court or to produce evidence.

subsidy A government grant of money.

suffrage The right to vote.

supports The attitudes and actions of people that sustain and buttress the political system at all levels and allow it to continue to work.

supremacy clause The clause in Article VI of the Constitution declaring that the Constitution and the laws of Congress are "the supreme Law of the Land" and shall prevail over any conflicting state constitutions or laws.

suspension of the rules A procedure permitted four times a month under the rules of the House of Representatives, which allows any bill to be debated if two-thirds of the members who are voting agree.

system maintenance The process of keeping a diverse, unwieldy, institution, such as the House of Representatives, functioning.

tariff A federal tax on imports.

teller vote A vote in the Committee of the Whole in which members file down the aisle of the House and are counted.

third party A minor party that is an alternative to the two major parties; for example, the Know-Nothings of the 1850s, a party that exploited fear of Irish immigrants and other "foreigners," or the Populists of the 1890s, a protest party of Western farmers favoring "free silver."

ticket-splitter A voter who may be a Republican or Democrat, but who occasionally votes for a candidate of another party.

tombstone voters Persons who vote illegally by using the names of deceased voters.

town meeting An annual meeting held in the spring in many New England towns, at which the townspeople come together to elect a board of selectmen and to discuss local policy questions. The town meeting has become a symbol of participatory democracy.

transnational relations Contacts, coalitions, and interactions across national boundaries—such as personal contacts or business relationships—that are not controlled by the central foreign policy organs of governments.

triangle A powerful alliance of mutual benefit among an agency or unit of the government, an interest group, and a committee or subcommittee of Congress. Also called an iron triangle or a subgovernment.

Truman Doctrine As enunciated by President Truman, a doctrine declaring that American security and world peace depended on United States protection for the "free peoples of the world."

trustee Concept of the British Statesman Edmund Burke that a legislator should act according to his own conscience.

unanimous consent A Senate procedure under which the objections of a single senator can prevent a bill from being called up for consideration from the legislative calendar.

unicameral legislature A legislature with only one house.

union shop A place of work in which any person may be hired provided he or she joins the union within a specified time.

unitary system of government A centralized system of government, such as that of France, where most of the important policy decisions are made by a central government.

United Nations A world organization founded in 1945 for the purpose of collectively keeping the peace and working for the betterment of humanity.

unit rule A procedure at national political conventions which in some cases allowed the majority of a state delegation to cast the state's entire vote.

universe The total group from which poll takers select a random sample in order to measure public opinion.

unreasonable searches and seizures Searches prohibited by the Fourth Amendment, often because they take place without a search warrant issued by a court.

vanishing marginals An electoral trend in which the number of unsafe, marginal districts in House elections appears to be declining.

veto Disapproval of a bill by a chief executive, such as the President, or a state governor.

Virginia Plan A plan offered at the Constitutional Convention of 1787, and favored by the large states, which called for a two-house legislature, the lower house chosen by the people and the upper house chosen by the lower; and a national executive and a national judiciary chosen by the legislature.

War Powers Resolution A law passed by Congress in 1973 that sets a time limit on the use of combat forces abroad by a President.

welfare state A government like that of the United States that exercises responsibility for the welfare of its citizens in such areas as social security, housing, and education.

whips Legislative leaders of each party who are responsible for rounding up party members for important votes.

whistle-blowers Government employees who publicly expose evidence of official waste or corruption that they have learned about in the course of their duties.

winner-take-all primaries Presidential primaries in which the victorious candidate could win all of a state's convention delegates, no matter how slim the margin of victory.

Zero-Base Budgeting (ZBB) A management system instituted by President Carter that sought to examine the need for existing programs as if they were being proposed for the first time.

INDEX

Page numbers in *italics* refer to figures and tables.

A

Abington School District v. *Schempp*, 111n
ABM. *See* Antiballistic missiles
Abortion laws: and Medicaid payments, 148, 180, 469; opposition to, 148–49, 209, 481, 489; Supreme Court decision on, 29, 107, 147–48, 171, 479, 481, 485
Abourezk, James, 453, 454
Abraham, Henry J., 125n, 475, 475n, 482n, 485n, 488n
Abscam, 430, 500–01
ACTION, 539, 586
Adams, Charles F., Jr., 81n
Adams, Charles Francis, 34n, 46n
Adams, John, 30–31, 35n, 46, 49, 113, 222, 475; on American Revolution, 34; on Vice Presidency, 377
Adams, John Quincy, 240, 334, 334n
Adams, Samuel, 35, 47
Adams, Sherman, 374, 385
Adams v. *Williams,* 116n
Addonizio, Hugh, 506
Adversary system of justice, 501, 510
Advertising: fraudulent, 94, 415; by interest groups, 206–07; in political campaigns, 22, 251, 254–56, 265, 271–72, 275–78, 284, 289, 293; television and radio costs, 197, 275, 287, 290. *See also* Media, mass
Affirmative action programs, 29, 167–69, 172, 468, 479
Afghanistan: Soviet invasion of, 7, 320, 322, 355, 516, 517, 521, 526, 538, 546, 554, 556–57
AFL-CIO, 568–69; Committee on Political Education (COPE) of, 205, 284, 569; and Democratic party, 205, 570; and expelling of Teamsters, 570; as interest group, 75, 203, 205
Africa, 127, 520; and cultural heritage of black Americans, 153; new nations of, 48–49, 68, 167, 523, 538, 541
Afroyim v. *Rusk,* 127, 127n
Agency for International Development (AID), 534, 538–39, 540
Agnew, Spiro T., 377, 387n; and attacks on news media, 195, 377, 380; criminal charges and conviction of, 377–78; resigna-
tion of as Vice President, 56, 225, 378, 385, 387; on Vice Presidency, 377
Agriculture, 71, 399, 516; agrarian discontent and minor parties, 224; farm bloc of, 21; federal aid to, 562, 566, 567–68, 600. *See also* Farm workers
Aid to Families with Dependent Children (AFDC), 583
Airline industry, 231, 565, 566; deregulation of, 416, 427
Air pollution, 23, 73, 592, 593, 600, 608, 617, 621, 630. *See also* Pollution of environment
Alabama, 76, 163; Freedom Riders in, 160; *Scottsboro* case, 73, 73n; voting in, 304n, 324
Alabama, University of, 65, 156
Alaska, 72, 137, 164, 337n, 615; constitution of, 611; voting in, 329
Albert, Carl, 387
Albertson v. *Subversive Activities Control Board,* 114n
Alexander, Herbert E., 255n, 275n, 283n, 287n, 289
Alexander v. *Holmes County Board of Education,* 157n
Alien and Sedition acts (1798), 49, 113
Allard, Robert E., 489n
Allen, James, 454
Allen, Richard V., 259, 376, 532, 533
Allen, Robert S., 477n
Allied Chemical Corporation, 591
Allport, Floyd, 177–78, 178n
Almond, Gabriel A., 542, 542n
Amendments to the Constitution, 27, 50, 54–58; amending process, 52–53, *53, 54*; Civil War, 42n, 55, 154; convention method, 53; proposed ERA, 56–57, 57n, 144–46, 171; proposed for balanced budget, 53; proposed for direct election of President, 52, 335; proposed on District of Columbia, 57; proposed to end one person, one vote principle, 53, 336–37, 481. *See also* Bill of Rights; individual amendments
American Automobile Association (AAA), 207
American Bar Association (ABA), 75, 488
American Broadcasting Company (ABC), 196, 277; 1980 election exit poll of, 304n, 325n
American Civil Liberties Union (ACLU), 109
American Communications Association v. *Douds,* 95n
American Federation of Labor (AFL), 568–69
American Federation of Labor–Congress of Industrial Organizations. *See* AFL-CIO
American Independent party, 226, 231–33, 252, 316n
American Indian Movement (AIM); at Wounded Knee, 137–38
American Indians, 21n, 134, 136–38, 164, 171
American Institute of Public Opinion. *See* Gallup poll
American Medical Association (AMA), 75, 215; and lobbying, 205, 431; Political Action Committee (AMPAC) of, 205; Republican-oriented, 205
American Nazi Party, 108–09
American Revolution, 30, 32, 34–36, 48, 153, 192
Americans for Indian Opportunity, 136
Amtrak, 401, 566
Anderson, John B., 8, 189, 226, 231, 233, 248, 251, 252, 274–75, 278, 285n, 286, 290, 316, 321, 322, *322,* 323, 324–25, 342
Anderson, Martin, 259, 376
Annapolis conference (1786), 37
Anson, Robert Sam, 530
Antiballistic missiles (ABMs), 550–51; and SALT talks, 551, 553, 558
Antifederalists, 47, 58
Anti-Masons, 231, 252
Antiwar movement: and CIA, 535; at Democratic National Convention (1968), 496, 496n, 497, and justice system, 94, 471; students in, 12, 117, 179, 542. *See also* Vietnam war: protests against
Apodaca, Jerry, 141
Apodaca v. *Oregon,* 505n
Appalachia, 585
Arab-Israeli wars: of 1973, 541, 592; Six-Day War (1967), 541
Arab states: and oil, 520, 526, 592; and OPEC, 6, 531, 595, 596
Arendt, Hannah, 395, 395n
Argersinger v. *Hamlin,* 123, 123n, 124n
Armed forces, 353, 371, 599; unification of, 547, 558. *See also* Department of Defense; Military establishment; President: as Commander in Chief
Arms: control and disarmament, 540, 552–54, 556, 558; race, 521, 550, 552, 558; right to bear, 54, 58, 125n; sale of, 362, 556. *See also* Nuclear weapons

Arms Control and Disarmament Agency, 540
Armstrong, Scott, 482n, 483, 485n, 508n
Arthur, Chester A., 418
Articles of Confederation (1781–1789), 35–38, 47, 58, 68, 353
Asia, 520; and immigration quotas, 127; new nations of, 48–49, 68, 167, 523, 538, 541
Associated Milk Producers, Inc. (AMPI), 203–04
Associated Press v. *Walker,* 105n
Atlanta, Georgia, 337, 621, 626–27, 632; black mayor elected in, 169, 633; MARTA system of, 630
Atomic Energy Act (1954), 88
Atomic bomb, 360. *See also* Nuclear weapons
Attica (state prison), 494, 495
Attorney General, 498–99, 510; and civil rights, 163, 327n; and FBI, 500. *See also* Department of Justice
Attucks, Crispus, 153
Australian ballot (secret), 330
Automobile industry, 566; and environment, 592, 593; and federal safety standards, 565, 578, 580; and Nader, 565, 577–78; regulations affecting, 394
Avrech, Mark, 487

B

Bachrach, Peter, 200n
Badillo, Herman, 144
Bagdikian, Ben H., 585, 585n
Bail Reform Act (1966), 502–03
Bail system, 54, 125n, 130, 502–03, 509, 510
Bain, Richard C., 246n, 248n, 250n
Baker, Bobby, 451, 451n
Baker, Charles W., 336
Baker, Howard H., Jr., 231, 321, 452
Baker, James A. III, 259, 373
Baker v. *Carr,* 336, 336n, 477n, 615, 615n
Bakke, Allan, 29, 168–69, 172. *See also* Affirmative action
Baldwin, James, 133, 133n, 151–52, 152n
Baldwin v. *New York,* 505n
Ball, George W., 556–57, 557n
Baltimore, Maryland, 622, 623
Banfield, Edward C., 622, 622n, 632, 632n
Banking. *See* Federal Reserve System
Baratz, Morton S., 200n
Barber, James David, 388, 388n, 389
Barceló, Carlos Romero, 143
Barenblatt v. *United States,* 458n
Barnburners, 231
Barnet, Richard J., 520–21, 521n
Barone, Michael, 446n
Barrett, Edward L., Jr., 490–91, 491n
Barron v. *Baltimore,* 123, 123n
Barry, Marion, 151
Bartlett, E. L., 590n
Baxter, Sandra, 297, 297n, 305n
Bayh, Birch, 210–11
Beal, Richard S., 279
Beame, Abraham, 631

Beaney, William M., 478n
Beard, Charles A., 45, 45n
Becker, Carl L., 30, 31n, 240
Becklund, Laurie, 140
Begin, Menachem, 276
Bellei, Aldo Mario, 127
Benanti v. *United States,* 118n
Bender, Paul, 101n
Benitez, Andrew, 141
Bennett, W. Lance, 178, 178n, 190n, 192n
Benton v. *Maryland,* 125, 125n
Berelson, Bernard, 300n, 301n
Berger, Raoul, 384n
Berger v. *New York,* 118n
Berns, Walter, 70n
Bernstein, Carl, 98, 381
Betts v. *Brady,* 122n
Beyle, Thad L., 612, 612n
Biaggi, Mario, 278
Bibby, John F., 286n
Bickel, Alexander M., 90, 90n
Bill of attainder, 51
Bill of Rights, 26, 54, 54n, 58, 92n, 128, 475; absent from original Constitution, 47, 92; applied to the states, 54, 71, 93, 123–25, 125n, 131, 478; English influence on, 32; and rights of accused, 54, 119–23, 477–78; Supreme Court interpretations of, 89–131. *See also* individual amendments and freedoms
Binkley, Wilfred E., 222n
Biological weapons, 552–53
Birmingham, Alabama: church bombing in, 161; civil rights demonstrations in, 160
Birth control: pills, congressional investigation of, 436; programs, 19
Bish, Robert L., 638n
Bishop, Joseph W., Jr., 480n
Black, Hugo, 89, 95, 95n, 96, 110–11, 122, 130, 480, 480n, 485, 509n
Black Americans, 21n; and affirmative action, 168–69, 468; African heritage of, 153; in American history, 153–54; and black power, 99, 166–67, 470; and busing issue, 157–59; citizenship for, 55, 154, 171; and Civil Rights Act of 1964, 161, 167–68, 169; and community control, 166; in Congress, 21, 169, 172, 438, 460, 465; and Constitutional amendments, 42n, 55, 56, 154; as convention delegates, 243, 244, 245; disadvantages of federalism for, 62; economic and political gains of, 132, 133, 152, 169–70, 172; education of, 133, 158, 169; employment of, 133, 161, 169, 624, 630; and framers of Constitution, 44–45, 154; and housing, 133, 162, 169, 479; income of, 135; on integration and separation, 167; and interest groups, 214–15, 437; and "Jim Crow" laws, 154, 154n, 155; lynchings of, 155, 155n, 192; as mayors, 21, 169, 506, 633, 637; middle class, 132, 152; migrated to cities, 21, 152, 606, 622–23; migrated to suburbs, 170, 304, 607, 623–24; party affiliation of, 180, 219, 225, 229, 252, 342; political participation of, 50,

164–65; poverty of, 132–33, 152, 170, 171, 172, 585; in prisons, 494, 495; and school desegregation, 64–65, 133, 155–59; struggle for equality of, 16, 23, 44–45, 132–36, 151–53, 167, 169, 172; unemployment of, 133, 170; and urban riots, 7, 23, 165–66, 192, 470, 585; voter behavior and participation of, 169, 297–98, 304, 307, 325; and voting rights, 46, 55, 56, 161, 162, *162,* 163–64, *164,* 165, 172, 297–98, 321, 328, 342; youth, 133. *See also* Civil rights; Civil rights movement; Slavery; Slums: ghettos in
Blackmun, Harry Andrew, 470, 478, 483, 485
Blackstone, Sir William, 32
Blaine, James G., 267–68
Block grants, 77, 78, 83, *84, 85,* 87
Blue-collar workers, 135, 170, 180, 219, 258, 438
Board of Education v. *Allen,* 112n
Bolling, Richard, 431–32, 432n, 446
Bonafede, Dom, 369n
B-1 bomber program, 555–56
Boorstin, Daniel J., 26, 26n, 35n
Boston, Massachusetts, 622, 623; busing conflict in, 157–58
Boston Massacre (1770), 153
Bowen, Bruce D., 188n
Bowen, Catherine Drinker, 38n, 39n, 40, 41, 41n
Boyd, William J. D., 339n
Bradley, Omar, 548
Brady, James S., 379
Brady v. *United States,* 501n
Brandeis, Louis D., 106, 130, 476, 485
Branzburg v. *Hayes,* 99n
Brennan, William J., Jr., 103, 117, 144, 478, 482, 483
Brethren, The, 481–82, 482n, 483, 484–85
Brewer v. *Williams,* 121, 122n
Brezhnev, Leonid I., 526, 553
Bribery, 204–05, 429–30, 433, 613. *See also* Corruption and scandal
Briggs, Ellis O., 403
Broadcasting industry, 231; and FCC, 100–01, 399, 565; and obscene material, 101; and Supreme Court, 100–01
Brock, Bill, 234–35
Broder, David S., 191n, 279n, 280, 280n
Brooke, Edward W., 186
Brookings Institution, 80–81, 246, 248
Brooks, Jack, 80
Brown, Dee, 137n
Brown, Edmund G. (Pat), 279
Brown, Harold, 406
Brown, Linda Carol, 155, 157
Brown, Robert E., 45, 45n
Brown, Thad A., 306n
Brown v. *Board of Education of Topeka, Kansas,* 29n, 133, 155–56, 156n, 157, 158–59, 172, 477, 477n
Bryan, William Jennings, 224
Bryant, Anita, 150
Bryce, James, 177, 177n, 249

Intelligence agencies, 536; abuses by, 348, 390, 398, 535, 537; investigations into, 433, 436, 535, 537–38. *See also* Central Intelligence Agency; Federal Bureau of Investigation

Intercontinental ballistic missiles. *See* ICBMs

Interest groups: and bureaucracy, 399, 401–02, 413, 426; and city government, 634; and Congress, 202–05, *206*, 207–13, 431, 433, 436–37, 444, 449, 456, 466, 575, 629; defined, 201; in a democracy, 12, 213–15; and executive branch, 213; and federalism, 62–63, 75, 87; functions of, 213–15, 216; and grass-roots pressure, 207, 213, 216; and lobbying, 202–05, 216; mass propaganda of, 206–07, 208, 210–11, 216; membership of, 202, 214, 216, 292; and minorities, 214–15, 216, 437; operations of, 202–12; political action committees (PACs) of, 209–12, 216, 288, 289, 291; political parties as mediators between, 221, 249; public, 208–09, 214–15; regulation of, 212–13; single-issue, 6, 209, 212, 216, 289, 437; spending by, 203–05; and state government, 613; tax advantages of, 575; types of, 201; uses and abuses of, 63, 213–15. *See also* Client groups; Lobbying

Internal Revenue Service (IRS): political use of, 193, 383, 385, 429

Internal Security Act (1950, McCarran Act), 114

International Bank for Reconstruction and Development (World Bank), 538

International Communications Agency (ICA), 74, 534, 539, 540

International Development Cooperation Agency, 538

International Telephone and Telegraph Corporation (ITT), 564

Interstate commerce, 71, 74

Interstate Commerce Commission (ICC), 415, 417, 565, 566

Interstate relations, 72–73

In the Matter of Samuel Winship, 501n

Iran, 515, 526, 596; American hostages freed from, 5, 6, 324, 356, 514, 515n; American hostages in, 8, 9, 176, 265, 267, 271, 319–20, 322, 355, 364, 369, 406, 514–15, 516, 517, 521, 526, 531, 538, 542, 546, 554, 556–67; American rescue mission in, 322, 362, 515, 533; and CIA, 536; revolution in, 7, 514

Iraq, 515, 526, 596

Irish Americans, 233, 233n, 303, 623

Irvin v. *Dowd,* 97n

Isolationism, 521–22

Israel, 61, 180, 520, 527, 541, 543, 548, 552

Italian Americans, 180, 303, 507, 623

J

Jackson, Andrew, 192, 222, 240, 353, 378, 387, 418, 475

Jackson, Henry, 527

Jackson, Jesse, 165

Jackson, Robert H., 110, 125, 156, 156n, 473, 473n, 475n, 480, 480n, 509, 509n

Jacksonian democracy, 222, 613

Jacob, Herbert, 615n, 617n

Jacobellis v. *Ohio,* 104n

Jacobs, Jane, 625

Jacquet, Constant H., Jr., 21n

Japan, 360, 519, 522, 552, 567

Japanese Americans, 363

Jarvis, Howard A., 609

Jascalevich, Dr. Mario, 99

Jaworski, Leon, 367, 498

Jay, John, 47, 477

Jefferson, Thomas, 42n, 113, 417–18, 475, 521; on Constitution, 45, 57; and Declaration of Independence, 10, 30–32, 35, 48; and Democratic-Republicans, 222; in election of 1800, 52, 334n; on freedom of religion, 109; on Presidency, 377, 387; on press, 281; on Vice Presidency, 377

Jehovah's Witnesses, 110

Jenkins v. *Anderson,* 122n

Jenkins v. *Georgia,* 104n

Jennings, M. Kent, 179, 179n

Jenrette, John W., Jr., 430

Jensen, Merrill, 36, 36n

Jews, 21, 623; discrimination against, 135; and Israel, 543; political affiliation of, 180, 229, 252, 302, 342; as voters, 297, 302, 305, 325, 325n, 543

"Jim Crow" laws, 154, 154n, 155

Johnson, Andrew, 384, 385

Johnson, Lyndon B., 352, 378n, 379; and ABM program, 550–51; and bureaucracy, 423; and cabinet, 372; and CIA, 536; and Civil Rights Act of 1964, 161; and "creative federalism," 67; credibility gap of, 543; death of, 358; and death of Kennedy, 360, 378, 386; declined to run in 1968, 176, 225, 251, 319n. 346, 525, 542; domestic policies in, 101, 112, 376, 434, 489, 579; foreign policies, 528, 530; Great Society program of, 8, 67, 74, 229, 363, 440, 561, 588–89, 626; and Humphrey's 1968 campaign, 266; informal advisers of, 372, 378; and National Security Council, 532; 1964 campaign and election of, 225, 271–72, 301, 307, 308, 340, 340n, 451n; personality of, 374, 451; on Presidency, 352, 354, 359; as President, 358, 371, 386, 388; and press, 380; and protection for candidates, 266; as Senate majority leader, 434, 451; Supreme Court appointments of, 480, 480n; and Tonkin Gulf resolution, 271, 361, 363, 530, 543; and urban riots, 165; and Vietnam war, 176, 250–51, 271, 340, 340n, 346, 361, 363, 364, 372, 407, 407n, 432, 525; and Voting Rights Act, 163; war on poverty of, 18, 423, 585–86, 599; White House staff of, 78, 374; and wiretapping, 119

Johnson, Richard M., 334n

Johnson v. *Louisiana,* 505n

Joint Chiefs of Staff, 547; and ABM program,

550; and Bay of Pigs invasion, 406; and Cuban missile crisis, 547–48; and hostage rescue, 406

Joint Economic Committee, 571

Jones, Harry W., 489n

Jones v. *Mayer,* 162n

Jordan, Hamilton, 185, 260, 374

Judges, 488–89; in criminal court, 501–03, 509; merit appointment of, 488, 510; and politics, 616

Judicial branch, 509; powers of, under Constitution, 43–44, 52, 58. *See also* Criminal justice system; Supreme Court; individual courts

Judicial review, 44, 45, 52, 58, 473–76, 510, 611, 616

Judiciary Act (1789), 475

Juries: and capital punishment, 503; and confessions, 121; and juvenile offenders, 505; and news media, 97; trial by, 33, 52, 54, 58, 124, 125n, 504–05; verdicts by, 505. *See also* Grand juries

Justices of the Supreme Court. *See* Supreme Court

Juvenile delinquency, 505

K

Kahn, Herman, 550, 550n

Kaiser Aluminum and Chemical Corporation, 169

Kalmbach, Herbert W., 382

Kansas-Nebraska Act (1854), 223

Kassebaum, Nancy, 149, 438

Kastigar v. *United States,* 121n

Katz v. *United States,* 118, 118n

Kaufman, Herbert, 634n

Kearns, Doris, 363

Keech, William R., 247, 247n

Kefauver, Estes, 241n, 247n

Kelley, Clarence M., 500

Kelley, Stanley, Jr., 279, 279n

Kellie family, James, 97

Kelly, Alfred H., 70n

Kelly, Richard, 430

Kemp, Jack, 571

Kennan, George, 522, 532, 532n

Kennedy, Edward M., 229, 278, 367, 595; and national health insurance, 588; 1980 primary campaign of, 75, 243–44, 247, 263, 319, *319,* 320, 516, 572

Kennedy, Eugene, 75n

Kennedy, John F., 439n, 352; assassination of, 7, 56, 97, 161, 192, 225, 264, 346, 357–58, 360, 378, 386, 431; and Bay of Pigs, 361, 406, 543; on black Americans, 171; and bureaucracy, 350, 404, 405; and cabinet, 372; and civil rights, 161; and Congress, 366, 477; in Congress, 435, 445, 451; and Cuban missile crisis, 351, 376, 519; debates with Nixon, 272–73; defense policies, 540, 549; on democracy, 16, 16n; domestic policies, 112, 167, 579; foreign policies, 389n, 529; on individual rights, 91; meeting with

244; student movements for, 159–60; suffrage for, 164, 172; unemployment of, 584; and urban poverty, 133, 135; and women, 149. *See also* Women; individual minorities

Minutemen missiles, 544, 548, 552

Miranda v. *Arizona,* 120, 120n, 121–22, 131, 478, 479, 481n, 487

MIRV (Multiple Independently Targetable Reentry Vehicle), 550, 551

Mississippi: murder of civil rights workers in, 161; voting in, 161, 304n, 324

Mississippi, University of, 65, 156

Missouri plan, 489

Mitchell, John, 118; and Watergate, 28n, 381, 383, 384, 471

Mitchell, Parren, 460

Mitchell v. *Bindrim,* 106n

Mobile, Alabama, 165

Model Cities program, 626–27

Mondale, Walter F., 273, 387n; in 1980 election, 278, 321; on Vice Presidency, 377

Monetary policy. *See* Economic policy: monetary

Monopoly, 563–64, 600

Monroe, James, 92, 222

Monroe Doctrine, 522

Montesquieu, 14, 43, 43n

Montgomery, Alabama: bus boycott in, 159; march to, 163

Moral Majority, 207

Morgan v. *Commonwealth of Virginia,* 416n

Morison, Samuel Eliot, 32–33, 33n

Morland, Howard, 88, 90, 90n

Mormons, 110

Morrill Act (1862), 588

Morris, Gouverneur, 38, 42, 353, 443

Morris, Dr. J. Anthony, 425

Mosher, Frederick C., 406, 406n

Mosher, Lawrence, 565n

Moss, Frank E., 101

Motor Carrier Act (1980), 417

Moyers, Bill, 374

Moynihan, Daniel P., 541, 584n, 585, 585n

Muckrakers: and business, 201

Müller, Ronald E., 520–21, 521n

Mumford, Lewis, 622, 622n, 628, 628n

Municipal Assistance Corporation ("Big Mac"), 631

Muñoz Marin, Luis, 143

Murphy, John M., 430

Murphy, Thomas P., 636–37, 637n

Murphy, Walter F., 481, 481n, 484n

Murray v. *Curlett,* 111n

Muskie, Edmund, 374, 533, 593

MX missiles, 552

Myers, Michael O., 430

Myers v. *United States,* 360n

My Lai, 486–87

Myrdal, Gunnar, 152, 152n, 153, 153n

N

NAACP. *See* National Association for the Advancement of Colored People

Nader, Ralph, 208, 213, 424, 565, 600; and General Motors, 577, 577n, 578

Nardone v. *United States,* 118n

NASA. *See* National Aeronautics and Space Administration

Nathan, Richard P., 81n

National Advisory Commission on Civil Disorders, 165–66

National Aeronautics and Space Administration (NASA), 395, 403–04, 413, 590

National Association for the Advancement of Colored People (NAACP), 155, 159

National Bank of the United States, 69–70

National Broadcasting Company (NBC), 196, 239, 277, 331

National Broadcasting Co. v. *United States,* 100n

National Commission on the Causes and Prevention of Violence, 167, 489–90

National Conservative Political Action Committee (NCPAC), 210, 288, 437

National conventions, 45, 220, 223, 234, 238–48, 252; compromises at, 240; cost and financing of, 285, 286; credentials committees at, 241; dark horses at, 240, 246; decision making at, 245–47; delegates to, 237, 241, 242–45, 247, 252, 330; future of, 247–48; and national committees, 234, 252; nominating a presidential candidate at, 234, 240–48, 252; open, 243–44; and platform, 234, 241, 252; and public opinion polls, 247; selecting a vice-presidential candidate at, 234, 241, 241n, 252; television coverage of, 238–40, 251, 272, 272n; types of nominations made by, 246. *See also* Democratic National Conventions; Republican National Conventions

National Defense Education Act (1958), 588

National Education Association (NEA), 590

National Environmental Policy Act (1969), 594

National Foreign Intelligence Board, 536

National Guard, 64–65, 156, 163, 611

National Industrial Recovery Act, 71

Nationalism: in new nations, 48–49, 523

National Labor Relations Act (1935), 71, 140, 569, 600

National Labor Relations Board (NLRB), 416, 569

National Labor Relations Board v. *Jones & Laughlin Steel Corp.,* 71n

National League of Cities v. *Usery,* 71n, 419n

National Mediation Board, 569

National Organization for Women (NOW), 149

National origins of Americans, 20–21, 21n

National Railroad Passenger Corporation (Amtrak), 401, 566

National Rifle Association, 207, 209

National Right to Life Committee, 149, 209

National Science Foundation, 590

National security: abuses of, in a democracy, 16, 519, 521, 538; and bureaucracy, 419; and civil liberties, 113–14, 116, 118–19, 521; and classification of documents, 102;

and defense establishment, 518, 545, 547; and domestic policy, 521, 527, 537–38, 557; and freedom of information, 102; and freedom of the press, 89; in nuclear age, 74, 518, 519–20, 558; and President, 102, 348, 374, 390, 527, 531–32, 535, 537, 538; and Watergate, 16, 382. *See also* Central Intelligence Agency; Department of Defense; Foreign policy: and national security

National Security Act (1947), 375, 531, 536, 547, 558

National Security Agency (NSA), 74, 536, 547

National Security Council (NSC), 375–76, 531–32, 533, 534, 558; and CIA, 535–36; and State Department, 374, 533, 534, 538

National Socialist Party v. *Village of Skokie,* 109n

National Student Association, 536

National Women's Political Caucus, 149

Nation building process, 49–50

Natural gas: controls on, 596; deregulation of, 202, 209, 453, 454, 597

Natural resources: federal aid for, 84, 87. *See also* Environmental movement

Natural rights, 31–32, 472

Nava, Julian, 141

Navajo Indians, 110, 136

Near v. *Minnesota,* 89n, 124n

Nebraska Press Association v. *Stuart,* 97n

Negative income tax, 584

Negre v. *Larsen,* 110n

Nerve gases, 552–53

Neuborne, Burt, 101n

Neustadt, Richard E., 359, 359n, 366n, 369n, 370, 370n, 373n, 378n, 404n, 409, 409n, 425n, 528, 528n

Neutron bomb, 552

Newark, New Jersey: black mayor elected in, 169, 506, 633; organized crime in, 506; riots in, 165

New Deal, 86, 224, 229, 309, 340, 341, 355, 391, 569, 571, 600; and federal powers of, 66, 74; social welfare programs of, 66, 397, 561, 562, 584; and Supreme Court decisions, 66, 71, 476–77, 563. *See also* Roosevelt, Franklin D.

New Frontier, 225, 229

New Hampshire, 33, 47, 324, 609n, 615; primaries in, 247, 262, 320, 321

New Jersey Plan, 40, 58

Newspaper: citizen access to, 96; colonial, 34; decline in number of, 198–99; and election campaigns, 96, 280–82, *282,* 290; and libel, 105–06; political division of, *282;* political endorsements of, 281–82; and public opinion, 195, 198–99, 206. *See also* Media, mass; Press

New York City, New York, 115, 514, 593, 621, 622; crime in, 493; criminal courts in, 502; fiscal crisis of, 64, 66, 618, 631–32; government of, 618, 632; labor unions in, 618, 632; minorities in, 143; newspapers of, 199; organized crime in, 506, 507; police corruption in, 506; politics in, 14, 180,

Sheatsley, Paul B., 358n
Shelton, Frank, 316n
Sheppard v. *Maxwell,* 97, 97n
Sherman, Roger, 41
Sherman Antitrust Act (1890), 563
Sherwood, Robert E., 269n
Shipler, David K., 625n
Sidey, Hugh, 359, 371n, 530
Silberman, Charles E., 152, 152n
Sindler, Allan P., 226, 226n
Sioux Indians, 137
Sirica, John J., 382, 383
Sixteenth Amendment, 55, 481, 481n, 575
Sixth Amendment, 54, 98, 119, 120, 124
Skokie, Illinois, 108–09
Skolnick, Jerome H., 167n
Slavery, 153; in colonial America, 33; and Constitution, 41–42, 44–45, 58, 154; and Declaration of Independence, 30; outlawed by Thirteenth Amendment, 42n. 55; as political issue, 223, 223n
Sloan v. *Lemon,* 112n
Slums, 136, 545, 585, 622, 639; and crime, 492–93, 509, 622, 625; ghettos, 23, 133, 135, 143, 152, 165–66, 169, 493, 585, 608, 626, 630; higher prices in, 578–79; housing in, 624–28; and police corruption, 506; schools of, 158; urban renewal projects in, 626–27
Small Business Administration (SBA), 396, 566–67
Smith, Alfred E., 224, 308
Smith Act (1940), 95, 113
Smith v. *Goguen,* 94n
Snail darter, 594, 594n
Snepp v. *United States,* 102, 102n, 469n
Sobul, DeAnne, 110n
Social change: and Warren Court, 470. *See also* Political system: and changing society
Social class: and criminal justice, 489; and interest groups, 214; of political leaders, 438; and public opinion, 179–80, 215; and social welfare programs, 180; and voting, 297, 299, 301, 305, 342. *See also* individual classes
Social security, 10, 71, 74n, 229, 237, 275, 278, 394, 562, 577, 581–84, 587, 588, 599, 600; monthly payments under, 396, 575, 580, 581, 581n, *582;* and Supplemental Security Income, 580, 583, 584; taxes for, 574, 581–82
Social Security Act (1935), 581, 583, 600
Social welfare programs: and Constitution, 561–62, 599; cost of, 581–82, 587, 588, 600; criticism of, 74, 562, 577, 581, 583–84, 586, 599; and federal government, 8, 74, 237, 346, 355, 391, 560–61, 562, 572, 577, 580–88, 599, 600; of New Deal, 66, 229, 397, 561, 562, 584; in New York City, 631; and politics, 562, 577, 581; public assistance, 10, 16, 74, 84, 87, 237, 577, 580, 581, 583–84, 599, 600, 606, 608; and public opinion, 74, 180, 562, 577, 581, 583–84, 588, 588n; reform of, 351, 391, 560, 584; and states, 560; taxation for, 562,

574, 581–82, 583, 599, 600. *See also* Democratic party: and social welfare programs; individual programs
Sorauf, Frank J., 219, 219n, 220, 236–37, 237n
Sorensen, Theodore C., 406n
South, the: black migration from, 152; and civil rights legislation, 161–64, 434, 454; and Constitutional Convention compromise, 41–42, 44; and federalism, 62; population increase in, 19; Republican gains in, 229, *230,* 264, 304, 309, 325, 617; and school desegregation, 64–65, 156–57, 172, 477, 611; segregation in, 154–55, 159–61; voter rights and registration in, 56, 161, 162, *162,* 163–64, *164,* 165, 169, 172, 298, 327, 327n, 328; welfare benefits in, 583. *See also* Democratic party: in the South
South Carolina, 30, 33, 47, 262, 334, 612; voting in, 163, 164
Southeast Asia, 351, 436, 525, 530, 545–46, 548. *See also* Vietnam war
Southeastern Promotions, Ltd. v. *Conrad,* 105n
Southern Christian Leadership Conference (SCLC), 159
Soviet Union, 14, 21, 61; and China, 523; and Cold War, 113, 519, 522; and Cuban missile crisis, 519; and détente, 516, 526; and Eastern Europe, 274, 516; economy of, and arms race, 521; embargo of grain sales to, 516, 568; expansion of influence of, 522–23, 526; Nixon's trip to, 267, 521, 526, 553; as nuclear power, 353, 523, 525, 540, 544–45, 548, 550–53, 557; outlawed biological weapons, 553; recognition of, 365–66; and SALT, 294, 516, 526, 540, 551–52, 553–54, 558; signed Nonproliferation Treaty, 552; signed nuclear test ban treaty, 552, 558; and Sputnik, 548, 588, 590; and United Nations, 540–41; and United States, 520, 522, 523, 525, 526, 537, 541, 557; and Vladivostok accord, 551, 553; and wheat deal, 568. *See also* Afghanistan: Soviet invasion of
Spanish-American War, 522
Spencer, Stuart, 259
Spencer-Roberts (campaign managers), 279
Spenkelink, John Arthur, 504
Spoils system, 418
Sproul, Kathleen, 246n
Sputnik, 548, 588, 590
Stack, Robert, 276
Staggers Rail Act (1980), 417, 566
Standard Metropolitan Statistical Areas (SMSA), 606n. *See also* Metropolitan areas
Stanford Daily, 117
Stang, David P., 496n
Stanley, Robert Eli, 107
Stanley v. *Georgia,* 107n
Stare decisis principle, 472
State government, 10, 293, 556, 606–17; aid to education, 112–13, 129–30, 560; Bill of Rights applied to, 54, 71, 93, 123–25, 125n, 131, 478; bureaucracy of, 399, 408, *409,* 419, 424, 426, 608, 610, 613; and

business, 476, 563, 609; constitutions of, 609, 610–11, 612, 613, 616, 618, 639; federal aid to, 67, 77–86, 583, 599, 607, 609, 613, 638; and federal government, 52, 63, 69–72; and federalism, 43, 60–67, 75, 76–77, 86, 608, 617; and housing, 560; income and expenditures of, 84–85, 608–09, *610;* initiatives for amendments in, 611; interstate relations, 72–73; and labor, 569; and local governments, 71–72, 83, 85–86, 87, 607–08, 618, 638; policy outcomes in, 76–77; responsibilities of, 43, 609–10, 639; and social welfare programs, 560, 580, 583, 587; taxation by, 572, 608–09; and unemployment insurance, 583; urban problems of, 608, 610, 611, 620–21. *See also* Federalism; Governors; Political parties, state
State laws, 610; abortion, 148; capital punishment, 503, 610; discrimination against women in, 144–45, 148; election, 284; judicial review of, 611, 616; for nominating process, 329; suffrage, 327, 327n, 330
State legislatures, 47, 242, 610–11, 613–14, *614,* 615; and amending Constitution, 53; conservative character of, 79, 615; corruption in, 613; and interest groups, 613; public opinion of, 613; and reapportionment, 53, 235, 336–37, 435, 469, 613, 615; structure of, 613–15; suburban representation in, 21, 615, 620
States' rights: and Supreme Court, 69–71, 476; and Tenth Amendment, 70–71
Steel mills: strike threat, 363
Steiner, Gilbert, 581, 581n
Stennis, John, 400
Sternlieb, Dr. George, 634
Stevens, John Paul, 115, 470, 478
Stevenson, Adlai E., 241n, 247n, 272, 306, 308
Steward Machine Co. v. *Davis,* 71n
Stewart, Potter, 98, 99, 104, 117, 118, 121, 470, 478, 483, 487
Stimpson, George, 56n
Stimson, James A., 442, 442n
Stock market, 565, 576; crash, 224, 576
Stokes, Donald E., 183n, 298n, 303n, 307n, 312n, 331n, 339n, 442n
Stone, Harlan Fiske, 71, 96, 477, 484, 485
Stone v. *Powell,* 117n
"Stop and frisk" rulings, 116, 479
Stouffer, Samuel A., 180n
Strategic Air Command (SAC), 544–45, 552
Strauss, Robert S., 260
Strunk v. *United States,* 126n
Student movements, 12, 128; antiwar, 12, 117, 179, 542; for minorities, 159–60
Students: constitutional rights of, 94–95; and election campaigns, 258, 259; and government, 9–10; as interest group, 12, 201; loans for, 10, 588, 589; and Nader, 208. *See also* Youth
Suburbs, 133, 608, 620n, 634–37; black migration to, 170, 304, 607; busing in, 158; conflict between cities and, 607, 620–21,

Voter participation *(Continued)*
in, 297–98, *298, 299,* 342; of youth, 297, 329
Voter registration, 259, 297, 330; in South, 161, 162, *162,* 163–64, *164,* 298
Voting, 220, 326; absentee, 327; ballots for, 330–31, *332;* and democracy, 11, 15, 201, 292–93, 341; by machine, 331; patterns, 308–16, 324. *See also* Suffrage
Voting Rights Act (1965), 163–65, 172, 298, 327, 327n, 328, *328*

W

Wages: controls on, 562, 571, 572, 577; minimum, 569, 600; voluntary guidelines, 571, 572
Wagner, Robert F., 569
Waldheim, Kurt, 541
Waldo, Dwight, 397–98, 398n
Walker, Daniel, 497n
Wallace, George C., 65, 156, 163, 617; 1968 campaign of, 226, 231–33, 264, 324, 335; shooting of, 264, 431
Waltz, Kenneth N., 542, 542n, 543, 543n
Walz, Frederick, 111
Walz v. *Tax Commission of the City of New York,* 111n, 112n
War, 517, 556; biological and chemical weapons, 552; and economic controls, 572; guerrilla, 545, 549; limited, 353–54, 518, 545, 549–50. *See also* Arms; Congress, war powers of; Nuclear war; President, war powers of
War Powers Resolution (1973), 44, 348, 351, 354, 361–62, 368n, 370, 391, 392, 432, 435, 464, 465, 529, 558
Warren, Charles, 39n, 42n
Warren, Earl, 92, 92n, 125, 469–70, 477, 485, 508, 509; and Eisenhower, 480; on free speech, 94–95; on rights of accused, 119–20; on school desegregation, 155–56, 172
Warren, Robert W., 88–89
Warren Commission, 192, 378, 386
Warren Court, 469–70, 476, 477–78, 508; and anti-Communist legislation, 478; and obscenity, 478; public opinion of, 470; and reapportionment, 469, 476, 477; and rights of accused, 119–20, 125–26, 131, 469, 476, 477–78, 481; and school desegregation, 155–56, 172, 469, 477; and school prayers, 469, 478
Warsaw Pact, 523
Washington, George, 36, 47, 67, 67n, 179; in American Revolution, 35, 153; at Constitutional Convention, 38, 40, 41, 43; and isolationism, 521; and political parties, 222; as President, 45, 48, 49, 56, 352, 353, 387, 417; and Whiskey Rebellion, 360
Washington state, 150, 171, 609n; American Indians in, 137; voting in, 329
Washington, D.C., 151, 593, 622; black mayor elected in, 169, 633; crime in, 493; gay rights rally in, 151; March on, 160–61;

Metro system of, 630; riots in, 165. *See also* District of Columbia
Washington Post, 66, 98, 121, 161, 165, 195, 196, 198, 203, 270, 276, 280, 381, 424, 431, 595
Washington v. *Texas,* 124n
Watergate scandal, 9, 225, 381–84, 533; abuse of executive power in, 7, 16, 24, 27, 383, 385, 429, 543; break-in at Democratic headquarters, 28, 116, 270, 341, 367, 379, 381–82, 385, 429, 498, 536; burglary of Ellsberg's psychiatrist, 116; and campaign finance reforms, 283, 290; and CIA, 381, 382–83, 385, 429, 500, 536; and Congress, 436; cover-up, 28, 98, 341, 367, 382, 383, 429, 471, 498, 543; enemies list, 383, 385; and executive privilege, 366–67; and FBI, 383, 385, 429, 499, 500, 536; Gallup poll on, 270n; and Justice Department, 471, 498; and national security, 16, 382; and 1972 elections, 197, 270, 270n, 271; Nixon as unindicted co-conspirator, 360, 471; and Nixon tapes, 27–28, 367, 381, 383, 385, 424, 429, 457, 471, 473–74, 480, 498; and Plumbers, 382, 385, 521, 536; and Presidency, 348; and press, 98, 196, 283; and public opinion, 176, 248, 270n, 471, 498; Senate hearings on, 29, 197, 283, 341, 367, 383, 424, 452, 457; special prosecutor for, 367, 383, 471, 474, 498; and Supreme Court, 27–28, 367, 383, 471, 474, 480, 498n; trials and convictions in, 270–71, 374, 382, 383, 384, 425, 471, 474; and White House staff, 270, 271, 374; and wiretapping, 270, 382–83, 521. *See also* Nixon, Richard M.: impeachment investigation of
Water pollution, 23, 73, 591, 592, 593–94, 600
Water Pollution Control Act (1972), 593–94
Watkins v. *United States,* 458n
Watson, Jack H., Jr., 83
Wattenberg, Ben J., 19n, 21n, 341n
Watts riot, 165
Weather Underground, 192
Weaver, James B., 224
Weaver, Paul, 335n
Weber, Brian, 169. *See also* Affirmative action
Weber, Max, 397
Webster, William, 500
Wedge, Bryant, 389n
Weeks v. *United States,* 17n
Weems, Parson, 179
Weinberg v. *Prichard,* 337n
Weintraub, Boris, 450n
Weisband, Edward, 362n, 464, 464n
Weisberg, Herbert F., 188n, 192n
Weiss, Ted, 151
Welfare program. *See* Social welfare programs: public assistance
Welsh, William, 234n
Welsh v. *United States,* 109, 109n
Weltner, Charles L., 626–27
Wendelken, Martin, 316n
Wertheimer, Fred, 212, 212n

Wesberry v. *Sanders,* 337, 337n
West, the: politics in, 223–24, 309; population increase in, 19
Westerfield, H. Bradford, 522n
Westin, Alan F., 118n
West Virginia, 110, 286; poverty in, 62–63
West Virginia Board of Education v. *Barnette,* 110n, 125n
Whigs, 222, 222n, 223, 226, 252
Whiskey Rebellion, 360
Whitaker and Baxter (campaign managers), 279
White, Byron R., 94, 99, 101, 106, 470, 478, 483
White, Theodore H., 230, 230n, 264n, 272, 272n, 273, 273n, 281n
White, William S., 434, 434n, 450, 450n
White Americans, 21, 477; and busing issue, 157–59; migrated to cities, 607; migrated to suburbs, 21, 158, 589, 607, 621, 623–24, 634–35, 640; political affiliation of, 229, 230, 252, 309; and racism, 23, 64–65, 133–34, 135, 152, 156, 165–66, 170, 233, 622–23, 624, 627
White v. *Regester,* 337n
Whitehurst, Carol A., 147, 147n
Wiesner, Jerome B., 549
Wilbern, York, 638n
Wildavsky, Aaron B., 261, 261n, 266, 266n, 281n, 406, 406n
Williams, Robert Anthony, 121
Williams v. *Florida,* 505n
Williams v. *North Carolina* cases, 72, 72n
Willkie, Wendell L., 246
Wills, Frank, 380
Wilson, James, 40, 42, 353, 475
Wilson, James Q., 408n, 497n, 609n, 632, 632n
Wilson, Woodrow, 44, 224, 353, 366, 373, 380, 385, 387, 388, 454–55, 455n, 522
Winters, Glenn R., 489n
Winters, Richard F., 77n
Wiretapping: and CIA, 535; and civil rights, 117–19, 126, 130, 479, 521; and FBI, 118; and Fourth Amendment, 118; and law enforcement, 118; ordered by Nixon, 118, 382, 385, 521; of organized crime, 506; and Watergate, 270, 382–83, 521
Wirthlin, Richard B., 184, 185, 186, 257, 279–80
Wise, David, 101n, 404n, 406n, 530n, 538n
Witcover, Jules, 422n, 537n
Wolff v. *Rice,* 117n
Wolfinger, Raymond E., 237n, 297n, 473n
Wolfson, Louis E., 480n
Wolman v. *Walter,* 113n
Wolston v. *Reader's Digest,* 106, 106n
Women, 144–50; and abortion, 147–49, 171; appointed as judges, 488, 510; in Congress, 149, 438, 465; as convention delegates, 149, 243, 244, 245; and day-care, 170; discrimination against, 144–50, 171, 218; and the draft, 144–45, 179, 546; and the family, 145, 147; in federal bureaucracy, 146–47; income of, compared with men, 135, 146,

146, 147, 171; in labor force, 145–47, 147; laws for protection of, 144–45; lesbians, rights of, 149; and minorities, 149; political gains of, 149, 180; political participation of, 50; proposed ERA for, 56–57, 57n, 144–46, 171; suffrage for, 27, 33, 46, 55, 295, 327, 342; voting behavior and participation of, 295, 297, 304–05, 305n, 325

Women's Liberation movement, 135, 144, 171

Wood v. *Ohio,* 122n

Woodson v. *North Carolina,* 503n

Woodward, Bob, 98, 381, 482n, 483, 485n, 508n

World Bank, 538

Wounded Knee: occupation of, 137–38

Y

Yadlosky, Elizabeth, 328n

Yarborough, Ralph, 386

Yates v. *United States,* 114n

Young, Donald, 377n

Youngblood, Rufus, 386

Youngstown Sheet and Tube Co. v. *Sawyer,* 363n

Youths, 5, 135; as convention delegates, 243, 244, 245; crime by, 493; in criminal justice system, 505; and Democratic party, 229, 252; and knowledge of issues, 191; unemployment of, 170, 560; voter participation of, 297, 329

Z

Zamora, Fernando Rodriguez, 122

Zero-Base Budgeting (ZBB), 423

Ziegler, Ronald L., 270, 379

Zingale, Nancy, 261n

Zorach v. *Clauson,* 112n

Zurcher v. *Stanford Daily,* 117n

2
3
D 4
E 5
F 6
G 7
H 8
I 9
J 0